Interpreting Literature

"...the two great esthetic problems ...of communication and ...of value"
—W. H. AUDEN

Preliminaries to Literary Judgment:
Interpreting Literature

FIFTH EDITION

K. L. KNICKERBOCKER University of Tennessee   **H. WILLARD RENINGER** University of Northern Iowa

HOLT, RINEHART AND WINSTON, INC. NEW YORK, CHICAGO, SAN FRANCISCO, ATLANTA, DALLAS, MONTREAL, TORONTO

Library of Congress Cataloging in Publication Data

Knickerbocker, Kenneth Leslie, ed.
   Interpreting literature.

   1. Literature—Collections.   I. Reninger, Harry
Willard,   joint ed.   II. Title.   III. Title: Preliminaries to literary judgment.

PN6014.K57   1974   808.8   73–10247

ISBN: 0–03–005416–8

4 5 6 7   071   9 8 7 6 5 4 3 2 1

ACKNOWLEDGMENTS

This constitutes the copyright page as legally required by rights and permissions agreements.

For the materials copyrighted by authors, publishers, and agents, the editors are indebted to
the following:

Atheneum Publishers, Inc. for "The Dover Bitch"
from *The Hard Hours* by Anthony Hecht. Copyright © 1960 by Anthony E. Hecht. Reprinted by
permission of Atheneum Publishers. Appeared
originally in *Transatlantic Review*.

James Baldwin for permission to reprint "Exodus."

Lincoln Barnett for permission to reprint "Tennessee Williams" from *Life Magazine,* February 16,
1948.

Barricade Music, Inc. for "Crucifixion" by Phil
Ochs. Copyright 1966, Barricade Music, Inc.
(ASCAP) All Rights Reserved. Used by per-
mission.

Black World for "To the Mercy Killers," copyright
© September 1966 by *Negro Digest*. Reprinted
by permission of *Black World* and Dudley Randall.

The Beloit Poetry Journal and The University of
Tennessee Press for permission to reprint "The
Garden" by Stephen Mooney.

The Bobbs-Merrill Company, Inc. for "A Poem for
Black Hearts" from *Black Magic Poetry 1961–
1967,* copyright © 1969, by LeRoi Jones, reprinted by permission of the publisher, The
Bobbs-Merrill Company, Inc.

Chilton Book Company for permission to reprint
"Amazing Grace" from *Amazing Grace* by Robert
Drake. Copyright © 1965 by Robert Drake. Used
with permission of Chilton Book Company, Philadelphia and New York, and the author.

Columbia University Press for permission to reprint sketch of Edward Gibbon from *The Columbia Encyclopedia,* Second Edition.

Combine Music Corporation for "Sunday Mornin'
Comin' Down" and "Me and Bobby McGee,"
both copyright © 1969 by Combine Music Corporation. International copyright secured. All
rights reserved.

Corinth Books, Inc. for "Preface to a Twenty Vol-
ume Suicide Note," copyright © 1961 by LeRoi
Jones. Reprinted by permission of Corinth
Books.

Frank Marshall Davis for permission to reprint
"Roosevelt Smith."

J. M. Dent and Sons, Ltd., for permission to reprint
"The Lagoon" by Joseph Conrad.

Acknowledgments are continued on p. 896.

DEDICATED TO OUR AUTHORS

WHO HAVE DIED SINCE THE APPEARANCE OF THE FIRST EDITION

W. H. Auden 1907–1973
Bertolt Brecht 1898–1956
Albert Camus* 1913–1960
E. E. Cummings 1894–1962
Floyd Dell 1887–1969
John Dos Passos 1896–1970
Walter Prichard Eaton 1878–1957
T. S. Eliot* 1888–1965
William Faulkner* 1897–1962
Robert Frost 1874–1963
Ernest Hemingway* 1899–1961
Aldous Huxley 1894–1963
Shirley Jackson 1919–1965
Randall Jarrell 1914–1965
Robinson Jeffers 1887–1962
Joseph Wood Krutch 1893–1970
Percy Lubbock 1879–1965

Thomas Mann* 1875–1955
W. Somerset Maugham 1874–1965
Stephen Mooney 1915–1971
Ogden Nash 1902–1971
Alfred Noyes 1880–1958
Frank O'Connor 1903–1966
Dorothy Parker 1893–1967
Ezra Pound 1885–1972
Bertrand Russell* 1872–1970
Carl Sandburg 1878–1967
John Steinbeck* 1902–1968
Wallace Stevens 1879–1955
Ruth Suckow 1892–1960
James Thurber 1894–1961
William Carlos Williams 1883–1963

* Nobel Prize Award.

PREFACE

Have you practiced so long
   to learn to read?
Have you felt so proud
   to get at the meaning
   of poems?
   WALT WHITMAN, "Song of Myself"

In the preparation of this volume we have kept our eyes steadily on the student-reader. Editorial devices and selection of material have been guided by this concentration on both the abilities and the limitations of students when they are faced with a piece of imaginative writing. We believe that most students regard imaginative literature as a conspiracy against their mental and emotional peace. Their minds are accustomed to work best at a literal—that is, a servile—level. They are in a very real sense shackled. We are convinced that in most instances these shackles can be broken, that literal minds can be liberated. We know, of course, that a key figure in this process of liberation is the instructor and that a book's effectiveness—ours or anyone else's—must depend in great part upon the wisdom and enthusiasm of those who teach. It has been our chief purpose to provide a readily teachable book.

The principles that have guided our editorial work may be briefly indicated. First of all we have so far as possible allowed literature to speak for itself. In "General Preliminaries," for example, we call on literature to define itself so that the reader may see and know what literature is and not simply be told what it is. In "Fiction: Preliminaries," instead of laying down rules for short stories, we present a story that shows many of the rules in action. In "Biography: Preliminaries," we ask the reader to see for himself the literary characteristics of autobiographical and biographical writing. The same procedure is followed in the preliminaries to the sections on poetry, drama, and the essay.

The second principle that guided us—a corollary of the first—was to delay comment on a literary technique or characteristic until a demonstration of the technique or characteristic actually appeared in one of the selections. In "The Essay: Preliminaries," for example, we are able to illustrate the sharp distinction between two kinds of essays, but on the basis of our excerpts from Lamb and Huxley we cannot appropriately say anything demonstrable about the structure of essays. As soon as we reach the full-length essay, however, we have an illustration of structure and can show its importance to the essay.

Our procedure in this respect explains why we use the term "Preliminaries" instead of "Introduction" for the essays that precede the various sections. Each section as a whole —"Preliminaries," the selections, comments, and questions—constitutes an introduction to the type of literature it contains.

The third principle was that all technical terms should be explained as soon as used. Furthermore, since sections of this book may be used out of the order given, we have not hesitated to repeat definitions of terms that reoccur in the various sections. We think that these occasional repetitions will be a convenience and an aid to the reader in fixing certain terms in his mind. Each definition is shaped to be applied to the form being considered.

Finally, we have offered in each section a body of material without comment or questions. We have done this so that whatever has been learned may be independently applied.

The selections have been chosen with two considerations in mind. First, we have offered at the beginning of each section the sort of material that may be readily understood and immediately enjoyed. Secondly, we have followed the simpler selections with progressively more difficult selections. This progression is most apparent in the section on poetry, where proceeding from the simple to the difficult is most important. In general, stories emphasizing plot precede those emphasizing character in the section on fiction. Two one-act plays precede nine full-length plays in the section on drama. Anecdotes precede biographical sketches in the section on biography. The essay begins with short and light bits of speculation and moves on to heavier fare.

PREFACE TO THE FIFTH EDITION

In its four editions *Interpreting Literature* has maintained its focus on literature that is teachable. The fifth edition does not depart from this fundamental. We have not been concerned with fads, with causes, with biases. We are concerned with the eternally relevant, whether the pieces representing this sort of relevance were written centuries ago or yesterday. The older literature has something to say to our times, and the best of the younger literature also speaks to us. We have sought a balance between the old and the young.

In addition to the regular Contents and Index, we are providing in this edition an organization of selections according to theme. This sort of cross-referencing will suggest innumerable ideas for writing and class discussions. Although the Thematic Contents is extensive, the controlling topics are clearly subject to all sorts of modifications. Many selections will illustrate more than one theme. Teachers and students will be free, of course, to create other topics and to rearrange our arrangement in any way that may seem appropriate.

Fiction features the storytellers of the twentieth century, largely because short narratives have a relatively brief history. Hemingway, Steinbeck, Faulkner, Mann, Camus (all Nobel Prize winners) are some of the moderns, along with Oates, Ellison, Baldwin, Hughes, O'Connor, Wright. Fiction now offers twenty-nine stories and includes D. H. Lawrence's poetic novella "The Man Who Died."

Poetry has been expanded from 210 poems to 236, a fact of not much importance in itself. Noteworthy, however, is the inclusion of poems reflecting the rhythms of our times, rhythms heard long ago in early folk ballads and now given new expression. The current troubadours fit lyric to music, or, just as likely, music to lyrics. We present a number of the lyrics. Teachers with access to sound equipment can demonstrate how effective is, say, "Sunday Mornin' Comin' Down," written by Kris Kristofferson and sung by Johnny Cash. Besides Kristofferson, eleven other singer-poets are represented: Bob Dylan, Fred Foster, Leonard Cohen, Tom Paxton, Richard Fariña, Peter Seeger, Donovan Leitch, Phil Ochs, Carl Oglesby, Jack Blanchard, Johnny Hartford. Three older anonymous ballads are included: "Frankie and Johnny," "The Wabash Cannon Ball," and "On Top of Old Smoky."

Some older poets are new to our book: William Cartwright, John Clare, Oscar Wilde. T. S. Eliot's "The Cultivation of Christmas Trees"—one of this poet's most sensitive poems—is added as a foil for "The Love Song of J. Alfred Prufrock" and "The Hollow Men."

The section on Drama, thoroughly revised and expanded for the Fourth Edition, has been retained.

Biography has been somewhat reduced. Only two new selections have been added: Douglass's "A Child's Reasoning" and Sylvia Plath's "The last thing I wanted was infinite security. . . ." The piece by Douglass adds to an understanding of Hayden's poem "Frederick Douglass" and the Plath piece relates to two of her poems (see section on Poetry). Some essays have been dropped and six new ones added: Thurber's "A Unicorn in the Garden," Ellison's "Brave Words for a Startling Occasion," Arthur P. Davis's "Trends in Negro American Literature (1940–1965)," Graves and McBain's "Electric Orphic Circuit," Baldwin's "Notes for a Hypothetical Novel," and Hough's "Lawrence's Quarrel with Christianity: 'The Man Who Died.'" The selection by Thurber offers a prime example of satire. The remainder of the new essays deal with literature: Ellison and Baldwin with the novel, Davis with poetry and fiction (a glance at drama) of black writers, Graves and McBain with the new minstrelsy (see the section on Poetry), and Hough with the novella "The Man Who Died" (see Fiction).

We are grateful for help from a number of individuals. We are especially indebted to Dr. David R. Bluhm, Professor of Religion and Philosophy, University of Northern Iowa, for his indispensable scholarly assistance in clarifying philosophical and biblical references in Frost's "A Masque of Reason," Lawrence's "The Man Who Died," Eliot's "The Cultivation of Christmas Trees," and other selections including Pound's "Ballad of the Goodly Fere." Dr. Mary Richards, The University of Tennessee at Knoxville, has performed many small but significant services that deserve our gratitude. Other colleagues at Tennessee have offered random, lunchtime suggestions that have been accepted. As with previous editions, there have been outside readers, unknown to us, who have microscopically scanned our book and sent their helpful analyses to Holt editors, who passed these on to us. These critics include: James Antonioli, El Camino College; Donald E. Barnett, University of Georgia; G. E. DeWitt, Long Beach City College; Nick Aaron Ford, Morgan State College; Charles B. Harris, Illinois State University; Joan D. Humphries, University of Georgia; Robert Earl Kipp, Jr., Brevard Community College; Nora B. Leitch, Lamar University; Crawford B. Lindsay, Tennessee State University–Nashville; J. L. Mitchum, Tennessee Technological University; Michael Squires, Virginia Polytechnic Institute and State University; Thomas W. Teer, Wingate College; Cleo Congrady and Pat Klopp, Alvin Junior College; Annette Chamberlin, Melissa Croker, and Nancy Prickett, Gadsden State Junior College; Robert Felgar and Evelyn McMillan, Jacksonville State University.

Mrs. Bonita Bryant, Bibliographer at the University of Northern Iowa Library and Miss Eleanor Goehring of the University of Tennessee Library have solved many stubborn problems for us. Mrs. Joyce Smith, administrative secretary at the University of Tennessee, has made the mechanics of editing run smoothly.

K.L.K.

H.W.R.

Knoxville, Tennessee
Cedar Falls, Iowa
January 1974

CONTENTS

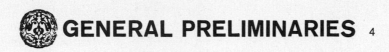

GENERAL PRELIMINARIES   4

FICTION   12

THE LANGUAGE OF POETRY   269

THE COMMENT ON EXPERIENCE:
FROM SENSUOUS EXPERIENCE TO DOMINANT ATTITUDE   291

HUMAN VALUES AND THE CRITICISM OF EXPERIENCE: PHILOSOPHICAL POEMS 299

THE DIMENSIONS OF POETIC EXPERIENCE   324

# DRAMA   416

PRELIMINARIES   416

BIOGRAPHY 740

PRELIMINARIES 740

APPENDIX 887

FROM ARISTOTLE'S "POETICS" 887

INDEX OF AUTHORS AND TITLES 901

INDEX OF LITERARY AND CRITICAL TERMS 908

THEMATIC CONTENTS*

The Individual: The Psychological Problem

THE WORTH OF THE INDIVIDUAL

SELF-LOVE AND SELF-DELUSION

LOVE BETWEEN MAN AND WOMAN

---

* The editors recognize the difficulty of classifying works of literature, especially imaginative literature that by its very nature is suggestive, connotative, and fictional. This thematic classification is meant only to suggest clusters of works each of which has the same general theme approached from differing points of view. We have resisted the temptation to place some works in more than one category feeling that overclassification could be more confusing than helpful to some readers. We leave that interesting project to the resourceful reader to enjoy in his own way and on his own responsibility.

LOVE AS HEALER AND DESTROYER

TOWARD SELF-KNOWLEDGE AND THE SEARCH FOR ONE'S IDENTITY

PROBLEMS OF THE SEXES

HUMOR, WIT, AND THE DELIGHT OF THE SENSES

SATIRICAL THRUSTS AT HUMAN FOIBLES OR SOCIAL INEQUITIES

The Individual, Society, and the State:
The Social Problem

WHAT HUMANKIND HAS MADE OF ITSELF

THE CONFLICT OF FREEDOM AND AUTHORITARIANISM

THE INHUMANITY OF HUMAN BEINGS

THE SPIRITUAL DEGENERATION OF THE AGE

THE DEBATE OVER VALUES: WHAT WILL THE FUTURE BRING?

THE NECESSARY IDENTIFICATION OF THE INDIVIDUAL WITH HUMANITY

The Individual, Nature, and the Universe: Philosophical and Religious Problems

NATURE AND THE UNIVERSE AS SOURCES OF RELIGIOUS FEELING AND KNOWLEDGE

THE STRUGGLE WITH THE NATURE OF FAITH, TRUTH, AND THE UNKNOWN

HUMAN RESPONSES TO DEITY

ATTITUDES TOWARD DEATH, JUDGMENT DAY, IMMORTALITY, AND PARADISE

ATTITUDES TOWARD THE MEANING OF LIFE

The Functions of Literature

Interpreting Literature

GENERAL PRELIMINARIES

". . . we may come to realize that the two essential facts about a work of art, that it is contemporary with its own time and that it is contemporary with ours, are not opposed but complementary facts."

—NORTHROP FRYE

We are concerned here with three basic questions: (1) What is the difference between utilitarian and creative literature? (2) What are the devices used by writers to create the forms of creative literature? (3) What kind of truth, or reality, do we find in creative literature, and how is such truth created? The purpose of this introductory essay is to explore the elemental answers to these questions as preparation for understanding the nature and uses of literature.

It is possible to find many of the answers to such basic questions in the literature itself. We have a classic precedent in Aristotle to support us. As preparation for writing his *Poetics** (often regarded as the fountainhead of all criticism of tragedy), Aristotle attended the Greek theater, analyzed the plays *and* the spectators' reactions, and used his observations to give us his theory of the ideal, or best, structure of tragedy in his *Poetics*. In other words, the Greek plays helped Aristotle to answer his questions about the nature and uses of tragedy.

Let us adopt a similar method. In a very real sense let us ask the kinds of literature to define themselves. In doing so we shall acquire some common ground and common literary vocabulary to help us understand and savor the literary experiences as we move through this volume. Only confusion will result if we use terms like *imagery, symbol,* and *creative literature* before they are defined as they emerge from the literature itself.

UTILITARIAN LITERATURE: LITERAL TRUTH

As sound is the medium of music and color the medium of painting, language is the medium of literature. The only purpose of language is to communicate something—anything—from one person to another. Throughout the centuries the various literary forms—poem, essay, short story—have been invented by writers to serve their needs. There the simplicity ends because men and their lives can be very complex. But whether simple or complex, whether impersonal or personal, every writer is communicating whatever is real to him, and this reality is *his* truth. As we shall see in the extracts on the next few pages, the kind of reality, or truth, varies with

* See p. 887.

the literary form, and from writer to writer.

Here is an example of utilitarian literature written by Thomas Henry Huxley (see "The Nature of an Hypothesis," p. 800):

When our means of observation of any natural fact fail to carry us beyond a certain point, it is perfectly legitimate, and often extremely useful, to make a supposition as to what we should see, if we could carry direct observation a step farther. A supposition of this kind is called an *hypothesis,* and the value of any hypothesis depends upon the extent to which reasoning upon the assumption that it is true enables us to account for the phenomena with which it is concerned.

What has Huxley done, and how has he done it? His subject is the hypothesis, sometimes called an assumption, used to explain a group of established facts. Huxley's paragraph is a definition, or explanation, of the nature and value of an hypothesis. The remainder of his essay demonstrates, by example, how the hypothesis is used. The essay is a useful definition for anyone interested in the nature of an hypothesis, and is therefore utilitarian literature.

To communicate his information Huxley has used a series of literal, abstract, declarative sentences; except for the words *carry* and *step* the paragraph is barren of imagery. These sentences are called propositions, statements embodying practical experience and observation. Their truth is called scientific or empirical, and these propositions *about* such experience are sometimes defined as "anything which can be said to be true or false." Such literature is called utilitarian because it is useful in the practical affairs of men. It was invented to present information objectively and impersonally. Let us keep in mind that a proposition is truth *about* something: we shall return to this idea later. (For further discussion of Huxley's method, see p. 800.)

THE TRANSITION TO CREATIVE LITERATURE

One way to learn why Huxley's essay is called utilitarian literature is to compare it with a different kind of essay, Emerson's "Self-Reliance." Here are a few of Emerson's sentences:

To believe your own thought, to believe that what is true for you in your private heart is true for all men,—that is genius. Speak your latent conviction, and it shall be the universal sense; for the inmost in due time becomes the outmost, and our first thought is rendered back to us by the trumpets of the Last Judgment. Familiar as the voice of the mind is to each, the highest merit we ascribe to Moses, Plato and Milton is that they set at naught books and traditions, and spoke not what men, but what *they* thought. A man should learn to detect and watch that gleam of light which flashes across his mind from within, more than the lustre of the firmament of bards and sages. Yet he dismisses without notice his thought, because it is his. In every work of genius we recognize our own rejected thoughts; they come back to us with a certain alienated majesty. . . . Trust thyself: every heart vibrates to that iron string.

Again we ask our questions: What has Emerson done, and how has he done it? His tone, or his attitude toward his subject, suggests that he is offering more than information for some utilitarian purpose. We feel that his attitudes are deeply involved with something of supreme importance to him. Emerson's subject is the importance of self-reliance as a human value, and for Emerson this subject is far more important than a material value. Unlike Huxley, his purpose is not only to inform, but also to arouse and persuade: he urges us to embrace the doctrine of self-reliance and to participate in its consequences.

To communicate his meaning Emerson, like Huxley, has used a series of propositions, but he has used something more, and *in that more lies Emerson's approach into creative literature.* This something more is Emerson's personal, urgent tone, mentioned before, his imagery and allusions, figures of speech, symbols, and sentence rhythms. These are the devices of poetry, and we therefore call Emerson's essay *poetic prose.* Indeed, practiced readers of Emerson know he thinks like a poet, as the complete "Self-Reliance" will testify. Note Emerson's use of images:

A man should learn to detect and watch that gleam of light which flashes across his mind from within, more than the lustre of the firmament of bards and sages.

Paraphrased literally, the sentence could read as Huxley might have written it:

A man should learn to rely on his own intuitive perception more than on the notable ideas of the past.

This literal, abstract paraphrase speaks *about* something, but Emerson's poetic imagery requires us to *experience* the little scene in concrete, lifelike terms, and we therefore participate in the scene. The "intuitive perception" becomes a "gleam of light which flashes across his mind," and we see the lighted revelation which is brighter than the "lustre of the firmament of bards and sages." Emerson's allusions to "Moses, Plato and Milton" are rich in suggestion, as is the figure (personification) of our rejected thoughts coming back to us with "alienated majesty." The image of the "iron string" becomes a symbol that *stands for* the integrity of the self which Emerson never tires of celebrating. Many of Emerson's sentences fall naturally into free-verse units, as this one:

In every work of genius
We recognize our own rejected thoughts;
They come back to us
With a certain alienated majesty. . . .

Unlike Huxley's *abstract* impersonal prose, Emerson's *concrete* poetic prose translates his abstract ideas into imagery, and we identify ourselves personally with his own experiences and values. We shall again see poetry at work in another kind of situation when we later examine *Othello.* (For further discussion of the poet's method, see "Poetry: Preliminaries," p. 236. See also MacLeish's poem, "Ars Poetica," p. 286, for his belief that poetry is not true as a theory or a proposition is true, but that poetry should be its own witness for its own kind of truth by presenting experience as *experience.*)

The essay as a form, then, can look in either direction: it can present impersonal truth and empirical experience (one kind of reality for the writer) in abstract propositions as Huxley does, or it can present personal convictions (another kind of reality for the writer) in poetic prose as Emerson does. Reading an essay like "Self-Reliance" is our first step into understanding and enjoying creative literature. (For further discussion of the essayist's method, see "The Essay: Preliminaries," p. 800.)

Our next step is reading biography. But to reproduce here a short passage from a full-length work would hardly illustrate biography's method and subject matter, so we refer ourselves to W. Somerset Maugham's "Brandy" (p. 745), a complete anecdote which can be read in a few minutes.

Maugham's anecdote has raised the two basic questions once more: What has Maugham done, and how has he done it? The anecdote concerns itself primarily with two characters, Martell and the narrator. It presents a true-to-life episode with an unforeseen conclusion and one or two comments on the human situation. Maugham uses the devices of action (narrative), character, scene, and dialogue, and a touch of symbolism. These are the devices of creative literature, but nevertheless the anecdote is not fiction, and the reasons therefor will help us to understand the exact nature of both biography and creative literature.

The subject of a biography is an actual person, and a biography's truth lies (1) in the accuracy of empirical fact collected about the person, and (2) in the interpretation made of those facts. Biography, then, is a form of history, *subject to its methods and limitations*. The value of both biography and history lies in their truthfulness to actual life; neither has any other serious reason for existing. The biographer collects the facts of a person's life from birth to death: these facts constitute empirical truth—objective, impersonal information. The biographer's selection and arrangement of these facts constitute an *interpretation* which is subjective truth. In five biographies of Walt Whitman we therefore have five somewhat different Whitmans.

We are now prepared to make a careful distinction between biography and creative literature, especially fiction and drama.

The biographer may—and most legitimately does—use some of the devices of fiction or drama, and yet write neither. If the biographer possesses integrity, he is limited by the nature of his subject—his character—as dictated by the known facts. He can, of course, select a few facts of a life, write a biography in the form of a novel, and emerge with neither biography nor fiction. Ordinarily he strives to portray a particular and unique character, to delineate the qualities which make that personality different from any other. The great biographies of men and women have followed this pattern. If a biographer's subject becomes a symbol or the epitome of a whole generation or class of men, it is usually accidental, not purposely designed. Further, the biographer is not bound to explain cause and effect in the action of his subject; he is bound by a time sequence only. Indeed, some of the most extraordinary actions of extraordinary men seem to be inexplicable. The biographer may offer solutions and apparent reasons, but his successor is likely to offer different ones. And finally, the biographer is not bound by credibility. It's all very well for us to exclaim about an act of, say, Charles II, "I don't see how it *really* happened!"—but the biographer can ignore our skepticism by pointing to the documents which verify the act. Indeed, the very incredibility of some of his acts helped to make Charles II what he was.

The story writer and dramatist, however, are (1) *not* limited by known facts. These writers create facts and characters for their own purposes. (2) The creative writer *is* bound to explain cause and effect if his characters' motives are to mean anything. (3) A creative writer's violation of credibility *would* vitiate the impact of his story. (For further discussion of the biographer's method, see "Biography: Preliminaries," p. 740.)

CREATIVE LITERATURE: SYMBOLIC TRUTH

What would happen if a writer depended solely on invented characters and events and not on impersonal, historical facts? Suppose he created (hence the term *creative literature*) the whole poem, story, or play, from beginning to end? What truth would exist? The practical man devoted to empirical facts and the search for useful information is likely to answer, "None at all" —but let us follow our original plan by investigating for ourselves.

Except for certain descriptive and lyric poems, the very essence of creative literature is *character* involved either in external action (outside himself) or internal action (within himself). What this character *is*, and *why* he does what he does mark the distinction between creative and noncreative literature (informational literature based on verifiable empirical facts). Let us test this statement by examining *Othello* (p. 455).

The principal characters are Othello, Desdemona, and Iago. Regardless of what else Shakespeare does, he must make these characters and *their world* credible to us. How has he done it? Suppose we begin by using a passage from the play to help answer the question. In the scenes preceding this passage "honest" Iago has by sheer duplicity finally convinced Othello that Desdemona has committed adultery with Cassio, and Othello at this moment may remember the warning Desdemona's father, Brabantio, offered him:

> Look to her, Moor, if thou hast eyes to see.
> She has deceiv'd her father, and may thee.
>
> (I. iii. 395–396.)

Othello now confronts Desdemona:

DESDEMONA Upon my knees, what doth your
    speech import?
I understand a fury in your words,
But not the words.
OTHELLO Why, what art thou?
DESDEMONA Your wife, my lord; your true and
    loyal wife. . . .
Heaven doth truly know it.
OTHELLO Heaven truly knows that thou art
    false as hell.
DESDEMONA To whom, my lord? With whom?
    How am I false?
OTHELLO Ah, Desdemon! Away! away! away!
DESDEMONA Alas the heavy day! Why do you
    weep? . . .
OTHELLO Had it pleased Heaven
To try me with affliction, had they rain'd
All kinds of sores and shames on my bare
    head,
Steeped me in poverty to the very lips,
Given to captivity me and my utmost hopes,
I should have found in some place of my soul
A drop of patience. But, alas, to make me
A fixed figure for the time of scorn
To point his slow and moving finger at!
Yet could I bear that too; well, very well.
But there where I have garnered up my heart,
Where either I must live or bear no life,
The fountain from the which my current runs,
Or else dries up—to be discarded thence,
Or keep it as a cistern for foul toads
To knot and gender in—turn thy complexion
    there,
Patience, thou young and rose-lipped
    cherubin!
I here look grim as hell!

    (IV. ii. 46–93.)

What has Shakespeare accomplished with this passage, especially with Othello's cry of the heart? Unlike the essayist and biographer who, with occasional exceptions, make literal statements *about* the nature of a character, Shakespeare has Othello present himself, giving the reader (or observer at the play) the opportunity to identify himself with Othello. Why in poetry? Because poetry is a language capable of saying some things unsayable in any other way* (see "The Language of Poetry," p. 269). According to some qualified critics, Othello's lines are the key to the depth of the tragedy. This commanding figure of impeccable integrity who has been tried with the world's afflictions of poverty and captivity which he has borne with patience and final poise is now struck down where he has garnered up his heart, where he must either live or die. In short, his faith, his very inner being, has been destroyed. The imagery "a cistern for foul toads/ To knot and gender in" is almost too tragic to bear, as Shakespeare means it to be. Our participation in this poetic passage created through imagery, rhythm, and emotion is active, not passive. Instead of merely looking and listening, we are invited to help create the scene in our imagination. As we read, *we* can create the gestures and facial expressions; *we* can feel the collapse of Othello's soul. We participate in Othello's inner world, and to cause us to do so is a basic function of creative literature.

We still have to answer our final question, what kind of reality, or truth, is to be found in creative literature, and how is it created? *Symbolic truth* is the customary label, although such labels as representative truth, universal truth, and artistic truth are used, and each label describes an element of the nature of this kind of truth. *The creation of this kind of truth is a unique and fascinating phenomenon in creative literature and, however labeled, it is the fundamental justification for all serious literary art.*

The careful examination of almost any work of creative literature (poem, story, or play) will uncover its literal truth and its symbolic truth, often called its literal and symbolic levels of meaning. This distinction means that the writer

---

* See Sanders, "An Introduction to *Othello*," p. 867, for a quotation from Ellis-Fermŏr on the function of poetry, especially imagery, in drama.

has used the literal truth, or literal sense, to *stand for*—to express by implication or indirection—something more universal in place and time than the literal sense of his work.* For example: William Allen White is supposed to have said, "I was never a Socialist in my youth so as not to be a Republican in my old age." Frost wrote:

> I never dared be radical when young
> For fear it would make me conservative when old.

White's timely statement in political terms has been converted by Frost to a timeless comment on the nature of human beings. Socialist and Republican in White's sense could and undoubtedly will pass away, but human nature as Frost conceives it is likely to remain constant. In fiction and drama symbolic truth can emerge from the setting, exposition, characters, action, and poetry if any, but the essential symbolic truth usually comes from the characters in action, and because such action expresses more than its literal meaning, it has been called *symbolic action.*

To explain these matters we return to some of the differences between biography and *Othello.* The biographer's facts and characters are empirically true: they exist in an actual way in an actual locality in actual time. The biographer *starts* with the collected facts about an actual person and works *toward* an interpretation of that person's life. The empirical (verifiable) facts sternly dictate the kind of person who emerges from the biography.

Othello, on the other hand, is a "fiction," the result of Shakespeare's imagination, shaped by a theme perhaps as old as civilization. Creative literature is also called imaginative literature because the writer, to dramatize the theme and to make it articulate in terms of lifelike action, may begin with a controlling theme and then imagine (create) a situation and characters governed by certain motives. An older technique as found in Aesop's fables was used to "illustrate" an abstract truth to make the truth, or lesson, arresting and palatable.** But dramatic technique invites (actually requires?) us to *participate* in the consequences of the theme for the human soul by creating an *illusion of reality* that can be more real than much of life itself. Here lies the unique paradox of symbolic truth: How can an illusion of reality be more real than reality itself? As some wit has put it, truth may be stranger than fiction, but fiction can be truer than [literal] truth.

Unlike the biographer who begins with actual facts about an actual person, Shakespeare may have begun with a theme which shaped the nature of the plot, characters, poetry, and symbolism. The general theme of *Othello* can be read as the destruction of the human soul through the destruction of faith ("But there, where I have garnered up my heart,/ Where either I must live, or bear no life. . . .").*** But the play cannot be read as a fable by Aesop is read. Shakespeare has qualified and sharpened this theme by creating a specific situation with well-defined characters controlled by specific motives. From this dramatized qualification of the theme emerges the symbolic truth. How is it accomplished?

The literal level of *Othello* is found in the story's facts, the kind of story offered in handbooks such as Marchette Chute's *Stories from Shakespeare.**** But the "story" of *Othello* is, emphatically, not the play because we cannot *experience* the story as poetic drama, and we therefore miss most of the symbolic action. The question is, then, how does Shakespeare take us from the literal to the symbolic level of meaning?

---

* Perhaps more technically stated, symbolic truth is philosophical, generalized truth dramatized through the particulars of human personality. Surely Aristotle is talking about a similar idea when he says that poetry, or creative literature, "is a more philosophical and higher thing than history; for poetry tends to express the universal, history the particular. By the universal I mean how a person of a certain type will on occasion speak or act, according to the law of probability or necessity; and it is this universality at which poetry aims. . . ." See *Poetics,* IX, p. 890.

** Aesop's "The Fox and the Grapes" promotes the moral, "too much cunning overreaches itself."
*** This is not to say that another reading of the play would not locate a different theme. *Othello* can be read as a study in evil by concentrating on Iago who is probably the most unrelieved symbol of evil in all Shakespeare. When this "honest" smiling spider determines to make a net of Desdemona's goodness to "enmesh them all," can we conceive of a more vile sin against humanity? For another and very thoughtful interpretation of the play see Sanders, "An Introduction to *Othello*," p. 867.
**** New York: Mentor Books, 1959.

We can look first at the setting and atmosphere. As he often does, Shakespeare involves us immediately with the prevailing atmosphere. In the opening scene we are confronted with Iago's hatred of Cassio, his injured vanity, the poison he pours into Roderigo's ears, and his easy confession,

> . . . I will wear my heart upon my sleeve
> For daws to peck at. I am not what I am.
> (I. i. 86–87.)

Here is the suggestion of the power of evil and the perverted human values represented by Iago.

As the action develops, Iago plans a triple play: He will bring Othello down, square accounts with Cassio, and rob Roderigo of his money. And through it all rings the symbolic, ironic refrain "honest Iago" to represent the duplicity of evil. These kinds of symbols make their contribution to symbolic meaning as they appear repeatedly throughout the play, but the most revealing ones appear in the characters and the plot, or structure of action.

Consider Iago and Othello. Shakespeare has shaped these characters for his own purposes and made them dramatic symbols. Actually the characters do not exist, yet within the play they "exist" because they represent people like themselves who do exist. Iago whose determination to rid himself of his frustrations at any evil cost to others is a composite representative of all Iagos; and likewise Othello whose loss of faith has destroyed him. The point is this: Shakespeare has taken an abstract concept of two kinds of men, and by the devices of poetry and drama he has presented the characters of Iago and Othello so realistically that they exist in our imagination as symbols of what each represents in the real world.

As the play unfolds, the principal characters make moral choices which bring certain consequences. On the literal level these characters are the agents of Shakespeare's will, but on the symbolic level of action (hence, symbolic truth) they represent certain human tendencies or moral and immoral currents of human action. Once Shakespeare had constructed his total action and had determined the final consequences of that action, his problem was to make the play credible (probable, not merely possible*) and representative of the human situation. Shakespeare solves his problem by the inevitability of his plot which depends on cause and effect, life-*like* characters, and poetry which reveals each soul's depth, nobility, and degradation.

Therefore the literal facts, the characters, and the action in *Othello* are true if we believe they represent an actuality which *could* be true. We ask, would two personalities like Iago and Othello with their motives, confronted with their kind of situation have acted as they did? If we answer yes, *Othello* is true, and its truth we call symbolic truth which has emerged from all the symbols working together to rise above the play's literal, surface action. (For further discussion of the creative writer's method, see Fiction: Preliminaries," p. 12, for the story writer's method, and for the dramatist's method, see "Drama: Preliminaries," p. 416.)

The reader who wishes to explore the concepts of creative literature more fully may want to investigate the critics whose essays appear in this book. Camus's "Nobel Prize Acceptance Speech" (p. 823) is a contemporary commentary on the writer's relation to morals, justice, and liberty, and should be read with his story "The Guest" (p. 174). De Quincey's "The Literature of Knowledge and the Literature of Power" (p. 808) is valuable as a direct extension of the distinction made above between utilitarian literature (literature of knowledge) and creative literature (literature of power). Cowley's "Criticism: A Many-Windowed House" (p. 817) investigates the various critical approaches to literature and offers his own. Auden's "Reading" (p. 813), written in the *pensée* tradition, ranges through literature, writers, and critics. And finally, Huxley's "Music at Night" (p. 810) develops, among other matters, a basic idea that no student of literature should ever forget: Using Shakespeare as an example he says, "Nobody's 'own words,' except those of Shakespeare himself, can possibly 'express' what Shakespeare meant. The substance of a work of art is inseparable from its form: its truth and beauty are two and yet, mysteriously one." In a very real sense the burden of Huxley's final sentence is one of the basic burdens of this book.

* See Aristotle's *Poetics*, IX, p. 890, for discussion of this distinction.

FICTION

"The meagre satisfaction that [man] can extract
from reality leaves him starving."
—SIGMUND FREUD

PRELIMINARIES

The storyteller is the perennial delight of mankind. As he begins, we are immediately confronted with people—characters, the most interesting thing in the world. We may be entertained by the unusual turn of events (plot); we may be given a fresh insight into human personality (character); or we may be offered a penetrating comment on the human situation (theme). The meaning of plot, character, and theme is determined, we shall later discover, by the storyteller's *attitude* toward the facts he relates.

But why should we take seriously a story whose characters and action have never existed? We accept as authentic most biography and history, but why should we attend to something invented, made up? This is a fair question, most often asked by the practical, hardheaded person who gives his devotion to facts. We shall search for the answer by employing one of the basic principles of this book: We shall ask a few storytellers to provide the answer as we examine their work. We begin with John Galsworthy.

Quality

JOHN GALSWORTHY
1867–1933

I knew him from the days of my extreme youth, because he made my father's boots; inhabiting with his elder brother two little shops let into one, in a small by-street—now no more, but then most fashionably placed in the West End.

That tenement had a certain quiet distinction; there was no sign upon its face that he made for any of the Royal Family—merely his own German name of Gessler Brothers; and in the window a few pairs of boots. I remember that it always troubled me to account for those unvarying boots in the window, for he made only what was ordered, reaching nothing down, and it seemed so inconceivable that what he made could ever have failed to fit. Had he bought them to put there? That, too, seemed inconceivable. He would never have tolerated in his house leather on which he had not worked himself. Besides, they were too beautiful—the pair of pumps, so inexpressibly slim, the patent leathers with cloth tops, making water come into one's mouth, the tall brown riding-boots with marvellous sooty glow, as if, though new, they had been worn a hundred years. Those pairs could only have been made by one who saw before him the Soul of Boot—so truly were they prototypes incarnating the very spirit of all footgear. These thoughts, of course, came to me later, though even when I was promoted to him, at the age of perhaps fourteen, some inkling haunted me of the dignity of himself and brother. For to make boots—such boots as he made—seemed to me then, and still seems to me, mysterious and wonderful.

I remember well my shy remark, one day, while stretching out to him my youthful foot:

"Isn't it awfully hard to do, Mr. Gessler?"

And his answer, given with a sudden smile from out of the sardonic redness of his beard: "Id is an Ardt!"

Himself, he was a little as if made from leather, with his yellow crinkly face, and crinkly reddish hair and beard, and neat folds slanting down his cheeks to the corners of his mouth, and his guttural and one-toned voice; for leather is a sardonic substance, and stiff and slow of purpose. And that was the character of his face, save that his eyes, which were grey-blue, had in them the simple gravity of one secretly possessed by the Ideal. His elder brother was so very like him—though watery, paler in every way, with a great industry—that sometimes in early days I was not quite sure of him until the interview was over. Then I knew that it was he, if the words, "I will ask my brudder," had not been spoken; and that, if they had, it was his elder brother.

When one grew old and wild and ran up bills, one somehow never ran them up with Gessler Brothers. It would not have seemed becoming to go in there and stretch out one's foot to that blue iron-spectacled glance, owing him for more than—say—two pairs, just the comfortable reassurance that one was still his client.

For it was not possible to go to him very often—his boots lasted terribly, having something beyond the temporary—some, as it were, essence of boot stitched into them.

One went in, not as into most shops, in the mood of: "Please serve me, and let me go!" but restfully, as one enters a church; and, sitting on the single wooden chair, waited—for there was never anybody there. Soon, over the top edge of that sort of well—rather dark, and smelling soothingly of leather—which formed the shop, there would be seen his face, or that of his elder brother, peering down. A guttural sound, and the tip-tap of bast slippers beating the narrow wooden stairs, and he would stand before one without coat, a little bent, in leather apron, with sleeves turned back, blinking—as if awakened from some dream of boots, or like an owl surprised in daylight and annoyed at this interruption.

And I would say: "How do you do, Mr. Gessler? Could you make me a pair of Russia leather boots?"

Without a word he would leave me, retiring whence he came, or into the other portion of the shop, and I would continue to rest in the wooden chair, inhaling the incense of his trade. Soon he would come back, holding in his thin, veined hand a piece of gold-brown leather. With eyes fixed on it, he would remark: "What a beautiful biece!" When I, too, had admired it, he would speak again. "When do you wand dem?" And I would answer: "Oh! As soon as you conveniently can." And he would say: "To-morrow fordnighd?" Or if he were his elder brother: "I will ask my brudder!"

Then I would murmur: "Thank you! Good-morning, Mr. Gessler." "Goot-morning!" he would reply, still looking at the leather in his hand. And as I moved to the door, I would hear the tip-tap of his bast slippers restoring him,

up the stairs, to his dream of boots. But if it were some new kind of footgear that he had not yet made me, then indeed he would observe ceremony—divesting me of my boot and holding it long in his hand, looking at it with eyes at once critical and loving, as if recalling the glow with which he had created it, and rebuking the way in which one had disorganized this masterpiece. Then, placing my foot on a piece of paper, he would two or three times tickle the outer edges with a pencil and pass his nervous fingers over my toes, feeling himself into the heart of my requirements.

I cannot forget that day on which I had occasion to say to him: "Mr. Gessler, that last pair of town walking-boots creaked, you know."

He looked at me for a time without replying, as if expecting me to withdraw or qualify the statement, then said:

"Id shouldn'd 'ave greaked."

"It did, I'm afraid."

"You goddem wed before dey found demselves?"

"I don't think so."

At that he lowered his eyes, as if hunting for memory of those boots, and I felt sorry I had mentioned this grave thing.

"Zend dem back!" he said; "I will look at dem."

A feeling of compassion for my creaking boots surged up in me, so well could I imagine the sorrowful long curiosity of regard which he would bend on them.

"Zome boods," he said slowly, "are bad from birdt. If I can do noding wid dem, I dake dem off your bill."

Once (once only) I went absently-mindedly into his shop in a pair of boots bought in an emergency at some large firm's. He took my order without showing me any leather, and I could feel his eyes penetrating the inferior integument of my foot. At last he said:

"Dose are nod my boods."

The tone was not one of anger, nor of sorrow, not even of contempt, but there was in it something quiet that froze the blood. He put his hand down and pressed a finger on the place where the left boot, endeavoring to be fashionable, was not quite comfortable.

"Id 'urds you dere," he said. "Dose big virms 'ave no self-respect. Drash!" And then, as if something had given way within him, he spoke long and bitterly. It was the only time I ever heard him discuss the conditions and hardships of his trade.

"Dey get id all," he said, "dey get id by ad-verdisement, nod by work. Dey dake it away from us, who lofe our boods. Id gomes to this— bresently I haf no work. Every year id gets less —you will see." And looking at his lined face I saw things I had never noticed before, bitter things and bitter struggle—and what a lot of grey hairs there seemed suddenly in his red beard!

As best I could, I explained the circumstances of the purchase of those ill-omened boots. But his face and voice made so deep an impression that during the next few minutes I ordered many pairs. Nemesis fell! They lasted more ter-ribly than ever. And I was not able conscien-tiously to go to him for nearly two years.

When at last I went I was surprised to find that outside one of the two little windows of his shop another name was painted, also that of a bootmaker—making, of course, for the Royal Family. The old familiar boots, no longer in dignified isolation, were huddled in the single window. Inside, the now contracted well of the one little shop was more scented and darker than ever. And it was longer than usual, too, before a face peered down, and the tip-tap of the bast slippers began. At last he stood before me, and gazing through those rusty iron spec-tacles, said:

"Mr. ——, isn'd it?"

"Ah! Mr. Gessler," I stammered, "but your boots are really *too* good, you know! See, these are quite decent still!" And I stretched out to him my foot. He looked at it.

"Yes," he said, "beople do nod wand good boods, id seems."

To get away from his reproachful eyes and voice I hastily remarked: "What have you done to your shop?"

He answered quietly: "Id was too exbensif. Do you wand some boods?"

I ordered three pairs, though I had only wanted two, and quickly left. I had, I do not know quite what feeling of being part, in his mind, of a conspiracy against him; or not per-haps so much against him as against his idea of boot. One does not, I suppose, care to feel like that; for it was again many months before my next visit to his shop, paid, I remember, with the feeling: "Oh! well, I can't leave the old boy— so here goes! Perhaps it'll be his elder brother!"

For his elder brother, I knew, had not char-acter enough to reproach me, even dumbly.

And, to my relief, in the shop there did ap-pear to be his elder brother, handling a piece of leather.

"Well, Mr. Gessler," I said, "how are you?"

He came close, and peered at me.

"I am breddy well," he said slowly, "but my elder brudder is dead."

And I saw that it was indeed himself—but how aged and wan! And never before had I heard him mention his brother. Much shocked, I murmured: "Oh! I am sorry!"

"Yes," he answered, "he was a good man, he made a good bood; but he is dead." And he touched the top of his head, where the hair had suddenly gone as thin as it had been on that of his poor brother, to indicate, I suppose, the cause of death. "He could nod ged over losing de oder shop. Do you wand any boods?" And he held up the leather in his hand: "Id's a beaudi-ful biece."

I ordered several pairs. It was very long be-fore they came—but they were better than ever. One simply could not wear them out. And soon after that I went abroad.

It was over a year before I was again in Lon-don. And the first shop I went to was my old friend's. I had left a man of sixty, I came back to one of seventy-five, pinched and worn and tremulous, who genuinely, this time, did not at first know me.

"Oh! Mr. Gessler," I said, sick at heart; "how splendid your boots are! See, I've been wearing this pair nearly all the time I've been abroad; and they're not half worn out, are they?"

He looked long at my boots—a pair of Russia leather, and his face seemed to regain steadi-ness. Putting his hand on my instep, he said:

"Do dey vid you here? I 'ad drouble wid dat bair, I remember."

I assured him that they had fitted beautifully.

"Do you wand any boods?" he said. "I can make dem quickly; id is a slack dime."

I answered: "Please, please! I want boots all round—every kind!"

"I will make a vresh model. Your food must be bigger." And with utter slowness, he traced round my foot, and felt my toes, only once look-ing up to say:

"Did I dell you my brudder was dead?"

To watch him was painful, so feeble had he grown; I was glad to get away.

I had given those boots up, when one evening they came. Opening the parcel, I set the four pairs out in a row. Then one by one I tried them on. There was no doubt about it. In shape and fit, in finish and quality of leather, they were the best he had ever made me. And in the mouth of one of the town walking-boots I found his bill. The amount was the same as usual, but it gave me quite a shock. He had never before sent it in till quarter day. I flew downstairs and wrote a cheque, and posted it at once with my own hand.

A week later, passing the little street, I thought I would go in and tell him how splendidly the new boots fitted. But when I came to where his shop had been, his name was gone. Still there, in the window, were the slim pumps, the patent leathers with cloth tops, the sooty riding boots.

I went in, very much disturbed. In the two little shops—again made into one—was a young man with an English face.

"Mr. Gessler in?" I said.

He gave me a strange, ingratiating look.

"No, sir," he said, "no. But we can attend to anything with pleasure. We've taken the shop over. You've seen our name, no doubt, next door. We make for some very good people."

"Yes, yes," I said; "but Mr. Gessler?"

"Oh!" he answered; "dead."

"Dead! But I only received these boots from him last Wednesday week."

"Ah!" he said; 'a shockin' go. Poor old man starved 'imself."

"Good God!"

"Slow starvation, the doctor called it! You see he went to work in such a way! Would keep the shop on; wouldn't have a soul touch his boots except himself. When he got an order, it took him such a time. People won't wait. He lost everybody. And there he'd sit, goin' on and on— I will say that for him—not a man in London made a better boot! But look at the competition! He never advertised! Would 'ave the best leather, too, and do it all 'imself. Well, there it is. What could you expect with his ideas?"

"But starvation—!"

"That may be a bit flowery, as the sayin' is— but I know myself he was sittin' over his boots day and night, to the very last. You see I used to watch him. Never gave 'imself time to eat; never had a penny in the house. All went in rent and leather. How he lived so long I don't know. He regular let his fire go out. He was a character. But he made good boots."

"Yes," I said, "he made good boots."

FIRST IMPRESSIONS

Perhaps our first question about this or any other story is, do we like it? Our immediate answer comes from our first impressions and can be called a *natural* response. But experience has taught us that our first impressions about life, people, and literature can be exceedingly misleading, and thoughtful men have therefore devised many ways of critically examining their impressions. To examine anything we must have a framework of ideas about its nature and function: the buyer of a used car, for example, better have a pretty sound notion of the structure of the automobile before he determines its real value. Likewise, the reader of fiction should have a sound notion of the structure and function of the short story or novel before he accepts its influence on his life. Both the buyer of a car and the reader of fiction should have a method of analysis to confirm or reject first impressions, particularly emotional ones.

The chief reason for analyzing a story is to assure us that our total reading experience has been *provided by the story*. Our analysis tests the accuracy of our response; it protects us against uncritical stock responses (p. 243); and it helps us to suspend judgment until the story is understood as a complete whole.

With the suggested method of analysis found below, we can test our first impressions of "Quality," and better still we can, in the process, be developing a method of analysis of our own. One reason, surely, for analyzing literature is finally to make every reader his own qualified critic.

THE BASIC QUESTION

We can begin our exploration, or analysis, of Galsworthy's story by asking the question, what happens to whom and why? This question directs our attention to the fundamental matters of fiction. *What happens?* asks for a consideration of *plot,* or the structure of action; *to whom?* asks for a consideration of the *characters;* and *why?* requires us to investigate the story's *theme* which controls and shapes the meaning of the characters' action. To keep this basic question constantly in mind will show us how Galsworthy has worked to achieve his final meaning, and of course that meaning is precisely what we are after.

THE FACTS OF THE STORY

To think clearly about the story we must first have a firm command of the facts of the story—we must know what happens to whom on the literal level. Unless the literal facts of the story are clearly understood before further analysis begins, we are likely to misconstrue the story's total meaning. This book will repeatedly emphasize this principle because its violation misinterprets imaginative literature. At the moment we shall postpone asking why these things happened to the Gessler brothers—let us take one thing at a time to be sure of our ground. The facts of the story can be stated as follows.

For many years Gessler Brothers had made and sold boots in "two little shops let into one," a tenement which had "a certain quiet distinction." Because the younger brother dealt with the customers, it is through him that we see the character and integrity of these brothers as men and bootmakers. For him the making of boots was an ideal and an art, and the boots were therefore both utilitarian and aesthetic masterpieces. They "lasted terribly" long, and their beauty was "mysterious and wonderful."

But now the big firms of bootmakers were diminishing Gesslers' trade by advertising,

according to the younger brother, and not by good work. They were forced to abandon one of their two shops to another bootmaker who represented the new regime of advertising and quick service. This blow brought death to the elder brother, but the younger brother doggedly refused to meet the new "competition" and continued to use the best leather and to produce boots of supreme quality. He finally died of "slow starvation" and his shop was taken over by his brisk competitor. It is significant that the last boots he made immediately before his death were, according to the narrator, "the best he had ever made me."

The basic facts of any story may be made more manageable by the use of a device called an *action line* (see the chart at page bottom) which clearly shows their sequence.

The account of the facts of the story, which resembles a newspaper notice of the troubles and failure of Gessler Brothers, is known as a *paraphrase* on the literal level. But in making the paraphrase we have raised some questions. Unless Galsworthy's story means more than the paraphrase includes, does the story deserve further consideration? The paraphrase has omitted a good deal, and we sense that the real meaning will be found in these omissions. Why has Galsworthy caused these facts to move in this sequence? What is Galsworthy's *attitude* toward the failure of the Gessler brothers? In short, to know the *surface* action is not enough: what is the *symbolic* action, or the artistic truth of the story—the kind of truth we contemplated in "General Preliminaries"?

WARNINGS

Because no single method of analysis will reveal the meaning of all stories, each one must be attacked on its own grounds and interpreted within its own terms of construction. There are, of course, certain principles of fiction which do

For years Gessler Brothers had made fine boots. For	Big firms now furnish new competition.	They give up part of their shop to a new firm.	Surviving Gessler refuses	He dies of slow
them bootmaking was an art.	Gesslers' trade is diminished.	Elder Gessler dies of the blow.	to compromise his art.	starvation.

remain constant, but even these must be applied with tact and discrimination by the reader as interpreter. We should greet with skepticism such dogmatic doctrines as, "All stories must have a plot," or "The conflicts in stories must always be resolved," or "Virtue should always be rewarded, and evil punished." We may finally accept such doctrines, but we must not begin with them. Let us begin by discussing a story. Let us look first for the basic devices by which Galsworthy has transformed the facts of his story into a piece of fictional art with meaning.

Like other writers of fiction, Galsworthy has created his own characters, placed them on his own fictional stage, and caused them to act to some purpose. But in doing so he was forced to make some decisions which can be found embodied in his story. If we can locate these decisions and determine *why* he made them, the meaning of the story should become clear.

Suppose we try to get at the matter this way: if we were to set up a motion-picture camera on a busy, city-street intersection and shoot the scene for half an hour, we would have a documentary film, but no art. Why? Because the action and characters would be purely accidental, without purpose, form, and specific meaning. Since Galsworthy's story does have these characteristics, we know he must have made certain decisions regarding the course his story was to take. His story was no accident.

AUTHOR'S CONTROLLING THEME

Every good story is shaped by a controlling theme, or idea. This controlling theme selects and arranges everything which goes into the story—the characters, the action, the resolution of the conflict, and anything else used by the writer to dramatize his total meaning. As we read a story, its theme is usually revealed to us by degrees as the story moves to its conclusion.

We find our first clue to Galsworthy's theme in his title: his general theme or subject is quality. But as the story unfolds, the theme becomes more sharply defined. Whose quality? How does it shape the story's action? What are its consequences in the lives of the principal characters? To answer these questions Galsworthy begins to dramatize his theme through the actions and responses of Gessler, and the story is on its way.

It is apparent that Galsworthy has written a serious story, a thoughtful interpretation of an aspect of humanity. In a serious writer such an interpretation emerges from his world view, or his philosophy of life, which is his accounting of the meaning of existence. He has therefore a scale of values, and above all he makes a distinction between quantitative and qualitative values. The artist, regardless of his medium, is deeply involved with the quality of experience. His general subject is the quality of human nature, and his evaluation of any specific human experience is his truth or, if you disagree with him, his bias. As we move on through our examination of Galsworthy's story we shall observe the influence of his scale of values, or his attitude toward the facts of the story.

THE SHAPING DEVICES OF FICTION

Plot, or the Structure of Action

We have said before that Galsworthy has created his own characters, placed them on his own stage, and caused them to act to some purpose. Here, we are especially concerned with that word *act*. Whatever else a storywriter does, he must present characters in action, an action which is designed to dramatize a fully realized theme, a situation, a character—in fact, anything the writer wishes to dramatize, or to make concrete in terms of action. This action can take more than one form: it can be violent and obvious like Othello's murder of Desdemona; it can be a lovers' embrace like Romeo and Juliet's; or it can be the inward action of lovers' affection like Queen Victoria's and Albert's. Whatever form the action takes, its function is to dramatize the event for the reader.

The word *plot* has been used to indicate almost any kind of action found in a story, including the closed plot, the open plot, and straight narrative with little or no serious complication. (For further discussion of plot, see p. 23.) Generally, whatever means is used to dramatize the writer's purpose is called plot, or the structure of action.

Most stories emphasize plot, character, or theme, and we shall later meet stories which are notable for one of the three. What of Galsworthy's "Quality"? Let us refer again to the story's action line (p. 16). Galsworthy has used a rather slight, closed plot which runs the customary course of complication, conflict, climax, and denouement (resolution). The story's external action can be described in this way: the complication appears when Gesslers' trade is diminished; the conflict appears between the Gesslers and the big firm when they lose one of their two shops; the climax arrives when the surviving Gessler can no longer make a living; and the denouement, or resolution, comes with Gessler's death and the success of the big firm. The story does depend on plot, but we see that the significant action and conflict actually lie within Gessler himself—which means that Galsworthy is using his plot to reveal character. He is doing even more: he is using plot and character to reveal his theme. The story is an excellent example, as we shall see more fully later, of how the basic elements of a story work together harmoniously to produce a significant interpretation of some phase of life.

Before leaving this matter of plot, we can profitably clarify the uses of the word *dramatic*. It can mean one of three things. One sense of the word has been implied directly above: it is used to make a distinction between the essay which presents abstract ideas and the story which presents a theme concretely through characters in action. Students often refer to Professor ——who dramatizes his ideas in the classroom, meaning that he illustrates the sense of his abstract ideas with concrete examples in action. All stories by their very nature have this kind of dramatic quality. The word *dramatic* is used also to mean the dramatic method used in a scene where characters present themselves with their own words. Hemingway's "A Clean, Well-Lighted Place" (p. 42) uses the dramatic scene almost exclusively. And finally, the word is used to indicate the tension created by the conflict of the characters in action. The action is dramatic, we say, when we are stirred emotionally and suspended in a state of expectancy.

Character

We return once more to our statement that Galsworthy has created his characters and has caused them to act to some purpose. This time we are especially interested in that word *character*. The nature and use of characters in any story are determined by the purpose of the writer.

Galsworthy presents a conflict over quality, and his characters therefore represent in one way or another the terms of the conflict. This conflict, as we have seen, is both external and internal: external, between Gessler Brothers and the big firm; and internal, within the younger Gessler himself. The external conflict could have been represented by type characters only but, because Galsworthy chose to dramatize an inner conflict as well, at least one character must be individualized to make the inner conflict understandable and credible.

In a serious story like Galsworthy's one of the uses of character is to dramatize the moral choices made by the author. When Gessler is faced with a declining trade, he is forced to make a decision. Shall he maintain his ideal of making boots or shall he cheapen his product and meet the new competition? Gessler has uncommon personal integrity and his boots must not represent merely a price on the open market; they must represent him as a workman. His boots in a very real sense are Gessler. Gessler's choice must therefore be basically a moral choice, not merely a profit-and-loss choice. Galsworthy has created a character who is required by his very nature to make the moral choice he made. That is, the choice is motivated by the created character, which means, of course, that Galsworthy made the choice when he created Gessler who helps to dramatize Galsworthy's theme. We have here a concrete example of what is meant by the parts of a story working harmoniously to reveal meaning,

Any story's credibility depends on the consistency of each one of its characters. This is more true of the short story than of the novel because there is rarely time enough in the former to permit the development of, or changes in, characters. Once Galsworthy has defined the terms of the conflict over quality and has established the meaning or temper of each character, the action moves to its inevitable conclusion. Suppose that Gessler had compromised his art and had met the new competition. Would that action have been inevitable or credible? Had he done so, the story's structure would have collapsed.

Symbolism

As we continue to penetrate beneath the surface of Galsworthy's story we see that the meaning of his symbolism must not escape us. His basic symbols are his characters, the finished boots, and even the raw leather itself. In fact, Gessler, his boots, and his leather are actually a compound symbol which stands for an uncompromising ideal. Speaking of the boots on display in Gessler's window, Galsworthy says,

> Those pairs could only have been made by one who saw before him the Soul of Boot— so truly were they prototypes incarnating the very spirit of all footgear.

This is a reference, of course, to Plato's idealism, and Galsworthy is saying in effect that Gessler attempted to make copies of the Ideal Boot. If we recall Matthew Arnold's saying that culture is *a study of perfection,* Gessler becomes a symbol of a rich philosophical and literary tradition. When a character is used as a symbol, regardless of how much of an individual he may be, he represents more than himself, and in that more lie the richness and universality of the story. The truth of this statement will be demonstrated when we discuss the full, or symbolic, meaning of "Quality."

Narrator's Point of View: Who Shall Tell the Story?

To make the story credible as fiction the author must establish some authority outside himself who will objectify and make a representative truth of the author's theme or personal bias. The author must disentangle himself from the web of his personal experience and not permit his personality to stand between the representative truth (p. 7) of the story and the reader. Writers have devised ways of establishing an authority outside themselves, one of which is to create a narrator whose point of view controls the entire story. What he knows, sees, and feels dominates everything. The "I" in a story may, of course, be the author, but nevertheless the author must make it appear as if the "I" were the authority for the story.

Galsworthy has used a first-person narrator who speaks in the past tense and who tells only what he has seen and experienced. Because he says in effect, "I saw it all," this point of view carries a good deal of authority. And by confronting us with a witness, Galsworthy helps to achieve his illusion of reality.

This witness has observed the Gessler broth-ers since his boyhood. He first bought boots from them "at the age of perhaps fourteen," and years later saw them defeated and disappear in death. Moreover, he seems to be sensitive to human values, and he understands the ideal which motivates Gessler. Could Galsworthy's credibility and the illusion of reality have been so convincingly achieved by another kind of narrator? Suppose the "young man with the English face" had told the story? Or the president of the "big firm"? To tell so much with so few words apparently required a visible witness whose authority is implicit in his presence and his basic understanding of Gessler.

Panorama and Scene

The narrator's point of view focuses our attention on whatever the author wishes us to hear and see. Joseph Conrad has said, "My task which I am trying to achieve is, by the power of the written word to make you hear, to make you feel —it is, before all, to make you *see.*" To make us see, most writers of fiction use a blend of panorama and scene. Panorama gives us the comprehensive, extensive view, and scene gives us the close-up, or intensive view. Henry James calls them *pictorial* and *picture.* The movies use these two views constantly to focus our attention one way or the other.

The *panoramic* view is usually presented through exposition and description, and it greatly helps to establish the atmosphere and tone (see p. 21) of the story. Here are Galsworthy's opening sentences:

> I knew him from the days of my extreme youth, because he made my father's boots; inhabiting with his elder brother two little shops let into one; in a small by-street—now no more, but then most fashionably placed in the West End.
> That tenement had a certain quiet distinction; there was no sign upon its face that he made for any of the Royal Family— merely his own German name of Gessler Brothers; and in the window a few pairs of boots. . . . Had he bought them to put there? . . . He would never have tolerated in his house leather on which he had not worked himself.

The focus here is comprehensive: The West End of London, the street, the two shops, the window, the shoes, and finally a suggestion of the character of the younger brother. This description of the Gesslers' environment does at least three things almost simultaneously: it describes the Gesslers' character; it establishes the tone of the story—Galsworthy's attitude toward the facts of the story; and it establishes the authority of the narrator. These three things together help to create the atmosphere which will guide our interpretation of every character and action to follow.

When we are to meet Gessler face to face, the narrator shifts the focus from panorama to scene:

> I remember well my shy remark, one day, while stretching out to him my youthful foot:
> "Isn't it awfully hard to do, Mr. Gessler?"
> And his answer, given with a sudden smile from out of the sardonic redness of his beard: "Id is an Ardt!"

The focus here is the close-up, like the focus of a scene in drama. Through dialogue the characters present and interpret themselves with little or no comment by the narrator. Galsworthy uses dialogue and scene whenever he wishes us to feel and hear the intense quality of Gessler's idealism and his scorn for shoddy workmanship. Examining a pair of boots made by a large firm, Gessler reveals himself:

> "Id 'urds you dere," he said. "Dose big virms 'ave no self-respect. Drash!" And then as if something had given away within him, he spoke long and bitterly. . . .
> "Dey get id all," he said, "dey get id by **adverdisement, nod by work.**"

If the devices of panorama and scene seem to be pretty obvious, perhaps the effects achieved by them are not. Good art is usually deceivingly simple until we examine it closely.

Closely related to focus is a factor known as *aesthetic distance*, sometimes called *psychic,* or *artistic, distance*, which helps to control the intensity and kind of attention the reader is asked to give to the story, especially to its dramatic scenes (close-ups). It helps to determine how near the author should bring the reader to the scene. Art is not life: art re-creates a phase of life for a specific purpose. Art selects, emphasizes, and interprets a phase of life to direct the observer's attention to it in some significant way. The question of how close the observer should be brought into the dramatic scenes of a story (or of a play) becomes very important if the author is to make the story credible—and if he fails to make it credible, all is lost (see "Credibility and the Illusion of Reality," p. 21). The good author desires the reader to participate in the story's action but not to the extent of losing himself in his emotional reaction. The reader must be able to contemplate and feel the action almost simultaneously. If the distance between him and the action is too great, he cannot participate in the feeling; if the distance is too little, he cannot contemplate the intellectual content of the action. He must neither stand off to smile at pure invention, nor must he wallow in the intense emotional experience of the characters. Aesthetic distance, in short, contributes to making a story art. A good story is not a slice of emotional life dramatized to overwhelm us, to give us "a good cry," or to violate our sensibilities as was done in one moving picture. In the final scene a character dies in childbirth, but the movie's focus was so close and detailed that some observers were forced to leave the theater before the scene ran its course. This focus was a gross violation of aesthetic distance, and the scene as art was therefore shattered. The scene did have life, but it was not credible as art. It is entirely reasonable, of course, for a writer to violate this principle to achieve some desirable effect necessary to realize his total purpose, as Shakespeare does in *King Lear* when Gloucester's eyes are plucked out. But for Shakespeare to have included this mutilation scene as a shocker and end in itself would have been artistically false.

Aesthetic distance is also the distance the author himself keeps from the action and characters in his story. He designs his form to permit the action and characters to speak for themselves, to obliterate himself as a person. Such writing is sometimes called *objective* as opposed to *subjective* writing in which the person and personality of the author are clearly apparent. Such objectivity is one of the tenets of naturalism in fiction, and is identified with the dramatic method as we see it operating in Hemingway's "A Clean, Well-Lighted Place" (p. 42). The point to be made here for our purposes is that whether aesthetic distance is used to name the distance the author himself keeps from the story's action, or to name the distance the reader is kept from the action, the result is likely to be the same: to represent life *in art,* not to reproduce life's bare actualism.

THE RESULTS OF THE SHAPING DEVICES

Credibility and the Illusion of Reality

We now return to a question asked at the beginning of this section: why do we read and take seriously, or accept as authentic, a story whose characters and action have never existed? Some answers will be suggested in this section, but one thing is incontestably clear: regardless of the writer's brilliance and depth, regardless of the dexterity used in employing the devices of fiction already mentioned, if the writer fails to make the story credible, the story will fail. Many philosophers of art (aestheticians) have made similar comments about all art. For example: "There is . . . absolutely no test of good drawing or painting except the capacity of the artist to make us believe. . . . So . . . we demand of every novel and play, every dramatic and narrative poem, that it create the semblance of reality." *

When we approach a story we must, in Coleridge's words, exercise a "willing suspension of disbelief." We do not ask, did this thing really happen? When we demand something that really happened, we go to history and biography (see "Biography: Preliminaries," p. 740). When we begin a story we suspend our skepticism of its actual, literal truth, and ask at the story's end, *could* this thing have happened? The tests for the truth of history and biography are irrelevant for the truth of fiction. This distinction has been enunciated at least since Aristotle (384–322 B.C.) observed

> that it is not the function of the poet [the imaginative writer] to relate what has happened, but what may happen,—what is possible according to the law of probability or necessity. . . . Poetry [imaginative literature], therefore, is more philosophical and a higher thing than history: for poetry tends to express the universal, history the particular . . . and it is this universality at which poetry aims. . . .
> (*Poetics,* IX, see page 890.)

* DeWitt H. Parker, *The Analysis of Art,* New Haven, Conn.: Yale University Press, 1926, p. 6.

The key words here are *probability* and *universality.* (See "General Preliminaries," p. 6, for a discussion of symbolic truth.) To dramatize some specific truth found universally in mankind or in a given civilization—not the truth of an isolated occurrence—the writer is free to be false to the actual in order to be true to the general, the universal. But in devising his fiction he must make it probable, *not* merely possible; within its own terms of construction it must be credible, believeable. The story must create the illusion of reality from beginning to end. How is this done?

How does Galsworthy do it? In many ways with many devices. By using a first-person narrator who has witnessed the actions of the Gesslers, and who has worn their boots; by confronting us with characters who present themselves in their own characteristic words; but most of all by properly motivating the actions of the characters to make the plot, or the structure of action, move to its *probable* and inevitable conclusion. That is, Galsworthy is saying, given these characters including the Gesslers in this situation according to these circumstances, it is entirely probable that this story would happen in this way.

Is all this so mysterious? Hardly. What do we mean by saying "Truth is stranger than fiction"? We simply mean that any story whose aim is universal truth based on "the law of probability or necessity" cannot rely on the strange, isolated occurrence. If the story relied on such, no sane reader would believe what happens in the story even though it could be proved true in life. We confirm the accuracy of this point of view whenever we read a newspaper account of a strange occurrence and find ourselves saying, "If it hadn't happened, I wouldn't believe it. Incredible, isn't it?" It may seem to be incredible, but it is true. In fiction, however, a situation must seem to be credible or it cannot be accepted as true.

Tone and Atmosphere

We remind ourselves again that the basic, shaping force of Galsworthy's story is his attitude toward the story's literal facts. Gessler makes fine boots; he refuses to compromise his ideal; he dies of slow starvation; the big firm takes over his shops. What does Galsworthy think of all this? Where shall we look beyond the matters already discussed above to find out? We can examine his tone and atmosphere, less tangible than plot, characters, theme, and symbolism, but perhaps the most potent and revealing of all.

In a very real sense Galsworthy's tone *is* his attitude toward the facts of the story. When someone in real life speaks, we attend not only to what he says, but also to the tone or attitude he takes toward what he is saying. In a story we listen for the tone of the author's voice in the same way. "Written words," said Joseph Conrad, "have their accent, too."

What does Galsworthy think about Gessler's ideal, and what is his attitude toward his fate? Gessler is treated with the most sensitive consideration, as if Galsworthy were exhibiting something very uncommon in the human scene. For example:

> But if it were some new kind of footgear that he had not yet made me, then indeed he would observe ceremony—divesting me of my boot and holding it long in his hand, looking at it with eyes at once critical and loving, as if recalling the glow with which he had created it, and rebuking the way in which one had disorganized this masterpiece.

In an interesting and instructive way Galsworthy has demonstrated how important it is to maintain a consistent tone throughout a story. When "Quality" was first published, the last sentence read:

> And I turned and went out quickly, for I did not want that youth to know that I could hardly see.

Later, this sentence was eliminated. Why? Apparently because it violated the story's tone by introducing sentimentality in the narrator for which there is no motivation.

Atmosphere is sometimes used to mean the setting of a story, or the physical environment in which the action takes place. In many stories, including Galsworthy's, atmosphere means psychological as well as physical environment. The two opening paragraphs of Galsworthy's story provide this psychological atmosphere which gives direction to his attitudes and values.

The value of tone and atmosphere working together lies in their powerful and subtle suggestiveness. Galsworthy's tone and atmosphere come through mostly by indirection, and we know without his ever saying so that Gessler's fate is more than a personal tragedy. We feel, as we say, the enveloping tragedy, and we know it will spread, not end, with Gessler's death.

Tone is then, as we shall see again in the section on poetry, a figure of speech because it permeates the entire story and helps to interpret the symbolic action as distinguished from the mere surface action of the plot. We are now prepared to examine the symbolic action of "Quality."

The Meaning of the Story: The Parts and the Whole

The unremitting quality of Gessler Brothers moves through three actions which approximate three scenes in a one-act play. Galsworthy's attitude toward the three actions is established early by the title and the two opening paragraphs. The references to "quality," to the Gesslers' tenement that had a "certain, quiet distinction," and to "those unvarying boots in the window" that "could only have been made by one who saw before him the Soul of Boot," all clearly reveal Galsworthy's respect for the Gessler "Ideal."

The first action presents the Gesslers pursuing their " 'Ardt,' " exercising extreme care with their customers' needs, and at peace with their world except for the complication introduced by the new competition of the big firms. Gessler Brothers had been for years the symbol of quality and persevering workmanship. These men had fused making a *living* with making a *life*, and their boots therefore represented their intrinsic character. When they offered a pair of boots to a customer, they offered themselves. When the narrator complains about a pair that creaked, Gessler says, " 'Zome boods . . . are bad from birdt. If I can do noding wid dem, I dake dem off your bill.' " There were no written guarantees carefully modified in small print: there was only Gessler Brothers, and that was enough.

The second action presents the pivotal event, the crisis in Gessler when he is forced by the big firms to decide whether to maintain his quality or meet the new competition. For Gessler this problem is basically moral, not economic. He does not make a living with his left hand and moral decisions with his right. The whole man makes all decisions, and his decision to maintain his quality followed from his moral integrity as the night the day. He knew in advance of their coming what the consequences of his decision would be: his business would decline, it would finally fail—but he would not compromise his Ideal. The quality was maintained to the end, and the last boots he made for the narrator were "in shape and fit, in finish and quality of leather . . . the best he had ever made me."

The third action presents the resolution of the crisis, or the consequence of Gessler's decision: his economic failure, his death, and the success of the new firm that bought his shops. Perhaps the basic question to be answered is, what was defeated? Two men or what they stood for?

To answer these questions we move to the symbolic level of meaning in the story. Because Gessler refused to compromise his ideal, he won a personal, moral victory, but his death symbolizes the defeat of something larger than himself, a defeat which constitutes a tragedy more far-reaching than his personal end. His death symbolizes a blow against the preindustrial practice of combining making a living with making a life. It symbolizes an attack on the personal responsibility taken by the artisan for his work. For Gessler there was no such thing as an economic morality apart from a personal morality. Gessler symbolizes the absorption of material values by human values. (For a brief discussion of these two kinds of value, see "Human Values and the Criticism of Experience," p. 299.) The larger tragedy of the story appears when the symbol is reversed, when human values are absorbed by material values, when boots are made to sell, as Gessler himself says, " 'by advertisement, nod by work,' " instead of being a joy forever to both the maker as artist and the buyer.

Comment on Further Fictional Practices

The examination of "Quality" has not, of course, revealed all the standard devices and practices used by short-story writers, to say nothing of the many unconventional ones. Galsworthy has used the devices of first-person narrator and closed plot, but there are other kinds of narrators and plots which produce results quite different from Galsworthy's. While we review the steps already taken to analyze "Quality," we shall investigate other fictional practices as appropriate. Before we begin, one principle should be fixed in mind: *No device or practice in a story is good or bad except as its use makes it so; any device should be judged according to its effectiveness in the story.* Wharton's "Roman Fever" (p. 26) is radically different from "Quality," and to judge Wharton's story by Galsworthy's technique would be unspeakably insensitive to the entire cause-and-effect problem in fiction.

1. THE FACTS OF THE STORY. Our first step was to locate the facts of "Quality" to understand its literal level. All analysis begins there if we wish to be clearheaded about the rest of it. This act freed us to examine Galsworthy's devices, to see what he had done with the facts, to define his attitude toward them, and to discover what symbolic meaning he had derived from them. To locate the literal facts is, then, the initial step into almost any story. If the exception appears in the form of pure symbolism (see 5, p. 24), it will be revealed as an exception because in looking for the literal facts we shall find none.

2. AUTHOR'S CONTROLLING THEME. Theme has been defined as the controlling idea which has determined everything Galsworthy has done in his story. Theme may mean a definite intellectual concept, as it does in Mann's "The Infant Prodigy," or it may indicate a highly complex situation, as for example in Faulkner's "A Rose for Emily." In general, the value of a story does not lie in its theme but rather in what the writer has done with it. The same general theme of the growing pains experienced by young people is used by Flannery O'Connor and Algren, yet both stories (in this volume) develop and dramatize the theme in different ways. The theme of a story can usually be defined in a crisp abstraction, but the abstraction should never be accepted as the total meaning of a substantial story.

3. PLOT, OR THE STRUCTURE OF ACTION. Although "Quality" has a closed plot, Galsworthy uses plot chiefly to reveal character. Many other writers, however, use closed plots for other reasons. This type of plot, with its definite resolution of conflict, is usually found in mystery stories and in stories, such as Maupassant's "La Mère Sauvage," which have an obvious thesis whose truth the writer attempts to demonstrate.

The open plot has little or no resolution. Certain writers of serious stories, such as Chekhov in "On the Road," may believe that resolutions cannot be found for many of our basic conflicts; they may refuse the formula of the closed plot because they reject on philosophical grounds a finished interpretation of a complicated world.

Steinbeck rejects it in "The Chrysanthemums," and Hemingway in "A Clean, Well-Lighted Place" simply ignores it in favor of the dramatic, simple narrative. Except when a reader is looking for sheer entertainment and amusement, he has good reason to suspect a story which relies heavily on plot, especially the story with a trick ending whose plot machinery grinds audibly.

4. CHARACTER. "Quality" is a judicious blend of plot, character, and theme, but many, if not most, stories rely mainly on one of the three. Character studies such as Wright's "Bright and Morning Star" rely chiefly, of course, on fully drawn characters and very little on plot or theme.

At the other extreme, in a story predominantly of plot, the characters may be little more than types, sometimes no more than pawns, used to create suspense or horror or a situation. Likewise, sometimes in a story predominantly of theme, the characters resemble counters moved about in such a way as to prove the theme. Does Kafka's "A Hunger Artist" entirely avoid the use of characters as pawns?

There is, of course, always the middle ground, occupied, for example, by Gessler in "Quality" and by Liharev in Chekhov's "On the Road." These characters, rounded individuals, are types of humanity in the symbolic sense: they stand for groups of individuals and therefore achieve universality.

5. SYMBOLISM. Symbolism can appear almost anywhere in fiction: in characters, plots, natural objects, man-made objects, and situations. When a symbol is worked through an entire story, it can be used as an integrating device by which many facts are fused and made meaningful in some basic and comprehensive way. Characters are used to symbolize abstract ideas, as Gessler symbolizes quality, or a psychological state such as we find in Ellison's "King of the Bingo Game." As we have seen in "General Preliminaries," the symbol is in a sense the basic device of most imaginative literature.

6. NARRATOR'S POINT OF VIEW. In "Quality" the authority for telling the story is vested in the narrator by Galsworthy to convert the facts of the story into a credible, universal truth. The many kinds of narrators have been variously named and classified, but the basic kinds can perhaps be reduced to four.

First, there is the *first-person narrator*, as used by Galsworthy, who has the authority of an intimate witness, one who is himself involved in the action. In some stories the narrator is the principal character who describes with unchallenged authority his own sensations and ideas. Such a narrator can invest a story with uncommon credibility, but the device has its obvious limitations because the narrator can know and understand only what his temperament and talent permit.

Second, there is the *dramatic narrator* who effaces himself almost completely, as he does in Hemingway's "A Clean, Well-Lighted Place." This narrator resembles the playwright whose characters present themselves with little or no comment by the narrator. Modified in one way or another, this narrative device is very popular in current fiction because, perhaps, it gives the effect of impersonal objectivity and appeals to the scientific temper of our time.

Third, there is the *third-person limited narrator* who comes by his knowledge through natural means only, as he does in Maupassant's "La Mère Sauvage," Steinbeck's "The Chrysanthemums," and many others. Such a narrator is sometimes called a *roving narrator* who can be anywhere at any time except within the minds of the characters. In a sense he is omniscient with his omniscience artfully concealed.

And last, there is the *third-person omniscient narrator* who knows everything and can be at any place at any time without having to explain his presence. Such a device gives the author extraordinary flexibility, particularly because he can look into the minds of his characters and report their thoughts and sensations. Maugham's "The Colonel's Lady" uses such a narrator in a very special and effective manner.

Rarely is any one of these devices used exclusively in any single story. Salinger's "For Esmé —With Love and Squalor" deliberately uses two kinds of narrator to achieve a desired effect.

Is there a best kind of narrator? The best narrator best fulfills the purposes of the author, and we judge the efficacy of a narrator as we judge all other elements in a story—according to the consequences he produces in the story.

7. PANORAMA AND SCENE. The function of these two devices is to permit a necessary shift in focus. "Quality" uses both as appropriate to the purpose, but some stories rely on one or the other almost exclusively. The use of panorama is sometimes much more subtle than readers may

recognize, including as it does setting and atmosphere. In "The Lagoon," Conrad's panoramic use of nature becomes a method of interpreting the meaning of the story's action.

Scene, as we found in "Quality," is the focus of the close-up. Perhaps no story in this volume uses scenes quite so effectively as Chekhov's "On the Road," unless it is Hemingway's "A Clean, Well-Lighted Place." Chekhov's use of scene seems to have more depth than Hemingway's because, perhaps, his understanding of the motives of humanity is more penetrating.

8. CREDIBILITY AND THE ILLUSION OF REALITY. There are various levels of credibility, in fact, about five. "Quality" is credible on the realistic level, chiefly because the plot, characters, theme, setting, and atmosphere are all entirely probable on natural grounds. The meaning of this statement should become clearer as we examine the remaining levels.

Hughes's mixture of fantasy and realism in "On the Road" is one step removed from the realistic level.

A story like Kafka's "A Hunger Artist" is another step away from the realistic level because it veers toward, but does not seriously enter, the supernatural level.

The fourth and fifth levels of credibility are at times so closely merged in the same story as to make them appear as one level, although the use of one is possible without the other. We shall call them the symbolic and the supernatural levels. Poe's "Ligeia" (not included in this volume) is an example of the merger, an uncommonly successful one.

A story (or poem such as Eliot's "The Waste Land") which uses the symbolic level exclusively, or almost so, is incomprehensible unless the symbols are clearly understood. When symbols are used in a story told on the realistic level of credibility, they are defined by the context of the story; this is not necessarily true of a story which is credible only on the symbolic level. Such a story is credible if its theme is comprehensible and its tone consistent, but to attempt to apply the test of the realistic level to such a story is to misconceive the nature of the story's art.

9. TONE AND ATMOSPHERE. Consistency of tone and atmosphere is without question one of the basic necessities of a good story, especially if the story is satiric or ironic. If satire and irony are revealed by broad exaggeration, tone and atmosphere may seem to make only a minor contribution; but if the satire and irony are subtle and perhaps profound, consistency of tone and atmosphere is indispensable. A close study of Chekhov's "On the Road" reveals how delicately yet positively he has worked to maintain an especially consistent tone: one major slip could have reduced the story to confusion.

10. THE MEANING OF THE STORY: THE PARTS AND THE WHOLE. A reader may be acute and discriminating, but his real test centers in this area. Like any organism, the meaning of a story is always more than the sum of its parts. One of the cardinal errors in the interpretation of imaginative literature is accepting a part for the whole. The meaning of "Quality" does not lie in Gessler alone: it lies in the interaction of Gessler with everything else in the story. This principle of interpretation is often violated, and unless the principle is carefully observed, Tolstoy's "Three Deaths," for example, can be easily misinterpreted and some of the symbolism in this story may escape all except the most discriminating readers.

First, master all the facts of a story, and then determine what has been done with *all* of them. There is no short cut to the precise interpretation of fiction, poetry, or drama, but there is tremendous pleasure in mastering the approaches.

A Note on the Novel

Most of the preceding observations concerning the structure of the short story can also be applied to the novel. Although the greater length of the novel gives the reader increased responsibilities, particularly in fusing all the parts of the novel to make the complete whole of his focus and comprehension, the basic devices in both forms remain much the same. Like the short story, the novel uses the devices already discussed to transform the facts of the story into a piece of fictional art with meaning. The basic reading problem, then, is quite the same for both the short story and the novel, namely, to learn to read the forms. (See p. 209 for observations on the novella.)

What Makes a Good Story?

Fortunately, there is no single formula to guarantee excellence. Fortunately indeed, because if there were, the fascinating variety in stories would be lost, and the formula would quickly bring boredom. Some readers demand entertainment of stories; other readers demand ideas, or interesting characters, or action, plot, and suspense. All such demands are reasonable, but if a reader demands, says, suspense and finds none, the story is not necessarily a failure. Suspense would have been quite ridiculous in Galsworthy's "Quality"; indeed, he dissipated all hope for it in his opening paragraph.

In our search for excellence, we may begin with one fairly stable assumption: *We should judge all the elements in a story according to the consequences they produce in the story.* Plot, character, theme, suspense—none of these things are good or bad except as their use makes them so. All good creative writers seek to use the right means to bring the desired ends. We therefore ask of every story, has it been told well? Is it a piece of *literary art* whose technique and subject matter are fused to produce a meaningful whole? Such questions will at least reduce the temptation to condemn escape literature for its want of philosophy, and parable literature for its want of sheer entertainment. There are twenty-nine stories in this volume and twenty-nine ways of telling them. Let us begin by judging every story within its own terms of construction, within its own frame of accomplishment. Some tellings may be better than others, and we shall look to this matter as we go along. We shall look to another ingredient also, a final and indispensable matter: Having decided how well a story has been told, we shall ask about its value and its truth to humanity.

Roman Fever

EDITH WHARTON
1862–1937

Edith Wharton's "Roman Fever" differs from Galsworthy's "Quality" in many ways. Meaning in stories can be controlled and made manifest variously—through plot, character, theme, symbol, irony, tone, and so on. "Quality" is a blend of plot, character, and theme, but our analysis above has shown the basic importance to Galsworthy of theme, as the story's title indicates. "Roman Fever" is quite a different matter. Readers who look exclusively for philosophical ideas may find too few, and other readers who look for subtle character analysis may find too little, but readers who enjoy the revelation of character and theme through plot will be richly rewarded. The sudden revelation of character made credible is perhaps Wharton's chief technical achievement here.

1

From the table at which they had been lunching two American ladies of ripe but well-cared-for middle age moved across the lofty terrace of the Roman restaurant and, leaning on its parapet, looked first at each other, and then down on the outspread glories of the Palatine[1] and the Forum, with the same expression of vague but benevolent approval.

As they leaned there a girlish voice echoed up gaily from the stairs leading to the court below. "Well, come along, then," it cried, not to them but to an invisible companion, "and let's leave the young things to their knitting"; and a voice as fresh laughed back: "Oh, look here, Babs, not actually *knitting*—" "Well, I mean figuratively," rejoined the first. "After all, we haven't left our poor parents much else to do . . ." and at that point the turn of the stairs engulfed the dialogue.

The two ladies looked at each other again, this time with a tinge of smiling embarrassment, and the smaller and paler one shook her head and coloured slightly.

"Barbara!" she murmured, sending an unheard rebuke after the mocking voice in the stairway.

The other lady, who was fuller, and higher in colour, with a small determined nose supported by vigorous black eyebrows, gave a good-humoured laugh. "That's what our daughters think of us!"

Her companion replied by a deprecating gesture. "Not of us individually. We must remember that. It's just the collective modern idea of Mothers. And you see—" Half guiltily she drew

[1] Palace of the Roman Caesars.

from her handsomely mounted black handbag a twist of crimson silk run through by two fine knitting needles. "One never knows," she murmured. "The new system has certainly given us a good deal of time to kill; and sometimes I get tired just looking—even at this." Her gesture was now addressed to the stupendous scene at their feet.

The dark lady laughed again, and they both relapsed upon the view, contemplating it in silence, with a sort of diffused serenity which might have been borrowed from the spring effulgence of the Roman skies. The luncheon-hour was long past, and the two had their end of the vast terrace to themselves. At its opposite extremity a few groups, detained by a lingering look at the outspread city, were gathering up guidebooks and fumbling for tips. The last of them scattered, and the two ladies were alone on the air-washed height.

"Well, I don't see why we shouldn't just stay here," said Mrs. Slade, the lady of the high colour and energetic brows. Two derelict basket-chairs stood near, and she pushed them into the angle of the parapet, and settled herself in one, her gaze upon the Palatine. "After all, it's still the most beautiful view in the world."

"It always will be, to me," assented her friend Mrs. Ansley, with so slight a stress on the "me" that Mrs. Slade, though she noticed it, wondered if it were not merely accidental, like the random underlinings of old-fashioned letter-writers.

"Grace Ansley was always old-fashioned," she thought; and added aloud, with a retrospective smile: "It's a view we've both been familiar with for a good many years. When we first met here we were younger than our girls are now. You remember?"

"Oh, yes, I remember," murmured Mrs. Ansley, with the same undefinable stress.—"There's that head-waiter wondering," she interpolated. She was evidently far less sure than her companion of herself and of her rights in the world.

"I'll cure him of wondering," said Mrs. Slade, stretching her hand toward a bag so discreetly opulent-looking as Mrs. Ansley's. Signing to the head-waiter, she explained that she and her friend were old lovers of Rome, and would like to spend the end of the afternoon looking down on the view—that is, if it did not disturb the

service? The head-waiter, bowing over her gratuity, assured her that the ladies were most welcome, and would be still more so if they would condescend to remain for dinner. A full-moon night, they would remember. . . .

Mrs. Slade's black brows drew together, as though references to the moon were out-of-place and even unwelcome. But she smiled away her frown as the head-waiter retreated. "Well, why not? We might do worse. There's no knowing, I suppose, when the girls will be back. Do you even know back from *where*? I don't!"

Mrs. Ansley again coloured slightly. "I think those young Italian aviators we met at the Embassy invited them to fly to Tarquinia[2] for tea. I suppose they'll want to wait and fly back by moonlight."

"Moonlight—moonlight! What a part it still plays. Do you suppose they're as sentimental as we were?"

"I've come to the conclusion that I don't in the least know what they are," said Mrs. Ansley. "And perhaps we didn't know much more about each other."

"No; perhaps we didn't."

Her friend gave her a shy glance. "I never should have supposed you were sentimental, Alida."

"Well, perhaps I wasn't." Mrs. Slade drew her lids together in retrospect; and for a few moments the two ladies, who had been intimate since childhood, reflected how little they knew each other. Each one, of course, had a label ready to attach to the other's name; Mrs. Delphin Slade, for instance, would have told herself, or any one who asked her, that Mrs. Horace Ansley, twenty-five years ago, had been exquisitely lovely—no, you wouldn't believe it, would you? . . . though, of course, still charming, distinguished. . . . Well, as a girl she had been exquisite; far more beautiful than her daughter Barbara, though certainly Babs, according to the new standards at any rate, was more effective—had more *edge*, as they say. Funny where she got it, with those two nullities as parents. Yes; Horace Ansley was—well, just the duplicate of his wife. Museum specimens of old New York. Good-looking, irreproachable, ex-

[2] Town in central Italy.

emplary. Mrs. Slade and Mrs. Ansley had lived opposite each other—actually as well as figuratively—for years. When the drawing-room curtains in No. 20 East 73rd Street were renewed, No. 23, across the way, was always aware of it. And of all the movings, buyings, travels, anniversaries, illnesses—the tame chronicle of an estimable pair. Little of it escaped Mrs. Slade. But she had grown bored with it by the time her husband made his big *coup* in Wall Street, and when they bought in upper Park Avenue had already begun to think: "I'd rather live opposite a speak-easy for a change; at least one might see it raided." The idea of seeing Grace raided was so amusing that (before the move) she launched it at a woman's lunch. It made a hit, and went the rounds—she sometimes wondered if it had crossed the street, and reached Mrs. Ansley. She hoped not, but didn't much mind. Those were the days when respectability was at a discount, and it did the irreproachable no harm to laugh at them a little.

A few years later, and not many months apart, both ladies lost their husbands. There was an appropriate exchange of wreaths and condolences, and a brief renewal of intimacy in the half-shadow of their mourning; and now, after another interval, they had run across each other in Rome, at the same hotel, each of them the modest appendage of a salient daughter. The similarity of their lot had again drawn them together, lending itself to mild jokes, and the mutual confession that, if in old days it must have been tiring to "keep up" with daughters, it was now, at times, a little dull not to.

No doubt, Mrs. Slade reflected, she felt her unemployment more than poor Grace ever would. It was a big drop from being the wife of Delphin Slade to being his widow. She had always regarded herself (with a certain conjugal pride) as his equal in social gifts, as contributing her full share to the making of the exceptional couple they were: but the difference after his death was irremediable. As the wife of the famous corporation lawyer, always with an international case or two on hand, every day brought its exciting and unexpected obligation: the impromptu entertaining of eminent colleagues from abroad, the hurried dashes on legal business to London, Paris or Rome, where the entertaining was so handsomely reciprocated; the amusement of hearing in her wake: "What, that handsome woman with the good clothes and the eyes is Mrs. Slade—*the* Slade's wife? Really? Generally the wives of celebrities are such frumps."

Yes; being *the* Slade's widow was a dullish business after that. In living up to such a husband all her facilities had been engaged; now she had only her daughter to live up to, for the son who seemed to have inherited his father's gifts had died suddenly in boyhood. She had fought through that agony because her husband was there, to be helped and to help; now, after the father's death, the thought of the boy had become unbearable. There was nothing left but to mother her daughter; and dear Jenny was such a perfect daughter that she needed no excessive mothering. "Now with Babs Ansley I don't know that I *should* be so quiet," Mrs. Slade sometimes half-enviously reflected; but Jenny, who was younger than her brilliant friend, was that rare accident, an extremely pretty girl who somehow made youth and prettiness seem as safe as their absence. It was all perplexing—and to Mrs. Slade a little boring. She wished that Jenny would fall in love—with the wrong man, even; that she might have to be watched, outmanoeuvred, rescued. And instead, it was Jenny who watched her mother, kept her out of draughts, made sure that she had taken her tonic. . . .

Mrs. Ansley was much less articulate than her friend, and her mental portrait of Mrs. Slade was slighter, and drawn with fainter touches. "Alida Slade's awfully brilliant; but not as brilliant as she thinks," would have summed it up; though she would have added, for the enlightenment of strangers, that Mrs. Slade had been an extremely dashing girl; much more so than her daughter, who was pretty, of course, and clever in a way, but had none of her mother's—well, "vividness," some one had once called it. Mrs. Ansley would take up current words like this, and cite them in quotation marks, as unheard-of audacities. No; Jenny was not like her mother. Sometimes Mrs. Ansley thought Alida Slade was disappointed; on the whole she had had a sad life. Full of failures and mistakes; Mrs. Ansley had always been rather sorry for her. . . .

So these two ladies visualized each other, each through the wrong end of her little telescope.

2

For a long time they continued to sit side by side without speaking. It seemed as though, to both, there was a relief in laying down their somewhat futile activities in the presence of the vast Memento Mori[3] which faced them. Mrs. Slade sat quite still, her eyes fixed on the golden slope of the Palace of the Caesars, and after a while Mrs. Ansley ceased to fidget with her bag, and she too sank into meditation. Like many intimate friends, the two ladies had never before had occasion to be silent together, and Mrs. Ansley was slightly embarrassed by what seemed, after so many years, a new stage in their intimacy, and one with which she did not yet know how to deal.

Suddenly the air was full of that deep clangour of bells which periodically covers Rome with a roof of silver. Mrs. Slade glanced at her wristwatch. "Five o'clock already," she said, as though surprised.

Mrs. Ansley suggested interrogatively: "There's bridge at the Embassy at five." For a long time Mrs. Slade did not answer. She appeared to be lost in contemplation, and Mrs. Ansley thought the remark had escaped her. But after a while she said, as if speaking out of a dream: "Bridge, did you say? Not unless you want to. . . . But I don't think I will, you know."

"Oh, no," Mrs. Ansley hastened to assure her. "I don't care to at all. It's so lovely here; and so full of old memories, as you say." She settled herself in her chair, and almost furtively drew forth her knitting. Mrs. Slade took sideway note of this activity, but her own beautifully cared-for hands remained motionless on her knee.

"I was just thinking," she said slowly, "what different things Rome stands for to each generation of travellers. To our grandmothers, Roman fever; to our mothers, sentimental dangers—how we used to be guarded!—to our daughters, no more dangers than the middle of Main Street. They don't know it—but how much they're missing!"

The long golden light was beginning to pale, and Mrs. Ansley lifted her knitting a little closer to her eyes. "Yes; how we were guarded!"

"I always used to think," Mrs. Slade continued, "that our mothers had a much more difficult job than our grandmothers. When Roman fever stalked the streets it must have been comparatively easy to gather in the girls at the danger hour; but when you and I were young, with such beauty calling us, and the spice of disobedience thrown in, and no worse risk than catching cold during the cool hour after sunset, the mothers used to be put to it to keep us in—didn't they?"

She turned again toward Mrs. Ansley, but the latter had reached a delicate point in her knitting. "One, two, three—slip two; yes, they must have been," she assented, without looking up.

Mrs. Slade's eyes rested on her with a deepened attention. "She can knit—in the face of *this!* How like her. . . ."

Mrs. Slade leaned back, brooding, her eyes ranging from the ruins which faced her to the long green hollow of the Forum, the fading glow of the church fronts beyond it, and the outlying immensity of the Colosseum. Suddenly she thought: "It's all very well to say that our girls have done away with sentiment and moonlight. But if Babs Ansley isn't out to catch that young aviator—the one who's a Marchese—then I don't know anything. And Jenny has no chance beside her. I know that too. I wonder if that's why Grace Ansley likes the two girls to go everywhere together? My poor Jenny as a foil—!" Mrs. Slade gave a hardly audible laugh, and at the sound Mrs. Ansley dropped her knitting.

"Yes?"

"I—oh, nothing. I was only thinking how your Babs carries everything before her. That Campolieri boys is one of the best matches in Rome. Don't look so innocent, my dear—you know he is. And I was wondering, ever so respectfully, you understand . . . wondering how two such exemplary characters as you and Horace had managed to produce anything quite so dynamic." Mrs. Slade laughed again, with a touch of asperity.

Mrs. Ansley's hands lay inert across her needles. She looked straight out at the great accumulated wreckage of passion and splendour at her feet. But her small profile was almost expressionless. At length she said: "I think you overrate Babs, my dear."

Mrs. Slade's tone grew easier. "No; I don't. I appreciate her. And perhaps envy you. Oh, my

---

[3] An object, usually emblematic, used as a reminder of death.

girl's perfect; if I were a chronic invalid I'd—well, I think I'd rather be in Jenny's hands. There must be times . . . but there! I always wanted a brilliant daughter . . . and never quite understood why I got an angel instead."

Mrs. Ansley echoed her laugh in a faint murmur. "Babs is an angel too."

"Of course—of course! But she's got rainbow wings. Well, they're wandering by the sea with their young men; and here we sit . . . and it all brings back the past a little too acutely."

Mrs. Ansley had resumed her knitting. One might almost have imagined (if one had known her less well, Mrs. Slade reflected) that, for her also, too many memories rose from the lengthening shadows of those august ruins. But no; she was simply absorbed in her work. What was there for her to worry about? She knew that Babs would almost certainly come back engaged to the extremely eligible Campolieri. "And she'll sell the New York house, and settle down near them in Rome, and never be in their way . . . she's much too tactful. But she'll have an excellent cook, and just the right people in for bridge and cocktails . . . and a perfectly peaceful old age among her grandchildren."

Mrs. Slade broke off this prophetic flight with a recoil of self-disgust. There was no one of whom she had less right to think unkindly than of Grace Ansley. Would she never cure herself of envying her? Perhaps she had begun too long ago.

She stood up and leaned against the parapet, filling her troubled eyes with the tranquillizing magic of the hour. But instead of tranquillizing her the sight seemed to increase her exasperation. Her gaze turned toward the Colosseum. Already its golden flank was drowned in purple shadow, and above it the sky curved crystal clear, without light or colour. It was the moment when afternoon and evening hang balanced in mid-heaven.

Mrs. Slade turned back and laid her hand on her friend's arm. The gesture was so abrupt that Mrs. Ansley looked up, startled.

"The sun's set. You're not afraid, my dear?"

"Afraid—?"

"Of Roman fever or pneumonia? I remember how ill you were that winter. As a girl you had a very delicate throat, hadn't you?"

"Oh, we're all right up here. Down below, in the Forum, it does get deathly cold, all of a sudden . . . but not here."

"Ah, of course you know because you had to be so careful." Mrs. Slade turned back to the parapet. She thought: "I must make one more effort not to hate her." Aloud she said: "Whenever I look at the Forum from up here, I remember that story about a great-aunt of yours, wasn't she? A dreadfully wicked great-aunt?"

"Oh, yes; Great-aunt Harriet. The one who was supposed to have sent her young sister out to the Forum after sunset to gather a night-blooming flower for her album. All our great-aunts and grandmothers used to have albums of dried flowers."

Mrs. Slade nodded. "But she really sent her because they were in love with the same man—"

"Well, that was the family tradition. They said Aunt Harriet confessed it years afterward. At any rate, the poor little sister caught the fever and died. Mother used to frighten us with the story when we were children."

"And you frightened *me* with it, that winter when you and I were here as girls. The winter I was engaged to Delphin."

Mrs. Ansley gave a faint laugh. "Oh, did I? Really frightened you? I don't believe you're easily frightened."

"Not often; but I was then. I was easily frightened because I was too happy. I wonder if you know what that means?"

"I—yes. . . ." Mrs. Ansley faltered.

"Well, I suppose that was why the story of your wicked aunt made such an impression on me. And I thought: 'There's no more Roman fever, but the Forum is deathly cold after sunset—especially after a hot day. And the Colosseum's even colder and damper.'"

"The Colosseum—?"

"Yes. It wasn't easy to get in, after the gates were locked for the night. Far from easy. Still, in those days it could be managed; it *was* managed, often. Lovers met there who couldn't meet elsewhere. You knew that?"

"I—I daresay. I don't remember."

"You don't remember? You don't remember going to visit some ruins or other one evening, just after dark, and catching a bad chill? You were supposed to have gone to see the moon rise. People always said that expedition was what caused your illness."

There was a moment's silence; then Mrs. Ansley rejoined: "Did they? It was all so long ago."

"Yes. And you got well again—so it didn't matter. But I suppose it struck your friends—the reason given for your illness, I mean—because everybody knew you were so prudent on account of your throat, and your mother took such care of you. . . . You *had* been out late sight-seeing, hadn't you, that night?"

"Perhaps I had. The most prudent girls aren't always prudent. What made you think of it now?"

Mrs. Slade seemed to have no answer ready. But after a moment she broke out: "Because I simply can't bear it any longer—!"

Mrs. Ansley lifted her head quickly. Her eyes were wide and very pale. "Can't bear what?"

"Why—your not knowing that I've always known why you went."

"Why I went—?"

"Yes. You think I'm bluffing, don't you? Well, you went to meet the man I was engaged to—and I can repeat every word of the letter that took you there."

While Mrs. Slade spoke Mrs. Ansley had risen unsteadily to her feet. Her bag, her knitting and gloves, slid in a panic-stricken heap to the ground. She looked at Mrs. Slade as though she were looking at a ghost.

"No, no—don't," she faltered out.

"Why not? Listen, if you don't believe me. 'My one darling, things can't go on like this. I must see you alone. Come to the Colosseum immediately after dark tomorrow. There will be somebody to let you in. No one whom you need fear will suspect'—but perhaps you've forgotten what the letter said?"

Mrs. Ansley met the challenge with an unexpected composure. Steadying herself against the chair she looked at her friend, and replied: "No; I know it by heart too."

"And the signature? 'Only *your* D.S.' Was that it? I'm right, am I? That was the letter that took you out that evening after dark?"

Mrs. Ansley was still looking at her. It seemed to Mrs. Slade that a slow struggle was going on behind the voluntarily controlled mask of her small quiet face. "I shouldn't have thought _e had herself so well in hand," Mrs. Slade _cted, almost resentfully. But at this moment

Mrs. Ansley spoke. "I don't know how you knew. I burnt that letter at once."

"Yes; you would, naturally—you're so prudent!" The sneer was open now. "And if you burnt the letter you're wondering how on earth I know what was in it. That's it, isn't it?"

Mrs. Slade waited, but Mrs. Ansley did not speak.

"Well, my dear, I know what was in that letter because I wrote it!"

"You wrote it?"

"Yes."

The two women stood for a minute staring at each other in the last golden light. Then Mrs. Ansley dropped back into her chair. "Oh," she murmured, and covered her face with her hands.

Mrs. Slade waited nervously for another word or movement. None came, and at length she broke out: "I horrify you."

Mrs. Ansley's hands dropped to her knee. The face they uncovered was streaked with tears. "I wasn't thinking of you. I was thinking—it was the only letter I ever had from him!"

"And I wrote it. Yes; I wrote it! But I was the girl he was engaged to. Did you happen to remember that?"

Mrs. Ansley's head drooped again. "I'm not trying to excuse myself . . . I remembered. . . ."

"And still you went?"

"Still I went."

Mrs. Slade stood looking down on the small bowed figure at her side. The flame of her wrath had already sunk, and she wondered why she had ever thought there would be any satisfaction in inflicting so purposeless a wound on her friend. But she had to justify herself.

"You do understand? I'd found out—and I hated you, hated you. I knew you were in love with Delphin—and I was afraid; afraid of you, of your quiet ways, your sweetness . . . your . . . well, I wanted you out of the way, that's all. Just for a few weeks; just till I was sure of him. So in a blind fury I wrote that letter . . . I don't know why I'm telling you now."

"I suppose," said Mrs. Ansley slowly, "it's because you've always gone on hating me."

"Perhaps. Or because I wanted to get the whole thing off my mind." She paused. "I'm glad you destroyed the letter. Of course I never thought you'd die."

Mrs. Ansley relapsed into silence, and Mrs.

Slade, leaning above her, was conscious of a strange sense of isolation, of being cut off from the warm current of human communion. "You think me a monster!"

"I don't know. . . . It was the only letter I had, and you say he didn't write it?"

"Ah, how you care for him still!"

"I cared for the memory," said Mrs. Ansley.

Mrs. Slade continued to look down on her. She seemed physically reduced by the blow—as if, when she got up, the wind might scatter her like a puff of dust. Mrs. Slade's jealousy suddenly leapt up again at the sight. All these years the woman had been living on that letter. How she must have loved him, to treasure the mere memory of its ashes! The letter of the man her friend was engaged to. Wasn't it she who was the monster?

"You tried your best to get him away from me, didn't you? But you failed; and I kept him. That's all."

"Yes. That's all."

"I wish now I hadn't told you. I'd no idea you'd feel about it as you do; I thought you'd be amused. It all happened so long ago, as you say; and you must do me the justice to remember that I had no reason to think you'd ever taken it seriously. How could I, when you were married to Horace Ansley two months afterward? As soon as you could get out of bed your mother rushed you off to Florence and married you. People were rather surprised—they wondered at its being done so quickly; but I thought I knew. I had an idea you did it out of *pique*—to be able to say you'd got ahead of Delphin and me. Girls have such silly reasons for doing the most serious things. And your marrying so soon convinced me that you'd never really cared."

"Yes. I suppose it would," Mrs. Ansley assented.

The clear heaven overhead was emptied of all its gold. Dusk spread over it, abruptly darkening the Seven Hills. Here and there lights began to twinkle through the foliage at their feet. Steps were coming and going on the deserted terrace—waiters looking out of the doorway at the head of the stairs, then reappearing with trays and napkins and flasks of wine. Tables were moved, chairs straightened. A feeble string of electric lights flickered out. Some vases of faded flowers were carried away, and brought back replenished. A stout lady in a dustcoat suddenly appeared, asking in broken Italian if any one had seen the elastic band with her stick under the table at which she had lunched, the waiters assisting.

The corner where Mrs. Slade and Mrs. Ansley sat was still shadowy and deserted. For a long time neither of them spoke. At length Mrs. Slade began again: "I suppose I did it as a sort of joke—"

"A joke?"

"Well, girls are ferocious sometimes, you know. Girls in love especially. And I remember laughing to myself all that evening at the idea that you were waiting around there in the dark, dodging out of sight, listening for every sound, trying to get in—. Of course I was upset when I heard you were ill afterward."

Mrs. Ansley had not moved for a long time. But now she turned slowly toward her companion. "But I didn't wait. He'd arranged everything. He was there. We were let in at once," she said.

Mrs. Slade sprang up from her leaning position. "Delphin there? They let you in? Ah, now you're lying!" she burst out with violence.

Mrs. Ansley's voice grew clearer, and full of surprise. "But of course he was there. Naturally he came—"

"Came? How did he know he'd find you there? You must be raving!"

Mrs. Ansley hesitated, as though reflecting. "But I answered the letter. I told him I'd be there. So he came."

Mrs. Slade flung her hands up to her face. "Oh, God—you answered! I never thought of your answering. . . ."

"It's odd you never thought of it, if you wrote the letter."

"Yes. I was blind with rage."

Mrs. Ansley rose, and drew her fur scarf about her. "It is cold here. We'd better go. . . . I'm sorry for you," she said, as she clasped the fur about her throat.

The unexpected words sent a pang through Mrs. Slade. "Yes; we'd better go." She gathered up her bag and cloak. "I don't know why you should be sorry for me," she muttered.

Mrs. Ansley stood looking away from her toward the dusky secret mass of the Colosseum.

"Well—because I didn't have to wait that night."

Mrs. Slade gave an unquiet laugh. "Yes; I was beaten there. But I oughtn't to begrudge it to you, I suppose. At the end of all these years. After all, I had everything; I had him for twenty-five years. And you had nothing but that one letter that he didn't write."

Mrs. Ansley was again silent. At length she turned toward the door of the terrace. She took a step, and turned back, facing her companion.

"I had Barbara," she said, and began to move ahead of Mrs. Slade toward the stairway.

Comments and Questions

"Roman Fever" is in the tradition of the well-made story characterized by a highly compressed structure of action which moves to its inevitable conclusion without author comment, without interruption of any kind, and providing no more intensity than the situation will bear. Wharton has chosen a single subject and has embodied it in a dramatic situation to permit the characters to develop and speak for themselves. The resolution of the story is reserved for the final sentence, and if credibility is therefore not to be violated, the plot structure must be logically impeccable. Yet, the plot seems not to be contrived—as such plots so often are—to guarantee the final surprise. The story relies, then, on plot to reveal character, theme, and final meaning. What does Wharton accomplish with this technique?

The story, if nothing more, is good entertainment. Mrs. Ansley's triumph comes as a dramatic surprise which is itself a subtle kind of humor and delight, and we may be tempted to classify the story as escape literature, enjoyed once and then dismissed. But a little reflection may prove otherwise. There is something arresting in the story's tone—Wharton's implied attitude toward the dramatic situation of the two women. If we are delighted with the final sentence, we are sympathetic with Mrs. Ansley, as Wharton

intended us to be. But why? Hardly because our sportsmanship relishes a victory of the demure little Grace Ansley over the aggressive, self-assured Alida Slade. Surely Wharton has provided us with something more than a game—her tone tells us that.

It is often remarked that a second or third reading of a story is one test of its excellence. We may have been taken in by the excitement of the first reading; or we may have missed basic implications which give the story substantial status. As we read Wharton's story again, some statements become more arresting. Mrs. Slade to Mrs. Ansley: " 'I was wondering, ever so respectfully, you understand . . . wondering how two such exemplary characters as you and Horace had managed to produce anything quite so dynamic [as Barbara].' Mrs. Slade laughed again, with a touch of asperity." Mrs. Slade again: " 'I always wanted a brilliant daughter . . . and never quite understood why I got an angel instead.' " The serious aspect of the story appears, of course, in Mrs. Slade's self-assumed superiority over Mrs. Ansley, and yet she cannot quite endure the paradox (see "Figure and Symbol," p. 282) of Mrs. Ansley's inferiority producing the brilliant Barbara while her own superiority produces only Jenny. The story's final sentence therefore accomplishes a good deal. This revelation releases the irony (see "The Misreading of Poems," p. 240) which now envelops Mrs. Slade whose sense of superiority crashes before the real superiority of Mrs. Ansley—and the irony is compounded because Mrs. Slade, as well as the reader, experiences the irony.

1. This brief interpretation has omitted many important aspects of the story. Despite the humor found in the final sentence, the story has its measure of pathos. Consider Mrs. Slade's final speech, and then describe what her sensations must have been after the final blow.

2. Any story that relies chiefly on plot must stand or fall on the author's ability to achieve credibility. Do you find any serious flaws? Why did Mrs. Slade write the letter to Mrs. Ansley? How does Wharton make Mrs. Ansley's having Barbara credible?—does Aunt Harriet help to explain matters?

Everything That Rises Must Converge

FLANNERY O'CONNOR
1925–1964

This story provides, among other things, a challenge to one's ability to read fiction as imaginative literature, as an art. Two basic questions confront most readers. Is the title ironic? Is the race problem central to the story or only peripheral? The answers to these questions have generated a good deal of critical debate.

Because of O'Connor's multiple interests, her Southern experience and background, and her deeply religious nature and readings in theology, the meaning of her stories has become uncommonly controversial. As one sympathetic critic points out, some readers find "her as another member of the Southern Gothic School"; some "Roman Catholic critics . . . were often pleased to claim this staunch daughter of their Communion as their own especial property . . . in the tradition of 'modern Catholic writers' "; while other critics, "declining to tag Miss O'Connor with such convenient labels, and conceding her gift for the comic, expressed distaste for what seemed her undue emphasis on the grotesque . . . and the unnecessary theological intrusions into the body of her fiction." Instead of such excursions by critics into the extrinsic causes of her fiction, what she really needed, according to this critic, "was a good liberating from literary critics unwilling to grant her the primary concession, according to Henry James, due any artist—an acceptance by the reader of her *donnée*,"* or the set of assumptions upon which her fiction proceeds. That is, it is time that she be regarded first as an artist and that her stories be examined as works of art instead of as veiled religious or Southern doctrine.

The excursions into the causes of O'Connor's fiction have been plentiful as readers have looked for the meaning of "Everything That Rises Must Converge." O'Connor offers

us some help: "Justice is justice and should not be appealed to along racial lines. The problem is not abstract for the Southerner, it's concrete; he sees it in terms of persons, not races—which way of seeing does away with easy answers. I have tried to touch this subject by way of fiction only once—in a story called 'Everything That Rises Must Converge.' "**

She leaves no doubt about the kind of personal and public world Mrs. Chestny lives in as contrasted with her son Julian's personal and public world. "She lived," says the narrator, "according to the laws of her own fantasy world, outside of which [Julian] had never seen her set foot." Julian is determined to avoid her fantasy world and to come to grips with the reality of his own existence. The conflict between him and his mother brings tragedy to both of them. So the question remains, what is the nature of their "convergence"? Is it ironic or otherwise?

Her doctor had told Julian's mother that she must lose twenty pounds on account of her blood pressure, so on Wednesday nights Julian had to take her downtown on the bus for a reducing class at the Y. The reducing class was designed for working girls over fifty, who weighed from 165 to 200 pounds. His mother was one of the slimmer ones, but she said ladies did not tell their age or weight. She would not ride the buses by herself at night since they had been integrated, and because the reducing class was one of her few pleasures, necessary for her health, and *free*, she said Julian could at least put himself out to take her, considering all she did for him. Julian did not like to consider all she did for him, but every Wednesday night he braced himself and took her.

She was almost ready to go, standing before the hall mirror, putting on her hat, while he, his hands behind him, appeared pinned to the door frame, waiting like Saint Sebastian for the arrows to begin piercing him. The hat was new and had cost her seven dollars and a half. She kept saying, "Maybe I shouldn't have paid that for it. No, I shouldn't have. I'll take it off and

* Robert Drake, *Flannery O'Connor, A Critical Essay*, Grand Rapids, Mich.: William B. Eerdmans, Publisher, 1966, p. 6.

** From a letter to Sister M. Bernetta Quinn, July 27, 1963.

return it tomorrow. I shouldn't have bought it."

Julian raised his eyes to heaven. "Yes, you should have bought it," he said. "Put it on and let's go." It was a hideous hat. A purple velvet flap came down on one side of it and stood up on the other; the rest of it was green and looked like a cushion with the stuffing out. He decided it was less comical than jaunty and pathetic. Everything that gave her pleasure was small and depressed him.

She lifted the hat one more time and set it down slowly on top of her head. Two wings of gray hair protruded on either side of her florid face, but her eyes, sky-blue, were as innocent and untouched by experience as they must have been when she was ten. Were it not that she was a widow who had struggled fiercely to feed and clothe and put him through school and who was supporting him still, "until he got on his feet," she might have been a little girl that he had to take to town.

"It's all right, it's all right," he said. "Let's go." He opened the door himself and started down the walk to get her going. The sky was a dying violet and the houses stood out darkly against it, bulbous liver-colored monstrosities of a uniform ugliness though no two were alike. Since this had been a fashionable neighborhood forty years ago, his mother persisted in thinking they did well to have an apartment in it. Each house had a narrow collar of dirt around it in which sat, usually, a grubby child. Julian walked with his hands in his pockets, his head down and thrust forward and his eyes glazed with the determination to make himself completely numb during the time he would be sacrificed to her pleasure.

The door closed and he turned to find the dumpy figure, surmounted by the atrocious hat, coming toward him. "Well," she said, "you only live once and paying a little more for it, I at least won't meet myself coming and going."

"Some day I'll start making money," Julian said gloomily—he knew he never would—"and you can have one of those jokes whenever you take the fit." But first they would move. He visualized a place where the nearest neighbors would be three miles away on either side.

"I think you're doing fine," she said, drawing on her gloves. "You've only been out of school a year. Rome wasn't built in a day."

She was one of the few members of the Y reducing class who arrived in hat and gloves and who had a son who had been to college. "It takes time," she said, "and the world is in such a mess. This hat looked better on me than any of the others, though when she brought it out I said, 'Take that thing back. I wouldn't have it on my head,' and she said, 'Now wait till you see it on,' and when she put it on me, I said, 'We-ull,' and she said, 'If you ask me, that hat does something for you and you do something for the hat, and besides,' she said, 'with that hat, you won't meet yourself coming and going.'"

Julian thought he could have stood his lot better if she had been selfish, if she had been an old hag who drank and screamed at him. He walked along, saturated in depression, as if in the midst of his martyrdom he had lost his faith. Catching sight of his long, hopeless, irritated face, she stopped suddenly with a grief-stricken look, and pulled back on his arm. "Wait on me," she said. "I'm going back to the house and take this thing off and tomorrow I'm going to return it. I was out of my head. I can pay the gas bill with that seven-fifty."

He caught her arm in a vicious grip. "You are not going to take it back," he said. "I like it."

"Well," she said, "I don't think I ought . . ."

"Shut up and enjoy it," he muttered, more depressed than ever.

"With the world in the mess it's in," she said, "it's a wonder we can enjoy anything. I tell you, the bottom rail is on the top."

Julian sighed.

"Of course," she said, "if you know who you are, you can go anywhere." She said this every time he took her to the reducing class. "Most of them in it are not our kind of people," she said, "but I can be gracious to anybody. I know who I am."

"They don't give a damn for your graciousness," Julian said savagely. "Knowing who you are is good for one generation only. You haven't the foggiest idea where you stand now or who you are."

She stopped and allowed her eyes to flash at him. "I most certainly do know who I am," she said, "and if you don't know who you are, I'm ashamed of you."

"Oh hell," Julian said.

"Your great-grandfather was a former governor of this state," she said. "Your grandfather was a prosperous landowner. Your grandmother was a Godhigh."

"Will you look around you," he said tensely, "and see where you are now?" and he swept his arm jerkily out to indicate the neighborhood, which the growing darkness at least made less dingy.

"You remain what you are," she said. "Your great-grandfather had a plantation and two hundred slaves."

"There are no more slaves," he said irritably.

"They were better off when they were," she said. He groaned to see that she was off on that topic. She rolled onto it every few days like a train on an open track. He knew every stop, every junction, every swamp along the way, and knew the exact point at which her conclusion would roll majestically into the station: "It's ridiculous. It's simply not realistic. They should rise, yes, but on their own side of the fence."

"Let's skip it," Julian said.

"The ones I feel sorry for," she said, "are the ones that are half white. They're tragic."

"Will you skip it?"

"Suppose we were half white. We would certainly have mixed feelings."

"I have mixed feelings now," he groaned.

"Well let's talk about something pleasant," she said. "I remember going to Grandpa's when I was a little girl. Then the house had double stairways that went up to what was really the second floor—all the cooking was done on the first. I used to like to stay down in the kitchen on account of the way the walls smelled. I would sit with my nose pressed against the plaster and take deep breaths. Actually the place belonged to the Godhighs but your grandfather Chestny paid the mortgage and saved it for them. They were in reduced circumstances," she said, "but reduced or not, they never forgot who they were."

"Doubtless that decayed mansion reminded them," Julian muttered. He never spoke of it without contempt or thought of it without longing. He had seen it once when he was a child before it had been sold. The double stairways had rotted and been torn down. Negroes were living in it. But it remained in his mind as his mother had known it. It appeared in his dreams regularly. He would stand on the wide porch, listening to the rustle of oak leaves, then wander through the high-ceilinged hall into the parlor that opened onto it and gaze at the worn rugs and faded draperies. It occurred to him that it was he, not she, who could have appreciated it. He preferred its threadbare elegance to anything he could name and it was because of it that all the neighborhoods they had lived in had been a torment to him—whereas she had hardly known the difference. She called her insensitivity "being adjustable."

"And I remember the old darky who was my nurse, Caroline. There was no better person in the world. I've always had a great respect for my colored friends," she said. "I'd do anything in the world for them and they'd . . ."

"Will you for God's sake get off that subject?" Julian said. When he got on a bus by himself, he made it a point to sit down beside a Negro, in reparation as it were for his mother's sins.

"You're mighty touchy tonight," she said. "Do you feel all right?"

"Yes I feel all right," he said. "Now lay off."

She pursed her lips. "Well, you certainly are in a vile humor," she observed. "I just won't speak to you at all."

They had reached the bus stop. There was no bus in sight and Julian, his hands still jammed in his pockets and his head thrust forward, scowled down the empty street. The frustration of having to wait on the bus as well as ride on it began to creep up his neck like a hot hand. The presence of his mother was borne in upon him as she gave a pained sigh. He looked at her bleakly. She was holding herself very erect under the preposterous hat, wearing it like a banner of her imaginary dignity. There was in him an evil urge to break her spirit. He suddenly unloosened his tie and pulled it off and put it in his pocket.

She stiffened. "Why must you look like *that* when you take me to town?" she said. "Why must you deliberately embarrass me?"

"If you'll never learn where you are," he said, "you can at least learn where I am."

"You look like a—thug," she said.

"Then I must be one," he murmured.

"I'll just go home," she said. "I will not bother you. If you can't do a little thing like that for me . . ."

Rolling his eyes upward, he put his tie back on. "Restored to my class," he muttered. He thrust his face toward her and hissed, "True culture is in the mind, the *mind*," he said, and tapped his head, "the mind."

"It's in the heart," she said, "and in how you do things and how you do things is because of who you *are*."

"Nobody in the damn bus cares who you are."

"I care who I am," she said icily.

The lighted bus appeared on top of the next hill and as it approached, they moved out into the street to meet it. He put his hand under her elbow and hoisted her up on the creaking step. She entered with a little smile, as if she were going into a drawing room where everyone had been waiting for her. While he put in the tokens, she sat down on one of the broad front seats for three which faced the aisle. A thin woman with protruding teeth and long yellow hair was sitting on the end of it. His mother moved up beside her and left room for Julian beside herself. He sat down and looked at the floor across the aisle where a pair of thin feet in red and white canvas sandals were planted.

His mother immediately began a general conversation meant to attract anyone who felt like talking. "Can it get any hotter?" she said and removed from her purse a folding fan, black with a Japanese scene on it, which she began to flutter before her.

"I reckon it might could," the woman with the protruding teeth said, "but I know for a fact my apartment couldn't get no hotter."

"It must get the afternoon sun," his mother said. She sat forward and looked up and down the bus. It was half filled. Everybody was white. "I see we have the bus to ourselves," she said. Julian cringed.

"For a change," said the woman across the aisle, the owner of the red and white canvas sandals. "I come on one the other day and they were thick as fleas—up front and all through."

"The world is in a mess everywhere," his mother said. "I don't know how we've let it get in this fix."

"What gets my goat is all those boys from good families stealing automobile tires," the woman with the protruding teeth said. "I told my boy, I said you may not be rich but you been raised right and if I ever catch you in any such mess, they can send you on to the reformatory. Be exactly where you belong."

"Training tells," his mother said. "Is your boy in high school?"

"Ninth grade," the woman said.

"My son just finished college last year. He wants to write but he's selling typewriters until he gets started," his mother said.

The woman leaned forward and peered at Julian. He threw her such a malevolent look that she subsided against the seat. On the floor across the aisle there was an abandoned newspaper. He got up and got it and opened it out in front of him. His mother discreetly continued the conversation in a lower tone but the woman across the aisle said in a loud voice, "Well that's nice. Selling typewriters is close to writing. He can go right from one to the other."

"I tell him," his mother said, "that Rome wasn't built in a day."

Behind the newspaper Julian was withdrawing into the inner compartment of his mind where he spent most of his time. This was a kind of mental bubble in which he established himself when he could not bear to be a part of what was going on around him. From it he could see out and judge but in it he was safe from any kind of penetration from without. It was the only place where he felt free of the general idiocy of his fellows. His mother had never entered it but from it he could see her with absolute clarity.

The old lady was clever enough and he thought that if she had started from any of the right premises, more might have been expected of her. She lived according to the laws of her own fantasy world, outside of which he had never seen her set foot. The law of it was to sacrifice herself for him after she had first created the necessity to do so by making a mess of things. If he had permitted her sacrifices, it was only because her lack of foresight had made them necessary. All of her life had been a struggle to act like a Chestny without the Chestny goods, and to give him everything she thought a Chestny ought to have; but since, said she, it was fun to struggle, why complain? And when you had won, as she had won, what fun to look back on the hard times! He could not forgive her that she had enjoyed the struggle and that she thought *she* had won.

What she meant when she said she had won was that she had brought him up successfully and had sent him to college and that he had turned out so well—good looking (her teeth had gone unfilled so that his could be straightened), intelligent (he realized he was too intelligent to be a success), and with a future ahead of him (there was of course no future ahead of him). She excused his gloominess on the grounds that he was still growing up and his radical ideas on his lack of practical experience. She said he didn't yet know a thing about "life," that he hadn't even entered the real world—when already he was as disenchanted with it as a man of fifty.

The further irony of all this was that in spite of her, he had turned out so well. In spite of going to only a third-rate college, he had, on his own initiative, come out with a first-rate education; in spite of growing up dominated by a small mind, he had ended up with a large one; in spite of all her foolish views, he was free of prejudice and unafraid to face facts. Most miraculous of all, instead of being blinded by love for her as she was for him, he had cut himself emotionally free of her and could see her with complete objectivity. He was not dominated by his mother.

The bus stopped with a sudden jerk and shook him from his meditation. A woman from the back lurched forward with little steps and barely escaped falling in his newspaper as she righted herself. She got off and a large Negro got on. Julian kept his paper lowered to watch. It gave him a certain satisfaction to see injustice in daily operation. It confirmed his view that with a few exceptions there was no one worth knowing within a radius of three hundred miles. The Negro was well dressed and carried a briefcase. He looked around and then sat down on the other end of the seat where the woman with the red and white canvas sandals was sitting. He immediately unfolded a newspaper and obscured himself behind it. Julian's mother's elbow at once prodded insistently into his ribs. "Now you see why I won't ride on these busses by myself," she whispered.

The woman with the red and white canvas sandals had risen at the same time the Negro sat down and had gone further back in the bus and taken the seat of the woman who had got off. His mother leaned forward and cast her an approving look.

Julian rose, crossed the aisle, and sat down in the place of the woman with the canvas sandals. From this position, he looked serenely across at his mother. Her face had turned an angry red. He stared at her, making his eyes the eyes of a stranger. He felt his tension suddenly lift as if he had openly declared war on her.

He would have liked to get in conversation with the Negro and to talk with him about art or politics or any subject that would be above the comprehension of those around them, but the man remained entrenched behind his paper. He was either ignoring the change of seating or had never noticed it. There was no way for Julian to convey his sympathy.

His mother kept her eyes fixed reproachfully on his face. The woman with the protruding teeth was looking at him avidly as if he were a type of monster new to her.

"Do you have a light?" he asked the Negro.

Without looking away from his paper, the man reached in his pocket and handed him a packet of matches.

"Thanks," Julian said. For a moment he held the matches foolishly. A NO SMOKING sign looked down upon him from over the door. This alone would not have deterred him; he had no cigarettes. He had quit smoking some months before because he could not afford it. "Sorry," he muttered and handed back the matches. The Negro lowered the paper and gave him an annoyed look. He took the matches and raised the paper again.

His mother continued to gaze at him but she did not take advantage of his momentary discomfort. Her eyes retained their battered look. Her face seemed to be unnaturally red, as if her blood pressure had risen. Julian allowed no glimmer of sympathy to show on his face. Having got the advantage, he wanted desperately to keep it and carry it through. He would have liked to teach her a lesson that would last her a while, but there seemed no way to continue the point. The Negro refused to come out from behind his paper.

Julian folded his arms and looked stolidly before him, facing her but as if he did not see her, as if he had ceased to recognize her existence. He visualized a scene in which, the bus having reached their stop, he would remain in his seat and when she said, "Aren't you going to get off?" he would look at her as at a stranger who had rashly addressed him. The corner they got off on was usually deserted, but it was well lighted and it would not hurt her to walk by herself the four blocks to the Y. He decided to wait until the time came and then decide whether or not he would let her get off by herself. He would have to be at the Y at ten to bring her back, but he could leave her wondering if he was going to show up. There was no reason for her to think she could always depend on him.

He retired again into the high-ceilinged room sparsely settled with large pieces of antique furniture. His soul expanded momentarily but then he became aware of his mother across from him and the vision shriveled. He studied her coldly. Her feet in little pumps dangled like a child's and did not quite reach the floor. She was training on him an exaggerated look of reproach. He felt completely detached from her. At that moment he could with pleasure have slapped her as he would have slapped a particularly obnoxious child in his charge.

He began to imagine various unlikely ways by which he could teach her a lesson. He might make friends with some distinguished Negro professor or lawyer and bring him home to spend the evening. He would be entirely justified but her blood pressure would rise to 300. He could not push her to the extent of making her have a stroke, and moreover, he had never been successful at making any Negro friends. He had tried to strike up an acquaintance on the bus with some of the better types, with ones that looked like professors or ministers or lawyers. One morning he had sat down next to a distinguished-looking dark brown man who had answered his questions with a sonorous solemnity but who had turned out to be an undertaker. Another day he had sat down beside a cigar-smoking Negro with a diamond ring on his finger, but after a few stilted pleasantries, the Negro had rung the buzzer and risen, slipping two lottery tickets into Julian's hand as he climbed over him to leave.

He imagined his mother lying desperately ill and his being able to secure only a Negro doctor for her. He toyed with that idea for a few minutes and then dropped it for a momentary vision of himself participating as a sympathizer in a sit-in demonstration. This was possible but he did not linger with it. Instead, he approached the ultimate horror. He brought home a beautiful suspiciously Negroid woman. Prepare yourself, he said. There is nothing you can do about it. This is the woman I've chosen. She's intelligent, dignified, even good, and she's suffered and she hasn't thought it *fun*. Now persecute us, go ahead and persecute us. Drive her out of here, but remember, you're driving me too. His eyes were narrowed and through the indignation he had generated, he saw his mother across the aisle, purple-faced, shrunken to the dwarf-like proportions of her moral nature, sitting like a mummy beneath the ridiculous banner of her hat.

He was tilted out of his fantasy again as the bus stopped. The door opened with a sucking hiss and out of the dark a large, gaily dressed, sullen-looking colored woman got on with a little boy. The child, who might have been four, had on a short plaid suit and a Tyrolean hat with a blue feather in it. Julian hoped that he would sit down beside him and that the woman would push in beside his mother. He could think of no better arrangement.

As she waited for her tokens, the woman was surveying the seating possibilities—he hoped with the idea of sitting where she was least wanted. There was something familiar-looking about her but Julian could not place what it was. She was a giant of a woman. Her face was set not only to meet opposition but to seek it out. The downward tilt of her large lower lip was like a warning sign: DON'T TAMPER WITH ME. Her bulging figure was encased in a green crepe dress and her feet overflowed in red shoes. She had on a hideous hat. A purple velvet flap came down on one side of it and stood up on the other; the rest of it was green and looked like a cushion with the stuffing out. She carried a mammoth red pocketbook that bulged throughout as if it were stuffed with rocks.

To Julian's disappointment, the little boy climbed up on the empty seat beside his mother. His mother lumped all children, black and white, into the common category, "cute," and she thought little Negroes were on the whole cuter than little white children. She smiled at the little boy as he climbed on the seat.

Meanwhile the woman was bearing down upon the empty seat beside Julian. To his annoyance, she squeezed herself into it. He saw his mother's face change as the woman settled herself next to him and he realized with satisfaction that this was more objectionable to her than it was to him. Her face seemed almost gray and there was a look of dull recognition in her eyes, as if suddenly she had sickened at some awful confrontation. Julian saw that it was because she and the woman had, in a sense, swapped sons. Though his mother would not realize the symbolic significance of this, she would feel it. His amusement showed plainly on his face.

The woman next to him muttered something unintelligible to herself. He was conscious of a kind of bristling next to him, a muted growling like that of an angry cat. He could not see anything but the red pocketbook upright on the bulging green thighs. He visualized the woman as she had stood waiting for her tokens—the ponderous figure, rising from the red shoes upward over the solid hips, the mammoth bosom, the haughty face, to the green and purple hat.

His eyes widened.

The vision of the two hats, identical, broke upon him with the radiance of a brilliant sunrise. His face was suddenly lit with joy. He could not believe that Fate had thrust upon his mother such a lesson. He gave a loud chuckle so that she would look at him and see that he saw. She turned her eyes on him slowly. The blue in them seemed to have turned a bruised purple. For a moment he had an uncomfortable sense of her innocence, but it lasted only a second before principle rescued him. Justice entitled him to laugh. His grin hardened until it said to her as plainly as if he were saying aloud: Your punishment exactly fits your pettiness. This should teach you a permanent lesson.

Her eyes shifted to the woman. She seemed unable to bear looking at him and to find the woman preferable. He became conscious again of the bristling presence at his side. The woman was rumbling like a volcano about to become active. His mother's mouth began to twitch slightly at one corner. With a sinking heart, he saw incipient signs of recovery on her face and realized that this was going to strike her suddenly as funny and was going to be no lesson at all. She kept her eyes on the woman and an amused smile came over her face as if the

woman were a monkey that had stolen her hat. The little Negro was looking up at her with large fascinated eyes. He had been trying to attract her attention for some time.

"Carver!" the woman said suddenly. "Come heah!"

When he saw that the spotlight was on him at last, Carver drew his feet up and turned himself toward Julian's mother and giggled.

"Carver!" the woman said. "You heah me? Come heah!"

Carver slid down from the seat but remained squatting with his back against the base of it, his head turned slyly around toward Julian's mother, who was smiling at him. The woman reached a hand across the aisle and snatched him to her. He righted himself and hung backwards on her knees, grinning at Julian's mother. "Isn't he cute?" Julian's mother said to the woman with the protruding teeth.

"I reckon he is," the woman said without conviction.

The Negress yanked him upright but he eased out of her grip and shot across the aisle and scrambled, giggling wildly, onto the seat beside his love.

"I think he likes me," Julian's mother said, and smiled at the woman. It was the smile she used when she was being particularly gracious to an inferior. Julian saw everything lost. The lesson had rolled off her like rain on a roof.

The woman stood up and yanked the little boy off the seat as if she were snatching him from contagion. Julian could feel the rage in her at having no weapon like his mother's smile. She gave the child a sharp slap across his leg. He howled once and then thrust his head into her stomach and kicked his feet against her shins. "Be-have," she said vehemently.

The bus stopped and the Negro who had been reading the newspaper got off. The woman moved over and set the little boy down with a thump between herself and Julian. She held him firmly by the knee. In a moment he put his hands in front of his face and peeped at Julian's mother through his fingers.

"I see yoooooooo!" she said and put her hand in front of her face and peeped at him.

The woman slapped his hand down. "Quit yo' foolishness," she said, "before I knock the living Jesus out of you!"

Julian was thankful that the next stop was theirs. He reached up and pulled the cord. The woman reached up and pulled it at the same time. Oh my God, he thought. He had the terrible intuition that when they got off the bus together, his mother would open her purse and give the little boy a nickel. The gesture would be as natural to her as breathing. The bus stopped and the woman got up and lunged to the front, dragging the child, who wished to stay on, after her. Julian and his mother got up and followed. As they neared the door, Julian tried to relieve her of her pocketbook.

"No," she murmured, "I want to give the little boy a nickel."

"No!" Julian hissed. "No!"

She smiled down at the child and opened her bag. The bus door opened and the woman picked him up by the arm and descended with him, hanging at her hip. Once in the street she set him down and shook him.

Julian's mother had to close her purse while she got down the bus step but as soon as her feet were on the ground, she opened it again and began to rummage inside. "I can't find but a penny," she whispered, "but it looks like a new one."

"Don't do it!" Julian said fiercely between his teeth. There was a streetlight on the corner and she hurried to get under it so that she could better see into her pocketbook. The woman was heading off rapidly down the street with the child still hanging backward on her hand.

"Oh little boy!" Julian's mother called and took a few quick steps and caught up with them just beyond the lamppost. "Here's a bright new penny for you," and she held out the coin, which shone bronze in the dim light.

The huge woman turned and for a moment stood, her shoulders lifted and her face frozen with frustrated rage, and stared at Julian's mother. Then all at once she seemed to explode like a piece of machinery that had been given one ounce of pressure too much. Julian saw the black fist swing out with the red pocketbook. He shut his eyes and cringed as he heard the woman shout, "He don't take nobody's pennies!" When he opened his eyes, the woman was disappearing down the street with the little boy staring wide-eyed over her shoulder. Julian's mother was sitting on the sidewalk.

"I told you not to do that," Julian said angrily. "I told you not to do that!"

He stood over her for a minute, gritting his teeth. Her legs were stretched out in front of her and her hat was on her lap. He squatted down and looked her in the face. It was totally expressionless. "You got exactly what you deserved," he said. "Now get up."

He picked up her pocketbook and put what had fallen out back in it. He picked the hat up off her lap. The penny caught his eye on the sidewalk and he picked that up and let it drop before her eyes into the purse. Then he stood up and leaned over and held his hands out to pull her up. She remained immobile. He sighed. Rising above them on either side were black apartment buildings, marked with irregular rectangles of light. At the end of the block a man came out of a door and walked off in the opposite direction. "All right," he said, "suppose somebody happens by and wants to know why you're sitting on the sidewalk?"

She took the hand and, breathing hard, pulled heavily up on it and then stood for a moment, swaying slightly as if the spots of light in the darkness were circling around her. Her eyes, shadowed and confused, finally settled on his face. He did not try to conceal his irritation. "I hope this teaches you a lesson," he said. She leaned forward and her eyes raked his face. She seemed trying to determine his identity. Then, as if she found nothing familiar about him, she started off with a headlong movement in the wrong direction.

"Aren't you going on to the Y?" he asked.

"Home," she muttered.

"Well, are we walking?"

For answer she kept going. Julian followed along, his hands behind him. He saw no reason to let the lesson she had had go without backing it up with an explanation of its meaning. She might as well be made to understand what had happened to her. "Don't think that was just an uppity Negro woman," he said. "That was the whole colored race which will no longer take your condescending pennies. That was your black double. She can wear the same hat as you, and to be sure," he added gratuitously (because he thought it was funny), "it looked better on her than it did on you. What all this means," he said, "is that the old world is gone. The old manners are obsolete and your graciousness is not worth a damn." He thought bitterly of the house that had been lost for him. "You aren't who you think you are," he said.

She continued to plow ahead, paying no attention to him. Her hair had come undone on one side. She dropped her pocketbook and took no notice. He stooped and picked it up and handed it to her but she did not take it.

"You needn't act as if the world had come to an end," he said, "because it hasn't. From now on you've got to live in a new world and face a few realities for a change. Buck up," he said, "it won't kill you."

She was breathing fast.

"Let's wait on the bus," he said.

"Home," she said thickly.

"I hate to see you behave like this," he said. "Just like a child. I should be able to expect more of you." He decided to stop where he was and make her stop and wait for a bus. "I'm not going any farther," he said, stopping. "We're going on the bus."

She continued to go on as if she had not heard him. He took a few steps and caught her arm and stopped her. He looked into her face and caught his breath. He was looking into a face he had never seen before. "Tell Grandpa to come get me," she said.

He stared, stricken.

"Tell Caroline to come get me," she said.

Stunned, he let her go and she lurched forward again, walking as if one leg were shorter than the other. A tide of darkness seemed to be sweeping her from him. "Mother!" he cried. "Darling, sweetheart, wait!" Crumpling, she fell to the pavement. He dashed forward and fell at her side, crying, "Mamma, Mamma!" He turned her over. Her face was fiercely distorted. One eye, large and staring, moved slightly to the left as if it had become unmoored. The other remained fixed on him, raked his face again, found nothing and closed.

"Wait here, wait here!" he cried and jumped up and began to run for help toward a cluster of lights he saw in the distance ahead of him. "Help, help!" he shouted, but his voice was thin, scarcely a thread of sound. The lights drifted farther away the faster he ran and his feet moved numbly as if they carried him nowhere. The tide of darkness seemed to sweep him back to her, postponing from moment to moment his entry into the world of guilt and sorrow.

A Clean, Well-Lighted Place

ERNEST HEMINGWAY
1899–1961

It was late and everyone had left the café except an old man who sat in the shadow the leaves of the tree made against the electric light. In the day time the street was dusty, but at night the dew settled the dust and the old man liked to sit late because he was deaf and now at night it was quiet and he felt the difference. The two waiters inside the café knew that the old man was a little drunk, and while he was a good client they knew that if he became too drunk he would leave without paying, so they kept watch on him.

"Last week he tried to commit suicide," one waiter said.

"Why?"

"He was in despair."

"What about?"

"Nothing."

"How do you know it was nothing?"

"He has plenty of money."

They sat together at a table that was close against the wall near the door of the café and looked at the terrace where the tables were all empty except where the old man sat in the shadow of the leaves of the tree that moved slightly in the wind. A girl and a soldier went by in the street. The street light shone on the brass number on his collar. The girl wore no head covering and hurried beside him.

"The guard will pick him up," one waiter said.

"What does it matter if he gets what he's after?"

"He had better get off the street now. The guard will get him. They went by five minutes ago."

The old man sitting in the shadow rapped on his saucer with his glass. The younger waiter went over to him.

"What do you want?"

The old man looked at him. "Another brandy," he said.

"You'll be drunk," the waiter said. The old man looked at him. The waiter went away.

"He'll stay all night," he said to his colleague. "I'm sleepy now. I never get into bed before three o'clock. He should have killed himself last week."

The waiter took the brandy bottle and another saucer from the counter inside the café and marched out to the old man's table. He put down the saucer and poured the glass full of brandy.

"You should have killed yourself last week," he said to the deaf man. The old man motioned with his finger. "A little more," he said. The waiter poured on into the glass so that the brandy slopped over and ran down the stem into the top saucer of the pile. "Thank you," the old man said. The waiter took the bottle back inside the café. He sat down at the table with his colleague again.

"He's drunk now," he said.

"He's drunk every night."

"What did he want to kill himself for?"

"How should I know."

"How did he do it?"

"He hung himself with a rope."

"Who cut him down?"

"His niece."

"Why did they do it?"

"Fear for his soul."

"How much money has he got?"

"He's got plenty."

"He must be eighty years old."

"Anyway I should say he was eighty."

"I wish he would go home. I never get to bed before three o'clock. What kind of hour is that to go to bed?"

"He stays up because he likes it."

"He's lonely. I'm not lonely. I have a wife waiting in bed for me."

"He had a wife once too."

"A wife would be no good to him now."

"You can't tell. He might be better with a wife."

"His niece looks after him. You said she cut him down."

"I know."

"I wouldn't want to be that old. An old man is a nasty thing."

"Not always. This old man is clean. He drinks without spilling. Even now, drunk. Look at him."

"I don't want to look at him. I wish he would go home. He has no regard for those who must work."

The old man looked from his glass across the square, then over at the waiters.

"Another brandy," he said, pointing to his glass. The waiter who was in a hurry came over.

"Finished," he said, speaking with that omission of syntax stupid people employ when talking to drunken people or foreigners. "No more tonight. Close now."

"Another," said the old man.

"No. Finished." The waiter wiped the edge of the table with a towel and shook his head.

The old man stood up, slowly counted the saucers, took a leather coin purse from his pocket and paid for the drinks, leaving half a peseta tip.

The waiter watched him go down the street, a very old man walking unsteadily but with dignity.

"Why didn't you let him stay and drink?" the unhurried waiter asked. They were putting up the shutters. "It is not half-past two."

"I want to go home to bed."

"What is an hour?"

"More to me than to him."

"An hour is the same."

"You talk like an old man yourself. He can buy a bottle and drink at home."

"It's not the same."

"No, it is not," agreed the waiter with a wife. He did not wish to be unjust. He was only in a hurry.

"And you? You have no fear of going home before your usual hour?"

"Are you trying to insult me?"

"No, hombre, only to make a joke."

"No," the waiter who was in a hurry said, rising from pulling down the metal shutters. "I have confidence. I am all confidence."

"You have youth, confidence, and a job," the older waiter said. "You have everything."

"And what do you lack?"

"Everything but work."

"You have everything I have."

"No. I have never had confidence and I am not young."

"Come on. Stop talking nonsense and lock up."

"I am of those who like to stay late at the café," the older waiter said. "With all those who do not want to go to bed. With all those who need a light for the night."

"I want to go home and into bed."

"We are of two different kinds," the older waiter said. He was now dressed to go home. "It is not only a question of youth and confidence although those things are very beautiful. Each night I am reluctant to close up because there may be some one who needs the café."

"Hombre, there are bodegas open all night long."

"You do not understand. This is a clean and pleasant café. It is well lighted. The light is very good and also, now, there are shadows of the leaves."

"Good night," said the younger waiter.

"Good night," the other said. Turning off the electric light he continued the conversation with himself. It is the light of course but it is necessary that the place be clean and pleasant. You do not want music. Certainly you do not want music. Nor can you stand before a bar with dignity although that is all that is provided for these hours. What did he fear? It was not fear or dread. It was a nothing that he knew too well. It was all a nothing and a man was nothing too. It was only that and light was all it needed and a certain cleanness and order. Some lived in it and never felt it but he knew it all was nada y pues nada y nada y pues nada.[1] Our nada who art in nada, nada be thy name thy kingdom nada thy will be nada in nada as it is in nada. Give us this nada our daily nada and nada us our nada as we nada our nadas and nada us not into nada but deliver us from nada; pues nada. Hail nothing full of nothing, nothing is with thee.[2] He smiled and stood before a bar with a shining steam pressure coffee machine.

"What's yours?" asked the barman.

"Nada."

"Otro loco mas,"[3] said the barman and turned away.

"A little cup," said the waiter.

The barman poured it for him.

"The light is very bright and pleasant but the bar is unpolished," the waiter said.

The barman looked at him but did not answer. It was too late at night for conversation.

"You want another copita?"[4] the barman asked.

"No, thank you," said the waiter and went out. He disliked bars and bodegas. A clean, well-lighted café was a very different thing. Now, without thinking further, he would go home to his room. He would lie in the bed and finally, with daylight, he would go to sleep. After all, he said to himself, it is probably only insomnia. Many must have it.

Comments

The problem here, as found in so many Hemingway stories, is to discover how he manages to make apparently so little come to so much. A basic concern of every literary artist is to devise a technique, a literary form, to fashion the meaning of the situation he is exploring. No modern writer has worked more diligently to develop such a literary technique than Hemingway.

Ralph Ellison, author of the story "King of the Bingo Game" (p. 55) and the celebrated novel *Invisible Man* (1952), says about Hemingway: "In the end . . . it is the quality of his art which is primary. . . . And it was through this struggle with form that he became the master, the culture hero, whom we have come to know and admire." In a letter (February 4, 1930) to one of the editors of this book Hemingway comments on that struggle: "I have some 40 drafts of the last chapter [of *A Farewell to Arms*]—may have destroyed others. This process proves nothing as far as I know except that I worked over and over it to get it right. . . . This process of transmitting your sensations and imagination, etc. from yourself, complete, to the person reading is what constitutes the discipline of prose."

What disciplines has Hemingway used to create "A Clean, Well-Lighted Place," one of the shortest stories in the English language and one of Hemingway's favorites?

---

[1] "nada y pues nada . . .": nothing and then nothing . . .   [2] "Our nada who art in nada. . . . nothing is with thee.": an ironic prayer.   [3] One more crazy person.

[4] Usually a small drink of wine.

On the surface level we have a simple tale with three principal characters, but its implications, like those in Hemingway's *The Old Man and the Sea* (1952), can be as profound as the reader has insight. The scene is a Spanish cafe very late at night where an old man is having a drink while an old waiter and a young one discuss him. Except when the old waiter closes the cafe and goes to a bar for a drink, there is no action, much less suspense, whatever.

The story is a triumph of meaning expressed through dramatic tone and symbolism. Hemingway uses the dramatic method (see "Plot," p. 17) to permit the characters to present themselves. The story is actually a little one-act play with the author comment almost totally absent. Further, most of the customary exposition and author comment are embodied in the dialogue (for which Hemingway is justly famous), and the key facts are merely touched upon, rarely accented. The story is highly compressed: hardly a wasted word and every word counts. All this means that the reader participates in a drama which requires him to contribute to its understanding. Whatever tension the story possesses is created by the conflict between the old and young waiter as they regard the old man drinking in his loneliness. The symbolism? Each character represents a value system, a basic attitude toward life, and the word *nada,* or *nothing,* finally becomes the basic symbol upon which the meaning of the story turns.

It is easy to say, as one critic has said, "The story is about nothing, and we know that from the start. . . . the style itself tells us that there is no meaning in life." But this preemptive judgment hardly considers the importance of the cafe as a substitute for home as understood by the old waiter. And he understands even more: the value of affection, of communication among men, and that love is necessary to self-realization and simple dignity to the end. These things are precisely what the young waiter does not understand, and the old waiter's *ironic* prayer makes perfectly clear that the story is about Something very important to sensitive men and women. How else account for the final paragraph where the old man says to himself, "After all . . . it is probably only insomnia. Many must have it." Insomnia? Surely, an ironic name for loneliness and loss of identity, as Hemingway means it to be.

The Drunkard

FRANK O'CONNOR [1]
1903–1966

It was a terrible blow to Father when Mr. Dooley on the terrace died. Mr. Dooley was a commercial traveller with two sons in the Dominicans and a car of his own, so socially he was miles ahead of us, but he had no false pride. Mr. Dooley was an intellectual, and, like all intellectuals the thing he loved best was conversation, and in his own limited way Father was a well-read man and could appreciate an intelligent talker. Mr. Dooley was remarkably intelligent. Between business acquaintances and clerical contacts, there was very little he didn't know about what went on in town, and evening after evening he crossed the road to our gate to explain to Father the news behind the news. He had a low, palavering voice and a knowing smile, and Father would listen in astonishment, giving him a conversational lead now and again, and then stump triumphantly in to Mother with his face aglow and ask: "Do you know what Mr. Dooley is after telling me?" Ever since, when somebody has given me some bit of information off the record I have found myself on the point of asking: "Was it Mr. Dooley told you that?"

Till I actually saw him laid out in his brown shroud with the rosary beads entwined between his waxy fingers I did not take the report of his death seriously. Even then I felt there must be a catch and that some summer evening Mr. Dooley must reappear at our gate to give us the lowdown on the next world. But Father was very upset, partly because Mr. Dooley was about one age with himself, a thing that always gives a distinctly personal turn to another man's demise; partly because now he would have no one to tell him what dirty work was behind the latest scene at the Corporation. You could count on your fingers the number of men in Blarney Lane

[1] Pen name for Michael O'Donovan.

who read the papers as Mr. Dooley did, and none of these would have overlooked the fact that Father was only a labouring man. Even Sullivan, the carpenter, a mere nobody, thought he was a cut above Father. It was certainly a solemn event.

"Half past two to the Curragh," Father said meditatively, putting down the paper.

"But you're not thinking of going to the funeral?" Mother asked in alarm.

" 'Twould be expected," Father said, scenting opposition. "I wouldn't give it to say to them."

"I think," said Mother with suppressed emotion, "it will be as much as anyone will expect if you go to the chapel with him."

("Going to the chapel," of course, was one thing, because the body was removed after work, but going to a funeral meant the loss of a half-day's pay.)

"The people hardly know us," she added.

"God between us and all harm," Father replied with dignity, "we'd be glad if it was our own turn."

To give Father his due, he was always ready to lose a half day for the sake of an old neighbour. It wasn't so much that he liked funerals as that he was a conscientious man who did as he would be done by; and nothing could have consoled him so much for the prospect of his own death as the assurance of a worthy funeral. And, to give Mother her due, it wasn't the half-day's pay she begrudged, badly as we could afford it.

Drink, you see, was Father's great weakness. He could keep steady for months, even for years, at a stretch, and while he did he was as good as gold. He was first up in the morning and brought the mother a cup of tea in bed, stayed at home in the evenings and read the paper; saved money and bought himself a new blue serge suit and bowler hat. He laughed at the folly of men who, week in week out, left their hard-earned money with the publicans; and sometimes, to pass an idle hour, he took pencil and paper and calculated precisely how much he saved each week through being a teetotaller. Being a natural optimist he sometimes continued this calculation through the whole span of his prospective existence and the total was breath-taking. He would die worth hundreds.

If I had only known it, this was a bad sign; a sign he was becoming stuffed up with spiritual pride and imagining himself better than his neighbours. Sooner or later, the spiritual pride grew till it called for some form of celebration. Then he took a drink—not whisky, of course; nothing like that—just a glass of some harmless drink like lager beer. That was the end of Father. By the time he had taken the first he already realized that he had made a fool of himself, took a second to forget it and a third to forget that he couldn't forget, and at last came home reeling drunk. From this on it was "The Drunkard's Progress," as in the moral prints. Next day he stayed in from work with a sick head while Mother went off to make his excuses at the works, and inside a fortnight he was poor and savage and despondent again. Once he began he drank steadily through everything down to the kitchen clock. Mother and I knew all the phases and dreaded all the dangers. Funerals were one.

"I have to go to Dunphy's to do a half-day's work," said Mother in distress. "Who's to look after Larry?"

"I'll look after Larry," Father said graciously. "The little walk will do him good."

There was no more to be said, though we all knew I didn't need anyone to look after me, and that I could quite well have stayed at home and looked after Sonny, but I was being attached to the party to act as a brake on Father. As a brake I had never achieved anything, but Mother still had great faith in me.

Next day, when I got home from school, Father was there before me and made a cup of tea for both of us. He was very good at tea, but too heavy in the hand for anything else; the way he cut bread was shocking. Afterwards, we went down the hill to the church, Father wearing his best blue serge and a bowler cocked to one side of his head with the least suggestion of the masher. To his great joy he discovered Peter Crowley among the mourners. Peter was another danger signal, as I knew well from certain experiences after Mass on Sunday morning: a mean man, as Mother said, who only went to funerals for the free drinks he could get at them. It turned out that he hadn't even known Mr. Dooley! But Father had a sort of contemptuous regard for him as one of the foolish people who wasted their good money in public-houses when they could be saving it. Very little of his own money Peter Crowley wasted!

It was an excellent funeral from Father's point of view. He had it all well studied before we set off after the hearse in the afternoon sunlight.

"Five carriages!" he exclaimed. "Five carriages and sixteen covered cars! There's one alderman, two councillors and 'tis unknown how many priests. I didn't see a funeral like this from the road since Willie Mack, the publican, died."

"Ah, he was well liked," said Crowley in his husky voice.

"My goodness, don't I know that?" snapped Father. "Wasn't the man my best friend? Two nights before he died—only two nights—he was over telling me the goings-on about the housing contract. Them fellows in the Corporation are night and day robbers. But even I never imagined he was as well connected as that."

Father was stepping out like a boy, pleased with everything: the other mourners, and the fine houses along Sunday's Well. I knew the danger signals were there in full force: a sunny day, a fine funeral, and a distinguished company of clerics and public men were bringing out all the natural vanity and flightiness of Father's character. It was with something like genuine pleasure that he saw his old friend lowered into the grave; with the sense of having performed a duty and the pleasant awareness that however much he would miss poor Mr. Dooley in the long summer evenings, it was he and not poor Mr. Dooley who would do the missing.

"We'll be making tracks before they break up," he whispered to Crowley as the grave-diggers tossed in the first shovelfuls of clay, and away he went, hopping like a goat from grassy hump to hump. The drivers, who were probably in the same state as himself, though without months of abstinence to put an edge on it, looked up hopefully.

"Are they nearly finished, Mick?" bawled one.

"All over now bar the last prayers," trumpeted Father in the tone of one who brings news of great rejoicing.

The carriages passed us in a lather of dust several hundred yards from the public-house, and Father, whose feet gave him trouble in hot weather, quickened his pace, looking nervously over his shoulder for any sign of the main body of mourners crossing the hill. In a crowd like that a man might be kept waiting.

When we did reach the pub the carriages were drawn up outside, and solemn men in black ties were cautiously bringing out consolation to mysterious females whose hands reached out modestly from behind the drawn blinds of the coaches. Inside the pub there were only the drivers and a couple of shawly women. I felt if I was to act as a brake at all, this was the time, so I pulled Father by the coattails.

"Dadda, can't we go home now?" I asked.

"Two minutes now," he said, beaming affectionately. "Just a bottle of lemonade and we'll go home."

This was a bribe, and I knew it, but I was always a child of weak character. Father ordered lemonade and two pints. I was thirsty and swallowed my drink at once. But that wasn't Father's way. He had long months of abstinence behind him and an eternity of pleasure before. He took out his pipe, blew through it, filled it, and then lit it with loud pops, his eyes bulging above it. After that he deliberately turned his back on the pint, leaned one elbow on the counter in the attitude of a man who did not know there was a pint behind him, and deliberately brushed the tobacco from his palms. He had settled down for the evening. He was steadily working through all the important funerals he had ever attended. The carriages departed and the minor mourners drifted in till the pub was half full.

"Dadda," I said, pulling his coat again, "can't we go home now?"

"Ah, your mother won't be in for a long time yet," he said benevolently enough. "Run out in the road and play, can't you?"

It struck me as very cool, the way grown-ups assumed that you could play all by yourself on a strange road. I began to get bored as I had so often been bored before. I knew Father was quite capable of lingering there till nightfall. I knew I might have to bring him home, blind drunk, down Blarney Lane, with all the old women at their doors, saying: "Mick Delaney is on it again." I knew that my mother would be half crazy with anxiety; that next day Father wouldn't go out to work; and before the end of the week she would be running down to the pawn with the clock under her shawl. I could never get over the lonesomeness of the kitchen without a clock.

I was still thirsty. I found if I stood on tiptoe I could just reach Father's glass, and the idea occurred to me that it would be interesting to know what the contents were like. He had his back to it and wouldn't notice. I took down the glass and sipped cautiously. It was a terrible disappointment. I was astonished that he could even drink such stuff. It looked as if he had never tried lemonade.

I should have advised him about lemonade but he was holding forth himself in great style. I heard him say that bands were a great addition to a funeral. He put his arms in the position of someone holding a rifle in reverse and hummed a few bars of Chopin's Funeral March. Crowley nodded reverently. I took a longer drink and began to see that porter might have its advantages. I felt pleasantly elevated and philosophic. Father hummed a few bars of the Dead March in *Saul*. It was a nice pub and a very fine funeral, and I felt sure that poor Mr. Dooley in Heaven must be highly gratified. At the same time I thought they might have given him a band. As Father said, bands were a great addition.

But the wonderful thing about porter was the way it made you stand aside, or rather float aloft like a cherub rolling on a cloud, and watch yourself with your legs crossed, leaning against a bar counter, not worrying about trifles but thinking deep, serious, grown-up thoughts about life and death. Looking at yourself like that, you couldn't help thinking after a while how funny you looked, and suddenly you got embarrassed and wanted to giggle. But by the time I had finished the pint, that phase too had passed; I found it hard to put back the glass, the counter seemed to have grown so high. Melancholia was supervening again.

"Well," Father said reverently, reaching behind him for his drink, "God rest the poor man's soul, wherever he is!" He stopped, looked first at the glass, and then at the people round him. "Hello," he said in a fairly good-humoured tone, as if he were just prepared to consider it a joke, even if it was in bad taste, "who was at this?"

There was silence for a moment while the publican and the old women looked first at Father and then at his glass.

"There was no one at it, my good man," one of the women said with an offended air. "Is it robbers you think we are?"

"Ah, there's no one here would do a thing like that, Mick," said the publican in a shocked tone.

"Well, someone did it," said Father, his smile beginning to wear off.

"If they did, they were them that were nearer it," said the woman darkly, giving me a dirty look; and at the same moment the truth began to dawn on Father. I suppose I must have looked a bit starry-eyed. He bent and shook me.

"Are you all right, Larry?" he asked in alarm.

Peter Crowley looked down at me and grinned.

"Could you beat that?" he exclaimed in a husky voice.

I could, and without difficulty. I started to get sick. Father jumped back in holy terror that I might spoil his good suit, and hastily opened the back door.

"Run! run! run!" he shouted.

I saw the sunlit wall outside with the ivy overhanging it, and ran. The intention was good but the performance was exaggerated, because I lurched right into the wall, hurting it badly, as it seemed to me. Being always very polite, I said "Pardon" before the second bout came on me. Father, still concerned for his suit, came up behind and cautiously held me while I got sick.

"That's a good boy!" he said encouragingly. "You'll be grand when you get that up."

Begor, I was not grand! Grand was the last thing I was. I gave one unmerciful wail out of me as he steered me back to the pub and put me sitting on the bench near the shawlies. They drew themselves up with an offended air, still sore at the suggestion that they had drunk his pint.

"God help us!" moaned one, looking pityingly at me, "isn't it the likes of them would be fathers?"

"Mick," said the publican in alarm, spraying sawdust on my tracks, "that child isn't supposed to be in here at all. You'd better take him home quick in case a bobby would see him."

"Merciful God!" whimpered Father, raising his eyes to heaven and clapping his hands silently as he only did when distraught, "what misfortune was on me? Or what will his mother say? . . . If women might stop at home and look after their children themselves!" he added in a snarl for the benefit of the shawlies. "Are them carriages all gone, Bill?"

"The carriages are finished long ago, Mick," replied the publican.

"I'll take him home," Father said despairingly. . . . "I'll never bring you out again," he threatened me. "Here," he added, giving me the clean handkerchief from his breast pocket, "put that over your eye."

The blood on the handkerchief was the first indication I got that I was cut, and instantly my temple began to throb and I set up another howl.

"Whisht, whisht, whisht!" Father said testily, steering me out the door. "One'd think you were killed. That's nothing. We'll wash it when we get home."

"Steady now, old scout!" Crowley said, taking the other side of me. "You'll be all right in a minute."

I never met two men who knew less about the effects of drink. The first breath of fresh air and the warmth of the sun made me groggier than ever and I pitched and rolled between wind and tide till Father started to whimper again.

"God Almighty, and the whole road out! What misfortune was on me didn't stop at my work! Can't you walk straight?"

I couldn't. I saw plain enough that, coaxed by the sunlight, every woman old and young in Blarney Lane was leaning over her half-door or sitting on her doorstep. They all stopped gabbling to gape at the strange spectacle of two sober, middle-aged men bringing home a drunken small boy with a cut over his eye. Father, torn between the shamefast desire to get me home as quick as he could, and the neighbourly need to explain that it wasn't his fault, finally halted outside Mrs. Roche's. There was a gang of old women outside a door at the opposite side of the road. I didn't like the look of them from the first. They seemed altogether too interested in me. I leaned against the wall of Mrs. Roche's cottage with my hands in my trousers pockets, thinking mournfully of poor Mr. Dooley in his cold grave on the Curragh, who would never walk down the road again, and, with great feeling, I began to sing a favourite song of Father's.

Though lost to Mononia and cold in the grave
He returns to Kincora no more.

"Wisha, the poor child!" Mrs. Roche said. "Haven't he a lovely voice, God bless him!"

That was what I thought myself, so I was the more surprised when Father said "Whisht!" and raised a threatening finger at me. He didn't seem to realize the appropriateness of the song, so I sang louder than ever.

"Whisht, I tell you!" he snapped, and then tried to work up a smile for Mrs. Roche's benefit. "We're nearly home now. I'll carry you the rest of the way."

But, drunk and all as I was, I knew better than to be carried home ignominiously like that.

"Now," I said severely, "can't you leave me alone? I can walk all right. 'Tis only my head. All I want is a rest."

"But you can rest at home in bed," he said viciously, trying to pick me up, and I knew by the flush on his face that he was very vexed.

"Ah, Jasus," I said crossly, "what do I want to go home for? Why the hell can't you leave me alone?"

For some reason the gang of old women at the other side of the road thought this very funny. They nearly split their sides over it. A gassy fury began to expand in me at the thought that a fellow couldn't have a drop taken without the whole neighbourhood coming out to make game of him.

"Who are ye laughing at?" I shouted, clenching my fists at them. "I'll make ye laugh at the other side of yeer faces if ye don't let me pass."

They seemed to think this funnier still; I had never seen such ill-mannered people.

"Go away, ye bloody bitches!" I said.

"Whisht, whisht, whisht, I tell you!" snarled Father, abandoning all pretence of amusement and dragging me along behind him by the hand. I was maddened by the women's shrieks of laughter. I was maddened by Father's bullying. I tried to dig in my heels but he was too powerful for me, and I could only see the women by looking back over my shoulder.

"Take care or I'll come back and show ye!" I shouted. "I'll teach ye to let decent people pass. Fitter for ye to stop at home and wash yeer dirty faces."

" 'Twill be all over the road," whimpered Father. "Never again, never again, not if I lived to be a thousand!"

To this day I don't know whether he was forswearing me or the drink. By way of a song suitable to my heroic mood I bawled "The Boys of Wexford," as he dragged me in home. Crowley, knowing he was not safe, made off and Father undressed me and put me to bed. I couldn't sleep because of the whirling in my head. It was very unpleasant, and I got sick again. Father came in with a wet cloth and mopped up after me. I lay in a fever, listening to him chopping sticks to start a fire. After that I heard him lay the table.

Suddenly the front door banged open and Mother stormed in with Sonny in her arms, not her usual gentle, timid self, but a wild, raging woman. It was clear that she had heard it all from the neighbours.

"Mick Delaney," she cried hysterically, "what did you do to my son?"

"Whisht, woman, whisht, whisht!" he hissed, dancing from one foot to the other. "Do you want the whole road to hear?"

"Ah," she said with a horrifying laugh, "the road knows all about it by this time. The road knows the way you filled your unfortunate innocent child with drink to make sport for you and that other rotten, filthy brute."

"But I gave him no drink," he shouted, aghast at the horrifying interpretation the neighbours had chosen to give his misfortune. "He took it while my back was turned. What the hell do you think I am?"

"Ah," she replied bitterly, "everyone knows what you are now. God forgive you, wasting our hard-earned few ha'pence on drink, and bringing up your child to be a drunken corner-boy like yourself."

Then she swept into the bedroom and threw herself on her knees by the bed. She moaned when she saw the gash over my eye. In the kitchen Sonny set up a loud bawl on his own, and a moment later Father appeared in the bedroom door with his cap over his eyes, wearing an expression of the most intense self-pity.

"That's a nice way to talk to me after all I went through," he whined. "That's a nice accusation, that I was drinking. Not one drop of drink crossed my lips the whole day. How could it when he drank it all? I'm the one that ought to be pitied, with my day ruined on me, and I after being made a show for the whole road."

But next morning, when he got up and went out quietly to work with his dinner-basket, Mother threw herself on me in the bed and kissed me. It seemed it was all my doing, and I was being given a holiday till my eye got better.

"My brave little man!" she said with her eyes shining. "It was God did it you were there. You were his guardian angel."

The Chrysanthemums
JOHN STEINBECK
1902–1968

The high grey-flannel fog of winter closed off the Salinas Valley from the sky and from all the rest of the world. On every side it sat like a lid on the mountains and made of the great valley a closed pot. On the broad, level land floor the gang plows bit deep and left the black earth shining like metal where the shares had cut. On the foothill ranches across the Salinas River, the yellow stubble fields seemed to be bathed in pale cold sunshine, but there was no sunshine in the valley now in December. The thick willow scrub along the river flamed with sharp and positive yellow leaves.

It was a time of quiet and of waiting. The air was cold and tender. A light wind blew up from the southwest so that the farmers were mildly hopeful of a good rain before long; but fog and rain do not go together.

Across the river, on Henry Allen's foothill ranch there was little work to be done, for the hay was cut and stored and the orchards were plowed up to receive the rain deeply when it should come. The cattle on the higher slopes were becoming shaggy and rough-coated.

Elisa Allen, working in her flower garden, looked down across the yard and saw Henry, her husband, talking to two men in business suits. The three of them stood by the tractor shed, each man with one foot on the side of the little Fordson. They smoked cigarettes and studied the machine as they talked.

Elisa watched them for a moment and then went back to her work. She was thirty-five. Her face was lean and strong and her eyes were as clear as water. Her figure looked blocked and heavy in her gardening costume, a man's black hat pulled low down over her eyes, clodhopper shoes, a figured print dress almost completely covered by a big corduroy apron with four big pockets to hold the snips, the trowel and scratcher, the seeds and the knife she worked with. She wore heavy leather gloves to protect her hands while she worked.

She was cutting down the old year's chrysanthemum stalks with a pair of short and powerful scissors. She looked down toward the men by the tractor shed now and then. Her face was eager and mature and handsome; even her work with the scissors was over-eager, over-powerful. The chrysanthemum stems seemed too small and easy for her energy.

She brushed a cloud of hair out of her eyes with the back of her glove, and left a smudge of earth on her cheek in doing it. Behind her stood the neat white farm house with red geraniums close-banked around it as high as the windows. It was a hard-swept looking little house, with hard-polished windows, and a clean mud-mat on the front steps.

Elisa cast another glance toward the tractor shed. The strangers were getting into their Ford coupe. She took off a glove and put her strong fingers down into the forest of new green chrysanthemum sprouts that were growing around the old roots. She spread the leaves and looked down among the close-growing stems. No aphids were there, no sowbugs or snails or cutworms. Her terrier fingers destroyed such pests before they could get started.

Elisa started at the sound of her husband's voice. He had come near quietly, and he leaned over the wire fence that protected her flower garden from cattle and dogs and chickens.

"At it again," he said. "You've got a strong new crop coming."

Elisa straightened her back and pulled on the gardening glove again. "Yes. They'll be strong this coming year." In her tone and on her face there was a little smugness.

"You've got a gift with things," Henry observed. "Some of those yellow chrysanthemums you had this year were ten inches across. I wish you'd work out in the orchard and raise some apples that big."

Her eyes sharpened. "Maybe I could do it, too. I've a gift with things, all right. My mother had it. She could stick anything in the ground and make it grow. She said it was having planters' hands that knew how to do it."

"Well, it sure works with flowers," he said.

"Henry, who were those men you were talking to?"

"Why, sure, that's what I came to tell you. They were from the Western Meat Company. I sold those thirty head of three-year-old steers. Got nearly my own price, too."

"Good," she said. "Good for you."

"And I thought," he continued, "I thought how it's Saturday afternoon, and we might go into Salinas for dinner at a restaurant, and then

to a picture show—to celebrate, you see."

"Good," she repeated. "Oh, yes. That will be good."

Henry put on his joking tone. "There's fights tonight. How'd you like to go to the fights?"

"Oh, no," she said breathlessly. "No, I wouldn't like fights."

"Just fooling, Elisa. We'll go to a movie. Let's see. It's two now. I'm going to take Scotty and bring down those steers from the hill. It'll take us maybe two hours. We'll go in town about five and have dinner at the Cominos Hotel. Like that?"

"Of course I'll like it. It's good to eat away from home."

"All right, then. I'll go get up a couple of horses."

She said, "I'll have plenty of time to transplant some of these sets, I guess."

She heard her husband calling Scotty down by the barn. And a little later she saw the two men ride up the pale yellow hillside in search of the steers.

There was a little square sandy bed kept for rooting the chrysanthemums. With her trowel she turned the soil over and over, and smoothed it and patted it firm. Then she dug ten parallel trenches to receive the sets. Back at the chrysanthemum bed she pulled out the little crisp shoots, trimmed off the leaves of each one with her scissors and laid it on a small orderly pile.

A squeak of wheels and plod of hoofs came from the road. Elisa looked up. The country road ran along the dense bank of willows and cottonwoods that bordered the river, and up this road came a curious vehicle, curiously drawn. It was an old spring-wagon, with a round canvas top on it like the cover of a prairie schooner. It was drawn by an old bay horse and a little grey-and-white burro. A big stubble-bearded man sat between the cover flaps and drove the crawling team. Underneath the wagon, between the hind wheels, a lean and rangy mongrel dog walked sedately. Words were painted on the canvas, in clumsy, crooked letters. "Pots, pans, knives, sisors, lawn mores, Fixed." Two rows of articles, and the triumphantly definitive "Fixed" below. The black paint had run down in little sharp points beneath each letter.

Elisa, squatting on the ground, watched to see the crazy, loose-jointed wagon pass by. But it didn't pass. It turned into the farm road in front of her house, crooked old wheels skirling and squeaking. The rangy dog darted from between the wheels and ran ahead. Instantly the two ranch shepherds flew out at him. Then all three stopped, and with stiff and quivering tails, with taut straight legs, with ambassadorial dignity, they slowly circled, sniffing daintily. The caravan pulled up to Elisa's wire fence and stopped. Now the newcomer dog, feeling outnumbered, lowered his tail and retired under the wagon with raised hackles and bared teeth.

The man on the wagon seat called out, "That's a bad dog in a fight when he gets started."

Elisa laughed. "I see he is. How soon does he generally get started?"

The man caught up her laughter and echoed it heartily. "Sometimes not for weeks and weeks," he said. He climbed stiffly down, over the wheel. The horse and the donkey drooped like unwatered flowers.

Elisa saw that he was a very big man. Although his hair and beard were greying, he did not look old. His worn black suit was wrinkled and spotted with grease. The laughter had disappeared from his face and eyes the moment his laughing voice ceased. His eyes were dark, and they were full of the brooding that gets in the eyes of teamsters and of sailors. The calloused hands he rested on the wire fence were cracked, and every crack was a black line. He took off his battered hat.

"I'm off my general road, ma'am," he said. "Does this dirt road cut over across the river to the Los Angeles highway?"

Elisa stood up and shoved the thick scissors in her apron pocket. "Well, yes, it does, but it winds around and then fords the river. I don't think your team could pull through the sand."

He replied with some asperity, "It might surprise you what them beasts can pull through."

"When they get started?" she asked.

He smiled for a second. "Yes. When they get started."

"Well," said Elisa, "I think you'll save time if you go back to the Salinas road and pick up the highway there."

He drew a big finger down the chicken wire and made it sing. "I ain't in any hurry, ma'am. I go from Seattle to San Diego and back every year. Takes all my time. About six months each way. I aim to follow nice weather."

Elisa took off her gloves and stuffed them in the apron pocket with the scissors. She touched the under edge of her man's hat, searching for fugitive hairs. "That sounds like a nice kind of a way to live," she said.

He leaned confidentially over the fence. "Maybe you noticed the writing on my wagon. I mend pots and sharpen knives and scissors. You got any of them things to do?"

"Oh, no," she said quickly. "Nothing like that." Her eyes hardened with resistance.

"Scissors is the worst thing," he explained. "Most people just ruin scissors trying to sharpen 'em, but I know how. I got a special tool. It's a little bobbit kind of thing, and patented. But it sure does the trick."

"No. My scissors are all sharp."

"All right, then. Take a pot," he continued earnestly, "a bent pot, or a pot with a hole. I can make it like new so you don't have to buy no new ones. That's a saving for you."

"No," she said shortly. "I tell you I have nothing like that for you to do."

His face fell to an exaggerated sadness. His voice took on a whining undertone. "I ain't had a thing to do today. Maybe I won't have no supper tonight. You see I'm off my regular road. I know folks on the highway clear from Seattle to San Diego. They save their things for me to sharpen up because they know I do it so good and save them money."

"I'm sorry," Elisa said irritably. "I haven't anything for you to do."

His eyes left her face and fell to searching the ground. They roamed about until they came to the chrysanthemum bed where she had been working. "What's them plants, ma'am?"

The irritation and resistance melted from Elisa's face. "Oh, those are chrysanthemums, giant whites and yellows. I raise them every year, bigger than anybody around here."

"Kind of a long-stemmed flower? Looks like a quick puff of colored smoke?" he asked.

"That's it. What a nice way to describe them."

"They smell kind of nasty till you get used to them," he said.

"It's a good bitter smell," she retorted, "not nasty at all."

He changed his tone quickly. "I like the smell myself."

"I had ten-inch blooms this year," she said.

The man leaned farther over the fence. "Look.

I know a lady down the road a piece, has got the nicest garden you ever seen. Got nearly every kind of flower but no chrysantheums. Last time I was mending a copper-bottom washtub for her (that's a hard job but I do it good), she said to me, 'If you ever run acrost some nice chrysantheums I wish you'd try to get me a few seeds.' That's what she told me."

Elisa's eyes grew alert and eager. "She couldn't have known much about chrysanthemums. You can raise them from seed, but it's much easier to root the little sprouts you see there."

"Oh," he said. "I s'pose I can't take none to her, then."

"Why yes you can," Elisa cried. "I can put some in damp sand, and you can carry them right along with you. They'll take root in the pot if you keep them damp. And then she can transplant them."

"She'd sure like to have some, ma'am. You say they're nice ones?"

"Beautiful," she said. "Oh, beautiful." Her eyes shone. She tore off the battered hat and shook out her dark pretty hair. "I'll put them in a flower pot, and you can take them right with you. Come into the yard."

While the man came through the picket gate Elisa ran excitedly along the geranium-bordered path to the back of the house. And she returned carrying a big red flower pot. The gloves were forgotten now. She kneeled on the ground by the starting bed and dug up the sandy soil with her fingers and scooped it into the bright new flower pot. Then she picked up the little pile of shoots she had prepared. With her strong fingers she pressed them into the sand and tamped around them with her knuckles. The man stood over her. "I'll tell you what to do," she said. "You remember so you can tell the lady."

"Yes, I'll try to remember."

"Well, look. These will take root in about a month. Then she must set them out, about a foot apart in good rich earth like this, see?" She lifted a handful of dark soil for him to look at. "They'll grow fast and tall. Now remember this: In July tell her to cut them down, about eight inches from the ground."

"Before they bloom?" he asked.

"Yes, before they bloom." Her face was tight with eagerness. "They'll grow right up again. About the last of September the buds will start."

She stopped and seemed perplexed. "It's the budding that takes the most care," she said hesitantly. "I don't know how to tell you." She looked deep into his eyes, searchingly. Her mouth opened a little, and she seemed to be listening. "I'll try to tell you," she said. "Did you ever hear of planting hands?"

"Can't say I have, ma'am."

"Well, I can only tell you what it feels like. It's when you're picking off the buds you don't want. Everything goes right down into your fingertips. You watch your fingers work. They do it themselves. You can feel how it is. They pick and pick the buds. They never make a mistake. They're with the plant. Do you see? Your fingers and the plant. You can feel that, right up your arm. They know. They never make a mistake. You can feel it. When you're like that you can't do anything wrong. Do you see that? Can you understand that?"

She was kneeling on the ground looking up at him. Her breast swelled passionately.

The man's eyes narrowed. He looked away self-consciously. "Maybe I know," he said. "Sometimes in the night in the wagon there——"

Elisa's voice grew husky. She broke in on him, "I've never lived as you do, but I know what you mean. When the night is dark—why, the stars are sharp-pointed and there's quiet. Why, you rise up and up! Every pointed star gets driven into your body. It's like that. Hot and sharp and—lovely."

Kneeling there, her hand went out toward his legs in the greasy black trousers. Her hesitant fingers almost touched the cloth. Then her hand dropped to the ground. She crouched low like a fawning dog.

He said, "It's nice, just like you say. Only when you don't have no dinner, it ain't."

She stood up then, very straight, and her face was ashamed. She held the flower pot out to him and placed it gently in his arms. "Here. Put it in your wagon, on the seat, where you can watch it. Maybe I can find something for you to do."

At the back of the house she dug in the can pile and found two old and battered aluminum saucepans. She carried them back and gave them to him. "Here, maybe you can fix these."

His manner changed. He became professional. "Good as new I can fix them." At the back of his wagon he set a little anvil, and out of an oily tool box dug a small machine hammer. Elisa came through the gate to watch him while he pounded out the dents in the kettles. His mouth grew sure and knowing. At a difficult part of the work he sucked his under-lip.

"You sleep right in the wagon?" Elisa asked.

"Right in the wagon, ma'am. Rain or shine I'm dry as a cow in there."

"It must be nice," she said. "It must be very nice. I wish women could do such things."

"It ain't the right kind of a life for a woman."

Her upper lip raised a little, showing her teeth. "How do you know? How can you tell?" she said.

"I don't know, ma'am," he protested. "Of course I don't know. Now here's your kettles, done. You don't have to buy no new ones."

"How much?"

"Oh, fifty cents'll do. I keep my prices down and my work good. That's why I have all them satisfied customers up and down the highway."

Elisa brought him a fifty-cent piece from the house and dropped it in his hand. "You might be surprised to have a rival some time. I can sharpen scissors, too. And I can beat the dents out of little pots. I could show you what a woman might do."

He put his hammer back in the oily box and shoved the little anvil out of sight. "It would be a lonely life for a woman, ma'am, and a scarey life, too, with animals creeping under the wagon all night." He climbed over the singletree, steadying himself with a hand on the burro's white rump. He settled himself in the seat, picked up the lines. "Thank you kindly, ma'am," he said. "I'll do like you told me; I'll go back and catch the Salinas road."

"Mind," she called, "if you're long in getting there, keep the sand damp."

"Sand, ma'am? . . . Sand? Oh, sure. You mean around the chrysanthemums. Sure I will." He clucked his tongue. The beasts leaned luxuriously into their collars. The mongrel dog took his place between the back wheels. The wagon turned and crawled out the entrance road and back the way it had come, along the river.

Elisa stood in front of her wire fence watching the slow progress of the caravan. Her shoulders were straight, her head thrown back, her eyes half-closed, so that the scene came vaguely into them. Her lips moved silently, forming the words

"Good-bye—good-bye." Then she whispered, "That's a bright direction. There's a glowing there." The sound of her whisper startled her. She shook herself free and looked about to see whether anyone had been listening. Only the dogs had heard. They lifted their heads toward her from their sleeping in the dust, and then stretched out their chins and settled asleep again. Elisa turned and ran hurriedly into the house.

In the kitchen she reached behind the stove and felt the water tank. It was full of hot water from the noonday cooking. In the bathroom she tore off her soiled clothes and flung them into the corner. And then she scrubbed herself with a little block of pumice, legs and thighs, loins and chest and arms, until her skin was scratched and red. When she had dried herself she stood in front of a mirror in her bedroom and looked at her body. She tightened her stomach and threw out her chest. She turned and looked over her shoulder at her back.

After a while she began to dress, slowly. She put on her newest underclothing and her nicest stockings and the dress which was the symbol of her prettiness. She worked carefully on her hair, penciled her eyebrows and rouged her lips.

Before she was finished she heard the little thunder of hoofs and the shouts of Henry and his helper as they drove the red steers into the corral. She heard the gate bang shut and set herself for Henry's arrival.

His step sounded on the porch. He entered the house calling, "Elisa, where are you?"

"In my room, dressing. I'm not ready. There's hot water for your bath. Hurry up. It's getting late."

When she heard him splashing in the tub, Elisa laid his dark suit on the bed, and shirt and socks and tie beside it. She stood his polished shoes on the floor beside the bed. Then she went to the porch and sat primly and stiffly down. She looked toward the river road where the willow-line was still yellow with frosted leaves so that under the high grey fog they seemed a thin band of sunshine. This was the only color in the grey afternoon. She sat unmoving for a long time. Her eyes blinked rarely.

Henry came banging out of the door, shoving his tie inside his vest as he came. Elisa stiffened and her face grew tight. Henry stopped short and looked at her. "Why—why, Elisa. You look so nice!"

"Nice? You think I look nice? What do you mean by 'nice'?"

Henry blundered on. "I don't know. I mean you look different, strong and happy."

"I am strong? Yes, strong. What do you mean 'strong'?"

He looked bewildered. "You're playing some kind of a game," he said helplessly. "It's a kind of a play. You look strong enough to break a calf over your knee, happy enough to eat it like a watermelon."

For a second she lost her rigidity. "Henry! Don't talk like that. You didn't know what you said." She grew complete again. "I'm strong," she boasted. "I never knew before how strong."

Henry looked down toward the tractor shed, and when he brought his eyes back to her, they were his own again. "I'll get out the car. You can put on your coat while I'm starting."

Elisa went into the house. She heard him drive to the gate and idle down his motor, and then she took a long time to put on her hat. She pulled it here and pressed it there. When Henry turned the motor off she slipped into her coat and went out.

The little roadster bounced along on the dirt road by the river, raising the birds and driving the rabbits into the brush. Two cranes flapped heavily over the willow-line and dropped into the river-bed.

Far ahead on the road Elisa saw a dark speck. She knew.

She tried not to look as they passed it, but her eyes would not obey. She whispered to herself sadly, "He might have thrown them off the road. That wouldn't have been much trouble, not very much. But he kept the pot," she explained. "He had to keep the pot. That's why he couldn't get them off the road."

The roadster turned a bend and she saw the caravan ahead. She swung full around toward her husband so she could not see the little covered wagon and the mismatched team as the car passed them.

In a moment it was over. The thing was done. She did not look back.

She said loudly, to be heard above the motor, "It will be good, tonight, a good dinner."

"Now you're changed again," Henry com-

plained. He took one hand from the wheel and patted her knee. "I ought to take you in to dinner oftener. It would be good for both of us. We get so heavy out on the ranch."

"Henry," she asked, "could we have wine at dinner?"

"Sure we could. Say! That will be fine."

She was silent for a while; then she said, "Henry, at those prize fights, do the men hurt each other very much?"

"Sometimes a little, not often. Why?"

"Well, I've read how they break noses, and blood runs down their chests. I've read how the fighting gloves get heavy and soggy with blood."

He looked around at her. "What's the matter, Elisa? I didn't know you read things like that." He brought the car to a stop, then turned to the right over the Salinas River bridge.

"Do any women ever go to the fights?" she asked.

"Oh, sure, some. What's the matter, Elisa? Do you want to go? I don't think you'd like it, but I'll take you if you really want to go."

She relaxed limply in the seat. "Oh, no. No. I don't want to go. I'm sure I don't." Her face was turned away from him. "It will be enough if we can have wine. It will be plenty." She turned up her coat collar so he could not see that she was crying weakly—like an old woman.

King of the Bingo Game
RALPH ELLISON
1914–

This story was published in 1944 when Ellison was thirty years old, and it preceded his celebrated novel, *Invisible Man* (1952), by eight years. In 1965 the magazine *Book Week* asked 200 authors, critics, and editors to determine according to their collective judgment the most distinguished writers and the most distinguished novel published in America between 1945 and 1965. Of the more than 10,000 novels, *Invisible Man* was judged to be "the most distinguished single work," and Ellison was given sixth place among novelists, one place above Norman Mailer and two above Hemingway. Concerning *Invisible Man* Ellison wrote: "Indeed, if I were asked in all seriousness just what I considered to be the chief significance of *Invisible Man* as a fiction, I would reply: Its experimental attitude, and its attempt to return to the mood of personal moral responsibility for democracy which typified the best of our nineteenth-century fiction. . . . I came to believe that the writers of that period took a much greater responsibility for the condition of democracy and, indeed, their works were imaginative projections of the conflicts within the human heart which arose when the sacred principles of the Constitution and the Bill of Rights clashed with the practical exigencies of human greed and fear, hate and love. . . . Whenever we as Americans have faced serious crises we have returned to fundamentals; this, in brief, is what I have tried to do."* Undoubtedly Ellison's basic concern in this statement is that writers should take a personal moral responsibility for the condition of democracy, and this Ellison has done in very large measure.

"King of the Bingo Game" and "Flying Home" (1944) are often said to be his best short stories, and in them he clearly accepts his moral responsibility for the condition of democracy. The larger, deeper issue in "King of the Bingo Game" is the Negro's condition and place in American democracy, as issue which permeates most of American Negro literature.** The desperate young Negro who tries to win in the bingo game of life as arranged by the whites is defeated, and the consequences of this defeat is, as Ellison dramatizes here and in the *Invisible Man,* a violation of the Constitution and the Bill of Rights. Just who is the King of the bingo game? Ellison provides his answer.

The woman in front of him was eating roasted peanuts that smelled so good that he could barely contain his hunger. He could not

* For Ellison's complete essay, "Brave Words for a Startling Occasion," see p. 825.
** See stories by Richard Wright (p. 121), Langston Hughes (p. 144), and James Baldwin (p. 196).

even sleep and wished they'd hurry and begin the bingo game. There, on his right, two fellows were drinking wine out of a bottle wrapped in a paper bag, and he could hear soft gurgling in the dark. His stomach gave a low, gnawing growl. "If this was down South," he thought, "all I'd have to do is lean over and say, 'Lady, gimme a few of those peanuts, please ma'am,' and she'd pass me the bag and never think nothing of it." Or he could ask the fellows for a drink in the same way. Folks down South stuck together that way; they didn't even have to know you. But up here it was different. Ask somebody for something, and they'd think you were crazy. Well, I ain't crazy. I'm just broke, 'cause I got no birth certificate to get a job, and Laura 'bout to die 'cause we got no money for a doctor. But I ain't crazy. And yet a pinpoint of doubt was focused in his mind as he glanced toward the screen and saw the hero stealthily entering a dark room and sending the beam of a flashlight along a wall of bookcases. This is where he finds the trapdoor, he remembered. The man would pass abruptly through the wall and find the girl tied to a bed, her legs and arms spread wide, and her clothing torn to rags. He laughed softly to himself. He had seen the picture three times, and this was one of the best scenes.

On his right the fellow whispered wide-eyed to his companion, "Man, look a-yonder!"

"Damn!"

"Wouldn't I like to have her tied up like that . . ."

"Hey! That fool's letting her loose!"

"Aw, man, he loves her."

"Love or no love!"

The man moved impatiently beside him, and he tried to involve himself in the scene. But Laura was on his mind. Tiring quickly of watching the picture he looked back to where the white beam filtered from the projection room above the balcony. It started small and grew large, specks of dust dancing in its whiteness as it reached the screen. It was strange how the beam always landed right on the screen and didn't mess up and fall somewhere else. But they had it all fixed. Everything was fixed. Now suppose when they showed that girl with her dress torn the girl started taking off the rest of her clothes, and when the guy came in he didn't untie her but kept her there and went to taking off his own clothes? *That* would be something to see. If a picture got out of hand like that those guys up there would go nuts. Yeah, and there'd be so many folks in here you couldn't find a seat for nine months? A strange sensation played over his skin. He shuddered. Yesterday he'd seen a bedbug on a woman's neck as they walked out into the bright street. But exploring his thigh through a hole in his pocket he found only goose pimples and old scars.

The bottle gurgled again. He closed his eyes. Now a dreamy music was accompanying the film and train whistles were sounding in the distance, and he was a boy again walking along a railroad trestle down South, and seeing the train coming, and running back as fast as he could go, and hearing the whistle blowing, and getting off the trestle to solid ground just in time, with the earth trembling beneath his feet, and feeling relieved as he ran down the cinder-strewn embankment onto the highway, and looking back and seeing with terror that the train had left the track and was following him right down the middle of the street, and all the white people laughing as he ran screaming . . .

"Wake up there, buddy! What the hell do you mean hollering like that? Can't you see we trying to enjoy this here picture?"

He stared at the man with gratitude.

"I'm sorry, old man," he said. "I musta been dreaming."

"Well, here, have a drink. And don't be making no noise like that, damn!"

His hands trembled as he tilted his head. It was not wine, but whiskey. Cold rye whiskey. He took a deep swoller, decided it was better not to take another, and handed the bottle back to its owner.

"Thanks, old man," he said.

Now he felt the cold whiskey breaking a warm path straight through the middle of him, growing hotter and sharper as it moved. He had not eaten all day, and it made him light-headed. The smell of the peanuts stabbed him like a knife, but he got up and found a seat in the middle aisle. But no sooner did he sit than he saw a row of intense-faced young girls, and he got up again, thinking, "You chicks musta been Lindy-hopping somewhere." He found a seat several rows ahead as the lights came on, and he saw the screen disappear behind a heavy red and gold curtain; then the curtain rising, and the man with the microphone and a uniformed attendant coming on the stage.

He felt for his bingo cards, smiling. The guy at the door wouldn't like it if he knew about his having *five* cards. Well, not everyone played the bingo game; and even with five cards he didn't have much of a chance. For Laura, though, he had to have faith. He studied the cards, each with its different numerals, punching the free center hole in each and spreading them neatly across his lap; and when the light faded he sat slouched in his seat so that he could look from his cards to the bingo wheel with but a quick shifting of his eyes.

Ahead, at the end of the darkness, the man with the microphone was pressing a button attached to a long cord and spinning the bingo wheel and calling out the number each time the wheel came to rest. And each time the voice rang out his finger raced over the cards for the number. With five cards he had to move fast. He became nervous; there were too many cards, and the man went too fast with his grating voice. Perhaps he should just select one and throw the others away. But he was afraid. He became warm. Wonder how much Laura's doctor would cost? Damn that, watch the cards! And with despair he heard the man call three in a row which he missed on all five cards. This way he'd never win. . .

When he saw the row of holes punched across the third card, he sat paralyzed and he heard the man call three more numbers before he stumbled forward, screaming.

"Bingo! Bingo!"

"Let that fool up there," someone called.

"Get up there, man!"

He stumbled down the aisle and up the steps to the stage into a light so sharp and bright that for a moment it blinded him, and he felt that he had moved into the spell of some strange, mysterious power. Yet it was as familiar as the sun, and he knew it was the perfectly familiar bingo.

The man with the microphone was saying something to the audience as he held out his card. A cold light flashed from the man's finger as the card left his hand. His knees trembled. The man stepped closer, checking the card against the numbers chalked on the board. Suppose he had made a mistake? The pomade on the man's hair made him feel faint, and he backed away. But the man was checking the card over the microphone now, and he had to stay. He stood tense, listening.

"Under the O, forty-four," the man chanted. Under the I, seven. Under the G, three. Under the B, ninety-six. Under the N, thirteen!"

His breath came easier as the man smiled at the audience.

"Yessir, ladies and gentlemen, he's one of the chosen people!"

The audience rippled with laughter and applause.

"Step right up to the front of the stage."

He moved slowly forward, wishing that the light was not so bright.

"To win tonight's jackpot of $36.90 the wheel must stop between the double zero, understand?"

He nodded, knowing the ritual from the many days and nights he had watched the winners march across the stage to press the button that controlled the spinning wheel and receive the prizes. And now he followed the instructions as though he'd crossed the slippery stage a million prize-winning times.

The man was making some kind of a joke, and he nodded vacantly. So tense had he become that he felt a sudden desire to cry and shook it away. He felt vaguely that his whole life was determined by the bingo wheel; not only that which would happen now that he was at last before it, but all that had gone before, since his birth, and his mother's birth and the birth of his father. It had always been there, even though he had not been aware of it, handing out the unlucky cards and numbers of his days. The feeling persisted, and he started quickly away. I better get down from here before I make a fool of myself, he thought.

"Here, boy," the man called. "You haven't started yet."

Someone laughed as he went hesitantly back.

"Are you all reet?"

He grinned at the man's jive talk, but no words would come, and he knew it was not a convincing grin. For suddenly he knew that he stood on the slippery brink of some terrible embarrassment.

"Where are you from, boy?" the man asked.

"Down South."

"He's from down South, ladies and gentlemen," the man said. "Where from? Speak right into the mike."

"Rocky Mont," he said. "Rock' Mont, North Car'lina."

"So you decided to come down off the mountain to the U.S.," the man laughed. He felt that the man was making a fool of him, but then something cold was placed in his hand, and the lights were no longer behind him.

Standing before the wheel he felt alone, but that was somehow right, and he remembered his plan. He would give the wheel a short quick twirl. Just a touch of the button. He had watched it many times, and always it came close to double zero when it was short and quick. He steeled himself; the fear had left, and he felt a profound sense of promise, as though he were about to be repaid for all the things he'd suffered all his life. Trembling, he pressed the button. There was a whirl of lights, and in a second he realized with finality that though he wanted to, he could not stop. It was as though he held a high-powered line in his naked hand. His nerves tightened. As the wheel increased its speed it seemed to draw him more and more into his power, as though it held his fate; and with it came a deep need to submit, to whirl, to lose himself in its swirl of color. He could not stop it now, he knew. So let it be.

The button rested snuggly in his palm where the man had placed it. And now he became aware of the man beside him, advising him through the microphone, while behind the shadowy audience hummed with noisy voices. He shifted his feet. There was still that feeling of helplessness within him, making part of him desire to turn back, even now that the jackpot was right in his hand. He squeezed the button until his fist ached. Then, like the sudden shriek of a subway whistle, a doubt tore through his head. Suppose he did not spin the wheel long enough? What could he do, and how could he tell? And then he knew, even as he wondered, that as long as he pressed the button, he could control the jackpot. He and only he could determine whether or not it was to be his. Not even the man with the microphone could do anything about it now. He felt drunk. Then, as though he had come down from a high hill into a valley of people, he heard the audience yelling.

"Come down from there, you jerk!"

"Let somebody else have a chance . . ."

"Ole Jack thinks he done found the end of the rainbow . . ."

The last voice was not unfriendly, and he turned and smiled dreamily into the yelling mouths. Then he turned his back squarely on them.

"Don't take too long, boy," a voice said.

He nodded. They were yelling behind him. Those folks did not understand what had happened to him. They had been playing the bingo game day in and night out for years, trying to win rent money or hamburger change. But not one of those wise guys had discovered this wonderful thing. He watched the wheel whirling past the numbers and experienced a burst of exaltation: This is God! This is the really truly God! He said it aloud, "This is God!"

He said it with such absolute conviction that he feared he would fall fainting into the footlights. But the crowd yelled so loud that they could not hear. Those fools, he thought. I'm here trying to tell them the most wonderful secret in the world, and they're yelling like they gone crazy. A hand fell upon his shoulder.

"You'll have to make a choice now, boy. You've taken too long."

He brushed the hand violently away.

"Leave me alone, man. I know what I'm doing!"

The man looked surprised and held on to the microphone for support. And because he did not wish to hurt the man's feelings he smiled, realizing with a sudden pang that there was no way of explaining to the man just why he had to stand there pressing the button forever.

"Come here," he called tiredly.

The man approached, rolling the heavy microphone across the stage.

"Anybody can play this bingo game, right?" he said.

"Sure, but . . ."

He smiled, feeling inclined to be patient with this slick looking white man with his blue sport shirt and his sharp gabardine suit.

"That's what I thought," he said. "Anybody can win the jackpot as long as they get the lucky number, right?"

"That's the rule, but after all . . ."

"That's what I thought," he said. "And the big prize goes to the man who knows how to win it?"

The man nodded speechlessly.

"Well then, go on over there and watch me win like I want to. I ain't going to hurt nobody," he said, "and I'll show you how to win. I mean to show the whole world how it's got to be done."

And because he understood, he smiled again to let the man know that he held nothing against him for being white and impatient. Then he refused to see the man any longer and stood pressing the button, the voices of the crowd reaching him like sounds in distant streets. Let them yell. All the Negroes down there were just ashamed because he was black like them. He smiled inwardly, knowing how it was. Most of the time he was ashamed of what Negroes did himself. Well, let them be ashamed for something this time. Like him. He was like a long thin black wire that was being stretched and wound upon the bingo wheel; wound until he wanted to scream; wound, but this time himself controlling the winding and the sadness and the shame, and because he did, Laura would be all right. Suddenly the lights flickered. He staggered backwards. Had something gone wrong? All this noise. Didn't they know that although he controlled the wheel, it also controlled him, and unless he pressed the button forever and forever and ever it would stop, leaving him high and dry, dry and high on this hard high slippery hill and Laura dead? There was only one chance; he had to do whatever the wheel demanded. And gripping the button in despair, he discovered with surprize that it imparted a nervous energy. His spine tingled. He felt a certain power.

Now he faced the raging crowd with defiance, its screams penetrating his eardrums like trumpets shrieking from a juke-box. The vague faces glowing in the bingo lights gave him a sense of himself that he had never known before. He was running the show, by God! They had to react to him, for he was their luck. This is *me*, he thought. Let the bastards yell. Then someone was laughing inside him, and he realized that somehow he had forgotten his own name. It was a sad, lost feeling to lose your name, and a crazy thing to do. That name had been given him by the white man who had owned his grandfather a long lost time ago down South. But maybe those wise guys knew his name.

"Who am I?" he screamed.

"Hurry up and bingo, you jerk!"

They didn't know either, he thought sadly. They didn't even know their own names, they were all poor nameless bastards. Well, he didn't need that old name; he was reborn. For as long as he pressed the button he was The-man-who-pressed-the-button-who-held-the-prize-who-was-the-King-of-Bingo. That was the way it was, and he'd have to press the button even if nobody understood, even though Laura did not understand.

"Live!" he shouted.

The audience quieted like the dying of a huge fan.

"Live, Laura, baby. I got holt of it now, sugar. Live!"

He screamed it, tears streaming down his face. "I got nobody but YOU!"

The screams tore from his very guts. He felt as though the rush of blood to his head would burst out in baseball seams of small red droplets, like a head beaten by police clubs. Bending over he saw a trickle of blood splashing the toe of his shoe. With his free hand he searched his head. It was his nose. God, suppose something has gone wrong? He felt that the whole audience had somehow entered him and was stamping his feet in his stomach and he was unable to throw them out. They wanted the prize, that was it. They wanted the secret for themselves. But they'd never get it; he would keep the bingo wheel whirling forever, and Laura would be safe in the wheel. But would she? It had to be, because if she were not safe the wheel would cease to turn; it could not go on. He had to get away, *vomit* all, and his mind formed an image of himself running with Laura in his arms down the tracks of the subway just ahead of an A train, running desperately *vomit* with people screaming for him to come out but knowing no way of leaving the tracks because to stop would bring the train crushing down upon him and to attempt to leave across the other tracks would mean to run into a hot third rail as high as his waist which threw blue sparks that blinded his eyes until he could hardly see.

He heard singing and the audience was clapping its hands.

Shoot the liquor to him, Jim, boy!
Clap-clap-clap
Well a-calla the cop
He's blowing his top!
Shoot the liquor to him, Jim, boy!

Bitter anger grew within him at the singing.

They think I'm crazy. Well let 'em laugh. I'll do what I got to do.

He was standing in an attitude of intense listening when he saw that they were watching something on the stage behind him. He felt weak. But when he turned he saw no one. If only his thumb did not ache so. Now they were applauding. And for a moment he thought that the wheel had stopped. But that was impossible, his thumb still pressed the button. Then he saw them. Two men in uniform beckoned from the end of the stage. They were coming toward him, walking in step, slowly, like a tap-dance team returning for a third encore. But their shoulders shot forward, and he backed away, looking wildly about. There was nothing to fight them with. He had only the long black cord which led to a plug somewhere back stage, and he couldn't use that because it operated the bingo wheel. He backed slowly, fixing the men with his eyes as his lips stretched over his teeth in a tight, fixed grin; moved toward the end of the stage and realizing that he couldn't go much further, for suddenly the cord became taut and he couldn't afford to break the cord. But he had to do something. The audience was howling. Suddenly he stopped dead, seeing the men halt, their legs lifted as in an interrupted step of a slow-motion dance. There was nothing to do but run in the other direction and he dashed forward, slipping and sliding. The men fell back, surprised. He struck out violently going past.

"Grab him!"

He ran, but all too quickly the cord tightened, resistingly, and he turned and ran back again. This time he slipped them, and discovered by running in a circle before the wheel he could keep the cord from tightening. But this way he had to flail his arms to keep the men away. Why couldn't they leave a man alone? He ran, circling.

"Ring down the curtain," someone yelled. But they couldn't do that. If they did the wheel flashing from the projection room would be cut off. But they had him before he could tell them so, trying to pry open his fist, and he was wrestling and trying to bring his knees into the fight and holding on to the button, for it was his life. And now he was down, seeing a foot coming down, crushing his wrist cruelly, down, as he saw the wheel whirling serenely above.

"I can't give up," he screamed. Then quietly,

in a confidential tone, "Boys, I really can't give it up."

It landed hard against his head. And in the blank moment they had it away from him, completely now. He fought them trying to pull him up from the stage as he watched the wheel spin slowly to a stop. Without surprise he saw it rest at double-zero.

"You see," he pointed bitterly.

"Sure, boy, sure, it's O. K.," one of the men said smiling.

And seeing the man bow his head to someone he could not see, he felt very, very happy; he would receive what all the winners received.

But as he warmed in the justice of the man's tight smile he did not see the man's slow wink, nor see the bow-legged man behind him step clear of the swiftly descending curtain and set himself for a blow. He only felt the dull pain exploding in his skull, and he knew even as it slipped out of him that his luck had run out on the stage.

A Bottle of Milk for Mother

NELSON ALGREN
1909–

I feel I am of them—
I belong to those convicts and prostitutes
*   myself,*
And henceforth I will not deny them—
For how can I deny myself? [1]

—WHITMAN

Two months after the Polish Warriors S.A.C. had had their heads shaved, Bruno Lefty Bicek got into his final difficulty with the Racine Street police. The arresting officers and a reporter from the *Dziennik Chicagoski* were grouped about the captain's desk when the boy was urged forward into the room by Sergeant Adamovitch, with two fingers wrapped about the boy's broad belt: a full-bodied boy wearing a worn and sleeveless blue work shirt grown too tight across the shoulders; and the shoulders themselves with a loose swing to them. His skull

[1] From "You Felons on Trial in Courts."

and face were shining from a recent scrubbing, so that the little bridgeless nose glistened between the protective points of the cheekbones. Behind the desk sat Kozak, eleven years on the force and brother to an alderman. The reporter stuck a cigarette behind one ear like a pencil.

"We spotted him followin' the drunk down Chicago—" Sergeant Comiskey began.

Captain Kozak interrupted. "Let the jackroller tell us how he done it hisself."

"I ain't no jackroller." [2]

"What are you doin' here, then?"

Bicek folded his naked arms.

"Answer me. If you ain't here for jackrollin' it must be for strong-arm robb'ry—'r you one of them Chicago Av'noo moll-buzzers?" [3]

"I ain't that neither."

"C'mon, c'mon. I seen you in here before— what were you up to, followin' that poor old man?"

"I ain't been in here before."

Neither Sergeant Milano, Comiskey, nor old Adamovitch moved an inch; yet the boy felt the semicircle about him drawing closer. Out of the corner of his eye he watched the reporter undoing the top button of his mangy raccoon coat, as though the barren little query room were already growing too warm for him.

"What were you doin' on Chicago Av'noo in the first place when you live up around Division? Ain't your own ward big enough you have to come down here to get in trouble? What do you *think* you're here for?"

"Well, I was just walkin' down Chicago like I said, to get a bottle of milk for Mother, when the officers jumped me. I didn't even see 'em drive up, they wouldn't let me say a word, I got no idea what I'm here for. I was just doin' a errand for Mother 'n—"

"All right, son, you want us to book you as a pickup 'n hold you overnight, is that it?"

"Yes sir."

"What about this, then?"

Kozak flipped a spring-blade knife with a five-inch blade onto the police blotter; the boy resisted an impulse to lean forward and take it. His own double-edged double-jointed spring-

[2] One who knocks out (rolls) a person to rob him of money (jack).   [3] A man, usually a gangster, who lives with (buzzes) a girl friend (moll), sometimes a prostitute.

blade cuts-all genuine Filipino twisty-handled all-American gut-ripper.

"Is it yours or ain't it?"

"Never seen it before, Captain."

Kozak pulled a billy out of his belt, spread the blade across the bend of the blotter before him, and with one blow clubbed the blade off two inches from the handle. The boy winced as though he himself had received the blow. Kozak threw the broken blade into a basket and the knife into a drawer.

"Know why I did that, son?"

"Yes sir."

"Tell me."

" 'Cause it's three inches to the heart."

"No. 'Cause it's against the law to carry more than three inches of knife. C'mon, Lefty, tell us about it. 'N it better be good."

The boy began slowly, secretly gratified that Kozak appeared to know he was the Warriors' first-string left-hander: maybe he'd been out at that game against the Knothole Wonders the Sunday he'd finished his own game and then had relieved Dropkick Kodadek in the sixth in the second. Why hadn't anyone called him "Iron-Man Bicek" or "Fireball Bruno" for that one?

"Everythin' you say can be used against you," Kozak warned him earnestly. "Don't talk unless you want to." His lips formed each syllable precisely.

Then he added absently, as though talking to someone unseen, "We'll just hold you on an open charge till you do."

And his lips hadn't moved at all.

The boy licked his own lips, feeling a dryness coming into his throat and a tightening in his stomach. "We seen this boobatch with his collar turned inside out cash'n his check by Konstanty Stachula's Tonsorial Palace of Art on Division. So I followed him a way, that was all. Just break'n the old monotony was all. Just a notion, you might say, that come over me. I'm just a neighborhood kid, Captain."

He stopped as though he had finished the story. Kozak glanced over the boy's shoulder at the arresting officers and Lefty began again hurriedly.

"Ever' once in a while he'd pull a little single-shot of Scotch out of his pocket, stop a second t' toss it down, 'n toss the bottle at the car tracks. I picked up a bottle that didn't bust but there wasn't a spider left in 'er, the boobatch'd drunk her dry. 'N do you know, he had his pockets *full* of them little bottles? 'Stead of buyin' hisself a fifth in the first place. Can't understand a man who'll buy liquor that way. Right before the corner of Walton 'n Noble he popped into a hallway. That was Chiney-Eye-the-Princinct-Captain's hallway, so I popped right in after him. Me'n Chiney-Eye 'r just like that." The boy crossed two fingers of his left hand and asked innocently, "Has the alderman been in to straighten this out, Captain?"

"What time was all this, Lefty?"

"Well, some of the street lamps was lit awready 'n I didn't see nobody either way down Noble. It'd just started spitt'n a little snow 'n I couldn't see clear down Walton account of Wojciechowski's Tavern bein' in the way. He was a old guy, a dino you. He couldn't speak a word of English. But he started in cryin' about how every time he gets a little drunk the same old thing happens to him 'n he's gettin' fed up, he lost his last three checks in the very same hallway 'n it's gettin' so his family don't believe him no more . . ."

Lefty paused, realizing that his tongue was going faster than his brain. He unfolded his arms and shoved them down his pants pockets; the pants were turned up at the cuffs and the cuffs were frayed. He drew a colorless cap off his hip pocket and stood clutching it in his left hand.

"I didn't take him them other times, Captain," he anticipated Kozak.

"Who did?"

Silence.

"What's Benkowski doin' for a livin' these days, Lefty?"

"Just nutsin' around."

"What's Nowogrodski up to?"

"Goes wolfin' on roller skates by Riverview. The rink's open all year round."

"Does he have much luck?"

"Never turns up a hair. They go by too fast."

"What's that evil-eye up to?"

Silence.

"You know who I mean. Idzikowski."

"The Finger?"

"You know who I mean. Don't stall."

"He's hexin' fights, I heard."

"Seen Kodadek lately?"

"I guess. A week 'r two 'r a month ago."

"What was *he* up to?"

"Sir?"

"What was Kodadek doin' the last time you seen him?"

"You mean Dropkick? He was nutsin' around."

"Does he nuts around drunks in hallways?"

Somewhere in the room a small clock or wrist watch began ticking distinctly.

"Nutsin' around ain't jackrollin'."

"You mean Dropkick ain't a jackroller but you are."

The boy's blond lashes shuttered his eyes.

"All right, get ahead with your lyin' a little faster."

Kozak's head came down almost neckless onto his shoulders, and his face was molded like a flatiron, the temples narrow and the jaws rounded. Between the jaws and the open collar, against the graying hair of the chest, hung a tiny crucifix, slender and golden, a shade lighter than his tunic's golden buttons.

"I told him I wasn't gonna take his check, I just needed a little change, I'd pay it back someday. But maybe he didn't understand. He kept hollerin' how he lost his last check, please to let him keep this one. 'Why you drink'n it all up, then,' I put it to him, 'if you're that anxious to hold onto it?' He gimme a foxy grin then 'n pulls out four of them little bottles from four different pockets, 'n each one was a different kind of liquor. I could have one, he tells me in Polish, which do I want, 'n I slapped all four out of his hands. All four. I don't like to see no full-grown man drinkin' that way. A Polak hillbilly he was, 'n certain'y no citizen."

" 'Now let me have that change,' I asked him, 'n that wasn't so much t' ask. I don't go around just lookin' fcr trouble, Captain. 'N my feet was slop-full of water 'n snow. I'm just a neighborhood fella. But he acted like I was gonna kill him 'r somethin'. I got one hand over his mouth 'n a half nelson behind him 'n talked polite-like in Polish in his ear, 'n he began sweatin' 'n tryin' t' wrench away on me. 'Take it easy,' I asked him. 'Be reas'nable, we're both in this up to our necks now.' 'N he wasn't drunk no more then, 'n he was plenty t' hold onto. You wouldn't think a old boobatch like that'd have so much stren'th left in him, boozin' down Division night after night, year after year, like he didn't have no

home to go to. He pulled my hand off his mouth 'n started hollerin', '*Mlody bandyta! Mlody bandyta!*' 'n I could feel him slippin'. He was just too strong fer a kid like me to hold—"

"Because you were reach'n for his wallet with the other hand?"

"Oh no. The reason I couldn't hold him was my right hand had the nelson 'n I'm not so strong there like in my left 'n even my left ain't what it was before I thrun it out pitchin' that doubleheader."

"So you kept the rod in your left hand?"

The boy hesitated. Then: "Yes sir." And felt a single drop of sweat slide down his side from under his armpit. Stop and slide again down to the belt.

"What did you get off him?"

"I tell you, I had my hands too full to get *anythin'*—that's just what I been tryin' to tell you. I didn't get so much as one of them little singleshots for all my trouble."

"How many slugs did you fire?"

"Just one, Captain. That was all there was in 'er. I didn't really fire, though. Just at his feet. T' scare him so's he wouldn't jump me. I fired in self-defense. I just wanted to get out of there." He glanced helplessly around at Comiskey and Adamovitch. "You do crazy things sometimes, fellas—well, that's all I was doin'."

The boy caught his tongue and stood mute. In the silence of the query room there was only the scraping of the reporter's pencil and the unseen wrist watch. "I'll ask Chiney-Eye if it's legal, a reporter takin' down a confession, that's my out," the boy thought desperately, and added aloud, before he could stop himself: " 'N beside I had to show him—"

"Show him what, son?"

Silence.

"Show him what, Left-hander?"

"That I wasn't just another greenhorn sprout like he thought."

"Did he say you were just a sprout?"

"No. But I c'd tell. Lots of people think I'm just a green kid. I show 'em. I guess I showed 'em now all right." He felt he should be apologizing for something and couldn't tell whether it was for strong-arming a man or for failing to strong-arm him.

"I'm just a neighborhood kid. I belonged to the Keep-Our-City-Clean Club at St. John

Cant'us. I told him polite-like, like a Polish-American citizen, this was Chiney-Eye-a-Friend-of-Mine's hallway. 'No more after this one,' I told him. 'This is your last time gettin' rolled, old man. After this I'm pertectin' you, I'm seein' to it nobody touches you—but the people who live here don't like this sort of thing goin' on any more'n you 'r I do. There's gotta be a stop to it, old man—'n we all gotta live, don't we?' That's what I told him in Polish."

Kozak exchanged glances with the prim-faced reporter from the *Chicagoski*, who began cleaning his black tortoise-shell spectacles hurriedly yet delicately, with the fringed tip of his cravat. They depended from a black ribbon; he snapped them back onto his beak.

"You shot him in the groin, Lefty. He's dead."

The reporter leaned slightly forward, but perceived no special reaction and so relaxed. A pretty comfy old chair for a dirty old police station, he thought lifelessly. Kozak shaded his eyes with his gloved hand and looked down at his charge sheet. The night lamp on the desk was still lit, as though he had been working all night; as the morning grew lighter behind him lines came out below his eyes, black as though packed with soot, and a curious droop came to the St. Bernard mouth.

"You shot him through the groin—zip." Kozak's voice came, flat and unemphatic, reading from the charge sheet as though without understanding. "Five children. Stella, Mary, Grosha, Wanda, Vincent. Thirteen, ten, six, six, and one two months. Mother invalided since last birth, name of Rose. WPA fifty-five dollars. You told the truth about *that*, at least."

Lefty's voice came in a shout: "You know *what*? That bullet must of bounced, that's what!"

"Who was along?"

"I was singlin'. Lone-wolf stuff." His voice possessed the first faint touch of fear.

"You said, 'We seen the man.' Was he a big man? How big a man was he?"

"I'd judge two hunerd twenty pounds," Comiskey offered, "at least. Fifty pounds heavier 'n this boy, just about. 'N half a head taller."

"Who's 'we,' Left-hander?"

"Captain, I said, 'We seen.' Lots of people, fellas, seen him is all I meant, cashin' his check by Stachula's when the place was crowded. Konstanty cashes checks if he knows you. Say, I even know the project that old man was on, far as that

goes, because my old lady wanted we should give up the store so's I c'd get on it. But it was just me done it, Captain."

The raccoon coat readjusted his glasses. He would say something under a by-line like "This correspondent has never seen a colder gray than that in the eye of the wanton killer who arrogantly styles himself the *lone wolf of Potomoc Street*." He shifted uncomfortably, wanting to get farther from the wall radiator but disliking to rise and push the heavy chair.

"Where was that bald-headed pal of yours all this time?"

"Don't know the fella, Captain. Nobody got hair any more around the neighborhood, it seems. The whole damn Triangle went 'n got army haircuts by Stachula's."

"Just you 'n Benkowski, I mean. Don't be afraid, son—we're not tryin' to ring in anythin' you done afore this. Just this one you were out cowboyin' with Benkowski on; were you help'n him 'r was he help'n you? Did you 'r him have the rod?"

Lefty heard a Ford V-8 pull into the rear of the station, and a moment later the splash of the gas as the officers refueled. Behind him he could hear Milano's heavy breathing. He looked down at his shoes, carefully buttoned all the way up and tied with a double bowknot. He'd have to have new laces mighty soon or else start tying them with a single bow.

"That Benkowski's sort of a toothless monkey used to go on at the City Garden at around a hundred an' eighteen pounds, ain't he?"

"Don't know the fella well enough t' say."

"Just from seein' him fight once 'r twice is all. 'N he wore a mouthpiece, I couldn't tell about his teeth. Seems to me he came in about one thirty-three, if he's the same fella you're thinkin' of, Captain."

"I guess you fought at the City Garden once 'r twice yourself, ain't you?"

"Oh, once 'r twice."

"How'd you make out, Left'?"

"Won 'em both on K.O.s. Stopped both fights in the first. One was against that boogie from the Savoy. If he woulda got up I woulda killed him fer life. Fer Christ I would. I didn't know I could hit like I can."

"With Benkowski in your corner both times?"

"Oh no, sir."

"That's a bloodsuck'n lie. I seen him in your

corner with my own eyes the time you won off Cooney from the C.Y.O. He's your manager, jackroller."

"I didn't say he wasn't."

"You said he wasn't secondin' you."

"He don't."

"Who does?"

"The Finger."

"You told me the Finger was your hexman. Make up your mind."

"He does both, Captain. He handles the bucket 'n sponge 'n between he fingers the guy I'm fightin', 'n if it's close he fingers the ref 'n judges. Finger, he never lost a fight. He waited for the boogie outside the dressing room 'n pointed him clear to the ring. He win that one for me awright." The boy spun the frayed greenish cap in his hand in a concentric circle about his index finger, remembering a time when the cap was new and had earlaps. The bright checks were all faded now, to the color of worn pavement, and the earlaps were tatters.

"What possessed your mob to get their heads shaved, Lefty?"

"I strong-armed him myself, I'm rugged as a bull." The boy began to swell his chest imperceptibly; when his lungs were quite full he shut his eyes, like swimming under water at the Oak Street beach, and let his breath out slowly, ounce by ounce.

"I didn't ask you that. I asked you what happened to your hair."

Lefty's capricious mind returned abruptly to the word "possessed" that Kozak had employed. That had a randy ring, sort of: "What possessed you boys?"

"I forgot what you just asked me."

"I asked you why you didn't realize it'd be easier for us to catch up with your mob when all of you had your heads shaved."

"I guess we figured there'd be so many guys with heads shaved it'd be harder to catch a finger than if we all had hair. But that was some accident all the same. A fella was gonna lend Ma a barber chair 'n go fifty-fifty with her shavin' all the Polaks on P'tom'c Street right back of the store, for relief tickets. So she started on me, just to show the fellas, but the hair made her sicker 'n ever 'n back of the store's the only place she got to lie down 'n I hadda finish the job myself.

"The fellas begun giv'n me a Christ-awful razzin' then, ever' day. God oh God, wherever I went around the Triangle, all the neighborhood fellas 'n little niducks 'n old-time hoods by the Broken Knuckle, whenever they seen me they was pointin' 'n laughin' 'n sayin', 'Hi, Baldy Bicek!' So I went home 'n got the clippers 'n the first guy I seen was Bibleback Watrobinski, you wouldn't know him. I jumps him 'n pushes the clip right through the middle of his hair—he ain't had a haircut since the alderman got indicted you—'n then he took one look at what I done in the drugstore window 'n we both bust out laughin' 'n laughin', 'n fin'lly Bible says I better finish what I started. So he set down on the curb 'n I finished him. When I got all I could off that way I took him back to the store 'n heated water 'n shaved him close 'n Ma couldn't see the point at all.

"Me 'n Bible prowled around a couple days 'n here come Catfoot Nowogrodski from Fry Street you, out of Stachula's with a spanty-new sideburner haircut 'n a green tie. I grabbed his arms 'n let Bible run it through the middle just like I done him. Then it was Catfoot's turn, 'n we caught Chester Chekhovka fer *him*, 'n fer Chester we got Cowboy Okulanis from by the Nort'-western Viaduct you, 'n fer him we got Mustang, 'n fer Mustang we got John from the Joint, 'n fer John we got Snake Baranowski, 'n we kep' right on goin' that way till we was doin' guys we never seen before even, Wallios 'n Greeks 'n a Flip from Clark Street he musta been, walkin' with a white girl we done it to. 'N fin'lly all the sprouts in the Triangle start comin' around with their heads shaved, they want to join up with the Baldheads A.C., they called it. They thought it was a club you.

"It got so a kid with his head shaved could beat up on a bigger kid because the big one'd be a-scared to fight back hard, he thought the Baldheads'd get him. So that's why we changed our name then, that's why we're not the Warriors any more, we're the Baldhead True American Social 'n Athletic Club.

"I played first for the Warriors when I wasn't on the mound," he added cautiously, "'n I'm enterin' the Gold'n Gloves next year 'less I go to collitch instead. I went to St. John Cant'us all the way through. Eight' grade, that is. If I keep on gainin' weight I'll be a hunerd ninety-eight this time next year 'n be five-foot-ten—I'm a fair-sized light-heavy right this minute. That's what in England they call a cruiser weight you."

He shuffled a step and made as though to unbutton his shirt to show his proportions. But Adamovitch put one hand on his shoulders and slapped the boy's hand down. He didn't like this kid. This was a low-class Polak.[4] He himself was a high-class Polak because his name was Adamovitch and not Adamowski. This sort of kid kept spoiling things for the high-class Polaks by always showing off instead of just being good citizens like the Irish. That was why the Irish ran the City Hall and Police Department and the Board of Education and the Post Office while the Polaks stayed on relief and got drunk and never got anywhere and had everybody down on them. All they could do like the Irish, old Adamovitch reflected bitterly, was to fight under Irish names to get their ears knocked off at the City Garden.

"That's why I want to get out of this jam," this one was saying beside him. "So's it don't ruin my career in the rope' arena. I'm goin' straight. This has sure been one good lesson fer me. Now I'll go to a big-ten collitch 'n make good you."

Now, if the college-coat asked him, "What big-ten college?" he'd answer something screwy like "The Boozological Stoodent-Collitch." That ought to set Kozak back awhile, they might even send him to a bug doc. He'd have to be careful —not *too* screwy. Just screwy enough to get by without involving Benkowski.

He scuffed his shoes and there was no sound in the close little room save his uneasy scuffing; square-toed boy's shoes, laced with a button-hook. He wanted to look more closely at the reporter but every time he caught the glint of the fellow's glasses he felt awed and would have to drop his eyes; he'd never seen glasses on a string like that before and would have given a great deal to wear them a moment. He took to looking steadily out of the barred window behind Kozak's head, where the January sun was glowing sullenly, like a flame held steadily in a fog. Heard an empty truck clattering east on Chicago, sounding like either a '38 Chevvie or a '37 Ford dragging its safety chain against the car tracks; closed his eyes and imagined sparks flashing from the tracks as the iron struck, bounced, and struck again. The bullet had bounced too. Wow.

[4] A person of Polish birth or descent; sometimes used disparagingly, but not in the context above.

"What do you think we ought to do with a man like you, Bicek?"

The boy heard the change from the familiar "Lefty" to "Bicek" with a pang; and the dryness began in his throat again.

"One to fourteen is all I can catch fer manslaughter." He appraised Kozak as coolly as he could.

"You like farm work the next fourteen years? Is that okay with you?"

"I said that's all I could get, at the most. This is a first offense 'n self-defense too. I'll plead the unwritten law."

"Who gave you *that* idea?"

"Thought of it myself. Just now. You ain't got a chance to send me over the road 'n you know it."

"We can send you to St. Charles, Bicek. 'N transfer you when you come of age. Unless we can make it first-degree murder."

The boy ignored the latter possibility.

"Why, a few years on a farm'd true me up fine. I planned t' cut out cigarettes 'n whisky anyhow before I turn pro—a farm'd be just the place to do that."

"By the time you're released you'll be thirty-two, Bicek—too late to turn pro then, ain't it?"

"I wouldn't wait that long. Hungry Piontek-from-by-the-Warehouse you, he lammed twice from that St. Charles farm. 'N Hungry don't have all his marbles even. He ain't even a citizen."

"Then let's talk about somethin' you couldn't lam out of so fast 'n easy. Like the chair. Did you know that Bogatski from Noble Street, Bicek? The boy that burned last summer, I mean."

A plain-clothes man stuck his head in the door and called confidently: "That's the man, Captain. That's the man."

Bicek forced himself to grin good-naturedly. He was getting pretty good, these last couple days, at grinning under pressure. When a fellow got sore he couldn't think straight, he reflected anxiously. And so he yawned in Kozak's face with deliberateness, stretching himself as effortlessly as a cat.

"Captain, I ain't been in serious trouble like this before . . ." he acknowledged, and paused dramatically. He'd let them have it straight from the shoulder now: "So I'm mighty glad to be so close to the alderman. Even if he is indicted."

There. Now they know. He'd told them.

"You talkin' about my brother, Bicek?"

The boy nodded solemnly. Now they knew who they had hold of at last.

The reporter took the cigarette off his ear and hung it on his lower lip. And Adamovitch guffawed.

The boy jerked toward the officer: Adamovitch was laughing openly at him. Then they were all laughing openly at him. He heard their derision, and a red rain danced one moment before his eyes; when the red rain was past, Kozak was sitting back easily, regarding him with the expression of a man who has just been swung at and missed and plans to use the provocation without undue haste. The captain didn't look like the sort who'd swing wildly or hurriedly. He didn't look like the sort who missed. His complacency for a moment was as unbearable to the boy as Adamovitch's guffaw had been. He heard his tongue going, trying to regain his lost composure by provoking them all.

"Hey, Stingywhiskers!" He turned on the reporter. "Get your Eversharp goin' there, write down I plugged the old rumpot, write down Bicek carries a rod night 'n day 'n don't care where he points it. You, I go around slappin' the crap out of whoever I feel like—"

But they all remained mild, calm, and unmoved: for a moment he feared Adamovitch was going to pat him on the head and say something fatherly in Polish.

"Take it easy, lad," Adamovitch suggested. "You're in the query room. We're here to help you, boy. We want to see you through this thing so's you can get back to pugging. You just ain't letting us help you, son."

Kozak blew his nose as though that were an achievement in itself, and spoke with the false friendliness of the insurance man urging a fleeced customer toward the door.

"Want to tell us where you got that rod now, Lefty?"

"I don't want to tell you anything." His mind was setting hard now, against them all. Against them all in here and all like them outside. And the harder it set, the more things seemed to be all right with Kozak: he dropped his eye to his charge sheet now and everything was all right with everybody. The reporter shoved his notebook into his pocket and buttoned the top button of his coat as though the questioning were over.

It was all too easy. They weren't going to ask him anything more, and he stood wanting them to. He stood wishing them to threaten, to shake their heads ominously, wheedle and cajole and promise him mercy if he'd just talk about the rod.

"I ain't mad, Captain. I don't blame you men either. It's your job, it's your bread 'n butter to talk tough to us neighborhood fellas—every'-body got to have a racket, 'n yours is talkin' tough." He directed this last at the captain, for Comiskey and Milano had left quietly. But Kozak was studying the charge sheet as though Bruno Lefty Bicek were no longer in the room. Nor anywhere at all.

"I'm still here," the boy said wryly, his lip twisting into a dry and bitter grin.

Kozak looked up, his big, wind-beaten, impassive face looking suddenly to the boy like an autographed pitcher's mitt he had once owned. His glance went past the boy and no light of recognition came into his eyes. Lefty Bicek felt a panic rising in him: a desperate fear that they weren't going to press him about the rod, about the old man, about his feelings. "Don't look at me like I ain't nowheres," he asked. And his voice was struck flat by fear.

Something else! The time he and Dropkick had broken into a slot machine! The time he and Casey had played the attention racket and made four dollars! Something! Anything else!

The reporter lit his cigarette.

"Your case is well disposed of," Kozak said, and his eyes dropped to the charge sheet forever.

"I'm born in this country. I'm educated here—"

But no one was listening to Bruno Lefty Bicek any more.

He watched the reporter leaving with regret—at least the guy could have offered him a drag—and stood waiting for someone to tell him to go somewhere now, shifting uneasily from one foot to the other. Then he started slowly, backward, toward the door: he'd make Kozak's tell Adamovitch to grab him. Halfway to the door he turned his back on Kozak.

There was no voice behind him. Was this what "well disposed of" meant? He turned the knob and stepped confidently into the corridor; at the end of the corridor he saw the door that opened into the courtroom, and his heart began shaking his whole body with the impulse to make a run for it. He glanced back and Adamovitch was five yards behind, coming up catfooted like only an old man who has been a citizen-dress man can come up catfooted, just far enough behind and just casual enough to make it appear unimportant whether the boy made a run for it or not.

The Lone Wolf of Potomac Street waited miserably, in the long unlovely corridor, for the sergeant to thrust two fingers through the back of his belt. Didn't they realize that he might have Dropkick and Catfoot and Benkowski with a submachine gun in a streamlined cream-colored roadster right down front, that he'd zigzag through the courtroom onto the courtroom fire escape and—swish—down off the courtroom roof three stories with the chopper still under his arm and through the car's roof and into the driver's seat? Like that George Raft did that time he was innocent at the Chopin, and cops like Adamovitch had better start ducking when Lefty Bicek began making a run for it. He felt the fingers thrust overfamiliarly between his shirt and his belt.

A cold draft came down the corridor when the door at the far end opened; with the opening of the door came the smell of disinfectant from the basement cells. Outside, far overhead, the bells of St. John Cantius were beginning. The boy felt the winding steel of the staircase to the basement beneath his feet and heard the whining screech of a Chicago Avenue streetcar as it paused on Ogden for the traffic lights and then screeched on again, as though a cat were caught beneath its back wheels. Would it be snowing out there still? he wondered, seeing the white-washed basement walls.

"Feel all right, son?" Adamovitch asked in his most fatherly voice, closing the cell door while thinking to himself: "The kid don't *feel* guilty is the whole trouble. You got to make them *feel* guilty or they'll never get to church at all. A man who goes to church without feeling guilty for *something* is wasting his time, I say." Inside the cell he saw the boy pause and go down on his knees in the cell's gray light. The boy's head turned slowly toward him, a pious oval in the dimness. Old Adamovitch took off his hat.

"This place'll rot down 'n mold over before

Lefty Bicek starts prayin', boobatch. Prays, squeals, 'r bawls. So run along 'n I'll see you in hell with yer back broke. I'm lookin' for my cap I dropped is all."

Adamovitch watched him crawling forward on all fours, groping for the pavement-colored cap; when he saw Bicek find it he put his own hat back on and left feeling vaguely dissatisfied.

He did not stay to see the boy, still on his knees, put his hands across his mouth and stare at the shadowed wall.

Shadows were there within shadows.

"I knew I'd never get to be twenty-one anyhow," Lefty told himself softly at last.

In the Region of Ice

JOYCE CAROL OATES
1938–

Sister Irene was a tall, deft woman in her early thirties. What one could see of her face made a striking impression—serious, hard gray eyes, a long slender nose, a face waxen with thought. Seen at the right time, from the right angle, she was almost handsome. In her past teaching positions she had drawn a little upon the fact of her being young and brilliant and also a nun, but she was beginning to grow out of that.

This was a new university and an entirely new world. She had heard—of course it was true—that the Jesuit administration of this school had hired her at the last moment to save money and to head off the appointment of a man of dubious religious commitment. She had prayed for the necessary energy to get her through this first semester. She had no trouble with teaching itself; once she stood before a classroom she felt herself capable of anything. It was the world immediately outside the classroom that confused and alarmed her, though she let none of this show—the cynicism of her colleagues, the indifference of many of the students, and, above all, the looks she got that told her nothing much would be expected of her because she was a nun. This took energy, strength. At times she had the idea that she was on trial and that the excuses she made to herself about her discomfort were only the common excuses made by guilty people. But in front of a class she had no time to worry about herself or the conflicts in her mind. She became, once and for all, a figure existing only for the benefit of others, an instrument by which the facts were communicated.

About two weeks after the semester began, Sister Irene noticed a new student in her class. He was slight and fair-haired, and his face was blank, but not blank by accident, blank on purpose, suppressed and restricted into a dumbness that looked hysterical. She was prepared for him before he raised his hand, and when she saw his arm jerk, as if he had at last lost control of it, she nodded to him without hesitation.

"Sister, how can this be reconciled with Shakespeare's vision in *Hamlet?* How can these opposing views be in the same mind?"

Students glanced at him, mildly surprised. He did not belong in the class, and this was mysterious, but his manner was urgent and blind.

"There is no need to reconcile opposing views," Sister Irene said, leaning forward against the podium. "In one play Shakespeare suggests one vision, in another play another; the plays are not simultaneous creations, and even if they were, we never demand a logical—"

"We must demand a logical consistency," the young man said. "The idea of education is itself predicated upon consistency, order, sanity—"

He had interrupted her, and she hardened her face against him—for his sake, not her own, since she did not really care. But he noticed nothing. "Please see me after class," she said.

After class the young man hurried up to her.

"Sister Irene, I hope you didn't mind my visiting today. I'd heard some things, interesting things," he said. He stared at her, and something in her face allowed him to smile. "I . . . could we talk in your office? Do you have time?"

They walked down to her office. Sister Irene sat at her desk, and the young man sat facing her; for a moment they were self-conscious and silent.

"Well, I suppose you know—I'm a Jew," he said.

Sister Irene stared at him. "Yes?" she said.

"What am I doing at a Catholic university, huh?" He grinned. "That's what you want to know."

She made a vague movement of her hand to show that she had no thoughts on this, nothing at all, but he seemed not to catch it. He was sitting on the edge of the straight-backed chair. She saw that he was young but did not really look young. There were harsh lines on either side of his mouth, as if he had misused that youthful mouth somehow. His skin was almost as pale as hers, his eyes were dark and not quite in focus. He looked at her and through her and around her, as his voice surrounded them both. His voice was a little shrill at times.

"Listen, I did the right thing today—visiting your class! God, what a lucky accident it was; some jerk mentioned you, said you were a good teacher—I thought, what a laugh! These people know about good teachers here? But yes, listen, yes, I'm not kidding—you are good. I mean that."

Sister Irene frowned. "I don't quite understand what all this means."

He smiled and waved aside her formality, as if he knew better. "Listen, I got my BA. at Columbia, then I came back here to this crappy city. I mean, I did it on purpose, I wanted to come back. I wanted to. I have my reasons for doing things. I'm on a three-thousand-dollar fellowship," he said, and waited for that to impress her. "You know, I could have gone almost anywhere with that fellowship, and I came back home here—my home's in the city—and enrolled here. This was last year. This is my second year. I'm working on a thesis, I mean I was, my master's thesis—but the hell with that. What I want to ask you is this: Can I enroll in your class, is it too late? We have to get special permission if we're late."

Sister Irene felt something nudging her, some uneasiness in him that was pleading with her not to be offended by his abrupt, familiar manner. He seemed to be promising another self, a better self, as if his fair, childish, almost cherubic face were doing tricks to distract her from what his words said.

"Are you in English studies?" she asked.

"I was in history. Listen," he said, and his mouth did something odd, drawing itself down into a smile that made the lines about it deepen like knives, "listen, they kicked me out."

He sat back, watching her. He crossed his legs. He took out a package of cigarettes and offered her one. Sister Irene shook her head, staring at his hands. They were small and stubby and might have belonged to a ten-year-old, and the nails were a strange near-violet color. It took him awhile to extract a cigarette.

"Yeah, kicked me out. What do you think of that?"

"I don't understand."

"My master's thesis was coming along beautifully, and then this bastard—I mean, excuse me, this professor, I won't pollute your office with his name—he started making criticisms, he said some things were unacceptable, he—" The boy leaned forward and hunched his narrow shoulders in a parody of secrecy. "We had an argument. I told him some frank things, things only a broad-minded person could hear about himself. That takes courage, right? He didn't have it! He kicked me out of the master's program, so now I'm coming into English. Literature is greater than history; European history is one big pile of garbage. Sky-high. Filth and rotting corpses, right? Aristotle says that poetry is higher than history; he's right; in your class today I suddenly realized that this is my field, Shakespeare, only Shakespeare is—"

Sister Irene guessed that he was going to say that only Shakespeare was equal to him, and she caught the moment of recognition and hesitation, the half-raised arm, the keen, frowning forehead, the narrowed eyes; then he thought better of it and did not end the sentence. "The students in your class are mainly negligible, I can tell you that. You're new here, and I've been here a year—I would have finished my studies last year but my father got sick, he was hospitalized, I couldn't take exams and it was a mess —but I'll make it through English in one year or drop dead. I can do it, I can do anything. I'll take six courses at once—" He broke off, breathless. Sister Irene tried to smile. "All right then, it's settled? You'll let me in? Have I missed anything so far?"

He had no idea of the rudeness of his question. Sister Irene, feeling suddenly exhausted, said, "I'll give you a syllabus of the course."

"Fine! Wonderful!"

He got to his feet eagerly. He looked through the schedule, muttering to himself, making favorable noises. It struck Sister Irene that she was making a mistake to let him in. There were these moments when one had to make an intelligent decision. . . . But she was sympathetic

with him, yes. She was sympathetic with something about him.

She found out his name the next day: Allen Weinstein.

After this she came to her Shakespeare class with a sense of excitement. It became clear to her at once that Weinstein was the most intelligent student in her class. Until he had enrolled, she had not understood what was lacking, a mind that could appreciate her own. Within a week his jagged, protean mind had alienated the other students, and though he sat in the center of the class, he seemed totally alone, encased by a miniature world of his own. When he spoke of the "frenetic humanism of the High Renaissance," Sister Irene dreaded the raised eyebrows and mocking smiles of the other students, who no longer bothered to look at Weinstein. She wanted to defend him, but she never did, because there was something rude and dismal about his knowledge; he used it like a weapon, talking passionately of Nietzsche and Goethe and Freud until Sister Irene would be forced to close discussion.

In meditation, alone, she often thought of him. When she tried to talk about him to a young nun, Sister Carlotta, everything sounded gross. "But no, he's an excellent student," she insisted. "I'm very grateful to have him in class. It's just that . . . he thinks ideas are real." Sister Carlotta, who loved literature also, had been forced to teach grade-school arithmetic for the last four years. That might have been why she said, a little sharply, "You don't think ideas are real?"

Sister Irene acquiesced with a smile, but of course she did not think so: only reality is real.

When Weinstein did not show up for class on the day the first paper was due, Sister Irene's heart sank, and the sensation was somehow a familiar one. She began her lecture and kept waiting for the door to open and for him to hurry noisily back to his seat, grinning an apology toward her—but nothing happened.

If she had been deceived by him, she made herself think angrily, it was as a teacher and not as a woman. He had promised her nothing.

Weinstein appeared the next day near the steps of the liberal arts building. She heard someone running behind her, a breathless exclamation: "Sister Irene!" She turned and saw him, panting and grinning in embarrassment. He wore a dark-blue suit with a necktie, and he looked, despite his childish face, like a little old man; there was something oddly precarious and fragile about him. "Sister Irene, I owe you an apology, right?" He raised his eyebrows and smiled a sad, forlorn, yet irritatingly conspiratorial smile. "The first paper—not in on time, and I know what your rules are. . . . You won't accept late papers, I know—that's good discipline, I'll do that when I teach too. But, unavoidably, I was unable to come to school yesterday. There are many—many—" He gulped for breath, and Sister Irene had the startling sense of seeing the real Weinstein stare out at her, a terrified prisoner behind the confident voice. "There are many complications in family life. Perhaps you are unaware—I mean—"

She did not like him, but she felt this sympathy, something tugging and nagging at her the way her parents had competed for her love so many years before. They had been whining, weak people, and out of their wet need for affection, the girl she had been (her name was Yvonne) had emerged stronger than either of them, contemptuous of tears because she had seen so many. But Weinstein was different; he was not simply weak—perhaps he was not weak at all—but his strength was confused and hysterical. She felt her customary rigidity as a teacher begin to falter. "You may turn your paper in today if you have it," she said, frowning.

Weinstein's mouth jerked into an incredulous grin. "Wonderful! Marvelous!" he said. "You are very understanding, Sister Irene, I must say. I must say . . . I didn't expect, really . . ." He was fumbling in a shabby old briefcase for the paper. Sister Irene waited. She was prepared for another of his excuses, certain that he did not have the paper, when he suddenly straightened up and handed her something. "Here! I took the liberty of writing thirty pages instead of just fifteen," he said. He was obviously quite excited; his cheeks were mottled pink and white. "You may disagree violently with my interpretation—I expect you to, in fact I'm counting on it—but let me warn you, I have the exact proof, right here in the play itself!" He was thumping at a book, his voice growing louder and shriller.

Sister Irene, startled, wanted to put her hand over his mouth and soothe him.

"Look," he said breathlessly, "may I talk with you? I have a class now I hate, I loathe, I can't bear to sit through! Can I talk with you instead?"

Because she was nervous, she stared at the title page of the paper: " 'Erotic Melodies in *Romeo and Juliet*' by Allen Weinstein, Jr."

"All right?" he said. "Can we walk around here? Is it all right? I've been anxious to talk with you about some things you said in class."

She was reluctant, but he seemed not to notice. They walked slowly along the shaded campus paths. Weinstein did all the talking, of course, and Sister Irene recognized nothing in his cascade of words that she had mentioned in class. "The humanist must be committed to the totality of life," he said passionately. "This is the failing one finds everywhere in the academic world! I found it in New York and I found it here and I'm no ingénu, I don't go around with my mouth hanging open—I'm experienced, look, I've been to Europe, I've lived in Rome! I went everywhere in Europe except Germany, I don't talk about Germany . . . Sister Irene, think of the significant men in the last century, the men who've changed the world! Jews, right? Marx, Freud, Einstein! Not that I believe Marx, Marx is a madman . . . and Freud, no, my sympathies are with spiritual humanism. I believe that the Jewish race is the exclusive . . . the exclusive, what's the word, the exclusive means by which humanism will be extended. . . . Humanism begins by excluding the Jew, and now," he said with a high, surprised laugh, "the Jew will perfect it. After the Nazis, only the Jew is authorized to understand humanism, its limitations and its possibilities. So, I say that the humanist is committed to life in its totality and not just to his profession! The religious person is totally religious, he is his religion! What else? I recognize in you a humanist and a religious person—"

But he did not seem to be talking to her or even looking at her.

"Here, read this," he said. "I wrote it last night." It was a long free-verse poem, typed on a typewriter whose ribbon was worn out.

"There's this trouble with my father, a wonderful man, a lovely man, but his health—his strength is fading, do you see? What must it be to him to see his son growing up? I mean, I'm a man now, he's getting old, weak, his health is bad—it's hell, right? I sympathize with him. I'd do anything for him, I'd cut open my veins, anything for a father—right? That's why I wasn't in school yesterday," he said, and his voice dropped for the last sentence, as if he had been dragged back to earth by a fact.

Sister Irene tried to read the poem, then pretended to read it. A jumble of words dealing with "life" and "death" and "darkness" and "love." "What do you think?" Weinstein said nervously, trying to read it over her shoulder and crowding against her.

"It's very . . . passionate," Sister Irene said.

This was the right comment; he took the poem back from her in silence, his face flushed with excitement. "Here, at this school, I have few people to talk with. I haven't shown anyone else that poem." He looked at her with his dark, intense eyes, and Sister Irene felt them focus upon her. She was terrified at what he was trying to do—he was trying to force her into a human relationship.

"Thank you for your paper," she said, turning away.

When he came the next day, ten minutes late, he was haughty and disdainful. He had nothing to say and sat with his arms folded. Sister Irene took back with her to the convent a feeling of betrayal and confusion. She had been hurt. It was absurd, and yet— She spent too much time thinking about him, as if he were somehow a kind of crystallization of her own loneliness; but she had no right to think so much of him. She did not want to think of him or of her loneliness. But Weinstein did so much more than think of his predicament; he embodied it, he acted it out, and that was perhaps why he fascinated her. It was as if he were doing a dance for her, a dance of shame and agony and delight, and so long as he did it, she was safe. She felt embarrassment for him, but also anxiety; she wanted to protect him. When the dean of the graduate school questioned her about Weinstein's work, she insisted that he was an "excellent" student, though she knew the dean had not wanted to hear that.

She prayed for guidance, she spent hours on her devotions, she was closer to her vocation than she had been for some years. Life at the convent became tinged with unreality, a misty distortion that took its tone from the glowering skies of the city at night, identical smokestacks ranged against the clouds and giving to the sky the excrement of the populated and successful earth. This city was not her city, this world was not her world. She felt no pride in knowing this, it was a fact. The little convent was not like an island in the center of this noisy world, but rather a kind of hole or crevice the world did not bother with, something of no interest. The convent's rhythm of life had nothing to do with the world's rhythm, it did not violate or alarm it in any way. Sister Irene tried to draw together the fragments of her life and synthesize them somehow in her vocation as a nun: she was a nun, she was recognized as a nun and had given herself happily to that life, she had a name, a place, she had dedicated her superior intelligence to the Church, she worked without pay and without expecting gratitude, she had given up pride, she did not think of herself but only of her work and her vocation, she did not think of anything external to these, she saturated herself daily in the knowledge that she was involved in the mystery of Christianity.

A daily terror attended this knowledge, however, for she sensed herself being drawn by that student, that Jewish boy, into a relationship she was not ready for. She wanted to cry out in fear that she was being forced into the role of a Christian, and what did that mean? What could her studies tell her? What could the other nuns tell her? She was alone, no one could help; he was making her into a Christian, and to her that was a mystery, a thing of terror, something others slipped on the way they slipped on their clothes, casually and thoughtlessly, but to her a magnificent and terrifying wonder.

For days she carried Weinstein's paper, marked A, around with her; he did not come to class. One day she checked with the graduate office and was told that Weinstein had called in to say his father was ill and that he would not be able to attend classes for a while. "He's strange, I remember him," the secretary said. "He missed all his exams last spring and made a lot of trouble. He was in and out of here every day."

So there was no more of Weinstein for a while, and Sister Irene stopped expecting him to hurry into class. Then, one morning, she found a letter from him in her mailbox.

He had printed it in black ink, very carefully, as if he had not trusted handwriting. The return address was in bold letters that, like his voice, tried to grab onto her: Birchcrest Manor. Somewhere north of the city. "Dear Sister Irene," the block letters said, "I am doing well here and have time for reading and relaxing. The Manor is delightful. My doctor here is an excellent, intelligent man who has time for me, unlike my former doctor. If you have time, you might drop in on my father, who worries about me too much, I think, and explain to him what my condition is. He doesn't seem to understand. I feel about this new life the way that boy, what's his name, in *Measure for Measure*, feels about the prospects of a different life; you remember what he says to his sister when she visits him in prison, how he is looking forward to an escape into another world. Perhaps you could *explain* this to my father and he would stop worrying." The letter ended with the father's name and address, in letters that were just a little too big. Sister Irene, walking slowly down the corridor as she read the letter, felt her eyes cloud over with tears. She was cold with fear, it was something she had never experienced before. She knew what Weinstein was trying to tell her, and the desperation of his attempt made it all the more pathetic; he did not deserve this, why did God allow him to suffer so?

She read through Claudio's speech to his sister, in *Measure for Measure:*[1]

Ay, but to die, and go we know not where;
To lie in cold obstruction[2] *and to rot;*
This sensible warm motion[3] *to become*
A kneaded clod;[4] *and the delighted spirit*
To bathe in fiery floods, or to reside
In thrilling[5] *region of thick-ribbèd ice,*
To be imprison'd in the viewless[6] *winds*
And blown with restless violence round about
The pendent world; or to be worse than worst
Of those that lawless and incertain thought
Imagine howling! 'Tis too horrible!
The weariest and most loathed worldly life
That age, ache, penury, and imprisonment

Can lay on nature is a paradise
To what we fear of death.

Sister Irene called the father's number that day. "Allen Weinstein residence, who may I say is calling?" a woman said, bored. "May I speak to Mr. Weinstein? It's urgent—about his son," Sister Irene said. There was a pause at the other end. "You want to talk to his mother, maybe?" the woman said. "His mother? Yes, his mother, then. Please. It's very important."

She talked with this strange, unsuspected woman, a disembodied voice that suggested absolutely no face, and insisted upon going over that afternoon. The woman was nervous, but Sister Irene, who was a university professor, after all, knew enough to hide her own nervousness. She kept waiting for the woman to say, "Yes, Allen has mentioned you . . ." but nothing happened.

She persuaded Sister Carlotta to ride over with her. This urgency of hers was something they were all amazed by. They hadn't suspected that the set of her gray eyes could change to this blurred, distracted alarm, this sense of mission that seemed to have come to her from nowhere. Sister Irene drove across the city in the late afternoon traffic, with the high whining noises from residential streets where trees were being sawed down in pieces. She understood now the secret, sweet wildness that Christ must have felt, giving himself for man, dying for the billions of men who would never know of him and never understand the sacrifice. For the first time she approached the realization of that great act. In her troubled mind the city traffic was jumbled and yet oddly coherent, an image of the world that was always out of joint with what was happening in it, its inner history struggling with its external spectacle. This sacrifice of Christ's, so mysterious and legendary now, almost lost in time—it was that by which Christ transcended both God and man at one moment, more than man because of his fate to do what no other man could do, and more than God because no god could suffer as he did. She felt a flicker of something close to madness.

She drove nervously, uncertainly, afraid of missing the street and afraid of finding it too, for while one part of her rushed forward to confront these people who had betrayed their son, another part of her would have liked noth-

[1] III. i. 118–132. [2] Obstruction: i.e., stiff and cold. [3] This sensible warm motion: this feeling, living body. [4] Kneaded clod; i.e., turned into earth. [5] Thrilling: freezing. [6] Viewless: invisible.

ing so much as to be waiting as usual for the summons to dinner, safe in her room. . . . When she found the street and turned onto it, she was in a state of breathless excitement. Here lawns were bright green and marred with only a few leaves, magically clean, and the houses were enormous and pompous, a mixture of styles: ranch houses, colonial houses, French country houses, white-bricked wonders with curving glass and clumps of birch trees somehow encircled by white concrete. Sister Irene stared as if she had blundered into another world. This was a kind of heaven, and she was too shabby for it.

The Weinstein's house was the strangest one of all: it looked like a small Alpine lodge, with an inverted-V-shaped front entrance. Sister Irene drove up the black-topped driveway and let the car slow to a stop; she told Sister Carlotta she would not be long.

At the door she was met by Weinstein's mother, a small, nervous woman with hands like her son's. "Come in, come in," the woman said. She had once been beautiful, that was clear, but now in missing beauty she was not handsome or even attractive but looked ruined and perplexed, the misshapen swelling of her white-blond professionally set hair like a cap lifting up from her surprised face. "He'll be right in. Allen?" she called, "our visitor is here." They went into the living room. There was a grand piano at one end and an organ at the other. In between were scatterings of brilliant modern furniture in conversational groups, and several puffed-up white rugs on the polished floor. Sister Irene could not stop shivering.

"Professor, it's so strange, but let me say when the phone rang I had a feeling—I had a feeling," the woman said, with damp eyes. Sister Irene sat, and the woman hovered about her. "Should I call you Professor? We don't . . . you know . . . we don't understand the technicalities that go with—Allen, my son, wanted to go here to the Catholic school; I told my husband why not? Why fight? It's the thing these days, they do anything they want for knowledge. And he had to come home, you know. He couldn't take care of himself in New York, that was the beginning of the trouble. . . . Should I call you Professor?"

"You can call me Sister Irene."

"Sister Irene?" the woman said, touching her throat in awe, as if something intimate and unexpected had happened.

Then Weinstein's father appeared, hurrying. He took long, impatient strides. Sister Irene stared at him and in that instant doubted everything—he was in his fifties, a tall, sharply handsome man, heavy but not fat, holding his shoulders back with what looked like an effort, but holding them back just the same. He wore a dark suit and his face was flushed, as if he had run a long distance.

"Now," he said, coming to Sister Irene and with a precise wave of his hand motioning his wife off, "now, let's straighten this out. A lot of confusion over that kid, eh?" He pulled a chair over, scraping it across a rug and pulling one corner over, so that its brown underside was exposed. "I came home early just for this, Libby phoned me. Sister, you got a letter from him, right?"

The wife looked at Sister Irene over her husband's head as if trying somehow to coach her, knowing that this man was so loud and impatient that no one could remember anything in his presence.

"A letter—yes—today—"

"He says what in it? You got the letter, eh? Can I see it?"

She gave it to him and wanted to explain, but he silenced her with a flick of his hand. He read through the letter so quickly that Sister Irene thought perhaps he was trying to impress her with his skill at reading. "So?" he said, raising his eyes, smiling, "so what is this? He's happy out there, he says. He doesn't communicate with us any more, but he writes to you and says he's happy—what's that? I mean, what the hell is that?"

"But he isn't happy. He wants to come home," Sister Irene said. It was so important that she make him understand that she could not trust her voice; goaded by this man, it might suddenly turn shrill, as his son's did. "Someone must read their letters before they're mailed, so he tried to tell me something by making an allusion to—"

"What?"

"—an allusion to a play, so that I would know. He may be thinking suicide, he must be very unhappy—"

She ran out of breath. Weinstein's mother

had begun to cry, but the father was shaking his head jerkily back and forth. "Forgive me, Sister, but it's a lot of crap, he needs the hospital, he needs help—right? It costs me fifty a day out there, and they've got the best place in the state, I figure it's worth it. He needs help, that kid, what do I care if he's unhappy? He's unbalanced!" he said angrily. "You want us to get him out again? We argued with the judge for two hours to get him in, an acquaintance of mine. Look, he can't control himself—he was smashing things here, he was hysterical. They need help, lady, and you do something about it fast! You do something! We made up our minds to do something and we did it! This letter—what the hell is this letter? He never talked like that to us!"

"But he means the opposite of what he says—"

"Then he's crazy! I'm the first to admit it." He was perspiring, and his face had darkened. "I've got no pride left this late. He's a little bastard, you want to know? He calls me names, he's filthy, got a filthy mouth—that's being smart huh? They give him a big scholarship for his filthy mouth? I went to college too, and I got out and knew something, and I for Christ's sake did something with it; my wife is an intelligent woman, a learned woman, would you guess she does book reviews for the little newspaper out here? Intelligent isn't crazy—crazy isn't intelligent. Maybe for you at the school he writes nice papers and gets an A, but out here, around the house, he can't control himself, and we got him committed!"

"But—"

"We're fixing him up, don't worry about it!" He turned to his wife. "Libby, get out of here, I mean it. I'm sorry, but get out of here, you're making a fool of yourself, go stand in the kitchen or something, you and the goddamn maid can cry on each other's shoulders. That one in the kitchen is nuts too, they're all nuts. Sister," he said, his voice lowering, "I thank you immensely for coming out here. This is wonderful, your interest in my son. And I see he admires you —that letter there. But what about that letter? If he did want to get out, which I don't admit —he was willing to be committed, in the end he said okay himself—if he wanted out I wouldn't do it. Why? So what if he wants to come back? The next day he wants something

else, what then? He's a sick kid, and I'm the first to admit it."

Sister Irene felt that sickness spread to her. She stood. The room was so big it seemed it must be a public place; there had been nothing personal or private about their conversation. Weinstein's mother was standing by the fireplace, sobbing. The father jumped to his feet and wiped his forehead in a gesture that was meant to help Sister Irene on her way out. "God, what a day," he said, his eyes snatching at hers for understanding, "you know—one of those days all day long? Sister, I thank you a lot. There should be more people in the world who care about others, like you. I mean that."

On the way back to the convent, the man's words returned to her, and she could not get control of them; she could not even feel anger. She had been pressed down, forced back, what could she do? Weinstein might have been watching her somehow from a barred window, and he surely would have understood. The strange idea she had had on the way over, something about understanding Christ, came back to her now and sickened her. But the sickness was small. It could be contained.

About a month after her visit to his father, Weinstein himself showed up. He was dressed in a suit as before, even the necktie was the same. He came right into her office as if he had been pushed and could not stop.

"Sister," he said, and shook her hand. He must have seen fear in her because he smiled ironically. "Look, I'm released. I'm let out of the nut house. Can I sit down?"

He sat. Sister Irene was breathing quickly, as if in the presence of an enemy who does not know he is an enemy.

"So, they finally let me out. I heard what you did. You talked with him, that was all I wanted. You're the only one who gave a damn. Because you're a humanist and a religious person, you respect . . . the individual. Listen," he said, whispering, "it was hell out there! Hell Birchcrest Manor! All fixed up with fancy chairs and *Life* magazines lying around—and what do they do to you? They locked me up, they gave me shock treatments! Shock treatments, how do you like that, it's discredited by everybody now —they're crazy out there themselves, sadists. They locked me up, they gave me hypodermic shots, they didn't treat me like a human being! Do you know what that is," Weinstein demanded savagely, "not to be treated like a human being? They made me an animal—for fifty dollars a day! Dirty filthy swine! Now I'm an outpatient because I stopped swearing at them. I found somebody's bobby pin, and when I wanted to scream I pressed it under my fingernail and it stopped me—the screaming went inside and not out—so they gave me good reports, those sick bastards. Now I'm an outpatient and I can walk along the street and breathe in the same filthy exhaust from the buses like all you normal people! Christ," he said, and threw himself back against the chair.

Sister Irene stared at him. She wanted to take his hand, to make some gesture that would close the aching distance between them. "Mr. Weinstein—"

"Call me Allen!" he said sharply.

"I'm very sorry—I'm terribly sorry—"

"My own parents committed me, but of course they didn't know what it was like. It was hell," he said thickly, "and there isn't any hell except what other people do to you. The psychiatrist out there, the main shrink, he hates Jews, too, some of us were positive of that, and he's got a bigger nose than I do, a real beak." He made a noise of disgust. "A dirty bastard, a sick, dirty, pathetic bastard—all of them. Anyway, I'm getting out of here, and I came to ask you a favor."

"What do you mean?"

"I'm getting out. I'm leaving. I'm going up to Canada and lose myself. I'll get a job, I'll forget everything, I'll kill myself maybe—what's the difference? Look, can you lend me some money?"

"Money?"

"Just a little! I have to get to the border, I'm going to take a bus."

"But I don't have any money—"

"No money?" He stared at her. "You mean—you don't have any? Sure you have some!"

She stared at him as if he had asked her to do something obscene. Everything was splotched and uncertain before her eyes.

"You must . . . you must go back," she said, "you're making a—"

"I'll pay it back. Look, I'll pay it back, can you go to where you live or something and get it? I'm in a hurry. My friends are sons of bitches: one of them pretended he didn't see me yesterday—I stood right in the middle of the sidewalk and yelled at him, I called him some appropriate names! So he didn't see me, huh? You're the only one who understands me, you understand me like a poet, you—"

"I can't help you, I'm sorry—I . . ."

He looked to one side of her and flashed his gaze back, as if he could control it. He seemed to be trying to clear his vision.

"You have the soul of a poet," he whispered, "you're the only one. Everybody else is rotten! Can't you lend me some money, ten dollars maybe? I have three thousand in the bank, and I can't touch it! They take everything away from me, they make me into an animal. . . . You know I'm not an animal, don't you? Don't you?"

"Of course," Sister Irene whispered.

"You could get money. Help me. Give me your hand or something, touch me, help me—please. . . ." He reached for her hand and she drew back. He stared at her and his face seemed about to crumble, like a child's. "I want something from you, but I don't know what—I want something!" he cried. "Something real! I want you to look at me like I was a human being, is that too much to ask? I have a brain, I'm alive, I'm suffering—what does that mean? Does that mean nothing? I want something real and not this phony Christian love garbage—it's all in the books, it isn't personal—I want something real—look. . . ."

He tried to take her hand again, and this time she jerked away. She got to her feet. "Mr. Weinstein," she said, "please—"

"You! You nun!" he said scornfully, his mouth twisted into a mock grin. "You nun! There's nothing under that ugly outfit, right? And you're not particularly smart even though you think you are; my father has more brains in his foot than you—"

He got to his feet and kicked the chair.

"You bitch!" he cried.

She shrank back against her desk as if she thought he might hit her, but he only ran out of the office.

Weinstein: the name was to become disembodied from the figure, as time went on. The semester passed, the autumn drizzle turned into snow, Sister Irene rode to school in the morning and left in the afternoon, four days a week, anonymous in her black winter cloak, quiet and stunned. University teaching was an anonymous task, each day dissociated from the rest, with no necessary sense of unity among the teachers: they came and went separately and might for a year miss a colleague who left his office five minutes before they arrived, and it did not matter.

She heard of Weinstein's death, his suicide by drowning, from the English Department secretary, a handsome white-haired woman who kept a transistor radio on her desk. Sister Irene was not surprised; she had been thinking of him as dead for months. "They identified him by some special television way they have now," the secretary said. "They're shipping the body back. It was up in Quebec. . . ."

Sister Irene could feel a part of herself drifting off, lured by the plains of white snow to the north, the quiet, the emptiness, the sweep of the Great Lakes up to the silence of Canada. But she called that part of herself back. She could only be one person in her lifetime. That was the ugly truth, she thought, that she could not really regret Weinstein's suffering and death; she had only one life and had already given it to someone else. He had come too late to her. Fifteen years ago, perhaps, but not now.

She was only one person, she thought, walking down the corridor in a dream. Was she safe in this single person, or was she trapped? She had only one identity. She could make only one choice. What she had done or hadn't done was the result of that choice, and how was she guilty? If she could have felt guilt, she thought, she might at least have been able to feel something.

Cruel and Barbarous Treatment

MARY McCARTHY
1912–

She could not bear to hurt her husband. She impressed this on the Young Man, on her confidants, and finally on her husband himself. The thought of Telling Him actually made her heart

turn over in a sudden and sickening way, she said. This was true, and yet she knew that being a potential divorcee was deeply pleasurable in somewhat the same way that being an engaged girl had been. In both cases, there was at first a subterranean courtship, whose significance it was necessary to conceal from outside observers. The concealment of the original, premarital courtship had, however, been a mere superstitious gesture, briefly sustained. It had also been, on the whole, a private secretiveness, not a partnership of silence. One put one's family and one's friends off the track because one was still afraid that the affair might not come out right, might not lead in a clean, direct line to the altar. To confess one's aspirations might be, in the end, to publicize one's failure. Once a solid understanding had been reached, there followed a short intermission of ritual bashfulness, in which both parties awkwardly participated, and then came the Announcement.

But with the extramarital courtship, the deception was prolonged where it had been ephemeral, necessary where it had been frivolous, conspiratorial where it had been lonely. It was, in short, serious where it had been dilettantish. That it was accompanied by feelings of guilt, by sharp and genuine revulsions, only complicated and deepened its delights, by abrading the sensibilities, and by imposing a sense of outlawry and consequent mutual dependence upon the lovers. But what this interlude of deception gave her, above all, she recognized, was an opportunity, unparalleled in her experience, for exercising feelings of superiority over others. For her husband she had, she believed, only sympathy and compunction. She got no fun, she told the Young Man, out of putting horns on her darling's head, and never for a moment, she said, did he appear to her as the comic figure of the cuckolded husband that one saw on the stage. (The Young Man assured her that his own sentiments were equally delicate, that for the wronged man he felt the most profound respect, tinged with consideration.) It was as if by the mere act of betraying her husband, she had adequately bested him; it was supererogatory for her to gloat, and, if she gloated at all, it was over her fine restraint in not-gloating, over the integrity of her moral sense, which allowed her to preserve even while engaged in sinfulness the acute realization of sin and shame.

Her overt superiority feelings she reserved for her friends. Lunches, and teas, which had been time killers, matters of routine, now became perilous and dramatic adventures. The Young Man's name was a bright, highly explosive ball which she bounced casually back and forth in these feminine tête-à-têtes. She would discuss him in his status of friend of the family, speculate on what girls he might have, attack him or defend him, anatomize him, keeping her eyes clear and impersonal, her voice empty of special emphasis, her manner humorously detached. *While all the time . . . !*

Three times a week or oftener, at lunch or tea, she would let herself tremble thus on the exquisite edge of self-betrayal, involving her companions in a momentous game whose rules and whose risks only she herself knew. The Public Appearances were even more satisfactory. To meet at a friend's house by design and to register surprise, to strike just the right note of young-matronly affection at cocktail parties, to treat him formally as "my escort" at the theater during intermissions—these were triumphs of stage management, more difficult of execution, more nerve-racking than the lunches and teas, because *two* actors were involved. His overardent glance must be hastily deflected; his too-self-conscious reading of his lines must be entered in the debit of her ledger of love, in anticipation of an indulgent accounting in private.

The imperfections of his performance were, indeed, pleasing to her. Not, she thought, because his impetuosities, his gaucheries, demonstrated the sincerity of his passion for her, nor because they proved him a new hand at this game of intrigue, but rather because the high finish of her own acting showed off well in comparison. "I should have gone on the stage," she could tell him gaily, "or been a diplomat's wife or an international spy," while he would admiringly agree. Actually, she doubted whether she could ever have been an actress, acknowledging that she found it more amusing and more gratifying to play herself than to interpret any character conceived by a dramatist. In these private theatricals it was her own many-faceted nature that she put on exhibit, and the audience, in this case unfortunately limited to two, could applaud both her skill of projection and intrinsic variety. Furthermore, this was a play in which

the *donnée*[1] was real, and the penalty for a missed cue or an inopportune entrance was, at first anyway, unthinkable.

She loved him, she knew, for being a bad actor, for his docility in accepting her tender, mock-impatient instruction. Those superiority feelings were fattening not only on the gullibility of her friends, but also on the comic flaws of her lover's character, and on the vulnerability of her lover's position. In this particular hive she was undoubtedly queen bee.

The Public Appearances were not exclusively duets. They sometimes took the form of a trio. On these occasions the studied and benevolent carefulness which she always showed for her husband's feelings served a double purpose. She would affect a conspicuous domesticity, an affectionate conjugal demonstrativeness, would sprinkle her conversation with "Darlings," and punctuate it with pats and squeezes till her husband would visibly expand and her lover plainly and painfully shrink. For the Young Man no retaliation was possible. These endearments of hers were sanctioned by law, usage, and habit; they belonged to her role of wife and could not be condemned or paralleled by a young man who was himself unmarried. They were clear provocations, but they could not be called so, and the Young Man preferred not to speak of them. *But she knew. . . .* Though she was aware of the sadistic intention of these displays, she was not ashamed of them, as she was sometimes twistingly ashamed of the hurt she was preparing to inflict on her husband. Partly she felt that they were punishments which the Young Man richly deserved for the wrong he was doing her husband, and that she herself in contriving them was acting, quite fittingly, both as judge and accused. Partly, too, she believed herself justified in playing the fond wife, whatever the damage to her lover's ego, because, in a sense, she actually was a fond wife. She *did* have these feelings, she insisted, whether she was exploiting them or not.

Eventually, however, her reluctance to wound her husband and her solicitude for his pride were overcome by an inner conviction that her love affair must move on to its next preordained

[1] A set of assumptions upon which a play or a story is built.

stage. The possibilities of subterranean courtship had been exhausted; it was time for the
Announcement. She and the Young Man began
to tell each other in a rather breathless and
literary style that the Situation Was Impossible,
and Things Couldn't Go On This Way Any
Longer. The ostensible meaning of the flurried
laments was that, under present conditions, they
were not seeing enough of each other, that their
hours together were too short and their periods
of separation too dismal, that the whole business of deception had become morally distasteful to them. Perhaps the Young Man really believed these things; she did not. For the first
time, she saw that the virtue of marriage as an
institution lay in its public character. Private
cohabitation, long continued, was, she concluded, a bore. Whatever the coziness of isolation, the warm delights of having a secret, a
love affair finally reached the point where it
needed the glare of publicity to revive the interest of its protagonists. Hence, she thought,
the engagement parties, the showers, the big
church weddings, the presents, the receptions.
These were simply socially approved devices by
which the lovers got themselves talked about.
The gossip-value of a divorce and remarriage
was obviously far greater than the gossip-value
of a mere engagement, and she was now ready,
indeed hungry, to hear What People Would
Say.

The lunches, the teas, the Public Appearances were getting a little flat. It was not, in the
end, enough to be a Woman With A Secret, if
to one's friends one appeared to be a woman
without a secret. The bliss of having a secret
required, in short, the consummation of telling
it, and she looked forward to the My-dear-I-had-
no-idea's, the I-thought-you-and-Bill-were-so-
happy-together's, the How-did-you-keep-it-so-
dark's with which her intimates would greet her
announcement. The audience of two no longer
sufficed her; she required a larger stage. She
tried it first, a little nervously, on two or three
of her closest friends, swearing them to secrecy.
"Bill must hear it first from me," she declared.
"It would be too terrible for his pride if he
found out afterwards that the whole town knew
it before he did. So you mustn't tell, even later
on, that I told you about this today. I felt I had
to talk to someone." After these lunches she

would hurry to a phone booth to give the Young
Man the gist of the conversation, just as a reporter, sent to cover a fire, telephones in to the
city desk. "She certainly was surprised," she
could always say with a little gush of triumph.
"But she thinks it's fine." *But did they actually?*
She could not be sure. Was it possible that she
sensed in these luncheon companions, her dearest friends, a certain reserve, a certain unex-
pressed judgment?

It was a pity, she reflected, that she was so
sensitive to public opinion. "I couldn't really
love a man," she murmured to herself once, "if
everybody didn't think he was wonderful." Everyone seemed to like the Young Man, of course.
But still. . . . She was getting panicky, she
thought. Surely it was only common sense that
nobody is admired by everybody. And even if a
man were universally despised, would there not
be a kind of defiant nobility in loving him in
the teeth of the whole world? There would, certainly, but it was a type of heroism that she
would scarcely be called upon to practice, for
the Young Man was popular, he was invited
everywhere, he danced well, his manners were
ingratiating, he kept up intellectually. But was
he not perhaps *too* amiable, *too* accommodat-
ing? Was it for this that her friends seemed
silently to criticize him?

At this time a touch of acridity entered into
her relations with the Young Man. Her indulgent
scoldings had an edge to them now, and it grew
increasingly difficult for her to keep her make-
believe impatience from becoming real. She
would look for dark spots in his character and
drill away at them as relentlessly as a dentist
at a cavity. A compulsive didacticism possessed
her: no truism of his, no cliché, no ineffectual
joke could pass the rigidity of her censorship.
And, hard as she tried to maintain the character of charming schoolmistress, the Young Man,
she saw, was taking alarm. She suspected that,
frightened and puzzled, he contemplated flight.
She found herself watching him with scientific
interest, speculating as to what course he would
take, and she was relieved but faintly disappointed when it became clear that he ascribed
her sharpness to the tension of the situation
and had decided to stick it out.

The moment had come for her to tell her
husband. By this single, cathartic act, she

would, she believed, rid herself of the doubts and anxieties that beset her. If her husband were to impugn the Young Man's character, she could answer his accusations and at the same time discount them as arising from jealousy. From her husband, at least, she might expect the favor of an open attack to which she could respond with the prepared defense that she carried, unspoken, about with her. Further, she had an intense, childlike curiosity as to How Her Husband Would Take It, a curiosity which she disguised for decency's sake as justifiable apprehension. The confidences already imparted to her friends seemed like pale dress rehearsals of the supreme confidence she was about to make. Perhaps it was toward this moment that the whole affair had been tending, for this moment that the whole affair had been designed. This would be the ultimate testing of her husband's love, its final, rounded, quintessential expression. Never, she thought, when you live with a man do you feel the full force of his love. It is gradually rationed out to you in an impure state, compounded with all the other elements of daily existence, so that you are hardly sensible of receiving it. There is no single point at which it is concentrated; it spreads out into the past and the future until it appears as a nearly imperceptible film over the surface of your life. Only face to face with its own annihilation could it show itself wholly, and, once shown, drop into the category of completed experiences.

She was not disappointed. She told him at breakfast in a fashionable restaurant, because, she said, he would be better able to control his feelings in public. When he called at once for the check, she had a spasm of alarm lest in an excess of brutality or grief he leave her there alone, conspicuous, and, as it were, unfulfilled. But they walked out of the restaurant together and through the streets, hand in hand, tears streaming, "unchecked," she whispered to herself, down their faces. Later they were in the Park, by an artificial lake, watching the ducks swim. The sun was very bright, and she felt a kind of superb pathos in the careful and irrelevant attention they gave to the pastoral scene. This was, she knew, the most profound, the most subtle, the most idyllic experience of her life. All the strings of her nature were, at last, vibrant. She was both doer and sufferer:

she inflicted pain and participated in it. And she was, at the same time, physician, for, as she was the weapon that dealt the wound, she was also the balm that could assuage it. Only she could know the hurt that engrossed him, and it was to her that he turned for the sympathy she had ready for him. Finally, though she offered him his discharge slip with one hand, with the other she beckoned him to approach. She was wooing him all over again, but wooing him to a deeper attachment than he had previously experienced, to an unconditional surrender. She was demanding his total understanding of her, his compassion, and his forgiveness. When at last he answered her repeated and agonized I-love-you's by grasping her hand more tightly and saying gently, "I know," she saw that she had won him over. She had drawn him into a truly mystical union. Their marriage was complete.

Afterwards everything was more prosaic. The Young Man had to be telephoned and summoned to a conference *à trois*,[2] a conference, she said, of civilized, intelligent people. The Young Man was a little awkward, even dropped a tear or two, which embarrassed everyone else, but what after all, she thought, could you expect? He was in a difficult position; his was a thankless part. With her husband behaving so well, indeed, so gallantly, the Young Man could not fail to look a trifle inadequate. The Young Man would have preferred it, of course, if her husband had made a scene, had bullied or threatened her, so that he himself might have acted the chivalrous protector. She, however, did not hold her husband's heroic courtesy against him: in some way, it reflected credit on herself. The Young Man, apparently, was expecting to Carry Her Off, but this she would not allow. "It would be too heartless," she whispered when they were alone for a moment. "We must all go somewhere together."

So the three went out for a drink, and she watched with a sort of desperation her husband's growing abstraction, the more and more perfunctory attention he accorded the conversation she was so bravely sustaining. "He is bored," she thought. "He is going to leave." The prospect of being left alone with the Young Man seemed suddenly unendurable. If her hus-

[2] Of three.

band were to go now, he would take with him the third dimension that had given the affair depth, and abandon her to a flat and vulgar love scene. Terrified, she wondered whether she had not already prolonged the drama beyond its natural limits, whether the confession in the restaurant and the absolution in the Park had not rounded off the artistic whole, whether the sequel of divorce and remarriage would not, in fact, constitute an anticlimax. Already she sensed that behind her husband's good manners an ironical attitude toward herself had sprung up. Was it possible that he had believed that they would return from the Park and all would continue as before? It was conceivable that her protestations of love had been misleading, and that his enormous tenderness toward her had been based, not on the idea that he was giving her up, but rather on the idea that he was taking her back—with no questions asked. If that were the case, the telephone call, the conference, and the excursion had in his eyes been a monstrous *gaffe*,[3] a breach of sensibility and good taste, for which he would never forgive her. She blushed violently. Looking at him again, she thought he was watching her with an expression which declared: I have found you out: now I know what you are like. For the first time, she felt him utterly alienated.

When he left them she experienced the letdown she had feared but also a kind of relief. She told herself that it was as well that he had cut himself off from her: it made her decision simpler. There was now nothing for her to do but to push the love affair to its conclusion, whatever that might be, and this was probably what she most deeply desired. Had the poignant intimacy of the Park persisted, she might have been tempted to drop the adventure she had begun and return to her routine. But that was, looked at coldly, unthinkable. For if the adventure would seem a little flat after the scene in the Park, the resumption of her marriage would seem even flatter. If the drama of the triangle had been amputated by her confession, the curtain had been brought down with a smack on the drama of wedlock.

And, as it turned out, the drama of the triangle was not quite ended by the superficial rupture of her marriage. Though she had left

her husband's apartment and been offered shelter by a confidante, it was still necessary for her to see him every day. There were clothes to be packed, and possessions to be divided, love letters to be reread and mementoes to be wept over in common. There were occasional passionate, unconsummated embraces; there were endearments and promises. And though her husband's irony remained, it was frequently vulnerable. It was not, as she had at first thought, an armor against her, but merely a sword, out of *Tristan and Isolde*,[4] which lay permanently between them and enforced discretion.

They met often, also, at the houses of friends, for, as she said, "What can I do? I know it's not tactful, but we all know the same people. You can't expect me to give up my friends." These Public Appearances were heightened in interest by the fact that these audiences, unlike the earlier ones, had, as it were, purchased librettos,[5] and were in full possession of the intricacies of the plot. She preferred, she decided, the evening parties to the cocktail parties, for there she could dance alternately with her lover and her husband to the accompaniment of subdued gasps on the part of the bystanders.

This interlude was at the same time festive and heartrending: her only dull moments were the evenings she spent alone with the Young Man. Unfortunately, the Post-Announcement period was only too plainly an interlude and its very nature demanded that it be followed by something else. She could not preserve her anomalous status indefinitely. It was not decent and, besides, people would be bored. From the point of view of one's friends, it was all very well to entertain a Triangle as a novelty; to cope with it as a permanent problem was a different matter. Once they had all three gotten drunk, and there was a scene, and, though everyone talked about it afterwards, her friends were, she thought, a little colder, a little more critical. People began to ask her when she was going to Reno. Furthermore, she noticed that her husband was getting a slight edge in popu-

---

[3] A social blunder; a *faux pas,* literally a false step.

[4] An opera by Wagner based on the Celtic tragic story of two lovers whose love is denied consummation. In the opera a sword separates them to enforce resistance to temptation.   [5] An operatic text; the plot.

larity over the Young Man. It was natural, of course, that everyone should feel sorry for him, and be especially nice. *But yet. . . .*

When she learned from her husband that he was receiving invitations from members of her own circle, invitations in which she and the Young Man were unaccountably not included, she went at once to the station and bought her ticket. Her good-by to her husband, which she had privately allocated to her last hours in town, took place prematurely, two days before she was to leave. He was rushing off to what she inwardly feared was a Gay Weekend in the country; he had only a few minutes; he wished her a pleasant trip; and he would write, of course. His highball was drained while her glass still stood half full; he sat forward nervously on his chair; and she knew herself to be acting the Ancient Mariner,[6] but her dignity would not allow her to hurry. She hoped that he would miss his train for her, but he did not. He left her sitting in the bar, and that night the Young Man could not, as he put it, do a thing with her. There was nowhere, absolutely nowhere, she said passionately, that she wanted to go, nobody she wanted to see, nothing she wanted to do. "You need a drink," he said with the air of a diagnostician. "A drink," she answered bitterly. "I'm sick of the drinks we've been having. Gin, whisky, rum, what else is there?" He took her into a bar, and she cried, but he bought her a fancy mixed drink, something called a Ramos gin fizz, and she was a little appeased because she had never had one before. Then some friends came in, and they all had another drink together, and she felt better. "There," said the Young Man, on the way home, "don't I know what's good for you? Don't I know how to handle you?" "Yes," she answered in her most humble and feminine tones, but she knew that they had suddenly dropped into a new pattern, that they were no longer the cynosure of a social group, but merely another young couple with an evening to pass, another young couple looking desperately for entertainment, wondering whether to call on a married couple or to drop in somewhere for a drink. This time the Young Man's prescription had worked, but

[6] The character in Coleridge's poem who delays a wedding guest to tell his mysterious tale; hence, one who delays another for his own purposes.

it was pure luck that they had chanced to meet someone they knew. A second or a third time they would scan the faces of the other drinkers in vain, would order a second drink and surreptitiously watch the door, and finally go out alone, with a quite detectable air of being unwanted.

When, a day and a half later, the Young Man came late to take her to the train, and they had to run down the platform to catch it, she found him all at once detestable. He would ride to 125th Street with her, he declared in a burst of gallantry, but she was angry all the way because she was afraid there would be trouble with the conductor. At 125th Street, he stood on the platform blowing kisses to her and shouting something that she could not hear through the glass. She made a gesture of repugnance, but, seeing him flinch, seeing him weak and charming and incompetent, she brought her hand reluctantly to her lips and blew a kiss back. The other passengers were watching, she was aware, and though their looks were doting and not derisive, she felt herself to be humiliated and somehow vulgarized. When the train began to move, and the Young Man began to run down the platform after it, still blowing kisses and shouting alternately, she got up, turned sharply away from the window and walked back to the club car. There she sat down and ordered a whisky and soda.

There were a number of men in the car, who looked up in unison as she gave her order, but, observing that they were all the middle-aged, small-business-men who "belonged" as inevitably to the club car as the white-coated porter and the leather-bound *Saturday Evening Post*, she paid them no heed. She was now suddenly overcome by a sense of depression and loss that was unprecedented for being in no way dramatic or pleasurable. In the last half hour she had seen clearly that she would never marry the Young Man, and she found herself looking into an insubstantial future with no signpost to guide her. Almost all women, she thought, when they are girls never believe that they will get married. The terror of spinsterhood hangs over them from adolescence on. Even if they are popular they think that no one really interesting will want them enough to marry them. Even if they get engaged they are afraid that something will go wrong, something will intervene. When they do get married it seems to them a sort of miracle, and, after they have been married for a time, though in retrospect the whole process looks perfectly natural and inevitable, they retain a certain unarticulated pride in the wonder they have performed. Finally, however, the terror of spinsterhood has been so thoroughly exorcised that they forget ever having been haunted by it, and it is at this stage that they contemplate divorce. "How could I have forgotten?" she said to herself and began to wonder what she would do.

She could take an apartment by herself in the Village. She would meet new people. She would entertain. But, she thought, if I have people in for cocktails, there will always come the moment when they have to leave, and I will be alone and have to pretend to have another engagement in order to save embarrassment. If I have them to dinner, it will be the same thing, but at least I will not have to pretend to have an engagement. I shall give dinners. Then, she thought, there will be the cocktail parties, and, if I go alone, I shall always stay a little too late, hoping that a young man or even a party of people will ask me to dinner. And if I fail, if no one asks me, I shall have the ignominy of walking out alone, trying to look as if I had somewhere to go. Then there will be the evenings at home with a good book when there will be no reason at all for going to bed, and I shall perhaps sit up all night. And the mornings when there will be no point in getting up, and I shall perhaps stay in bed till dinnertime. There will be the dinners in tearooms with other unmarried women, tearooms because women alone look conspicuous and forlorn in good restaurants. And then, she thought, I shall get older.

She would never, she reflected angrily, have taken this step, had she felt that she was burning her bridges behind her. She would never have left one man unless she had had another to take his place. But the Young Man, she now saw, was merely a sort of mirage which she had allowed herself to mistake for an oasis. "If the Man," she muttered, "did not exist, the Moment would create him." This was what had happened to her. She had made herself the victim of an imposture. But, she argued, with an access of cheerfulness, if this were true, if

out of the need of a second, a new, husband she had conjured up the figure of one, she had possibly been impelled by unconscious forces to behave more intelligently than appearances would indicate. She was perhaps acting out in a sort of hypnotic trance a ritual whose meaning had not yet been revealed to her, a ritual which required that, first of all, the Husband be eliminated from the cast of characters. Conceivably, she was designed for the role of *femme fatale*,[7] and for such a personage considerations of safety provisions against loneliness and old age, were not only philistine but irrelevant. She might marry a second, a third, a fourth time, or she might never marry again. But, in any case, for the thrifty bourgeois love-insurance, with its daily payments of patience, forbearance, and resignation, she was no longer eligible. She would be, she told herself delightedly, a bad risk.

She was, or soon would be, a Young Divorcee, and the term still carried glamor. Her divorce decree would be a passport conferring on her the status of citizeness of the world. She felt gratitude toward the Young Man for having unwittingly effected her transit into a new life. She looked about her at the other passengers. Later she would talk to them. They would ask, of course, where she was bound for; that was the regulation opening move of train conversations. But it was a delicate question what her reply should be. To say "Reno" straight out would be vulgar; it would smack of confidences too cheaply given. Yet to lie, to say "San Francisco" for instance, would be to cheat herself, to minimize her importance, to mislead her interlocutor into believing her an ordinary traveler with a commonplace destination. There must be some middle course which would give information without appearing to do so, which would hint at a *vie galante*[8] yet indicate a barrier of impeccable reserve. It would probably be best, she decided, to say "West" at first, with an air of vagueness and hesitation. Then, when pressed, she might go so far as to say "Nevada." But no farther.

[7] Fatal woman; woman regarded as man's fate; a prominent theme in Romantic literature.   [8] The gallant, gay life free of conventional encumbrance.

A Rose for Emily

WILLIAM FAULKNER
1897–1962

1

When Miss Emily Grierson died, our whole town went to her funeral: the men through a sort of respectful affection for a fallen monument, the women mostly out of curiosity to see the inside of her house, which no one save an old manservant—a combined gardener and cook—had seen in at least ten years.

It was a big, squarish frame house that had once been white, decorated with cupolas and spires and scrolled balconies in the heavily lightsome style of the seventies, set on what had once been our most select street. But garages and cotton gins had encroached and obliterated even the august names of that neighborhood; only Miss Emily's house was left, lifting its stubborn and coquettish decay above the cotton wagons and the gasoline pumps—an eyesore among eyesores. And now Miss Emily had gone to join the representatives of those august names where they lay in the cedar-bemused cemetery among the ranked and anonymous graves of Union and Confederate soldiers who fell at the battle of Jefferson.[1]

Alive, Miss Emily had been a tradition, a duty and a care; a sort of hereditary obligation upon the town, dating from that day in 1894 when Colonel Sartoris, the mayor—he who fathered the edict that no Negro woman should appear on the streets without an apron—remitted her taxes, the dispensation dating from the death of her father on into perpetuity. Not that Miss Emily would have accepted charity. Colonel Sartoris invented an involved tale to the effect that Miss Emily's father had loaned money to the town, which the town, as a matter of business, preferred this way of repaying. Only a man of Colonel Sartoris' generation and thought could have invented it, and only a woman could have believed it.

When the next generation, with its more modern ideas, became mayors and aldermen, this arrangement created some little dissatisfaction. On the first of the year they mailed her a tax notice. February came, and there was no reply. They wrote her a formal letter, asking her to call at the sheriff's office at her convenience. A week later the mayor wrote her himself, offering to call or send his car for her and received in reply a note on paper of an archaic shape, in a thin flowing calligraphy in faded ink, to the effect that she no longer went out at all. The tax notice was also enclosed, without comment.

They called a special meeting of the Board of Aldermen. A deputation waited upon her, knocked at the door through which no visitor had passed since she ceased giving china-painting lessons eight or ten years earlier. They were admitted by the old Negro into a dim hall from which a stairway mounted into still more shadow. It smelled of dust and disuse—a close, dank smell. The Negro led them into the parlor. It was furnished in heavy, leather-covered furniture. When the Negro opened the blinds of one window, they could see that the leather was cracked; and when they sat down, a faint dust rose sluggishly about their thighs, spinning with slow motes in the single sun-ray. On a tarnished gilt easel before the fireplace stood a crayon portrait of Miss Emily's father.

They rose when she entered—a small, fat woman in black, with a thin gold chain descending to her waist and vanishing into her belt, leaning on an ebony cane with a tarnished gold head. Her skeleton was small and spare; perhaps that was why what would have been merely plumpness in another was obesity in her. She looked bloated, like a body long submerged in motionless water, and of that pallid hue. Her eyes, lost in the fatty ridges of her face, looked like two small pieces of coal pressed into a lump of dough as they moved from one face to another while the visitors stated their errand.

She did not ask them to sit. She just stood in the door and listened quietly until the spokesman came to a stumbling halt. Then they could hear the invisible watch ticking at the end of the gold chain.

Her voice was dry and cold. "I have no taxes in Jefferson. Colonel Sartoris explained it to me. Perhaps one of you can gain access to the city records and satisfy yourselves."

"But we have. We are the city authorities, Miss Emily. Didn't you get a notice from the sheriff, signed by him?"

---

[1] Faulkner's name for Oxford, Mississippi.

"I received a paper, yes," Miss Emily said. "Perhaps he considers himself the sheriff . . . I have no taxes in Jefferson."

"But there is nothing on the books to show that, you see. We must go by the—"

"See Colonel Sartoris. I have no taxes in Jefferson."

"But, Miss Emily—"

"See Colonel Sartoris." (Colonel Sartoris had been dead almost ten years.) "I have no taxes in Jefferson. Tobe!" The Negro appeared. "Show these gentlemen out."

2

So she vanquished them, horse and foot, just as she had vanquished their fathers thirty years before about the smell. That was two years after her father's death and a short time after her sweetheart—the one we believed would marry her—had deserted her. After her father's death she went out very little; after her sweetheart went away, people hardly saw her at all. A few of the ladies had the temerity to call, but were not received, and the only sign of life about the place was the Negro man—a young man then —going in and out with a market basket.

"Just as if a man—any man—could keep a kitchen properly," the ladies said; so they were not surprised when the smell developed. It was another link between the gross, teeming world and the high and mighty Griersons.

A neighbor, a woman, complained to the mayor, Judge Stevens, eighty years old.

"But what will you have me do about it, madam?" he said.

"Why, send her word to stop it," the woman said. "Isn't there a law?"

"I'm sure that won't be necessary," Judge Stevens said. "It's probably just a snake or a rat that nigger of hers killed in the yard. I'll speak to him about it."

The next day he received two more complaints, one from a man who came in diffident deprecation. "We really must do something about it, Judge. I'd be the last one in the world to bother Miss Emily, but we've got to do something." That night the Board of Aldermen met —three graybeards and one younger man, a member of the rising generation.

"It's simple enough," he said. "Send her word to have her place cleaned up. Give her a certain time to do it in, and if she don't . . ."

"Dammit, sir," Judge Stevens said, "will you accuse a lady to her face of smelling bad?"

So the next night, after midnight, four men crossed Miss Emily's lawn and slunk about the house like burglars, sniffing along the base of the brickwork and at the cellar openings while one of them performed a regular sowing motion with his hand out of a sack slung from his shoulder. They broke open the cellar door and sprinkled lime there, and in all the outbuildings. As they recrossed the lawn, a window that had been dark was lighted and Miss Emily sat in it, the light behind her, and her upright torso motionless as that of an idol. They crept quietly across the lawn and into the shadow of the locusts that lined the street. After a week or two the smell went away.

That was when people had begun to feel really sorry for her. People in our town, remembering how old lady Wyatt, her great-aunt, had gone completely crazy at last, believed that the Griersons held themselves a little too high for what they really were. None of the young men were quite good enough for Miss Emily and such. We had long thought of them as a tableau, Miss Emily a slender figure in white in the background, her father a spraddled silhouette in the foreground, his back to her and clutching a horsewhip, the two of them framed by the back-flung front door. So when she got to be thirty and was still single, we were not pleased exactly, but vindicated; even with insanity in the family she wouldn't have turned down all of her chances if they had really materialized.

When her father died, it got about that the house was all that was left to her; and in a way, people were glad. At last they could pity Miss Emily. Being left alone, and a pauper, she had become humanized. Now she too would know the old thrill and the old despair of a penny more or less.

The day after his death all the ladies prepared to call at the house and offer condolence and aid, as is our custom. Miss Emily met them at the door, dressed as usual and with no trace of grief on her face. She told them that her father was not dead. She did that for three days, with the ministers calling on her, and the doctors, trying to persuade her to let them dispose of the body. Just as they were about to resort to law and force, she broke down, and they buried her father quickly.

We did not say she was crazy then. We believed she had to do that. We remembered all the young men her father had driven away, and we knew that with nothing left, she would have to cling to that which had robbed her, as people will.

3

She was sick for a long time. When we saw her again, her hair was cut short, making her look like a girl, with a vague resemblance to those angels in colored church windows—sort of tragic and serene.

The town had just let the contracts for paving the sidewalks, and in the summer after her father's death they began the work. The construction company came with niggers and mules and machinery, and a foreman named Homer Barron, a Yankee—a big, dark, ready man, with a big voice and eyes lighter than his face. The little boys would follow in groups to hear him cuss the niggers, and the niggers singing in time to the rise and fall of picks. Pretty soon he knew everybody in town. Whenever you heard a lot of laughing anywhere about the square, Homer Barron would be in the center of the group. Presently we began to see him and Miss Emily on Sunday afternoons driving in the yellow-wheeled buggy and the matched team of bays from the livery stable.

At first we were glad that Miss Emily would have an interest, because the ladies all said, "Of course a Grierson would not think seriously of a Northerner, a day laborer." But there were still others, older people, who said that even grief could not cause a real lady to forget *noblesse oblige*[2]—without calling it *noblesse oblige*. They just said, "Poor Emily. Her kinsfolk should come to her." She had some kin in Alabama; but years ago her father had fallen out with them over the estate of old lady Wyatt, the crazy woman, and there was no communication between the two families. They had not even been represented at the funeral.

And as soon as the old people said, "Poor Emily," the whispering began. "Do you suppose it's really so?" they said to one another. "Of course it is. What else could . . ." This behind their hands; rustling of craned silk and satin

2 The obligation of the noble.

behind jalousies closed upon the sun of Sunday afternoon as the thin, swift clop-clop-clop of the matched team passed: "Poor Emily."

She carried her head high enough—even when we believed that she was fallen. It was as if she demanded more than ever the recognition of her dignity as the last Grierson; as if it had wanted that touch of earthiness to reaffirm her imperviousness. Like when she bought the rat poison, the arsenic. That was over a year after they had begun to say "Poor Emily," and while the two female cousins were visiting her.

"I want some poison," she said to the druggist. She was over thirty then, still a slight woman, though thinner than usual, with cold, haughty black eyes in a face the flesh of which was strained across the temples and about the eye-sockets as you imagine a lighthouse-keeper's face ought to look. "I want some poison," she said.

"Yes, Miss Emily. What kind? For rats and such? I'd recom—"

"I want the best you have. I don't care what kind."

The druggist named several. "They'll kill anything up to an elephant. But what you want is—"

"Arsenic," Miss Emily said. "Is that a good one?"

"Is . . . arsenic? Yes, ma'am. But what you want—"

"I want arsenic."

The druggist looked down at her. She looked back at him, erect, her face like a strained flag. "Why, of course," the druggist said. "If that's what you want. But the law requires you to tell what you are going to use it for."

Miss Emily just stared at him, her head tilted back in order to look him eye for eye, until he looked away and went and got the arsenic and wrapped it up. The Negro delivery boy brought her the package; the druggist didn't come back. When she opened the package at home there was written on the box, under the skull and bones: "For rats."

4

So the next day we all said, "She will kill herself"; and we said it would be the best thing. When she had first begun to be seen with Homer Barron, we had said, "She will marry him." Then we said, "She will persuade him yet," because Homer himself had remarked—he liked men, and it was known that he drank with the younger men in the Elks' Club—that he was not a marrying man. Later we said, "Poor Emily" behind the jalousies as they passed on Sunday afternoon in the glittering buggy, Miss Emily with her head high and Homer Barron with his hat cocked and a cigar in his teeth, reins and whip in a yellow glove.

Then some of the ladies began to say that it was a disgrace to the town, and a bad example to the young people. The men did not want to interfere, but at last the ladies forced the Baptist minister—Miss Emily's people were Episcopal—to call upon her. He would never divulge what happened during that interview, but he refused to go back again. The next Sunday they again drove about the streets, and the following day the minister's wife wrote to Miss Emily's relations in Alabama.

So she had blood-kin under her roof again and we sat back to watch developments. At first nothing happened. Then we were sure that they were to be married. We learned that Miss Emily had been to the jeweler's and ordered a man's toilet set in silver, with the letters H. B. on each piece. Two days later we learned that she had bought a complete outfit of men's clothing, including a nightshirt, and we said, "They are married." We were really glad. We were glad because the two female cousins were even more Grierson than Miss Emily had ever been.

So we were not surprised when Homer Barron—the streets had been finished some time since—was gone. We were a little disappointed that there was not a public blowing-off, but we believed that he had gone on to prepare for Miss Emily's coming, or to give her a chance to get rid of the cousins. (By that time it was a cabal, and we were all Miss Emily's allies to help circumvent the cousins). Sure enough. after another week they departed. And, as we had expected all along, within three days Homer Barron was back in town. A neighbor saw the Negro man admit him at the kitchen door at dusk one evening.

And that was the last we saw of Homer Barron. And of Miss Emily for some time. The Negro man went in and out with the market basket, but the front door remained closed. Now and then we would see her at a window for a moment, as the men did that night when they sprinkled the lime, but for almost six months she did not appear on the streets. Then we knew that this was to be expected too; as if that quality of her father which had thwarted her woman's life so many times had been too virulent and too furious to die.

When we next saw Miss Emily, she had grown fat and her hair was turning gray. During the next few years it grew grayer and grayer until it attained an even pepper-and-salt iron-gray, when it ceased turning. Up to the day of her death at seventy-four it was still that vigorous iron-gray, like the hair of an active man.

From that time on her front door remained closed, save for a period of six or seven years, when she was about forty, during which she gave lessons in china-painting. She fitted up a studio in one of the downstairs rooms, where the daughters and grand-daughters of Colonel Sartoris' contemporaries were sent to her with the same regularity and in the same spirit that they were sent to church on Sundays with a twenty-five cent piece for the collection plate. Meanwhile her taxes had been remitted.

The newer generation became the backbone and the spirit of the town, and the painting pupils grew up and fell away and did not send their children to her with boxes of color and tedious brushes and pictures cut from the ladies' magazines. The front door closed upon the last one and remained closed for good. When the town got free postal delivery, Miss Emily alone refused to let them fasten the metal numbers above her door and attach a mailbox to it. She would not listen to them.

Daily, monthly, yearly we watched the Negro grow grayer and more stooped, going in and out with the market basket. Each December we sent her a tax notice, which would be returned by the post office a week later, unclaimed. Now and then we would see her in one of the downstairs windows—she had evidently shut up the top floor of the house—like the carven torso of an idol in a niche, looking or not looking at us, we could never tell which. Thus she passed from generation to generation—dear, inescapable, impervious, tranquil, and perverse.

And so she died. Fell ill in the house filled with dust and shadows, with only a doddering Negro man to wait on her. We did not even know she was sick; we had long since given up trying to get any information from the Negro. He talked to no one, probably not even to her, for his voice had grown harsh and rusty, as if from disuse.

She died in one of the downstairs rooms, in a heavy walnut bed with a curtain, her gray head propped on a pillow yellow and moldy with age and lack of sunlight.

5

The Negro met the first of the ladies at the front door and let them in, with their hushed, sibilant voices and their quick, curious glances, and then he disappeared. He walked right through the house and out the back and was not seen again.

The two female cousins came at once. They held the funeral on the second day, with the town coming to look at Miss Emily beneath a mass of bought flowers, with the crayon face of her father musing profoundly above the bier and the ladies sibilant and macabre; and the very old men—some in their brushed Confederate uniforms—on the porch and the lawn, talking of Miss Emily as if she had been a contemporary of theirs, believing that they had danced with her and courted her perhaps, confusing time with its mathematical progression, as the old do, to whom all the past is not a diminishing road but, instead, a huge meadow which no winter ever quite touches, divided from them now by the narrow bottleneck of the most recent decade of years.

Already we knew that there was one room in that region above stairs which no one had seen in forty years, and which would have to be forced. They waited until Miss Emily was decently in the ground before they opened it.

The violence of breaking down the door seemed to fill this room with pervading dust. A thin, acrid pall as of the tomb seemed to lie everywhere upon this room decked and furnished as for a bridal: upon the valance curtains of faded rose color, upon the rose-shaded lights, upon the dressing table, upon the delicate array of crystal and the man's toilet things backed with tarnished silver, silver so tarnished that the monogram was obscured. Among them lay a collar and tie, as if they had just been removed, which, lifted, left upon the surface a pale crescent in the dust. Upon a chair hung the suit,

carefully folded; beneath it the two mute shoes and the discarded socks.

The man himself lay in the bed.

For a long while we just stood there, looking down at the profound and fleshless grin. The body had apparently once lain in the attitude of an embrace, but now the long sleep that outlasts love, that conquers even the grimace of love, had cuckolded him. What was left of him, rotted beneath what was left of the nightshirt, had become inextricable from the bed in which he lay; and upon him and upon the pillow beside him lay that even coating of the patient and biding dust.

Then we noticed that in the second pillow was the indentation of a head. One of us lifted something from it, and leaning forward, that faint and invisible dust dry and acrid in the nostrils, we saw a long strand of iron-gray hair.

La Mère Sauvage[1]
GUY DE MAUPASSANT
1850–1893

Like most of Maupassant's stories, this one has been praised for its compression and suggestiveness, and for the management of detail and economy of means. Indeed, the author's objective, matter-of-fact tone, and simple narrative technique may trap the reader on the literal level until he examines the meaning of the rabbit and the stone, especially the meaning of the final sentence, "And I picked up a little stone, still blackened by the flames," which not only explains the transformation of the mother but also reveals Maupassant's universal theme of the effect of the brutality of war on human beings.

I had not been at Virelogne for fifteen years. I went back there in the autumn, to shoot with my friend Serval, who had at last rebuilt his château, which had been destroyed by the Prussians.

I loved that district very much. It is one of those corners of the world which have a sensu-

[1] The Savage Mother.

ous charm for the eyes. You love it with a bodily love. We, whom the country seduces, we keep tender memories for certain springs, for certain woods, for certain pools, for certain hills, seen very often, and which have stirred us like joyful events. Sometimes our thoughts turn back towards a corner in a forest, or the end of a bank, or an orchard powdered with flowers, seen but a single time, on some gay day; yet remaining in our hearts like the images of certain women met in the street on a spring morning, with bright transparent dresses; and leaving in soul and body an unappeased desire which is not to be forgotten, a feeling that you have just rubbed elbows with happiness.

At Virelogne I loved the whole countryside, dotted with little woods, and crossed by brooks which flashed in the sun and looked like veins, carrying blood to the earth. You fished in them for crawfish, trout, and eels! Divine happiness! You could bathe in places, and you often found snipe among the high grass which grew along the borders of these slender watercourses.

I was walking, lightly as a goat, watching my two dogs ranging before me. Serval, a hundred metres to my right, was beating a field of lucern. I turned the thicket which forms the boundary of the wood of Sandres, and I saw a cottage in ruins.

All of a sudden, I remembered it as I had seen it the last time, in 1869, neat, covered with vines, with chickens before the door. What is sadder than a dead house, with its skeleton standing upright, bare and sinister?

I also remembered that in it, one very tiring day, the good woman had given me a glass of wine to drink, and that Serval had then told me the history of its inhabitants. The father, an old poacher, had been killed by the gendarmes. The son, whom I had once seen, was a tall, dry fellow who also passed for a ferocious destroyer of game. People called them *"les Sauvage."*

Was that a name or a nickname?

I hailed Serval. He came up with his long strides like a crane.

I asked him:

"What's become of those people?"

And he told me this story:

When war was declared, the son Sauvage, who was then thirty-three years old, enlisted, leaving his mother alone in the house. People did not pity the old woman very much because she had money; they knew it.

But she remained quite alone in that isolated dwelling so far from the village, on the edge of the wood. She was not afraid, however, being of the same strain as her menfolk; a hardy old woman, tall and thin, who laughed seldom, and with whom one never jested. The women of the fields laugh but little in any case; that is men's business, that! But they themselves have sad and narrowed hearts, leading a melancholy, gloomy life. The peasants learn a little boisterous merriment at the tavern, but their helpmates remain grave, with countenances which are always severe. The muscles of their faces have never learned the movements of the laugh.

La Mère Sauvage continued her ordinary existence in her cottage, which was soon covered by the snows. She came to the village once a week, to get bread and a little meat; then she returned into her house. As there was talk of wolves, she went out with a gun upon her back —her son's gun, rusty, and with the butt worn by the rubbing of the hand; and she was strange to see, the tall "Sauvage," a little bent, going with slow strides over the snow, the muzzle of the piece extending beyond the black headdress, which pressed close to her head and imprisoned her white hair, which no one had ever seen.

One day a Prussian force arrived. It was billeted upon the inhabitants, according to the property and resources of each. Four were allotted to the old woman, who was known to be rich.

They were four great boys with blond skin, with blond beards, with blue eyes, who had remained stout notwithstanding the fatigues which they had endured already, and who also, though in a conquered country, had remained kind and gentle. Alone with this aged woman, they showed themselves full of consideration, sparing her, as much as they could, all expenses and fatigue. They would be seen, all four of them, making their toilet around the well, of a morning, in their shirt-sleeves, splashing with great swishes of water, under the crude daylight of the snowy weather, their pink-white Northman's flesh, while La Mère Sauvage went and came, making ready the soup. Then they would be seen cleaning the kitchen, rubbing the tiles, splitting wood, peeling potatoes, doing up all the housework, like four good sons about their mother.

But the old woman thought always of her own, so tall and thin, with his hooked nose and his brown eyes and his heavy mustache which made a roll of black hairs upon his lip. She asked each day of each of the soldiers who were installed beside her hearth:

"Do you know where the French Marching Regiment No. 23 was sent? My boy is in it."

They answered, "No, not know, not know at all." And, understanding her pain and her uneasiness (they, who had mothers too, there at home), they rendered her a thousand little services. She loved them well, moreover, her four enemies, since the peasantry feels no patriotic hatred; that belongs to the upper class alone. The humble, those who pay the most, because they are poor, and because every new burden crushes them down; those who are killed in masses, who make the true cannon's-meat, because they are so many; those, in fine, who suffer most cruelly the atrocious miseries of war, because they are the feeblest, and offer least resistance—they hardly understand at all those bellicose ardors, that excitable sense of honor, or those pretended political combinations which in six months exhaust two nations, the conqueror with the conquered.

They said on the countryside in speaking of the Germans of La Mère Sauvage:

"There are four who have found a soft place."

Now, one morning, when the old woman was alone in the house, she perceived far off on the plain a man coming towards her dwelling. Soon she recognized him; it was the postman charged to distribute the letters. He gave her a folded paper, and she drew out of her case the spectacles which she used for sewing; then she read:

MADAME SAUVAGE,—The present letter is to tell you sad news. Your boy Victor was killed yesterday by a shell which near cut him in two. I was just by, seeing that we stood next each other in the company, and he would talk to me about you to let you know on the same day if anything happened to him.

I took his watch, which was in his pocket, to bring it back to you when the war is done.

I salute you very friendly.

CÉSAIRE RIVOT
Soldier of the 2nd class, March. Reg. No. 23

The letter was dated three weeks back.

She did not cry at all. She remained motionless, so seized and stupefied that she did not even suffer as yet. She thought: "V'la Victor who is killed now." Then little by little the tears mounted to her eyes, and the sorrow caught her heart. The ideas came to her, one by one, dreadful, torturing. She would never kiss him again, her child, her big boy, never again! The gendarmes had killed the father, the Prussians had killed the son. He had been cut in two by a cannon-ball. She seemed to see the thing, the horrible thing: the head falling, the eyes open, while he chewed the corner of his big mustache as he always did in moments of anger.

What had they done with his body afterwards? If they had only let her have her boy back as they had given her back her husband—with the bullet in the middle of his forehead!

But she heard a noise of voices. It was the Prussians returning from the village. She hid her letter very quickly in her pocket, and she received them quietly, with her ordinary face, having had time to wipe her eyes.

They were laughing, all four, delighted, since they brought with them a fine rabbit—stolen, doubtless—and they made signs to the old woman that there was to be something good to eat.

She set herself to work at once to prepare breakfast; but when it came to killing the rabbit, her heart failed her. And yet it was not the first. One of the soldiers struck it down with a blow of his fist behind the ears.

The beast once dead, she separated the red body from the skin; but the sight of the blood which she was touching, and which covered her hands, of the warm blood which she felt cooling and coagulating, made her tremble from head to foot; and she kept seeing her big boy cut in two, and quite red also, like this still-palpitating animal.

She set herself at table with the Prussians, but she could not eat, not even a mouthful. They devoured the rabbit without troubling themselves about her. She looked at them askance, without speaking, ripening a thought, and with a face so impassible that they perceived nothing.

All of a sudden she said: "I don't even know your names, and here's a whole month that we've been together." They understood, not without difficulty, what she wanted, and told their names. That was not sufficient; she had them written for her on a paper, with the addresses of their families, and, resting her spectacles on her great nose, she considered that strange handwriting, then folded the sheet and put it in her pocket, on top of the letter which told her of the death of her son.

When the meal was ended, she said to the men:

"I am going to work for you."

And she began to carry up hay into the loft where they slept.

They were astonished at her taking all this trouble; she explained to them that thus they would not be so cold; and they helped her. They heaped the trusses of hay as high as the straw roof; and in that manner they made a sort of great chamber with four walls of fodder, warm and perfumed, where they should sleep splendidly.

At dinner, one of them was worried to see that La Mère Sauvage still ate nothing. She told him that she had the cramps. Then she kindled a good fire to warm herself up, and the four Germans mounted to their lodging-place by the ladder which served them every night for this purpose.

As soon as they closed the trap, the old woman removed the ladder, then opened the outside door noiselessly, and went back to look for more bundles of straw, with which she filled her kitchen. She went barefoot in the snow, so softly that no sound was heard. From time to time she listened to the sonorous and unequal snoring of the four soldiers who were fast asleep.

When she judged her preparations to be sufficient, she threw one of the bundles into the fireplace, and when it was alight she scattered it all over the others. Then she went outside again and looked.

In a few seconds the whole interior of the cottage was illumined with a violent brightness and became a dreadful brasier, a gigantic fiery furnace, whose brilliance spouted out of the narrow window and threw a glittering beam upon the snow.

Then a great cry issued from the summit of the house; it was a clamor of human shriekings, heart-rending calls of anguish and of fear. At last, the trap having fallen in, a whirlwind of fire shot up into the loft, pierced the straw roof, rose to the sky like the immense flame of a torch; and all the cottage flared.

Nothing more was heard therein but the crackling of the fire, the crackling sound of the walls, the falling of the rafters. All of a sudden the roof fell in, and the burning carcass of the dwelling hurled a great plume of sparks into the air, amid a cloud of smoke.

The country, all white, lit up by the fire, shone like a cloth of silver tinted with red.

A bell, far off, began to toll.

The old 'Sauvage" remained standing before her ruined dwelling, armed with her gun, her son's gun, for fear lest one of those men might escape.

When she saw that it was ended, she threw her weapon into the brasier. A loud report rang back.

People were coming, the peasants, the Prussians.

They found the woman seated on the trunk of a tree, calm and satisfied.

A German officer, who spoke French like a son of France, demanded of her:

"Where are your soldiers?"

She extended her thin arm towards the red heap of fire which was gradually going out, and she answered with a strong voice:

"There!"

They crowded round her. The Prussian asked:

"How did it take fire?"

She said:

"It was I who set it on fire."

They did not believe her, they thought that the sudden disaster had made her crazy. So, while all pressed round and listened, she told the thing from one end to the other, from the arrival of the letter to the last cry of the men who were burned with her house. She did not forget a detail of all which she had felt, nor of all which she had done.

When she had finished, she drew two pieces of paper from her pocket, and, to distinguish them by the last glimmers of the fire, she again adjusted her spectacles; then she said, showing one: "That, that is the death of Victor." Showing the other, she added, indicating the red ruins with a bend of the head: "That, that is their names, so that you can write home." She calmly held the white sheet out to the officer, who held her by the shoulders, and she continued:

"You must write how it happened, and you must say to their mothers that it was I who did that, Victoire Simon, la Sauvage! Do not forget."

The officer shouted some orders in German.

They seized her, they threw her against the walls of her house, still hot. Then twelve men drew quickly up before her, at twenty paces. She did not move. She had understood; she waited.

An order rang out, followed instantly by a long report. A belated shot went off by itself, after the others.

The old women did not fall. She sank as though they had mowed off her legs.

The Prussian officer approached her. She was almost cut in two, and in her withered hand she held her letter bathed with blood.

My friend Serval added:

"It was by way of reprisal that the Germans destroyed the château of the district, which belonged to me."

As for me, I thought of the mothers of those four gentle fellows burned in the house; and of the atrocious heroism of that other mother shot against the wall.

And I picked up a little stone, still blackened by the flames.

On the Road

ANTON CHEKHOV
1860–1904

*"Upon the breast of a gigantic crag,
A golden cloudlet rested for one night."*
—LERMONTOV[1]

In the room which the tavern keeper, the Cossack Semyon Tchistopluy, called the "travellers' room," that is kept exclusively for travellers, a tall, broad-shouldered man of forty was sitting at the big unpainted table. He was asleep with his elbows on the table and his head leaning on his fist. An end of tallow candle, stuck into an old pomatum pot, lighted up his light brown beard, his thick, broad nose, his sunburnt cheeks and the thick, black eyebrows overhanging his closed eyes. . . . The nose and the cheeks and the eyebrows, all the features, each taken separately, were coarse and heavy, like the furni-

ture and the stove in the "travellers' room," but taken all together they gave the effect of something harmonious and even beautiful. Such is the lucky star, as it is called, of the Russian face: the coarser and harsher its features the softer and more good-natured it looks. The man was dressed in a gentleman's reefer jacket, shabby, but bound with wide new braid, a plush waistcoat, and full black trousers thrust into big high boots.

On one of the benches, which stood in a continuous row along the wall, a girl of eight, in a brown dress and long black stockings, lay asleep on a coat lined with fox. Her face was pale, her hair was flaxen, her shoulders were narrow, her whole body was thin and frail, but her nose stood out as thick and ugly a lump as the man's. She was sound asleep, and unconscious that her semicircular comb had fallen off her head and was cutting her cheek.

The "travellers' room" had a festive appearance. The air was full of the smell of freshly scrubbed floors, there were no rags hanging as usual on the line that ran diagonally across the room, and a little lamp was burning in the corner over the table, casting a patch of red light on the ikon of St. George the Victorious.[2] From the ikon stretched on each side of the corner a row of cheap oleographs, which maintained a strict and careful gradation in the transition from the sacred to the profane. In the dim light of the candle end and the red ikon lamp the pictures looked like one continuous stripe, covered with blurs of black. When the tiled stove, trying to sing in unison with the weather, drew in the air with a howl, while the logs, as though waking up, burst into bright flame and hissed angrily, red patches began dancing on the log walls, and over the head of the sleeping man could be seen first the Elder Seraphim,[3] then the Shah Nasir-ed-Din,[4] then a fat, brown baby with goggle eyes, whispering in the ear of a young girl with an extraordinarily blank, and indifferent face. . . .

Outside a storm was raging. Something frantic and wrathful, but profoundly unhappy, seemed to be flinging itself about the tavern with the ferocity of a wild beast and trying to break

---

[1] Mikhail Yurievich Lermontov (1814–1841), Russian poet and novelist, was called the "poet of the Caucasus" because he was twice exiled there.

[2] Historical and mythological religious character.
[3] Literally, Elder Angel.   [4] Famous jester of Turkish legend.

in. Banging at the doors, knocking at the windows and on the roof, scratching at the walls, it alternately threatened and besought, then subsided for a brief interval, and then with a gleeful, treacherous howl burst into the chimney, but the wood flared up, and the fire, like a chained dog, flew wrathfully to meet its foe, a battle began, and after it—sobs, shrieks howls of wrath. In all of this there was the sound of angry misery and unsatisfied hate, and the mortified impatience of something accustomed to triumph.

Bewitched by this wild, inhuman music the "travellers' room" seemed spellbound forever, but all at once the door creaked and the potboy, in a new print shirt, came in. Limping on one leg, and blinking his sleepy eyes, he snuffed the candle with his fingers, put some more wood on the fire and went out. At once from the church, which was three hundred paces from the tavern, the clock struck midnight. The wind played with the chimes as with the snowflakes; chasing the sounds of the clock it whirled them round and round over a vast space, so that some strokes were cut short or drawn out in long, vibrating notes, while others were completely lost in the general uproar. One stroke sounded as distinctly in the room as though it had chimed just under the window. The child, sleeping on the foxskin, started and raised her head. For a minute she stared blankly at the dark window, at Nasir-ed-Din over whom a crimson glow from the fire flickered at that moment, then she turned her eyes upon the sleeping man.

"Daddy," she said.

But the man did not move. The little girl knitted her brow angrily, lay down, and curled up her legs. Someone in the tavern gave a loud, prolonged yawn. Soon afterwards there was the squeak of the swing door and the sound of indistinct voices. Someone came in, shaking the snow off, and stamping in felt boots which made a muffled thud.

"What is it?" a woman's voice asked languidly.

"Mademoiselle Ilovaisky has come, . . ." answered a bass voice.

Again there was the squeak of the swing door. Then came the roar of the wind rushing in. Someone, probably the lame boy, ran to the door leading to the "travellers' room," coughed deferentially, and lifted the latch.

"This way, lady, please," said a woman's voice in dulcet tones. "It's clean in here, my beauty. . . ."

The door was opened wide and a peasant with a beard appeared in the doorway, in the long coat of a coachman, plastered all over with snow from head to foot, and carrying a big trunk on his shoulder. He was followed into the room by a feminine figure, scarcely half his height, with no face and no arms, muffled and wrapped up like a bundle and also covered with snow. A damp chill, as from a cellar, seemed to come to the child from the coachman and the bundle, and the fire and the candles flickered.

"What nonsense!" said the bundle angrily. "We could go perfectly well. We have only nine more miles to go, mostly by the forest, and we should not get lost. . . ."

"As for getting lost, we shouldn't, but the horses can't go on, lady!" answered the coachman. "And it is Thy Will, O Lord! As though I had done it on purpose!"

"God knows where you have brought me. . . . Well, be quiet. . . . There are people asleep here, it seems. You can go. . . ."

The coachman put the portmanteau on the floor, and as he did so, a great lump of snow fell off his shoulders. He gave a sniff and went out.

Then the little girl saw two little hands come out from the middle of the bundle, stretch upwards and begin angrily disentangling the network of shawls, kerchiefs, and scarves. First a big shawl fell on the ground, then a hood, then a white knitted kerchief. After freeing her head, the traveller took off her pelisse and at once shrank to half the size. Now she was in a long, grey coat with big buttons and bulging pockets. From one pocket she pulled out a paper parcel, from the other a bunch of big, heavy keys, which she put down so carelessly that the sleeping man started and opened his eyes. For some time he looked blankly round him as though he didn't know where he was, then he shook his head, went to the corner and sat down. . . . The newcomer took off her greatcoat, which made her shrink to half her size again, she took off her big felt boots, and sat down, too.

By now she no longer resembled a bundle: she was a thin little brunette of twenty, as slim as a snake, with a long white face and curly hair. Her nose was long and sharp, her chin, too, was long and sharp, her eyelashes were long, the corners of her mouth were sharp, and, thanks to this general sharpness, the expression of her face was biting. Swathed in a closely fitting black dress with a mass of lace at her neck and sleeves, with sharp elbows and long pink fingers, she recalled the portraits of mediaeval English ladies. The grave concentration of her face increased this likeness.

The lady looked round at the room, glanced sideways at the man and the little girl, shrugged her shoulders, and moved to the window. The dark windows were shaking from the damp west wind. Big flakes of snow glistening in their whiteness lay on the window frame, but at once disappeared, borne away by the wind. The savage music grew louder and louder. . . .

After a long silence the little girl suddenly turned over, and said angrily, emphasizing each word:

"Oh, goodness, goodness, how unhappy I am! Unhappier than anyone!"

The man got up and moved with little steps to the child with a guilty air, which was utterly out of keeping with his huge figure and big beard.

"You are not asleep, dearie?" he said, in an apologetic voice. "What do you want?"

"I don't want anything, my shoulder aches! You are a wicked man, Daddy, and God will punish you! You'll see He will punish you."

"My darling, I know your shoulder aches, but what can I do, dearie?" said the man, in the tone in which men who have been drinking excuse themselves to their stern spouses. "It's the journey has made your shoulder ache, Sasha. To-morrow we shall get there and rest, and the pain will go away. . . ."

"To-morrow, to-morrow. . . . Every day you say to-morrow. We shall be going on another twenty days."

"But we shall arrive to-morrow, dearie, on your father's word of honour. I never tell a lie, but if we are detained by the snowstorm it is not my fault."

"I can't bear any more, I can't, I can't!"

Sasha jerked her leg abruptly and filled the room with an unpleasant wailing. Her father made a despairing gesture, and looked hopelessly toward the young lady. The latter shrugged her shoulders, and hesitatingly went up to Sasha.

"Listen, my dear," she said, "it is no use crying. It's really naughty; if your shoulder aches it can't be helped."

"You see, Madam," said the man quickly, as though defending himself, "we have not slept for two nights, and have been travelling in a revolting conveyance. Well, of course, it is natural she should be ill and miserable, . . . and then, you know, we had a drunken driver, our portmanteau has been stolen . . . the snowstorm all the time, but what's the use of crying, Madam? I am exhausted, though, by sleeping in a sitting position, and I feel as though I were drunk. Oh, dear! Sasha, and I feel sick as it is, and then you cry!"

Then man shook his head, and with a gesture of despair sat down.

"Of course you mustn't cry," said the young lady. "It's only little babies cry. If you are ill, dear, you must undress and go to sleep. . . Let us take off your things!"

When the child had been undressed and pacified a silence reigned again. The young lady seated herself at the window, and looked round wonderingly at the room of the inn, at the ikon, at the stove. . . . Apparently the room and the little girl with the thick nose, in her short boy's nightgown, and the child's father, all seemed strange to her. This strange man was sitting in a corner; he kept looking about him helplessly, as though he were drunk, and rubbing his face with the palm of his hand. He sat silent, blinking, and judging from his guilty-looking figure it was difficult to imagine that he would soon begin to speak. Yet he was the first to begin. Stroking his knees, he gave a cough, laughed, and said:

"It's a comedy, it really is. . . . I look and I cannot believe my eyes: for what devilry has destiny driven us to this accursed inn? What did she want to show by it? Life sometimes performs such 'salto mortale,'[5] one can only stare and blink in amazement. Have you come from far, Madam?"

"No, not from far," answered the young lady. "I am going from our estate, fifteen miles from here, to our farm, to my father and brother. My name is Ilovaisky, and the farm is called Ilovaiskoe. It's nine miles away. What unpleasant weather!"

"It couldn't be worse."

[5] Mortal leap; deadly jump.

The lame boy came in and stuck a new candle in the pomatum pot.

"You might bring us the samovar, boy," said the man, addressing him.

"Who drinks tea now?" laughed the boy. "It is a sin to drink tea before mass. . . ."

"Never mind, boy, you won't burn in hell if we do. . . ."

Over the tea the new acquaintances got into conversation.

Mlle. Ilovaisky learned that her companion was called Grigory Petrovitch Liharev, that he was the brother of the Liharev who was Marshal of Nobility in one of the neighbouring districts, and he himself had once been a landowner, but had "run through everything in his time." Liharev learned that her name was Marya Mihailovna, that her father had a huge estate, but that she was the only one to look after it as her father and brother looked at life through their fingers, were irresponsible, and were too fond of harriers.

"My father and brother are all alone at the farm," she told him, brandishing her fingers (she had the habit of moving her fingers before her pointed face as she talked, and after every sentence moistened her lips with her sharp little tongue). "They, I mean men, are an irresponsible lot, and don't stir a finger for themselves. I can fancy there will be no one to give them a meal after the fast! We have no mother, and we have such servants that they can't lay the tablecloth properly when I am away. You can imagine their condition now! They will be left with nothing to break their fast, while I have to stay here all night. How strange it all is."

She shrugged her shoulders, took a sip from her cup, and said:

"There are festivals that have a special fragrance: at Easter, Trinity and Christmas there is a peculiar scent in the air. Even unbelievers are fond of those festivals. My brother, for instance, argues that there is no God, but he is the first to hurry to Matins at Easter."

Liharev raised his eyes to Mlle. Ilovaisky and laughed.

"They argue that there is no God," she went on, laughing too, "but why is it, tell me, all the celebrated writers, the learned men, clever people generally, in fact, believe towards the end of their life?"

"If man does not know how to believe when

he is young, Madam, he won't believe in his old age if he is ever so much of a writer."

Judging from Liharev's cough he had a bass voice, but, probably from being afraid to speak aloud, or from exaggerated shyness, he spoke in a tenor. After a brief pause he heaved a sigh and said:

"The way I look at it is that faith is a faculty of the spirit. It is just the same as a talent, one must be born with it. So far as I can judge by myself, by the people I have seen in my time, and by all that is done around us, this faculty is present in Russians in its highest degree. Russian life presents us with an uninterrupted succession of convictions and aspirations, and if you care to know, it has not yet the faintest notion of lack of faith or scepticism. If a Russian does not believe in God, it means he believes in something else."

Liharev took a cup of tea from Mlle. Ilovaisky, drank off half in one gulp, and went on:

"I will tell you about myself. Nature has implanted in my breast an extraordinary faculty for belief. Whisper it not to the night, but half my life I was in the ranks of the Atheists and Nihilists,[6] but there was not one hour in my life in which I ceased to believe. All talents, as a rule, show themselves in early childhood, and so my faculty showed itself when I could still walk upright under the table. My mother liked her children to eat a great deal, and when she gave me food she used to say: 'Eat! Soup is the great thing in life!' I believed, and ate the soup ten times a day, ate like a shark, ate till I was disgusted and stupefied. My nurse used to tell me fairy tales, and I believed in house-spirits, in wood-elves, and in goblins of all kinds. I used sometimes to steal corrosive sublimate from my father, sprinkle it on cakes, and carry them up to the attic that the house-spirits, you see, might eat them and be killed. And when I was taught to read and understand what I read, then there was a fine to-do. I ran away to America and went off to join the brigands, and wanted to go into a monastery, and hired boys to torture me for being a Christian. And note that my faith was always active, never

[6] Believer in Nihilism (Lat. *nihil*, nothing), a movement that appeared in Russia about 1850 aimed at the annihilation of many beliefs and institutions; happiness was to be the only law.

dead. If I was running away to America I was not alone, but seduced someone else, as great a fool as I was, to go with me, and was delighted when I was nearly frozen outside the town gates and when I was thrashed; if I went to join the brigands I always came back with my face battered. A most restless childhood, I assure you! And when they sent me to the high school and pelted me with all sorts of truths—that is, that the earth goes round the sun, or that white light is not white, but is made up of seven colours—my poor little head began to go round! Everything was thrown into a whirl in me: Navin who made the sun stand still, and my mother who in the name of the Prophet Elijah[7] disapproved of lightning conductors, and my father who was indifferent to the truths I had learned. My enlightenment inspired me. I wandered about the house and stables like one possessed, preaching my truths, was horrified by ignorance, glowed with hatred for anyone who saw in white light nothing but white light. . . . But all that's nonsense and childishness. Serious, so to speak, manly enthusiasms began only at the university. You have, no doubt, Madam, taken your degree somewhere?"

"I studied at Novotcherkask at the Don Institute."

"Then you have not been to a university? So you don't know what science means. All the sciences in the world have the same passport, without which they regard themselves as meaningless . . . the striving towards truth! Every one of them, even pharmacology, has for its aim not utility, not the alleviation of life, but truth. It's remarkable! When you set to work to study any science, what strikes you first of all is its beginning. I assure you there is nothing more attractive and grander, nothing is so staggering, nothing takes a man's breath away like the beginning of any science. From the first five or six lectures you are soaring on wings of the brightest hopes, you already seem to yourself to be welcoming truth with open arms. And I gave myself up to science, heart and soul, passionately, as to the woman one loves. I was its slave; I found it the sun of my existence, and asked for no other.

I studied day and night without rest, ruined myself over books, wept when before my eyes men exploited science for their own personal ends. But my enthusiasm did not last long. The trouble is that every science has a beginning but not an end, like a recurring decimal. Zoology has discovered 35,000 kinds of insects, chemistry reckons 60 elements. If in time tens of noughts can be written after these figures, zoology and chemistry will be just as far from their end as now, and all contemporary scientific work consists in increasing these numbers. I saw through this trick when I discovered the 35,001st and felt no satisfaction. Well, I had no time to suffer from disillusionment, as I was soon possessed by a new faith. I plunged into Nihilism, with its manifestoes, its 'black divisions,' and all the rest of it. I 'went to the people,' worked in factories, worked as an oiler, as a barge hauler. Afterwards, when wandering over Russia, I had a taste of Russian life, I turned into a fervent devotee of that life. I loved the Russian people with poignant intensity, I loved their God and believed in Him, and in their language, their creative genius. . . . And so on, and so on. . . . I have been a Slavophile[8] in my time, I used to pester Aksakov[9] with letters, and I was a Ukrainophile, and an archaeologist, and a collector of specimens of peasant art. . . . I was enthusiastic over ideas, people, events, places . . . my enthusiasm was endless! Five years ago I was working for the abolition of private property; my last creed was non-resistance to evil."

Sasha gave an abrupt sigh and began moving. Liharev got up and went to her.

"Won't you have some tea, dearie?" he asked tenderly.

"Drink it yourself," the child answered rudely.

Liharev was disconcerted, and went back to the table with a guilty step.

"Then you have had a lively time," said Mlle. Ilovaisky; "you have something to remember."

"Well, yes, it's all very lively when one sits over tea and chatters to a kind listener, but you should ask what that liveliness has cost me! What price have I paid for the variety of my life? You see, Madam, I have not held my con-

---

[7] See *I Kings,* 18, especially verse 38: "Then the fire of the Lord fell. . . ." The point here is that Liharev's mother disapproved of lightning rods because they distorted God's purposes.

[8] Lover of Slav civilization.   [9] Sergei Aksakov (1791–1859), a Russian novelist.

victions like a German doctor of philosophy, *zierlichmännerlich*,[10] I have not lived in solitude, but every conviction I have had has bound my back to the yoke, has torn my body to pieces. Judge, for yourself. I was wealthy like my brothers, but now I am a beggar. In the delirium of my enthusiasm I smashed up my own fortune and my wife's—a heap of other people's money. Now I am forty-two, old age is close upon me, and I am homeless, like a dog that has dropped behind its waggon at night. All my life I have not known what peace meant, my soul has been in continual agitation, distressed even by its hopes . . . I have been wearied out with heavy irregular work, have endured privation, have five times been in prison, have dragged myself across the provinces of Archangel and of Toblosk . . . it's painful to think of it! I have lived, but in my fever I have not even been conscious of the process of life itself. Would you believe it, I don't remember a single spring, I never noticed how my wife loved me, how my children were born. What more can I tell you? I have been a misfortune to all who have loved me. . . . My mother has worn mourning for me all these fifteen years, while my proud brothers, who have had to wince, to blush, to bow their heads, to waste their money on my account, have come in the end to hate me like poison."

Liharev got up and sat down again.

"If I were simply unhappy I should thank God," he went on without looking at his listener. "My personal unhappiness sinks into the background when I remember how often in my enthusiasms I have been absurd, far from the truth, unjust, cruel, dangerous! How often I have hated and despised those whom I ought to have loved, and *vice versa*. I have changed a thousand times. One day I believe, fall down and worship, the next I flee like a coward from the gods and friends of yesterday, and swallow in silence the 'scoundrel!' they hurl after me. God alone has seen how often I have wept and bitten my pillow in shame for my enthusiasms. Never once in my life have I intentionally lied or done evil, but my conscience is not clear! I cannot even boast, Madam, that I have no one's life upon my conscience, for my wife died before my eyes, worn

[10] Elegantly man-like, or in a culturally mannered way.

out by my reckless activity. Yes, my wife! I tell you they have two ways of treating women nowadays. Some measure women's skulls to prove woman is inferior to man, pick out her defects to mock at her, to look original in her eyes, and to justify their sensuality. Others do their utmost to raise women to their level, that is, force them to learn by heart the 35,000 species, to speak and write the same foolish things as they speak and write themselves."

Liharev's face darkened.

"I tell you that woman has been and always will be the slave of man," he said in a bass voice, striking his fist on the table. "She is soft, tender wax which a man always moulds into anything he likes. . . . My God! for the sake of some trumpery masculine enthusiasm she will cut off her hair, abandon her family, die among strangers! . . . among the ideas for which she has sacrificed herself there is not a single feminine one. . . . An unquestioning, devoted slave! I have not measured skulls, but I say this from hard, bitter experience: the proudest, most independent women, if I have succeeded in communicating to them my enthusiasm, have followed me without criticism, without question, and have done anything I chose; I have turned a nun into a Nihilist who, as I heard afterwards, shot a gendarme; my wife never left me for a minute in my wanderings, and like a weather-cock changed her faith in step with my changing enthusiasms."

Liharev jumped up and walked up and down the room.

"A noble, sublime slavery!" he said, clasping his hands. "It is just in it that the highest meaning of woman's life lies! Of all the fearful medley of thoughts and impressions accumulated in my brain from my association with women my memory, like a filter, has retained no ideas, no clever saying, no philosophy, nothing but that extraordinary resignation to fate, that wonderful mercifulness, forgiveness of everything."

Liharev clenched his fists, stared at a fixed point, and with a sort of passionate intensity, as though he were savouring each word as he uttered it, hissed through his clenched teeth:

"That . . . that great-hearted fortitude, faithfulness unto death, poetry of the heart. . . . The meaning of life lies in just that unrepining martyrdom, in the tears which would soften a stone, in the boundless, all-forgiving love which brings light and warmth into the chaos of life. . . ."

Mlle. Ilovaisky got up slowly, took a step towards Liharev, and fixed her eyes upon his face. From the tears that glittered on his eye-lashes, from his quivering, passionate voice, from the flush on his cheeks, it was clear to her that women were not a chance, not a simple subject of conversation. They were the object of his new enthusiasm, or, as he said himself, his new faith! For the first time in her life she saw a man carried away, fervently believing. With his gesticulations, with his flashing eyes he seemed to her mad, frantic, but there was a feeling of such beauty in the fire of his eyes, in his words, in all the movements of his huge body, that without noticing what she was doing she stood facing him as though rooted to the spot, and gazed into his face with delight.

"Take my mother," he said, stretching out his hand to her with an imploring expression on his face, "I poisoned her existence, according to her ideas disgraced the name of Liharev, did her as much harm as the most malignant enemy, and what do you think? My brothers give her little sums for holy bread and church services, and outraging her religious feelings, she saves that money and sends it in secret to her erring Grig-ory. This trifle alone elevates and ennobles the soul far more than all the theories, all the clever sayings and the 35,000 species. I can give you thousands of instances. Take you, even, for in-stance! With tempest and darkness outside you are going to your father and your brother to cheer them with your affection in the holiday, though very likely they have forgotten and are not thinking of you. And, wait a bit, and you will love a man and follow him to the North Pole. You would, wouldn't you?"

"Yes, if I loved him."

"There, you see," cried Liharev delighted, and he even stamped with his foot. "Oh dear! How glad I am that I have met you! Fate is kind to me, I am always meeting splendid people. Not a day passes but one makes acquaintance with somebody one would give one's soul for. There are ever so many more good people than bad in this world. Here, see, for instance, how openly and from our hearts we have been talk-ing as though we had known each other a hun-dred years. Sometimes, I assure you, one re-strains oneself for ten years and holds one's tongue, is reserved with one's friends and one's wife, and meets some cadet in a train and bab-bles one's whole soul out to him. It is the first time I have the honour of seeing you, and yet I have confessed to you as I have never confessed in my life. Why is it?"

Rubbing his hands and smiling good-hu-mouredly Liharev walked up and down the room, and fell to talking about women again. Meanwhile they begin ringing for matins.

"Goodness," wailed Sasha. "He won't let me sleep with his talking!"

"Oh, yes!" said Liharev, startled. "I am sorry, darling, sleep, sleep. . . . I have two boys be-sides her," he whispered. "They are living with their uncle, Madam, but this one can't exist a day without her father. She's wretched, she complains, but she sticks to me like a fly to honey. I have been chattering too much, Ma-dam, and it would do you no harm to sleep. Wouldn't you like me to make up a bed for you?"

Without waiting for permission he shook the wet pelisse, stretched it on a bench, fur side up-wards, collected various shawls and scarves, put the overcoat folded up into a roll for a pillow, and all this he did in silence with a look of devout reverence, as though he were not han-dling a woman's rags, but the fragments of holy vessels. There was something apologetic, em-barrassed about his whole figure, as though in the presence of a weak creature he felt ashamed of his height and strength. . . .

When Mlle. Ilovaisky had lain down, he put out the candle and sat down on a stool by the stove.

"So, Madam," he whispered, lighting a fat cigarette and puffing the smoke into the stove. "Nature has put into the Russian an extraordi-nary faculty for belief, a searching intelligence, and the lift of speculation, but all that is reduced to ashes by irresponsibility, laziness, and dreamy frivolity. . . . Yes. . . ."

She gazed wonderingly into the darkness, and saw only a spot of red on the ikon and the flicker of the light of the stove on Liharev's face. The darkness, the chime of the bells, the roar of the storm, the lame boy, Sasha with her fretful-ness, unhappy Liharev and his sayings—all this was mingled together, and seemed to grow into one huge impression, and God's world seemed to her fantastic, full of marvels and magical forces. All that she had heard was ringing in her ears, and human life presented itself to her as a beautiful poetic fairy tale without an end.

The immense impression grew and grew, clouded consciousness, and turned into a sweet dream. She was asleep, though she saw the little ikon lamp and a big nose with the light playing on it.

She heard the sound of weeping.

"Daddy, darling," a child's voice was tenderly entreating, "let's go back to uncle! There is a Christmas-tree there! Styopa and Kolya are there!"

"My darling, what can I do?" a man's bass persuaded softly. "Understand me! Come, understand!"

And the man's weeping blended with the child's. This voice of human sorrow, in the midst of the howling of the storm, touched the girl's ear with such sweet human music that she could not bear the delight of it, and wept too. She was conscious afterwards of a big, black shadow coming softly up to her, picking up a shawl that had dropped on to the floor and carefully wrapping it round her feet.

Mlle. Ilovaisky was awakened by a strange uproar. She jumped up and looked about her in astonishment. The deep blue dawn was looking in at the window half-covered with snow. In the room there was a grey twilight, through which the stove and the sleeping child and Nasir-ed-Din stood out distinctly. The stove and the lamp were both out. Through the wide-open door she could see the big tavern room with a counter and chairs. A man, with a stupid, gipsy face and astonished eyes, was standing in the middle of the room in a puddle of melting snow, holding a big red star on a stick. He was surrounded by a group of boys, motionless as statues, and plastered over with snow. The light shone through the red paper of the star, throwing a glow of red on their wet faces. The crowd was shouting in disorder, and from its uproar Mlle. Ilovaisky could make out only one couplet:

"Hi, you little Russian lad,
Bring your sharp knife,
We will kill the Jew, we will kill him,
The son of tribulation. . . ."

Liharev was standing near the counter, looking feelingly at the singers and tapping his feet in time. Seeing Mlle. Ilovaisky, he smiled all over his face and came up to her. She smiled too.

"A happy Christmas!" he said. "I saw you slept well."

She looked at him, said nothing, and went on smiling.

After the conversation in the night he seemed to her not tall and broad shouldered, but little, just as the biggest steamer seems to us a little thing when we hear that it has crossed the ocean.

"Well, it is time for me to set off," she said. "I must put on my things. Tell me where you are going now?

"I? To the station of Klinushki, from there to Sergievo, and from Sergievo, with horses, thirty miles to the coal mines that belong to a horrid man, a general called Shashkovsky. My brothers have got me the post of superintendent there. . . . I am going to be a coal miner."

"Stay, I know those mines. Shashkovsky is my uncle, you know. But . . . what are you going there for?" asked Mlle. Ilovaisky, looking at Liharev in surprise.

"As superintendent. To superintend the coal mines."

"I don't understand!" she shrugged her shoulders. "You are going to the mines. But you know, it's the bare steppe, a desert, so dreary that you couldn't exist a day there! It's horrible coal, no one will buy it, and my uncle's a maniac, a despot, a bankrupt. . . . You won't get your salary!"

"No matter," said Liharev, unconcernedly. "I am thankful even for coal mines."

She shrugged her shoulders, and walked about the room in agitation.

"I don't understand, I don't understand," she said, moving her fingers before her face. "It's impossible, and . . . and irrational! You must understand that it's . . . it's worse than exile. It is a living tomb! O Heavens!" she said hotly, going up to Liharev and moving her fingers before his smiling face; her upper lip was quivering, and her sharp face turned pale, "Come, picture it, the bare steppe, solitude. There is no one to say a word to there, and you . . . are enthusiastic over women! Coal mines . . . and women!"

Mlle. Ilovaisky was suddenly ashamed of her heat and, turning away from Liharev, walked to the window.

"No, no, you can't go there," she said,

moving her fingers rapidly over the pane.

Not only in her heart, but even in her spine she felt that behind her stood an infinitely unhappy man, lost and outcast, while he, as though he were unaware of his unhappiness, as though he had not shed tears in the night, was looking at her with a kindly smile. Better he should go on weeping! She walked up and down the room several times in agitation, then stopped short in a corner and sank into thought. Liharev was saying something, but she did not hear him. Turning her back on him she took out of her purse a money note, stood for a long time crumpling it in her hand, and looking round at Liharev, blushed and put it in her pocket.

The coachman's voice was heard through the door. With a stern concentrated face she began putting on her things in silence. Liharev wrapped her up, chatting gaily, but every word he said lay on her heart like a weight. It is not cheering to hear the unhappy or the dying jest.

When the transformation of a live person into a shapeless bundle had been completed, Mlle. Ilovaisky looked for the last time round the "travellers' room," stood a moment in silence, and slowly walked out. Liharev went to see her off. . . .

Outside, God alone knows why, the winter was raging still. Whole clouds of big soft snowflakes were whirling restlessly over the earth, unable to find a resting-place. The horses, the sledge, the trees, a bull tied to a post, all were white and seemed soft and fluffy.

"Well, God help you," muttered Liharev, tucking her into the sledge. "Don't remember evil against me. . . ."

She was silent. When the sledge started, and had to go round a huge snowdrift, she looked back at Liharev with an expression as though she wanted to say something to him. He ran up to her, but she did not say a word to him, she only looked at him through her long eyelashes with little specks of snow on them.

Whether his finely intuitive soul were really able to read that look, or whether his imagination deceived him, it suddenly began to seem to him that with another touch or two that girl would have forgiven him his failures, his age, his desolate position, and would have followed him without question or reasonings. He stood a long while as though rooted to the spot, gazing at the tracks left by the sledge runners. The snowflakes greedily settled on his hair, his beard, his shoulders. . . . Soon the track of the runners had vanished, and he himself covered with snow, began to look like a white rock, but still his eyes kept seeking something in the clouds of snow.

Comments and Questions

As we continue with our study of the short story, we must not lose sight of the basic matters while we, of necessity, move among the technical matters of story construction. We recall our earlier statement that although we are giving a good deal of attention to form, we must never lose sight of our ultimate goal, which is *to comprehend the values and reality explored by any piece of writing.*

We still keep in mind our question, what makes a good short story? As we look back —Galsworthy, Hemingway, Steinbeck, Faulkner—have we found a *great* short story? How would we make the distinction between a good and a great one? Perhaps we can help ourselves to find that distinction by trying to answer questions like these about Chekhov's story:

1. What are the principal devices used by Chekhov to transform the facts of his story into a piece of fictional art with meaning? Has he relied chiefly on plot, character, or theme? Panorama or scene? What kind of a narrator? Does the symbolism, if any, help to give the story its most fundamental meaning? In what ways do the tone and atmosphere help to make clear Chekhov's meaning? These questions concern technique and form; they are ways of getting into a discussion of the story's meaning. To know the answers to the questions is not to know very much, but to know the *meaning* of the answers is to know a great deal about the meaning of the story.

2. Let us drive more deeply into the heart of our problem: Is the story a good or a great one? Is Chekhov a mechanic only who can fit parts together, or is he an artist? To put the question another way: Is the story a satisfactory technical performance or is

the technique *used* to dramatize a penetrating interpretation of life? Have you ever heard a pianist or violinist who gave a brilliant technical performance, yet left you unmoved—a technician but no artist? How would you classify Chekhov?

3. It has been said that the whole purpose of art is to get below the surface meaning of life. Does Chekhov get there? Does the story have two or three dimensions? Support your opinion by evidence from the story.

4. Is Chekhov unusually sensitive to human personality and character? Do we *know* Liharev and Mlle. Ilovaisky?

5. What is the significance of the snowstorm? The story begins and ends with the storm. Is this an accident, decoration, or symbolism?

The Colonel's Lady

W. SOMERSET MAUGHAM
1874–1965

All this happened two or three years before the outbreak of the war.

The Peregrines were having breakfast. Though they were alone and the table was long they sat at opposite ends of it. From the walls George Peregrine's ancestors, painted by the fashionable painters of the day, looked down upon them. The butler brought in the morning post. There were several letters for the Colonel, business letters, *The Times* and a small parcel for his wife Evie. He looked at his letters and then, opening *The Times*, began to read it. They finished breakfast and rose from the table. He noticed that his wife hadn't opened the parcel.

"What's that?" he asked.

"Only some books."

"Shall I open it for you?"

"If you like."

He hated to cut string and so with some difficulty untied the knots.

"But they're all the same," he said when he had unwrapped the parcel. "What on earth d'you want six copies of the same book for?" He opened one of them. "Poetry." Then he looked at the title page. *When Pyramids Decay*, he read, by E. K. Hamilton. Eva Katherine Hamilton: that was his wife's maiden name. He looked at her with smiling surprise. "Have you written a book, Evie? You are a slyboots."

"I didn't think it would interest you very much. Would you like a copy?"

"Well, you know poetry isn't much in my line, but—yes, I'd like a copy; I'll read it. I'll take it along to my study. I've got a lot to do this morning."

He gathered up *The Times*, his letters and the book and went out. His study was a large and comfortable room, with a big desk, leather armchairs and what he called "trophies of the chase" on the walls. In the bookshelves were works of reference, books on farming, gardening, fishing and shooting, and books on the last war, in which he had won an M.C. and a D.S.O. For before his marriage he had been in the Welsh Guards. At the end of the war he retired and settled down to the life of a country gentleman in the spacious house, some twenty miles from Sheffield, which one of his forebears had built in the reign of George III. George Peregrine had an estate of some fifteen hundred acres which he managed with ability; he was a justice of the peace and performed his duties conscientiously. During the season he rode to hounds two days a week. He was a good shot, a golfer and though now a little over fifty could still play a hard game of tennis. He could describe himself with propriety as an all-round sportsman.

He had been putting on weight lately, but was still a fine figure of a man; tall, with grey curly hair, only just beginning to grow thin on the crown, frank blue eyes, good features and a high colour. He was a public-spirited man, chairman at any number of local organizations and, as became his class and station, a loyal member of the Conservative party. He looked upon it as his duty to see to the welfare of the people on his estate and it was a satisfaction to him to know that Evie could be trusted to tend the sick and succour the poor. He had built a cottage hospital on the outskirts of the village and paid the wages of a nurse out of his own pocket. All he asked of the recipients of his bounty was that at elections, county or general, they should vote for his candidate. He was a friendly man, affable to his inferiors, considerate with his tenants and popular with the neighbouring gentry. He would have been pleased and at the same time slightly embarrassed if someone had told him he was a jolly good fellow. That was what he wanted to be. He desired no higher praise.

It was hard luck that he had no children. He would have been an excellent father, kindly but strict, and would have brought up his sons as a gentleman's sons should be brought up, sent them to Eton, you know, taught them to fish, shoot and ride. As it was, his heir was a nephew, son of his brother killed in a motor accident, not a bad boy, but not a chip off the old block, no, sir, far from it; and would you believe it, his fool of a mother was sending him to a co-educational school. Evie had been a sad disappointment to him. Of course she was a lady, and she had a bit of money of her own; she managed the house uncommonly well and she was a good hostess. The village people adored her. She had been a pretty young thing when he married her, with a creamy skin, light brown hair and a trim figure, healthy, too, and not a bad tennis player; he couldn't understand why she'd had no children; of course she was faded now, she must be getting on for five and forty; her skin was drab, her hair had lost its sheen and she was as thin as a rail. She was always neat and suitably dressed, but she didn't seem to bother how she looked; she wore no makeup and didn't even use lipstick; sometimes at night when she dolled herself up for a party you could tell that once she'd been quite attractive, but ordinarily she was—well, the sort of woman you simply didn't notice. A nice woman, of course, a good wife, and it wasn't her fault if she was barren, but it was tough on a fellow who wanted an heir of his own loins; she hadn't any vitality, that's what was the matter with her. He supposed he'd been in love with her when he asked her to marry him, at least sufficiently in love for a man who wanted to marry and settle down, but with time he discovered that they had nothing much in common. She didn't care about hunting, and fishing bored her. Naturally they'd drifted apart. He had to do her the justice to admit that she'd never bothered him. There'd been no scenes. They had no quarrels. She seemed to take it for granted that he should go his own

way. When he went up to London now and then she never wanted to come with him. He had a girl there, well, she wasn't exactly a girl, she was thirty-five if she was a day, but she was blonde and luscious and he only had to wire ahead of time and they'd dine, do a show and spend the night together. Well, a man, a healthy normal man had to have some fun in his life. The thought crossed his mind that if Evie hadn't been such a good woman she'd have been a better wife; but it was not the sort of thought that he welcomed and he put it away from him.

George Peregrine finished his *Times* and being a considerate fellow rang the bell and told the butler to take the paper to Evie. Then he looked at his watch. It was half-past ten and at eleven he had an appointment with one of his tenants. He had half an hour to spare.

"I'd better have a look at Evie's book," he said to himself.

He took it up with a smile. Evie had a lot of highbrow books in her sitting-room, not the sort of books that interested him, but if they amused her he had no objection to her reading them. He noticed that the volume he now held in his hand contained no more than ninety pages. That was all to the good. He shared Edgar Allan Poe's opinion that poems should be short. But as he turned the pages he noticed that several of Evie's had long lines of irregular length and didn't rhyme. He didn't like that. At his first school, when he was a little boy, he remembered learning a poem that began: *The boy stood on the burning deck*, and later, at Eton, one that started: *Ruin seize thee, ruthless king;* and then there was Henry V; they'd had to take that one half. He stared at Evie's pages with consternation.

"That's not what I call poetry," he said.

Fortunately it wasn't all like that. Interspersed with the pieces that looked so odd, lines of three or four words and then a line of ten or fifteen, there were little poems, quite short, that rhymed, thank God, with the lines all the same length. Several of the pages were just headed with the word *Sonnet*, and out of curiosity he counted the lines; there were fourteen of them. He read them. They seemed all right, but he didn't quite know what they were all about. He repeated to himself: *Ruin seize thee, ruthless king.*

"Poor Evie," he sighed.

At that moment the farmer he was expecting

was ushered into the study, and putting the book down he made him welcome. They embarked on their business.

"I read your book, Evie," he said as they sat down to lunch. "Jolly good. Did it cost you a packet to have it printed?"

"No, I was lucky. I sent it to a publisher and he took it."

"Not much money in poetry, my dear," he said in his good-natured, hearty way.

"No, I don't suppose there is. What did Bannock want to see you about this morning?"

Bannock was the tenant who had interrupted his reading of Evie's poems.

"He's asked me to advance the money for a pedigree bull he wants to buy. He's a good man and I've half a mind to do it."

George Peregrine saw that Evie didn't want to talk about her book and he was not sorry to change the subject. He was glad she had used her maiden name on the title page; he didn't suppose anyone would ever hear about the book, but he was proud of his own unusual name and he wouldn't have liked it if some damned penny-a-liner had made fun of Evie's effort in one of the papers.

During the few weeks that followed he thought it tactful not to ask Evie any questions about her venture into verse and she never referred to it. It might have been a discreditable incident that they had silently agreed not to mention. But then a strange thing happened. He had to go to London on business and he took Daphne out to dinner. That was the name of the girl with whom he was in the habit of passing a few agreeable hours whenever he went to town.

"Oh, George," she said, "is that your wife who's written a book they're all talking about?"

"What on earth d'you mean?"

"Well, there's a fellow I know who's a critic. He took me out to dinner the other night and he had a book with him. 'Got anything for me to read?' I said. 'What's that?' 'Oh, I don't think that's your cup of tea,' he said, 'It's poetry, I've just been reviewing it.' 'No poetry for me,' I said. 'It's about the hottest stuff I ever read, he said. 'Selling like hot cakes. And it's damned good.'"

"Who's the book by?" asked George.

"A woman called Hamilton. My friend told

me that wasn't her real name. He said her real name was Peregrine. 'Funny,' I said, 'I know a fellow called Peregrine.' 'Colonel in the army,' he said. 'Lives near Sheffield.'"

"I'd just as soon you didn't talk about me to your friends," said George with a frown of vexation.

"Keep your shirt on, dearie. Who'd you take me for? I just said, 'It's not the same one.'" Daphne giggled. "My friend said: 'They say he's a regular Colonel Blimp.'"

George had a keen sense of humour.

"You could tell them better than that," he laughed. "If my wife had written a book I'd be the first to know about it, wouldn't I?"

"I suppose you would."

Anyhow the matter didn't interest her and when the Colonel began to talk of other things she forgot about it. He put it out of his mind too. There was nothing to it, he decided, and that silly fool of a critic had just been pulling Daphne's leg. He was amused at the thought of her tackling that book because she had been told it was hot stuff and then finding it just a lot of stuff cut up into unequal lines.

He was a member of several clubs and next day he thought he'd lunch at one in St. James's Street. He was catching a train back to Sheffield early in the afternoon. He was sitting in a comfortable armchair having a glass of sherry before going into the dining-room when an old friend came up to him.

"Well, old boy, how's life?" he said. "How d'you like being the husband of a celebrity?"

George Peregrine looked at his friend. He thought he saw an amused twinkle in his eyes.

"I don't know what you're talking about," he answered.

"Come off it, George. Everyone knows E. K. Hamilton is your wife. Not often a book of verse has a success like that. Look here, Henry Dashwood is lunching with me. He'd like to meet you."

"Who the devil is Henry Dashwood and why should he want to meet me?"

"Oh, my dear fellow, what do you do with yourself all the time in the country? Henry's about the best critic we've got. He wrote a wonderful review on Evie's book. D'you mean to say she didn't show it to you?"

Before George could answer his friend had

called a man over. A tall, thin man, with a high forehead, a beard, a long nose and a stoop, just the sort of man whom George was prepared to dislike at first sight. Introductions were effected. Henry Dashwood sat down.

"Is Mrs. Peregrine in London by any chance? I should very much like to meet her," he said.

"No, my wife doesn't like London. She prefers the country," said George stiffly.

"She wrote me a very nice letter about my review. I was pleased. You know, we critics get more kicks than halfpence. I was simply bowled over by her book. It's so fresh and original, very modern without being obscure. She seems to be as much at her ease in free verse as in classical metres." Then because he was a critic he thought he should criticize. "Sometimes her ear is a trifle at fault, but you can say the same of Emily Dickinson. There are several of those short lyrics of hers that might have been written by Landor."

All this was gibberish to George Peregrine. The man was nothing but a disgusting highbrow. But the Colonel had good manners and he answered with proper civility. Henry Dashwood went on as though he hadn't spoken.

"But what makes the book so outstanding is the passion that throbs in every line. So many of these young poets are so anaemic, cold, bloodless, dully intellectual, but here you have real naked, earthy passion; of course deep, sincere emotion like that is tragic—ah, my dear Colonel, how right Heine was when he said that the poet makes little songs out of his great sorrows. You know, now and then, as I read and re-read those heart-rending pages I thought of Sappho."

This was too much for George Peregrine and he got up.

"Well, it's jolly nice of you to say such nice things about my wife's little book. I'm sure she'll be delighted. But I must bolt, I've got to catch a train and I want to get a bite of lunch."

"Damned fool," he said irritably to himself as he walked upstairs to the dining-room.

He got home in time for dinner and after Evie had gone to bed he went into his study and looked for her book. He thought he'd just glance through it again to see for himself what they were making such a fuss about, but he couldn't find it. Evie must have taken it away.

"Silly," he muttered.

He'd told her he thought it jolly good. What more could a fellow be expected to say? Well, it didn't matter. He lit his pipe and read the *Field* till he felt sleepy. But a week or so later it happened that he had to go into Sheffield for the day. He lunched there at his club. He had nearly finished when the Duke of Haverel came in. This was the great local magnate and of course the Colonel knew him, but only to say how d'you do to; and he was surprised when the Duke stopped at his table.

"We're so sorry your wife couldn't come to us for the week-end," he said, with a sort of shy cordiality. "We're expecting rather a nice lot of people."

George was taken aback. He guessed that the Haverels had asked him and Evie over for the week-end and Evie, without saying a word to him about it, had refused. He had the presence of mind to say he was sorry too.

"Better luck next time," said the Duke pleasantly and moved on.

Colonel Peregrine was very angry and when he got home he said to his wife:

"Look here, what's this about our being asked over to Haverel? Why on earth did you say we couldn't go? We've never been asked before and it's the best shooting in the county."

"I didn't think of that. I thought it would only bore you."

"Damn it all, you might at least have asked me if I wanted to go."

"I'm sorry."

He looked at her closely. There was something in her expression that he didn't quite understand. He frowned.

"I suppose *I* was asked?" he barked.

Evie flushed a little.

"Well, in point of fact you weren't."

"I call it damned rude of them to ask you without asking me."

"I suppose they thought it wasn't your sort of party. The Duchess is rather fond of writers and people like that, you know. She's having Henry Dashwood, the critic, and for some reason he wants to meet me."

"It was damned nice of you to refuse, Evie."

"It's the least I could do," she smiled. She hesitated a moment. "George, my publishers want to give a little dinner party for me one day towards the end of the month and of course they want you to come too."

"Oh, I don't think that's quite my mark. I'll

come up to London with you if you like. I'll find someone to dine with."

Daphne.

"I expect it'll be very dull, but they're making rather a point of it. And the day after, the American publisher who's taken my book is giving a cocktail party at Claridge's. I'd like you to come to that if you wouldn't mind."

"Sounds like a crashing bore, but if you really want me to come I'll come."

"It would be sweet of you."

George Peregrine was dazed by the cocktail party. There were a lot of people. Some of them didn't look so bad, a few of the women were decently turned out, but the men seemed to him pretty awful. He was introduced to everybody as Colonel Peregrine, E. K. Hamilton's husband, you know. The men didn't seem to have anything to say to him, but the women gushed.

"You *must* be proud of your wife. Isn't it *wonderful?* You know, I read it right through at a sitting, I simply couldn't put it down, and when I'd finished I started again at the beginning and read it right through a second time. I was simply *thrilled.*"

The English publisher said to him:

"We've not had a success like this with a book of verse for twenty years. I've never seen such reviews."

The American publisher said to him:

"It's swell. It'll be a smash hit in America. You wait and see."

The American publisher had sent Evie a great spray of orchids. Damned ridiculous, thought George. As they came in, people were taken up to Evie and it was evident that they said flattering things to her, which she took with a pleasant smile and a word or two of thanks. She seemed a trifle flushed with excitement, but seemed quite at her ease. Though he thought the whole thing a lot of stuff and nonsense, George noted with approval that his wife was carrying it off in just the right way.

"Well, there's one thing," he said to himself, "you can see she's a lady and that's a damned sight more than you can say of anyone else here."

He drank a good many cocktails. But there was one thing that bothered him. He had a notion that some of the people he was introduced to looked at him in a rather funny sort of way, he couldn't quite make out what it meant, and

once when he strolled by two women who were sitting together on a sofa he had the impression that they were talking about him and after he passed he was almost certain they tittered. He was very glad when the party came to an end.

In the taxi on their way back to their hotel Evie said to him:

"You were wonderful, dear. You made quite a hit. The girls simply raved about you; they thought you so handsome."

"Girls," he said bitterly. "Old hags."

"Were you bored, dear?"

"Stiff."

She pressed his hand in a gesture of sympathy.

"I hope you won't mind if we wait and go down by the afternoon train. I've got some things to do in the morning."

"No, that's all right. Shopping?"

"I do want to buy one or two things, but I've got to go and be photographed. I hate the idea, but they think I ought to be. For America, you know."

He said nothing. But he thought. He thought it would be a shock to the American public when they saw the portrait of the homely, dessicated little woman who was his wife. He'd always been under the impression that they liked glamour in America.

He went on thinking and next morning when Evie had gone out he went to his club and up to the library. There he looked up recent numbers of *The Times Literary Supplement,* the *New Statesman* and the *Spectator.* Presently he found reviews of Evie's book. He didn't read them very carefully, but enough to see that they were extremely favourable. Then he went to the bookseller's in Piccadilly where he occasionally bought books. He'd made up his mind that he had to read this damned thing of Evie's properly, but he didn't want to ask her what she'd done with the copy she'd given him. He'd buy one for himself. Before going in he looked in the window and the first thing he saw was a display of *When Pyramids Decay.* Damned silly title! He went in. A young man came forward and asked if he could help him.

"No, I'm just having a look round." It embarrassed him to ask for Evie's book and he thought he'd find it for himself and then take it to the salesman. But he couldn't see it anywhere and at last, finding the young man near him, he said in a carefully casual tone: "By the way, have you got a book called *When Pyramids Decay?*"

"The new edition came in this morning. I'll get a copy."

In a moment the young man returned with it. He was a short, rather stout young man, with a shock of untidy carroty hair and spectacles. George Peregrine, tall, upstanding, very military, towered over him.

"Is this a new edition then?" he asked.

"Yes, sir. The fifth. It might be a novel the way it's selling."

George Peregrine hesitated a moment.

"Why d'you suppose it's such a success? I've always been told no one reads poetry."

"Well, it's good, you know. I've read it me-self." The young man, though obviously cultured, had a slight Cockney accent, and George quite instinctively adopted a patronizing attitude. "It's the story they like. Sexy, you know, but tragic."

George frowned a little. He was coming to the conclusion that the young man was rather impertinent. No one had told him anything about there being a story in the damned book and he had not gathered that from reading the reviews. The young man went on.

"Of course it's only a flash in the pan, if you know what I mean. The way I look at it, she was sort of inspired like by a personal experience, like Housman was with *The Shropshire Lad.* She'll never write anything else."

"How much is the book?" said George coldly to stop his chatter. "You needn't wrap it up, I'll just slip it in my pocket."

The November morning was raw and he was wearing a greatcoat.

At the station he bought the evening papers and magazines and he and Evie settled themselves comfortably in opposite corners of a first-class carriage and read. At five o'clock they went along to the restaurant car to have tea and chatted a little. They arrived. They drove home in the car which was waiting for them. They bathed, dressed for dinner, and after dinner Evie, saying she was tired out, went to bed. She kissed him, as was her habit, on the forehead. Then he went into the hall, took Evie's book out of his greatcoat pocket and going into the study began to read it. He didn't read verse very easily and though he read with attention, every word

of it, the impression he received was far from clear. Then he began at the beginning again and read it a second time. He read with increasing malaise, but he was not a stupid man and when he had finished he had a distinct understanding of what it was all about. Part of the book was in free verse, part in conventional metres, but the story it related was coherent and plain to the meanest intelligence. It was the story of a passionate love affair between an older woman, married, and a young man. George Peregrine made out the steps of it as easily as if he had been doing a sum in simple addition.

Written in the first person, it began with the tremulous surprise of the woman, past her youth, when it dawned upon her that the young man was in love with her. She hesitated to believe it. She thought she must be deceiving herself. And she was terrified when on a sudden she discovered that she was passionately in love with him. She told herself it was absurd; with the disparity of age between them nothing but unhappiness could come to her if she yielded to her emotion. She tried to prevent him from speaking, but the day came when he told her that he loved her and forced her to tell him that she loved him too. He begged her to run away with him. She couldn't leave her husband, her home; and what life could they look forward to, she an ageing woman, he so young? How could she expect his love to last? She begged him to have mercy on her. But his love was impetuous. He wanted her, he wanted her with all his heart, and at last trembling, afraid, desirous, she yielded to him. Then there was a period of ecstatic happiness. The world, the dull, humdrum world of every day, blazed with glory. Love songs flowed from her pen. The woman worshipped the young, virile body of her lover. George flushed darkly when she praised his broad chest and slim flanks, the beauty of his legs and the flatness of his belly.

Hot stuff, Daphne's friend had said. It was that all right. Disgusting.

There were sad little pieces in which she lamented the emptiness of her life when, as must happen, he left her, but they ended with a cry that all she had to suffer would be worth it for the bliss that for a while had been hers. She wrote of the long, tremulous nights they passed together and the languor that lulled them to sleep in one another's arms. She wrote of the rapture of brief stolen moments when, braving all danger, their passion overwhelmed them and they surrendered to its call.

She thought it would be an affair of a few weeks, but miraculously it lasted. One of the poems referred to three years having gone by without lessening the love that filled their hearts. It looked as though he continued to press her to go away with him, far away, to a hill town in Italy, a Greek island, a walled city in Tunisia, so that they could be together always, for in another of the poems she besought him to let things be as they were. Their happiness was precarious. Perhaps it was owing to the difficulties they had to encounter and the rarity of their meetings that their love had retained for so long its first enchanting ardour. Then on a sudden the young man died. How, when or where George could not discover. There followed a long, heartbroken cry of bitter grief, grief she could not indulge in, grief that had to be hidden. She had to be cheerful, give dinner parties and go out to dinner, behave as she had always behaved, though the light had gone out of her life and she was bowed down with anguish. The last poem of all was a set of four short stanzas in which the writer, sadly resigned to her loss, thanked the dark powers that rule man's destiny that she had been privileged at least for a while to enjoy the greatest happiness that we poor human beings can ever hope to know.

It was three o'clock in the morning when George Peregrine finally put the book down. It had seemed to him that he heard Evie's voice in every line; over and over again he came upon turns of phrase he had heard her use, there were details that were as familiar to him as to her; there was no doubt about it; it was her own story she had told, and it was as plain as anything could be that she had had a lover and her lover had died. It was not anger so much that he felt, nor horror or dismay, though he was dismayed and he was horrified, but amazement. It was as inconceivable that Evie should have had a love affair, and a wildly passionate one at that, as that the trout in a glass case over the chimney piece in his study, the finest he had ever caught, should suddenly wag its tail. He understood now the meaning of the amused look he had seen in the eyes of that man he had spoken with at the club, he understood why Daphne when she was talking about the book had seemed to be enjoying a private joke, and why those two women at the cocktail party had tittered when he strolled past them.

He broke out into a sweat. Then on a sudden he was seized with fury and he jumped up to go and awake Evie and ask her sternly for an explanation. But he stopped at the door. After all what proof had he? A book. He remembered that he'd told Evie he thought it jolly good. True, he hadn't read it, but he'd pretended he had. He would look a perfect fool if he had to admit that.

"I must watch my step," he muttered.

He made up his mind to wait for two or three days and think it all over. Then he'd decide what to do. He went to bed, but he couldn't sleep for a long time.

"Evie," he kept on saying to himself, "Evie, of all people."

They met at breakfast next morning as usual. Evie was as she always was, quiet, demure and self-possessed, a middle-aged woman who made no effort to look younger than she was, a woman who had nothing of what he still called It. He looked at her as he hadn't looked at her for years. She had her usual placid serenity. Her pale blue eyes were untroubled. There was no sign of guilt on her candid brow. She made the same little casual remarks she always made.

"It's nice to get back to the country again after those two hectic days in London. What are you going to do this morning?"

It was incomprehensible.

Three days later he went to see his solicitor. Henry Blane was an old friend of George's as well as his lawyer. He had a place not far from Peregrine's and for years they had shot over one another's preserves. For two days a week he was a busy country gentleman and for the other five a busy lawyer in Sheffield. He was a tall, robust fellow, with a boisterous manner and a jovial laugh, which suggested that he liked to be looked upon essentially as a sportsman and a good fellow and only incidentally as a lawyer. But he was shrewd and worldly-wise.

"Well, George, what's brought you here today?" he boomed as the Colonel was shown into his office. "Have a good time in London? I'm taking my missus up for a few days next week. How's Evie?"

"It's about Evie I've come to see you," said Peregrine, giving him a suspicious look. "Have you read her book?"

His sensitivity had been sharpened during those last days of troubled thought and he was conscious of a faint change in the lawyer's expression. It was as though he were suddenly on his guard.

"Yes, I've read it. Great success, isn't it? Fancy Evie breaking out into poetry. Wonders will never cease."

George Peregrine was inclined to lose his temper.

"It's made me look a perfect damned fool."

"Oh, what nonsense, George! There's no harm in Evie's writing a book. You ought to be jolly proud of her."

"Don't talk such rot. It's her own story. You know it and everyone else knows it. I suppose I'm the only one who doesn't know who her lover was."

"There is such a thing as imagination, old boy. There's no reason to suppose the whole thing isn't just made up."

"Look here, Henry, we've known one another all our lives. We've had all sorts of good times together. Be honest with me. Can you look me in the face and tell me you believe it's a made-up story?"

Henry Blane moved uneasily in his chair. He was disturbed by the distress in old George's voice.

"You've got no right to ask me a question like that. Ask Evie."

"I daren't," George answered after an anguished pause. "I'm afraid she'd tell me the truth."

There was an uncomfortable silence.

"Who was the chap?"

Henry Blane looked at him straight in the eye.

"I don't know, and if I did I wouldn't tell you."

"You swine. Don't you see what a position I'm in? Do you think it's very pleasant to be made absolutely ridiculous?"

The lawyer lit a cigarette and for some moments silently puffed it.

"I don't see what I can do for you," he said at last.

"You've got private detectives you employ, I suppose. I want you to put them on the job and let them find everything out."

"It's not very pretty to put detectives on one's wife, old boy; and besides, taking for granted for a moment that Evie had an affair, it was a good many years ago and I don't suppose it would be possible to find a thing. They seem to have covered their tracks pretty carefully."

"I don't care. You put the detectives on. I want to know the truth."

"I won't, George. If you're determined to do that you'd better consult someone else. And look here, even if you got evidence that Evie had been unfaithful to you what would you do with it? You'd look rather silly divorcing your wife because she'd committed adultery ten years ago."

"At all events I could have it out with her."

"You can do that now, but you know just as well as I do that if you do she'll leave you. D'you want her to do that?"

George gave him an unhappy look.

"I don't know. I always thought she'd been a damned good wife to me. She runs the house perfectly, we never have any servant trouble; she's done wonders with the garden and she's splendid with all the village people. But damn it, I have my self-respect to think of. How can I go on living with her when I know that she was grossly unfaithful to me?"

"Have you always been faithful to her?"

"More or less, you know. After all we've been married for nearly twenty-four years and Evie was never much for bed."

The solicitor slightly raised his eyebrows, but George was too intent on what he was saying to notice.

"I don't deny that I've had a bit of fun now and then. A man wants it. Women are different."

"We only have men's word for that," said Henry Blane, with a faint smile.

"Evie's absolutely the last woman I'd have suspected of kicking over the traces. I mean, she's a very fastidious, reticent woman. What on earth made her write the damned book?"

"I suppose it was a very poignant experience and perhaps it was a relief to her to get it off her chest like that."

"Well, if she had to write it why the devil didn't she write it under an assumed name?"

"She used her maiden name. I suppose she

thought that was enough and it would have been if the book hadn't had this amazing boom."

George Peregrine and the lawyer were sitting opposite one another with a desk between them. George, his elbow on the desk, his cheek resting on his hand, frowned at his thought.

"It's so rotten not to know what sort of a chap he was. One can't even tell if he was by way of being a gentleman. I mean, for all I know he may have been a farmhand or a clerk in a lawyer's office."

Henry Blane did not permit himself to smile and when he answered there was in his eyes a kindly, tolerant look.

"Knowing Evie so well I think the probabilities are that he was all right. Anyhow I'm sure he wasn't a clerk in my office."

"It's been such a shock to me," the Colonel sighed. "I thought she was fond of me. She couldn't have written that book unless she hated me."

"Oh, I don't believe that. I don't think she's capable of hatred."

"You're not going to pretend that she loves me."

"No."

"Well, what does she feel for me?"

Henry Blane leaned back in his swivel chair and looked at George reflectively.

"Indifference, I should say."

The Colonel gave a little shudder and reddened.

"After all, you're not in love with her, are you?"

George Peregrine did not answer directly.

"It's been a great blow to me not to have any children, but I've never let her see that I think she's let me down. I've always been kind to her. Within reasonable limits I've tried to do my duty by her."

The lawyer passed a large hand over his mouth to conceal the smile that trembled on his lips.

"It's been such an awful shock to me," Peregrine went on. "Damn it all, even ten years ago Evie was no chicken, and God knows she wasn't much to look at. It's so ugly." He sighed deeply. "What would *you* do in my place?"

"Nothing."

George Peregrine drew himself bolt upright in his chair and he looked at Henry with the stern, set face that he must have worn when he inspected his regiment.

"I can't overlook a thing like this. I've been made a laughing-stock. I can never hold up my head again."

"Nonsense," said the lawyer sharply, and then in a pleasant, kindly manner: "Listen, old boy: the man's dead; it all happened a long while back. Forget it. Talk to people about Evie's book, rave about it, tell 'em how proud you are of her. Behave as though you had so much confidence in her, you *knew* she could never have been unfaithful to you. The world moves so quickly and people's memories are so short. They'll forget."

"I shan't forget."

"You're both middle-aged people. She probably does a great deal more for you than you think and you'd be awfully lonely without her. I don't think it matters if you don't forget. It'll be all to the good if you can get it into that thick head of yours that there's a lot more in Evie than you ever had the gumption to see."

"Damn it all, you talk as if *I* was to blame."

"No, I don't think you were to blame, but I'm not so sure that Evie was either. I don't suppose she wanted to fall in love with this boy. D'you remember those verses right at the end? The impression they gave me was that though she was shattered by his death, in a strange sort of way she welcomed it. All through she'd been aware of the fragility of the tie that bound them. He died in the full flush of his first love and had never known that love so seldom endures; he'd only known its bliss and beauty. In her own bitter grief she found solace in the thought that he'd been spared all sorrow."

"All that's a bit above my head, old boy. I see more or less what you mean."

George Peregrine stared unhappily at the inkstand on the desk. He was silent and the lawyer looked at him with curious, yet sympathetic eyes.

"Do you realize what courage she must have had never by a sign to show how dreadfully unhappy she was?" he said gently.

Colonel Peregrine sighed.

"I'm broken. I suppose you're right; it's no good crying over spilt milk and it would only make things worse if I made a fuss."

"Well?"

George Peregrine gave a pitiful little smile.

"I'll take your advice. I'll do nothing. Let them think me a damned fool and to hell with them. The truth is, I don't know what I'd do without Evie. But I'll tell you what, there's one thing I shall never understand till my dying day: What in the name of heaven did the fellow ever see in her?"

Comments and Questions

It is uncommonly profitable to compare the method and results of Chekhov's "On the Road" (p. 92) with those of Maugham's story. Each writer has a method and subject quite different from the other's. Maugham is critical of Chekhov's method and results, particularly because Chekhov does not rely on plot, because, from Maugham's point of view, he tells no story. "If you try to tell one of his stories," says Maugham, "you will find that there is nothing to tell." For Maugham, apparently Chekhov's stories have a middle, but no beginning or end. Here, Maugham could be commenting about "On the Road": "If you could take two or three persons, describe their mutual relations and leave it at that, why then it wasn't hard to write a story. . . ." Both Chekhov and Maugham have had a tremendous influence on the short story, and it would be naive to conclude that one is right, the other wrong. As Henry James said, "The House of Fiction has . . . not one window, but a million. . . ."

1. The tone and atmosphere of "On the Road" and "The Colonel's Lady" are quite different. How does each writer achieve them, and with what results? This is a large question, and requires a comprehensive, thoughtful answer. Perhaps the answers to the following questions will help.

2. In what ways does Maugham comment on the action of the story? Consider especially his *indirect* comments; for example, the scene in which Peregrine meets the critic Dashwood. We seem to have a clear idea about Maugham's attitude toward his characters—are we so clear about Chekhov's attitude?

3. Assuming that you enjoyed both stories, describe what you enjoyed about each one. Does the word *enjoy* exactly describe your reaction to *both* stories?

4. We recognize that Chekhov's structure of action differs considerably from Maugham's. Is one better than the other or is each one designed to produce different and *justifiable* results?

5. Is one author more serious than the other, or is it simply that one is Russian and the other British? If the latter part of this question is quite meaningless to you, state your case. Did you laugh at all as you read either story? If we laugh at a serious story, do we discredit it?

For Esmé— With Love and Squalor

J. D. SALINGER
1919—

Just recently, by air mail, I received an invitation to a wedding that will take place in England on April 18th. It happens to be a wedding I'd give a lot to be able to get to, and when the invitation first arrived, I thought it might just be possible for me to make the trip abroad, by plane, expenses be hanged. However, I've since discussed the matter rather extensively with my wife, a breathtakingly level-headed girl, and we've decided against it—for one thing, I'd completely forgotten that my mother-in-law is looking forward to spending the last two weeks in April with us. I really don't get to see Mother Grencher terribly often, and she's not getting any younger. She's fifty-eight. (As she'd be the first to admit.)

All the same, though, wher*ever* I happen to be, I don't think I'm the type that doesn't even lift a finger to prevent a wedding from flatting. Accordingly, I've gone ahead and jotted down a few revealing notes on the bride as I knew her almost six years ago. If my notes should cause the groom, whom I haven't met, an uneasy moment or two, so much the better. Nobody's aiming to please, here. More, really, to edify, to instruct.

In April of 1944, I was among some sixty American enlisted men who took a rather specialized pre-Invasion training course, directed by British Intelligence, in Devon, England. And as I look back, it seems to me that we were fairly unique, the sixty of us, in that there wasn't one good mixer in the bunch. We were all essentially letter-writing types, and when we spoke to each other out of the line of duty, it was usually to ask somebody if he had any ink he wasn't using. When we weren't writing letters or attending classes, each of us went pretty much his own way. Mine usually led, on clear days, in scenic circles around the countryside. Rainy days, I generally sat in a dry place and read a book, often just an axe length away from a ping-pong table.

The training course lasted three weeks, ending on a Saturday, a very rainy one. At seven that last night, our whole group was scheduled to entrain for London, where, as rumor had it, we were to be assigned to infantry and airborne divisions mustered for the D Day landings. By three in the afternoon, I'd packed all my belongings into my barrack bag, including a canvas gasmask container full of books I'd brought over from the Other Side. (The gas mask itself I'd slipped through a porthole of the *Mauretania* some weeks earlier, fully aware that if the enemy ever *did* use gas I'd never get the damn thing on in time.) I remember standing at an end window of our Quonset hut for a very long time, looking out at the slanting, dreary rain, my trigger finger itching imperceptibly, if at all. I could hear behind my back the uncomradely scratching of many fountain pens on many sheets of V-mail paper. Abruptly, with nothing special in mind, I came away from the window and put on my raincoat, cashmere muffler, galoshes, woolen gloves, and overseas cap (the last of which, I'm still told, I wore at an angle all my own—slightly down over both ears). Then, after synchronizing my wristwatch with the clock in the latrine, I walked down the long, wet cobblestone hill into town. I ignored the flashes of lightning all around me. They either had your number on them or they didn't.

In the center of town, which was probably the wettest part of town, I stopped in front of a church to read the bulletin board, mostly because the featured numerals, white on black, had caught my attention but partly because, after three years in the Army, I'd become addicted to reading bulletin boards. At three-fifteen, the board stated, there would be children's-choir practice. I looked at my wristwatch, then back

at the board. A sheet of paper was tacked up, listing the names of the children expected to attend practice. I stood in the rain and read all the names, then entered the church.

A dozen or so adults were among the pews, several of them bearing pairs of small-size rubbers, soles up, in their laps. I passed along and sat down in the front row. On the rostrum, seated in three compact rows of auditorium chairs, were about twenty children, mostly girls, ranging in age from about seven to thirteen. At the moment, their choir coach, an enormous woman in tweeds, was advising them to open their mouths wider when they sang. Had anyone, she asked, ever heard of a little dickeybird that *dared* to sing his charming song without first opening his little beak wide, wide, wide? Apparently nobody ever had. She was given a steady, opaque look. She went on to say that she wanted *all* her children to absorb the *meaning* of the words they sang, not just *mouth* them, like silly-billy parrots. She then blew a note on her pitch pipe, and the children, like so many underage weight-lifters, raised their hymnbooks.

They sang without instrumental accompaniment—or, more accurately in their case, without any interference. Their voices were melodious and unsentimental, almost to the point where a somewhat more denominational man than myself might, without straining, have experienced levitation. A couple of the very youngest children dragged the tempo a trifle, but in a way that only the composer's mother could have found fault with. I had never heard the hymn, but I kept hoping it was one with a dozen or more verses. Listening, I scanned all the children's faces but watched one in particular, that of the child nearest me, on the end seat in the first row. She was about thirteen, with straight ash-blond hair of ear-lobe length, an exquisite forehead, and blasé eyes that, I thought, might very possibly have counted the house. Her voice was distinctly separate from the other children's voices, and not just because she was seated nearest me. It had the best upper register, the sweetest-sounding, the surest, and it automatically led the way. The young lady, however, seemed slightly bored with her own singing ability, or perhaps just with the time and place; twice, between verses, I saw her yawn. It was a ladylike yawn, a closed-mouth yawn, but you couldn't miss it; her nostril wings gave her away.

The instant the hymn ended, the choir coach began to give her lengthy opinion of people who can't keep their feet still and their lips sealed tight during the minister's sermon. I gathered that the singing part of the rehearsal was over, and before the coach's dissonant speaking voice could entirely break the spell the children's singing had cast, I got up and left the church.

It was raining even harder. I walked down the street and looked through the window of the Red Cross recreation room, but soldiers were standing two and three deep at the coffee counter, and, even through the glass, I could hear ping-pong balls bouncing in another room. I crossed the street and entered a civilian tearoom, which was empty except for a middle-aged waitress, who looked as if she would have preferred a customer with a dry raincoat. I used a coat tree as delicately as possible, and then sat down at a table and ordered tea and cinnamon toast. It was the first time all day that I'd spoken to anyone. I then looked through all my pockets, including my raincoat, and finally found a couple of stale letters to reread, one from my wife, telling me how the service at Schrafft's Eighty-eighth Street had fallen off, and one from my mother-in-law, asking me to please send her some cashmere yarn first chance I got away from "camp."

While I was still on my first cup of tea, the young lady I had been watching and listening to in the choir came into the tearoom. Her hair was soaking wet, and the rims of both ears were showing. She was with a very small boy, unmistakably her brother, whose cap she removed by lifting it off his head with two fingers, as if it were a laboratory specimen. Bringing up the rear was an efficient-looking woman in a limp felt hat—presumably their governess. The choir member, taking off her coat as she walked across the floor, made the table selection—a good one, from my point of view, as it was just eight or ten feet directly in front of me. She and the governess sat down. The small boy, who was about five, wasn't ready to sit down yet. He slid out of and discarded his reefer; then, with the dead-pan expression of a born heller, he methodically went about annoying his governess by pushing in and pulling out his chair several times, watching her face. The governess, keeping her voice down, gave him two or three orders to sit down and, in effect, stop the monkey business, but it was only when his sister spoke to him that he came around and applied the small of his back to his chair seat. He immediately picked up his napkin and put it on his head. His sister removed it, opened it, and spread it out on his lap.

About the time their tea was brought, the choir member caught me staring over at her party. She stared back at me, with those house-counting eyes of hers, then, abruptly, gave me a small, qualified smile. It was oddly radiant, as certain small, qualified smiles sometimes are. I smiled back, much less radiantly, keeping my upper lip down over a coal-black G.I. temporary filling showing between two of my front teeth. The next thing I knew, the young lady was standing, with enviable poise, beside my table. She was wearing a tartan dress—a Campbell tartan,[1] I believe. It seemed to me to be a wonderful dress for a very young girl to be wearing on a rainy, rainy day. "I thought Americans despised tea," she said.

It wasn't the observation of a smart aleck but that of a truth-lover or a statistics-lover. I replied that some of us never drank anything *but* tea. I asked her if she'd care to join me.

"Thank you," she said. "Perhaps for just a fraction of a moment."

I got up and drew a chair for her, the one opposite me, and she sat down on the forward quarter of it, keeping her spine easily and beautifully straight. I went back—almost hurried back—to my own chair, more than willing to hold up my end of a conversation. When I was seated, I couldn't think of anything to say, though. I smiled again, still keeping my coal-black filling under concealment. I remarked that it was certainly a terrible day out.

"Yes; quite," said my guest, in the clear, unmistakable voice of a small-talk detester. She placed her fingers flat on the table edge, like someone at a séance, then, almost instantly, closed her hands—her nails were bitten down to the quick. She was wearing a wristwatch, a military-looking one that looked rather like a navigator's chronograph. Its face was much too large for her slender wrist. "You were at choir practice," she said matter-of-factly. "I saw you."

[1] Scottish plaid textile identifying the Campbell clan.

I said I certainly had been, and that I had heard her voice singing separately from the others. I said I thought she had a very fine voice.

She nodded. "I know. I'm going to be a professional singer."

"Really? Opera?"

"Heavens, no. I'm going to sing jazz on the radio and make heaps of money. Then, when I'm thirty, I shall retire and live on a ranch in Ohio." She touched the top of her soaking-wet head with the flat of her hand. "Do you know Ohio?" she asked.

I said I'd been through it on the train a few times but that I didn't really know it. I offered her a piece of cinnamon toast.

"No, thank you," she said. "I eat like a bird, actually."

I bit into a piece of toast myself, and commented that there's some mighty rough country around Ohio.

"I know. An American I met told me. You're the eleventh American I've met."

Her governess was now urgently signalling her to return to her own table—in effect, to stop bothering the man. My guest, however, calmly moved her chair an inch or two so that her back broke all possible further communication with the home table. "You go to that secret Intelligence school on the hill, don't you?" she inquired coolly.

As security-minded as the next one, I replied that I was visiting Devonshire for my health.

"*Really*," she said, "I wasn't quite born yesterday, you know."

I said I'd bet she hadn't been, at that. I drank my tea for a moment. I was getting a trifle posture-conscious and I sat up somewhat straighter in my seat.

"You seem quite intelligent for an American," my guest mused.

I told her that was a pretty snobbish thing to say, if you thought about it at all, and that I hoped it was unworthy of her.

She blushed—automatically conferring on me the social poise I'd been missing. "Well. Most of the Americans I've seen act like animals. They're forever punching one another about, and insulting everyone, and—You know what one of them did?"

I shook my head.

"One of them threw an empty whiskey bottle through my aunt's window. *Fortunately*, the window was open. But does that sound very intelligent to you?"

It didn't especially, but I didn't say so. I said that many soldiers, all over the world, were a long way from home, and that few of them had had many real advantages in life. I said I'd thought that most people could figure that out for themselves.

"Possibly," said my guest, without conviction. She raised her hand to her wet head again, picked at a few limp filaments of blond hair, trying to cover her exposed ear rims. "My hair is soaking wet," she said. "I look a fright." She looked over at me. "I have quite wavy hair when it's dry."

"I can see that, I can see you have."

"Not actually curly, but quite wavy," she said. "Are you married?"

I said I was.

She nodded. "Are you very deeply in love with your wife? Or am I being too personal?"

I said that when she was, I'd speak up.

She put her hands and wrists farther forward on the table, and I remember wanting to do something about that enormous-faced wristwatch she was wearing—perhaps suggest that she try wearing it around her waist.

"Usually, I'm not terribly gregarious," she said, and looked over at me to see if I knew the meaning of the word. I didn't give her a sign, though, one way or the other. "I purely came over because I thought you looked extremely lonely. You have an extremely sensitive face."

I said she was right, that I *had* been feeling lonely, and that I was very glad she'd come over.

"I'm training myself to be more compassionate. My aunt says I'm a terribly cold person," she said and felt the top of her head again. "I live with my aunt. She's an extremely kind person. Since the death of my mother, she's done everything within her power to make Charles and me feel adjusted."

"I'm glad."

"Mother was an extremely intelligent person. Quite sensuous, in many ways." She looked at me with a kind of fresh acuteness. "Do you find me terribly cold?"

I told her absolutely not—very much to the contrary, in fact. I told her my name and asked for hers.

She hesitated. "My first name is Esmé. I don't think I shall tell you my full name, for the moment. I have a title and you may just be impressed by titles. Americans are, you know."

I said I didn't think I would be, but that it might be a good idea, at that, to hold onto the title for a while.

Just then, I felt someone's warm breath on the back of my neck. I turned around and just missed brushing noses with Esmé's small brother. Ignoring me, he addressed his sister in a piercing treble: "Miss Megley said you must come and finish your tea!" His message delivered, he retired to the chair between his sister and me, on my right. I regarded him with high interest. He was looking very splendid in brown Shetland shorts, a navy-blue jersey, white shirt, and striped necktie. He gazed back at me with immense green eyes. "Why do people in films kiss sideways?" he demanded.

"Sideways?" I said. It was a problem that had baffled me in my own childhood. I said I guessed it was because actors' noses are too big for kissing anyone head on.

"His name is Charles," Esmé said. "He's extremely brilliant for his age."

"He certainly has green eyes. Haven't you, Charles?"

Charles gave me the fishy look my question deserved, then wriggled downward and forward in his chair till all of his body was under the table except his head, which he left, wrestler's-bridge style, on the chair seat. "They're orange," he said in a strained voice, addressing the ceiling. He picked up a corner of the tablecloth and put it over his handsome, deadpan little face.

"Sometimes he's brilliant and sometimes he's not," Esmé said. "Charles, do sit up!"

Charles stayed right where he was. He seemed to be busy holding his breath.

"He misses our father very much. He was s-l-a-i-n in North Africa."

I expressed regret to hear it.

Esmé nodded. "Father adored him." She bit reflectively at the cuticle of her thumb. "He looks very much like my mother—Charles, I mean. I look exactly like my father." She went on biting at her cuticle. "My mother was quite a passionate woman. She was an extrovert. Father was an introvert. They were quite well mated, though, in a superficial way. To be quite candid, Father really needed more of an intellectual companion than Mother was. He was an extremely gifted genius."

I waited, receptively, for further information, but none came. I looked down at Charles, who was now resting the side of his face on his chair seat. When he saw that I was looking at him, he closed his eyes, sleepily, angelically, then stuck out his tongue—an appendage of startling length—and gave out what in *my* country would have been a glorious tribute to a myopic baseball umpire. It fairly shook the tearoom.

"Stop that," Esmé said, clearly unshaken. "He saw an American do it in a fish-and-chips queue, and now he does it whenever he's bored. Just stop it, now, or I shall send you directly to Miss Megley."

Charles opened his enormous eyes, as a sign that he'd heard his sister's threat, but otherwise didn't look especially alerted. He closed his eyes again, and continued to rest the side of his face on the chair seat.

I mentioned that maybe he ought to save it —meaning the Bronx cheer—till he started using his title regularly. That is, if he had a title, too.

Esmé gave me a long, faintly clinical look. "You have a dry sense of humor, haven't you?" she said—wistfully. "Father said I have no sense of humor at all. He said I was unequipped to meet life because I have no sense of humor."

Watching her, I lit a cigarette and said I didn't think a sense of humor was of any use in a real pinch.

"Father said it was."

This was a statement of faith, not a contradiction, and I quickly switched horses. I nodded and said her father had probably taken the long view, while I was taking the short (whatever *that* meant).

"Charles misses him exceedingly," Esmé said, after a moment. "He was an exceedingly lovable man. He was extremely handsome, too. Not that one's appearance matters greatly, but he was. He had terribly penetrating eyes, for a man who was intransically kind."

I nodded. I said I imagined her father had had quite an extraordinary vocabulary.

"Oh, yes; quite," said Esmé. "He was an archivist—amateur, of course."

At that point, I felt an importunate tap, almost a punch, on my upper arm, from Charles's direction. I turned to him. He was sitting in a fairly normal position in his chair now, except that he had one knee tucked under him. "What did one wall say to the other wall?" he asked shrilly. "It's a riddle!"

I rolled my eyes reflectively ceilingward and repeated the question aloud. Then I looked at Charles with a stumped expression and said I gave up.

"Meet you at the corner!" came the punch line, at top volume.

It went over biggest with Charles himself. It struck him as unbearably funny. In fact, Esmé had to come around and pound him on the back, as if treating him for a coughing spell. "Now, stop that," she said. She went back to her own seat. "He tells that same riddle to everyone he meets and has a fit every single time. Usually he drools when he laughs. Now, just stop, please."

"It's one of the best riddles I've heard, though," I said, watching Charles, who was very gradually coming out of it. In response to this compliment, he sank considerably lower in his chair and again masked his face up to the eyes with a corner of the tablecloth. He then looked at me with his exposed eyes, which were full of slowly subsiding mirth and the pride of someone who knows a really good riddle or two.

"May I inquire how you were employed before entering the Army?" Esmé asked me.

I said I hadn't been employed at all, that I'd only been out of college a year but that I liked to think of myself as a professional short-story writer.

She nodded politely. "Published?" she asked.

It was a familiar but always touchy question, and one that I didn't answer just one, two, three. I explained how most editors in America were a bunch—

"My father wrote beautifully," Esmé interrupted. "I'm saving a number of his letters for posterity."

I said that sounded like a very good idea. I happened to be looking at her enormous-faced, chronographic-looking wristwatch again. I asked if it had belonged to her father.

She looked down at her wrist solemnly. "Yes, it did," she said. "He gave it to me just before Charles and I were evacuated." Self-consciously, she took her hands off the table, saying, "Purely as a momento, of course." She guided the con-

versation in a different direction. "I'd be extremely flattered if you'd write a story exclusively for me sometime. I'm an avid reader."

I told her I certainly would, if I could. I said that I wasn't terribly prolific.

"It doesn't have to be terribly prolific! Just so that it isn't childish and silly." She reflected. "I prefer stories about squalor."

"About what?" I said, leaning forward.

"Squalor. I'm extremely interested in squalor."

I was about to press her for more details, but I felt Charles pinching me, hard, on my arm. I turned to him, wincing slightly. He was standing right next to me. "What did one wall say to the other wall?" he asked, not unfamiliarly.

"You asked him that," Esmé said. "Now, stop it."

Ignoring his sister, and stepping up on one of my feet, Charles repeated the key question. I noticed that his necktie knot wasn't adjusted properly. I slid it up into place, then, looking him straight in the eye, suggested, "Meetcha at the corner?"

The instant I'd said it, I wished I hadn't. Charles's mouth fell open. I felt as if I'd struck it open. He stepped down off my foot and, with white-hot dignity, walked over to his own table, without looking back.

"He's furious," Esmé said. "He has a violent temper. My mother had a propensity to spoil him. My father was the only one who didn't spoil him."

I kept looking over at Charles, who had sat down and started to drink his tea, using both hands on the cup. I hoped he'd turn around, but he didn't.

Esmé stood up. "*Il faut que je parte aussi,*" she said, with a sigh. "Do you know French?"

I got up from my own chair, with mixed feelings of regret and confusion. Esmé and I shook hands; her hand, as I'd suspected, was a nervous hand, damp at the palm. I told her, in English, how very much I'd enjoyed her company.

She nodded. "I thought you might," she said. "I'm quite communicative for my age." She gave her hair another experimental touch. "I'm dreadfully sorry about my hair," she said. "I've probably been hideous to look at."

"Not at all! As a matter of fact, I think a lot of the wave is coming back already."

She quickly touched her hair again. "Do you think you'll be coming here again in the immediate future?" she asked. "We come here every Saturday, after choir practice."

I answered that I'd like nothing better but that, unfortunately, I was pretty sure I wouldn't be able to make it again.

"In other words, you can't discuss troop movements," said Esmé. She made no move to leave the vicinity of the table. In fact, she crossed one foot over the other and, looking down, aligned the toes of her shoes. It was a pretty little execution, for she was wearing white socks and her ankles and feet were lovely. She looked up at me abruptly. "Would you like me to write to you?" she asked, with a certain amount of color in her face. "I write extremely articulate letters for a person my—"

"I'd love it." I took out pencil and paper and wrote down my name, rank, serial number, and A.P.O.[2] number.

"I shall write to you first," she said, accepting it, "so that you don't feel *com*promised in any way." She put the address into a pocket of her dress. "Goodbye," she said, and walked back to her own table.

I ordered another pot of tea and sat watching the two of them till they, and the harassed Miss Megley, got up to leave. Charles led the way out, limping tragically, like a man with one leg several inches shorter than the other. He didn't look over at me. Miss Megley went next, then Esmé, who waved to me. I waved back, half getting up from my chair. It was a strangely emotional moment for me.

Less than a minute later, Esmé came back into the tearoom, dragging Charles behind her by the sleeve of his reefer. "Charles would like to kiss you goodbye," she said.

I immediately put down my cup, and said that was very nice, but was she *sure?*

"Yes," she said, a trifle grimly. She let go Charles's sleeve and gave him a rather vigorous push in my direction. He came forward, his face livid, and gave me a loud, wet smacker just below the right ear. Following this ordeal, he started to make a beeline for the door and a less sentimental way of life, but I caught the half belt at the back of his reefer, held on to it, and asked him, "What did one wall say to the other wall?"

2 Army Post Office.

His face lit up. "Meet you at the corner!" he shrieked, and raced out of the room, possibly in hysterics.

Esmé was standing with crossed ankles again. "You're quite sure you won't forget to write that story for me?" she asked. "It doesn't have to be *exclusive*ly for me. It can—"

I said there was absolutely no chance that I'd forget. I told her that I'd never written a story for anybody, but that it seemed like exactly the right time to get down to it.

She nodded. "Make it extremely squalid and moving," she suggested. "Are you at all acquainted with squalor?"

I said not exactly but that I was getting better acquainted with it, in one form or another, all the time, and that I'd do my best to come up to her specifications. We shook hands.

"Isn't a pity that we didn't meet under less extenuating circumstances?"

I said it was, I said it certainly was.

"Goodbye," Esmé said. "I hope you return from the war with all your faculties intact."

I thanked her, and said a few other words, and then watched her leave the tearoom. She left it slowly, reflectively, testing the ends of her hair for dryness.

This is the squalid, or moving, part of the story, and the scene changes. The people change, too. I'm still around, but from here on in, for reasons I'm not at liberty to disclose, I've disguised myself so cunningly that even the cleverest reader will fail to recognize me.

It was about ten-thirty at night in Gaufurt, Bavaria, several weeks after V-E Day. Staff Sergeant X was in his room on the second floor of the civilian home in which he and nine other American soldiers had been quartered, even before the armistice. He was seated on a folding wooden chair at a small, messy-looking writing table, with a paperback overseas novel open before him, which he was having great trouble reading. The trouble lay with him, not the novel. Although the men who lived on the first floor usually had first grab at the books sent each month by Special Services, X usually seemed to be left with the book he might have selected himself. But he was a young man who had not come through the war with all his faculties intact, and for more than an hour he had been triple-reading paragraphs, and now he was doing it to the sentences. He suddenly closed the book, without marking his place. With his hand, he shielded his eyes for a moment against the harsh, watty glare from the naked bulb over the table.

He took a cigarette from a pack on the table and lit it with fingers that bumped gently and incessantly against one another. He sat back a trifle in his chair and smoked without any sense of taste. He had been chain-smoking for weeks. His gums bled at the slightest pressure of the tip of his tongue, and he seldom stopped experimenting; it was a little game he played, sometimes by the hour. He sat for a moment smoking and experimenting. Then, abruptly, familiarly, and, as usual, with no warning, he thought he felt his mind dislodge itself and teeter, like insecure luggage on an overhead rack. He quickly did what he had been doing for weeks to set things right: he pressed his hands hard against his temples. He held on tight for a moment. His hair needed cutting, and it was dirty. He had washed it three or four times during his two weeks' stay at the hospital in Frankfort on the Main, but it had got dirty again on the long, dusty jeep ride back to Gaufurt. Corporal Z, who had called for him at the hospital, still drove a jeep combat-style, with the windshield down on the hood, armistice or no armistice. There were thousands of new troops in Germany. By driving with his windshield down, combat-style, Corporal Z hoped to show that he was not one of them, that not by a long shot was he some new son of a bitch in the E.T.O.[3]

When he let go of his head, X began to stare at the surface of the writing table, which was a catchall for at least two dozen unopened letters and at least five or six unopened packages, all addressed to him. He reached behind the debris and picked out a book that stood against the wall. It was a book by Goebbels, entitled "Die Zeit Ohne Beispiel." [4] It belonged to the thirty-eight-year-old, unmarried daughter of the family that, up to a few weeks earlier, had been living in the house. She had been a low official in the Nazi Party, but high enough, by Army

Regulations standards, to fall into an automatic-arrest category. X himself had arrested her. Now, for the third time since he had returned from the hospital that day, he opened the woman's book and read the brief inscription on the flyleaf. Written in ink, in German, in a small, hopelessly sincere handwriting, were the words "Dear God, life is hell." Nothing led up to or away from it. Alone on the page, and in the sickly stillness of the room, the words appeared to have the stature of an uncontestable, even classic indictment. X stared at the page for several minutes, trying, against heavy odds, not to be taken in. Then, with far more zeal than he had done anything in weeks, he picked up a pencil stub and wrote down under the inscription, in English, "Fathers and teachers, I ponder 'What is hell?' I maintain that it is the suffering of being unable to love." He started to write Dostoevski's name under the inscription, but saw—with fright that ran through his whole body—that what he had written was almost entirely illegible. He shut the book.

He quickly picked up something else from the table, a letter from his older brother in Albany. It had been on his table even before he had checked into the hospital. He opened the envelope, loosely resolved to read the letter straight through, but read only the top half of the first page. He stopped after the words "Now that the g.d. war is over and you probably have a lot of time over there, how about sending the kids a couple of bayonets or swastikas . . ." After he'd torn it up, he looked down at the pieces as they lay in the wastebasket. He saw that he had overlooked an enclosed snapshot. He could make out somebody's feet standing on a lawn somewhere.

He put his arms on the table and rested his head on them. He ached from head to foot, all zones of pain seemingly interdependent. He was rather like a Christmas tree whose lights, wired in series, must all go out if even one bulb is defective.

The door banged open, without having been rapped on. X. raised his head, turned it, and saw Corporal Z standing in the door. Corporal Z had been X's jeep partner and constant companion from D Day straight through five campaigns of the war. He lived on the first floor

---

[3] European Theater of Operations.   [4] "The Epoch Without Precedent."

and he usually came up to see X when he had a few rumors or gripes to unload. He was a huge, photogenic young man of twenty-four. During the war, a national magazine had photographed him in Hürtgen Forest; he had posed, more than just obligingly, with a Thanksgiving turkey in each hand. "Ya writin' letters?" he asked X. "Its' spooky in here, for Chrissake." He preferred always to enter a room that had the overhead light on.

X turned around in his chair and asked him to come in, and to be careful not to step on the dog.

"The what?"

"Alvin. He's right under your feet, Clay. How 'bout turning on the goddam light?"

Clay found the overhead-light switch, flicked it on, then stepped across the puny, servant's-size room and sat down on the edge of the bed, facing his host. His brick-red hair, just combed, was dripping with the amount of water he required for satisfactory grooming. A comb with a fountain-pen clip protruded, familiarly, from the right-hand pocket of his olive-drab shirt. Over the left-hand pocket he was wearing the Combat Infantrymen's Badge (which, technically, he wasn't authorized to wear), the European Theatre ribbon, with five bronze stars in it (instead of a lone silver one, which was the equivalent of five bronze ones), and the pre-Pearl Harbor service ribbon. He sighed heavily and said, "Christ almighty." It means nothing: it was Army. He took a pack of cigarettes from his shirt pocket, tapped one out, then put away the pack and rebuttoned the pocket flap. Smoking, he looked vacuously around the room. His look finally settled on the radio. "Hey," he said. "They got this terrific show comin' on the radio in a coupla minutes. Bob Hope, and everybody."

X, opening a fresh pack of cigarettes, said he had just turned the radio off.

Undarkened, Clay watched X trying to get a cigarette lit. "Jesus," he said, with spectator's enthusiasm, "you oughta see your goddam hands. Boy, have you got the shakes. Ya know that?"

X got his cigarette lit, nodded, and said Clay had a real eye for detail.

"No kidding, hey. I goddam near fainted when I saw you at the hospital. You looked like a goddam *corpse*. How much weight ya lose? How many pounds? Ya know?"

"I don't know. How was your mail when I was gone? You heard from Loretta?"

Loretta was Clay's girl. They intended to get married at their earliest convenience. She wrote to him fairly regularly, from a paradise of triple exclamation points and inaccurate observations. All through the war, Clay had read all Loretta's letters aloud to X, however intimate they were —in fact, the more intimate, the better. It was his custom, after each reading, to ask X to plot out or pad out the letter of reply, or to insert a few impressive words in French or German.

"Yeah, I had a letter from her yesterday. Down in my room. Show it to ya later," Clay said, listlessly. He sat up straight on the edge of the bed, held his breath, and issued a long, resonant belch. Looking just semi-pleased with the achievement, he relaxed again. "Her goddam brother's gettin' outa the Navy on account of his hip," he said. "He's got this hip, the bastard." He sat up again and tried for another belch, but with below-par results. A jot of alertness came into his face. "Hey. Before I forget. We gotta get up at five tomorrow and drive to Hamburg or someplace. Pick up Eisenhower jackets for the whole detachment."

X, regarding him hostilely, stated that he didn't want an Eisenhower jacket.

Clay looked surprised, almost a trifle hurt, "Oh, they're good! They look good. How come?"

"No reason. Why do we have to get up at five? The war's over, for God's sake."

"I don't know—we gotta get back before lunch. They got some new forms in we gotta fill out before lunch. . . . I asked Bulling how come we couldn't fill 'em out tonight—he's *got* the goddam forms right on his desk. He don't want to open the envelopes yet, the son of a bitch."

The two sat quiet for a moment, hating Bulling.

Clay suddenly looked at X with new—higher—interest than before. "Hey," he said. "Did you know the goddam side of your face is jumping all over the place?"

X said he knew all about it, and covered his tic with his hand.

Clay stared at him for a moment, then said, rather vividly, as if he were the bearer of exceptionally good news, "I wrote Loretta you had a nervous breakdown."

"Oh?"

"Yeah. She's interested as hell in all that stuff. She's majoring in psychology." Clay stretched himself out on the bed, shoes included. "You know what she said? She says nobody gets a nervous breakdown just from the war and all. She says you probably were unstable like, your whole goddam life."

X bridged his hand over his eyes—the light over the bed seemed to be blinding him—and said that Loretta's insight into things was always a joy.

Clay glanced over at him. "Listen, ya bastard," he said. "She knows a goddam sight more psychology than *you* do."

"Do you think you can bring yourself to take your stinking feet off my bed?" X asked.

Clay left his feet where they were for a few don't-tell-me-where-to-put-my-feet seconds, then swung them around to the floor and sat up. "I'm goin' downstairs anyway. They got the radio on in Walker's room." He didn't get up from the bed, though. "Hey, I was just tellin' that new son of a bitch, Bernstein, downstairs. Remember that time I and you drove into Valognes, and we got shelled for about two goddam hours, and that goddam cat I shot that jumped up on the hood of the jeep when we were layin' in that hole? Remember?"

"Yes—don't start that business with that cat again, Clay, God damn it. I don't want to hear about it."

"No, all I mean is I wrote Loretta about it. She and the whole psychology class discussed it. In class and all. The goddam professor and everybody."

"That's fine. I don't want to hear about it, Clay."

"No, you know the reason I took a pot shot at it, Loretta says? She says I was temporarily insane. No kidding. From the shelling and all."

X threaded his fingers, once, through his dirty hair, then shielded his eyes against the light again. "You weren't insane. You were simply doing your duty. You killed that pussycat in as manly a way as anybody could've, under the circumstances."

Clay looked at him suspiciously. "What the hell are you talkin' about?"

"That cat was a spy. You *had* to take a pot shot at it. It was a very clever German midget dressed up in a cheap fur coat. So there was absolutely nothing brutal, or cruel, or dirty, or even—"

"God damn it!" Clay said, his lips thinned. "Can't you ever be *sincere?*"

X suddenly felt sick, and he swung around in his chair and grabbed the wastebasket—just in time.

When he had straightened up and turned toward his guest again, he found him standing, embarrassed, halfway between the bed and the door. X started to apologize, but changed his mind and reached for his cigarettes.

"C'mon down and listen to Hope on the radio, hey," Clay said, keeping his distance but trying to be friendly over it. "It'll do ya good. I mean it."

"You go ahead, Clay. . . . I'll look at my stamp collection."

"Yeah? You got a stamp collection? I didn't know you—"

"I'm only kidding."

Clay took a couple of slow steps toward the door. "I may drive over to Ehstadt later," he said. "They got a dance. It'll probably last till around two. Wanna go?"

"No, thanks. . . . I may practice a few steps in the room."

"O.K. G'night! Take it easy, now, for Chrissake." The door slammed shut, then instantly opened again. "Hey, O.K. if I leave a letter to Loretta under your door? I got some German stuff in it. Willya fix it up for me?"

"Yes. Leave me alone now, God damn it."

"Sure," said Clay. "You know what my mother wrote me? She wrote me she's glad you and I were together all the whole war. In the same jeep and all. She says my letters are a helluva lot more intelligent since we been goin' around together."

X looked up and over at him, and said, with great effort, "Thanks. Tell her thanks for me."

"I will. G'night!" The door slammed shut, this time for good.

X sat looking at the door for a long while, then turned his chair around toward the writing table and picked up his portable typewriter from the floor. He made space for it on the messy table surface, pushing aside the collapsed pile of unopened letters and packages. He thought if he wrote a letter to an old friend of his in New York, there might be some quick, however slight, therapy in it for him. But he couldn't insert his notepaper into the roller properly, his fingers were shaking so violently now. He put his hands down at his sides for a minute, then tried again, but finally crumpled the notepaper in his hand.

He was aware that he ought to get the wastebasket out of the room, but instead of doing anything about it, he put his arms on the typewriter and rested his head again, closing his eyes.

A few throbbing minutes later, when he opened his eyes, he found himself squinting at a small, unopened package wrapped in green paper. It had probably slipped off the pile when he had made space for the typewriter. He saw that it had been readdressed several times. He could make out, on just one side of the package, at least three of his old A.P.O. numbers.

He opened the package without any interest, without even looking at the return address. He opened it by burning the string with a lighted match. He was more interested in watching the string burn all the way down than in opening the package, but he opened it, finally.

Inside the box, a note, written in ink, lay on top of a small object wrapped in tissue paper. He picked out the note and read it.

17, —— ROAD,
——, DEVON
JUNE 7, 1944

DEAR SERGEANT X,

I hope you will forgive me for having taken 38 days to begin our correspondence but, I have been extremely busy as my aunt has undergone streptococcus of the throat and nearly perished and I have been justifiably saddled with one responsibility after another. However I have thought of you frequently and of the extremely pleasant afternoon we spent in each other's company on April 30, 1944 between 3:45 and 4:15 P.M. in case it slipped your mind.

We are all tremendously excited and overawed about D Day and only hope that it will bring about the swift termination of the war and a method of existence that is ridiculous to say the least. Charles and I are both quite concerned about you; we hope you were not among those who made the first initial assault upon the Cotentin Peninsula. Were you? Please reply as speedily as possible. My warmest regards to your wife.

Sincerely yours,
ESMÉ

P.S. I am taking the liberty of enclosing my wristwatch which you may keep in your possession for the duration of the conflict. I did not observe whether you were wearing one during our brief association, but this one is extremely waterproof and shock-proof as well as having many other virtues among which one can tell at what velocity one is walking if one wishes. I am quite certain that you will use it to greater advantage in these difficult days than I ever can and that you will accept it as a lucky talisman.

Charles, whom I am teaching to read and write and whom I am finding an extremely intelligent novice, wishes to add a few words. Please write as soon as you have the time and inclination.

HELLO HELLO HELLO HELLO HELLO HELLO HELLO HELLO HELLO HELLO LOVE AND KISSES CHALES

It was a long time before X could set the note aside, let alone lift Esmés' father's wristwatch out of the box. When he did finally lift it out, he saw that its crystal had been broken in transit. He wondered if the watch was otherwise undamaged, but he hadn't the courage to wind it and find out. He just sat with it in his hand for another long period. Then, suddenly, almost ecstatically, he felt sleepy.

You take a really sleepy man, Esmé, and he *al*ways stands a chance of again becoming a man with all his fac—with all his f-a-c-u-l-t-i-e-s intact.

Comments and Questions

Two matters are immediately clear about Salinger's story: the technique is unusual, and the meaning does not lie on the surface. Perhaps you have already developed the valuable habit of asking questions about a piece of creative literature to probe its depth. Why does Salinger use his unusual time arrangement? He begins, really, at the end of the story in April 1950, shifts quickly to April 30, 1944, moves to August 1945, backs up to June 7, 1944 (Esmé's letter), and moves ahead again to August. We shall not get to the heart of the matter unless we keep ourselves properly placed in time. Why does the story have two parts, each with a different kind of a narrator? Does Charles have an important function in the story or is he simply comic relief? What does the title mean? Why love *and* squalor? How is Esmé's precocity related to the title? Why does the first narrator say, "Nobody's aiming to please, here. More, really, to edify, to instruct"? There are adequate signposts along the way.

The first narrator has promised Esmé in 1944 to write her a story about squalor. For six years he had not done so, but now (1950) that he cannot attend her wedding, he is moved, in mitigation, to write the story. The narrator is young in 1944, out of college a year, and a lonely American soldier in England. Esmé *is* precocious (and moreover she is English, not American), sensitive, and reads his temper and needs accurately. She leaves him with the words, " 'I hope you return from the war with all your faculties intact.' " "It was," he says, "a strangely emotional moment for me."

The narrator now "disguises" himself as Sergeant X to increase the aesthetic distance (p. 20) which removes much of the intimacy created in the first scene in the tearoom. The second scene must be presented more objectively (with a third-person narrator) to prevent the first-person narrator from appearing maudlin. The intimate tone in the first half of the story would have been a false note in the second half. The maneuver is neatly executed, to Salinger's credit. The squalor the first-person narrator promised to write about is now his (Sergeant X's) own, and the faculties which Esmé hoped would be kept "intact" have been "dislodged." Esmé's letter, the watch (presented "as a lucky talisman"), and Charles's healthy burst of sentiment arrive almost too late, but Esmé, "you take a really sleepy man . . . and he *al*ways stands a chance of again becoming a man with all his fac—with all his f-a-c-u-l-t-i-e-s intact." We are brought full circle back to the title, "To Esmé—with Love . . . ," the spiritual therapy for the squalor of war.

1. We should not overlook the distinct difference between the style of the first half and that of the second half of the story. What does each style contribute to the tone of the story?

2. Why does Salinger have Esmé describe her father and mother—how does this knowledge help us to find the story's meaning?

Bright and Morning Star
RICHARD WRIGHT
1908–1960

I

She stood with her black face some six inches from the moist windowpane and wondered when on earth would it ever stop raining. It might keep up like this all week, she thought. She heard rain droning upon the roof and high up in the wet sky her eyes followed the silent rush of a bright shaft of yellow that swung from the airplane beacon in far off Memphis. Momently she could see it cutting through the rainy dark; it would hover a second like a gleaming sword above her head, then vanish. She sighed, troubling, Johnny-Boys been trampin in this slop all day wid no decent shoes on his feet. . . . Through the window she could see the rich black earth sprawling outside in the night. There was more rain than the clay could soak up; pools stood everywhere. She yawned and mumbled: "Rains good n bad. It kin make seeds bus up thu the ground, er it kin bog things down lika watah-soaked coffin." Her hands were folded loosely over her stomach and the hot air of the kitchen traced a filmy vein of sweat on her forehead. From the cook stove came the soft singing of burning wood and now and then a throaty bubble rose from a pot of simmering greens.

"Shucks, Johnny-Boy coulda let somebody else do all tha runnin in the rain. Theres others bettah fixed fer it than he is. But, naw! Johnny-Boy ain the one t trust nobody t do nothin. Hes gotta do it *all* hissef. . . ."

She glanced at a pile of damp clothes in a

zinc tub. Waal, Ah bettah git t work. She turned, lifted a smoothing iron with a thick pad of cloth, touched a spit-wet finger to it with a quick, jerking motion: *smiiitz!* Yeah; its hot! Stooping, she took a blue work-shirt from the tub and shook it out. With a deft twist of her shoulders she caught the iron in her right hand; the fingers of her left hand took a piece of wax from a tin box and a frying sizzle came as she smeared the bottom. She was thinking of nothing now; her hands followed a life-long ritual of toil. Spreading a sleeve, she ran the hot iron to and fro until the wet cloth became stiff. She was deep in the midst of her work when a song rose up out of the far off days of her childhood and broke through half-parted lips:

> *Hes the Lily of the Valley, the Bright n Mawnin Star*
> *Hes the Fairest of Ten Thousand t ma soul . . .*

A gust of wind dashed rain against the window. Johnny-Boy oughta c mon home n eat his suppah. Aw, Lawd! Itd be fine ef Sug could eat wid us tonight! Itd be like ol times! Mabbe aftah all it wont be long fo he comes back. Tha lettah Ah got from im last week said *Don give up hope.* . . . Yeah; we gotta live in hope. Then both of her sons, Sug and Johnny-Boy, would be back with her.

With an involuntary nervous gesture, she stopped and stood still, listening. But the only sound was the lulling fall of rain. Shucks, ain no usa me ackin this way, she thought. Ever time they gits ready to hol them meetings Ah gits jumpity. Ah been a lil scared ever since Sug went t jail. She heard the clock ticking and looked. Johnny-Boys a *hour* late! He sho must be havin a time doin all tha trampin, trampin thu the mud. . . . But her fear was a quiet one; it was more like an intense brooding than a fear; it was a sort of hugging of hated facts so closely that she could feel their grain, like letting cold water run over her hand from a faucet on a winter morning.

She ironed again, faster now, as if she felt the more she engaged her body in work the less she would think. But how could she forget Johnny-Boy out there on those wet fields rounding up white and black Communists for a meeting tomorrow? And that was just what Sug had been doing when the sheriff had caught him, beat him, and tried to make him tell who and where his comrades were. Po Sug! They sho musta beat the boy somethin awful! But, thank Gawd, he didnt talk! He ain no weaklin, Sug ain! Hes been lion-hearted all his life long.

That had happened a year ago. And now each time those meetings came around the old terror surged back. While shoving the iron a cluster of toiling days returned; days of washing and ironing to feed Johnny-Boy and Sug so they could do party work; days of carrying a hundred pounds of white folks' clothes upon her head across fields sometimes wet and sometimes dry. But in those days a hundred pounds was nothing to carry carefully balanced upon her head while stepping by instinct over the corn and cotton rows. The only time it had seemed heavy was when she had heard of Sug's arrest. She had been coming home one morning with a bundle upon her head, her hands swinging idly by her sides, walking slowly with her eyes in front of her, when Bob, Johnny-Boy's pal, had called from across the fields and had come and told her that the sheriff had got Sug. That morning the bundle had become heavier than she could ever remember.

And with each passing week now, though she spoke of it to no one, things were becoming heavier. The tubs of water and the smoothing iron and the bundles of clothes were becoming harder to lift, with her back aching so; and her work was taking longer, all because Sug was gone and she didn't know just when Johnny-Boy would be taken too. To ease the ache of anxiety that was swelling her heart, she hummed, then sang softly:

> *He walks wid me, He talks wid me*
> *He tells me Ahm His own. . . .*

Guiltily, she stopped and smiled. Looks like Ah jus cant seem t fergit them ol songs, no mattah how hard Ah tries. . . . She had learned them when she was a little girl living and working on a farm. Every Monday morning from the corn and cotton fields the slow strains had floated from her mother's lips, lonely and haunting; and later, as the years had filled with gall, she had learned their deep meaning. Long hours of scrubbing floors for a few cents a day had taught her who Jesus was, what a great boon it was to cling to Him, to be like Him and suffer without a mumbling word. She had poured the yearning of her life into the songs, feeling buoyed with a faith beyond this world. The figure of the Man nailed in agony to the Cross, His burial in a cold grave, His transfigured Resurrection, His being breath and clay, God and Man—all had focused her feelings upon an imagery which had swept her life into a wondrous vision.

But as she had grown older, a cold white mountain, the white folks and their laws, had swum into her vision and shattered her songs and their spell of peace. To her that white mountain was temptation, something to lure her from her Lord, a part of the world God had made in order that she might endure it and come through all the stronger, just as Christ had risen with greater glory from the tomb. The days crowded with trouble had enhanced her faith and she had grown to love hardship with a bitter pride; she had obeyed the laws of the white folks with a soft smile of secret knowing.

After her mother had been snatched up to heaven in a chariot of fire, the years had brought her a rough workingman and two black babies, Sug and Johnny-Boy, all three of whom she had wrapped in the charm and magic of her vision. Then she was tested by no less than God; her man died, a trial which she bore with the strength shed by the grace of her vision; finally even the memory of her man faded into the vision itself, leaving her with two black boys growing tall, slowly into manhood.

Then one day grief had come to her heart when Johnny-Boy and Sug had walked forth demanding their lives. She had sought to fill their eyes with her vision, but they would have none of it. And she had wept when they began to boast of the strength shed by a new and terrible vision.

But she had loved them, even as she loved them now; bleeding, her heart had followed them. She could have done no less, being an old woman in a strange world. And day by day her sons had ripped from her startled eyes her old vision, and image by image had given her a new one, different, but great and strong enough to fling her into the light of another grace. The wrongs and sufferings of black men had taken the place of Him nailed to the Cross; the meager beginning of the party had become another Resurrection; and the hate of those who would

destroy her new faith had quickened in her a hunger to feel how deeply her new strength went.

"Lawd, Johnny-Boy," she would sometimes say, "Ah jus wan them white folks t try t make me tell *who* is *in* the party n who *ain!* Ah jus wan em t try, Ahll show em somethin they never thought a black woman could have!"

But sometimes like tonight, while lost in the forgetfulness of work, the past and the present would become mixed in her; while toiling under a strange star for a new freedom the old songs would slip from her lips with their beguiling sweetness.

The iron was getting cold. She put more wood into the fire, stood again at the window and watched the yellow blade of light cut through the wet darkness. Johnny-Boy ain here yit. . . . Then, before she was aware of it, she was still, listening for sounds. Under the drone of rain she heard the slosh of feet in mud. Tha ain Johnny-Boy. She knew his long, heavy footsteps in a million. She heard feet come on the porch. Some woman. . . . She heard bare knuckles knock three times, then once. Thas some of them comrades! She unbarred the door, cracked it a few inches, and flinched from the cold rush of damp wind.

"Whos tha?"

"Its me!"

"Who?"

"Me, Reva!"

She flung the door open.

"Lawd, chile, c mon in!"

She stepped to one side and a thin, blond-haired white girl ran through the door; as she slid the bolt she heard the girl gasping and shaking her wet clothes. Somethings wrong! Reva wouldna walked a mil t mah house in all this slop fer nothin! That gals stuck onto Johnny-Boy. Ah wondah ef anythin happened t im?

"Git on inter the kitchen, Reva, where its warm."

"Lawd, Ah sho is wet!"

"How yuh reckon yuhd be, in all tha rain?"

"Johnny-Boy ain here *yit?*" asked Reva.

"Naw! N ain no usa yuh worryin bout im. Jus yuh git them shoes off! Yuh wanna ketch yo deatha col?" She stood looking absently. Yeah; its somethin about the party er Johnny-Boy thas gone wrong. Lawd, Ah wondah ef her pa knows how she feels bout Johnny-Boy?

"Honey, yuh hadn't oughta come out in sloppy weather like this."

"Ah had t come, An Sue."

She led Reva to the kitchen.

"Git them shoes off n git close t the stove so yuhll git dry!"

"An Sue, Ah got somethin t tell yuh . . ."

The words made her hold her breath. Ah bet its somethin bout Johnny-Boy!

"Whut, honey?"

"The sheriff wuz by our house tonight. He come t see pa."

"Yeah?"

"He done got word from somewheres about tha meetin tomorrow."

"Is it Johnny-Boy, Reva?"

"Aw, naw, An Sue! Ah ain hearda word bout im. Ain yuh seen im tonight?"

"He ain come home t eat yit."

"Where kin he be?"

"Lawd knows, chile."

"Somebodys gotta tell them conrades that meetings off," said Reva. "The sheriffs got men watchin our house. Ah had t slip out t git here widout em followin me."

"Reva?"

"Hunh?"

"Ahma ol woman n Ah wans yuh t tell me the truth."

"Whut, An Sue?"

"Yuh ain tryin t fool me, is yuh?"

"*Fool* yuh?"

"Bout Johnny-Boy?"

"Lawd, naw, An Sue!"

"Ef theres anythin wrong jus tell me, chile. Ah kin stan it."

She stood by the ironing board, her hands as usual folded loosely over her stomach, watching Reva pull off her water-clogged shoes. She was feeling that Johnny-Boy was already lost to her; she was feeling the pain that would come when she knew it for certain; and she was feeling that she would have to be brave and bear it. She was like a person caught in a swift current of water and knew where the water was sweeping her and did not want to go on but had to go on to the end.

"It ain nothin bout Johnny-Boy, An Sue," said Reva. "But we gotta do somethin er we'll all git inter trouble."

"How the sheriff know about tha meetin?"

"Thas whut pa wants t know."

"Somebody done turned Judas."

"Sho looks like it."

"Ah bet it wuz some of them new ones," she said.

"Its hard t tell," said Reva.

"Lissen, Reva, yuh oughta stay here n git dry, but yuh bettah git back n tell yo pa Johnny-Boy ain here n Ah don know when hes gonna show up. *Some*bodys gotta tell them comrades t stay erway from yo pas house."

She stood with her back to the window, looking at Reva's wide, blue eyes. Po critter! Gotta go back thu all tha slop! Though she felt sorry for Reva, not once did she think that it would not have to be done. Being a woman, Reva was not suspect; she would *have* to go. It was just as natural for Reva to go back through the cold rain as it was for her to iron night and day, or for Sug to be in jail. Right now, Johnny-Boy was out there on those dark fields trying to get home. Lawd, don let em git im tonight! In spite of herself her feelings became torn. She loved her son and, loving him, she loved what he was trying to do. Johnny-Boy was happiest when he was working for the party, and her love for him was for his happiness. She frowned, trying hard to fit something together in her feelings: for her to try to stop Johnny-Boy was to admit that all the toil of years meant nothing; and to let him go meant that sometime or other he would be caught, like Sug. In facing it this way she felt a little stunned, as though she had come suddenly upon a blank wall in the dark. But outside in the rain were people, white and black, whom she had known all her life. Those people depended upon Johnny-Boy, loved him and looked to him as a man and leader. Yeah; hes gotta keep on; he cant stop now. . . . She looked at Reva; she was crying and pulling her shoes back on with reluctant fingers.

"Whut yuh carryin on tha way fer, chile?"

"Yuh done los Sug, now yuh sending Johnny-Boy . . ."

"Ah got t, honey."

She was glad she could say that. Reva believed in black folks and not for anything in the world would she falter before her. In Reva's trust and acceptance of her she had found her first feelings of humanity; Reva's love was her refuge from shame and degradation. If in the early days of her life the white mountain had driven her back from the earth, then in her last days Reva's love was drawing her toward it, like the beacon that swung through the night outside. She heard Reva sobbing.

"Hush, honey!"

"Mah brothers in jail too! Ma cries ever day . . .

"Ah know, honey."

She helped Reva with her coat; her fingers felt the scant flesh of the girl's shoulder. She don git ernuff t eat, she thought. She slipped her arms around Reva's waist and held her close for a moment.

"Now, yuh stop that cryin."

"A-a-ah c-c-cant hep it. . . ."

"Everythingll be awright; Johnny-Boyll be back."

"Yuh think so?"

"Sho, chile. Cos he will."

Neither of them spoke again until they stood in the doorway. Outside they could hear water washing through the ruts of the street.

"Be sho n send Johnny-Boy t tell the folks t stay erway from pas house," said Reva.

"Ahll tell im. Don yuh worry."

"Good-bye!"

"Good-bye!"

Leaning against the door jamb, she shook her head slowly and watched Reva vanish through the falling rain.

II

She was back at her board, ironing, when she heard feet sucking in the mud of the back yard; feet she knew from long years of listening were Johnny-Boy's. But tonight, with all the rain and fear, his coming was like a leaving, was almost more than she could bear. Tears welled to her eyes and she blinked them away. She felt that he was coming so that she could give him up; to see him now was to say good-bye. But it was a good-bye she knew she could never say; they were not that way toward each other. All day long they could sit in the same room and not speak; she was his mother and he was her son. Most of the time a nod or a grunt would carry all the meaning that she wanted to convey to him, or he to her. She did not even turn her head when she heard him come stomp-ing into the kitchen. She heard him pull up a chair, sit, sigh, and draw off his muddy shoes; they fell to the floor with heavy thuds. Soon the kitchen was full of the scent of his drying socks and his burning pipe. Tha boys hongry! She paused and looked at him over her shoulder; he was puffing at his pipe with his head tilted back and his feet propped up on the edge of the stove; his eyelids drooped and his wet clothes steamed from the heat of the fire. Lawd, tha boy gits mo like his pa every day he lives, she mused, her lips breaking in a slow, faint smile. Hols tha pipe in his mouth just like his pa usta hol his. Wondah how they woulda got erlong ef his pa hada lived? They oughta liked each other, they so mucha like. She wished there could have been other children besides Sug, so Johnny-Boy would not have to be so much alone. A man needs a woman by his side. . . . She thought of Reva; she liked Reva; the brightest glow her heart had ever known was when she had learned that Reva loved Johnny-Boy. But beyond Reva were cold white faces. Ef theys caught it means *death*. . . . She jerked around when she heard Johnny-Boy's pipe clatter to the floor. She saw him pick it up, smile sheepishly at her, and wag his head.

"Gawd, Ahm sleepy," he mumbled.

She got a pillow from her room and gave it to him.

"Here," she said.

"Hunh," he said, putting the pillow between his head and the back of the chair.

They were silent again. Yes, she would have to tell him to go back out into the cold rain and slop; maybe to get caught; maybe for the last time; she didn't know. But she would let him eat and get dry before telling him that the sheriff knew of the meeting to be held at Lem's tomorrow. And she would make him take a big dose of soda before he went out; soda always helped to stave off a cold. She looked at the clock. It was eleven. Theres time yit. Spreading a newspaper on the apron of the stove, she placed a heaping plate of greens upon it, a knife, a fork, a cup of coffee, a slab of cornbread, and a dish of peach cobbler.

"Yo suppahs ready," she said.

"Yeah," he said.

He did not move. She ironed again. Presently, she heard him eating. When she could no longer hear his knife tickling against the edge of the plate, she knew he was through. It was almost twelve now. She would let him rest a little while longer before she told him. Till one er'clock, mabbe. Hes so tired. . . . She finished her ironing, put away the board, and stacked the clothes in her dresser drawer. She poured herself a cup of black coffee, drew up a chair, sat down and drank.

"Yuh almos dry," she said, not looking around.

"Yeah," he said, turning sharply to her.

The tone of voice in which she had spoken had let him know that more was coming. She drained her cup and waited a moment longer.

"Reva wuz here."

"Yeah?"

"She lef bout a hour ergo."

"Whut she say?"

"She said old man Lem hada visit from the sheriff today."

"Bout the meetin?"

She saw him stare at the coals glowing red through the crevices of the stove and run his fingers nervously through his hair. She knew he was wondering how the sheriff had found out. In the silence he would ask a wordless question and in the silence she would answer wordlessly. Johnny-Boys too trustin, she thought. Hes trying to make the party big n hes takin in folks fastern he kin git t know em. You cant trust ever white man yuh meet. . . .

"Yuh know, Johnny-Boy, yuh been takin in a lotta them white folks lately . . ."

"Aw, ma!"

"But, Johnny-Boy . . ."

"Please, don't talk t me bout tha now, ma."

"Yuh ain t ol t lissen n learn, son," she said.

"Ah know whut yuh gonna say, ma. N yuh wrong. Yuh cant judge folks just by how yuh feel bout em n by how long yuh done knowed em. Ef we start that we wouldnt have *nobody* in the party. When folks pledge they word t be with us, then we gotta take em in. Wes too weak to be choosy."

He rose abruptly, rammed his hands into his pockets, and stood facing the window; she looked at his back in a long silence. She knew his faith; it was deep. He had always said that black men could not fight the rich bosses alone; a man could not fight with every hand against him. But he believes so hard hes blind, she thought. At odd times they had had these arguments before; always she would be pitting her feelings against the hard necessity of his thinking, and always she would lose. She shook her head. Po Johnny-Boy; he don know . . .

"But ain nona our folks tol, Johnny-Boy," she said.

"How yuh know?" he asked. His voice came low and with a tinge of anger. He still faced the window and now and then the yellow blade of light flicked across the sharp outline of his black face.

"Cause Ah know em," she said.

"*Any*body mighta tol," he said.

"It wuznt nona *our* folks," she said again.

She saw his hand sweep in a swift arc of disgust.

"*Our* folks! Ma, who in Gawds name is *our* folks?"

"The folks we wuz born n raised wid, son. The folks we *know!*"

"We cant make the party grow tha way, ma."

"It mighta been Booker," she said.

"Yuh don know."

". . . er Blattberg . . ."

"Fer Chrissakes!"

". . . er any of the fo-five others whut joined las week."

"Ma, yuh just don wan me t go out tonight," he said.

"Yo ol ma wans yuh t be careful, son."

"Ma, when yuh start doubtin folks in the party, then there ain no end."

"Son, Ah knows ever black man n woman in this parta the country," she said, standing too. "Ah watched em grow up; Ah even heped birth n nurse some of em; Ah knows em *all* from way back. There ain none of em that *coulda* tol! The folks Ah know jus don open they dos n ast death t walk in! Son, it wuz some of them *white* folks! Yuh just mark mah word n wait n see!"

"Why is it gotta be *white* folks?" he asked. "Ef they tol, then theys just Judases, thas all."

"Son, look at whuts befo yuh."

He shook his head and sighed.

"Ma, Ah done tol yuh a hundred times. Ah cant see white n Ah cant see black," he said. "Ah sees rich men n Ah sees po men."

She picked up his dirty dishes and piled them in a pan. Out of the corners of her eyes she saw him sit and pull on his wet shoes. Hes goin! When she put the last dish away he was standing fully dressed, warming his hands over the stove. Jus a few mo minutes now n hell be gone, like Sug, mabbe. Her throat tightened. This black mans fight takes *ever*thin! Looks like Gawd put us in this world jus t beat us down!

"Keep this, ma," he said.

She saw a crumpled wad of money in his outstretched fingers.

"Naw, yuh keep it. Yuh might need it."

"It ain mine, ma. It berlongs t the party."

"But, Johnny-Boy, yuh might hafta go er-way!"

"Ah kin make out."

"Don fergit yosef too much, son."

"Ef Ah don come back theyll need it."

He was looking at her face and she was looking at the money.

"Yuh keep tha," she said slowly. "Ahll give em the money."

"From where?"

"Ah got some."

"Where yuh git it from?"

She sighed.

"Ah been savin a dollah a week fer Sug ever since hes been in jail."

"Lawd, ma!"

She saw the look of puzzled love and wonder in his eyes. Clumsily, he put the money back into his pocket.

"Ahm gone," he said.

"Here; drink this glass of soda watah."

She watched him drink, then put the glass away.

"Waal," he said.

"Take the stuff outta yo pockets!"

She lifted the lid of the stove and he dumped all the papers from his pocket into the fire. She followed him to the door and made him turn round.

"Lawd, yuh tryin to maka revolution n yuh cant even keep yo coat buttoned." Her nimble fingers fastened his collar high around his throat. "There!"

He pulled the brim of his hat low over his eyes. She opened the door and with the suddenness of the cold gust of wind that struck her face, he was gone. She watched the black fields and the rain take him, her eyes burning. When the last faint footstep could no longer be heard, she closed the door, went to her bed, lay down, and pulled the cover over her while fully dressed. Her feelings coursed with the rhythm of the rain: Hes gone! Lawd, Ah *knows* hes gone! Her blood felt cold.

III

She was floating in a grey void somewhere between sleeping and dreaming and then suddenly she was wide awake, hearing and feeling in the same instant the thunder of the door crashing in and a cold wind filling the room. It was pitch black and she stared, resting on her elbows, her mouth open, not breathing, her ears full of the sound of tramping feet and booming voices. She knew at once: They lookin fer im! Then, filled with her will, she was on her feet, rigid, waiting, listening.

"The lamps burnin!"

"Yuh see her?"

"Naw!"

"Look in the kitchen!"

"Gee, this place smells like niggers!"

"Say, somebodys here er been here!"

"Yeah; theres fire in the stove!"

"Mabbe hes been here n gone?"

"Boy, look at these jars of jam!"

"Niggers make good jam!"

"Git some bread!"

"Heres some cornbread!"

"Say, lemme git some!"

"Take it easy! Theres plenty here!"

"Ahma take some of this stuff home!"

"Look, heres a pota greens!"

"N some hot cawffee!"

"Say, yuh guys! C mon! Cut it out! We didn't come here fer a feas!"

She walked slowly down the hall. They lookin fer im, but they ain got im yit! She stopped in the doorway, her gnarled, black hands as always folded over her stomach, but tight now, so tightly the veins bulged. The kitchen was crowded with white men in glistening raincoats. Though the lamp burned, their flashlights still glowed in red fists. Across her floor she saw the muddy track of their boots.

"Yuh white folks git outta mah house!"

There was a quick silence; every face turned toward her. She saw a sudden movement, but did not know what it meant until something hot and wet slammed her squarely in the face. She gasped, but did not move. Calmly, she wiped the warm, greasy liquor of greens from her eyes with her left hand. One of the white men had thrown a handful of greens out of the pot at her.

"How they taste, ol bitch?"

"Ah ast yuh t git outta mah house!"

She saw the sheriff detach himself from the crowd and walk toward her.

"Now, Anty . . ."

"White man, don yuh *Anty* me!"

"Yuh ain got the right sperit!"

"Sperit hell! Yuh git these men outta mah house!"

"Yuh ack like yuh don like it!"

"Naw, Ah don like it, n yuh knows dam waal Ah don!"

"What yuh gonna do about it?"

"Ahm telling yuh t git outta mah house!"

"Gittin sassy?"

"Ef telling yuh t git outta mah house is sass, then Ahm sassy!"

Her words came in a tense whisper; but beyond, back of them, she was watching, thinking, judging the men.

"Listen, Anty," the sheriff's voice came soft and low. "Ahm here t hep yuh. How come yuh wanna ack this way?"

"Yuh ain never heped yo *own* sef since yuh been born," she flared. "How kin the likes of yuh hep me?"

One of the white men came forward and stood directly in front of her.

"Lissen, nigger woman, yuh talkin t *white* men!"

"Ah don care who Ahm talkin t!"

"Yuhll wish some day yuh did!"

"Not t the likes of yuh!"

"Yuh need somebody t teach yuh how t be a good nigger!"

"*Yuh* cant teach it t me!"

"Yuh gonna change yo tune."

"Not longs mah bloods warm!"

"Don git smart now!"

"Yuh git outta mah house!"

"Spose we don go?" the sheriff asked.

They were crowded around her. She had not moved since she had taken her place in the doorway. She was thinking only of Johnny-Boy as she stood there giving and taking words; and she knew that they, too, were thinking of Johnny-Boy. She knew they wanted him, and her heart was daring them to take him from her.

"Spose we don go?" the sheriff asked again.

"Twenty of yuh runnin over one ol woman! Now, ain yuh white men glad yuh so brave?"

The sheriff grabbed her arm.

"C mon, now! Yuh don did ernuff sass fer one night. Wheres tha nigger son of yos?"

"Don't yuh wished yuh knowed?"

"Yuh wanna git slapped?"

"Ah ain never seen one of yo kind that wuznt too low fer . . ."

The sheriff slapped her straight across her face with his open palm. She fell back against a wall and sank to her knees.

"Is tha whut white men do t nigger women?"

She rose slowly and stood again, not even touching the place that ached from his blow, her hands folded over her stomach.

"Ah ain never seen one of yo kind tha wuznt too low fer . . ."

He slapped her again; she reeled backward several feet and fell on her side.

"Is tha whut we too low to do?"

She stood before him again, dry-eyed, as though she had not been struck. Her lips were numb and her chin was wet with blood.

"Aw, let her go! Its the nigger we wan!" said one.

"Wheres that nigger son of yos?" the sheriff asked.

"Find im," she said.

"By Gawd, ef we hafta find im well kill im!"

"He wont be the only nigger yuh ever killed," she said.

She was consumed with a bitter pride. There was nothing on this earth, she felt then, that they could not do to her but that she could take. She stood on a narrow plot of ground from which she would die before she was pushed. And then it was, while standing there feeling warm blood seeping down her throat, that she gave up Johnny-Boy, gave him up to the white folks. She gave him up because they had come tramping into her heart demanding him, thinking they could get him by beating her, thinking they could scare her into making her tell where he was. She gave him up because she wanted them to know that they could not get what they wanted by bluffing and killing.

"Wheres this meetin gonna be?" the sheriff asked.

"Don yuh wish yuh knowed?"

"Ain there gonna be a meetin?"

"How come yuh astin me?"

"There *is* gonna be a meetin," said the sheriff. "Is it?"

"Ah gotta great mind t choke it outta yuh!"

"Yuh so smart," she said.

"We ain playing wid yuh!"

"Did Ah say yuh wuz?"

"Tha nigger son of yos is erroun here somewheres n Ah aim to find im," said the sheriff. "Ef yuh tell us where he is n ef he talks, mabbe hell git off easy. But ef we hafta find im, well kill im! Ef we hafta find im, then yuh git a sheet t put over im in the mawnin, see? Git yuh a sheet, cause hes gonna be dead!"

"He wont be the only nigger yuh ever killed," she said again.

The sheriff walked past her. The others followed. Yuh didnt git whut yuh wanted! she thought exultingly. N yuh ain gonna *never* git it! Hotly, something arched in her to make them feel the intensity of her pride and freedom; her heart groped to turn the bitter hours of her life into words of a kind that would make them feel that she had taken all they had done to her in stride and could still take more. Her faith surged so strongly in her she was all but blinded. She walked behind them to the door, knotting and twisting her fingers. She saw them step to the muddy ground. Each whirl of the yellow beacon revealed glimpses of slanting rain. Her lips moved, then she shouted:

"Yuh didnt git whut yuh wanted! N yuh ain gonna nevah git it!"

The sheriff stopped and turned; his voice came low and hard.

"Now, by Gawd, thas ernuff outta yuh!"

"Ah know when Ah done said ernuff!"

"Aw, naw, yuh don!" he said. "Yuh don know when yuh done said ernuff, but Ahma teach yuh ternight!"

He was up the steps and across the porch with one bound. She backed into the hall, her eyes full on his face.

"Tell me when yuh gonna stop talkin!" he said, swinging his fist.

The blow caught her high on the cheek; her eyes went blank; she fell flat on her face. She felt the hard heel of his wet shoes coming into her temple and stomach.

"Lemma hear yuh talk some mo!"

She wanted to, but could not; pain numbed

and choked her. She lay still and somewhere out of the grey void of unconsciousness she heard someone say: *Aw fer chrissakes leave her erlone, its the nigger we wan. . . .*

IV

She never knew how long she had lain huddled in the dark hallway. Her first returning feeling was of a nameless fear crowding the inside of her, then a deep pain spreading from her temple downward over her body. Her ears were filled with the drone of rain and she shuddered from the cold wind blowing through the door. She opened her eyes and at first saw nothing. As if she were imagining it, she knew she was half lying and half sitting in a corner against a wall. With difficulty she twisted her neck and what she saw made her hold her breath—a vast white blur was suspended directly above her. For a moment she could not tell if her fear was from the blur or if the blur was from her fear. Gradually the blur resolved itself into a huge white face that slowly filled her vision. She was stone still, conscious really of the effort to breathe, feeling somehow that she existed only by the mercy of that white face. She had seen it before; its fear had gripped her many times; it had for her the fear of all the white faces she had ever seen in her life. *Sue . . .* As from a great distance, she heard her name being called. She was regaining consciousness now, but the fear was coming with her. She looked into the face of a white man, wanting to scream out for him to go; yet accepting his presence because she felt she had to. Though some remote part of her mind was active, her limbs were powerless. It was as if an invisible knife had split her in two, leaving one half of her lying there helpless, while the other half shrank in dread from a forgotten but familiar enemy. *Sue its me Sue its me . . .* Then all at once the voice came clearly.

"Sue, its me! Its Booker!"

And she heard an answering voice speaking inside of her. Yeah, its Booker . . . The one whut just joined . . . She roused herself, struggling for full consciousness; and as she did so she transferred to the person of Booker the nameless fear she felt. It seemed that Booker towered above her as a challenge to her right to exist upon the earth.

"Yuh awright?"

She did not answer; she started violently to her feet and fell.

"Sue, yuh hurt!"

"Yeah," she breathed.

"Where they hit yuh?"

"Its mah head," she whispered.

She was speaking even though she did not want to; the fear that had hold of her compelled her.

"They beat yuh?"

"Yeah."

"Them bastards! Them Gawddam bastards!"

She heard him saying it over and over; then she felt herself being lifted.

"Naw!" she gasped.

"Ahma take yuh t the kitchen!"

"Put me down!"

"But yuh cant stay here like this!"

She shrank in his arms and pushed her hands against his body; when she was in the kitchen she freed herself, sank into a chair, and held tightly to its back. She looked wonderingly at Booker. There was nothing about him that should frighten her so, but even that did not ease her tension. She saw him go to the water bucket, wet his handkerchief, wring it, and offer it to her. Distrustfully, she stared at the damp cloth.

"Here; put this on yo fohead . . ."

"Naw!"

"C mon; itll make yuh feel bettah!"

She hesitated in confusion. What right had she to be afraid when someone was acting as kindly as this toward her? Reluctantly, she leaned forward and pressed the damp cloth to her head. It helped. With each passing minute she was catching hold of herself, yet wondering why she felt as she did.

"Whut happened?"

"Ah don know."

"Yuh feel bettah?"

"Yeah."

"Who all wuz here?"

"Ah don know," she said again.

"Yo head still hurt?"

"Yeah."

"Gee, Ahm sorry."

"Ahm awright," she sighed and buried her face in her hands.

She felt him touch her shoulder.

"Sue, Ah got some bad news fer yuh . . ."

She knew; she stiffened and grew cold. It had happened; she stared dry-eyed, with compressed lips.

"Its mah Johnny-Boy," she said.

"Yeah; Ahm awful sorry t hafta tell yuh this way. But Ah thought yuh oughta know . . ."

Her tension eased and a vacant place opened up inside of her. A voice whispered, Jesus, hep me!

"W-w-where is he?"

"They got im out t Foleys Woods trying t make him tell who the others is."

"He ain gonna tell," she said. "They jus as waal kill im, cause he ain gonna nevah tell."

"Ah hope he don," said Booker. "But he didnt have a chance t tell the others. They grabbed im just as he got t the woods."

Then all the horror of it flashed upon her; she saw flung out over the rainy countryside an array of shacks where white and black comrades were sleeping; in the morning they would be rising and going to Lem's; then they would be caught. And that meant terror, prison, and death. The comrades would have to be told; she would have to tell them; she could not entrust Johnny-Boy's work to another, and especially not to Booker as long as she felt toward him as she did. Gripping the bottom of the chair with both hands, she tried to rise; the room blurred and she swayed. She found herself resting in Booker's arms.

"Lemma go!"

"Sue, yuh too weak t walk!"

"Ah gotta tell em!" she said.

"Set down, Sue! Yuh hurt! Yuh sick!"

When seated, she looked at him helplessly.

"Sue, lissen! Johnny-Boys caught. Ahm here. Yuh tell me who they is n Ahll tell em."

She stared at the floor and did not answer. Yes; she was too weak to go. There was no way for her to tramp all those miles through the rain tonight. But should she tell Booker? If only she had somebody like Reva to talk to! She did not want to decide alone; she must make no mistake about this. She felt Booker's fingers pressing on her arm and it was as though the white mountain was pushing her to the edge of a sheer height; she again exclaimed inwardly. Jesus, hep me! Booker's white face was at her side, waiting. Would she be doing right to tell him? Suppose she did not tell and then the comrades were caught? She could not ever forgive herself for doing a thing like that. But maybe she was wrong; maybe her fear was what Johnny-Boy had always called "jus foolishness." She remembered his saying, Ma, we cant make the party grow ef we start doubtin everbody. . . .

"Tell me who they is, Sue, n Ahll tell em. Ah just joined n Ah don know who they is."

"Ah don know who they is," she said.

"Yuh *gotta* tell me who they is, Sue!"

"Ah tol yuh Ah don know!"

"Yuh *do* know! C mon! Set up n talk!"

"Naw!"

"Yuh wan em all t git *killed?*"

She shook her head and swallowed. Lawd, Ah don believe in this man!

"Lissen, Ahll call the names n yuh tell me which ones is in the party n which ones ain, see?"

"Naw!"

"Please, Sue!"

"Ah don know," she said.

"Sue, yuh ain doin right by em. Johnny-Boy wouldnt wan yuh t be this way. Hes out there holdin up his end. Les hol up ours . . ."

"Lawd, Ah don know . . ."

"Is yuh scared a me cause Ahm *white?* Johnny-Boy ain like tha. Don let all the work we don go fer nothin."

She gave up and bowed her head in her hands.

"Is it Johnson? Tell me, Sue?"

"Yeah," she whispered in horror, a mounting horror of feeling herself being undone.

"Is it Green?"

"Yeah."

"Murphy?"

"Lawd, Ah don know!"

"Yuh gotta tell me, Sue!"

"Mistah Booker, please leave me erlone . . ."

"Is it Murphy?"

She answered yes to the names of Johnny-Boy's comrades; she answered until he asked her no more. Then she thought, How he know the sheriffs men is watching Lems house? She stood up and held onto her chair, feeling something sure and firm within her.

"How yuh know about Lem?"

"Why . . . How Ah know?"

"Whut yuh doin here this tima night? How yuh know the sheriff got Johnny-Boy?"

"Sue, don yuh believe in me?"

She did not, but she could not answer. She stared at him until her lips hung open; she was searching deep within herself for certainty.

"You meet Reva?" she asked.

"Reva?"

"Yeah; Lems gal?"

"Oh, yeah. Sho, Ah met Reva."

"She tell yuh?"

She asked the question more of herself than of him; she longed to believe.

"Yeah," he said softly. "Ah reckon Ah oughta be goin t tell em now."

"Who?" she asked. "Tell *who?*"

The muscles of her body were stiff as she waited for his answer; she felt as though life depended upon it.

"The comrades," he said.

"Yeah," she sighed.

She did not know when he left; she was not looking or listening. She just suddenly saw the room empty and from her the thing that had made her fearful was gone.

V

For a space of time that seemed to her as long as she had been upon the earth, she sat huddled over the cold stove. One minute she would say to herself, They both gone now; Johnny-Boy n Sug . . . Mabbe Ahll never see em ergin. Then a surge of guilt would blot out her longing. "Lawd, Ah shouldna tol!" she mumbled. "But no man kin be so low-down as to do a thing like that . . ." Several times she had an impulse to try to tell the comrades herself; she was feeling a little better now. But what good would that do? She had told Booker the names. He jus couldnt be a Judas to po folks like us . . . He *couldn't!*

"An Sue!"

Thas Reva! Her heart leaped with an anxious gladness. She rose without answering and limped down the dark hallway. Through the open door, against the background of rain, she saw Reva's face lit now and then to whiteness by the whirling beams of the beacon. She was about to call, but a thought checked her, Jesus, hep me! Ah gotta tell her bout Johnny-Boy . . . Lawd, Ah cant!

"An Sue, yuh there?"

"C mon in, chile!"

She caught Reva and held her close for a moment without speaking.

"Lawd, Ahm sho glad yuh here," she said at last.

"Ah thought somethin had happened t yuh," said Reva, pulling away. "Ah saw the do open . . . Pa told me to come back n stay wid yuh tonight . . ." Reva paused and started, "W-w-whuts the mattah?"

She was so full of having Reva with her that she did not understand what the question meant.

"Hunh?"

"Yo neck . . ."

"Aw, it ain nothin, chile. C mon in the kitchen."

"But theres blood on yo neck!"

"The sheriff wuz here . . ."

"Them fools! Whut they wanna bother yuh fer? Ah could kill em! So hep me Gawd, Ah could!"

"It ain nothin," she said.

She was wondering how to tell Reva about Johnny-Boy and Booker. Ahll wait a lil while longer, she thought. Now that Reva was here, her fear did not seem as awful as before.

"C mon, lemma fix you head, An Sue. Yuh hurt."

They went to the kitchen. She sat silent while Reva dressed her scalp. She was feeling better now; in just a little while she would tell Reva. She felt the girl's fingers pressing gently upon her head.

"That hurt?"

"A lil, chile."

"Yuh po thing."

"It ain nothin."

"Did Johnny-Boy come?"

She hesitated.

"Yeah."

"He done gone t tell the others?"

Reva's voice sounded so clear and confident that it mocked her. Lawd, Ah cant tell this chile . . .

"Yuh tol im, didnt yuh, An Sue?"

"Y-y-yeah . . ."

"Gee! Thas good! Ah tol pa he didnt hafta worry ef Johnny-Boy got the news. Mabbe thingsll come out awright."

"Ah hope . . ."

She could not go on; she had gone as far as she could. For the first time that night she began to cry.

"Hush, An Sue! Yuh awways been brave. Itll be awright!"

"Ain nothing awright, chile. The worls jus too much fer us, Ah reckon."

"Ef yuh cry that way itll make me cry."

She forced herself to stop. Naw; Ah cant carry on this way in fronta Reva . . . Right now she had a deep need for Reva to believe in her. She watched the girl get pine-knots from behind the stove, rekindle the fire, and put on the coffee pot.

"Yuh wan some cawffee?" Reva asked.

"Naw, honey."

"Aw, c mon, An Sue."

"Jusa lil, honey."

"Thas the way to be. Oh, say, Ah fergot," said Reva, measuring out spoonsful of coffee. "Pa tol me t tell yuh t watch out fer tha Booker man. Hes a stool."

She showed not one sign of outward movement or expression, but as the words fell from Reva's lips she went limp inside.

"Pa tol me soon as Ah got back home. He got word from town . . ."

She stopped listening. She felt as though she had been slapped to the extreme outer edge of life, into a cold darkness. She knew now what she had felt when she had looked up out of her fog of pain and had seen Booker. It was the image of all the white folks, and the fear that went with them, that she had seen and felt during her lifetime. And again, for the second time that night, something she had felt had come true. All she could say to herself was, Ah didnt like im! Gawd knows, Ah didnt! Ah tol Johnny-Boy it wuz some of them white folks . . .

"Here; drink yo cawffee . . ."

She took the cup; her fingers trembled, and the steaming liquid spilt onto her dress and leg.

"Ahm sorry, An Sue!"

Her leg was scalded, but the pain did not bother her.

"Its awright," she said.

"Wait; lemma put some lard on tha burn!"

"It don hurt."

"Yuh worried bout somethin."

"Naw, honey."

"Lemma fix yuh so mo cawffee."

"Ah don wan nothin now, Reva."

"Waal, buck up. Don be tha way . . ."

They were silent. She heard Reva drinking. No; she would not tell Reva; Reva was all she had left. But she had to do something, some way, somehow. She was undone too much as it was; and to tell Reva about Booker or Johnny-Boy was more than she was equal to; it would be too coldly shameful. She wanted to be alone and fight this thing out with herself.

"Go t bed, honey. Yuh tired."

"Nah; Ahm awright, An Sue."

She heard the bottom of Reva's empty cup clank against the top of the stove. Ah *got* t make her go t bed! Yes; Booker would tell the names of the comrades to the sheriff. If she could only stop him some way! That was the answer, the point, the star that grew bright in the morning of new hope. Soon, maybe half an hour from now, Booker would reach Foleys Woods. Hes boun t go the long way, cause he don know no short cut, she thought. Ah could wade the creek n beat im there. . . . But what would she do after that?

"Reva, honey, go t bed. Ahm awright. Yuh need res."

"Ah ain sleepy, An Sue."

"Ah knows whuts bes fer yuh, chile. Yuh tired n wet."

"Ah wanna stay up wid yuh."

She forced a smile and said:

"Ah don think they gonna hurt Johnny-Boy . . ."

"Fer *real*, An Sue?"

"Sho, honey."

"But Ah wanna wait up wid yuh."

"Thas mah job, honey. Thas what a mas fer, t wait up fer her chillun."

"Good night, An Sue."

"Good night, honey."

She watched Reva pull up and leave the kitchen; presently she heard the shucks in the mattress whispering, and she knew that Reva had gone to bed. She was alone. Through the cracks of the stove she saw the fire dying to grey ashes; the room was growing cold again. The yellow beacon continued to flit past the window and the rain still drummed. Yes; she was alone; she had done this awful thing alone; she must find some way out, alone. Like touching a festering sore, she put her finger upon that moment when she had shouted her defiance

to the sheriff, when she had shouted to feel her strength. She had lost Sug to save others; she had let Johnny-Boy go to save others; and then in a moment of weakness that came from too much strength she had lost all. If she had not shouted to the sheriff, she would have been strong enough to have resisted Booker; she would have been able to tell the comrades herself. Something tightened in her as she remembered and understood the fit of fear she had felt on coming to herself in the dark hallway. A part of her life she thought she had done away with forever had had hold of her then. She had thought the soft, warm past was over; she had thought that it did not mean much when now she sang: *"Hes the Lily of the Valley, the Bright n Mawnin Star"* . . . The days when she had sung that song were the days when she had not hoped for anything on this earth, the days when the cold mountain had driven her into the arms of Jesus. She had thought that Sug and Johnny-Boy had taught her to forget Him, to fix her hope upon the fight of black men for freedom. Through the gradual years she had believed and worked with them, had felt strength shed from the grace of their terrible vision. That grace had been upon her when she had let the sheriff slap her down; it had been upon her when she had risen time and again from the floor and faced him. But she had trapped herself with her own hunger; to water the long, dry thirst of her faith; her pride had made a bargain which her flesh could not keep. Her having told the names of Johnny-Boy's comrades was but an incident in a deeper horror. She stood up and looked at the floor while call and counter-call, loyalty and counter-loyalty struggled in her soul. Mired she was between two abandoned worlds, living, but dying without the strength of the grace that either gave. The clearer she felt it the fuller did something well up from the depths of her for release; the more urgent did she feel the need to fling into her black sky another star, another hope, one more terrible vision to give her the strength to live and act. Softly and restlessly she walked about the kitchen, feeling herself naked against the night, the rain, the world; and shamed whenever the thought of Reva's love crossed her mind. She lifted her empty hands and looked at her writhing fingers. Lawd, whut kin Ah do now? She could still wade the creek and get to Foleys Woods before Booker. And then what? How could she manage to see Johnny-Boy or Booker? Again she heard the sheriff's threatening voice: Git yuh a sheet, cause hes gonna be dead! The sheet! Thas it, the *sheet!* Her whole being leaped with will; the long years of her life bent toward a moment of focus, a point. Ah kin go wid mah sheet! Ahll be doin whut he said! Lawd Gawd in Heaven, Ahma go lika nigger woman wid mah windin sheet t git mah dead son! But then what? She stood straight and smiled grimly; she had in her heart the whole meaning of her life; her entire personality was poised on the brink of a total act. Ah know! Ah *know!* She thought of Johnny-Boy's gun in the dresser drawer. Ahll hide the gun in the sheet n go aftah Johnny-Boys body. . . . She tiptoed to her room, eased out the dresser drawer, and got a sheet. Reva was sleeping; the darkness was filled with her quiet breathing. She groped in the drawer and found the gun. She wound the gun in the sheet and held them both under her apron. Then she stole to the bedside and watched Reva. Lawd, hep her! But mabbe shes bettah off. This had t happen sometime . . . She n Johnny-Boy couldna been together in this here South . . . N Ah couldnt tell her about Booker. Itll come out awright n she wont nevah know. Reva's trust would never be shaken. She caught her breath as the shucks in the mattress rustled dryly; then all was quiet and she breathed easily again. She tiptoed to the door, down the hall, and stood on the porch. Above her the yellow beacon whirled through the rain. She went over muddy ground, mounted a slope, stopped and looked back at her house. The lamp glowed in her window, and the yellow beacon that swung every few seconds seemed to feed it with light. She turned and started across the fields, holding the gun and sheet tightly, thinking, Po Reva . . . Po critter . . . Shes fas ersleep . . .

VI

For the most part she walked with her eyes half shut, her lips tightly compressed, leaning her body against the wind and the driving rain, feeling the pistol in the sheet sagging cold and heavy in her fingers. Already she was getting wet; it seemed that her feet found every puddle of water that stood between the corn rows.

She came to the edge of the creek and paused wondering at what point was it low. Taking the sheet from under her apron, she wrapped the gun in it so that her finger could be upon the trigger. Ahll cross here, she thought. At first she did not feel the water; her feet were already wet. But the water grew cold as it came up to her knees; she gasped when it reached her waist. Lawd, this creeks high! When she had passed the middle, she knew that she was out of danger. She came out of the water, climbed a grassy hill, walked on, turned a bend and saw the lights of autos gleaming ahead. Yeah; theys still there! She hurried with her head down. Wondah did Ah beat im here? Lawd, Ah *hope* so! A vivid image of Booker's white face hovered a moment before her eyes and a surging will rose up in her so hard and strong that it vanished. She was among the autos now. From nearby came the hoarse voices of the men.

"Hey, yuh!"

She stopped, nervously clutching the sheet. Two white men with shotguns came toward her.

"Whut in hell yuh doin out here?"

She did not answer.

"Didnt yuh hear somebody speak t yuh?"

"Ahm comin aftah mah son," she said humbly.

"Yo *son?*"

"Yessuh."

"What yo son doin out here?"

"The sheriffs got im."

"Holy Scott! Jim, its the niggers ma!"

"Whut yuh got there?" asked one.

"A sheet."

"A *sheet?*"

"Yessuh."

"Fer whut?"

"The sheriff tol me to bring a sheet t git his body."

"Waal, waal . . ."

"Now, ain tha somethin?"

The white men looked at each other.

"These niggers sho love one ernother," said one.

"N tha ain no lie," said the other.

"Take me t the sheriff" she begged.

"Yuh ain givin us *orders,* is yuh?"

"Nawsuh."

"Well take yuh when wes good n ready."

"Yessuh."

"So yuh wan his body?"

"Yessuh."

"Waal, he ain dead yit."

"They gonna kill im," she said.

"Ef he talks they wont."

"He ain gonna talk," she said.

"How yuh know?"

"Cause he ain."

"We got ways of makin niggers talk."

"Yuh ain got no way fer im."

"Yuh thinka lot of that black Red, don yuh?"

"Hes mah son."

"Why don yuh teach im some sense?"

"Hes mah son," she said again.

"Lissen, ol nigger woman, yuh stand there wid yo hair white. Yuh got bettah sense than t believe tha niggers kin make a revolution . . ."

"A black republic," said the other one, laughing.

"Take me t the sheriff," she begged.

"Yuh his ma," said one. "Yuh kin make im talk n tell whose in this thing wid im."

"He ain gonna talk," she said.

"Don yuh wan im t live?"

She did not answer.

"C mon, les take her t Bradley."

They grabbed her arms and she clutched hard at the sheet and gun; they led her toward the crowd in the woods. Her feelings were simple; Booker would not tell; she was there with the gun to see to that. The louder became the voices of the men the deeper became her feeling of wanting to right the mistake she had made; of wanting to fight her way back to solid ground. She would stall for time until Booker showed up. Oh, ef theyll only lemma git close t Johnny-Boy! As they led her near the crowd she saw white faces turning and looking at her and heard a rising clamor of voices.

"Whose tha?"

"A nigger woman!"

"Whut she doin out here?"

"This is his ma!" called one of the men.

"Whut she wan?"

"She brought a sheet t cover his body!"

"He ain dead yit!"

"They tryin to make im talk!"

"But he will be dead soon ef he don open up!"

"Say, look! The niggers ma brought a sheet t cover up his body!"

"Now, ain that sweet?"

"Mabbe she wans t hol a prayer meetin!"

"Did she git a preacher?"

"Say, go git Bradley!"

"O.K.!"

The crowd grew quiet. They looked at her curiously; she felt their cold eyes trying to detect some weakness in her. Humbly, she stood with the sheet covering the gun. She had already accepted all that they could do to her.

The sheriff came.

"So yuh brought yuh sheet, hunh?"

"Yessuh," she whispered.

"Looks like them slaps we gave yuh learned yuh some sense, didnt they?"

She did not answer.

"Yuh don need tha sheet. Yo son ain dead yit," he said, reaching toward her.

She backed away, her eyes wide.

"Naw!"

"Now, lissen, Anty!" he said. "There ain no use in yuh ackin a fool! Go in there n tell tha nigger son of yos t tell us whos in this wid im, see? Ah promise we wont kill im ef he talks. We'll let im git outta town."

"There ain nothing Ah kin tell im," she said.

"Yuh wan us to kill im?"

She did not answer. She saw someone lean toward the sheriff and whisper.

"Bring her erlong," the sheriff said.

They led her to a muddy clearing. The rain streamed down through the ghostly glare of the flashlights. As the men formed a semi-circle she saw Johnny-Boy lying in a trough of mud. He was tied with rope; he lay hunched and one side of his face rested in a pool of black water. His eyes were staring questioningly at her.

"Speak t im," said the sheriff.

If she could only tell him why she was here! But that was impossible; she was close to what she wanted and she stared straight before her with compressed lips.

"Say, nigger!" called the sheriff, kicking Johnny-Boy. "Heres yo ma!"

Johnny-Boy did not move or speak. The sheriff faced her again.

"Lissen, Anty," he said. "Yuh got mo say wid im than anybody. Tell im t talk n hava chance. Whut he wanna pertect the other niggers n white folks fer?"

She slid her finger about the trigger of the gun and looked stonily at the mud.

"Go t him," said the sheriff.

She did not move. Her heart was crying out to answer the amazed question in Johnny-Boy's eyes. But there was no way now.

"Waal, yuhre astin fer it. By Gawd, we gotta way to *make* yuh talk t im," he said, turning away. "Sam, Tim, git one of them logs n turn that nigger upside-down n put his legs on it!"

A murmur of assent ran through the crowd. She bit her lips; she knew what that meant.

"Yuh wan yo nigger son crippled?" she heard the sheriff ask.

She did not answer. She saw them roll the log up; they lifted Johnny-Boy and laid him on his face and stomach, then they pulled his legs over the log. His kneecaps rested on the sheer top of the log's back and the toes of his shoes pointed groundward. So absorbed was she in watching that she felt that it was she who was being lifted and made ready for torture.

"Git a crowbar!" said the sheriff.

A tall, lank man got a crowbar from a nearby auto and stood over the log. His jaws worked slowly on a wad of tobacco.

"Now, its up t yuh, Anty," the sheriff said. "Tell the man whut to do!"

She looked into the rain. The sheriff turned.

"Mebba she think wes playin. Ef she don say nothin, then break em at the kneecaps!"

"O.K., Sheriff!"

She stood waiting for Booker. Her legs felt weak; she wondered if she would be able to wait much longer. Over and over she said to herself, Ef he came now Ahd kill em both!

"She ain sayin nothin, Sheriff!"

"Waal, Gawddammit, let im have it!"

The crowbar came down and Johnny-Boy's body lunged in the mud and water. There was a scream. She swayed, holding tight to the gun and sheet.

"Hol im! Git the other leg!"

The crowbar fell again. There was another scream.

"Yuh break em?" asked the sheriff.

The tall man lifted Johnny-Boy's legs and let them drop limply again, dropping rearward from the kneecaps. Johnny-Boy's body lay still. His head had rolled to one side and she could not see his face.

"Jus lika broke sparrow wing," said the man, laughing softly.

Then Johnny-Boy's face turned to her; he screamed.

"Go way, ma! Go way!"

It was the first time she had heard his voice since she had come out to the woods; she all but lost control of herself. She started violently forward, but the sheriff's arm checked her.

"Aw, naw! Yuh had yo chance!" He turned to Johnny-Boy. "She kin go ef yuh talk."

"Mistah, he ain gonna talk," she said.

"Go way, ma!" said Johnny-Boy.

"Shoot im! Don make im suffah so," she begged.

"He'll either talk or he'll never hear yuh ergin," the sheriff said. "Theres other things we kin do t im."

She said nothing.

"Whut yuh come here fer, ma?" Johnny-Boy sobbed.

"Ahm gonna split his eardrums," the sheriff said. "Ef yuh got anythin to say t im yuh bettah say it *now!*"

She closed her eyes. She heard the sheriff's feet sucking in mud. Ah could save im! She opened her eyes; there were shouts of eagerness from the crowd as it pushed in closer.

"Bus em, Sheriff!"

"Fix im so he cant hear!"

"He knows how t do it, too!"

"He busted a Jew boy tha way once!"

She saw the sheriff stoop over Johnny-Boy, place his flat palm over one ear and strike his fist against it with all his might. He placed his palm over the other ear and struck again. Johnny-Boy moaned, his head rolling from side to side, his eyes showing white amazement in a world without sound.

"Yuh wouldnt talk t im when yuh had the chance," said the sheriff. "Try n talk now."

She felt warm tears on her cheeks. She longed to shoot Johnny-Boy and let him go. But if she did that they would take the gun from her, and Booker would tell who the others were. Lawd, hep me! The men were talking loudly now, as though the main business was over. It seemed ages that she stood there watching Johnny-Boy roll and whimper in his world of silence.

"Say, Sheriff, heres somebody lookin fer yuh!"

"Who is it?"

"Ah don know!"

"Bring em in!"

She stiffened and looked around wildly, holding the gun tight. Is tha Booker? Then she held still, feeling that her excitement might betray her. Mabbe Ah kin shoot em both! Mabbe Ah kin shoot *twice!* The sheriff stood in front of her, waiting. The crowd parted and she saw Booker hurrying forward.

"Ah know em all, Sheriff!" he called.

He came full into the muddy clearing where Johnny-Boy lay.

"Yuh mean yuh got the names?"

"Sho! The ol nigger . . ."

She saw his lips hang open and silent when he saw her. She stepped forward and raised the sheet.

"Whut . . ."

She fired, once; then, without pausing, she turned, hearing them yell. She aimed at Johnny-Boy, but they had their arms around her, bearing her to the ground, clawing at the sheet in her hand. She glimpsed Booker lying sprawled in the mud, on his face, his hands stretched out before him; then a cluster of yelling men blotted him out. She lay without struggling, looking upward through the rain at the white faces above her. And she was suddenly at peace; they were not a white mountain now; they were not pushing her any longer to the edge of life. Its awright . . .

"She shot Booker!"

"She hada gun in the sheet!"

"She shot im right thu the head!"

"Whut she shoot im fer?"

"Kill the bitch!"

"Ah *thought* somethin wuz wrong bout her!"

"Ah wuz fer givin it t her from the firs!"

"Thas whut yuh git fer treatin a nigger nice!"

"Say, Bookers dead!"

She stopped looking into the white faces, stopped listening. She waited, giving up her life before they took it from her; she had done what she wanted. Ef only Johnny-Boy . . . She looked at him; he lay looking at her with tired eyes. Ef she could only tell im! But he lay already buried in a grave of silence.

"Whut yuh kill im fer, hunh?"

It was the sheriff's voice; she did not answer.

"Mabbe she wuz shootin at yuh, Sheriff?"

"Whut yuh kill im fer?"

She felt the sheriff's foot come into her side; she closed her eyes.

"Yuh black bitch!"

"Let her have it!"

"Yuh reckon she foun out bout Booker?"

"She mighta."

"Jesus Chris, whut yuh dummies *waitin* on!"

"Yeah; kill her!"

"Kill em *both!*"

"Let her know her nigger sons dead firs!"

She turned her head toward Johnny-Boy; he lay looking puzzled in a world beyond the reach of voices. At leas he cant hear, she thought.

"C mon, let im have it."

She listened to hear what Johnny-Boy could not. They came, two of them, one right behind the other: so close together that they sounded like one shot. She did not look at Johnny-Boy now; she looked at the white faces of the men, hard and wet in the glare of the flashlights.

"Yuh hear tha, nigger woman?"

"Did tha surprise im? Hes in hell now wonderin whut hit im!"

"C mon! Give it t her, Sheriff!"

"Lemma shoot her, Sheriff! It wuz mah pal she shot!"

"Awright, Pete! Thas fair ernuff!"

She gave up as much of her life as she could before they took it from her. But the sound of the shot and the streak of fire that tore its way through her chest forced her to live again, intensely. She had not moved, save for the slight jarring impact of the bullet. She felt the heat of her own blood warming her cold, wet back. She yearned suddenly to talk. "Yuh didnt git whut yuh wanted! N yuh ain gonna nevah git it! Yuh didnt kill me; Ah come here by mahsef . . ." She felt rain falling into her wide-open, dimming eyes and heard faint voices. Her lips moved soundlessly. *Yuh didnt git yuh didn't yuh didnt . . .* Focused and pointed she was, buried in the depths of her star, swallowed in its peace and strength; and not feeling her flesh growing cold, cold as the rain that fell from the invisible sky upon the doomed living and the dead that never dies.

Three Deaths

LEO TOLSTOY
1828–1910

1

It was autumn. Two carriages were driving at a rapid trot along the highroad. In the foremost sat two women. One was a lady, thin and pale; the other, her maid, was plump, with shining, red cheeks. Her short, coarse hair stood out under her faded hat; her red hand, in a torn glove, kept hurriedly putting it tidy; her high bosom, covered with a tapestry kerchief, was eloquent of health; her quick, black eyes watched out of the window the fields flying past, then glanced timidly at her mistress, then shifted uneasily about the corners of the carriage. Just before the maid's nose swung the lady's hat, hanging from the rack above; on her lap lay a puppy. Her feet were kept from the floor by the boxes that stood on the carriage floor, and could be faintly heard knocking on them through the shaking of the springs and the rattling of the windows.

With her hands clasped on her knees and her eyes closed, the lady swayed feebly to and fro on the cushions that had been put at her back, and with a slight frown she coughed inwardly. On her head she wore a white nightcap, and a light blue kerchief was tied on her soft, white neck. A straight parting, retreating under her cap, divided her fair, pomaded, exceedingly flat hair, and there was a dry, deathlike look about the whiteness of the skin of this wide parting. The faded, yellowish skin hung loose on her delicate and beautiful features and was flushed on her cheeks. Her lips were dry and restless, her eyelashes were thin and straight, and her cloth travelling cloak fell in straight folds over her sunken bosom. Though her eyes were closed, the lady's face expressed fatigue, irritation, and habitual suffering. A footman was dozing on the box, one elbow on the rail of the seat. The driver, hired from the posting-station, shouted briskly to the four sturdy, sweating horses, and looked round now and then at the other driver, who called to him from behind on the coach. Smoothly and rapidly the wheels made their broad, parallel tracks along the chalky mud of the road. The sky was gray and cold; a damp mist was falling over the fields and the road. The carriage was close, and smelt of eau de Cologne and dust. The sick woman stretched her head back and slowly opened her eyes. Her large, handsome, dark eyes were very bright.

"Again," she said, her beautiful, thin hand nervously thrusting away a corner of the maid's cloak which was just brushing against her knees, and her mouth twitched painfully. Matryosha gathered up her cloak in both hands, lifted it up on her lap, and edged further away. Her blooming face flushed bright red. The sick woman's fine dark eyes kept eager watch on the servant's actions. She leaned with both hands on the seat and tried to raise herself, so as to be sitting higher; but her strength failed her. Her mouth twitched and her whole face worked with an expression of helpless, wrathful irony. "You might at least help me! . . . Ah, you needn't! I can do it myself, only be so good as not to lay your bundles, bags, or whatever they are behind me, please! You had better not touch me if you're so awkward!"

The lady shut her eyes, and rapidly raising her eyelids again glanced at the maid. Matryosha was staring at her and biting her red underlip. A heavy sigh rose from the sick woman's chest, but changed to a cough before it was uttered. She turned away, frowning, and clutched at her chest with both hands. When the cough was over, she closed her eyes again and sat without stirring. The carriage and the coach drove into a village. Matryosha put her stout arm out from under her kerchief and crossed herself.

"What is it?" asked the lady.

"A station, madam."

"What do you cross yourself for, I ask?"

"A church, madam."

The sick woman turned towards the window, and began slowly crossing herself, her great eyes fastened on the big village church as the carriage drove by it.

The two carriages stopped together at the station. The sick woman's husband and the doctor got out of the other carriage and came up to her.

"How do you feel?" asked the doctor, taking her pulse.

"Well, how are you, my dear—not tired?" asked her husband, in French. "Wouldn't you like to get out?"

Matryosha, gathering up her bundles, squeezed into a corner so as not to be in their way as they talked.

"Just the same," answered the lady. "I won't get out."

Her husband stayed a little while beside the carriage, then went into the station-house. Matryosha got out of the carriage and ran on tiptoe through the mud to the gates.

"If I am ill, it's no reason you shouldn't have your lunch," the invalid said with a faint smile to the doctor, who was standing at the carriage window.

"None of them care anything about me," she added to herself, as soon as the doctor had moved with sedate step away from her and run at a trot up the steps of the station-house. "They are all right, so they don't care. O my God!"

"Well, Eduard Ivanovich," said her husband, meeting the doctor and rubbing his hands, with a cheery smile. "I've ordered the case of wine to be brought in. What do you say to a bottle?"

"I shouldn't say no," answered the doctor.

"Well, how is she?" the husband asked with a sigh, lifting his eyebrows and dropping his voice.

"I have told you she can't possibly get as far as Italy; if she reaches Moscow it will be a wonder, especially in this weather."

"What are we to do! Oh my God! my God!" The husband put his hand over his eyes. "Put it here," he added to the servant who brought in the case of wine.

"You should have kept her at home," the doctor answered, shrugging his shoulders.

"But tell me, what could I do?" protested the husband. "I did everything I could, you know, to keep her. I talked to her of our means, and of the children whom we should have to leave behind, and of my business—she won't hear a word of anything. She makes plans for her life abroad as though she were strong and well. And to tell her of her position would be the death of her."

"But death has hold of her already, you ought to know it, Vasily Dmitrich. A person can't live without lungs, and the lungs can't grow again. It's distressing and terrible, but what's one to do? My duty and yours is simply to see that her end should be as easy as possible. It's the priest who is needed now."

"O my God! But conceive my position, having to speak to her of the last sacrament. Come what will, I can't tell her. You know how good she is."

"You must try, all the same, to persuade her to wait till the roads are frozen," said the doctor, shaking his head significantly, "or we may have a disaster on the road."

"Aksyusha, hey, Aksyusha!" shrieked the stationmaster's daughter, flinging a jacket over her head, and stamping on the dirty back steps of the station; "let's go and have a look at the lady from Shirkin; they say she's being taken abroad for her lungs. I've never seen what people look like in consumption."

Aksyusha darted out at the doorway, and arm in arm they ran by the gate. Slackening their pace, they walked by the carriage, and peeped in at the lowered window. The sick woman turned her head towards them, but noticing their curiosity, she frowned and turned away.

"My gra-a-cious!" said the stationmaster's daughter, turning her head away quickly. "Such a wonderful beauty as she was, and what does she look like now. Enough to frighten one, really. Did you see, did you see, Aksyusha?"

"Yes, she is thin!" Aksyusha assented. "Let's go by and get another look at her, as though we were going to the well. She turned away before I'd seen her properly. I am sorry for her, Masha!"

"And the mud's awful!" answered Masha, and both ran back to the gate.

"I've grown frightful, it seems," thought the invalid. "Ah, to make haste, to make haste to get abroad, then I shall soon be better!"

"Well, how are you, my dear?" said her husband, still munching as he came up to the carriage.

"Always that invariable question," thought the sick woman, "and he goes on eating too!"

"Just the same," she muttered through her teeth.

"Do you know, my dear, I'm afraid the journey will be bad for you in this weather, and Eduard Ivanovich says so too. Hadn't we better turn back?"

She kept wrathfully silent.

"The weather will change, and the roads perhaps will be hard, and that would make it better for you; and then we would all go together."

"Excuse me. If I hadn't listened to you long ago, I should be in Berlin by now and should be quite well."

"That couldn't be helped, my angel; it was out of the question, as you know! But now, if you would wait for a month, you would be ever so much better. I should have settled my business, and we could take the children."

"The children are quite well, and I am not."

"But consider, my dear, with this weather if you get worse on the road . . . there, at any rate, you're at home."

"And if I am at home? . . . To die at home?"

the sick woman answered hotly. But the word "die" evidently terrified her; she bent an imploring, questioning look upon her husband. He dropped his eyes and did not speak. The sick woman's mouth puckered all at once like a child's, and tears dropped from her eyes. Her husband buried his face in his handkerchief, and walked away from the carriage without speaking.

"No, I am going," said the sick woman, lifting her eyes towards heaven, and she fell to whispering disconnected words. "My God, what for?" she said, and the tears flowed more freely. For a long while she prayed fervently, but there was still the same pain and tightness on her chest. The sky, the fields, and the road were just as gray and cheerless; and the same autumn mist, neither thicker nor clearer, hung over the mud of the road, the roofs of the huts, the carriage and the sheepskin coats of the drivers, who were greasing and harnessing a carriage, chatting together in their vigorous, merry voices.

2

The horses were put in the shafts; but the driver lingered. He went into the drivers' hut. It was hot and stifling, dark and oppressive in the hut; there was a smell of human beings, baking bread, and cabbage, and sheepskins. There were several drivers in the room: the cook was busy at the stove; on the top of the stove lay a sick man wrapped in sheepskins.

"Uncle Fyodor! hey, Uncle Fyodor!" said the driver as he came into the room. He was a young fellow, in a sheepskin coat with a whip stuck in his belt, and he was addressing the sick man.

"What do you want Fedya for, you windbag?" one of the drivers interposed. "They are waiting for you in the carriage."

"I want to ask him for his boots; I've worn mine out," answered the young fellow, tossing back his hair and straightening the gloves in his belt. "Is he asleep? Hey, Uncle Fyodor?" he repeated, going up to the stove.

"What?" a weak voice was heard in reply, and a thin face with a red beard bent over from the stove. A big, wasted, white hand, covered with hair, pulled up a coat on the bony shoulder in the dirty shirt. "Give me a drink, brother; what do you want?"

The young man handed him a dipper of water.

"Well, Fedya," he said, hesitating, "you won't be wanting your new boots now; give them to me; you won't be going out, you know."

Pressing his weary head to the shining dipper, and wetting his scanty, hanging mustaches in the turbid water, the sick man drank feebly and eagerly. His tangled beard was not clean, his sunken, lusterless eyes were lifted with an effort to the young man's face. When he had finished drinking he tried to lift his hand to wipe his wet lips, but he could not, and he wiped them on the sleeve of the coat. Without uttering a sound, but breathing heavily through his nose, he looked straight into the young man's eyes, trying to rally his strength.

"Maybe you've promised them to someone already?" said the young man; "if so, never mind. The thing is, it's soaking wet outside, and I've got to go out on a job; and I said to myself, why, I'll ask Fedya for his boots, he'll not need them, for sure. If you are likely to need them yourself, say so."

There was a gurgle and a rattle in the sick man's throat; he bent over and was choked by a deep, stifling cough.

"He need them!" the cook cried out in sudden anger, filling the whole hut with her voice. "He's not got off the stove these two months! Why, he coughs fit to split himself; it makes me ache inside simply to hear him. How could he want boots? He won't wear new boots to be buried! And time he was, too, long ago—God forgive me the sin! Why, he coughs fit to split himself. He ought to be moved into another hut, or somewhere! There are hospitals, I've heard say, for such in the town; he takes up the whole place, and what's one to do? One hasn't room to turn around. And then they expect me to keep the place clean!"

"Hi, Seryoga! go and take your seat; the gentry are waiting," the stationmaster shouted at the door.

Seryoga would have gone away without waiting for an answer, but the sick man's eyes, while he was coughing, had told him he wanted to answer.

"You take the boots, Seryoga," said he, stifling the cough and taking breath a minute. "Only buy me a stone when I die, do you hear?" he added huskily.

"Thanks, uncle, so I'll take them; and as to the stone, ay, ay, I'll buy it."

"There, lads, you hear?" the sick man managed to articulate, and again he bent over and began choking.

"All right, we heard," said one of the drivers. "Go along, Seryoga, or the overseer will be running after you again. The lady from Shirkin is ill."

Seryoga quickly pulled off his torn boots, which were much too large for him, and thrust them under a bench. Uncle Fyodor's new boots fitted his feet perfectly, and Seryoga went out to the carriage looking at them.

"What grand boots! let me grease them for you," said a driver with the greasepot in his hand, as Seryoga got on the box and picked up the reins. "Did he give them to you for nothing?"

"Why, are you jealous?" answered Seryoga, getting up and shaking down the skirts of his coat about his legs. "Hi, get up, my darlings!" he shouted to the horses, brandishing the whip, and the two carriages, with their occupants, boxes, and baggage, rolled swiftly along the wet road, and vanished into the gray autumn mist.

The sick driver remained lying on the stove in the stifling hut. Unrelieved by coughing, he turned over on the other side with an effort, and was quiet. All day till evening, men were coming and going and dining in the hut; there was no sound from the sick man. At nightfall, the cook clambered up onto the stove and reached across his legs to get a sheepskin. "Don't you be angry with me, Nastasya," said the sick man; "I shall soon clear out of your place."

"That's all right, that's all right; why, I didn't mean it," muttered Nastasya. "But what is it that's wrong with you, uncle? Tell me about it."

"All my inside's wasted away. God knows what it is."

"My word! and does your throat hurt when you cough!"

"It hurts me all over. My death is at hand—that's what it is. Oh, oh, oh!" moaned the sick man.

"Cover your legs up like this," said Nastasya, pulling a coat over him as she crept off the stove.

A night-light glimmered dimly all night in the hut. Nastasya and some ten drivers lay on the floor and the benches asleep, and snoring loudly. The sick man alone moaned faintly, coughed, and turned over on the stove. Towards morning he became quite still.

"A queer dream I had in the night," said the cook, stretching next morning in the half-light. "I dreamed that Uncle Fyodor got down from the stove and went out to chop wood. 'Nastasya,' says he, 'I'll split you some'; and I says to him, 'How can you chop wood?' and he snatches up the axe and starts chopping so fast, so fast that the chips were flying. 'Why,' says I, 'you were ill, weren't you?' 'No,' says he, 'I'm all right,' and he swings the axe, so that it gave me quite a fright. I screamed out and waked up. Isn't he dead, perhaps? Uncle Fyodor! Hey, uncle!"

Fyodor made no sound in reply.

"May be he is dead. I'll get up and see," said one of the drivers who was awake.

A thin hand, covered with reddish hairs, hung down from the stove; it was cold and pale.

"I'll go and tell the overseer. He's dead, seemingly," said the driver.

Fyodor had no relations—he had come from distant parts. The next day he was buried in the new graveyard beyond the copse, and for several days after Nastasya told every one of the dream she had had, and how she had been the first to discover that Uncle Fyodor was dead.

3

Spring had come. Streams of water hurried gurgling between the frozen dung-heaps in the wet streets of the town. The people moving to and fro were gayly dressed and gayly chattering. Behind the fences of the little gardens the buds on the trees were swelling, and their branches rustled faintly in the fresh breeze. Everywhere there was a running and a dripping of clear drops. . . . The sparrows chattered incoherently, and fluttered to and fro on their little wings. On the sunny side, on fences, trees, and houses, all was movement. There was youth and gladness in the sky and on the earth and in the heart of man. In one of the principal streets there was straw lying in front of a large house; in the house lay the dying woman who had been hastening abroad.

At the closed door of her room stood the patient's husband and her cousin, an elderly woman; on a sofa sat a priest with downcast eyes, holding something wrapped up in his stole. In a corner an old lady, the patient's mother, lay in an armchair, weeping bitterly. Near her stood a maid holding a clean pocket-handkerchief in readiness for the old lady when she should ask for it. Another maid was rubbing the old lady's temples with something and blowing on her gray head under her cap.

"Well, Christ be with you, my dear," said the husband to the elderly woman who was standing with him at the door; "she has such confidence in you, you know so well how to talk to her; go in, and have a good talk with her." He would have opened the door; but the cousin restrained him, put her handkerchief several times to her eyes, and shook her head.

"Come, now, I don't look as if I had been crying, I think," she said, and opening the door herself, she went into the sickroom.

The husband was in great excitement, and seemed utterly distraught. He walked towards the old lady, but stopped short a few paces from her, turned, walked about the room, and went up to the priest. The priest looked at him, raised his eyebrows heavenwards, and sighed. His thick, grizzled beard turned upwards too, and then sank again.

"My God! my God!" said the husband.

"There is nothing one can do," said the priest, and again his brows and his beard were elevated and drooped again.

"And her mother here!" the husband said, almost in despair. "She will never be able to bear this! She loves her, she loves her so that she . . . I don't know. If you, father, would attempt to soothe her and to persuade her to go out of this room."

The priest rose and went to the old lady.

"True it is, that none can sound the depths of a mother's heart," said he; "but God is merciful."

The old lady's face began suddenly twitching, and she sobbed hysterically.

"God is merciful," the priest went on, when she was a little calmer. "In my parish, I must tell you, there was a man ill, much worse than Marya Dmitryevna, and a simple artisan cured him with herbs in a very short time. And this same artisan is in Moscow now, indeed. I told Vasily Dmitryevich—he might try him. Any

way, it would be a comfort to the sick woman. To God all things are possible."

"No, she can't live," said the old lady; "if it could have been me, but God takes her." And her hysterics grew so violent that she fainted.

The sick woman's husband hid his face in his hands, and ran out of the room.

The first person that met him in the corridor was a boy of six, who was running at full speed after a little girl younger than himself.

"Shouldn't I take the children to see their mamma?" asked the nurse.

"No, she doesn't want to see them. It upsets her."

The boy stood still for a moment, staring intently into his father's face, then suddenly kicking up his foot, with a merry shriek he ran on.

"I'm pretending she's my black horse, papa!" shouted the boy, pointing to his sister.

Meanwhile in the next room the cousin was sitting by the sick woman's bedside, and trying by skillfully leading up to the subject to prepare her for the idea of death. The doctor was at the other window mixing a draught.

The sick woman, in a white dressing-gown, sat propped up with pillows in bed, and gazed at the cousin without speaking.

"Ah, my dear," she said, suddenly interrupting her, "don't try to prepare me. Don't treat me as a child. I am a Christian. I know all about it. I know I haven't long to live; I know that if my husband would have listened to me sooner, I should have been in Italy, and perhaps, most likely indeed, should have been quite well. Everyone told him so. But it can't be helped, it seems that it was God's will. We are all great sinners, I know that; but I put my trust in God's mercy: He will forgive all, surely, all. I try to understand myself. I, too, have sinned greatly, my dear. But, to make up, how I have suffered. I have tried to bear my sufferings with patience. . . ."

"Then may I send for the priest, my dear? You will feel all the easier after the sacrament," said the cousin. The sick woman bowed her head in token of assent. "God forgive me, a sinner!" she murmured.

The cousin went out and beckoned to the priest.

"She is an angel!" she said to the husband with tears in her eyes. The husband began to weep; the priest went in at the door; the old lady was still unconscious, and in the outer room there was a complete stillness. Five minutes later the priest came out, and taking off his stole smoothed back his hair.

"Thank God, the lady is calmer now," he said; "she wants to see you."

The cousin and the husband went in. The sick woman was weeping quietly, gazing at the holy picture.

"I congratulate you, my dear," said her husband.

"Thank you! How happy I am now, what unspeakable joy I am feeling!" said the sick woman, and a faint smile played about her thin lips. "How merciful is God! Is it not true? Is He not merciful and almighty?" And again with eyes full of tears she gazed at the holy picture in eager prayer.

Then suddenly something seemed to recur to her mind. She beckoned her husband to her.

"You never will do what I ask," she said in a weak, irritable voice.

Her husband, craning his neck forward, listened submissively.

"What is it, my dear?"

"How often I've told you those doctors don't know anything; there are plain women healers, who work cures. . . . The priest told me . . . an artisan . . . send for him."

"For whom, my dear?"

"My God, he won't understand anything!" . . .

And the sick woman frowned and covered her eyes. The doctor went up and took her hand. The pulse was growing perceptibly weaker and weaker. He made a sign to the husband. The sick woman noticed this gesture and looked around in alarm. The cousin turned away, and burst into tears.

"Don't cry, don't torture yourself and me," said the sick woman. "That destroys all the calm left me."

"You are an angel!" said the cousin, kissing her hand.

"No, kiss me here, it's only the dead who are kissed on the hand. My God! my God!"

The same evening the sick woman was a corpse, and the corpse lay in a coffin in the drawing-room of the great house. The doors of the big room were closed, and in it a deacon sat alone, reading the Psalms of David aloud in a rhythmic, nasal tone. The bright light of the wax candles in the tall silver candlesticks fell on the pale brow of the dead woman, on the heavy, waxen hands and the stonelike folds of the shroud, that jutted up horribly at the knees and toes. The deacon read on rhythmically without taking in the meaning of his own words, and the words echoed and died away strangely in the still room. From time to time the sounds of children's voices and the tramp of their feet came from a far-away room.

" 'Hidest thou thy face, they are troubled,' " the psalm-reader boomed; " 'thou takest away their breath, they die and return to their dust. Thou sendest forth thy spirit, they are created; and thou renewest the face of the earth. The glory of the Lord shall endure for ever.' "

The face of the dead woman was stern and solemn. Nothing stirred the pure, cold brow and the firmly set lips. She was all attention. But did she even now understand those grand words?

4

A month later a stone chapel was raised over the dead woman's grave. But there was still no stone over the driver's grave, and there was nothing but the bright green grass over the mound, which was the only sign of a man's past existence.

"You will be sinning, Seryoga," the cook at the station said one day, "if you don't buy a stone for Fyodor. You were always saying it was winter, but now why don't you keep your word? I was by at the time. He's come back once already to ask you for it; if you don't buy it, he'll come again and stifle you."

"Why, did I say I wasn't going to?" answered Seryoga; "I'll buy a stone as I said I would; I'll buy one for a silver rouble and a half. I've not forgotten, but it must be fetched, you know. As soon as I've a chance to go to the town I'll buy it."

"You might put a cross up anyway," put in an old driver, "or else it's a downright shame. You're wearing the boots."

"Where's one to get a cross? You wouldn't cut one out of a log of firewood?"

"What are you talking about? You can't hew it out of a log. You take an axe and go early in the morning into the copse; you can cut a cross there. An aspen or something you can fell. And it'll make a fine wooden monument too. Or else you'll have to go and stand the forester a drink of vodka. One doesn't want to have to give him a drink for every trifle. The other day I broke a splinter-bar; I cut myself a first-rate new one, and no one said a word to me."

In the early morning, when it was hardly light, Seryoga took his axe and went into the wood. Over all lay a chill, even-colored veil of still-falling dew, not lighted up by the sun. The east was imperceptibly growing clearer, reflecting its faint light on the arch of sky covered with fine clouds. Not a blade of grass below, not a leaf on the topmost twig stirred. The stillness of the forest was only broken at intervals by the sound of wings in a tree or a rustle on the ground. Suddenly a strange sound, not one of nature's own, rang out and died away on the edge of the forest. But again the sound was heard, and began to be repeated at regular intervals near the trunk of the motionless trees. One of the treetops began shaking in a strange way; its sappy leaves whispered something; and a warbler that had been perched on one of its branches fluttered round it twice, and uttering a whistle and wagging its tail, settled on another tree.

The sound of the axe was more and more muffled, the sappy, white chips flew out on the dewy grass, and a faint crackling sound followed each blow. The tree shuddered all over, bowed, and quickly stood up straight again, trembling in dismay on its roots. For a moment all was still, but again the tree bent; a crack was heard in its trunk, and with a snapping of twigs its branches dropped, and it crashed down with its top on the damp earth. The sound of the axe and of steps died away. The warbler whistled and flew up higher. The branch in which it had caught its wings shook for a little while in all its leaves, then became still like the rest. The trees displayed their motionless branches more gladly than ever in the newly opened space.

The first beams of the sun, piercing the delicate cloud, shone out in the sky and darted over the earth. The mist began rolling in waves in the hollows; the dew glittered sparkling on the green grass; the translucent clouds turned white, and floated in haste across the blue sky. The birds flitted to and fro in the thickets and twittered some happy song, like mad things. The sappy leaves whispered joyously and calmly on the treetops, and the branches of the living trees, slowly, majestically, swayed above the fallen dead tree.

On the Road
LANGSTON HUGHES
1902–1967

Hughes, often regarded as "America's senior Negro professional literary man," believes that his purpose as a writer is "to explain and illuminate the Negro condition in America." One of Hughes's most knowledgeable critics and a Negro poet (see p. 406 for two of his poems), James A. Emanuel, believes that " 'On the Road' is artistically among the top five or six of Hughes's many stories" and "is a richly symbolic fusion of dream and reality, using well over two hundred precisely patterned images." In talking to the writer Kay Boyle about the story, Hughes commented:

All I had in mind was cold, hunger, a strange town at night . . . and a black vagabond named Sargeant against white snow, cold people, hard doors, trying to go somewhere, but too tired and hungry to make it—hemmed in on the ground by the same people who hemmed Christ in by rigid rituals surrounding a man-made cross. It developed as a kind of visual picture-story out of night, snow, man, church, police, cross, doors becoming bars, then ending with a man shaking the bars, but Christ at least free on the precarious road—His destination Kansas City, being a half-way point across the country. . . .

I was writing of the little man. . . . I was writing, too, of Jesus as a human being whose meaning sometimes has been lost through the organization of the church. . . . The function of religion in daily life, as the Reverend [Martin Luther] King has made it function, is what I was talking about. . . . Sargeant had done as much for Jesus in getting Him down off the cross as Jesus had done for Sargeant

in showing him that even the Saviour of men had nowhere to go except to push on. . . .
—Quoted in James A. Emanuel, *Langston Hughes*, New York: Twayne Publishers, Inc., 1967, pp. 93–94.

He was not interested in the snow. When he got off the freight, one early evening during the depression, Sargeant never even noticed the snow. But he must have felt it seeping down his neck, cold, wet, sopping in his shoes. But if you had asked him, he wouldn't have known it was snowing. Sargeant didn't see the snow, not even under the bright lights of the main street, falling white and flaky against the night. He was too hungry, too sleepy, too tired.

The Reverend Mr. Dorset, however, saw the snow when he switched on his porch light, opened the front door of his parsonage, and found standing there before him a big black man with snow on his face, a human piece of night with snow on his face—obviously unemployed.

Said the Reverend Mr. Dorset before Sargeant even realized he'd opened his mouth: "I'm sorry. No! Go right on down this street four blocks and turn to your left, walk up seven and you'll see the Relief Shelter. I'm sorry. No!" He shut the door.

Sargeant wanted to tell the holy man that he had already been to the Relief Shelter, been to hundreds of relief shelters during the depression years, the beds were always gone and supper was over, the place was full, and they drew the color line anyhow. But the minister said, "No," and shut the door. Evidently he didn't want to hear about it. And he *had* a door to shut.

The big black man turned away. And even yet he didn't see the snow, walking right into it. Maybe he sensed it, cold, wet, sticking to his jaws, wet on his black hands, sopping in his shoes. He stopped and stood on the sidewalk hunched over—hungry, sleepy, cold—looking up and down. Then he looked right where he was—in front of a church. Of course! A church! Sure, right next to a parsonage, certainly a church.

It had *two* doors.

Broad, white steps in the night all snowy white. Two high arched doors with slender stone pillars on either side. And way up, a round lacy window with a stone crucifix in the middle and Christ on the crucifix in stone. All this was pale in the street lights, solid and stony pale in the snow.

Sargeant blinked. When he looked up the snow fell into his eyes. For the first time that night he *saw* the snow. He shook his head. He shook the snow from his coat sleeves, felt hungry, felt lost, felt not lost, felt cold. He walked up the steps of the church. He knocked at the door. No answer. He tried the handle. Locked. He put his shoulder against the door and his long black body slanted like a ramrod. He pushed. With loud rhythmic grunts, like the grunts in a chain-gang song, he pushed against the door.

"I'm tired . . . Huh! . . . Hongry . . . Uh! . . . I'm sleepy . . . Huh! I'm cold . . . I got to sleep somewheres," Sargeant said. "This here is a church, ain't it? Well, uh!"

He pushed against the door.

Suddenly, with an undue cracking and squeaking, the door began to give way to the tall black Negro who pushed ferociously against the door.

By now two or three white people had stopped in the street, and Sargeant was vaguely aware of some of them yelling at him concerning the door. Three or four more came running, yelling at him.

"Hey!" they said. "Hey!"

"Un-huh," answered the big tall Negro, "I know it's a white folks' church, but I got to sleep somewhere." He gave another lunge at the door. "Huh!"

And the door broke open.

But just when the door gave way, two white cops arrived in a car, ran up the steps with their clubs and grabbed Sargeant. But Sargeant for once had no intention of being pulled or pushed away from the door.

Sargeant grabbed, but not for anything so weak as a broken door. He grabbed for one of the tall stone pillars beside the door, grabbed at it and caught it. And held it. The cops pulled and Sargeant pulled. Most of the people in the street got behind the cops and helped them pull.

"A big black unemployed Negro holding onto our church!" thought the people. "The idea!"

The cops began to beat Sargeant over the head, and nobody protested. But he held on.

And then the church fell down.[1]

Gradually, the big stone front of the church fell down, the walls and the rafters, the crucifix and the Christ. Then the whole thing fell down, covering the cops and the people with bricks and stones and debris. The whole church fell down in the snow.

Sargeant got out from under the church and went walking on up the street with the stone pillar on his shoulder. He was under the impression that he had buried the parsonage and the Reverend Mr. Dorset who said, "No!" So he laughed, and threw the pillar six blocks up the street and went on.

Sargeant thought he was alone, but listening to the crunch, crunch, crunch on the snow of his own footsteps, he heard other footsteps, too, doubling his own. He looked around and there was Christ walking along beside him, the same Christ that had been on the cross on the church —still stone with a rough stone surface, walking along beside him just like he was broken off the cross when the church fell down.

"Well, I'll be dogged," said Sargeant. "This here's the first time I ever seed you off the cross."

"Yes," said Christ, crunching his feet in the snow. "You had to pull the church down to get me off the cross."

"You glad?" said Sargeant.

"I sure am," said Christ.

They both laughed.

"I'm a hell of a fellow, ain't I?" said Sargeant. "Done pulled the church down!"

"You did a good job," said Christ. "They have kept me nailed on a cross for nearly two thousand years."

"Whee-ee-e!" said Sargeant. "I know you are glad to get off."

"I sure am," said Christ.

They walked on in the snow. Sargeant looked at the man of stone.

"And you been up there two thousand years?"

"I sure have," Christ said.

"Well, if I had a little cash," said Sargeant, "I'd show you around a bit."

[1] Reminiscent of Samson's pulling down the pillars of the temple where the great feast of the Philistine god Dagon was held. See *Judges*, 16:28–31.

"I been around," said Christ.

"Yeah, but that was a long time ago."

"All the same," said Christ, "I've been around."

They walked on in the snow until they came to the railroad yards. Sargeant was tired, sweating and tired.

"Where you goin'?" Sargeant said, stopping by the tracks. He looked at Christ. Sargeant said, "I'm just a bum on the road. How about you? Where you goin'?"

"God knows," Christ said, "but I'm leavin' here."

They saw the red and green lights of the railroad yard half veiled by the snow that fell out of the night. Away down the track they saw a fire in a hobo jungle.

"I can go there and sleep," Sargeant said.

"You can?"

"Sure," said Sargeant. "That place ain't got no doors."

Outside the town, along the tracks, there were barren trees and bushes below the embankment, snow-gray in the dark. And down among the trees and bushes there were makeshift houses made out of boxes and tin and old pieces of wood and canvas. You couldn't see them in the dark, but you knew they were there if you'd ever been on the road, if you had ever lived with the homeless and hungry in a depression.

"I'm side-tracking," Sargeant said. "I'm tired."

"I'm gonna make it on to Kansas City," said Christ.

"O.K.," Sargeant said. "So long!"

He went down into the hobo jungle and found himself a place to sleep. He never did see Christ no more. About six A.M. a freight came by. Sargeant scrambled out of the jungle with a dozen or so more hoboes and ran along the track, grabbing at the freight. It was dawn, early dawn, cold and gray.

"Wonder where Christ is by now?" Sargeant thought. "He must-a gone on way on down the road. He didn't sleep in this jungle."

Sargeant grabbed the train and started to pull himself up into a moving coal car, over the edge of a wheeling coal car. But strangely enough, the car was full of cops. The nearest cop rapped Sargeant soundly across the knuckles with his night stick. Wham! Rapped his big black hands for clinging to the top of the car.

Wham! But Sargeant did not turn loose. He clung on and tried to pull himself into the car. He hollered at the top of his voice, "Damn it, lemme in this car!"

"Shut up," barked the cop. "You crazy coon!" He rapped Sargeant across the knuckles and punched him in the stomach. "You ain't out in no jungle now. This ain't no train. You in jail."

Wham! across his bare black fingers clinging to the bars of his cell. Wham! between the steel bars low down against his shins.

Suddenly Sargeant realized that he really was in jail. He wasn't on no train. The blood of the night before had dried on his face, his head hurt terribly, and a cop outside in the corridor was hitting him across the knuckles for holding onto the door, yelling and shaking the cell door.

"They must-a took me to jail for breaking down the door last night," Sargeant thought, "that church door."

Sargeant went over and sat on a wooden bench against the cold stone wall. He was emptier than ever. His clothes were wet, clammy cold wet, and shoes sloppy with snow water. It was just about dawn. There he was, locked up behind a cell door, nursing his bruised fingers.

The bruised fingers were his, but not the *door*.

Not the *club*, but the fingers.

"You wait," mumbled Sargeant, black against the jail wall. "I'm gonna break down this door, too."

"Shut up—or I'll paste you one," said the cop.

"I'm gonna break down this door," yelled Sargeant as he stood up in his cell.

Then he must have been talking to himself because he said, "I wonder where Christ's gone? I wonder if he's gone to Kansas City?"

The Lagoon

JOSEPH CONRAD
1857–1924

The white man, leaning with both arms over the roof of the little house in the stern of the boat, said to the steersman:

"We will pass the night in Arsat's clearing. It is late."

The Malay only grunted, and went on looking fixedly at the river. The white man rested his chin on his crossed arms and gazed at the wake of the boat. At the end of the straight avenue of forests cut by the intense glitter of the river, the sun appeared unclouded and dazzling, poised low over the water that shone smoothly like a band of metal. The forests, somber and dull, stood motionless and silent on each side of the broad stream. At the foot of big, towering trees, trunkless nipa palms rose from the mud of the bank, in bunches of leaves enormous and heavy, that hung unstirring over the brown swirl of eddies. In the stillness of the air every tree, every leaf, every bough, every tendril of creeper and every petal of minute blossoms seemed to have been bewitched into an immobility perfect and final. Nothing moved on the river but the eight paddles that rose flashing regularly, dipped together with a single splash; while the steersman swept right and left with a periodic and sudden flourish of his blade describing a glinting semicircle above his head. The churned-up water frothed alongside with a confused murmur. And the white man's canoe, advancing upstream in the short-lived disturbance of its own making, seemed to enter the portals of a land from which the very memory of motion had forever departed.

The white man, turning his back upon the setting sun, looked along the empty and broad expanse of the sea-reach. For the last three miles of its course the wandering, hesitating river, as if enticed irresistibly by the freedom of an open horizon, flows straight into the sea, flows straight to the east—to the east that harbors both light and darkness. Astern of the boat the repeated call of some bird, a cry discordant and feeble, skipped along over the smooth water and lost itself, before it could reach the other shore, in the breathless silence of the world.

The steersman dug his paddle into the stream, and held hard with stiffened arms, his body thrown forward. The water gurgled aloud; and suddenly the long straight reach seemed to pivot on its center, the forests swung in a semicircle, and the slanting beams of sunset touched the broadside of the canoe with a fiery glow, throwing the slender and distorted shadows of its crew upon the streaked glitter of the river. The white man turned to look ahead. The course of the boat had been altered at right angles to the stream, and the carved dragon head of its prow was pointing now at a gap in the fringing bushes of the bank. It glided through, brushing the overhanging twigs, and disappeared from the river like some slim and amphibious creature leaving the water for its lair in the forests.

The narrow creek was like a ditch: tortuous, fabulously deep; filled with gloom under the thin strip of pure and shining blue of the heaven. Immense trees soared up, invisible behind the festooned draperies of creepers. Here and there, near the glistening blackness of the water, a twisted root of some tall tree showed amongst the tracery of small ferns, black and dull, writhing and motionless, like an arrested snake. The short words of the paddlers reverberated loudly between the thick and somber walls of vegetation. Darkness oozed out from between the trees, through the tangled maze of the creepers, from behind the great fantastic and unstirring leaves; the darkness, mysterious and invincible; the darkness scented and poisonous of impenetrable forests.

The men poled in the shoaling water. The creek broadened, opening out into a wide sweep of a stagnant lagoon. The forests receded from the marshy bank, leaving a level strip of bright green, reedy grass to frame the reflected blueness of the sky. A fleecy pink cloud drifted high above, trailing the delicate coloring of its image under the floating leaves and the silvery blossoms of the lotus. A little house, perched on high piles, appeared black in the distance. Near it, two tall nibong palms, that seemed to have come out of the forests in the background, leaned slightly over the ragged roof, with a suggestion of sad tenderness and care in the droop of their leafy and soaring heads.

The steersman, pointing with his paddle, said, "Arsat is there. I see his canoe fast between the piles."

The polers ran along the sides of the boat glancing over their shoulders at the end of the day's journey. They would have preferred to spend the night somewhere else than on this lagoon of weird aspect and ghostly reputation. Moreover, they disliked Arsat, first as a stranger, and also because he who repairs a ruined house, and dwells in it, proclaims that he is not afraid to live amongst the spirits that haunt the places abandoned by mankind. Such a man can disturb the course of fate by glances or words; while his familiar ghosts are not easy to propitiate by casual wayfarers upon whom they long to wreak the malice of their human master. White men care not for such things, being unbelievers and in league with the Father of Evil, who leads them unharmed through the invisible dangers of this world. To the warnings of the righteous they oppose an offensive pretense of disbelief. What is there to be done?

So they thought, throwing their weight on the end of their long poles. The big canoe glided on swiftly, noiselessly, and smoothly, towards Arsat's clearing, till, in a great rattling of poles thrown down, and the loud murmurs of "Allah by praised!" it came with a gentle knock against the crooked piles below the house.

The boatmen with uplifted faces shouted discordantly, "Arsat! O Arsat!" Nobody came. The white man began to climb the rude ladder giving access to the bamboo platform before the house. The juragan of the boat said sulkily, "We will cook in the sampan, and sleep on the water."

"Pass my blankets and the basket," said the white man, curtly.

He knelt on the edge of the platform to receive the bundle. Then the boat shoved off, and the white man, standing up, confronted Arsat, who had come out through the low door of his hut. He was a man young, powerful, with broad chest and muscular arms. He had nothing on but his sarong. His head was bare. His big, soft eyes stared eagerly at the white man, but his voice and demeanor were composed as he asked, without any words of greeting:

"Have you medicine, Tuan?"

"No," said the visitor in a startled tone. "No. Why? Is there sickness in the house?"

"Enter and see," replied Arsat, in the same calm manner, and turning short round, passed again through the small doorway. The white man, dropping his bundles, followed.

In the dim light of the dwelling he made out on a couch of bamboos a woman stretched on her back under a broad sheet of red cotton cloth. She lay still, as if dead; but her big eyes, wide open, glittered in the gloom, staring upwards at the slender rafters, motionless and unseeing. She was in a high fever, and evidently unconscious. Her cheeks were sunk slightly, her lips were partly open, and on the young face there was the ominous and fixed expression—the absorbed, contemplating expression of the unconscious who are going to die. The two men stood looking down at her in silence.

"Has she been long ill?" asked the traveler.

"I have not slept for five nights," answered the Malay, in a deliberate tone. "At first she heard voices calling her from the water and struggled against me who held her. But since the son of today rose she hears nothing—she hears not me. She sees nothing. She sees not me—ME!"

He remained silent for a minute, then asked softly:

"Tuan, will she die?"

"I fear so," said the white man, sorrowfully. He had known Arsat years ago, in a far country in times of trouble and danger, when no friendship is to be despised. And since his Malay friend had come unexpectedly to dwell in the hut on the lagoon with a strange woman, he had slept many times there, in his journeys up and down the river. He liked the man who knew how to keep faith in council and how to fight without fear by the side of his white friend. He liked him—not so much perhaps as a man likes his favorite dog—but still he liked him well enough to help and ask no questions, to think sometimes vaguely and hazily in the midst of his own pursuits, about the lonely man and the long-haired woman with audacious face and triumphant eyes, who lived together hidden by the forests—alone and feared.

The white man came out of the hut in time to see the enormous conflagration of sunset put out by the swift and stealthy shadows that, rising like a black and impalpable vapor above the treetops, spread over the heaven, extinguishing the crimson glow of floating clouds and the red brilliance of departing daylight. In a few moments all the stars came out above the intense blackness of the earth and the great lagoon gleaming suddenly with reflected lights resembled an oval patch of night sky flung down into the hopeless and abysmal night of the wilderness. The white man had some supper out of the basket, then collecting a few sticks that lay about the platform, made up a small fire, not for warmth, but for the sake of the smoke, which would keep off the mosquitoes. He wrapped himself in the blankets and sat with his back against the reed wall of the house, smoking thoughtfully.

Arsat came through the doorway with noiseless steps and squatted down by the fire. The white man moved his outstretched legs a little.

"She breathes," said Arsat in a low voice, anticipating the expected question. "She breathes and burns as if with a great fire. She speaks not; she hears not—and burns!"

He paused for a moment, then asked in a quiet, incurious tone:

"Tuan . . . will she die?"

The white man moved his shoulders uneasily and muttered in a hesitating manner:

"If such is her fate."

"No, Tuan," said Arsat, calmly. "If such is my fate. I hear, I see, I wait. I remember. . . . Tuan, do you remember the old days? Do you remember my brother?"

"Yes," said the white man. The Malay rose suddenly and went in. The other, sitting still outside, could hear the voice in the hut. Arsat said: "Hear me! Speak!" His words were succeeded by a complete silence. "O Diamelen!" he cried, suddenly. After that cry there was a deep sigh. Arsat came out and sank down again in his old place.

They sat in silence before the fire. There was no sound within the house, there was no sound near them; but far away on the lagoon they could hear the voices of the boatmen ringing fitful and distinct on the calm water. The fire in the bows of the sampan shone faintly in the distance with a hazy red glow. Then it died out. The voices ceased. The land and the water slept invisible, unstirring and mute. It was as though there had been nothing left in the world but the glitter of stars streaming, ceaseless and vain, through the black stillness of the night.

The white man gazed straight before him into the darkness with wide-open eyes. The fear and fascination, the inspiration and the wonder of death—of death near, unavoidable; and unseen, soothed the unrest of his race and stirred the most indistinct, the most intimate of his thoughts. The ever-ready suspicion of evil, the gnawing suspicion that lurks in our hearts, flowed out into the stillness round him—into the stillness profound and dumb, and made it appear untrustworthy and infamous, like the placid and impenetrable mask of an unjustifiable violence. In that fleeting and powerful disturbance of his being the earth enfolded in the starlight peace became a shadowy country of inhuman strife, a battlefield of phantoms terrible and charming, august or ignoble, struggling ardently for the possession of our helpless hearts. An unquiet and mysterious country of inextinguishable desires and fears.

A plaintive murmur rose in the night; a murmur saddening and startling, as if the great solitudes of surrounding woods had tried to whisper into his ear the wisdom of their immense and lofty indifference. Sounds hesitating and vague floated in the air round him, shaped themselves slowly into words; and at last flowed on gently in a murmuring stream of soft and monotonous sentences. He stirred like a man waking up and changed his position slightly. Arsat, motionless and shadowy, sitting with bowed head under the stars, was speaking in a low and dreamy tone:

". . . for where can we lay down the heaviness of our trouble but in a friend's heart? A man must speak of war and of love. You, Tuan, know what war is, and you have seen me in time of danger seek death as other men seek life! A writing may be lost; a lie may be written; but what the eye has seen is truth and remains in the mind!"

"I remember," said the white man, quietly. Arsat went on with mournful composure:

"Therefore I shall speak to you of love. Speak in the night. Speak before both night and love are gone—and the eye of day looks upon my sorrow and my shame; upon my blackened face; upon my burnt-up heart."

A sigh, short and faint, marked an almost imperceptible pause, and then his words flowed on, without a stir, without a gesture.

"After the time of trouble and war was over and you went away from my country in the pursuit of your desires, which we, men of the islands, cannot understand, I and my brother became again, as we had been before, the sword bearers of the Ruler. You know we were men of family, belonging to a ruling race, and more fit than any to carry on our right shoulder the emblem of power. And in the time of prosperity Si Dendring showed us favor, as we, in time of sorrow, had showed to him the faithfulness of our courage. It was a time of peace. A time of deer hunts and cock fights; of idle talks and foolish squabbles between men whose bellies are full and weapons are rusty. But the sower watched the young rice shoots grow up without

fear, and the traders came and went, departed lean and returned fat into the river of peace. They brought news, too. Brought lies and truth mixed together, so that no man knew when to rejoice and when to be sorry. We heard from them about you also. They had seen you here and had seen you there. And I was glad to hear, for I remembered the stirring times, and I always remembered you, Tuan, till the time came when my eyes could see nothing in the past, because they had looked upon the one who is dying there—in the house."

He stopped to exclaim in an intense whisper, "O Mara bahia! O Calamity!" then went on speaking a little louder:

"There's no worse enemy and no better friend than a brother, Tuan, for one brother knows another, and in perfect knowledge is strength for good or evil. I loved my brother. I went to him and told him that I could see nothing but one face, hear nothing but one voice. He told me: 'Open your heart so that she can see what is in it—and wait. Patience is wisdom. Inchi Midah may die or our Ruler may throw off his fear of a woman!' . . . I waited! . . . You remember the lady with the veiled face, Tuan, and the fear of our Ruler before her cunning and temper. And if she wanted her servant, what could I do? But I fed the hunger of my heart on short glances and stealthy words. I loitered on the path to the bathhouses in the daytime, and when the sun had fallen behind the forest I crept along the jasmine hedges of the women's courtyard. Unseeing, we spoke to one another through the scent of flowers, through the veil of leaves, through the blades of long grass that stood still before our lips; so great was our prudence, so faint was the murmur of our great longing. The time passed swiftly . . . and there were whispers amongst women—and our enemies watched—my brother was gloomy, and I began to think of killing and of a fierce death. . . . We are of a people who take what they want—like you whites. There is a time when a man should forget loyalty and respect. Might and authority are given to rulers, but to all men is given love and strength and courage. My brother said, 'You shall take her from their midst. We are two who are like one.' And I answered, 'Let it be soon, for I find no warmth in sunlight that does not shine upon her.' Our time came when the Ruler and all the great people went to the mouth of the river to fish by torchlight. There were hundreds of boats, and on the white sand, between the water and the forests, dwellings of leaves were built for the households of the Rajahs. The smoke of cooking fires was like a blue mist of the evening, and many voices rang in it joyfully. While they were making the boats ready to beat up the fish, my brother came to me and said, 'Tonight!' I looked to my weapons, and when the time came our canoe took its place in the circle of boats carrying the torches. The lights blazed on the water, but behind the boats there was darkness. When the shouting began and the excitement made them like mad we dropped out. The water swallowed our fire, and we floated back to the shore that was dark with only here and there the glimmer of embers. We could hear the talk of slave girls amongst the sheds. Then we found a place deserted and silent. We waited there. She came. She came running along the shore, rapid and leaving no trace, like a leaf driven by the wind into the sea. My brother said gloomily, 'Go and take her; carry her into our boat.' I lifted her in my arms. She panted. Her heart was beating against my breast. I said, 'I take you from those people. You came to the cry of my heart, but my arms take you into my boat against the will of the great!' 'It is right,' said my brother. 'We are men who take what we want and can hold it against many. We should have taken her in daylight.' I said, 'Let us be off'; for since she was in my boat I began to think of our Ruler's many men. 'Yes. Let us be off,' said my brother. 'We are cast out and this boat is our country now—and the sea is our refuge.' He lingered with his foot on the shore, and I entreated him to hasten, for I remembered the strokes of her heart against my breast and thought that two men cannot withstand a hundred. We left, paddling downstream close to the bank; and as we passed by the creek where they were fishing, the great shouting had ceased, but the murmur of voices was loud like the humming of insects flying at noonday. The boats floated, clustered together, in the red light of torches, under a black roof of smoke; and men talked of their sport. Men that boasted, and praised, and jeered—men that would have been our friends in the morning, but on that night were already our enemies. We paddled swiftly past. We had no more friends in the country of our birth. She sat in the middle of the canoe with covered face; silent as she is now; unseeing as she is now—and I had no regret at what I was leaving because I could hear her breathing close to me—as I can hear her now."

He paused, listened with his ear turned to the doorway, then shook his head and went on:

"My brother wanted to shout the cry of challenge—one cry only—to let the people know we were freeborn robbers who trusted our arms and the great sea. And again I begged him in the name of our love to be silent. Could I not hear her breathing close to me? I knew the pursuit would come quick enough. My brother loved me. He dipped his paddle without a splash. He only said, 'There is half a man in you now—the other half is in that woman. I can wait. When you are a whole man again, you will come back with me here to shout defiance. We are sons of the same mother.' I made no answer. All my strength and all my spirit were in my hands that held the paddle—for I longed to be with her in a safe place beyond the reach of men's anger and of women's spite. My love was so great, that I thought it could guide me to a country where death was unknown, if I could only escape from Inchi Midah's fury and from our Ruler's sword. We paddled with haste, breathing through our teeth. The blades bit deep into the smooth water. We passed out of the river; we flew in clear channels amongst the shallows. We skirted the black coast; we skirted the sand beaches where the sea speaks in whispers to the land; and the gleam of white sand flashed back past our boat, so swiftly she ran upon the water. We spoke not. Only once I said, 'Sleep, Diamelen, for soon you may want all your strength.' I heard the sweetness of her voice, but I never turned my head. The sun rose and still we went on. Water fell from my face like rain from a cloud. We flew in the light and heat. I never looked back, but I knew that my brother's eyes, behind me, were looking steadily ahead, for the boat went as straight as a bushman's dart, when it leaves the end of the sumpitan. There was no better paddler, no better steersman than my brother. Many times, together, we had won races in that canoe. But we never had put out our strength as we did then—then, when for the last time we paddled together! There was no braver or stronger man in our country than my brother. I could not spare the strength to turn my head and look at him, but every moment I heard the hiss of his breath getting louder behind me. Still he did not speak. The sun was high. The heat clung to my back like a flame of fire. My ribs were ready to burst, but I could no longer get enough air into my chest. And then I felt I must cry out with my last breath, 'Let us rest!' . . . 'Good!' he answered; and his voice was firm. He was strong. He was brave. He knew not fear and no fatigue . . . My brother!"

A murmur powerful and gentle, a murmur vast and faint; the murmur of trembling leaves, of stirring boughs, ran through the tangled depths of the forests, ran over the starry smoothness of the lagoon, and the water between the piles lapped the slimy timber once with a sudden splash. A breath of warm air touched the two men's faces and passed on with a mournful sound—a breath loud and short like an uneasy sign of the dreaming earth.

Arsat went on in an even, low voice.

"We ran our canoe on the white beach of a little bay close to a long tongue of land that seemed to bar our road; a long wooded cape going far into the sea. My brother knew that place. Beyond the cape a river has its entrance, and through the jungle of that land there is a narrow path. We made a fire and cooked rice. Then we lay down to sleep on the soft sand in the shade of our canoe, while she watched. No sooner had I closed my eyes than I heard her cry of alarm. We leaped up. The sun was halfway down the sky already, and coming in sight in the opening of the bay we saw a prau manned by many paddlers. We knew it at once; it was one of our Rajah's praus. They were watching the shore, and saw us. They beat the gong, and turned the head of the prau into the bay. I felt my heart become weak within my breast. Diamelen sat on the sand and covered her face. There was no escape by sea. My brother laughed. He had the gun you had given him, Tuan, before you went away, but there was only a handful of powder. He spoke to me quickly: 'Run with her along the path. I shall keep them back, for they have no firearms, and landing in the face of a man with a gun is certain death for some. Run with her. On the other side of that wood there is a fisherman's house—and a canoe. When I have fired all the shots I will follow. I am a great runner, and before they can come

up we shall be gone. I will hold out as long as I can, for she is but a woman—that can neither run nor fight, but she has your heart in her weak hands.' He dropped behind the canoe. The prau was coming. She and I ran, and as we rushed along the path I heard shots. My brother fired—once—twice—and the booming of the gong ceased. There was silence behind us. That neck of land is narrow. Before I heard my brother fire the third shot I saw the shelving shore, and I saw the water again; the mouth of a broad river. We crossed a grassy glade. We ran down to the water. I saw a low hut above the black mud, and a small canoe hauled up. I heard another shot behind me. I thought, 'That is his last charge.' We rushed down to the canoe; a man came running from the hut, but I leaped on him, and we rolled together in the mud. Then I got up, and he lay still at my feet. I don't know whether I had killed him or not. I and Diamelen pushed the canoe afloat. I heard yells behind me, and I saw my brother run across the glade. Many men were bounding after him. I took her in my arms and threw her into the boat, then leaped in myself. When I looked back I saw that my brother had fallen. He fell and was up again, but the men were closing round him. He shouted, 'I am coming!' The men were close to him. I looked. Many men. Then I looked at her. Tuan, I pushed the canoe! I pushed it into deep water. She was kneeling forward looking at me, and I said, 'Take your paddle,' while I struck the water with mine. Tuan, I heard him cry. I heard him cry my name twice; and I heard voices shouting, 'Kill! Strike!' I never turned back. I heard him calling my name again with a great shriek, as when life is going out together with the voice—and I never turned my head. My own name! . . . My brother! Three times he called—but I was not afraid of life. Was she not there in that canoe? And could I not with her find a country where death is forgotten—where death is unknown!"

The white man sat up. Arsat rose and stood, an indistinct and silent figure above the dying embers of the fire. Over the lagoon a mist drifting and low had crept, erasing slowly the glittering images of the stars. And now a great expanse of white vapor covered the land: it flowed cold and gray in the darkness, eddied in noiseless whirls round the tree trunks and about the platform of the house, which seemed to float upon a restless and impalpable illusion of a sea. Only far away the tops of the trees stood outlined on the twinkle of heaven, like a somber and forbidding shore—a coast deceptive, pitiless and black.

Arsat's voice vibrated loudly in the profound peace.

"I had her there! I had her! To get her I would have faced all mankind. But I had her —and—"

His words went out ringing into the empty distances. He paused, and seemed to listen to them dying away very far—beyond help and beyond recall. Then he said quietly:

"Tuan, I loved my brother."

A breath of wind made him shiver. High above his head, high above the silent sea of mist the drooping leaves of the palms rattled together with a mournful and expiring sound. The white man stretched his legs. His chin rested on his chest, and he murmured sadly without lifting his head:

"We all love our brothers."

Arsat burst out with an intense whispering violence:

"What did I care who died? I wanted peace in my own heart."

He seemed to hear a stir in the house—listened—then stepped in noiselessly. The white man stood up. A breeze was coming in fitful puffs. The stars shone paler as if they had retreated into the frozen depths of immense space. After a chill gust of wind there were a few seconds of perfect calm and absolute silence. Then from behind the black and wavy line of the forests a column of golden light shot up into the heavens and spread over the semicircle of the eastern horizon. The sun had risen. The mist lifted, broke into drifting patches, vanished into thin flying wreaths; and the unveiled lagoon lay, polished and black, in the heavy shadows at the foot of the wall of trees. A white eagle rose over it with a slanting and ponderous flight, reached the clear sunshine and appeared dazzlingly brilliant for a moment, then soaring higher, became a dark and motionless speck before it vanished into the blue as if it had left the earth forever. The white man, standing gazing upwards before the doorway, heard in the

hut a confused and broken murmur of distracted words ending with a loud groan. Suddenly Arsat stumbled out with outstretched hands, shivered, and stood still for some time with fixed eyes. Then he said:

"She burns no more."

Before his face the sun showed its edge above the treetops rising steadily. The breeze freshened; a great brilliance burst upon the lagoon, sparkled up the rippling water. The forests came out of the clear shadows of the morning, became distinct, as if they had rushed nearer—to stop short in a great stir of leaves, of nodding boughs, of swaying branches. In the merciless sunshine the whisper of unconscious life grew louder, speaking in an incomprehensible voice round the dumb darkness of that human sorrow. Arsat's eyes wandered slowly, then stared at the rising sun.

"I can see nothing," he said half aloud to himself.

"There is nothing," said the white man, moving to the edge of the platform and waving his hand to his boat. A shout came faintly over the lagoon and the sampan began to glide towards the abode of the friend of ghosts.

"If you want to come with me, I will wait all the morning," said the white man, looking away upon the water.

"No, Tuan," said Arsat, softly. "I shall not eat or sleep in this house, but I must first see my road. Now I can see nothing—see nothing! There is no light and no peace in the world; but there is death—death for many. We are sons of the same mother—and I left him in the midst of enemies; but I am going back now."

He drew a long breath and went on in a dreamy tone:

"In a little while I shall see clear enough to strike—to strike. But she has died, and . . . now . . . darkness."

He flung his arms wide open, let them fall along his body, then stood still with unmoved face and stony eyes, staring at the sun. The white man got down into his canoe. The polers ran smartly along the sides of the boat, looking over their shoulders at the beginning of a weary journey. High in the stern, his head muffled up in white rags, the juragan sat moody, letting his paddle trail in the water. The white man, leaning with both arms over the grass roof of the little cabin, looked back at the shining ripple of the boat's wake. Before the sampan passed out of the lagoon into the creek he lifted his eyes. Arsat had not moved. He stood lonely in the searching sunshine; and he looked beyond the great light of a cloudless day into the darkness of a world of illusions.

Questions

1. What advantages are there in having the Malay Arsat tell the story?

2. Analyze Conrad's style sufficiently to describe its contribution to the atmosphere of the story. In what way does the atmosphere help to reveal the story's meaning?

3. The setting, too, is important: Why is the story titled "The Lagoon"?

4. What symbols are found in Conrad's description of nature? Are they helpful in determining the story's meaning?

5. What does Arsat mean by referring to " 'my sorrow and my shame . . . my blackened face . . . my burnt-up heart' "?

6. Is the death of Diamelen Arsat's punishment for having betrayed his brother? Or is the matter not quite that simple?

The Infant Prodigy

THOMAS MANN
1875–1955

The early environment and parental influence of Mann stimulated his thinking about the nature of the artist, society's regard and lack of regard for him, and especially the opposition of artist and businessman. As Mann's sensibilities matured and sharpened, he became a critic of European culture, and the results of his probing are found in his novel *The Magic Mountain* (*Der Zauberberg*), 1924, often regarded as one of the great novels of our century. Both the novel and "The Infant Prodigy" depend greatly on symbolism for their deepest meaning which warns the reader that the story below demands his concentrated attention. By using a very young artist for his central character, Mann is able to dramatize the abnormality of both artist and audience. " 'We are all infant prodigies, we artists,' " says "the girl with untidy hair and swinging arms."

The infant prodigy entered. The hall became quiet.

It became quiet and then the audience began to clap, because somewhere at the side a leader of mobs, a born organizer, clapped first. The audience had heard nothing yet, but they applauded; for a mighty publicity organization had heralded the prodigy and people were already hypnotized, whether they knew it or not.

The prodigy came from behind a splendid screen embroidered with Empire garlands and great conventionalized flowers, and climbed nimbly up to the steps of the platform, diving into the applause as into a bath; a little chilly and shivering, but yet as though into a friendly element. He advanced to the edge of the platform and smiled as though he were about to be photographed; he made a shy, charming gesture of greeting, like a little girl.

He was dressed entirely in white silk, which the audience found enchanting. The little white jacket was fancifully cut, with a sash underneath it, and even his shoes were made of white silk. But against the white socks his bare little legs stood out quite brown; for he was a Greek boy.

He was called Bibi Saccellaphylaccas. And such indeed was his name. No one knew what Bibi was the pet name for, nobody but the impresario, and he regarded it as a trade secret. Bibi had smooth black hair reaching to his shoulders; it was parted on the side and fastened back from the narrow domed forehead by a little silk bow. His was the most harmless childish countenance in the world, with an unfinished nose and guileless mouth. The area beneath his pitch-black mouselike eyes was already a little tired and visibly lined. He looked as though he were nine years old but was really eight and was given out for seven. It was hard to tell whether to believe this or not. Probably everybody knew better and still believed it, as happens about so many things. The average man thinks that a little falseness goes with beauty. Where should we get any excitement out of our daily life if we were not willing to pretend a bit? And the average man is quite right, in his average brains!

The prodigy kept on bowing until the applause died down, then he went up to the grand piano, and the audience cast a last look at its programmes. First came a *Marche solonnelle,* then a *Rêverie,* and then *Le Hibou et les moineaux*—all by Bibi Saccellaphylaccas. The whole programme was by him, they were all his compositions. He could not score them, of course, but he had them all in his extraordinary little head and they possessed real artistic significance, or so it said, seriously and objectively, in the programme. The programme sounded as though the impresario had wrested these concessions from his critical nature after a hard struggle.

The prodigy sat down upon the resolving stool and felt with his feet for the pedals, which were raised by means of a clever device so that Bibi could reach them. It was Bibi's own piano, he took it everywhere with him. It rested upon wooden trestles and its polish was somewhat marred by the constant transportation—but all that only made things more interesting.

Bibi put his silk-shod feet on the pedals; then he made an artful little face, looked straight ahead of him, and lifted his right hand. It was a brown, childish little hand; but the wrist was strong and unlike a child's, with well-developed bones.

Bibi made his face for the audience because he was aware that he had to entertain them a little. But he had his own private enjoyment in the thing too, an enjoyment which he could never convey to anybody. It was that prickling delight, that secret shudder of bliss, which ran through him every time he sat at an open piano—it would always be with him. And here was the keyboard again, these seven black and white octaves, among which he had so often lost himself in abysmal and thrilling adventures—and yet it always looked as clean and untouched as a newly washed blackboard. This was the realm of music that lay before him. It lay spread out like an inviting ocean, where he might plunge in and blissfully swim, where he might let himself be borne and carried away, where he might go under in night and storm, yet keep the mastery: control, ordain—he held his right hand poised in the air.

A breathless stillness reigned in the room— the tense moment before the first note came. . . . How would it begin? It began so. And

Bibi, with his index finger, fetched the first note out of the piano, a quite unexpectedly powerful first note in the middle register, like a trumpet blast. Others followed, an introduction developed—the audience relaxed.

The concert was held in the palatial hall of a fashionable first-class hotel. The walls were covered with mirrors framed in gilded arabesques, between frescoes of the rosy and fleshly school. Ornamental columns supported a ceiling that displayed a whole universe of electric bulbs, in clusters darting a brilliance far brighter than day and filling the whole space with thin, vibrating golden light. Not a seat was unoccupied, people were standing in the side aisles and at the back. The front seats cost twelve marks; for the impresario believed that anything worth having was worth paying for. And they were occupied by the best society, for it was in the upper classes, of course, that the greatest enthusiasm was felt. There were even some children, with their legs hanging down demurely from their chairs and their shining eyes staring at their gifted little white-clad contemporary.

Down in front on the left side sat the prodigy's mother, an extremely obese woman with a powdered double chin and a feather on her head. Beside her was the impresario, a man of oriental appearance with large gold buttons on his conspicuous cuffs. The princess was in the middle of the front row—a wrinkled, shrivelled little old princess but still a patron of the arts, especially everything full of sensibility. She sat in a deep, velvet-upholstered arm-chair, and a Persian carpet was spread before her feet. She held her hands folded over her grey striped-silk breast, put her head on one side, and presented a picture of elegant composure as she sat looking up at the performing prodigy. Next to her sat her lady-in-waiting, in a green striped-silk gown. Being only a lady-in-waiting she had to sit up very straight in her chair.

Bibi ended in a grand climax. With what power this wee manikin belaboured the keyboard! The audience could scarcely trust its ears. The march theme, an infectious, swinging tune, broke out once more, fully harmonized, bold and showy; with every note Bibi flung himself back from the waist as though he were marching in a triumphal procession. He ended *fortissimo,* bent over, slipped sideways off the stool, and stood with a smile awaiting the applause.

And the applause burst forth, unanimously, enthusiastically; the child made his demure little maidenly curtsy and people in the front seat thought: "Look what slim little hips he has! Clap! clap! Hurrah, bravo, little chap, Saccophylax or whatever your name is! Wait, let me take off my gloves—what a little devil of a chap he is!"

Bibi had to come out three times from behind the screen before they would stop. Some latecomers entered the hall and moved about looking for seats. Then the concert continued. Bibi's *Rêverie* murmured its numbers, consisting almost entirely of arpeggios, above which a bar of melody rose now and then, weak-winged. Then came *Le Hibou et les moineaux*. This piece was brilliantly successful, it made a strong impression; it was an effective childhood fantasy, remarkably well envisaged. The bass represented the owl, sitting morosely rolling his filmy eyes; while in the treble the impudent, half-frightened sparrows chirped. Bibi received an ovation when he finished, he was called out four times. A hotel page with shiny buttons carried up three great laurel wreaths onto the stage and proffered them from one side while Bibi nodded and expressed his thanks. Even the princess shared in the applause, daintily and noiselessly pressing her palms together.

Ah, the knowing little creature understood how to make people clap! He stopped behind the screen, they had to wait for him; lingered a little on the steps of the platform, admired the long streamers on the wreaths—although actually such things bored him stiff by now. He bowed with the utmost charm, he gave the audience plenty of time to have itself out, because applause is valuable and must not be cut short. "*Le Hibou* is my drawing card," he thought—this expression he had learned from the impresario. "Now I will play the fantasy, it is a lot better than *Le Hibou*, of course, especially the C-sharp passage. But you idiots dote on the *Hibou*, though it is the first and silliest thing I wrote." He continued to bow and smile.

Next came a *Méditation* and then an *Étude* —the programme was quite comprehensive. The *Méditation* was very like the *Rêverie*—which was nothing against it—and the *Étude* displayed all of Bibi's virtuosity, which naturally fell a little short of his inventiveness. And then the *Fantaisie*. This was his favourite; he varied it a little each time, giving himself free rein and sometimes surprising even himself, on good evenings, by his own inventiveness.

He sat and played, so little, so white and shining, against the great black grand piano, elect and alone, above that confused sea of faces, above the heavy, insensitive mass soul, upon which he was labouring to work with his individual, differentiated soul. His lock of soft black hair with the white silk bow had fallen over his forehead, his trained and bony little wrists pounded away, the muscles stood out visibly on his brown childish cheeks.

Sitting there he sometimes had moments of oblivion and solitude, when the gaze of his strange little mouselike eyes with the big rings beneath them would lose itself and stare through the painted stage into space that was peopled with strange vague life. Then out of the corner of his eye he would give a quick look back into the hall and be once more with his audience.

"Joy and pain, the heights and the depths— that is my *Fantaisie*," he thought lovingly. "Listen, here is the C-sharp passage." He lingered over the approach, wondering if they would notice anything. But no, of course not, how should they? And he cast his eyes up prettily at the ceiling so that at least they might have something to look at.

All these people sat there in their regular rows, looking at the prodigy and thinking all sorts of things in their regular brains. An old gentleman with a white beard, a seal ring on his finger and a bulbous swelling on his bald spot, a growth if you like, was thinking to himself: "Really, one ought to be ashamed." He had never got any further than "Ah, thou dearest Augustin" on the piano, and here he sat now, a grey old man, looking on while this little hop-o'-my-thumb performed miracles. Yes, yes, it is a gift of God, we must remember that. God grants His gifts, or He withholds them, and there is no shame in being an ordinary man. Like with the Christ Child.—Before a child one may kneel without feeling ashamed. Strange that thoughts like these should be so satisfying —he would even say so sweet, if it was not too silly for a tough old man like him to use the word. That was how he felt, anyhow.

Art . . . the business man with the parrot-nose was thinking. "Yes, it adds something cheerful to life, a little good white silk and a little tumty-ti-ti-tum. Really he does not play so badly. Fully fifty seats, twelve marks apiece, that makes six hundred marks—and everything else besides. Take off the rent of the hall, the lighting and the programmes, you must have fully a thousand marks profit. That is worth while."

That was Chopin he was just playing, thought the piano-teacher, a lady with a pointed nose; she was of an age when the understanding sharpens as the hopes decay. "But not very original—I will say that afterwards, it sounds well. And his hand position is entirely amateur. One must be able to lay a coin on the back of the hand—I would use a ruler on him."

Then there was a young girl, at that self-conscious and chlorotic time of life when the most ineffable ideas come into the mind. She was thinking to herself: "What is it he is playing? It is expressive of passion, yet he is a child. If he kissed me it would be as though my little brother kissed me—no kiss at all. Is there such a thing as passion all by itself, without any earthly object, a sort of child's-play of passion? What nonsense! If I were to say such things aloud they would just be at me with some more codliver oil. Such is life."

An officer was leaning against a column. He looked on at Bibi's success and thought: "Yes, you are something and I am something, each in his own way." So he clapped his heels together and paid to the prodigy the respect which he felt to be due to all the powers that be.

Then there was a critic, an elderly man in a shiny black coat and turned-up trousers splashed with mud. He sat in his free seat and thought: "Look at him, this young beggar of a Bibi. As an individual he has still to develop, but as a type he is already quite complete, the artist *par excellence*. He has in himself all the artist's exaltation and his utter worthlessness, his charlatanry and his sacred fire, his burning contempt and his secret raptures. Of course I can't write all that, it is too good. Of course, I should have been an artist myself if I had not seen through the whole business so clearly."

Then the prodigy stopped playing and a perfect storm arose in the hall. He had to come out again and again from behind his screen. The man with the shiny buttons carried up more wreaths: four laurel wreaths, a lyre made of violets, a bouquet of roses. He had not arms enough to convey all these tributes, the impresario himself mounted the stage to help him. He hung a laurel wreath round Bibi's neck, he tenderly stroked the black hair—and suddenly as though overcome he bent down and gave the prodigy a kiss, a resounding kiss, square on the mouth. And then the storm became a hurricane. That kiss ran through the room like an electric shock, it went direct to peoples' marrow and made them shiver down their backs. They were carried away by a helpless compulsion of sheer noise. Loud shouts mingled with the hysterical clapping of hands. Some of Bibi's commonplace little friends down there waved their handkerchiefs. But the critic thought: "Of course that kiss had to come—it's a good old gag. Yes, good Lord, if only one did not see through everything quite so clearly—"

And so the concert drew to a close. It began at half past seven and finished at half past eight. The platform was laden with wreaths and two little pots of flowers stood on the lamp-stands of the piano. Bibi played as his last number his *Rhapsodie grecque*, which turned into the Greek national hymn at the end. His fellow-countrymen in the audience would gladly have sung it with him if the company had not been so august. They made up for it with a powerful noise and hullabaloo, a hot-blooded national demonstration. And the aging critic was thinking: "Yes, the hymn had to come too. They have to exploit every vein—publicity cannot afford to neglect any means to its end. I think I'll criticize that as inartistic. But perhaps I am wrong, perhaps that is the most artistic thing of all. What is the artist? A jack-in-the-box. Criticism is on a higher plane. But I can't say that." And away he went in his muddy trousers.

After being called out nine or ten times the prodigy did not come any more from behind the screen but went to his mother and the impresario down in the hall. The audience stood about among the chairs and applauded and pressed forward to see Bibi close at hand. Some of them wanted to see the princess too. Two dense circles formed, one round the prodigy, the other round the princess, and you could actually not tell which of them was receiving more homage. But the court lady was commanded to go over to Bibi; she smoothed down his silk jacket a bit to make it look suitable for a court function, led him by the arm to the princess, and solemnly indicated to him that he was to kiss the royal hand. "How do you do it, child?" asked the princess. "Does it come into your head of itself when you sit down?" *"Oui, madame,"* answered Bibi. To himself he thought: "Oh, what a stupid old princess!" Then he turned round shyly and un-courtierlike and went back to his family.

Outside in the cloak-room there was a crowd. People held up their numbers and received with open arms, furs, shawls, and galoshes. Somewhere among her acquaintances the piano-teacher stood making her critique. "He is not very original," she said audibly and looked about her.

In front of one of the great mirrors an elegant young lady was being arrayed in her evening cloak and fur shoes by her brothers, two lieutenants. She was exquisitely beautiful, with her steel-blue eyes and her clean-cut, well-bred face. A really noble dame. When she was ready she stood waiting for her brothers. "Don't stand so long in front of the glass, Adolf," she said softly to one of them, who could not tear himself away from the sight of his simple, good-looking young features. But Lieutenant Adolf thinks: What cheek! He would button his overcoat in front of the glass, just the same. Then they went out on the street where the arc-lights gleamed cloudily through the white mist. Lieutenant Adolf struck up a little nigger-dance on the frozen snow to keep warm, with his hands in his slanting overcoat pockets and his collar turned up.

A girl with untidy hair and swinging arms, accompanied by a gloomy-faced youth, came out just behind them. A child! she thought. A charming child. But in there he was an awe-inspiring . . . and aloud in a toneless voice she said: "We are all infant prodigies, we artists."

"Well, bless my soul!" thought the old gentleman who had never got further than Augustin on the piano, and whose wen was now concealed by a top hat. "What does all that mean? She sounds very oracular." But the gloomy youth understood. He nodded his head slowly.

Then they were silent and the untidy-haired girl gazed after the brothers and sister. She rather despised them, but she looked after them until they had turned the corner.

Eveline

JAMES JOYCE
1882–1941

She sat at the window watching the evening invade the avenue. Her head was leaned against the window curtains and in her nostrils was the odour of dusty cretonne. She was tired.

Few people passed. The man out of the last house passed on his way home; she heard his footsteps clacking along the concrete pavement and afterwards crunching on the cinder path before the new red houses. One time there used to be a field there in which they used to play every evening with other people's children. Then a man from Belfast bought the field and built houses in it—not like their little brown houses but bright brick houses with shining roofs. The children of the avenue used to play together in that field—the Devines, the Waters, the Dunns, little Keogh the cripple, she and her brothers and sisters. Ernest, however, never played: he was too grown up. Her father used often to hunt them in out of the field with his blackthorn stick; but usually little Keogh used to keep *nix* and call out when he saw her father coming. Still they seemed to have been rather happy then. Her father was not so bad then; and besides, her mother was alive. That was a long time ago; she and her brothers and sisters were all grown up; her mother was dead. Tizzie Dunn was dead, too, and the Waters had gone back to England. Everything changes. Now she was going to go away like the others, to leave her home.

Home! She looked round the room, reviewing all its familiar objects which she had dusted once a week for so many years, wondering where on earth all the dust came from. Perhaps she would never see again those familiar objects from which she had never dreamed of being divided. And yet during all those years she had never found out the name of the priest whose yellowing photograph hung on the wall above the broken harmonium beside the coloured print of the promises made to Blessed Margaret Mary Alacoque. He had been a school friend of her father. Whenever he showed the photograph to a visitor her father used to pass it with a casual word:

"He is in Melbourne now."

She had consented to go away, to leave her home. Was that wise? She tried to weigh each side of the question. In her home anyway she had shelter and food; she had those whom she had known all her life about her. Of course she had to work hard, both in the house and at business. What would they say of her in the Stores when they found out that she had run away with a fellow? Say she was a fool, perhaps; and her place would be filled up by advertisement. Miss Gavan would be glad. She had always had an edge on her, especially whenever there were people listening.

"Miss Hill, don't you see these ladies are waiting?"

"Look lively, Miss Hill, please."

She would not cry many tears at leaving the Stores.

But in her new home, in a distant unknown country, it would not be like that. Then she would be married—she, Eveline. People would treat her with respect then. She would not be treated as her mother had been. Even now, though she was over nineteen, she sometimes felt herself in danger of her father's violence. She knew it was that that had given her the palpitations. When they were growing up he had never gone for her, like he used to go for Harry and Ernest, because she was a girl; but latterly he had begun to threaten her and say what he would do to her only for her dead mother's sake. And now she had nobody to protect her. Ernest was dead and Harry, who was in the church decorating business, was nearly always down somewhere in the country. Besides, the invariable squabble for money on Saturday nights had begun to weary her unspeakably. She always gave her entire wages—seven shillings—and Harry always sent up what he could but the trouble was to get any money from her father. He said she used to squander the money, that she had no head, that he wasn't going to give her his hard earned money to throw about the streets, and much more, for he was usually fairly bad on Saturday night. In the end he would give her the money and ask her had she any intention of buying Sunday's dinner. Then she had to rush out as quickly as she could and do her marketing, holding her black leather purse tightly in her hand as she elbowed her way through the crowds and returning home late under her load of provisions. She had hard work to keep the house together and to see that the two young children who had been left to her charge went to school regularly and got their meals regularly. It was hard work—a hard life—but now that she was about to leave it she did not find it a wholly undesirable life.

She was about to explore another life with Frank. Frank was very kind, manly, open-hearted. She was to go away with him by the night-boat to be his wife and to live with him in Buenos Ayres where he had a home waiting for her. How well she remembered the first time she had seen him; he was lodging in a house on the main road where she used to visit. It seemed a few weeks ago. He was standing at the gate, his peaked cap pushed back on his head and his hair tumbled forward over a face of bronze. Then they had come to know each other. He used to meet her outside the Stores every evening and see her home. He took her to see *The Bohemian Girl*[1] and she felt elated as she sat in an unaccustomed part of the theatre with him. He was awfully fond of music and sang a little. People knew that they were courting and, when he sang about the lass that loves a sailor, she always felt pleasantly confused. He used to call her Poppens out of fun. First of all it had been an excitement for her to have a fellow and then she had begun to like him. He had tales of distant countries. He had started as a deck boy at a pound a month on a ship of the Allan Line going out to Canada. He told her the names of the ships he had been on and the names of the different services. He had sailed through the Straits of Magellen and he told her stories of the terrible Patagonians. He had fallen on his feet in Buenos Ayres, he said, and had come over to the old country just for a holiday. Of course, her father had found out the affair and had forbidden her to have anything to say to him.

"I know these sailor chaps," he said.

One day he had quarrelled with Frank and after that she had to meet her lover secretly.

The evening deepened in the avenue. The white of two letters in her lap grew indistinct. One was to Harry; the other was to her father. Ernest had been her favourite but she liked Harry too. Her father was becoming old lately, she noticed; he would miss her. Sometimes he could be very nice. Not long before, when she

---

[1] A light opera by M. W. Balfe, 1843.

had been laid up for a day, he had read her out a ghost story and made toast for her at the fire. Another day, when their mother was alive, they had all gone for a picnic to the Hill of Howth. She remembered her father putting on her mother's bonnet to make the children laugh.

Her time was running out but she continued to sit by the window, leaning her head against the window curtain, inhaling the odour of dusty cretonne. Down far in the avenue she could hear a street organ playing. She knew the air. Strange that it should come that very night to remind her of the promise to her mother, her promise to keep the home together as long as she could. She remembered the last night of her mother's illness; she was again in the close dark room at the other side of the hall and outside she heard a melancholy air of Italy. The organ-player had been ordered to go away and given sixpence. She remembered her father strutting back into the sickroom saying:

"Damned Italians! coming over here!"

As she mused the pitiful vision of her mother's life laid its spell on the very quick of her being—that life of commonplace sacrifices closing in final craziness. She trembled as she heard again her mother's voice saying constantly with foolish insistence:

"Derevaun Seraun! Derevaun Seraun!"

She stood up in a sudden impulse of terror. Escape! She must escape! Frank would save her. He would give her life, perhaps love, too. But she wanted to live. Why should she be unhappy? She had a right to happiness. Frank would take her in his arms, fold her in his arms. He would save her.

She stood among the swaying crowd in the station at the North Wall. He held her hand and she knew that he was speaking to her, saying something about the passage over and over again. The station was full of soldiers with brown baggages. Through the wide doors of the sheds she caught a glimpse of the black mass of the boat, lying in beside the quay wall, with il-lumined portholes. She answered nothing. She felt her cheek pale and cold and, out of a maze of distress, she prayed to God to direct her, to show her what was her duty. The boat blew a long mournful whistle into the mist. If she went, to-morrow she would be on the sea with Frank, steaming towards Buenos Ayres. Their passage

had been booked. Could she still draw back after all he had done for her? Her distress awoke a nausea in her body and she kept moving her lips in silent fervent prayer.

A bell clanged upon her heart. She felt him seize her hand:

"Come!"

All the seas of the world tumbled about her heart. He was drawing her into them: he would drown her. She gripped with both hands at the iron railing.

"Come!"

No! No! No! It was impossible. Her hands clutched the iron in frenzy. Amid the seas she sent a cry of anguish!

"Eveline! Evvy!"

He rushed beyond the barrier and called to her to follow. He was shouted at to go on but he still called to her. She set her white face to him, passive, like a helpless animal. Her eyes gave him no sign of love or farewell or recognition.

The Magic Barrel

BERNARD MALAMUD
1914–

Not long ago there lived in uptown New York, in a small, almost meager room, though crowded with books, Leo Finkle, a rabbinical student in the Yeshivah University. Finkle, after six years of study, was to be ordained in June and had been advised by an acquaintance that he might find it easier to win himself a congregation if he were married. Since he had no present prospects of marriage, after two tormented days of turning it over in his mind, he called in Pinye Salzman, a marriage broker whose two-line advertisement he had read in the *Forward*.

The matchmaker appeared one night out of the dark fourth-floor hallway of the graystone rooming house where Finkle lived, grasping a black, strapped portfolio that had been worn thin with use. Salzman, who had been long in the business, was of slight but dignified build, wearing an old hat, and an overcoat too short and tight for him. He smelled frankly of fish, which he loved to eat, and although he was missing a few teeth, his presence was not displeasing because of an amiable manner curiously contrasted with mournful eyes. His voice, his lips, his wisp of beard, his bony fingers were animated, but gave him a moment of repose and his mild blue eyes revealed a depth of sadness, a characteristic that put Leo a little at ease although the situation, for him, was inherently tense.

He at once informed Salzman why he had asked him to come, explaining that his home was in Cleveland, and that but for his parents, who had married comparatively late in life, he was alone in the world. He had for six years devoted himself almost entirely to his studies, as a result of which, understandably, he had found himself without time for a social life and the company of young women. Therefore he thought it the better part of trial and error—of embarrassing fumbling—to call in an experienced person to advise him on these matters. He remarked in passing that the function of the marriage broker was ancient and honorable, highly approved in the Jewish community, because it made practical the necessary without hindering joy. Moreover, his own parents had been brought together by a matchmaker. They had made, if not a financially profitable marriage—since neither had possessed any worldly goods to speak of—at least a successful one in the sense of their everlasting devotion to each other. Salzman listened in embarrassed surprise, sensing a sort of apology. Later, however, he experienced a glow of pride in his work, an emotion that had left him years ago, and he heartily approved of Finkle.

The two went to their business. Leo had led Salzman to the only clear place in the room, a table near a window that overlooked the lamplit city. He seated himself at the matchmaker's side but facing him, attempting by an act of will to suppress the unpleasant tickle in his throat. Salzman eagerly unstrapped his portfolio and removed a loose rubber band from a thin packet of much-handled cards. As he flipped through them, a gesture and sound that physically hurt Leo, the student pretended not to see and gazed steadfastly out the window. Although it was still February, winter was on its last legs, signs of which he had for the first time in years begun to notice. He now observed the round white moon, moving high in the sky through a cloud menagerie, and watched with half-open mouth as it penetrated a huge hen, and dropped out of her like an egg laying itself. Salzman, though pretending through eyeglasses he had just slipped on, to be engaged in scanning the writing on the cards, stole occasional glances at the young man's distinguished face, noting with pleasure the long, severe scholar's nose, brown eyes heavy with learning, sensitive yet ascetic lips, and a certain, almost hollow quality of the dark cheeks. He gazed around at shelves upon shelves of books and let out a soft, contented sigh.

When Leo's eyes fell upon the cards, he counted six spread out in Salzman's hand.

"So few?" he asked in disappointment.

"You wouldn't believe me how much cards I got in my office," Salzman replied. "The drawers are already filled to the top, so I keep them now in a barrel, but is every girl good for a new rabbi?"

Leo blushed at this, regretting all he had revealed of himself in a curriculum vitae he had sent to Salzman. He had thought it best to acquaint him with his strict standards and specifications, but in having done so, felt he had told the marriage broker more than was absolutely necessary.

He hesitantly inquired, "Do you keep photographs of your clients on file?"

"First comes family, amount of dowry, also what kind promises," Salzman replied, unbuttoning his tight coat and settling himself in the chair. "After comes pictures, rabbi."

"Call me Mr. Finkle. I'm not yet a rabbi."

Salzman said he would, but instead called him doctor, which he changed to rabbi when Leo was not listening too attentively.

Salzman adjusted his horn-rimmed spectacles, gently cleared his throat and read in an eager voice the contents of the top card:

"Sophie P. Twenty-four years. Widow one year. No children. Educated high school and two years college. Father promises eight thousand dollars. Has wonderful wholesale business. Also real estate. On the mother's side comes teachers, also one actor. Well known on Second Avenue."

Leo gazed up in surprise. "Did you say a widow?"

"A widow don't mean spoiled, rabbi. She lived with her husband maybe four months. He was a sick boy she made a mistake to marry him."

"Marrying a widow has never entered my mind."

"This is because you have no experience. A widow, especially if she is young and healthy like this girl, is a wonderful person to marry. She will be thankful to you the rest of her life. Believe me, if I was looking now for a bride, I would marry a widow."

Leo reflected, then shook his head.

Salzman hunched his shoulders in an almost imperceptible gesture of disappointment. He placed the card down on the wooden table and began to read another:

"Lily H. High school teacher. Regular. Not a substitute. Has savings and new Dodge car. Lived in Paris one year. Father is successful dentist thirty-five years. Interested in professional man. Well Americanized family. Wonderful opportunity."

"I knew her personally," said Salzman. "I wish you could see this girl. She is a doll. Also very intelligent. All day you could talk to her about books and theyater and what not. She also knows current events."

"I don't believe you mentioned her age?"

"Her age?" Salzman said, raising his brows. "Her age is thirty-two years."

Leo said after a while, "I'm afraid that seems a little too old."

Salzman let out a laugh. "So how old are you, rabbi?"

"Twenty-seven."

"So what is the difference, tell me, between twenty-seven and thirty-two? My own wife is seven years older than me. So what did I suffer? —Nothing. If Rothschild's a daughter wants to marry you, would you say on account of her age, no?"

"Yes," Leo said dryly.

Salzman shook off the no in the yes. "Five years don't mean a thing. I give you my word that when you will live with her for one week you will forget her age. What does it mean five years—that she lived more and knows more than somebody who is younger? On this girl, God bless her, years are not wasted. Each one that it comes makes better the bargain."

"What subject does she teach in high school?"

"Languages. If you heard the way she speaks French, you will think it is music. I am in the business twenty-five years, and I recommend her with my whole heart. Believe me, I know what I'm talking, rabbi."

"What's on the next card?" Leo said abruptly.

Salzman reluctantly turned up the third card:

"Ruth K. Nineteen years. Honor student. Father offers thirteen thousand cash to the right bridegroom. He is a medical doctor. Stomach specialist with marvelous practice. Brother in law owns own garment business. Particular people."

Salzman looked as if he had read his trump card.

"Did you say nineteen?" Leo asked with interest.

"On the dot."

"Is she attractive?" He blushed. "Pretty?"

Salzman kissed his finger tips. "A little doll. On this I give you my word. Let me call the father tonight and you will see what means pretty."

But Leo was troubled. "You're sure she's that young?"

"This I am positive. The father will show you the birth certificate."

"Are you positive there isn't something wrong with her?" Leo insisted.

"Who says there is wrong?"

"I don't understand why an American girl her age should go to a marriage broker."

A smile spread over Salzman's face.

"So for the same reason you went, she comes."

Leo flushed. "I am pressed for time."

Salzman, realizing he had been tactless, quickly explained. "The father came, not her. He wants she should have the best, so he looks around himself. When we will locate the right boy he will introduce him and encourage. This makes a better marriage than if a young girl without experience takes for herself. I don't have to tell you this."

"But don't you think this young girl believes in love?" Leo spoke uneasily.

Salzman was about to guffaw but caught himself and said soberly, "Love comes with the right person, not before."

Leo parted dry lips but did not speak. Noticing that Salzman had snatched a glance at the next card, he cleverly asked, "How is her health?"

"Perfect," Salzman said, breathing with difficulty. "Of course, she is a little lame on her right foot from an auto accident that it happened to her when she was twelve years, but nobody notices on account she is so brilliant and also beautiful."

Leo got up heavily and went to the window. He felt curiously bitter and upbraided himself for having called in the marriage broker. Finally, he shook his head.

"Why not?" Salzman persisted, the pitch of his voice rising.

"Because I detest stomach specialists."

"So what do you care what is his business? After you marry her do you need him? Who says he must come every Friday night in your house?"

Ashamed of the way the talk was going, Leo dismissed Salzman, who went home with heavy, melancholy eyes.

Though he had felt only relief at the marriage broker's departure, Leo was in low spirits the next day. He explained it as arising from Salzman's failure to produce a suitable bride for him. He did not care for his type of clientele. But when Leo found himself hesitating whether to seek out another matchmaker, one more polished than Pinye, he wondered if it could be—his protestations to the contrary, and although he honored his father and mother—that he did not, in essence, care for the matchmaking institution? This thought he quickly put out of mind yet found himself still upset. All day he ran around in the woods—missed an important appointment, forgot to give out his laundry, walked out of a Broadway cafeteria without paying and had to run back with the ticket in his hand; had even not recognized his landlady in the street when she passed with a friend and courteously called out, "A good evening to you, Doctor Finkle." By nightfall, however, he had regained sufficient calm to sink his nose into a book and there found peace from his thoughts.

Almost at once there came a knock on the door. Before Leo could say enter, Salzman, commercial cupid, was standing in the room. His face was gray and meager, his expression hungry, and he looked as if he would expire on his feet. Yet the marriage broker managed, by some trick of the muscles, to display a broad smile.

"So good evening. I am invited?"

Leo nodded, disturbed to see him again, yet unwilling to ask the man to leave.

Beaming still, Salzman laid his portfolio on the table. "Rabbi, I got for you tonight good news."

"I've asked you not to call me rabbi. I'm still a student."

"Your worries are finished. I have for you a first-class bride."

"Leave me in peace concerning this subject." Leo pretended lack of interest.

"The world will dance at your wedding."

"Please, Mr. Salzman, no more."

"But first must come back my strength," Salzman said weakly. He fumbled with the portfolio straps and took out of the leather case an oily paper bag, from which he extracted a hard, seeded roll and a small, smoked white fish. With a quick motion of his hand he stripped the fish out of its skin and began ravenously to chew. "All day in a rush," he muttered.

Leo watched him eat.

"A sliced tomato you have maybe?" Salzman hesitantly inquired.

"No."

The marriage broker shut his eyes and ate. When he had finished he carefully cleaned up the crumbs and rolled up the remains of the fish, in the paper bag. His spectacled eyes roamed the room until he discovered, amid some piles of books, a one-burner gas stove. Lifting his hat he humbly asked, "A glass tea you got, rabbi?"

Conscience-stricken, Leo rose and brewed the tea. He served it with a chunk of lemon and two cubes of lump sugar, delighting Salzman.

After he had drunk his tea, Salzman's strength and good spirits were restored.

"So tell me, rabbi," he said amiably, "you considered some more the three clients I mentioned yesterday?"

"There was no need to consider."

"Why not?"

"None of them suits me."

"What then suits you?"

Leo let it pass because he could give only a confused answer.

Without waiting for a reply, Salzman asked, "You remember this girl I talked to you—the high school teacher?"

"Age thirty-two?"

But, surprisingly, Salzman's face lit in a smile. "Age twenty-nine."

Leo shot him a look. "Reduced from thirty-two?"

"A mistake," Salzman avowed. "I talked today

with the dentist. He took me to his safety deposit box and showed me the birth certificate. She was twenty-nine years last August. They made her a party in the mountains where she went for her vacation. When her father spoke to me the first time I forgot to write the age and I told you thirty-two, but now I remember this was a different client, a widow."

"The same one you told me about? I thought she was twenty-four?"

"A different. Am I responsible that the world is filled with widows?"

"No, but I'm not interested in them, nor for that matter, in school teachers."

Salzman pulled his clasped hands to his breast. Looking at the ceiling he devoutly exclaimed, "Yiddishe kinder, what can I say to somebody that he is not interested in high school teachers? So what then you are interested?"

Leo flushed but controlled himself.

"In what else will you be interested," Salzman went on, "if you not interested in this fine girl that she speaks four languages and has personally in the bank ten thousand dollars? Also her father guarantees further twelve thousand. Also she has a new car, wonderful clothes, talks on all subjects, and she will give you a first-class home and children. How near do we come in life to paradise?"

"If she's so wonderful, why wasn't she married ten years ago?"

"Why?" said Salzman with a heavy laugh. "—Why? Because she is *partikiler*. That is why. She wants the *best*."

Leo was silent, amused at how he had entangled himself. But Salzman had aroused his interest in Lily H., and he began seriously to consider calling on her. When the marriage broker observed how intently Leo's mind was at work on the facts he had supplied, he felt certain they would soon come to an agreement.

Late Saturday afternoon, conscious of Salzman, Leo Finkle walked with Lily Hirschorn along Riverside Drive. He walked briskly and erectly, wearing with distinction the black fedora he had that morning taken with trepidation out of the dusty hat box on his closet shelf, and the heavy black Saturday coat he had thoroughly whisked clean. Leo also owned a walking stick, a present from a distant relative, but quickly put temptation aside and did not use it.

Lily, petite and not unpretty, had on something signifying the approach of spring. She was au courant, animatedly, with all sorts of subjects, and he weighed her words and found her surprisingly sound—score another for Salzman, whom he uneasily sensed to be somewhere around, hiding perhaps high in a tree along the street, flashing the lady signals with a pocket mirror; or perhaps a cloven-hoofed Pan, piping nuptial ditties as he danced his invisible way before them, strewing wild buds on the wall and purple grapes in their path, symbolizing fruit of a union, though there was of course still none.

Lily startled Leo by remarking, "I was thinking of Mr. Salzman, a curious figure, wouldn't you say?"

Not certain what to answer, he nodded.

She bravely went on, blushing. "I for one am grateful for his introducing us. Aren't you?"

He courteously replied, "I am."

"I mean," she said with a little laugh—and it was all in good taste, or at least gave the effect of being not in bad—"do you mind that we came together so?"

He was not displeased with her honesty, recognizing that she meant to set the relationship aright, and understanding that it took a certain amount of experience in life, and courage, to want to do it quite that way. One had to have some sort of past to make that kind of beginning.

He said that he did not mind. Salzman's function was traditional and honorable—valuable for what it might achieve, which, he pointed out, was frequently nothing.

Lily agreed with a sigh. They walked on for a while and she said after a long silence, again with a nervous laugh, "Would you mind if I asked you something a little bit personal? Frankly, I find the subject fascinating." Although Leo shrugged, she went on half embarrassedly, "How was it that you came to your calling? I mean was it a sudden passionate inspiration?"

Leo, after a time, slowly replied, "I was always interested in the Law."

"You saw revealed in it the presence of the Highest?"

He nodded and changed the subject. "I understand that you spent a little time in Paris, Miss Hirschorn?"

"Oh, did Mr. Salzman tell you, Rabbi Finkle?" Leo winced but she went on, "It was ages ago and almost forgotten. I remember I had to return for my sister's wedding."

And Lily would not be put off. "When," she asked in a trembly voice, "did you become enamored of God?"

He stared at her. Then it came to him that she was talking not about Leo Finkle, but of a total stranger, some mystical figure, perhaps even passionate prophet that Salzman had dreamed up for her—no relation to the living or dead. Leo trembled with rage and weakness. The trickster had obviously sold her a bill of goods, just as he had him, who'd expected to become acquainted with a young lady of twenty-nine, only to behold, the moment he laid eyes upon her strained and anxious face, a woman past thirty-five and aging rapidly. Only his self control had kept him this long in her presence.

"I am not," he said gravely, "a talented religious person," and in seeking words to go on, found himself possessed by shame and fear. "I think," he said in a strained manner, "that I came to God not because I loved Him, but because I did not."

This confession he spoke harshly because its unexpectedness shook him.

Lily wilted. Leo saw a profusion of loaves of bread go flying like ducks high over his head, not unlike the winged loaves by which he had counted himself to sleep last night. Mercifully, then, it snowed, which he would not put past Salzman's machinations.

He was infuriated with the marriage broker and swore he would throw him out of the room the minute he reappeared. But Salzman did not come that night, and when Leo's anger had subsided, an unaccountable despair grew in its place. At first he thought this was caused by his disappointment in Lily, but before long it became evident that he had involved himself with Salzman without a true knowledge of his own intent. He gradually realized—with an emptiness that seized him with six hands—that he had called in the broker to find him a bride because he was incapable of doing it himself. This terrifying insight he had derived as a result of his meeting and conversation with Lily Hirschorn. Her probing questions had somehow irritated him into revealing—to himself more than her—the true nature of his relationship to God,

and from that it had come upon him, with shocking force, that apart from his parents, he had never loved anyone. Or perhaps it went the other way, that he did not love God so well as he might, because he had not loved man. It seemed to Leo that his whole life stood starkly revealed and he saw himself for the first time as he truly was—unloved and loveless. This bitter but somehow not fully unexpected revelation brought him to a point of panic, controlled only by extraordinary effort. He covered his face with his hands and cried.

The week that followed was the worst of his life. He did not eat and lost weight. His beard darkened and grew ragged. He stopped attending seminars and almost never opened a book. He seriously considered leaving the Yeshivah, although he was deeply troubled at the thought of the loss of all his years of study—saw them like pages torn from a book, strewn over the city—and at the devastating effect of this decision upon his parents. But he had lived without knowledge of himself, and never in the Five Books[1] and all the Commentaries—mea culpa[2] —had the truth been revealed to him. He did not know where to turn, and in all this desolating loneliness there was no *to whom,* although he often thought of Lily but not once could bring himself to go downstairs and make the call. He became touchy and irritable, especially with his landlady, who asked him all manner of personal questions; on the other hand, sensing his own disagreeableness, he waylaid her on the stairs and apologized abjectly, until mortified, she ran from him. Out of this, however, he drew the consolation that he was a Jew and that a Jew suffered. But gradually, as the long and terrible week drew to a close, he regained his composure and some idea of purpose in life: to go on as planned. Although he was imperfect, the ideal was not. As for his quest for a bride, the thought of continuing afflicted him with anxiety and heartburn, yet perhaps with this new knowledge of himself he would be more successful than in the past. Perhaps love would now come to him and a bride to that love. And for this sanctified seeking who needed a Salzman?

[1] The *Megilloth:* Song of Solomon, Ruth, Lamentations. Ecclesiastes, and Esther.   [2] Through my fault.

The marriage broker, a skeleton with haunted eyes, returned that very night. He looked, withal, the picture of frustrated expectancy—as if he had steadfastly waited the week at Miss Lily Hirschorn's side for a telephone call that never came.

Casually coughing, Salzman came immediately to the point: "So how did you like her?"

Leo's anger rose and he could not refrain from chiding the matchmaker: "Why did you lie to me, Salzman?"

Salzman's pale face went dead white, the world had snowed on him.

"Did you not state that she was twenty- nine?" Leo insisted.

"I give you my word—"

"She was thirty-five, if a day. *At least* thirty-five."

"Of this don't be too sure. Her father told me—"

"Never mind. The worst of it was that you lied to her."

"How did I lie to her, tell me?"

"You told her things about me that weren't true. You made me out to be more, consequently less than I am. She had in mind a totally different person, a sort of semi-mystical Wonder Rabbi."

"All I said, you was a religious man."

"I can imagine."

Salzman sighed. "This is my weakness that I have," he confessed. "My wife says to me I shouldn't be a salesman, but when I have two fine people that they would be wonderful to be married, I am so happy that I talk too much." He smiled wanly. "This is why Salzman is a poor man."

Leo's anger left him. "Well, Salzman, I'm afraid that's all."

The marriage broker fastened hungry eyes on him.

"You don't want any more a bride?"

"I do," said Leo, "but I have decided to seek her in a different way. I am no longer interested in an arranged marriage. To be frank, I now admit the necessity of premarital love. That is, I want to be in love with the one I marry."

"Love?" said Salzman, astounded. After a moment he remarked, "For us, our love is our life, not for the ladies. In the ghetto they—"

"I know, I know," said Leo. "I've thought of it often. Love, I have said to myself, should be a by-product of living and worship rather than its own end. Yet for myself I find it necessary to establish the level of my need and fulfill it."

Salzman shrugged but answered, "Listen, rabbi, if you want love, this I can find for you also. I have such beautiful clients that you will love them the minute your eyes will see them."

Leo smiled unhappily. "I'm afraid you don't understand."

But Salzman hastily unstrapped his portfolio and withdrew a manila packet from it.

"Pictures," he said, quickly laying the envelope on the table.

Leo called after him to take the pictures away, but as if on the wings of the wind, Salzman had disappeared.

March came. Leo had returned to his regular routine. Although he felt not quite himself yet —lacked energy—he was making plans for a more active social life. Of course it would cost something, but he was an expert in cutting corners; and when there were no corners left he would make circles rounder. All the while Salzman's pictures had lain on the table, gathering dust. Occasionally as Leo sat studying, or enjoying a cup of tea, his eyes fell on the manila envelope, but he never opened it.

The days went by and no social life to speak of developed with a member of the opposite sex —it was difficult, given the circumstances of his situation. One morning Leo toiled up the stairs to his room and stared out the window at the city. Although the day was bright his view of it was dark. For some time he watched the people in the street below hurrying along and then turned with a heavy heart to his little room. On the table was the packet. With a sudden relentless gesture he tore it open. For a half-hour he stood by the table in a state of excitement, examining the photographs of the ladies Salzman had included. Finally, with a deep sigh he put them down. There were six, of varying degrees of attractiveness, but look at them long enough and they all became Lily Hirschorn: all past their prime, all starved behind bright smiles, not a true personality in the lot. Life, despite their frantic yoohooings, had passed them by; they were pictures in a brief case that stank of fish. After a while, however, as Leo attempted to return the photographs into the envelope, he found in it another, a snapshot of the type taken by a machine for a quarter. He gazed at it a moment and let out a cry.

Her face deeply moved him. Why, he could at first not say. It gave him the impression of youth—spring flowers, yet age—a sense of having been used to the bone, wasted; this came from the eyes, which were hauntingly familiar, yet absolutely strange. He had a vivid impression that he had met her before, but try as he might he could not place her although he could almost recall her name, as if he had read it in her own handwriting. No, this couldn't be; he would have remembered her. It was not, he affirmed, that she had an extraordinary beauty—no, though her face was attractive enough; it was that *something* about her moved him. Feature for feature, even some of the ladies of the photographs could do better; but she leaped forth to his heart —had *lived,* or wanted to—more than just wanted, perhaps regretted how she had lived— had somehow deeply suffered: it could be seen in the depths of those reluctant eyes, and from the way the light enclosed and shone from her, and within her, opening realms of possibility: this was her own. Her he desired. His head ached and eyes narrowed with the intensity of his gazing, then as if an obscure fog had blown up in the mind, he experienced fear of her and was aware that he had received an impression, somehow, of evil. He shuddered, saying softly, it is thus with us all. Leo brewed some tea in a small pot and sat sipping it without sugar, to calm himself. But before he had finished drinking, again with excitement he examined the face and found it good: good for Leo Finkle. Only such a one could understand him and help him seek whatever he was seeking. She might, perhaps, love him. How she had happened to be among the discards in Salzman's barrel he could never guess, but he knew he must urgently go find her.

Leo rushed downstairs, grabbed up the Bronx telephone book, and searched for Salzman's home address. He was not listed, nor was his office. Neither was he in the Manhattan book. But Leo remembered having written down the address on a slip of paper after he had read Salzman's advertisement in the "personals" column of the *Forward.* He ran up to his room and tore through his papers, without luck. It was exasperating. Just when he needed the match-

maker he was nowhere to be found. Fortunately Leo remembered to look in his wallet. There on a card he found his name written and a Bronx address. No phone number was listed, the reason—Leo now recalled—he had originally communicated with Salzman by letter. He got on his coat, put a hat on over his skull cap and hurried to the subway station. All the way to the far end of the Bronx he sat on the edge of his seat. He was more than once tempted to take out the picture and see if the girl's face was as he remembered it, but he refrained, allowing the snapshot to remain in his inside coat pocket, content to have her so close. When the train pulled into the station he was waiting at the door and bolted out. He quickly located the street Salzman had advertised.

The building he sought was less than a block from the subway, but it was not an office building, nor even a loft, nor a store in which one could rent office space. It was a very old tenement house. Leo found Salzman's name in pencil on a soiled tag under the bell and climbed three dark flights to his apartment. When he knocked, the door was opened by a thin, asthmatic, gray-haired woman, in felt slippers.

"Yes?" she said, expecting nothing. She listened without listening. He could have sworn he had seen her, too, before but knew it was an illusion.

"Salzman does he live here? Pinye Salzman," he said, "the matchmaker?"

She stared at him a long minute. "Of course."

He felt embarrassed. "Is he in?"

"No." Her mouth, though left open, offered nothing more.

"The matter is urgent. Can you tell me where his office is?"

"In the air." She pointed upward.

"You mean he has no office?" Leo asked.

"In his socks."

He peered into the apartment. It was sunless and dingy, one large room divided by a half-open curtain, beyond which he could see a sagging metal bed. The near side of a room was crowded with rickety chairs, old bureaus, a three-legged table, racks of cooking utensils, and all the apparatus of a kitchen. But there was no sign of Salzman or his magic barrel, probably also a figment of the imagination. An odor of frying fish made Leo weak to the knees.

"Where is he?" he insisted. "I've got to see your husband."

At length she answered, "So who knows where he is? Every time he thinks a new thought he runs to a different place. Go home, he will find you."

"Tell him Leo Finkle."

She gave no sign she had heard.

He walked downstairs, depressed.

But Salzman, breathless, stood waiting at his door.

Leo was astounded and overjoyed. "How did you get here before me?"

"I rushed."

"Come inside."

They entered. Leo fixed tea, and a sardine sandwich for Salzman. As they were drinking he reached behind him for the packet of pictures and handed them to the marriage broker.

Salzman put down his glass and said expectantly, "You found somebody you like?"

"Not among these."

The marriage broker turned away.

"Here is the one I want." Leo held forth the snapshot.

Salzman slipped on his glasses and took the picture into his trembling hand. He turned ghastly and let out a groan.

"What's the matter?" cried Leo.

"Excuse me. Was an accident this picture. She isn't for you."

Salzman frantically shoved the manila packet into his portfolio. He thrust the snapshot into his pocket and fled down the stairs.

Leo, after momentary paralysis, gave chase and cornered the marriage broker in the vestibule. The landlady made hysterical outcries but neither of them listened.

"Give me back the picture, Salzman."

"No." The pain in his eyes was terrible.

"Tell me who she is then."

"This I can't tell you. Excuse me."

He made to depart, but Leo, forgetting himself, seized the matchmaker by his tight coat and shook him frenziedly.

"Please," sighed Salzman. "*Please.*"

Leo ashamedly let him go. "Tell me who she is," he begged. "It's very important for me to know."

"She is not for you. She is a wild one—wild, without shame. This is not a bride for a rabbi."

"What do you mean wild?"

"Like an animal. Like a dog. For her to be poor was a sin. This is why to me she is dead now."

"In God's name, what do you mean?"

"Her I can't introduce to you," Salzman cried.

"Why are you so excited?"

"Why, he asks," Salzman said, bursting into tears. "This is my baby, my Stella, she should burn in hell."

Leo hurried up to bed and hid under the covers. Under the covers he thought his life was through. Although he soon fell asleep he could not sleep her out of his mind. He woke, beating his breast. Though he prayed to be rid of her, his prayers went unanswered. Through days of torment he endlessly struggled not to love her; fearing success, he escaped it. He then concluded to convert her to goodness, himself to God. The idea alternately nauseated and exalted him.

He perhaps did not know that he had come to a final decision until he encountered Salzman in a Broadway cafeteria. He was sitting alone at a rear table, sucking the bony remains of a fish. The marriage broker appeared haggard, and transparent to the point of vanishing.

Salzman looked up at first without recognizing him. Leo had grown a pointed beard and his eyes were weighted with wisdom.

"Salzman," he said, "love has at last come to my heart."

"Who can love from a picture?" mocked the marriage broker.

"It is not impossible."

"If you can love her, then you can love anybody. Let me show you some new clients that they just sent me their photographs. One is a little doll."

"Just her I want," Leo murmured.

"Don't be a fool, doctor. Don't bother with her."

"Put me in touch with her, Salzman," Leo said humbly. "Perhaps I can be of service."

Salzman had stopped eating and Leo understood with emotion that it was now arranged.

Leaving the cafeteria, he was, however, afflicted by a tormenting suspicion that Salzman had planned it all to happen this way.

Leo was informed by letter that she would meet him on a certain corner, and she was there one spring night, waiting under a street lamp. He appeared, carrying a small bouquet of violets and rosebuds. Stella stood by the lamp post, smoking. She wore white with red shoes, which fitted his expectations, although in a troubled moment he had imagined the dress red, and only the shoes white. She waited uneasily and shyly. From afar he saw that her eyes—clearly her father's—were filled with desperate innocence. He pictured, in her, his own redemption. Violins and lit candles revolved in the sky. Leo ran forward with flowers outthrust.

Around the corner, Salzman, leaning against a wall, chanted prayers for the dead.

The Lottery

SHIRLEY JACKSON
1919–1965

Although this story was published before the appearance of what has come to be known as the literature of the absurd,* nevertheless the temptation to read "The Lottery" as part of this literary movement is compelling. In discussing the military draft lottery** Max Lerner says, "It is a game in which a third of the players are bound to lose, another third to win and the in-between third sentenced for a spell to uncertainty. I am speaking of the lottery drawing which pulled all 366 possible birthdays out of a big jar in a random sequence that decided the draft future of over 800,000 young Americans." And then Lerner adds a philosophical note: "We go through life on the assumption that it makes some sort of rational sense, but constantly we have to face the element of the absurd in it. To all the absurdities of the human condition the young men must now add this wild absurdity of having their fate decided by a random drawing of a birthdate which was accidental to start with." Lerner's comments serve as an appropriate way of identifying Jackson's "The Lottery" with the literature of the absurd.

The morning of June 27th was clear and sunny, with the fresh warmth of a full-summer day; the flowers were blossoming profusely and the grass was richly green. The people of the village began to gather in the square, between the post office and the bank, around ten o'clock; in some towns there were so many people that the lottery took two days and had to be started on June 26th, but in this village, where there were only about three hundred people, the whole lottery took less than two hours, so it could begin at ten o'clock in the morning and still be through in time to allow the villagers to get home for noon dinner.

The children assembled first, of course. School was recently over for the summer, and the feeling of liberty sat uneasily on most of them; they tended to gather together quietly for a while before they broke into boisterous play, and their talk was still of the classroom and the teacher, of books and reprimands. Bobby Martin had already stuffed his pockets full of stones, and the other boys soon followed his example, selecting the smoothest and roundest stones; Bobby and Harry Jones and Dickie Delacroix—the villagers pronounced this name "Dellacroy"—eventually made a great pile of stones in one corner of the square and guarded it against the raids of the other boys. The girls stood aside, talking among themselves, looking over their shoulders at the boys, and the very small children rolled in the dust or clung to the hands of their older brothers or sisters.

Soon the men began to gather, surveying their own children, speaking of planting and rain, tractors and taxes. They stood together, away from the pile of stones in the corner, and their jokes were quiet and they smiled rather than laughed. The women, wearing faded house

* For a definition and discussion of the literature of the absurd, see Esslin's essay, "The Absurdity of the Absurd," (p. 882) which is the Introduction to his book, *The Theatre of the Absurd*, New York: Doubleday and Co., 1961. See also the headnote to Camus, "The Guest" (p. 174); to Sartre, "The Wall" (p. 186); and to Frisch, "Biedermann and the Firebugs" (p. 709). These two stories and the play are identified with the literature of the absurd as is Kafka's story, "A Hunger Artist" (p. 181).
** *Miami Herald*, December 5, 1969.

dresses and sweaters, came shortly after their menfolk. They greeted one another and exchanged bits of gossip as they went to join their husbands. Soon the women, standing by their husbands, began to call to their children, and the children came reluctantly, having to be called four or five times. Bobby Martin ducked under his mother's grasping hand and ran, laughing, back to the pile of stones. His father spoke up sharply, and Bobby came quickly and took his place between his father and his oldest brother.

The lottery was conducted—as were the square dances, the teen-age club, the Halloween program—by Mr. Summers, who had time and energy to devote to civic activities. He was a round-faced, jovial man and he ran the coal business, and people were sorry for him, because he had no children and his wife was a scold. When he arrived in the square, carrying a black wooden box, there was a murmur of conversation among the villagers, and he waved and called, "Little late today, folks." The postmaster, Mr. Graves, followed him, carrying a three-legged stool, and the stool was put in the center of the square and Mr. Summers set the black box down on it. The villagers kept their distance, leaving a space between themselves and the stool, and when Mr. Summers said, "Some of you fellows want to give me a hand?" there was a hesitation before two men, Mr. Martin and his oldest son, Baxter, came forward to hold the box steady on the stool while Mr. Summers stirred up the papers inside it.

The original paraphernalia for the lottery had been lost long ago, and the black box now resting on the stool had been put into use even before Old Man Warner, the oldest man in town, had been born. Mr. Summers spoke frequently to the villagers about making a new box, but no one liked to upset even as much tradition as there was represented by the black box. There was a story that the present box had been made with some pieces of the box that had preceded it, the one that had been constructed when the first people settled down to make a village here. Every year, after the lottery, Mr. Summers began talking again about a new box, but every year the subject was allowed to fade off without anything's being done. The black box grew shabbier each year; by now it was no longer completely black but splintered badly along one side to show the original wood color, and in some places faded or stained.

Mr. Martin and his oldest son, Baxter, held the black box securely on the stool until Mr. Summers had stirred the papers thoroughly with his hand. Because so much of the ritual had been forgotten or discarded, Mr. Summers had been successful in having slips of paper substituted for the chips of wood that had been used for generations. Chips of wood, Mr. Summers had argued, had been all very well when the village was tiny, but now that the population was more than three hundred and likely to keep on growing, it was necessary to use something that would fit more easily into the black box. The night before the lottery, Mr. Summers and Mr. Graves made up the slips of paper and put them in the box, and it was then taken to the safe of Mr. Summers' coal company and locked up until Mr. Summers was ready to take it to the square next morning. The rest of the year, the box was put away, sometimes one place, sometimes another: it had spent one year in Mr. Graves's barn and another year underfoot in the post office, and sometimes it was set on a shelf in the Martin grocery and left there.

There was a great deal of fussing to be done before Mr. Summers declared the lottery open. There were the lists to make up—of heads of families, heads of households in each family, members of each household in each family. There was the proper swearing-in of Mr. Summers by the postmaster, as the official of the lottery; at one time, some people remembered, there had been a recital of some sort, performed by the official of the lottery, a perfunctory, tuneless chant that had been rattled off duly each year; some people believed that the official of the lottery used to stand just so when he said or sang it, others believed that he was supposed to walk among the people, but years and years ago this part of the ritual had been allowed to lapse. There had been, also, a ritual salute, which the official of the lottery had had to use in addressing each person who came up to draw from the box, but this also changed with time, until now it was felt necessary only for the official to speak to each person approaching. Mr. Summers was very good at all this; in his clean white shirt and blue jeans, with one hand resting carelessly on the black box, he seemed very proper and important as he talked interminably to Mr. Graves and the Martins.

Just as Mr. Summers finally left off talking and turned to the assembled villagers, Mrs. Hutchinson came hurriedly along the path to the square, her sweater thrown over her shoulders, and slid into place in the back of the crowd. "Clean forgot what day it was," she said to Mrs. Delacroix, who stood next to her, and they both laughed softly. "Thought my old man was out back stacking wood," Mrs. Hutchinson went on, "and then I looked out the window and the kids was gone, and then I remembered it was the twenty-seventh and came a-running." She dried her hands on her apron, and Mrs. Delacroix said, "You're in time though. They're still talking away up there."

Mrs. Hutchinson craned her neck to see through the crowd and found her husband and children standing near the front. She tapped Mrs. Delacroix on the arm as a farewell and began to make her way through the crowd. The people separated good-humoredly to let her through; two or three people said, in voices just loud enough to be heard across the crowd, "Here comes your Missus, Hutchinson," and "Bill, she made it after all." Mrs. Hutchinson reached her husband, and Mr. Summers, who had been waiting, said cheerfully, "Thought we were going to have to get on without you, Tessie." Mrs. Hutchinson said, grinning, "Wouldn't have me leave m'dishes in the sink, now, would you, Joe?" and soft laughter ran through the crowd as the people stirred back into position after Mrs. Hutchinson's arrival.

"Well, now," Mr. Summers said soberly, "guess we better get started, get this over with, so's we can go back to work. Anybody ain't here?"

"Dunbar," several people said, "Dunbar, Dunbar."

Mr. Summers consulted his list. "Clyde Dunbar," he said. "That's right. He's broke his leg, hasn't he. Who's drawing for him?"

"Me, I guess," a woman said, and Mr. Summers turned to look at her. "Wife draws for her husband," Mr. Summers said. "Don't you have a grown boy to do it for you, Janey?" Although Mr. Summers and everyone else in the village knew the answer perfectly well, it was the busi-

ness of the official of the lottery to ask such questions formally. Mr. Summers waited with an expression of polite interest while Mrs. Dunbar answered.

"Horace's not but sixteen yet," Mrs. Dunbar said regretfully. "Guess I gotta fill in for the old man this year."

"Right," Mr. Summers said. He made a note on the list he was holding. Then he asked, "Watson boy drawing this year?"

A tall boy in the crowd raised his hand. "Here," he said. "I'm drawing for m'mother and me." He blinked his eyes nervously and ducked his head as several voices in the crowd said things like "Good fellow, Jack," and "Glad to see your mother's got a man to do it."

"Well," Mr. Summers said, "guess that's everyone. Old Man Warner make it?"

"Here," a voice said, and Mr. Summers nodded.

A sudden hush fell on the crowd as Mr. Summers cleared his throat and looked at the list. "All ready?" he called. "Now, I'll read the names—heads of families first—and the men come up and take a paper out of the box. Keep the paper folded in your hand without looking at it until everyone has had a turn. Everything clear?"

The people had done it so many times that they only half listened to the directions; most of them were quiet, wetting their lips, not looking around. Then Mr. Summers raised one hand high and said, "Adams." A man disengaged himself from the crowd and came forward. "Hi, Steve," Mr. Summers said, and Mr. Adams said, "Hi, Joe." They grinned at one another humorlessly and nervously. Then Mr. Adams reached into the black box and took out a folded paper. He held it firmly by one corner as he turned and went hastily back to his place in the crowd, where he stood a little apart from his family, not looking down at his hand.

"Allen," Mr. Summers said. "Anderson . . . Bentham."

"Seems like there's no time at all between lotteries any more," Mrs. Delacroix said to Mrs. Graves in the back row. "Seems like we got through with the last one only last week."

"Time sure goes fast," Mrs. Graves said.

"Clark. . . . Delacroix."

"There goes my old man." Mrs. Delacroix

said. She held her breath while her husband went forward.

"Dunbar," Mr. Summers said, and Mrs. Dunbar went steadily to the box while one of the women said, "Go on, Janey," and another said, "There she goes."

"We're next," Mrs. Graves said. She watched while Mr. Graves came around from the side of the box, greeted Mr. Summers gravely, and selected a slip of paper from the box. By now, all through the crowd there were men holding the small folded papers in their large hands, turning them over and over nervously. Mrs. Dunbar and her two sons stood together, Mrs. Dunbar holding the slip of paper.

"Harburt. . . . Hutchinson."

"Get up there, Bill," Mrs. Hutchinson said, and the people near her laughed.

"Jones."

"They do say," Mr. Adams said to Old Man Warner, who stood next to him, "that over in the north village they're talking of giving up the lottery."

Old Man Warner snorted. "Pack of crazy fools," he said. "Listening to the young folks, nothing's good enough for *them*. Next thing you know, they'll be wanting to go back to living in caves, nobody work any more, live *that* way for a while. Used to be a saying about 'Lottery in June, corn be heavy soon.' First thing you know, we'd all be eating stewed chickweed and acorns. There's *always* been a lottery," he added petulantly. "Bad enough to see young Joe Summers up there joking with everybody."

"Some places have already quit lotteries," Mrs. Adams said.

"Nothing but trouble in *that*," Old Man Warner said stoutly. "Pack of young fools."

"Martin." And Bobby Martin watched his father go forward. "Overdyke. . . . Percy."

"I wish they'd hurry," Mrs. Dunbar said to her older son. "I wish they'd hurry."

"They're almost through," her son said.

"You get ready to run tell Dad," Mrs. Dunbar said.

Mr. Summers called his own name and then stepped forward precisely and selected a slip from the box. Then he called, "Warner."

"Seventy-seventh year I been in the lottery," Old Man Warner said as he went through the crowd. "Seventy-seventh time."

"Watson." The tall boy came awkwardly through the crowd. Someone said, "Don't be nervous, Jack," and Mr. Summers said, "Take your time, son."

"Zanini."

After that, there was a long pause, a breathless pause, until Mr. Summers, holding his slip of paper in the air, said, "All right, fellows." For a minute, no one moved and then all the slips of paper were opened. Suddenly, all the women began to speak at once, saying, "Who is it?" "Who's got it?" "Is it the Dunbars?" "Is it the Watsons?" Then the voices began to say, "It's Hutchinson. It's Bill." "Bill Hutchinson's got it."

"Go tell your father," Mrs. Dunbar said to her older son.

People began to look around to see the Hutchinsons. Bill Hutchinson was standing quiet, staring down at the paper in his hand. Suddenly, Tessie Hutchinson shouted to Mr. Summers, "You didn't give him time enough to take any paper he wanted. I saw you. It wasn't fair!"

"Be a good sport, Tessie," Mrs. Delacroix called, and Mrs. Graves said, "All of us took the same chance."

"Shut up, Tessie." Bill Hutchinson said.

"Well, everybody," Mr. Summers said, "that was done pretty fast, and now we've got to be hurrying a little more to get done in time." He consulted his next list. "Bill," he said, "you draw for the Hutchinson family. You got any other households in the Hutchinsons?"

"There's Don and Eva," Mrs. Hutchinson yelled. "Make *them* take their chance!"

"Daughters draw with their husbands' families, Tessie," Mr. Summers said gently. "You know that as well as anyone else."

"It wasn't *fair*," Tessie said.

"I guess not, Joe," Bill Hutchinson said regretfully. "My daughter draws with her husband's family, that's only fair. And I've got no other family except the kids."

"Then, as far as drawing for families is concerned, it's you," Mr. Summers said in explanation, "and as far as drawing for households is concerned, that's you, too. Right?"

"Right," Bill Hutchinson said.

"How many kids, Bill?" Mr. Summers asked formally.

"Three," Bill Hutchinson said. "There's Bill, Jr., and Nancy, and little Dave. And Tessie and me."

"All right, then," Mr. Summers said. "Harry, you got their tickets back?"

Mr. Graves nodded and held up the slips of paper. "Put them in the box, then," Mr. Summers directed. "Take Bill's and put it in."

"I think we ought to start over," Mrs. Hutchinson said, as quietly as she could. "I tell you it wasn't *fair*. You didn't give him time enough to choose. Everybody saw that."

Mr. Graves had selected the five slips and put them in the box, and he dropped all the papers but those onto the ground, where the breeze caught them and lifted them off.

"Listen, everybody," Mrs. Hutchinson was saying to the people around her.

"Ready, Bill?" Mr. Summers asked, and Bill Hutchinson, with one quick glance around at his wife and children, nodded.

"Remember," Mr. Summers said, "take the slips and keep them folded until each person has taken one. Harry, you help little Dave." Mr. Graves took the hand of the little boy, who came willingly with him up to the box. "Take a paper out of the box, Davy," Mr. Summers said. Davy put his hand into the box and laughed. "Take just *one* paper," Mr. Summers said. "Harry, you hold it for him." Mr. Graves took the child's hand and removed the folded paper from the tight fist and held it while little Dave stood next to him and looked up at him wonderingly.

"Nancy next," Mr. Summers said. Nancy was twelve, and her school friends breathed heavily as she went forward, switching her skirt, and took a slip daintily from the box. "Bill, Jr.," Mr. Summers said, and Billy, his face red and his feet overlarge, nearly knocked the box over as he got a paper out. "Tessie," Mr. Summers said. She hesitated for a minute, looking around defiantly, and then set her lips and went up to the box. She snatched a paper out and held it behind her.

"Bill," Mr. Summers said, and Bill Hutchinson reached into the box and felt around, bringing his hand out at last with the slip of paper in it.

The crowd was quiet. A girl whispered. "I hope it's not Nancy," and the sound of the whisper reached the edges of the crowd.

"It's not the way it used to be," Old Man Warner said clearly. "People ain't the way they used to be."

"All right," Mr. Summers said. "Open the papers. Harry, you open little Dave's."

Mr. Graves opened the slip of paper and there was a general sigh through the crowd as he held it up and everyone could see that it was blank. Nancy and Bill, Jr., opened theirs at the same time, and both beamed and laughed, turning around to the crowd and holding their slips of paper above their heads.

"Tessie," Mr. Summers said. There was a pause, and then Mr. Summers looked at Bill Hutchinson, and Bill unfolded his paper and showed it. It was blank.

"It's Tessie," Mr. Summers said, and his voice was hushed. "Show us her paper, Bill."

Bill Hutchinson went over to his wife and forced the slip of paper out of her hand. It had a black spot on it, the black spot Mr. Summers had made the night before with the heavy pencil in the coal-company office. Bill Hutchinson held it up, and there was a stir in the crowd.

"All right, folks," Mr. Summers said. "Let's finish quickly."

Although the villagers had forgotten the ritual and lost the original black box, they still remembered to use stones. The pile of stones the boys had made earlier was ready; there were stones on the ground with the blowing scraps of paper that had come out of the box. Mrs. Delacroix selected a stone so large she had to pick it up with both hands and turned to Mrs. Dunbar. "Come on," she said. "Hurry up."

Mrs. Dunbar had small stones in both hands, and she said, gasping for breath, "I can't run at all. You'll have to go ahead and I'll catch up with you."

The children had stones already, and someone gave little Davy Hutchinson a few pebbles.

Tessie Hutchinson was in the center of a cleared space by now, and she held her hands out desperately as the villagers moved in on her. "It isn't fair," she said. A stone hit her on the side of the head.

Old Man Warner was saying, "Come on, come on, everyone." Steve Adams was in the front of the crowd of villagers, with Mrs. Graves beside him.

"It isn't fair, it isn't right," Mrs. Hutchinson screamed, and then they were upon her.

The Guest

ALBERT CAMUS
1913–1960

This story is identified with the contemporary literature of the absurd, and that absurdity Camus defines: "A world that can be explained by reasoning, however faulty, is a familiar world. But in a universe that is suddenly deprived of illusions and of light, man feels a stranger. His is an irremediable exile, because he is deprived of memories of a lost homeland as much as he lacks the hope of a promised land to come. This divorce between man and his life, the actor and his setting, truly constitutes the feeling of Absurdity." (Quoted by Esslin, p. 882.) Yet Camus could say, "I am not a painter of the Absurd. . . . What else have I done but reflect on an idea I found current in the streets? That I nourished this idea, like the rest of my generation, goes without saying. But I have kept my distance in order to treat it and determine its logic. . . ." By keeping his distance he finally found hope, not despair, by exploring life as it is instead of relying on rationalizations about the meaning of the universe. "Who," he said as he accepted the Nobel Prize (p. 823), ". . . could expect of [the writer] ready-made solutions and moral codes? Truth is mysterious, elusive, ever to be won anew. . . . Consequently, what writer would dare, with a clear conscience, to become a preacher of virtue? As for me, I must say once more that I am far from all that."

We are warned, then, that the use of conventional morals acceptable to society at least in theory if not always in practice will not properly interpret Camus's story, or for that matter his celebrated short novel *The Stranger* (1942) which can be read as a satire on judging conduct by inflexible moral standards. An understanding of Daru's compassion and of society's irrationality in "The Guest," rather than a rationalized ethic, will bring us closer to Camus's meaning. The title, "The Guest," is significant: Why does Daru treat a murderer as he does? Camus's fiction is often called enigmatic, and for the reader who contemplates no ethic other than his own, it probably is. To help dissipate the mystery see Camus's "Nobel Prize Acceptance Speech," p. 823, and Esslin's "The Absurdity of the Absurd," p. 882.

The schoolmaster was watching the two men climb toward him. One was on horseback, the other on foot. They had not yet tackled the abrupt rise leading to the schoolhouse built on the hillside. They were toiling onward, making slow progress in the snow, among the stones, on the vast expanse of the high, deserted plateau. From time to time the horses stumbled. Without hearing anything yet, he could see the breath issuing from the horse's nostrils. One of the men, at least, knew the region. They were following the trail although it had disappeared days ago under a layer of dirty white snow. The schoolmaster calculated that it would take them half an hour to get onto the hill. It was cold; he went back into the school to get a sweater.

He crossed the empty, frigid classroom. On the blackboard the four rivers of France, drawn with four different colored chalks, had been flowing toward their estuaries for the past three days. Snow had suddenly fallen in mid-October after eight months of drought without the transition of rain, and the twenty pupils, more or less, who lived in the villages scattered over the plateau had stopped coming. With fair weather they would return. Daru now heated only the single room that was his lodging, adjoining the classroom and giving also onto the plateau to the east. Like the class windows, his window looked to the south too. On that side the school was a few kilometers from the point where the plateau began to slope toward the south. In clear weather could be seen the purple mass of the mountain range where the gap opened onto the desert.

Somewhat warmed, Daru returned to the window from which he had first seen the two men. They were no longer visible. Hence they must have tackled the rise. The sky was not so dark, for the snow had stopped falling during the night. The morning had opened with a dirty light which had scarcely become brighter as the ceiling of clouds lifted. At two in the afternoon it seemed as if the day were merely beginning. But still this was better than those three days when the thick snow was falling amidst unbroken darkness with little gusts of wind that rattled the double door of the classroom. Then Daru had spent long hours in his room, leaving it only to go to the shed and feed the chickens or get some coal. Fortunately the delivery truck from Tadjid, the nearest village to the north, had brought his supplies two days before the blizzard. It would return in forty-eight hours.

Besides, he had enough to resist a siege, for the little room was cluttered with bags of wheat that the administration left as a stock to distribute to those of his pupils whose families had suffered from the drought. Actually they had all been victims because they were all poor. Every day Daru would distribute a ration to the children. They had missed it, he knew, during these bad days. Possibly one of the fathers or big brothers would come this afternoon and he could supply them with grain. It was just a matter of carrying them over to the next harvest. Now shiploads of wheat were arriving from France and the worst was over. But it would be hard to forget that poverty, that army of ragged ghosts wandering in the sunlight, the plateaus burned to a cinder month after month, the earth shriveled up little by little, literally scorched, every stone bursting into dust under one's foot. The sheep had died then by thousands and even a few men, here and there, sometimes without anyone's knowing.

In contrast with such poverty, he who lived almost like a monk in his remote schoolhouse, nonetheless satisfied with the little he had and with the rough life, had felt like a lord with his whitewashed walls, his narrow couch, his unpainted shelves, his well, and his weekly provision of water and food. And suddenly this snow, without warning, without the foretaste of rain. This is the way the region was, cruel to live in, even without men—who didn't help matters either. But Daru had been born here. Everywhere else, he felt exiled.

He stepped out onto the terrace in front of the schoolhouse. The two men were now halfway up the slope. He recognized the horseman as Balducci, the old gendarme he had known for a long time. Balducci was holding on the end of a rope an Arab who was walking behind him with hands bound and head lowered. The gendarme waved a greeting to which Daru did not reply, lost as he was in contemplation of the Arab dressed in a faded blue jellaba, his feet in sandals but covered with socks of heavy raw wool, his head surmounted by a narrow, short *chèche*. They were approaching. Balducci was holding back his horse in order not to hurt the Arab, and the group was advancing slowly.

Within earshot, Balducci shouted: "One hour to do the three kilometers from El Ameur!" Daru did not answer. Short and square in his thick sweater, he watched them climb. Not once had the Arab raised his head. "Hello," said Daru when they got up onto the terrace. "Come in and warm up." Balducci painfully got down from his horse without letting go the rope. From under his bristling mustache he smiled at the schoolmaster. His little dark eyes, deep-set under a tanned forehead, and his mouth surrounded with wrinkles made him look attentive and studious. Daru took the bridle, led the horse to the shed, and came back to the two men, who were now waiting for him in the school. He led them into his room. "I am going to heat up the classroom," he said. "We'll be more comfortable there." When he entered the room again, Balducci was on the couch. He had undone the rope tying him to the Arab, who had squatted near the stove. His hands still bound, the *chèche* pushed back on his head, he was looking toward the window. At first Daru noticed only his huge lips, fat, smooth, almost Negroid; yet his nose was straight, his eyes were dark and full of fever. The *chèche* revealed an obstinate forehead and, under the weathered skin now rather discolored by the cold, the whole face had a restless and rebellious look that struck Daru when the Arab, turning his face toward him, looked him straight in the eyes. "Go into the other room," said the schoolmaster, "and I'll make you some mint tea." "Thanks," Balducci said. "What a chore! How I long for retirement." And addressing his prisoner in Arabic: "Come on, you." The Arab got up and, slowly, holding his bound wrists in front of him, went into the classroom.

With the tea, Daru brought a chair. But Balducci was already enthroned on the nearest pupil's desk and the Arab had squatted against the teacher's platform facing the stove, which stood between the desk and the window. When he held out the glass of tea to the prisoner, Daru hesitated at the sight of his bound hands. "He might perhaps be untied." "Sure," said Balducci. "That was for the trip." He started to get to his feet. But Daru, setting the glass on the floor, had knelt beside the Arab. Without saying anything, the Arab watched him with his feverish eyes. Once his hands were free, he rubbed his swollen wrists against each other, took the glass of tea, and sucked up the burning liquid in swift little sips.

"Good," said Daru. "And where are you headed?"

Balducci withdrew his mustache from the tea. "Here, son."

"Odd pupils! And you're spending the night?"

"No. I'm going back to El Ameur. And you will deliver this fellow to Tinguit. He is expected at police headquarters."

Balducci was looking at Daru with a friendly little smile.

"What's this story?" asked the schoolmaster. "Are you pulling my leg?"

"No, son. Those are the orders."

"The orders? I'm not . . ." Daru hesitated, not wanting to hurt the old Corsican. "I mean, that's not my job."

"What! What's the meaning of that? In wartime people do all kinds of jobs."

"Then I'll wait for the declaration of war!" Balducci nodded.

"O.K. But the orders exist and they concern you too. Things are brewing, it appears. There is talk of a forthcoming revolt. We are mobilized, in a way."

Daru still had his obstinate look.

"Listen, son," Balducci said. "I like you and you must understand. There's only a dozen of us at El Ameur to patrol throughout the whole territory of a small department and I must get back in a hurry. I was told to hand this guy over to you and return without delay. He couldn't be kept there. His village was beginning to stir; they wanted to take him back. You must take him to Tinguit tomorrow before the day is over. Twenty kilometers shouldn't faze a husky fellow like you. After that, all will be over. You'll come back to your pupils and your comfortable life."

Behind the wall the horse could be heard snorting and pawing the earth. Daru was looking out the window. Decidedly, the weather was clearing and the light was increasing over the snowy plateau. When all the snow was melted, the sun would take over again and once more would burn the fields of stone. For days, still, the unchanging sky would shed its dry light on the solitary expanse where nothing had any connection with man.

"After all," he said, turning around toward Balducci, "what did he do?" And, before the gendarme had opened his mouth, he asked: "Does he speak French?"

"No, not a word. We had been looking for him for a month, but they were hiding him. He killed his cousin."

"Is he against us?"

"I don't think so. But you can never be sure."

"Why did he kill?"

"A family squabble, I think. One owed the other grain, it seems. It's not at all clear. In short, he killed his cousin with a billhook. You know, like a sheep, *kreezk!*"

Balducci made the gesture of drawing a blade across his throat and the Arab, his attention attracted, watched him with a sort of anxiety. Daru felt a sudden wrath against the man, against all men with their rotten spite, their tireless hates, their blood lust.

But the kettle was singing on the stove. He served Balducci more tea, hesitated, then served the Arab again, who, a second time, drank avidly. His raised arms made the jellaba fall open and the schoolmaster saw his thin, muscular chest.

"Thanks, kid," Balducci said. "And now, I'm off."

He got up and went toward the Arab, taking a small rope from his pocket.

"What are you doing?" Daru asked dryly.

Balducci, disconcerted, showed him the rope.

"Don't bother."

The old gendarme hesitated. "It's up to you. Of course, you are armed?"

"I have my shotgun."

"Where?"

"In the trunk."

"You ought to have it near your bed."

"Why? I have nothing to fear."

"You're crazy, son. If there's an uprising, no one is safe, we're all in the same boat."

"I'll defend myself. I'll have time to see them coming."

Balducci began to laugh, then suddenly the mustache covered the white teeth.

"You'll have time? O.K. That's just what I was saying. You have always been a little cracked. That's why I like you, my son was like that."

At the same time he took out his revolver and put it on the desk.

"Keep it; I don't need two weapons from here to El Ameur."

The revolver shone against the black paint of the table. When the gendarme turned toward him, the schoolmaster caught the smell of leather and horseflesh.

"Listen, Balducci," Daru said suddenly, "every bit of this disgusts me, and first of all your fellow here. But I won't hand him over. Fight, yes, if I have to. But not that."

The old gendarme stood in front of him and looked at him severely.

"You're being a fool," he said slowly. "I don't like it either. You don't get used to putting a rope on a man even after years of it, and you're even ashamed—yes, ashamed. But you can't let them have their way."

"I won't hand him over," Daru said again.

"It's an order, son, and I repeat it."

"That's right. Repeat to them what I've said to you: I won't hand him over."

Balducci made a visible effort to reflect. He looked at the Arab and at Daru. At last he decided.

"No, I won't tell them anything. If you want to drop us, go ahead; I'll not denounce you. I have an order to deliver the prisoner and I'm doing so. And now you'll just sign this paper for me."

"There's no need. I'll not deny that you left him with me."

"Don't be mean with me. I know you'll tell the truth. You're from hereabouts and you are a man. But you must sign, that's the rule."

Daru opened his drawer, took out a little square bottle of purple ink, the red wooden penholder with the "sergeant-major" pen he used for making models of penmanship, and signed. The gendarme carefully folded the paper and put it into his wallet. Then he moved toward the door.

"I'll see you off," Daru said.

"No," said Balducci. "There's no use being polite. You insulted me."

He looked at the Arab, motionless in the same spot, sniffed peevishly, and turned away toward the door. "Good-by, son," he said. The door shut behind him. Balducci appeared suddenly outside the window and then disappeared. His footsteps were muffled by the snow. The horse stirred on the other side of the wall and several chickens fluttered in fright. A moment later Balducci reappeared outside the window leading the horse by the bridle. He walked toward the little rise without turning around and disappeared from sight with the horse following him. A big stone could be heard bouncing down. Daru walked back toward the prisoner, who, without stirring, never took his eyes off him. "Wait," the schoolmaster said in Arabic and went toward the bedroom. As he was going through the door, he had a second thought, went to the desk, took the revolver, and stuck it in his pocket. Then, without looking back, he went into his room.

For some time he lay on his couch watching the sky gradually close over, listening to the silence. It was this silence that had seemed painful to him during the first days here, after the war. He had requested a post in the little town at the base of the foothills separating the upper plateaus from the desert. There, rocky walls, green and black to the north, pink and lavender to the south, marked the frontier of eternal summer. He had been named to a post farther north, on the plateau itself. In the beginning, the solitude and the silence had been hard for him on these wastelands peopled only by stones. Occasionally, furrows suggested cultivation, but they had been dug to uncover a certain kind of stone good for building. The only plowing here was to harvest rocks. Elsewhere a thin layer of soil accumulated in the hollows would be scraped out to enrich paltry village gardens. This is the way it was: bare rock covered three quarters of the region. Towns sprang up, flourished, then disappeared; men came by, loved one another or fought bitterly, then died. No one in this desert, neither he nor his guest, mattered. And yet, outside this desert neither of them, Daru knew, could have really lived.

When he got up, no noise came from the

classroom. He was amazed at the unmixed joy he derived from the mere thought that the Arab might have fled and that he would be alone with no decision to make. But the prisoner was there. He had merely stretched out between the stove and the desk. With eyes open, he was staring at the ceiling. In that position, his thick lips were particularly noticeable, giving him a pouting look. "Come," said Daru. The Arab got up and followed him. In the bedroom, the schoolmaster pointed to a chair near the table under the window. The Arab sat down without taking his eyes off Daru.

"Are you hungry?"

"Yes," the prisoner said.

Daru set the table for two. He took flour and oil, shaped a cake in a frying-pan, and lighted the little stove that functioned on bottled gas. While the cake was cooling, he went out to the shed to get cheese, eggs, dates, and condensed milk. When the cake was done he set it on the window sill to cool, heated some condensed milk diluted with water, and beat up the eggs into an omelette. In one of his motions he knocked against the revolver stuck in his right pocket. He set the bowl down, went into the classroom, and put the revolver in his desk drawer. When he came back to the room, night was falling. He put on the light and served the Arab. "Eat," he said. The Arab took a piece of the cake, lifted it eagerly to his mouth, and stopped short.

"And you?" he asked.

"After you. I'll eat too."

The thick lips opened slightly. The Arab hesitated, then bit into the cake determinedly.

The meal over, the Arab looked at the schoolmaster. "Are you the judge?"

"No, I'm simply keeping you until tomorrow."

"Why do you eat with me?"

"I'm hungry."

The Arab fell silent. Daru got up and went out. He brought back a folding bed from the shed, set it up between the table and the stove, perpendicular to his own bed. From a large suitcase which, upright in a corner, served as a shelf for papers, he took two blankets and arranged them on the camp bed. Then he stopped, felt useless, and sat down on his bed. There was nothing more to do or to get ready. He had to look at this man. He looked at him, therefore, trying to imagine his face bursting with rage.

He couldn't do so. He could see nothing but the dark yet shining eyes and the animal mouth.

"Why did you kill him?" he asked in a voice whose hostile tone surprised him.

The Arab looked away.

"He ran away. I ran after him."

He raised his eyes to Daru again and they were full of a sort of woeful interrogation. "Now what will they do to me?"

"Are you afraid?"

He stiffened, turning his eyes away.

"Are you sorry?"

The Arab stared at him openmouthed. Obviously he did not understand. Daru's annoyance was growing. At the same time he felt awkward and self-conscious with his big body wedged between the two beds.

"Lie down there," he said impatiently. "That's your bed."

The Arab didn't move. He called to Daru:

"Tell me!"

The schoolmaster looked at him.

"Is the gendarme coming back tomorrow?"

"I don't know."

"Are you coming with us?"

"I don't know. Why?"

The prisoner got up and stretched out on top of the blankets, his feet toward the window. The light from the electric bulb shone straight into his eyes and he closed them at once.

"Why?" Daru repeated, standing beside the bed.

The Arab opened his eyes under the blinding light and looked at him, trying not to blink.

"Come with us," he said.

In the middle of the night, Daru was still not asleep. He had gone to bed after undressing completely; he generally slept naked. But when he suddenly realized that he had nothing on, he hesitated. He felt vulnerable and the temptation came to him to put his clothes back on. Then he shrugged his shoulders; after all, he wasn't a child and, if need be, he could break his adversary in two. From his bed he could observe him, lying on his back, still motionless with his eyes closed under the harsh light. When Daru turned out the light, the darkness seemed to coagulate all of a sudden. Little by little, the night came back to life in the window where the starless sky was stirring gently. The schoolmaster soon made out the body lying at his feet.

The Arab did not move, but his eyes seemed open. A faint wind was prowling around the schoolhouse. Perhaps it would drive away the clouds and the sun would reappear.

During the night the wind increased. The hens fluttered a little and then were silent. The Arab turned over on his side with his back to Daru, who thought he heard him moan. Then he listened for his guest's breathing, become heavier and more regular. He listened to that breath so close to him and mused without being able to go to sleep. In this room where he had been sleeping alone for a year, this presence bothered him. But it bothered him also by imposing on him a sort of brotherhood he knew well but refused to accept in the present circumstances. Men who share the same rooms, soldiers or prisoners, develop a strange alliance as if, having cast off their armor with their clothing, they fraternized every evening, over and above their differences, in the ancient community of dream and fatigue. But Daru shook himself; he didn't like such musings, and it was essential to sleep.

A little later, however, when the Arab stirred slightly, the schoolmaster was still not asleep. When the prisoner made a second move, he stiffened, on the alert. The Arab was lifting himself slowly on his arms with almost the motion of a sleepwalker. Seated upright in bed, he waited motionless without turning his head toward Daru, as if he were listening attentively. Daru did not stir; it had just occurred to him that the revolver was still in the drawer of his desk. It was better to act at once. Yet he continued to observe the prisoner, who, with the same slithery motion, put his feet on the ground, waited again, then began to stand up slowly. Daru was about to call out to him when the Arab began to walk, in a quite natural but extraordinarily silent way. He was heading toward the door at the end of the room that opened into the shed. He lifted the latch with precaution and went out, pushing the door behind him but without shutting it. Daru had not stirred. "He is running away," he merely thought. "Good riddance!" Yet he listened attentively. The hens were not fluttering; the guest must be on the plateau. A faint sound of water reached him, and he didn't know what it was until the Arab again stood framed in the doorway, closed the door carefully, and came back to bed with-

out a sound. Then Daru turned his back on him and fell asleep. Still later he seemed, from the depths of his sleep, to hear furtive steps around the schoolhouse. "I'm dreaming! I'm dreaming!" he repeated to himself. And he went on sleeping.

When he awoke, the sky was clear; the loose window let in a cold, pure air. The Arab was asleep, hunched up under the blankets now, his mouth open, utterly relaxed. But when Daru shook him, he started dreadfully, staring at Daru with wild eyes as if he had never seen him and such a frightened expression that the schoolmaster stepped back. "Don't be afraid. It's me. You must eat." The Arab nodded his head and said yes. Calm had returned to his face, but his expression was vacant and listless.

The coffee was ready. They drank it seated together on the folding bed as they munched their pieces of the cake. Then Daru led the Arab under the shed and showed him the faucet where he washed. He went back into the room, folded the blankets and the bed, made his own bed and put the room in order. Then he went through the classroom and out onto the terrace. The sun was already rising in the blue sky; a soft, bright light was bathing the deserted plateau. On the ridge the snow was melting in spots. The stones were about to reappear. Crouched on the edge of the plateau, the schoolmaster looked at the deserted expanse. He thought of Balducci. He had hurt him, for he had sent him off in a way as if he didn't want to be associated with him. He could still hear the gendarme's farewell and, without knowing why, he felt strangely empty and vulnerable. At that moment, from the other side of the schoolhouse, the prisoner coughed. Daru listened to him almost despite himself and then, furious, threw a pebble that whistled through the air before sinking into the snow. That man's stupid crime revolted him, but to hand him over was contrary to honor. Merely thinking of it made him smart with humiliation. And he cursed at one and the same time his own people who had sent him this Arab and the Arab too who had dared to kill and not managed to get away. Daru got up, walked in a circle on the terrace, waited motionless, and then went back into the schoolhouse.

The Arab, leaning over the cement floor of the shed, was washing his teeth with two fingers.

Daru looked at him and said: "Come." He went back into the room ahead of the prisoner. He slipped a hunting-jacket on over his sweater and put on walking-shoes. Standing, he waited until the Arab had put on his *chèche* and sandals. They went into the classroom and the schoolmaster pointed to the exit, saying: "Go ahead." The fellow didn't budge. "I'm coming," said Daru. The Arab went out. Daru went back into the room and made a package of pieces of rusk, dates, and sugar. In the classroom, before going out, he hesitated a second in front of his desk, then crossed the threshold and locked the door. "That's the way," he said. He started toward the east, followed by the prisoner. But, a short distance from the schoolhouse, he thought he heard a slight sound behind them. He retraced his steps and examined the surroundings of the house; there was no one there. The Arab watched him without seeming to understand. "Come on," said Daru.

They walked for an hour and rested beside a sharp peak of limestone. The snow was melting faster and faster and the sun was drinking up the puddles at once, rapidly cleaning the plateau, which gradually dried and vibrated like the air itself. When they resumed walking, the ground rang under their feet. From time to time a bird rent the space in front of them with a joyful cry. Daru breathed in deeply the fresh morning light. He felt a sort of rapture before the vast familiar expanse, now almost entirely yellow under its dome of blue sky. They walked an hour more, descending toward the south. They reached a level height made up of crumbly rocks. From there on, the plateau sloped down, eastward, toward a low plain where there were a few spindly trees and, to the south, toward outcroppings of rock that gave the landscape a chaotic look.

Daru surveyed the two directions. There was nothing but the sky on the horizon. Not a man could be seen. He turned toward the Arab, who was looking at him blankly. Daru held out the package to him. "Take it," he said. "There are dates, bread, and sugar. You can hold out for two days. Here are a thousand francs too." The Arab took the package and the money but kept his full hands at chest level as if he didn't know what to do with what was being given him. "Now look," the schoolmaster said as he pointed in the direction of the east, "there's the way

to Tinguit. You have a two-hour walk. At Tinguit you'll find the administration and the police. They are expecting you." The Arab looked toward the east, still holding the package and the money against his chest. Daru took his elbow and turned him rather roughly toward the south. At the foot of the height on which they stood could be seen a faint path. "That's the trail across the plateau. In a day's walk from here you'll find pasturelands and the first nomads. They'll take you in and shelter you according to their law." The Arab had now turned toward Daru and a sort of panic was visible in his expression. "Listen," he said. Daru shook his head: "No, be quiet. Now I'm leaving you." He turned his back on him, took two long steps in the direction of the school, looked hesitantly at the motionless Arab, and started off again. For a few minutes he heard nothing but his own step resounding on the cold ground and did not turn his head. A moment later, however, he turned around. The Arab was still there on the edge of the hill, his arms hanging now, and he was looking at the schoolmaster. Daru felt something rise in his throat. But he swore with impatience, waved vaguely, and started off again. He had already gone some distance when he again stopped and looked. There was no longer anyone on the hill.

Daru hesitated. The sun was now rather high in the sky and was beginning to beat down on his head. The schoolmaster retraced his steps, at first somewhat uncertainly, then with decision. When he reached the little hill, he was bathed in sweat. He climbed it as fast as he could and stopped, out of breath, at the top. The rock-fields to the south stood out sharply against the blue sky, but on the plain to the east a steamy heat was already rising. And in that slight haze, Daru, with heavy heart, made out the Arab walking slowly on the road to prison.

A little later, standing before the window of the classroom, the schoolmaster was watching the clear light bathing the whole surface of the plateau, but he hardly saw it. Behind him on the blackboard, among the winding French rivers, sprawled the clumsily chalked-up words he had just read: "You handed over our brother. You will pay for this." Daru looked at the sky, the plateau, and, beyond, the invisible lands stretching all the way to the sea. In this vast landscape he had loved so much, he was alone.

A Hunger Artist

FRANZ KAFKA
1883–1924

This story is an allegory in the sense that the symbols which are embodied in characters, events, and natural objects represent ideas. In most allegory, as for example John Bunyan's *The Pilgrim's Progress,* 1678, the symbols can be translated into equivalents which remain constant throughout the story. But in "A Hunger Artist" Kafka has used his symbols to produce more than one level of meaning, each one used to dramatize a different theme. Is the story "about" the artist in an alien society, "about" religion—or possibly both and even more? On the problem of reading Kafka, Albert Camus offers some help: "The whole art of Kafka consists in forcing the reader to reread. . . . Sometimes there is a double possibility of interpretation. . . . This is what the author wanted. But it would be wrong to try to interpret everything in Kafka in detail. A symbol is always in general and, however precise its translation, an artist can restore to it only its movement: there is no word-for-word rendering" (*The Myth of Sisyphus,* 1955).

During these last decades the interest in professional fasting has markedly diminished. It used to pay very well to stage such great performances under one's own management, but today that is quite impossible. We live in a different world now. At one time the whole town took a lively interest in the hunger artist; from day to day of his fast the excitement mounted; everybody wanted to see him at least once a day; there were people who bought season tickets for the last few days and sat from morning till night in front of his small barred cage; even in the nighttime there were visiting hours, when the whole effect was heightened by torch flares; on fine days the cage was set out in the open air, and then it was the children's special treat to see the hunger artist; for their elders he was often just a joke that happened to be in fashion, but the children stood open-mouthed, holding each other's hands for greater security, marveling at

him as he sat there pallid in black tights, with his ribs sticking out so prominently, not even on a seat but down among straw on the ground, sometimes giving a courteous nod, answering questions with a constrained smile, or perhaps stretching an arm through the bars so that one might feel how thin it was, and then again withdrawing deep into himself, paying no attention to anyone or anything, not even to the all-important striking of the clock that was the only piece of furniture in his cage, but merely staring into vacancy with half-shut eyes, now and then taking a sip from a tiny glass of water to moisten his lips.

Besides casual onlookers there were also relays of permanent watchers selected by the public, usually butchers, strangely enough, and it was their task to watch the hunger artist day and night, three of them at a time, in case he should have some secret recourse to nourishment. This was nothing but a formality, instituted to reassure the masses, for the initiates knew well enough that during his fast the artist would never in any circumstances, not even under forcible compulsion, swallow the smallest morsel of food; the honor of his profession forbade it. Not every watcher, of course, was capable of understanding this, there were often groups of night watchers who were very lax in carrying out their duties and deliberately huddled together in a retired corner to play cards with great absorption, obviously intending to give the hunger artist the chance of a little refreshment, which they supposed he could draw from some private hoard. Nothing annoyed the artist more than such watchers; they made him miserable; they made his fast seem unendurable; sometimes he mastered his feebleness sufficiently to sing during their watch for as long as he could keep going, to show them how unjust their suspicions were. But that was of little use; they only wondered at his cleverness in being able to fill his mouth even while singing. Much more to his taste were the watchers who sat close up to the bars, who were not content with the dim night lighting of the hall but focused him in the full glare of the electric pocket torch given them by the impresario. The harsh light did not trouble him at all. In any case he could never sleep properly, and he could always drowse a little, whatever the light, at any hour, even when the hall was thronged with noisy onlookers. He was quite happy at the prospect of spending a sleepless night with such watchers; he was ready to exchange jokes with them, to tell them stories out of his nomadic life, anything at all to keep them awake and demonstrate to them again that he had no eatables in his cage and that he was fasting as not one of them could fast. But his happiest moment was when the morning came and an enormous breakfast was brought them, at his expense, on which they flung themselves with the keen appetite of healthy men after a weary night of wakefulness. Of course there were people who argued that this breakfast was an unfair attempt to bribe the watchers, but that was going rather too far, and when they were invited to take on a night's vigil without a breakfast, merely for the sake of the cause, they made themselves scarce, although they stuck stubbornly to their suspicions.

Such suspicions, anyhow, were a necessary accompaniment to the profession of fasting. No one could possibly watch the hunger artist continuously, day and night, and so no one could produce first-hand evidence that the fast had really been rigorous and continuous; only the artist himself could know that; he was therefore bound to be the sole completely satisfied spectator of his own fast. Yet for other reasons he was never satisfied; it was not perhaps mere fasting that had brought him to such skeleton thinness that many people had regretfully to keep away from his exhibitions, because the sight of him was too much for them, perhaps it was dissatisfaction with himself that had worn him down. For he alone knew, what no other initiate knew, how easy it was to fast. It was the easiest thing in the world. He made no secret of this, yet people did not believe him; at the best they set him down as modest, most of them, however, thought he was out for publicity or else was some kind of cheat who found it easy to fast because he had discovered a way of making it easy, and then had the impudence to admit the fact, more or less. He had to put up with all that, and in the course of time had got used to it, but his inner dissatisfaction always rankled, and never yet, after any term of fasting —this must be granted to his credit—had he left the cage of his own free will. The longest period of fasting was fixed by his impresario at forty days, beyond that term he was not allowed to

go, not even in great cities, and there was good reason for it, too. Experience had proved that for about forty days the interest of the public could be stimulated by a steadily increasing pressure of advertisement, but after that the town began to lose interest, sympathetic support began notably to fall off; there were of course local variations as between one town and another or one country and another, but as a general rule forty days marked the limit. So on the fortieth day the flower-bedecked cage was opened, enthusiastic spectators filled the hall, a military band played, two doctors entered the cage to measure the results of the fast, which were announced through a megaphone, and finally two young ladies appeared, blissful at having been selected for the honor, to help the hunger artist down the few steps leading to a small table on which was spread a carefully chosen invalid repast. And at this very moment the artist always turned stubborn. True, he would entrust his bony arms to the outstretched helping hands of the ladies bending over him, but stand up he would not. Why stop fasting at this particular moment, after forty days of it? He had held out for a long time, an illimitably long time; why stop now, when he was in his best fasting form, or rather, not quite in his best fasting form? Why should he be cheated of the fame he would get for fasting longer, for being not only the record hunger artist of all time, which presumably he was already, but for beating his own record by a performance beyond human imagination, since he felt that there were no limits to his capacity for fasting? His public pretended to admire him so much, why should it have so little patience with him; if he could endure fasting longer, why shouldn't the public endure it? Besides, he was tired, he was comfortable sitting in the straw, and now he was supposed to lift himself to his full height and go down to a meal the very thought of which gave him a nausea that only the presence of the ladies kept him from betraying, and even that with an effort. And he looked up into the eyes of the ladies who were apparently so friendly and in reality so cruel, and shook his head, which felt too heavy on its strengthless neck. But then there happened yet again what always happened. The impresario came forward, without a word—for the band made speech impossible

—lifted his arms in the air above the artist, as if inviting Heaven to look down upon its creature here in the straw, this suffering martyr, which indeed he was, although in quite another sense; grasped him round the emaciated waist, with exaggerated caution, so that the frail condition he was in might be appreciated; and committed him to the care of the blenching ladies, not without secretly giving him a shaking so that his legs and body tottered and swayed. The artist now submitted completely; his head lolled on his breast as if it had landed there by chance; his body was hollowed out; his legs in a spasm of self-preservation clung close to each other at the knees, yet scraped on the ground as if it were not really solid ground, as if they were only trying to find solid ground; and the whole weight of his body, a featherweight after all, relapsed onto one of the ladies, who, looking round for help and panting a little —this post of honor was not at all what she had expected it to be—first stretched her neck as far as she could to keep her face at least free from contact with the artist, then finding this impossible, and her more fortunate companion not coming to her aid but merely holding extended on her own trembling hand the little bunch of knucklebones that was the artist's, to the great delight of the spectators burst into tears and had to be replaced by an attendant who had long been stationed in readiness. Then came the food, a little of which the impresario managed to get between the artist's lips, while he sat in a kind of half-fainting trance, to the accompaniment of cheerful patter designed to distract the public's attention from the artist's condition; after that, a toast was drunk to the public, supposedly prompted by a whisper from the artist in the impresario's ear; the band confirmed it with a mighty flourish, the spectators melted away, and no one had any cause to be dissatisfied with the proceedings, no one except the hunger artist himself, he only, as always.

So he lived for many years, with small regular intervals of recuperation, in visible glory, honored by the world, yet in spite of that troubled in spirit, and all the more troubled because no one would take his trouble seriously. What comfort could he possibly need? What more could he possibly wish for? And if some good-natured person, feeling sorry for him, tried to console him by pointing out that his melancholy was probably caused by fasting, it could happen, especially when he had been fasting for some time, that he reacted with an outburst of fury and to the general alarm began to shake the bars of his cage like a wild animal. Yet the impresario had a way of punishing these outbreaks which he rather enjoyed putting into operation. He would apologize publicly for the artist's behavior, which was only to be excused, he admitted, because of the irritability caused by fasting; a condition hardly to be understood by well-fed people; then by natural transition he went on to mention the artist's equally incomprehensible boast that he could fast for much longer than he was doing; he praised the high ambition, the good will, the great self-denial undoubtedly implicit in such a statement; and then quite simply countered it by bringing out photographs, which were also on sale to the public, showing the artist on the fortieth day of a fast lying in bed almost dead from exhaustion. This perversion of the truth, familiar to the artist though it was, always unnerved him afresh and proved too much for him. What was a consequence of the premature ending of his fast was here presented as the cause of it! To fight against this lack of understanding, against a whole world of non-understanding, was impossible. Time and again in good faith he stood by the bars listening to the impresario, but as soon as the photographs appeared he always let go and sank with a groan back on to his straw, and the reassured public could once more come close and gaze at him.

A few years later when the witnesses of such scenes called them to mind, they often failed to understand themselves at all. For meanwhile the aforementioned change in public interest had set in; it seemed to happen almost overnight; there may have been profound causes for it, but who was going to bother about that; at any rate the pampered hunger artist suddenly found himself deserted one fine day by the amusement seekers, who went streaming past him to other more favored attractions. For the last time the impresario hurried him over half Europe to discover whether the old interest might still survive here and there; all in vain; everywhere, as if by secret agreement, a positive revulsion from professional fasting was in evidence. Of course it could not really have sprung up so suddenly as all that, and many premonitory symptoms which had not been sufficiently remarked or suppressed during the rush and glitter of success now came retrospectively to mind, but it was now too late to take any countermeasures. Fasting would surely come into fashion again at some future date, yet that was no comfort for those living in the present. What, then, was the hunger artist to do? He had been applauded by thousands in his time and could hardly come down to showing himself in a street booth at village fairs, and as for adopting another profession, he was not only too old for that but too fanatically devoted to fasting. So he took leave of the impresario, his partner in an unparalleled career, and hired himself to a large circus; in order to spare his own feelings he avoided reading the conditions of his contract.

A large circus with its enormous traffic in replacing and recruiting men, animals and apparatus can always find a use for people at any time, even for a hunger artist, provided of course that he does not ask too much, and in this particular case anyhow it was not only the artist who was taken on but his famous and long-known name as well; indeed considering the peculiar nature of his performance, which was not impaired by advancing age, it could not be objected that here was an artist past his prime, no longer at the height of his professional skill, seeking a refuge in some quiet corner of a circus; on the contrary, the hunger artist averred that he could fast as well as ever, which was entirely credible; he even alleged that if he were allowed to fast as he liked, and this was at once promised him without more ado, he could astound the world by establishing a record never yet achieved, a statement which certainly provoked a smile among the other professionals, since it left out of account the change in public opinion, which the hunger artist in his zeal conveniently forgot.

He had not, however, actually lost his sense of the real situation and took it as a matter of course that he and his cage should be stationed, not in the middle of the ring as a main attraction, but outside, near the animal cages, on a site that was after all easily accessible. Large and gaily painted placards made a frame for the cage and announced what was to be seen inside it. When the public came thronging out in the intervals to see the animals, they could hardly avoid passing the hunger artist's cage and stopping there for a moment, perhaps they might even have stayed longer had not those pressing behind them in the narrow gangway, who did not understand why they should be held up on their way towards the excitements of the menagerie, made it impossible for anyone to stand gazing quietly for any length of time. And that was the reason why the hunger artist, who had of course been looking forward to these visiting hours as the main achievement of his life, began instead to shrink from them. At first he could hardly wait for the intervals; it was exhilarating to watch the crowds come streaming his way, until only too soon—not even the most obstinate self-deception, clung to almost consciously, could hold out against the fact—the conviction was borne in upon him that these people, most of them, to judge from their actions, again and again, without exception, were all on their way to the menagerie. And the first sight of them from the distance remained the best. For when they reached his cage he was at once deafened by the storm of shouting and abuse that arose from the two contending factions, which renewed themselves continuously, of those who wanted to stop and stare at him—he soon began to dislike them more than the others—not out of real interest but only out of obstinate self-assertiveness, and those who wanted to go straight on to the animals. When the first great rush was past, the stragglers came along, and these, whom nothing could have prevented from stopping to look at him as long as they had breath, raced past with long strides, hardly even glancing at him, in their haste to get to the menagerie in time. And all too rarely did it happen that he had a stroke of luck, when some father of a family fetched up before him with his children, pointed a finger at the hunger artist and explained at length what the phenomenon meant, telling stories of earlier years when he himself had watched similar but much more thrilling performances, and the children, still rather uncomprehending, since neither inside nor outside school had they been sufficiently prepared for this lesson—what did they care about fasting?—yet showed by the brightness of their intent eyes that new and better times might be coming. Perhaps, said the hunger artist to himself many a time, things would be a little better if his cage were set not quite so near the menagerie. That made it too easy for people to make their choice, to say nothing of what he suffered from the stench of the menagerie, the animals' restlessness by night, the carrying past of raw lumps of flesh for the beasts of prey, the roaring at feeding times, which depressed him continually. But he did not dare to lodge a complaint with the management; after all, he had the animals to thank for the troops of people who passed his cage, among whom there might always be one here and there to take an interest in him, and who could tell where they might seclude him if he called attention to his existence and thereby to the fact that, strictly speaking, he was only an impediment on the way to the menagerie.

A small impediment, to be sure, one that grew steadily less. People grew familiar with the strange idea that they could be expected, in times like these, to take an interest in a hunger artist, and with this familiarity the verdict went out against him. He might fast as much as he could, and he did so; but nothing could save him now, people passed him by. Just try to explain to anyone the art of fasting! Anyone who has no feeling for it cannot be made to understand it. The fine placards grew dirty and illegible, they were torn down; the little notice board telling the number of fast days achieved, which at first was changed carefully every day, had long stayed at the same figure, for after the first few weeks even this small task seemed pointless to the staff; and so the artist simply fasted on and on, as he had once dreamed of doing, and it was no trouble to him, just as he had always foretold, but no one counted the days, no one, not even the artist himself, knew what records he was already breaking, and his heart grew heavy. And when once in a time some leisurely passer-by stopped, made merry over the old figure on the board and spoke of swindling, that was in its way the stupidest lie ever invented by indifference and inborn malice, since it was not the hunger artist who was cheating; he was working honestly, but the world was cheating him of his reward.

Many more days went by, however, and that too came to an end. An overseer's eye fell on the cage one day and he asked the attendants why this perfectly good stage should be left standing there unused with dirty straw inside it; nobody knew, until one man, helped out by the notice board, remembered about the hunger artist. They poked into the straw with sticks and found him in it. "Are you still fasting?" asked the overseer. "When on earth do you mean to stop?" "Forgive me, everybody," whispered the hunger artist; only the overseer, who had his ear to the bars, understood him. "Of course," said the overseer, and tapped his forehead with a finger to let the attendants know what state the man was in, "we forgive you." "I always wanted you to admire my fasting," said the hunger artist. "We do admire it," said the overseer, affably. "But you shouldn't admire it," said the hunger artist. "Well, then we don't admire it," said the overseer, "but why shouldn't we admire it?" "Because I have to fast, I can't help it," said the hunger artist. "What a fellow you are," said the overseer, "and why can't you help it?" "Because," said the hunger artist, lifting his head a little and speaking, with his lips pursed, as if for a kiss, right into the overseer's ear, so that no syllable might be lost, "because I couldn't find the food I liked. If I had found it, believe me, I should have made no fuss and stuffed myself like you or anyone else." These were his last words, but in his dimming eyes remained the firm though no longer proud persuasion that he was still continuing to fast.

"Well, clear this out now!" said the overseer, and they buried the hunger artist, straw and all. Into the cage they put a young panther. Even the most insensitive felt it refreshing to see this wild creature leaping around the cage that had so long been dreary. The panther was all right. The food he liked was brought him without hesitation by the attendants; he seemed not even to miss his freedom; his noble body, furnished almost to the bursting point with all that it needed, seemed to carry freedom around with it too; somewhere in his jaws it seemed to lurk; and the joy of life streamed with such ardent passion from his throat that for the onlookers it was not easy to stand the shock of it. But they braced themselves, crowded round the cage, and did not want ever to move away.

The Wall

JEAN-PAUL SARTRE
1905–

Sartre's story is commonly read as a dramatization of some basic aspects of existentialism,* a theory of existence which emerged in France after World War II and helped to generate the literature of the absurd of the new lost generation. (See the headnote for Camus's "The Guest," p. 174.) Existentialism is essentially a philosophy of revolt against nineteenth-century rationalism which perceived and understood reality through the intellect. It rejects such speculation about reality and finds reality in the experience of the individual. It finds no purpose or meaning inherent in the universe, and leaves morality to the individual who must arrive at his own code through experience. As Albert Camus observes, "The fact that certain great novelists have chosen to write in terms of images rather than of arguments reveals a great deal about a certain kind of thinking common to them all, a conviction of the futility of all explanatory principles, and of the instructive message of sensory impressions." And Sartre, sometimes referred to as the High Priest of existentialism, speaking of Camus says, he "is very much at peace within disorder. Nature's obstinate blindness probably irritates him, but it comforts him as well. Its irrationality is only a negative thing. The absurd man is a humanist; he knows only the good things in the world." These two quotations put together seem to arrive at the heart of existentialism: the futility of trying to explain life through reason, and the irrationality of nature and the universe. (See Frost's "The Trial by Existence," p. 332, and "A Masque of

* The serious student who wishes to explore existentialism will find these sources helpful: Jean-Paul Sartre, *Existentialism*, New York: Philosophical Library; London: Methuen and Company, 1947. Walter Kaufmann, *Existentialism from Dostoevsky to Sartre*, Cleveland and New York: Meridian Books, 1956, pp. 287–311. Esslin's "The Absurdity of the Absurd" (p. 882) shows the influence of existentialism on drama, especially through Sartre and Albert Camus.

Reason," p. 358; and Hardy's "Hap," p. 322.)

The setting of "The Wall" is the Spanish Civil War of 1936–1939. The story belongs to Pablo Ibbieta, the narrator, who is probably the voice of Sartre. The question is, why does Pablo die differently from Tom Steinbock and Juan Mirbal? He could have probably saved his life by betraying Ramon Gris. Why does Pablo finally say, "I laughed so hard the tears came to my eyes"? The answer lies, of course, in the kind of absurd world Pablo has experienced, the kind the existentialist rejects.

They pushed us into a large white room and my eyes began to blink because the light hurt them. Then I saw a table and four fellows seated at the table, civilians, looking at some papers. The other prisoners were herded together at one end and we were obliged to cross the entire room to join them. There were several I knew, and others who must have been foreigners. The two in front of me were blond with round heads. They looked alike. I imagine they were French. The smaller one kept pulling at his trousers, out of nervousness.

This lasted about three hours. I was dog-tired and my head was empty. But the room was well-heated, which struck me as rather agreeable; we had not stopped shivering for twenty-four hours. The guards led the prisoners in one after the other in front of the table. Then the four fellows asked them their names and what they did. Most of the time that was all—or perhaps from time to time they would ask such questions as: "Did you help sabotage the munitions?" or, "Where were you on the morning of the ninth and what were you doing?" They didn't even listen to the replies, or at least they didn't seem to. They just remained silent for a moment and looked straight ahead, then they began to write. They asked Tom if it was true he had served in the International Brigade. Tom couldn't say he hadn't because of the papers they had found in his jacket. They didn't ask Juan anything, but after he told them his name, they wrote for a long while.

"It's my brother José who's the anarchist," Juan said. "You know perfectly well he's not here now. I don't belong to any party. I never did take part in politics." They didn't answer.

Then Juan said, "I didn't do anything. And I'm not going to pay for what the others did."

His lips were trembling. A guard told him to stop talking and led him away. It was my turn.

"Your name is Pablo Ibbieta?"

I said yes.

The fellow looked at his papers and said, "Where is Ramon Gris?"

"I don't know."

"You hid him in your house from the sixth to the nineteenth."

"I did not."

They continued to write for a moment and the guards led me away. In the hall, Tom and Juan were waiting between two guards. We started walking. Tom asked one of the guards, "What's the idea?" "How do you mean?" the guard asked. "Was that just the preliminary questioning, or was that the trial?" "That was the trial," the guard said. "So now what? What are they going to do with us?" The guard answered drily, "The verdict will be told you in your cell."

In reality, our cell was one of the cellars of the hospital. It was terribly cold there because it was very drafty. We had been shivering all night long and it had hardly been any better during the day. I had spent the preceding five days in a cellar in the archbishop's palace, a sort of dungeon that must have dated back to the Middle Ages. There were lots of prisoners and not much room, so they housed them just anywhere. But I was not homesick for my dungeon. I hadn't been cold there, but I had been alone, and that gets to be irritating. In the cellar I had company. Juan didn't say a word; he was afraid, and besides, he was too young to have anything to say. But Tom was a good talker and knew Spanish well.

In the cellar there were a bench and four straw mattresses. When they led us back we sat down and waited in silence. After a while Tom said, "Our goose is cooked."

"I think so too," I said. "But I don't believe they'll do anything to the kid."

Tom said, "They haven't got anything on him. He's the brother of a fellow who's fighting, and that's all."

I looked at Juan. He didn't seem to have heard.

Tom continued, "You know what they do in Saragossa? They lay the guys across the road and then they drive over them with trucks. It was a Moroccan deserter who told us that. They say it's just to save ammunition."

I said, "Well, it doesn't save gasoline."

I was irritated with Tom; he shouldn't have said that.

He went on, "There are officers walking up and down the roads with their hands in their pockets, smoking, and they see that it's done right. Do you think they'd put 'em out of their misery? Like hell they do. They just let 'em holler. Sometimes as long as an hour. The Moroccan said the first time he almost puked."

"I don't believe they do that here," I said, "unless they really are short of ammunition."

The daylight came in through four air vents and a round opening that had been cut in the ceiling, to the left, and which opened directly onto the sky. It was through this hole, which was ordinarily closed by means of a trapdoor, that they unloaded coal into the cellar. Directly under the hole, there was a big pile of coal dust; it had been intended for heating the hospital, but at the beginning of the war they had evacuated the patients and the coal had stayed there unused; it even got rained on from time to time, when they forgot to close the trapdoor.

Tom started to shiver. "God damn it," he said, "I'm shivering. There, it is starting again."

He rose and began to do gymnastic exercises. At each movement, his shirt opened and showed his white, hairy chest. He lay down on his back, lifted his legs in the air and began to do the scissors movement. I watched his big buttocks tremble. Tom was tough, but he had too much fat on him. I kept thinking that soon bullets and bayonet points would sink into that mass of tender flesh as though it were a pat of butter.

I wasn't exactly cold, but I couldn't feel my shoulders or my arms. From time to time, I had the impression that something was missing and I began to look around for my jacket. Then I would suddenly remember they hadn't given me a jacket. It was rather awkward. They had taken our clothes to give them to their own soldiers and had left us only our shirts and these cotton trousers the hospital patients wore in mid-summer. After a moment, Tom got up and sat down beside me, breathless.

"Did you get warmed up?"

"Damn it, no. But I'm all out of breath."

Around eight o'clock in the evening, a Major came in with two falangists.[1]

"What are the names of those three over there?" he asked the guard.

"Steinbock, Ibbieta and Mirbal," said the guard.

The Major put on his glasses and examined his list.

"Steinbock—Steinbock . . . Here it is. You are condemned to death. You'll be shot tomorrow morning."

He looked at his list again.

"The other two, also," he said.

"That's not possible," said Juan. "Not me."

The Major looked at him with surprise. "What's your name?"

"Juan Mirbal."

"Well, your name is here," said the Major, "and you're condemned to death."

"I didn't do anything," said Juan.

The Major shrugged his shoulders and turned toward Tom and me.

"You are both Basque?"[2]

"No, nobody's Basque."

He appeared exasperated.

"I was told there were three Basques. I'm not going to waste my time running after them. I suppose you don't want a priest?"

We didn't even answer.

Then he said, "A Belgian doctor will be around in a little while. He has permission to stay with you all night."

He gave a military salute and left.

"What did I tell you?" Tom said. "We're in for something swell."

"Yes," I said. "It's a damned shame for the kid."

I said that to be fair, but I really didn't like the kid. His face was too refined and it was disfigured by fear and suffering, which had twisted all his features. Three days ago, he was just a kid with a kind of affected manner some people like. But now he looked like an aging fairy, and I thought to myself he would never be young again, even if they let him go. It

wouldn't have been a bad thing to show him a little pity, but pity makes me sick, and besides, I couldn't stand him. He hadn't said anything more, but he had turned gray. His face and hands were gray. He sat down again and stared, round-eyed, at the ground. Tom was good-hearted and tried to take him by the arm, but the kid drew himself away violently and made an ugly face. "Leave him alone," I said quietly. "Can't you see he's going to start to bawl?" Tom obeyed regretfully. He would have liked to console the kid; that would have kept him occupied and he wouldn't have been tempted to think about himself. But it got on my nerves. I had never thought about death, for the reason that the question had never come up. But now it had come up, and there was nothing else to do but think about it.

Tom started talking. "Say, did you ever bump anybody off?" he asked me. I didn't answer. He started to explain to me that he had bumped off six fellows since August. He hadn't yet realized what we were in for, and I saw clearly he didn't *want* to realize it. I myself hadn't quite taken it in. I wondered if it hurt very much. I thought about the bullets; I imagined their fiery hail going through my body. All that was beside the real question; but I was calm, we had all night in which to realize it. After a while Tom stopped talking and I looked at him out of the corner of my eye. I saw that he, too, had turned gray and that he looked pretty miserable. I said to myself, "It's starting." It was almost dark, a dull light filtered through the air vents across the coal pile and made a big spot under the sky. Through the hole in the ceiling I could already see a star. The night was going to be clear and cold.

The door opened and two guards entered. They were followed by a blond man in a tan uniform. He greeted us.

"I'm the doctor," he said. "I've been authorized to give you any assistance you may require in these painful circumstances."

He had an agreeable, cultivated voice.

I said to him, "What are you going to do here?"

"Whatever you want me to do. I shall do everything in my power to lighten these few hours."

"Why did you come to us? There are lots of others: the hospital's full of them."

---

[1] A member of the Spanish Phalanx, a fascist organization. [2] One of a people of obscure origin inhabiting the western Pyrenees on the Bay of Biscay.

"I was sent here," he answered vaguely. "You'd probably like to smoke, wouldn't you?" he added suddenly. "I've got some cigarettes and even some cigars."

He passed around some English cigarettes and some *puros*,[3] but we refused them. I looked him straight in the eye and he appeared uncomfortable.

"You didn't come here out of compassion," I said to him. "In fact, I know who you are. I saw you with some fascists in the barracks yard the day I was arrested."

I was about to continue, when all at once something happened to me which surprised me: the presence of this doctor had suddenly ceased to interest me. Usually, when I've got hold of a man I don't let go. But somehow the desire to speak had left me. I shrugged my shoulders and turned away. A little later, I looked up and saw he was watching me with an air of curiosity. The guards had sat down on one of the mattresses. Pedro, the tall thin one, was twiddling his thumbs, while the other one shook his head occasionally to keep from falling asleep.

"Do you want some light?" Pedro suddenly asked the doctor. The other fellow nodded, "Yes." I think he was not over-intelligent, but doubtless he was not malicious. As I looked at his big, cold, blue eyes, it seemed to me the worst thing about him was his lack of imagination. Pedro went out and came back with an oil lamp which he set on the corner of the bench. It gave a poor light, but it was better than nothing; the night before we had been left in the dark. For a long while I stared at the circle of light the lamp threw on the ceiling. I was fascinated. Then, suddenly, I came to, the light circle paled, and I felt as if I were being crushed under an enormous weight. It wasn't the thought of death, and it wasn't fear; it was something anonymous. My cheeks were burning hot and my head ached.

I roused myself and looked at my two companions. Tom had his head in his hands and only the fat, white nape of his neck was visible. Juan was by far the worst off; his mouth was wide open and his nostrils were trembling. The doctor came over to him and touched him on the shoulder, as though to comfort him; but his eyes remained cold. Then I saw the Belgian slide his hand furtively down Juan's arm to his wrist. Indifferent, Juan let himself be handled. Then, as though absent-mindedly, the Belgian laid three fingers over his wrist; at the same time, he drew away somewhat and managed to turn his back to me. But I leaned over backward and saw him take out his watch and look at it a moment before relinquishing the boy's wrist. After a moment, he let the inert hand fall and went and leaned against the wall. Then, as if he had suddenly remembered something very important that had to be noted down immediately, he took a notebook from his pocket and wrote a few lines in it. "The son-of-a-bitch," I thought angrily. "He better not come and feel my pulse; I'll give him a punch in his dirty jaw."

He didn't come near me, but I felt he was looking at me. I raised my head and looked back at him. In an impersonal voice, he said, "Don't you think it's frightfully cold here?"

He looked purple with cold.

"I'm not cold," I answered him.

He kept looking at me with a hard expression. Suddenly I understood, and I lifted my hands to my face. I was covered with sweat. Here, in this cellar, in mid-winter, right in a draft, I was sweating. I ran my fingers through my hair, which was stiff with sweat; at the same time, I realized my shirt was damp and sticking to my skin. I had been streaming with perspiration for an hour, at least, and had felt nothing. But this fact hadn't escaped that Belgian swine. He had seen the drops rolling down my face and had said to himself that it showed an almost pathological terror; and he himself had felt normal and proud of it because he was cold. I wanted to get up and go punch his face in, but I had hardly started to make a move before my shame and anger had disappeared. I dropped back into the bench with indifference.

I was content to rub my neck with my handkerchief because now I felt the sweat dripping from my hair onto the nape of my neck and that was disagreeable. I soon gave up rubbing myself, however, for it didn't do any good; my handkerchief was already wringing wet and I was still sweating. My buttocks, too, were sweating, and my damp trousers stuck to the bench.

Suddenly, Juan said, "You're a doctor, aren't you?"

"Yes," said the Belgian.

"Do people suffer—very long?"

[3] A cigar.

"Oh! When . . . ? No, no," said the Belgian, in a paternal voice, "it's quickly over."

His manner was as reassuring as if he had been answering a paying patient.

"But I . . . Somebody told me—they often have to fire two volleys."

"Sometimes," said the Belgian, raising his head, "it just happens that the first volley doesn't hit any of the vital organs."

"So then they have to reload their guns and aim all over again?" Juan thought for a moment, then added hoarsely, "But that takes time!"

He was terribly afraid of suffering. He couldn't think about anything else, but that went with his age. As for me, I hardly thought about it any more and it certainly was not fear of suffering that made me perspire.

I rose and walked toward the pile of coal dust. Tom gave a start and looked at me with a look of hate. I irritated him because my shoes squeaked. I wondered if my face was as putty-colored as his. Then I noticed that he, too, was sweating. The sky was magnificent; no light at all came into our dark corner and I had only to lift my head to see the Big Bear. But it didn't look the way it had looked before. Two days ago, from my cell in the archbishop's palace, I could see a big patch of sky and each time of day brought back a different memory. In the morning, when the sky was a deep blue, and light, I thought of beaches along the Atlantic; at noon, I could see the sun, and I remembered a bar in Seville where I used to drink manzanilla[4] and eat anchovies and olives; in the afternoon, I was in the shade, and I thought of the deep shadow which covers half of the arena while the other half gleams in the sunlight: it really gave me a pang to see the whole earth reflected in the sky like that. Now, however, no matter how much I looked up in the air, the sky no longer recalled anything. I liked it better that way. I came back and sat down next to Tom. There was a long silence.

Then Tom began to talk in a low voice. He had to keep talking, otherwise he lost his way in his own thoughts. I believe he was talking to me, but he didn't look at me. No doubt he was afraid to look at me, because I was gray and sweating. We were both alike and worse than mirrors for each other. He looked at the Belgian, the only one who was alive.

"Say, do you understand? I don't."

Then I, too, began to talk in a low voice. I was watching the Belgian.

"Understand what? What's the matter?"

"Something's going to happen to us that I don't understand."

There was a strange odor about Tom. It seemed to me that I was more sensitive to odors than ordinarily. With a sneer, I said, "You'll understand, later."

"That's not so sure," he said stubbornly. "I'm willing to be courageous, but at least I ought to know . . . Listen, they're going to take us out into the courtyard. All right. The fellows will be standing in line in front of us. How many of them will there be?"

"Oh, I don't know. Five, or eight. Not more."

"That's enough. Let's say there'll be eight of them. Somebody will shout 'Shoulder arms!' and I'll see all eight rifles aimed at me. I'm sure I'm going to feel like going through the wall. I'll push against the wall as hard as I can with my back, and the wall won't give in. The way it is in a nightmare. . . . I can imagine all that. Ah, if you only knew how well I can imagine it!"

"Skip it!" I said. "I can imagine it too."

"It must hurt like the devil. You know they aim at your eyes and mouth so as to disfigure you," he added maliciously. "I can feel the wounds already. For the last hour I've been having pains in my head and neck. Not real pains —it's worse still: They're the pains I'll feel to-morrow morning. And after that, then what?"

I understood perfectly well what he meant, but I didn't want to seem to understand. As for the pains, I, too, felt them all through my body, like a lot of little gashes. I couldn't get used to them, but I was like him, I didn't think they were very important.

"After that," I said roughly, "you'll be eating daisies."

He started talking to himself, not taking his eyes off the Belgian, who didn't seem to be listening to him. I knew what he had come for, and that what we were thinking didn't interest him. He had come to look at our bodies, our bodies which were dying alive.

"It's like in a nightmare," said Tom. "You want to think of something, you keep having the impression you've got it, that you're going to un-

---

[4] A pale aromatic dry Spanish sherry wine.

derstand, and then it slips away from you, it eludes you and it's gone again. I say to myself, afterwards, there won't be anything. But I don't really understand what that means. There are moments when I almost do—and then it's gone again. I start to think of the pains, the bullets, the noise of the shooting. I am a materialist, I swear it; and I'm not going crazy, either. But there's something wrong. I see my own corpse. That's not hard, but it's *I* who see it, with *my* eyes. I'll have to get to the point where I think —where I think I won't see anything more. I won't hear anything more, and the world will go on for the others. We're not made to think that way, Pablo. Believe me, I've already stayed awake all night waiting for something. But this is not the same thing. This will grab us from behind, Pablo, and we won't be ready for it."

"Shut up," I said. "Do you want me to call a father confessor?"

He didn't answer. I had already noticed that he had a tendency to prophesy and call me "Pablo" in a kind of pale voice. I didn't like that very much, but it seems all the Irish are like that. I had a vague impression that he smelled of urine. Actually, I didn't like Tom very much, and I didn't see why, just because we were going to die together, I should like him any better. There are certain fellows with whom it would be different—with Ramon Gris, for instance. But between Tom and Juan, I felt alone. In fact, I liked it better that way. With Ramon I might have grown soft. But I felt terribly hard at that moment, and I wanted to stay hard.

Tom kept on muttering, in a kind of absent-minded way. He was certainly talking to keep from thinking. Naturally, I agreed with him, and I could have said everything he was saying. It's not *natural* to die. And since I was going to die, nothing seemed natural any more: neither the coal pile, nor the bench, nor Pedro's dirty old face. Only it was disagreeable for me to think the same things Tom thought. And I knew perfectly well that all night long, within five minutes of each other, we would keep on thinking things at the same time, sweating or shivering at the same time. I looked at him sideways and, for the first time, he seemed strange to me. He had death written on his face. My pride was wounded. For twenty-four hours I had lived side by side with Tom, I had listened to him, I had talked to him, and I knew we had nothing in

common. And now we were as alike as twin brothers, simply because we were going to die together. Tom took my hand without looking at me.

"Pablo, I wonder . . . I wonder if it's true that we just cease to exist."

I drew my hand away.

"Look between your feet, you dirty dog."

There was a puddle between his feet and water was dripping from his trousers.

"What's the matter?" he said, frightened.

"You're wetting your pants," I said to him.

"It's not true," he said furiously. "I can't be . . . I don't feel anything."

The Belgian had come closer to him. With an air of false concern, he asked, "Aren't you feeling well?"

Tom didn't answer. The Belgian looked at the puddle without comment.

"I don't know what that is," Tom said savagely, "but I'm not afraid. I swear to you, I'm not afraid."

The Belgian made no answer. Tom rose and went to a corner. He came back, buttoning his fly, and sat down, without a word. The Belgian was taking notes.

We were watching the doctor. Juan was watching him too. All three of us were watching him because he was alive. He had the gestures of a living person, the interests of a living person; he was shivering in this cellar the way living people shiver; he had an obedient, well-fed body. We, on the other hand, didn't feel our bodies any more—not the same way, in any case. I felt like touching my trousers, but I didn't dare to. I looked at the Belgian, well-planted on his two legs, master of his muscles—and able to plan for tomorrow. We were like three shadows deprived of blood; we were watching him and sucking his life like vampires.

Finally he came over to Juan. Was he going to lay his hand on the nape of Juan's neck for some professional reason, or had he obeyed a charitable impulse? If he had acted out of charity, it was the one and only time during the whole night. He fondled Juan's head and the nape of his neck. The kid let him do it, without taking his eyes off him. Then, suddenly, he took hold of the doctor's hand and looked at it in a funny way. He held the Belgian's hand between his own two hands and there was nothing pleasing about them, those two gray paws squeezing that fat red hand. I sensed what was going to happen and Tom must have sensed it, too. But all the Belgian saw was emotion, and he smiled paternally. After a moment, the kid lifted the big red paw to his mouth and started to bite it. The Belgian drew back quickly and stumbled toward the wall. For a second, he looked at us with horror. He must have suddenly understood that we were not men like himself. I began to laugh, and one of the guards started up. The other had fallen asleep with his eyes wide open, showing only the whites.

I felt tired and over-excited at the same time. I didn't want to think any more about what was going to happen at dawn—about death. It didn't make sense, and I never got beyond just words, or emptiness. But whenever I tried to think about something else I saw the barrels of rifles aimed at me. I must have lived through my execution twenty times in succession; one time I thought it was the real thing; I must have dozed off for a moment. They were dragging me toward the wall and I was resisting; I was imploring their pardon. I woke with a start and looked at the Belgian. I was afraid I had cried out in my sleep. But he was smoothing his mustache; he hadn't noticed anything. If I had wanted to, I believe I could have slept for a while. I had been awake for the last forty-eight hours, and I was worn out. But I didn't want to lose two hours of life. They would have had to come and wake me at dawn. I would have followed them, drunk with sleep, and I would have gone off without so much as "Gosh!" I didn't want it that way, I didn't want to die like an animal. I wanted to understand. Besides, I was afraid of having nightmares. I got up and began to walk up and down and, so as to think about something else, I began to think about my past life. Memories crowded in on me, helter-skelter. Some were good and some were bad—at least that was how I had thought of them *before*. There were faces and happenings. I saw the face of a little *novillero*[5] who had gotten himself horned during the *Feria*,[6] in Valencia. I saw the face of one of my uncles, of Ramon Gris. I remembered all kinds of things that had happened: how I had been on strike for three

months in 1926, and had almost died of hunger. I recalled a night I had spent on a bench in Granada; I hadn't eaten for three days, I was nearly wild, I didn't want to give up the sponge. I had to smile. With what eagerness I had run after happiness, and women, and liberty! And to what end? I had wanted to liberate Spain, I admired Py Margall, I had belonged to the anarchist movement, I had spoken at public meetings. I took everything as seriously as if I had been immortal.

At that time I had the impression that I had my whole life before me, and I thought to myself, "It's all a god-damned lie." Now it wasn't worth anything because it was finished. I wondered how I had ever been able to go out and have a good time with girls. I wouldn't have lifted my little finger if I had ever imagined that I would die like this. I saw my life before me, finished, closed, like a bag, and yet what was inside was not finished. For a moment I tried to appraise it. I would have liked to say to myself, "It's been a good life." But it couldn't be appraised, it was only an outline. I had spent my life writing checks on eternity, and had understood nothing. Now, I didn't miss anything. There were a lot of things I might have missed: the taste of manzanilla, for instance, or the swims I used to take in summer in a little creek near Cadiz. But death had taken the charm out of everything.

Suddenly the Belgian had a wonderful idea.

"My friends," he said to us, "if you want me to—and providing the military authorities give their consent—I could undertake to deliver a word or some token from you to your loved ones. . . ."

Tom growled, "I haven't got anybody."

I didn't answer. Tom waited for a moment, then he looked at me with curiosity. "Aren't you going to send any message to Concha?"

"No."

I hated that sort of sentimental conspiracy. Of course, it was my fault, since I had mentioned Concha the night before, and I should have kept my mouth shut. I had been with her for a year. Even as late as last night, I would have cut my arm off with a hatchet just to see her again for five minutes. That was why I had mentioned her. I couldn't help it. Now I didn't care any more about seeing her. I hadn't anything more to say to her. I didn't even want to hold her in my

[5] An aspiring bullfighter who has not yet attained the rank of matador.   [6] A local religious holiday.

arms. I loathed my body because it had turned gray and was sweating—and I wasn't even sure that I didn't loathe hers too. Concha would cry when she heard about my death; for months she would have no more interest in life. But still it was I who was going to die. I thought of her beautiful, loving eyes. When she looked at me something went from her to me. But I thought to myself that it was all over; if she looked at me *now* her gaze would not leave her eyes, it would not reach out to me. I was alone.

Tom too, was alone, but not the same way. He was seated astride his chair and had begun to look at the bench with a sort of smile, with surprise, even. He reached out his hand and touched the wood cautiously, as though he were afraid of breaking something, then he drew his hand back hurriedly, and shivered. I wouldn't have amused myself touching that bench, if I had been Tom, that was just some more Irish play-acting. But somehow it seemed to me too that the different objects had something funny about them. They seemed to have grown paler, less massive than before. I had only to look at the bench, the lamp or the pile of coal dust to feel I was going to die. Naturally, I couldn't think clearly about my death, but I saw it everywhere, even on the different objects, the way they had withdrawn and kept their distance, tactfully, like people talking at the bedside of a dying person. It was *his own death* Tom had just touched on the bench.

In the state I was in, if they had come and told me I could go home quietly, that my life would be saved, it would have left me cold. A few hours, or a few years of waiting are all the same, when you've lost the illusion of being eternal. Nothing mattered to me any more. In a way, I was calm. But it was a horrible kind of calm—because of my body. My body—I saw with its eyes and I heard with its ears, but it was no longer I. It sweat and trembled independently, and I didn't recognize it any longer. I was obliged to touch it and look at it to know what was happening to it, just as if it had been someone else's body. At times I still felt it, I felt a slipping, a sort of headlong plunging, as in a falling airplane, or else I heard my heart beating. But this didn't give me confidence. In fact, everything that came from my body had something damned dubious about it. Most of the time it was silent, it stayed put and I didn't feel any-

thing other than a sort of heaviness, a loathsome presence against me. I had the impression of being bound to an enormous vermin.

The Belgian took out his watch and looked at it.

"It's half-past-three," he said.

The son-of-a-bitch! He must have done it on purpose. Tom jumped up. We hadn't yet realized the time was passing. The night surrounded us like a formless, dark mass; I didn't even remember it had started.

Juan started to shout. Wringing his hands, he implored, "I don't want to die! I don't want to die!"

He ran the whole length of the cellar with his arms in the air, then he dropped down onto one of the mattresses, sobbing. Tom looked at him with dismal eyes and didn't even try to console him any more. The fact was, it was no use; the kid made more noise than we did, but he was less affected, really. He was like a sick person who defends himself against his malady with a high fever. When there's not even any fever left, it's much more serious.

He was crying. I could tell he felt sorry for himself; he was thinking about death. For one second, one single second, I too felt like crying, crying out of pity for myself. But just the contrary happened. I took one look at the kid, saw his thin, sobbing shoulders, and I felt I was inhuman. I couldn't feel pity for these others or for myself. I said to myself, "I want to die decently."

Tom had gotten up and was standing just under the round opening looking out for the first signs of daylight. I was determined, I wanted to die decently, and I only thought about that. But underneath, ever since the doctor had told us the time, I felt time slipping, flowing by, one drop at a time.

It was still dark when I heard Tom's voice.

"Do you hear them?"

"Yes."

People were walking in the courtyard.

"What the hell are they doing? After all, they can't shoot in the dark."

After a moment, we didn't hear anything more. I said to Tom, "There's the daylight."

Pedro got up yawning, and came and blew out the lamp. He turned to the man beside him. "It's hellish cold."

The cellar had grown gray. We could hear shots at a distance.

"It's about to start," I said to Tom. "That must be in the back courtyard."

Tom asked the doctor to give him a cigarette. I didn't want any; I didn't want either cigarettes or alcohol. From that moment on, the shooting didn't stop.

"Can you take it in?" Tom said.

He started to add something, then he stopped and began to watch the door. The door opened and a lieutenant came in with four soldiers. Tom dropped his cigarette.

"Steinbock?"

Tom didn't answer. Pedro pointed him out.

"Juan Mirbal?"

"He's the one on the mattress."

"Stand up," said the Lieutenant.

Juan didn't move. Two soldiers took hold of him by the armpits and stood him up on his feet. But as soon as they let go of him he fell down.

The soldiers hesitated a moment.

"He's not the first one to get sick," said the Lieutenant. "You'll have to carry him, the two of you. We'll arrange things when we get there." He turned to Tom. "All right, come along."

Tom left between two soldiers. Two other soldiers followed, carrying the kid by his arms and legs. He was not unconscious; his eyes were wide open and tears were rolling down his cheeks. When I started to go out, the Lieutenant stopped me.

"Are you Ibbieta?"

"Yes."

"You wait here. They'll come and get you later on."

They left. The Belgian and the two jailers left too, and I was alone. I didn't understand what had happened to me, but I would have liked it better if they had ended it all right away. I heard the volleys at almost regular intervals; at each one, I shuddered. I felt like howling and tearing my hair. But instead, I gritted my teeth and pushed my hands deep into my pockets, because I wanted to stay decent.

An hour later, they came to fetch me and took me up to the first floor in a little room which smelt of cigar smoke and was so hot it seemed to me suffocating. Here there were two officers sitting in comfortable chairs, smoking, with papers spread out on their knees.

"Your name is Ibbieta?"

"Yes."

"Where is Ramon Gris?"

"I don't know."

The man who questioned me was small and stocky. He had hard eyes behind his glasses.

"Come nearer," he said to me.

I went nearer. He rose and took me by the arms, looking at me in a way calculated to make me go through the floor. At the same time he pinched my arms with all his might. He didn't mean to hurt me; it was quite a game; he wanted to dominate me. He also seemed to think it was necessary to blow his fetid breath right into my face. We stood like that for a moment, only I felt more like laughing than anything else. It takes a lot more than that to intimidate a man who's about to die: it didn't work. He pushed me away violently and sat down again.

"It's your life or his," he said. "You'll be allowed to go free if you tell us where he is."

After all, these two bedizened fellows with their riding crops and boots were just men who were going to die one day. A little later than I, perhaps, but not a great deal. And there they were, looking for names among their papers, running after other men in order to put them in prison or do away with them entirely. They had their opinions on the future of Spain and on other subjects. Their petty activities seemed to me to be offensive and ludicrous. I could no longer put myself in their place. I had the impression they were crazy.

The little fat fellow kept looking at me, tapping his boots with his riding crop. All his gestures were calculated to make him appear like a spirited, ferocious animal.

"Well? Do you understand?"

"I don't know where Gris is," I said. "I thought he was in Madrid."

The other officer lifted his pale hand indolently. This indolence was also calculated. I saw through all their little tricks, and I was dumbfounded that men should still exist who took pleasure in that kind of thing.

"You have fifteen minutes to think it over," he said slowly. "Take him to the linen-room, and bring him back here in fifteen minutes. If he continues to refuse, he'll be executed at once."

They knew what they were doing. I had spent the night waiting. After that, they had made me wait another hour in the cellar, while they shot Tom and Juan, and now they locked me in the linen-room. They must have arranged the whole thing the night before. They figured that sooner or later people's nerves wear out and they hoped to get me that way.

They made a big mistake. In the linen-room I sat down on a ladder because I felt very weak, and I began to think things over. Not their proposition, however. Naturally I knew where Gris was. He was hiding in his cousins' house, about two miles outside of the city. I knew, too, that I would not reveal his hiding place, unless they tortured me (but they didn't seem to be considering that). All that was definitely settled and didn't interest me in the least. Only I would have liked to understand the reasons for my own conduct. I would rather die than betray Gris. Why? I no longer liked Ramon Gris. My friendship for him had died shortly before dawn along with my love for Concha, along with my own desire to live. Of course I still admired him —he was hard. But it was not for that reason I was willing to die in his place; his life was no more valuable than mine. No life was of any value. A man was going to be stood up against a wall and fired at till he dropped dead. It didn't make any difference whether it was I or Gris or somebody else. I knew perfectly well he was more useful to the Spanish cause than I was, but I didn't give a God damn about Spain or anarchy, either; nothing had any importance now. And yet, there I was. I could save my skin by betraying Gris and I refused to do it. It seemed more ludicrous to me than anything else; it was stubbornness.

I thought to myself, "Am I hard-headed!" And I was seized with a strange sort of cheerfulness.

They came to fetch me and took me back to the two officers. A rat darted out under our feet and that amused me. I turned to one of the falangists and said to him, "Did you see that rat?"

He made no reply. He was gloomy, and took himself very seriously. As for me, I felt like laughing, but I restrained myself because I was afraid that if I started, I wouldn't be able to stop. The falangist wore mustaches. I kept after him, "You ought to cut off those mustaches, you fool."

I was amused by the fact that he let hair grow all over his face while he was still alive.

He gave me a kind of half-hearted kick, and I shut up.

"Well," said the fat officer, "have you thought things over?"

I looked at them with curiosity, like insects of a very rare species.

"I know where he is," I said. "He's hiding in the cemetery. Either in one of the vaults, or in the gravediggers' shack."

I said that just to make fools of them. I wanted to see them get up and fasten their belts and bustle about giving orders.

They jumped to their feet.

"Fine. Moles, go ask Lieutenant Lopez for fifteen men. And as for you," the little fat fellow said to me, "if you've told the truth, I don't go back on my word. But you'll pay for this, if you're pulling our leg."

They left noisily and I waited in peace, still guarded by the falangists. From time to time I smiled at the thought of the face they were going to make. I felt dull and malicious. I could see them lifting up the gravestones, or opening the doors of the vaults one by one. I saw the whole situation as though I were another person: the prisoner determined to play the hero, the solemn falangists with their mustaches and the men in uniform running around among the graves. It was irresistibly funny.

After half an hour, the little fat fellow came back alone. I thought he had come to give the order to execute me. The others must have stayed in the cemetery.

The officer looked at me. He didn't look at all foolish.

"Take him out in the big courtyard with the others," he said. "When military operations are over, a regular tribunal will decide his case."

I thought I must have misunderstood.

"So they're not—they're not going to shoot me?" I asked.

"Not now, in any case. Afterwards, that doesn't concern me."

I still didn't understand.

"But why?" I said to him.

He shrugged his shoulders without replying, and the soldiers led me away. In the big courtyard there were a hundred or so prisoners, women, children and a few old men. I started to walk around the grass plot in the middle. I felt absolutely idiotic. At noon we were fed in the dining hall. Two or three fellows spoke to me. I must have known them, but I didn't answer. I didn't even know where I was.

Toward evening, about ten new prisoners were pushed into the courtyard. I recognized Garcia, the baker.

He said to me, "Lucky dog! I didn't expect to find you alive."

"They condemned me to death," I said, "and then they changed their minds. I don't know why."

"I was arrested at two o'clock," Garcia said.

"What for?"

Garcia took no part in politics.

"I don't know," he said. "They arrest everybody who doesn't think the way they do."

He lowered his voice.

"They got Gris."

I began to tremble.

"When?"

"This morning. He acted like a damned fool. He left his cousins' house Tuesday because of a disagreement. There were any number of fellows who would have hidden him, but he didn't want to be indebted to anybody any more. He said, 'I would have hidden at Ibbieta's, but since they've got him, I'll go hide in the cemetery.'"

"In the cemetery?"

"Yes. It was the god-damnedest thing. Naturally they passed by there this morning; that had to happen. They found him in the gravediggers' shack. They opened fire at him and they finished him off."

"In the cemetery!"

Everything went around in circles, and when I came to I was sitting on the ground. I laughed so hard the tears came to my eyes.

Exodus

JAMES BALDWIN
1924–

Although one of the younger authors represented in this book, James Baldwin has nevertheless expressed himself in a variety of literary forms using an even greater variety of subjects all investigated with a moral force and sincerity not entirely common in

our time. It is difficult to read any work of his without feeling the authenticity woven into the fabric of his essays, short stories, and novels. The essays of *Notes of a Native Son* (1955) and *Nobody Knows My Name* (1961) emerge from the depth of his personal experience in Negro life. More recently he has published a far-ranging commentary on the struggle of the Negro in general, but most specifically of himself, to find his identity. The title, *No Name in the Street* (1972), is taken from *Job,* 18:17–18:

His remembrance shall perish from the earth,
And he shall have no name in the street.
He shall be driven from light into darkness,
And chased out of the world.

Baldwin's "Exodus" is the story of Florence's determination, almost regardless of the cost, to free herself of the white psychology that has dominated her people. Her dilemma, to remain with her mother Rachel until her mother dies or to leave the South for New York to escape her mother's fate, is the key symbol of the story. It is Florence's Exodus that hangs in the balance. The background of her mother's life is well-known to Florence—entirely too well-known—, and almost a story in itself. Baldwin's low-key method of telling the story could be a powerful influence on any sensitve reader who expects a condemnation of the Southern whites tinged with hatred. But since every fact of the mother's life is easily documented, we find the artist exploring the psychological effects of those facts instead of writing propaganda. If the reader feels as Florence feels, the artist in Baldwin is probably soberly content.

I

She had always seemed to Florence the oldest woman in the world—for she often spoke of Florence and Gabriel as the children of her old age; and she had been born, innumerable years ago, during slavery, on a plantation in another state. On this plantation she had grown up, one of the field workers, for she was very tall and strong; and by-and-by she had married, and raised children, all of whom had been taken from her, one by sickness, and two by auction, and one whom she had not been allowed to call her own, who had been raised in the master's house. When she was a woman grown, well past thirty as she reckoned it, with one husband buried—but the master had given her another—armies, plundering and burning, had come from the North to set them free. This was in answer to the prayers of the faithful, who had never ceased, both day and night, to cry out for deliverance.

For it had been the will of God that they should hear, and pass it, thereafter, one to another, the story of the Hebrew children, who had been held in bondage in the land of Egypt;[1] and how the Lord had heard their groaning, and how His heart was moved; and how He bid them wait but a little season till He should send deliverance. She had known this story, so it seemed, from the day that she was born. And while life ran, rising in the morning before the sun came up, standing and bending in the fields when the sun was high, crossing the fields homeward while the sun went down at the gates of heaven far away—hearing the whistle of the foreman, and his eerie cry across the fields; in the whiteness of winter when hogs and turkeys and geese were slaughtered, and lights burned bright in the big house, and Bathsheba, the cook, sent over in a napkin bits of ham and chicken and cakes left over by the white folks, in all that befell, in her joys—her pipe in the evening, her man at night, the children she suckled, and guided on their first short steps—and in her tribulations, death, and parting, and the lash; she did not forget that deliverance was promised, and would surely come. She had only to endure and trust in God. She knew that the big house, the house of pride where the white folks lived, would come down: it was written in the Word of God. And they, who walked so proudly now, yet had not fashioned, for themselves, or their children, so sure a foundation as was hers. They walked on the edge of a steep place and their eyes were sightless—God would cause them to rush down, as the herd of swine had once rushed down, into the sea. For all that they were so beautiful, and took their ease, she knew them, and she pitied

them, who would have no covering in the great day of His wrath.

Yet, she told her children, God was just, and He struck no people without first giving many warnings. God gave men time, but all the times were in His hand, and, one day, the time to forsake evil and do good would all be finished: then only the whirlwind, death riding on the whirlwind, awaited those people who had forgotten God. In all the days that she was growing up, signs failed not, but none heeded. *Slaves done riz*, was whispered in the cabin, and at the master's gate: slaves in another county had fired the master's house and fields, and dashed their children to death against the stones. *Another slave in hell*, Bethsheba might say one morning, shooing the pickaninnies away from the great porch: a slave had killed his master, or his overseer, and had gone down to hell to pay for it. *I ain't got long to stay here*, someone crooned beside her in the fields: who would be gone by morning on his journey North. All these signs, like the plagues with which the Lord had afflicted Egypt, only hardened the hearts of these people against the Lord. They thought the lash would save them, and they used the lash; or the knife, or the gallows, or the auction block; they thought that kindness would save them, and the master and mistress came down, smiling, to the cabins, making much of the pickaninnies, and bearing gifts. These were great days, and they all, black and white, seemed happy together. But when the Word has gone forth from the mouth of God nothing can turn it back.

The word was fulfilled one morning before she was awake. Many of the stories her mother told meant nothing to Florence, she knew them for what they were, tales told by an old black woman in a cabin in the evening to distract her children from their cold and hunger. But the story of this day she was never to forget, it was a day like the day for which she lived. There was a great running and shouting, said her mother, everywhere outside, and, as she opened her eyes to the light of that day, so bright, she said, and cold, she was certain that the judgment trump had sounded. While she still sat, amazed, and wondering what, on the judgment day, would be the best behavior, in rushed Bathsheba, and behind her many tumbling children, and field hands, and house niggers, all together, and Bath-

[1] See *Exodus*, Israel in bondage: 1:1–22; 2:1–25. God delivers His people from Egypt: 3:1–14.

sheba shouted, "Rise up, rise up, Sister Rachel, and see the Lord's deliverance! He done brought us out of Egypt, just like He promised, and we's free at last!"

Bathsheba grabbed her, tears running down her face, she, dressed in the clothes in which she had slept, walked to the door to look out on the new day God had given them.

On that day she saw the proud house humbled, green silk and velvet blowing out of windows, and the garden trampled by many horsemen, and the big gates open. The master and mistress, and their kin, and one child she had borne were in that house—which she did not enter. Soon it occurred to her that there was no reason any more to tarry here. She tied her things in a cloth, which she put on her head, and walked out through the big gate, never to see that country any more.

And this, as Florence grew, became her deep ambition: to walk out one morning through the cabin door, never to return. . . .

II

In 1900, when she was twenty-six, Florence walked out through the cabin door. She had thought to wait until her mother, who was so ill now that she no longer stirred out of bed, should be buried—but suddenly she knew that she would wait no longer, the time had come. She had been working as cook and serving girl for a large white family in town, and it was on the day that her master proposed that she become his concubine that she knew that her life among these wretched had come to its destined end. She left her employment that same day (leaving behind her a most vehement conjugal bitterness) and with part of the money which, with cunning, cruelty, and sacrifice, she had saved over a period of years, bought a railroad ticket to New York. When she bought it, in a kind of scarlet rage, she held, like a talisman at the back of her mind, the thought: "I can give it back, I can sell it. This don't mean I got to go." But she knew that nothing could stop her.

And it was this leave-taking which came to stand, in Florence's latter days, and with many another witness, at her bedside. Gray clouds obscured the sun that day, and outside the cabin

window she saw that mist still covered the ground. Her mother lay in bed, awake; she was pleading with Gabriel,[2] who had been out drinking the night before, and who was not really sober now, to mend his ways and come to the Lord. And Gabriel, full of the confusion, and pain, and guilt which were his whenever he thought of how he made his mother suffer, but which became nearly insupportable when she taxed him with it, stood before the mirror, head bowed, buttoning his shirt. Florence knew that he could not unlock his lips to speak; he could not say Yes to his mother, and to the Lord; and he could not say No.

"Honey," their mother was saying, "don't you *let* your old mother die without you look her in the eye and tell her she going to see you in glory. You hear me, boy?"

In a moment, Florence thought with scorn, tears would fill his eyes, and he would promise to "do better." He had been promising to "do better" since the day he had been baptized.

She put down her bag in the center of the hateful room.

"Ma," she said, "I'm going. I'm a-going this morning."

Now that she had said it, she was angry with herself for not having said it the night before, so that they would have had time to be finished with their weeping and their arguments. She had not trusted herself to withstand, the night before; but now there was almost no time left. The center of her mind was filled with the image of the great, white clock at the railway station, on which the hands did not cease to move.

"You going where?" her mother asked, sharply. But she knew that her mother had understood, had, indeed, long before this moment, known that this moment would come. The astonishment with which she stared at Florence's bag was not altogether astonishment, but a startled, wary attention. A danger imagined had

[2] It is significant that the mother's (Rachel's) son is given the biblical name Gabriel, meaning "God is mighty," but her daughter is given the name Florence which is customarily identified with bloom and prosperity. His mother had named him Gabriel apparently with great hope, a hope later dashed by his sins, giving his name an ironical twist. For Gabriel see *Luke,* 1:19, 26–38.

become present and real, and her mother was already searching for a way to break Florence's will. All this Florence, in a moment, knew, and it made her stronger. She watched her mother, waiting.

But at the tone of his mother's voice, Gabriel, who had scarcely heard Florence's announcement, so grateful had he been that something had occurred to distract from him his mother's attention, dropped his eyes, and saw Florence's traveling bag. And he repeated his mother's question in a stunned, angry voice, understanding it only as the words hit the air:

"Yes, girl. Where you think you going?"

"I'm going," she said, "to New York. I got my ticket."

And her mother watched her. For a moment no one said a word. Then, Gabriel, in a changed and frightened voice, asked:

"And when you done decide that?"

She did not look at him, nor answer his question. She continued to watch her mother. "I got my ticket," she repeated. "I'm going on the morning train."

"Girl," asked her mother, quietly, "is you sure you know what you's doing?"

She stiffened, seeing in her mother's eyes a mocking pity. "I'm a woman grown," she said. "I know what I'm doing."

"And you going," cried Gabriel, "this morning—just like that? And you going to walk off and leave your mother—just like that?"

"You hush," she said, turning to him for the first time; "she got you, ain't she?"

This was indeed, she realized, as he dropped his eyes, the bitter, troubling point. He could not endure the thought of being left alone with his mother, with nothing whatever to put between himself and his guilty love. With Florence gone, time would have swallowed up all his mother's children, except himself; and *he*, then, must make amends for all the pain that she had borne, and sweeten her last moments with all his proofs of love. And his mother required of him one proof only, that he tarry no longer in sin. With Florence gone, his stammering time, his playing time, contracted with a bound to the sparest interrogative second; when he must stiffen himself, and answer to his mother, and all the host of heaven, Yes, or No.

Florence smiled inwardly a small, malicious smile, watching his slow bafflement, and panic, and rage; and she looked at her mother again. "She got you," she repeated. "She don't need me."

"You going North," her mother said, then. "And when you reckon on coming back?"

"I don't reckon on coming back," she said.

"You come crying back soon enough," said Gabriel, with malevolence, "soon as they whip your butt up there four or five times."

She looked at him again. "Just don't you try to hold your breath till then, you hear?"

"Girl," said her mother, "you mean to tell me the devil's done made your heart so hard you can just leave your mother on her dying bed, and you don't care if you don't never see her in this world no more? Honey, you can't tell me you done got so evil as all that?"

She felt Gabriel watching her to see how she would take this question—the question, which, for all her determination, she had dreaded most to hear. She looked away from her mother, and straightened, catching her breath, looking outward through the small, cracked window. There, outside, beyond the slowly rising mist, and farther off than her eyes could see, her life awaited her. The woman on the bed was old, her life was fading as the mist rose. She thought of her mother as already in the grave; and she would not let herself be strangled by the hands of the dead.

"I'm going, Ma," she said. "I got to go."

Her mother leaned back, face upward to the light, and began to cry. Gabriel moved to Florence's side and grabbed her arm. She looked up into his face and saw that his eyes were full of tears.

"You can't go," he said. "You can't go. You can't go and leave your mother thisaway. She need a woman, Florence, to help look after her. What she going to do here, all alone with me?"

She pushed him from her and moved to stand over her mother's bed.

"Ma," she said, "don't be like that. Ain't a blessed thing for you to cry about so. Ain't a thing can happen to me up North can't happen to me here. God's everywhere, Ma. Ain't no need to worry."

She knew that she was mouthing words; and she realized suddenly that her mother scorned to dignify these words with her attention. She had granted Florence the victory—with a promptness which had the effect of making Florence, however dimly and unwillingly, wonder if her victory was real; and she was not weeping for her daughter's future; she was weeping for the past, and weeping in an anguish in which Florence had no part. And all of this filled Florence with a terrible fear, which was immediately transformed into anger.

"Gabriel can take care of you," she said, her voice shaking with malice; "Gabriel ain't never going to leave you. Is you, boy?" and she looked at him. He stood, stupid with bewilderment and grief, a few inches from the bed. "But me," she said, "I got to go." She walked to the center of the room again, and picked up her bag.

"Girl," Gabriel whispered, "ain't you got no feelings at *all?*"

"*Lord!*" her mother cried; and at the sound her heart turned over; she and Gabriel, arrested, stared at the bed. "Lord, Lord, Lord! Lord, have mercy on my sinful daughter! Stretch out your hand and hold her back from the lake that burns forever! Oh, my Lord, my Lord!" and her voice dropped, and broke, and tears ran down her face. "Lord, I done my best with all the children what you give me. Lord, have mercy on my children, and my children's children."

"Florence,' said Gabriel, "please don't go. Please don't go. You ain't really fixing to go and leave her like this?"

Tears stood suddenly in her own eyes, though she could not have said what she was crying for. "Leave me be," she said to Gabriel, and picked up her bag again. She opened the door; the cold morning air came in. "Good-by," she said. And then to Gabriel: "Tell her I said good-by." She walked through the cabin door and down the short steps into the frosty yard. Gabriel watched her, standing magnetized between the door and the weeping bed. Then, as her hand was on the gate, he ran before her, and slammed the gate shut.

"Girl, where you going? What you doing? You reckon on finding some men up North to dress you in pearls and diamonds?"

Violently, she opened the gate and moved out into the road. He watched her with his jaw hanging, until the dust and the distance swallowed her up.

The Horse-Dealer's Daughter

D. H. LAWRENCE
1885–1930

The theme of this story, at first titled "The Miracle," can be read as the regeneration, even the transfiguration as Lawrence calls it, of two lives through unexpected love. This theme is more fully explored in his novel *Women in Love,* 1920. Lawrence's use of the word *transfiguration* in "The Horse Dealer's Daughter" to describe the experience of Mabel Pevin carries humanistic religious overtones which are most significantly a part of his concept of love between man and woman. The clinical treatment of sex found in some fiction of the last two or three decades would have found no sympathetic response in Lawrence. See the headnote for Lawrence's novella, "The Man Who Died," page 209.

"Well, Mabel, and what are you going to do with yourself?" asked Joe, with a foolish flippancy. He felt quite safe himself. Without listening for an answer, he turned aside, worked a grain of tobacco to the tip of his tongue, and spat it out. He did not care about anything, since he felt safe himself.

The three brothers and the sister sat round the desolate breakfast table, attempting some sort of desultory consultation. The morning's post had given the final tap to the family fortune, and all was over. The dreary dining-room itself, with its heavy mahogany furniture, looked as if it were waiting to be done away with.

But the consultation amounted to nothing. There was a strange air of ineffectuality about the three men, as they sprawled at table, smoking and reflecting vaguely on their own condition. The girl was alone, a rather short, sullen-looking young woman of twenty-seven. She did not share the same life as her brothers. She would have been good-looking, save for the impassive fixity of her face, "bulldog," as her brothers called it.

There was a confused trampling of horses' feet outside. The three men all sprawled round in their chairs to watch. Beyond the dark holly-bushes that separated the strip of lawn from the highroad, they could see a cavalcade of shire horses swinging out of their own yard, being taken for exercise. This was the last time. These were the last horses that would go through their hands. The young men watched with critical, callous look. They were all frightened at the collapse of their lives, and the sense of disaster in which they were involved left them no inner freedom.

Yet they were three fine, well-set fellows enough. Joe, the eldest, was a man of thirty-three, broad and handsome in a hot, flushed way. His face was red, he twisted his black moustache over a thick finger, his eyes were shallow and restless. He had a sensual way of uncovering his teeth when he laughed, and his bearing was stupid. Now he watched the horses with a glazed look of helplessness in his eyes, a certain stupor of downfall.

The great draught-horses swung past. They were tied head to tail, four of them, and they heaved along to where a lane branched off from the highroad, planting their great hoofs floutingly in the fine black mud, swinging their great rounded haunches sumptuously, and trotting a few sudden steps as they were led into the lane, round the corner. Every movement showed a massive, slumbrous strength, and a stupidity which held them in subjection. The groom at the head looked back, jerking the leading rope. And the cavalcade moved out of sight up the lane, the tail of the last horse, bobbed up tight and stiff, held out taut from the swinging great haunches as they rocked behind the hedges in a motion like sleep.

Joe watched with glazed hopeless eyes. The horses were almost like his own body to him. He felt he was done for now. Luckily he was engaged to a woman as old as himself, and therefore her father, who was steward of a neighbouring estate, would provide him with a job. He would marry and go into harness. His life was over, he would be a subject animal now.

He turned uneasily aside, the retreating steps of the horses echoing in his ears. Then with foolish recklessness, he reached for the scraps of bacon-rind from the plates, and making a faint whistling sound, flung them to the terrier that lay against the fender. He watched the dog swallow them, and waited till the creature looked into his eyes. Then a faint grin came on his face, and in a high, foolish voice he said:

"You won't get much more bacon, shall you, you little bitch?"

The dog faintly and dismally wagged its tail, then lowered its haunches, circled round, and lay down again.

There was another helpless silence at the table. Joe sprawled uneasily in his seat, not willing to go till the family conclave was dissolved. Fred Henry, the second brother, was erect, clean-limbed, alert. He had watched the passing of the horses with more sang-froid. If he was an animal, like Joe, he was an animal which controls, not one which is controlled. He was master of any horse, and he carried himself with a well-tempered air of mastery. But he was not master of the situations of life. He pushed his coarse brown moustache upwards, off his lip, and glanced irritably at his sister, who sat impassive and inscrutable.

"You'll go and stop with Lucy for a bit, shan't you?" he asked. The girl did not answer.

"I don't see what else you can do," persisted Fred Henry.

"Go as a skivvy," Joe interpolated laconically. The girl did not move a muscle.

"If I was her, I should go in training for a nurse," said Malcolm, the youngest of them all. He was the baby of the family, a young man of twenty-two, with a fresh, jaunty *museau*.[1]

But Mabel did not take any notice of him. They had talked at her and round her for so many years, that she hardly heard them at all.

The marble clock on the mantelpiece softly chimed the half-hour, the dog rose uneasily from the hearthrug and looked at the party at the breakfast table. But still they sat on in ineffectual conclave.

"Oh, all right," said Joe suddenly, apropos of nothing. "I'll get a move on."

He pushed back his chair, straddled his knees with a downward jerk, to get them free, in horsey fashion, and went to the fire. Still he did not go out of the room; he was curious to know what the others would do or say. He began to charge his pipe, looking down at the dog and saying, in a high, affected voice:

"Going wi' me? Going wi' me are ter? Tha'rt

[1] Face.

goin' further tha that counts on just now, dost hear?"

The dog faintly wagged its tail, the man stuck out his jaw and covered his pipe with his hands, and puffed intently, losing himself in the tobacco, looking down all the while at the dog with an absent brown eye. The dog looked up at him in mournful distrust. Joe stood with his knees stuck out, in real horsey fashion.

"Have you had a letter from Lucy?" Fred Henry asked of his sister.

"Last week," came the neutral reply.

"And what does she say?"

There was no answer.

"Does she *ask* you to go and stop there?" persisted Fred Henry.

"She says I can if I like."

"Well, then, you'd better. Tell her you'll come on Monday."

This was received in silence.

"That's what you'll do then, is it?" said Fred Henry in some exasperation.

But she made no answer. There was a silence of futility and irritation in the room. Malcolm grinned fatuously.

"You'll have to make up your mind between now and next Wednesday," said Joe loudly, "or else find yourself lodgings on the kerbstone."

The face of the young woman darkened, but she sat on immutable.

"Here's Jack Fergusson!" exclaimed Malcolm, who was looking aimlessly out of the window.

"Where?" exclaimed Joe, loudly.

"Just gone past."

"Coming in?"

Malcolm craned his neck to see the gate.

"Yes," he said.

There was a silence. Mabel sat on like one condemned, at the head of the table. Then a whistle was heard from the kitchen. The dog got up and barked sharply. Joe opened the door and shouted:

"Come on."

After a moment a young man entered. He was muffled up in overcoat and a purple woollen scarf, and his tweed cap, which he did not remove, was pulled down on his head. He was of medium height, his face was rather long and pale, his eyes looked tried.

"Hello, Jack! Well, Jack!" exclaimed Malcolm and Joe. Fred Henry merely said, "Jack."

"What's doing?" asked the newcomer, evidently addressing Fred Henry.

"Same. We've got to be out by Wednesday. Got a cold?"

"I have—got it bad, too."

"Why don't you stop in?"

"*Me* stop in? When I can't stand on my legs, perhaps I shall have a chance." The young man spoke huskily. He had a slight Scotch accent.

"It's a knock-out, isn't it," said Joe, boisterously, "if a doctor goes round croaking with a cold. Looks bad for the patients, doesn't it?"

The young doctor looked at him slowly.

"Anything the matter with *you*, then?" he asked sarcastically.

"Not as I know of. Damn your eyes, I hope not. Why?"

"I thought you were very concerned about the patients, wondered if you might be one yourself."

"Damn it, no, I've never been patient to no flaming doctor, and hope I never shall be," returned Joe.

At this point Mabel rose from the table, and they all seemed to become aware of her existence. She began putting the dishes together. The young doctor looked at her, but did not address her. He had not greeted her. She went out of the room with the tray, her face impassive and unchanged.

"When are you off then, all of you?" asked the doctor.

"I'm catching the eleven-forty," replied Malcolm. "Are you goin' down wi' th' trap, Joe?"

"Yes, I've told you I'm going down wi' th' trap, haven't I?"

"We'd better be getting her in then. So long, Jack, if I don't see you before I go," said Malcolm, shaking hands.

He went out, followed by Joe, who seemed to have his tail between his legs.

"Well, this is the devil's own," exclaimed the doctor, when he was left alone with Fred Henry. "Going before Wednesday, are you?"

"That's the orders," replied the other.

"Where, to Northampton?"

"That's it."

"The devil," exclaimed Fergusson, with quiet chagrin.

And there was silence between the two.

"All settled up, are you?" asked Fergusson.

"About."

There was another pause.

"Well, I shall miss yer, Freddy, boy," said the young doctor.

"And I shall miss thee, Jack," returned the other.

"Miss you like hell," mused the doctor.

Fred Henry turned aside. There was nothing to say. Mabel came in again, to finish clearing the table.

"What are *you* going to do, then, Miss Pervin?" asked Fergusson. "Going to your sister's, are you?"

Mabel looked at him with her steady, dangerous eyes, that always made him uncomfortable, unsettling his superficial ease.

"No," she said.

"Well, what in the name of fortune *are* you going to do? Say what you mean to do," cried Fred Henry, with futile intensity.

But she only averted her head, and continued her work. She folded the white table-cloth, and put on the chenille cloth.

"The sulkiest bitch that ever trod!" muttered her brother.

But she finished her task with perfectly impassive face, the young doctor watching her interestedly all the while. Then she went out.

Fred Henry stared after her, clenching his lips, his blue eyes fixing in sharp antagonism, as he made a grimace of sour exasperation.

"You could bray her into bits, and that's all you'd get out of her," he said in a small, narrowed tone.

The doctor smiled faintly.

"What's she *going* to do, then?" he asked.

"Strike me if *I* know!" returned the other.

There was a pause. Then the doctor stirred.

"I'll be seeing you to-night, shall I?" he said to his friend.

"Ay—where's it to be? Are we going over to Jessdale?"

"I don't know. I've got a cold on me. I'll come round to the Moon and Stars, anyway."

"Let Lizzie and May miss their night for once, eh?"

"That's it—if I feel as I do now."

"All's one—"

The two young men went through the passage and down to the back door together. The house was large, but it was servantless now, and desolate. At the back was a small bricked houseyard, and beyond that a big square, gravelled fine and red, and having stables on two sides. Sloping, dank, winter-dark fields stretched away on the open sides.

But the stables were empty. Joseph Pervin, the father of the family, had been a man of no education, who had become a fairly large horse dealer. The stables had been full of horses, there was a great turmoil and come-and-go of horses and of dealers and grooms. Then the kitchen was full of servants. But of late things had declined. The old man had married a second time, to retrieve his fortune. Now he was dead and everything was gone to the dogs, there was nothing but debt and threatening.

For months, Mabel had been servantless in the big house, keeping the home together in penury for her ineffectual brothers. She had kept house for ten years. But previously it was with unstinted means. Then, however brutal and coarse everything was, the sense of money had kept her proud, confident. The men might be foul-mouthed, the women in the kitchen might have bad reputations, her brothers might have illegitimate children. But so long as there was money, the girl herself felt established, and brutally proud, reserved.

No company came to the house, save dealers and coarse men. Mabel had no associates of her own sex, after her sister went away. But she did not mind. She went regularly to church, she attended to her father. And she lived in the memory of her mother, who had died when she was fourteen, and whom she had loved. She had loved her father, too, in a different way, depending upon him, and feeling secure in him, until at the age of fifty-four he married again. And then she had set hard against him. Now he had died and left them all hopelessly in debt.

She had suffered badly during the period of poverty. Nothing, however, could shake the curious, sullen, animal pride that dominated each member of the family. Now, for Mabel, the end had come. Still she would not cast about her. She would follow her own way just the same. She would always hold the keys of her own situation. Mindless and persistent, she endured from day to day. Why should she think? Why should she answer anybody! It was enough that this was the end, and there was no way out. She need not pass any more darkly along the main street of the small town, avoiding every eye. She need not demean herself any more, going into the shops and buying the cheapest food. This was at an end. She thought of nobody, not even of herself. Mindless and persistent, she seemed in a sort of ecstasy to be coming nearer to her fulfillment, her own glorification, approaching her dead mother, who was glorified.

In the afternoon she took a little bag, with shears and sponge and a small scrubbing brush, and went out. It was a grey, wintry day, with saddened, dark green fields and an atmosphere blackened by the smoke of foundries not far off. She went quickly, darkly along the causeway, heeding nobody, through the town to the churchyard.

There she always felt secure, as if no one could see her, although as a matter of fact she was exposed to the stare of everyone who passed along under the churchyard wall. Nevertheless, once under the shadow of the great looming church, among the graves, she felt immune from the world, reserved within the thick churchyard wall as in another country.

Carefully she clipped the grass from the grave, and arranged the pinky white, small chrysanthemums in the tin cross. When this was done, she took an empty jar from a neighbouring grave, brought water, and carefully, most scrupulously sponged the marble headstone and the coping-stone.

It gave her sincere satisfaction to do this. She felt in immediate contact with the world of her mother. She took minute pains, went through the park in a state bordering on pure happiness, as if in performing this task she came into a subtle, intimate connection with her mother. For the life she followed here in the world was far less real than the world of death she inherited from her mother.

The doctor's house was just by the church. Fergusson, being a mere hired assistant, was slave to the country-side. As he hurried now to attend the outpatients in the surgery, glancing across the graveyard with his quick eye, he saw the girl at her task at the grave. She seemed so intent and remote, it was like looking into another world. Some mystical element was touched in him. He slowed down as he walked, catching her as if spell-bound.

She lifted her eyes, feeling him looking. Their eyes met. And each looked away again at once, each feeling, in some way, found out by the other. He lifted his cap and passed on down the road. There remained distinct in his consciousness, like a vision, the memory of her face, lifted from the tombstone in the churchyard, and looking at him with slow, large, portentous eyes. It *was* portentous, her face. It seemed to mesmerize him. There was a heavy power in her eyes which laid hold of his whole being, as if he had drunk some powerful drug. He had been feeling weak and done before. Now the life came back into him, he felt delivered from his own fretted, daily self.

He finished his duties at the surgery as quickly as might be, hastily filling up the bottles of the waiting people with cheap drugs. Then, in perpetual haste, he set off again to visit several cases in another part of his round, before teatime. At all times he preferred to walk if he could, but particularly when he was not well. He fancied the motion restored him.

The afternoon was falling. It was grey, deadened, and wintry, with a slow, moist, heavy coldness sinking in and deadening all the faculties. But why should he think or notice? He hastily climbed the hill and turned across the dark green fields, following the black cinder-track. In the distance, across a shallow dip in the country, the small town was clustered like smouldering ash, a tower, a spire, a heap of low, raw, extinct houses. And on the nearest fringe of the town, sloping into the dip, was Oldmeadow, the Pervins' house. He could see the stables and the outbuildings distinctly, as they lay towards him on the slope. Well, he would not go there many more times! Another resource would be lost to him, another place gone; the only company he cared for in the alien, ugly little town he was losing. Nothing but work, drudgery, constant hastening from dwelling to dwelling among the colliers and the iron-workers. It wore him out, but at the same time he had a craving for it. It was a stimulant to him to be in the homes of the working people, moving as it were through the innermost body of their life. His nerves were excited and gratified. He could come so near, into the very lives of the rough, inarticulate, powerfully emotional men and women. He grumbled, he said he hated the hellish hole. But as a matter of fact it excited him, the contact with the rough, strongly-feeling people was a stimulant applied direct to his nerves.

Below Oldmeadow, in the green, shallow, soddened hollow of fields, lay a square, deep pond. Roving across the landscape, the doctor's quick eye detected a figure in black passing through the gate of the field, down towards the pond. He looked again. It would be Mabel Pervin. His mind suddenly became alive and attentive.

Why was she going down there? He pulled up on the path on the slope above, and stood staring. He could just make sure of the small black figure moving in the hollow of the failing day. He seemed to see her in the midst of such obscurity, that he was like a clairvoyant, seeing rather with the mind's eye than with ordinary sight. Yet he could see her positively enough, whilst he kept his eye attentive. He felt, if he looked away from her, in the thick, ugly falling dusk, he would lose her altogether.

He followed her minutely as she moved, direct and intent, like something transmitted rather than stirring in voluntary activity, straight down the field towards the pond. There she stood on the bank for a moment. She never raised her head. Then she waded slowly into the water.

He stood motionless as the small black figure walked slowly and deliberately towards the centre of the pond, very slowly, gradually moving deeper into the motionless water, and still moving forward as the water got up to her breast. Then he could see no more in the dusk of the dead afternoon.

"There!" he exclaimed. "Would you believe it?"

And he hastened straight down, running over the wet, soddened fields, pushing through the hedges, down into the depression of callous wintry obscurity. It took him several minutes to come to the pond. He stood on the bank, breathing heavily. He could see nothing. His eyes seemed to penetrate the dead water. Yes, perhaps that was the dark shadow of her black clothing beneath the surface of the water.

He slowly ventured into the pond. The bottom was deep, soft clay, he sank in, and the water clasped dead cold round his legs. As he stirred he could smell the cold, rotten clay that fouled up into the water. It was objectionable in his lungs. Still, repelled and yet not heeding, he moved deeper into the pond. The cold water rose over his thighs, over his loins, upon his abdomen. The lower part of his body was all sunk in the hideous cold element. And the bottom was so deeply soft and uncertain he was afraid of pitching with his mouth underneath. He could not swim, and was afraid.

He crouched a little, spreading his hands under the water and moving them round, trying to feel for her. The dead cold pond swayed upon his chest. He moved again, a little deeper, and again, with his hands underneath, he felt all around under the water. And he touched her clothing. But it evaded his fingers. He made a desperate effort to grasp it.

And so doing he lost his balance and went under, horribly, suffocating in the foul earthy water, struggling madly for a few moments. At last, after what seemed an eternity, he got his footing, rose again into the air and looked around. He gasped, and knew he was in the world. Then he looked at the water. She had risen near him. He grasped her clothing, and drawing her nearer, turned to take his way to land again.

He went very slowly, carefully, absorbed in the slow progress. He rose higher, climbing out of the pond. The water was now only about his legs; he was thankful, full of relief to be out of the clutches of the pond. He lifted her and staggered on to the bank, out of the horror of wet, grey clay.

He laid her down on the bank. She was quite unconscious and running with water. He made the water come from her mouth, he worked to restore her. He did not have to work very long before he could feel the breathing begin again in her; she was breathing naturally. He worked a little longer. He could feel her live beneath his hands; she was coming back. He wiped her face, wrapped her in his overcoat, looked round into the dim, dark grey world, then lifted her and staggered down the bank and across the fields.

It seemed an unthinkably long way, and his burden so heavy he felt he would never get to the house. But at last he was in the stable-yard, and then in the house-yard. He opened the door and went into the house. In the kitchen he laid her down on the hearthrug, and called. The house was empty. But the fire was burning in the grate.

Then again he kneeled to attend her. She was breathing regularly, her eyes were wide open and as if conscious, but there seemed something missing in her look. She was conscious in herself, but unconscious of her surroundings.

He ran upstairs, took blankets from a bed, and put them before the fire to warm. Then he removed her saturated, earthy-smelling clothing, rubbed her dry with a towel, and wrapped her naked in the blankets. Then he went into the dining-room, to look for spirits. There was a little whisky. He drank a gulp himself, and put some into her mouth.

The effect was instantaneous. She looked full into his face, as if she had been seeing him for some time, and yet had only just become conscious of him.

"Dr. Fergusson?" she said.

"What?" he answered.

He was divesting himself of his coat, intending to find some dry clothing upstairs. He could not bear the smell of the dead, clayey water, and he was mortally afraid for his own health.

"What did I do?" she asked.

"Walked into the pond," he replied. He had begun to shudder like one sick, and could hardly attend to her. Her eyes remained full on him, he seemed to be going dark in his mind, looking back at her helplessly. The shuddering became quieter in him, the life came back in him, dark and unknowing, but strong again.

"Was I out of my mind?" she asked, while her eyes were fixed on him all the time.

"Maybe, for the moment," he replied. He felt quiet, because his strength had come back. The strange fretful strain had left him.

"Am I out of my mind now?" she asked.

"Are you?" he reflected a moment. "No," he answered truthfully. "I don't see that you are." He turned his face aside. He was afraid now, because he felt dazed, and felt dimly that her power was stronger than his, in this issue. And she continued to look at him fixedly all the time. "Can you tell me where I shall find some dry things to put on?" he asked.

"Did you dive into the pond for me?" she asked.

"No," he answered. "I walked in. But I went in overhead as well."

There was silence for a moment. He hesitated. He very much wanted to go upstairs to get into dry clothing. But there was another desire in him. And she seemed to hold him. His will seemed to have gone to sleep, and left him, standing there slack before her. But he felt warm inside himself. He did not shudder at all, though his clothes were sodden on him.

"Why did you?" she asked.

"Because I didn't want you to do such a foolish thing," he said.

"It wasn't foolish," she said, still gazing at him as she lay on the floor, with a sofa cushion under her head. "It was the right thing to do. *I* knew best, then."

"I'll go and shift these wet things," he said. But still he had not the power to move out of her presence, until she sent him. It was as if she had the life of his body in her hands, and he could not extricate himself. Or perhaps he did not want to.

Suddenly she sat up. Then she became aware of her own immediate condition. She felt the blankets about her, she knew her own limbs. For a moment it seemed as if her reason were going. She looked round, with wild eye, as if seeking something. He stood still with fear. She saw her clothing scattered.

"Who undressed me?" she asked, her eyes resting full and inevitable on his face.

"I did," he replied, "to bring you round."

For some moments she sat and gazed at him awfully, her lips parted.

"Do you love me, then?" she asked.

He only stood and stared at her, fascinated. His soul seemed to melt.

She shuffled forward on her knees, and put her arms round him, round his legs, as he stood there, pressing her breasts against his knees and thighs, clutching him with strange, convulsive certainty, pressing his thighs against her, drawing him to her face, her throat, as she looked up at him with flaring, humble eyes of transfiguration, triumphant in first possession.

"You love me," she murmured, in strange transport, yearning and triumphant and confident. "You love me. I know you love me, I know."

And she was passionately kissing his knees, through the wet clothing, passionately and indiscriminately kissing his knees, his legs, as if unaware of everything.

He looked down at the tangled wet hair, the wild, bare, animal shoulders. He was amazed, bewildered, and afraid. He had never thought of loving her. He had never wanted to love her. When he rescued her and restored her, he was a doctor, and she was a patient. He had no single personal thought of her. Nay, this introduction of the personal element was very distasteful to him, a violation of his professional honour. It was horrible to have her there embracing his knees. It was horrible. He revolted from it, violently. And yet—and yet—he had not the power to break away.

She looked at him again, with the same supplication of powerful love, and that same transcendent, frightening light of triumph. In view of the delicate flame which seemed to come from her face like a light, he was powerless. And yet he had never intended to love her. He had never intended. And something stubborn in him could not give way.

"You love me," she repeated, in a murmur of deep, rhapsodic assurance. "You love me."

Her hands were drawing him, drawing him down to her. He was afraid, even a little horrified. For he had, really, no intention of loving her. Yet her hands were drawing him towards her. He put out his hand quickly to steady himself, and grasped her bare shoulder. A flame seemed to burn the hand that grasped her soft shoulder. He had no intention of loving her: his whole will was against his yielding. It was horrible. And yet wonderful was the touch of her shoulders, beautiful the shining of her face. Was she perhaps mad? He had a horror of yielding to her. Yet something in him ached also.

He had been staring away at the door, away from her. But his hand remained on her shoulder. She had gone suddenly very still. He looked down at her. Her eyes were now wide with fear, with doubt, the light was dying from her face, a shadow of terrible greyness was returning. He could not bear the touch of her eyes' question upon him, and the look of death behind the question.

With an inward groan he gave way, and let his heart yield towards her. A sudden gentle smile came on his face. And her eyes, which never left his face, slowly, slowly filled with tears. He watched the strange water rise in her eyes, like some slow fountain coming up. And his heart seemed to burn and melt away in his breast.

He could not bear to look at her any more. He dropped on his knees and caught her head with his arms and pressed her face against his throat. She was very still. His heart, which seemed to have broken, was burning with a kind of agony in his breast. And he felt her slow, hot tears wetting his throat. But he could not move.

He felt the hot tears wet his neck and the hollows of his neck, and he remained motionless, suspended through one of man's eternities. Only now it had become indispensable to him to have her face pressed close to him; he could never let her go again. He could never let her head go away from the close touch of his arm. He wanted to remain like that for ever, with his heart hurting him in a pain that was also life to him. Without knowing, he was looking down on her damp, soft brown hair.

Then, as it were suddenly, he smelt the horrid stagnant smell of that water. And at the same moment she drew away from him and looked at him. Her eyes were wistful and unfathomable. He was afraid of them, and he fell to kissing her, not knowing what he was doing. He wanted her eyes not to have that terrible, wistful, unfathomable look.

When she turned her face to him again, a faint delicate flush was glowing, and there was again dawning that terrible shining of joy in her eyes, which really terrified him, and yet which he now wanted to see, because he feared the look of doubt still more.

"You love me?" she said, rather faltering.

"Yes." The word cost him a painful effort. Not because it wasn't true. But because it was too newly true, the *saying* seemed to tear open again his newly-torn heart. and he hardly wanted it to be true, even now.

She lifted her face to him, and he bent forward and kissed her on the mouth, gently, with the one kiss that is an eternal pledge. And as he kissed her his heart strained again in his breast. He never intended to love her. But now it was over. He had crossed over the gulf to her, and all that he had left behind had shrivelled and become void.

After the kiss, her eyes again slowly filled with tears. She sat still, away from him, with her face drooped aside, and her hands folded in her lap. The tears fell slowly. There was complete silence. He too sat there motionless and silent on the hearthrug. The strange pain of his heart that was broken seemed to consume him. That he should love her? That this was love! That he should be ripped open in this way! Him, a doctor! How they would all jeer if they knew! It was agony to him to think they might know.

In the curious naked pain of the thought he looked again to her. She was sitting there drooped into a muse. He saw a tear fall, and his heart flared hot. He saw for the first time that one of her shoulders was quite uncovered, one arm bare, he could see one of her small breasts; dimly, because it had become almost dark in the room.

"Why are you crying?" he asked, in an altered voice.

She looked up at him, and behind her tears the consciousness of her situation for the first time brought a dark look of shame to her eyes.

"I'm not crying, really," she said, watching him half frightened.

He reached his hand, and softly closed it on her bare arm.

"I love you! I love you!" he said in a soft, low vibrating voice, unlike himself.

She shrank, and dropped her head. The soft, penetrating grip of his hand on her arm distressed her. She looked up at him.

"I want to go," she said. "I want to go and get you some dry things."

"Why?" he said. "I'm all right."

"But I want to go," she said. "And I want you to change your things."

He released her arm, and she wrapped herself in the blanket, looking at him rather frightened. And still she did not rise.

"Kiss me," she said wistfully.

He kissed her, but briefly, half in anger.

Then, after a second, she rose nervously, all mixed up in the blanket. He watched her in her confusion, as she tried to extricate herself and wrap herself up so that she could walk. He watched her relentlessly, as she knew. And as she went, the blanket trailing, and as he saw a glimpse of her feet and her white leg, he tried to remember her as she was when he had wrapped her in the blanket. But then he didn't want to remember, because she had been nothing to him then, and his nature revolted from remembering her as she was when she was nothing to him.

A tumbling, muffled noise from within the dark house startled him. Then he heard her voice: —"There are the clothes." He rose and went to the foot of the stairs, and gathered up the garments she had thrown down. Then he came back to the fire, to rub himself down and dress. He grinned at his own appearance when he had finished.

The fire was sinking, so he put on coal. The house was now quite dark, save for the light of a street-lamp that shone in faintly from beyond the holly trees. He lit the gas with matches he found on the mantelpiece. Then he emptied the pockets of his own clothes, and threw all his wet things in a heap into the scullery. After which he gathered up her sodden clothes, gently, and put them in a separate heap on the copper-top in the scullery.

It was six o'clock on the clock. His own watch had stopped. He ought to go back to the surgery. He waited, and still she did not come down. So he went to the foot of the stairs and called.

"I shall have to go."

Almost immediately he heard her coming down. She had on her best dress of black voile, and her hair was tidy, but still damp. She looked at him—and in spite of herself, smiled.

"I don't like you in those clothes," she said.

"Do I look a sight?" he answered.

They were shy of one another.

"I'll make you some tea," she said.

"No, I must go."

"Must you?" And she looked at him again with the wide, strained, doubtful eyes. And again, from the pain of his breast, he knew how he loved her. He went and bent to kiss her, gently, passionately, with his heart's painful kiss.

"And my hair smells so horrible," she murmured in distraction. "And I'm so awful, I'm so awful. Oh, no, I'm too awful." And she broke into bitter, heart-broken sobbing. "You can't want to love me, I'm horrible."

"Don't be silly, don't be silly," he said, trying to comfort her, kissing her, holding her in his arms. "I want you, I want to marry you, we're going to be married, quickly, quickly—tomorrow if I can."

But she only sobbed terribly, and cried:

"I feel awful. I feel awful. I feel I'm horrible to you."

"No, I want you, I want you," was all he

answered, blindly, with that terrible intonation which frightened her almost more than her horror lest he should *not* want her.

THE NOVELLA

Literary theory and literary criticism are often plagued by imprecise terms because literature and the other arts defy exact classification and description, especially abstract description. The basic forms of fiction are usually referred to as the short story, the short novel, and the novel. But the very word *short* raises many questions. How short, or limited, must a novel be to be a short novel? And how much shorter to be a short story? Surely the number of pages involved can hardly be the only answer, for who is to determine the dividing lines? Is Hemingway's *The Old Man and the Sea* a long short story, a short novel, or a novel? Melville's *Benito Cereno*, which was gathered into his *Piazza Tales*, has been labeled all three over the years, yet Melville called it a tale which may be the right simplifying solution after all.

These three classifications—the short story, the short novel, and the novel—are perhaps better defined by the scope, or range, of the work instead of by counting the number of words or pages. Scope involves such matters as the amount of time represented in the work, the number of characters, the philosophical content, and perhaps above all the complexity of the situation in the work. Ordinarily the more complex the situation the more detail is required to present the complexity, and detail requires space which lengthens the work. Under these circumstances Lawrence's "The Man Who Died" or Conrad's "Heart of Darkness" are short novels, and Hemingway's "A Clean, Well-Lighted Place" (p. 42) and Hughes's "On the Road" (p. 144) are short stories. These are rather clear-cut decisions, but how to classify, say, Wright's "Bright and Morning Star" (p. 121) or Hemingway's *The Old Man and the Sea?*

In recent years the term *novella* has been revived especially by departments of English to represent the short novel, and novella courses and novella anthologies have flourished by the dozen. We are often told that the term *novella*

is used to represent the early tales of the Italian and French writers as, for example Boccaccio's *Decameron* and Marguerite of Valois' *Heptameron*. That our term *novel* emerged from *novella* to represent the form of fiction we now read is obvious, and our present use of *novella* can be explored in Lawrence's "The Man Who Died."

The Man Who Died

D. H. LAWRENCE
1885–1930

Painter, short-story writer, novelist, poet, essayist, and critic, David Herbert Lawrence was a controversial figure from the beginning to the end of his career. If artistic versatility is a gauge of genius, surely he had genius in good measure.

But now a little more than forty years after his death—so often the experience of controversial authors—the tumult and the shouting dies, and scholars, critics, and general readers take a closer look at Lawrence's art. One of the basic reasons for this new emphasis on his literary art is described by the critic Mark Spilka: "But the critical renaissance [fostered by the New Critics and their close reading of literary works, including John Crowe Ransom, Cleanth Brooks, and Robert Penn Warren] . . . has rescued Lawrence from the possessive memorialists, sex cultists, hostile liberals, and religious purists who destroyed his reputation in the Thirties." * Perhaps the greatest single force in establishing Lawrence's present reputation is the British critic F. R. Leavis who flatly states that "The great English novelists are Jane Austen, George Eliot, Henry James, and Joseph Conrad . . . ," at which point he asks, "Is there no name later than Conrad's to be included in the great tradition? There is, I am convinced, one: D. H. Lawrence. Lawrence, in the English language, was the

* Mark Spilka, ed., *D. H. Lawrence, A Collection of Critical Essays*, Englewood Cliffs, N. J.: Prentice-Hall, Inc., 1963, p. 1.

great genius of our time (I mean the age, or climatic phase, following Conrad's)." *

Along with many other works by Lawrence, "The Man Who Died" has more recently enjoyed a critical understanding which was denied the story during his lifetime. Graham Hough's critical essay, "Lawrence's Quarrel with Christianity: 'The Man Who Died' " (found on page 875), has been a clarifying statement of the meaning of this novella since 1957, twenty-eight years after the novella was first published. Hough and other critics have helped to answer and sometimes destroy charges that the story is "heretical" and "irreligious" although during his lifetime Lawrence insisted that "primarily I am a passionately religious man, and my novels must be written from the depth of my religious experience. That I must keep to, because I can only work like that." Like Whitman,** Lawrence was charged with sex-obsession to which he replied (as Whitman did in different terms) that "the sensual passions and mysteries are equally sacred with the spiritual mysteries and passions. Who would deny it anymore? The only thing unbearable is the degradation, the prostitution of the living mysteries in us." Concerning pornography Lawrence says it is "the attempt to insult sex, to do dirt on it. . . . In the degraded human being the deep instincts have gone dead. . . . It happens when the psyche deteriorates, and the profound controlling instincts collapse. Then sex is dirt and dirt is sex, and the sexual excitement becomes playing with dirt. . . ."

There have been many attempts, literary and otherwise, to humanize Jesus, to see him as a natural man among other men and women. Ezra Pound's poem, "Ballad of the Goodly Fere" (found on page 374), gives us a rather unconventional Jesus who is nevertheless surprisingly supported by the scriptures. "The Man Who Died" goes further, and as Hough points out, the story "is simply what Lawrence first called it—a story of the Resurrection, deriving much of its strength from its

background of the Gospel narrative, passing over into a more rootless fantasy* as this recedes into the distance. Its theme is the necessity of rejecting the Christian love-ideal for a man who has really risen from the flesh. And right or wrong, we recognize this as an integral part of the Lawrencean thesis." The story, continues Hough, can be seen "not as the story of a particular man at a particular time, but as an allegory of the course of Christian civilization." So as usual Lawrence has not hesitated to employ the surface action of fiction to symbolize something very basic to humanity which could hardly have been said in any other way.

Part I

There was a peasant near Jerusalem who acquired a young gamecock which looked a shabby little thing, but which put on brave feathers as spring advanced, and was resplendent with arched and orange neck by the time the fig-trees were letting out leaves from their end-tips.

This peasant was poor, he lived in a cottage of mud-brick, and had only a dirty little inner courtyard with a tough fig-tree for all his territory. He worked hard among the vines and olives and wheat of his master, then came home to sleep in the mud-brick cottage by the path. But he was proud of his young rooster. In the shut-in yard were three shabby hens which laid small eggs, shed the few feathers they had, and made a disproportionate amount of dirt. There was also, in a corner under a straw roof, a dull donkey that often went out with the peasant to work, but sometimes stayed at home. And there was the peasant's wife, a black-browed young woman who did not work too hard. She threw a little grain, or the remains of the porridge mess, to the fowls, and she cut green fodder with a sickle, for the ass.

The young cock grew to a certain splendour. By some freak of destiny, he was a dandy rooster, in that dirty little yard with three patchy hens. He learned to crane his neck and give shrill

* F. R. Leavis, *The Great Tradition*, New York: New York University Press, 1963, pp. 1 and 23.
** See his "Song of Myself," p. 343, 11. 40–47.

* See Langston Hughes's "On the Road" (p. 144) for another story that combines fantasy with realism to forge symbolic meaning.

answers to the crowing of other cocks, beyond the walls, in a world he knew nothing of. But there was a special fiery colour to his crow, and the distant calling of the other cocks roused him to unexpected outbursts.

"How he sings," said the peasant, as he got up and pulled his day-shirt over his head.

"He is good for twenty hens," said the wife.

The peasant went out and looked with pride at his young rooster. A saucy, flamboyant bird, that has already made the final acquaintance of the three tattered hens. But the cockerel was tipping his head, listening to the challenge of far-off unseen cocks, in the unknown world. Ghost voices, crowing at him mysteriously out of limbo. He answered with a ringing defiance, never to be daunted.

"He will surely fly away one of these days," said the peasant's wife.

So they lured him with grain, caught him, though he fought with all his wings and feet, and they tied a cord round his shank, fastening it against the spur; and they tied the other end of the cord to the post that held up the donkey's straw pent-roof.

The young cock, freed, marched with a prancing stride of indignation away from the humans, came to the end of his string, gave a tug and a hitch of his tied leg, fell over for a moment, scuffled frantically on the unclean earthen floor, to the horror of the shabby hens, then with a sickening lurch, regained his feet, and stood to think. The peasant and the peasant's wife laughed heartily, and the young cock heard them. And he knew, with a gloomy, foreboding kind of knowledge, that he was tied by the leg.

He no longer pranched and ruffled and forged his feathers. He walked within the limits of his tether sombrely. Still he gobbled up the best bits of food. Still, sometimes, he saved an extra-best bit for his favourite hen of the moment. Still he pranced with quivering, rocking fierceness upon such of his harem as came nonchalantly within range, and gave off the invisible lure. And still he crowed defiance to the cock-crows that showered up out of limbo, in the dawn.

But there was now a grim voracity in the way he gobbled his food, and a pinched triumph in the way he seized upon the shabby hens. His voice, above all, had lost the full gold of its clangour. He was tied by the leg and he knew it. Body, soul and spirit were tied by that string.

Underneath, however, the life in him was grimly unbroken. It was the cord that should break. So one morning, just before the light of dawn, rousing from his slumbers with a sudden wave of strength, he leaped forward on his wings, and the string snapped. He gave a wild strange squawk, rose in one lift to the top of the wall, and there he crowed a loud and splitting crow. So loud, it woke the peasant.

At the same time, at the same hour before dawn, on the same morning, a man awoke from a long sleep in which he was tied up. He woke numb and cold, inside a carved hole in the rock. Through all the long sleep his body had been full of hurt, and it was still full of hurt. He did not open his eyes. Yet he knew that he was awake, and numb, and cold, and rigid, and full of hurt, and tied up. His face was banded with cold bands, his legs were bandaged together. Only his hands were loose.

He could move if he wanted: he knew that. But he had no want. Who would want to come back from the dead? A deep, deep nausea stirred in him, at the premonition of movement. He resented already the fact of the strange, incalculable moving that had already taken place in him: the moving back into consciousness. He had not wished it. He had wanted to stay outside, in the place where even memory is stone dead.

But now, something had returned to him, like a returned letter, and in that return he lay overcome with a sense of nausea. Yet suddenly his hands moved. They lifted up, cold, heavy and sore. Yet they lifted up, to drag away the cloth from his face, and to push at the shoulder bands. Then they fell again, cold, heavy, numb, and sick with having moved even so much, unspeakably unwilling to move further.

With his face cleared, and his shoulders free, he lapsed again, and lay dead, resting on the cold nullity of being dead. It was the most desirable. And almost, he had it complete: the utter cold nullity of being outside.

Yet when he was most nearly gone, suddenly, driven by an ache at the wrists, his hands rose and began pushing at the bandages of his knees, his feet began to stir, even while his breast lay cold and dead still.

And at last, the eyes opened. On to the dark. The same dark! yet perhaps there was a pale chink, of the all-disturbing light, prizing open the pure dark. He could not lift his head. The eyes closed. And again it was finished.

Then suddenly he leaned up, and the great world reeled. Bandages fell away. And narrow walls of rock closed upon him, and gave the new anguish of imprisonment. There were chinks of light. With a wave of strength that came from revulsion, he leaned forward, in that narrow well of rock, and leaned frail hands on the rock near the chinks of light.

Strength came from somewhere, from revulsion; there was a crash and a wave of light, and the dead man was crouching in his lair, facing the animal onrush of light. Yet it was hardly dawn. And the strange, piercing keenness of daybreak's sharp breath was on him. It meant full awakening.

Slowly, slowly he crept down from the cell of rock, with the caution of the bitterly wounded. Bandages and linen and perfume fell away, and he crouched on the ground against the wall of rock, to recover oblivion. But he saw his hurt feet touching the earth again, with unspeakable pain, the earth they had meant to touch no more, and he saw his thin legs that had died, and pain unknowable, pain like utter bodily disillusion, filled him so full that he stood up, with one torn hand on the ledge of the tomb.

To be back! To be back again, after all that! He saw the linen swathing-bands fallen round his dead feet, and stooping, he picked them up, folded them, and laid them back in the rocky cavity from which he had emerged. Then he took the perfumed linen sheet, wrapped it round him as a mantle, and turned away, to the wanness of the chill dawn.

He was alone; and having died, was even beyond loneliness.

Filled still with the sickness of unspeakable disillusion, the man stepped with wincing feet down the rocky slope, past the sleeping soldiers, who lay wrapped in their woollen mantles under the wild laurels. Silent, on naked scarred feet, wrapped in a white linen shroud, he glanced down for a moment on the inert, heap-like bodies of the soldiers. They were repulsive, a slow squalor of limbs, yet he felt a certain compassion. He passed on towards the road, lest they should wake.

Having nowhere to go, he turned from the city that stood on her hills. He slowly followed the road away from the town, past the olives, under which purple anemones were drooping in the chill of dawn, and rich-green herbage was pressing thick. The world, the same as ever, the natural world, thronging with greenness, a nightingale winsomely, wistfully, coaxingly calling from the bushes beside a runnel of water, in the world, the natural world of morning and evening, forever undying, from which he had died.

He went on, on scarred feet, neither of this world nor of the next. Neither here nor there, neither seeing nor yet sightless, he passed dimly on, away from the city and its precincts, wondering why he should be travelling, yet driven by a dim, deep nausea of disillusion, and a resolution of which he was not even aware.

Advancing in a kind of half-consciousness under the dry stone wall of the olive orchard, he was roused by the shrill wild crowing of a cock just near him, a sound which made him shiver as if electricity had touched him. He saw a black and orange cock on a bough above the road, then running through the olives of the upper level, a peasant in a gray woollen shirt-tunic. Leaping out of greenness, came the black and orange cock with the red comb, his tail-feathers streaming lustrous.

"O stop him, Master!" called the peasant. "My escaped cock!"

The man addressed, with a sudden flicker of smile, opened his great white wings of a shroud in front of the leaping bird. The cock fell back with a squawk and a flutter, the peasant jumped forward, there was a terrific beating of wings, and whirring of feathers, then the peasant had the escaped cock safely under his arm, its wings shut down, its face crazily craning forward, its round eyes goggling from its white chops.

"It's my escaped cock!" said the peasant, soothing the bird with his left hand, as he looked perspiringly up into the face of the man wrapped in white linen.

The peasant changed countenance, and stood transfixed, as he looked into the dead-white face of the man who had died. That dead-white face, so still, with the black beard growing on it as if in death; and those wide-open black sombre eyes, that had died! and those washed scars on the waxy forehead! The slow-blooded man of the field let his jaw drop, in childish inability to meet the situation.

"Don't be afraid," said the man in the shroud. "I am not dead. They took me down too soon. So I have risen up. Yet if they discover me, they will do it all over again. . . ."

He spoke in a voice of old disgust. Humanity! Especially humanity in authority! There was only one thing it could do. He looked with black, indifferent eyes into the quick, shifty eyes of the peasant. The peasant quailed, and was powerless under the look of deathly indifference, and strange cold resoluteness. He could only say the one thing he was afraid to say:

"Will you hide in my house, Master?"

"I will rest there. But if you tell anyone, you know what will happen. You will have to go before a judge."

"Me! I shan't speak. Let us be quick!"

The peasant looked round in fear, wondering sulkily why he had let himself in for this doom. The man with scarred feet climbed painfully up to the level of the olive garden, and followed by the sullen, hurrying peasant across the green wheat among the olive trees. He felt the cool silkiness of the young wheat under his feet that had been dead, and the roughishness of its separate life was apparent to him. At the edges of rocks, he saw the silky, silvery-haired buds of the scarlet anemone bending downwards. And they too were in another world. In his own world he was alone, utterly alone. These things around him were in a world that had never died. But he himself had died, or had been killed from out of it, and all that remained now was the great void nausea of utter disillusion.

They came to a clay cottage, and the peasant waited dejectedly for the other man to pass.

"Pass!" he said. "Pass! We have not been seen."

The man in white linen entered the earthen room, taking with him the aroma of strange perfumes. The peasant closed the door, and passed through the inner doorway into the yard, where the ass stood within the high walls, safe from being stolen. There the peasant, in great disquietude, tied up the cock. The man with the waxen face sat down on a mat near the hearth, for he was spent and barely conscious. Yet he heard outside the whispering of the peasant to his wife, for the woman had been watching from the roof.

Presently they came in, and the woman hid her face. She poured water, and put bread and dried figs on a wooden platter.

"Eat, Master!" said the peasant. "Eat! No one has seen."

But the stranger had no desire for food. Yet he moistened a little bread in the water, and ate it, since life must be. But desire was dead in him, even for food and drink. He had risen without desire, without even the desire to live, empty save for the all-overwhelming disillusion that lay like nausea where his life had been. Yet perhaps, deeper even than disillusion, was a desireless resoluteness, deeper even than consciousness.

The peasant and his wife stood near the door, watching. They saw with terror the livid wounds on the thin waxy hands and the thin feet of the stranger, and the small lacerations in the still dead forehead. They smelled with terror the scent of rich perfumes that came from him, from his body. And they looked at the fine, snowy, costly linen. Perhaps really he was a dead king, from the region of terrors. And he was still cold and remote in the region of death, with perfumes coming from his transparent body as if from some strange flower.

Having with difficulty swallowed some of the moistened bread, he lifted his eyes to them. He saw them as they were: limited, meagre in their life, without any splendour of gesture and of courage. But they were what they were, slow inevitable parts of the natural world. They had no nobility, but fear made them compassionate.

And the stranger had compassion on them again, for he knew that they would respond best to gentleness, giving back a clumsy gentleness again.

"Do not be afraid," he said to them gently. "Let me stay a little while with you. I shall not stay long. And then I shall go away forever. But do not be afraid. No harm will come to you through me."

They believed him at once, yet the fear did not leave them. And they said:

"Stay, Master, while ever you will. Rest! Rest quietly!"

But they were afraid.

So he let them be, and the peasant went away with the ass. The sun had risen bright, and in the dark house with the door shut, the man was again as if in the tomb. So he said to the woman, "I would lie in the yard."

And she swept the yard for him, and laid him a mat, and he lay down under the wall in the morning sun. There he saw the first green leaves spurting like flames from the ends of the enclosed fig-tree, out of the bareness to the sky of spring above. But the man who had died could not look, he only lay quite still in the sun, which was not yet too hot, and had no desire in him, not even to move. But he lay with his thin legs in the sun, his black perfumed hair falling into the hollows of his neck, and his thin colourless arms utterly inert. As he lay there, the hens clucked and scratched, and the escaped cock, caught and tied by the leg again, cowered in a corner.

The peasant woman was frightened. She came peeping, and, seeing him never move, feared to have a dead man in the yard. But the sun had grown stronger, he opened his eyes and looked at her. And now she was frightened of the man who was alive, but spoke nothing.

He opened his eyes, and saw the world again bright as glass. It was life, in which he had no share any more. But it shone outside him, blue sky, and a bare fig-tree with little jets of green leaf. Bright as glass, and he was not of it, for desire had failed.

Yet he was there, and not extinguished. The day passed in a kind of coma, and at evening he went into the house. The peasant man came home, but he was frightened, and had nothing to say. The stranger too ate of the mess of beans, a little. Then he washed his hands and turned to the wall, and was silent. The peasants were silent too. They watched their guest sleep. Sleep was so near death he could still sleep.

Yet when the sun came up, he went again to lie in the yard. The sun was the one thing that drew him and swayed him, and he still wanted to feel the cool air of morning in his nostrils, see the pale sky overhead. He still hated to be shut up.

As he came out, the young cock crowed. It was a diminished, pinched cry, but there was that in the voice of the bird stronger than chagrin. It was the necessity to live, and even to cry out the triumph of life. The man who had died stood and watched the cock who had escaped and been caught, ruffling himself up, rising forward on his toes, throwing up his head, and parting his beak in another challenge from life to death. The brave sounds rang out, and though they were diminished by the cord round the bird's leg, they were not cut off. The man who had died looked nakedly on life, and saw a vast resoluteness everywhere flinging itself up in stormy or subtle wave-crests, foam-tips emerging out of the blue invisible, a black and orange cock or the green flame-tongues out of the extremes of the fig-tree. They came forth, these things and creatures of spring, glowing with desire and with assertion. They came like crests of foam, out of the blue flood of the invisible desire, out of the vast invisible sea of strength, and they came coloured and tangible, evanescent, yet deathless in their coming. The man who had died looked on the great swing into existence of things that had not died, but he saw no longer their tremulous desire to exist and to be. He heard instead their ringing, ringing, defiant challenge to all other things existing.

The man lay still, with eyes that had died now wide open and darkly still, seeing the everlasting resoluteness of life. And the cock, with the flat, brilliant glance, glanced back at him, with a bird's half-seeing look. And always the man who had died saw not the bird alone, but the short, sharp wave of life of which the bird was the crest. He watched the queer, beaky motion of the creature as it gobbled into itself the scraps of food; its glancing of the eye of life, ever alert and watchful, overweening and cautious, and the voice of its life, crowing triumph and assertion, yet strangled by a cord of circumstance. He seemed to hear the queer speech of very life, as the cock triumphantly imitated the clucking of the favourite hen, when she had laid an egg, a clucking which still had, in the male bird, the hollow chagrin of the cord round his leg. And when the man threw a bit of bread to the cock, it called with an extraordinary cooing tenderness, tousling and saving the morsel for the hens. The hens ran up greedily, and carried the morsel away beyond the reach of the string.

Then, walking complacently after them, suddenly the male bird's leg would hitch at the end of his tether, and he would yield with a kind of collapse. His flag fell, he seemed to diminish, he would huddle in the shade. And he was young, his tail-feathers, glossy as they were, were not fully grown. It was not till evening again that the tide of life in him made him forget. Then when his favourite hen came strolling unconcernedly near him, emitting the lure, he pounced on her with all his feathers vibrating. And the man who had died watched the unsteady, rocking vibration of the bent bird, and it was not the bird he saw, but one wave-tip of life overlapping for a minute another, in the tide of the swaying ocean of life. And the destiny of life seemed more fierce and compulsive to him even than the destiny of death. The doom of death was a shadow compared to the raging destiny of life, the determined surge of life.

At twilight the peasant came home with the ass, and he said: "Master! It is said that the body was stolen from the garden, and the tomb is empty, and the soldiers are taken away, accursed Romans! And the women are there to weep."

The man who had died looked at the man who had not died.

"It is well," he said. "Say nothing, and we are safe."

And the peasant was relieved. He looked rather dirty and stupid, and even as much flaminess as that of the young cock, which he had tied by the leg, would never glow in him. He was without fire. But the man who had died thought to himself: "Why, then, should he be lifted up? Clods of earth are turned over for refreshment, they are not to be lifted up. Let the earth remain earthy, and hold its own against the sky. I was wrong to seek to lift it up. I was wrong to try to interfere. The ploughshare of devastation will be set in the soil of Judaea, and the life of this peasant will be overturned like the sods of the field. No man can save the earth from tillage. It is tillage, not salvation. . . ."

So he saw the man, the peasant, with compassion; but the man who had died no longer wished to interfere in the soul of the man who had not died, and who could never die, save to return to earth. Let him return to earth in his own good hour, and let no one try to interfere when the earth claims her own.

So the man with scars let the peasant go from him, for the peasant had no re-birth in him. Yet the man who had died said to himself: "He is my host."

And at dawn, when he was better, the man who had died rose up, and on slow, sore feet retraced his way to the garden. For he had been betrayed in a garden, and buried in a garden. And as he turned round the screen of laurels, near the rock-face, he saw a woman hovering by the tomb, a woman in blue and yellow. She peeped again into the mouth of the hole, that was like a deep cupboard. But still there was nothing. And she wrung her hands and wept. And as she turned away, she saw the man in white, standing by the laurels, and she gave a cry, thinking it might be a spy, and she said:

"They have taken him away!"

So he said to her:

"Madeleine!"[1]

Then she reeled as if she would fall, for she knew him. And he said to her:

"Madeleine! Do not be afraid. I am alive. They took me down too soon, so I came back to life. Then I was sheltered in a house."

She did not know what to say, but fell at his feet to kiss them.

"Don't touch me, Madeleine," he said. "Not yet! I am not yet healed and in touch with men."

So she wept because she did not know what to do. And he said:

"Let us go aside, among the bushes, where we can speak unseen."

So in her blue mantle and her yellow robe, she followed him among the trees, and he sat down under a myrtle bush. And he said:

"I am not yet quite come to. Madeleine, what is to be done next?"

"Master!" she said. "Oh, we have wept for you! And will you come back to us?"

"What is finished is finished, and for me the end is past," he said. "The stream will run till no more rains fill it, then it will dry up. For me, that life is over."

"And will you give up your triumph?" she said sadly.

"My triumph," he said, "is that I am not dead. I have outlived my mission, and know no more of it. It is my triumph. I have survived the day and the death of my interference, and am still a man. I am young still, Madeleine, not even come to middle age. I am glad all that is over. It had to be. But now I am glad it is over, and the day of my interference is done. The teacher

[1] Mary Magdelene. See *Luke*, 7:37–50; *Matthew*, 27:56, 61; 28:1–7; and *Mark*, 16:9–10.

and the saviour are dead in me; now I can go about my business, into my own single life."

She heard him, and did not fully understand. But what he said made her feel disappointed.

"But you will come back to us?" she said, insisting.

"I don't know what I shall do," he said. "When I am healed, I shall know better. But my mission is over, and my teaching is finished, and death has saved me from my own salvation. Oh, Madeleine, I want to take my single way in life, which is my portion. My public life is over, the life of my self-importance. Now I can wait on life, and say nothing, and have no one betray me. I wanted to be greater than the limits of my hands and feet, so I brought betrayal on myself. And I know I wronged Judas, my poor Judas.[2] For I have died, and now I know my own limits. Now I can live without striving to sway others any more. For my reach ends in my finger-tips, and my stride is no longer than the ends of my toes.[3] Yet I would embrace multitudes, I who have never truly embraced even one. But Judas and the high priests saved me from my own salvation, and soon I can turn to my destiny like a bather in the sea at dawn, who has just come down to the shore alone."

"Do you want to be alone henceforward?" she asked. "And was your mission nothing? Was it all untrue?"

"Nay!" he said. "Neither were your lovers in the past nothing. They were much to you, but you took more than you gave. Then you came to me for salvation from your own excess. And I, in my mission, I too ran to excess. I gave more than I took, and that also is woe and vanity. So Pilate and the high priests[4] saved me from my own excessive salvation. Don't run to excess now in living, Madeleine. It only means another death."

She pondered bitterly, for the need for excessive giving was in her, and she could not bear to be denied.

"And will you not come back to us?" she said. "Have you risen for yourself alone?"

He heard the sarcasm in her voice, and looked at her beautiful face which still was dense with excessive need for salvation from the woman she had been, the female who had caught men at her will. The cloud of necessity was on her, to be saved from the old, wilful Eve, who had embraced many men and taken more than she gave. Now the other doom was on her. She wanted to give without taking. And that, too, is hard, and cruel to the warm body.

"I have not risen from the dead in order to seek death again," he said.

She glanced up at him, and saw the weariness settling again on his waxy face, and the vast disillusion in his dark eyes, and the underlying indifference. He felt her glance, and said to himself:

"Now my own followers will want to do me to death again, for having risen up different from their expectation."

"But you will come to us, to see us, us who love you?" she said.

He laughed a little and said:

"Ah, yes." Then he added, "Have you a little money? Will you give me a little money? I owe it."

She had not much, but it pleased her to give it to him.

"Do you think," he said to her, "that I might come and live with you in your house?"

She looked up at him with large blue eyes, that gleamed strangely.

"Now?" she said, with peculiar triumph.

And he, who shrank now from triumph of any sort, his own or another's, said:

"Not now! Later, when I am healed, and . . . and I am in touch with the flesh."

The words faltered in him. And in his heart he knew he would never go to live in her house. For the flicker of triumph had gleamed in her eyes; the greed of giving. But she murmured in a humming rapture:

"Ah, you know I would give up everything to you."

"Nay!" he said. "I didn't ask that."

---

[2] See *Matthew*, 26:14–50 which includes: "Then one of the twelve [disciples], called Judas Iscariot, went unto the chief priests, And said *unto them*, What will ye give me, and I will deliver him unto you? And they covenanted with him for thirty pieces of silver. . . . Now he that betrayed him gave them a sign, saying, Whomsoever I shall kiss, that same is he; hold him fast. And forthwith he came to Jesus, and said, Hail Master; and kissed him."   [3] "For my reach ends in my finger-tips": an interesting negation of the celebrated lines in Browning's "Andrea del Sarto":

Ah, but a man's reach should exceed his grasp,
Or what's a heaven for?

[4] Pilate and the high priests: see *Matthew*, 27.

A revulsion from all the life he had known came over him again, the great nausea of disillusion, and the spear-thrust through his bowels. He crouched under the myrtle bushes, without strength. Yet his eyes were open. And she looked at him again, and she saw that it was not the Messiah. The Messiah had not risen. The enthusiasm and the burning purity were gone, and the rapt youth. His youth was dead. This man was middle-aged and disillusioned, with a certain terrible indifference, and a resoluteness which love would never conquer. This was not the Master she had so adored, the young, flamy, unphysical exalter of her soul. This was nearer to the lovers she had known of old, but with a greater indifference to the personal issue, and a lesser susceptibility.

She was thrown out of the balance of her rapturous, anguished adoration. This risen man was the death of her dream.

"You should go now," he said to her. "Do not touch me, I am in death. I shall come again here, on the third day. Come if you will, at dawn. And we will speak again."

She went away, perturbed and shattered. Yet as she went, her mind discarded the bitterness of the reality, and she conjured up rapture and wonder, that the Master was risen and was not dead. He was risen, the Saviour, the exalter, the wonder-worker! He was risen, but not as man; as pure God, who should not be touched by flesh, and who should be rapt away into Heaven. It was the most glorious and most ghostly of the miracles.

Meanwhile the man who had died gathered himself together at last, and slowly made his way to the peasant's house. He was glad to go back to them, and away from Madeleine and his own associates. For the peasants had the inertia of earth and would let him rest, and as yet, would put no compulsion on him.

The woman was on the roof, looking for him. She was afraid that he had gone away. His presence in the house had become like gentle wine to her. She hastened to the door, to him.

"Where have you been?" she said. "Why did you go away?"

"I have been to walk in a garden, and I have seen a friend, who gave me a little money. It is for you."

He held out his thin hand, with the small amount of money, all that Madeleine could give him. The peasant's wife's eyes glistened, for money was scarce, and she said:

"Oh, Master! And is it truly mine?"

"Take it!" he said. "It buys bread, and bread brings life."

So he lay down in the yard again, sick with relief at being alone again. For with the peasants he could be alone, but his own friends would never let him be alone. And in the safety of the yard, the young cock was dear to him, as it shouted in the helpless zest of life, and finished in the helpless humiliation of being tied by the leg. This day the ass stood swishing her tail under the shed. The man who had died lay down and turned utterly away from life, in the sickness of death in life.

But the woman brought wine and water, and sweetened cakes, and roused him, so that he ate a little, to please her. The day was hot, and as she crouched to serve him, he saw her breasts sway from her humble body, under her smock. He knew she wished he would desire her, and she was youngish, and not unpleasant. And he, who had never known a woman, would have desired her if he could. But he could not want her, though he felt gently towards her soft, crouching, humble body. But it was her thoughts, her consciousness, he could not mingle with. She was pleased with the money, and now she wanted to take more from him. She wanted the embrace of his body. But her little soul was hard, and short-sighted, and grasping, her body had its little greed, and no gentle reverence of the return gift. So he spoke a quiet, pleasant word to her, and turned away. He could not touch the little, personal body, the little, personal life of this woman, nor in any other. He turned away from it without hesitation.

Risen from the dead, he had realised at last that the body, too, has its little life, and beyond that, the greater life. He was virgin, in recoil from the little, greedy life of the body. But now he knew that virginity is a form of greed; and that the body rises again to give and to take, to take and to give, ungreedily. Now he knew that he had risen for the woman, or women, who knew the greater life of the body, not greedy to give, not greedy to take, and with whom he could mingle his body. But having died, he was patient, knowing there was time, an eternity of time. And he was driven by no greedy desire, either to give himself to others, or to grasp anything for himself. For he had died.

The peasant came home from work, and said:

"Master, I thank you for the money. But we did not want it. And all I have is yours."

But the man who had died was sad, because the peasant stood there in the little, personal body, and his eyes were cunning and sparkling with the hope of greater rewards in money, later on. True, the peasant had taken him in free, and had risked getting no reward. But the hope was cunning in him. Yet even this was as men are made. So when the peasant would have helped him to rise, for night had fallen, the man who had died said:

"Don't touch me, brother. I am not yet risen to the Father."[5]

The sun burned with greater splendour, and burnished the young cock brighter. But the peasant kept the string renewed, and the bird was a prisoner. Yet the flame of life burned up to a sharp point in the cock, so that it eyed askance and haughtily the man who had died. And the man smiled and held the bird dear, and he said to it:

"Surely thou art risen to the Father, among birds." And the young cock, answering, crowed.

When at dawn on the third morning the man went to the garden, he was absorbed, thinking of the greater life of the body, beyond the little, narrow, personal life. So he came through the thick screen of laurel and myrtle bushes, near the rock, suddenly, and he saw three women near the tomb. One was Madeleine, and one was the woman who had been his mother, and third was a woman he knew, called Joan. He looked up, and saw them all, and they saw him, and they were all afraid.

He stood arrested in the distance, knowing they were there to claim him back, bodily. But he would in no wise return to them. Pallid, in the shadow of a gray morning that was blowing to rain, he saw them, and turned away. But Madeleine hastened towards him.

"I did not bring them," she said. "They have come of themselves. See, I have brought you money! . . . Will you not speak to them?"

She offered him some gold pieces and he took them, saying:

"May I have this money? I shall need it. I cannot speak to them, for I am not yet ascended to the Father. And I must leave you now."

"Ah! Where will you go?" she cried.

He looked at her, and saw she was clutching for the man in him who had died and was dead, the man of his youth and his mission, of his chastity and his fear, of his little life, his giving without taking.

"I must go to my Father!" he said.

"And you will leave us? There is your mother!" she cried, turning round with the old anguish, which yet was sweet to her.

"But now I must ascend to my Father," he said, and he drew back into the bushes, and so turned quickly, and went away, saying to himself:

"Now I belong to no one and have no connection, and mission or gospel is gone from me. Lo! I cannot make even my own life, and what have I to save? . . . I can learn to be alone."

So he went back to the peasant's house, to the yard where the young cock was tied by the leg, with a string. And he wanted no one, for it was best to be alone; for the presence of people made him lonely. The sun and the subtle salve of spring healed his wounds, even the gaping wound of disillusion through his bowels was closing up. And his need of men and women, his fever to have them and to be saved by them, this too was healing in him. Whatever came of touch between himself and the race of men, henceforth, should come without trespass or compulsion. For he said to himself:

"I tried to compel them to live, so they compelled me to die. It is always so, with compulsion. The recoil kills the advance. Now is my time to be alone."

Therefore he went no more to the garden, but lay still and saw the sun, or walked at dusk across the olive slopes, among the green wheat, that rose a palm-breadth higher every sunny day. And always he thought to himself:

"How good it is to have fulfilled my mission, and to be beyond it. Now I can be alone, and leave all things to themselves, and the fig-tree[6]

---

[5] Graham Hough observes in his essay (p. 875) "that in Lawrence's mythology the Father was also the Flesh."

[6] See *Matthew*, 21:19–22.

may be barren if it will, and the rich may be rich.[7] My way is my own alone."

So the green jets of leaves unspread on the fig-tree, with the bright, translucent, green blood of the tree. And the young cock grew brighter, more lustrous with the sun's burnishing; yet always tied by the leg with a string. And the sun went down more and more in pomp, out of the gold and red-flushed air. The man who had died was aware of it all, and he thought:

"The Word is but the midge that bites at evening. Man is tormented with words like midges, and they follow him right into the tomb. But beyond the tomb they cannot go. Now I have passed the place where words can bite no more and the air is clear, and there is nothing to say, and I am alone within my own skin, which is the walls of all my domain."

So he healed of his wounds, and enjoyed his immortality of being alive without fret. For in the tomb he had slipped that noose which we call care. For in the tomb he had left his striving self, which cares and asserts itself. Now his uncaring self healed and became whole within his skin, and he smiled to himself with pure aloneness, which is one sort of immortality.

Then he said to himself: "I will wander the earth, and say nothing. For nothing is so marvellous as to be alone in the phenomenal world, which is raging, and yet apart. And I have not seen it, I was too much blinded by my confusion within it. Now I will wander among the stirring of the phenomenal world, for it is the stirring of all things among themselves which leaves me purely alone."

So he communed with himself, and decided to be a physician. Because the power was still in him to heal any man or child who touched his compassion. Therefore he cut his hair and his beard after the right fashion, and smiled to himself. And he bought himself shoes, and the right mantle, and put the right cloth over his head, hiding all the little scars. And the peasant said:

"Master, will you go forth from us?"

"Yes, for the time is come for me to return to men."

So he gave the peasant a piece of money, and said to him:

[7] See *Mark*, 10:17–23.

"Give me the cock that escaped and is now tied by the leg. For he shall go forth with me."

So for a piece of money the peasant gave the cock to the man who had died, and at dawn the man who had died set out into the phenomenal world, to be fulfilled in his own loneliness in the midst of it. For previously he had been too much mixed up in it. Then he had died. Now he must come back, to be alone in the midst. Yet even now he did not go quite alone, for under his arm, as he went, he carried the cock, whose tail fluttered gaily behind, and who craned his head excitedly, for he too was adventuring out for the first time into the wider phenomenal world, which is the stirring of the body of cocks also. And the peasant woman shed a few tears, but then went indoors, being a peasant, to look again at the pieces of money. And it seemed to her, a gleam came out of the pieces of money, wonderful.

The man who had died wandered on, and it was a sunny day. He looked around as he went, and stood aside as the pack-train passed by, towards the city. And he said to himself:

"Strange is the phenomenal world, dirty and clean together! And I am the same. Yet I am apart! And life bubbles variously. Why should I have wanted it to bubble all alike? What a pity I preached to them! A sermon is so much more likely to cake into mud, and to close the fountains, than is a psalm or a song. I made a mistake. I understand that they executed me for preaching to them. Yet they could not finally execute me, for now I am risen in my own aloneness, and inherit the earth, since I lay no claim on it. And I will be alone in the seethe of all things; first and foremost, forever, I shall be alone. But I must toss this bird into the seethe of phenomena, for he must ride his wave. How hot he is with life! Soon, in some place, I shall leave him among the hens. And perhaps one evening, I shall meet a woman who can lure my risen body, yet leave me my aloneness. For the body of my desire has died, and I am not in touch anywhere. Yet how do I know! All at least is life. And this cock gleams with bright aloneness, though he answers the lure of hens. And I shall hasten on to that village on the hill ahead of me; already I am tired and weak, and want to close my eyes to everything."

Hastening a little with the desire to have finished going, he overtook two men going slowly, and talking. And being soft-footed, he heard they were speaking of himself. And he remembered them, for he had known them in his life, the life of his mission. So he greeted them, but did not disclose himself in the dusk, and they did not know him. He said to them:

"What then of him who would be king, and was put to death for it?"

They answered suspiciously: "Why ask you of him?"

"I have known him, and thought much about him," he said.

So they replied: "He has risen."

"Yea! And where is he, and how does he live?"

"We know not, for it is not revealed. Yet he is risen, and in a little while will ascend unto the Father."

"Yea! And where then is his Father?"

"Know ye not? You are then of the Gentiles! The Father is in Heaven, above the cloud and the firmament."

"Truly? Then how will he ascend?"

"As Elijah[8] the Prophet, he shall go up in a glory."

"Even into the sky."

"Into the sky."

"Then is he not risen in the flesh?"

"He is risen in the flesh."

"And will he take flesh up into the sky?"

"The Father in Heaven will take him up."

The man who had died said no more, for his say was over, and words beget words, even as gnats. But the man asked him: "Why do you carry a cock?"

"I am a healer," he said, "and the bird hath virtue."

"You are not a believer?"

"Yea! I believe the bird is full of life and virtue."

They walked on in silence after this, and he felt they disliked his answer. So he smiled to himself, for a dangerous phenomenon in the world is a man of narrow belief, who denies the right of his neighbour to be alone. And as they came to the outskirts of the village, the man who had died stood still in the gloaming and said in his old voice:

"Know ye me not?"

And they cried in fear: "Master!"

"Yea!" he said, laughing softly. And he turned suddenly away, down a side lane, and was gone under the wall before they knew.

So he came to an inn where the asses stood in the yard. And he called for fritters, and they were made for him. So he slept under a shed. But in the morning he was wakened by a loud crowing, and his cock's voice ringing in his ears. So he saw the rooster of the inn walking forth to battle, with his hens, a goodly number, behind him. Then the cock of the man who had died sprang forth, and a battle began between the birds. The man of the inn ran to save his rooster, but the man who had died said:

"If my bird wins I will give him thee. And if he lose, thou shalt eat him."

So the birds fought savagely, and the cock of the man who had died killed the common cock of the yard. Then the man who had died said to his young cock:

"Thou at least hast found thy kingdom, and the females to thy body. Thy aloneness can take on splendour, polished by the lure of thy hens."[9]

And he left his bird there, and went on deeper into the phenomenal world, which is a vast complexity of entanglements and allurements. And he asked himself a last question:

"From what, and to what, could this infinite whirl be saved?"

So he went his way, and was alone. But the way of the world was past belief, as he saw the strange entanglement of passions and circumstance and compulsion everywhere, but always the dread insomnia of compulsion. It was fear, the ultimate fear of death, that made men mad. So always he must move on, for if he stayed, his neighbours wound the strangling of their fear and bullying round him. There was nothing he could touch, for all, in a mad assertion of the ego, wanted to put a compulsion on him,

---

[8] *II Kings*, 2:11: ". . . behold, *there appeared* a chariot of fire, and horses of fire . . . and Elijah went up by a whirlwind into heaven."

[9] This paragraph which concludes the scene of the cock fight brings to point the parallel Lawrence has been drawing of Jesus and the cock: each is looking for freedom to pursue his own destiny in the natural world.

and violate his intrinsic solitude. It was the mania of cities and societies and hosts, to lay a compulsion upon a man, upon all men. For men and women alike were mad with the egoistic fear of their own nothingness. And he thought of his own mission, how he had tried to lay the compulsion of love on all men. And the old nausea came back on him. For there was no contact without a subtle attempt to inflict a compulsion. And already he had been compelled even into death. The nausea of the old wound broke out afresh, and he looked again on the world with repulsion, dreading its mean contacts.

Part II

The wind came cold and strong from inland, from the invisible snows of Lebanon. But the temple, facing south and west, towards Egypt, faced the splendid sun of winter as he curved down towards the sea, the warmth and radiance flooded in between the pillars of painted wood. But the sea was invisible, because of the trees, though its dashing sounded among the hum of pines. The air was turning golden to afternoon. The woman who served Isis[10] stood in her yellow robe, and looked up at the steep slopes coming down to the sea, where the olive-trees silvered under the wind like water splashing. She was alone save for the goddess. And in the winter afternoon the light stood erect and magnificent off the invisible sea, filling the hills of the coast. She went towards the sun, through the grove of Mediterranean pine-trees and evergreen oaks, in the midst of which the temple stood, on a little, tree-covered tongue of land between two bays.

It was only a very little way, and then she stood among the dry trunks of the outermost pines, on the rocks under which the sea smote and sucked, facing the open where the bright sun gloried in winter. The sea was dark, almost indigo, running away from the land, and crested with white. The hand of the wind brushed it strangely with shadow, as it brushed the olives of the slopes with silver. And there was no boat out.

[10] For a discussion of the Lady and priestess of Isis see Hough's essay, p. 875.

The three boats were drawn high up on the steep shingle of the little bay, by the small gray tower. Along the edge of the shingle ran a high wall, inside which was a garden occupying the brief flat of the bay, then rising in terraces up the steep slope of the coast. And there, some little way up, within another wall, stood the low white villa, white and alone as the coast, overlooking the sea. But higher, much higher up, where the olives had given way to pine-trees again, ran the coast road, keeping to the height to be above the gullies that came down to the bays.

Upon it all poured the royal sunshine of the January afternoon. Or rather, all was part of the great sun, glow and substance and immaculate loneliness of the sea, and pure brightness.

Crouching in the rocks above the dark waters, which only swung up and down, two slaves, half naked, were dressing pigeons for the evening meal. They pierced the throat of a blue, live bird, and let the drops of blood fall into the heaving sea, with curious concentration. They were performing some sacrifice, or working some incantation. The woman of the temple, yellow and white and alone like a winter narcissus, stood between the pines of the small, humped peninsula where the temple secretly hid, and watched.

A black-and-white pigeon, vividly white, like a ghost escaped over the low dark sea, sped out, caught the wind, tilted, rode, soared and swept over the pine-trees, and wheeled away, a speck, inland. It had escaped. The priestess heard the cry of the boy slave, a garden slave of about seventeen. He raised his arms to heaven in anger as the pigeon wheeled away, naked and angry and young he held out his arms. Then he turned and seized the girl in an access of rage, and beat her with his fist that was stained with pigeon's blood. And she lay down with her face hidden, passive and quivering. The woman who owned them watched. And as she watched, she saw another onlooker, a stranger, in a low, broad hat, and a cloak of gray homespun, a dark bearded man standing on the little causeway of a rock that was the neck of her temple peninsula. By the blowing of his dark-gray cloak she saw him. And he saw her, on the rocks like a white-and-yellow narcissus, because of the flutter of her white linen tunic, below the yellow mantle of wool. And both of them watched the two slaves.

The boy suddenly left off beating the girl. He crouched over her, touching her, trying to make her speak. But she lay quite inert, face down on the smoothed rock. And he put his arms round her and lifted her, but she slipped back to earth like one dead, yet far too quickly for anything dead. The boy, desperate, caught her by the hips and hugged her to him, turning her over there. There she seemed inert, all her fight was in her shoulders. He twisted her over, intent and unconscious, and pushed his hands between her thighs, to push them apart. And in an instant he was covering her in the blind, frightened frenzy of a boy's first passion. Quick and frenzied his young body quivered naked on hers, blind, for a minute. Then it lay quite still, as if dead.

And then, in terror, he peeped up. He peeped round, and drew slowly to his feet, adjusting his loin-rag. He saw the stranger, and then he saw, on the rocks beyond, the lady of Isis, his mistress. And as he saw her, his whole body shrank and cowed, and with a strange cringing motion he scuttled lamely towards the door in the wall.

The girl sat up and looked after him. When she had seen him disappear, she too looked round. And she saw the stranger and the priestess. Then with a sullen movement she turned away, as if she had seen nothing, to the four dead pigeons and the knife, which lay there on the rock. And she began to strip the small feathers, so that they rose on the wind like dust.

The priestess turned away. Slaves! Let the overseer watch them. She was not interested. She went slowly through the pines again, back to the temple, which stood in the sun in a small clearing at the centre of the tongue of land. It was a small temple of wood, painted all pink and white and blue, having at the front four wooden pillars rising like stems to the swollen lotus-bud of Egypt at the top, supporting the roof and open, spiky lotus-flowers of the outer frieze, which went round under the eaves. Two low steps of stone led up to the platform before the pillars, and the chamber behind the pillars was open. There a low stone altar stood, with a few embers in its hollow, and the dark stain of blood in its end groove.

She knew her temple so well, for she had built it at her own expense, and tended it for seven years. There it stood, pink and white, like a flower in the little clearing, backed by blackish evergreen oaks; and the shadow of afternoon was already washing over its pillarbases.

She entered slowly, passing through to the dark inner chamber, lighted by a perfumed oil-flame. And once more she pushed shut the door, and once more she threw a few grains of incense on a brazier before the goddess, and once more she sat down before her goddess, in the almost-darkness, to muse, to go away into the dreams of the goddess.

It was Isis; but not Isis, Mother of Horus. It was Isis Bereaved, Isis in Search. The goddess, in painted marble, lifted her face and strode, one thigh forward through the frail fluting of her robe, in the anguish of bereavement and of search. She was looking for the fragments of the dead Osiris, dead and scattered asunder, dead, torn apart, and thrown in fragments over the wide world. And she must find his hands and his feet, his heart, his thighs, his head, his belly, she must gather him together and fold her arms round the re-assembled body till it became warm again, and roused to life, and could embrace her, and could fecundate her womb. And the strange rapture and anguish of search went on through the years, as she lifted her throat and her hollowed eyes looked inward, in the tormented ecstasy of seeking, and the delicate navel of her bud-like belly showed through the frail, girdled robe with the eternal asking, asking, of her search. And through the years she found him bit by bit, heart and head and limbs and body. And yet she had not found the last reality, the final clue to him, that alone could bring him really back to her. For she was Isis of the subtle lotus, the womb which waits submerged and in bud, waits for the touch of that other inward sun that streams its rays from the loins of the male Osiris.

This was the mystery the woman had served alone for seven years, since she was twenty, till now she was twenty-seven. Before, when she was young, she had lived in the world, in Rome in Ephesus, in Egypt. For her father had been one of Anthony's captains and comrades, had fought with Anthony and had stood with him when Caesar was murdered, and through to the days of shame. Then he had come again across to Asia, out of favour with Rome, and had been killed in the mountains beyond Lebanon. The widow, having no favour to hope for from Octavius, had retired to her small property on the coast under Lebanon, taking her daughter from the world, a girl of nineteen, beautiful but unmarried.

When she was young the girl had known Caesar, and had shrunk from his eagle-like rapacity. The golden Anthony had sat with her many a half-hour, in the splendour of his great limbs and glowing manhood, and talked with her of the philosophies and the gods. For he was fascinated as a child by the gods, though he mocked at them, and forgot them in his own vanity. But he said to her:

"I have sacrificed two doves for you, to Venus, for I am afraid you make no offering to the sweet goddess. Beware you will offend her. Come, why is the flower of you so cool within? Does never a ray nor a glance find its way through? Ah, come, a maid should open to the sun, when the sun leans towards her to caress her."

And the big, bright eyes of Anthony laughed down on her, bathing her in his glow. And she felt the lovely glow of his male beauty and his amorousness bathe all her limbs and her body. But it was as he said: the very flower of her womb was cool, was almost cold, like a bud in shadow of frost, for all the flooding of his sunshine. So Anthony, respecting her father, who loved her, had left her.

And it had always been the same. She saw many men, young and old. And on the whole, she liked the old ones best, for they talked to her still and sincere, and did not expect her to open like a flower to the sun of their maleness. Once she asked a philosopher: "Are all women born to be given to men?" To which the old man answered slowly:

"Rare women wait for the re-born man. For the lotus, as you know, will not answer to all the bright heat of the sun. But she curves her dark, hidden head in the depths, and stirs not. Till, in the night, one of these rare, invisible suns that have been killed and shine no more, rises among the stars in unseen purple, and like the violet, sends its rare, purple rays out into the night. To these the lotus stirs as to a caress, and rises upwards through the flood, and lifts up her bent head, and opens with an expansion such as no other flower knows, and spreads her

sharp rays of bliss, and offers her soft, gold depths such as no other flower possesses, to the penetration of the flooding, violet-dark sun that has died and risen and makes no show. But for the golden brief day-suns of show such as Anthony, and for the hard winter suns of power, such as Caesar, the lotus stirs not, nor will ever stir. Those will only tear open the bud. Ah, I tell you, wait for the re-born and wait for the bud to stir."

So she waited. For all the men were soldiers or politicians in the Roman spell, assertive, manly, splendid apparently, but of an inward meanness, an inadequacy. And Rome and Egypt alike had left her alone, unroused. And she was a woman to herself, she would not give herself for a surface glow, nor marry for reasons. She would wait for the lotus to stir.

And then, in Egypt, she had found Isis, in whom she spelled her mystery. She had brought Isis to the shores of Sidon, and lived with her in the mystery of search; whilst her mother, who loved affairs, controlled the small estate and the slaves with a free hand.

When the woman had roused from her muse and risen to perform the last brief ritual to Isis, she replenished the lamp and left the sanctuary, locking the door. In the outer world, the sun had already set, and twilight was chill among the humming trees, which hummed still, though the wind was abating.

A stranger in a dark, broad hat rose from the corner of the temple steps, holding his hat in the wind. He was dark-faced, with a black pointed beard. "O Madam, whose shelter may I implore?" he said to the woman, who stood in her yellow mantle on a step above him, beside a pink-and-white painted pillar. Her face was rather long and pale, her dusky blond hair was held under a thin gold net. She looked down on the vagabond with indifference. It was the same she had seen watching the slaves.

"Why come you down from the road?" she asked.

"I saw the temple like a pale flower on the coast, and would rest among the trees of the precincts, if the lady of the goddess permits."

"It is Isis in Search," she said, answering his first question.

"The goddess is great," he replied.

She looked at him still with mistrust. There was a faint remote smile in the dark eyes lifted to her, though the face was hollow with suffering. The vagabond divined her hesitation, and was mocking her.

"Stay here upon the steps," she said. "A slave will show you the shelter."

"The lady of Egypt is gracious."

She went down the rocky path of the humped peninsula, in her gilded sandals. Beautiful were her ivory feet, beneath the white tunic, and above the saffron mantle her dusky-blond head bent as with endless musings. A woman entangled in her own dream. The man smiled a little, half-bitterly, and sat again on the step to wait, drawing his mantle round him, in the cold twilight.

At length a slave appeared, also in hodden gray.

"Seek ye the shelter of our lady?" he said insolently.

"Even so."

"Then come."

With the brusque insolence of a slave waiting on a vagabond, the young fellow led through the trees and down into a little gully in the rock, where, almost in darkness, was a small cave, with a litter of the tall heaths that grew on the waste places of the coast, under the stone-pines. The place was dark, but absolutely silent from the wind. There was still a faint odour of goats.

"Here sleep!" said the slave. "For the goats come no more on this half-island. And there is water!" He pointed to a little basin of rock where the maidenhair fern fringed a dripping mouthful of water.

Having scornfully bestowed his patronage, the slave departed. The man who had died climbed out to the tip of the peninsula, where the wave thrashed. It was rapidly getting dark, and the stars were coming out. The wind was abating for the night. Inland, the steep grooved upslope was dark to the long wavering outline of the crest against the translucent sky. Only now and then, a lantern flickered towards the villa.

The man who had died went back to the shelter. There he took bread from his leather pouch, dipped it in the water of the tiny spring, and slowly ate. Having eaten and washed his mouth, he looked once more at the bright stars in the pure windy sky, then settled the heath for his bed. Having laid his hat and his sandals aside, and put his pouch under his cheek for a pillow,

he slept, for he was very tired. Yet during the night the cold woke him, pinching wearily through his weariness. Outside was brilliantly starry, and still windy. He sat and hugged himself in a sort of coma, and towards dawn went to sleep again.

In the morning the coast was still chill in shadow, though the sun was up behind the hills, when the woman came down from the villa towards the goddess. The sea was fair and pale blue, lovely in newness, and at last the wind was still. Yet the waves broke white in the many rocks, and tore in the shingle[11] of the little bay. The woman came slowly, towards her dream. Yet she was aware of an interruption.

As she followed the little neck of rock on to her peninsula, and climbed the slope between the trees to the temple, a slave came down and stood, making his obeisance. There was a faint insolence in his humility. "Speak!" she said.

"Lady, the man is there, he still sleeps. Lady, may I speak?"

"Speak!" she said, repelled by the fellow.

"Lady, the male is an escaped malefactor."

The slave seemed to triumph in imparting the unpleasant news.

"By what sign?"

"Behold his hands and feet! Will the lady look on him?"

"Lead on!"

The slave led quickly over the mound of the hill down to the tiny ravine. There he stood aside, and the woman went into the crack towards the cave. Her heart beat a little. Above all she must preserve her temple inviolate.

The vagabond was asleep with his cheek on his scrip, his mantle wrapped round him, but his bare, soiled feet curling side by side, to keep each other warm, and his hand lying loosely clenched in sleep. And in the pale skin of his feet, usually covered by sandalstraps, she saw the scars, and in the palm of the loose hand.

She had no interest in men, particularly in the servile class. Yet she looked at the sleeping face. It was worn, hollow, and rather ugly. But, a true priestess, she saw the other kind of beauty in it, the sheer stillness of the deeper life. There was even a sort of majesty in the dark brows, over the still, hollow cheeks. She saw that his black hair, left long, in contrast to the Roman

[11] Pebbled beach.

fashion, was touched with gray at the temples, and the black pointed beard had threads of gray. But that must be suffering or misfortune, for the man was young. His dusky skin had the silvery glisten of youth still.

There was a beauty of much suffering, and the strange calm candour of finer life in the whole delicate ugliness of the face. For the first time, she was touched on the quick at the sight of a man, as if the tip of a fine flame of living had touched her. It was the first time. Men had roused all kinds of feeling in her, but never had touched her with the flame-tip of life.

She went back under the rock to where the slave waited.

"Know!" she said. "This is no malefactor, but a free citizen of the east. Do not disturb him. But when he comes forth, bring him to me; tell him I would speak with him."

She spoke coldly, for she found slaves invariably repellant, a little repulsive. They were so embedded in the lesser life, and their appetites and their small consciousness were a little disgusting. So she wrapped her dream round her, and went to the temple, where a slave-girl brought winter roses and jasmine, for the altar. But to-day, even in her ministrations, she was disturbed.

The sun rose over the hill, sparkling, the light fell triumphantly on the little pine-covered peninsula of the coast, and on the pink temple, in the pristine newness. The man who had died woke up, and put on his sandals. He put on his hat too, slung his scrip under his mantle, and went out, to see the morning in all its blue and its new gold. He glanced at the little yellow-and-white narcissus sparkling gaily in the rocks. And he saw the slave waiting for him like a menace.

"Master!" said the slave. "Our lady would speak with you at the house of Isis."

"It is well," said the wanderer.

He went slowly, staying to look at the pale blue sea like a flower in unruffled bloom, and the white fringes among the rocks, like white rock-flowers, the hollow slopes sheering up high from the shore, gray with olive-trees and green with bright young wheat, and set with the white small villa. All fair and pure in the January morning.

The sun fell on the corner of the temple, he sat down on the step in the sunshine, in the infinite patience of waiting. He had come back to life, but not the same life that he had left, the life of little people and the little day. Reborn, he was in the other life, the greater day of the human consciousness. And he was alone and apart from the little day, and out of contact with the daily people. Not yet had he accepted the irrevocable noli me tangere[12] which separates the re-born from the vulgar. The separation was absolute, as yet here at the temple he felt peace, the hard, bright pagan peace with hostility of slaves beneath.

The woman came into the dark inner doorway of the temple, from the shrine, and stood there, hesitating. She could see the dark figure of the man, sitting in that terrible stillness that was portentous to her, had something almost menacing in its patience.

She advanced across the outer chamber of the temple, and the man, becoming aware of her, stood up. She addressed him in Greek, but he said:

"Madam, my Greek is limited. Allow me to speak vulgar Syrian."

"Whence come you? Whither go you?" she asked, with a hurried preoccupation of a priestess.

"From the east beyond Damascus—and I go west as the road goes," he replied slowly.

She glanced at him with sudden anxiety and shyness.

"But why do you have the marks of a malefactor?" she asked abruptly.

"Did the Lady of Isis spy upon me in my sleep?" he asked, with a gray weariness.

"The slave warned me—your hands and feet —" she said.

He looked at her. Then he said:

"Will the Lady of Isis allow me to bid her farewell, and go up to the road?"

The wind came in a sudden puff, lifting his mantle and his hat. He put up his hand to hold the brim, and she saw again the thin brown hand with its scar.

"See! The scar!" she said, pointing.

"Even so!" he said. "But farewell, and to Isis my homage and my thanks for sleep."

He was going. But she looked up at him with her wondering blue eyes.

[12] Noli me tangere": as defined below, touch me not.

"Will you not look at Isis?" she said, with sudden impulse. And something stirred in him, like pain.

"Where then?" he said.

"Come!"

He followed her into the inner shrine, into the almost-darkness. When his eyes got used to the faint glow of the lamp, he saw the goddess striding like a ship, eager in the swirl of her gown, and he made his obeisance.

"Great is Isis!" he said. "In her search she is greater than death. Wonderful is such walking in a woman, wonderful the goal. All men praise thee, Isis, thou greater than the mother unto man."

The woman of Isis heard, and threw incense on the brazier. Then she looked at the man.

"Is it well with thee here?" she asked him. "Has Isis brought thee home to herself?"

He looked at the priestess in wonder and trouble.

"I know not," he said.

But the woman was pondering that this was the lost Osiris. She felt it in the quick of her soul. And her agitation was intense.

He would not stay in the close, dark, perfumed shrine. He went out again to the morning, to the cold air. He felt something approaching to touch him, and all his flesh was still woven with pain and the wild commandment: Noli me tangere! Touch me not! Oh, don't touch me!

The woman followed into the open with timid eagerness. He was moving away.

"Oh stranger, do not go! O stay awhile with Isis!"

He looked at her, at her face open like a flower, as if a sun had risen in her soul. And again his loins stirred.

"Would you detain me, girl of Isis?" he said.

"Stay! I am sure you are Osiris!" she said.

He laughed suddenly. "Not yet!" he said. Then he looked at her wistful face. "But I will sleep another night in the cave of the goats, if Isis wills it," he added.

She put her hands together with a priestess's childish happiness.

"Ah! Isis will be glad!" she said.

So he went down to the shore, in great trouble, saying to himself: "Shall I give myself into this touch? Shall I give myself into this touch? Men have tortured me to death with their touch.

Yet this girl of Isis is a tender flame of healing. I am a physician, yet I have no healing like the flame of this tender girl. The flame of this tender girl! Like the first pale crocus of the spring. How could I have been blind to the healing and the bliss in the crocus-like body of a tender woman! Ah, tenderness! More terrible and lovely than the death I died—"

He pried small shell-fish from the rocks, and ate them with relish and wonder for the simple taste of the sea. And inwardly, he was tremulous, thinking: "Dare I come into touch? For this is further than death. I have dared to let them lay hands on me and put me to death. But dare I come into this tender touch of life? Oh, this is harder—"

But the woman went into the shrine again, and sat rapt in pure muse, through the long hours, watching the swirling stride of the yearning goddess, and the navel of the budlike belly, like a seal on the virgin urge of the search. And she gave herself to the woman-flow and to the urge of Isis in Search.

Towards sundown she went on the peninsula to look for him. And she found him gone towards the sun, as she had gone the day before, and sitting on the pine-needles at the foot of the tree, where she had stood when first she saw him. Now she approached tremulously and slowly, afraid lest he did not want her. She stood near him unseen, till suddenly he glanced up at her from under his broad hat, and saw the westering sun on her netted hair. He was startled, yet he expected her.

"Is that your home?" he said, pointing to the white low villa on the slope of olives.

"It is my mother's house. She is a widow, and I am her only child."

"And are these all her slaves?"

"Except those that are mine."

Their eyes met for a moment.

"Will you too sit to see the sun go down?" he said.

He had not risen to speak to her. He had known too much pain. So she sat on the dry brown pine-needles, gathering her saffron mantle round her knees. A boat was coming in, out of the open glow into the shadow of the bay, and slaves were lifting small nets, their babble coming off the surface of the water.

"And this is home to you," he said.

"But I serve Isis in Search," she replied.

He looked at her. She was like a soft, musing cloud, somehow remote. His soul smote him with passion and compassion.

"Mayst thou find thy desire, maiden," he said, with sudden earnestness.

"And art thou not Osiris?" she asked.

He flushed suddenly.

"Yes, if thou wilt heal me!" he said. "For the death aloofness is still upon me, and I cannot escape it."

She looked at him for a moment in fear, from the soft blue sun of her eyes. Then she lowered her head, and they sat in silence in the warmth and glow of the western sun: the man who had died, and the woman of the pure search.

The sun was curving down to the sea, in grand winter splendour. It fell on the twinkling, naked bodies of the slaves, with their ruddy broad hams and their small black heads, as they ran spreading the nets on the pebble beach. The all-tolerant Pan[13] watched over them. All-tolerant Pan should be their god for ever.

The woman rose as the sun's rim dipped, saying:

"If you will stay, I shall send down victual and covering."

"The lady your mother, what will she say?"

The woman of Isis looked at him strangely, but with a tinge of misgiving.

"It is my own," she said.

"It is good," he said, smiling faintly, and foreseeing difficulties.

He watched her go, with her absorbed, strange motion of the self-dedicate. Her dun head was a little bent, the white linen swung about her ivory ankles. And he saw the naked slaves stand to look at her, with a certain wonder, and even a certain mischief. But she passed intent through the door in the wall, on the bay.

The man who had died sat on at the foot of the tree overlooking the strand, for on the little shore everything happened. At the small stream

[13] Pan (Gr. all, everything) the god of pastures, forests, flocks, and herds of Greek mythology, and also the personification of deity displayed in creation and pervading all things. Hence the doctrine of pantheism (*pan* + *theist*) equates God with the forces and laws of the universe—God all and everywhere. Pan is the subject of two of Elizabeth Barrett Browning's poems, "The Dead Pan" and "A Musical Instrument"; and of Robert Browning's poem, "Pan and Luna."

which ran in round the corner of the property wall, women slaves were still washing linen, and now and again came the hollow chock! chock! chock! as they beat it against the smooth stones, in the dark little hollow of the pool. There was a smell of olive-refuse on the air; and sometimes still the faint rumble of the grindstone that was milling the olives, inside the garden, and the sound of the slave calling to the ass at the mill. Then through the doorway a woman stepped, a gray-haired woman in a mantle of whitish wool, and there followed her a bare-headed man in a toga, a Roman: probably her steward or overseer. They stood on the high shingle above the sea, and cast round a rapid glance. The broad-hammed, ruddy-bodied slaves bent absorbed and abject over the nets, picking them clean, the women washing linen thrust their palms with energy down on the wash, the old slave bent absorbed at the water's edge, washing the fish and the polyps of the catch. And the woman and the overseer saw it all, in one glance. They also saw, seated at the foot of the tree on the rocks of the peninsula, the strange man silent and alone. And the man who had died saw that they spoke of him. Out of the little sacred world of the peninsula he looked on the common world, and saw it still hostile.

The sun was touching the sea, across the tiny bay stretched the shadow of the opposite humped headland. Over the shingle, now blue and cold in shadow, the elderly woman trod heavily, in shadow too, to look at the fish spread in the flat basket of the old man crouching at the water's edge: a naked old slave with fat hips and shoulders, on whose soft, fairish-orange body the last sun twinkled, then died. The old slave continued cleaning the fish absorbedly, not looking up: as if the lady were the shadow of twilight falling on him.

Then from the gateway stepped two slave-girls with flat baskets on their heads, and from one basket the terra-cotta wine-jar and the oil-jar poked up, leaning slightly. Over the massive shingle, under the wall, came the girls, and the woman of Isis in her saffron mantle stepped in twilight after them. Out at sea, the sun still shone. Here was shadow. The mother with gray head stood at the sea's edge and watched the daughter, all yellow and white, with dun blond[14]

[14] Dusky blond, contrasting colors.

head, swinging unseeing and unheeding after the slave-girls, towards the neck of rock of the peninsula; the daughter, travelling in her absorbed other-world. And not moving from her place, the elderly mother watched that procession of three file up the rise of the headland, between the trees, and disappear, shut in by trees. No slave had lifted a head to look. The gray-haired woman still watched the trees where her daughter had disappeared. Then she glanced again at the foot of the tree, where the man who had died was still sitting, inconspicuous now, for the sun had left him; and only the far blade of the sea shone bright. It was evening. Patience! Let destiny move!

The mother plodded with a stamping stride up the shingle: not long and swinging and rapt, like the daughter, but short and determined. Then down the rocks opposite came two naked slaves trotting with huge bundles of dark green on their shoulders, so their broad, naked legs twinkled underneath like insects' legs, and their heads were hidden. They came trotting across the shingle, heedless and intent on their way, when suddenly the man, the Roman-looking overseer, addressed them, and they stopped dead. They stood invisible under their loads, as if they might disappear altogether, now they were arrested. Then a hand came out and pointed to the peninsula. Then the two green-heaped slaves trotted on, towards the temple precincts. The gray-haired woman joined the man, and slowly the two passed through the door again, from the shingle of the sea to the property of the villa. Then the old, fat-shouldered slave rose, pallid in the shadow, with his tray of fish from the sea, and the women rose from the pool, dusky and alive, piling the wet linen in a heap on to the flat baskets, and the slaves who had cleaned the net gathered its whitish folds together. And the old slave with the fish basket on his shoulder, and the women slaves with the heaped baskets of wet linen on their heads, and the two slaves with the folded net, and the slave with oars on his shoulders, and the boy with the folded sail on his arm, gathered in a naked group near the door, and the man who had died heard the low buzz of their chatter. Then as the wind wafted cold, they began to pass through the door.

It was the life of the little day, the life of little people. And the man who had died said to himself: "Unless we encompass it in the greater day, and set the little life in the circle of the greater life, all is disaster."

Even the tops of the hills were in shadow. Only the sky was still upwardly radiant. The sea was a vast milky shadow. The man who had died rose a little stiffly, and turned into the grove.

There was no one at the temple. He went on to his lair in the rock. There, the slave-men had carried out the old heath of the bedding, swept the rock floor, and were spreading with nice art the myrtle, then the rougher heath, then the soft, bushy heath-tips on top, for a bed. Over it all they put a well-tanned white ox-skin. The maids had laid folded woollen covers at the head of the cave, and the wine-jar, the oil-jar, a terra-cotta drinking-cup, and a basket containing bread, salt, cheese, dried figs and eggs stood neatly arranged. There was also a little brazier of charcoal. The cave was suddenly full, and a dwelling-place.

The woman of Isis stood in the hollow by the tiny spring.

Only one slave at a time could pass. The girl-slaves waited at the entrance to the narrow place. When the man who had died appeared, the woman sent the girls away. The men-slaves still arranged the bed, making the job as long as possible. But the woman of Isis dismissed them too. And the man who had died came to look at his house.

"Is it well?" the woman asked him.

"It is very well," the man replied. "But the lady, your mother, and he who is no doubt the steward, watched while the slaves brought the goods. Will they not oppose you?"

"I have my own portion! Can I not give of my own? Who is going to oppose me and the gods?" she said, with a certain soft fury, touched with exasperation. So that he knew that her mother would oppose her, and that the spirit of the little life would fight against the spirit of the greater. And he thought: "Why did the woman of Isis relinquish her portion in the daily world? She should have kept her goods fiercely!"

"Will you eat and drink?" she said. "On the ashes are warm eggs. And I will go up to the meal at the villa. But in the second hour of the night I shall come down to the temple. O, then, will you come too to Isis?" She looked at him, and a queer glow dilated her eyes. This was her dream, and it was greater than herself. He could not bear to thwart her or hurt her in the least thing now. She was in the full glow of her woman's mystery.

"Shall I wait at the temple?" he said.

"O, wait at the second hour and I shall come." He heard the humming supplication in her voice and his fibres quivered.

"But the lady, your mother?" he said gently.

The woman looked at him, startled.

"She will not thwart me!" she said.

So he knew that the mother would thwart the daughter, for the daughter had left her goods in the hands of her mother, who would hold fast to this power.

But she went, and the man who had died lay reclining on his couch, and ate the eggs from the ashes, and dipped his bread in oil, and ate it, for his flesh was dry: and he mixed wine and water, and drank. And so he lay still, and the lamp made a small bud of light.

He was absorbed and enmeshed in new sensations. The woman of Isis was lovely to him, not so much in form, as in the wonderful womanly glow of her. Suns beyond suns had dipped her in mysterious fire, the mysterious fire of a potent woman, and to touch her was like touching the sun. Best of all was her tender desire for him, like sunshine, so soft and still.

"She is like sunshine upon me," he said to himself, stretching his limbs. "I have never before stretched my limbs in such sunshine as her desire for me. The greatest of all gods granted me this."

At the same time he was haunted by the fear of the outer world. "If they can, they will kill us," he said to himself. "But there is a law of the sun which protects us."

And again he said to himself: "I have risen naked and branded. But if I am naked enough for this contact, I have not died in vain. Before I was clogged."

He rose and went out. The night was chill and starry, and of a great wintery splendour. "There are destinies of splendour," he said to the night, "after all our doom of littleness and meanness and pain."

So he went up silently to the temple, and waited in darkness against the inner wall, looking out on a gray darkness, stars, and rims of trees. And he said again to himself: "There are destinies of splendour, and there is a greater power."

So at last he saw the light of her silk lanthorn swinging, coming intermittent between the trees, yet coming swiftly. She was alone, and near, the light softly swishing on her mantle-hem. And he trembled with fear and with joy, saying to himself: "I am almost more afraid of this touch than I was of death. For I am more nakedly exposed to it."

"I am here, Lady of Isis," he said softly out of the dark.

"Ah!" she cried, in fear also, yet in rapture. For she was given to her dream.

She unlocked the door of the shrine, and he followed after her. Then she latched the door shut again. The air inside was warm and close and perfumed. The man who had died stood by the closed door, and watched the woman. She had come first to the goddess. And dim-lit, the goddess-statue stood surging forward, a little fearsome like a great woman-presence urging.

The priestess did not look at him. She took off her saffron mantle and laid it on a low couch. In the dim light she was bare armed, in her girdled white tunic. But she was still hiding herself away from him. He stood back in shadow, and watched her slowly fan the brazier and fling on incense. Faint clouds of sweet aroma arose on the air. She turned to the statue in the ritual of approach, softly swaying forward with a slight lurch, like a moored boat, tipping towards the goddess.

He watched the strange rapt woman, and he said to himself: "I must leave her alone in her rapture, her female mysteries." So she tipped in her strange forward-swaying rhythm before the goddess. Then she broke into a murmur of Greek, which he could not understand. And, as she murmured, her swaying softly subsided, like a boat on a sea that grows still. And as he watched her, he saw her soul in its aloneness, and its female difference. He said to himself: "How different she is from me, how strangely different! She is afraid of me, and my male difference. She is getting herself naked and clear of her fear. How sensitive and softly alive she is, with a life so different from mine! How beautiful with a soft strange courage, of life, so different from my courage of death! What a beautiful thing, like the heart of a rose, like the core of a flame. She is making herself completely penetrable. Ah! how terrible to fail her, or to trespass on her!"

She turned to him, her face glowing from the goddess.

"You are Osiris, aren't you?" she said naïvely.

"If you will," he said.

"Will you let Isis discover you? Will you not take off your things?"

He looked at the woman, and lost his breath. And his wounds, and especially the death-wound through his belly, began to cry again.

"It has hurt so much!" he said. "You must forgive me if I am still held back."

But he took off his cloak and his tunic, and went naked towards the idol, his breast panting with the sudden terror of overwhelming pain, memory of overwhelming pain, and grief too bitter.

"They did me to death!" he said in excuse of himself, turning his face to her for a moment.

And she saw the ghost of the death in him, as he stood there thin and stark before her, and suddenly she was terrified, and she felt robbed. She felt the shadow of the gray, grisly wing of death triumphant.

"Ah, Goddess," he said to the idol, in the vernacular. "I would be so glad to live, if you would give me my clue again."

For here again he felt desperate, faced by the demand of life, and burdened still by his death.

"Let me anoint you!" the woman said to him softly. "Let me anoint the scars! Show me, and let me anoint them!"

He forgot his nakedness in this re-evoked old pain. He sat on the edge of the couch, and she poured a little ointment into the palm of his hand. And as she chafed his hand, it all came back, the nails, the holes, the cruelty, the unjust cruelty against him who had offered only kindness. The agony of injustice and cruelty came over him again, as in his death-hour. But she chafed the palm, murmuring: "What was torn becomes a new flesh, what was a wound is full of fresh life; this scar is the eye of the violet."

And he could not help smiling at her, in her naïve priestess's absorption. This was her dream, and he was only a dream-object to her. She would never know or understand what he was. Especially she would never know the death that was gone before in him. But what did it matter? She was different. She was woman: her life and her death were different from his. Only she was good to him.

When she chafed his feet with oil and tender, tender healing, he could not refrain from saying to her:

"Once a woman washed my feet with tears, and wiped them with her hair, and poured on precious ointment." [15]

The woman of Isis looked up at him from her earnest work, interrupted again.

"Were they hurt then?" she said. "Your feet?"

"No, no! It was while they were whole."

"And did you love her?"

"Love had passed in her. She only wanted to serve," he replied. "She had been a prostitute."

"And did you let her serve you?" she asked.

"Yea."

"Did you let her serve you with the corpse of her love?"

"Ay!"

Suddenly it dawned on him: "I asked them all to serve me with the corpse of their love. And in the end I offered them only the corpse of my love. This is my body—take and eat[16]—my corpse—"

A vivid shame went through him. "After all," he thought, "I wanted them to love with dead bodies. If I had kissed Judas with live love, perhaps he would never have kissed me with death. Perhaps he loved me in the flesh, and I willed that he should love me bodylessly, with the corpse of love—"

There dawned on him the reality of the soft warm love which is in touch, and which is full of delight. "And I told them, blessed are they that mourn," he said to himself. "Alas, if I mourned even this woman here, now I am in death, I should have to remain dead, and I want so much to live. Life has brought me to this woman with warm hands. And her touch is more to me now than all my words. For I want to live—"

[15] Mary Magdelene; see footnote 1, p. 215.

[16] *Matthew,* 26:26: "And as they were eating, Jesus took bread, and blessed *it,* and brake *it,* and gave *it* to the disciples, and said, Take, eat; this is my body."

"Go then to the goddess!" she said softly, gently pushing him towards Isis. And as he stood there dazed and naked as an unborn thing, he heard the woman murmuring to the goddess, murmuring, murmuring with a plaintive appeal. She was stooping now, looking at the scar in the soft flesh of the socket of his side, a scar deep and like an eye sore with endless weeping, just in the soft socket above the hip. It was here that his blood had left him, and his essential seed. The woman was trembling softly and murmuring in Greek. And he in the recurring dismay of having died, and in the anguished perplexity of having tried to force life, felt his wounds crying aloud, and the deep places of the body howling again: "I have been murdered, and I lent myself to murder. They murdered me, but I lent myself to murder—"

The woman, silent now, but quivering, laid oil in her hand and put her palm over the wound in his right side. He winced, and the wound absorbed his life again, as thousands of times before. And in the dark, wild pain and panic of his consciousness rang only one cry: "Oh, how can she take this death out of me? How can she take me from this death? She can never know! She can never understand! She can never equal it! . . ."

In silence, she softly rhythmically chafed the scar with oil. Absorbed now in her priestess's task, softly, softly gathering power, while the vitals of the man howled in panic. But as she gradually gathered power, and passed in a girdle round him to the opposite scar, gradually warmth began to take the place of the cold terror, and he felt: "I am going to be warm again, and I am going to be whole! I shall be warm like the morning. I shall be a man. It doesn't need understanding. It needs newness. She brings me newness—"

And he listened to the faint, ceaseless wail of distress of his wounds, sounding as if for ever under the horizons of his consciousness. But the wail was growing dim, more dim.

He thought of the woman toiling over him: "She does not know! She does not realise the death in me. But she has another consciousness. She comes to me from the opposite end of the night."

Having chafed all his lower body with oil, having worked with her slow intensity of a priestess, so that the sound of his wounds grew dimmer and dimmer, suddenly she put her breast against the wound in his left side, and her arms round him, folding over the wound in his right side, and she pressed him to her, in a power of living warmth, like the folds of a river. And the wailing died out altogether, and there was a stillness, and darkness in his soul, unbroken dark stillness, wholeness.

Then slowly, slowly, in the perfect darkness of his inner man, he felt the stir of something coming. A dawn, a new sun. A new sun was coming up in him, in the perfect inner darkness of himself. He waited for it breathless, quivering with a fearful hope . . . "Now I am not myself, I am something new . . ."

And as it rose, he felt, with a cold breath of disappointment, the girdle of the living woman slip down from him, the warmth and the glow slipped from him, leaving him stark. She crouched, spent, at the feet of the goddess, hiding her face.

Stooping, he laid his hand softly on her warm, bright shoulder, and the shock of desire went through him, shock after shock, so that he wondered if it were another sort of death; but full of magnificence.

Now all his consciousness was there in the crouching, hidden woman. He stooped beside her and caressed her softly, blindly, murmuring inarticulate things. And his death and his passion of sacrifice were all as nothing to him now, he knew only the crouching fulness of the woman there, the soft white rock of life. . . . "On this rock I built my life." The deep-folded, penetrable rock of the living woman! The woman, hiding her face. Himself bending over, powerful and new like dawn.

He crouched to her, and he felt the blaze of his manhood and his power rise up in his loins, magnificent.

"I am risen!"

Magnificent, blazing indomitable in the depths of his loins, his own sun dawned, and sent its fire running along his limbs, so that his face shone unconsciously.

He untied the string on the linen tunic, and slipped the garment down, till he saw the white glow of her white-gold breasts. And he touched them, and he felt his life go molten. "Father!" he said, "why did you hide this from me?" And he touched her with the poignancy of wonder, and the marvellous piercing transcendence of desire. "Lo!" he said, "this is beyond prayer." It was the deep, interfolded warmth, warmth living and penetrable, the woman, the heart of the rose! "My mansion is the intricate warm rose, my joy is this blossom!"

She looked up at him suddenly, her face like a lifted light, wistful, tender, her eyes like many wet flowers. And he drew her to his breast with a passion of tenderness and consuming desire, and the last thought: "My hour is upon me, I am taken unawares—"

So he knew her, and was one with her.

Afterwards, with a dim wonder, she touched the great scars in his sides with her finger-tips, and said:

"But they no longer hurt?"

"They are suns!" he said. "They shine from your touch. They are my atonement with you."

And when they left the temple, it was the coldness before dawn. As he closed the door, he looked again at the goddess, and he said: "Lo, Isis is a kindly goddess; and full of tenderness. Great gods are warm-hearted, and have tender goddesses."

The woman wrapped herself in her mantle and went home in silence, sightless, brooding like the lotus softly shutting again, with its gold core full of fresh life. She saw nothing, for her own petals were a sheath to her. Only she thought: "I am full of Osiris. I am full of the risen Osiris! . . ."

But the man looked at the vivid stars before dawn, as they rained down to the sea, and the dog-star green towards the sea's rim. And he thought: "How plastic it is, how full of curves and folds like an invisible rose of dark-petalled openness that shows where the dew touches its darkness! How full it is, and great beyond all gods. How it leans around me, and I am part of it, the great rose of Space. I am like a grain of its perfume, and the woman is a grain of its beauty. Now the world is one flower of many petalled darknesses, and I am in its perfume as in a touch."

So, in the absolute stillness and fulness of touch, he slept in his cave while the dawn came. And after the dawn, the wind rose and brought a storm, with cold rain. So he stayed in his cave in the peace and the delight of being in touch, delighting to hear the sea, and the rain on the earth, and to see one white-and-gold narcissus

bowing wet, and still wet. And he said: "This is the great atonement, the being in touch. The gray sea and the rain, the wet narcissus and the woman I wait for, the invisible Isis and the unseen sun are all in touch, and at one."

He waited at the temple for the woman, and she came in the rain. But she said to him:

"Let me sit awhile with Isis. And come to me, will you come to me, in the second hour of night?"

So he went back to the cave and lay in stillness and in the joy of being in touch, waiting for the woman who would come with the night, and consummate again the contact. Then when night came the woman came, and came gladly, for her great yearning too was upon her, to be in touch, to be in touch with him, nearer.

So the days came, and the nights came, and days came again, and the contact was perfected and fulfilled. And he said: "I will ask her nothing, not even her name, for a name would set her apart."

And she said to herself: "He is Osiris. I wish to know no more."

Plum-blossom blew from the trees, the time of the narcissus was past, anemones lit up the ground and were gone, the perfume of bean-field was in the air. All changed, the blossom of the universe changed its petals and swung round to look another way. The spring was fulfilled, a contact was established, the man and the woman were fulfilled of one another, and departure was in the air.

One day he met her under the trees, when the morning sun was hot, and the pines smelled sweet, and on the hills the last pear-bloom was scattering. She came slowly towards him, and in her gentle lingering, her tender hanging back from him, he knew a change in her.

"Hast thou conceived?" he asked her.

"Why?" she said.

"Thou art like a tree whose green leaves follow the blossom, full of sap. And there is a withdrawing about thee."

"It is so," she said. "I am with young by thee. Is it good?"

"Yea!" he said. "How should it not be good? So the nightingale calls no more from the valley-bed. But where wilt thou bear the child, for I am naked of all but life."

"We will stay here," she said.

"But the lady, your mother?"

A shadow crossed her brow. She did not answer.

"What when she knows?" he said.

"She begins to know."

"And would she hurt you?"

"Ah, not me! What I have is all my own. And I shall be big with Osiris. . . . But thou, do you watch her slaves."

She looked at him, and the peace of her maternity was troubled by anxiety.

"Let not your heart be troubled!" he said. "I have died the death once."

So he knew the time was come again for him to depart. He would go alone, with his destiny. Yet not alone, for the touch would be upon him, even as he left his touch on her. And invisible suns would go with him.

Yet he must go. For here on the bay the little life of jealousy and property was resuming sway again, as the suns of passionate fecundity relaxed their sway. In the name of property, the widow and her slaves would seek to be revenged on him for the bread he had eaten, and the living touch he had established, the woman he had delighted in. But he said: "Not twice! They shall not now profane the touch in me. My wits against theirs."

So he watched. And he knew they plotted. So he moved from the little cave, and found another shelter, a tiny cove of sand by the sea, dry and secret under the rocks.

He said to the woman:

"I must go now soon. Trouble is coming to me from the slaves. But I am a man, and the world is open. But what is between us is good, and is established. Be at peace. And when the nightingale calls again from your valley-bed, I shall come again, sure as Spring."

She said: "O don't go! Stay with me on half the island, and I will build a house for you and me under the pine-trees by the temple, where we can live apart."

Yet she knew that he would go. And even she wanted the coolness of her own air around her, and the release from anxiety.

"If I stay," he said, "they will betray me to the Romans and to their justice. But I will never be betrayed again. So when I am gone, live in peace with the growing child. And I shall come

again; all is good between us, near or apart. The suns come back in their seasons: and I shall come again."

"Do not go yet," she said. "I have set a slave to watch at the neck of the peninsula. Do not go yet, till the harm shows."

But as he lay in his little cove, on a calm, still night, he heard the soft knock of oars, and the bump of a boat against the rock. So he crept out to listen. And he heard the Roman overseer say:

"Lead softly to the goat's den. And Lysippus shall throw the net over the malefactor while he sleeps, and we will bring him before justice, and the Lady of Isis shall know nothing of it . . ."

The man who had died caught a whiff of flesh from the oiled and naked slaves as they crept up, then the faint perfume of the Roman. He crept nearer the sea. The slave who sat in the boat sat motionless, holding the oars, for the sea was quite still. And the man who had died knew him.

So out of the deep cleft of a rock he said, in a clear voice:

"Art thou not that slave who possessed the maiden under the eyes of Isis? Art thou not the youth? Speak!"

The youth stood up in the boat in terror. His movement sent the boat bumping against the rock. The slave sprang out in wild fear, and fled up the rocks. The man who had died quickly seized the boat and stepped in, and pushed off. The oars were yet warm with the unpleasant warmth of the hands of the slaves. But the man pulled slowly out, to get into the current which set down the coast, and would carry him in silence. The high coast was utterly dark against the starry night. There was no glimmer from the peninsula: the priestess came no more at night. The man who had died rowed slowly on, with the current, and laughed to himself: "I have sowed the seed of my life and my resurrection, and put my touch forever upon the choice woman of this day, and I carry her perfume in my flesh like essence of roses. She is dear to me in the middle of my being. But the gold and flowing serpent is coiling up again, to sleep at the root of my tree.

"So let the boat carry me. To-morrow is another day."

POETRY

. . . is "news that stays news"
—EZRA POUND

The verse is mine but friend, when you declaim it,
It seems like yours, so grievously you maim it.
—MARTIAL

PRELIMINARIES

Stopping by Woods on a Snowy Evening
ROBERT FROST
1874–1963

Whose woods these are I think I know.
His house is in the village though;
He will not see me stopping here
To watch his woods fill up with snow.

My little horse must think it queer   5
To stop without a farmhouse near
Between the woods and frozen lake
The darkest evening of the year.

He gives his harness bells a shake
To ask if there is some mistake.   10
The only other sound's the sweep
Of easy wind and downy flake.

The woods are lovely, dark, and deep.
But I have promises to keep,
And miles to go before I sleep,   15
And miles to go before I sleep.

The definitions of poetry, the hymns of praise, and the essays on the nature of poetry would cram the shelves of any modest public library and overflow onto the floors as well. Good talk about poetry is nevertheless rare, and even the best of it will rest lightly on fallow ground until we ourselves have learned how to penetrate the inner life of a few poems. We cannot be talked into enjoying the pleasures of poetry, but we can bring ourselves to such pleasures by learning to understand individual poems.

"General Preliminaries" (p. 4) implies that each type of literature has a structure of its own.

If we wish to understand the structure of a poem, it seems sensible to begin by examining one. We shall learn much about poetry in general if we can discover exactly what Frost has done and how he has done it.

The Plain Sense of a Poem

As we read Frost's poem for the first time, a certain kind of sense comes through to us almost immediately. This sense we shall call the poem's plain sense, sometimes called literal sense or literal meaning. The plain sense gives us the literal facts of a poem, and with such facts all understanding of a poem begins, but does *not* end.

The plain sense of Frost's poem tells us that the speaker, returning home at dusk in his one-horse sleigh, stops to enjoy the peace and solitude of the occasion: the snow is falling softly, the woods are inviting, there is no other human being to break the silence. But the horse finds no reason for stopping: it is growing dark, there is no house in sight, and the miles stretch before them. Reflecting on his horse's impatience, the speaker concedes that he should move on to keep the commitments he has made.

But in drawing the plain sense from the poem we have raised many questions. Unless this poem means more than the paraphrase above includes, does the poem merit further consideration? Will another kind of approach to the poem reveal meanings not yet located? These and other questions we must answer if we are to understand the poem fully. Let us note before we proceed that paraphrasing the poem helped to raise the questions about the poem's fullest meaning. Unless the plain sense is clearly understood before further analysis of a poem begins, the reader is likely to misconstrue the total meaning of the poem.

Imagery

A little closer reading of the poem shows us that Frost is depending on our ability to see and hear imaginatively. When he uses such words as *woods* and *horse,* he depends on our ability to see the real woods and horse. When the horse "gives his harness bells a shake," and when we are told that

> The only other sound's the sweep
> Of easy wind and downy flake,

the poet depends on our ability to hear these sounds. Contrary to some popular opinion, there is no mystery in imagery. Its function in poetry is identical with its function in everyday speech: it presents to the reader his concrete world of things, and recalls the sight and sound and feel of them. With imagery the poet peoples and furnishes the world of his poem, and causes us to experience that world as directly and unmistakably as we experience life itself. Indeed, it is sometimes said that imagery is the very basis of poetry, and as we proceed we shall observe the force of this assertion. (For further exploration of imagery, see "Imagery," p. 277.)

Figurative Language

A still closer reading of Frost's poem shows that he has used some of his imagery in a special way. When we read that

> My little horse must think it queer
> To stop without a farmhouse near,

we suspect that this is no ordinary horse. And when we read further that

> He gives his harness bells a shake
> To ask if there is some mistake,

we know that this is a very special horse, one that asks questions. At this point in our attempt to understand the poem we are moving from the plain sense to the figurative sense of the poem. The speaker in the poem is not alone, as he seemed to be in the first stanza, and we sense a conflict of some sort between him and the horse. The horse, having been given some human characteristics, becomes in a sense a human being and challenges the speaker in some significant way. By comparing the horse with a human being, the poet has described him figuratively.

There are other figures in the poem, as in the lines,

> The only other sound's the *sweep*
> Of *easy* wind and *downy* flake,

in which both the wind and snow are described figuratively, not literally. The wind moves gracefully, easily, with the curving, hushed motion of an unseen broom; and the snowflakes are as soft as the down, or fluffy feathers, on a young bird.

It is customary at this point in most books on the nature of poetry to describe in abstract terms the reason for using figurative language. Suppose we forego this temptation and permit the poem itself to tell us. Perhaps the poem can answer the question most often asked by students and general readers alike: "Why doesn't the poet say what he *means?* If by downy flake he means soft flake, why doesn't he say so?" Such questions are usually asked impatiently, as if only poets resorted to figures of speech. But our everyday speech is peppered (!) with figures of speech. We "go on a lark," "lead a dog's life," "smell a rat," "stumble in our thinking," and "walk the straight and narrow path." Aren't we saying what we mean? We are saying exactly what we mean, and so is Frost. The word *soft* is too general: there is also soft steel and soft wood. How soft is soft? We know how soft Frost's flakes are: they are as soft as down—about as soft as soft can be.

The figure of speech not only says exactly what the poet means, *it also invites the reader to help to say it.* To understand what Frost means by "downy flake," we must transfer the relevant characteristics from the down of birds to the snowflakes. This is an imaginative act, not a passive acceptance. *The figure requires us to participate in the life of the poem.* (For further exploration of figures, see "Figure and Symbol," p. 282.)

Symbolism

We now return to Frost's little horse. The poet has described the horse figuratively by giving him certain characteristics of a person. The horse thinks it queer "to stop without a farmhouse near," and he therefore asks "if there is some mistake" about this stopping. He is challenging the "impractical" sense of the driver with his own horse sense. When the writer uses one thing to stand for another we call it a symbol. The horse stands for horse sense, and operates as a symbol in the poem, as we shall observe later.

Not all figures of speech contain symbols, and not all symbols in a poem are embedded in figures of speech. (For further explanation of this distinction, see "Figure and Symbol," p. 282.) The horse is a figure and a symbol, but what about the "woods," the "promises," and the "miles"? These things are not figuratively described but they could be symbols. And if they are, what do they stand for? Why is the driver of the horse tempted to interrupt his journey by watching the woods fill up with snow? Why does he regard them as "lovely, dark and deep"? To whom has he given "promises," and what kind of promises? And while we are bearing down on this seemingly innocent little poem, questioning every literal stroke of the poet's pen, let us ask what kind of "miles" are meant. And is the "sleep" only temporary or permanent?

Perhaps these questions have already suggested that many symbols in poetry have been made conventional through long use. Just as the handclasp in everyday life stands for friendliness, the word *dark* or *darkest* in poetry may stand for something unknown or forbidding or secretive, perhaps even tragic. The title of Arthur Koestler's novel, *Darkness at Noon*, is completely symbolic, and suggests that some tragedy throws its shadow over our century. Here a warning is appropriate: such words as *darkness, noon, light, black,* and *white* are not always used symbolically. How, then, do we know when they are so used? Symbols are identified and their meaning made clear by the full context of the poem. In fact, this principle determines the meaning of all the elements in every poem. It can be stated this way: *the whole poem helps to determine the meaning of its parts, and, in turn, each part helps to determine the meaning of the whole poem.*

The Meaning of a Poem: The Parts and the Whole

As the first step in understanding a poem, we have seen how helpful it is to make a paraphrase of its plain sense. We are now in a position to make a different kind of paraphrase, one that includes the figurative-symbolic meaning of the poem. We are seeing again the method used in all creative literature (as we saw in "General Preliminaries"), a method we have already seen operate in fiction. As we begin, we keep in mind imagery, figurative language, and symbolism. We should enjoy this detective work, determined to let nothing important escape us.

Frost's imagery gives us the life-texture of the situation and makes it credible, or believable. Within this context of reality we can think and feel as we do in real life: we can participate in the life of the poem. But in order to do so we must understand the relationships of the imagery, figures, and symbols: their relationships make the symbolic meaning of the poem.

Why is the driver tempted to interrupt his journey? Is it because nature has invited him to her communion? The solitude and peace of the woods softly filling with snow tempt him to leave off this moving from place to place—to what end is all this journeying? The woods, "lovely, dark and deep," invite him to leave the traffic of the world on "the darkest evening of the year," the time of his life when his personal burdens weigh most heavily upon him.* But the dramatic device of the horse shows us the conflict within the man: shall he yield to this temptation or move on to fulfill his promises? The noise of the harness bells breaks his reverie, and asks for his decision.

Having come so far in this symbolic interpretation of the poem, it is no longer possible to regard the "promises," the "miles," and the "sleep" as mere literal facts.

The last stanza,

> The woods are lovely, dark and deep.
> But I have promises to keep,
> And miles to go before I sleep,
> And miles to go before I sleep,

can therefore be paraphrased by saying that the driver consents to move on, to forego entering a world of his own, because he has promises and responsibilities to fulfill to humanity during the years before he dies. Interpreted figuratively, these lines reconcile the conflict within the driver. This conflict is a condition which exists in most, if not all, human beings, and for this reason we say that Frost's poem has universal value, or universality.

* Some readers have found a death wish in this poem. In a public lecture at the State University of Iowa, April 13, 1959, Frost stated explicitly that the poem "is not concerned with death." His statement, of course, does not settle the matter. Nevertheless the tension in the poem is surely between the horse and the driver, and they hardly represent life and death.

Rhythm and Rhyme

There are other elements, not yet mentioned, which Frost has used to fashion the total meaning of his poem. It is sometimes difficult for readers to believe that such matters as rhythm and rhyme are used to convey meaning. Popular opinion regards them as troublesome technical matters of interest to the specialist only, or at best as ornaments on the poetic Christmas tree. Once again let us forego the customary abstract definitions of such matters and let the poet's practice provide the instruction.

After all we have now discovered about Frost's compact, sensitive lyric, we can hardly suspect him of decorating his poem with the trinkets of rhythm and rhyme to exhibit his cleverness. Here, it should be made very clear that poetry should be spoken aloud: poetry is speech, and the voice, or tone, of the poet communicates his attitude toward the facts of the poem. Unless we *hear* Frost's lines being spoken aloud, all of our observations below will miss the mark.

A very old definition of poetry regards it as a fusion of sound and sense.* Note that word *fusion:* not a mechanical combination, but a fusion, a melting together of sound and sense. In our paraphrase of the figurative meaning of the poem above, we apparently discussed the sense while ignoring the sound. But—now the secret comes out—this was not so. Experienced readers of poetry know that the division is impossible because as one reads for sense he is either consciously or unconsciously being influenced by the sound. Hence before our paraphrase of the poem had been started, the sound of the poem had already done its work, exerting its influence on the writer of the paraphrase. Now let us see just how skillful Frost has been.

As we read the poem aloud, we hear and feel the movement within each line. In a good poem the right sound is fused with the right sense, thus:

Whose woods these are I think I know.
His house is in the vil-lage though.

Now let us change the word order but not the words themselves:

I think I know whose woods these are
Though his house is in the village.

Here, the wrong sound has distorted the sense.

As we read Frost's arrangement aloud we hear the four pulsations or beats in each line. Because there are four beats we call the line *tetrameter* (tetra = four), a line of· four feet. We hear also that each foot contains two syllables, the first one unstressed and the second one stressed (whose woods), which foot we call *iambic*. The iambic foot is acknowledged to be the most natural rhythm in colloquial English, that is, in our familiar, everyday spoken language. Compare Frost's lines with these (read them aloud):

'Twas the night before Christ-mas, when all
    through the house,
Not a crea-ture was stir-ring, not e-ven a
    mouse.

This anapestic rhythm is appropriate to give us the feel of galloping reindeer and the excitement of Christmas Eve, but it is hardly appropriate for the colloquial expression with which Frost speaks to us directly, simply, and naturally. It should be clear, then, that his rhythm is not a decoration, but rather a basic element in the poem's structure.

A brief examination of Frost's rhyme scheme will show how consciously and purposefully it must have been chosen. It runs:

. . . know	a	b	c	d
. . . though	a	b	c	d
. . . here	b	c	d	d
. . . snow	a	b	c	d

One of the purposes of rhyme is to tie the sense together with sound. Note, then, three important consequences of Frost's rhyme scheme. First, three of the four lines in each stanza (except the last stanza) rhyme; hence, these stanzas are very compact sound-and-sense units. Second, the *third* line in each stanza always rhymes with the *first* line in the following stanza; hence the sound helps to pass the sense from one stanza to the next. And third, in the last stanza all four lines rhyme; hence, the sound is brought to rest

* As Pope put it, "The sound must seem an Echo to the sense" (p. 269). Frost speaks of "the sound of sense."

just as the reconciliation of the conflict within the driver is brought to rest, and as he will be brought to rest upon his arrival at home. And note particularly that the symbols involved in the rhyming words *deep*, *keep*, and *sleep* are the key symbols which finally reveal the full meaning of the poem. (For further explanation of the functions of rhythm and rhyme, see "Rhythm and Rhyme," p. 269.)

Are we ready to say that these matters are accidents or pretty decorations or troublesome technical matters outside the full meaning of Frost's poem? Hardly. Frost has demonstrated to us the truth of Stephen Spender's acute remark that "a poem *means* the sum of everything which it *is*. . . ." (See Spender's essay, "On Teaching Modern Poetry," p. 837.) The sum of everything which Frost's poem *is* contains more than we have already located, but we have located and discussed the poem's basic factors, the factors which must be understood in order to interpret the meaning of almost any poem.

What Have We Learned?

We have learned that a poem is a living organism which contains the necessary elements of its own life. If "a poem *means* the sum of everything which it *is*," we must not only understand everything in the poem: we must be aware of all its parts as they work together to make the total meaning of the poem. If the poem is a good one, and this is surely one test, every element in it contributes to its meaning.

We have learned further that a poem has at least two levels of meaning: the literal level and the figurative-symbolic level. We have seen that a poem suggests much more than it says literally: like lovers' conversation, a poem gives out hints of extensive meanings along the way. Students often refer to the figurative meaning as the hidden meaning, as if the poet had set out to hide his meaning in order to make the poem difficult. Ordinarily, poets have outgrown the game of hide-and-seek, but they do write figuratively for such reasons as Frost has already demonstrated.

And we have learned that a poem possesses a concentration and intensity which help to make it memorable. *The right word in the right place, the intimate fusion of sound and sense, and the economy of rich suggestion are virtues of the structure of most poetry.*

THE MISREADING OF POEMS

Most misreadings of poems come from the reader's failure to realize that there are many languages within the English language, such as the languages of science, history, journalism, and, of course, the language of poetry itself. By using *language* in this sense we mean a unified pattern of words including certain specific devices to communicate a very specific meaning. Poetry has such a language of its own. For example, when Frost says,

My little horse must think it queer
To stop without a farmhouse near,

we immediately sense the language of poetry, not of science or history, because of the devices of rhythm (iambic tetrameter), rhyme (*queer-near*), figurative language (a horse that thinks), and symbol (a horse that stands for practical sense as against the impractical sense of the driver).

It is best, of course, to learn in a positive way what to look for in a poem, and what to do with what we find, but nevertheless we may save ourselves some difficulty if we first identify a few blind alleys to be avoided.

To illustrate some basic causes of misreading a poem, suppose we begin by examining a few student comments on the following poem.

North Labrador
HART CRANE
1899–1932

A land of leaning ice
Hugged by plaster-grey arches of sky,
Flings itself silently
Into eternity.

"Has no one come here to win you,   5
Or left you with the faintest blush
Upon your glittering breasts?
Have you no memories, O Darkly Bright?"

Cold-hushed, there is only the shifting of
    moments

That journey toward no Spring—   10
No birth, no death, no time nor sun
In answer.

Failure on the Literal Level *

Incredible as it may seem, the failures on this level are legion. Few readers admit guilt, yet most of us are sinners. One reader of "North Labrador" read *Spring* (l. 10) as running water, and asked why the word had been capitalized. It is easy to smile at this error, but even practiced readers are victims of similar kinds of mistakes. We can avoid failure on the literal level by asking questions like these about every poem: *Who* is speaking to whom? *What* is the situation in the poem? *Where* are we geographically, and in time? Further, the literal level is determined by applying the same basic disciplines we use in reading prose: we should seek to understand the sentence structure—the very grammar—the vocabulary (how many failures here!), the pronouns (especially *its*), and even the punctuation. Elementary? Yes, and indispensable. True, the full meaning of a poem does not end with its literal sense, but neither will figurative meaning begin without it.

Failure to Rise to the Figurative Level

Having examined "North Labrador," three readers commented as follows. "I think this poem is rather stupid. It is quite evident that no one could survive on a sheet of ice. But the author does ask the question, 'why has no one settled here?' There seems to be little point to it." Despite that slight stirring in his third sentence, this reader is truly shackled, and even the second stanza which compares North Labrador to a woman does no more than to shake his prose chains. Another reader begins to worry about those chains: "I like the arrangement of this poem. It leaves one with thoughts about it, and I wonder just what is meant." Still another reader threatens to break loose and rise to the figurative level: "The words [images] in this one caught my attention first—they are quite descriptive and put me in a mood. I can see the

* For a demonstration of the difference between the literal and figurative levels as found, for example, in Frost's "Stopping by Woods on a Snowy Evening," see "The Plain Sense of a Poem," p. 236, and compare "The Meaning of a Poem," p. 238.

cold desolation, the colorlessness, and can feel the moments plodding by with a pointless, 'toward no Spring,' sameness." This reader is on his way to poetic liberation. When he sees that the entire poem is literally about North Labrador but figuratively about the utter loneliness and emotional starvation of the human heart, he will have learned a basic lesson in the reading of poems.

To rise to the figurative level of a poem requires imagination, or the ability to perceive comparisons—to understand, for example, that Hart Crane is making a comment on humanity by talking about North Labrador. Crane had seen the dramatic comparison with his imagination, and he has therefore used certain aspects of North Labrador to comment on a tragic situation in the human heart.

Failure to Recognize Irony

Many readers, churning with good spirits and ready to accept their world at face value, are likely to accept irony at face value, too. The failure to recognize irony is closely related to the failure to rise to the figurative level because irony, like simile and metaphor, is a figure of speech. Yet it is a special kind of figure because it relies more on *contrast* than on comparison, and consequently the poet depends on the reader to bring a special knowledge to the ironical statement to understand the contrast. In extended pieces of literature, of course, the author himself may provide the necessary special knowledge.

When Burns writes,

My love is like a red red rose,

he is emphasizing the comparison, not the contrast, between the loved one and the beauties of the rose. But when Sandburg writes in *The People, Yes* (p. 313),

"The czar has eight million men with guns
     and bayonets.
"Nothing can happen to the czar.
"The czar is the voice of God and shall live
     forever.
"Turn and look at the forest of steel and
     cannon
"Where the czar is guarded by eight million
     soldiers.
"Nothing can happen to the czar,"

he is emphasizing the contrast between the czar and the voice of God that shall live forever. With our knowledge of what did happen to the czar we understand Sandburg's irony in having the speaker naively believe that "nothing can happen to the czar" because he "is guarded by eight million soldiers." And the irony is further compounded by the suggestion that the voice of God will live forever because of the protection of guns and bayonets.

The title of Eliot's poem, "The Love Song of J. Alfred Prufrock" (p. 304), is ironic for the reader if he catches the suggestion of a prude dressed in a frock coat (a Prince Albert) contemplating the act of love-making. "Love Song" is intended to recall the sensations of love songs long admired, and the reader may remember two famous lines from a Shakespearian sonnet (p. 278):

Love alters not with his brief hours and
weeks,
But bears it out even to the edge of doom.

Prufrock's love song tells us why he hovers on the edge of doom, but hardly for the reasons offered by Shakespeare. By such a contrast Eliot exposes Prufrock's frustration: Eliot's use of the word *love* is ironic because Prufrock is capable only of self-love.

As a poetic device irony accomplishes some valuable effects for the poet. He can profess a restraint and detachment while often his emotions are intensely aroused. This posture plus the double meaning of the irony are likely to appeal to the sophisticated intelligence of readers who come to feel that they and the poet share recondite meanings obscure to less perceptive minds. Irony, indeed, has enjoyed a long philosophical career, and its enjoyment is a mark of the mature mind. It produces an unmistakable tone in a poem, and tone itself, we shall come to see later, becomes a figure of speech as it pervades an entire poem. (See "Figure and Symbol," p. 282.)

Preconceptions About the Nature of Poetry

One of the most persistent preconceptions holds that a poem must contain ideas, penetrating abstractions about the meaning of life—or,

the reverse, a poem must be "pure" and never "soiled" with "thought." * Either position disqualifies a huge share of the world's distinguished poetry, and this act alone should alert us to the untenable dogmatism. *Must* we make a decision between Dryden's "A Song for St. Cecilia's Day, 1687" (p. 329) and Coleridge's "Kubla Khan" (p. 335)? The judgment of the years says no.

Another preconception can become a little militant at times against pessimism. One reader of Crane's "North Labrador" writes that "This one appears to be on the gloomy side of things and it didn't appeal to me at all." This statement is closely allied to another reader's comment, "I don't think I am a better person for having read it." These preconceptions, too, would disqualify another huge share of the world's poems. We shall come to see that the fine poets do not arbitrarily decree that either optimism or pessimism is superior, nor do they assume that the proper function of a poem is to offer morals in capsule form. "North Labrador," for example, is actually a religious poem in the deepest sense, but Crane includes no explicitly stated prescription for happiness here or for salvation later. His comment appears by indirection and inference: the isolated soul who "journeys toward no Spring" is a cold, tragic soul who has been cut off from the warmth of love and affection. But Crane feels no responsibility for spelling out the prescription by adding another stanza saying, "Don't be like that—avoid it at all cost!" Beware of judging a poem by its optimism or pessimism. It is better to ask, is the poem true? Does it enlarge my understanding and sympathies?

Preconceptions in favor of or against one doctrine or another can produce curious results in the reading of poems. Some readers constantly search for the confirming doctrine; they are determined to find what they already believe. This attitude of mind used as an approach to poems can bring unfortunate consequences. It may violate the poem's meaning to make it conform to the reader's belief. It is comfortable to have a great poet on our side, and the temptation to

---

* For a defense of this latter position, see the Introduction by George Moore to his *An Anthology of Pure Poetry.* New York: Liveright Publishing Corporation, 1924.

stretch him into place is not always resisted, but the art of the poem may be undervalued if the poem fails to confirm the reader's belief. Milton's *Paradise Lost* suffered this fate when T. S. Eliot found Milton's theology unpalatable, although, to Eliot's credit, he later recanted. Or this attitude of mind may overpraise the art of the poem if the poem does confirm the reader's belief.

The last-mentioned preconception is perhaps the most difficult to correct because it is quite natural—but still wrong—to accept without critical examination a poem's art simply because we agree with the poem's point of view. Forty-nine college students still without instruction in poetry on the college level were asked to judge seven poems which ranged from very good to bad. Thirty students commented favorably on the poorest poem of the seven, titled "A Visit to Mom and Dad," and five students thought it to be the best of the lot. After six weeks of experience in analyzing and judging many poems, these readers changed their opinion radically concerning the value of "A Visit to Mom and Dad" because they had learned that no subject, however close to their hearts, necessarily makes a good poem. (See "The Language of Poetry," especially p. 269, for a demonstration of this principle.)

These readers were victims of what is known as *stock response*. To facilitate everyday living most of us gather a pattern of attitudes and a hierarchy of values by which we make decisions, issue opinions, and guide our everyday behavior. We are likely to react quickly against certain ideas and key words and in favor of others, sometimes without examining the context of the idea or key word. Debaters, candidates for office, and advertisers make a conscious study of our stock responses, and play the human console accordingly. And so do some writers of verse. In his poem, "Edgar A. Guest Considers 'The Old Woman Who Lived in a Shoe' and the Good Old Verities at the Same Time" (p. 251), Untermeyer satirizes Guest's way of appealing to our stock responses (the "Good Old Verities" are our generalized notions about children, parents, the home, sacrifice).

But we should be very clear about the relationship of stock responses and poems. There is nothing inherently wrong with stock responses. The point is, *what has the poet done with them?*

The good poet—the poet devoted to his art—tries to furnish within the poem itself the attitudes and reasons for our participating in his belief. The poor poet simply pushes buttons marked "God," "Country," "Mom," and "Dad," and gives us no fresh experience, no insights, no "temporary stay against confusion." The logical question is: if the poet has no more to offer than his rhyming of our stock responses, why should he write?

Other preconceptions which sidetrack readers have to do with the sound of a poem, its form, and even its length. "North Labrador" brought such comments as these: "It's choppy. I prefer things that read a little smoother." Another reader: "I don't care for this style of writing." Another: "It's awfully short." But still another reader disagrees: "This reads easily and sounds like poetry should." These contradictory comments emerge from a failure to understand one of the basic principles of all poems: the poet selects the means (the technical devices) to produce his desired end. The sound and sense of a good poem are a fusion, an organic whole, and we must first comprehend the whole before we judge the means, or the technical matters. We shall soon see that Frost's "Departmental" (p. 250) is choppy, and that Burns's "Sweet Afton" (p. 249) is smoother and more flowing. And we shall see, too, that if either poem had the other's rhythm, both poems would be quite meaningless, indeed a little silly.

The only serviceable cure for the preconceptions brought to the reading of poems is to refuse to accept or reject *any* part of a poem until after the poem's totality has been mastered. Briefly, we should not read *into* poems; we should read *out* of poems whatever the poets have put into them. Once we have completely surrounded a poem's meaning it is our privilege to use the poem for any purpose whatever: as a document in the history of sensibility, as a confirmation or denial of the value of some sensuous experience or idea—but *not* before we have surrounded the poem's meaning. There is simply no other way.*

---

* For a revealing study of the causes of the misreadings of poems see I. A. Richards, *Practical Criticism, a Study of Literary Judgment.* New York: Harcourt Brace Jovanovich, Inc., 1929 and 1952.

My Last Duchess
Ferrara

ROBERT BROWNING
1812–1889

Now that we have absorbed some initial instruction on the reading of poetry, including some pitfalls to be avoided, suppose we put our preliminary knowledge to work on a poem. Browning's influence on the new twentieth-century poetry is now well known; he is indeed very much a "modern." "My Last Duchess" is a concentrated little dramatic scene in which the Duke describes his own character through his words and actions. Although the poem is a dramatic monologue, we can easily supply the conversation that has taken place between the Duke and his listener, the Count's emissary.

That's my last Duchess painted on the wall
Looking as if she were alive. I call
That piece a wonder, now: Frà Pandolf's hands
Worked busily a day, and there she stands.
Will't please you sit and look at her? I said   5
"Frà Pandolf" by design, for never read
Strangers like you that pictured countenance,
The depth and passion of its earnest glance,
But to myself they turned (since none puts by
The curtain I have drawn for you, but I)   10
And seemed as they would ask me, if they durst,
How such a glance came there; so, not the first
Are you to turn and ask thus. Sir, 'twas not
Her husband's presence only, called that spot
Of joy into the Duchess' cheek: perhaps   15
Frà Pandolf chanced to say, "Her mantle laps
Over my lady's wrist too much," or "Paint
Must never hope to reproduce the faint
Half-flush that dies along her throat." Such stuff
Was courtesy, she thought, and cause enough   20
For calling up that spot of joy. She had
A heart—how shall I say?—too soon made glad,
Too easily impressed; she liked whate'er
She looked on, and her looks went everywhere.
Sir, 'twas all one! My favor at her breast,   25
The dropping of the daylight in the West,
The bough of cherries some officious fool
Broke in the orchard for her, the white mule
She rode with round the terrace—all and each

Would draw from her alike the approving
    speech,   30
Or blush, at least. She thanked men,—good! but
    thanked
Somehow—I know not how—as if she ranked
My gift of a nine-hundred-years-old name
With anybody's gift. Who'd stoop to blame
This sort of trifling? Even had you skill   35
In speech—(which I have not)—to make your
    will
Quite clear to such an one, and say, "Just this
Or that in your disgusts me; here you miss,
Or there exceed the mark"—and if she let
Herself be lessoned so, nor plainly set   40
Her wits to yours, forsooth, and made excuse,
—E'en then would be some stooping; and I
    choose
Never to stoop. Oh, sir, she smiled, no doubt,
Whene'er I passed her; but who passed without
Much the same smile? This grew; I gave com-
    mands;   45
Then all smiles stopped together. There she
    stands
As if alive. Will't please you rise? We'll meet
The company below then. I repeat,
The Count your master's known munificence
Is ample warrant that no just pretence   50
Of mine for dowry will be disallowed;
Though his fair daughter's self, as I avowed
At starting, is my object. Nay, we'll go
Together down, sir. Notice Neptune, though,
Taming a sea-horse, thought a rarity,   55
Which Claus of Innsbruck cast in bronze for me!

Analytical Dialogue on "My Last Duchess"

The following Dialogue on "My Last Duchess" is one way of analyzing a poem, that is, accounting for all the important matters which make the poem meaningful. This conversation between a student and his professor actually contains about nineteen principles which when observed help us to read poems accurately. The first principle appears in the opening comment by A: he has stated, very briefly, the plain, or literal, sense of the poem. He knows what the poem is "about."

But Z refuses to allow the poem to rest there, and the analysis is under way. What other principles of accurate reading can be found?

---

z: You have read the poem?

a: Yes, and I think I understand it fairly well. It's about a Duke who had his wife killed because she was too pleasant to everybody.

z: If that's all there is to it, why do so many people enjoy—and remember—this poem?

a: It's sensational; I suppose that's why.

z: Perhaps, but in essence the story is common-place. Newspapers every day carry accounts of murders committed for the slightest reasons. "Husband Has Wife Killed Because She Smiled at Everybody"—such a headline and the story would get passing attention, but few people would paste the account into a scrap-book. There must be something else to make this bit of writing memorable. Shall we see if we can find out what it is?

a: All right. Where do we start?

z: With the title. Anything worth noting about the title? What does "Last" mean? Does it mean final?

a: Certainly not. The Duke's going to have another duchess. Probably "Last" means former or latest.

z: Latest? Would that meaning imply that the Duke might have had another duchess—or several other duchesses—before the last one?

a: I don't know.

z: Well, neither do I, and since such an idea has no bearing on the poem as it is told, suppose we discard it.

a: I have no objection. Besides I want you to know that I looked up Ferrara: it's a place in Italy, northern Italy.

z: Good. That gives us something to go on, doesn't it? Ferrara is a real place. The speaker is an Italian duke, and the subject of his remarks is his former wife. Now if we want to be orderly about our inquiry, we ought to know to whom the Duke is speaking.

a: I didn't find that out until near the end of the poem when the Duke mentioned a count as the master of the person the Duke is talking to. He evidently was visiting the Duke to make marriage arrangements for the Count's daughter. I felt sorry for her.

z: You should. Actually the daughter of the Count is the real object of all the Duke's talk, isn't she?

a: How do you know?

z: Because the Duke obviously is not talking at random; he's not revealing his arrogance and cruelty for the fun of hearing himself talk. He is issuing a sharp, clear warning: "This is precisely the way my former duchess conducted herself; I did not attempt to school her in proper behavior; I choose never to stoop; I do not intend to stoop to my next Duchess; but if you like, here is a warning to her." Since it is unlikely that the Count would resist a ducal connection for his daughter, one may hope that he and his daughter were given a verbatim report of the Duke's comments.

a: I read somewhere that the stop before the painting of the Duchess was simply part of an art tour with the pause before Neptune as another part of the tour.

z: Does that interpretation fit the facts? What were the Duke and the Count's emissary doing immediately *before* the poem opens?

a: They were discussing the proposed wedding and how much dowry the Count would provide. The lines about the dowry come near the end of the poem—lines 48 to 53 beginning with the words, "I repeat."

z: And where were they going after settling this question?

a: To "meet the company below."

z: Do you think it likely that an art tour would be sandwiched between these two actions? Isn't it more likely that the deliberate pause before the portrait was planned by the Duke in advance as *part* of the negotiations for the hand of the Count's daughter?

a: Let me ask you a question: Why didn't the poem end as the Duke and the emissary descend the stairs? What's the significance of Neptune taming a sea horse?

z: A much debated question. Some critics make a parallel between the Duke and Neptune: the Duke tamed a wife as Neptune tamed a sea horse. Is there any difficulty here?

a: Sounds plausible to me—but wait a minute: the Duke really didn't tame his wife, did he? He didn't make any effort to tame her; he simply removed her without warning. I would say the parallel breaks down.

z: Agreed. Other critics say that the bronze

statue and the portrait were equally interest-ing as art forms. I think this interpretation is only partly true. The Duke must have realized that in talking of his last Duchess there had inevitably been "some stooping," some con-descension, a curious sort of charitableness, a touch of magnanimity. He was relieved to be done with the warning. He could return to casualness and hope that the reference to the bronze would be linked to the portrait as sim-ply another work of art. And it may be that having used the portrait to point a moral and adorn a tale, he himself could *now* classify the portrait as simply another of his art treasures. You look skeptical.

A: I feel skeptical. The poem doesn't say all that, does it?

Z: No.

A: Why doesn't it?

Z: Because you, along with millions of other readers, would not enjoy being told every-thing in a-b-c fashion. The poet could have made his lines as clear as

Thirty days hath September,
April, June, and November.

These are useful lines but not very absorbing.

A: Nevertheless, I don't like puzzles.

Z: Unless you can solve them?

A: Yes.

Z: A good poem is an open puzzle—all the parts are there, and some of the fun is in putting them firmly together. This poet, for example, wanted you and me to enter into the character of a cold, arrogant, devious, observing, sus-picious, scheming, all-powerful husband. He had confidence that you could provide these adjectives even though he uses none of them himself. He wanted you to speculate about the Duchess, too. Do you know anything about women?

A: Not much.

Z: Do you think you would like the Duchess?

A: Yes, I think so. She was easygoing and popu-lar, I imagine, with everybody except her husband.

Z: Any more adjectives for her?

A: You might call her charming, genial, and I imagine she was pretty. She was democratic. She could blush easily, which shows she was sensitive.

Z: Good. But did she have any fault, any blind spot?

A: She didn't pay enough attention to her hus-band?

Z: Why didn't she?

A: How should I know?

Z: Do you recall how close an observer the hus-band was? He knew when his wife smiled and why, and when she blushed; and he could re-peat the phrases or describe the actions which would call forth these genial responses.

A: Maybe she didn't notice that he was watch-ing her, or maybe she felt so innocent that she didn't notice. You mean her weakness was a blindness to her husband watching her? That isn't a weakness.

Z: Doubtless even if she had studied her hus-band's expression she would have seen little warning in its monotonous impassiveness. But what did she lack which women pride them-selves on having?

A: A woman's intuition?

Z: Precisely. "All smiles stopped together"— that is, suddenly and finally. No hint of the Duke's displeasure ever reached the Duchess until it was too late. If she had had intuition, she . . .

A: Excuse me for interrupting, but didn't you say this was to be an orderly discussion? We began with the title, and that's as far as we went in orderliness.

Z: But haven't we been *essentially* well orga-nized? We analyzed the title, then the speaker, then the person spoken of. We mentioned the person spoken to, and we set forth the real purpose of the Duke's remarks. We haven't said much about setting. How much do we know about that?

A: Much. The country is Italy, the city Ferrara, and the local address, the palace of the Duke. As I see it, the Duke and emissary have stopped at the head of a stairway, marble, I think, but the poet doesn't say so. There the Duke draws back curtains and reveals a por-trait. He steps back and sits down with the emissary—on a bench of some sort. I suppose, possibly like those in museums. After the Duke finishes, they rise and go down the stairs together.

Z: Why together?

A: Because the Duke is feeling in good spirits;

everything is going well and he feels democratic.

z: That's the chief reason. Another is that the emissary is entitled to be treated as his master, the Count, would have been treated. Are we ready for a straightforward statement of the poem's contents, including the action before the poem opened—the antecedent action?

A: We ought to be ready. Please proceed.

z: The proud Duke of Ferrara, dissatisfied with the indiscriminate geniality of his wife, puts her away, and later decides to negotiate with a Count for the hand of his daughter. The emissary of the Count arrives at the ducal residence and goes into conference with the Duke over marriage terms. At the conclusion of a friendly talk, the Duke uses the portrait of his last Duchess as the pretext for warning his duchess-to-be of the conduct expected of her. The warning delivered, the conferees go to meet the Duke's guests, who perhaps were assembled to hear the news of the betrothal. Anything left out?

A: That is the story, all right. Do you suppose that was the form the story had when the poet sat down to write?

z: An important and observant question. I think almost surely the poet worked from the straightforward story, his raw materials. Details and arrangement make the poem. We cannot say how much material he discarded, but all surplusage is gone. Give these same basic materials to any number of writers and the result will be any number of versions, some of which might be excellent, but none, one feels, superior to this poem.

A: I can see that. He might have told us more about Frà Pandolf—a smooth flatterer. Or the emissary might have been in love with the Count's daughter and—

z: Hold on! You've jumped the fence, and that way lies Tristan and Isolde.

A: Who?

z: Never mind. You might look them up sometime and see how many versions there are of *that* affair. Now, I want you to consider for a moment the problems our poet faced, and the artistic tact he used in solving them.

A: Do we have to do this?

z: No, but you have entered very well into one level of enjoyment, and I thought you might like to try, briefly, another level—the level of technical artistry.

A: Sounds forbidding, but go ahead.

z: For one thing, the poet deliberately imposed upon himself the limitations of the dramatic monologue.

A: Please define. I know your habits on examinations.

z: The dramatic monologue is the name given to poems in which a single speaker talks aloud to one or more listeners. If there are no listeners, by the way, the speaker is indulging in dramatic soliloquy. There are enough ordinary difficulties in telling a story, but the difficulties of the dramatic monologue are extraordinary.

A: It doesn't look so terribly difficult. It flows so easily that at first I didn't even notice the rhymes. But I grant the difficulty. Why did the poet choose this form?

z: The results of great art always look easy. As for your question, the poet must have decided that this was the one effective way *for him* to tell his story. Since we agree that he was successful, we are likely to agree that he chose the right form. Shall we list some of the "handicaps" which the poet imposed upon himself?

A: If you wish.

z: Will you name the first and perhaps most obvious one?

A: I defer to you. You have my permission to name the whole list.

z: I'll name the first, and you will then be able to name the second. One, the poet excluded himself from the poem—no comments, no moral. All dramatic writers do this, more or less. Two?

A: He doesn't say how to read the poem, is that it?

z: Yes. He omits stage directions. Few dramatic writers do that. This means that within a short speech he must include the setting (time and place), the exposition, and the antecedent action, all in such a natural way that these elements are absorbed into the forward motion of the poem. Three, he had to watch the time element with special care. He could allow the Duke to be greatly skilled in speech—in spite of the Duke's protests to the contrary—but a long speech at the particular time would have been out of character. Four?

A: Four, if you please.

z: This is most important. The Duke had to say things which would reveal his true (cruel) nature, and yet the reader must believe that this particular character would actually say such things. Here the motivation must be strong and convincing. As we have already seen, the motivation—a warning to the Count's daughter—is strong and convincing.

A: The poem is believable all right. Would you call this a great poem?

z: One measure—not the only measure—of a poem's validity is its staunchness before searching questions. By this test the poem is great. An inferior poem would not fare so well.

So far we have been concerned to note how the figurative-symbolic level develops from the literal level of a poem. The first poem below is the Latin original; the second is a literal translation of it; and the third poem shows us what Jonson made of the original. It should not be assumed, of course, that Jonson was obligated to render the Latin poem into English in a slavish way; had he tried to do so the Latin rhythms and idiom would have defeated him poetically (artistically). To note the differences between the second and third poems teaches us much about the nature of poetry. What makes Jonson's poem poetry? If you read Latin readily, why not convert Catullus' poem to your own poetic version?

Carmen V, Ad Lesbiam
G. VALERIUS CATULLUS
84?–54 B.C.

Vivamus, mea Lesbia, atque amemus,
Rumoresque senum severiorum
Omnes unius aestimemus assis.
Soles occidere et redire possunt:
Nobis, cum semel occidit brevis lux,   5
Nox est perpetua una dormienda.
Da mi basia mille, deinde centum,
Dein mille altera, dein secunda centum,
Dein usque altera mille, deinde centum:

Dein, cum milia multa fecerimus,   10
Conturbabimus illa, ne sciamus,
Aut ne quis malus invidere possit,
Cum tantum sciat esse basiorum.

To Lesbia

Let us live, my Lesbia, and let us love,
And let us estimate all the gossip of prudish
     old men
As worth only a penny.
Suns can set and then rise again,
But as for us, when once our brief light
     sets,   5
There is only an everlasting night of sleep.
Give me a thousand kisses, then a hundred,
Then another thousand, then a second
     hundred,
Then still another thousand, then a
     hundred:
Then after we shall have run up many
     thousands,   10
We shall confuse the count, so that we do
     not know it,
And no wicked person may be able to put
     the evil eye on us,
When he knows that our kisses were just so
     many.

Come, My Celia
BEN JONSON
1572–1637

Come, my Celia, let us prove
While we may the sports of love;
Time will not be ours forever,
He at length our good will sever.
Spend not then his gifts in vain;   5
Suns that set may rise again,
But if once we lose this light,
'Tis with us perpetual night.
Why should we defer our joys?
Fame and rumor are but toys.   10
Cannot we delude the eyes
Of a few poor household spies?
Or his easier ears beguile,
So removèd by our wile?

'Tis no sin love's fruit to steal;   15
But the sweet theft to reveal,
To be taken, to be seen,
These have crimes accounted been.

TONE AND THE PLEASURES OF POETRY *

One of the open secrets of this book lies in the belief that readers cannot be required or forced to enjoy poetry, much less to understand it. But we can be led into understanding by first reading good poems whose meaning and structure are quite immediately clear, especially if the poems give us a good-natured jolt or touch some universal feeling or attitude. Our immediate concern is to feel the delight of the fusion of *sound and sense*. The following poems have been chosen because the fusion can be immediately felt. No reader, however, is expected to enjoy every good poem he reads regardless of his skill in reading poems: our past experiences, backgrounds, and temperaments will help and hinder enjoyment of poems, so if you can find even two or three of these poems that come alive for you, you are on your way.

One more word about sound and sense. The poet has made the fusion, and we must read both sound and sense simultaneously. Read each poem *aloud*, and *let it have its way with you*. Will you be one-and-twenty, or have you been one-and-twenty? In either case Housman has a twinkling word for you.

When I Was One-and-Twenty
A. E. HOUSMAN
1859–1936

When I was one-and-twenty
    I heard a wise man say,
"Give crowns and pounds and guineas

* See Auden's essay "Reading" (p. 813) for comments on the pleasures of poetry; for example, "Pleasure is by no means an infallible critical guide, but it is the least fallible."

But not your heart away;
Give pearls away and rubies   5
    But keep your fancy free."
But I was one-and-twenty,
    No use to talk to me.

When I was one-and-twenty
    I heard him say again,   10
"The heart out of the bosom
    Was never given in vain;
'Tis paid with sighs a-plenty
    And sold for endless rue."
And I am two-and-twenty,   15
    And oh, 'tis true, 'tis true.

Housman's problem here was to make us *feel* the jaunty cocksureness of the young speaker in the poem who ignores the wise man's advice until the speaker's own experience confirms it. Housman could have told us he was jaunty and cocksure, but Housman has the speaker present himself to exhibit his jaunty cocksureness. How did Housman accomplish this? By having the sound—the rhythm, rhyme, and the clipped words—help to interpret the sense. Each line has only three feet (trimeter); each line's rhythm is well-nigh perfect (*sure*, like the young man); most words have only one syllable (clipped, jaunty); and the rhyme is repetitious—like the speaker until he grows into wisdom. The character of the speaker is clear because the sound has prepared us for a fuller sense of the poem.

Let us now hear a completely different fusion of sound and sense in Burns's poem.

Sweet Afton
ROBERT BURNS
1759–1796

Flow gently, sweet Afton! among thy green
                braes,[1]
Flow gently, I'll sing thee a song in thy praise;
My Mary's asleep by thy murmuring stream,
Flow gently, sweet Afton, disturb not her dream.

Thou stock-dove whose echo resounds through
                the glen,   5

[1] Banks.

Ye wild whistling blackbirds in yon thorny den,
Thou green-crested lapwing, thy screaming for-
    bear,
I charge you, disturb not my slumbering fair.

How lofty, sweet Afton, thy neighboring hills,
Far marked with the courses of clear, winding
    rills;   10
There daily I wander as noon rises high,
My flocks and my Mary's sweet cot [2] in my eye.

How pleasant thy banks and green valleys below,
Where, wild in the woodlands, the primroses
    blow;
There oft, as mild ev'ning weeps over the lea, 15
The sweet-scented birk [3] shades my Mary and
    me.

Thy crystal stream, Afton, how lovely it glides,
And winds by the cot where my Mary resides;
How wanton thy waters her snowy feet lave,
As, gathering sweet flowerets, she stems thy
    clear wave.   20

Flow gently, sweet Afton, among thy green
    braes,
Flow gently sweet river, the theme of my lays;[4]
My Mary's asleep by thy murmuring stream,
Flow gently, sweet Afton, disturb not her dream.

Burns's problem here was to make us feel the mood of the speaker generated by his loved one, so the poet has employed the devices of his art—rhythm, rhyme, word sounds (onomatopoeia), and stanza form. With these devices he has accomplished a good deal. The sentiments of the speaker flow gently and tenderly as the river flows, and the tone of the poem is reminiscent of a tenderness muted and enriched by time. The flowing quality is produced by the four-footed line (tetrameter) with most feet having three syllables accented on the third syllable (anapestic foot), as in the first line:

Flŏw gént|lў swēet Af|tŏn ămóng|thў green
    braés

Yet the couplets (*braes-praise; stream-dream*) present a series of disciplined sentiments which do not disappear in the strong force of the flowing rhythm. The poem's emotion is therefore measured, gentle, and yet strong as if it would match time in eternity.

Poems, we see, *do* speak for themselves *if we know how to listen*, but Frost's poem now speaks in a radically different manner.

Departmental
ROBERT FROST
1874–1963

An ant on the table cloth
Ran into a dormant moth
Of many times his size.
He showed not the least surprise.
His business wasn't with such.   5
He gave it scarcely a touch,
And was off on his duty run.
Yet if he encountered one
Of the hive's enquiry squad
Whose work is to find out God   10
And the nature of time and space,
He would put him onto the case.
Ants are a curious race;
One crossing with hurried tread
The body of one of their dead   15
Isn't given a moment's arrest—
Seems not even impressed.
But he no doubt reports to any
With whom he crosses antennae,
And they no doubt report   20
To the higher up at court.
Then word goes forth in Formic:
"Death's come to Jerry McCormic,
Our selfless forager Jerry.
Will the special Janizary[1]   25
Whose office it is to bury
The dead of the commissary
Go bring him home to his people.
Lay him in state on a sepal.
Wrap him for shroud in a petal.   30
Embalm him with ichor of nettle.
This is the word of your Queen."
And presently on the scene
Appears a solemn mortician;
And taking formal position,   35

---

[2] Small house; cottage.   [3] Birch.   [4] Song.   [1] A soldier of an elite corps.

With feelers calmly atwiddle,
Seizes the dead by the middle,
And heaving him high in air,
Carries him out of there.
No one stands round to stare.   40
It is nobody else's affair.

It couldn't be called ungentle.
But how thoroughly departmental.

This poem is a satire on our modern tendency to accept only individual responsibility in life instead of accepting some responsibility for the whole social structure. Literally Frost is talking about ants, but figuratively he is satirizing men. Satire is usually a light, sprightly form of ridi-cule, and Frost's *technical* problem was therefore to make us feel the force of his short jabs, needling, against our fragmentizing of life. By using the devices of the short, clipped line (trimeter) and the couplet form, and by ending many lines with abrupt stops (*report-court; Formic-McCormic; atwiddle-middle*), we see and feel these efficient little ants (men) scurrying to their single duties looking neither to the right nor left. And note that when Frost wants to rub the satire in, he rhymes three and even four successive lines (*space-case-race; air-there-stare-affair*). Perhaps we feel a little punch-drunk at the end of the poem.

If we are now alive to the various results of poets fusing sound and sense expertly, the following poems may provide us with a good deal of pleasure.

Edgar A. Guest Considers "The Old Woman Who Lived in a Shoe" and the Good Old Verities at the Same Time
LOUIS UNTERMEYER
1885–

Edgar A. Guest (1881–1959) wrote popular sentimental and moralistic verse especially for the *Detroit Free Press* which was syndicated throughout the United States. Untermeyer is satirizing the dead imagery, the monotonous rhythms, and particularly the stock responses used by Guest to snare the uncritical reader. (For discussion of stock response see p. 243.)

It takes a heap o' children to make a home that's true,
And home can be a palace grand or just a plain old shoe;
But if it has a mother dear and a good old dad or two,
Why, that's the sort of good old home for good old me and you.

Of all the institutions this side the Vale of Rest   5
Howe'er it be it seems to me a good old mother's best;
And fathers are a blessing, too, they give the place a tone;
In fact each child should try and have some parents of his own.

The food can be quite simple; just a sop of milk and bread
Are plenty when the kiddies know it's time to go to bed.   10
And every little sleepy-head will dream about the day
When he can go to work because a Man's Work is his Play.

And, oh, how sweet his life will seem, with nought to make him cross;
And he will never watch the clock and always mind the boss.
And when he thinks (as may occur), this thought will please him best: 15
That ninety million think the same—including

EDDIE GUEST

A Bird Came down the Walk

EMILY DICKINSON
1830–1886

A Bird came down the Walk—
He did not know I saw—
He bit an Angleworm in halves
And ate the fellow, raw,

And then he drank a Dew   5
From a convenient Grass—
And then hopped sidewise to the Wall
To let a Beetle pass—

He glanced with rapid eyes
That hurried all around—   10
They looked like frightened Beads, I thought—
He stirred His Velvet Head

Like one in danger, Cautious,
I offered him a Crumb
And he unrolled his feathers   15
And rowed him softer home—

Than Oars divide the Ocean,
Too silver for a seam—
Or Butterflies, off Banks of Noon
Leap, plashless as they swim.   20

THE ENDURING BALLAD
STORY BALLADS *

Barbra Allen

ANONYMOUS

In London City where I once did dwell, there's where I got my learning,
I fell in love with a pretty young girl, her name was Barbra Allen.
I courted her for seven long years, she said she would not have me;
Then straightaway home as I could go and liken to a dying.

I wrote her a letter on my death bed, I wrote it slow and moving;   5
"Go take this letter to my old true love and tell her I am dying."
She took the letter in her lily-white hand, she read it slow and moving;
"Go take this letter back to him, and tell him I am coming."

As she passed by his dying bed she saw his pale lips quivering;
"No better, no better I'll ever be until I get Barbra Allen."   10
As she passed by his dying bed; "You're very sick and almost dying,
No better, no better you will ever be, for you can't get Barbra Allen."

As she went down the long stair steps she heard the death bell toning,
And every bell appeared to say, "Hard-hearted Barbra Allen!"
As she went down the long piney walk she heard some small birds singing,   15
And every bird appeared to say, "Hard-hearted Barbra Allen!"

She looked to the East, she looked to the West, she saw the pale corpse coming,
"Go bring them pale corpse unto me, and let me gaze upon them.

* For more poems in the ballad tradition not included in this section see Burns, "Sweet Afton" (p. 249);
"John Barleycorn: A Ballad" (p. 333); Moore, "Believe Me, If All Those Endearing Young Charms" (p.
276); "Western Wind, When Wilt Thou Blow?" (p. 324); and "Jolly Good Ale and Old" (p. 324).

Oh, mama, mama, go make my bed, go make it soft and narrow!
Sweet Willie died today for me, I'll die for him tomorrow!"   20

They buried Sweet Willie in the old church yard, they buried Miss Barbra beside him;
And out of his grave there sprang a red rose, and out of hers a briar.
They grew to the top of the old church tower, they could not grow any higher,
They hooked, they tied in a true love's knot, red rose around the briar.

Sir Patrick Spens
ANONYMOUS

The king sits in Dumferling toune,
  Drinking the blude-reid wine:
"Oh whar will I get guid sailor,
  To sail this schip of mine?"

Up and spak an eldern knicht,[1]   5
  Sat at the kings richt kne:
"Sir Patrick Spens is the best sailor
  That sails upon the se."

The king has written a braid [2] letter,
  And signd it wi his hand,   10
And sent it to Sir Patrick Spens,
Was walking on the sand.

The first line that Sir Patrick red,
  A loud lauch lauched he;
The next line that Sir Patrick red,   15
  The teir blinded his ee.

"O wha is this has don this deid,
  This ill deid don to me,
To send me out this time o' the yeir,
  To sail upon the se!   20

"Mak hast, mak haste, my mirry men all,
  Our guid schip sails the morne."
"O say na sae,[3] my master deir,
  For I feir a deadlie storme.

"Late, late yestreen I saw the new moone,   25
  Wi the auld moone in hir arme,
And I feir, I feir, my deir master,
  That we will cum to harme."

O our Scots nobles wer richt laith[4]

To weet their cork-heild schoone,[5]   30
Bot lang owre[6] a' the play wer playd,
  Thair hats they swam aboone.[7]

O lang, lang may their ladies sit,
  Wi their fans into their hand,
Or eir[8] they se Sir Patrick Spens   35
  Cum sailing to the land.

O lang, lang may the ladies stand,
  Wi their gold kems[9] in their hair,
Waiting for their ain[10] deir lords,
  For they'll se thame na mair.   40

Haf owre, half owre[11] to Aberdour,
  It's fiftie fadom[12] deip,
And thair lies guid Sir Patrick Spens,
  Wi the Scots lords at his feit.

Comments and Questions

This poem, like "Barbra Allen," is an anonymous folk, or popular, ballad whose "final" shape includes the alterations which were made as the ballad passed from generation to generation. Like all literary forms, the ballad emerged to serve a purpose, and the purpose of the ballad seems to have been to celebrate, lament, or commemorate some dramatic incident which probably affected the community at the time.

1. Of the many versions of this old Scottish ballad, this one seems to have become the best established, perhaps because of its brevity, compression, and dramatic intensity. It is, in effect, a short story. What are the facts of the story?

2. This ballad has a surprising number of characteristics of the modern short story.

[5] Cork-heeled shoes.   [6] Before.   [7] Above.
[8] Before.   [9] Combs.   [10] Own.
[11] Halfway over.   [12] Fathom.

[1] Knight.   [2] Stately.   [3] Not so.   [4] Loath.

Consider the narrator's point of view, panorama and scene, character portrayal, and dramatic elements. (For a discussion of these terms see "Fiction: Preliminaries" p. 12.) Note particularly the relative absence of author comment.

3. In what way does the tone of this ballad differ from that of "Barbra Allen"?

4. Note the metrical structure of "Sir Patrick Spens." It is written in conventional ballad stanza, the first and third lines having four feet (tetrameter), the second and fourth lines having three feet (trimeter),

written mostly in iambic meter (the king), and with a rhyme scheme of *abcb*. This form is sometimes called a classic structure and is quite different of course from the structure found in "Barbra Allen" which has roughly seven feet in each line, written in broken iambic meter. It is tempting to ask which ballad has the better technique, but it is sounder to ask, does each technique serve well the meaning of the poem? What is your opinion? Consider question 3 again before you conclude.

5. Compare "Sir Patrick Spens" with Pound's "Ballad of the Goodly Free" (p. 374) and note the similar metrical effect.

Frankie and Johnny
ANONYMOUS

Frankie and Johnny were lovers, great God how
    they could love!
Swore to be true to each other, true as the stars
    up above.
He was her man, but he done her wrong.

Frankie she was his woman, everybody knows.
She spent her forty dollars for Johnny a suit of
    clothes.   5
He was her man, but he done her wrong.

Frankie and Johnny went walking, Johnny in his
    brand new suit.
"O good Lawd," said Frankie, "but don't my
    Johnny look cute?"
He was her man, but he done her wrong.

Frankie went down to the corner, just for a
    bucket of beer.   10

Frankie said, "Mr. Bartender, has my loving
    Johnny been here?
He is my man, he wouldn't do me wrong."

"I don't want to tell you no story. I don't want
    to tell you no lie,
But your Johnny left here an hour ago with that
    lousy Nellie Blye.
He is your man, but he's doing you wrong."   15

Frankie went back to the hotel, she didn't go
    there for fun,
For under her red kimono she toted a forty-four
    gun.
He was her man, but he done her wrong.

Frankie went down to the hotel and looked in
    the window so high,
And there was her loving Johnny a-loving up
    Nellie Blye.   20
He was her man, but he was doing her wrong.

Frankie threw back her kimono, took out that
    old forty-four.
Root-a-toot-toot, three times she shot, right
    through the hardwood door.
He was her man, but he was doing her wrong.

Johnny grabbed off his Stetson, crying, "O
    Frankie don't shoot!"   25
Frankie pulled that forty-four, went root-a-toot-
    toot-toot-toot.
He was her man, but he done her wrong.

"Roll me over gently, roll me over slow,
Roll me on my right side, for my left side hurts
    me so,
I was her man, but I done her wrong."   30

With the first shot Johnny staggered, with the
    second shot he fell;
When the last bullet got him, there was a new
    man's face in hell.
He was her man, but he done her wrong.

"O, bring out your rubber-tired hearses, bring
    out your rubber-tired hacks;
Gonna take Johnny to the graveyard and ain't
    gonna bring him back.   35
He was my man, but he done me wrong."

"O, put me in that dungeon, put me in that cell,
Put me where the northeast wind blows from
    the southeast corner of hell.
I shot my man, cause he done me wrong!"

The Wabash Cannon Ball
ANONYMOUS

From the great Atlantic Ocean to the wide Pacific Shore,
From the ones we leave behind us to the ones we see once more,
She's mighty tall and handsome, and quite well known by all,
How we love the choo choo of the Wabash Cannon Ball.

Hear the bell and whistle calling,   5
Hear the wheels that go "clack clack,"
Hear the roaring of the engine,
As she rolls along the track.
The magic of the railroad wins hearts of one and all,
As we reach our destination on the Wabash Cannon Ball.   10

Listen to the rhythmic jingle and the rumble and the roar,
As she glides along the woodlands thro' the hills and by the shore.
You hear the mighty engine and pray that it won't stall,
While we safely travel on the Wabash Cannon Ball.

Hear the bell and whistle calling, etc.   15

She was coming from Atlanta on a cold December day,
As she rolled into the station, I could hear a woman say:
"He's mighty big and handsome, and sure did make me fall,
"He's a-coming tow'rd me on the Wabash Cannon Ball."

Hear the bell and whistle calling, etc.   20

On Top of Old Smoky
ANONYMOUS

On top of old Smoky,
All cover'd with snow,
I lost my true lover,
For courtin' too slow.

A-courtin's a pleasure,   5
A-flirtin's a grief,
A false-hearted lover—
Is worse than a thief.

For a thief, he will rob you,
And take what you have,   10
But a false-hearted lover —
Sends you to your grave.

She'll hug you and kiss you,
And tell you more lies,

Than the ties on the railroad,   15
Or the stars in the skies.

Meet Me in the Green Glen
JOHN CLARE
1793–1864

This poem and the ones to follow are called literary ballads, or art ballads, conscious imitations of the popular, folk ballad. The ballads we have already read are primitive poems that survive because of their singing quality and their frank projection of elementary emotions; they have the charm of being understood immediately, of striking home without study. Now enters the professional poet.

Love, meet me in the green glen,
  Beside the tall elm-tree,
Where the sweetbrier smells so sweet agen;[1]
  There come with me,
    Meet me in the green glen.   5

Meet me at the sunset
  Down in the green glen,
Where we've often met
  By hawthorn-tree and foxes' den,
    Meet me in the green glen.   10

Meet me in the green glen,
  By sweetbrier bushes there;
Meet me by your own sen,[2]
  Where the wild thyme blossoms fair.
    Meet me in the green glen.   15

Meet me by the sweetbrier,
  By the mole-hill swelling there;
When the west glows like a fire
  God's crimson bed is there.
    Meet me in the green glen.   20

Comments

This lyric is helpful in interpreting Robert Penn Warren's recent novel, *Meet Me in the Green Glen* (New York: Random House, Inc., 1971). The lyric's theme expresses the hope of the central character Cassie Spottwood who can be seen as a symbol of all mankind who would meet love in the green glen of happiness.

La Belle Dame sans Merci

JOHN KEATS
1795–1821

Oh, what can ail thee, knight-at-arms,
  Alone and palely loitering?
The sedge has withered from the lake,
  And no birds sing.

Oh, what can ail thee, knight-at-arms,   5
  So haggard and so woe-begone?

The squirrel's granary is full,
  And the harvest's done.

I see a lily on thy brow,
  With anguish moist and fever dew;   10
And on thy cheeks a fading rose
  Fast withereth too.

"I met a lady in the meads,
  Full beautiful—a faery's child;
Her hair was long, her foot was light,   15
  And her eyes were wild.

"I made a garland for her head,
  And bracelets too, and fragrant zone;[1]
She looked at me as she did love,
  And made sweet moan.   20

"I set her on my pacing steed,
  And nothing else saw all day long;
For sideways would she lean, and sing
  A faery's song.

"She found me roots of relish sweet,   25
  And honey wild, and manna-dew,
And sure in language strange she said,
  'I love thee true.'

"She took me to her elfin grot,
  And there she wept, and sighed full sore,   30
And there I shut her wild, wild eyes,
  With kisses four.

"And there she lullèd me asleep,
  And there I dreamed—ah! woe betide!—
The latest dream I ever dreamed   35
  On the cold hill side.

"I saw pale kings and princes too,
  Pale warriors, death-pale were they all,
They cried—'La Belle Dame sans Merci
  Hath thee in thrall!'   40

"I saw their starved lips in the gloam,
  With horrid warning gapèd wide;
And I awoke, and found me here
  On the cold hill's side.

"And this is why I sojourn here   45
  Alone and palely loitering,

---

[1] Again.   [2] Self.

[1] Girdle, sash.

Though the sedge is withered from the lake,
    And no birds sing."

Comments and Questions

1. The title announces the ballad's general theme, the beautiful lady without pity. What is the specific theme? This is the most complex and self-conscious ballad we have yet read, and it includes more symbolism than we have yet encountered. What does the lady symbolize?

2. Who are the two speakers in the poem? How do lines 1–12 sustain or complement the remainder of the poem?

3. We note in passing that Keats's stanza form is similar to that in "Sir Patrick Spens" (p. 253). Can you hazard an explanation of why Keats's form differs in some respects from the other?

The Seven Ages of Man
WILLIAM SHAKESPEARE
1564–1616

                All the world's a stage,
And all the men and women merely players.
They have their exits and their entrances,
And one man in his time plays many parts,
His acts being seven ages. At first the infant, 5
Mewling[1] and puking in the nurse's arms.
Then the whining schoolboy, with his satchel
And shining morning face, creeping like snail
Unwillingly to school. And then the lover,
Sighing like furnace, with a woeful ballad [2] 10
Made to his mistress' eyebrow. Then a soldier,
Full of strange oaths and bearded like the pard,[3]
Jealous in honor,[4] sudden and quick in quarrel,
Seeking the bubble reputation[5]
Even in the cannon's mouth. And then the
                justice, 15
In fair round belly with good capon lined,[6]
With eyes severe and beard of formal cut,

Full of wise saws[7] and modern instances;[8]
And so he plays his part. The sixth age shifts
Into the lean and slippered Pantaloon,[9] 20
With spectacles on nose and pouch on side;
His youthful hose, well saved, a world too wide
For his shrunk shank, and his big manly voice,
Turning again toward childish treble, pipes
And whistles in his sound. Last scene of all, 25
That ends this strange eventful history,
Is second childishness and mere oblivion,
Sans[10] teeth, sans eyes, sans taste, sans every-
                thing.
                —*As You Like It*, II. vii. 139–166

The Seven Spiritual Ages
of Mrs. Marmaduke Moore
OGDEN NASH
1902–1971

Mrs. Marmaduke Moore, at the age of ten
(Her name was Jemima Jevons then),
Was the quaintest of little country maids.
Her pigtails slapped on her shoulderblades;
She fed the chickens, and told the truth 5
And could spit like a boy through a broken
                tooth.
She could climb a tree to the topmost perch,
And she used to pray in the Methodist church.

At the age of twenty her heart was pure,
And she caught the fancy of Mr. Moore. 10
He broke his troth (to a girl named Alice),
And carried her off to his city palace,
Where she soon forgot her childhood piety
And joined in the orgies of high society.
Her voice grew English, or, say, Australian, 15
And she studied to be an Episcopalian.

At thirty our lives are still before us,
But Mr. Moore had a friend in the chorus.
Connubial bliss was overthrown
And Mrs. Moore now slumbered alone. 20
Hers was a nature that craved affection;
She gave herself up to introspection; ·

---

[1] Whimpering.   [2] Poem.   [3] Leopard.   [4] Sensitive about honor.   [5] As quickly burst as a bubble.   [6] Magistrate bribed with a chicken.

[7] Sayings.   [8] Commonplace illustrations.   [9] The foolish old man of Italian comedy.   [10] Without.

Then, finding theosophy rather dry,
Found peace in the sweet Bahai and Bahai.

Forty? and still an abandoned wife. 25
She felt old urges stirring to life.
She dipped her locks in a bowl of henna
And booked a passage through to Vienna.
She paid a professor a huge emolument
To demonstrate what his ponderous volume
    meant. 30
Returning, she preached to the unemployed
The gospel according to St. Freud.

Fifty! she haunted museums and galleries,
And pleased young men by augmenting their
    salaries.
Oh, it shouldn't occur, but it does occur, 35
That poets are made by fools like her.
Her salon was full of frangipani,
Roumanian, Russian and Hindustani,
And she conquered par as well as bogey
By reading a book and going Yogi. 40

Sixty! and time was on her hands—
Maybe remorse and maybe glands.
She felt a need for a free confession
To publish each youthful indiscretion,
And before she was gathered to her mothers, 45
To compare her sinlets with those of others,
Mrs. Moore gave a joyous whoop,
And immersed herself in the Oxford group.

That is the story of Mrs. Moore,
As far as it goes. But of this I'm sure— 50
When seventy stares her in the face
She'll have found some other state of grace.
Mohammed may be her Lord and master,
Or Zeus, or Mithros, or Zoroaster.
For when a lady is badly sexed 55
God knows what God is coming next.

the ballad of chocolate Mabbie
GWENDOLYN BROOKS
1917—

It was Mabbie without the grammar school
    gates.
And Mabbie was all of seven.
And Mabbie was cut from a chocolate bar.
And Mabbie thought life was heaven.

The grammar school gates were the pearly
    gates, 5
For Willie Boone went to school.
When she sat by him in history class
Was only her eyes were cool.

It was Mabbie without the grammer school gates
Waiting for Willie Boone. 10
Half hour after the closing bell!
He would surely be coming soon.

Oh, warm is the waiting for joys, my dears!
And it cannot be too long.
Oh, pity the little poor chocolate lips 15
That carry the bubble of song!

Out came the saucily bold Willie Boone.
It was woe for our Mabbie now.
He wore like a jewel a lemon-hued lynx
With sand-waves loving her brow. 20

It was Mabbie alone by the grammer school
    gates.
Yet chocolate companions had she:
Mabbie on Mabbie with hush in the heart.
Mabbie on Mabbie to be.

Molly Means
MARGARET A. WALKER
1915—

Old Molly Means was a hag and a witch;
Chile of the devil, the dark, and sitch.
Her heavy hair hung thick in ropes
And her blazing eyes was black as pitch.
Imp at three and wench at 'leben 5
She counted her husbands to the number seben.
  O Molly, Molly, Molly Means
  There goes the ghost of Molly Means.

Some say she was born with a veil on her face
So she could look through unnatchal space 10
Through the future and through the past
And charm a body or an evil place
And every man could well despise
The evil look in her coal black eyes.
  Old Molly, Molly, Molly Means 15
  Dark is the ghost of Molly Means.

And when the tale begun to spread
Of evil and of holy dread:
Her black-hand arts and her evil powers
How she cast her spells and called the dead, 20
The younguns was afraid at night
And the farmers feared their crops would blight.
   Old Molly, Molly, Molly Means
   Cold is the ghost of Molly Means.

Then one dark day she put a spell 25
On a young gal-bride just come to dwell
In the lane just down from Molly's shack
And when her husband coming riding back
His wife was barking like a dog
And on all fours like a common hog. 30
   O Molly, Molly, Molly Means
   Where is the ghost of Molly Means?

The neighbors come and they went away
And said she'd die before break of day
But her husband held her in his arms 35
And swore he'd break the wicked charms,
He'd search all up and down the land
And turn the spell on Molly's hand.
   O Molly, Molly, Molly Means
   Sharp is the ghost of Molly Means. 40

So he rode all day and he rode all night
And at the dawn he come in sight
Of a man who said he could move the spell
And cause the awful thing to dwell
On Molly Means, to bark and bleed 45
Till she died at the hands of her evil deed.
   Old Molly, Molly, Molly Means
   This is the ghost of Molly Means.

Sometimes at night through the shadowy trees
She rides along on a winter breeze. 50

You can hear her holler and whine and cry.
Her voice is thin and her moan is high,
And her cackling laugh or her barking cold
Bring terror to the young and old.
   O Molly, Molly, Molly Means 55
   Lean is the ghost of Molly Means.

THE RETURN OF THE MINSTREL: NEW FOLK AND COUNTRY BALLADS

The return of the minstrel, formerly a musical entertainer or traveling poet of the later Middle Ages, has become a national and international phenomenon during the last two decades. Recordings of these minstrels' songs are bought by the millions, and the performers entertain huge audiences in concert halls and millions of enthusiasts every week by radio and television. The folk ballad has a long and persistent tradition, and its resurgence may be a symbol of something very important in contemporary life, something too important to be ignored by the official literati of the poetic world. For an excellent examination and historical explanation of this movement see Barbara Farris Graves and Donald J. McBain's essay, "Electric Orphic Circuit" (p. 831), which has been taken from their book, *Lyric Voices, Approaches to the Poetry of Contemporary Song* (New York: John Wiley and Sons, Inc., 1972). The book contains many of the best of these lyrics, and the serious reader would do well to make the book his own.

Another valuable book, one which investigates the evolution of the lyric, is C. Day Lewis's *The Lyric Impulse* (Cambridge: Harvard University Press, 1965); chapter 5, "Country Lyrics," is especially valuable.

Sunday Mornin' Comin' Down
KRIS KRISTOFFERSON
1936—

    Well, I woke up Sunday mornin'
      with no way to hold my head that didn't hurt;
    And the beer I had for breakfast wasn't bad,
      so I had one more for dessert;
    Then I fumbled in my closet
      through my clothes and found my cleanest dirty shirt;

5

Then I washed my face, and combed my hair,
    and stumbled down the stairs to meet the day.

I'd smoked my mind the night before
    with cigarettes and songs I'd been pickin';   10
But I lit my first and watched a small kid
    playing with a can that he was kickin';
Then I walked across the empty street and caught
    the Sunday smell of someone fryin' chicken;
And it took me back to somethin' that   15
    I'd lost somewhere somehow along the way.

On the Sunday mornin' sidewalk, I'm wishin, Lord, that I was stoned,
  'Cause there's something in a Sunday that makes a body feel alone;
And there's nothing short of dyin' that's half as lonesome as the sound
  On the sleeping city sidewalk; and Sunday mornin' comin' down.   20

In the park I saw a daddy
    with a laughing little girl that he was swingin';
And I stopped beside a Sunday school
    and listened to the song they were singin';
Then I headed down the street,   25
    and somewhere far away a lonely bell was ringin';
And it echoed thru the canyon
    like a disappearing dream of yesterday.

On the Sunday mornin' sidewalk, I'm wishin', Lord, that I was stoned,
  'Cause there's something in a Sunday that make a body feel alone;   30
And there's nothing short of dyin' that's half as lonesome as the sound
  On the sleeping city sidewalk; and Sunday mornin' comin' down.

Me and Bobby McGee

KRIS KRISTOFFERSON and
FRED FOSTER
1936–
1931–

Busted flat in Baton Rouge,
Headin' for the trains;
Feelin' nearly faded as my jeans,
Bobby thumbed a diesel down
Just before it rained;   5
Took us all the way to New Orleans.

I took my harpoon out
    of my dirty, red bandana
And was blowin' sad,
    while Bobby sang the blues;

With them windshield wipers slappin' time
    and Bobby clappin' hands
We fin'ly sang up ev'ry song that driver
    knew.   10

Freedom's just another word for nothin' left to
    lose,
    Nothin' ain't worth nothin',
        but it's free;
    Feelin good was easy, Lord,
      When Bobby sang the blues;
And feelin' good was good enough for me, 15
    Good enough for me and Bobby McGee.

From the coal mines of Kentucky
To the California sun,
Bobby shared the secrets of my soul;
Standin' right beside me, Lord,   20

Through everything I done,
And every night she kept me from the cold.

Then somewhere near Salinas,
    Lord, I let her slip away
Lookin' for the home   25
    I hope she'll find;
And I'd trade all of my tomorrows
    for a single yesterday,
Holdin' Bobby's body next to mine.

Freedom's just another word for nothin' left to
        lose,
    Nothin' left is all she left for me;   30
    Feeling good was easy, Lord,
    When Bobby sang the blues;
    Nothin' left is all she left for me;
And buddy that was good was good enough for
        me,
    Good enough for me and Bobby McGee.   35

Stories of the Street [1]

LEONARD COHEN
1934–

The stories of the street are mine
The Spanish voices laugh
The Cadillacs go creeping down
Through the night and the poison gas.
I lean from my window sill   5
In this old hotel I chose
One hand on my suicide
One hand on the rose.

I know you've heard it's over now
And war must surely come   10
The cities they are broke in half
And the middle men are gone.
But let me ask you one more time
O, children of the dust,
All these hunters who are shrieking now   15
Do they speak for us?

And where do all these highways go
Now that we are free?
Why are the armies marching still
That were coming home to me?   20
O, lady with your legs so fine

O, stranger at your wheel
You are locked into your suffering
And your pleasures are the seal.

The age of lust is giving birth   25
And both the parents ask
The nurse to tell them fairy tales
On both sides of the glass
Now the infant with his cord
Is hauled in like a kite   30
And one eye filled with blueprints
One eye filled with night.

O, come with me my little one
And we will find that farm
And grow us grass and apples there   35
And keep all the animals warm.
And if by chance I wake at night
And I ask you who I am
O, take me to the slaughter house
I will wait there with the lamb.   40

With one hand on a hexagram
And one hand on a girl
I balance on a wishing well
That all men call the world.
We are so small between the stars   45
So large against the sky
And lost among the subway crowds
I try to catch your eye.

Hey, That's No Way to Say Goodbye [1]

LEONARD COHEN
1934–

I loved you in the morning
Our kisses deep and warm,
Your head upon the pillow
Like a sleepy golden storm.
Yes, many loved before us   5
I know that we are not new,
In city and in forest
They smiled like me and you,
But now it's come to distances
And both of us must try,   10
Your eyes are soft with sorrow,
Hey, that's no way to say goodbye.

I'm not looking for another
As I wander in my time,
Walk me to the corner   15
Our steps will always rhyme,
You know my love goes with you
As your love stays with me,
It's just the way it changes
Like the shoreline and the sea,   20
But let's not talk of love or chains
And things we can't untie,
Your eyes are soft with sorrow,
Hey, that's no way to say goodbye.

I loved you in the morning   25
Our kisses deep and warm,
Your head upon the pillow
Like a sleepy golden storm.
Yes, many loved before us
I know that we are not new,   30
In city and in forest
They smiled like me and you,
But let's not talk of love or chains
And things we can't untie,
Your eyes are soft with sorrow,   35
Hey, that's no way to say goodbye.

I Give You the Morning [1]
TOM PAXTON
1937–

Ever again the morning creeps
Across your shoulder.
Through the frosted window pane
The sun grows bolder.
Your hair flows down your pillow,   5
You're still dreaming,
   I think I'll wake you now and hold you,
   Tell you again the things I told you,
   Behold, I give you the morning,
   I give you the day.   10

Through the waving curtain wall
The sun is streaming.
Far behind your flickering eyelids
You're still dreaming.
You're dreaming of the good times,   15
And you're smiling.
   I think I'll wake you now and hold you,

Tell you again the things I told you.
Behold, I give you the morning,
I give you the day.   20

Close beneath our window sill,
The earth is humming.
Like an eager Christmas child,
The day is coming.
Listen to the morning song   25
It's singing.
   I think I'll wake you now and hold you,
   Tell you again the things I told you.
   Behold, I give you the morning,
   I give you the day.   30

Like an antique ballroom fan,
Your eyelids flutter.
Sunlight streams across your eyes
Through open shutter.
Now I think you're ready for the journey.   35
   I think I'll wake you now and hold you,
   Tell you again the things I told you.
   Behold, I give you the morning,
   I give you the day.

Celebration for a Grey Day
RICHARD FARIÑA
1937–1966

Be quiet now and still. Be unafraid:
That hiss and garden tinkle is the rain,
That face you saw breathe on the window pane
Was just a startled cat with eyes of jade—
Cats worry in the rain, you know, and are
    afraid.   5
The nervous laugh that creeps into our room
Is throated in a voice beyond the door.
We hear it once and then no more,
A distant echo tumbling from its loom.
Our time is measured in another room.   10

We know days pass away because we're told.
We lie alone and sense the reeling earth.
(You whisper in my ear it had some worth)
And I learn to keep you from the cold.
There are so many things that must be told.   15
I speak of lost regimes and distant times,
And mooneyed children whirling in the womb,
And legless beggars prophesying doom,
And afternoons of rain spun into rhyme.
(The patter of the rainfall marks our time.)   20

As does the waning moon. Or muted sun.
As do the nodding gods who ride the sea.
For even now, alone and still with me,
You sense the bonds that cannot be undone:
Our pulse is in the rain and moon and sun,   25
We take our breaths together and are one.

Where Have All the Flowers Gone? [1]

PETER SEEGER
1919–

Where have all the flowers gone?
Long time passing
Where have all the flowers gone?
Long time ago
Where have all the flowers gone?   5
Young girls have picked them, every one.
Oh, when will they ever learn?
Oh, when will they ever learn?

Where have all the young girls gone?
Long time passing   10
Where have all the young girls gone?
Long time ago
Where have all the young girls gone?
They've taken husbands, every one.
Oh, when will they ever learn?   15
Oh, when will they ever learn?

Where have all the husbands gone?
Long time passing
Where have all the husbands gone?
Long time ago   20
Where have all the husbands gone?
Gone for soldiers, every one.
Oh, when will they ever learn?
Oh, when will they ever learn?

Where have all the soldiers gone?   25
Long time passing
Where have all the soldiers gone?
Long time ago
Where have all the soldiers gone?
Gone to graveyards, every one.   30
Oh, when will they ever learn?
Oh, when will they ever learn?

Where have all the graveyards gone?
Long time passing
Where have all the graveyards gone?   35
Long time ago
Where have all the graveyards gone?
They're covered with flowers, every one.
Oh, when will they ever learn?
Oh, when will they ever learn?   40

Where have all the flowers gone?
Long time passing
Where have all the flowers gone?
Long time ago
Where have all the flowers gone?   45
Young girls have picked them, every one.
Oh, when will they ever learn?
Oh, when will they ever learn?

Sad-Eyed Lady of the Lowlands

BOB DYLAN
1941–

With your mercury mouth in the missionary
          times
And your eyes like smoke and your prayers like
          rhymes
And your silver cross and your voice like chimes
Oh, who among them do they think could bury
          you?
With your pockets well-protected at last   5
And your streetcar visions which you place on
          the grass
And your flesh like silk and your face like glass
Who among them could they get to carry you?

Sad-eyed lady of the lowlands
Where the sad-eyed prophet says that no man
          comes   10
My warehouse eyes my Arabian drums
Should I leave them by your gate
Or sad-eyed lady, should I wait?

With your sheets like metal and your belt like
          lace
And your deck of cards missing the jack and the
          ace   15
And your basement clothes and your hollow face
Who among them can think he could outguess
          you?
With your silhouette when the sunlight dims
Into your eyes where the moonlight swims

And your matchbook songs and your gypsy
    hymns   20
Who among them would try to impress you?

Sad-eyed lady of the lowlands
Where the sad-eyed prophet says that no man
    comes
My warehouse eyes my Arabian drums
Should I leave them by your gate   25
Or, sad-eyed lady, should I wait?

The kings of Tyrus with their convict list
Are waiting in line for their geranium kiss
And you wouldn't know it would happen like
    this
But who among them really wants just to kiss
    you   30
With your childhood flames on your midnight
    rug
And your Spanish manners and your mother's
    drugs
And your cowboy mouth and your curfew plugs
Who among them do you think could resist you?

Sad-eyed lady of the lowlands   35
Where the sad-eyed prophet says that no man
    comes
My warehouse eyes my Arabian drums
Should I leave them by your gate
Or, sad-eyed lady, should I wait?

Oh, the farmers and the business men they all
    did decide   40
To show you the dead angels that they used to
    hide
But why did they pick you to sympathize with
    their side
How could they ever mistake you?
They wish you'd accepted the blame for the
    farm,
But with the sea at your feet and the phony false
    alarm   45
And with the child of a hoodlum wrapped up in
    your arms,
How could they ever have persuaded you?

Sad-eyed lady of the lowlands
Where the sad-eyed prophet says that no man
    comes
My warehouse eyes my Arabian drums   50
Should I leave them by your gate
Or, sad-eyed lady, should I wait?

With your sheet metal memory of Cannery Row
And your magazine husband who one day just
    had to go
And your gentleness now which you just can't
    help but show   55
Who among them do you think would employ
    you?
Now, you stand with your thief; you're on his
    parole
With your holy medallion which your fingertips
    fold
And your saint-like face and your ghost-like soul
Who among them could ever think he could
    destroy you?   60

Sad-eyed lady of the lowlands
Where the sad-eyed prophet says that no man
    comes
My warehouse eyes my Arabian drums
Should I leave them by your gate
Or, sad-eyed lady, should I wait?   65

All Along the Watchtower
BOB DYLAN
1941–

"There must be some way out of here,"
said the joker to the thief.
"There's too much confusion,
I can't get no relief."

"Bus'nessmen, they drink my wine,   5
plowmen dig my earth;
none of them along the line
know what any of it is worth."

"No reason to get excited,"
the thief he kindly spoke.   10
"There are many here among us
who feel that life is but a joke."

"But, you and I, we've been thru that,
and this is not our fate;
so, let us not talk falsely now,   15
the hour is getting late."

All along the watchtower,
princes kept the view,
while all the women came and went,
barefoot servants, too.   20

Outside in the distance,
a wildcat did growl.
Two riders were approaching.
The wind began to howl.

Hampstead Incident

DONOVAN LEITCH [1]
1946–

Standing by the Everyman
Digging the rigging on my sails
Rain fell through sounds of harpsichords
Through the spell of fairly tales

The heath was hung in magic mists   5
And gentle dripping glades
I'll taste the tastes until my mind
Drifts from this scene and fades

In the nighttime

Crystals sparkle in the grass   10
I polish them with thought
On my lash there in my eye
A star of light is caught

Fortunes told in grains of sand
Here I am is all I know   15
Can be stuck in children's hair
Everywhere I go

In the nighttime
In the nighttime

Gypsy is the clown of love   20
I paint his face a smile
Anyone we ever make
We always make in style

Strange young girls with radar screens
And hands as quick as pain   25
I want just now later on maybe
And even then I'll wait

In the nighttime
In the nighttime

Standing by the Everyman   30
Digging the rigging on my sails
Rain fell through sounds of harpsichords
Through the spell of fairy tales

The heath was hung in magic mists
And gentle dripping glades   35
I'll taste the tastes until my mind
Drifts from this scene and fades

In the nighttime
In the nighttime

The Lullaby of Spring

DONOVAN LEITCH [1]
1946–

rain has showered far her drip
splash and trickle running
plant has flowered in the sand
shell and pebble sunning

so begins another spring   5
green leaves and of berries
chiff-chaff eggs are painted by
motherbird eating cherries

in a misty tangled sky
fast a wind is blowing   10
in a newborn rabbit's heart
river life is flowing

so begins another spring
green leaves and of berries
chiff-chaff eggs are painted by   15
motherbird eating cherries

from the dark and whetted soil
petals are unfolding
from the stony village kirk[2]
easter bells of old ring   20

so begins another spring
green leaves and of berries
chiff-chaff eggs are painted by
motherbird eating cherries

---

[1] Better known as Donovan.

[1] Better known as Donovan.   [2] Church.

Crucifixion

PHIL OCHS
1940–

And the night comes again to the circle-studded
    sky
The stars settle slowly, in loneliness they lie
Till the universe explodes as a falling star is
    raised
The planets are paralyzed, the mountains are
    amazed
But they all glow brighter from the brilliance
    of the blaze   5
With the speed of insanity, then, he dies.

In the green fields of turning a baby is born
His cries crease the wind and mingle with the
    morn
An assault upon the order, the changing of the
    guard
Chosen for a challenge that's hopelessly hard   10
And the only single sign is the sighing of the
    stars
But to the silence of distance they're sworn.

So dance, dance, dance
Teach us to be true
Come dance, dance, dance   15
'Cause we love you.

Images of innocence charge him to go on
But the decadence of history is looking for a
    pawn
To a nightmare of knowledge he opens up the
    gate
A blinding revelation is served upon his plate   20
That beneath the greatest love is a hurricane of
    hate
And God help the critic of the dawn.

So he stands on the sea and he shouts to the
    shore
But the louder that he screams the longer he's
    ignored
For the wine of oblivion is drunk to the dregs   25
And the merchants of the masses almost have to
    be begged
Till the giant is aware that someone's pulling
    at his leg
And someone is tapping at the door.

So dance, dance, dance

Teach us to be true   30
Come dance, dance, dance
'Cause we love you.

Then his message gathers meaning and it
    spreads across the land
The rewarding of the fame is the following of
    the man
But ignorance is everywhere and people have
    their way   35
And success is an enemy to the losers of the day
In the shadows of the churches who knows what
    they pray
And blood is the language of the band.

The Spanish bulls are beaten, the crowd is soon
    beguiled
The matador is beautiful, a symphony of style   40
Excitement is ecstatic, passion places bets
Gracefully he bows to ovations that he gets
But the hands that are applauding are slippery
    with sweat
And saliva is falling from their smiles.

So dance, dance, dance   45
Teach us to be true
Come dance, dance, dance
'Cause we love you.

Then this overflow of life is crushed into a liar
The gentle soul is ripped apart and tossed into
    the fire   50
It's the burial of beauty, it's the victory of night
Truth becomes a tragedy limping from the light
The heavens are horrified, they stagger from the
    sight
And the cross is trembling with desire.

They say they can't believe it, it's a sacrilegious
    shame   55
Now who would want to hurt such a hero of
    the game
But you know I predicted it, I knew he had to
    fall
How did it happen, I hope his suffering was
    small
Tell me every detail, I've got to know it all
And do you have a picture of the pain?   60

So dance, dance, dance
Teach us to be true
Come dance, dance, dance
'Cause we love you.

Time takes her toll and the memory fades   65
But his glory is growing in the magic that he
  made
Reality is ruined, there is nothing more to fear
The drama is distorted to what they want to hear
Swimming in their sorrow in the twisting of a
  tear
As they wait for the new thrill parade.   70

The eyes of the rebel have been branded by the
  blind
To the safety of sterility the threat has been
  refined
The child was created to the slaughter house
  he's led
So good to be alive when the eulogies are read
The climax of emotion, the worship of the
  dead   75
As the cycle of sacrifice unwinds.

So dance, dance, dance
Teach us to be true
Come dance, dance, dance
'Cause we love you.   80

And the night comes again to the circle-studded
  sky
The stars settle slowly, in loneliness they lie
Till the universe explodes as a falling star is
  raised
The planets are paralyzed, the mountains are
  amazed
But they all glow brighter from the brilliance
  of the blaze   85
With the speed of insanity, then, he dies.

Black Panther

CARL OGLESBY
1935–

I warned you things were crumbling
You could feel the storm in the air
You just showed me your Japanese umbrella
So cool, so debonair

Icecubes tinkled   5
The conversation strayed
To cocktail observations
On the one who was trying to pray

I cried in the name of your Jesus
Beware the big-time brass   10
You just stood there with your lollipop eyes
Like stoned on a kilo of grass

Oh the panther with the burning wound
Has found your perfume trail
You sit there tolling your I Ching changes   15
And you won't even open your special-delivery
  mail

Oh the panther gonna get your mama
Oh the panther gonna love your lamb
Spaced out of your mind on your dime horo-
  scope
You got the virgin going down on the ram   20

Don't you know your garden is weedy
Don't you know your vineyards are bare
Dry well, poison water,
And your stallion is eating your mare

Well footman, footman, better shut the gates   25
Make sure the windows are closed
I told you baby that was just not enough
You just sat in your swing sniffing your rose

Footman, footman, better bring his coach
Better bring round this young man's cape   30
Seems to me it's about time he should leave
He's had a bit much of that old vino veritas
  grape

But the footman, he just stands there
Just looks you cold up and down
So you tell him, Boy, don't get insolent   35
And you try not to notice his frown

Then you feel yourself growing weary
And you hear a strange breathing at your side
Well maybe you better hurry up baby
Better find yourself some place to hide   40

Then the trees, they turn into husbands
The roses turn into wives
The night comes down, it's black panther town
The children turn into knives

Well, I warned you in the morning   45
You would never make high noon
You just swiveled around like some satisfied
  woman
Crooning your personal tunes

But now that your fine lips are bleeding
And you burn from a thousand rapes   50
And your bare body is learning
The name of the game and the stakes

You'll remember the way back to human
You'll remember the way back to soul
You'll remember the way it all come down   55
You'll pick up your ruins and go down one more
      road

Tennessee Bird Walk [1]

JACK BLANCHARD
1930–

Take away the trees, and the birds all have to sit upon the ground, uum,
Take away their wings, and the birds will have to walk to get around.
And take away the bird baths and dirty birds will soon be everywhere,
Take away their feathers, and the birds will walk around in underwear,
Take away their chirp, and the birds will have to whisper when they sing,   5
And take away their common sense, and they'll be headed southward
      in the Spring.

Oh, remember me, my darling,
When Spring is in the air,
And the baldheaded birds are whispering everywhere,
You can see them walking southward in their dirty underwear,   10
That's Tennessee bird walk.

How about some trees, so the birds won't have to sit upon the ground, uum,
How about some wings, so the birds won't have to walk to get around.
And how about a bird bath or two, so the birds will all be clean,
How about some feathers, so their underwear no longer can be seen,   15
How about a chirp, so the birds won't have to whisper when they sing,
And how about some common sense, so they won't be blocking traffic
      in the Spring.

Oh, remember me, my darling,
When Spring is in the air,
And the baldheaded birds are whispering everywhere,   20
You can see them walking southward in their dirty underwear,
That's Tennessee bird walk.

Gentle on My Mind [1]

JOHNNY HARTFORD
1937–

It's knowing that your door is always open and your path is free to walk,
That makes me tend to leave my sleeping bag rolled up and stashed behind
      your couch,
And it's knowing that I'm not shackled by forgotten words and bonds

And the ink stains that have tried upon some line,
That keeps you in the backroads by the rivers of my memory that keeps   5
         you ever
Gentle on my mind.

It's not clinging to the rocks and ivy planted on their columns now that binds me
Or something that somebody said because they thought we fit together walkin',
It's just knowing that the world will not be cursing or forgiving when I walk along
Some railroad track and find   10
That you're moving on the backroads by the rivers of my memory and for hours
You're just gentle on my mind.

Though the wheat fields and the clothes lines and junkyards and the highways
Come between us
And some other woman crying to her mother 'cause she turned and I was gone.   15
I still run in silence, tears of joy might stain my face and summer sun might
Burn me 'til I'm blind
But not to where I cannot see you walkin' on the backroads by the rivers flowing
Gentle on my mind.

I dip my cup of soup from the gurglin' cracklin' caldron in some train yard   20
My beard a rough'ning coal pile and a dirty hat pulled low across my face.
Through cupped hands 'round a tin can I pretend I hold you to my breast and find
That you're waving from the backroads by the rivers of my memory ever smilin'
Ever gentle on my mind.

THE LANGUAGE OF POETRY

If we are to understand and enjoy all that good poems offer us, we should know what to look for. The person who says that "I don't know much about poetry, but I know what I like," should say rather that he likes only what he knows and understands, which is obviously too little. Self-defense may be human, but as a learning process it can be fatal.

We have already said there are many languages within the English language—the language of science, of journalism, of history, of philosophy (p. 240). True, all of these languages have some basic things in common which make them English instead of French or German, such as grammatical structure and vocabulary. If we read that "North Labrador is a land of ice covered by grey sky, a silence where time has no meaning," the description is clear to anyone schooled in the basic devices of the English language. But when Hart Crane says (p. 240) that North Labrador is

  A land of leaning ice
Hugged by plaster-grey arches of sky [that]

Flings itself silently
Into eternity,

we know that special language devices are being used to create a special kind of comment on North Labrador. We have already been introduced to the basic devices in "Poetry: Preliminaries" (p. 236), but the time has now arrived to explore them more thoroughly to prepare us for some penetrating poems yet to come. In a very real sense we need the right keys to unlock the many corridors of poetic experience.

RHYTHM AND RHYME: THE PROPER FUSION OF SOUND AND SENSE

Pope saw clearly that

  True ease in writing comes from art, not
         chance,
  As those move easiest who have learn'd to
         dance.
  'Tis not enough no harshness gives offense,
  The sound must seem an Echo to the sense.
      —"An Essay on Criticism," ll. 362–365

Rhythm and rhyme, the basis of sound, are used to convey *meaning* in poetry. Most readers readily acknowledge that they can produce delightful effects for their own sake, as they do for some readers in Poe's "The Bells," but it is not usually understood that rhythm and rhyme actually help in shaping the meaning of a poem. The popular myth runs: the *idea* must be put into some form or frame, of course, but the idea is really the important matter—as if the idea has been put into a fancy basket to be delivered to the reader in appropriate style. A brief demonstration of this erroneous approach to poems may be more substantial than a book of arguments.

Evening

GEORGE WASHINGTON DOANE
1799–1859

Softly now the light of day
Fades upon my sight away;
Free from care, from labor free,
Lord, I would commune with Thee:

Thou, whose all-pervading eye,   5
   Naught escapes, without, within,
Pardon each infirmity,
   Open fault and secret sin.

Soon, for me, the light of day
Shall forever pass away;   10
Then, from sin and sorrow free,
Take me, Lord, to dwell with Thee:

Thou, who, sinless, yet hast known
   All of man's infirmity;
Then from Thine eternal throne,   15
   Jesus, look with pitying eye.

This poem presents a perfectly sound religious idea, acceptable to thousands of readers regardless of their sectarian doctrine. The first stanza says roughly that with the fading of "the light of day" the poet "would commune" with God.

The second stanza asks omniscient God to pardon the speaker's sins. The third stanza includes a nice touch by now using "the light of day" to mean life. When this light passes forever away, the speaker wishes to dwell with God, free from earthly sin and sorrow. The last stanza asks God, sinless though He is, to look with pity upon man's earthly infirmity.

The poem contains humility, and a distaste for all sins which bring sorrow—who would quarrel with such sentiments? Do such sentiments make a good *poem*? A brief examination of its rhythm and rhyme will help to answer the question.

Note the rhyme scheme:

    aabb   *cdcd*   *aabb*   *ecec*
  (couplets)   (couplets)

Does there seem to be any reason why stanzas 1 and 3 only should be written in couplets? If we examine the *logic* of the poem, stanzas 3 and 4 should be reversed, permitting the poem to come to rest with the line,

Take me, Lord, to dwell with Thee.

With this structure, the exact repetition of the rhymes in stanzas 1 and 4 would have real point by bringing to rest the tone which opens the poem in stanza 1. We note further that most of the rhymes are hackneyed and trite: *day* calls for *away*, *free* calls for *Thee*, and so on. Instead of awakening our sensibilities and surprising us with the fresh word, the rhymes discourage our expectancy, and the sense of the poem slips through our lulled wits. Line 3 seems to be especially awkward, beginning and ending with the same word, *free*, which rhymes with Thee in line 4.

The entire poem, save the last line, is written in monotonous tetrameter. Hardly the slightest variation exists except in the last line, where it is the least appropriate if we assume that the function of the last line is to bring the action to rest. Further, the monotonous regularity of the accented beat sometimes accents unimportant words: *upon*, line 2; *would*, line 4. To summarize, the poem is not memorable, condensed, or rigidly organized; and the religious idea, *which could have been made a religious experience* for the reader, lies dormant and ineffective.

A Good-Night
FRANCIS QUARLES
1592–1644

Close now thine eyes and rest secure;
Thy soul is safe enough, thy body sure;
   He that loves thee, he that keeps
And guards thee, never slumbers, never sleeps.
The smiling conscience in a sleeping breast   5
   Has only peace, has only rest;
   The music and the mirth of kings
Are all but very discords, when she sings;
   Then close thine eyes and rest secure;
No sleep so sweet as thine, no rest so sure.   10

The idea in this religious poem can be simply stated: a free conscience brings the peace and security provided by God. It requires no subtle analysis, however, to discover the shaping influences of rhythm and rhyme which have helped to make the poem so superior to the paraphrase.

Although the lyric is written in five couplets which could have been monotonous, the poet has provided a good deal of variation in only ten lines. Note that the first line of each couplet is tetrameter, and the second line pentameter except the third couplet—the middle couplet—which is reversed to break the rhythmic regularity. Note further that although the poem uses an iambic foot, the accent in the first foot does not always come on the second syllable. To *read* the accent on the second syllable of lines 1, 3, 6, and 10 would certainly violate their meaning. Note the difference in lines 3 and 4:

He that loves thee, he that keeps
And guards thee, never slumbers, never sleeps.

In one respect at least the rhyme scheme is especially appropriate. The sense of the poem has to do with restful security, and the rhyme helps to produce such an effect in the reader by closing the poem with the same sound that opened it, *secure-sure.* That is, the sound actually helps to interpret the sense. If further proof is necessary, suppose we change the word order a bit in the first four lines:

Close thine eyes now and rest secure;
Thy body is sure, thy soul safe enough;

He that keeps, he that loves thee
And guards thee, never sleeps, never slumbers.

The sense is still there—or is it?

The Emergent Tone

We are not concerned with exhibiting the extreme subtleties in the fusion of sound and sense in poetry, nor are we encouraging anyone to underestimate their importance. We wish to make clear that rhythm and rhyme help to shape the exact meaning of a poem. They help to establish the tone, which is in effect the poet's attitude toward the sense, or facts, of the poem, and *the reader must allow the tone to help him interpret the poem.* (See comments on Burns's "Sweet Afton," p. 249.) He must read the poem aloud and listen for the poet's voice, his attitude, because that attitude has shaped the meaning of the entire poem. Some readers have misunderstood, for example, Donne's "Go and Catch a Falling Star," calling it bitter and cynical because they have ignored Donne's tone (see p. 298 for the poem and comments). Tone is less tangible than image and figure (indeed, we borrow a term from music to describe it), but no less real. We shall see when we consider figures of speech and symbols (p. 282) that tone can actually become a figure of speech when the *entire* poem is meaningful only on the figurative level.

The Shaping Mechanics of Verse

Because poetry is an art, many people are irritated with the phrase "the mechanics of verse." "What does it matter"—the objection runs—"whether the line is iambic or trochaic, tetrameter or pentameter? I don't want to write poetry; I just want to read it." The argument seems to make good sense until we press that word *read* a little. Whether or not we read a poem aloud, we must be able to "hear" and feel its rhythms as well as to understand its sense. In a good poem the fusion of rhythm and sense is there, and we must read the fusion, not rhythm *or* sense, to experience the whole poem. To emphasize the rhythm as we read produces singsong; to emphasize the sense loses the poet's tone and attitude. To read both rhythm and sense simultaneously requires an elementary knowledge of the *foot,* the *line,* and the *stanza.*

THE FOOT. This is the smallest unit of stressed and unstressed syllables to appear in verse. An elementary knowledge includes four kinds of feet.

1. *Iamb:* One unstressed and one stressed syllable, as in dĕlíght. This line is composed of iambic feet:

Hŏw smáll | ă párt | ŏf tíme | thĕy sháre

2. *Anapest:* Two unstressed and one stressed syllable, as in **underneath**. This line is composed chiefly of anapestic feet:

Ĭt wăs mán|y̆ ănd mán|y̆ ă yeár | ă̆gó

3. *Trochee:* One stressed and one unstressed syllable, as in **happen** and **trochee**. This line is composed of trochaic feet:

Shóuld yŏu | ásk mĕ | whénce thĕse |

stóriĕs

4. *Dactyl:* One stressed and two unstressed syllables, as in Míchĭgăn and élĕphănt. This line is composed of dactylic feet:

Táke hĕr úp | ténderly̆

THE LINE. The line, called also *a verse*, determines the basic rhythmical pattern of the poem, and provides a principle of order for the sense. Lines are named according to the number of feet they possess, as follows:

> One foot—monometer
> Two feet—dimeter
> Three feet—trimeter
> Four feet—tetrameter
> Five feet—pentameter
> Six feet—hexameter
> Seven feet—heptameter
> Eight feet—octameter

Lines are therefore described according to the *kind* and *number* of feet they possess. For example, the line used to illustrate iambic meter is called *iambic tetrameter:*

Hŏw smáll | ă párt | ŏf tíme | thĕy sháre
   1.   2.   3.   4.

This line is *dactylic dimeter:*

Táke hĕr úp | ténderly̆
  1.   2.

Most poems, like most of those we have already read, have lines composed of from three to five feet because these units of verse best serve the sense communicated by most poets. Poe's "The Raven" is an exception with its octameter line because the poet is working for a special tone and is using internal rhyme (p. 273) to help achieve his tone. His octameter line can be seen actually as two tetrameter units which are sometimes rhymed:

Ónce ŭp|ŏn ă | mídnĭght | dreáry̆, || whíle Ĭ | póndĕred, | weák ănd | weáry̆

Now that we have come so far in our brief analysis of the foot and the line, we see that few poems are written exclusively with the same line or even the same foot. To avoid monotony, to achieve special effects, and—most important—to fuse the sound and sense, poets employ many kinds of variations. Although we have scanned the line from "The Raven" as "regular" trochaic octameter verse, we do not read it that way because the resulting sound would violate the sense. We actually read the line something like this:

Ónce ŭp″|ŏn ă | mídnĭght | dreáry̆, | whíle Ĭ | póndĕred, | weák″ ănd | weáry̆

There are, then, actually two degrees of stress, called primary (′) and secondary (″), which are made necessary by the poem's sense.

Another kind of variation in the line is made by substituting one kind of foot for another. The substitution of the anapestic foot for the iambic foot is found in Bryant's "Green River":

Whĕn breéz|ĕs ăre sóft | ănd skíes | ăre fáir, Ĭ steál | ăn hoúr | frŏm stúd|y̆ ănd cáre

Note another kind of substitution, dimeter for tetrameter, in Waller's "Song" (p. 293):

> Go, love|ly Rose,
> Tell her | that wastes | her time | and me,
> That now | she knows
> When I | resem|ble her | to thee
> How sweet | and fair | she seems | to be.

Because everyone does not read poetry the same way—not even highly qualified readers—

we should be extremely reluctant to draw dogmatic generalizations about the scansion of any poem. Almost every serious poem has both metrical and rhetorical rhythm unless it is written in free verse (see p. 274). There is movement of sound and movement of sense in every poem, and generally some compromise between the two must be made if the total meaning of the poem is not to be violated. This statement is especially true of poems with rhyme, and even more true of poems with internal rhyme. The reading of poems, especially aloud, is an accomplished art, but it will not be accomplished unless the reader knows what goes on in the poem.

RHYME. Rhyme is perhaps the most obvious technical device in poetry, yet its effects can be most subtle. Like all other devices, it is used for a specific purpose in each poem, and to judge its usefulness we must understand that purpose. The limerick depends heavily on rhyme:

> There once was a man from Nantucket
> Who kept all his cash in a bucket;
>   But his daughter, named Nan,
>   Ran away with a man,
> And as for the bucket, Nantucket.

Some limericks combine a substantial subject with humor as does this one that plays with Einstein's famous theory of relativity:

> There was a young lady named Bright,
> Whose speed was far faster than light;
>   She set out one day
>   In a relative way,
> And returned home the previous night.

Rhyme is used here to produce a humorous effect by emphasizing the element of surprise. The use of rhyme in Blake's "The Tiger" (p. 294) is more subtle:

> Tiger! Tiger! burning bright
> In the forests of the night,
> What immortal hand or eye
> Could frame thy fearful symmetry?

The rhyme *bright-night* suggests a paradox, or an apparent contradiction which upon close examination proves to be true. The rhyme *eye-symmetry* is even more subtle in its suggestion that an immortal eye, really unknown to us and by suggestion part of the "night," frames this symmetry, fearful because, by suggestion, it, too, is part of the "night." To hit the rhymes in "The Tiger" as we are expected to do in the limerick

would violate the poem's meaning. In fact, by alternating a perfect rhyme, *bright-night*, with an imperfect rhyme, *eye-symmetry*, Blake has discouraged us from over-emphasizing the rhymes in the stanza.

There are many kinds of rhymes, used to achieve different purposes. The principal rhymes are *perfect* and *imperfect*, subdivided as follows:

Masculine (perfect): final accented syllables rhyme.

> *lie-die; resist-consist*

Feminine or Multiple (perfect): rhyming accented syllables are followed by identical unaccented syllables:

> *raven-craven; comparison-garrison*

Sprung or near-rhyme (imperfect): similar but not identical vowels rhyme:

> *blood-good; strong-unstrung;
> eye-symmetry*

Rhyme is found in two positions:

End-rhyme: at the end of the lines, the usual position, as in "The Tiger."

Internal rhyme: within the line.

> The splendor *falls* on castle *walls*

STANZA FORM. A stanza is a pattern of lines which usually presents a unit of poetic experience. If the poem is composed of two or more stanzas, the pattern is generally repeated. There are many variations, of course, in stanza form, but we shall note only the standard forms which appear most frequently in American and English poetry. An alert reader will, of course, examine the stanza in any poem to determine how and why it helps to shape the poem's meaning. As we become more experienced in reading poetry —and more conditioned by standard stanza forms—certain expectancies are established in us which help to interpret the various forms.

Heroic Couplet: two rhymed iambic pentameter lines; each couplet is usually a complete unit, as in Pope:

> Hope springs eternal in the human breast;
> Man never is, but always to be, blessed.
> —"An Essay on Man"

The couplet is not confined to iambic pentameter lines; Jonson, for example, uses iambic tetrameter in "Come, My Celia" (p. 248):

Come, my Celia, let us prove
While we may the sports of love;
Time will not be ours forever,
He at length our good will sever.

Swinburne uses anapestic pentameter couplets in a chorus of "Atalanta in Calydon";

We have seen thee, O Love, thou art fair;
    thou art goodly, O Love;
Thy wings make light in the air as the wings
    of a dove.

Ballad Stanza: four-line iambic, alternately tetrameter and trimeter, rhyming *abcb*, as in "Sir Patrick Spens" (p. 253):

The king sits in Dumferling toune,
    Drinking the blude-reid wine:
"O whar will I get guid sailor,
    To sail this schip of mine?"

The Sonnet: fourteen iambic pentameter lines, grouped variously according to the purpose of the poet.

The *Italian,* sometimes called *Petrarchan* or *legitimate,* has two parts: an octet, or eight lines, rhyming *abbaabba;* and a sestet, or six lines, using new rhymes, rhyming *cdcdcd* or some other combination. Wordsworth's "Composed upon Westminster Bridge" (p. 295) and Milton's "On His Blindness' (p. 297) are sonnets in the Italian form.

The *English,* sometimes called the *Shakespearian,* sonnet has three four-line units, or quatrains, and a concluding couplet, rhyming, *ababcdcdefefgg.* Drayton's "Since There's No Help" (p. 297) and the sonnets by Shakespeare, of course, are examples of the English form.

Usually, but not necessarily, the octet of a sonnet presents a problem or conflict, and the sestet offers a resolution or simply a comment on the conflict. Frost observed with characteristic humor that after the eighth line a sonnet takes a turn for better or worse. (See pp. 295–298 for six sonnets and further commentary on the sonnet form.)

The Spenserian Stanza: devised by Edmund Spenser (1552–1599) and used in *The Faerie Queene,* contains nine lines, eight of iambic pentameter, and the last of iambic hexameter (an Alexandrine), rhyming *ababbcbcc.* Because of the excellent effects it can be made to produce, this stanza form seems to be forever fresh and useful.

Blank Verse: iambic pentameter verse free from rhyme, the metrical line which seems to fit best the natural rhythms of our language. Shakespeare used it in his plays (*Othello,* p. 455), Milton chose it for *Paradise Lost,* T. S. Eliot gave it to the present-day stage in *The Cocktail Party,* and Frost used it with extraordinary effectiveness in "A Masque of Reason" (p. 358).

Free Verse: Free verse—not to be confused with blank verse—is verse which does not adhere to any exact metrical pattern. Although much of the world's poetry is written in free verse, sometimes called *vers libre,* many handbooks and textbooks on poetry give it a wide berth as if the whole matter were of little importance or not quite respectable.

There are both good and bad metrical verse and free verse, but the sins of one are not the virtues of the other. Bad metrical verse is perfectly, monotonously, and mechanically regular; bad free verse is rhetorically undisciplined and formless. Writers of good metrical verse resort to many variations, as we have seen, and the more they use, the closer they come to free verse. Writers of good free verse use a firm rhetorical discipline which often approximates a metrical form, and the firmer the rhetorical discipline the closer it comes to metrical verse. Are the differences between the two following passages very marked?

To be or not to be: that is the question:
Whether 'tis nobler in the mind to suffer
The slings and arrows of outrageous fortune,
Or to take arms against a sea of troubles,
And by opposing end them. To die, to
    sleep—   5
No more; and by a sleep to say we end
The heart-ache and the thousand natural
    shocks
That flesh is heir to; 't is a consummation
Devoutly to be wish'd. . . .
        —Shakespeare, *Hamlet*

This, this is he; softly a while;
Let us not break in upon him.
O change beyond report, thought, or belief!
See how he lies at random, carelessly diffused,
With languished head unpropt,
As one past hope, abandoned,
And by himself given over,
In slavish habit, ill-fitted weeds

O'er-worn and soiled.
Or do my eyes misrepresent? Can this be
   he,   10
That heroic, that renowned,
Irresistible Samson? whom, unarmed,
No strength of man, or fiercest wild beast,
   could withstand;
Who tore the lion as the lion tears the kid;
Ran on embattled armies clad in iron,   15
And, weaponless himself,
Made arms ridiculous, useless the forgery
Of brazen shield and spear, the hammered
   cuirass,
Chalybean-tempered steel, and frock of mail
Adamantean proof. . . .   20
          —Milton, *Samson Agonistes*

Both these passages are shaped by a firm rhetorical discipline. Shakespeare is using blank verse liberally varied to permit the sense to strike home. To attempt to read any line metrically simply violates the sense; for example:

The heart-ache and the thousand natural

   shocks

Rhetorically, it scans something like this:

The heart-ache and the thousand natural

   shocks

Although the passage from Milton is written in free verse, the metrical verse often shows itself (lines 5, 6, 8, 9, and so on), and the rhetorical discipline never falters. It seems quite pointless to ask, is metrical verse superior to free verse? It seems better to ask, does the verse form properly shape the meaning of the poem?

The rhythm of good free verse is the rhythm of thought. Much so-called "poetic prose" is actually free verse written in prose form. We all know "Psalm 23," King James Version, in its prose form; it is easily converted:

The Lord is my shepherd;
I shall not want.

He maketh me to lie down in green pastures:
He leadeth me beside the still waters.
He restoreth my soul: 5
He leadeth me in the paths of righteousness
For his name's sake.
Yea, though I walk

Through the valley of the shadow of death,
I will fear no evil: 10
For thou art with me;
Thy rod and thy staff
They comfort me.

Thou preparest a table before me
In the presence of mine enemies: 15
Thou anointest my head with oil;
My cup runneth over.

Surely goodness and mercy shall follow me
All the days of my life:
And I will dwell in the house of the Lord 20
For ever.

As we ask ourselves some questions about the poems to follow, perhaps we can observe the appropriate uses of metrical and free verse.

My Heart Leaps Up
WILLIAM WORDSWORTH
1770–1850

My heart leaps up when I behold
   A rainbow in the sky:
So was it when my life began;
So is it now I am a man;
So be it when I shall grow old,   5
   Or let me die!
The Child is father of the Man;
And I could wish my days to be
Bound each to each by natural piety.

Comments and Questions

1. Although Wordsworth uses metrical verse, the poem is, compared to a sonnet, quite irregular in form. All lines are written in iambic meter, but note that they vary from dimeter to pentameter. Note further that the rhyme scheme is somewhat unusual: *abccabcdd*. We do not ask, is it right for Wordsworth to depart from the more regular forms? The question is, does the poem's irregular form shape the poem's meaning? Does the sound help to interpret the sense? The poem's form is certainly no accident. Why is line 6 the shortest, and line 9 the longest? Why do the last two lines rhyme?

Why do lines 1 and 5 rhyme, and lines 2 and 6? The answers to these questions are related to the total experience provided by the poem.

2. How good a poem is it?

3. What do you think Freud might have said about the line, "The Child is father of the Man"?

Poets to Come
WALT WHITMAN
1819–1892

Poets to come! orators, singers, musicians to come!
Not to-day is to justify me and answer what I am for,
But you, a new brood, native, athletic, continental, greater than before known,
Arouse! for you must justify me.

I myself but write one or two indicative words for the future,   5
I but advance a moment only to wheel and hurry back in the darkness.

I am a man who, sauntering along without fully stopping, turns a casual look upon you
      and then averts his face,
Leaving it to you to prove and define it,
Expecting the main things from you.

Comments and Questions

1. We ask the same basic question of Whitman's poem that we asked of Wordsworth's: Does the poem's free-verse form help to interpret the sense? How do the lines of varying length help to communicate Whitman's attitude toward the facts of the poem? Why is line 7 the longest and most supple, and line 9 the shortest?

2. Do the lines move with the rhythm of thought in the poem? Support your opinion with evidence from the poem.

Believe Me, If All Those Endearing Young Charms
THOMAS MOORE
1779–1852

Believe me, if all those endearing young charms,
  Which I gaze on so fondly today,
Were to change by tomorrow, and fleet in my
    arms,
  Like fairy-gifts fading away,
Thou wouldst still be adored, as this moment
    thou art,   5
  Let thy loveliness fade as it will,
And around the dear ruin each wish of my
    heart
  Would entwine itself verdantly still.

It is not while beauty and youth are thine own,
  And thy cheeks unprofaned by a tear,   10
That the fervor and faith of a soul can be known,
  To which time will but make thee more dear;
No, the heart that has truly loved never forgets,
  But as truly loves on to the close,
As the sun-flower turns on her god, when he
    sets,   15
  The same look which she turned when he rose.

Comments and Questions

1. The regularity of Moore's lyric—a brief subjective and musical poem—is apparent:

the foot is anapestic, the lines alternate between tetrameter and trimeter, and the rhyme scheme has a definite pattern (*ababcdcd*, and so on). Compared with "My Heart Leaps Up" and "Poets to Come," is Moore's poem dull and monotonous, or does his form help shape the meaning of the poem?

2. The poem, we said, is a lyric. Does this fact help to account for its form?

3. How good a poem is it?

Easter Wings
GEORGE HERBERT
1593–1633

It is interesting to note a device used by a few seventeenth-century poets: the form of the poem below speaks for itself. Joseph Addison (1672–1719) called this sort of thing "false wit," which we may translate as false poetic form. What is your opinion? For a more subtle example of the use of typography as a means to an effect, see Cummings' "Among Crumbling People," p. 290.

Lord, who createdst man in wealth and store,
  Though foolishly he lost the same,
    Decaying   more   and   more
      Till   he   became
        Most   poor;   5
        With   thee
      Oh,   let   me   rise
    As   larks,   harmoniously,
  And   sing   this   day   thy   victories;
Then shall the fall further the flight in me.   10

My   tender   age   in   sorrow   did   begin;
  And   still   with   sicknesses   and   shame
    Thou   didst   so   punish   sin,
      That   I   became
        Most   thin.   15
        With   thee
      Let   me   combine,
  And feel this day thy victory;
  For   if   I   imp   my   wing   on   thine,
Affliction shall advance the flight in me.   20

IMAGERY

There are in general two ways of speaking: abstractly and concretely. If we say "George is an honest, just man with a good deal of integrity," we have described him with abstract terms. If we say "As George was following the stranger, he saw the stranger's pocketbook slip to the sidewalk, he picked it up, quickened his step, and returned it to him"—we have described George with concrete terms. In the first statement we have spoken *about* George; in the second statement we have allowed George's *act to speak* for George himself. In the first statement we testify to his honesty; in the second statement the act testifies for him, and it may be the more convincing. The second statement illustrates the basic method of the creative writer, especially the poet.

In the second statement we "image" or—as we say—we imagine George's act. We see it all happen because of the concrete details involved: *stranger, pocketbook, sidewalk,* and *step.* Such words are called *imagery* in a poem because they bring real, concrete life into it; they represent the life that the poet wants the reader to experience. Except in poorly constructed, superficial poems, these images are not mere decorations—they are in great part a poet's *method* of thinking. This principle we must understand if we are to enter the inner life of a good poem, and not to enter it is to bypass the poem's higher level, the figurative level of meaning.

Some poems rely almost exclusively on imagery for their meaning, as we shall see when we later explore MacLeish's "You, Andrew Marvell" (p. 279). Poets can rely on images for meaning if the images are carefully *selected* (not the approximate image, but the *exact* image) and *arranged* because we think naturally in images as children constantly demonstrate. The third-grade child who wrote,

Six little pigs sitting on a fence,
Not one of them had any sense,

was thinking in images because it is our natural way. Note how our mind searches for meaning by grouping these images: *table, bottle, cabinet, glasses, alcohol, men*—and we see a barroom. Yet, note what happens when we add only two more images: *test tube, Bunsen burner.* The *regrouped* images become a laboratory because the last two images alter the *grouped* meaning of the first six.*

In that little demonstration of how we think in images there are many lessons for the readers of poems, but for our purposes here chiefly these: we must understand the poem as an organic whole—we must allow the meaning of each image to come clear in its natural setting with all the other images. And we must make sure that all the images are included in our interpretation of the poem's meaning. We are driven back to our basic principle ("Poetry: Preliminaries," p. 236): the whole poem helps to determine the meaning of its parts, and, in turn, each part helps to determine the meaning of the whole. When we interpret a poem's imagery, the observance of this principle is imperative.

We are now in a position to understand why imagery is the life of a good poem. With imagery the poet allows life to present itself, and we can hear, see, smell, feel, and touch experience. As we read the following poem, we are immediately involved with sense experience—concrete life itself.

I Taste a Liquor Never Brewed
EMILY DICKINSON
1830–1886

I taste a liquor never brewed—
From Tankards scooped in Pearl—
Not all the Frankfort Berries
Yield such an Alcohol!

Inebriate of Air—am I— 5
And Debauchee of Dew—
Reeling—thro endless summer days—
From inns of Molten Blue—

When "Landlords" turn the drunken Bee
Out of the Foxglove's door— 10
When Butterflies—renounce their "drams"—
I shall but drink the more!

* For a psychological explanation of the creative process, see Norman R. F. Maier and H. Willard Reninger, *A Psychological Approach to Literary Criticism.* New York: Appleton-Century-Crofts, 1933, esp. chap. III.

Till Seraphs swing their snowy Hats—
And Saints—to windows run—
To see the little Tippler 15
From Manzanilla come!

Comments

Through images—many of which are also figures and symbols—this poem presents a theme which, as such, is never mentioned directly. The "liquor never brewed" is the exhilarating aspect of nature in which we participate by entering Emily Dickinson's sensuous world, and we participate fully because the images are fresh and unusual. "Scooped in Pearl," "inebriate of Air," and "reeling . . . from inns of Molten Blue" are not the worn counters of expression. They are sharp, concrete, arresting sense impressions which communicate meaning, quite unforgettably.

We see, then, that the purpose of imagery is to communicate meaning, not merely to serve as a graceful embellishment. If we understand this distinction before we investigate imagery further, our study can become a genuine pleasure instead of an academic chore. Many of the poems in this section use imagery in striking and original ways and, read carefully, they can help to cultivate our sensitivity to imagery as communication. For most poets imagery actually becomes a way of thinking, or of translating abstractions into concrete experience. Indeed, imagery is the chief means the poet has of creating reality —*his* own sense of the reality of the inner and outer world and their relationships. Here are Shakespeare and Donne thinking in images.

Sonnet 116: Let Me Not to the Marriage of True Minds
WILLIAM SHAKESPEARE
1564–1616

Let me not to the marriage of true minds
Admit impediments. Love is not love
Which alters when it alteration finds,

Or bends with the remover to remove.
Oh, no! it is an ever-fixed mark 5
That looks on tempests and is never shaken;
It is the star to every wandering bark,
Whose worth's unknown, although his height be
    taken.
Love's not Time's fool, though rosy lips and
    cheeks
Within his bending sickle's compass come; 10
Love alters not with his brief hours and weeks,
But bears it out even to the edge of doom.
    If this be error and upon me proved,
    I never writ, nor no man ever loved.

images and figures. To realize just how
powerfully suggestive Donne's images are,
try to state the plain sense of the poem in
literal language only. What are the basic
images, and how does Donne relate them to
define the sensation of love?

2. What is the tone of the poem? Is Donne
serious about this idea of love or is there a
trace of extravagance in the poem?

3. Donne is well known for his technical
dexterity. Does it serve or override the sense
in this poem? Is the poem merely technically
admirable or does it also present a valuable
experience?

The Good-Morrow
JOHN DONNE
1572–1631

I wonder by my troth, what thou and I
Did, till we loved? Were we not weaned till then,
But sucked on country pleasures, childishly?
Or snorted we in the seven sleepers' den?
'Twas so; but this, all pleasures fancies be. 5
If ever any beauty I did see,
Which I desired, and got, 'twas but a dream of
    thee.

And now good morrow to our waking souls,
Which watch not one another out of fear;
For love all love of other sights controls, 10
And makes one little room an everywhere.
Let sea-discoverers to new worlds have gone,
Let maps to other, worlds on worlds have shown;
Let us possess one world, each hath one, and is
    one.

My face in thine eye, thine in mine appears, 15
And true plain hearts do in the faces rest;
Where can we find two better hemispheres
Without sharp north, without declining west?
Whatever dies was not mixed equally;
If our two loves be one, or thou and I 20
Love so alike that none do slacken, none can die.

Comments and Questions

1. Much like Shakespeare's "Sonnet 116,"
this poem is a definition of love presented in

On Donne's Poetry[1]
SAMUEL TAYLOR COLERIDGE
1772–1834

With Donne, whose muse on dromedary trots,
Wreathe iron pokers into true-love knots;
Rhyme's sturdy cripple, fancy's maze and clue,
Wit's forge and fire-blast, meaning's press and
    screw.

You, Andrew Marvell
ARCHIBALD MacLEISH
1892–

And here face down beneath the sun
And here upon earth's noonward height
To feel the always coming on
The always rising of the night:

To feel creep up the curving east 5
The earthy chill of dusk and slow
Upon those under lands the vast
And ever climbing shadow grow

And strange at Ectaban the trees
Take leaf by leaf the evening strange 10

[1] In addition to Donne's "The Good-Morrow" above,
see also his "Go and Catch a Falling Star," p. 298;
"Holy Sonnet, VII," p. 320; and "Woman's Constancy," p. 326.

The flooding dark about their knees
The mountains over Persia change

And now at Kermanshah the gate
Dark empty and the withered grass
And through the twilight now the late   15
Few travelers in the westward pass

And Baghdad darken and the bridge
Across the silent river gone
And through Arabia the edge
Of evening widen and steal on   20

And deepen on Palmyra's street
The wheel rut in the ruined stone
And Lebanon fade out and Crete
High through the clouds and overblown

And over Sicily the air   25
Still flashing with the landward gulls
And loom and slowly disappear
The sails above the shadowy hulls

And Spain go under and the shore
Of Africa the gilded sand   30
And evening vanish and no more
The low pale light across that land

Nor now the long light on the sea:

And here face downward in the sun
To feel how swift how secretly   35
The shadow of the night comes on. . .

Comments and Questions

Edwin Arlington Robinson called this poem "really a magical thing." It must be read aloud three or four times in a leisurely way to appreciate Robinson's comment. What produces the magic? Many poetic devices working together, of course, not the least of them the imagery. The title is undoubtedly a reference to Marvell's "To His Coy Mistress" (p. 301), particularly to such well-known lines as:

> But at my back I always hear
> Time's wingéd chariot hurrying near;

And yonder all before us lie
Deserts of vast eternity.

These lines and MacLeish's poem are concerned with the relentless movement of time —thieving time, as the Elizabethans called it. Note that the sound never diminishes until the last line, and the suspense is evenly distributed from beginning to end, helped along by the relentless stress of almost perfect (regular) iambic meter. The tone of the poem is one of restrained resignation and perhaps profound regret.

To get at the specific meaning of the poem —a meaning more specific than that of relentless time—we must account for the first and last stanzas which are quite different from others with their specific references to cities and countries. Where is the "here," the vantage point from which the poet speaks and feels this relentless time? Some readers have felt that "here" means MacLeish's native land, America, and the poet has confirmed it.[*] Working with this clue, can we read the poem as saying that young America will someday also experience the ravages of time as the older countries have? We may now return to the tremendous importance of the images, important because they seem to answer the question affirmatively. Note how the images move from "noonward height" in the first stanza to these images in the following stanzas: "the earthy chill," "the flooding dark," "the withered grass," "Spain go under," and "evening vanish." And finally, line 34 repeats the image in line 1, implying that America, too, will have its withered grass and its evening vanish. It is important to recognize that MacLeish has not offered his argument in some logical frame; he has depended upon his images to make us feel the force of his specific theme. This technique is quite characteristic of much modern poetry, depending as it does so heavily on imagery and unusual symbolism.

---

[*] Norman C. Stageberg and Wallace L. Anderson, *Poetry as Experience.* New York: American Book Company, 1952, p. 465.

Spring and Fall:
to a young child
GERARD MANLEY HOPKINS
1844–1889

Márgarét, are you gríeving
Over Goldengrove[1] unleaving?
Léaves, líke the things of man, you
With your fresh thoughts care for, can you?
Áh, ás the heart grows older   5
It will come to such sights colder
By and by, nor spare a sigh
Though worlds of wanwood leafmeal lie;
And yet you will weep and know why.
Now no matter, child, the name: 10
Sórrow's spríngs áre the same.
Nor mouth had, no nor mind, expressed
What heart heard of, ghost guessed:[2]
It ís the blight man was born for,
It is Margaret you mourn for.   15

Comments and Questions

1. This poem will not be understood or enjoyed through hurried reading, but the subtle fusion of sound and sense can be enjoyed if we first understand the poem's literal sense. The sense is actually not difficult, but it is highly concentrated: every word counts, and every line moves the sense along without interruption. Put the literal sense into writing, and account for every phrase in the poem. How did you interpret line 9? Note that the poet stresses *will*, not *weep*. The first word in lines 14 and 15 is very important, and line 15 summarizes the meaning of the poem.

2. Perhaps you have already discovered how thoroughly fused the sound and sense are. Note the rhyme in the first couplet: how does it contribute to meaning? What is the relationship of the first and last couplets? Note especially the rhyme *born for—mourn for.*

[1] Literally an estate in Wales, near Llansa in Flintshire; figuratively a color of vanishing youth.
[2] Ll. 12–13. *I Corinthians*, 2:9 and 13: "But as it is written, Eye hath not seen, nor ear heard, neither have entered into the heart of man, the things which God hath prepared for them that love him." "Which things also we speak, not in the words which man's wisdom teacheth, but which the Holy Ghost teacheth; comparing spiritual things with spiritual." Also *Isaiah*, 64:4:

For since the beginning of the world *men* have
    not heard, nor perceived by the ear,
Neither hath the eye seen, O God, besides thee,
What he hath prepared for him that waiteth
    for him. . . .

Neither Out Far nor in Deep
ROBERT FROST
1874–1963

The people along the sand
All turn and look one way.
They turn their backs on the land.
They look at the sea all day.

As long as it takes to pass   5
A ship keeps raising its hull;
The wetter ground like glass
Reflects a standing gull.

The land may vary more;
But whatever the truth may be—   10
The water comes ashore,
And the people look at the sea.

They cannot look out far.
They cannot look in deep.
But when was that ever a bar   15
To any watch they keep?

Comments and Questions

In this poem the plain sense, the rhyme scheme, the rhythm, the images—in fact, everything seems to be simple. By this time, however, we have had enough experience with poems to suspect that Frost's little poem means something more than meets the eye, and we recall that our analysis of his "Stopping by Woods on a Snowy Evening" ("Poetry: Preliminaries," p. 236) found the something more in his figures and symbols. Like so many of Frost's poems, the one above is disarmingly simple, but let us arm ourselves just the same. The following sub-section, "Figure and Symbol," will explore these matters: we use this poem to introduce the problems.

Frost's figures and symbols here are quite conventional, made so by repeated use and time. As usual, we come to figures and symbols through the images, and the central images here are "people," "land," "sea," and "watch." Practiced readers have developed the habit of asking questions of poems, whatever questions a poem seems to raise. Who are these "people"? Because they are completely unidentified, they must represent (see the symbol appear?) all of us, humanity. Why do "they turn their back on the land" and all "look at the sea"? The clue to the answer lies in line 10: they are looking for truth. Why do they look to the sea for it—is there no truth to be found on the land? The land gives us our bearings and represents the known, but the sea is limitless and mysterious to the eye and represents the unknown, exciting the imagination. We scrutinize the unknown, and little by little extract more meaning from it, but our progress toward the great, final answers is small ("they cannot look out far") because their subtleties are too great ("they cannot look in deep"). Nevertheless, the human race keeps the watch and continues to scrutinize the unknown, and there is hope ("the water comes ashore") that we shall know more and more about our destiny.

It is not entirely uncommon for some readers who really enjoy poems to protest at this point, asking in good faith, "*Must* we scatter the beauty of this little poem by all this analysis—is it really necessary to read all this *into* [note well, *into*] the poem?" The answer to this impatient question is not simple, and if the questioner is impatient enough, the answer is never adequate. A preliminary answer says it all depends on what is meant by "the beauty of this little poem." If a reader is satisfied with the sound and the harmony of the images, for him that is beauty enough. But there is no reason why this reader should legislate for other readers who find beauty, too, in the meaningful truth provided by the poem's figures and symbols. Such is the beginning of the answer to the impatient question; we hope a fuller answer will be found in

the subsection to follow. (See Spender's "On Teaching Modern Poetry," p. 837, for commentary on this controversy.)

FIGURE AND SYMBOL

Now that we have seen how images bring concrete life (sensuous experience) into a poem, and how poets think naturally with them (as we all do), we are prepared to see how poets use these images in special ways, sometimes to say things which can be said in no other way.

Figures and symbols are images used in a particular way to explore the less known through the known. Joseph Conrad describes an old Chinese shipowner as having "a face like an ancient lemon." The images in this figure are the face and the lemon, the first unknown to us, the second well known. Our imagination is required to transfer the *revelant* characteristics of the ancient lemon to the face, and we "see" it as wrinkled, jaundiced, dried-up, oval-shaped, and toughened by time—but the irrelevant characteristic of the lemon we allow to drop away. That is, we must make the proper association between the face and the lemon, and when someone insists on transferring the complete lemon or no lemon at all to the face, we say he has no imagination. For such a person poetry is simply an empty art because he cannot interpret figurative meaning. (See p. 241 on "Failure to Rise to the Figurative Level.")

Conrad could have used the adjectives mentioned above (*wrinkled, jaundiced*) instead of the figure; he could have described the Chinese face with a paragraph, but he would have lost his economy of means and concentrated suggestiveness provided by the figure. But figures can be used even on a higher level to communicate experience which cannot be communicated in any other way. To communicate the subtleties of the love experience has always placed a tremendous burden on language and the poets, and we therefore find love poems rife with figures (and symbols—see below) of all kinds. On falling deeply in love how would you explain and describe the exact shades and depths of feeling to a person who had never experienced such love? With abstract terms? Try it, and despair. We are quickly forced into a series of figures to compare the love experiences with other experiences which are somewhat related to love:

"Shall I compare thee to a summer's day?"
(Shakespeare, p. 325)

"My love is like a red red rose."
(Burns, p. 333)

Figures were not concocted as decorations: poetic necessity was originally the mother of communicative invention.

Poetry, then, understood in its most basic sense does not mean merely a collection of rhymes, rhythms and images: it is actually a way of thinking and feeling (E. E. Cummings would probably write *thinkfeeling* and he would be right) used to explore the unknown. Writers of prose as well as poets use this method, and here is Vernon Louis Parrington, scholar and master of figurative language, speaking of Herman Melville:

The golden dreams of transcendental faith, that buoyed up Emerson and gave hope to Thoreau, turned to ashes in his mouth; the white gleams of mysticism that now and then lighted up his path died out and left him in darkness.

Like Melville, Macbeth saw his own dreams perish; when he saw his darkness coming, Shakespeare makes him say:

Tomorrow, and tomorrow, and tomorrow,
Creeps in this petty pace from day to day
To the last syllable of recorded time;
And all our yesterdays have lighted fools
The way to dusty death. Out, out, brief candle!
Life's but a walking shadow, a poor player
That struts and frets his hour upon the stage
And then is heard no more. It is a tale
Told by an idiot, full of sound and fury,
Signifying nothing.
—*Macbeth*, V. v. 19–28

A full analysis and explanation of everything said by Shakespeare in these ten lines would require many prose pages. Why is this so?

The answer lies in the nature of Shakespeare's figurative language, especially in its economy and tremendous suggestiveness. Shakespeare could have had Macbeth tell us simply that life is meaningless—why did he use ten lines to tell us that? (Such a question is sometimes asked impatiently by the literal mind.) Because Shakespeare wants to participate in Macbeth's tragic flash of insight by having us transfer the relevant characteristics of *petty pace, last syllable, dusty death, brief candle, a walking shadow, a player that struts and frets* to Macbeth's feeling about life at this moment. These images we understand, and when Shakespeare uses them as figures too, we understand Macbeth. This act of transference we call the *imaginative process:* in our mind, life for Macbeth is *as* meaningless as a shadow, a fretting player, an idiot's tale. Is it any wonder that Macbeth cries, "Out, out, brief candle!" when its flickering light signifies nothing to be lived for?

Kinds of Figures

We are so accustomed to figures of speech in our everyday reading and conversation that unpracticed readers of poems sometimes overlook some figures and read them literally. It is best therefore to have the kinds of figures in mind, and to add their names to our critical vocabulary. Figurative language is sometimes called metaphorical language, or simply metaphor because its Greek ancestor *metapherein* means to carry meaning beyond its literal meaning (*meta* = beyond + *pherein* = to bring—that is, to bring beyond). Regardless, then, of the *kind* of figure we observe, its basic function is always to carry meaning from the literal to the figurative level.

Simile: a stated comparison, introduced by *like* or *as.* For example, "My love is like a red red rose." "There is no frigate like a book."

Metaphor: an implied comparison, with *like* or *as* omitted. For example, "Life's but a walking shadow"—instead of saying "Life is *like* a walking shadow."

Personification: giving human characteristics to an object, animal, or an abstract idea. Personification is a metaphor, of course, in the sense that there is an implied comparison between a non-human thing and a human being. For example, "There Honor comes, a pilgrim gray"; "My little horse must think it queer / To stop without a farmhouse near."

Synecdoche: using a part for the whole. For example, "Fifty winters [years] passed him by." Or using the whole for the part: for example, "the halcyon year"—meaning summer.

Metonymy: describing one thing by using the term for another thing closely associated with it.

For example, "the crown" used for "the king."

Hyperbole: an exaggeration used for special effect. For example, "Drink to me only with thine eyes"; "Go and catch a falling star."

Irony: a statement whose real meaning is completely opposed to its professed, or surface meaning. (See p. 241.) For example, " 'The czar is the voice of God and shall live forever.' "

Paradox: a statement whose surface, obvious meaning seems to be illogical, even absurd, but which makes good sense upon closer examination. For example: speaking of humanity Somerset Maugham observed, "the normal is the rarest thing in the world." Another example, Christ "lives that death may die." One more, "He couldn't find it because he knew where it was." Donne is famous for his paradoxes; see "The Canonization" (p. 326) for his paradoxical proof that unholy lovers are saints. Irony, of course, is related to paradox because in each surface meaning is never the real meaning, and hence both rely on an indirect method, a well-established device in poetry.

Dead Metaphor: a metaphor which has lost its figurative meaning through endless use. For example, "the back of the chair"; "the face of the clock."

Allusion: a reference to some well-known place, event, or person. Not a comparison in the exact sense, but a figure in the sense that it implies more than its narrow meaning. For example: "No! I am not Prince Hamlet, nor was meant to be"; "Miniver loved the Medici"; "There is a stubborn torch that flames from Marathon to Concord."

The Entire Poem as Figure: a poem which can be understood and enjoyed on the literal level, but when properly interpreted *as a whole* is completely figurative. There are many examples in this book: Frost's "Departmental" (p. 250), Herrick's "Delight in Disorder" (p. 327), and so on. It is not argued that such poems should be read literally only, but only that they can be, just as *Gulliver's Travels* and *Alice in Wonderland* can be read as stories without implications.

Tone: in some serious treatments of the relation of tone to meaning in poems, it is often implied that tone is actually an extended figure of speech. For example, more than an occasional reader misinterprets Donne's "Go and Catch a Falling Star" because he misreads Donne's tone

and calls the poem bitter or cynical. (See p. 298 for the poem and relevant comments on this problem.)

Symbol

A symbol, defined most simply, is one thing used to stand for, to represent, another thing. A lion stands for strength and courage; a lamb stands for gentleness; a burning torch held aloft stands for liberty. The word's Greek ancestor is *symballein,* meaning to compare by throwing together. A symbol is therefore a figure of speech although there is a technical difference between the two which should be understood in order to identify the *kinds* of symbol in poems.

If Shakespeare had written,

Life's like a walking shadow,

he would have used a simile because the comparison is *stated.* He did write,

Life's but a walking shadow,

and he therefore used a metaphor which *implies* the comparison without explicitly stating it, but note that both terms of the figure, *life* and *shadow,* are still present in the metaphor. If Shakespeare had dropped one term, *life,* and had used only *shadow* to stand for life, he would have used a symbol.

A symbol, however, is not necessarily related to metaphor. It can stand on its own feet by representing through continued use and common understanding a simple object or a complex pattern of associations or ideas. When we use the Cross to represent Christianity, we do not imply that the Cross is *like* Christianity; we simply say it stands for it, and the device works because the association is universally understood. When Frost says in "Birches,"

I'd like to go [*toward* heaven] by climbing a
    birch tree.
And climb black branches up a snow-white
    trunk,

almost any reader of poems should sense that Frost is up to something with those *"black branches"* and that *"snow-white* trunk." And of course he is. The *"snow-white* trunk" stands for the ideal which reaches toward heaven, and the black branches are life's dark realities we shall have to climb *over* and *with* to complete the climb to the top of the ideal. These are *conven-*

tional symbols, made so by use and time, recognized by practiced readers of poetry.

But some poets depart from conventional symbols to invent their own for their special purposes because, we assume, the conventional symbols will not properly communicate new sensations in a new age. Such symbols are called *arbitrary* or *personal* symbols, and must be understood in the poem's complete context, not by any previous mutual understanding between poet and reader. A good deal of "modern" poetry relies heavily on textual symbolism, and it accounts for some of the obscurity some readers find in modern poetry. When Eliot begins "The Love Song of J. Alfred Prufrock" (p. 304) with these lines,

> Let us go then, you and I,
> When the evening is spread out aginst the
>   sky
> Like a patient etherised upon a table,

the explanation of his symbols must be found in the remainder of the poem, not in any conventional meaning of patients who are etherized upon tables.

Genuine understanding of metaphor and symbol will not be achieved, however, through theoretical explanations: let us examine them in action in the poems that follow.

There Is No Frigate Like a Book

EMILY DICKINSON
1830–1886

There is no Frigate like a Book
To take us Lands away
Nor any Coursers like a Page
Of prancing Poetry—
This Travel may the poorest take   5
Without offence of Toll—
How frugal is the Chariot
That bears the Human soul.

Comments

The reader unable to read figurative language would find this poem incomprehen-

sible. Structurally and rhetorically the poem is simple, but unless we can visualize a book as a "ship" taking us to new intellectual and emotional "lands," and a page as a spirited "horse," no amount of abstract explanation will help us to understand the poem. Because the poem's structure is simple, the poem readily reveals the basic problem in reading poetry; but regardless of the complexity of a poem's structure and rhetoric, unless we can interpret the meaning of image, figure, and symbol, no amount of work on structure will make the poem clear. Even at the risk of laboring the obvious, this principle must be made absolutely clear: it is repeatedly overlooked even by practiced readers.

Morning at the Window

T. S. ELIOT
1888–1965

They are rattling breakfast plates in basement
        kitchens,
And along the trampled edges of the street
I am aware of the damp souls of housemaids
Sprouting despondently at area gates.

The brown waves of fog toss up to me   5
Twitsed faces from the bottom of the street,
And tear from a passer-by with muddy skirts
An aimless smile that hovers in the air
And vanishes along the level of the roofs.

Comments and Questions

Except for a few images, Eliot's poem appears to be written in plain statement. The literal situation is simple: the speaker is perhaps looking from a second-floor window or balcony as he sees and hears the movements and noises appropriate to the neighborhood's morning activities. Breakfast plates rattle, housemaids appear at the gates, waves of fog rise to reveal faces in the street, faces with problems in them, and the fog vanishes over the roofs. But the unusual images press for meaning—they tell us this literal reading will not do. Why the "basement" kitchens? Why the "trampled edges" of the street? Why the "damp souls" and why do they "sprout" despondently? We go back to the title, suspecting we have been trapped by irony. Morning is a conventional symbol of hope and energy, but neither is in this poem. As we account for the brown (stained) waves of fog, the twisted (abnormal, perverted) faces, the aimless smile whose owner has lost his bearings, we see that Eliot finds humanity living in the slums—this, we understand, is our morning now whose hope and energy have vanished over the roofs of the world. We shall meet more of Eliot's theme —the degeneration of our time—in "The Love Song of J. Alfred Prufrock" (p. 304), and "The Hollow Men" (p. 376).

But note the sharp precision of the scene in the poem—no plain statement, no abstractions, no message wrapped up and labeled in the final line, no stale figures and symbols. What does Eliot depend on instead? The poem below will tell us—an acknowledged manifesto of modern poetry.

Ars Poetica

ARCHIBALD MacLEISH
1892–

A poem should be palpable and mute
As a globed fruit,

Dumb
As old medallions to the thumb,
Silent as the sleeve-worn stone   5
Of casement ledges where the moss has grown—

A poem should be wordless
As the flight of birds.

*

A poem should be motionless in time
As the moon climbs,   10

Leaving, as the moon releases
Twig by twig the night-entangled trees,

Leaving, as the moon behind the winter leaves,
Memory by memory the mind—

A poem should be motionless in time   15
As the moon climbs.

*

A poem should be equal to:
Not true.

For all the history of grief
An empty doorway and a maple leaf.   20

For love
The leaning grasses and two lights above the
          sea—

A poem should not mean
But be.

Comments and Questions

Ars poetica means the art of poetry, or, in this case, MacLeish's definition of a poem. We can assume that he is describing what he means by a good poem as contrasted, say, with a lecture or perhaps an essay.

In presenting his *ars poetica* as a poem MacLeish assumed a double responsibility: he must not only make the sense of the poem describe a poem, but he must also cause this poem to be an example of the kind of poem of which he approves.

The poem has stimulated a good deal of controversy, especially the final "couplet." What does the poem mean—what, according to MacLeish, is a good poem? The structure, a series of couplets (except lines 13–14 and 21–22), is not complicated, so the difficulty must be chiefly in the figures and symbols, especially in the paradoxes (see p. 284).

The poem has three principal divisions, lines 1–8, 9–16, and 17–end; each division presents a basic principle of a good poem. First, "a poem should be palpable and mute" (dumb, silent, wordless). Literally, this dictum is nonsense, but MacLeish is not speaking literally—and *no* poem, he is saying by implication, ever should. A poem should speak concretely (palpably) through images, by presenting things which speak silently for themselves. That is, the poet should not talk about things in some general abstract way; he should permit things to speak for themselves. The "globed fruit," the "old medallions," the "casement ledges," and the "flight of birds" will tell their own stories by their presence. The reader must find the meaning of the thing in the thing itself.

Second (lines 9–16), a poem should be timeless and universal in its attitudes, timeless as the moon is timeless and as memories are. An event is always timely, but the meaning of an event in human terms is timeless and universal.

The third division of the poem (lines 17– end) seems to give the most difficulty although its meaning has already been partially explained in the previous lines. "A poem should be equal to" the experience presented *as experience* in the whole poem, and "not true" as a theory or a propositional truth is true—not merely abstractly true. A poem's truth should be self-evident as it emerges from the poem's images which represent experience, not a labored truth sustained by argument. "A poem should not mean" as an argument means, but should "be" its own witness for its own kind of truth. Commenting on the nature of art, without directly mentioning "Ars Poetica," MacLeish seems to put the poem's meaning into prose:

> Art is a method of dealing with our experience of this world, which makes that experience, *as* experience, recognizable to the spirit. . . . Art is not a technique for extracting truths. . . . Art is an organization of experience in terms of experience, the purpose of which is the recognition of experience. ["A poem should be equal to: / Not true."] It is an interpreter between ourselves and that which has happened to us, the purpose of which is to make legible what it is that has happened. . . . It is an organization of experience comprehensible not in terms of something else, but of itself; not in terms of significance, but of itself; not in terms of truth even, but of itself. ["A poem should not mean / But be."] The truth of a work of art is the truth of its organization. It has no other truth." *

When Stephen Spender says that "a poem *means* the sum of everything which it *is* . . . ,"

* *A Time to Speak.* Boston: Houghton Mifflin Company, 1940, pp. 84–85.

he is saying much the same thing. (See Spender's essay, "On teaching Modern Poetry," p. 837.)

For our immediate purposes the value of Mac-Leish's poem lies in his explanation and use of a method used by many modern poets, including T. S. Eliot and others whom we shall read later. This method—to summarize briefly for the moment—relies chiefly on textual symbols, compound images, and communication by association, rather than on logical structure.

The Cambridge Ladies
E. E. CUMMINGS
1894–1962

As we have moved progressively through the poems by Moore, Dickinson, Eliot, and MacLeish, we have moved away from the older poetry with its conventional techniques and attitudes into the newer, modern poetry. We have learned that the language (the poetic devices of symbol, rhythm, and sound) of Dickinson is somewhat different from Moore's language; and that the language of Eliot is sharply different from the poetic language used by both Moore and Dickinson. We have, in short, been involved with a *reading* problem—which means a problem of *understanding*.

Many qualified readers believe that the most celebrated modern poetic innovator is E. E. Cummings. Although he has never achieved the almost universal popularity of a Frost, Cummings has appealed especially to young people. One Cummings biographer, Charles Norman, reports that "when Cummings went to Bennington College in Vermont to give a reading, the entire audience of girls rose as he mounted the platform and chanted . . . in unison his poem 'Buffalo Bill's.' "

On first meeting Cummings' poetry the reader is likely to assume that he is confronted with the whims of a dabbler who delights in linguistic pyrotechnics in order to confuse and astonish a public he does not deserve. But the young who are slow to accept the chains of conventional grammatical and rhetorical practice (as Hemingway, Dos Passos, and Faulkner refuse to do) are ready to consider Hemingway's argument that "there is a fourth and fifth dimension that can be gotten" in prose—and, implies Cummings, in poetry, too. In short, there is no reason to believe that conventionally accepted textbook language forms, regardless of how "liberal" and "descriptive," are adequate to communicate all personal, subjective experience, especially the intensely personal experience of a Cummings. The basic question for the creative writer is not, is this language pattern "acceptable"? The question is, how far may language be stretched and distorted to communicate my experience and still reach the sensibilities of the enlightened reader? Shakespeare took some chances, Eliot took them, and Cummings took even greater chances (of not being understood—there is no other criterion involved) and at times he was downright reckless. Actually, the only question for the *reader* confronted by language is, at what point am I lost? Under such circumstances it is obvious that Cummings has not written for the language-shackled reader, and only insofar as the reader is willing to explore experience not expressed in bread-and-butter forms can he be happy with Cummings' poems.*

Let us now examine three of Cummings' poems. The first poem is a sonnet which is somewhat unconventional; the second poem is more unconventional; and the third poem represents Cummings at his liberated best.

---

the Cambridge ladies who live in furnished souls
are unbeautiful and have comfortable minds
(also, with the church's protestant blessings
daughters, unscented shapeless spirited)
they believe in Christ and Longfellow, both
    dead,   5
are invariably interested in so many things—
at the present writing one still finds
delighted fingers knitting for the is it Poles?

---

* For a perceptive explanation of Cummings' technique see Ralph J. Mills, Jr., "The Poetry of Innocence: Notes on E. E. Cummings," *English Journal*, Nov. 1959, pp. 433–442.

perhaps. While permanent faces coyly bandy
scandal of Mrs. N and Professor D   10
.... the Cambridge ladies do not care, above
Cambridge if sometimes in its box of
sky lavender and cornerless, the
moon rattles like a fragment of angry candy

Comments and Questions

It is easy to become impatient with Cummings, and although some of his poems may deserve our impatience, his best ones teach us in the most extraordinary way the importance of the fusion of sound and sense, and the contribution technique (the devices of poetry working together) makes to meaning.

"The Cambridge Ladies" is one of his more conventional poems, but still an appropriate one to sharpen our wits on. Cummings calls the poem a sonnet, but when we compare it with Shakespeare's "Sonnet 18" (p. 325), the differences are apparent. True, Cummings sonnet has fourteen lines, but the rhyme scheme in the octet is quite irregular for the form; the sestet is a little unusual; and the rhythm is only roughly iambic pentameter. Compared to Shakespeare's sonnet, Cummings' threatens to become shapeless with each succeeding beat, as if it would run off its track on the next curve. Is his sonnet therefore inferior? Not if we recall one of our basic principles: no device is good or bad in a poem except as its use makes it so. The tone (Cummings attitude toward his subject) of his sonnet is radically different from Shakespeare's, and Cummings' devices, working together, produce the tone he wants us to hear.

Are the Cambridge ladies local specimens only or do they finally symbolize certain traits in a type of woman? What do they believe in; what are their spiritual resources (always the concern of the artist)? Surely the tone is satiric, and it helps us to interpret the meaning of every image, figure, and symbol. Instead of having free souls to embrace spiritual values wherever found, their souls are dull ("unbeautiful") rooms already furnished (by family and religious inheritance) in which their minds can live "comfortably" without fear of the new, original, or challenging. They believe in the *dead* Christ and Longfellow. Christ alive (T. S. Eliot's "tiger" in his poem "Gerontion") would indeed threaten the complacency of these Cambridge ladies; and Cummings' placing Longfellow—a symbol of Harvard's earlier Genteel Tradition—against a tremendous spiritual force like Christ throws into sharp relief the decadence of the ladies. They knit for—"is it Poles?" It does not matter for whom because knitting is socially fashionable at the moment (the war effort?). They fill their empty minds with scandal, an excitement used as a substitute for adventures they fear to touch themselves. What can we make of the last four lines? Cummings' satiric thrust against the ladies' superficiality helps us to find their lives lived in a neat little box scented with lavender, shielded from life's bruises by round corners. And if the moon—a conventional symbol of love, mystery, and adventures—has been reduced *within* their box to the ladies' size to be regarded by these children as candy, we should express no surprise to hear the moon's protest rattle in anger against its confinement.

Is the sonnet really shapeless compared to Shakespeare's? Not if each has a shape appropriate to fusing the poem's sound and sense. The even-flowing lines of Shakespeare are not appropriate for Cummings' satiric jabs, and our being jolted by the sound prepares us to *experience* the sense of the sonnet—we *feel* the sense as well as comprehend it intellectually.

Pity This Busy Monster, Manunkind

E. E. CUMMINGS
1894–1962

pity this busy monster,manunkind,

not.   Progress is a comfortable disease:
your victim(death and life safely beyond)

plays with the bigness of his littleness
—electrons deify one razorblade   5
into a mountainrange;lenses extend

unwish through curving wherewhen till unwish
returns on its unself.
        A world of made
is not a world of born—pity poor flesh

and trees,poor stars and stones,but never this 10
fine specimen of hypermagical

ultraomnipotence.   We doctors know

a hopeless case if—listen:there's a hell
of a good universe next door;let's go

Comments

This unconventional sonnet is a satire on humanity. The creature manunkind (mankind, humankind, and man unkind), surrounded by his world and universe, never gets beyond the image of himself as he rummages around in his little circle of materialism ("plays with the bigness of his littleness"). The heart of his tragedy,

              lenses extend
   unwish through curving wherewhen till unwish
   returns on its unself,

comes clear if we understand that "curving wherewhen" ("where" as space and "when" as time) refers to Einstein's concept of "space-time" as a single dimension. When in his "A Masque of Reason" (p. 358), II. 159–161) Frost's character God says to Job,

        You got your age reversed
  When time was found to be a space dimension
  That could, like any space, be turned around in?

Frost is using the same Einstein concept. Man, then, says Cummings, looking out at the universe through his telescopes, only "returns on its unself" instead of extending the self beyond its "hypermagical ultraomnipotence."

Among Crumbling People

E. E. CUMMINGS
1894–1962

a
  mong crum
        bling people(a
long ruined streets
hither and)softly   5

thither between (tumb
ling)
    houses(as
the kno

wing spirit prowls,its   10
nose winces
before a dissonance of

Rish and Foses)
        until
            (finding one's self   15
at some distance from the
crooked town)a

harbour fools the sea(
while
    emanating the triple   20
starred

Hotel du Golf . . . that notable structure
or ideal edifice . . . situated or established
. . . far from the noise of waters
                    :)one's   25

eye perceives
        (as the ego approaches)
painfully sterilized contours;
within

which   30
"ladies&gentlemen"
—under

glass—
are:
asking.   35

?each
oth?
er

rub,
!berg;   40
:uestions

Comments

We see at a glance that this is one of Cummings' less conventional poems. Either the strange form helps to interpret its meaning or we have been hoodwinked. The key to both its meaning and form lies in the first line: the people are crumbling, for reasons given in the poem, as the form itself crumbles away in the last ten lines. The plain, literal sense seems to be this: The knowing spirit prowls along ruined streets among crumbling people and their houses, wincing before the incompatible odors of fish and roses ("Rish and Foses") until the spirit finds in the Hotel du Golf an "ideal edifice" with "sterilized contours," inhabitants who live "under glass," asking each other ("rubber") questions without point or meaning.

But to find the poem's full meaning we must understand how the various devices help to interpret its figurative meaning. For example, note the combined effect of the irregular lines and the parentheses. Lines 1–3 are themselves dropping off, and the knowing spirit prowls around and among the parentheses. We read *outside* the parentheses that the spirit moves "among crumbling people . . . softly thither between . . . houses"; but we read *within* the parentheses that the spirit moves "along ruined streets hither and . . . tumbling. . . ." The purpose of such devices is apparently to cause us to *experience* this ruined topsy-turvy world that the knowing (critical, evaluating) spirit investigates and finds wanting. We find another device in Cummings' use of the slurred " 'ladies&gentlemen' " to show the lack of discrimination and taste in another kind of crumbling people, those who live "under glass" in "sterilized contours." These people are exhibited as dead specimens in showcases whose inner life has disintegrated.

The effect of the poem, then, is to cause us to experience through this unusual fusion of sound, sense, *and* the typographical form of the poem on the page two kinds of people: those who live among external ruins (streets, houses, incompatible odors), and those who live with their own internal ruins—their soulless lives.

THE COMMENT ON EXPERIENCE: FROM SENSUOUS EXPERIENCE TO DOMINANT ATTITUDE

Some wit has said that poetry is the art of saying something by saying something else just as good. He was thinking, of course, of the poet's use of figures of speech and symbolism. But the wit really missed the point by failing to see that poetry is the art of saying something that can hardly be said in any other way. Poetic language is not a substitute for some other language with which the poet could make things clearer were he less obstinate and aesthetic. Poetic language exists simply because no other language has been found to communicate our attitudes and feelings toward certain kinds of experience.

In this section we shall begin with poems that contain little or no comment—poems of sensuous experience—and pass along to poems with increasingly more comment. Our purpose is not merely to classify poems according to the degree of comment they possess. *We use this device to make us sensitive to whatever is happening within the poem, to make us aware of the kind of experience the poet has provided*. And, certainly not least, to demonstrate that one kind of poem is not superior to another because it happens to present a sensuous experience or an intellectual experience which appeals immediately to our temperament or prejudices. We should recognize such prejudices when we hear it said, "nature poetry is the best poetry," or "philosophical poetry is best because philosophy is the highest wisdom." A student of poetry may finally adopt such an attitude or other, but let us not begin wih it. Let us begin with an attitude that focuses our attention on the *experience* and *quality of art* in each poem. Our prejudices will develop fast enough without encouragement; we require no course or book to point the way.

Some poets have presented their objects with little or no comment, as Emerson has done in "The Snow-Storm," while others have used some object as a basis for their comment, making the comment instead of the object the life of the poem, as Jonson has done in "Song, to Celia" (p. 292). Other poets have gone beyond to the object-comment combination by using a situation or animal as a symbol, as Blake has used an animal as a symbol of raw life force (interpreted by some readers as evil) in "The Tiger" (p. 294).

As we approach the middle of this section, the poems will include attitudes which are more prominently implied or stated than they are in the earlier poems. Some readers will say that the poems contain more ideas, and are therefore more valuable than poems of sensuous experience like Emerson's "The Snow-Storm."

It is easy to become dogmatic about the relation of poetry to ideas—to thought, philosophy, and the meaning of life. The greatest poetry, says one group, is philosophical poetry, and they produce as their proof such poems as Milton's *Paradise Lost,* Tennyson's "In Memoriam," and Jeffers' "Meditation on Saviors." The finest poetry, counters another group, is "pure poetry" by which they mean poetry of sensuous experience never "soiled" with "thought." Fortunately for those of us who would roam freely through the entire history of poetry, choosing as we go, no school of critics has ever successfully legislated for or against one kind of poetry. Every decade or so such legislation is attempted, of course, as, for example, at present John Donne and his brother metaphysicians are brought forward as the heroes, while Shelley and his brother romantics are permitted to languish. Not even Shakespeare escapes the legislators, and we read with some astonishment that *Hamlet* is an "artistic failure." We should not frown upon the legislators because another group always takes their place, and the new agitation is stimulating while it lasts even though their wine making is at times only the production of new bottles with loose corks.

Perhaps we can avoid the confusions created by the dogmatic legislators of successive generations by reminding ourselves of two or three basic matters we have already examined a little. Through the centuries good poets have explored and commented upon almost every phase of experience regardless of the winds of critical doctrine which have howled around them. The winds blow away and the poems remain. The moral here is obvious: each one of us tries to understand—absorb, digest, assimilate—the experiences provided by hundreds of poems, and we call those experiences good which make some substantial contribution to our expanding personal sensibilities and to our awareness of the world around us. Further, we remind ourselves that the quality of a poem is first determined by its artistic qualities—that it should be first judged as a poem, not as an idea or argument. And further, in this poetic realm of subjective experience each one of us must become his own critic who finally establishes his own hierarchy of poems. If we permit someone else to make the hierarchy, we shall not know who we are, and to know who we are is the final lesson of the humanities, including poetry.

The Snow-Storm
RALPH WALDO EMERSON
1803–1882

Announced by all the trumpets of the sky,
Arrives the snow, and, driving o'er the fields,
Seems nowhere to alight: the whited air
Hides hills and woods, the river, and the heaven,
And veils the farm-house at the garden's end.   5
The sled and traveller stopped, the courier's feet
Delayed, all friends shut out, the housemates sit
Around the radiant fireplace, enclosed
In a tumultuous privacy of storm.

Come see the north wind's masonry,   10
Out of an unseen quarry evermore
Furnished with tile, the fierce artificer
Curves his white bastions with projected roof
Round every windward stake, or tree, or door.
Speeding, the myriad-handed, his wild work   15
So fanciful, so savage, nought cares he
For number or proportion. Mockingly,
On coop or kennel he hangs Parian wreaths;
A swan-like form invests the hidden thorn;
Fills up the farmer's lane from wall to wall,   20
Maugre the farmer's sighs; and at the gate
A tapering turret overtops the work.
And when his hours are numbered, and the
        world
Is all his own, retiring, as he were not,

Leaves, when the sun appears, astonished Art   25
To mimic in slow structures, stone by stone,
Built in an age, the mad wind's night-work,
The frolic architecture of the snow.

Song, to Celia
BEN JONSON
1572–1637

Drink to me only with thine eyes,
    And I will pledge with mine;
Or leave a kiss but in the cup
    And I'll not look for wine.
The thirst that from the soul doth rise   5
    Doth ask a drink divine;
But might I of Jove's nectar sup,
    I would not change for thine.

I sent thee late a rosy wreath,
    Not so much honoring thee   10
As giving it a hope that there
    It could not withered be;
But thou thereon didst only breathe,
    And sent'st it back to me;
Since when it grows, and smells, I swear,   15
    Not of itself but thee!

Comments and Questions

1. This poem has been set to music, and you may have known it first as a song. What qualities of the poem provide its *inherent* music?

2. Like Browning's "My Last Duchess" (p. 244) the poem is a dramatic lyric. What makes it dramatic?

3. Does the poem present sensuous experience exclusively, or has Jonson included some comment on experience? Confirm your opinion with evidence from the poem.

To Daffodils
ROBERT HERRICK
1591–1674

Fair daffodils, we weep to see
    You haste away so soon;
As yet the early-rising sun

Has not attained his noon.
    Stay, stay,   5
  Until the hasting day
    Has run
  But to the even-song;
And having prayed together, we
  Will go with you along.   10

We have short time to stay, as you;
  We have as short a spring,
As quick a growth to meet decay,
  As you, or anything.
    We die   15
  As your hours do, and dry
    Away
  Like to the summer's rain,
Or as the pearls of morning's dew,
  Ne'er to be found again.   20

Rose Aylmer

WALTER SAVAGE LANDOR
1775–1864

Ah, what avails the sceptred race,
  Ah, what the form divine!
What every virtue, every grace!
  Rose Aylmer, all were thine.

Rose Aylmer, who these wakeful eyes   5
  May weep, but never see,
A night of memories and of sighs
  I consecrate to thee.

Candles

CONSTANTINE P. CAVAFY
1863–1933

The days of our future stand before us
like a row of little lighted candles—
golden, warm, and lively little candles.

The days gone by remain behind us,
a mournful line of burnt-out candles;   5
the nearest ones are still smoking,
cold candles, melted and bent.

I do not want to look at them; their form saddens
  me,
and it saddens me to recall their first light.
I look ahead at my lighted candles.   10

I do not want to turn back, lest I see and shudder—
how quickly the somber line lengthens,
how quickly the burnt-out candles multiply.

Song

EDMUND WALLER
1606–1687

  Go, lovely Rose,
Tell her that wastes her time and me,
  That now she knows,
When I resemble her to thee,
How sweet and fair she seems to be.   5

  Tell her that's young,
And shuns to have her graces spied,
  That hadst thou sprung
In deserts where no men abide,
Thou must have uncommended died.   10

  Small is the worth
Of beauty from the light retir'd:
  Bid her come forth,
Suffer herself to be desir'd,
And not blush so to be admir'd.   15

  Then die, that she
The common fate of all things rare
  May read in thee,
How small a part of time they share,
That are so wondrous sweet and fair.   20

Comments

In some of the poems in this section we have found not only descriptions of natural objects and people but comments on them as well. Waller's poem goes even further by including an argument. The lover has observed the delicacy of the rose and the speed with which it fades. Looking for an argument to persuade the woman he loves, he uses the rose as an example of a natural object which exhibits its brief delicacy for the admiration of men. This is the lover's generalization, and with it he bids his lady to

Suffer herself to be desir'd,
And not blush so to be admir'd.

Perhaps we can locate the art in the poem by recognizing what makes the poem persuasive. The method is not the debater's—the appeal is hardly to the rational intellect. Waller relies chiefly on the emotional appeal generated by the sound—the music—which *moves* us to consider or accept the sense, or the abstract argument. The art of the poem requires us to participate in the lover's feelings, and in a sense we become the lover, moved by his urgency.

The Tiger

WILLIAM BLAKE
1757–1827

Tiger! Tiger! burning bright
In the forests of the night,
What immortal hand or eye
Could frame thy fearful symmetry?

In what distant deeps or skies   5
Burnt the fire of thine eyes?
On what wings dare he aspire?
What the hand dare seize the fire?

And what shoulder, and what art,
Could twist the sinews of thy heart?   10
And when thy heart began to beat,
What dread hand? and what dread feet?

What the hammer? what the chain?
In what furnace was thy brain?
What the anvil? What dread grasp   15
Dare its deadly terrors clasp?

When the stars threw down their spears,
And watered heaven with their tears,
Did he smile his work to see?
Did he who made the Lamb make thee?   20

Tiger! Tiger! burning bright
In the forests of the night,

What immortal hand or eye,
Dare frame thy fearful symmetry?

The Lamb

WILLIAM BLAKE
1757–1827

Little Lamb, who made thee?
Dost thou know who made thee?
Gave thee life, and bid thee feed,
By the stream and o'er the mead;
Gave thee clothing of delight,   5
Softest clothing, woolly, bright;
Gave thee such a tender voice,
Making all the vales rejoice?
Little Lamb, who made thee?
Dost thou know who made thee?   10

Little Lamb, I'll tell thee,
Little Lamb, I'll tell thee:
He is callèd by thy name,
For he calls himself a Lamb.
He is meek, and he is mild;   15
He became a little child.
I a child, and thou a lamb,
We are callèd by his name.
Little Lamb, God bless thee!
Little Lamb, God bless thee!   20

Comments and Questions

1. As line 20 of "The Tiger" indicates, Blake's two poems can be considered profitably as companion pieces. Both poems, of course, have a symbolic level of meaning. Describe the meaning of each symbol.

2. Considered together, how do the poems complement each other? In what way does Blake suggest that some thoughtful conclusion should emerge from his questioning?

To a Waterfowl

WILLIAM CULLEN BRYANT
1794–1878

Whither, midst falling dew,
While glow the heavens with the last steps of day,

Far, through their rosy depths, dost thou pursue
   Thy solitary way?

Vainly the fowler's eye   5
Might mark thy distant flight to do thee wrong,
As, darkly seen against the crimson sky,
   Thy figure floats along.

Seek'st thou the plashy brink
Of weedy lake, or marge of river wide,   10
Or where the rocking billows rise and sink
   On the chafed ocean-side?

There is a Power whose care
Teaches thy way along that pathless coast—
The desert and illimitable air—   15
   Lone wandering, but not lost.

All day thy wings have fanned,
At that far height, the cold, thin atmosphere,
Yet stoop not, weary, to the welcome land,
   Though the dark night is near.   20

And soon that toil shall end;
Soon shalt thou find a summer home, and rest,
And scream among thy fellows; reeds shall bend,
   Soon, o'er thy sheltered nest.

Thou'rt gone, the abyss of heaven   25
Hath swallowed up thy form; yet, on my heart
Deeply has sunk the lesson thou hast given,
   And shall not soon depart.

He who, from zone to zone,
Guides through the boundless sky thy certain
      flight,   30
In the long way that I must tread alone,
   Will lead my steps aright.

Comments and Questions

1. Bryant has here used an old device of drawing a lesson from nature. If there is a Power that directs the waterfowl safely to home and rest, the same Power, concludes the speaker, "will lead my steps aright." Regardless of your agreement or disagreement with Bryant's theme, what do you think of his explicitly labeling his theme a "lesson"? Bryant wrote during a period when delivering explicit messages in poetic form was fashionable,* but if we can believe MacLeish's "Ars Poetica" (p. 286) and the practice of most modern poets, messages are to be perceived but not heard—implied but not stated—and certainly not labeled. What is your view of the matter?

2. Note the somewhat unusual metrical structure of the stanzas: the first and fourth lines contain three feet (trimeter), and the second and third lines contain five feet (pentameter). The rhyme scheme is *abab*. How does this structure of sound help to create the tone of the poem?

Composed upon Westminster Bridge

WILLIAM WORDSWORTH
1770–1850

We now examine six sonnets which provide us with various kinds of experiences. We remind ourselves that the sonnet generally, but not always, presents a situation in the octet, and disposes of it in one way or another in the sestet. The form is therefore quite appropriate for presenting some phase of sensuous experience in the octet, and for commenting on, or expressing ideas about, that experience in the sestet. (See p. 274 for sonnet forms.)

Earth has not anything to show more fair;
Dull would he be of soul who could pass by
A sight so touching in its majesty;
This city now doth, like a garment, wear
The beauty of the morning; silent, bare,   5
Ships, towers, domes, theatres, and temples lie
Open unto the fields, and to the sky;
All bright and glittering in the smokeless air.
Never did sun more beautifully steep
In his first splendor, valley, rock, or hill;   10
Ne'er saw I, never felt, a calm so deep!
The river glideth at his own sweet will:

* For another example see the final stanza of Longfellow's "The Village Blacksmith." Longfellow was a contemporary of Bryant.

Dear God! The very houses seem asleep;
And all that mighty heart is lying still!

Comments and Questions

This sonnet gives us an opportunity to consider some questions often asked by students and readers in general. The questions run like these: Must we always grasp a poem like an orange to squeeze every last drop of subtle meaning from it? Can't we just *enjoy* a poem? Must we drive all the fun out of poetry with this everlasting search for meaning?

These are fair questions; suppose we try to answer them with the help of Wordsworth's sonnet.

The sonnet provides us with many levels of appreciation, just as a rich experience in life does. Many readers have called the sonnet beautiful undoubtedly because it provides a very satisfying sensuous experience: the liquid sound of rhythm and rhyme, the clear images of nature, the simple but dignified diction, and the structure on the literal level which is quite easily understood, all combine to give us a valuable experience. Once we have placed ourselves on the bridge and have absorbed this lovely picture of London lying still at full dawn, we can understand the natural resentment expressed by some readers against an analysis to find the sonnet's meaning. On this sensuous level the sonnet is quite clear and certainly of great value. But should these readers try to legislate against any further meaning the sonnet possesses any more than the philosophical readers should try to legislate against the sensuous readers? When students ask, can't we just enjoy the poem? the answer is a resounding yes—but we should ask further, how *many* ways can the poem be enjoyed? That, too, is a fair question. Perhaps we can help to find the answer by asking a few other questions.

1. We have already admitted that the poem provides a lovely experience; some readers have called it "charming," "enchanting." How would you describe your experience?

2. Wordsworth's images are undoubtedly partly responsible for our favorable sensuous reaction—lines 6–8, for example, are strik-ing. A picture so packed with images would probably have little unity unless it had a central image. Does the sonnet have one?

3. Suppose we assume that the central image is in lines 4–5:

This city now doth, like a garment, wear
The beauty of the morning. . . .

Why has Wordsworth personified the city? Have you noted particularly line 14?

4. What is the nature of the garment? "The beauty of the morning," Wordsworth says, by which he means nature. Perhaps the garment is a symbol which stands for a special kind of Nature. Perhaps the "smokeless air," contrasted with the smoke and grime of normal city atmosphere, is a symbol of purity of spirit which pervades the entire scene. Does the tone of the poem seem to be religious?

5. Is there any reason why the sonnet cannot be enjoyed on more than one level of appreciation and understanding? Is there any reason why these levels should not be coordinated to arrive at the *full* meaning of the poem?

Sonnet 29: When in Disgrace with Fortune and Men's Eyes
WILLIAM SHAKESPEARE
1564–1616

When in disgrace with fortune and men's eyes,
I all alone beweep my outcast state
And trouble deaf heaven with my bootless[1] cries
And look upon myself and curse my fate,
Wishing me like to one more rich in hope,   5
Featured like him, like him with friends possessed,
Desiring this man's art [2] and that man's scope,[3]
With what I most enjoy contented least;
Yet in these thoughts myself almost despising,
Haply I think on thee, and then my state,   10
Like to the lark at break of day arising
From sullen earth, sings hymns at heaven's gate;
   For thy sweet love remembered such wealth brings

[1] Futile.   [2] Skill.   [3] Range of opportunity.

That then I scorn to change my state with
    kings.

Sonnet 30: When to the Sessions of Sweet Silent Thought

WILLIAM SHAKESPEARE
1564–1616

When to the sessions of sweet silent thought[1]
I summon up remembrance of things past,
I sigh the lack of many a thing I sought,
And with old woes new wail my dear time's
    waste.
Then can I drown an eye, unused to flow,   5
For precious friends hid in death's dateless[2]
    night,
And weep afresh love's long-since canceled woe,
And moan the expense of many a vanished
    sight—[3]
Then can I grieve at grievances foregone,[4]
And heavily from woe to woe tell o'er   10
The sad account of fore-bemoaned moan,
Which I new pay as if not paid before.
    But if the while I think on thee, dear friend,
    All losses are restored and sorrows end.

Since There's No Help

MICHAEL DRAYTON
1563–1631

Since there's no help, come let us kiss and part—
Nay, I have done, you get no more of me;
And I am glad, yea, glad with all my heart,
That thus so cleanly I myself can free.
Shake hands for ever, cancel all our vows,   5
And when we meet at any time again,
Be it not seen in either of our brows
That we one jot of former love retain.
Now at the last gasp of Love's latest breath,
When, his pulse failing, Passion speechless
    lies,   10
When Faith is kneeling by his bed of death,

[1] L. 1: see *Othello*, III. iii. 138 ff. (p. 479).
[2] Endless.   [3] Lament the cost of lost objects.
[4] Past distresses.

And Innocence is closing up his[1] eyes,
    —Now if thou wouldst, when all have given
        him over,
    From death to life thou might'st him yet
        recover.

On His Blindness

JOHN MILTON
1608–1674

When I consider how my light is spent
Ere half my days in this dark world and wide,
And that one talent which is death to hide
Lodged with me useless, though my soul more
    bent
To serve therewith my Maker, and present   5
My true account, lest he returning chide;
"Doth God exact day-labor, light denied?"
I fondly[1] ask. But Patience, to prevent
That murmur, soon replies, "God doth not need
Either man's work or his own gifts. Who best   10
Bear his mild yoke, they serve him best. His
    state
Is kingly: thousands at his bidding speed,
And post o'er land and ocean without rest;
They also serve who only stand and wait."

Comments and Questions

1. The five sonnets we have now read indicate that the poets have used the form to present personal matters, and to draw conclusions from their experiences. Milton's blindness was a tremendous blow to his poetic aspirations, and when total blindness came in 1652, *Paradise Lost* was still to be written. Can you find evidences of Milton's struggle within himself in the *rhetorical* and *metrical* structure of the sonnet? Compare his sonnet with Wordsworth's "Composed upon Westminster Bridge" above; how does the sound of each differ from the other?

2. The word *talent* in line 3 can be related to *Matthew*, 25: 14–30. What is your conclusion about Milton's meaning?

[1] Love's.
[1] Foolishly.

Ozymandias[1]

PERCY BYSSHE SHELLEY
1792–1822

I met a traveler from an antique land
Who said: Two vast and trunkless legs of stone
Stand in the desert. Near them, on the sand,
Half sunk, a shattered visage lies, whose frown,
And wrinkled lip, and sneer of cold command,   5
Tell that its sculptor well those passions read
Which yet survive, stamped on these lifeless
     things,
The hand that mocked them, and the heart that
     fed:
And on the pedestal these words appear:
"My name is Ozymandias, King of Kings: 10
Look on my works, ye Mighty, and despair!"
Nothing beside remains. Round the decay
Of that colossal wreck, boundless and bare
The lone and level sands stretch far away.

Comments and Questions

1. It has been said that this sonnet "is an ironic poem on the vanity and futility of a tyrant's power." What is your opinion of the comment?

2. Does the sonnet express a universal truth? Confirm your opinion with evidence from the poem.

Go and Catch a Falling Star

JOHN DONNE
1572–1631

Go and catch a falling star,
    Get with child a mandrake root,
Tell me where all past years are,
    Or who cleft the devil's foot,
Teach me to hear mermaids singing,   5
Or to keep off envy's stinging,
       And find
       What wind
Serves to advance an honest mind.

[1] Ramses II (1295–1225 B.C.), Pharaoh of Egypt, whose statue at Thebes bore the inscription: "I am Ozymandias, king of kings: if anyone wishes to know what I am and where I lie, let him surpass me in some of my exploits."

If thou be'st born to strange sights,   10
    Things invisible to see,
Ride ten thousand days and nights
    Till age snow white hairs on thee,
Thou, when thou return'st, wilt tell me
All strange wonders that befell thee,   15
       And swear
       No where
Lives a woman true and fair.

If thou find'st one, let me know;
    Such a pilgrimage were sweet.   20
Yet do not; I would not go,
    Though at next door we might meet.
Though she were true when you met her,
And last till you write your letter,
       Yet she   25
       Will be
False, ere I come, to two or three.

Comments

With Donne's poem we are confronted with a fascinating example of poetic sophistication.

If his poem is to be interpreted rightly, we must be sensitive to its *tone.* Certainly if the tone is missed or violated by the reader, the poem will be badly misconstrued—and has been, repeatedly, by unpracticed readers. Donne wrote in the Elizabethan Age (the English Renaissance), a period when poetry was used to comment on almost everything from the most serious aspects of religion to inconsequential personal feuds. Elizabethan poets, being men first and poets afterwards (Heaven applaud!), debated endlessly the place and value of woman. Indeed, a courtier of the time, professional poet or not, was expected to have among his many accomplishments the ability to turn a few pretty verses in favor of his lady. In time, of course, many such poems became conventionalized as the ladies became idealized, and part of the convention consisted of placing the lady beyond reach while the lover languished in pain. Here is Sir Philip Sidney (1554–1586) languishing:

Loving in truth, and fain in verse my love
    to show,
    That she, dear she, might take some plea-
    sure of my pain,

Pleasure might cause her read, reading
    might make her know,
Knowledge might pity win, and pity grace
    obtain,—
I sought fit words to paint the blackest face
    of woe. . . .

Donne revolted against this tradition, and "Go and Catch a Falling Star" is part of the revolt (see also his "Woman's Constancy," p. 326). But to have shown his displeasure in some boorish heavy-handed way would have been no part of Donne's temperament, and he therefore uses a jaunty, bantering tone simply to redress the lack of balance in the convention of his time. Donne's friendly contemporary critics would praise the poem for its "wit," not meaning humor as we use the word, but meaning the "swift play and flash of mind" and the poetic skill to make the poet's theme sharp and memorable. We may disagree with Donne's theme, but what reader can ignore or forget the poem? To call it "bitter" or "cynical" is to miss the poem completely. Its tone is quite otherwise except for the reader who is the victim of his stock responses (see p. 243).

The entire poem is actually a figure of speech, in this case *hyperbole* (see p. 284), or an extravagant statement used for a particular effect. The poem is a tall tale rendered in superb images and sophisticated tone. To comprehend such a tone and place it in proper perspective is simply part of an educated person's equipment: in the adult world he will meet the attitude repeatedly.

Sonnet 130: My Mistress' Eyes Are Nothing Like the Sun

WILLIAM SHAKESPEARE
1564–1616

My mistress' eyes are nothing like the sun;
Coral is far more red than her lips' red:
If snow be white, why then her breasts are dun;
If hairs be wires, black wires grow on her head.
I have seen roses damask'd,[1] red and
    white,   5

But no such roses see I in her cheeks;
And in some perfumes is there more delight
Than in the breath that from my mistress reeks.
I love to hear her speak, yet well I know
That music hath a far more pleasing
    sound: 10
I grant I never saw a goddess go,—
My mistress, when she walks, treads on the
    ground.
    And yet, by heaven, I think my love as rare
    As any she[2] belied with false compare.

Comments and Questions

We see that Shakespeare, too, had some comments to make on the poetic convention of idealizing women. Why does he purposely hack out some of these rough lines (l. 4 especially) and violate our ears with ugly stabs? Why does he resort to words like *dun* and *reeks*?

HUMAN VALUES AND THE CRITICISM OF EXPERIENCE: PHILOSOPHICAL POEMS

Almost all poetry is in one sense or another a criticism, or an evaluation, of experience. In some poems the criticism is only implied, at times quite subtly; in others it is boldly stated.

If we stop to consider the nature and interests of the artist, regardless of his medium, it should surprise no one that he is usually critical of his age. By critical we mean that in exploring human experience he tries to sift the genuine and enduring from the shoddy and vulgar to erect a hierarchy of values. Above all, the artist is interested in *human values*. The phrase is often used but seldom defined.

The nature of these human values should be found in the poems, but perhaps we can prepare ourselves a little to recognize them as we come upon them later. There are two kinds of basic values, means values and end values. If we say that a house is worth $15,000, we are speaking of a means value because the house is a means to an end—the good life. All material things—

[1] Variegated.

[2] Woman.

land, food, clothing, automobiles—possess means values, or, as they are more frequently called, material values.

The consequences which accrue from using these material things we call living, or life, which we label good, mediocre, or bad, according to our basis of judgment, or our philosophy of life. We ask, what is the good life? Suppose we say it is the consequence of the whole man, body and spirit, living successfully with one's self, with society, and with the universe. The values which emerge from such a life we call end values, or human values. They are the values most prized by the artist, including the poet. Think back, for a moment, over the poems we have already read: what have the poets been interested in, means values or end values? Have they explored food, clothing, automobiles, material property, riches? Not often, of course; but when they have, what was their *attitude* toward them? Think of Frost's "Neither Out Far Nor in Deep" (p. 281) and Shelley's "Ozymandias" (p. 298). The burden of these poems is the *ends* in life; they ask the implied question, what shall we live *for*? Thoreau answered when he said, "the cost of a thing is the amount of what I will call life which is required to be exchanged for it. . . ." *

The artist—whether poet, painter, sculptor, or composer—does at least two things: he explores the inner world of personality, the essential man; and he records the consequences on the individual man of his having lived in any given civilization. Poems are the products of poets confronted by their environment, and the poems become value judgments on that environment. The poems of previous times therefore become documents or depositories where the human values of former ages are found.

We have implied above that man is confronted with three inescapable things: *himself*, *society*, and *the universe*. The poems to follow explore these relationships.

THE INDIVIDUAL: PSYCHOLOGICAL VALUES

These values emerge when the poet explores the nature and worth of the individual, and espe-

* *Walden*, ch. 1.

cially when the individual must struggle with conflicts within himself. The poet is immensely interested in the personal and spiritual resources of the individual, and many poets seem to find the world's most basic tragedy in our lack of them.

Miniver Cheevy
EDWIN ARLINGTON ROBINSON
1869–1935

Miniver Cheevy, child of scorn,
  Grew lean while he assailed the seasons;
He wept that he was ever born,
  And he had reasons.

Miniver loved the days of old   5
  When swords were bright and steeds were
        prancing;
The vision of a warrior bold
  Would set him dancing.

Miniver sighed for what was not,
  And dreamed, and rested from his
        labors;   10
He dreamed of Thebes and Camelot,
  And Priam's neighbors.

Miniver mourned the ripe renown
  That made so many a name so fragrant;
He mourned Romance, now on the town,   15
  And Art, a vagrant.

Miniver loved the Medici,
  Albeit he had never seen one;
He would have sinned incessantly
  Could he have been one.   20

Miniver cursed the commonplace
  And eyed a khaki suit with loathing;
He missed the medieval grace
  Of iron clothing.

Miniver scorned the gold he sought,   25
  But sore annoyed was he without it;

Miniver thought, and thought, and thought,
  And thought about it.

Miniver Cheevy, born too late,
  Scratched his head and kept on thinking; 30
Miniver coughed, and called it fate,
  And kept on drinking.

Comments

Robinson, a failure in practical affairs for years, was unusually sensitive to personal failure and frustration. Miniver is used as a symbol of all the Minivers in the world who because of their psychological structure cannot reconcile themselves to the realities of their environment. Miniver is a romantic in the sense that for him the heroic world lies in the past. What is the poet's attitude toward Miniver, what are his assumptions and their consequences in the poem?

Two attitudes are apparent: the poet is sympathetic with Miniver, yet he smiles at the humor and irony, albeit tragic, of his predicament. Many practical people would condemn Miniver as a lazy vagrant without ambition. Robinson sees further: he is too wise psychologically to be trapped by making a complicated situation simple. He knows that the predicament of the Minivers in the world is not simple. Miniver's problem is not social or philosophical, but rather psychological in the sense that Robinson apparently believes that Miniver's temperament prevents him from reconciling himself to a modern, industrial society. Miniver was simply "born too late," his temperament is his "fate," and no amount of "thinking" finds a solution for him. What, then, is Miniver to do? He "kept on drinking" —not literally only, of course, but figuratively; he kept on escaping to a romantic world in which he could live.

Robinson's basic assumption is that men— men like Miniver at least—do what they must do, what they are temperamentally equipped to do. This interpretation of human character, begun as a psychological investigation, soon attaches itself to philosophical speculation and becomes a part of a long philosophical tradition summarized by the phrase, "Character is fate."

To His Coy Mistress
ANDREW MARVELL
1621–1678

The three poems to follow explore man's deepest and most crucial emotion, the love experience. Marvell's "To His Coy Mistress" reflects the survival of the Elizabethan notion of thieving time (see also MacLeish's "You, Andrew Marvell," p. 279) as it touches love; Browning's "A Toccata of Galuppi's" (p. 302) reflects a Victorian conflict in the love experience; and Eliot's "The Love Song of J. Alfred Prufrock" (p. 304) reflects a modern view of frustration. All three poems finally go beyond the love experience as such to comment on basic human values which belong to no age or century alone. It is this universal meaning that we finally look for by reading the *totality* of each poem as a figure of speech—as a symbol.

Had we but world enough, and time,
This coyness, Lady, were no crime.
We would sit down and think which way
To walk and pass our long love's day.
Thou by the Indian Ganges' side   5
Shouldst rubies find: I by the tide
Of Humber would complain. I would
Love you ten years before the Flood,
And you should, if you please, refuse
Till the conversion of the Jews.   10
My vegetable love should grow
Vaster than empires, and more slow;
An hundred years should go to praise
Thine eyes and on thy forehead gaze;
Two hundred to adore each breast,   15
But thirty thousand to the rest;
An age at least to every part,
And the last age should show your heart.
For, Lady, you deserve this state,
Nor would I love at lower rate.   20
  But at my back I always hear
Time's wingèd chariot hurrying near;
And yonder all before us lie
Deserts of vast eternity.
Thy beauty shall no more be found,   25
Nor, in thy marble vault, shall sound

My echoing song; then worms shall try
That long preserved virginity,
And your quaint honor turn to dust,
And into ashes all my lust: 30
The grave's a fine and private place,
But none, I think, do there embrace.

　　Now therefore, while the youthful hue
Sits on thy skin like morning dew
And while thy willing soul transpires   35
At every pore with instant fires,
Now let us sport us while we may,
And now, like amorous birds of prey,
Rather at once our time devour
Than languish in his slow-chapt power.   40
Let us roll all our strength and all
Our sweetness up into one ball,
And tear our pleasures with rough strife
Thorough[1] the iron gates of life:
Thus, though we cannot make our sun   45
Stand still, yet we will make him run.

[1] Through.

Comments

The plain sense of this poem is clear enough, coming to us in three parts: Had we but time enough, says the lover to his desired, your coyness (prolonging the chase) would be appropriate and exciting—anticipation is greater than realization (ll. 1–20). But, argues the lover, time is against this leisurely approach to consummation (ll. 21–32), and therefore let us devour rather than languish (ll. 33–end). The poem, then, is an argument much like Waller's "Song" ("Go, lovely Rose," p. 293), and as such is impeccably logical, but in the realm of love logic is quite useless. The persuasion must come from the art of the poem which moves us to accept the abstract argument. The basic devices are hyperbole (exaggeration), the impatience of the lover created by the crisp couplets in short lines, and the images of rich emotional content. We may agree with the lover's argument not merely because he is logical, but because we *participate* in his emotional need and urgency which are common to us all.

A Toccata of Galuppi's

ROBERT BROWNING
1812–1889

I
Oh, Galuppi, Baldassaro, this is very sad to find!
I can hardly misconceive you; it would prove me deaf and blind;
But although I take your meaning, 'tis with such a heavy mind!

II
Here you come with your old music, and here's all the good it brings.
What, they lived once thus at Venice where the merchants were the kings,   5
Where St. Mark's is, where the Doges used to wed the sea with rings?

III
Ay, because the sea's the street there; and 'tis arched by . . . what you call
. . . Shylock's bridge with houses on it, where they kept the carnival:
I was never out of England—it's as if I saw it all!

IV
Did young people take their pleasure when the sea was warm in May?   10
Balls and masks begun at midnight, burning ever to mid-day
When they made up fresh adventures for the morrow, do you say?

V

Was a lady such a lady, cheeks so round and lips so red,—
On her neck the small face buoyant, like a bell-flower on its bed,
O'er the breast's superb abundance where a man might base his head?   15

VI

Well, and it was graceful of them they'd break talk off and afford
—She, to bite her mask's black velvet, he, to finger on his sword,
While you sat and played Toccatas, stately at the clavichord?

VII

What? Those lesser thirds so plaintive, sixths diminished, sigh on sigh,
Told them something? Those suspensions, those solutions—"Must we die?"   20
Those commiserating sevenths—"Life might last! we can but try!"

VIII

"Were you happy?"—"Yes."—"And are you still as happy?"—'Yes. And you?"
—"Then, more kisses!"—"Did *I* stop them, when a million seemed so few?"
Hark! the dominant's persistence, till it must be answered to!

IX

So an octave struck the answer. Oh, they praised you, I dare say!   25
"Brave Galuppi! that was music! good alike at grave and gay!
I can always leave off talking, when I hear a master play."

X

Then they left you for their pleasure: till in due time, one by one,
Some with lives that came to nothing, some with deeds as well undone,
Death came tacitly and took them where they never see the sun.   30

XI

But when I sit down to reason, think to take my stand nor swerve,
While I triumph o'er a secret wrung from nature's close reserve,
In you come with your cold music, till I creep thro' every nerve.

XII

Yes, you, like a ghostly cricket, creaking where a house was burned—
"Dust and ashes, dead and done with, Venice spent what Venice earned!   35
The soul, doubtless, is immortal—where a soul can be discerned.

XIII

"Yours for instance, you know physics, something of geology,
Mathematics are your pastime; souls shall rise in their degree;
Butterflies may dread extinction,—you'll not die, it cannot be!

XIV

"As for Venice and its people merely born to bloom and drop,   40
Here on earth they bore their fruitage, mirth and folly were the crop;
What of soul was left, I wonder, when the kissing had to stop?

XV

"Dust and ashes!" So you creak it, and I want the heart to scold.
Dear dead women, with such hair, too—what's become of all the gold
Used to hang and brush their bosoms? I feel chilly and grown old.   45

Comments and Questions

Few poems demonstrate so well as this one the contribution which sound makes to sense. Browning's musical education began early, and he remained devoted to music throughout his life, as his poetry testifies. Baldassare Galuppi (1706–1785) was a famous Venetian composer of light operas, church music, sonatas, and toccatas. If "A Toccata of Galuppi's" is read aloud with sympathy and understanding, the characteristics of the toccata are quite apparent. It is a composition written for the organ or clavichord (forerunner of the modern piano), characterized by brilliant full chords and running passages, free fantasia style, and quite unrestrained by any fixed form. The word *toccata* is the past participle of Italian *toccare*, to touch, meaning that the instrument is touched, not played, which produces the effect of a series of rapid tones touched but not held. Life is quickly conjured up and quickly fades away.

To enable us to see that Browning is actually using the toccata in more than one way, we should fix the facts of the poem clearly in mind. The scientific Englishman whose reliance on reason has caused him to look askance at love and the emotions is moved by Galuppi's toccata to reconsider his devotion to reason and science. Although he has never been out of England, the music paints pictures of old Venice in his mind, Venice the traditional harbor of love and romance—"it's as if I saw it all!" The questions he asks in stanzas IV–VI clearly indicate that his reliance on reason is shaken. The music causes him to hear the young couple discussing the meaning of the music to them (VII–IX): they are made to feel that although death will finally overtake them, they can try to pursue their love and frivolity—that the attempt will be at least a temporary reward. Knowing that the lovers did go to their death, he puts them away with soft, regretful words (X), but the music still persists to challenge his failure to rely on love and affection regardless of how fleeting they seem to be (XI–XIV): his rationalizing will not sustain him, and he feels "chilly and grown old." Briefly, he has missed the essence of life and knows it (XV).

1. As usual, a statement of the facts of a poem omits much of the essential poetic experience. How deeply is the Englishman really moved by the music? Explain the meaning of the music's comment in stanza XIII. What do the butterflies and mathematics symbolize?

2. The poem is, of course, actually a dramatic dialogue. Have you any idea how we can get at Browning's attitude toward the antagonists? The answer to this question lies partly in the tone of the poem, and its tone is greatly determined by Browning's use of the toccata's characteristics in his metrical structure. To put the question another way, to what extent does the sound help to interpret the sense? Confirm your opinion with specific evidence from the poem.

3. Is the Englishman related to Prufrock in any way (see below)?

The Love Song of J. Alfred Prufrock
T. S. ELIOT
1888–1965

*S'io credessi che mia risposta fosse
a persona che mai tornasse al mondo,
questa fiamma staria senza più scosse.
Ma per ciò che giammai di questo fondo
non tornò vivo alcun, s'i'odo il vero,
senza tema d'infamia ti rispondo.*[1]

Let us go then, you and I,
When the evening is spread out against the sky
Like a patient etherised upon a table;
Let us go, through certain half-deserted streets,
The muttering retreats   5
Of restless nights in one-night cheap hotels
And sawdust restaurants with oyster-shells:
Streets that follow like a tedious argument
Of insidious intent
To lead you to an overwhelming question . . .   10

---

[1] If I believed that my answer might belong
To anyone who ever returned to the world,
This flame would leap no more.
But since, however, from these depths
No one ever returns alive, if I know the truth,
Then without fear of infamy I answer you.
                    Dante, *Inferno*, xxvii, 61–66.

Oh, do not ask 'What is it?'
Let us go and make our visit.

In the room the women come and go
Talking of Michelangelo.

The yellow fog that rubs its back upon the
    window-panes,   15
The yellow smoke that rubs its muzzle on the
    window-panes,
Licked its tongue into the corners of the
    evening,
Lingered upon the pools that stand in drains,
Let fall upon its back the soot that falls from
    chimneys,
Slipped by the terrace, made a sudden leap,   20
And seeing that it was a soft October night,
Curled once about the house, and fell asleep.

And indeed there will be time
For the yellow smoke that slides along the street
Rubbing its back upon the window-panes;   25
There will be time, there will be time
To prepare a face to meet the faces that you
    meet;
There will be time to murder and create,
And time for all the works and days of hands
That lift and drop a question on your plate;   30
Time for you and time for me,
And time yet for a hundred indecisions,
And for a hundred visions and revisions,
Before the taking of a toast and tea.

In the room the women come and go   35
Talking of Michelangelo.

And indeed there will be time
To wonder, 'Do I dare?' and, 'Do I dare?'
Time to turn back and descend the stair,
With a bald spot in the middle of my hair—   40
(They will say: 'How his hair is growing thin!')
My morning coat, my collar mounting firmly to
    the chin,
My necktie rich and modest, but asserted by a
    simple pin—
(They will say: 'But how his arms and legs are
    thin!')
Do I dare   45
Disturb the universe?
In a minute there is time
For decisions and revisions which a minute will
    reverse.

For I have known them all already, known them
    all—
Have known the evenings, mornings, after-
    noons,   50
I have measured out my life with coffee spoons;
I know the voices dying with a dying fall
Beneath the music from a farther room.
    So how should I presume?

And I have known the eyes already, known them
    all—   55
The eyes that fix you in a formulated phrase,
And when I am formulated, sprawling on a pin,
When I am pinned and wriggling on the wall,
Then how should I begin
To spit out all the butt-ends of my days and
    ways?   60
    And how should I presume?

And I have known the arms already, known
    them all—
Arms that are braceleted and white and bare
(But in the lamplight, downed with light brown
    hair!)
Is it perfume from a dress   65
That makes me so digress?
Arms that lie along a table, or wrap about a
    shawl.
    And should I then presume?
    And how should I begin?

    .   .   .   .   .

Shall I say, I have gone at dusk through narrow
    streets   70
And watched the smoke that rises from the pipes
Of lonely men in shirt-sleeves, leaning out of
    windows? . . .

I should have been a pair of ragged claws
Scuttling across the floors of silent seas.

    .   .   .   .   .

And the afternoon, the evening, sleeps so peace-
    fully!   75
Smoothed by long fingers,
Asleep . . . tired . . . or it malingers,
Stretched on the floor, here beside you and me.
Should I, after tea and cakes and ices,

Have the strength to force the moment to its
    crisis? 80
But though I have wept and fasted, wept and
    prayed,
Though I have seen my head (grown slightly
    bald) brought in upon a platter,
I am no prophet—and here's no great matter;
I have seen the moment of my greatness flicker,
And I have seen the eternal Footman hold my
    coat, and snicker, 85
And in short, I was afraid.

And would it have been worth it, after all,
After the cups, the marmalade, the tea,
Among the porcelain, among some talk of you
    and me,
Would it have been worth while, 90
To have bitten off the matter with a smile,
To have squeezed the universe into a ball [2]
To roll it towards some overwhelming question,
To say: 'I am Lazarus, come from the dead,
Come back to tell you all, I shall tell you all'— 95
If one, settling a pillow by her head,
    Should say: 'That is not what I meant at all.
    That is not it, at all.'

And would it have been worth it, after all,
Would it have been worth while, 100
After the sunsets and the dooryards and the
    sprinkled streets,
After the novels, after the teacups, after the
    skirts that trail along the floor—
And this, and so much more?—
It is impossible to say just what I mean!
But as if a magic lantern threw the nerves in
    patterns on a screen: 105
Would it have been worth while
If one, settling a pillow or throwing off a shawl,
And turning toward the window, should say:
    'That is not it at all,
    That is not what I meant, at all.' 110

    . . . . .

No! I am not Prince Hamlet, nor was meant to
    be;
Am an attendant lord, one that will do
To swell a progress, start a scene or two,
Advise the prince; no doubt, an easy tool,

[2] See Marvell's "To His Coy Mistress," ll. 41–42,
p. 301.

Deferential, glad to be of use, 115
Politic, cautious, and meticulous;
Full of high sentence, but a bit obtuse;
At times, indeed, almost ridiculous—
Almost, at times, the Fool.

I grow old . . I grow old . . . 120
I shall wear the bottoms of my trousers rolled.

Shall I part my hair behind? Do I dare to eat
    a peach?
I shall wear white flannel trousers, and walk
    upon the beach.
I have heard the mermaids singing, each to each.

I do not think that they will sing to me. 125

I have seen them riding seaward on the waves
Combing the white hair of the waves blown back
When the wind blows the water white and black.

We have lingered in the chambers of the sea
By sea-girls wreathed with seaweed red and
    brown 130
Till human voices wake us, and we drown.

Comments

What we learned about modern poetry from reading MacLeish's "Ars Poetica" (p. 286) will help us to read Eliot's poem. Four matters are very important. First, most of Eliot's symbols are textual (personal). They are not conventional symbols whose meanings are immediately apparent; they must be understood in the complete text of the poem. Second, Eliot does not provide transitions between the scenes of his story; whatever logical sequence exists is implied, not stated. Note the absence of any conventional transition, for example, between lines 12 and 13. The transitions are implicit in the meaning of the poem. Third, Eliot uses the method of dramatic opposition, and this method, once understood, will help us to make the transitions between apparently unrelated scenes. Prufrock is opposed to Michaelangelo, John the Baptist, Lazarus, Shakespeare, in order to contrast sharply the great values of the past with those represented by Prufrock. And fourth, Eliot uses a method he calls the "objective correlative" by which he dramatizes sensations, emotions, and feelings through "a set of objects, a situation, a chain of events. . . ." For example, instead of having Prufrock tell us directly that he has wasted his life in frivolous activity, Eliot has him say, "I have measured out my life with coffee spoons," and we participate in Prufrock's emotion of frustration. By correlating Prufrock's frustration with the objective act of measuring out his life in useless activity, Eliot dramatizes Prufrock's sensations.

Two facts about the poem should help us get started: it is a soliloquy, and the title is ironic. The action takes place in Prufrock's mind where Eliot objectifies Prufrock's neurotic self. The love song is a far cry from those we have read by Shakespeare, Herrick, Marvell, Landor, and others. The poem is in effect a psychological self-analysis of a man who is incapable of love, physically and spiritually, who cannot "force the moment to its crisis," who is "in short . . . afraid." He is a man divided, like Hamlet, but unlike Hamlet he never welds himself together for any heroic action; he does not "Have the strength to force the moment to its crisis."

Sonnet 55: Not Marble, nor the Gilded Monuments

WILLIAM SHAKESPEARE
1564–1616

Not marble, nor the gilded monuments
Of princes, shall outlive this powerful rhyme;
But you shall shine more bright in these contents[1]
Than unswept stone,[2] besmeared with sluttish time.
When wasteful war shall statues overturn,   5
And broils[3] root out the work of masonry,
Nor Mars his sword nor war's quick fire shall burn
The living record of your memory.
'Gainst death and all-oblivious enmity

[1] Verses.   [2] Stone monument unswept by time.
[3] Tumult.

Shall you pace forth; your praise shall still find room   10
Even in the eyes of all posterity
That wear this world out to the ending doom.[4]
  So, till the judgment[5] that yourself arise,
  You live in this, and dwell in lovers' eyes.

Comments

Love poetry, always dominant in the history of literature, is of course an exploration of psychological values. Nothing is more personal than the love experience, nothing operates with greater impact on personality, nothing is so subtle in its influence on human character. In this sonnet Shakespeare's attitude toward love is highly complimentary. Let us compare his attitude with MacLeish's below.

"Not Marble nor the Gilded Monuments"

ARCHIBALD MacLEISH
1892–

The praisers of women in their proud and beautiful poems,
Naming the grave mouth and the hair and the eyes,
Boasted those they love should be forever remembered:
These were lies.

The words sound but the face in the Istrian[1] sun is forgotten.   5
The poet speaks but to her dead ears no more.
The sleek throat is gone—and the breast that was troubled to listen:
Shadow from door.

Therefore I will not praise your knees nor your fine walking
Telling you men shall remember your name as long   10

[4] Last Judgment.   [5] Till Judgment Day.
[1] Istria, a peninsula in northeast "Sunny Italy."

As lips move or breath is spent or the iron of
    English
Rings from a tongue.

I shall say you were young, and your arms
    straight, and your mouth scarlet:
I shall say you will die and none will remember
    you:
Your arms change, and none remember the swish
    of your garments,   15
Nor the click of your shoe.

Not with my hand's strength, not with difficult
    labor
Springing the obstinate words to the bones of
    your breast
And the stubborn line to your young stride and
    the breath to your breathing
And the beat to your haste   20
Shall I prevail on the hearts of unborn men to
    remember.

(What is a dead girl but a shadowy ghost
Or a dead man's voice but a distant and vain
    affirmation
Like dream words most)

Therefore I will not speak of the undying glory
    of women.   25
I will say you were young and straight and your
    skin fair
And you stood in the door and the sun was a
    shadow of leaves on your shoulders
And a leaf on your hair—

I will not speak of the famous beauty of dead
    women:
I will say the shape of a leaf lay once on your
    hair.   30
Till the world ends and the eyes are out and the
    mouths broken
Look! It is there!

THE INDIVIDUAL AND SOCIETY: SOCIAL VALUES

Social values are likely to emerge from poetry whenever a poet explores the relationships of the individual and society, especially when the needs of the individual differ from the demands of society. Although social values have appeared in the poetry of every age, they have become more prominent since the convergence of modern democracy, industrial civilization, and modern science. In the older agrarian societies, personal and social morals tended to coalesce, but in our industrial civilization private and public morals seem to grow further apart, and the repercussions of this conflict find their way into imaginative literature.

The poems in this subsection are concerned chiefly with the theme of a democratic morality which always honors, of course, the dignity of the individual and the preservation of his social rights and responsibilities.

Lines Written in Early Spring
WILLIAM WORDSWORTH
1770–1850

I heard a thousand blended notes,
While in a grove I sate reclined,
In that sweet mood when pleasant thoughts
Bring sad thoughts to the mind.

To her fair works did Nature link   5
The human soul that through me ran;
And much it grieved my heart to think
What man has made of man.

Through primrose tufts, in that green bower,
The periwinkle trailed its wreaths;   10
And 'tis my faith that every flower
Enjoys the air it breathes.

The birds around me hopped and played,
Their thoughts I cannot measure:—
But the least motion which they made,   15
It seemed a thrill of pleasure.

The budding twigs spread out their fan,
To catch the breezy air;
And I must think, do all I can,
That there was pleasure there.   20

If this belief from heaven be sent,
If such be Nature's holy plan,
Have I not reason to lament
What man has made of man?

Wordsworth seems to have raised the right question. The poets to follow furnish a variety of comments on what man has made of man.

The Dinner-Party

AMY LOWELL
1874–1925

FISH

"So . . ." they said,
With their wine-glasses delicately poised,
Mocking at the thing they cannot understand.
"So . . . " they said again,
Amused and insolent.   5
The silver on the table glittered,
And the red wine in the glasses
Seemed the blood I had wasted
In a foolish cause.

GAME

The   gentleman   with   the   grey-and-black
        whiskers   10
Sneered languidly over his quail.
Then my heart flew up and labored,
Then I burst from my own holding
And hurled myself forward.
With straight blows I beat upon him,   15
Furiously, with red-hot anger, I thrust against
        him.
But my weapon slithered over his polished sur-
        face,
And I recoiled upon myself,
Panting.

DRAWING-ROOM

In a dress all softness and half-tones,   20
Indolent and half-reclined,
She lay upon a couch,
With the firelight reflected in her jewels.
But her eyes had no reflection,
They swam in a grey smoke,   25
The smoke of smoldering ashes,
The smoke of her cindered heart.

COFFEE

They sat in a circle with their coffee-cups.
One dropped in a lump of sugar,
One stirred with a spoon.   30
I saw them as a circle of ghosts
Sipping blackness out of beautiful china,
And mildly protesting against my coarseness
In being alive.

TALK

They took dead men's souls   35
And pinned them on their breasts for ornament;
Their cuff-links and tiaras
Were gems dug from a grave;
They   were   ghouls   battening   on   exhumed
        thoughts;
And I took a green liqueur from a servant   40
So that he might come near me
And give me the comfort of a living thing.

ELEVEN O'CLOCK

The front door was hard and heavy,
It shut behind me on the house of ghosts.
I flattened my feet on the pavement   45
To feel it solid under me;
I ran my hand along the railings
And shook them,
And pressed their pointed bars
Into my palms.   50
The hurt of it reassured me,
And I did it again and again
Until they were bruised.
When I woke in the night
I laughed to find them aching,   55
For only living flesh can suffer.

Comments and Questions

The poet assumes that a democratic morality, discussed briefly above (p. 308), is a valuable code to live by. She assumes that social well-being, or the happiness of humanity, depends upon the sympathetic contact of all members of the community. The guests at the dinner party act upon no such assumption, and their violation of the democratic morality creates certain consequences exhibited in the poem. The guests' feeling of class superiority denies them not only sympathy for humanity, but—and more important —it perverts their own humanity as well. Their tragedy lies in their being unable to see that their attitude toward mankind corrupts themselves.

1. In what ways does the technique in this poem resemble that used in Eliot's "The Love Song of J. Alfred Prufrock" (p. 304)? Consider the use of image, symbol, and especially dramatic opposition.

2. What is the full meaning of the last line in the poem?

Centennial of Shiloh[1]

NANCY PRICE
1925–

Now Shiloh seems as old as Marathon;
each battle wears the other's somber face.
With names like watchfires: Waterloo, Verdun,
Troy, Hastings, Dunkirk, Crecy, Lexington,
the   ancient   slaughters   keep   an   austere
                         grace.   5

Naked as youths by Michelangelo
engraved on battlefields, or winged like birds,
or submarine as fish, men still would know
death when they saw him. Through the night at
                         Shiloh
the dying sang; everyone knew the words.   10

For the kilomegaton voice, the bombsight eye

[1] Shiloh: The site in Tennessee of a famous battle of the United States Civil War, April 6–7, 1862.

where are the words, the tune we can recall?
One hundred years from Shiloh cities die
under the faceless, detonated sky
where death spreads like a cloud, a drifting
                         pall   15
that has no name, no human shape at all.

Comments and Questions

A perceptive critic writes about this poem:

> The point of the poem is that, until the present, battle's "somber face" has always had at least an "austere grace." Even in its brutality, war remained comprehensible and in a way personal. But now the voice of battle speaks with a kilomegaton of force, the eye is that of the bombsight, and the death-dealing radioactive cloud is ". . . a drifting pall/ that has no name, no human shape at all." Hardly anything could better suggest the dreadful apocalypse of a world whose values have depreciated to a point where an atomic war is possible.*

1. On one level, then, we learn from the poem how the tragedy of war has been driven more deeply into the life of mankind. Is there another level of meaning in the poem?

2. The phrases, "the faceless, detonated sky" and "no human shape at all" are powerfully suggestive. Is war itself used as a symbol to suggest what is happening to modern man in peace as well as in war? Is *the* upsetting symbol "faceless"? We see again the penetration of the symbol in poetry.

* Edwin J. Maurer, *Midwest, A Literary Review*, Spring 1964.

Movie Actress

KARL SHAPIRO
1913–

I sit a queen, and am no widow, and shall see no sorrow

She is young and lies curved on the velvety floor of her fame
Like a prize-winning cat on a mirror of fire and oak,
And her dreams are as black as the Jew who uncovered her name;

She is folded in magic and hushed in the pride of her cloak
Which is woven of worship like silk for the hollows of eyes   5
That are raised in the dark to her image that shimmered and spoke;

And she speaks in her darkness alone and her emptiness cries
Till her voice is as shuddering tin in the wings of a stage,
And her beauty seems wrong as the wig of a perfect disguise;

She is sick with the shadow of shadow, diseased with the rage   10
Of the whiteness of light and the heat of interior sun,
And she faints like a pauper to carry the weight of her wage;

She is coarse with the honors of power, the duties of fun
And amazed at the regions of pleasure where skill is begun.

Shine, Republic
ROBINSON JEFFERS
1887–1962

The quality of these trees, green height; of the sky, shining; of water, a clear flow; of
        the rock, hardness
And reticence: each is noble in its quality. The love of freedom has been the quality
        of Western man.

There is a stubborn torch that flames from Marathon to Concord, its dangerous beauty
        binding three ages
Into one time; the waves of barbarism and civilization have eclipsed but have never
        quenched it.

For the Greeks the love of beauty, for Rome of ruling; for the present age the pas-
        sionate love of discovery;   5
But in one noble passion we are one; and Washington, Luther, Tacitus, Aeschylus,
        one kind of man.

And you, America, that passion made you. You were not born to prosperity, you were
        born to love freedom.
You did not say "en masse," you said "independence." But we cannot have all the
        luxuries and freedom also.

Freedom is poor and laborious; that torch is not safe but hungry, and often requires
        blood for its fuel.
You will tame it against it burn too clearly, you will hood it like a kept hawk, you will
        perch it on the wrist of Caesar.   10

But keep the tradition, conserve the forms, the observances, keep the spot sore. Be
        great, carve deep your heel-marks.
The states of the next age will no doubt remember you, and edge their love of free-
        dom with contempt of luxury.

Comments and Questions

1. It has been said that "the proper study of Americans is liberty." Roughly, Jeffers' poem says the same thing, but what *precisely* does the poem say?

2. Stanza 4 contains attitudes which Jeffers expresses in many poems. Is he right?

Shine, Perishing Republic

ROBINSON JEFFERS
1887–1962

While this America settles in the mould of its vulgarity, heavily thickening to empire,
And protest, only a bubble in the molten mass, pops and sighs out, and the mass hardens,

I sadly smiling remember that the flower fades to make fruit, the fruit rots to make
        earth.
Out of the mother; and through the spring exultances, ripeness and decadence; and
        home to the mother.

You making haste haste on decay; not blameworthy; life is good, be it stubbornly long
        or suddenly   5
A mortal splendor: meteors are not needed less than mountains: shine, perishing
        republic.

But for my children, I would have them keep their distance from the thickening center;
        corruption
Never has been compulsory, when the cities lie at the monster's feet there are left the
        mountains.

And boys, be in nothing so moderate as in love of man, a clever servant, insufferable
        master.
There is the trap that catches noblest spirits, that caught—they say—God, when he
        walked on earth.   10

Comments and Questions

The British writer W. Somerset Maugham (1874–1965) is reported to have said, "If a nation values anything more than freedom, it will lose its freedom; and if it is comfort or money that it values more, it will lose that, too." This statement can be used as a steppingstone from Jeffers' "Shine, Republic" to his poem above. In the latter poem Jeffers finds America on the way to empire because she has given up the "passion" for freedom that has made her. Students of Jeffers recognize his basic pattern of belief in this area as something like this: Civilizations have always risen and inevitably fallen, this cycle always moving from east to west. (See Oswald Spengler's *The Decline of the West*, 1918–1922, a book which is said to have influenced Jeffers.) Why do civilizations fall? Freedom and wealth are irreconcilable, according to Jeffers, because man is driven by desire (self-love) to achieve power over his fellow man, and he will sell his freedom to achieve it. Men and their nations therefore travel the cycle of freedom, desire, wealth, loss of freedom, and ruin. Men then travel westward—as the Pilgrims and others did in the early seventeenth century; they fight to regain their freedom, win it, and travel the cycle to ruin once more. The implication of the two poems above is clear: America is next.

1. Is agreement with Jeffers' point of view necessary to the enjoyment of his art?

2. What are the essential characteristics of his art as they differ from those of almost all other poems in this section? Jeffers has said that "a tidal recurrence is the one essential quality of the speech of poetry." How appropriate is Jeffers' free verse in the two poems above? If it illustrates his quoted statement, show how.

3. Note how Jeffers thinks in images, and how logically those images progress from line to line. Trace this progress of image-thinking through "Shine, Perishing Republic." (You may want to read one other poem by Jeffers, "Shine, Empire," which, with the two poems just quoted, form a little trilogy. It hardly possesses the poetic quality of the other two, but it does conclude the matter for Jeffers.)

From The People, Yes

CARL SANDBURG
1878–1967

The passages have been taken from Carl Sandburg's long poem, *The People, Yes.* Walt Whitman, who asked repeatedly for a poet to represent the common people, said that "Literature, strictly considered, has never recognized the People. . . . I know of nothing more rare, even in this country, than a fit scientific estimate and reverent appreciation of the People. . . .," Whitman would have welcomed Sandburg.

The People, Yes can be read, for the most part, as a soliloquy spoken by the people. Sandburg has presented in free-verse lines the attitudes, hopes, and in some instances the actual talk of common folk. We shall recognize many of our common proverbs although we may not have realized before the extent of their poetic quality.

Section 1

From the four corners of the earth,
from corners lashed in wind
and bitten with rain and fire,
from places where the winds begin
and fogs are born with mist children,   5
tall men from tall rocky slopes came
and sleepy men from sleepy valleys,
their women tall, their women sleepy,
with bundles and belongings,
with little ones babbling, "Where to now?   10
   what next?"

The people of the earth, the family of man,
wanted to put up something proud to look at,
a tower from the flat land of earth
on up through the ceiling into the top of the sky.

And the big job got going,   15
   the caissons and pilings sunk,

floors, walls and winding staircases
aimed at the stars high over,
aimed to go beyond the ladders of the moon.

And God Almighty could have struck them dead   20
or smitten them deaf and dumb.

And God was a whimsical fixer.
God was an understanding Boss
with another plan in mind,
And suddenly shuffled all the languages,   25
    changed the tongues of men
    so they all talked different
And the masons couldn't get what the hodcarriers said,
The helpers handed the carpenters the wrong tools,
Five hundred ways to say, "Who are you?"
Changed ways of asking, "Where do we go from here?"
Or of saying, "Being born is only the beginning,"   30
Or, "Would you just as soon sing as make that noise?"
Or, "What you don't know won't hurt you."
And the material-and-supply men started disputes
With the hauling gangs and the building trades
And the architects tore their hair over the blueprints   35
And the brickmakers and the mule skinners talked back
To the straw bosses who talked back to the superintendents
And the signals got mixed; the men who shovelled the bucket
Hooted the hoisting men—and the job was wrecked.

Some called it the Tower of Babel job[1]   40
And the people gave it many other names.
The wreck of it stood as a skull and a ghost,
a memorandum hardly begun,
swaying and sagging in tall hostile winds,
held up by slow friendly winds.   45

From *Section 29*

The people, yes—
Born with bones and heart fused in deep and violent secrets
Mixed from a bowl of sky blue dreams and sea slime facts—
A seething of saints and sinners, toilers, loafers, oxen, apes
In a womb of superstition, faith, genius, crime, sacrifice—   5
The one and only source of armies, navies, work-gangs,
The living flowing breath of the history of nations,
Of the little Family of Man hugging the little ball of Earth,
And a long hall of mirrors, straight, convex and concave,
Moving and endless with scrolls of the living,   10
Shimmering with phantoms flung from the past,
Shot over with lights of babies to come, not yet here.

[1] See p. 408, footnote 2 for comment on the Tower of Babel.

From *Section 30*

We'll see what we'll see.
Time is a great teacher.
Today me and tomorrow maybe you.
This old anvil laughs at many broken hammers.
What is bitter to stand against today may be sweet to remember tomorrow.   5
Fine words butter no parsnips. Moonlight dries no mittens.
Whether the stone bumps the jug or the jug bumps the stone it is bad for the jug.
One hand washes the other and both wash the face.
Better leave the child's nose dirty than wring it off.
We all belong to the same big family and have the same smell.   10
Handling honey, tar or dung some of it sticks to the fingers.
      The liar comes to believe his own lies.
He who burns himself must sit on the blisters.
      God alone understands fools.
The dumb mother understands the dumb child.   15
To work hard, to live hard, to die hard, and then to go to hell after all would be too
      damned hard.
You can fool all the people part of the time and part of the people all the time but you
      can't fool all the people all of the time.
It takes all kinds of people to make a world.

What is bred in the bone will tell.
Between the inbreds and the cross-breeds the argument goes on.   20
You can breed them up as easy as you can breed them down.
"I don't know who my ancestors were," said a mongrel, "but we've been descend-
      ing for a long time."
"My ancestors," said the Cherokee-blooded Oklahoman, "didn't come over in the
      Mayflower but we was there to meet the boat."

From *Section 31*

"Your low birth puts you beneath me,"
said Harmodius, Iphicrates replying,
"The difference between us is this.
   My family begins with me.
   Yours ends with you."   5

From *Section 41*

"Why did the children
put beans in their ears
when the one thing we told the children
they must not do
was put beans in their ears?"   5

"Why did the children
pour molasses on the cat
when the one thing we told the children
they must not do
was pour molasses on the cat?"   10

From *Section 50*

"Isn't that an iceberg on the horizon, Captain?"
"Yes, Madam."
"What if we get in a collision with it?"
"The iceberg, Madam, will move right along as though nothing had happened."

From *Section 86*

The people, yes, the people,
Until the people are taken care of one way or another,
Until the people are solved somehow for the day and hour,
Until then one hears "Yes but the people what about the people?"
Sometimes as though the people is a child to be pleased or fed   5
Or again a hoodlum you have to be tough with
And seldom as though the people is a caldron and a reservoir
Of the human reserves that shape history. . . .

"The czar has eight million men with guns and bayonets.
"Nothing can happen to the czar.   10
"The czar is the voice of God and shall live forever.
"Turn and look at the forest of steel and cannon
"Where the czar is guarded by eight million soldiers.
"Nothing can happen to the czar."
They said that for years and in the summer of 1914   15
In the year of Our Lord Nineteen Hundred and Fourteen
As a portent and an assurance they said with owl faces:
    "Nothing can happen to the czar."
Yet the czar and his bodyguard of eight million vanished
And the czar stood in a cellar before a little firing squad   20
And the command of fire was given
And the czar stepped into regions of mist and ice
The czar travelled into an ethereal uncharted siberia
While two kaisers also vanished from thrones
Ancient and established in blood and iron—   25
Two kaisers backed by ten million bayonets
Had their crowns in a gutter, their palaces mobbed.
    In fire, chaos, shadows,
In hurricanes beyond foretelling of probabilities,
In the shove and whirl of unforeseen combustions   30
    The people, yes, the people,
Move eternally in the elements of surprise,
Changing from hammer to bayonet and back to hammer,
The hallelujah chorus forever shifting its star soloists.

From *Section 107*

    The people will live on.
The learning and blundering people will live on.
    They will be tricked and sold and again sold
And go back to the nourishing earth for rootholds,
    The people so peculiar in renewal and comeback,   5
    You can't laugh off their capacity to take it.
The mammoth rests between his cyclonic dramas. . . .

This old anvil laughs at many broken hammers.
   There are men who can't be bought.
   The fireborn are at home in fire.   10
   The stars make no noise.
   You can't hinder the wind from blowing.
   Time is a great teacher.
   Who can live without hope?
In the darkness with a great bundle of grief the people march.   15
In the night, and overhead a shovel of stars for keeps, the people march:
                             "Where to? what next?"

The Gift Outright[1]

ROBERT FROST
1874–1963

In Frost's "An Extemporaneous Talk for Students" (p. 806) he says that this poem "is my story of the revolutionary war. . . . The dream was to occupy the land with character—that's another way to put it—to occupy a new land with character."

The land was ours before we were the land's.
She was our land more than a hundred years
Before we were her people. She was ours
In Massachusetts, in Virginia,
But we were England's, still colonials,   5
Possessing what we still were unpossessed by,
Possessed by what we now no more possessed.
Something we were withholding made[2] us weak
Until we found out that it was ourselves
We were withholding from our land of living,   10
And forthwith found salvation in surrender.
Such as we were we gave ourselves outright
(The deed of gift was many deeds of war)
To the land vaguely realizing westward,
But still unstoried, artless, unenhanced,   15
Such as she was, such as she would become.

[1] Read by Frost at the inauguration of John F. Kennedy as President of the United States, January 20, 1961.   [2] Although *made* is used in Frost's *Complete Poems* (Holt, Rinehart and Winston,

Carl Hamblin

EDGAR LEE MASTERS
1868–1950

The press of the Spoon River *Clarion* was
    wrecked,
And I was tarred and feathered,
For publishing this on the day the Anarchists
    were hanged in Chicago:
"I saw a beautiful woman with bandaged eyes
Standing on the steps of a marble temple.   5
Great multitudes passed in front of her,
Lifting their faces to her imploringly.
In her left hand she held a sword.
She was brandishing the sword,
Sometimes striking a child, again a
       laborer,   10
Again a slinking woman, again a lunatic.
In her right hand she held a scale;
Into the scale pieces of gold were tossed
By those who dodged the strokes of the sword.
A man in a black gown read from a manu-
    script: 15
'She is no respecter of persons.'
Then a youth wearing a red cap
Leaped to her side and snatched away the band-
    age.
And lo, the lashes had been eaten away
From the oozy eye-lids;   20
The eye-balls were seared with a milky mucus;
The madness of a dying soul
Was written on her face—
But the multitude saw why she wore the band-
    age."

1967, p. 467), Frost used *left* when he read the poem at President Kennedy's inauguration.

The Eagle That Is Forgotten[1]

VACHEL LINDSAY
1879–1931

(JOHN P. ALTGELD, BORN DECEMBER 30, 1847; DIED MARCH 12, 1902)

Sleep softly . . . eagle forgotten . . . under the stone.
Time has its way with you there, and the clay has its own.

"We have buried him now," thought your foes, and in secret rejoiced.
They made a brave show of their mourning, their hatred unvoiced.
They had snarled at you, barked at you, foamed at you day after day.   5
Now you were ended. They praised you, . . . and laid you away.

The others that mourned you in silence and terror and truth,
The widow bereft of her crust, and the boy without youth,
The mocked and the scorned and the wounded, the lame and the poor
That should have remembered forever, . . . remember no more.   10

Where are those lovers of yours, on what name do they call
The lost, that in armies wept over your funeral pall?
They call on the names of a hundred high-valiant ones,
A hundred white eagles have risen the sons of your sons,
The zeal in their wings is a zeal that your dreaming began   15
The valor that wore out your soul in the service of man.

Sleep softly, . . . eagle forgotten, . . . under the stone,
Time has its way with you there and the clay has its own.
Sleep on, O brave-hearted, O wise man, that kindled the flame—
To live in mankind is far more than to live in a name,   20
To live in mankind, far, far more . . . than to live in a name.

[1] As Governor of Illinois, Altgeld pardoned three anarchist leaders convicted of inciting the Haymarket Riot (May 4, 1886) in Chicago, referred to in Masters' "Carl Hamblin" (p. 317).

"THE TRIAL BY EXISTENCE": METAPHYSICAL VALUES

For many of our most fundamental and searching questions about life we have answers whose truth can be demonstrated beyond doubt. We no longer must *assume,* for example, that certain causes bring certain diseases; we *know* that such-and-such germs cause certain diseases. Science has provided the exact knowledge. But for other fundamental and searching questions we have no answers which can be verified beyond doubt. For example: Was the universe planned by a supreme being or was it an accident? Is death final or a passage to another life? What is the essential character of nature, and what can we learn from it?—is it something to follow, ignore or repel? Are we the victims of forces over which we have no control, or do we have some measure of free will? To summarize: What is the meaning of life? Is there any more basic question?

Where do we go for answers? It is possible to go to a branch of philosophy called metaphysics: no need to shy from a word which is quite easily understood. The word is of Greek origin, *meta*—beyond and *physikos*—external nature. That is, when we ask questions whose answers are to be looked for beyond the demonstrable knowledge grounded in physical or natural causes, we go to metaphysics. Metaphysics is the source of our *assumptions* about life, and we all live by certain assumptions whether or not we realize it. In religion we call them articles of faith. For example, if we assume that our earthly sins are punishable after death, certain consequences in our behavior are likely to follow immediately. If we assume no freedom to direct our own actions (freedom of will), other consequences are likely to follow, and so on.

Are you tempted to argue that such matters hardly concern you, that you know very well what to live for, and that nature and the universe can take care of themselves? True, they will take care of themselves, and of you, too—but will you be satisfied with the results? Will you be prepared to meet and absorb those results gracefully?

When verifiable scientific knowledge runs dry, we do not stop asking questions: in fact, some of the most important questions are still to be asked, and man has always insisted upon looking for answers. We shall see this insistence in the poets to follow. From its beginnings poetry has pursued metaphysical problems, and poets are often referred to as prophets. The Greek poets and dramatists dealt with the metaphysical and religious questions of their day; Milton's *Paradise Lost* is built on a pattern of metaphysical assumptions; and the poems below are nothing if not metaphysical in their implications.

The Secret Sits

ROBERT FROST
1874–1963

We dance round in a ring and suppose,
But the Secret sits in the middle and knows.

Truth

JAMES HEARST
1900–

How the devil do I know
if there are rocks in your field,
plow it and find out.
If the plow strikes something

harder than earth, the point   5
shatters at a sudden blow
and the tractor jerks sidewise
and dumps you off the seat—
because the spring hitch
isn't set to trip quickly enough   10
and it never is—probably
you hit a rock. That means
the glacier emptied his pocket
in your field as well as mine,
but the connection with a thing   15
is the only truth that I know of,
so plow it.

Because I Could Not Stop for Death

EMILY DICKINSON
1830–1886

Because I could not stop for Death—
He kindly stopped for me—
The Carriage held but just Ourselves—
And Immortality.

We slowly drove—He knew no haste   5
And I had put away
My labor and my leisure too,
For His Civility—

We passed the School, where Children strove
At Recess—in the Ring—   10
We passed the Fields of Gazing Grain—
We passed the Setting Sun—

Or rather—He passed Us—
The Dews drew quivering and chill—
For only Gossamer, my Gown—   15
My Tippet—only Tulle—

We paused before a House that seemed
A Swelling of the Ground—
The Roof was scarcely visible—
The Cornice—in the Ground—   20

Since then—'tis Centuries—and yet
Feels shorter than the Day
I first surmised the Horses Heads
Were toward Eternity—

Comments

We are all compelled finally to take some attitude toward death, and poets, too, have pursued the theme relentlessly. The conventional attitude toward death is often somber, awed, and hushed, but Emily Dickinson's attitude is hardly conventional. Death is here represented as the driver of a chariot who courts the lady by taking her for a drive; they are alone except for the passenger Immortality—what company could be more appropriate? Is the poet equating death with love? It seems so, but note that this idea is not pushed to sentimentality. Instead of drawing a commonplace moral from the situation she has created, she simply presents the situation. She presents it, in fact, a little ironically: death, in his "Civility," "kindly" stops for his beloved who puts aside both her "labor" and her "leisure." Could the arrival of death be more natural, less awesome? Stanzas 3–5 give us the sensation of passing from life to eternity, and finally (stanza 6) the realization that we were headed for eternity from the beginning of our life. Can we say that the poet's attitude toward death is sane and normal? She makes the process of passing from life to death seem natural, inevitable, and appropriate to life as we know it. At least, this is her assumption about the nature of death, and we are left free to contemplate it. We are left also, let it be said, with a beautiful poetic experience, regardless of our attitude toward her assumption.

Holy Sonnet, VII: At the Round Earth's Imagined Corners

JOHN DONNE
1572–1631

At the round earth's imagined corners,[1] blow
Your trumpets, angels; and arise, arise
From death, you numberless infinities
Of souls, and to your scattered bodies go;

[1] The earth conceived of as having four corners.

All whom the flood did, and fire shall o'er-
throw,   5
All whom war, dearth, age, agues, tyrannies,
Despair, law, chance hath slain, and you whose
eyes
Shall behold God and never taste death's woe.
But let them sleep, Lord, and me mourn a space,
For if above all these, my sins abound,   10
'Tis late to ask abundance of thy grace
When we are there; here on this lowly ground [2]
Teach me how to repent; for that's as good
As if thou'hadst sealed my pardon with thy
blood.[3]

Comments and Questions

As usual, Donne has used a highly concentrated rhetorical structure which must be read carefully, including the syntax on the literal level. For his poetic purposes, Donne invokes the angels to blow their trumpets to summon the dead to Judgment Day. The "numberless infinities of souls" are expected to return to their "scattered bodies" to be judged: some shall be condemned to "fire" and others "shall behold God and never taste death's woe." The octet is Donne's method of projecting himself, imaginatively, into Judgment Day, and this imaginative act causes him to consider his own sins, and by implication the earthly sins of all of us. Shall we rely on God's grace on Judgment Day, or repent and dissolve our sins here on earth? The implication of the poem is that we should do the latter.

1. What are Donne's two basic metaphysical assumptions?

2. If you cannot accept the assumption of Judgment Day as a reality, is the poem valueless to you? This question admits of at least two answers. We can say, of course, that agreement with a poem's meaning is not necessary to the appreciation of the poem as a *poem.* Let us assume that the sonnet is a fine poem, good art. Now, if we disagree with Donne's metaphysical assumption of Judgment Day, can we agree with the poem's meaning on the psychological level? Is it necessary—to put our point into nontheological terms—to accept the image of Judg-

[2] The earth.   [3] Christ's crucifixion.

ment Day to agree with Donne's second assumption that sins should be dissolved before death?

Brahma

RALPH WALDO EMERSON
1803–1882

If the red slayer think he slays,
  Or if the slain think he is slain,
They know not well the subtle ways
  I keep, and pass, and turn again.

Far or forgot to me is near;   5
  Shadow and sunlight are the same;
The vanished gods to me appear;
  And one to me are shame and fame.

They reckon ill who leave me out;
  When me they fly, I am the wings;   10
I am the doubter and the doubt,
  And I the hymn the Brahmin sings.

The strong gods pine for my abode,
  And pine in vain the sacred Seven;[1]
But thou, meek lover of the good!   15
  Find me, and turn thy back on heaven.

Comments and Questions

"Brahma" has troubled many Western readers for over a century although the Asian Indian student seems to absorb it with little difficulty.* The poem is one more attempt to understand the relationships among God, man (body *and* soul), and nature. It is one more attempt of the finite mind which is lim-

[1] The highest saints in Brahminism, none of them Brahma.
* The editors are indebted to S. P. Misra, Professor of English and Head of the Department of English and Modern European Languages, Gorakhpur University, India; and to Mrs. Mavis Ulrick, Senior Lecturer in English, Baikunthi Devi Kanya College, Agra, India, a visiting teacher of English at the University of Northern Iowa, 1963–1964, for help with this poem. "Brahma" is probably the best-known and most-analyzed American poem in the Indian universities today.

ited by space and time to place itself in infinity which, of course, is not limited by space and time.

"Brahma" is a fusion of Hindu religion and Emerson's Transcendentalism. Its paradoxes (see p. 284) all come from the basic assumption of the unity of all existence: that God (Brahma), man, the soul, and nature are *one,* and if the reader of the poem will keep in mind the *image of the circle* to represent this unity, he is on his way. This unity, or circle, Emerson calls "the perfect whole,"** meaning as he says,

Line in nature is not found;
Unit and universe are round. . . . ("Uriel")

Emerson can therefore say about each one of us as he says of himself, "the currents of the Universal Being circulate through me; I am part or parcel of God." Hence, as the paradoxes of the poem indicate, there is no death, no distance, no time, no fragments of God, man, and nature. Instead there is harmony of all, no beginning, no end—the circle. Such things as distance and time have been invented by man to administer his daily life, but they must be laid aside to penetrate his nature and destiny.

1. All this is not to say that we can understand this poem through a trance or mystical osmosis. There are facts and concrete references to be understood. Who is Brahma?—simply to substitute your God may not be the answer. Who are the sacred Seven? And why seven? Why not eight?—is there something significant about the *number* seven? Why *"meek* lover of the good"? It is not necessary to guess the meaning of these references: we can *know.*

2. Why should Brahma advise us to turn our back on "heaven"? Is Brahma's heaven of a different kind? If the sacred Seven, each with a planet as a heaven for himself, pine for Brahma's abode, what do they pine for?

3. For help in answering that question we can go to the Hindu *Bhagavadgītā* (c. fifth century B.C.), a popular religious and philosophical poem: "He who does work for Me, he who looks upon Me as his goal, he who

** See Emerson's "Each and All" (p. 340), especially the final line.

worships Me, free from attachment, he who is free from enmity to all creatures, he goes to me. . . ." (XI, 55). One interpreter, S. Radhakrishnan, observes: "This verse is the substance of the whole teaching of the *Gīta*. We must carry out our duties, directing the spirit to God and with detachment from all interest in the things of the world and free from enmity towards any living being." Could Brahma's abode be immortality, not merely personal immortality, but rather the continuity of all life? Confirm your answer with reference to the *entire* poem.

Hap[1]
THOMAS HARDY
1840–1928

If but some vengeful god would call to me
From up the sky, and laugh: "Thou suffering
      thing,
Know that thy sorrow is my ecstasy,
That thy love's loss is my hate's profiting!"
Then would I bear it, clench myself, and die,   5
Steeled by the sense of ire unmerited;
Half-eased in that a Powerfuller than I
Had willed and meted me the tears I shed.

But not so. How arrives it joy lies slain,
And   why   unblooms   the   best   hope   ever
      sown?   10
—Crass Casualty obstructs the sun and rain,
And dicing Time for gladness casts a moan. . . .
These purblind Doomsters had as readily strown
Blisses about my pilgrimage as pain.

The Trial by Existence[1]
ROBERT FROST
1874–1963

[1]
Even the bravest that are slain
   Shall not dissemble their surprise
On waking to find valor reign,
   Even as on earth, in paradise;

[1] Chance, haphazard.
[1] See *John*, 3:13, 6:61 ff; and *Ephesians*, 4:1 ff.

And where they sought without the sword   5
   Wide fields of asphodel fore'er,
To find that the utmost reward
   Of daring should be still to dare.

[2]
The light of heaven falls whole and white
   And is not shattered into dyes,   10
The light for ever is morning light;
   The hills are verdured pasture-wise;
The angel hosts with freshness go,
   And seek with laughter what to brave—
And binding all is the hushed snow   15
   Of the far-distant breaking wave.

[3]
And from a clifftop is proclaimed
   The gathering of the souls for birth,
The trial by existence named,
   The obscuration upon earth.   20
And the slant spirits trooping by
   In streams and cross- and counter-streams
Can but give ear to that sweet cry
   For its suggestion of what dreams!

[4]
And the more loitering are turned   25
   To view once more the sacrifice
Of those who for some good discerned
   Will gladly give up paradise.
And a white shimmering concourse rolls
   Toward the throne to witness there   30
The speeding of devoted souls
   Which God makes His especial care.

[5]
And none are taken but who will,
   Having first heard the life read out
That opens earthward, good and ill,   35
   Beyond the shadow of a doubt;
And very beautifully God limns,
   And tenderly, life's little dream,
But naught extenuates or dims,
   Setting the thing that is supreme.   40

[6]
Nor is there wanting in the press
   Some spirit to stand simply forth,
Heroic in its nakedness,
   Against the uttermost of earth.
The tale of earth's unhonored things   45
   Sounds nobler there than 'neath the sun;

And the mind whirls and the heart sings,
    And a shout greets the daring one.

[7]

But always God speaks at the end:
    "One thought in agony of strife   50
The bravest would have by for friend,
    The memory that he chose the life;
But the pure fate to which you go
    Admits no memory of choice,
Or the woe were not earthly woe   55
    To which you give the assenting voice."

[8]

And so the choice must be again,
    But the last choice is still the same;
And the awe passes wonder then,
    And a hush falls for all acclaim.   60
And God has taken a flower of gold
    And broken it, and used therefrom
The mystic link to bind and hold
    Spirit to matter till death come.

[9]

'Tis of the essence of life here,   65
    Though we choose greatly, still to lack
The lasting memory at all clear,
    That life has for us on the wrack
Nothing but what we somehow chose;
    Thus are we wholly stripped of pride   70
In the pain that has but one close,
    Bearing it crushed and mystified.

Comments and Questions

We have seen above how Emerson and Hardy have met the question of the meaning of life. Emerson would have us find its meaning by finding God within ourselves; Hardy finds no meaning that a rational man can accept; and Frost rejects the metaphysics of both of them.

For Frost, as for many of us, the meaning of life is a big question mark. In a poem published years after the appearance of "The Trial by Existence," Frost could conclude that "the strong are saying nothing until they see."* We recall his couplet (p. 319):

We dance round in a ring and suppose,
But the Secret sits in the middle and knows.

Nevertheless, he keeps after the Secret to find at least "enough to go on." Regardless

* See p. 358 for the poem.

of our opinion of Hardy's conclusion in "Hap," he raises the dogging question,

How arrives it joy lies slain,
And why unblooms the best hope ever sown?

"The Trial by Existence" is one of Frost's ways of getting at the question.

In few poems has he been so direct, and without a trace of his customary light satiric smile. Observe the conventional line and stanza form, and the scarcity of the Frost idiom and bantering tone. Here he seems to feel the need of all the conventional stability he can muster to support a metaphysic which would not appeal to an audience brought up on Longfellow. In one respect the tone is characteristic: Is he saying that with this poem *he* will stand "against the uttermost of earth"? He always has, and this poem may be part of his early creed, never later altered.

Suppose we regard the poem as a parable, or perhaps better a fable—a fictitious story used to illustrate certain assumptions and conclusions. Stanzas 3–8 present a little drama in six scenes; the other stanzas present Frost's assumptions and conclusions. The point of departure in his thinking is pretty clear: he intends to examine our easy assumption which holds that although life on earth is very often tragic and baffling, paradise will be quite a different matter.

In stanza 1 he is quick to say that "even the bravest that are slain" on earth should not be surprised to find *even* in paradise that "the utmost reward / Of daring should be still to dare." Stanza 2 describes heaven, and, by contrast, the earth. In heaven it is possible to see clearly and to understand the nature of things—there the secret becomes clear; but on earth the "light" *is* "shattered into dyes," and the whites, grays, and blacks intermingle to veil the secret.

The little drama in stanzas 3–8 is designed by Frost as a parable to illustrate his assumption about life, found in stanza 9. In stanza 3 the souls gather for birth, which is a joyous occasion for those who have endured the "trial by existence" and have returned to heaven (ll. 21–24). Stanzas 4 and 5 underscore the circumstances of "birth." The souls exercise freedom of choice: "for some good discerned" they "will gladly give up paradise." That the trial and "sacrifice" are freely chosen (the doctrine of free will as opposed to fatalism or determinism) is a cardinal assumption in the poem. Stanza 5 makes clear that no warning by God about "life's little dream" can diminish the enthusiasm of those who have chosen the trial. There is always the eager one, says stanza 6, ready to stand "against the uttermost of earth." God warns the departing souls (stanza 7) that part of their "earthly woe" will be in their not remembering they have chosen the trial. Stanza 8 rounds off the dramatic action of the parable as God the creator furnishes the "mystic link"—the pulse of life—to fuse the daring spirit and the willing flesh until death comes on earth.

Having finished his parable, Frost draws his conclusions from it in stanza 9: We are "crushed and mystified" by the "pain" of the "trial by existence" because we forget, or ignore, that the gift of free will includes the responsibilities for our choices. No need, implies Frost, for Hardy to shout abuse at "some vengeful god": whatever "life has for us on the wrack" there is "nothing but what we somehow chose."

1. The poem has at least a score of implications, as a thoughtful poem usually does. What evidence is there that Frost is not merely rationalizing but is getting at something important?

2. In lines 27–28 Frost says that the souls "for some good discerned / Will gladly give up paradise." Has the word "paradise" more than one meaning here?

3. What would J. Alfred Prufrock think of the notion of standing "against the uttermost of earth"? (See p. 304.)

Dying Speech of an Old Philosopher[1]
WALTER SAVAGE LANDOR
1775–1864

I strove with none, for none was worth my strife:
   Nature I loved, and, next to Nature, Art:

[1] Written on his seventy-fourth birthday, 1849.

I warm'd both hands before the fire of Life;
   It sinks; and I am ready to depart.

THE DIMENSIONS OF POETIC EXPERIENCE

Western Wind, When Wilt Thou Blow
ANONYMOUS

Western wind, when wilt thou blow,
The small rain down can rain?
Christ, if my love were in my arms,
And I in my bed again!

Jolly Good Ale and Old
ANONYMOUS

I cannot eat but little meat,
   My stomach is not good;
But sure I think that I can drink
   With him that wears a hood.
Though I go bare, take ye no care,   5
   I nothing am a-cold;
I stuff my skin so full within
   Of jolly good ale and old,

     Back and side go bare, go bare;
     Both foot and hand go cold;   10
     But, belly, God send thee good ale
       enough,
     Whether it be new or old.

I love no roast but a nut-brown toast,
   And a crab[1] laid in the fire;
A little bread shall do me stead;   15
   Much bread I not desire.
No frost nor snow, no wind, I trow,
   Can hurt me if I wold;
I am so wrapped and thoroughly lapped
   Of jolly good ale and old.   20
     Back and side go bare, go bare, etc.

[1] Crab apple.

And Tib, my wife, that as her life
  Loveth well good ale to seek,
Full oft drinks she till ye may see
  The tears run down her cheek: 25
Then doth she trowl to me the bowl
  Even as a maltworm should,
And saith, "Sweetheart, I took my part
  Of this jolly good ale and old."
      Back and side go bare, go bare, etc.   30

Now let them drink till they nod and wink,
  Even as good fellows should do;
They shall not miss to have the bliss
  Good ale doth bring men to;
And all poor souls that have scoured bowls   35
  Or have them lustily trolled,
God save the lives of them and their wives,
  Whether they be young or old.
      Back and side go bare, go bare;
      Both foot and hand go cold;   40
      But, belly, God send thee good ale
        enough,
      Whether it be new or old.

Sonnet 18: Shall I Compare Thee to a Summer's Day?

WILLIAM SHAKESPEARE
1564–1616

Shall I compare thee to a summer's day?
Thou art more lovely and more temperate:
Rough winds do shake the darling buds of May,
And summer's lease hath all too short a date:
Sometime too hot the eye of heaven shines,   5
And often is his gold complexion dimmed;
And every fair from fair sometime declines,[1]
By chance or nature's changing course un-
    trimmed;[2]
But thy eternal summer shall not fade
Nor lose possession of that fair thou owest;[3]   10
Nor shall Death brag thou wander'st in his shade,
When in eternal lines to time thou growest:
  So long as men can breathe, or eyes can see,
  So long lives this,[4] and this gives life to thee.

[1] Every beautiful thing finally loses its beauty.
[2] Stripped of gay apparel.   [3] Ownest.
[4] This poem.

Sonnet 33: Full Many a Glorious Morning Have I Seen

WILLIAM SHAKESPEARE
1564–1616

Full many a glorious morning have I seen
Flatter the mountain-tops with sovereign eye,
Kissing with golden face the meadows green,
Gilding pale streams with heavenly alchemy;
Anon permit the basest clouds to ride   5
With ugly rack [1] on his celestial face,
And from the forlorn world his visage hide,
Stealing unseen to west with this disgrace:
Even so my sun[2] one early morn did shine
With all-triumphant splendour on my brow;   10
But out, alack! he was but one hour mine;
The region[3] cloud hath mask'd him from me
    now.
  Yet him for this my love no whit disdaineth;
  Suns of the world may stain[4] when heaven's
    sun staineth.

Sonnet 73: That Time of Year Thou Mayst in Me Behold

WILLIAM SHAKESPEARE
1564–1616

That time of year thou mayst in me behold
When yellow leaves, or none, or few, do hang
Upon those boughs which shake against the cold,
Bare ruined choirs, where late the sweet birds
    sang.
In me thou seest the twilight of such day   5
As after sunset fadeth in the west;
Which by and by black night doth take away,
Death's second self, that seals up all in rest.
In me thou seest the glowing of such fire,
That [1] on the ashes of his[2] youth doth lie,   10
As the death-bed whereon it must expire,
Consum'd with that which it was nourished by.
  This thou perceiv'st, which makes thy love
    more strong.
  To love that well which thou must leave ere
    long.   15

[1] Storm clouds.   [2] My friend.   [3] Upper air,
not ground winds.   [4] Be obscured; become dim
or dull.
[1] As.   [2] Its.

Woman's Constancy

JOHN DONNE
1572–1631

Now thou hast loved me one whole day,
To-morrow when thou leav'st, what wilt thou
    say?
Wilt thou then antedate some new-made vow?
  Or say that now
We are not just those persons which we were? 5
Or, that oaths made in reverential fear
Of love, and his wrath, any may forswear?
Or, as true deaths true marriages untie,
So lovers' contracts, images of those,
Bind but till sleep, death's image,[1] them un-
    loose?   10
  Or, your own end to justify,
For having purposed change and falsehood, you
Can have no way but falsehood to be true?[2]
Vain lunatic, against these scapes I could
  Dispute and conquer, if I would;   15
  Which I abstain to do,
For by to-morrow, I may think so too.

The Canonization

JOHN DONNE
1572–1631

For God's sake hold your tongue, and let me
    love,
  Or chide my palsy, or my gout,
My five gray hairs, or ruined fortune flout,
  With wealth your state, your mind with arts
    improve,
    Take you a course, get you a place,[1]   5
    Observe his honor, or his grace,
Or the king's real, or his stampèd face.[2]
  Contemplate; what you will approve,
  So you will let me love.

Alas, alas, who's injured by my love?   10
  What merchant's ships have my sighs
    drowned?

Who says my tears have overflowed his ground?
  When did my colds a forward spring re-
    move?[3]
    When did the heats which my veins fill
    Add one more to the plaguey bill?[4]   15
Soldiers find wars, and lawyers find out still
  Litigious men, which quarrels move,
  Though she and I do love.

Call us what you will, we are made such by love;
  Call her one, me another fly,   20
We are tapers[5] too, and at our own cost die,[6]
  And we in us find the eagle and the dove.[7]
    The phoenix[8] riddle hath more wit
    By us; we two being one, are it.[9]
So to one neutral thing both sexes fit,   25
  We die and rise the same, and prove
  Mysterious by this love.

We can die by it, if not live by love,
  And if unfit for tombs and hearse
Our legend[10] be, it will be fit for verse; 30
  And if no piece or chronicle[11] we prove,
    We'll build in sonnets pretty rooms;
    As well a well-wrought urn becomes
The greatest ashes, as half-acre tombs,
  And by these hymns, all shall approve   35
  Us *canonized*[12] for love;

And thus invoke us; you whom reverend love
  Made one another's hermitage;
You, to whom love was peace, that now is rage;
  Who did the whole world's soul contract, and
    drove   40
    Into the glasses of your eyes
    (So made such mirrors, and such spies,
That they did all to you epitomize),
  Countries, towns, courts: beg from above
  A pattern[13] of your love!   45

---

[3] Delay.   [4] Weekly list of plague victims.
[5] Candles that burn out, die.   [6] *Die* has the secondary meaning of achieving consummation in sexual intercourse, as in ll. 26 and 28 also.   [7] *Eagle*,
strength; *dove*, purity.   [8] Fabulous bird of no
sex that rose immortal from its own ashes.   [9] We
die to rise as one love-wedded being.   [10] Story
of a saint's life.   [11] History.   [12] Made saints.
[13] Likeness, copy.

---

[1] Sleep which is an image of death.   [2] Ll. 12–13:
In your declaration of love, you must be false again
to rid yourself of the false declaration. That is,
one falsehood demands another.
[1] Office.   [2] As on a coin.

His Farewell to Sack[1]

ROBERT HERRICK
1591–1674

Farewell thou thing, time-past so known, so dear
To me, as blood to life and spirit; near,
Nay, thou more near than kindred, friend, man,
    wife,
Male to the female, soul to body, life
To quick action, or the warm soft side   5
Of the resigning, yet resisting bride.
The kiss of virgins, first fruits of the bed,
Soft speech, smooth touch, the lips, the maiden-
    head:
These, and a thousand sweets, could never be
So near, or dear, as thou wast once to me.   10
O thou, the drink of gods and angels! wine
That scatter'st spirit and lust, whose purest shine
More radiant than the summer's sunbeams
    shows;
Each way illustrious, brave, and like to those
Comets we see by night, whose shagg'd por-
    tents   15
Foretell the coming of some dire events;
Or some full flame which with a pride aspires,
Throwing about his wild and active fires.
'Tis thou, above nectar, O divinest soul!
Eternal in thyself, that canst control   20
That which subverts whole nature, grief and
    care,
Vexation of the mind, and damned despair.
'Tis thou alone who, with thy mystic fan,[2]
Work'st more than wisdom, art, or nature can
To rouse the sacred madness and awake   25
The frost-bound blood and spirits, and to make
Them frantic with thy raptures, flashing through
The soul like lightning, and as active too.
'Tis not Apollo[3] can, or those thrice three
Castalian sisters,[4] sing, if wanting thee.   30
Horace, Anacreon, both had lost their fame
Hadst thou not filled them with thy fire and
    flame.
Phœbean splendor! and thou Thespian spring!
Of which sweet swans must drink before they
    sing

Their true-paced numbers and their holy lays, 35
Which makes them worthy cedar and the bays.
But why, why longer do I gaze upon
Thee with the eye of admiration?
Since I must leave thee, and enforced, must say
To all thy witching beauties, Go, away!   40
But if thy whimp'ring looks do ask me why,
Then know that nature bids thee go, not I.
'Tis her erroneous self has made a brain
Uncapable of such a sovereign
As is thy powerful self. Prithee not smile,   45
Or smile more inly, lest thy looks beguile
My vows denounced in zeal, which thus much
    show thee,
That I have sworn but by thy looks to know thee.
Let others drink thee freely, and desire
Thee and their lips espoused, while I admire 50
And love thee, but not taste thee. Let my muse
Fail of thy former helps, and only use
Her inadult'rate strength; what's done by me
Hereafter, shall smell of the lamp, not thee.

Delight in Disorder

ROBERT HERRICK
1591–1674

A sweet disorder in the dress
Kindles in clothes a wantonness;
A lawn[1] about the shoulders thrown
Into a fine distraction,
An erring lace, which here and there   5
Enthralls the crimson stomacher,[2]
A cuff neglectful, and thereby
Ribands to flow confusedly,
A winning wave, deserving note,
In the tempestuous petticoat,   10
A careless shoe-string, in whose tie
I see a wild civility,
Do more bewitch me than when art [3]
Is too precise in every part.

---

[1] A dry Spanish wine, a favorite drink of the Elizabethans.   [2] Symbolic emblem in the festivals of
Bacchus.   [3] Symbol of the perfection of youthful manhood.   [4] The muses.

[1] Fine linen. as a scarf.   [2] Center front section
of a waist or underwaist or an unusually heavily embroidered or jeweled separate piece for the center
front of a bodice.   [3] *Art:* conscious effort to
achieve a desired effect.

Redemption

GEORGE HERBERT
1593–1633

Having been tenant long to a rich Lord,
   Not thriving, I resolvëd to be bold,
   And make a suit [1] unto him to afford
A new small-rented lease and cancel th' old.
In heaven at his manor I him sought.   5
   They told me there that he was lately gone
   About some land which he had dearly bought
Long since on earth, to take possessïon.
I straight returned, and knowing his great birth,
   Sought him accordingly in great resorts,   10
   In cities, theaters, gardens, parks, and courts.
At length I heard a ragged noise and mirth
   Of thieves and murderers; there I him espied,
   Who straight, Your suit is granted, said, and
      died.

On Shakespeare

JOHN MILTON
1608–1674

What needs my Shakespeare for his honor'd
    bones
The labor of an age in pilèd stones,
Or that his hallow'd relics should be hid
Under a star-ypointing[1] pyramid?
Dear son of memory, great heir of fame,   5
What need'st thou such weak witness of thy
    name?
Thou in our wonder and astonishment
Hast built thyself a livelong monument.
For whilst to th' shame of slow-endeavoring art
Thy easy numbers[2] flow, and that each heart   10
Hath from the leaves of thy unvalu'd [3] book
Those Delphic[4] lines with deep impression took,
Then thou, our fancy of itself bereaving,
Dost make us marble with too much conceiving,[5]
And so sepúlcher'd in such pomp does lie,   15
That kings for such a tomb would wish to die.

---

[1] Request.
[1] Old English for star-pointing.   [2] Verses.   [3] Invaluable.   [4] Inspired.   [5] Imagining.

On Time

JOHN MILTON
1608–1674

Fly envious Time, till thou run out thy race,
Call on the lazy leaden-stepping hours,
Whose speed is but the heavy Plummet's pace;
And glut thy self with what thy womb devours,
Which is no more than what is false and vain,   5
And merely mortal dross;
So little is our loss,
So little is thy gain.
For when as each thing bad thou hast entomb'd,
And last of all, thy greedy self consum'd,   10
Then long Eternity shall greet our bliss
With an individual kiss;
And Joy shall overtake us as a flood,
When every thing that is sincerely good
And perfectly divine,   15
With Truth, and Peace, and Love shall ever
    shine
About the supreme Throne
Of him, t'whose happy-making sight alone,
When once our heav'nly-guided soul shall climb,
Then all this Earthy grossness quit,   20
Attir'd with Stars, we shall for ever sit,
Triumphing over Death, and Chance, and thee
    O Time.

No Platonic Love

WILLIAM CARTWRIGHT
1611–1643

Some readers would call this early seventeenth-century poem amazingly modern although Chaucer (1340?–1400) would have absorbed it with ease. For a brief discussion of Cartwright's general point of view, see the comment on Donne's "Go and Catch a Falling Star," p. 298.

Tell me no more of minds embracing minds,
   And hearts exchanged for hearts;
That spirits spirits meet, as winds do winds,
   And mix their subtlest parts;
That two unbodied essences may kiss,   5
And then like angels, twist and feel one bliss.

I was that silly thing that once was wrought
  To practise this thin love;
I climbed from sex to soul, from soul to thought;
  But thinking there to move,   10
Headlong I rolled from thought to soul, and then
From soul I lighted at the sex again.

As some strict down-looked men pretend to fast
  Who yet in closets eat,
So lovers who profess they spirits taste,   15
  Feed yet on grosser meat;
I know they boast they souls to souls convey,
Howe'er they meet, the body is the way.

Come, I will undeceive thee: they that tread
  Those vain aerial ways   20
Are like young heirs and alchemists, misled
  To waste their wealth and days;
For searching thus to be forever rich,
They only find a med'cine for the itch.

To Lucasta, Going to the Wars

RICHARD LOVELACE
1618–1658

Tell me not, Sweet, I am unkind,
  That from the nunnery
Of thy chaste breast and quiet mind
  To war and arms I fly.

True, a new mistress now I chase,   5
  The first foe in the field;
And with a stronger faith embrace
  A sword, a horse, a shield.

Yet this inconstancy is such
  As thou too shalt adore;   10
I could not love thee, Dear, so much,
  Loved I not Honor more.

A Song for St. Cecilia's Day, 1687

JOHN DRYDEN
1631–1700

1
From harmony, from heav'nly harmony,
  This universal frame began;

When Nature underneath a heap
  Of jarring atoms lay,
  And could not heave her head,   5
The tuneful voice was heard from high;
  "Arise, ye more than dead."
Then cold and hot and moist and dry[1]
In order to their stations leap,
  And Music's pow'r obey.   10
From harmony, from heav'nly harmony,
  This universal frame began:
  From harmony to harmony
Through all the compass of the notes it ran,
The diapason closing full in man.   15

2
What passion cannot Music raise and quell!
  When Jubal[2] struck the corded shell,
  His listening brethren stood around,
  And, wond'ring, on their faces fell
  To worship that celestial sound.   20
Less than a god they thought there could not dwell
  Within the hollow of that shell
  That spoke so sweetly and so well.
What passion cannot Music raise and quell!

3
  The trumpet's loud clangor   25
    Excites us to arms
  With shrill notes of anger
    And mortal alarms.
  The double, double, double beat
    Of the thundering drum   30
    Cries: "Hark! the foes come;
Charge, charge, 'tis too late to retreat!"

4
  The soft complaining flute
  In dying notes discovers
  The woes of hopeless lovers,   35
Whose dirge is whispered by the warbling lute.

5
  Sharp violins proclaim
Their jealous pangs and desperation,
Fury, frantic indignation,
Depth of pains, and height of passion,   40
  For the fair, disdainful dame.

---

[1] The four elements of medieval physics of which all matter is made.   [2] "The father of all such as handle the harp and organ."—*Genesis*, 4:21.

6

But oh! what art can teach,
What human voice can reach
    The sacred organ's praise?
Notes inspiring holy love,   45
Notes that wing their heavenly ways
    To mend the choirs above.

7

Orpheus[3] could lead the savage race;
And trees unrooted left their place,
    Sequacious of [4] the lyre;   50
But bright Cecilia raised the wonder higher:
When to her organ vocal breath was given,
An angel heard, and straight appeared,
    Mistaking earth for heaven.

GRAND CHORUS

As from the power of sacred lays   55
  The spheres began to move,
And sung the great Creator's praise
  To all the blessed above;
So when the last and dreadful hour
This crumbling pageant shall devour,   60
The trumpet shall be heard on high,
The dead shall live, the living die,
And Music shall untune the sky.[5]

Elegy Written in a Country Churchyard

THOMAS GRAY
1716–1771

The Curfew tolls the knell of parting day,
  The lowing herd wind slowly o'er the lea,
The plowman homeward plods his weary way,
  And leaves the world to darkness and to me.

Now fades the glimmering landscape on the
      sight,   5

[3] Legendary Thracian musician, inventor of the lyre, whose skill caused animals, and even trees and rocks to follow him as he played.   [4] Following.
[5] When the trumpet of the Last Judgment shall sound and the whole world shall be destroyed, the music of the spheres will come to an end.

And all the air a solemn stillness holds,
  Save where the beetle wheels his droning flight,
    And drowsy tinklings lull the distant folds;

Save that from yonder ivy-mantled tower
  The moping owl does to the moon com-
      plain   10
Of such, as wandering near her secret bower,
  Molest her ancient solitary reign.

Beneath those rugged elms, that yew-tree's
      shade,
  Where heaves the turf in many a mould'ring
      heap.
Each in his narrow cell for ever laid,   15
  The rude Forefathers of the hamlet sleep.

The breezy call of incense-breathing Morn,
  The swallow twitt'ring from the straw-built
      shed,
The cock's shrill clarion, or the echoing horn,[1]
  No more shall rouse them from their lowly
      bed.   20

For them no more the blazing hearth shall burn,
  Or busy housewife ply her evening care:
No children run to lisp their sire's return,
  Or climb his knees the envied kiss to share.

Oft did the harvest to their sickle yield,   25
  Their furrow oft the stubborn glebe has broke;
How jocund did they drive their team afield!
  How bowed the woods beneath their sturdy
      stroke!

Let not Ambition mock their useful toil,
  Their homely joys, and destiny obscure;   30
Nor Grandeur hear with a disdainful smile
  The short and simple annals of the poor.

The boast of heraldry, the pomp of power,
  And all that beauty, all that wealth e'er gave,
Awaits[2] alike th' inevitable hour.   35
  The paths of glory lead but to the grave.

Nor you, ye Proud, impute to These the fault,
  If Memory o'er their Tomb no Trophies raise,

[1] Of the hunt, early in the morning.   [2] The subject of the verb *awaits* is *hour*.

Where through the long-drawn aisle and fretted
    vault
    The pealing anthem swells the note of
      praise.   40

Can storied urn[3] or animated [4] bust
    Back to its mansion call the fleeting breath?
Can Honor's voice provoke[5] the silent dust,
    Or Flattery soothe the dull cold ear of Death?

Perhaps in this neglected spot is laid   45
    Some heart once pregnant with celestial fire;
Hands, that the rod of empire might have
    swayed,
    Or waked to ecstasy the living lyre.

But Knowledge to their eyes her ample page
    Rich with the spoils of time did ne'er un-
      roll: 50
Chill Penury repressed their noble rage,[6]
    And froze the genial [7] current of the soul.

Full many a gem of purest ray serene,
    The dark unfathomed caves of ocean bear:
Full many a flower is born to blush unseen,   55
    And waste its sweetness on the desert air.

Some village-Hampden,[8] that with dauntless
    breast
    The little Tyrant of his fields withstood;
Some mute inglorious Milton here may rest,
    Some Cromwell guiltless of his country's
      blood.   60

Th' applause of list'ning senates to command,
    The threats of pain and ruin to despise,
To scatter plenty o'er a smiling land,
    And read their history in a nation's eyes,

Their lot forbade: not circumscribed alone   65
    Their growing virtues, but their crimes con-
      fined;
Forbade to wade through slaughter to a throne,
    And shut the gates of mercy on mankind,

The struggling pangs of conscious truth to hide
    To quench the blushes of ingenuous shame,   70
Or heap the shrine of Luxury and Pride
    With incense kindled at the Muse's flame.

Far from the madding crowd's ignoble strife,
    Their sober wishes never learned to stray;
Along the cool sequestered vale of life   75
    They kept the noiseless tenor of their way.

Yet ev'n these bones from insult to protect,
    Some frail memorial still erected nigh,
With uncouth rhymes and shapeless sculpture
    decked,
    Implores the passing tribute of a sigh.   80

Their name, their years, spelt by th' unlettered
    muse,
    The place of fame and elegy supply;
And many a holy text around she strews,
    That teach the rustic moralist to die.

For who to dumb Forgetfulness a prey,   85
    This pleasing anxious being e'er resigned,
Left the warm precincts of the cheerful day,
    Nor cast one longing ling'ring look behind?

On some fond breast the parting soul relies,
    Some pious drops the closing eye requires;   90
Ev'n from the tomb the voice of Nature cries,
    Ev'n in our Ashes live their wonted Fires.

For[9] thee, who mindful of th' unhonored Dead
    Dost in these lines their artless tale relate,
If chance,[10] by lonely contemplation led,   95
    Some kindred Spirit shall inquire thy fate,

Haply some hoary-headed Swain may say,
    "Oft have we seen him at the peep of dawn
Brushing with hasty steps the dews away
    To meet the sun upon the upland lawn.   100

"There at the foot of yonder nodding beech
    That wreathes its old fantastic roots so high,
His listless length at noontide would he stretch,
    And pore upon the brook that babbles by.

[3] Such as Keats describes in his "Ode on a Grecian Urn" (see p. 339).   [4] Lifelike.   [5] Call forth.   [6] Inspired mood.   [7] Creative.   [8] John Hampden (1594–1643) whose leadership in Parliament resisted the tyranny of Charles I.

[9] As for.   [10] If it should chance.

"Hard by yon wood, now smiling as in scorn, 105
   Mutt'ring his wayward fancies he would rove,
Now drooping, woeful wan, like one forlorn,
   Or crazed with care, or crossed in hopeless
      love.

"One morn I missed him on the customed hill,
   Along the heath and near his favorite
      tree; 110
Another came; nor yet beside the rill,
   Nor up the lawn, nor at the wood was he;

"The next with dirges due in sad array
   Slow through the church-way path we saw
      him borne.
Approach and read (for thou cans't read) the
   lay, 115
   Graved on the stone beneath yon agèd thorn."

THE EPITAPH

Here rests his head upon the lap of earth
   A youth to fortune and to fame unknown.
Fair Science frowned not on his humble birth,
   And Melancholy marked him for her own. 120

Large was his bounty, and his soul sincere,
   Heaven did a recompense as largely send:
He gave to Misery all he had, a tear,
   He gained from Heaven ('twas all he wished)
      a friend.

No further seek his merits to disclose, 125
   Or draw his frailties from their dread abode,
(There they alike in trembling hope repose)
   The bosom of his Father and his God.

The Little Black Boy
WILLIAM BLAKE
1757–1827

My mother bore me in the southern wild,
And I am black, but O! my soul is white;
White as an angel is the English child,
But I am black, as if bereav'd of light.

My mother taught me underneath a tree, 5
And sitting down before the heat of day,

She took me on her lap and kissed me,
And pointing to the east, began to say:

"Look on the rising sun: there God does live,
And gives his light, and gives his heat away; 10
And flowers and trees and beasts and men re-
   ceive
Comfort in morning, joy in the noonday.

"And we are put on earth a little space,
That we may learn to bear the beams of love;
And these black bodies and this sunburnt face 15
Is but a cloud, and like a shady grove.

"For when our souls have learn'd the heat to
   bear,
The cloud will vanish; we shall hear his voice,
Saying: 'Come out from the grove, my love and
   care,
And round my golden tent like lambs rejoice.'" 20

Thus did my mother say, and kissed me;
And thus I say to little English boy:
When I from black and he from white cloud
   free,
And round the tent of God like lambs we joy,

I'll shade him from the heat, till he can bear 25
To lean in joy upon our father's knee;
And then I'll stand and stroke his silver hair,
And be like him, and he will then love me.

Scoffers
WILLIAM BLAKE
1757–1827

Mock on, mock on, Voltaire, Rousseau,
Mock on, mock on; 'tis all in vain;
You throw the sand against the wind,
And the wind blows it back again.

And every sand becomes a gem, 5
Reflected in the beams divine;
Blown back, they blind the mocking eye,
But still in Israel's path they shine.

The atoms of Democritus
And Newton's particles of light   10
Are sands upon the Red Sea shore
Where Israel's tents do shine so bright.

My Love Is Like
a Red Red Rose
ROBERT BURNS
1759–1796

My love is like a red red rose
   That's newly sprung in June:
My love is like the melodie
   That's sweetly played in tune.

So fair art thou, my bonnie lass,   5
   So deep in love am I:
And I will love thee still, my dear,
   Till a' the seas gang dry.

Till a' the seas gang dry, my dear,
   And the rocks melt wi' the sun: 10
And I will love thee still, my dear,
   While the sands o' life shall run.

And fare thee weel, my only love,
   And fare thee weel awhile!
And I will come again, my love,   15
   Tho' it were ten thousand mile.

John Barleycorn: A Ballad
ROBERT BURNS
1759–1796

There were three Kings into the east
   Three Kings both great and high,
And they hae[1] sworn a solemn oath
   John Barleycorn should die.

They took a plough and ploughed him down,   5
   Put clods upon his head,
And they hae sworn a solemn oath
   John Barleycorn was dead.

[1] Have.

But the cheerfu' Spring came kindly on,
   And show'rs began to fall;   10
John Barleycorn got up again,
   And sore surprised them all.

The sultry suns of Summer came,
   And he grew thick and strong,
His head weel[2] armed wi' pointed spears,   15
   That no one should him wrong.

The sober Autumn entered mild,
   When he grew wan and pale;
His bending joints and drooping head
   Showed he began to fail.   20

His colour sickened more and more,
   He faded into age;
And then his enemies began
   To shew their deadly rage.

They've ta'en a weapon, long and sharp,   25
   And cut him by the knee;
Then tied him fast upon a cart,
   Like a rogue for forgerie.

They laid him down upon his back,
   And cudgelled him full sore;   30
They hung him up before the storm,
   And turned him o'er and o'er.

They fillèd up a darksome pit
   With water to the brim,
They heavèd in John Barleycorn,   35
   There let him sink or swim.

They laid him out upon the floor,
   To work him further woe,
And still, as signs of life appeared,
   They tossed him to and fro.   40

They wasted, o'er a scorching flame,
   The marrow of his bones;
But a miller used him worst of all,
   For he crushed him between the stones.

And they hae ta'en his very heart's blood,   45
   And drank it round and round;

[2] Well.

And still the more and more they drank,
   Their joy did more abound.

John Barleycorn was a hero bold,
   Of noble enterprise,   50
For if you do but taste his blood,
   'Twill make your courage rise;

'Twill make a man forget his woe;
   'Twill heighten all his joy:
'Twill make the widow's heart to sing,   55
   Tho' the tear were in her eye.

Then let us toast John Barleycorn,
   Each man a glass in hand;
And may his great posterity
   Ne'er fail in old Scotland.   60

I Wandered
Lonely as a Cloud
WILLIAM WORDSWORTH
1770–1850

I wandered lonely as a cloud
That floats on high o'er vales and hills,
When all at once I saw a crowd,
A host, of golden daffodils;
Beside the lake, beneath the trees,   5
Fluttering and dancing in the breeze.

Continuous as the stars that shine
And twinkle on the milky way,
They stretched in never-ending line
Along the margin of a bay: 10
Ten thousand saw I at a glance,
Tossing their heads in sprightly dance.

The waves beside them danced; but they
Out-did the sparkling waves in glee:
A poet could not but be gay,   15
In such a jocund company:
I gazed—and gazed—but little thought
What wealth the show to me had brought:

For oft, when on my couch I lie
In vacant or in pensive mood,   20
They flash upon that inward eye

Which is the bliss of solitude;
And then my heart with pleasure fills,
And dances with the daffodils.

It Is a Beauteous Evening
WILLIAM WORDSWORTH
1770–1850

It is a beauteous evening, calm and free;
The holy time is quiet as a nun
Breathless with adoration; the broad sun
Is sinking down in its tranquillity;
The gentleness of heaven broods o'er the sea: 5
Listen! the mighty Being is awake,
And doth with his eternal motion make
A sound like thunder—everlastingly.
Dear child! dear girl! that walkest with me here,
If thou appear untouched by solemn thought,   10
Thy nature is not therefore less divine:
Thou liest in Abraham's bosom all the year,
And worship'st at the Temple's inner shrine,
God being with thee when we know it not.

The World Is Too Much
with Us
WILLIAM WORDSWORTH
1770–1850

The world is too much with us; late and soon,
Getting and spending, we lay waste our powers;
Little we see in Nature that is ours;
We have given our hearts away, a sordid boon!
This Sea that bares her bosom to the moon;   5
The winds that will be howling at all hours,
And are up-gathered now like sleeping flowers;
For this, for everything, we are out of tune;
It moves us not.—Great God! I'd rather be
A Pagan suckled in a creed outworn;   10
So might I, standing on this pleasant lea,
Have glimpses that would make me less forlorn:
Have sight of Proteus rising from the sea;
Or hear old Triton[1] blow his wreathèd [2] horn.

[1] Sea gods of classical mythology. Proteus could assume any shape. Triton, son of Neptune, could raise and calm the waves by blasts on his conch-shell trumpet.   [2] Spiral.

Kubla Khan: Or a Vision in a Dream[1]

SAMUEL TAYLOR COLERIDGE
1772–1834

In Xanadu did Kubla Khan[2]
A stately pleasure-dome decree;
Where Alph, the sacred river, ran
Through caverns measureless to man
Down to a sunless sea.   5

So twice five miles of fertile ground
With walls and towers were girdled round:
And here were gardens bright with sinuous rills,
Where blossomed many an incense-bearing tree;
And here were forests ancient as the hills   10
Enfolding sunny spots of greenery.

But oh! that deep romantic chasm which slanted
Down the green hill athwart[3] a cedarn cover!
A savage place! as holy and enchanted
As e'er beneath a waning moon was haunted   15
By woman wailing for her demon-lover!
And from this chasm, with ceaseless turmoil seething,
As if this earth in fast thick pants were breathing
A mighty fountain momently[4] was forced:
Amid whose swift half-intermitted burst   20
Huge fragments vaulted like rebounding hail,
Or chaffy grain beneath the thresher's flail:
And 'mid these dancing rocks at once and ever
It flung up momently the sacred river.
Five miles meandering with a mazy motion   25
Through wood and dale the sacred river ran,
Then reached the caverns measureless to man,
And sank in tumult to a lifeless ocean:
And 'mid this tumult Kubla heard from far
Ancestral voices prophesying war!   30

    The shadow of the dome of pleasure
    Floated midway on the waves;
    Where was heard the mingled measure
    From the fountain and the caves.
It was a miracle of rare device,   35
A sunny pleasure-dome with caves of ice!

    A damsel with a dulcimer[5]
    In a vision once I saw:
    It was an Abyssinian maid,
    And on her dulcimer she played,   40
    Singing of Mount Abora.
    Could I revive with me
    Her symphony and song,
    To such a deep delight 'twould win me,
That with music loud and long,   45
I would build that dome in air,
That sunny dome! those caves of ice!
And all who heard should see them there,—
And all should cry, Beware! Beware!—
His flashing eyes, his floating hair!   50
Weave a circle round him thrice,
And close your eyes with holy dread,
For he on honey-dew hath fed,
And drunk the milk of Paradise.

[1] The poem was written in 1798, not 1797 as Coleridge erroneously states. A preface by the author explains the genesis and composition of the poem; "In the summer of the year of 1797 [1798], the Author, then in ill health, had retired to a lonely farm-house. . . . In consequence of a slight indisposition, an anodyne [it was opium] had been prescribed, from the effects of which he fell asleep in his chair at the moment that he was reading the following sentence, or words of the same substance, in 'Purchas's Pilgrimage': 'Here the Khan Kubla commanded a palace to be built, and a stately garden thereunto. And thus ten miles of fertile ground were enclosed with a wall.' The author continued for about three hours in a profound sleep, at least of the external senses, during which time he has the most vivid confidence, that he could not have composed less than from two to three hundred lines; if that indeed can be called composition in which all the images rose up before him as *things*, with a parallel production of the correspondent expressions, without any sensation or consciousness of effort. On awaking he appeared to himself to have a distinct recollection of the whole, and taking his pen, ink and paper, instantly and eagerly wrote down the lines that are here preserved. At this moment he was unfortunately called out by a person on business from Porlock, and detained by him above an hour, and on his return to his room, found, to his no small surprise and mortification, that though he still retained some vague and dim recollection of the general purport of the vision, yet, with the exception of some eight or ten scattered lines and images, all the rest had passed away like the images on the surface of a stream into which a stone has been cast, but, alas! without the after restoration of the latter!"   [2] Founder of the Mongol dynasty in China.

[3] Across.   [4] Continuously.   [5] Wire-stringed instrument played with light hammers in the hand.

She Walks in Beauty

GEORGE GORDON, LORD BYRON
1788–1824

She walks in beauty, like the night
  Of cloudless climes and starry skies;
And all that's best or dark and bright
  Meet in her aspect and her eyes:
Thus mellowed to that tender light   5
  Which heaven to gaudy day denies.

One shade the more, one day the less,
  Had half impaired the nameless grace
Which waves in every raven tress,
  Or softly lightens o'er her face;   10
Where thoughts serenely sweet express
  How pure, how dear, their dwelling-place.

And on that cheek, and o'er that brow,
  So soft, so calm, so eloquent,
The smiles that win, the tints that glow,   15
  But tell of days in goodness spent,
A mind at peace with all below,
  A heart whose love is innocent!

Prometheus[1]

GEORGE GORDON, LORD BYRON
1788–1824

1

Titan! to whose immortal eyes
  The sufferings of mortality,
  Seen in their sad reality,
Were not as things that gods despise;
What was thy pity's recompense?   5

A silent suffering, and intense;
The rock, the vulture, and the chain,
All that the proud can feel of pain,
The agony they do not show,
The suffocating sense of woe,   10
  Which speaks but in its loneliness,
And then is jealous lest the sky
Should have a listener, nor will sigh
  Until its voice is echoless.

2

Titan! to thee the strife was given   15
  Between the suffering and the will,
  Which torture where they cannot kill;
And the inexorable Heaven,
And the deaf tyranny of Fate,
The ruling principle of Hate,   20
Which for its pleasure doth create
The things it may annihilate,
Refused thee even the boon to die:
The wretched gift eternity
Was thine—and thou hast borne it well.   25
All that the Thunderer wrung from thee
Was but the menace which flung back
On him the torments of thy rack;
The fate thou didst so well foresee,
But would not to appease him tell;   30
And in thy Silence was his Sentence,
And in his Soul a vain repentance,
And evil dread so ill dissembled,
That in his hand the lightnings trembled.

3

Thy Godlike crime was to be kind,   35
  To render with thy precepts less
  The sum of human wretchedness,
And strengthen Man with his own mind;
But baffled as thou wert from high,
Still in thy patient energy,   40
In the endurance, and repulse
  Of thine impenetrable Spirit,
Which Earth and Heaven could not convulse,
  A mighty lesson we inherit:
Thou art a symbol and a sign   45
  To Mortals of their fate and force;
Like thee, Man is in part divine,
  A troubled stream from a pure source;
And Man in portions can foresee
His own funereal destiny;   50
His wretchedness, and his resistance,
And his sad unallied existence:
To which his Spirit may oppose

[1] Prometheus (Greek, "forethought") was employed
by Zeus to make men of mud and water, but pitying
them Prometheus stole fire from heaven and gave it
to them. Hence Prometheus (adj., Promethean) has
come to mean a benefactor of mankind. He is celebrated by Aeschylus, Shelley, Bridges, and other
writers. "Promethean heat," the divine spark, is used
by Shakespeare in *Othello,* V. ii. 14 (p. 500); and
"Promethean fire" in *Love's Labor's Lost,* IV. iii.
302–304:

  From women's eyes this doctrine I derive:
  They are the ground, the books, the academes,
  From whence doth spring the true Promethean
    fire.

Itself—an equal to all woes,
    And a firm will, and a deep sense,   55
Which even in torture can descry
    Its own concenter'd recompense,
Triumphant where it dares defy,
And making Death a Victory.

Ode to the West Wind

PERCY BYSSHE SHELLEY
1792–1822

I

O wild West Wind, thou breath of Autumn's
    being,
Thou, from whose unseen presence the leaves
    dead
Are driven, like ghosts from an enchanter fleeing,

Yellow, and black, and pale, and hectic red,
Pestilence-stricken multitudes: O thou,   5
Who chariotest to their dark wintry bed

The wingèd seeds, where they lie cold and low,
Each like a corpse within its grave, until
Thine azure sister[1] of the spring shall blow

Her clarion o'er the dreaming earth, and fill   10
(Driving sweet buds like flocks to feed in air)
With living hues and odours plain and hill;

Wild Spirit, which art moving everywhere;
Destroyer and preserver; hear, Oh hear!

II

Thou on whose stream, 'mid the steep sky's
    commotion,   15
Loose clouds like earth's decaying leaves are
    shed,
Shook from the tangled boughs of Heaven and
    Ocean,

Angels of rain and lightning: there are spread
On the blue surface of thine airy surge,
Like the bright hair uplifted from the head   20

Of some fierce Mænad,[2] even from the dim verge

Of the horizon to the zenith's height
The locks of the approaching storm. Thou dirge

Of thy dying year, to which this closing[3] night
Will be the dome of a vast sepulchre,   25
Vaulted with all thy congregated might

Of vapours, from whose solid atmosphere
Black rain, and fire, and hail will burst: Oh hear!

III

Thou who didst waken from his summer dreams
The blue Mediterranean, where he lay,   30
Lulled by the coil of his crystalline streams,

Beside a pumice[4] isle in Baiæ's[5] bay,
And saw in sleep old palaces and towers
Quivering within the wave's intenser day,

All overgrown with azure moss and flowers   35
So sweet, the sense faints picturing them! Thou
For whose path the Atlantic's level powers

Cleave themselves into chasms, while far below
The sea-blooms and the oozy woods which wear
The sapless foliage of the ocean, know   40

Thy voice, and suddenly grow gray with fear,
And tremble and despoil themselves: Oh hear!

IV

If I were a dead leaf thou mightest bear;
If I were a swift cloud to fly with thee;
A wave to pant beneath thy power, and share   45

The impulse of thy strength, only less free
Than thou, O uncontrollable! If even
I were as in my boyhood, and could be

The comrade of thy wanderings over heaven,
As then, when to outstrip thy skiey speed   50
Scarce seemed a vision; I would ne'er have
    striven

As thus with thee in prayer in my sore need.
Oh! lift me as a wave, a leaf, a cloud!
I fall upon the thorns of life! I bleed!

---

[1] The south wind.   [2] Nymph attending Bacchus; literally, a frenzied woman.

[3] Closing down on the world.   [4] *I.e.*, volcanic.
[5] Town by the sea, near Naples.

A heavy weight of hours has chained and
     bowed   55
One too like thee; tameless, and swift, and
     proud.

     V

Make me thy lyre, even as the forest is:
What if my leaves are falling like its own!
The tumult of thy mighty harmonies

Will take from both a deep, autumnal tone,   60
Sweet though in sadness. Be thou, spirit fierce,
My spirit! Be thou me, impetuous one!

Drive my dead thoughts over the universe
Like withered leaves to quicken a new birth!
And, by the incantation of this verse,   65

Scatter, as from an unextinguished hearth
Ashes and sparks, my words among mankind!
Be through my lips to unawakened earth

The trumpet of a prophecy! O, wind,
If Winter comes, can Spring be far behind?   70

On First Looking into Chapman's Homer

JOHN KEATS
1795–1821

Much have I traveled in the realms of gold,[1]
And many goodly states and kingdoms seen;
Round many western islands[2] have I been
Which bards in fealty to Apollo[3] hold.
Oft of one wide expanse had I been told   5
That deep-browed Homer ruled as his demesne;
Yet did I never breathe its pure serene
Till I heard Chapman speak out loud and bold:
Then felt I like some watcher of the skies
When a new planet swims into his ken;   10
Or like stout Cortez[4] when with eagle eyes
He stared at the Pacific—and all his men
Looked at each other with a wild surmise—
Silent, upon a peak in Darien.[5]

---

[1] Great literature.   [2] Modern European literature.
[3] God of poetry.   [4] Keats's error: it was Balboa.
[5] Isthmus of Panama.

Ode to a Nightingale

JOHN KEATS
1795–1821

   1

My heart aches, and a drowsy numbness pains
   My sense, as though of hemlock I had drunk,
Or emptied some dull opiate to the drains
   One minute past, and Lethe-wards had sunk:
'Tis not through envy of thy happy lot,   5
   But being too happy in thy happiness,—
      That thou, light-wingèd Dryad[1] of the trees,
        In some melodious plot
Of beechen green, and shadows numberless,
   Singest of summer in full-throated ease.   10

   2

O, for a draught of vintage! that hath been
   Cooled a long age in the deep-delvèd earth,
Tasting of Flora[2] and the country-green,
   Dance, and Provençal[3] song, and sunburnt
      mirth!
O for a beaker full of the warm South,   15
   Full of the true, the blushful Hippocrene,[4]
      With beaded bubbles winking at the brim,
        And purple-stainèd mouth;
      That I might drink, and leave the world
      unseen,
      And with thee fade away into the forest
      dim: 20

   3

Fade far away, dissolve, and quite forget
   What thou among the leaves hast never
      known,
The weariness, the fever, and the fret
   Here, where men sit and hear each other
      groan;
Where palsy shakes a few, sad, last gray hairs,   25
   Where youth grows pale, and spectre-thin,
      and dies;
      Where but to think is to be full of sorrow
        And leaden-eyed despairs,
Where Beauty cannot keep her lustrous eyes
      Or new Love pine at them beyond to-
      morrow.   30

---

[1] Tree nymph.   [2] Goddess of flowers.   [3] Provence, original home of the troubadours in southeastern France.   [4] Drinking from this fountain supposedly induced poetic inspiration.

4

Away! away! for I will fly to thee,
  Not charioted by Bacchus and his pards,[5]
But on the viewless wings of Poesy,
  Though the dull brain perplexes and retards:
Already with thee! tender is the night,   35
   And haply the Queen-Moon is on her throne,
    Clustered around by all her starry Fays;[6]
     But here there is no light,
   Save what from heaven is with the breezes
     blown
    Through verdurous glooms and winding
     mossy ways.   40

5

I cannot see what flowers are at my feet,
  Nor what soft incense hangs upon the boughs,
But, in embalmèd [7] darkness, guess each sweet
  Wherewith the seasonable month endows
The grass, the thicket, and the fruit-tree wild; 45
   White hawthorn, and the pastoral eglantine;
    Fast-fading violets covered up in leaves;
     And mid-May's eldest child,
   The coming musk-rose, full of dewy wine,
    The murmurous haunt of flies on summer
     eves.   50

6

Darkling I listen; and, for many a time
  I have been half in love with easeful Death,
Called him soft names in many a musèd rhyme,
  To take into the air my quiet breath;
Now more than ever seems it rich to die,   55
   To cease upon the midnight with no pain,
    While thou art pouring forth thy soul
     abroad
     In such an ecstasy!
   Still wouldst thou sing, and I have ears in
     vain—
    To thy high requiem become a sod.   60

7

Thou wast not born for death, immortal Bird!
  No hungry generations tread thee down;
The voice I hear this passing night was heard
  In ancient days by emperor and clown:
Perhaps the self-same song that found a path 65
   Through the sad heart of Ruth, when, sick for
    home,
    She stood in tears amid the alien corn;[8]

The same that oft-times hath
  Charmed magic casements, opening on the
    foam
    Of perilous seas, in faery lands forlorn.   70

8

Forlorn! the very word is like a bell
  To toll me back from thee to my sole self!
Adieu! the fancy cannot cheat so well
  As she is famed to do, deceiving elf.
Adieu! adieu! thy plaintive anthem fades 75
   Past the near meadows, over the still stream,
    Up the hill-side; and now 'tis buried deep
     In the next valley-glades:
   Was it a vision, or a waking dream?
    Fled is that music:—Do I wake or sleep? 80

Ode on a Grecian Urn

JOHN KEATS
1795–1821

1

Thou still unravished bride of quietness,
  Thou foster-child of silence and slow time,
Sylvan historian, who canst thus express
  A flowery tale more sweetly than our rime:
What leaf-fringed legend haunts about thy
    shape   5
   Of deities or mortals, or of both,
    In Tempe[1] or the dales of Arcady? [2]
What men or gods are these? What maidens
    loth?
   What mad pursuit? What struggles to escape?
    What pipes and timbrels? [3] What wild
     ecstasy?   10

2

Heard melodies are sweet, but those unheard
  Are sweeter; therefore, ye soft pipes, play on;
Not to the sensual[4] ear, but, more endeared,
  Pipe to the spirit ditties of no tone:
Fair youth, beneath the trees, thou canst not
    leave   15

---

[5] Leopards.   [6] Fairies.   [7] Fragrant.
[8] Ll. 66–67: see *Ruth*, 2.

[1] Valley in Thessaly.   [2] Central hill region in
southern Greece, long associated in poetry with pastoral life.   [3] Small drums or tambourines.   [4] Sensuous, physical, actual.

Thy song, nor ever can those trees be bare;
    Bold Lover, never, never canst thou kiss,
Though winning near the goal—yet, do not
        grieve;
    She cannot fade, though thou hast not thy
        bliss,
        Forever wilt thou love, and she be fair!   20

3

Ah, happy, happy boughs! That cannot shed
    Your leaves, nor ever bid the Spring adieu:
And, happy melodist, unwearièd,
    Forever piping songs forever new;
More happy love! more happy, happy love!   25
    Forever warm and still to be enjoy'd,
        Forever panting, and forever young;
All breathing human passion far above,
    That leaves a heart high-sorrowful and cloyed,
        A burning forehead, and a parching
            tongue.   30

4

Who are these coming to the sacrifice?
    To what green altar, O mysterious priest,
Lead'st thou that heifer lowing at the skies,
    And all her silken flanks with garlands drest?
What little town by river or sea shore,   35
    Or mountain-built with peaceful citadel,
        Is emptied of this folk, this pious morn?
And, little town, thy streets for evermore
    Will silent be; and not a soul to tell
        Why thou art desolate, can e'er return.   40

5

O Attic⁵ shape! Fair Attitude! with brede⁶
    Of marble men and maidens overwrought,
With forest branches and the trodden weed;
    Thou, silent form, dost tease us out of thought
As doth eternity: Cold Pastoral! ⁷   45
    When old age shall this generation waste,
        Thou shalt remain, in midst of other woe
Than ours, a friend to man, to whom thou sayst,
    "Beauty is truth, truth beauty,"—that is all
        Ye know on earth, and all ye need to
            know.   50

⁵ Of Attica, Athenian.   ⁶ Embroidery, braid.
⁷ Pastoral scene fired in cold marble or clay.

Each and All¹

RALPH WALDO EMERSON
1803–1882

Little thinks, in the field, yon red-cloaked clown
Of thee from the hill-top looking down;
The heifer that lows in the upland farm,
Far-heard, lows not thine ear to charm;
The sexton, tolling his bell at noon,   5
Deems not that great Napoleon
Stops his horse, and lists with delight,
Whilst his files sweep round yon Alpine height;
Nor knowest thou what argument
Thy life to thy neighbor's creed has lent.   10
All are needed by each one;
Nothing is fair or good alone.
I thought the sparrow's note from heaven,
Singing at dawn on the alder bough;
I brought him home, in his nest, at even;   15
He sings the song, but it cheers not now,
For I did not bring home the river and sky;
He sang to my ear—they sang to my eye.
The delicate shells lay on the shore;
The bubbles of the latest wave   20
Fresh pearls to their enamel gave,
And the bellowing of the savage sea
Greeted their safe escape to me.
I wiped away the weeds and foam,
I fetched my sea-born treasures home;   25
But the poor, unsightly, noisome things
Had left their beauty on the shore
With the sun and the sand and the wild uproar.
The lover watched his graceful maid,
As 'mid the virgin train she strayed,   30
Nor knew her beauty's best attire
Was woven still by the snow-white choir.
At last she came to his hermitage,
Like the bird from the woodlands to the cage;
The gay enchantment was undone,   35
A gentle wife, but fairy none.

¹ Emerson recorded the germinal idea of the poem:
"I remember when I was a boy going upon the
beach and being charmed with the colors and forms
of the shells. I picked up many and put them in my
pocket. When I got home I could find nothing that
I gathered—nothing but some dry, ugly mussel and
snail shells. Thence I learned that composition was
more important than the beauty of individual forms
to effect. On the shore they lay wet and social by
the sea and under the sky" (*Journals*, May 16,
1834).

Then I said, "I covet truth;
Beauty is unripe childhood's cheat;
I leave it behind with the games of youth":
As I spoke, beneath my feet   40
The ground-pine curled its pretty wreath,
Running over the club-moss burrs;
I inhaled the violet's breath;
Around me stood the oaks and firs;
Pine-cones and acorns lay on the ground;   45
Over me soared the eternal sky,
Full of light and of deity;
Again I saw, again I heard,
The rolling river, the morning bird;
Beauty through my senses stole;   50
I yielded myself to the perfect whole.[2]

The Conqueror Worm

EDGAR ALLAN POE
1809–1849

This poem first appeared in *Graham's Magazine,* January, 1843, and was later appropriately inserted by Poe in the second version of his story "Ligeia." Lady Ligeia is the first wife of the unnamed narrator, a passionate, intense woman of "astounding" learning who guided her husband, as he says, "through the chaotic world of metaphysical [not supported by empirical data] investigation . . . . onward to the goal of a wisdom too divinely precious not to be forbidden!" Her "passionate devotion [to him] amounted to idolatry," but on the day of her untimely death she gave him this poem "composed by herself" to read aloud, after which she cried, "O God! O Divine Father! shall these things be undeviatingly so? shall this conqueror be not once conquered?" The full implications of the poem, however, can be found best by reading Poe's story.

Lo! 'tis a gala night
    Within the lonesome latter years.
An angel throng, bewinged, bedight

2 See the commentary on Emerson's "Brahma" for discussion of "the perfect whole" (p. 321).

In veils, and drowned in tears,
Sit in a theatre to see   5
    A play of hopes and fears,
While the orchestra breathes fitfully
    The music of the spheres.[1]

Mimes,[2] in the form of God on high,
    Mutter and mumble low,   10
And hither and thither fly;
    Mere puppets they, who come and go
At bidding of vast formless things
    That shift the scenery to and fro,
Flapping from out their condor[3] wings   15
    Invisible Woe.

That motley drama—oh, be sure
    It shall not be forgot!
With its Phantom chased for evermore,
    By a crowd that seize it not,   20
Through a circle that ever returneth in
    To the self-same spot;
And much of Madness, and more of Sin,
    And Horror the soul of the plot.

But see, amid the mimic rout[4]   25
    A crawling shape intrude:
A blood-red thing that writhes from out
    The scenic solitude!
It writhes—it writhes! with mortal[5] pangs
    The mimes become its food,   30
And seraphs[6] sob at vermin fangs
    In human gore imbued.

Out—out are the lights—out all!
    And over each quivering form

1 According to legend the Greek Pythagoras (about the sixth century B.C.) discovered the perfect intervals (the octave, the fourth, and the fifth) in the course of experiments with vibrating strings. Supposedly this led him toward the doctrine that all things were literally numbers. If all things were numbers, it should be possible to find the "harmonies" associated with the entire universe. Thus the motion of the planets were "harmonies" also and the "physical" reality of the universe was associated with certain "perfect" sounds. So just as the soul is a "harmony" of the body, so the entire universe has a harmony, a "music" associated with its "soul."
2 Performers who communicate with gestures instead of words.   3 Carrion-eating vulture identified with death.   4 Masked dance.   5 Deadly.
6 Of the highest order of angels.

The curtain, a funeral pall, 35
  Comes down with the rush of a storm,
While the angels, all pallid and wan,
  Uprising, unveiling, affirm
That the play is the tragedy, "Man,"
  And its hero, the Conqueror Worm. 40

Break, Break, Break
ALFRED, LORD TENNYSON
1809–1892

Break, break, break,
  On thy cold gray stones, O Sea!
And I would that my tongue could utter
  The thoughts that arise in me.

O well for the fisherman's boy, 5
  That he shouts with his sister at play!
O well for the sailor lad,
  That he sings in his boat on the bay!

And the stately ships go on
  To their haven under the hill; 10
But O for the touch of a vanished hand,
  And the sound of a voice that is still!

Break, break, break,
  At the foot of thy crags, O Sea!
But the tender grace of a day that is dead 15
  Will never come back to me.

Tears, Idle Tears
ALFRED, LORD TENNYSON
1809–1892

Tears, idle tears, I know not what they mean,
Tears from the depth of some divine despair
Rise in the heart, and gather to the eyes,
In looking on the happy Autumn-fields,
And thinking of the days that are no more. 5

Fresh as the first beam glittering on a sail,
That brings our friends up from the underworld,
Sad as the last which reddens over one
That sinks with all we love below the verge;
So sad, so fresh, the days that are no more. 10

Ah, sad and strange as in dark summer dawns
The earliest pipe of half-awakened birds
To dying ears, when unto dying eyes
The casement slowly grows a glimmering square;
So sad, so strange, the days that are no more. 15

Dear as remembered kisses after death,
And sweet as those by hopeless fancy feigned
On lips that are for others; deep as love,
Deep as first love, and wild with all regret;
O Death in Life, the days that are no more! 20
(From *The Princess*)

The Eagle
ALFRED, LORD TENNYSON
1809–1892

He clasps the crag with crooked hands;
Close to the sun in lonely lands,
Ringed with the azure world, he stands.

The wrinkled sea beneath him crawls;
He watches from his mountain walls, 5
And like a thunderbolt he falls.

Porphyria's Lover
ROBERT BROWNING
1812–1889

The rain set early in to-night,
  The sullen wind was soon awake,
It tore the elm-tops down for spite,
  And did its worst to vex the lake:
  I listened with heart fit to break. 5
When glided in Porphyria; straight
  She shut the cold out and the storm,
And kneeled and made the cheerless grate
  Blaze up, and all the cottage warm;
  Which done, she rose, and from her form 10
Withdrew the dripping cloak and shawl,
  And laid her soiled gloves by, untied
Her hat and let the damp hair fall,
  And, last, she sat down by my side
  And called me. When no voice replied, 15
She put my arm about her waist,
  And made her smooth white shoulder bare,

And all her yellow hair displaced,
    And, stopping, made my cheek lie there,
    And spread, o'er all, her yellow hair,   20
Murmuring how she loved me—she
    Too weak, for all her heart's endeavor,
To set its struggling passion free
    From pride, and vainer ties dissever,
    And give herself to me forever.   25
But passion sometimes would prevail,
    Nor could to-night's gay feast restrain
A sudden thought of one so pale
    For love of her, and all in vain:
    So, she was come through wind and rain.   30
Be sure I looked up at her eyes
    Happy and proud; at last I knew
Porphyria worshipped me; surprise
    Made my heart swell, and still it grew
    While I debated what to do.   35
That moment she was mine, mine, fair,
    Perfectly pure and good: I found
A thing to do, and all her hair
    In one long yellow string I wound
    Three times her little throat around,   40
And strangled her. No pain felt she;
    I am quite sure she felt no pain.
As a shut bud that holds a bee,
    I warily oped her lids: again
    Laughed the blue eyes without a stain.   45
And I untightened next the tress
    About her neck; her cheek once more
Blushed bright beneath my burning kiss:
    I propped her head up as before,
    Only, this time my shoulder bore   50

Her head, which droops upon it still:
    The smiling rosy little head,
So glad it has its utmost will,
    That all it scorned at once is fled,
    And I, its love, am gained instead!   55
Porphyria's love: she guessed not how
    Her darling one wish would be heard.
And thus we sit together now,
    And all night long we have not stirred,
    And yet God has not said a word!   60

One's-Self I Sing

WALT WHITMAN
1819–1892

One's-Self I sing, a simple separate person,
Yet utter the word Democratic, the word En-
    Masse.

Of physiology from top to toe I sing,
Not physiognomy alone nor brain alone is worthy
    for the Muse. I say the Form complete
    is worthier far,
The Female equally with the Male I sing.   5

Of Life immense in passion, pulse, and power,
Cheerful, for freest action form'd under the laws
    divine,
The Modern Man I sing.

From Song of Myself [1]

WALT WHITMAN
1819–1892

1

I celebrate myself, and sing myself,
And what I assume you shall assume,
For every atom belonging to me as good belongs to you.

I loafe and invite my soul,
I lean and loafe at my ease observing a spear of summer grass.   5

My tongue, every atom of my blood, form'd from this soil, this air,
Born here of parents born here from parents the same, and their parents the same,

[1] Whitman regards himself as the voice of the divine average in humanity as ll. 2–3 make clear. The phrase "O divine average!" is used in his poem "Starting from Paumanok."

I, now thirty-seven years old in perfect health begin,
Hoping to cease not till death.

Creeds and schools in abeyance,   10
Retiring back a while sufficed at what they are, but never forgotten,
I harbor for good or bad, I permit to speak at every hazard,
Nature without check with original energy.[2]

2

Houses and rooms are full of perfumes, the shelves are crowded with perfumes,
I breathe the fragrance myself and know it and like it,   15
The distillation would intoxicate me also, but I shall not let it.[3]

The atmosphere is not a perfume, it has no taste of the distillation, it is odorless,
It is for my mouth forever, I am in love with it,
I will go to the bank by the wood and become undisguised and naked,
I am mad for it to be in contact with me.   20
The smoke of my own breath,
Echoes, ripples, buzz'd whispers, love-root, silk-thread, crotch and vine,
My respiration and inspiration, the beating of my heart, the passing of blood and air
        through my lungs,
The sniff of green leaves and dry leaves, and of the shore and dark-color'd sea-rocks,
        and of hay in the barn,
The sound of the belch'd words of my voice loos'd to the eddies of the wind,   25
A few light kisses, a few embraces, a reaching around of arms,
The play of shine and shade on the trees as the supple boughs wag,
The delight alone or in the rush of the streets, or along the fields and hill-sides,
The feeling of health, the full-noon trill, the song of me rising from bed and meeting
        the sun.

Have you reckon'd a thousand acres much? Have you reckon'd the earth much?   30
Have you practis'd so long to learn to read?
Have you felt so proud to get at the meaning of poems?
Stop this day and night with me and you shall possess the origin of all poems,[4]
You shall possess the good of the earth and sun, (there are millions of suns left.)
You shall no longer take things at second or third hand, nor look through the eyes of
        the dead, nor feed on the spectres in books,   35
You shall not look through my eyes either, nor take things from me,
You shall listen to all sides and filter them from your self.

3

I have heard what the talkers were talking, the talk of the beginning and the end,
But I do not talk of the beginning or the end.

There was never any more inception than there is now,   40
Nor any more youth or age than there is now,

---

[2] Ll. 10–13 are cardinal in Whitman's thought. As John Burroughs (1837–1921), American naturalist, friend to Whitman, and author of *Whitman, A Study* (1896) was quick to see, these lines present his single theme: reliance on absolute nature.   [3] Whitman rejects the artificial in order to embrace nature. See ll. 32–35.   [4] Because he insists on reading nature, not men's interpretation of nature. There is, of course, a good deal of mysticism in Whitman's own interpretation of nature.

And will never be any more perfection than there is now,
Nor any more heaven or hell than there is now.

Urge and urge and urge,
Always the procreant urge of the world.   45
Out of the dimness opposite equals advance, always substance and increase, always sex,
Always a knit of identity, always distinction, always a breed of life.

To elaborate is no avail, learn'd and unlearn'd feel that it is so.

Sure as the most certain sure, plumb in the uprights, well entretied,[5] braced in the
      beams,
Stout as a horse, affectionate, haughty, electrical,   50
I and this mystery here we stand.

Clear and sweet is my soul, and clear and sweet is all that is not my soul.

Lack one lacks both, and the unseen is proved by the seen,
Till that becomes unseen and receives proof in its turn.

Showing the best and dividing it from the worst age vexes age,   55
Knowing the perfect fitness and equanimity of things, while they discuss I am silent,
      and go bathe and admire myself.

Welcome is every organ and attribute of me, and of any man hearty and clean,
Not an inch nor a particle of an inch is vile, and none shall be less familiar than the
      rest.

I am satisfied—I see, dance, laugh, sing;
As the hugging and loving bed-fellow sleeps at my side through the night, and with-
      draws at the peep of the day with stealthy tread,
Leaving the baskets cover'd with white towels swelling the house with their plenty,   60
Shall I postpone my acceptation and realization and scream at my eyes,
That they turn from gazing after and down the road,
And forthwith cipher and show me to a cent,
Exactly the value of one and exactly the value of two, and which is ahead?   65

Years of the Modern
WALT WHITMAN
1819–1892

   This poem has been called Whitman's greatest vision, one that the United Nations hopes
to make a reality.

Years of the modern! years of the unperform'd!
Your horizon rises, I see it parting away for more august dramas,

[5] A carpenter's vernacular meaning "crossed-braced" as between two joists or walls.

I see not America only, not only Liberty's nation but other nations preparing,
I see tremendous entrances and exists, new combinations, the solidarity of races,
I see that force advancing with irresistible power on the world's stage,   5
(Have the old forces, the old wars, played their parts? are the acts suitable to them
      closed?)
I see Freedom, completely arm'd and victorious and very haughty, with Law on one
      side and Peace on the other,
A stupendous trio all issuing forth against the idea of caste;
What historic denouements are these we so rapidly approach?
I see men marching and countermarching by swift millions,   10
I see the frontiers and boundaries of the old aristocracies broken,
I see the landmarks of European kings removed,
I see this day the People beginning their landmarks, (all others give way;)
Never were such sharp questions ask'd as this day,
Never was average man, his soul, more energetic, more like a God,   15
Lo, how he urges and urges, leaving the masses no rest!
His daring foot is on land and sea everywhere, he colonizes the Pacific, the archi-
      pelagoes,
With the steamship, the electric telegraph, the newspaper, the wholesale engines of
      war,
With these and the world-spreading factories he interlinks all geography, all lands;
What whispers are these O lands, running ahead of you, passing under the seas?   20
Are all nations communing? is there going to be but one heart to the globe?
Is humanity forming en-masse? for lo, tyrants tremble, crowns grow dim,
The earth, restive, confronts a new era, perhaps a general divine war,
No one knows what will happen next, such portents fill the days and nights;
Years prophetical! the space ahead as I walk, as I vainly try to pierce it, is full of
      phantoms,   25
Unborn deeds, things soon to be, project their shapes around me,
This incredible rush and heat, this strange ecstatic fever of dreams O years!
Your dreams O years, how they penetrate through me! (I know not whether I sleep
      or wake;)
The perform'd America and Europe grow dim, retiring in shadow behind me,
The unperform'd, more gigantic than ever, advance, advance upon me.   30

Native Moments
WALT WHITMAN
1819–1892

Native moments—when you come upon me—ah you are here now,
Give me now libidinous joys only,
Give me the drench of my passions, give me life coarse and rank,
To-day I go consort with Nature's darlings, to-night too,
I am for those who believe in loose delights, I share the midnight orgies of young
      men,   5
I dance with the dancers, and drink with the drinkers,
The echoes ring with our indecent calls, I pick out some low person for my dearest
      friend,
He shall be lawless, rude, illiterate, he shall be one condemn'd by others for deeds done,

I will play a part no longer, why should I exile myself from my companions?
O you shunn'd persons, I at least do not shun you,   10
I come forthwith in your midst, I will be your poet,
I will be more to you than to any of the rest.

Spirit That Form'd This Scene
WALT WHITMAN
1819–1892

Written in Platte Cañon, Colorado

Spirit that form'd this scene,
These tumbled rock-piles grim and red,
These reckless heaven-ambitious peaks,
These gorges, turbulent-clear streams, this naked
    freshness,
These formless wild arrays, for reasons of their
    own,   5
I know thee, savage spirit—we have communed
    together,
Mine too such wild arrays, for reasons of their
    own;
Was 't charged against my chants they had for-
    gotten art? [1]
To fuse within themselves its rules precise and
    delicatesse? [2]
The lyrist's measur'd beat, the wrought-out tem-
    ple's grace—column and polish'd arch
    forgot?   10
But thou that revelest here—spirit that form'd
    this scene,
They have remember'd thee.

In Harmony with Nature
To a Preacher

MATTHEW ARNOLD
1822–1888

"In harmony with Nature"? Restless fool,
Who with such heat dost preach what were to
    thee,
When true, the last impossibility—
To be like Nature strong, like Nature cool!

[1] See "Song of Myself," ll. 14–20 (p. 343).
[2] False delicacy.

Know, man hath all which Nature hath, but
    more,   5
And in that *more* lie all his hopes of good.
Nature is cruel, man is sick of blood;
Nature is stubborn, man would fain adore;

Nature is fickle, man hath need of rest;
Nature forgives no debt, and fears no grave;   10
Man would be mild, and with safe conscience
    blest.

Man must begin, know this, where Nature ends;
Nature and man can never be fast friends.
Fool, if thou canst not pass her, rest her slave!

Comments

Arnold's poem is clearly part of the eternal controversy over man's relation to nature. Arnold's basic point of view, found in lines 5–8, has been widely quoted by the humanists against the naturalists. The controversy, as old as Greek thought, became especially virulent in England after the appearance of Darwin's *The Origin of Species* in 1859; and later (after World War I) the controversy became involved in the Neo-Humanist movement in the United States. For definitions of these points of view, see the *Encyclopaedia Britannica*.

Dover Beach
MATTHEW ARNOLD
1822–1888

The sea is calm tonight,
The tide is full, the moon lies fair
Upon the straits;—on the French coast, the light
Gleams and is gone; the cliffs of England stand,

Glimmering and vast, out in the tranquil bay. 5
Come to the window, sweet is the night air!
Only, from the long line of spray
Where the sea meets the moon-blanch'd land,
Listen! you hear the grating roar
Of pebbles which the waves draw back, and
    fling, 10
At their return, up the high strand,
Begin, and cease, and then again begin,
With tremulous cadence slow, and bring
The eternal note of sadness in.

Sophocles long ago 15
Heard it on the Aegean, and it brought
Into his mind the turbid ebb and flow
Of human misery; we
Find also in the sound a thought,
Hearing it by this distant northern sea. 20

The Sea of Faith
Was once, too, at the full, and round earth's
    shore
Lay like the folds of a bright girdle furl'd.
But now I only hear
Its melancholy, long, withdrawing roar, 25
Retreating, to the breath
Of the night-wind, down the vast edges drear
And naked shingles[1] of the world.

Ah, love, let us be true
To one another! for the world, which seems 30
To lie before us like a land of dreams,
So various, so beautiful, so new,
Hath really neither joy, nor love, nor light,
Nor certitude, nor peace, nor help for pain;
And we are here as on a darkling plain 35
Swept with confused alarms of struggle and
    flight,
Where ignorant armies clash by night.

And he said to her, "Try to be true to me,
And I'll do the same for you, for things are bad
All over, etc., etc." 5
Well now, I knew this girl. It's true she had read
Sophocles in a fairly good translation
And caught that bitter allusion to the sea,
But all the time he was talking she had in mind
The notion of what his whiskers would feel
    like 10
On the back of her neck. She told me later on
That after a while she got to looking out
At the lights across the channel, and really felt
    sad,
Thinking of all the wine and enormous beds
And blandishments in French and the per-
    fumes. 15
And then she got really angry. To have been
    brought
All the way down from London, and then be
    addressed
As a sort of mournful cosmic last resort
Is really tough on a girl, and she was pretty.
Anyway, she watched him pace the room 20
And finger his watch-chain and seem to sweat
    a bit,
And then she said one or two unprintable things.
But you mustn't judge her by that. What I mean
    to say is,
She's really all right. I still see her once in a
    while
And she always treats me right. We have a
    drink 25
And I give her a good time, and perhaps it's a
    year
Before I see her again, but there she is,
Running to fat, but dependable as they come.
And sometimes I bring her a bottle of *Nuit
    d' Amour.*[1]

The Dover Bitch
A Criticism of Life
(For Andrews Wanning)

ANTHONY HECHT
1922–

So there stood Matthew Arnold and this girl
With the cliffs of England crumbling away be-
    hind them,

[1] Pebbled beaches.

Tragic Memory
GEORGE MEREDITH
1828–1909

In our old shipwrecked days there was an hour,
When in the firelight steadily aglow,
Joined slackly, we beheld the red chasm grow
Among the clicking coals. Our library-bower

[1] Night of Love, a perfume.

That eve was left to us: and hushed we sat   5
As lovers to whom Time is whispering.
From sudden-opened doors we heard them sing:
The nodding elders mixed good wine with chat.
Well knew we that Life's greatest treasure lay
With us, and of it was our talk. "Ah, yes!   10
Love dies!" I said: I never thought it less.
She yearned to me that sentence to unsay.
Then when the fire domed blackening, I found
Her cheek was salt against my kiss, and swift
Up the sharp scale of sobs her breast did
              lift:—   15
Now am I haunted by that taste! that sound!

Internal Harmony

GEORGE MEREDITH
1828–1909

Assured of worthiness we do not dread
Competitors; we rather give them hail
And greeting in the lists where we may fail:
Must, if we bear an aim beyond the head!
My betters are my masters: purely fed   5
By their sustainment I likewise shall scale
Some rocky steps between the mount and vale;
Meanwhile the mark I have and I will wed.
So that I draw the breath of finer air,
Station is nought, nor footways laurel-strewn,   10
Nor rivals tightly belted for the race.
Good speed to them! My place is here or there;
My pride is that among them I have place:
And thus I keep this instrument in tune.

I Never Lost as Much

EMILY DICKINSON
1830–1886

I never lost as much but twice,
And that was in the sod.
Twice have I stood a beggar
Before the door of God!

Angels—twice descending   5
Reimbursed my store—
Burglar! Banker—Father!
I am poor once more!

Wild Nights—Wild Nights!

EMILY DICKINSON
1830–1886

Wild Nights—Wild Nights!
Were I with thee
Wild Nights should be
Our luxury!

Futile—the Winds—   5
To a Heart in port—
Done with the Compass—
Done with the Chart!

Rowing in Eden—
Ah, the Sea!   10
Might I but moor—Tonight—
In Thee!

The Soul Selects Her Own Society

EMILY DICKINSON
1830–1886

The Soul selects her own Society—
Then—shuts the Door—
To her divine Majority—
Present no more—

Unmoved—she notes the Chariots
              pausing—   5
At her low Gate—
Unmoved—an Emperor be kneeling
Upon her Mat—

I've known her—from an ample nation—
Choose One—   10
Then—close the Valves of her attention—
Like Stone—

Some Keep the Sabbath Going to Church

EMILY DICKINSON
1830–1886

Some keep the sabbath going to Church—
I keep it, staying at Home—

With a Bobolink for a Chorister—
And an Orchard, for a Dome—

Some keep the Sabbath in Surplice—   5
I just wear my Wings—
And instead of tolling the Bell, for Church,
Our little Sexton—sings.

God preaches, a noted Clergyman—
And the sermon is never long,   10
So instead of getting to Heaven, at last—
I'm going, all along.

For that last Onset—when the King
Be witnessed—in the Room—

I willed my Keepsakes—Signed away
What portion of me be   10
Assignable—and then it was
There interposed a Fly—

With Blue—uncertain stumbling Buzz—
Between the light—and me—
And then the Windows failed—and then   15
I could not see to see—

I Died for Beauty

EMILY DICKINSON
1830–1886

I died for Beauty—but was scarce
Adjusted in the Tomb
When One who died for Truth, was lain
In an adjoining Room—

He questioned softly "Why I failed"?   5
"For Beauty", I replied—
"And I—for Truth—Themself are One—
We Bretheren, are", He said—

And so, as Kinsmen, met a Night—
We talked between the Rooms—   10
Until the Moss had reached our lips—
And covered up—our names—

I Started Early—
Took My Dog

EMILY DICKINSON
1830–1886

I started Early—Took my Dog—
And visited the Sea—
The Mermaids in the Basement
Came out to look at me—

And Frigates—in the Upper Floor   5
Extended Hempen Hands—
Presuming Me to be a Mouse—
Aground—upon the Sands—

But no Man moved Me—till the Tide
Went past my simple Shoe—   10
And past my Apron—and my Belt
And past my Boddice—too—

And made as He would eat me up—
As wholly as a Dew
Upon a Dandelion's Sleeve—   15
And then—I started—too—

And He—He followed—close behind—
I felt His Silver Heel
Upon my Ancle—Then my Shoes
Would overflow with Pearl—   20

Until We met the Solid Town—
No One He seemed to know—
And bowing—with a Mighty look—
At me—The Sea withdrew—

I Heard a Fly Buzz—
When I Died

EMILY DICKINSON
1830–1886

I heard a Fly buzz—when I died—
The Stillness in the Room
Was like the Stillness in the Air—
Between the Heaves of Storm—

The Eyes around—had wrung them dry—   5
And Breaths were gathering firm

I Had Been Hungry, All the Years

EMILY DICKINSON
1830–1886

I had been hungry, all the Years—
My Noon had Come—to dine—
I trembling drew the Table near—
And touched the Curious Wine—

'Twas this on Tables I had seen—   5
When turning, hungry, Home
I looked in Windows, for the Wealth
I could not hope—for Mine—

I did not know the ample Bread—
'Twas so unlike the Crumb   10
The Birds and I, had often shared
In Nature's—Dining Room—

The Plenty hurt me—'twas so new—
Myself felt ill—and odd—
As Berry—of a Mountain Bush—   15
Transplanted—to the Road—

Nor was I hungry—so I found
That Hunger—was a way
Of Persons outside Windows—
The Entering—takes away—   20

I Like to See It Lap the Miles

EMILY DICKINSON
1830–1886

I like to see it lap the Miles—
And lick the Valleys up—
And stop to feed itself at Tanks—
And then—prodigious step

Around a Pile of Mountains—   5
And supercilious peer
In Shanties—by the sides of Roads—
And then a Quarry pare

To fit it's sides
And crawl between   10
Complaining all the while
In horrid—hooting stanza—
Then chase itself down Hill—

And neigh like Boanerges—
Then—prompter than a Star   15
Stop—docile and omnipotent
At it's own stable door—

A Narrow Fellow in the Grass

EMILY DICKINSON
1830–1886

A narrow Fellow in the Grass
Occasionally rides—
You may have met Him—did you not
His notice sudden is—

The Grass divides as with a Comb—   5
A spotted shaft is seen—
And then it closes at your feet
And opens further on—

He likes a Boggy Acre
A Floor too cool for Corn—   10
Yet when a Boy, and Barefoot—
I more than once at Noon

Have passed, I thought, a Whip lash
Unbraiding in the Sun
When stooping to secure it   15
It wrinkled, and was gone—

Several of Nature's People
I know, and they know me—
I feel for them a transport
Of cordiality—   20

But never met this Fellow
Attended, or alone
Without a tighter breathing
And Zero at the Bone—

He Preached upon "Breadth"

EMILY DICKINSON
1830–1886

He preached upon "Breadth" till it argued him
       narrow—
The Broad are too broad to define

And of "Truth" until it proclaimed him a Liar—
The Truth never flaunted a Sign—

Simplicity fled from his counterfeit presence   5
As Gold the Pyrites would shun—
What confusion would cover the innocent Jesus
To meet so enabled a Man!

My Life Closed Twice Before Its Close

EMILY DICKINSON
1830–1886

My life closed twice before its close;
It yet remains to see
If Immortality unveil
A third event to me,

So huge, so hopeless to conceive   5
As these that twice befel.
Parting is all we know of heaven,
And all we need of hell.

The Last Chrysanthemum

THOMAS HARDY
1840–1928

Why should this flower delay so long
    To show its tremulous plumes?
Now is the time of plaintive robin-song,
    When flowers are in their tombs.

Through the slow summer, when the sun   5
    Called to each frond and whorl
That all he could for flowers was being done,
    Why did it not uncurl?

It must have felt that fervid call
    Although it took no heed,   10
Waking but now, when leaves like corpses fall,
    And saps all retrocede.

Too late its beauty, lonely thing,
    The season's shine is spent,
Nothing remains for it but shivering   15
    In tempests turbulent.

Had it a reason for delay,
    Dreaming in witlessness
That for a bloom so delicately gay
    Winter would stay its stress?   20

—I talk as if the thing were born
    With sense to work its mind;
Yet it is but one mask of many worn
    By the Great Face behind.

In Tenebris, II

THOMAS HARDY
1840–1928

*Considerabam ad dexteram, et videbam; et non
erat qui cognosceret me. . . . Non est qui requirat
animam meam. Psalm cxlii.*[1]

[1] I looked on *my* right hand and beheld, but *there
was* no man that would know me . . . no man
cared for my soul. (King James Version)

When the clouds' swoln bosoms echo back the
        shouts of the many and strong
That things are all as they best may be, save a
        few to be right ere long,
And my eyes have not the vision in them to dis-
        cern what to these is so clear,
The blot seems straightway in me alone; one
        better he were not here.

The stout upstanders say, All's well with us;
        ruers have nought to rue!   5
And what the potent say so oft, can it fail to be
        somewhat true?
Breezily go they, breezily come; their dust
        smokes around their career,
Till I think I am one born out of due time, who
        has no calling here.

Their dawns bring lusty joys, it seems; their eve-
        nings all that is sweet;
Our times are blessed times, they cry: Life
        shapes it as most meet,   10
And nothing is much the matter; there are many
        smiles to a tear;
Then what is the matter is I, I say. Why should
        such an one be here? . . .

Let him in whose ears the low-voiced Best is
    killed by the clash of the First,
Who holds that if way to the Better there be, it
    exacts a full look at the Worst,
Who feels that delight is a delicate growth
    cramped by crookedness, custom, and
    fear,   15
Get him up and be gone as one shaped awry; he
    disturbs the order here.

The Man He Killed

THOMAS HARDY
1840–1928

"Had he and I but met
    By some old ancient inn,
We should have sat us down to wet
    Right many a nipperkin!

"But ranged as infantry,   5
    And staring face to face,
I shot at him as he at me,
    And killed him in his place.

"I shot him dead because—
    Because he was my foe,   10
Just so: my foe of course he was;
    That's clear enough; although

"He thought he'd 'list, perhaps,
    Off-hand like—just as I—
Was out of work—had sold his traps—   15
    No other reason why.

"Yes; quaint and curious war is!
    You shoot a fellow down
You'd treat if met where any bar is,
    Or help to half-a-crown."   20

The Windhover:[1]
To Christ Our Lord

GERARD MANLEY HOPKINS
1844–1889

    Definitions of terms in the poem can be helpful, but the exact shade of meaning of each basic term depends more than usual on the complete, highly figurative context of the entire poem.

I caught this morning morning's minion,[2] king-
    dom of daylight's dauphin,[3] dapple-dawn-drawn Falcon, in his riding
    Of the rolling level underneath him steady air, and striding
High there, how he rung upon the rein of a wimpling[4] wing
In his ecstasy! then off, off forth on swing,   5
    As a skate's heel sweeps smooth on a bow-bend: the hurl and gliding
    Rebuffed the big wind. My heart in hiding
Stirred for a bird,—the achieve of, the mastery of the thing!

Brute beauty and valour and act, oh, air, pride, plume, here
    Buckle![5] AND the fire that breaks from thee then, a billion

[1] A member of the falcon family popularly so named because of its habit of hovering in the air over one spot. Known in England as a kestrel; in the United States as a sparrow hawk.   [2] One highly favored, a darling.   [3] Literally heir to the throne; figuratively Christ, Son of God.   [4] Turning or twisting on the wing.   [5] Interpreted variously. Probably buckle together, to join together the heroic qualities in l. 9.

Times told lovelier, more dangerous, O my chevalier! [6]

No wonder of it: shéer plód makes plough down sillion[7]   10
Shine, and blue-bleak embers, ah my dear,
   Fall, gall themselves, and gash[8] gold-vermilion.

[6] Literally knight; figuratively Christ.   [7] A plough's furrow; the ridge between the furrows.   [8] Probably Christ's blood.

The Harlot's House

OSCAR WILDE
1856–1900

WE caught the tread of dancing feet,
We loitered down the moonlit street,
And stopped beneath the harlot's house.

Inside, above the din and fray,
We heard the loud musicians play   5
The "Treues Liebes Herb"[1] of Strauss.

Like strange mechanical grotesques,
Making fantastic arabesques,
The shadows raced across the blind.

We watched the ghostly dancers spin   10
To sound of horn and violin,
Like black leaves wheeling in the wind.

Like wire-pulled automatons,
Slim silhouetted skeletons
Went sidling through the slow quadrille.   15

They took each other by the hand,
And danced a stately saraband;
Their laughter echoed thin and shrill.

Sometimes a clockwork puppet pressed
A phantom lover to her breast,   20
Sometimes they seemed to try to sing.

Sometimes a horrible marionette
Came out, and smoked its cigarette
Upon the steps like a live thing.

Then, turning to my love, I said,   25
"The dead are dancing with the dead,
The dust is whirling with the dust."

[1] "Dear True Heart."

But she—she heard the violin,
And left my side and entered in:
Love passed into the house of lust.   30

Then suddenly the tune went false,
The dancers wearied of the waltz,
The shadows ceased to wheel and whirl.

And down the long and silent street,
The dawn, with silver-sandalled feet,   35
Crept like a frightened girl.

Harlem Dancer

CLAUDE McKAY
1890–1948

Applauding youths laughed with young prosti-
   tutes
And watched her perfect, half-clothed body
   sway;
Her voice was like the sound of blended flutes
Blown by black players on a picnic day.
She sang and danced on gracefully and calm,   5
The light gauze hanging loose about her form;
To me she seemed a proudly-swaying palm
Grown lovelier for passing through a storm.
Upon her swarthy neck black shiny curls
Luxuriant fell; and tossing coins in praise,   10
The wine-flushed, bold-eyed boys, and even the
   girls,
Devoured her shape with eager, passionate gaze;
But looking at her falsely-smiling face,
I knew her self was not in that strange place.

To an Athlete Dying Young

A. E. HOUSMAN
1859–1936

The time you won your town the race
We chaired you through the market-place;

Man and boy stood cheering by,
And home we brought you shoulder-high.

To-day, the road all runners come,   5
Shoulder-high we bring you home,
And set you at your threshold down,
Townsman of a stiller town.

Smart lad, to slip betimes away
From fields where glory does not stay,   10
And early though the laurel grows
It withers quicker than the rose.

Eyes the shady night has shut
Cannot see the record cut,
And silence sounds no worse than cheers   15
After earth has stopped the ears.

Now you will not swell the rout
Of lads that wore their honours out,
Runners whom renown outran
And the name died before the man.   20

So set, before its echoes fade,
The fleet foot on the sill of shade,
And hold to the low lintel up
The still-defended challenge-cup.

And round that early-laurelled head   25
Will flock to gaze the strengthless dead,
And find unwithered on its curls
The garland briefer than a girl's.

The Wild Swans at Coole

WILLIAM BUTLER YEATS
1865–1939

The trees in their autumn beauty,
The woodland paths are dry,
Under the October twilight the water
Mirrors a still sky;
Upon the brimming water among the stones   5
Are nine-and-fifty swans.

The nineteenth autumn has come upon me
Since I first made my count;
I saw, before I had well finished,

All suddenly mount   10
And scatter wheeling in great broken rings
Upon their clamorous wings.

I have looked upon those brilliant creatures,
And now my heart is sore.
All's changed since I, hearing at twilight,   15
The first time on this shore,
The bell-beat of their wings above my head,
Trod with a lighter tread.

Unwearied still, lover by lover,
They paddle in the cold   20
Companionable streams or climb the air;
Their hearts have not grown old;
Passion or conquest, wander where they will,
Attend upon them still.

But now they drift on the still water   25
Mysterious, beautiful;
Among what rushes will they build,
By what lake's edge or pool
Delight men's eyes when I awake some day
To find they have flown away?   30

The Second Coming

WILLIAM BUTLER YEATS
1865–1939

Turning and turning in the widening gyre[1]
The falcon cannot hear the falconer;
Things fall apart; the centre cannot hold;
Mere anarchy is loosed upon the world,
The blood-dimmed tide is loosed, and every-
                            where   5
The ceremony of innocence is drowned;
The best lack all conviction, while the worst
Are full of passionate intensity.

Surely some revelation is at hand;
Surely the Second Coming[2] is at hand   10
The Second Coming! Hardly are those words out
When a vast image out of *Spiritus Mundi*[3]

[1] Circular or spiral movement.   [2] Related to the
second coming of Christ is Yeats's conviction that
the approaching end of an historical cycle of 2000
years would bring a new age.   [3] Literally world
spirit. For Yeats it means the "general mind," or our
collective consciousness penetrating the future.

Troubles my sight: somewhere in sands of the
    desert
A shape with lion body and the head of a man,
A gaze blank and pitless as the sun,   15
Is moving its slow thighs, while all about it
Reel shadows of the indignant desert birds.
The darkness drops again; but now I know
That twenty centuries of stony sleep
Were vexed to nightmare by a rocking cradle,   20
And what rough beast, its hour come round at
    last,
Slouches towards Bethlehem to be born?

Among School Children
WILLIAM BUTLER YEATS
1865–1939

I

I walk through the long schoolroom ques-
    tioning; [1]
A kind old nun in a white hood replies;
The children learn to cipher and to sing,
To study reading-books and history,
To cut and sew, be neat in everything   5
In the best modern way—the children's eyes
In momentary wonder stare upon
A sixty-year-old smiling public man.

II

I dream of a Ledaean body,[2] bent
Above a sinking fire, a tale that she   10
Told of a harsh reproof, or trivial event
That changed some childish day to tragedy—
Told, and it seemed that our two natures blent
Into a sphere from youthful sympathy,
Or else, to alter Plato's parable,[3]   15
Into the yolk and white of the one shell.

III

And thinking of that fit of grief or rage
I look upon one child or t'other there
And wonder if she stood so at that age—
For even daughters of the swan can share   20
Something of every paddler's heritage—
And had that colour upon cheek or hair,
And thereupon my heart is driven wild:
She stands before me as a living child.

IV

Her present image floats into the mind—   25
Did Quattrocento[4] finger fashion it
Hollow of cheek as though it drank the wind
And took a mess of shadows for its meat?
And I though never of Ladaean kind
Had pretty plumage once—enough of that,   30
Better to smile on all that smile, and show
There is a comfortable kind of old scarecrow.

V

What youthful mother, a shape upon her lap
Honey of generation[5] had betrayed,
And that must sleep, shriek, struggle to es-
    cape   35
As recollection or the drug decide,
Would think her son, did she but see that shape
With sixty or more winters on its head,
A compensation for the pang of his birth,
Or the uncertainty of his setting forth?   40

VI

Plato thought nature but a spume that plays
Upon a ghostly paradigm of things;[6]
Soldier Aristotle played the taws
Upon the bottom of a king of kings;[7]

[1] Yeats was an Irish Senator (1922–1928) interested in reforming the educational system.   [2] As beautiful as Leda and Helen of Troy, her daughter (see l. 20) whose father, Zeus, in the form of a swan had possessed Leda. Yeats's poem "Leda and the Swan" celebrates the event.   [3] Plato's *Symposium* tells us that Zeus "cut men in two . . . as you might divide an egg with a hair," and hence "each of us when separated is but the indenture of a man, having one side only like a flat fish, and he is always looking for his other half."

[4] An Italian term used by the art historians to describe schools and styles of fifteenth-century painting as, for example, Botticelli's female figures.
[5] Yeats's note: "I have taken the 'honey of generation' from Porphyry's essay on 'The Cave of the Nymphs,' but find no warrant in Porphyry for considering it the 'drug' that destroys the 'recollection' of pre-natal freedom. He blamed a cup of oblivion given in the zodiacal sign of Cancer." Porphyry's original name was Malchus (232?–304?), Greek scholar and neoplatonic philosopher.   [6] Plato regarded physical reality as an imperfect representation of ideal reality (Plato's philosophy of idealism).   [7] The pupil of Plato, Aristotle nevertheless taught that our world does possess reality.

World-famous golden-thighed Pythagoras[8]   45
Fingered upon a fiddle-stick or strings
What a star sang and careless Muses heard:
Old clothes upon old sticks to scare a bird.[9]

VII

Both nuns and mothers worship images,
But those the candles light are not as those   50
That animate a mother's reveries,
But keep a marble or a bronze repose.
And yet they too break hearts—O Presences
That passion, piety or affection knows,
And that all heavenly glory symbolise—   55
O self-born mockers of man's enterprise;

VIII

Labour is blossoming or dancing where
The body is not bruised to pleasure soul,
Nor beauty born out of its own despair,
Nor blear-eyed wisdom out of midnight oil.   60
O chestnut-tree, great-rooted blossomer,
Are you the leaf, the blossom or the bole?
O body swayed to music, O brightening glance,
How can we know the dancer from the dance?

Mr. Flood's Party
EDWIN ARLINGTON ROBINSON
1869–1935

Old Eben Flood,[1] climbing alone one night
Over the hill between the town below
And the forsaken upland hermitage
That held as much as he should ever know
On earth again of home, paused warily.   5
The road was his with not a native near;
And Eben, having leisure, said aloud,
For no man else in Tilbury Town[2] to hear:
"Well, Mr. Flood, we have the harvest moon
Again, and we may not have many more;   10
The bird is on the wing, the poet says,

And you and I have said it here before.
Drink to the bird." He raised up to the light
The jug that he had gone so far to fill,
And answered huskily: "Well, Mr. Flood,   15
Since you propose it, I believe I will."

Alone, as if enduring to the end
A valiant armor of scarred hopes outworn,
He stood there in the middle of the road
Like Roland's ghost winding a silent horn.[3]   20
Below him, in the town among the trees,
Where friends of other days had honored him,
A phantom salutation of the dead
Rang thinly till old Eben's eyes were dim.

Then, as a mother lays her sleeping child   25
Down tenderly, fearing it may awake,
He set the jug down slowly at his feet
With trembling care, knowing that most things
        break;
And only when assured that on firm earth
It stood, as the uncertain lives of men   30
Assuredly did not, he paced away,
And with his hand extended paused again:

"Well, Mr. Flood, we have not met like this
In a long time; and many a change has come
To both of us, I fear, since last it was   35
We had a drop together. Welcome home!"
Convivially returning with himself,
Again he raised the jug up to the light;
And with an acquiescent quaver said:
"Well, Mr. Flood, if you insist, I might.   40

"Only a very little, Mr. Flood—
For auld lang syne. No more, sir; that will do."
So, for the time, apparently it did,
And Eben evidently thought so too;
For soon amid the silver loneliness   45
Of night he lifted up his voice and sang,
Secure, with only two moons listening
Until the whole harmonious landscape rang—

"For auld lang syne." The weary throat gave out,
The last word wavered, and the song was
        done.   50
He raised again the jug regretfully
And shook his head, and was again alone.

---

[8] Greek philosopher, whose later followers thought him a god with a golden thigh, taught the transmigration of souls (reincarnation), and that reality is found in the mathematical relationships which govern its order and harmony. Such mysticism intrigued Yeats.   [9] See l. 32.

[1] Ebb and flood, the passing of time.   [2] Though this happens to be Robinson's name for Gardiner, Maine where he was reared, the name is of no consequence.

[3] Hero of the tales in the Charlemagne cycle; the defender of the Christians against the Saracens. The implications in ll. 19–20 is that Eben, like Roland, sounds his horn only to find his friends dead.

There was not much that was ahead of him,
And there was nothing in the town below—
Where strangers would have shut the many
    doors   55
That many friends had opened long ago.

Comments

Robinson has written a number of psychological portraits including "Miniver Cheevy" (p. 300). For an excellent analysis of "Mr. Flood's Party" see Wallace L. Anderson, *Edwin Arlington Robinson: A Critical Introduction,* Boston: Houghton Mifflin Company, 1967, pp. 110–112.

The Strong Are Saying Nothing

ROBERT FROST
1874–1963

The soil now gets a rumpling soft and damp,
And small regard to the future of any weed.
The final flat of the hoe's approval stamp
Is reserved for the bed of a few selected seed.

There is seldom more than a man to a harrowed
    piece.   5
Men work alone, their lots plowed far apart,
One stringing a chain of seed in an open crease,
And another stumbling after a halting cart.

To the fresh and black of the squares of early
    mold

The leafless bloom of a plum is fresh and
    white;   10
Though there's more than a doubt if the weather
    is not too cold
For the bees to come and serve its beauty aright.

Wind goes from farm to farm in wave on wave,
But carries no cry of what is hoped to be.
There may be little or much beyond the
    grave,   15
But the strong are saying nothing until they see.

Acquainted with the Night

ROBERT FROST
1874–1963

I have been one acquainted with the night.
I have walked out in rain—and back in rain.
I have outwalked the furthest city light.

I have looked down the saddest city lane.
I have passed by the watchman on his beat   5
And dropped my eyes, unwilling to explain.

I have stood still and stopped the sound of feet
When far away an interrupted cry
Came over houses from another street,

But not to call me back or say good-by;   10
And further still at an unearthly height
One luminary clock against the sky

Proclaimed the time was neither wrong nor right.
I have been one acquainted with the night.

A Masque of Reason

ROBERT FROST
1874–1963

"The Trial by Existence" (p. 322) and "A Masque of Reason" are companion pieces through which Frost explores some of his basic metaphysical assumptions. Both poems are concerned with the trial of man on the earth, and our failure to find ultimate answers to the meaning of that trial which leaves us "bearing it crushed and mystified." True to Frost's belief that "everything written is as good as it is dramatic," both poems are little verse plays, especially "A Masque of Reason" with its four characters—and the warning is clear: its meaning emerges from the interaction of the characters' points of view, not from the assumptions of any single character regardless of his importance.

Frost thinks of "A Masque of Reason" as being a forty-third chapter (see the final line) for *The Book of Job* which implies either that he answers the question, "Why do the innocent suffer?" or that he pursues the question further with commentary of his own. In any event, knowing the basic events in *Job* will increase our understanding of Frost's poem, although a fresh and intimate reading of *Job* is urgently recommended.*

The "Prologue" to *Job* (chaps. 1–2) makes it clear that Satan has taunted God by arguing that the "perfect and upright" Job "fears God and eschews evil" only because "his substance is increased in the land." God accepts the challenge and permits Satan to test Job with afflictions. Reduced to abject poverty and with his children dead, Job suffers intensely from boils while his wife advises him to "curse God, and die." Later, three friends counsel and finally warn him to confess his sins. Job stoutly maintains his innocence, challenges God's justice, and yearns to meet God face to face to ask why an innocent man should suffer. God appears "out of the whirlwind," and Job, awed by God's presence and knowledge, repents of his belligerent challenge to God ("What is the Almighty, that we should serve him?" 21:15)—but not of the crimes falsely alleged by his friends—and is returned to prosperity. "A Masque of Reason" begins with Job still wondering what he had done "to deserve such pain" and waiting to "come to rest in an official verdict."

A fair oasis in the purest desert.
A man sits leaning back against a palm.
His wife lies by him looking at the sky.

Man	You're not asleep?	
Wife	No, I can hear you. Why?	
Man	I said the incense tree's on fire again.	5
Wife	You mean the Burning Bush?[1]	
Man	The Christmas Tree.	
Wife	I shouldn't be surprised.	
Man	The strangest light!	
Wife	There's a strange light on everything today.	
Man	The myrrh tree gives it. Smell the rosin burning?	
	The ornaments the Greek artificers	10
	Made for the Emperor Alexius,[2]	
	The Star of Bethlehem, the pomegranates,	
	The birds, seem all on fire with Paradise.	
	And hark, the gold enameled nightingales	
	Are singing. Yes, and look, the Tree is troubled.	15
	Someone's caught in the branches.	
Wife	So there is.	

---

* The serious student of *Job* will be rewarded by consulting *The Interpreter's Bible,* Nashville: Abingdon Press, vol. III (1954), pp. 877–1198, including the Text, Exegesis, and Exposition. For a briefer but excellent commentary, see *The Westminster Study Edition of the Holy Bible,* Philadelphia: The Westminster Press, 1948, pp. 638–690.

[1] *Exodus,* 3:2. The Angel of the Lord appeared to Moses "in a flame of fire out of the midst of a bush . . . and the bush was not consumed."   [2] Alexius Comnenus (1048–1118), first of the Comneni dynasty of Byzantine emperors.

Man	He can't get out.
Wife	He's loose! He's out!
	It's God.

I'd know Him by Blake's picture[3] anywhere.
Now what's He doing?

Man	Pitching throne, I guess,

Here by our atoll.

Wife	Something Byzantine.[4]	20

(The throne's a plywood flat, prefabricated,
That God pulls lightly upright on its hinges
And stands beside, supporting it in place.)

Perhaps for an Olympic Tournament,
Or Court of Love.

Man	More likely Royal Court—	25

Or Court of Law, and this is Judgment Day.
I trust it is. Here's where I lay aside
My varying opinion of myself
And come to rest in an official verdict.
Suffer yourself to be admired, my love,   30
As Waller says.[5]

Wife	Or not admired. Go over

And speak to Him before the others come.
Tell Him He may remember you: you're Job.

God	Oh, I remember well: you're Job, my Patient.

How are you now? I trust you're quite recovered,   35
And feel no ill effects from what I gave you.

Job [6]	Gave me in truth: I like the frank admission.

I am a name for being put upon.
But, yes, I'm fine, except for now and then
A reminiscent twinge of rheumatism.   40
The let-up's heavenly. You perhaps will tell us
If that is all there is to be of Heaven,
Escape from so great pains of life on earth
It gives a sense of let-up calculated
To last a fellow to Eternity.   45

God	Yes, by and by. But first a larger matter.

I've had you on my mind a thousand years
To thank you someday for the way you helped me
Establish once for all the principle
There's no connection man can reason out   50
Between his just deserts and what he gets.
Virtue may fail and wickedness succeed.
'Twas a great demonstration we put on.
I should have spoken sooner had I found

---

[3] A reference to William Blake's (1757–1827) engravings for the Bible, especially to one titled, "Then the Lord Answered Job out of the Whirlwind." Blake furnished engravings for many of his own books of poetry.   [4] From Byzantium, the ancient name of Constantinople. A reference to the ornate Byzantine architecture notable for such features as the circle, dome, and round arch. St. Sophia at Constantinople and St. Mark at Venice are examples of Byzantine architecture.   [5] "Song" ("Go, lovely rose"), p. 293.
[6] By referring to Job first as "Man," Frost is, of course, using Job as a symbol of mankind, a symbol frequently used in connection with *The Book of Job*.

55

The word I wanted. You would have supposed
One who in the beginning *was* the Word [7]
Would be in a position to command it.
I have to wait for words like anyone.
Too long I've owed you this apology
For the apparently unmeaning sorrow

60

You were afflicted with in those old days.
But it was of the essence of the trial
You shouldn't understand it at the time.
It had to seem unmeaning to have meaning.
And it came out all right. I have no doubt

65

You realize by now the part you played
To stultify the Deuteronomist [8]
And change the tenor of religious thought.
My thanks are to you for releasing me
From moral bondage to the human race.

70

The only free will there at first was man's,
Who could do good or evil as he chose.
I had no choice but I must follow him
With forfeits and rewards he understood—
Unless I liked to suffer loss of worship.

75

I had to prosper good and punish evil.
You changed all that. You set me free to reign.
You are the Emancipator of your God,
And as such I promote you to a saint. [9]

Job   You hear him, Thyatira: [10] we're a saint.

80

Salvation in our case is retroactive.
We're saved, we're saved, whatever else it means.

Jobs' Wife   Well, after all these years!

Job   This is my wife.

Job's Wife   If You're the deity I assume You are—
(I'd know You by Blake's picture anywhere)—

85

God   The best, I'm told, I ever have had taken.

Job's Wife   —I have a protest I would lodge with You.
I want to ask You if it stands to reason
That women prophets should be burned as witches
Whereas men prophets are received with honor.

90

Job   Except in their own country, Thyatira.

God   You're not a witch?

Job's Wife   No.

God   Have you ever been one?

Job   Sometimes she thinks she has and gets herself
Worked up about it. But she really hasn't—

---

[7] *John,* 1:1. "In the beginning was the Word, and the Word was with God, and the Word was God."
[8] The name given to the unknown writer of the six books of history following *Deuteronomy* who interprets the history of the Hebrew nation with the so-called "Deuteronomic formula" which holds that obedience to God's laws will bring prosperity while disobedience will bring material disaster to the nation. The formula was later used in the Wisdom books (*Job, Proverbs,* and *Ecclesiastes*) as the Wisdom formula," but now applied to the individual instead of the nation. Frost states the result of the formula in l. 76.   [9] Job had demonstrated his own integrity, but, more important to God, by proving that not all men "serve for pay" (l. 353), Job had vindicated God against Satan.   [10] Frost's name for Job's wife; she is given no name in the Bible.

Not in the sense of having to my knowledge 95
Predicted anything that came to pass.

Job's Wife The witch of Endor[11] was a friend of mine.

God You wouldn't say she fared so very badly.
I noticed when she called up Samuel 100
His spirit had to come. Apparently
A witch was stronger than a prophet there.

Job's Wife But she was burned for witchcraft.

God   That is not
Of record in my Note Book.[12]

Job's Wife   Well, she was.
And I should like to know the reason why.[13]

God There you go asking for the very thing 105
We've just agreed I didn't have to give.

(*The throne collapses. But He picks it up
And this time locks it up and leaves it.*)

Where has she been the last half hour or so?
She wants to know why there is still injustice.
I answer flatly: That's the way it is, 110
And bid my will avouch it like Macbeth.[14]
We may as well go back to the beginning
And look for justice in the case of Segub.[15]

Job Oh, Lord, Let's not go *back* to anything. 115

God Because your wife's past won't bear looking into?
In our great moment what did you do, Madam?
What did you try to make your husband say?[16]

Job's Wife No, let's not live things over. I don't care.
I stood by Job. I may have turned on You. 120
Job scratched his boils[17] and tried to think what he
Had done or not done to or for the poor.
The test is always how we treat the poor.
It's time the poor were treated by the state
In some ways not so penal as the poorhouse. 125
That's one thing more to put on Your agenda.
Job hadn't done a thing, poor innocent.[18]
I told him not to scratch: it made it worse.
If I said once I said a thousand times,
Don't scratch! And when, as rotten as his skin, 130
His tents blew all to pieces, I picked up
Enough to build him every night a pup tent
Around him so it wouldn't touch and hurt him.
I did my wifely duty. I should tremble!
All You can seem to do is lose Your temper 135
When reason-hungry mortals ask for reasons.[19]

[11] *I Samuel,* 28:3–25.   [12] Her death is not recorded in the Bible (God's "Note Book").   [13] See footnote 26 for l. 241.   [14] See *Macbeth,* III. i. 118–120.   [15] *I Kings,* 16:34. Frost's line implies that the sacrifice of Segub's life by his father, Hiel, cannot be defended. See also *Joshua,* 6:26.   [16] "Then said his wife unto him, Dost thou still retain thine integrity? curse God, and die." *Job,* 2:9.   [17] The Biblical term implies a terrible disease, perhaps elephantiasis, which disfigured Job's face and bred worms or maggots in his sores.   [18] As Job stoutly maintains throughout his afflictions. Why, he asks, should the innocent suffer?   [19] Thyatira believes that instead of giving Job reasons for his pain, God challenged him with questions to induce awe and reverence in him. See footnote 21 for l. 172.

Of course, in the abstract high singular
There isn't any universal reason;
And no one but a man would think there was.
You don't catch women trying to be Plato.   140
Still there must be lots of unsystematic
Stray scraps of palliative reason
It wouldn't hurt You to vouchsafe the faithful.
You thought it was agreed You needn't give them.
You thought to suit Yourself. I've not agreed   145
To anything with anyone.

Job   There, there,
You go to sleep. God must await events
As well as words.

Job's Wife   I'm serious. God's had
Aeons of time and still it's mostly women
Get burned for prophecy, men almost never.   150

Job   God needs time just as much as you or I
To get things done. Reformers fail to see that.
She'll go to sleep. Nothing keeps her awake
But physical activity I find.
Try to read to her and she drops right off.   155

God   She's beautiful.

Job   Yes, she was just remarking
She now felt younger by a thousand years
Than the day she was born.

God   That's about right,
I should have said. You got your age reversed
When time was found to be a space dimension[20]   160
That could, like any space, be turned around in?

Job   Yes, both of us: we saw to that at once.
But, God, I have a question too to raise.
(My wife gets in ahead of me with hers.)
I need some help about this reason problem   165
Before I am too late to be got right
As to what reasons I agree to waive.
I'm apt to string along with Thyatira.
God knows—or rather, You know (God forgive me)
I waived the reason for my ordeal—but—   170
I have a question even there to ask—
In confidence.[21] There's no one here but her,
And she's a woman: she's not interested
In general ideas and principles.

God   What are her interests, Job?

Job   Witch-women's rights.   175
Humor her there or she will be confirmed
In her suspicion You're no feminist.
You have it in for women, she believes.

---

[20] An oblique reference to Einstein's concept of "space-time" as a single dimension.   [21] Job is saying that when God "answered" him "out of the whirlwind" (38:1 to 41:34) Job was given no reasons for his ordeal. Nothing had been more urgent to Job than to meet God face to face (19:25–27; 23:3–5), and according to Frost, Job's (man's) urgency still exists.

Kipling invokes You as Lord God of Hosts.[22]
She'd like to know how You would take a prayer   180
That started off Lord God of Hostesses.

God   I'm charmed with her.
Job   Yes, I could see You were.
But to my question. I am much impressed
With what You say we have established.[23]
Between us, You and I.

God   I make you see?   185
It would be too bad if Columbus-like
You failed to see the worth of your achievement.

Job   You call it mine.
God   We groped it out together.
Any originality it showed
I give you credit for. My forte is truth,   190
Or metaphysics, long the world's reproach
For standing still in one place true forever;
While science goes self-superseding on.
Look at how far we've left the current science
Of Genesis behind. The wisdom there though,   195
Is just as good as when I uttered it.
Still, novelty has doubtless an attraction.

Job   So it's important who first thinks of things?
God   I'm a great stickler for the author's name.
By proper names I find I do my thinking.   200

Job's Wife   God, who invented earth?
Job   What, still awake?
God   Any originality it showed
Was of the Devil. He invented Hell,
False premises that are the original
Of all originality, the sin   205
That felled the angels, Wolsey should have said.[24]
As for the earth, we groped that out together,
Much as your husband Job and I together
Found out the discipline man needed most
Was to learn his submission to unreason;   210
And that for man's own sake as well as mine,
So he won't find it hard to take his orders
From his inferiors in intelligence
In peace and war—especially in war.

Job   So he won't find it hard to take his war.   215
God   You have the idea. There's not much I can tell you.
Job   All very splendid. I am flattered proud
To have been in on anything with You.
'Twas a great demonstration if You say so.
Though incidentally I sometimes wonder   220
Why it had had to be at my expense.

God   It had to be at somebody's expense.
Society can never think things out:

---

[22] Rudyard Kipling's (1865–1936) poem, "Recessional."   [23] See ll. 47–79. The point of view expressed in them does not appear in *Job*.   [24] See Shakespeare, *Henry VIII*. III. ii. 440–441.

It has to see them acted out by actors,
Devoted actors at a sacrifice— 225
The ablest actors I can lay my hands on.[25]
Is that your answer?

Job   No, for I have yet
To ask my question. We disparage reason.
But all the time it's what we're most concerned with.
There's will as motor and there's will as brakes. 230
Reason is, I suppose, the steering gear.
The will as brakes can't stop the will as motor
For very long. We're plainly made to go.
We're going anyway and may as well
Have some say as to where we're headed for; 235
Just as we will be talking anyway
And may as well throw in a little sense.
Let's do so now. Because I let You off
From telling me Your reason, don't assume
I thought You had none. Somewhere back 240
I knew You had one.[26] But this isn't it
You're giving me. You say we groped this out.
But if You will forgive me the irreverence,
It sounds to me as if You thought it out,
And took Your time to it. It seems to me 245
An afterthought, a long long afterthought.
I'd give more for one least beforehand reason
Than all the justifying ex-post-facto
Excuses trumped up by You for theologians.
The front of being answerable to no one 250
I'm with You in maintaining to the public.
But, Lord, we showed them what. The audience
Has all gone home to bed. The play's played out.
Come, after all these years—to satisfy me.
I'm curious. And I'm a grown-up man: 255
I'm not a child for You to put me off
And tantalize me with another "Oh, because."
You'd be the last to want me to believe
All Your effects were merely lucky blunders.
That would be unbelief and atheism. 260
The artist in me cries out for design.
Such devilish ingenuity of torture
Did seem unlike You, and I tried to think
The reason might have been some other person's.
But there is nothing You are not behind. 265
I did not ask then, but it seems as if
Now after all these years You might indulge me.
Why did You hurt me so? I am reduced
To ask flatly for a reason—outright.

---

[25] Ll. 222–226 do not constitute a random remark by Frost merely to interject a theory of his (although the remark *does* represent a factor in his poetic theory); some Bible commentators regard *Job* as a play whose function is as Frost describes it.   [26] Man's inevitable insistence on finding ordered sense in life, and especially the reasons for things understandable to man.

God	I'd tell you, Job—	
Job	All right, don't tell me then	270

If you don't want to. I don't want to know.
But what is all this secrecy about?
I fail to see what fun, what satisfaction
A God can find in laughing at how badly
Men fumble at the possibilities   275
When left to guess forever for themselves.
The chances are when there's so much pretense
Of metaphysical profundity
The obscurity's a fraud to cover nothing.
I've come to think no so-called hidden value's   280
Worth going after. Get down into things
It will be found there's no more given there
Than on the surface. If there ever was,
The crypt was long since rifled by the Greeks.
We don't know where we are, or who we are.   285
We don't know one another; don't know You;
Don't know what time it is. We don't know, don't we?
Who says we don't? Who got up these misgivings?
Oh, we know well enough to go ahead with.
I mean we seem to know enough to act on.   290
It comes down to a doubt about the wisdom
Of having children—after having had them,
So there is nothing we can do about it
But warn the children they perhaps should have none.
You could end this by simply coming out   295
And saying plainly and unequivocally
Whether there's any part of man immortal.
Yet You don't speak. Let fools bemuse themselves
By being baffled for the sake of being.
I'm sick of the whole artificial puzzle.[27]   300

Job's Wife	You won't get any answers out of God.	
God	My kingdom, what an outbreak!	
Job's Wife	Job is right.	

Your kingdom, yes, Your kingdom come on earth.
Pray tell me what does that mean. Anything?
Perhaps that earth is going to crack someday   305
Like a big egg and hatch a heaven out
Of all the dead and buried from their graves.
One simple little statement from the throne
Would put an end to such fantastic nonsense;[28]
And, too, take care of twenty of the four   310
And twenty freedoms on the party docket.
Or is it only four?[29] My extra twenty
Are freedoms from the need of asking questions.
(I hope You know the game called twenty questions.)
For instance, is there such a thing as Progress?   315

---

[27] See *Job*, 10:1 and 15.   [28] See *Revelation*, 20–21.   [29] Apparently a reference to the Four Freedoms proposed by President Franklin D. Roosevelt in his message to Congress (January 6, 1941): (1) freedom of speech and expression, (2) freedom of every person to worship God in his own way, (3) freedom from want, and (4) freedom from fear.

Job says there's no such thing as Earth's becoming
An easier place for man to save his soul in.
Except as a hard place to save his soul in,
A trial ground where he can try himself[30]
And find out whether he is any good,   320
It would be meaningless. It might as well
Be Heaven at once and have it over with.

God Two pitching on like this tend to confuse me.
One at a time, please. I will answer Job first.
I'm going to tell Job why I tortured him   325
And trust it won't be adding to the torture.
I was just showing off to the Devil, Job,
As is set forth in chapters One and Two.
(*Job takes a few steps pacing.*) Do you mind?
(*God eyes him anxiously.*)

Job   No. No, I mustn't.   330
'Twas human of You. I expected more
Than I could understand and what I get
Is almost less than I can understand.
But I don't mind. Let's leave it as it stood.
The point was it was none of my concern.   335
I stick to that. But talk about confusion!
How is that for a mix-up, Thyatira?
Yet I suppose what seems to us confusion
Is not confusion, but the form of forms,
The serpent's tail stuck down the serpent's throat,   340
Which is the symbol of eternity
And also of the way all things come round,
Or of how rays return upon themselves,
To quote the greatest Western poem yet.[31]
Though I hold rays deteriorate to nothing,   345
First white, then red, then ultra red, then out.[32]

God Job, you must understand my provocation.
The tempter comes to me and I am tempted.[33]
I'd had about enough of his derision
Of what I valued most in human nature.   350
He thinks he's smart. He thinks he can convince me
It is no different with my followers
From what it is with his. Both serve for pay.
Disinterestedness never did exist
And if it did, it wouldn't be a virtue.   355
Neither would fairness. You have heard the doctrine.
It's on the increase. He could count on no one:
That was his look out. I could count on you.
I wanted him forced to acknowledge so much.

[30] See "The Trial by Existence," p. 322.   [31] In conversation with one of the editors of this book (Nov. 19, 1960) Frost identified this poem as Emerson's "Uriel," especially ll. 21–24 which read: "'Line in nature is not found; / Unit and universe are round; In vain produced, all rays return; / Evil will bless, and ice will burn.'"   [32] This line might be read in this way: First a clear light (knowledge or reason), then the heat of argument with less light, then argument in anger, then neither—nothing.   [33] Satan had said to God, "Thou hast blessed the work of his [Job's] hands, and his substance is increased in the land. But put forth thy hand now, and touch all that he hath, and he will curse thee to thy face." *Job*, 1:10–11.

I gave you over to him, but with safeguards.　　　　　　　　　360
I took care of you. And before you died
I trust I made it clear I took your side
Against your comforters in their contention
You must be wicked to deserve such pain.
That's Browning and sheer Chapel Non-conformism.[34]　　365

Job　　God, please, enough for now. I'm in no mood
　　　　For more excuses.

God　　　　　　　　　What I mean to say:
　　　　Your comforters were wrong.[35]

Job　　　　　　　　　　　　Oh, that committee!

God　　I saw you had no fondness for committees.
　　　　Next time you find yourself pressed on to one　　　370
　　　　For the revision of the Book of Prayer
　　　　Put that in if it isn't in already:
　　　　Deliver us from committees. 'Twill remind me.
　　　　I would do anything for you in reason.

Job　　Yes, yes.

God　　　　　　You don't seem satisfied.

Job　　　　　　　　　　　　I am.　　　　　　　　　375

God　　You're pensive.

Job　　　　　　　　Oh, I'm thinking of the Devil.
　　　　You must remember he was in on this.
　　　　We can't leave him out.

God　　　　　　　　　　　No. No, we don't need to.
　　　　We're too well off.

Job　　　　　　　　Someday we three should have
　　　　A good old get-together celebration.　　　　　　380

God　　Why not right now?

Job　　　　　　　　　　We can't without the Devil.

God　　The Devil's never very far away.
　　　　He too is pretty circumambient.
　　　　He has but to appear. He'll come for me,
　　　　Precipitated from the desert air.　　　　　　　　385
　　　　Show yourself, son. I'll get back on my throne
　　　　For this I think. I find it always best
　　　　To be upon my dignity with him.

　　　　(*The Devil enters like a sapphire wasp*
　　　　That flickers mica wings. He lifts a hand　　　390
　　　　To brush away a disrespectful smile.
　　　　Job's wife sits up.)

---

[34] "Chapel Non-conformism" is a reference to certain Protestant sects (called also Dissenters and Non-cons) who refused the Church of England's Act of Uniformity ("unfeigned assent to all and everything contained in The Book of Common Prayer"). According to Frost's God the Nonconformists believe that pain is used to punish the wicked. L. 364, except for the first word, is an exact quotation from Browning's poem, " 'Childe Roland to the Dark Tower Came,' "—"He must be wicked to deserve such pain" (l. 84), a comment on a horribly ugly horse. Frost's God, then, is using Browning's line as a credo of the Nonconformists with whom, of course, Frost's God disagrees. 　　[35] Eliphaz, Bildad, and Zophar, whom Job calls "miserable comforters" (16:2), are rebuked by God for falsely accusing Job of crimes (42:7–8). They are used here by Frost to symbolize traditional habits of thought which neither Frost's God nor *Job's* God subscribes to. For the "comforters'" speeches, see *Job*, chaps. 4–31.

Job's Wife	Well, if we aren't all here,
	Including me, the only Dramatis
	Personae needed to enact the problem.
Job	We've waked her up.
Job's Wife	I haven't been asleep. 395
	I've heard what you were saying—every word.
Job	What did we say?
Job's Wife	You said the Devil's in it.
Job	She always claims she hasn't been asleep.
	And what else did we say?
Job's Wife	Well, what led up—
	Something about—(*The three men laugh.*) 400
	—The Devil's being God's best inspiration.
Job	Good, pretty good.
Job's Wife	Wait till I get my Kodak.
	Would you two please draw in a little closer?
	No—no, that's not a smile there. That's a grin.
	Satan, what ails you? Where's the famous tongue, 405
	Thou onetime Prince of Conversationists?
	This is polite society you're in
	Where good and bad are mingled everywhichway,
	And ears are lent to any sophistry
	Just as if nothing mattered but our manners. 410
	You look as if you either hoped or feared
	You were more guilty of mischief than you are.
	Nothing has been brought out that for my part
	I'm not prepared for or that Job himself
	Won't find a formula for taking care of. 415
Satan	Like the one Milton found to fool himself
	About his blindness.[36]
Job's Wife	Oh, he speaks! He *can* speak!
	That strain again! Give me excess of it! [37]
	As dulcet as a pagan temple gong!
	He's twitting us. Oh, by the way, you haven't 420
	By any chance a Lady Apple on you?
	I saw a boxful in the Christmas market.
	How I should prize one personally from you.
God	Don't *you* twit. He's unhappy. Church neglect
	And figurative use have pretty well 425
	Reduced him to a shadow of himself.
Job's Wife	*That* explains why he's so diaphanous
	And easy to see through. But where's he off to?
	I thought there were to be festivities
	Of some kind. We could have charades. 430
God	He has his business he must be about.
	Job mentioned him and so I brought him in
	More to give his reality its due
	Than anything.
Job's Wife	He's very real to me
	And always will be. Please don't go. Stay, stay 435

[36] See "On His Blindness," p. 297. Satin is equating the tragic blow of blindness which struck Milton in mid-career with Job's afflictions.   [37] Shakespeare, *Twelfth Night*, I. i. 1–4.

But to the evensong and having played
Together we will go with you along.[38]
There are who won't have had enough of you
If you go now. Look how he takes no steps!
He isn't really going, yet he's leaving.   440

Job   (*Who has been standing dazed with new ideas*)
He's on that tendency that like the Gulf Stream,
Only of sand not water, runs through here.
It has a rate distinctly different
From the surrounding desert; just today   445
I stumbled over it and got tripped up.

Job's Wife   Oh, yes, that tendency! Oh, do come off it.
Don't let it carry you away. I hate
A tendency. The minute you get on one
It seems to start right off accelerating.   450
Here, take my hand.

(*He takes it and alights*
In three quick steps as off an escalator.
The tendency, a long, long narrow strip
Of middle-aisle church carpet, sisal hemp,
Is worked by hands invisible off stage.)   455

I want you in my group beside the throne—
Must have you. There, that's just the right arrangement.
Now someone can light up the Burning Bush
And turn the gold enameled artificial birds on.
I recognize them. Greek artificers   460
Devised them for Alexius Comnenus.
That won't show in the picture. That's too bad.
Neither will I show. That's too bad moreover.
Now if you three have settled anything   465
You'd as well smile as frown on the occasion.[39]

(*Here endeth chapter forty-three of Job.*)

[38] See Herrick's poem, "To Daffodils," p. 292, ll. 8–10, for the source of ll. 435–437 above.   [39] Reminiscent of Voltaire's saying, "It is better to laugh than to hang oneself."

Sunday Morning[1]

WALLACE STEVENS *
1879–1955

I

Complacencies of the peignoir,[2] and late

Coffee and oranges in a sunny chair,
And the green freedom of a cockatoo
Upon a rug mingle to dissipate
The holy hush of ancient sacrifice.   5
She dreams a little, and she feels the dark
Encroachment of that old catastrophe,[3]
As a calm darkens among water-lights.
The pungent oranges and bright, green wings
Seem things in some procession of the dead,   10

[1] Double meaning: religious Sunday, and sun day as in ll. 2, 19–21, 91–97, 110. Stevens's basic question: where is the true paradise? The answer is found in the replies to the woman's troubled questionings.   [2] Negligee.
* For the third poem by Stevens in this book, "Anecdote of the Jar," see Ciardi's "Dialogue with the Audience," p. 848) in which he comments on Stevens and his poem.

[3] The crucifixion or possibly death in general.

Winding across wide water,[4] without sound.
The day is like wide water, without sound,
Stilled for the passing of her dreaming feet
Over the seas, to silent Palestine,
Dominion of the blood and sepulchre.[5]   15

II

Why should she give her bounty to the dead?
What is divinity if it can come
Only in silent shadows and in dreams?
Shall she not find in comforts of the sun,
In pungent fruit and bright, green wings, or
    else   20
In any balm or beauty of the earth,
Things to be cherished like the thought of
    heaven?
Divinity must live within herself:
Passions of rain, or moods in falling snow;
Grievings in loneliness, or unsubdued   25
Elations when the forest blooms; gusty
Emotions on wet roads on autumn nights;
All pleasures and all pains, remembering
The bough of summer and the winter branch.
These are the measures destined for her soul.   30

III

Jove[6] in the clouds had his inhuman birth.
No mother suckled him, no sweet land gave
Large-mannered motions to his mythy mind.
He moved among us, as a muttering king,
Magnificent, would move among his hinds,   35
Until our blood, commingling, virginal,
With heaven, brought such requital to desire
The very hinds discerned it, in a star.
Shall our blood fail? Or shall it come to be
The blood of paradise? And shall the earth   40
Seem all of paradise that we shall know?
The sky will be much friendlier then than now,
A part of labor and a part of pain,

And next in glory to enduring love,
Not this dividing and indifferent blue.   45

IV

She says, "I am content when wakened birds,
Before they fly, test the reality
Of misty fields, by their sweet questionings;
But when the birds are gone, and their warm
    fields
Return no more, where, then, is paradise?"   50
There is not any haunt of prophecy,
Nor any old chimera of the grave,
Neither the golden underground, nor isle
Melodious, where spirits gat[7] them home,
Nor visionary south, nor cloudy palm   55
Remote on heaven's hill, that has endured
As April's green endures; or will endure
Like her remembrance of awakened birds,
Or her desire for June and evening, tipped
By the consummation of the swallow's wings. 60

V

She says, "But in contentment I still feel
The need of some imperishable bliss."
Death is the mother of beauty;[8] hence from her,
Alone, shall come fulfilment to our dreams
And our desires. Although she strews the
    leaves   65
Of sure obliteration on our paths,
The path sick sorrow took, the many paths
Where triumph rang its brassy phrase, or love
Whispered a little out of tenderness,
She makes the willow shiver in the sun   70
For maidens who were wont to sit and gaze
Upon the grass, relinquished to their feet.
She causes boys to pile new plums and pears
On disregarded plate. The maidens taste
And stray impassioned in the littering leaves.   75

VI

Is there no change of death in paradise?
Does ripe fruit never fall? Or do the boughs
Hang always heavy in that perfect sky,
Unchanging, yet so like our perishing earth,
With rivers like our own that seek for seas   80
They never find, the same receding shores
That never touch with inarticulate pang?
Why set the pear upon those river-banks

---

[4] "And he showed me a pure river of water of life, clear as crystal, proceeding out of the throne of God and of the Lamb." *Revelation*, 22:1. ". . . . And whosoever will, let him take of the water of life freely." *Revelation*, 22:17.   [5] Ll. 14–15: Palestine, the Christian Holy Land, the scene of Christ's crucifixion (blood) and the tomb (sepulchre). [6] God of the sky and king of gods and men (Latin —Jupiter, Greek—Zeus). Milton in *Paradise Lost* makes Jove one of the fallen angels (i. 512).

[7] Got.   [8] A basic paradox of Stevens's.

Or spice the shores with odors of the plum?
Alas, that they should wear our colors there,   85
The silken weavings of our afternoons,
And pick the strings of our insipid lutes!
Death is the mother of beauty, mystical,
Within whose burning bosom we devise
Our earthly mothers waiting, sleeplessly.   90

VII

Supple and turbulent, a ring of men
Shall chant in orgy on a summer morn
Their boisterous devotion to the sun,
Not as a god, but as a god might be,
Naked among them, like a savage source.[9]   95
Their chant shall be a chant of paradise,
Out of their blood, returning to the sky;
And in their chant shall enter, voice by voice,
The windy lake wherein their lord delights,
The trees, like serafin,[10] and echoing hills,   100
That choir among themselves long afterward.
They shall know well the heavenly fellowship
Of men that perish and of summer morn.
And whence they came and whither they shall
        go
The dew upon their feet shall manifest.   105

VIII

She hears, upon that water[11] without sound,
A voice that cries, "The tomb in Palestine[12]
Is not the porch of spirits lingering.
It is the grave of Jesus, where he lay."
We live in an old chaos of the sun,   110
Or old dependency of day and night,
Or island solitude, unsponsored, free,
Of that wide water, inescapable.
Deer walk upon our mountains, and the quail
Whistle about us their spontaneous cries;   115
Sweet berries ripen in the wilderness;
And, in the isolation of the sky,
At evening, casual flocks of pigeons make
Ambiguous undulations as they sink,
Downward to darkness, on extended wings.   120

Peter Quince[1] at the Clavier
WALLACE STEVENS
1879–1955

I

Just as my fingers on these keys
Make music, so the selfsame sounds
On my spirit make a music, too.

Music is feeling, then, not sound;
And thus it is that what I feel,   5
Here in this room, desiring you,

Thinking of your blue-shadowed silk,
Is music. It is like the strain
Waked in the elders by Susanna.[2]

Of a green evening, clear and warm,   10
She bathed in her still garden, while
The red-eyed elders watching, felt

The basses of their beings throb
In witching chords, and their thin blood [3]
Pulse pizzicati[4] of Hosanna.   15

II

In the green water, clear and warm,
Susanna lay.
She searched
The touch of springs,
And found   20
Concealed imaginings.
She sighed,
For so much melody.

Upon the bank, she stood
In the cool   25
Of spent emotions.
She felt, among the leaves,
The dew
Of old devotions.

[9] Untamed, primitive (savage) source of energy?
[10] Seraphim (pl.), highest order of angels at God's throne. See Dickinson's "I Taste a Liquor Never Brewed," final stanza (p. 372).   [11] Again, the ebb and flow of generations as in l. 11.   [12] Ll. 107–112: the passage seems to mean that Jesus was but a man who like us was "unsponsored, free."

[1] Carpenter and poet of sorts in Shakespeare's *A Midsummer Night's Dream*.   [2] The story of Susanna and the Elders is conveniently found in *The Bible Designed to Be Read as Living Literature*, New York: Simon and Schuster (1936), pp. 858–862. As a part of the Apocrypha the story is rarely included in Protestant Bibles.   [3] A reference to the advanced age of the Elders.   [4] Creating sound by plucking instead of bowing the instrument.

She walked upon the grass, 30
Still quivering.
The winds were like her maids,
On timid feet,
Fetching her woven scarves,
Yet wavering. 35

A breath upon her hand
Muted the night.
She turned—
A cymbal crashed,
And roaring horns. 40

III

Soon, with a noise like tambourines,
Came her attendant Byzantines.

They wondered why Susanna cried
Against the elders by her side;

And as they whispered, the refrain 45
Was like a willow swept by rain.

Anon, their lamps' uplifted flame
Revealed Susanna and her shame.

And then, the simpering Byzantines
Fled, with a noise like tambourines. 50

IV

Beauty is momentary in the mind—[5]
The fitful tracing of a portal;
But in the flesh it is immortal.
The body dies; the body's beauty lives.
So evenings die, in their green going, 55
A wave, interminably flowing.
So gardens die, their meek breath scenting
The cowl of winter, done repenting.
So maidens die, to the auroral
Celebration of a maiden's choral. 60
Susanna's music touched the bawdy strings
Of those white elders; but, escaping,
Left only Death's ironic scraping.
Now, in its immortality, it plays
On the clear viol of her memory, 65
And makes a constant sacrament of praise.

[5] Ll. 51–58: Stevens's theory of beauty. See his
"Sunday Morning," l. 63: "Death is the mother of
beauty" (p. 371).

Piano

D. H. LAWRENCE
1885–1930

Softly, in the dusk, a woman is singing to me;
Taking me back down the vista of years, till I
    see
A child sitting under the piano, in the boom of
    the tingling strings
And pressing the small, poised feet of a mother
    who smiles as she sings.

In spite of myself the insidious mastery of
    song 5
Betrays me back, till the heart of me weeps to
    belong
To the old Sunday evenings at home, with win-
    ter outside
And hymns in the cozy parlor, the tinkling piano
    our guide.

So now it is vain for the singer to burst into
    clamor
With the great black piano appassionato. The
    glamor 10
Of childish days is upon me, my manhood is cast
Down in the flood of remembrance, I weep like
    a child for the past.

The Elephant Is Slow to Mate

D. H. LAWRENCE
1885–1930

The elephant, the huge old beast, is slow to
    mate;
he finds a female, they show no haste, they wait

for the sympathy in their vast shy hearts slowly,
    slowly to rouse
as they loiter along the river-beds and drink and
    browse

and dash in panic through the brake of forest
    with the herd, 5
and sleep in massive silence, and wake together,
    without a word.

So slowly the great hot elephant hearts grow full
    of desire,

and the great beasts mate in secret at last, hiding
    their fire.

Oldest they are and the wisest of beasts so they
    know at last
how to wait for the loneliest of feasts, for the full
    repast.   10

They do not snatch, they do not tear; their mas-
    sive blood
moves as the moon-tides, near, more near, till
    they touch in flood.

Ballad of the Goodly Fere[1]

EZRA POUND
1885–1972

*Simon Zelotes[2] speaketh it somewhile after the
    Crucifixion.*

[1]
Ha' we lost the goodliest fere o' all
For the priests and the gallows tree?
Aye lover he was of brawny men,
O' ships and the open sea.

[2]
When they came wi' a host to take Our Man   5
His smile was good to see;
"First let these go!" quo' our Goodly Fere,
"Or I'll see ye damned," says he.

[3]
Aye, he sent us out through the crossed high
    spears,
And the scorn of his laugh rang free;   10
"Why took ye not me when I walked about
Alone in the town?" says he.[3]

[4]
Oh, we drunk his "Hale" in the good red wine
When we last made company;

No capon priest was the Goodly Fere   15
But a man o' men was he.[4]

[5]
I ha' seen him drive a hundred men
Wi' a bundle o' cords swung free,
That they took the high and holy house
For their pawn and treasury.[5]   20

[6]
They'll no' get him a' in a book I think,
Though they write it cunningly;
No mouse of the scrolls[6] was the Goodly Fere
But aye loved the open sea.

[7]
If they think they ha' snared our Goodly
    Fere   25
They are fools to the last degree.
"I'll go to the feast," quo' our Goodly Fere,
"Though I go to the gallows tree." [7]

[8] [8]
"Ye ha' seen me heal the lame and blind,
And wake the dead," says he;   30
"Ye shall see one thing to master all:
'Tis how a brave man dies on the tree."

[9]
A son of God was the Goodly Fere
That bade us his brothers be.
I ha' seen him cow a thousand men.   35
I have seen him upon the tree.[9]

[10]
He cried no cry when they drave the nails
And the blood gushed hot and free;

[4] L. 16: see *Matthew*, 11:19 for confirmation. "No
capon priest," rather, a full-blooded male, as D. H.
Lawrence interprets the resurrected Christ in the
novella, "The Man Who Died" (p. 209).   [5] The
cleansing of the Temple: see *John*, 2:13–17.   [6] No
creeper through scriptures; instead a man who
fought for his principles.   [7] Christ was not
tricked; he entered Jerusalem knowing what would
happen. See *Matthew*, 16:21–23; 20:17–19.   [8] A
continuation of the prophecy in *Matthew* above. See
also *Luke*, 18:35–43.   [9] Stanzas 9 and 11: reference to the Nazareth incident where Christ's fellow Galileans "filled with wrath . . . rose up, and
thrust him out of the city, and led him unto the
brow of the hill . . . that they might cast him down
headlong. But he, passing through the midst of
them, went his own way." *Luke*, 4:28–30.

[1] *Fere:* literally a traveling comrade.   [2] A dis-
ciple of Christ (not to be confused with Simon
Peter; see *Acts*, 1:13) and one of the zealots (Zelotes) who bitterly opposed the Roman domination
of Palestine. In having us see Christ through Simon's
eyes, Pound provides a rather unconventional Christ
who is nevertheless surprisingly supported by the
scriptures.   [3] Christ challenges and needles his
captors; see *Matthew*, 26:55.

The hounds of the crimson sky gave tongue
But never a cry cried her.[10]

[11]
I ha' seen him cow a thousand men
On the hills o' Galilee;
They whined as he walked out calm between,
Wi' his eyes like the grey o' the sea,

[12]
Like the sea that brooks no voyaging   45
With the winds unleashed and free,
Like the sea that he cowed at Genseret
Wi' twey words spoke' suddently.[11]

[13]
A master of men was the Goodly Fere,
A mate of the wind and sea;   50
If they think they ha' slain our Goodly Fere
They are fools eternally.

[14]
I ha' seen him eat o' the honey-comb[12]
Sin' they nailed him to the tree.

Envoi (1919)
EZRA POUND
1885–1972

Go, dumb-born book,
Tell her that sang me once that song of Lawes;[1]
Hadst thou but song
As thou hast subjects known,
Then were there cause in thee that should con-
          done   5
Even my faults that heavy upon me lie,
And build her glories their longevity.

Tell her that sheds
Such treasure in the air,

Recking[2] naught else but that her graces give   10
Life to the moment,
I would bid them live
As roses might, in magic amber laid,[3]
Red overwrought with orange and all made
Onc substance and one colour   15
Braving time.

Tell her that goes
With song upon her lips
But sings not out the song, nor knows
The maker of it, some other mouth,   20
May be as fair as hers,
Might, in new ages, gain her worshippers,
When our two dusts with Waller's[4] shall be laid,
Siftings on siftings in oblivion,
Till change hath broken down   25
All things save Beauty alone.

Science[1]
ROBINSON JEFFERS
1887–1962

Man, introverted man, having crossed
In passage and but a little with the nature of
          things this latter century
Has begot giants; but being taken up
Like a maniac with self-love and inward con-
          flicts cannot manage his hybrids.
Being used to deal with edgeless dreams,   5
Now he's bred knives on nature turns them also
          inward: they have thirsty points
          though.
His mind forebodes his own destruction;
Actaeon[2] who saw the goddess naked among
          leaves and his hounds tore him.
A little knowledge, a pebble from the shingle,[3]
A drop from the oceans: who would have
          dreamed this infinitely little too
          much?[4]   10

[2] Caring for.   [3] To withstand time.   [4] See
footnote 1.
[1] Published years before the hydrogen bomb existed,
this poem can now be read as a tragic prophecy.
[2] Having seen Diana bathing while he was hunting,
Actaeon was changed by her into a stag and his
hounds tore him.   [3] Seashore.   [4] A century
earlier Hawthorne observed, ". . . and even heroism—so deadly a gripe is Science laying on our
noble possibilities—will become a matter of very
minor importance." ("Chiefly About War Matters,"
The Writings of Nathaniel Hawthorne, Boston and
New York, 1898, Riverside Edition, XII, 336.)

[10] See Matthew, 27:45, 51; Luke, 23:44–45.
[11] Genseret (Gennesaret in Luke, 5:1), another
name for Galilee. The words Christ spoke: "Peace,
be still," as in Mark, 4:39.   [12] Honey-comb:
see Luke, 24:42–49 which begins: "And they gave
him a piece of a broiled fish, and of a honeycomb."
[1] Henry Lawes (1596–1662), composer who set to
music Edmund Waller's "Song" (Go, lovely Rose"),
p. 293, songs by Shakespeare, and Milton's Comus.

The Bloody Sire[1]

ROBINSON JEFFERS
1887–1962

It is not bad. Let them play.
Let the guns bark and the bombing-plane
Speak his prodigious blasphemies.
It is not bad, it is high time,
Stark violence is still the sire of all the world's
    values.   5

What but the wolf's tooth whittled so fine
The fleet limbs of the antelope?
What but fear winged the birds, and hunger
Jeweled with such eyes the great goshawk's
    head?
Violence has been the sire of all the world's
    values.   10

Who would remember Helen's[2] face
Lacking the terrible halo of spears?
Who formed Christ but Herod[3] and Caesar,
The cruel and bloody victories of Caesar?
Violence, the bloody sire of all the world's
    values.   15

Never weep, let them play,
Old violence is not too old to beget new values.

The Hollow Men

T. S. ELIOT
1888–1965

Mistah Kurtz—he dead.[1]
        A penny for the Old Guy[2]

I

We are the hollow men
We are the stuffed men
Leaning together
Headpiece filled with straw. Alas!
Our dried voices, when   5
We whisper together
Are quiet and meaningless
As wind in dry grass
Or rats' feet over broken glass
In our dry cellar   10

Shape without form, shade without colour,
Paralysed force, gesture without motion;

Those who have crossed
With direct eyes, to death's other Kingdom
Remember us—if at all—not as lost   15
Violent souls, but only
As the hollow men
The stuffed men.

II

Eyes I dare not meet in dreams
In death's dream kingdom   20
These do not appear:
There, the eyes are
Sunlight on a broken column
There, is a tree swinging
And voices are   25
In the wind's singing
More distant and more solemn
Than a fading star.

---

[1] This poem, surely a contemporary comment on World War II, troubled Jeffers because he thinks poetry "is the worse for being timely"; but today, almost thirty-five years later, the poem threatens to become timeless. For a later companion poem, see Price, "Centennial of Shiloh," p. 310. [2] Undoubtedly a reference to Helen of Troy, wife of Menelaus, whose elopement with Paris brought about the siege and destruction of Troy. [3] Herod the Great (73?–4 B.C.) who destroyed the babes of Bethlehem (*Matthew*, 2:16).

[1] The epigraph, taken from Joseph Conrad's short novel *Heart of Darkness*, is an announcement of the death of the character Kurtz. He had gone into the Congo to gather ivory for his fortune, taking with him "moral ideas of some sort" to serve him as an "emissary of pity, and science, and progress." But in his eagerness to gather huge quantities of ivory, he allowed the natives to make a god of him and yielded also to other temptations including presiding "at certain midnight dances ending with unspeakable rites" that brought his degeneration and death. Before his death, however, Kurtz saw the "horror" of evil, affirmed it, and gained a "moral victory." The epigraph understood in the context of Eliot's poem suggests that we in our time, unlike Kurtz, will not cross "with direct eyes, to death's other Kingdom" because we hardly recognize the presence of the evil that engulfs us. [2] Guy Fawkes (1570–1606) was involved in the Gunpowder Plot to blow up the English Houses of Parliament, November 5, 1605; he was arrested, tried, and executed. November 5 is still celebrated in England by burning Fawkes in effigy while the children beg "a penny for the Old Guy."

Let me be no nearer
In death's dream kingdom   30
Let me also wear
Such deliberate disguises
Rat's coat, crowskin, crossed staves
In a field
Behaving as the wind behaves   35
No nearer—

Not that final meeting
In the twilight kingdom

    III
This is the dead land
This is cactus land   40
Here the stone images
Are raised, here they receive
The supplication of a dead man's hand
Under the twinkle of a fading star.

Is it like this   45
In death's other kingdom
Waking alone
At the hour when we are
Trembling with tenderness
Lips that would kiss   50
Form prayers to broken stone.

    IV
The eyes are not here
There are no eyes here
In this valley of dying stars
In this hollow valley   55
This broken jaw of our lost kingdoms

In this last of meeting places
We grope together
And avoid speech
Gathered on this beach of the tumid river   60

Sightless, unless
The eyes reappear
As the perpetual star
Multifoliate rose
Of death's twilight kingdom   65
The hope only
Of empty men.

    V
Here we go round the prickly pear
Prickly pear prickly pear
Here we go round the prickly pear   70
At five o'clock in the morning.

Between the idea
And the reality
Between the motion
And the act   75
Falls the Shadow
                For Thine is the Kingdom

Between the conception
And the creation
Between the emotion   80
And the response
Falls the Shadow
                Life is very long

Between the desire
And the spasm   85
Between the potency
And the existence
Between the essence
And the descent
Falls the Shadow   90
                For Thine is the Kingdom

For Thine is
Life is
For Thine is the

This is the way the world ends   95
This is the way the world ends
This is the way the world ends
Not with a bang but a whimper.

The Naming of Cats

T. S. ELIOT
1888–1965

The Naming of Cats is a difficult matter,
    It isn't just one of your holiday games;
You may think at first I'm as mad as a hatter
When I tell you, a cat must have THREE DIFFER-
        ENT NAMES.
First of all, there's the name that the family use
        daily,   5
    Such as Peter, Augustus, Alonzo or James,
Such as Victor or Jonathan, George or Bill
        Bailey—
    All of them sensible everyday names.
There are fancier names if you think they sound
        sweeter,

Some for the gentlemen, some for the
dames: 10
Such as Plato, Admetus, Electra, Demeter—
But all of them sensible everyday names.
But I tell you, a cat needs a name that's par-
ticular,
A name that's peculiar, and more dignified,
Else how can he keep up his tail perpen-
dicular,   15
Or spread out his whiskers, or cherish his
pride?
Of names of this kind, I can give you a quorum,
Such as Munkustrap, Quaxo, or Coricopat
Such as Bombalurina, or else Jellylorum—
Names that never belong to more than one
cat.   20
But above and beyond there's still one name left
over,
And that is the name that you never will
guess;
The name that no human research can dis-
cover—
But THE CAT HIMSELF KNOWS, and will never
confess.
When you notice a cat in profound medita-
tion,   25
The reason, I tell you, is always the same:
His mind is engaged in a rapt contemplation
Of the thought, of the thought, of the thought
of his name:
His ineffable effable
Effanineffable   30
Deep and inscrutable singular Name.

The Cultivation of Christmas[1] Trees

T. S. ELIOT
1888–1965

This poem, published rather late in Eliot's
life in 1954, thirty-seven years after "The
Love Song of J. Alfred Prufrock" (p. 304) and
twenty-five years after "The Hollow Men" (p.
376), states in a positive way Eliot's religious
beliefs which are stated indirectly and ironically in the two earlier poems. The poem
should be better known by those members
of the younger generation who now search
for spiritual stability to replace an ever-
fleeting materialism.

There are several attitudes towards Christmas,
Some of which we may disregard:
The social, the torpid, the patently commercial,[2]
The rowdy (the pubs being open till midnight),
And the childish—which is not that of the
child[3]   5
For whom the candle is a star, and the gilded
angel
Spreading its wings at the summit of the tree
Is not only a decoration, but an angel.
The child wonders at the Christmas Tree:
Let him continue in the spirit of wonder   10
At the Feast[4] as an event not accepted as a pre-
text;
So that the glittering rapture, the amazement
Of the first-remembered Christmas Tree,
So that the surprises, delight in new possessions
(Each one with its peculiar and exciting
smell),   15
The expectation of the goose or turkey
And the expected awe on its appearance,
So that the reverence and the gaiety
May not be forgotten in later experience,
In the bored habituation, the fatigue, the
tedium,   20
The awareness of death, the consciousness of
failure,
Or in the piety of the convert
Which may be tainted with a self-conceit
Displeasing to God and disrespectful to the
children

---

[1] Christmas: Christ's mass, a celebration of the
Eucharist (Gr. grateful, and akin to Gr. *chairein,* to
rejoice), a grateful rejoicing for the birth of Christ.
Hence the title can be read as the cultivation (annual renewal) of the rejoicing within ourselves, the
tree being a symbol of the event.

[2] Patently commercial: Openly, unabashedly materialistic. In "A Masque of Reason" (p. 358, ll. 5–8)
Frost uses the modern Christmas tree as a fraudu-
lent symbol of the true, original Christmas season.
[3] L. 5: "At the same time came the disciples unto
Jesus, saying, Who is the greatest in the kingdom
of heaven? And Jesus called a little child unto him,
and set him in the midst of them. And said, Verily
I say unto you, Except ye be converted, and become as little children, ye shall not enter into the
kingdom of heaven." *Matthew,* 18:1–4.   [4] Feast:
festival of the nativity, i.e., Christmas.

(And here I remember also with gratitude   25
St. Lucy,[5] her carol, and her crown of fire):[6]
So that before the end, the eightieth Christmas
(By "eightieth" meaning whichever is the last)
The accumulated memories of annual emotion
May be concentrated into a great joy   30
Which shall be also a great fear, as on the
     occasion
When fear came upon every soul:[7]
Because the beginning shall remind us of the
     end
And the first coming of the second coming.[8]

The Equilibrists

JOHN CROWE RANSOM
1888–

Full of her long white arms and milky skin
He had a thousand times remembered sin.
Alone in the press of people traveled he,
Minding her jacinth, and myrrh, and ivory.

Mouth he remembered: the quaint orifice   5
From which came heat that flamed upon the
     kiss,
Till cold words came down spiral from the head,
Grey doves from the officious tower illsped.

Body: it was a white field ready for love,
On her body's field, with the gaunt tower
     above,   10

[5] Swedish child Saint about thirteen years of age.
[6] Each year Sweden installs a Queen of Lights who
wears a crown of lighted candles. The "crown of
fire" probably refers to the fire of purification.
[7] Ll. 31–32. See *Luke,* 2:7–14 which says in part:
And Mary "brought forth her firstborn son. . . . And
there were in the same country shepherds abiding
in the field. . . . and the glory of the Lord shone
round about them; and they were sore afraid. And
the angel said unto them, Fear not. . . . For unto
you is born this day . . . a Saviour, which is Christ
the Lord."   [8] L. 34 can be read on at least two
levels: "first coming," the birth of Christ and of us;
"second coming," the resurrection of Christ and our
being born again, on earth and in heaven.

The lilies grew, beseeching him to take,
If he would pluck and wear them, bruise and
     break.

Eyes talking: Never mind the cruel words,
Embrace my flowers, but not embrace the
     swords.
But what they said, the doves came straightaway
     flying   15
And unsaid: Honor, Honor, they came crying.

Importunate her doves. Too pure, too wise,
Clambering on his shoulder, saying, Arise,
Leave me now, and never let us meet,
Eternal distance now command thy feet.   20

Predicament indeed, which thus discovers
Honor among thieves, Honor between lovers.
O such a little word is Honor, they feel!
But the grey word is between them cold as
     steel.

At length I saw these lovers fully were come   25
Into their torture of equilibrium;
Dreadfully had forsworn each other, and yet
They were bound each to each, and they did not
     forget.

And rigid as two painful stars, and twirled
About the clustered night their prison world,   30
They burned with fierce love always to come
     near,
But Honor beat them back and kept them clear.

Ah, the strict lovers, they are ruined now!
I cried in anger. But with puddled brow
Devising for those gibbeted and brave   35
Came I descanting: Man, what would you have?

For spin your period out, and draw your breath,
A kinder saeculum begins with Death.
Would you ascend to Heaven and bodiless
     dwell?
Or take your bodies honorless to Hell?   40

In Heaven you have heard no marriage is,
So white flesh tinder to your lecheries,
Your male and female tissue sweetly shaped
Sublimed away, and furious blood escaped.

Great lovers lie in Hell, the stubborn ones   45

Infatuate of the flesh upon the bones;
Stuprate, they rend each other when they kiss,
The pieces kiss again, no end to this.

But still I watched them spinning, orbited nice.
Their flames were not more radiant than their
    ice.   50
I dug in the quiet earth and wrought the tomb
And made these lines to memorize their doom:—

Epitaph

Equilibrists lie here; stranger, tread light;
Close, but untouching in each other's sight;
Mouldered the lips and ashy the tall skull,   55
Let them lie perilous and beautiful.

If We Must Die
CLAUDE McKAY
1890–1948

    When Winston Churchill addressed both Houses of Congress to attempt to urge the United States to enter World War II, he read this poem.

If we must die, let it not be like hogs
Hunted and penned in an inglorious spot,
While round us bark the mad and hungry dogs,
Making their mock at our accursèd lot.
If we must die, O let us nobly die,   5
So that our precious blood may not be shed
In vain; then even the monsters we defy
Shall be constrained to honor us though dead!
O kinsmen! we must meet the common foe!
Though far outnumbered let us show us
    brave,   10
And for their thousand blows deal one death-
    blow!
What though before us lies the open grave?
Like men we'll face the murderous, cowardly
    pack,
Pressed to the wall, dying, but fighting back!

The White House[1]
CLAUDE McKAY
1890–1948

Your door is shut against my tightened face,
And I am sharp as steel with discontent;
But I possess the courage and the grace
To bear my anger proudly and unbent.
The pavement slabs burn loose beneath my
    feet,   5
A chafing savage, down the decent street;
And passion rends my vitals as I pass,
Where boldly shines your shuttered door of glass.
Oh, I must search for wisdom every hour,
Deep in my wrathful bosom sore and raw,   10
And find in it the superhuman power
To hold me to the letter of your law!
Oh, I must keep my heart inviolate
Against the potent poison of your hate.

Speaking of Poetry
JOHN PEALE BISHOP
1892–1944

The ceremony must be found
That will wed Desdemona to the huge Moor.[1]

                   It is not enough—
To win the approval of the Senator
Or to outwit his disapproval; honest Iago   5
Can manage that: it is not enough. For then,
Though she may pant again in his black arms
(His weight resilient as a Barbary stallion's)
She will be found
When the ambassadors of the Venetian state
    arrive   10
Again smothered. These things have not been
    changed,
Not in three hundred years

1 "My title was symbolic . . . it had no reference to the official residence of the President of the United States. . . . The title 'White Houses' changed the whole symbolic intent and meaning of the poem, making it appear as if the burning ambition of the black malcontent was to enter white houses in general." Claude McKay: *A Long Way from Home* (1937), pp. 313–314.
1 *Othello*, p. 455.

(Tupping is still tupping
Though that particular word is obsolete.
Naturally, the ritual would not be in Latin.)

For though Othello had his blood from kings 15
His ancestry was barbarous, his ways African,
His speech uncouth. It must be remembered
That though he valued an embroidery—
Three mulberries proper on a silk like silver—
It was not for the subtlety of the stitches, 20
But for the magic in it. Whereas, Desdemona
Once contrived to imitate in needlework
Her father's shield, and plucked it out
Three times, to begin again, each time
With diminished colors. This is a small point 25
But indicative.

Desdemona was small and fair,

Delicate as a grasshopper
At the tag-end of summer: a Venetian
To her noble finger-tips.

O, it is not enough
That they should meet, naked, at dead of
night 30
In a small inn on a dark canal. Procurers
Less expert than Iago can arrange as much.

The ceremony must be found

Traditional, with all its symbols
Ancient as the metaphors in dreams; 35
Strange, with never before heard music; con-
tinuous
Until the torches deaden at the bedroom door.

Frescoes for Mr. Rockefeller's City[1]
ARCHIBALD MacLEISH
1892–

[1]

LANDSCAPE AS A NUDE

She lies on her left side her flank golden:
Her hair is burned black with the strong sun.
The scent of her hair is of rain in the dust on her shoulders:
She has brown breasts and the mouth of no other country.

Ah she is beautiful here in the sun where she lies:
She is not like the soft girls naked in vineyards
Nor the soft naked girls of the English islands
Where the rain comes in with the surf on an east wind:

Hers is the west wind and the sunlight: the west
Wind is the long clean wind of the continents—
The wind turning with earth, the wind descending
Steadily out of the evening and following on. 10

[1] Diego Rivera (1886–1957), the controversial Mexican artist who revived the techniques of fresco paint-ing, had painted murals for Rockefeller Center in New York City. Because of the implied criticism of capitalism, the murals were removed although Rivera was paid for his work. A similar controversy de-veloped while Rivera was painting murals in the Detroit Institute of Arts, but Edsel Ford who was pay-ing for the work defended the murals as art despite their satire on his father, Henry Ford. Thousands of petitioners supported Edsel Ford; the murals were completed and never removed. See E. B. White's "I Paint What I See" for satiric comment on the Rockefeller Center Controversy (p. 389).

The wind here where she lies is west: the trees
Oak ironwood cottonwood hickory: standing in
Great groves they roll on the wind as the sea would.   15
The grasses of Iowa Illinois Indiana

Run with the plunge of the wind as a wave tumbling.

Under her knees there is no green lawn of the Florentines:
Under her dusty knees is the corn stubble:
Her belly is flecked with the flickering light of the corn.   20

She lies on her left side her flank golden:
Her hair is burned black with the strong sun.
The scent of her hair is of dust and of smoke on her shoulders:
She has brown breasts and the mouth of no other country.

[2]

WILDWEST[2]

There were none of my blood in this battle: 25
There were Minneconjous, Sans Arcs, Brules,
Many nations of Sioux: they were few men galloping.

This would have been in the long days in June:
They were galloping well deployed under the plum-trees:
They were driving riderless horses: themselves they were few.   30

Crazy Horse had done it with few numbers.
Crazy Horse was small for a Lakota.
He was riding always alone thinking of something:

He was standing alone by the picket lines by the ropes:
He was young then, he was thirty when he died: 35
Unless there were children to talk he took no notice.

When the soldiers came for him there on the other side
On the Greasy Grass in the villages we were shouting
"Hoka Hey! Crazy Horse will be riding!"

They fought in the water: horses and men were drowning: 40
They rode on the butte: dust settled in sunlight:
Hoka Hey! they lay on the bloody ground.

No one could tell of the dead which man was Custer . . .
That was the end of his luck: by that river.
The soldiers beat him at Slim Buttes once: 45

[2] Black Elk's memories of Crazy Horse recorded by Neihardt.—MacLeish's note. Crazy Horse (c. 1849–1877), chief and military leader of the Sioux and Cheyenne Indians, helped Sitting Bull to demolish the forces of Major General George Custer in the Battle of Little Big Horn in Montana territory, 1876.

They beat him at Willow Creek when the snow lifted:
The last time they beat him was the Tongue.
He had only the meat he had made and of that little.

Do you ask why he should fight? It was his country:
My God should he not fight? It was his.   50
But after the Tongue there were no herds to be hunting:

He cut the knots of the tails and he led them in:
He cried out "I am Crazy Horse! Do not touch me!"
There were many soldiers between and the gun glinting . . .

And a Mister Josiah Perham of Maine had much of the   55
land Mister Perham was building the Northern Pacific
railroad that is Mister Perham was saying at lunch that

forty say fifty millions of acres in gift and
government grant outright ought to be worth a
wide price on the Board at two-fifty and   60

later a Mister Cooke had relieved Mister Perham and
later a Mister Morgan[3] relieved Mister Cooke:
Mister Morgan converted at prices current:

It was all prices to them: they never looked at it:
why should they look at the land? they were Empire Builders: 65
it was all in the bid and the asked and the ink on their books . . .

When Crazy Horse was there by the Black Hills
His heart would be big with the love he had for that country
And all the game he had seen and the mares he had ridden

And how it went out from you wide and clean in the sunlight   70

[3]

BURYING GROUND BY THE TIES

Ayee! Ai! This is heavy earth on our shoulders:
There were none of us born to be buried in this earth:
Niggers we were, Portuguese, Magyars,[4] Polacks:

We were born to another look of the sky certainly.
Now we lie here in the river pastures:
We lie in the mowings under the thick turf: 75

We hear the earth and the all-day rasp of the grasshoppers.
It was we laid the steel to this land from ocean to ocean:
It was we (if you know) put the U. P.[5] through the passes

---

[3] John Pierpont Morgan (1837–1913), financier, head of J. P. Morgan and Company, won control of the Northern Pacific Railroad from Edward Henry Harriman (1848–1909) whose methods of financing were called "indefensible" by the Interstate Commerce Commission. (See ll. 128–130).   [4] One of the dominant people of Hungary.   [5] Union Pacific Railroad.

Bringing her down into Laramie full load,   80
Eighteen mile on the granite anticlinal,
Forty-three foot to the mile and the grade holding:

It was we did it: hunkies of our kind.
It was we dug the caved-in holes for the cold water:
It was we built the gully spurs and the freight sidings: 85

Who would do it but we and the Irishmen bossing us?
It was all foreign-born men there were in this country:
It was Scotsmen, Englishmen, Chinese, Squareheads,[6] Austrians . . .

Ayee! but there's weight to the earth under it.
Not for this did we come out—to be lying here   90
Nameless under the ties in the clay cuts:

There's nothing good in the world but the rich will buy it:
Everything sticks to the grease of a gold note—
Even a continent—even a new sky!

Do not pity us much for the strange grass over us: 95
We laid the steel to the stone stock of these mountains:
The place of our graves is marked by the telegraph poles!

It was not to lie in the bottoms we came out
And the trains going over us here in the dry hollows . . .

[4]

OIL PAINTING OF THE ARTIST AS THE ARTIST

The plump Mr. Pl'f is washing his hands of America: 100
The plump Mr. Pl'f is in ochre with such hair:

America is in blue-black-grey-green-sandcolor.
America is a continent—many lands:

The plump Mr. Pl'f is washing his hands of America.
He is pictured at Pau on the place and his eyes glaring: 105

He thinks of himself as an exile[7] from all this,
As an émigré from his own time into history

(History being an empty house without owners
A practical man may get in by the privy stones:

The dead are excellent hosts, they have no objections   110
And once in he can nail the knob on the next one

---

[6] Scandinavians.   [7] A reference to the American expatriates who settled chiefly in France and Italy during the 1920s. Malcolm Cowley's *Exile's Return, A Literary Odyssey of the 1920's* (New York: The Viking Press, Inc., 1934, 1951) is a valuable study of the literary expatriates.

Living the life of a classic in bad air
With himself for the Past and his face in the glass for Posterity).

The Cinquecento[8] is nothing at all like Nome
Or Natchez or Wounded Knee or the Shenandoah.   115

Your vulgarity, Tennessee: your violence, Texas:
The rocks under your fields Ohio, Connecticut:

Your clay Missouri your clay: you have driven him out.
You have shadowed his life Appalachians, purple mountains.

There is much too much of your flowing, Mississippi: 120
He prefers a tidier stream with a terrace for trippers and

Cypresses mentioned in Horace or Henry James:
He prefers a country where everything carries the name of a

Countess or real king or an actual palace or
Something in Prose and the stock prices all in Italian.   125

There is more shade for an artist under a fig
Than under the whole rock range (he finds) of the Big Horns.

   [5]

EMPIRE BUILDERS[9]

THE MUSEUM ATTENDANT:

This is *The Making of America in Five Panels:*

This is Mister Harriman making America:
Mister-Harriman-is-buying-the-Union-Pacific-at-Seventy:
The Santa Fe is shining on his hair.   130

This is Commodore Vanderbilt making America:
Mister-Vanderbilt-is-eliminating-the-short-interest-in-Hudson:
Observe the carving on the rocking chair.

This is J. P. Morgan making America:
(The Tennessee Coal is behind to the left of the Steel Company.)   135
Those in mauve are braces he is wearing.

This is Mister Mellon making America:
Mister-Mellon-is-represented-as-a-symbolical-figure-in-aluminum-
Strewing-bank-stocks-on-a-burnished-stair.

---

[8] Sixteenth-century Italian Renaissance; often used as an epithet to imply inferior art.   [9] "The individualism of the Empire Builders, the kind of individualism which is all rights and no duties. . . ." (MacLeish,
A Time to Speak, Boston: Houghton Mifflin Company, 1940, p. 22.)

This is the Bruce is the Barton[10] making America: 140
Mister-Barton-is-selling-us-Doctor's-Deliciousest-Dentifrice.
This is he in beige with the canary.

You have just beheld the Makers making America:
This is The Making of America in Five Panels:
America lies to the west-southwest of the switch-tower;   145
There is nothing to see of America but land.

THE ORIGINAL DOCUMENT
UNDER THE PANEL PAINT:

"To Thos. Jefferson Esq. his obd't serv't
M. Lewis:[11] captain: detached:
                              Sir:
Having in mind your repeated commands in this matter,   150
And the worst half of it done and the streams mapped,

And we here on the back of this beach beholding the
Other ocean—two years gone and the cold

Breaking with rain for the third spring since St. Louis,
The crows at the fishbones on the frozen dunes,   155

The first cranes going over from south north,
And the river down by a mark of the pole since the morning,

And time near to return, and a ship (Spanish)
Lying in for the salmon: and fearing chance or the

Drought or the Sioux should deprive you of these discoveries—   160
Therefore we send by sea in this writing.

                              Above the
Platte there were long plains and a clay country:
Rim of the sky far off, grass under it,

Dung for the cook fires by the sulphur licks.
After that there were low hills and the sycamores,   165

And we poled up by the Great Bend in the skiffs:
The honey bees left us after the Osage River:

The wind was west in the evenings, and no dew and the
Morning Star larger and whiter than usual—

The winter rattling in the brittle haws.   170
The second year there was sage and the quail calling.

---

[10] Bruce Barton (1886–1967), advertising executive, and author of a best-selling book, *The Man Nobody Knows* (1925), which presents Jesus as a predecessor of the modern business man, "the most popular dinner guest in Jerusalem," whose parables were "the most powerful advertisements of all time."   [11] Meriwether Lewis of the Lewis and Clark expedition that established an overland route to the Pacific," 1803–1806. Jefferson was President at the time.

All that valley is good land by the river:
Three thousand miles and the clay cliffs and

Rue and beargrass by the water banks
And many birds and the brant going over and tracks of   175

Bear, elk, wolves, marten: the buffalo—
Numberless so that the cloud of their dust covers them:

The antelope fording the fall creeks, and the mountains and
Grazing lands and the meadow lands and the ground

Sweet and open and well-drained.
                              We advise you to   180
Settle troops at the forks and to issue licenses:

Many men will have living on these lands.
There is wealth in the earth for them all and the wood standing

And wild birds on the water where they sleep.
There is stone in the hills for the towns of a great people . . ."   185

You have just beheld the Makers Making America:

They screwed her scrawny and gaunt with their seven-year panics:
They bought her back on their mortgages old-whore-cheap:

They fattened their bonds at her breasts till the thin blood ran from them.
Men have forgotten how full clear and deep   190
The Yellowstone moved on the gravel and the grass grew
When the land lay waiting for her westward people!

[6]

BACKGROUND WITH REVOLUTIONARIES

And the corn singing Millennium!
Lenin! Millennium! Lennium!

When they're shunting the cars on the Katy[12] *a mile off* [13]   195
When they're shunting the cars when they're shunting the cars on the Katy
You can hear the clank of the couplings riding away.

Also Comrade Divine who writes of America
Most instructively having in 'Seventy-four
Crossed to the Hoboken side on the Barclay Street Ferry.   200

She sits on a settle in the State of North Dakota,
O she sits on a settle in the State of North Dakota,
She can hear the engines whistle over Iowa and Idaho.

[12] The Missouri-Kansas-Texas Railroad.   [13] Lines in italic type represent the American democratic voice; lines in roman type represent the satiric voice against communism.

Also Comrade Edward Remington Ridge
Who has prayed God since the April of 'Seventeen   205
To replace in his life his lost (M.E.) religion.

And The New York Daily Worker[14] *goes a'blowing over Arkansas,*
The New York Daily Worker *goes a'blowing over Arkansas,*
The grasses let it go along the Ozarks over Arkansas.

Even Comrade Grenadine Grilt who has tried since   210
August tenth for something to feel about strongly in
Verses—his personal passions having tired.

I can tell my land by the jays in the apple-trees,
Tell my land by the jays in the apple-trees,
I can tell my people by the blue-jays in the apple-trees.   215

Aindt you read in d' books you are all brudders?
D' glassic historic objective broves you are brudders!
You and d' Wops and d' Chinks you are all brudders!
Havend't you got it d' same ideology? Havend't you?

When it's yesterday in Oregon it's one A M in Maine   220
And she slides: and the day slides: and it runs: over us:
And the bells strike twelve strike twelve strike twelve
In Marblehead in Buffalo in Cheyenne in Cherokee:
Yesterday runs on the states like a crow's shadow.

For Marx has said to us, Workers what do you need?   225
And Stalin has said to us, Starvers what do you need?
You need the Dialectical Materialism![15]

She's a tough land under the corn, mister:
She has changed the bone in the cheeks of many races:
She has winced the eyes of the soft Slavs with her sun on them: 230
She has tried the fat from the round rumps of Italians:
Even the voice of the English has gone dry
And hard on the tongue and alive in the throat speaking.

She's a tough land under the oak-trees, mister:
It may be she can change the word in the book   235
As she changes the bone of a man's head in his children:
It may be that the earth and the men remain . . .

There is too much sun on the lids of my eyes to be listening.

---

[14] Newspaper that promotes the communist line.   [15] Marxian (Karl Marx, 1818–1883, author of *Das Kapital,* 3 vols., 1867, 1885, 1895) theory that maintains that all human phenomena (historical, social, economic, and psychological) should be interpreted in terms of physical or material causes.

I Paint What I See[1]

A Ballad of Artistic Integrity, on the Occasion of the Removal of Some Rather Expensive Murals from the RCA Building.

E. B. WHITE
1899–

"What do you paint, when you paint on a wall?"
  Said John D.'s grandson Nelson.
"Do you paint just anything there at all?
"Will there be any doves, or a tree in fall?
"Or a hunting scene, like an English hall?"   5

  "I paint what I see," said Rivera.

"What are the colors you use when you paint?"
  Said John D.'s grandson Nelson.
"Do you use any red in the beard of a saint?
"If you do, is it terribly red, or faint?   10
"Do you use any blue? Is it Prussian?"

  "I paint what I paint," said Rivera.

"Whose is that head that I see on my wall?"
  Said John D.'s grandson Nelson.
"Is it anyone's head whom we know, at all?   15
"A Rensselaer, or a Saltonstall?
"Is it Franklin D.? Is it Mordaunt Hall?
"Or is it the head of a Russian?"

  "I paint what I think," said Rivera.

"I paint what I paint, I paint what I see,   20
  "I paint what I think," said Rivera,
"And the thing that is dearest in life to me
"In a bourgeois hall is Integrity;
  "However . . .
"I'll take out a couple of people drinkin'   25
"And put in a picture of Abraham Lincoln;
"I could even give you McCormick's reaper
"And still not make my art much cheaper.
"But the head of Lenin has got to stay
"Or my friends will give me the bird today,   30
  "The bird, the bird, forever."

"It's not good taste in a man like me,"
  Said John D.'s grandson Nelson,

"To question an artist's integrity
"Or mention a practical thing like a fee,   35
"But I know what I like to a large degree,
  "Though art I hate to hamper;
"For twenty-one thousand conservative bucks
"You painted a radical. I say shucks,
  "I never could rent the offices—   40
  "The capitalistic offices.
"For this, as you know, is a public hall
"And people want doves, or a tree in fall,
"And though your art I dislike to hamper,
"I owe a *little* to God and Gramper,   45
  "And after all,
  "It's *my* wall . . ."

"We'll see if it is," said Rivera.

Anyone Lived in a Pretty How Town[1]

E. E. CUMMINGS
1894–1962

anyone lived in a pretty how town
(with up so floating many bells down)
spring summer autumn winter
he sang his didn't he danced his did.

Women and men (both little and small)   5
cared for anyone not at all
they sowed their isn't they reaped their same
sun moon stars rain

children guessed (but only a few
and down they forgot as up they grew   10
autumn winter spring summer)
that noone loved him more by more

when by now and tree by leaf
she laughed his joy she cried his grief
bird by snow and stir by still   15
anyone's any was all to her

someones married their everyones
laughed their cryings and did their dance

[1] See MacLeish's "Frescoes for Mr. Rockefeller's City," footnote 1 (p. 381), for comment on Diego Rivera (1886–1957), the Mexican painter.

[1] For commentary on Cummings' technique and three of his poems, see pp. 287–290.

(sleep wake hope and then) they
said their nevers they slept their dream   20

stars rain sun moon
(and only the snow can begin to explain
how children are apt to forget to remember
with up so floating many bells down)

one day anyone died i guess   25
(and noone stopped to kiss his face)
busy folk buried them side by side
little by little and was by was

all by all and deep by deep
and more by more they dream their sleep   30
noone and anyone earth by april
wish by spirit and if by yes.

Women and men (both dong and ding)
summer autumn winter spring
reaped their sowing and went their came   35
sun moon stars rain

To Brooklyn Bridge

HART CRANE
1899–1932

[1]
How many dawns, chill from his rippling rest
The seagull's wings shall dip and pivot him,
Shedding white rings of tumult, building high
Over the chained bay waters Liberty—

[2]
Then, with inviolate curve, forsake our eyes   5
As apparitional as sails that cross
Some page of figures to be filed away;
—Till elevators drop us from our day . . .

[3]
I think of cinemas, panoramic sleights
With multitudes bent toward some flashing
          scene   10
Never disclosed, but hastened to again,
Foretold to other eyes on the same screen;

[4]
And Thee, across the harbor, silver-paced
As though the sun took step of thee, yet left
Some motion ever unspent in thy stride,—   15
Implicitly thy freedom staying thee!

[5]
Out of some subway scuttle, cell or loft
A bedlamite speeds to thy parapets,
Tilting there momently, shrill shirt ballooning,
A jest falls from the speechless caravan.   20

[6]
Down Wall, from girder into street noon leaks,
A rip-tooth of the sky's acetylene;
All afternoon the cloud-flown derricks turn . . .
Thy cables breathe the North Atlantic still.

[7]
And obscure as that heaven of the Jews,   25
Thy guerdon . . . Accolade thou dost bestow
Of anonymity time cannot raise:
Vibrant reprieve and pardon thou dost show.

[8]
O harp and altar, of the fury fused,
(How could mere toil align thy choiring
          strings!)   30
Terrific threshold of the prophet's pledge,
Prayer of pariah, and the lover's cry,—

[9]
Again the traffic lights that skim thy swift
Unfractioned idiom, immaculate sigh of stars,
Beading thy path—condense eternity: 35
And we have seen night lifted in thine arms.

[10]
Under thy shadow by the piers I waited;
Only in darkness is thy shadow clear.
The City's fiery parcels all undone,
Already snow submerges an iron year . . .   40

[11]
O Sleepless as the river under thee,
Vaulting the sea, the prairies' dreaming sod,
Unto us lowliest sometime sweep, descend
And of the curveship lend a myth to God.

Comments

This poem is used by Crane as a "Proem," or preface, to his long poem, "The Bridge," the major effort of his brief career.

Crane has said that in the entire poem, "The Bridge," he was attempting to recreate the "Myth of America." He was much concerned about the future of America because, as he said, "I feel persuaded that here are destined to be discovered certain as yet undefined spiritual quantities. . . ." Brooklyn Bridge he made the symbol of America, the "threshold" of these spiritual quantities. The "Proem: To Brooklyn Bridge" is an invocation to and a eulogy of his basic symbol, Brooklyn Bridge.

From Harlem Gallery

MELVIN B. TOLSON
1900–1966

. . .
The night John Henry is born an ax
of lightning splits the sky,
and a hammer of thunder pounds the earth,
and the eagles and panthers cry!
. . .
Wafer Waite—   5
an ex-peon from the Brazos Bottoms,
who was in the M.-K.-T. station
when a dipping funnel
canyoned the Cotton Market Capital—
leaps to his feet and shouts,   10
"Didn't John Henry's Ma and Pa
get no warning?"

Hideho,
with the tolerance of Diogenes
naked in the market place on a frosty morning,   15
replies:
"Brother,
the tornado alarm became
tongue-tied."
. . .
John Henry—he says to his Ma and Pa: 20
"Get a gallon of barleycorn.
I want to start right, like a he-man child,
the night that I am born!"
. . .
The Zulu Club patrons whoop and stomp,
clap thighs and backs and knees: 25
the poet and the audience one,
each gears itself to please.

Says: "I want some ham hocks, ribs, and jowls,
a pot of cabbage and greens;
some hoecakes, jam, and buttermilk,   30
a platter of pork and beans!"

John Henry's Ma—she wrings her hands,
and his Pa—he scratches his head.
John Henry—he curses in giraffe-tall words,
flops over, and kicks down the bed.   35

He's burning mad, like a bear on fire—
so he tears to the riverside.
As he stoops to drink, Old Man River gets scared
and runs upstream to hide!

Some say he was born in Georgia—O Lord!　　　　　40
Some say in Alabam.
But it's writ on the rock at the Big Bend Tunnel:
"Lousyana was my home. So scram!"

. . .

The Zulu Club Wits
(dusky vestiges of the University Wits)　　　　　45
screech like a fanfare of hunting horns
when Hideho flourishes his hip-pocket bottle.

High as the ace of trumps,
an egghead says, " 'The artist is a strange bird,' Lenin says."
Dipping in every direction like a quaquaversal,　　　　　50
the M. C. guffaws: "Hideho, that swig would make
a squirrel spit in the eye of a bulldog!"

Bedlam beggars
at a poet's feast in a people's dusk of dawn counterpoint
protest and pride　　　　　55
in honky-tonk rhythms
hot as an ache in a cold hand warmed.
The creative impulse in the Zulu Club
leaps from Hideho's lips to Frog Legs' fingers,
like the electric fire from the clouds　　　　　60
that blued the gap between
Franklin's key and his Leyden jar.
A Creole co-ed from Basin Street by way of
Morningside Heights
—circumspect as a lady in waiting—　　　　　65
brushes my shattered cocktail glass into a tray.
Am I a Basilidian anchoret rapt in secret studies?
O spiritual, work-song, ragtime, blues, jazz—
consorts of
the march, quadrille, polka, and waltz!　　　　　70
Witness to a miracle
—I muse—
the birth of a blues,
the flesh
made of André Gide's　　　　　75
musique nègre!

. . .

I was born in Bitchville, Lousyana.
A son of Ham, I had to scram!
I was born in Bitchville, Lousyana.
so I ain't worth a T.B. damn!　　　　　80

. . .

My boon crony,

Vincent Aveline, sports editor
of the *Harlem Gazette,*
anchors himself at my table.
"What a night!" he groans. "*What* a night!"   85
. . . I wonder . . .
Was he stewed or not
when he sneaked Hideho's
Skid Row Ballads
from my walk-up apartment?   90
Then the You advises the I,
Every bookworm is a potential thief.

. . .

Ma taught me to pray. Pa taught me to grin.
It pays, Black Boy; oh, it pays!
So I pray to God and grin at the Whites   95
in seventy-seven different ways!

I came to Lenox Avenue.
Poor Boy Blue! Poor Boy Blue!
I came to Lenox Avenue,
but I find up here a Bitchville, too!   100

. . .

Like an explorer
on the deck of the *Albatross,*
ex-professor of philosophy, Joshua Nitze,
sounds the wet unknown;
then, in humor, he refreshes the Zulu Club Wits   105
with an anecdote on integration,
from the Athens of the Cumberland:
"A black stevedore bulked his butt
in a high-hat restaurant
not far from the bronze equestrian statue   110
of Andrew Jackson.
The ofay waitress hi-fied,
'What can I do for you, Mister?'
Imagine, if you can, Harlem nitwits,
a black man mistered by a white dame   115
in the Bible Belt of the pale phallus and the chalk clitoris!
The South quaked.
Gabriel hadn't high-Ced his horn,
nor the Africans invaded from Mars.
It was only the end-man's bones of Jeff Davis   120
rattling the *Dies Irae*
in the Hollywood Cemetery!
The Negro dock hand said,
'Ma'am, a platter of chitterlings.'
The ofay waitress smiled a blond dolichocephalic smile,   125
'That's not on the menu, Mister.'
Then the stevedore sneered:
'Night and day, Ma'am,
I've been telling Black Folks
you White Folks ain't ready for integration!' "   130

Snake in the Strawberries

JAMES HEARST
1900–

This lovely girl dressed in lambswool thoughts
dances a tune in the sunshine, a tune like a
    bright path
leading to that soft cloud curled up like a girl
in her sleep, but she stops at the strawberry bed
carrying nothing but joy in her basket and it
    falls   5
to the ground. O-h-h-h-h, her red lips round out
berries of sound but the berries under her feet
are not startled though they sway ever so slightly
as life long striped and winding congeals into
form, driving its red tongue into her breast   10
forever marking its presence and turning into a
    shiver
barely a thread of motion in the clusters of green
    leaves.
She stands now as cold as marble now with the
    thought
coiled around her, the image of her thought
    holding her
tightly in its folds for it is part of her now and
    dimly   15
like faint sobbing she knows that part of her
    crawls
forever among green leaves and light grasses, it
    is the same
shiver that shakes her now and now her hair
    tumbles slightly
and now she feels dishevelled but the spell
    breaks finally.
For the warm sun has not changed and maybe
    the tune   20
of her coming still floats in the air but the path
no longer ends in the cloud. She fills her basket
    taking
the richest ripe berries for this is what she came
    to do
she touches her breast a minute and then the
    ground
feeling beneath her fingers the coiled muscles   25
of a cold fear that seems so dark and secret
beside the warm colors of the sunlight
splashing like blood on the heaped fruit in her
    basket.

Miracles

ARNA BONTEMPS
1902–

Doubt no longer miracles,
this spring day makes it plain
a man may crumble into dust
and straightway live again.

A jug of water in the sun   5
will easy turn to wine
if love is stopping at the well
and love's brown arms entwine.

And you who think Him only man,
I tell you faithfully   10
that I have seen Christ clothed in rain
walking on the sea.

Reconnaissance

ARNA BONTEMPS
1902–

After the cloud embankments,
The lamentation of wind,
And the starry descent into time,
We came to the flashing waters and shaded our
    eyes
From the glare.   5

Alone with the shore and the harbor,
The stems of the cocoanut trees,
The fronds of silence and hushed music,
We cried for the new revelation
And waited for miracles to rise.   10

Where elements touch and merge,
Where shadows swoon like outcasts on the sand
And the tired moment waits, its courage gone—
There were we

In latitudes where storms are born.   15

Southern Mansion

ARNA BONTEMPS
1902–

Poplars are standing there still as death
And ghosts of dead men

Meet their ladies walking
Two by two beneath the shade
And standing on the marble steps.   5

There is a sound of music echoing
Through the open door
And in the field there is
Another sound tinkling in the cotton:
Chains of bondmen dragging on the ground.   10

The years go back with an iron clank,
A hand is on the gate,
A dry leaf trembles on the wall.
Ghosts are walking.
They have broken roses down   15
And poplars stand there still as death.

The Negro Mother
LANGSTON HUGHES
1902–1967

Children, I come back today
To tell you a story of the long dark way
That I had to climb, that I had to know
In order that the race might live and grow.
Look at my face—dark as the night—   5
Yet shining like the sun with love's true light.
I am the child they stole from the sand
Three hundred years ago in Africa's land.
I am the dark girl who crossed the wide sea
Carrying in my body the seed of the free.   10
I am the woman who worked in the field
Bringing the cotton and the corn to yield.
I am the one who labored as a slave,
Beaten and mistreated for the work that I gave—
Children sold away from me, husband sold,
        too.   15
No safety, no love, no respect was I due.
Three hundred years in the deepest South:
But God put a song and a prayer in my mouth.
God put a dream like steel in my soul.
Now, through my children, I'm reaching the
        goal.   20
Now, through my children, young and free,
I realize the blessings denied to me.
I couldn't read then. I couldn't write.
I had nothing, back there in the night
Sometimes, the valley was filled with tears,   25

But I kept trudging on through the lonely years.
Sometimes, the road was hot with sun,
But I had to keep on till my work was done:
I *had* to keep on! No stopping for me—
I was the seed of the coming Free.   30
I nourished the dream that nothing could
        smother
Deep in my breast—the Negro mother.
I had only hope then, but now through you,
Dark ones of today, my dreams must come true:
All you dark children in the world out there,   35
Remember my sweat, my pain, my despair.
Remember my years, heavy with sorrow—
And make of those years a torch for tomorrow.
Make of my past a road to the light
Out of the darkness, the ignorance, the night.   40
Lift high my banner out of the dust.
Stand like free men supporting my trust.
Believe in the right, let none push you back.
Remember the whip and the slaver's track.
Remember how the strong in struggle and
        strife   45
Still bar you the way, and deny you life—
But march ever forward, breaking down bars.
Look ever upward at the sun and the stars.
Oh, my dark children, may my dreams and my
        prayers
Impel you forever up the great stairs—   50
For I will be with you till no white brother
Dares keep down the children of the Negro
        mother.

For John Keats[1]
Apostle of Beauty
COUNTEE CULLEN
1903–1946

Not writ in water, nor in mist,
        Sweet lyric throat, thy name;
Thy singing lips that cold death kissed [2]
        Have seared his own with flame.

---

[1] Keats's poems are found on pp. 256, 338, and 339.
[2] Keats (1795–1821) suffered an untimely death.

From the Dark Tower
(To Charles S. Johnson)
COUNTEE CULLEN
1903–1946

We shall not always plant while others reap
The golden increment of bursting fruit,
Not always countenance, abject and mute,
That lesser men should hold their brothers
    cheap;
Not everlastingly while others sleep   5
Shall we beguile their limbs with mellow flute,
Not always bend to some more subtle brute;
We were not made eternally to weep.

The night whose sable breast relieves the stark,
White stars is no less lovely being dark,   10
And there are buds that cannot bloom at all
In light, but crumple, piteous, and fall;
So in the dark we hide the heart that bleeds,
And wait, and tend our agonizing seeds.

Yet Do I Marvel
COUNTEE CULLEN
1903–1946

I doubt not God is good, well-meaning, kind,
And did He stoop to quibble could tell why
The little buried mole continues blind,
Why flesh that mirrors Him must some day die,
Make plain the reason tortured Tantalus[1]   5
Is baited by the fickle fruit, declare
If merely brute caprice dooms Sisyphus[2]
To struggle up a never-ending stair.
Inscrutable His ways are, and immune
To catechism by a mind too strewn   10
With petty cares to slightly understand
What awful brain compels His awful hand.

[1] Tantalus. In Greek mythology, the son of Zeus and a Lydian king who divulged the secrets of the gods to mortals and was punished by being submerged up to the chin in a river of Hades with a tree of fruit above his head. Whenever he tried to eat the fruit or drink the water they moved just beyond his reach causing him agonizing thirst and hunger. The nature of his punishment gave us the word *tantalize*.
[2] Sisyphus. A legendary king of Corinth whose work in the world of shades is to roll a huge stone to the top of a hill where it constantly rolls back. Hence "a labor of Sisyphus" is endless and exhausting.

Yet do I marvel at this curious thing:
To make a poet black, and bid him sing!

The Fury
of Aerial Bombardment
RICHARD EBERHART
1904–

You would think the fury of aerial bombardment
Would rouse God to relent; the infinite spaces
Are still silent. He looks on shock-pried faces.
History, even, does not know what is meant.

You would feel that after so many centuries   5
God would give man to repent; yet he can kill
As Cain could, but with multitudinous will,
No farther advanced than in his ancient furies.

Was man made stupid to see his own stupidity?
Is God by definition indifferent, beyond us
    all?   10
Is the eternal truth man's fighting soul
Wherein the Beast ravens in its own avidity?

Of Van Wettering I speak, and Averill,
Names on a list, whose faces I do not recall
But they are gone to early death, who late in
    school   15
Distinguished the belt feed lever from the belt
    holding pawl.

The Day After Sunday
PHYLLIS McGINLEY
1905–

Always on Monday, God's in the morning papers,
    His Name is a headline, His Works are ru-
        mored abroad.
Having been praised by men who are movers
    and shapers,
    From prominent Sunday pulpits, newsworthy
    is God.

On page 27, just opposite Fashion Trends,   5
    One reads at a glance how He scolded the
        Baptists a little,
Was firm with the Catholics, practical with the
    Friends,
    To Unitarians pleasantly noncommittal.

In print are His numerous aspects, too: God
    smiling,
God vexed, God thunderous, God whose man-
    sions are pearl,   10
Political God, God frugal, God reconciling
    Himself with science, God guiding the Camp
    Fire Girl.

Always on Monday morning the press reports
    God as revealed to His vicars in various
    guises—
Benevolent, stormy, patient, or out of sorts.   15
    God knows which God is the God God recog-
    nizes.

Roosevelt Smith

FRANK MARSHALL DAVIS
1905–

You ask what happened to Roosevelt Smith

Well . . .

Conscience and the critics got him

Roosevelt Smith was the only dusky child born and bred in the village of Pine City,
    Nebraska

At college they worshipped the novelty of a black poet and predicted fame   5

At twenty-three he published his first book . . . the critics said he imitated Carl
    Sandburg, Edgar Lee Masters and Vachel Lindsay . . . they raved about a
    wealth of racial material and the charm of darky dialect

So for two years Roosevelt worked and observed in Dixie

At twenty-five a second book . . . Negroes complained about plantation scenes and
    said he dragged Aframerica's good name in the mire for gold . . . "Europe,"
    they said, "honors Dunbar for his 'Ships That Pass in the Night' [1] and not for
    his dialect which they don't understand"

For another two years Roosevelt strove for a different medium of expression

At twenty-seven a third book . . . The critics said the density of Gertrude Stein or
    T.S. Eliot hardly fitted the simple material to which a Negro had access   10

For another two years Roosevelt worked

At twenty-nine his fourth book . . . the critics said a Negro had no business initiating
    the classic forms of Keats, Browning and Shakespeare . . . "Roosevelt Smith,"

[1] A short romantic poem by Paul Laurence Dunbar (1872–1906) which, implies Davis, is honored in Europe because it has little or nothing to reflect the realities of Negro life as they are reflected in such poems by Dunbar as "A Death Song" and "When Malindy Sings." Further, Davis implies, the English would be impressed by Dunbar's title "Ships That Pass in the Night" because an English romantic novel with the same title (1893) written by Bearice Harraden had sold over a million copies.

they announced, "has nothing original and is merely a blackface white. His African heritage is a rich source should he use it"

So for another two years Roosevelt went into the interior of Africa

At thirty-one his fifth book . . . interesting enough, the critics said, but since it followed nothing done by any white poet it was probably just a new kind of prose

Day after the reviews came out Roosevelt traded conscience and critics for the leather pouch and bunions of a mail carrier and read in the papers until his death how little the American Negro had contributed to his nation's litera- ture . . .[2]   15

[2] See Dudley Randall's "Black Poet, White Critic," p. 401.

Lullaby[1]

W. H. AUDEN
1907–1973

Lay your sleeping head, my love,
Human on my faithless arm;
Time and fevers burn away
Individual beauty from
Thoughtful children, and the grave   5
Proves the child ephemeral:
But in my arms till break of day
Let the living creature lie,
Mortal, guilty, but to me
The entirely beautiful.   10

Soul and body have no bounds:
To lovers as they lie upon
Her tolerant enchanted slope
In their ordinary swoon,
Grave the vision Venus sends   15
Of supernatural sympathy,
Universal love and hope;
While an abstract insight wakes
Among the glaciers and the rocks
The hermit's carnal ecstasy.   20

Certainty, fidelity
On the stroke of midnight pass

[1] Editors have previously used "Lay Your Sleeping Head" as the title; Auden has now supplied one. He has made four word changes: 1. 20, *carnal* for *sensual;* 1. 34, *welcome* for *sweetness;* 1. 36, *our* for *the;* 1. 37, *find* for *see.* Any sensitive, critical reader of poetry would probably ask himself why Auden made the changes.

Like vibrations of a bell
And fashionable madmen raise
Their pedantic boring cry: 25
Every farthing of the cost,
All the dreaded cards foretell,
Shall be paid, but from this night
Not a whisper, not a thought,
Not a kiss nor look be lost.   30

Beauty, midnight, vision dies:
Let the winds of dawn that blow
Softly round your dreaming head
Such a day of welcome show
Eye and knocking heart may bless,   35
Find our mortal world enough;
Noons of dryness find you fed
By the involuntary powers,
Nights of insult let you pass
Watched by every human love.   40

Musée des Beaux Arts[1]

W. H. AUDEN
1907–1973

About suffering they were never wrong,
The Old Masters: how well they understood
Its human position; how it takes place
While someone else is eating or opening a win-
        dow or just walking dully along;
How, when the aged are reverently, passionately
        waiting   5
For the miraculous birth, there always must be

[1] Museum of Fine Arts.

Children who did not specially want it to hap-
pen, skating
On a pond at the edge of the wood:
They never forgot
That even the dreadful martyrdom must run its
course   10
Anyhow in a corner, some untidy spot
Where the dogs go on with their doggy life and
the torturer's horse
Scratches its innocent behind on a tree.
In Brueghel's *Icarus*,[2] for instance: how every-
thing turns away
Quite leisurely from the disaster; the ploughman
may   15
Have heard the splash, the forsaken cry,
But for him it was not an important failure; the
sun shone
As it had to on the white legs disappearing into
the green
Water; and the expensive delicate ship that must
have seen
Something amazing, a boy falling out of the
sky,   20
Had somewhere to get to and sailed calmly on.

The Unknown Citizen

W. H. AUDEN
1907–1973

(*To JS/07/M/378*
This Marble Monument
Is Erected by the State

He was found by the Bureau of Statistics to be
One against whom there was no official com-
plaint,
And all the reports on his conduct agree
That, in the modern sense of an old-fashioned
word, he was a saint,
For in everything he did he served the Greater
Community.   5
Except for the War till the day he retired
He worked in a factory and never got fired,

[2] A painting by the Flemish Pieter Brueghel (1525–
1569) in the Royal Museum in Brussels. Icarus,
flying with his father Daedalus, flew too close to the
sun which melted the wax holding on his wings, and
pitched him into the sea. The adjective *Icarian* has
come to mean soaring too high for safety.

But satisfied his employers, Fudge Motors Inc.
Yet he wasn't a scab[1] or odd in his views,
For his Union reports that he paid his dues,   10
(Our report on his Union shows it was sound)
And our Social Psychology workers found
That he was popular with his mates and liked a
drink.
The Press are convinced that he bought a paper
every day
And that his reactions to advertisements were
normal in every way.   15
Policies taken out in his name prove that he was
fully insured,
And his Health-card shows he was once in hospi-
tal but left it cured.
Both Producers Research and High-Grade Liv-
ing declare
He was fully sensible to the advantages of the
Instalment Plan
And had everything necessary to the Modern
Man,   20
A phonograph, a radio, a car and a frigidaire.
Our researchers into Public Opinion are content
That he held the proper opinions for the time of
year;
When there was peace, he was for peace; when
there was war, he went.
He was married and added five children to the
population,   25
Which our Eugenist [2] says was the right number
for a parent of his generation,
And our teachers report that he never interfered
with their education.
Was he free? Was he happy? The question is
absurd:
Had anything been wrong, we should certainly
have heard.

Dolor

THEODORE ROETHKE
1908–1963

I have known the inexorable sadness of pencils,
Neat in their boxes, dolor of pad and paper-
weight,

[1] A union member or nonmember disloyal to the
union during a strike.   [2] One versed in eugenics,
the science which aims at improving the human
race by controlling the hereditary qualities through
proper mating.

All the misery of manila folders and mucilage,
Desolation in immaculate public places,
Lonely reception room, lavatory, switchboard,   5
The unalterable pathos of basin and pitcher,
Ritual of multigraph, paper-clip, comma,
Endless duplication of lives and objects.

And I have seen dust from the walls of institu-
    tions,
Finer than flour, alive, more dangerous than
    silica,   10
Sift, almost invisible, through long afternoons of
    tedium,
Dripping a fine film on nails and delicate eye-
    brows,
Glazing the pale hair, the duplicate gray stan-
    dard faces.

The Landscape
near an Aerodrome
STEPHEN SPENDER
1909–

More beautiful and soft than any moth
With burring furred antennae feeling its huge
    path
Through dusk, the air liner with shut-off engines
Glides over suburbs and the sleeves set trailing
    tall
To point the wind. Gently, broadly, she falls,   5
Scarcely disturbing charted currents of air.

Lulled by descent, the travellers across sea
And across feminine land indulging its easy limbs
In miles of softness, now let their eyes trained
    by watching
Penetrate through dusk the outskirts of this
    town   10
Here where industry shows a fraying edge.
Here they may see what is being done.

Beyond the winking masthead light
And the landing ground, they observe the out-
    posts
Of work: chimneys like lank black fingers   15
Or figures, frightening and mad: and squat
    buildings
With their strange air behind trees, like women's
    faces

Shattered by grief. Here where few houses
Moan with faint light behind their blinds,
They remark the unhomely sense of complaint,
    like a dog   20
Shut out, and shivering at the foreign moon.

In the last sweep of love, they pass over fields
Behind the aerodrome, where boys play all day
Hacking dead grass: whose cries, like wild birds,
Settle upon the nearest roofs   25
But soon are hid under the loud city.
Then, as they land, they hear the tolling bell
Reaching across the landscape of hysteria,
To where, louder than all those batteries
And charcoaled towers against that dying
    sky,   30
Religion stands, the Church blocking the sun.

Comments

Spender's "On Teaching Modern Poetry" (p. 837) includes a good deal of comment on the nature of modern poetry, and the kinds of value to be found in it. The reader may find it profitable to consider Spender's poem in the light of his critical opinions.

Frederick Douglass[1]
ROBERT E. HAYDEN
1913–

When it is finally ours, this freedom, this liberty, this beautiful
and terrible thing, needful to man as air,

[1] Frederick Douglass (1817–1895), an early, powerful champion of emancipation and enfranchisement for Negroes, born a slave in Maryland, escaped (1838) to New York, and legally won his freedom in 1846. He became a poet, a distinguished antislavery orator and autobiographer, worked with William Lloyd Garrison on *The Liberator*, broke with Garrison in 1847, and launched his own weekly, *The North Star*, and later his *Frederick Douglass' Paper* and *Douglass' Monthly*. In a letter to his former master, Thomas Arnold, Douglass stated his position during the Civil War: "We are fighting for unity of idea, unity of sentiment, unity of object, unity of institutions, in which there will be no North, no South, no East, no West, no black, no white, but a solidarity of the nation, making every slave free, and every free man a voter."

usable as earth; when it belongs at last to all,
when it is truly instinct, brain matter, diastole,
    systole,
reflex action; when it is finally won; when it is
    more   5
than the gaudy mumbo jumbo of politicians:
this man, this Douglass, this former slave, this
    Negro
beaten to his knees, exiled, visioning a world
where none is lonely, more hunted, alien,
this man, superb in love and logic, this man   10
shall be remembered. Oh, not with statues'
    rhetoric,
not with legends and poems and wreaths of
    bronze alone,
but with the lives grown out of his life, the lives
fleshing his dream of the beautiful, needful thing.

Black Poet, White Critic[1]
DUDLEY RANDALL
1914–

A critic advises
not to write on controversial subjects
like freedom or murder,
but to treat universal themes
and timeless symbols   5
like the white unicorn.

A white unicorn?

Booker T. and W. E. B.[1]
DUDLEY RANDALL
1914–

"It seems to me," said Booker T.,
"It shows a mighty lot of cheek

To study chemistry and Greek
When Mister Charlie needs a hand
To hoe the cotton on his land,   5
And when Miss Ann looks for a cook,
Why stick your nose inside a book?"

"I don't agree," said W.E.B.,
"If I should have the drive to seek
Knowledge of chemistry or Greek,   10
I'll do it. Charles and Miss can look
Another place for hand or cook.
Some men rejoice in skill of hand,
And some in cultivating land,
But there are others who maintain   15
The right to cultivate the brain."

"It seems to me," said Booker T.,
"That all you folks have missed the boat
Who shout about the right to vote,
And spend vain days and sleepless nights   20
In uproar over civil rights.
Just keep your mouths shut, do not grouse,
But work, and save, and buy a house."

"I don't agree," said W.E.B.,
"For what can property avail   25
If dignity and justice fail.
Unless you help to make the laws,
They'll steal your house with trumped-up clause.
A rope's as tight, a fire as hot,
No matter how much cash you've got."   30

Author's note. Du Bois preferred the initials W. E. B.
This poem suggests (as good poems usually do) more than it explicitly says. A basic disagreement between Washington and Du Bois, who was twelve years younger than Washington, appeared when the Negroes began to settle in white Harlem about 1905, a result of the rise of black economic nationalism. Washington's National Negro Business League, founded in 1900 and identified with the Afro-American Realty Company, was a powerful influence on the Negro move into Harlem. Washington and his Negro business allies had become aggressive in economics but remained conservative in civil rights politics. Du Bois, disagreeing with this conservatism, believed that unless the Negro fought for and won his civil rights there was no guarantee that his new economic status would remain safe. Stanzas 2 and 3 in the poem present the opposing points of view, and line 32 tells us where the poet stands. For a full account of this disagreement consult Harold Cruse, *The Crisis of the Negro Intellectual*, New York: William Morrow and Co., 1967, especially pp. 11–63.

For further information on Douglass consult Philip S. Foner, *Frederick Douglass*, New York: Citadel Press, 1961; see also "A Child's Reasoning" by Douglass (p. 770).
[1] See Davis's "Roosevelt Smith," p. 397.
[1] Booker T. Washington (1856–1915) and Dr. William Edward Burghardt Du Bois (1868–1963)—

Speak soft, and try your little plan,
But as for me, I'll be a man."

"It seems to me," said Booker T.—

"I don't agree,"
Said W.E.B.   35

To the Mercy Killers
DUDLEY RANDALL
1914–

If ever mercy move you murder me,
I pray you, gentle killers, let me live.
Never conspire with death to set me free,
But let me know such life as pain can give.
Even though I be a clot, an aching clench,   5
A stub, a stump, a butt, a scab, a knob,
A roaring pain, a putrefying stench,
Still let me live so long as life shall throb.
Even though I be such traitor to myself
As beg to die, do not accomplice me.   10
Even though I seem not human, a mute shelf
Of glucose, bottled blood, machinery
To swell the lung and pump the heart—even so,
Do not put out my life. Let me still glow.

The Emancipators[1]
RANDALL JARRELL
1914–1965

When you[2] ground the lenses[3] and the moons[4]
      swam free
From that great wanderer; when the apple[5]
      shone

Like a sea-shell through your prism, voyager;[6]
When, dancing in pure flame, the Roman
      mercy,[7]
Your doctrines blew like ashes from your
      bones;[8]   5

Did you think, for an instant, past the numerals
Jellied in Latin[9] like bacteria in broth,
Snatched for by holy Europe like a sign?
Past sombre tables[10] inched out with the lives
Forgotten or clapped for by the wigged
      Societies?[11]   10

You guessed this? The earth's face altering with
      iron,
The smoke ranged like a wall against the day?
—The equations metamorphose into use: the
      free
Drag their slight bones from tenements to vote
To die with their children in your factories. 15

Man is born in chains,[12] and everywhere we see
      him dead.
On your earth they sell nothing but our lives.
You knew that what you died for was our deaths?
You learned, those years, that what men wish is
      Trade?
It was you who understood; it is we who
      change.[13]   20

---

[1] Jarrell observes: "Galileo, Newton, and Bruno are the great emancipators addressed in the first stanza. ..." *Selected Poems*, 1955, p. xiii.   [2] Galileo Galilei (1564–1642), Italian astronomer and physicist who supported Copernicus's (1473–1543) contention that the earth and planets revolve around the sun; regarded as heresy at the time.   [3] The telescope he made.   [4] Jupiter's satellites which he discovered (1610).   [5] Sir Isaac Newton (1642–1727); seeing an apple fall led him to the law of gravitation. Byron wrote:
When Newton saw an apple fall, he found,
In that slight startle from his contemplation. . . .
A mode of proving that the earth turned round,
In a most natural whirl called gravitation.
      Don Juan, X. I.
[6] Voyager through the realms of thought. Wordsworth's lines are found on Newton's statue in Trinity College, Cambridge:
The marble index of a mind for ever
Voyaging through strange seas of Thought alone.
      "The Prelude"
[7] Roman Catholic Church took Bruno's life before his soul was completely damned.   [8] Ll. 4–5: Giordano Bruno (*c.* 1548–1600), Italian philosopher, critic of Christianity, and supporter of the Copernican system (see footnote 2); burned at the stake for heresy.   [9] Probably scientific terms (numerals).   [10] Scientific formulas or charts.   [11] Royal Societies.   [12] "Man is born free, and everywhere he is in chains." Rousseau (1712–1778), *The Social Contract*, 1762.   [13] Final stanza: implies that the freedom man thought he had achieved is an illusion.

Second Air Force[1]

RANDALL JARRELL
1914–1965

Far off, above the plain the summer dries,
The great loops of the hangars sway like hills.
Buses and weariness and loss, the nodding sol-
    diers
Are wire, the bare frame building, and a pass
To what was hers; her head hides his square
    patch   5
And she thinks heavily: My son is grown.
She sees a world: sand roads, tar-paper barracks,
The bubbling asphalt of the runways, sage,
The dunes rising to the interminable ranges,
The dim flights moving over clouds like
    clouds.   10
The armorers[2] in their patched faded green,
Sweat-stiffened, banded with brass cartridges,
Walk to the line; their Fortresses, all tail,
Stand wrong and flimsy on their skinny legs,
And the crews climb to them clumsily as
    bears.   15
The head withdraws into its hatch (a boy's),
The engines rise to their blind laboring roar,
And the green, made beasts run home to air.
Now in each aspect death is pure.
(At twilight they wink over men like stars   20
And hour by hour, through the night, some see
The great lights floating in—from Mars, from
    Mars.)
How emptily the watchers see them gone.

They go, there is silence; the woman and her son
Stand in the forest of the shadows, and the
    light   25
Washes them like water. In the long-sunken city
Of evening, the sunlight stills like sleep
The faint wonder of the drowned; in the evening,
In the last dreaming light, so fresh, so old,
The soldiers pass like beasts, unquestioning,   30

And the watcher for an instant understands
What there is then no need to understand;
But she wakes from her knowledge, and her
    stare,
A shadow now, moves emptily among
The shadows learning in their shadowy fields   35
The empty missions.
                Remembering,
She hears the bomber calling, *Little Friend!*
To the fighter hanging in the hostile sky,
And sees the ragged flame eat, rib by rib,
Along the metal of the wing into her heart: 40
The lives stream out, blossom, and float steadily
To the flames of the earth, the flames
That burn like stars above the lands of men.

She saves from the twilight that takes everything
A squadron shipping, in its last parade—   45
Its dogs run by it, barking at the band—
A gunner walking to his barracks, half-asleep,
Starting at something, stumbling (above, invisi-
    ble,
The crews in the steady winter of the sky
Tremble in their wired fur); and feels for
    them   50
The love of life for life. The hopeful cells
Heavy with someone else's death, cold carriers
Of someone else's victory, grope past their lives
Into her own bewilderment: The years meant
    this?

But for them the bombers answer everything.   55

[1] Jarrell's note: "In 'Second Air Force' the woman visiting her son remembers what she has read on the front page of her newspaper the week before, a conversation between a bomber, in flames over Germany, and one of the fighters protecting it: 'Then I heard the bomber call me in: "Little Friend, Little Friend, I got two engines on fire. Can you see me, Little Friend?" I said, "I'm crossing right over you. Let's go home."'" *Selected Poems,* 1955, p. xvi.
[2] Fliers.

The Force That Through the Green Fuse Drives the Flower

DYLAN THOMAS
1914–1953

The force that through the green fuse drives the
    flower
Drives my green age; that blasts the roots of
    trees
Is my destroyer.
And I am dumb to tell the crooked rose
My youth is bent by the same wintry fever.   5

The force that drives the water through the rocks

Drives my red blood; that dries the mouthing
    streams
Turns mine to wax.
And I am dumb to mouth unto my veins
How at the mountain spring the same mouth
    sucks.   10

The hand that whirls the water in the pool
Stirs the quicksand; that ropes the blowing wind
Hauls my shroud sail.
And I am dumb to tell the hanging man
How of my clay is made the hangman's lime. 15

The lips of time leech to the fountain head;
Love drips and gathers, but the fallen blood
Shall calm her sores.
And I am dumb to tell a weather's wind
How time has ticked a heaven round the
    stars.   20

And I am dumb to tell the lover's tomb
How at my sheet goes the same crooked worm.

Do Not Go Gentle into That Good Night

DYLAN THOMAS
1914–1953

Do not go gentle into that good night,
Old age should burn and rave at close of day;
Rage, rage against the dying of the light.

Though wise men at their end know dark is
    right,
Because their words had forked no lightning
    they   5
Do not go gentle into that good night.

Good men, the last wave by, crying how bright
Their frail deeds might have danced in a green
    bay,
Rage, rage against the dying of the light.

Wild men who caught and sang the sun in
    flight,   10
And learn, too late, they grieved it on its way,
Do not go gentle into that good night.

Grave men, near death, who see with blinding
    sight

Blind eyes could blaze like meteors and be gay,
Rage, rage against the dying of the light.   15

And you, my father, there on the sad height,
Curse, bless, me now with your fierce tears, I
    pray.
Do not go gentle into that good night.
Rage, rage against the dying of the light.

Sorrow Is the Only Faithful One

OWEN DODSON
1914–

Sorrow is the only faithful one:
The lone companion clinging like a season
To its original skin no matter what the variations.

If all the mountains paraded
Eating the valleys as they went   5
And the sun were a coiffure on the highest peak,

Sorrow would be there between
The sparkling and the giant laughter
Of the enemy when the clouds come down to
    swim.

But I am less, unmagic, black,   10
Sorrow clings to me more than to doomsday
    mountains
Or erosion scars on a palisade.

Sorrow has a song like a leech
Crying because the sand's blood is dry
And the stars reflected in the lake   15

Are water for all their twinkling
And bloodless for all their charm.
I have blood, and a song.

Sorrow is the only faithful one.

For Malcolm X[1]

MARGARET A. WALKER
1915–

All you violated ones with gentle hearts;
You violent dreamers whose cries shout heart-
    break;

[1] See LeRoi Jones, "A Poem for Black Hearts," p.
412, for another poem on Malcolm X. See also *The
Autobiography of Malcolm X*, New York: Grove

Whose voices echo clamors of our cool capers,
And whose black faces have hollowed pits for
    eyes.
All you gambling sons and hooked children and
    bowery bums   5
Hating white devils and black bourgeoisie,
Thumbing your noses at your burning red suns,
Gather round this coffin and mourn your dying
    swan.

Snow-white moslem head-dress around a dead
    black face!
Beautiful were your sand-papering words against
    our skins!   10
Our blood and water pour from your flowing
    wounds.
You have cut open our breasts and dug scalpels
    in our brains.
When and Where will another come to take your
    holy place?
Old man mumbling in his dotage, or crying
    child, unborn?

kitchenette building

GWENDOLYN BROOKS
1917–

We are things of dry hours and the involuntary
    plan,
Grayed in, and gray. "Dream" makes a giddy
    sound, not strong
Like "rent," "feeding a wife," "satisfying a man."

But could a dream send up through onion fumes
Its white and violet, fight with fried potatoes 5
And yesterday's garbage ripening in the hall,
Flutter, or sing an aria down these rooms

Even if we were willing to let it in,
Had time to warm it, keep it very clean,
Anticipate a message, let it begin?   10

We wonder. But not well! not for a minute!
Since Number Five is out of the bathroom now,
We think of lukewarm water, hope to get in it.

The Egg Boiler

GWENDOLYN BROOKS
1917–

Being you, you cut your poetry from wood.
The boiling of an egg is heavy art.
You come upon it as an artist should,
With rich-eyed passion, and with straining heart.
We fools, we cut our poems out of air,   5
Night color, wind soprano, and such stuff.
And sometimes weightlessness is much to bear.
You mock it, though, you name it Not Enough.
The egg, spooned gently to the avid pan,
And left the strict three minutes, or the four,   10
Is your Enough and art for any man.
We fools give courteous ear—then cut some
    more,
Shaping a gorgeous Nothingness from cloud.
You watch us, eat your egg, and laugh aloud.

The Children of the Poor
1

GWENDOLYN BROOKS
1917–

People who have no children can be hard:
Attain a mail of ice and insolence:
Need not pause in the fire, and in no sense
Hesitate in the hurricane to guard.
And when wide world is bitten and bewarred 5
They perish purely, waving their spirits hence
Without a trace of grace or of offense
To laugh or fail, diffident, wonder-starred.
While through a throttling dark we others hear
The little lifting helplessness, the queer   10
Whimper-whine; whose unridiculous
Lost softness softly makes a trap for us.
And makes a curse. And makes a sugar of
The malocclusions, the inconditions of love.

Press, Inc., 1964, especially ch. 19; and *Malcolm X
Speaks, Selected Speeches and Statements*, ed.,
George Breitman, New York: Grove Press, Inc.,
1966. Malcolm X was assassinated in Harlem, Feb.
21, 1965. For a poem on the death of Martin Luther
King, Jr., see Stephen Mooney, "Assassination at
Memphis," p. 407.

Emmett Till[1]

JAMES A. EMANUEL
1921–

I hear a whistling
Through the water.
Little Emmett
Won't be still.
He keeps floating   5
Round the darkness,
Edging through
The silent chill.

Tell me, please,
That bedtime story   10
Of the fairy
River Boy
Who swims forever,
Deep in treasures,
Necklaced in   15
A coral toy.

A Pause for a Fine Phrase

JAMES A. EMANUEL
1921–

I meditate right off the page.
Quick memory and pleasing rage
And soothing slide of conscious mind
Move to the brink, and there I find
A meaning more than what you meant[1]   5
Gleaming in a corner bent
Right out of flooring that you laid
For stud and joist you never made.
The corner turns and comes to me,
Then something fits, and I am free   10
To lift my finger off the line
That you have made completely mine.

[1] Emmett Till was a fourteen-year-old black boy from Chicago who, when visiting relatives in Mississippi in 1955, was murdered and thrown into the Tallahatchie River for allegedly whistling at a white woman. The poet says about this poem, "I intended . . . to help make Emmett Till's name legendary in our nation's history, to make him 'swim forever' in the darkness of the American dream."
[1] L. 5 is reminiscent of Albert Camus saying, "Like great works, deep feelings always mean more than they are conscious of saying." *The Myth of Sisyphus,* 1955.

To the Western World[1]

LOUIS SIMPSON
1923–

This poem and Mooney's "Assassination at Memphis" (p. 407) can be read as companion pieces in the sense that they contrast the founding of the new American civilization by successive generations working and dying to "civilize the ground," and the slow erosion of American civilization by the fear of change which has inevitably brought hatred, violence, and death. Has America forgotten the wisdom of the ancient doctrine that the only permanent thing is change? Or as the Greek philosopher Heraclitus has put it, "the sun is new each day." Or as Emerson told his countrymen when he urged them in 1836 to break their chains with the past and to "enjoy an original relation to the universe," "the sun shines today also."

A siren sang, and Europe turned away
From the high castle and the shepherd's crook.
Three caravels[2] went sailing to Cathay[3]
On the strange ocean, and the captains shook
Their banners out across the Mexique Bay.   5

And in our early days we did the same.
Remembering our fathers in their wreck
We crossed the sea from Palos[4] where they came
And saw, enormous to the little deck,
A shore in silence waiting for a name.   10

The treasures of Cathay were never found.
In this America, this wilderness
Where the axe echoes with a lonely sound,
The generations labor to possess
And grave by grave we civilize the ground.   15

[1] Within his book of poems, *A Dream of Governors,* 1959, Simpson significantly places this poem in the section titled "My America."   [2] Sailing ship, especially a small fifteenth- and sixteenth-century ship with broad bows, high narrow poop, and lateen sails.   [3] The name given to a country in eastern Asia, approximating northern China, by Marco Polo (1254?–1324), a Venetian traveler and adventurer. He is the hero of Donn Byrne's novel *Messer Marco Polo,* 1921.   [4] Former seaport in southwest Spain on the Tinto River southeast of Huelva. Columbus sailed from there August 3, 1492.

Assassination at Memphis
STEPHEN MOONEY
1915–1971

And grave by grave we civilize the ground.[1]
—LOUIS SIMPSON

Although the occasion of this poem was the assassination of Martin Luther King, Jr., April 4, 1968, the poem suggests, especially lines 25–29, that something precious beyond Dr. King was destroyed. We see once more how the poet in all civilizations has used the timely event to explore what may finally become a timeless universal of history.

On tables not far from here
there is no salt.
Axes struck into the wood
as in a chopping-block.
And there are beds with no sheets,   5
mattresses with slits
showing cotton that oozes blood.
The drops are filled with axes.[2]
Who can be hungry?
The tables, the beds shrink to the size of
    toys,   10
thrown away, but the Salvation Army has van-
    ished.
And who can lie down to sleep?
This is the year of the axe
and the mattress.
    The bodies   15
    have crawled to the floor and
    out the window, and floated
    to the river and down
    to the artificial lakes.
    They are all gone under the dams   20
    and down into quicksand.

The trucks are silent
under other people's carports, the sun
drawn by magnets toward night and secrecy.
Strangers and enemies are watching   25
shows on television, dying for interruptions
that will explain who is guilty.

What has happened is the silence
of hearts moved only by death.

---

[1] The final line of "To the Western World" above.
[2] L. 8: the sharp, tragic imagery in this line may be a prophecy as we consider what *The Commercial Appeal* of Memphis said the morning after the assassination: "To many millions of American Negroes, Dr. Martin Luther King, Jr., was the prophet of their crusade for racial equality. He was their voice of anguish, their eloquence in humiliation, their battle cry for human dignity. He forged for them the weapons of nonviolence that withstood and blunted the ferocity of segregation." Note the contrasting use of "axe" in this line and in l. 13 of Simpson's poem.

The Garden
STEPHEN MOONEY
1915–1971

There is no evidence. But here was a marriage
In which the husband killed the wife—some-
    times
It goes the other way. It took him several years
Industriously pushing her ankle-deep
Into the greensward of the formal garden   5
While she, resisting statuesquely, grew genteel
Under the neighbors' eyes. "In fact, it's not
Unpleasant here," she sighed, and the ground
    rose up
Two inches higher on her legs.
                Nobody could dispute
That she was courteously cared for. Day after
    day   10
The clocks chimed on the landings of three
    flights
Of stairs, each waiting until the last one finished
To let the masculine bass bells sound one by one
Through open windows, clearly. Nourishing
    meals
Were brought to her on time.
                Naturally   15
She was bathed at night, after the moon went
    down.
Sometimes, faintly, someone passing
On the other side of the hedge would think he
    saw
The husband making love to her, and pause
To watch their shadows wrestle darkly,
    forming   20
A kind of fire that gives no light. The leaves
Would rustle, and the stranger would steal on,
Moved by faint expectations.
              One night she sank
Into the ground well past her knees; and now

She could touch the grass without bending
    over,   25
Feeling it under her fanned-out palms
Like close-cropped human hair. From this time
    on
She liked her situation better: As she learned
To hope for nothing, to remember nothing,
As she learned at last to wait, the trip down   30
Went faster. At once the legless torso
—Her husband's hands faithfully at her shoul-
    ders—
Became a bust, a head, a frontal bone,
A lost curl of hair. The final push
Happened in full day, when the lawn-
    sprinklers   35
Were making showers of wet light. Three birds
Flew through the spray, and rapid rainbows
Whirled all the light away.
                        Far off, the cockatoos
    Cried in the warning jungle. Fish
    Nibbled algae in the fragile ponds;   40
    And carelessly among remote Gibraltars
    Submerged in the Atlantic, a school
    Of eels swam through an open door
    Under a steep escarpment, out of mind.

As a Plane Tree by the Water[1]

ROBERT LOWELL
1917–

Darkness has called to darkness, and disgrace
Elbows about our windows in this planned
Babel of Boston[2] where our money talks

[1] "Blessed *is* the man that walketh not in the
    counsel of the ungodly . . .
    But his delight *is* in the law of the LORD . . .
    And he shall be like a tree planted by the rivers
    of water. . . ."
                        Psalm 1.
The Douai version of the Bible adds *plane* before
tree in the final line, meaning broad-leaved.
[2] A reference to the Tower of Babel, or Babylon,
which was the Old Testament man's supreme expression of self-will and pride in trying to build a
tower that would reach heaven and so place man on
a level with God. Noting this pride, God confounded
the builders' language to halt the building and scattered men "upon the face of all the earth." (*Genesis,*
11:1–9.) Likewise Boston, a "planned Babel" where
money multiplies the darkness.

And multiplies the darkness of a land
Of preparation[3] where the Virgin[4] walks   5
And roses spiral her enamelled face
Or fall to splinters on unwatered streets.
Our Lady of Babylon,[5] go by, go by,
I was once the apple of your eye;
Flies, flies[6] are on the plane tree, on the
    streets.   10

The flies, the flies, the flies of Babylon
Buzz in my ear-drums while the devil's long
Dirge of the people detonates the hour
For floating cities where his golden tongue
Enchants the masons of the Babel Tower   15
To raise tomorrow's city to the sun
That never sets upon these hell-fire streets
Of Boston, where the sunlight is a sword
Striking at the withholder of the Lord:
Flies, flies are on the plane tree, on the
    streets.   20

Flies strike the miraculous waters of the iced
Atlantic and the eyes of Bernadette
Who saw Our Lady standing in the cave
At Massabielle, saw her so squarely that
Her vision put out reason's eyes.[7] The grave   25
Is open-mouthed and swallowed up in Christ.[8]
O walls of Jericho! And all the streets
To our Atlantic wall are singing: "Sing,
Sing for the resurrection of the King." [9]
Flies, flies are on the plane tree, on the
    streets.   30

[3] A land of preparation for the next world; see
Hebrews, 11:13–16.   [4] The Virgin Mary; apparently an image of her is being carried (walks) in
an Easter procession.   [5] Used in contrast to the
Virgin; the great whore of Babylon (*Revelation,*
17:1–6, 18). Boston, the new Babylon.   [6] Symbol of the plaques; see *Exodus,* 8:20–24; 9:3, 6.
[7] Ll. 21–25: A reference to St. Bernadette (Soubir-
ous) who in 1859, at the age of fourteen, claimed
to have seen the Blessed Virgin in a cave in the
Massabielle rocks in the Pyrenees near Lourdes,
France. The cave contains a spring whose waters
have become "miraculous waters" of healing, a
shrine. The image of Bernadette is apparently being
carried in the Easter procession.   [8] Ll. 25–26:
The grave is open at this Eastertime, as witnessed
by the processional, and death is "swallowed up" by
Christ's victorious resurrection.   [9] The impreg-
nable, the walls of Jericho, has been taken; death
has been assailed and conquered by Christ. But not
so in Boston (l. 30).

The Dead in Europe

ROBERT LOWELL
1917–

After the planes unloaded, we fell down
Buried together, unmarried men and women;
Not crown of thorns,[1] not iron, not Lombard
    crown,[2]
Not grilled and spindle spires pointing to heaven
Could save us. Raise us, Mother,[3] we fell
      down   5
Here hugger-mugger in the jellied fire:[4]
Our sacred earth in our day was our curse.

Our Mother, shall we rise on Mary's day
In Maryland, wherever corpses married
Under the rubble, bundled together? Pray   10
For us whom the blockbusters married and bur-
    ied;
When Satan scatters us on Rising-day,[5]
O Mother, snatch our bodies from the fire:
Our sacred earth in our day was our curse.

Mother, my bones are trembling and I
      hear   15
The earth's reverberations and the trumpet[6]
Bleating into my shambles. Shall I bear,
(O Mary!) unmarried man and powder-puppet,
Witness to the Devil! Mary, hear,
O Mary, marry earth, sea, air and fire;   20
Our sacred earth in our day is our curse.

[1] The crown of thorns of Christ.   [2] Apparently
an ironic reference to the bankers and money lenders of Lombardy, established in Lombard Street,
London. The Lombard crown is a reference to the
Teutons who invaded Italy in 568 to establish a
kingdom. Lowell's reference is probably purposely
ambiguous.   [3] The Virgin Mary, mother of Christ.
[4] Jumbled in the bomb fire.   [5] The Last Judgment
(Judgment Day). "And I saw the dead, small and
great, stand before God; and the books were opened:
and another book was opened, which is *the book* of
life: and the dead were judged out of those things
which were written in the books, according to their
works. And the sea gave up the dead which were in
it; and death and hell delivered up the dead which
were in them: and they were judged every man
according to their works." *Revelation*, 20:12–13.
[6] Trumpets that wake the dead for the Last Judgment. See Donne's "Holy Sonnet, VII," p. 320.

The Goose Fish[1]

HOWARD NEMEROV
1920–

On the long shore, lit by the moon
To show them properly alone,
Two lovers suddenly embraced
So that their shadows were as one.
The ordinary night was graced   5
For them by the swift tide of blood
That silently they took at flood,
And for a little time they prized
    Themselves emparadised.

Then, as if shaken by stage-fright   10
Beneath the hard moon's bony light,
They stood together on the sand
Embarrassed in each other's sight
But still conspiring hand in hand,
Until they saw, there underfoot,   15
As though the world had found them out,
The goose fish turning up, though dead,
    His hugely grinning head.

There in the china light he lay,
Most ancient and corrupt and grey.   20
They hesitated at his smile,
Wondering what it seemed to say
To lovers who a little while
Before had thought to understand,
By violence upon the sand,   25
The only way that could be known
    To make a world their own.

It was a wide and moony grin
Together peaceful and obscene;
They knew not what he would express,   30
So finished a comedian
He might mean failure or success,
But took it for an emblem of
Their sudden, new and guilty love
To be observed by, when they kissed,   35
    That rigid optimist.

So he became their patriarch,
Dreadfully mild in the half-dark.
His throat that the sand seemed to choke,

[1] Local American name for the angler, a marine fish
three to five feet long that lies partly buried on the
bottom and attracts smaller fishes as prey with a lure
on its head and fleshy mouth appendages.

His picket teeth, these left their mark   40
But never did explain the joke
That so amused him, lying there
While the moon went down to disappear
Along the still and tilted track
    That bears the zodiac.   45

The Kiss
ANNE SEXTON
1928–

My mouth blooms like a cut.
I've been wronged all year, tedious
nights, nothing but rough elbows in them
and delicate boxes of Kleenex calling *crybaby
crybaby, you fool!*   5

Before today my body was useless.
Now it's tearing at its square corners.
It's tearing old Mary's garments off, knot by knot
and see—Now it's shot full of these electric bolts.
Zing! A resurrection!   10

Once it was a boat, quite wooden
and with no business, no salt water under it
and in need of some paint. It was no more
than a group of boards. But you hoisted her,
    rigged her.
She's been elected.   15

My nerves are turned on. I hear them like
musical instruments. Where there was silence
the drums, the strings are incurably playing. You
    did this.
Pure genius at work. Darling, the composer has
stepped into fire.   20

It Is a Spring Afternoon
ANNE SEXTON
1928–

Everything here is yellow and green.
Listen to its throat, its earthskin,

the bone dry voices of the peepers
as they throb like advertisements.
The small animals of the woods   5
are carrying their deathmasks
into a narrow winter cave.
The scarecrow has plucked out
his two eyes like diamonds
and walked into the village.   10
The general and the postman
have taken off their packs.
This has all happened before
but nothing here is obsolete.
Everything here is possible.   15

Because of this
perhaps a young girl has laid down
her winter clothes and has casually
placed herself upon a tree limb
that hangs over a pool in the river.   20
She has been poured out onto the limb,
low above the houses of the fishes
as they swim in and out of her reflection
and up and down the stairs of her legs.
Her body carries clouds all the way home.   25
She is overlooking her watery face
in the river where blind men
come to bathe at midday.

Because of this
the ground, that winter nightmare,   30
has cured its sores and burst
with green birds and vitamins.
Because of this
the trees turn in their trenches
and hold up little rain cups   35
by their slender fingers.
Because of this
a woman stands by her stove
singing and cooking flowers.
Everything here is yellow and green.   40

Surely spring will allow
a girl without a stitch on
to turn softly in her sunlight
and not be afraid of her bed.
She has already counted seven   45
blossoms in her green green mirror.
Two rivers combine beneath her.
The face of the child wrinkles
in the water and is gone forever.
The woman is all that can be seen   50
in her animal loveliness.

Her cherished and obstinate skin
lies deeply under the watery tree.
Everything is altogether possible
and the blind men can also see.   55

How they lean out from it
To touch truth. We presume to teach
But grow old and hang back from risk.   30
We ask our children: *What is love?*
And are, too, endlessly betrayed.

The Great Teachers[1]
ROBLEY WILSON, JR.
1930–

> *Love is not love*
> *Which alters when it alteration finds.*

It never bothered Socrates,
Who clustered close about him
His own images, ghostly togas
Milk-pure, frozen in flowing out.
The naive boys with crossed ankles   5
Rocked on their doubled fists,
The alert rows of them mirror
To the equanimities of love.

It never bothered Aristotle.
Thought was a sun his pupils   10
Tethered to like cavalries
Making a shambles of the past.
They brought him precious spoils
For the apartments of his mind;
Heavy with plunder, he divined   15
The blinded temperance of love.

It never bothered the Saviour
On the populous mountainsides,
Where the confusion of bared heads
Made like trees an orderly bowing.   20
If gospel truth sits oddly in
The mind, His vision meets
Upon some special confidence
The humble intersects of love.

It never bothers great teachers.   25
We learn them best when they are men
Poised on the sills of life, and see

[1] The poem was first published in *The Reporter*,
Sept. 22, 1966. The epigraph, taken from Shakespeare's "Sonnet 116" (p. 278), was added later.

War
ROBLEY WILSON, JR.
1930–

Sometimes I have wanted to go to war.
The stories are always good—Thermopylae
Was good, the Gallic campaigns were as good
As you could get against barbarians,
The Crusades were outright inspirational.   5

Everyone ought to go off to a war
Before he is too old to have the good
Of it. The people we call pacifist
Forget (or never learned) the power of it,
The sense of godliness killing provides.   10

Who would not want to be the angel, high
Over the enemy's cities with wings
Broad as the foreshadow of death? What boy
Cannot recall from his pitiless dreams
That carnage laid about him in his bed   15

Of adults and girls? War is for the young
And keeps them young; war is to make a man
Immortal; war is to subvert boredom
And the indiscriminacy of states.
Who favors war knows what liberty is.   20

Think about us. War would spare us the vice
Of guilt, the curse of inadequate love,
The remorse of aimlessness. War transforms;
It is a place to start from, props up pride,
Writes history. Out of war, art makes itself.   25

Sometimes I have wanted to go to war,
To turn flame in anyone's heart. Old names
Dazzle me: Alexander, Genghis Khan,
Caesar, Napoleon—will any man
Shrink from riding such splendor to his
                                grave?   30

Are you the one gone soft now over peace?
Nonsense. Woman has always profited
From men at war. Since time began, if you
Camp-followed any conqueror, you, too,
Could count a hundred lovers on the sand.   35

Two Views of a Cadaver Room

SYLVIA PLATH [1]
1932–1963

1

The day she visited the dissecting room
They had four men laid out, black as burnt
      turkey,
Already half unstrung. A vinegary fume
Of the death vats clung to them;
The white-smocked boys started working.   5
The head of his cadaver had caved in,
And she could scarcely make out anything
In that rubble of skull plates and old leather.
A sallow piece of string held it together.

In their jars the snail-nosed babies moon and
      glow.   10
He hands her the cut-out heart like a cracked
      heirloom.

2

In Brueghel's panorama of smoke and slaughter
Two people only are blind to the carrion army:
He, afloat in the sea of her blue satin
Skirts, sings in the direction   15
Of her bare shoulder, while she bends,
Fingering a leaflet of music, over him,
Both of them deaf to the fiddle in the hands
Of the death's-head shadowing their song.
These Flemish lovers flourish; not for long.   20

Yet desolation, stalled in paint, spares the little
      country
Foolish, delicate, in the lower right-hand corner.

[1] See ch. 7 from *The Bell Jar*, a fictionalized autobiography of Sylvia Plath, p. 777.

Suicide off Egg Rock

SYLVIA PLATH [1]
1932–1963

Behind him the hotdogs split and drizzled
On the public grills, and the ochreous salt flats,
Gas tanks, factory stacks—that landscape
Of imperfections his bowels were part of—
Rippled and pulsed in the glassy updraft.   5
Sun struck the water like a damnation.
No pit of shadow to crawl into,
And his blood beating the old tattoo
I am, I am, I am. Children
Were squealing where combers broke and the
      spindrift   10
Raveled wind-ripped from the crest of the wave.
A mongrel working his legs to a gallop
Hustled a gull flock to flap off the sandspit.

He smoldered, as if stone-deaf, blindfold,
His body beached with the sea's garbage,   15
A machine to breathe and beat forever.
Flies filing in through a dead skate's eyehole
Buzzed and assailed the vaulted brainchamber.
The words in his book wormed off the pages.
Everything glittered like blank paper.   20

Everything shrank in the sun's corrosive
Ray but Egg Rock on the blue wastage.
He heard when he walked into the water

The forgetful surf creaming on those ledges.

A Poem for Black Hearts[1]

LeROI JONES [2]
1934–

For Malcolm's eyes, when they broke
the face of some dumb white man. For
Malcolm's hands raised to bless us
all black and strong in his image
of ourselves, for Malcolm's words   5
fire darts, the victor's tireless

[1] See ch. 7 from *The Bell Jar*, a fictionalized autobiography of Sylvia Plath, p. 777.
[1] See Margaret A. Walker's poem, "For Malcolm X,"
p. 404, and the footnote to the poem.   [2] More
recently known as Imamu Amiri Baraka.

thrusts, words hung above the world
change as it may, he said it, and
for this he was killed, for saying,
and feeling, and being/change, all   10
collected hot in his heart, For Malcolm's
heart, raising us above our filthy cities,
for his stride, and his beat, and his address
to the grey monsters of the world, For Malcolm's
pleas for your dignity, black men, for your
    life,   15
black men, for the filling of your minds
with righteousness, For all of him dead and
gone and vanished from us, and all of him
    which
clings to our speech-black god of our time.
For all of him, and all of yourself, look up,   20
black man, quit stuttering and shuffling, look up,
black man, quit whining and stooping, for all of
    him,
For Great Malcolm a prince of the earth, let
    nothing in us rest
until we avenge ourselves for his death, stupid
    animals
that killed him, let us never breathe a pure
    breath if   25
we fail, and white men call us faggots till the
    end of
the earth.

Preface to a Twenty Volume Suicide Note

LeROI JONES [1]
1934–

Lately, I've become accustomed to the way
The ground opens up and envelops me
Each time I go out to walk the dog.
Or the broad edged silly music the wind
Makes when I run for a bus—   5

Things have come to that.

And now, each night I count the stars,
And each night I get the same number.
And when they will not come to be counted
I count the holes they leave.   10

Nobody sings anymore.

And then last night, I tiptoed up
To my daughter's room and heard her
Talking to someone, and when I opened
The door, there was no one there . . .   15
Only she on her knees,
Peeking into her own clasped hands.

[1] More recently known as Imamu Amiri Baraka.

DRAMA

In tragic life, Got wot,
No villain need be! Passions spin the plot:
We are betrayed by what is false within.
—GEORGE MEREDITH

PRELIMINARIES

A backward glance at the sections on fiction and poetry may recall to us many dramatic moments. We may have observed that the conversation of Mrs. Ansley and Mrs. Slade in "Roman Fever" was like a scene from a play; or that "My Last Duchess" is drama of a special sort. When we say *dramatic*, we may have in mind *intense*. If so, we have the right notion of the nature of drama, for although all forms of literature are concentrations or distillations of human experience, drama has its own peculiar intensity and rightly lends its name to other forms when they become especially vivid. We are not, then, unfamiliar with what is dramatic when we approach drama itself.

We know, too, that drama is simply one way of telling a story. All the terms which we have applied to fiction—plot, characters, setting, exposition, antecedent action, crisis, and others—apply equally well to drama. How drama tells a story may be seen most clearly in a representative specimen, a conventional one-act play by one of America's great dramatists. While reading, keep tab on your first impressions.

Ile
EUGENE O'NEILL
1888–1953

CHARACTERS

BEN, *the cabin boy*
THE STEWARD
CAPTAIN KEENEY
SLOCUM, *second mate*
MRS. KEENEY

JOE, *a harpooner*
Members of the crew of the steam whaler Atlantic Queen

SCENE: CAPTAIN KEENEY'S *cabin on board the steam whaling ship* Atlantic Queen—*a small, square compartment about eight feet high with a skylight in the center looking out on the poop deck. On the left [the stern of the ship] a long bench with rough cushions is built in against the wall. In front of the bench, a table. Over the bench, several curtained portholes.*

In the rear, left, a door leading to the CAPTAIN'S *sleeping quarters. To the right of the door a small organ, looking as if it were brand-new, is placed against the wall.*

On the right, to the rear, a marble-topped sideboard. On the sideboard, a woman's sewing basket. Farther forward, a doorway leading to the companionway, and past the officers' quarters to the main deck.

In the center of the room, a stove. From the middle of the ceiling a hanging lamp is suspended. The walls of the cabin are painted white.

There is no rolling of the ship, and the light which comes through the skylight is sickly and faint, indicating one of those gray days of calm when ocean and sky are alike dead. The silence is unbroken except for the measured tread of someone walking up and down on the poop deck overhead.

It is nearing two bells—one o'clock—in the afternoon of a day in the year 1895.

At the rise of the curtain there is a moment of intense silence. Then THE STEWARD *enters and commences to clear the table of the few dishes which still remain on it after the* CAPTAIN'S *dinner. He is an old, grizzled man dressed in dungaree pants, a sweater, and a woolen cap with earflaps. His manner is sullen and angry. He stops stacking up the plates and casts a quick glance upward at the skylight; then tiptoes over to the closed door in rear and listens with his ear pressed to the crack. What he hears makes his face darken and he mutters a furious curse. There is a noise from the doorway on the right and he darts back to the table.*

BEN *enters. He is an overgrown, gawky boy with a long, pinched face. He is dressed in sweater, fur cap, etc. His teeth are chattering with the cold and he hurries to the stove, where he stands for a moment shivering, blowing on his hands, slapping them against his sides, on the verge of crying.*

THE STEWARD [*In relieved tones—seeing who it is.*] Oh, 'tis you, is it? What're ye shiverin' 'bout? Stay by the stove where ye belong and ye'll find no need of chatterin'.

BEN It's c-c-cold. [*Trying to control his chattering teeth—derisively.*] Who d'ye think it were —the Old Man?

THE STEWARD [*Makes a threatening move— BEN shrinks away.*] None o' your lip, young un, or I'll learn ye. [*More kindly.*] Where was it ye've been all o' the time—the fo'c's'tle?

BEN Yes.

THE STEWARD Let the Old Man see ye up for'ard monkeyshinin' with the hands and ye'll get a hidin' ye'll not forget in a hurry.

BEN Aw, he don't see nothin'. [*A trace of awe in his tones—he glances upward.*] He just walks up and down like he didn't notice nobody—and stares at the ice to the no'th'ard.

THE STEWARD [*The same tone of awe creeping into his voice.*] He's always starin' at the ice. [*In a sudden rage, shaking his fist at the skylight.*] Ice, ice, ice! Damn him and damn the ice! Holdin' us in for nigh on a year—nothin' to see but ice—stuck in it like a fly in molasses!

BEN [*Apprehensively.*] Ssshh! He'll hear ye.

THE STEWARD [*Raging.*] Aye, damn him, and damn the Arctic seas, and damn this stinkin' whalin' ship of his, and damn me for a fool to ever ship on it! [*Subsiding as if realizing the uselessness of this outburst—shaking his head —slowly, with deep conviction.*] He's a hard man—as hard a man as ever sailed the seas.

BEN [*Solemnly.*] Aye.

THE STEWARD The two years we all signed up for are done this day. Blessed Christ! Two years o' this dog's life, and no luck in the fishin', and the hands half starved with the food runnin' low, rotten as it is; and not a sign of him turnin' back for home! [*Bitterly.*] Home! I begin to doubt if ever I'll set foot on land again. [*Excitedly.*] What is it he thinks he's goin' to do? Keep us all up here after our time is worked out till the last man of us is starved to death or frozen? We've grub enough hardly to last out the voyage back if we started now. What are the men goin' to do 'bout it? Did ye hear any talk in the fo'c's'tle?

BEN [*Going over to him—in a half-whisper.*] They said if he don't put back south for home today they're goin' to mutiny.

THE STEWARD [*With grim satisfaction.*] Mutiny? Aye, 'tis the only thing they can do; and serve him right after the manner he's treated them —'s if they weren't no better nor dogs.

BEN The ice is all broke up to s'uth'ard. They's clear water 's far 's you can see. He ain't got no excuse for not turnin' back for home, the men says.

THE STEWARD [*Bitterly.*] He won't look nowheres but no'th'ard where they's only the ice to see. He don't want to see no clear water. All he thinks on is gittin' the ile—'s if it was our fault he ain't had good luck with the whales. [*Shaking his head.*] I think the man's mighty nigh losin' his senses.

BEN [*Awed.*] D'you really think he's crazy?

THE STEWARD Aye, it's the punishment o' God on him. Did ye ever hear of a man who wasn't crazy do the things he does? [*Pointing to the door in rear.*] Who but a man that's mad would take his woman—and as sweet a woman as ever was—on a stinkin' whalin' ship to the Arctic seas to be locked in by the rotten ice for nigh on a year, and maybe lose her senses forever—for it's sure she'll never be the same again.

BEN [*Sadly.*] She useter be awful nice to me before—[*His eyes grow wide and frightened.*] she got—like she is.

THE STEWARD Aye, she was good to all of us. 'Twould have been hell on board without her; for he's a hard man—a hard, hard man—a driver if there ever were one. [*With a grim laugh.*] I hope he's satisfied now—drivin' her on till she's near lost her mind. And who could blame her? 'Tis a God's wonder we're not a ship full of crazed people—with the damned ice all the time, and the quiet so thick you're afraid to hear your own voice.

BEN [*With a frightened glance toward the door

on right.] She don't never speak to me no more—jest looks at me 's if she didn't know me.

THE STEWARD She don't know no one—but him. She talks to him—when she does talk—right enough.

BEN She does nothin' all day long now but sit and sew—and then she cries to herself without makin' no noise. I've seen her.

THE STEWARD Aye, I could hear her through the door a while back.

BEN [*Tiptoes over to the door and listens.*] She's cryin' now.

THE STEWARD [*Furiously—shaking his fist.*] God send his soul to hell for the devil he is! [*There is the noise of someone coming slowly down the companionway stairs.* THE STEWARD *hurries to his stacked-up dishes. He is so nervous from fright that he knocks off the top one, which falls and breaks on the floor. He stands aghast, trembling with dread.* BEN *is violently rubbing off the organ with a piece of cloth which he has snatched from his pocket.* CAPTAIN KEENEY *appears in the doorway on right and comes into the cabin, removing his fur cap as he does so. He is a man of about forty, around five-ten in height but looking much shorter on account of the enormous proportions of his shoulders and chest. His face is massive and deeply lined, with gray-blue eyes of a bleak hardness, and a tightly clenched, thin-lipped mouth. His thick hair is long and gray. He is dressed in a heavy blue jacket and blue pants stuffed into his sea-boots.*

He is followed into the cabin by the SECOND MATE, *a rangy six-footer with a lean weather-beaten face. The* MATE *is dressed about the same as the* CAPTAIN. *He is a man of thirty or so.*]

KEENEY [*Comes toward* THE STEWARD—*with a stern look on his face.* THE STEWARD *is visibly frightened and the stack of dishes rattle in his trembling hands.* KEENEY *draws back his fist and* THE STEWARD *shrinks away. The fist is gradually lowered and* KEENEY *speaks slowly.*] 'Twould be like hitting a worm. It is nigh on two bells, Mr. Steward, and this truck not cleared yet.

THE STEWARD [*Stammering.*] Y-y-yes, sir.

KEENEY Instead of doin' your rightful work ye've been below here gossipin' old woman's talk with that boy. [*To* BEN, *fiercely.*] Get out

o' this, you! Clean up the chart room. [BEN *darts past the* MATE *to the open doorway.*] Pick up that dish, Mr. Steward!

THE STEWARD [*Doing so with difficulty.*] Yes, sir.

KEENEY The next dish you break, Mr. Steward, you take a bath in the Bering Sea at the end of a rope.

THE STEWARD [*Tremblingly.*] Yes, sir. [*He hurries out. The* SECOND MATE *walks slowly over to the* CAPTAIN.]

MATE I warn't 'specially anxious the man at the wheel should catch what I wanted to say to you, sir. That's why I asked you to come below.

KEENEY [*Impatiently.*] Speak your say, Mr. Slocum.

MATE [*Unconsciously lowering his voice.*] I'm afeard there'll be trouble with the hands by the look o' things. They'll likely turn ugly, every blessed one o' them, if you don't put back. The two years they signed up for is up today.

KEENEY And d'you think you're tellin' me somethin' new, Mr. Slocum? I've felt it in the air this long time past. D'you think I've not seen their ugly looks and the grudgin' way they worked? [*The door in rear is opened and* MRS. KEENEY *stands in the doorway. She is a slight, sweet-faced little woman primly dressed in black. Her eyes are red from weeping and her face drawn and pale. She takes in the cabin with a frightened glance and stands as if fixed to the spot by some nameless dread, clasping and unclasping her hands nervously. The two men turn and look at her.*]

KEENEY [*With rough tenderness.*] Well, Annie?

MRS. KEENEY [*As if awakening from a dream.*] David, I— [*She is silent. The* MATE *starts for the doorway.*]

KEENEY [*Turning to him—sharply.*] Wait!

MATE Yes, sir.

KEENEY D'you want anything, Annie?

MRS. KEENEY [*After a pause, during which she seems to be endeavoring to collect her thoughts.*] I thought maybe—I'd go up on deck, David, to get a breath of fresh air. [*She stands humbly awaiting his permission. He and the* MATE *exchange a significant glance.*]

KEENEY It's too cold, Annie. You'd best stay below today. There's nothing to look at on deck—but ice.

MRS. KEENEY [*Monotonously.*] I know—ice, ice, ice! But there's nothing to see down here but these walls. [*She makes a gesture of loathing.*]

KEENEY You can play the organ, Annie.

MRS. KEENEY [*Dully.*] I hate the organ. It puts me in mind of home.

KEENEY [*A touch of resentment in his voice.*] I got it jest for you.

MRS. KEENEY [*Dully.*] I know. [*She turns away from them and walks slowly to the bench on left. She lifts up one of the curtains and looks through a porthole; then utters an exclamation of joy.*] Ah, water! Clear water! As far as I can see! How good it looks after all these months of ice! [*She turns around to them, her face transfigured with joy.*] Ah, now I must go up on the deck and look at it, David.

KEENEY [*Frowning.*] Best not today, Annie. Best wait for a day when the sun shines.

MRS. KEENEY [*Desperately.*] But the sun never shines in this terrible place.

KEENEY [*A tone of command in his voice.*] Best not today, Annie.

MRS. KEENEY [*Crumbling before this command —abjectly.*] Very well, David. [*She stands there staring straight before her as if in a daze. The two men look at her uneasily.*]

KEENEY [*Sharply.*] Annie!

MRS. KEENEY [*Dully.*] Yes, David.

KEENEY Me and Mr. Slocum has business to talk about—ship's business.

MRS KEENEY Very well, David. [*She goes slowly out, rear, and leaves the door three-quarters shut behind her.*]

KEENEY Best not have her on deck if they's goin' to be any trouble.

MATE Yes, sir.

KEENEY And trouble they's goin' to be. I feel it in my bones. [*Takes a revolver from the pocket of his coat and examines it.*] Got your'n?

MATE Yes, sir.

KEENEY Not that we'll have to use 'em—not if I know their breed of dog—just to frighten 'em up a bit. [*Grimly.*] I ain't never been forced to use one yit; and trouble I've had by land and by sea 's long as I kin remember, and will have till my dyin' day, I reckon.

MATE [*Hesitatingly.*] Then you ain't goin'—to turn back?

KEENEY Turn back! Mr. Slocum, did you ever hear o' me pointin' s'uth for home with only a measly four hundred barrel of ile in the hold?

MATE [*Hastily.*] No, sir—but the grub's gittin' low.

KEENEY They's enough to last a long time yit, if they're careful with it; and they's plenty o' water.

MATE They say it's not fit to eat—what's left; and the two years they signed on fur is up today. They might make trouble for you in the courts when we git home.

KEENEY To hell with 'em! Let them make what law trouble they kin. I don't give a damn 'bout the money. I've got to git the ile! [*Glancing sharply at the* MATE.] You ain't turnin' no damned sea-lawyer, be you, Mr. Slocum?

MATE [*Flushing.*] Not by a hell of a sight, sir.

KEENEY What do the fools want to go home fur now? Their share o' the four hundred barrel wouldn't keep 'em in chewin' terbacco.

MATE [*Slowly.*] They wants to git back to their folks an' things, I s'pose.

KEENEY [*Looking at him searchingly.*] 'N you want to turn back, too. [*The* MATE *looks down confusedly before his sharp gaze.*] Don't lie, Mr. Slocum. It's writ down plain in your eyes. [*With grim sarcasm.*] I hope, Mr. Slocum, you ain't agoin' to jine the men agin me.

MATE [*Indignantly.*] That ain't fair, sir, to say sich things.

KEENEY [*With satisfaction.*] I warn't much afeard o' that, Tom. You been with me nigh on ten year and I've learned ye whalin'. No man kin say I ain't a good master, if I be a hard one.

MATE I warn't thinkin' of myself, sir—'bout turnin' home, I mean. [*Desperately.*] But Mrs. Keeney, sir—seems like she ain't jest satisfied up here, ailin' like—what with the cold an' bad luck an' the ice an' all.

KEENEY [*His face clouding—rebukingly but not severely.*] That's my business, Mr. Slocum. I'll thank you to steer a clear course o' that. [*A pause.*] The ice'll break up soon to no'th'ard. I could see it startin' today. And when it goes and we git some sun Annie'll perk up. [*Another pause—then he bursts forth.*] It ain't the damned money what's keepin' me up in the Northern seas, Tom. But I can't go back to Homeport with a measly four hundred barrel of ile. I'd die fust. I ain't never come back home in all my days without a full ship. Ain't that truth?

MATE   Yes, sir; but this voyage you been ice-bound, an'—

KEENEY   [*Scornfully.*] And d'you s'pose any of 'em would believe that—any o' them skippers I've beaten voyage after voyage? Can't you hear 'em laughin' and sneerin'—Tibbots 'n' Harris 'n' Simms and the rest—and all o' Homeport makin' fun o' me? "Dave Keeney what boasts he's the best whalin' skipper out o' Homeport comin' back with a measly four hundred barrel of ile?" [*The thought of this drives him into a frenzy, and he smashes his fist down on the marble top of the sideboard.*] Hell! I got to git the ile, I tell you. How could I figger on this ice? It's never been so bad before in the thirty year I been acomin' here. And now it's breakin' up. In a couple o' days it'll be all gone. And they's whale here, plenty of 'em. I know they is and I ain't never gone wrong yit. I got to git the ile! I got to git it in spite of all hell, and by God, I ain't agoin' home till I do git it! [*There is the sound of subdued sobbing from the door in rear. The two men stand silent for a moment, listening. Then* KEENEY *goes over to the door and looks in. He hesitates for a moment as if he were going to enter—then closes the door softly.* JOE, *the harpooner, an enormous six-footer with a battered, ugly face, enters from right and stands waiting for the* CAPTAIN *to notice him.*]

KEENEY   [*Turning and seeing him.*] Don't be standin' there like a gawk, Harpooner. Speak up!

JOE   [*Confusedly.*] We want—the men, sir—they wants to send a depitation aft to have a word with you.

KEENEY   [*Furiously.*] Tell 'em to go to— [*Checks himself and continues grimly.*] Tell 'em to come. I'll see 'em.

JOE   Aye, aye, sir. [*He goes out.*]

KEENEY   [*With a grim smile.*] Here it comes, the trouble you spoke of, Mr. Slocum, and we'll make short shift of it. It's better to crush such things at the start than let them make headway.

MATE   [*Worriedly.*] Shall I wake up the First and Fourth, sir? We might need their help.

KEENEY   No, let them sleep. I'm well able to handle this alone, Mr. Slocum. [*There is the shuffling of footsteps from outside and five of the crew crowd into the cabin, led by* JOE. *All are dressed alike—sweaters, sea-boots, etc. They glance uneasily at the* CAPTAIN, *twirling their fur caps in their hands.*]

KEENEY   [*After a pause.*] Well? Who's to speak fur ye?

JOE   [*Stepping forward with an air of bravado.*] I be.

KEENEY   [*Eyeing him up and down coldly.*] So you be. Then speak your say and be quick about it.

JOE   [*Trying not to wilt before the* CAPTAIN's *glance and avoiding his eyes.*] The time we signed up for is done today.

KEENEY   [*Icily.*] You're tellin' me nothin' I don't know.

JOE   You ain't pintin' fur home yit, far 's we kin see.

KEENEY   No, and I ain't agoin' to till this ship is full of ile.

JOE   You can't go no further no'th with the ice afore ye.

KEENEY   The ice is breaking up.

JOE   [*After a slight pause during which the others mumble angrily to one another.*] The grub we're gittin' now is rotten.

KEENEY   It's good enough fur ye. Better men than ye are have eaten worse. [*There is a chorus of angry exclamations from the crowd.*]

JOE   [*Encouraged by this support.*] We ain't agoin' to work no more less you puts back for home.

KEENEY   [*Fiercely.*] You ain't, ain't you?

JOE   No; and the law courts'll say we was right.

KEENEY   To hell with your law courts! We're at sea now and I'm the law on this ship. [*Edging up toward the* HARPOONER.] And every mother's son of you what don't obey orders goes in irons. [*There are more angry exclamations from the crew.* MRS. KEENEY *appears in the doorway in rear and looks on with startled eyes. None of the men notice her.*]

JOE   [*With bravado.*] Then we're agoin' to mutiny and take the old hooker home ourselves. Ain't we, boys? [*As he turns his head to look at the others,* KEENEY's *fist shoots out to the side of his jaw.* JOE *goes down in a heap and lies there.* MRS. KEENEY *gives a shriek and hides her face in her hands. The men pull out their sheath knives and start a rush, but stop when they find themselves confronted by the revolvers of* KEENEY *and the* MATE.]

KEENEY   [*His eyes and voice snapping.*] Hold

still! [*The men stand huddled together in a sullen silence.* KEENEY's *voice is full of mockery.*] You've found out it ain't safe to mutiny on this ship, ain't you? And now git for'ard where ye belong, and—[*He gives* JOE's *body a contemptuous kick.*] drag him with you. And remember the first man of ye I see shirkin' I'll shoot dead as sure as there's a sea under us, and you can tell the rest the same. Git for'ard now! Quick! [*The men leave in cowed silence, carrying* JOE *with them.* KEENEY *turns to the* MATE *with a short laugh and puts his revolver back in his pocket.*] Best get up on deck, Mr. Slocum, and see to it they don't try none of their skulkin' tricks. We'll have to keep an eye peeled from now on. I know 'em.

MATE Yes, sir. [*He goes out, right.* KEENEY *hears his wife's hysterical weeping and turns around in surprise—then walks slowly to her side.*]

KEENEY [*Putting an arm around her shoulder—with gruff tenderness.*] There, there, Annie. Don't be afeard. It's all past and gone.

MRS. KEENEY [*Shrinking away from him.*] Oh, I can't bear it! I can't bear it any longer!

KEENEY [*Gently.*] Can't bear what, Annie?

MRS. KEENEY [*Hysterically.*] All this horrible brutality, and these brutes of men, and this terrible ship, and this prison cell of a room, and the ice all around, and the silence. [*After this outburst she calms down and wipes her eyes with her handkerchief.*]

KEENEY [*After a pause during which he looks down at her with a puzzled frown.*] Remember, I warn't hankerin' to have you come on this voyage, Annie.

MRS. KEENEY I wanted to be with you, David, don't you see? I didn't want to wait back there in the house all alone as I've been doing these last six years since we were married—waiting, and watching, and fearing—with nothing to keep my mind occupied—not able to go back teaching school on account of being Dave Keeney's wife. I used to dream of sailing on the great, wide, glorious ocean. I wanted to be by your side in the danger and vigorous life of it all. I wanted to see you the hero they make you out to be in Homeport. And instead— [*Her voice grows tremulous.*] all I find is ice and cold—and brutality! [*Her voice breaks.*]

KEENEY I warned you what it'd be, Annie. "Whalin' ain't no ladies' tea-party," I says to you, and "you better stay to home where you've got all your woman's comforts." [*Shaking his head.*] But you was so set on it.

MRS. KEENEY [*Wearily.*] Oh, I know it isn't your fault, David. You see, I didn't believe you. I guess I was dreaming about the old Vikings in the story books and I thought you were one of them.

KEENEY [*Protestingly.*] I done my best to make it as cozy and comfortable as could be. [MRS. KEENEY *looks around her in wild scorn.*] I even sent to the city for that organ for ye, thinkin' it might be soothin' to ye to be playin' it times when they was calms and things was dull like.

MRS. KEENEY [*Wearily.*] Yes, you were very kind, David. I know that. [*She goes to left and lifts the curtains from the porthole and looks out—then suddenly bursts forth:*] I won't stand it—I can't stand it—pent up by these walls like a prisoner. [*She runs over to him and throws her arms around him, weeping. He puts his arm protectingly over her shoulders.*] Take me away from here, David! If I don't get away from here, out of this terrible ship, I'll go mad! Take me home, David! I can't think any more. I feel as if the cold and the silence were crushing down on my brain. I'm afraid. Take me home!

KEENEY [*Holds her at arm's length and looks at her face anxiously.*] Best go to bed, Annie. You ain't yourself. You got fever. Your eyes look so strange like. I ain't never seen you look this way before.

MRS. KEENEY [*Laughing hysterically.*] It's the ice and the cold and the silence—they'd make any one look strange.

KEENEY [*Soothingly.*] In a month or two, with good luck, three at the most, I'll have her filled with ile and then we'll give her everything she'll stand and pint for home.

MRS. KEENEY But we can't wait for that—I can't wait. I want to get home. And the men won't wait. They want to get home. It's cruel, it's brutal for you to keep them. You must sail back. You've got no excuse. There's clear water to the south now. If you've a heart at all you've got to turn back.

KEENEY [*Harshly.*] I can't, Annie.

MRS. KEENEY Why can't you?

KEENEY A woman couldn't rightly understand my reason.

MRS. KEENEY [*Wildly.*] Because it's a stupid, stubborn reason. Oh, I heard you talking with the Second Mate. You're afraid the other captains will sneer at you because you didn't come back with a full ship. You want to live up to your silly reputation even if you do have to beat and starve men and drive me mad to do it.

KEENEY [*His jaw set stubbornly.*] It ain't that, Annie. Them skippers would never dare sneer to my face. It ain't so much what any one'd say—but— [*He hesitates, struggling to express his meaning.*] you see—I've always done it—since my first voyage as skipper. I always come back—with a full ship—and—it don't seem right not to—somehow. I been always first whalin' skipper out o' Homeport, and— Don't you see my meanin', Annie? [*He glances at her. She is not looking at him but staring dully in front of her, not hearing a word he is saying.*] Annie! [*She comes to herself with a start.*] Best turn in, Annie, there's a good woman. You ain't well.

MRS. KEENEY [*Resisting his attempts to guide her to the door in rear.*] David! Won't you please turn back?

KEENEY [*Gently.*] I can't, Annie—not yet awhile. You don't see my meanin'. I got to git the ile.

MRS. KEENEY It'd be different if you needed the money, but you don't. You've got more than plenty.

KEENEY [*Impatiently.*] It ain't the money I'm thinkin' of. D'you think I'm as mean as that?

MRS. KEENEY [*Dully.*] No—I don't know—I can't understand— [*Intensely.*] Oh, I want to be home in the old house once more and see my own kitchen again, and hear a woman's voice talking to me and be able to talk to her. Two years! It seems so long ago—as if I'd been dead and could never go back.

KEENEY [*Worried by her strange tone and the far-away look in her eyes.*] Best to go to bed, Annie. You ain't well.

MRS. KEENEY [*Not appearing to hear him.*] I used to be lonely when you were away. I used to think Homeport was a stupid, monotonous place. Then I used to go down on the beach, especially when it was windy and the breakers were rolling in, and I'd dream of the fine free life you must be leading. [*She gives a laugh which is half a sob.*] I used to love the sea then. [*She pauses; then continues with slow intensity:*] But now—I don't ever want to see the sea again.

KEENEY [*Thinking to humor her.*] 'Tis no fit place for a woman, that's sure. I was a fool to bring ye.

MRS. KEENEY [*After a pause—passing her hand over her eyes with a gesture of pathetic weariness.*] How long would it take us to reach home—if we started now?

KEENEY [*Frowning.*] 'Bout two months, I reckon, Annie, with fair luck.

MRS. KEENEY [*Counts on her fingers—then murmurs with a rapt smile.*] That would be August, the latter part of August, wouldn't it? It was on the twenty-fifth of August we were married, David, wasn't it?

KEENEY [*Trying to conceal the fact that her memories have moved him—gruffly.*] Don't you remember?

MRS. KEENEY [*Vaguely—again passes her hand over her eyes.*] My memory is leaving me—up here in the ice. It was so long ago. [*A pause— then she smiles dreamily.*] It's June now. The lilacs will be all in bloom in the front yard— and the climbing roses on the trellis to the side of the house—they're budding. [*She suddenly covers her face with her hands and commences to sob.*]

KEENEY [*Disturbed.*] Go in and rest, Annie. You're all wore out cryin' over what can't be helped.

MRS. KEENEY [*Suddenly throwing her arms around his neck and clinging to him.*] You love me, don't you, David?

KEENEY [*In amazed embarrassment at this outburst.*] Love you? Why d'you ask me such a question, Annie?

MRS. KEENEY [*Shaking him—fiercely.*] But you do, don't you, David? Tell me!

KEENEY I'm your husband, Annie, and you're my wife. Could there be aught but love between us after all these years?

MRS. KEENEY [*Shaking him again—still more fiercely.*] Then you do love me. Say it!

KEENEY [*Simply.*] I do, Annie.

MRS. KEENEY [*Shaking him again—her hands drop to her sides. KEENEY regards her anxiously. She passes her hand across her eyes and murmurs half to herself:*] I sometimes think if we could only have had a child. [KEENEY *turns away from her, deeply moved. She grabs his arm and turns him around to face her—intensely.*] And I've always been a good wife to you, haven't I, David?

KEENEY [*His voice betraying his emotion.*] No man has ever had a better, Annie.

MRS. KEENEY And I've never asked for much from you, have I, David? Have I?

KEENEY You know you could have all I got the power to give ye, Annie.

MRS. KEENEY [*Wildly.*] Then do this this once for my sake, for God's sake—take me home! It's killing me, this life—the brutality and cold and horror of it. I'm going mad. I can feel the threat in the air. I can hear the silence threatening me—day after gray day and every day the same. I can't bear it. [*Sobbing.*] I'll go mad, I know I will. Take me home, David, if you love me as you say. I'm afraid. For the love of God, take me home! [*She throws her arms around him, weeping against his shoulder. His face betrays the tremendous struggle going on within him. He holds her out at arm's length, his expression softening. For a moment his shoulders sag, he becomes old, his iron spirit weakens as he looks at her tear-stained face.*]

KEENEY [*Dragging out the words with an effort.*] I'll do it, Annie—for your sake—if you say it's needful for ye.

MRS. KEENEY [*Wild with joy—kissing him.*] God bless you for that, David! [*He turns away from her silently and walks toward the companionway. Just at that moment there is a clatter of footsteps on the stairs and the SECOND MATE enters the cabin.*]

MATE [*Excitedly.*] The ice is breakin' up to no'th'ard, sir. There's a clear passage through the floe, and clear water beyond, the lookout says. [KEENEY *straightens himself like a man coming out of a trance.* MRS. KEENEY *looks at the MATE with terrified eyes.*]

KEENEY [*Dazedly—trying to collect his thoughts.*] A clear passage? To no'th'ard?

MATE Yes, sir.

KEENEY [*His voice suddenly grim with determination.*] Then get her ready and we'll drive her through.

MATE Aye, aye, sir.

MRS. KEENEY [*Appealingly.*] David!

KEENEY [*Not heeding her.*] Will the men turn

to willin' or must we drag 'em out?

MATE They'll turn to willin' enough. You put the fear o' God into 'em, sir. They're meek as lambs.

KEENEY Then drive 'em—both watches. [*With grim determination.*] They's whale t'other side o' this floe and we're going to git 'em.

MATE Aye, aye, sir. [*He goes out hurriedly. A moment later there is the sound of scuffling feet from the deck outside and the MATE'S voice shouting orders.*]

KEENEY [*Speaking aloud to himself—derisively.*] And I was agoin' home like a yaller dog!

MRS. KEENEY [*Imploringly.*] David!

KEENEY [*Sternly.*] Woman, you ain't adoin' right when you meddle in men's business and weaken 'em. You can't know my feelin's. I got to prove a man to be a good husband for ye to take pride in. I got to git the ile, I tell ye.

MRS. KEENEY [*Supplicatingly.*] David! Aren't you going home?

KENNEY [*Ignoring this question—commandingly.*] You ain't well. Go and lay down a mite. [*He starts for the door.*] I got to git on deck. [*He goes out. She cries after him in anguish:*] David! [*A pause. She passes her hand across her eyes—then commences to laugh hysterically and goes to the organ. She sits down and starts to play wildly an old hymn.* KEENEY *reënters from the doorway to the deck and stands looking at her angrily. He comes over and grabs her roughly by the shoulder.*]

KEENEY Woman, what foolish mockin' is this? [*She laughs wildly and he starts back from her in alarm.*] Annie! What is it? [*She doesn't answer him.* KEENEY'S *voice trembles.*] Don't you know me, Annie? [*He puts both hands on her shoulders and turns her around so that he can look into her eyes. She stares up at him with a stupid expression, a vague smile on her lips. He stumbles away from her, and she commences softly to play the organ again.*]

KEENEY [*Swallowing hard—in a hoarse whisper, as if he had difficulty in speaking.*] You said—you was agoin' mad—God! [*A long wail is heard from the deck above.*] Ah bl-o-o-o-ow! [*A moment later the MATE'S face appears through the skylight. He cannot see MRS. KEENEY.*]

MATE [*In great excitement.*] Whales, sir—a

whole school of 'em—off the star'b'd quarter 'bout five miles away—big ones!

KEENEY [*Galvanized into action.*] Are you lowerin' the boats?

MATE Yes, sir.

KEENEY [*With grim decision.*] I'm acomin' with ye.

MATE Aye, aye, sir. [*Jubilantly.*] You'll git the ile now right enough, sir. [*His head is withdrawn and he can be heard shouting orders.*]

KEENEY [*Turning to his wife.*] Annie! Did you hear him? I'll get the ile. [*She doesn't answer or seem to know he is there. He gives a hard laugh, which is almost a groan.*] I know you're foolin' me, Annie. You ain't out of your mind —[*Anxiously.*] be you? I'll git the ile now right enough—jest a little while longer, Annie —then we'll turn hom'ard. I can't turn back now, you see that, don't ye? I've got to git the ile. [*In sudden terror.*] Answer me! You ain't mad, be you? [*She keeps on playing the organ, but makes no reply. The* MATE'S *face appears again through the skylight.*]

MATE All ready, sir. [KEENEY *turns his back on his wife and strides to the doorway, where he stands for a moment and looks back at her in anguish, fighting to control his feelings.*]

MATE Comin', sir?

KEENEY [*His face suddenly grown hard with determination.*] Aye. [*He turns abruptly and goes out.* MRS. KEENEY *does not appear to notice his departure. Her whole attention seems centered in the organ. She sits with half-closed eyes, her body swaying a little from side to side to the rhythm of the hymn. Her fingers move faster and faster and she is playing wildly and discordantly as*

[*The Curtain Falls.*]

FIRST IMPRESSIONS

All that a play is at the moment we read it and all that we are during the reading interact to produce our first impressions. (Compare "Fiction: Preliminaries," p. 12.) When we move away from what may be called *natural response* into conscious analysis of what we have read, two things are likely to happen: (1) the play changes; (2) we change. A new interaction takes place in which we act upon the play and the play acts upon us. The moment that we ask questions and attempt to answer them, we modify natural response and start analysis.

Natural response and conscious analysis are not completely separate processes. How separate they are depends greatly upon the reader. An untrained reader will passively allow what he is reading to act upon him; analysis for him is a separate process. The trained reader, even during the first reading, will begin applying analytical method which will modify his natural response. The point here, however, is that for the untrained and the trained reader analysis alone will yield the more complex meaning—and therefore the full pleasure—of a serious literary work.

Our natural response to *Ile* doubtless involves our attitude toward Captain Keeney. Do we like him? Probably not. Do we like Annie? Perhaps we do. The important question, however, is this one: Is our liking or disliking a character more, or less, significant than the credibility of the character? (Compare "Fiction: Preliminaries," p. 12.) Some of the best-drawn characters in literature are villains: Iago, for example, in *Othello*. We may dislike them on a moral level but like them as fully realized persons. In short, we need to warn ourselves that sympathy for Annie should not make us think of her as an artistically finer character than Captain Keeney, whom we may despise. Analysis will make this conclusion clear.

We should bear in mind that the analysis of *Ile* represents one approach, always with modifications, to the understanding of any play. *The Boor* (see p. 432), although different in almost every respect from *Ile*, offers an opportunity to use the method of analysis here suggested. The ten full-length plays are, of course, more complicated in structure than the one-act plays, but the same method of analysis will apply to them, too.

THE FACTS OF THE PLAY

We should first of all have before us the literal facts with which the play was built. These materials are not the play, but without a sure knowledge of them we cannot reach what is essential in the play.

In 1889 Annie, a schoolteacher with romantic notions of the sea, married Captain Keeney, the most successful whaling-boat skipper of Homeport. Childless after four years and imagining her husband's life at sea as free and venturesome compared to the monotonous life of Homeport, Annie won reluctant permission to accompany her husband on a voyage which began in June 1893. Before the voyage, Captain Keeney installed an organ in his cabin so that Annie might have the comfort of music during the long days ahead. Meager luck during the first year at sea played out completely when the *Atlantic Queen* became ice-locked in the Arctic Ocean and remained immovable until the exact day arrived ending the two-year contracts signed by the crew.

On this day, with the ice barrier broken to the south, the crew through a deputation demands on threat of mutiny that the ship be sailed homeward. Captain Keeney, with no intention of failing to get "ile" at whatever cost, knocks down the crew's spokesman and, with weapons, holds control of the ship. Annie, cured of all romantic notions of the sea and verging on madness, uses all her resources to force her husband to start for home. The final appeal to his love for her wins momentarily, but a report from the Second Mate that the ice to the north is broken and whales sighted returns Captain Kenney to his purpose of getting the "ile." Annie's mind gives way, and the play ends with Captain Keeney off after the whales and his wife wildly playing hymns on the organ.

Here are the materials. What does O'Neill make of this story? What do we make of it?

EXPOSITION AND ANTECEDENT ACTION

Exposition explains. It sets forth the information we need in order to understand the present action. If we look back at our summary of the play, we see that the first paragraph is straight exposition, an explanation of what has gone on before the play opened. Everything which occurred before the play opened is called *antecedent action* and is a part of the exposition. The playwright has the task of giving us as much of the exposition as possible through the medium of dialogue, dialogue which must be carefully motivated to appear casual and natural.

We need some information before the dialogue begins. The direct statements of the author are used chiefly to set the stage, to describe the characters, to indicate "stage business," and to direct the correct reading of the lines. He also gives us the key to what is antecedent action:

it is nearing two bells—one o'clock—in the afternoon of a day in the year 1895.

Here is our starting point. Everything which occurred before the moment indicated is antecedent action.

Before a word is spoken tension is established through a bit of stage business. (Stage business is action without dialogue.) The Steward—

. . . tiptoes over to the closed door in rear and listens with his ear pressed to the crack. What he hears makes his face darken and he mutters a furious curse.

What, we ask, is the significance of this action? We know that we have our first hint of the kind of play this is to be. Eavesdropping can be amusing, even farcical. The muttered curse, the tiptoeing give us warning of the play's tone. (Tone represents the author's attitude toward the facts of the play and determines how the play should be regarded by the reader.) Even before this, we as readers have taken heed of the author's serious intent in the words describing the atmosphere of the setting:

. . . the light which comes through the sky-light is sickly and faint, indicating one of those gray days of calm when ocean and sky are alike dead.

The tread of "someone walking up and down the poop deck" brings the monotony of sight and sound into unison. We are ready for a serious play, for perhaps a tragic play, before the first word is spoken.

Two minor characters, the Steward and Ben, appear first and talk naturally, yet economically, for our benefit. With their appearance the present action begins, even though the chief ingredient of their talk involves past action. In other words, exposition, antecedent action, and present action blend into one action. The cruel cold is made real by Ben's chattering speech. It is a fact of here and now. It is also a fact of the past and a portent of things to come. Ice and cold are prime factors. The Old Man (Captain Keeney) is "always starin' at the ice," says the Steward in awed tones. (Is it Ice versus Captain Keeney? we ask.) Then the Steward rages: "Ice, ice, ice! Damn him and damn the ice!" The past year of hardships is equally chargeable to the unyielding ice and to the unyielding Captain. Nothing can be done about the ice. What about the Captain? "What are the men goin' to do 'bout it?" asks the Steward. Ben replies: "They said if he don't put back south for home today they're goin' to mutiny." If this were to be a simple struggle between Captain and crew, we are now ready to meet the central character, "a hard man—as hard a man as ever sailed the seas."

The hardness of Captain Keeney, however, is to be given emphasis through his treatment of his wife, Annie. We must know what manner of woman she was and is. Ben attests: "She useter be awful nice to me before—[*His eyes grow wide and frightened.*] she got—like she is." The Steward adds: "'Twould have been hell on board without her." When Ben tiptoes to the door and hears Annie crying, we recall the Steward's action as the play opens. We have learned that Annie is a sweet, amiable person, in every way a contrast to her husband. We are now ready to meet Captain Keeney and later his wife.

Exposition, including references to antecedent action, does not stop of course with the introduction of the main characters. From the dialogue between Captain Keeney and the Second Mate, and between the Captain and his wife, we learn still more details as the present action moves forward. What we learn has already been summarized under "The Facts of the Play."

SETTING

Setting tells us where and when the action takes place and is correlated with the exposition. Setting is the *environment* of the play. (A similar term, *panorama,* is used in connection with short stories. See "Fiction: Preliminaries.") If we were in a theater to see *Ile,* the program would inform us that the action takes place in "Captain Keeney's cabin aboard the steam whaling vessel *Atlantic Queen*" and would add: "Time: afternoon of a day in the year 1895." That much information would be sufficient, since the remainder of the description serves as directions for staging which would be visible as soon as the curtain

went up. *As readers we must set our own stage.*

We are accustomed to this demand from a writer, for in reading fiction we were constantly aware of the background of the action. We note differences however, in that the dramatist must attend first of all to the setting of each scene, whereas the writer of short stories—or novels, or narrative poems—may intersperse descriptive passages as appropriate. We note, too, that the dramatist is crisp and precise in his description and confines himself for the most part to utilitarian prose. (George Bernard Shaw is an exception to this rule and frequently wrote novelistic plays. Even some of O'Neill's stage directions go beyond pure usefulness.) He is writing, not for a reader who might savor his style, but for a stage manager who will be expected to build the semblance of *"a small, square compartment about eight feet high with a skylight in the center looking out on the poop deck."*

Here, perhaps, we should ask: What difference does the setting make? Our answer, at first, is that the setting is important, and we cite the author's care in emphasizing the relation of the ice-bound ship to the characters. We are to be given a view of a microcosm, a little world, far removed and long removed from the larger world. We feel that we must understand the characters in relation to their restricted and unfavorable environment. In one sense, then, the setting, including the ice fields which have held the ship immovable, controls the characters and through them the action. We realize at once, however, that this answer may not be fully satisfactory. Would time and place have had the same effect on any other group of characters? Possibly not. We suspect that the setting of *Ile* simply tests characters which are already formed. We begin to suspect that setting represents something beyond itself, that it is in reality an *opposing force,* a symbol of challenge to man. Accepting the challenge, a man (or woman) may win or lose.

We see only the *"small, square compartment,"* but we know what is outside. The remainder of the ship is there with water to the south and ice to the north. To the north also are whales, the immediate goal. But do these things complete the setting? Are we looking at a true microcosm? Does the larger world have nothing to do with this smaller world? Clearly it does have much to do with it. In a sense the *Atlantic Queen* has invisible but powerful lines connecting it to Homeport. Homeport is part of the setting, a reality in the minds of every character. The men are desperate to complete the voyage and return even though to return without oil means a dead loss to them. Annie is frantic to "be home in the old house once more," to see her kitchen, to talk to women and to hear them talk. Yet, it is Homeport's ties with Captain Keeney that are strongest of all—he dares not go back unsuccessful, to occupy a position less exalted than "first whalin' skipper out o' Homeport." Part of the setting, then, is a place seen only in the mind's eyes of the characters and of the readers or observers of this play.

PLOT

The action in *Ile* is simple and straightforward. If in the beginning of our analysis it was useful to assemble a fairly detailed summary of the facts, it is equally necessary at this point to look at the essence of the action. Stripped of details, it is the story of a ship's captain who, in pursuit of whale oil, ignores hardships, subdues a mutinous crew, nearly succumbs to his wife's pleas, but reasserts himself in time to drive his wife mad and, apparently, in the end to win through to his goal. Except when the Captain knocks down the spokesman for the crew, the external action is limited to nothing more exciting than the dropping of a dish. Yet tension steadily mounts as we await the answer to the question: What course will Captain Keeney take?

Let us note first the dropping of the dish by the Steward. The agitation of the Steward at the approach of the Captain causes the accident. More important, after the Captain appears we

no longer have to depend on hearsay about his hardness and cruelty, we see cruelty in action:

[KEENEY *draws back his fist and* THE STEWARD *shrinks away. The fist is gradually lowered and* KEENEY *speaks slowly.*] 'Twould be like hitting a worm.

A moment later he adds:

The next dish you break, Mr. Steward, you take a bath in the Bering Sea at the end of a rope.

Here, then, is the hard man made real. We know now what to expect of him.

Before we proceed let us look at a diagram of the action. This diagram represents an "action line." Three separate interdependent conflicts are involved: Captain Keeney against natural forces (the Ice); Captain Keeney against the rights of men (the Crew); Captain Keeney against the claims of home and love (Annie).

Let us suppose that Captain Keeney upon being petitioned by his men had agreed to return home. Or suppose, on the other hand, everybody had agreed that getting the "ile" was the thing to do. Would either situation have made a play? Why not? Is it that we naturally dislike to see and hear people agree with each other? Is it that we prefer to witness a clash? We do enjoy a contest, and doubtless this is one good reason for emphasizing conflict. We must look further, however, for a basic answer to our reason for enjoying conflict. Agreement is an end, a result. Disagreement is a means to an end, an active process. Agreement is static; disagreement is dynamic. When agreement is reached, the struggle is over. Our first interest, then, must be centered in the struggle which will be resolved into some sort of agreement.

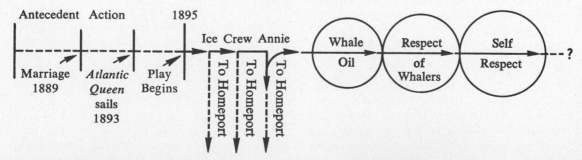

Action Line of *Ile*

Ile clearly depends upon disagreement or conflict. So many plays depend upon a clash of interests or personalities—clashes which may be expressed in talk or a blow, or may be waged within a character—that conflict is said to be the essence of drama. In reading *Ile* we are spectators of a combat in which the central figure, Captain Keeney, stands against all comers—the capricious Bering Sea, the crew, his wife. Will he win, and if he does, at what cost?

We have mentioned the word *crisis,* a useful term to describe a turning point. A play consists of one or more minor crises and one major crisis. The major crisis is the climax of the play. (Compare "Fiction: Preliminaries.") in *Ile* a minor crisis occurs when the crew through its deputation challenges Captain Keeney. Before the challenge we do not know the answers to such questions as these: Will Captain Keeney yield to a reasonable appeal? Will he yield to threats? Will he be forced to yield? As our diagram indicates, the Captain did not waver from his determined course; the men are vanquished and that question is settled. This settling of a question (or questions) constitutes a *minor resolution.* Agreement of a sort is reached.

No sooner is this minor crisis resolved than the action leading to the major crisis begins. Annie is more powerful than the men; Captain Keeney cannot settle this issue by a blow. He is apparently beaten:

> KEENEY—[*Dragging out the words with an effort.*] I'll do it, Annie—for your sake—if you say it's needful for ye.

For a brief moment disaster seems averted. We have hardly time to frame the question, Will Captain Keeney make good his promise? before we have the answer, an answer which clearly settles the major issue. The ice has broken, leaving a clear passage northward.

> KEENEY—[*His voice suddenly grim with determination.*] Then get her ready and we'll drive her through.

With this speech the issue is settled and the major resolution begins.

CHARACTERS

Our interest in how the play will come out is legitimate, but once we know the answer, other and more important questions confront us. Can the pursuit of whale oil, whether successful or not, be very important? Do we really care whether Captain Keeney wins or loses? Why should we care what happens to him or to Annie or to the crew of an obscure whaling ship? We have admiration for courage, of course, and pity for weakness. Are these emotions of admiration and pity stirred sufficiently to account for our concern? Perhaps. If the characters are credible, we see in them characteristics which we may call *universal qualities,* for we have seen these qualities in other people and detect them in ourselves.

Without Captain Keeney there would be no play, for he helps to create the forces that oppose him. The ice is a dread and a menace because he refuses to be beaten by it. The crew is mutinous because he makes them so. Annie becomes mad because in a real sense he wills that she shall go mad. We begin to see that the action, the plot, of this play is relatively unimportant. *Given these particular characters under these particular circumstances we realize that what happened must inevitably have happened.*

Is this, then, a character play? Certainly Captain Keeney is a man of strong will and single purpose, cruel, somber, destructive of anybody and anything which seeks to oppose him. Accustomed to winning through his ruthlessness, he has developed a contempt for lesser men and a determination never to hear "laughin' and sneerin'" at his expense. In direct conflict with his men he wins easily. "I know 'em," he says. Next he faces his distraught wife and bends to her appeal. We see a hint of softness, but it is the softness born of bewilderment and loss of words to explain his actions. He knows that he scorns the "ile" itself and the money it will bring. Why then, Annie wants to know, not turn homeward? Is he afraid of words from other whaling captains? Note the reply:

> It ain't so much what any one'd say—but—[*He hesitates, struggling to express his meaning.*] you see—I've always done it—since my first voyage as skipper. I always come back with a full ship—and—it don't seem right not to—somehow. I been always first whalin' skipper out o' Homeport, and—Don't you see my meanin', Annie?

Perhaps Annie did see his meaning, but to her

it was invalid. With this speech and others of like import, the play, we realize, takes on a significance beyond its literal meaning. Captain Keeney, Annie, the men, the ice wastes, Homeport fall into a pattern of universal significance. We have been reading a play in which each character is a symbol, each object something beyond itself. Older plays of this sort personified such abstractions as Vice, Virtue, Everyman. The personifications in *Ile* are not so clearcut, but we can identify them.

SYMBOLIC MEANING

Although Captain Keeney does not represent Everyman, he does stand for every man's deepest desire to excel. He is the fanatic who drives straight for his goal without swerving and with a ruthless disregard for those with tentative goals or those with insufficient will to draw a straight line. His force requires the submission of others: first, by a physical blow and the threat of a weapon, he wins his easiest victory; next, in a more difficult struggle, he bends to the power of human love but quickly regains his control and renounces his "weakness." The men who momentarily oppose him do not seek victory at any cost, though surely they would have won if they had so willed. They are the usual men, accustomed to go so far and not farther. One notes, however, that some will go farther than others. Mr. Slocum, the Second Mate, may someday become a Captain of Keeney's stamp. Joe the Harpooner, spokesman for the crew, has doubtless won his place by successfully asserting himself. All members of the "depitation" are chosen men. Always a man of some will can find submissiveness in men of feebler will.

Annie perhaps is the Usual Woman, kind, loving, appalled by cruelty. Her husband does not say, "*You* couldn't rightly understand my reason"; he does say, "A *woman* couldn't rightly understand my reason." Annie replies, "Because it's a stupid, stubborn reason." Yet, such stupid, stubborn reasons lie at the base of Captain Keeney's success, a success which had attracted Annie: "I wanted to see you the hero they make you out to be in Homeport." Does Captain Keeney suspect, perhaps know, that even his wife would not think him a hero if he turned back? Apparently so, for he says, "I got to prove

a man to be a good husband for ye to take pride in. I got to get the ile, I tell ye."

Homeport means what its name implies. For the men it represents release. For Annie it stands for sanity, for the normal, the warm, the safe things in life. For Captain Keeney it is a tribunal, a place of judgment to which at intervals he must return for the verdict. There must be no chance for an adverse decision. No excuses will do. He would not excuse another skipper; he does not expect, nor want, to be excused himself. The question will be: "Is your ship filled with oil?" The oil itself must be the answer.

In opposition to Homeport are the ice wastes of the Arctic seas. Droughts, floods, typhoons, earthquakes—there can be no malice in these, but when they touch man to his harm, he may shake his fist or go down on his knees. Captain Keeney could not strike down nor argue with nature. He could wait. The Usual Men and the Usual Women could wait, too, but not so long. The Ice Wastes won victory after victory down to the last man. Then, just as victory over the fanatic was about to go elsewhere, a cry rang out: "The ice is breakin' up to no'th'ard, sir." And in a moment: "Whales, sir—a whole school of 'em."

Has nature at last relented? Is this to be taken as an instance of reward for the persevering? Is this a happy ending? Hardly. If the ice had broken up a month before, all might have been well. If the ice had held fast a day longer, all might have been well. It is as though the Ice Wastes had played a closely calculated game with the end in view of mocking the fanatic. (Compare Creon's belated decision in *Antigone*, which begins on p. 438.) He will get his "ile." He will return to Homeport with a full ship and a mad wife. These things we know. Beyond these things we may speculate. Would the sort of price paid be too high even for a man like Captain Keeney? Would his pride remain in being "first whalin' skipper out o' Homeport"? We cannot be sure of the answers to these questions, but we can suspect that the struck target, in this instance, shattered into rubble.

APPLYING OUR OBSERVATIONS TO OTHER PLAYS

What we have observed about how a story is told in *Ile* may be applied, always with modifications, to other plays. It may be well to review our procedure by listing, point by point, the steps which we have taken.

1. We began with *first impressions.* As soon as you have completed a first reading of a play, take the time to examine what you think and feel about what you have read. Do you like the play? Before rereading the play, can you say *why* you liked it or did not like it? Were you amused, excited, depressed, apathetic as you read? Were you chiefly interested in the outcome? Or did the outcome matter less than the credibility of the persons involved? Did you find yourself thinking: "I know people like these characters"? On the other hand, did you say to yourself: "These characters are outside the range of my experience"? Such questions as these will help you to realize your first impressions.

2. The next step is to record the *facts of the play.* As we have seen in our analysis of *Ile,* the first event with any bearing on the present action of the play occurred six years before the play opened when Captain Keeney married Annie. We did not pick up this fact until late in the play. Your task, then, in assembling the facts is to look first of all for the chronological starting point and then to piece together a straightforward narrative. At the end of this process, you may be surprised to find how many significant facts, all bearing on a right interpretation, you overlooked during the first reading.

3. We have chosen to consider *exposition and antecedent* action next, but it would be just as convenient to consider setting at this point. Through gathering the facts, you have had to settle the matter of antecedent action. The exposition, partly through direct statement of the author and partly through dialogue, reveals the tone of the play. Is the tone serious, light, whimsical? How does the author intend that we shall regard his play? In what way does he let us know what our attitude should be? Do the stage directions establish the *atmosphere* and thereby prepare us for what may legitimately happen in such an atmosphere? Is the dialogue in keeping with the atmosphere? Is the action credible in relation to the characters and the atmosphere?

4. Next we have considered the *setting.* Playwrights normally must give careful attention to *time* and *place,* the two elements of setting. In *Ile* setting is of major significance though time,

but not *timing,* is of much less importance than place. The invisible setting, we have noted, plays a strong part in the drama. Setting is of much less consequence in *The Boor,* p. 432. The Greek convention of the unities of time and place (the action to occur in one place and within one day) reduces the significance of setting in *Antigone,* p. 438. The influence of setting on characters and plot in *Othello,* p. 455, is great even though to a modern reader it may not appear to be so. (See Norman Sanders' essay on *Othello,* pp. 867–875.) In *The Physician in Spite of Himself,* p. 506, Molière uses settings as mere backdrops against which the romping action can take place. The "coast town in southern Norway" —setting for *An Enemy of the People,* p. 523— could be any relatively provincial town, but settings for the individual scenes in Ibsen's play help reveal character and forward the action of the play. Shaw's *Arms and the Man,* p. 570, makes much of Bulgaria as its general setting and even more of stage props and devices to forward the satire. As the "Production Notes" *(The Glass Menagerie,* p. 602) prepared by Tennessee Williams show, setting is of crucial importance in bringing about a "closer approach to truth." One observes the detailed directions for staging and the author's overt interpretations, such as his comment on the "fire-escape" as "a touch of accidental poetic truth." (See p. 604.) Brecht, on the other hand, in his *The Caucasian Chalk Circle,* p. 636, leaves the matter of staging largely to the imagination of the reader, or, in the theater, to the ingenuity of the director. Time is an important factor in the Prologue and in the body of Brecht's play. In *The Visit,* p. 676. Duerrenmatt virtually makes a character of "the shabby and ruined" Central European town. As in Ibsen's play, it could be any town, but its desolation reflects a degradation from which the composite citizenry wishes to escape at any cost. Stage props play an extraordinarily significant part in Max Frisch's *Biedermann and The Firebugs,* p. 709. Biedermann lives in Everyman's house, a house, indeed, which is more than a house. The action of *A Raisin in the Sun* is in a real sense controlled by the setting, a living room that has "had to accommodate the living of too many people for too many years."

Key questions are these: Is the setting what it is simply because the characters are what they are? Or are the characters at least partly what they are because the setting is what it is? The function of the setting in relation to characters and plot can be determined by answering these questions.

5. The where and when of the play settled, we turn now to what happens, the *plot*. Here we note that the playwright—even the Absurdist who appears to eschew action—must be severely selective. In traditional plays every action must advance the play towards a minor crisis and point all minor crises towards the major crisis. A dish dropped, as in *Ile,* must have its significance. We may ask, then, what is the function of each act in relation to the crises? Next, is there a cause-and-effect relationship linking one action with the next? In *Ile,* Captain Keeney's conflict with the crew does not bring about the conflict with Annie. In other words, the second conflict does not grow out of the first. On the other hand, each action in *An Enemy of the People* grows out of a preceding action. Another question is this one: Is the action inevitable? To put it another way, does the action happen because the characters are what they are? If it does, the play is essentially a character play. The actions of Captain Keeney grow inevitably out of his character. What about the actions of Antigone? of Creon? of Othello? of Iago? of Laura? of Adzak? of Anton Schill? of Biedermann? of Lena Younger?

In examining the plot it is useful to construct an action line. Record on the line, with spaced dashes, the antecedent action; then at spaced intervals on an unbroken line indicate the minor crises which lead to the major crisis; end the line with the resolution of the final crisis, the *denouement.*

6. When we examine the *characters* of a play we find use for our total knowledge of human nature. Are the characters believable when tested by what we know of ourselves added to what we know about other human beings? Believability is relative, of course, and some characters come close to absolute believability, while others remain more or less distant. One probably does not doubt the reality of Captain Keeney. What of Smirnov, Haemon, Desdemona, Sganarelle, Dr. Stockmann, Raina, Tom Wingfield, Grusha, Claire Zachanassian, Sep Schmitz, Walter Lee Younger—to name almost at random one character from each of the other plays in this collection? Each character presents a fresh problem in credibility. An example of such a problem is Antigone. What she does and what she is are to be explained in part by reference to a whole system of mythology. Do we have to believe in the system of mythology in order to believe in Antigone? We face a different problem with Biedermann, who acts deceptively like an individual and yet becomes believable only if one is aware of the twentieth-century political forces which acted upon him.

For any play, we may ask: How *consistent* are the characters? What we are asking is, if a character has done this, would he also do that? Such a question is tricky. An element of inconsistency may be the most revealing trait in a character. Dr. Stockmann becomes more, not less, credible when his idealism is shown to be tarnished by arrogance. Dramatists, however, are wary of glaring inconsistencies, for the limits of time make it difficult to justify them.

7. Our last step is a *summing up*. What do all the parts mean? If the play has a general meaning, then it is certain that we have been involved with symbols. Do the characters stand simply for themselves or do they represent something beyond themselves? Does the play emphasize a theme, an idea, a way of life? If there is a theme, can you state it in a single sentence and then support that sentence with evidence from the play?

The foregoing suggestions for play analysis are by no means exhaustive. Little has been said, for example, about staging and the use of stage properties—*props*—those items which are referred to in the dialogue and which may be, as is the handkerchief in *Othello,* essential to the working out of the action. Of one thing every student can be certain: as authority over a play increases, pleasure also increases, even if in the end it turns into the negative fun of damning the play!

A NOTE ON SEEING PLAYS

Although there are closet dramas (plays to be read and not staged, such as Frost's "A Masque of Reason," p. 358), the vast majority of plays are written to be presented before an audience. In a very real sense, therefore, a play is not a complete work of art until it is acted out before an audience. An imaginative reader can do much toward staging the play in his own mind and, perhaps, even acting out the various parts. This sort of multiple role for the reader calls for a great deal of intellectual, even emotional, energy, but the rewards, though differing from those experienced in seeing a play, are great.

The Boor[1]

ANTON CHEKHOV
1860–1904

CHARACTERS

HELENA IVANOVNA POPOV, *a young widow, mistress of a country estate*
GRIGORI STEPANOVITCH SMIRNOV, *proprietor of a country estate*
LUKA, *servant of Mrs. Popov*
A gardener
A coachman
Several workmen

SCENE
The estate of MRS. POPOV

TIME
Late nineteenth century

SCENE: *A well-furnished reception-room in* MRS. POPOV's *home.* MRS. POPOV *is discovered in deep mourning, sitting upon a sofa, gazing steadfastly at a photograph.* LUKA *is also present.*

LUKA It isn't right, ma'am. You're wearing yourself out! The maid and the cook have gone looking for berries; everything that breathes is enjoying life, even the cat knows how to be happy—slips about the courtyard and catches birds—but you hide yourself here in the house as though you were in a cloister. Yes, truly, by actual reckoning you haven't left this house for a whole year.

MRS. POPOV And I shall never leave it—why should I? My life is over. He lies in his grave,

[1] A literal rendering of the title, from the Russian word *medved,* would be "The Bear."

and I have buried myself within these four walls. We are both dead.

LUKA There you are again! It's too awful to listen to, so it is! Nikolai Michailovitch is dead; it was the will of the Lord, and the Lord has given him eternal peace. You have grieved over it and that ought to be enough. Now it's time to stop. One can't weep and wear mourning forever! My wife died a few years ago. I grieved for her, I wept a whole month—and then it was over. Must one be forever singing lamentations? That would be more than your husband was worth! [*He sighs.*] You have forgotten all your neighbors. You don't go out and you receive no one. We live—you'll pardon me—like the spiders, and the good light of day we never see. All the livery is eaten by the mice—as though there weren't any more nice people in the world! But the whole neighborhood is full of gentlefolk. The regiment is stationed in Riblov—officers—simply beautiful! One can't see enough of them! Every Friday a ball, and military music every day. Oh, my dear, dear ma'am, young and pretty as you are, if you'd only let your spirits live—! Beauty can't last forever. When ten short years are over, you'll be glad enough to go out a bit and meet the officers—and then it'll be too late.

MRS. POPOV [*Resolutely.*] Please don't speak of these things again. You know very well that since the death of Nikolai Michailovitch my life is absolutely nothing to me. You think I live, but it only seems so. Do you understand? Oh, that his departed soul may see how I love him! I know, it's no secret to you; he was often unjust toward me, cruel, and—he wasn't faithful, but I shall be faithful to the grave and prove to him how *I* can love. There, in the Beyond, he'll find me the same as I was until his death.

LUKA What is the use of all these words, when you'd so much rather go walking in the garden or order Tobby or Welikan harnessed to the trap, and visit the neighbors?

MRS. POPOV [*Weeping.*] Oh!

LUKA Madam, dear Madam, what is it? In Heaven's name!

MRS. POPOV He loved Tobby so! He always drove him to the Kortschagins or the Vlassovs. What a wonderful horseman he was! How fine he looked when he pulled at the reins with all his might! Tobby, Tobby—give him an extra measure of oats to-day!

LUKA   Yes, ma'am. [*A bell rings loudly.*]

MRS. POPOV   [*Shudders.*] What's that? I am at home to no one.

LUKA   Yes, ma'am. [*A bell rings loudly.*]

MRS. POPOV   [*Gazing at the photograph.*] You shall see, Nikolai, how I can love and forgive! My love will die only with me—when my poor heart stops beating. [*She smiles through her tears.*] And aren't you ashamed? I have been a good, true wife, I have imprisoned myself and I shall remain true until death, and you—you—you're not ashamed of yourself, my dear monster! You quarrelled with me, left me alone for weeks—[LUKA *enters in great excitement.*]

LUKA   Oh, ma'am, someone is asking for you, insists on seeing you—

MRS. POPOV   You told him that since my husband's death I receive no one?

LUKA   I said so, but he won't listen, he says it is a pressing matter.

MRS. POPOV   I receive no one!

LUKA   I told him that, but he's a wildman, he swore and pushed himself into the room; he's in the dining-room now.

MRS. POPOV   [*Excitedly.*] Good. Show him in! The impudent—! [LUKA *goes out, center.*]

MRS. POPOV   What a bore people are! What can they want with me? Why do they disturb my peace? [*She sighs.*] Yes, it is clear I must enter a convent. [*Meditatively.*] Yes, a convent. [SMIRNOV *enters, followed by* LUKA.]

SMIRNOV   [*To* LUKA.] Fool, you make too much noise! You're an ass! [*Discovering* MRS. POPOV —*politely.*] Madam, I have the honor to introduce myself: Lieutenant in the Artillery, retired, country gentleman, Grigori Stepanovitch Smirnov! I'm compelled to bother you about an exceedingly important matter.

MRS. POPOV [*Without offering her hand.*] What is it you wish?

SMIRNOV   Your deceased husband, with whom I had the honor to be acquainted, left me two notes amounting to about twelve hundred rubles. Inasmuch as I have to pay the interest to-morrow on a loan from the Agrarian Bank, I should like to request, Madam, that you pay me the money today.

MRS. POPOV   Twelve hundred—and for what was my husband indebted to you?

SMIRNOV   He bought oats from me.

MRS. POPOV   [*With a sigh, to* LUKA.] Don't forget to give Tobby an extra measure of oats. [LUKA *goes out.*]

MRS. POPOV   [*To* SMIRNOV.] If Nikolai Michailovitch is indebted to you, I shall of course pay you, but I am sorry, I haven't the money to-day. To-morrow my manager will return from the city and I shall notify him to pay you what is due you, but until then I cannot satisfy your request. Furthermore, to-day it is just seven months since the death of my husband and I am not in a mood to discuss money matters.

SMIRNOV   And I am in the mood to fly up the chimney with my feet in the air if I can't lay hands on that interest to-morrow. They'll seize my estate!

MRS. POPOV   Day after to-morrow you will receive the money.

SMIRNOV   I don't need the money day after to-morrow, I need it to-day.

MRS. POPOV   I'm sorry I can't pay you to-day.

SMIRNOV   And I can't wait until day after to-morrow.

MRS. POPOV   But what can I do if I haven't it?

SMIRNOV   So you can't pay?

MRS. POPOV   I cannot.

SMIRNOV   Hm! Is that your last word?

MRS. POPOV   My last.

SMIRNOV   Absolutely?

MRS. POPOV   Absolutely.

SMIRNOV   Thank you. [*He shrugs his shoulders.*] And they expected me to stand for all that. The toll-gatherer just now met me in the road and asked me why I was always worrying? Why in Heaven's name shouldn't I worry? I need money, I feel the knife at my throat. Yesterday morning I left my house in the early dawn and called on all my debtors. If even one of them had paid his debt! I worked the skin off my fingers! The devil knows in what sort of Jew-inn I slept: in a room with a barrel of brandy! And now at last I come here, seventy versts from home, hope for a little money and all you give me is moods! Why shouldn't I worry?

MRS. POPOV   I thought I made it plain to you that my manager will return from town, and then you will get your money.

SMIRNOV   I did not come to see the manager, I came to see you. What the devil—pardon the language—do I care for your manager?

MRS. POPOV   Really, sir, I am not used to such language or such manners. I shan't listen to you any further. [*She goes out, left.*]

SMIRNOV   What can one say to that? Moods! Seven months since her husband died! Do I have to pay the interest or not? I repeat the question, have I to pay the interest or not? The husband is dead and all that; the manager is—the devil with him!—traveling somewhere. Now, tell me, what am I to do? Shall I run away from my creditors in a balloon? Or knock my head against a stone wall? If I call on Grusdev he chooses to be "not at home," Iroschevitch has simply hidden himself, I have quarrelled with Kurzin and came near throwing him out of the window, Masutov is ill and this woman has—moods! Not one of them will pay up! And all because I've spoiled them, because I'm an old whiner, dish-rag! I'm too tender-hearted with them. But wait! I allow nobody to play tricks with me, the devil with 'em all! I'll stay here and not budge until she pays! Brr! How angry I am, how terribly angry I am! Every tendon is trembling with anger and I can hardly breathe! I'm even growing ill! [*He calls out.*] Servant! [LUKA *enters.*]

LUKA   What is it you wish?

SMIRNOV   Bring me Kvas or water! [LUKA *goes out.*] Well, what can we do? She hasn't it on hand? What sort of logic is that? A fellow stands with the knife at his throat, he needs money, he is on the point of hanging himself, and she won't pay because she isn't in the mood to discuss money matters. Woman's logic! That's why I never liked to talk to women and why I dislike doing it now. I would rather sit on a powder barrel than talk with a woman. Brr!—I'm getting cold as ice, this affair has made me so angry. I need only to see such a romantic creature from a distance to get so angry that I have cramps in the calves! It's enough to make one yell for help! [*Enter* LUKA.]

LUKA   [*Hands him water.*] Madam is ill and is not receiving.

SMIRNOV   March! [LUKA *goes out.*] Ill and isn't receiving! All right, it isn't necessary. I won't receive, either! I'll sit here and stay until you bring that money. If you're ill a week, I'll sit here a week. If you're ill a year, I'll sit here a year. As Heaven is my witness, I'll get the money. You don't disturb me with your mourning—or with your dimples. We know these dimples! [*He calls out the window.*] Simon, unharness! We aren't going to leave right away. I am going to stay here. Tell them in the stable to give the horses some oats. The left horse has twisted the bridle again. [*Imitating him.*] Stop! I'll show you how. Stop! [*Leaves window.*] It's awful. Unbearable heat, no money, didn't sleep last night and now—mourning-dresses with moods. My head aches; perhaps I ought to have a drink. Ye-s, I must have a drink. [*Calling.*] Servant!

LUKA   What do you wish?

SMIRNOV   Something to drink! [LUKA *goes out.* SMIRNOV *sits down and looks at his clothes.*] Ugh, a fine figure. No use denying that. Dusty, dirty boots, unwashed, uncombed, straw on my vest—the lady probably took me for a highwayman. [*He yawns.*] It was a little impolite to come into a reception room with such clothes. Oh, well, no harm done. I'm not here as a guest. I'm a creditor. And there is no special costume for creditors.

LUKA   [*Entering with glass.*] You take great liberty, sir.

SMIRNOV   [*Angrily.*] What?

LUKA   I—I—I just—

SMIRNOV   Whom are you talking to? Keep quiet.

LUKA   [*Angrily.*] Nice mess! This fellow won't leave! [*He goes out.*]

SMIRNOV   Lord, how angry I am! Angry enough to throw mud at the whole world! I even feel ill! Servant! [MRS. POPOV *comes in with downcast eyes.*]

MRS. POPOV   Sir, in my solitude I have become unaccustomed to the human voice and I cannot stand the sound of loud talking. I beg you, please to cease disturbing my rest.

SMIRNOV   Pay me my money and I'll leave.

MRS. POPOV   I told you once, plainly, in your native tongue, that I haven't the money at hand; wait until day after to-morrow.

SMIRNOV   And I also had the honor of informing you in your native tongue that I need the money, not day after to-morrow, but to-day. If you don't pay me to-day I shall have to hang myself to-morrow.

MRS. POPOV   But what can I do if I haven't the money?

SMIRNOV   So you are not going to pay immediately? You're not?

MRS. POPOV   I cannot.

SMIRNOV Then I'll sit here until I get the money. [*He sits down.*] You will pay day after to-morrow? Excellent! here I stay until day after to-morrow. [*Jumps up.*] I ask you, do I have to pay the interest to-morrow or not? Or do you think I'm joking?

MRS. POPOV Sir, I beg of you, don't scream! This is not a stable.

SMIRNOV I'm not talking about stables, I'm asking you whether I have to pay that interest to-morrow or not?

MRS. POPOV You have no idea how to treat a lady.

SMIRNOV Oh, yes, I have.

MRS. POPOV No, you have not. You are an ill-bred, vulgar person. Respectable people don't speak so to ladies.

SMIRNOV How remarkable! How do you want one to speak to you? In French, perhaps! Madame, je vous prie? Pardon me for having disturbed you. What beautiful weather we are having to-day! And how this mourning becomes you! [*He makes a low bow with mock ceremony.*]

MRS. POPOV Not at all funny! I think it vulgar!

SMIRNOV [*Imitating her.*] Not at all funny—vulgar! I don't understand how to behave in the company of ladies. Madam, in the course of my life I have seen more women than you have sparrows. Three times have I fought duels for women, twelve I jilted and nine jilted me. There was a time when I played the fool, used honeyed language, bowed and scraped. I loved, suffered, sighed to the moon, melted in love's torments. I loved passionately, I loved to madness, loved in every key, chattered like a magpie on emancipation, sacrificed half my fortune in the tender passion, until now the devil knows I've had enough of it. Your obedient servant will let you lead him around by the nose no more. Enough! Black eyes, passionate eyes, coral lips, dimples in cheeks, moonlight whispers, soft, modest sighs—for all that, Madam, I wouldn't pay a kopeck! I am not speaking of present company, but of women in general; from the tiniest to the greatest, they are conceited, hypocritical, chattering, odious, deceitful from top to toe; vain, petty, cruel with a maddening logic and [*He strikes his forehead.*] in this respect, please excuse my frankness, but one sparrow is worth ten of the aforementioned petticoat-philoso-phers. When one sees one of the romantic creatures before him he imagines he is looking at some holy being, so wonderful that its one breath could dissolve him in a sea of a thousand charms and delights; but if one looks into the soul—it's nothing but a common crocodile. [*He seizes the arm-chair and breaks it in two.*] But the worst of all is that this crocodile imagines it is a masterpiece of creation, and that it has a monopoly on all the tender passions. May the devil hang me upside down if there is anything to love about a woman! When she is in love, all she knows is how to complain and shed tears. If the man suffers and makes sacrifices she swings her train about and tries to lead him by the nose. You have the misfortune to be a woman, and naturally you know woman's nature; tell me on your honor, have you ever in your life seen a woman who was really true and faithful? Never! Only the old and the deformed are true and faithful. It's easier to find a cat with horns or a white woodcock, than a faithful woman.

MRS. POPOV But allow me to ask, who is true and faithful in love? The man, perhaps?

SMIRNOV Yes, indeed! The man!

MRS. POPOV The man! [*She laughs sarcastically.*] The man true and faithful in love! Well, that is something *new!* [*Bitterly.*] How can you make such a statement? Men true and faithful! So long as we have gone thus far, I may as well say that of all the men I have known, my husband was the best; I loved him passionately with all my soul, as only a young, sensible woman may love; I gave him my youth, my happiness, my fortune, my life. I worshipped him like a heathen. And what happened? This best of men betrayed me in every possible way. After his death I found his desk filled with love-letters. While he was alive he left me alone for months—it is horrible even to think about it—he made love to other women in my very presence, he wasted my money and made fun of my feelings,—and in spite of everything, I trusted him and was true to him. And more than that: he is dead and I am still true to him. I have buried myself within these four walls and I shall wear this mourning to my grave.

SMIRNOV [*Laughing disrespectfully.*] Mourning! What on earth do you take me for? As if I didn't know why you wore this black domino and why you buried yourself within these four walls. Such a secret! So romantic! Some knight will pass the castle, gaze up at the windows and think to himself; "Here dwells the mysterious Tamara who, for love of her husband, has buried herself within four walls." Oh, I understand the art!

MRS. POPOV [*Springing up.*] What? What do you mean by saying such things to me?

SMIRNOV You have buried yourself alive, but meanwhile you have not forgotten to powder your nose!

MRS. POPOV How dare you speak so?

SMIRNOV Don't scream at me, please, I'm not the manager. Allow me to call things by their right names. I am not a woman, and I am accustomed to speak out what I think. So please don't scream.

MRS. POPOV I'm not screaming. It is you who are screaming. Please leave me, I beg of you.

SMIRNOV Pay me my money and I'll leave.

MRS. POPOV I won't give you the money.

SMIRNOV You won't? You won't give me my money?

MRS. POPOV I don't care what you do. You won't get a kopeck! Leave me!

SMIRNOV As I haven't the pleasure of being either your husband or your fiancé please don't make a scene. [*He sits down.*] I can't stand it.

MRS. POPOV [*Breathing hard.*] You are going to sit down?

SMIRNOV I already have.

MRS. POPOV Kindly leave the house!

SMIRNOV Give me the money.

MRS. POPOV I don't care to speak with impudent men. Leave! [*Pause.*] You aren't going?

SMIRNOV No.

MRS. POPOV No?

SMIRNOV No.

MRS. POPOV Very well. [*She rings the bell. Enter* LUKA.]

MRS. POPOV Luka, show the gentleman out.

LUKA [*Going to* SMIRNOV.] Sir, why don't you leave when you are ordered? What do you want?

SMIRNOV [*Jumping up.*] Whom do you think you are talking to? I'll grind you to powder.

LUKA [*Puts his hand to his heart.*] Good Lord! [*He drops into a chair.*] Oh, I'm ill, I can't breathe!

MRS. POPOV Where is Dascha? [*Calling.*] Dascha! Pelageja! Dascha! [*She rings.*]

LUKA They're all gone! I'm ill! Water!

MRS. POPOV [*To* SMIRNOV.] Leave! Get out!

SMIRNOV Kindly be a little more polite!

MRS. POPOV [*Striking her fists and stamping her feet.*] You are vulgar! You're a boor! A monster!

SMIRNOV What did you say?

MRS. POPOV I said you were a boor, a monster!

SMIRNOV [*Steps toward her quickly.*] Permit me to ask what right you have to insult me?

MRS. POPOV What of it? Do you think I am afraid of you?

SMIRNOV And you think that because you are a romantic creature you can insult me without being punished? I challenge you!

LUKA Merciful heaven! Water!

SMIRNOV We'll have a duel.

MRS. POPOV Do you think because you have big fists and a steer's neck I am afraid of you?

SMIRNOV I allow no one to insult me, and I make no exception because you are a woman, one of the "weaker sex!"

MRS. POPOV [*Trying to cry him down.*] Boor, boor, boor!

SMIRNOV It is high time to do away with the old superstition that it is only the man who is forced to give satisfaction. If there is equity at all let there be equity in all things. There's a limit!

MRS. POPOV You wish to fight a duel? Very well.

SMIRNOV Immediately.

MRS. POPOV Immediately. My husband had pistols. I'll bring them. [*She hurries away, then turns.*] Oh, what a pleasure it will be to put a bullet in your impudent head. The devil take you! [*She goes out.*]

SMIRNOV I'll shoot her down! I'm no fledgling, no sentimental young puppy. For me, there is no weaker sex!

LUKA Oh, sir! [*Falls to his knees.*] Have mercy on me, an old man, and go away. You have frightened me to death already, and now you want to fight a duel.

SMIRNOV [*Paying no attention.*] A duel. That's equity, emancipation. That way the sexes are made equal. I'll shoot her down as a matter of principle. What can a person say to such a woman? [*Imitating her.*] "The devil take you. I'll put a bullet in your impudent head." What can one say to that? She was angry, her eyes blazed, she accepted the challenge. On my honor, it's the first time in my life that I ever saw such a woman.

LUKA   Oh, sir. Go away. Go away!

SMIRNOV   That *is* a woman. I can understand her. A real woman. No shilly-shallying, but fire, powder, and noise! It would be a pity to shoot a woman like that.

LUKA   [*Weeping.*] Oh, sir, go away. [*Enter* MRS. POPOV.]

MRS. POPOV   Here are the pistols. But before we have our duel please show me how to shoot. I have never had a pistol in my hand before!

LUKA   God be merciful and have pity upon us! I'll go and get the gardener and the coachman. Why has this horror come to us? [*He goes out.*]

SMIRNOV   [*Looking at the pistols.*] You see, there are different kinds. There are special duelling pistols with cap and ball. But these are revolvers, Smith & Wesson, with ejectors; fine pistols! A pair like that cost at least ninety rubles. This is the way to hold a revolver. [*Aside.*] Those eyes, those eyes! A real woman!

MRS. POPOV   Like this?

SMIRNOV   Yes, that way. Then you pull the hammer back—so—then you aim—put your head back a little. Just stretch your arm out, please. So—then press your finger on the thing like that, and that is all. The chief thing is this: don't get excited, don't hurry your aim, and take care that your hand doesn't tremble.

MRS. POPOV   It isn't well to shoot inside; let's go into the garden.

SMIRNOV   Yes. I'll tell you now, I am going to shoot into the air.

MRS. POPOV   That is too much! Why?

SMIRNOV   Because—because. That's my business.

MRS. POPOV   You are afraid. Yes. A-h-h-h. No, no, my dear sir, no flinching! Please follow me. I won't rest until I've made a hole in that head I hate so much. Are you afraid?

SMIRNOV   Yes, I'm afraid.

MRS. POPOV   You are lying. Why won't you fight?

SMIRNOV   Because—because—I—like you.

MRS. POPOV   [*With an angry laugh.*] You like me! He dares to say he likes me! [*She points to the door.*] Go.

SMIRNOV   [*Laying the revolver silently on the table, takes his hat and starts. At the door he stops a moment gazing at her silently, then he approaches her, hesitating.*] Listen! Are you still angry? I was mad as the devil, but please understand me—how can I express myself? The thing is like this—such things are—[*He raises his voice.*] Now, is it my fault that you owe me money? [*Grasps the back of the chair, which breaks.*] The devil knows what breakable furniture you have! I like you! Do you understand? I—I'm almost in love!

MRS. POPOV   Leave! I hate you.

SMIRNOV   Lord! What a woman! I never in my life met one like her. I'm lost, ruined! I've been caught like a mouse in a trap.

MRS. POPOV   Go, or I'll shoot.

SMIRNOV   Shoot! You have no idea what happiness it would be to die in sight of those beautiful eyes, to die from the revolver in this little velvet hand! I'm mad! Consider it and decide immediately, for if I go now, we shall never see each other again. Decide—speak—I am a noble, a respectable man, have an income of ten thousand, can shoot a coin thrown into the air. I own some fine horses. Will you be my wife?

MRS. POPOV   [*Swings the revolver angrily.*] I'll shoot!

SMIRNOV   My mind is not clear—I can't understand. Servant—water! I have fallen in love like any young man. [*He takes her hand and she cries with pain.*] I love you! [*He kneels.*] I love you as I have never loved before. Twelve women I jilted, nine jilted me, but not one of them all have I loved as I love you. I am conquered, lost, I lie at your feet like a fool and beg for your hand. Shame and disgrace! For five years I haven't been in love; I thanked the Lord for it, and now I am caught, like a carriage tongue in another carriage. I beg for your hand! Yes, or no? Will you?— Good! [*He gets up and goes quickly to the door.*]

MRS. POPOV   Wait a moment!

SMIRNOV   [*Stopping.*] Well?

MRS. POPOV   Nothing. You may go. But—wait a moment. No, go on, go on. I hate you. Or— no: don't go. Oh, if you knew how angry I was, how angry! [*She throws the revolver on to the chair.*] My finger is swollen from this thing. [*She angrily tears her handkerchief.*] What are you standing there for? Get out!

SMIRNOV Farewell!

MRS. POPOV Yes, go. [*Cries out.*] Why are you going? Wait—no, go!! Oh, how angry I am! Don't come too near, don't come too near—er —come—no nearer.

SMIRNOV [*Approaching her.*] How angry I am with myself! Fall in love like a schoolboy, throw myself on my knees. I've got a chill! [*Strongly.*] I love you. This is fine—all I needed was to fall in love. To-morrow I have to pay my interest, the hay harvest has begun, and then you appear! [*He takes her in his arms.*] I can never forgive myself.

MRS. POPOV Go away! Take your hands off me! I hate you—you—this is—[*A long kiss. Enter LUKA with an ax, the gardener with a rake, the coachman with a pitch-fork, and workmen with poles.*]

LUKA [*Staring at the pair.*] Merciful Heavens! [*A long pause.*]

MRS. POPOV [*Dropping her eyes.*] Tell them in the stable that Tobby isn't to have any oats.

[*Curtain.*]

Comments and Questions

The Boor may be classified, somewhat hesitantly, as farce, which is exaggerated comedy with fun as its chief purpose. Hesitancy in adopting this classification is caused by the feeling that Chekhov, through his expert handling of the situation and the dialogue, almost convinces us that what happens could have happened and that the play is not devoid of meaning. He answers all questions, except, perhaps, this one: Is there enough time for the change in both Smirnov and Helena Popov to occur? One can muster a respectable answer that even here Chekhov provided evidence of reasonable probability. How long had the husband been dead? What loyalty did Helena really owe him? What evidence is there that the widow was already weary of her romantic self-sacrifice? As for Smirnov, how susceptible was he to the charms of women? Does his tirade against women identify him as only a pseudo-woman-hater? A case can be made that Smirnov was precisely the knight for whom the romantic Helena was receptively waiting.

The Boor was first published in 1888. One of the issues of the play—that women who aspire to the privileges of men must be willing to accept the responsibilities of men— could have been treated seriously, as it might be today by those who raise the battle cry for Women's Lib. Smirnov expresses the view of the male chauvinist pig when he describes "women in general" as "conceited, hypocritical, chattering, odious, deceitful from top to toe; vain, petty, cruel with a maddening logic. . . ." And Mrs. Popov responds in kind, calling Smirnov "vulgar . . . a boor! A monster!" She rises to liberation heights by eagerly agreeing to a duel.

1. Obviously, however, it is not necessary to take *The Boor* seriously. An interesting question is this: How do we know that Chekhov is not serious? The servant Luka weeps and cries out: "Why has this horror come to us?" If he takes to heart what is happening, why don't we?

2. Although *The Boor* is an entirely different sort of play from *Ile,* it will nevertheless respond to the same sort of analysis which we applied to *Ile.* Guided by the seven steps suggested before (pp. 430–431), examine the dramatic technique of *The Boor.*

3. After analyzing *The Boor,* contrast it step by step with *Ile.*

Antigone*
SOPHOCLES
496–406 B.C.

Antigone was written some twenty-four hundred years ago. Today it is still being performed, not simply as a curiosity but as a vital drama with ample modern significance.

If we follow our outline for reviewing a play, we shall see that *Antigone* requires only slightly different treatment from that accorded a modern play. Our *first impressions,*

* The translation based upon the text of Sir Richard C. Jebb has been somewhat modified by the editors and carefully checked and further modified by Professor Albert Rapp. We are deeply indebted to Professor Rapp for his assistance.

however, may be affected by a few technical details. It is best, therefore, to anticipate some of the questions which one would naturally ask upon first contact with Greek drama.

The first question involves the interrelationships of the characters. We need to know what Sophocles expected his audience to know about the family relationships of the royal house of Thebes. We may begin with Labdacus, the father of Laius. Laius married Jocasta and by her had a son, Oedipus, part of whose story is told in Sophocles' *Oedipus Rex.* Oedipus, under a curse of the gods, murdered his father without knowing that his victim was his father and then married Jocasta in ignorance that she was his mother. Oedipus and Jocasta had four children: two boys, Eteocles and Polynices; and two girls, Antigone and Ismene. Eteocles succeeded Oedipus as king of Thebes but was killed by his brother, Polynices, who, with six other champions, had come to Thebes to take the throne. In the duel Polynices also was killed. The throne passed then to Creon, who was the brother of Jocasta and, therefore, the uncle of Jocasta's and Oedipus' four children. Creon's wife was Eurydice and their children were Megareus and Haemon.

These relationships may be summarized in two diagrams:

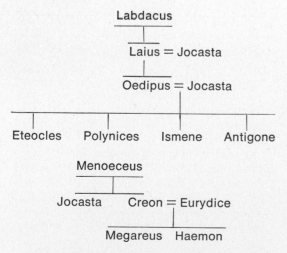

The second question involves the Chorus, a technique infrequently used in modern plays (but compare *The Caucasian Chalk Circle,* p. 636, *The Visit,* p. 676, and *Bieder-*

mann and the Firebugs, p. 709). You will see what functions are actually performed by the Chorus in *Antigone.* You will see that it does these things: (1) it provides as needed poetic interludes which suggest the passage of time; (2) it acts as spokesman for public opinion; (3) it occasionally is expository; (4) it helps to set the mood and to point up the universal significance of what is happening. You will note that it can be wise, and it can be stupid; that it vacillates and yet can make up its mind. In many ways it has all the virtues and vices of a general public.

With this much information available for reference, you should now be prepared to read this surprisingly modern play. Pronunciations of proper names used in the play are indicated in a listing on p. 454.

CHARACTERS

ANTIGONE ⎫ *daughters of Oedipus, former*
ISMENE ⎬ *king of Thebes*
CREON, *present king of Thebes*
EURYDICE, *wife of Creon*
HAEMON, *son of Creon and betrothed of Antigone*
TIRESIAS, *blind soothsayer*
GUARD, *assigned to watch unburied corpse of Polynices*
FIRST MESSENGER
SECOND MESSENGER
CHORUS OF THEBAN ELDERS

SCENE: *All dialogue is spoken before the Royal Palace at Thebes.* ISMENE *enters first, followed by* ANTIGONE.

ANTIGONE Ismene, sister, my own dear sister, do you know any evil, bequeathed to us by Oedipus, which Zeus will not fulfill while we live? Nothing painful is there, nothing ruinous, no shame, no dishonor, that I have not seen in your woes and mine. And now what of this new edict the King has just proclaimed to all Thebes? Do you know of it? Have you heard? Or has it been hidden from you that our friends are threatened with the doom of our enemies?

ISMENE No word of friends, Antigone, glad or painful, has come to me, since we two sisters lost two brothers, killed in one day by a two-fold blow. I know the Argive host withdrew last night; but more, good or bad, I know not.

ANTIGONE So I thought and therefore arranged to see you where you alone may hear.

ISMENE What is it? It is plain that you have dark news.

ANTIGONE Has not Creon destined our brothers, the one to honored burial, the other to unburied shame? Eteocles, they say, with due observance of right and custom, he has buried properly for joining honorably the dead below. But the body of Polynices—Creon has published to Thebes that none shall bury him, or mourn, but leave unwept, without a tomb, a welcome feast for birds. Such, I have heard, is the edict the good Creon has set forth for you and me—yes, for *me*—and is coming here to proclaim it clearly to those who have not heard, for it's a heavy matter, since whoever disobeys, his punishment is death by public stoning. [*Pause.*] You know it now, and you will soon show whether you are nobly bred or unworthy of a noble family.

ISMENE Poor sister—if all this is true, what could I do or undo?

ANTIGONE Will you help me do what must be done?

ISMENE What must be done? What do you mean?

ANTIGONE Will you help me lift the body?

ISMENE You would bury him?—when it is forbidden?

ANTIGONE I will do my part—and yours too, if you will not—for a brother. To him I will not be false.

ISMENE Would you dare when Creon has forbidden it?

ANTIGONE He has no right to keep me from my own.

ISMENE Antigone! Remember how our father perished, amid hate and scorn, when sins, self-revealed, moved him to strike out his eyes with his own hands; then the mother-wife, two names in one, with a twisted noose ended her life; and last, our two brothers—each killed by the other's hand. Now is it our turn? We two left all alone—think how we shall die more miserably than all the rest if we defy a king's decree or his powers. No, we must remember, first that we were born women and

should not strive with men; next, that we are ruled by the stronger and must obey in these things and even in worse ones. May the dead forgive me, but I must obey our ruler. It is foolish to do otherwise.

ANTIGONE I will not beg you. No, even if you offered now to help, you would not be welcome as my helper. Go your way. I will bury him and count it gain to die in doing that. I shall join a loved one, sinless my crime. I owe more allegiance to the dead than to the living, for with the dead I shall abide forever. But *you*—live on and disobey the laws of the gods.

ISMENE I intend no dishonor to the gods—but to defy the State—I am too weak for that.

ANTIGONE Such be your excuse. I go to heap earth on the brother whom I love.

ISMENE How I fear for you, Antigone!

ANTIGONE You need not. Be fearful for yourself.

ISMENE At least be careful. Tell no one your plan and neither will I.

ANTIGONE Announce it to all Thebes. I shall hate you even more if you don't.

ISMENE You have hot courage for a chilling act!

ANTIGONE My act will please where it counts most to please.

ISMENE Perhaps, but you are attempting what you cannot do.

ANTIGONE If my strength is not enough, at least I will have tried.

ISMENE A hopeless task should not be tried.

ANTIGONE If you continue talking in this way, I shall hate you and so will the dead! Leave me alone to suffer this dread thing. For I shall be suffering nothing as dreadful as a dishonorable death.

ISMENE Go, then, if you must, but remember no matter how foolish your deed, those who love you will love you still. [*Exit* ANTIGONE *left.* ISMENE *enters the Palace through one of the two side-doors.*]

[*Enter* CHORUS *of Theban elders.*]

CHORUS Beam of the sun, fairest light that ever dawned on Thebes of the seven gates, you have shone forth at last, eye of the golden day, arisen above Dirce's stream! The warrior of the white shield, who came from Argos in battle array, has been stirred by you to headlong flight.

He advanced against our land by reason of the vexed claims of Polynices; and, like a shrill-screaming eagle, he flew over our country, sheathed in snow-white wings, with an armed multitude and with plumage of helmets.

He paused above our homes; he ravened around our seven portals with spears athirst for blood; but he fled, before his jaws were glutted with gore or his fire had consumed our towers. Fierce was the noise of battle raised behind him as he wrestled with, but could not conquer, his dragon foe.

For Zeus utterly abhors the boast of a proud tongue; and when he beheld the Argives coming on in a great stream, their golden harness clanging, he smote with brandished fire one who was at that moment about to shout "Victory" from atop our ramparts.

Down to the earth with a crash fell the invader, torch in hand, he who but a moment before, in the frenzy of the mad attack, was blowing against us the blasts of his hot hate. But his threats fared not as he had hoped; and to our other foes the Wargod also dealt havoc, a mighty helper at our need.

For, seven invaders at seven gates, matched against seven, left a tribute of their bronze for Zeus who turned the battle; except for the two brothers, who crossed spears with each other and are sharers in a common death.

But since victory has come to us, let joy be ours in Thebes, city of the many chariots; let us enjoy forgetfulness after the recent wars, and let us visit all the temples of the gods with night-long dance and song; and may Bacchus be our leader, Bacchus whose dancing shakes the land of Thebes.

But behold, the king of the land comes, Creon, son of Menoeceus, our new ruler by the new fortunes that the gods have given; what matter is he pondering, that he has summoned this conference of elders to hear?

[*Enter* CREON, *from the central door of the Palace. Dressed as a king, he has with him two* ATTENDANTS.]

CREON   Sirs, the vessel of our State, after being tossed on wild waves, has once more been safely steadied by the gods: and you, of all the people, have been called here because I knew, first of all, how true and constant was your reverence for the royal power of Laius; and again, how, when Oedipus was ruler and then perished, you were still loyal to his chil-dren. Since then, his sons have fallen, each felled by the other, each stained with a brother's blood;—and now I possess the throne and all its powers, by right of near kinship to the dead.

No man can be fully known, in soul and spirit and mind, until he has been schooled in rule and law-giving. If the supreme ruler of a State does not seek the best counsel, I hold and have ever held such a person to be base. If one holds a friend of more worth to him than his fatherland, that person has no place in my regard. For I—Zeus, who sees everything, is my witness—I would not be silent if I saw ruin, instead of safety, coming to the citizens; the country's foes would never be friends of mine, for our country is the ship that bears us safe and we cannot have any friends unless the ship of state prospers in its voyage.

Such are the rules by which I guard the greatness of Thebes. In accord with these rules, I have published an edict to the citizens concerning the sons of Oedipus: that Eteocles, who fell fighting for our city, fighting with great courage, shall be entombed and favored with every rite that follows the noblest dead to their rest. But for his brother, Polynices, who came back from exile and sought to consume with fire the city of his fathers and the shrines of his father's gods, who sought to taste of kinsmen's blood and to lead the rest into slavery—touching this man, it has been proclaimed to our people that no one shall bury him or lament his death, but leave him unburied, a corpse for birds and dogs to eat, a ghastly, shameful sight.

Never, by deed of mine, shall the wicked stand in honor before the just, but whoever has good will towards Thebes, he shall be honored of me in both his life and death.

CHORUS   Such is your pleasure, Creon, son of Menoeceus, touching this city's foe and its friend. And you have the power to make good your order both for the dead and the living.

CREON   See, then, that my mandate is enforced.

CHORUS   Give this task to some younger man.

CREON   I don't mean that. Watchers of the corpse are at their posts.

CHORUS   What further then, do you have in mind?

CREON   That you do not side with breakers of these commands.

CHORUS   No man is foolish enough to be in love with death.

CREON   That would be the penalty. But always someone can be tempted to his ruin through love of gain.

[*Enter* GUARD.]

GUARD   O King, I will not say that I come breathless from speed, or that I have plied a nimble foot, for often my thoughts made me stop, and I would wheel around and start back. My mind was holding large discourse with me: "Fool, why hurry to your certain doom?" "Wretch, loitering again? And if Creon hears the story from someone else, will you not pay for it?" So debating, I went on my way without eagerness, and thus a short road was made long. At last, however, I have come hither—to you; and though what I will say may amount to little, I will say it, for I come holding tight to one hope: that I can suffer nothing but what is my fate.

CREON   And what makes you so fearful?

GUARD   First let me tell you about myself—I did not do the deed—I did not see the doer—it is not right that I should come to any harm.

CREON   You shrewdly build a fence around yourself. Clearly you must have strange news.

GUARD   Yes, truly. Dread news makes one pause.

CREON   Then tell it, will you, and so get you gone?

GUARD   Well, this is it—the corpse—someone has just given it burial and gone away—after sprinkling dry dust on the flesh, with other pious rites.

CREON   What do you say? What living man has dared do this?

GUARD   I know not. No mark of a pickaxe was seen there, no earth thrown up by mattock. The ground was hard and dry, unbroken, without track of wheels. Whoever did it left no trace. And when the first day-watchman showed it to us, dread wonder fell on all. The dead man was veiled from us—not really buried but strewn with dust, as by the hand of one who feared a curse. There was no evidence that any beast of prey or dog had come near him or torn him.

Then everyone began accusing everyone else and, without anyone to stop it, a fight nearly broke out. Every man was the accused, and no one was convicted but all denied any knowledge of the act. And we were ready to take red-hot iron in our hands—to walk through fire—to swear by the gods that we had not done the deed—that we knew nothing of the planning or the doing.

At last, when we had got nowhere with our searching, someone spoke who made all of us bow our heads in fright, for we could neither deny him nor escape misfortune if we obeyed. He said this deed must not be hidden but must be reported to you. And this seemed best; and the lot fell to me. So here I am—as unwelcome as unwilling, I know, for no man likes a bearer of bad news.

CHORUS   O King, think you by chance this deed might be the work of gods?

CREON   Stop, before your words fill me completely with anger and you be found not only old but foolish. You say what is not to be believed, that the gods are concerned with this corpse. Was it for high reward of trusty service that they hid his nakedness, the nakedness of one who came to burn their columned shrines and sacred treasures, to burn their land, and scatter its laws to the wind? Or do you imagine the gods honoring the wicked? It cannot be. No! From the first there were certain ones in this city that muttered against me, chafing at this edict, wagging their heads in secret; and kept not their necks bowed to the yoke like men contented with my rule.

It is by them, I am certain, that these have been lured and bribed to do the deed. No evil surpasses the power of money. Money lays cities low, drives men from their homes, misguides and warps honest souls till they do shameful things, and still teaches folks to practice villainies and to know every godless deed.

But the men who did this thing for hire have made it certain they shall pay the price. Now, as Zeus is my god, know this—I swear it: If you do not find the one who buried the corpse and bring him before me, death alone shall not be enough for you; before death, you will be tortured until you clear up this outrage. Your lesson will be to steal with sure knowledge of how bribes are won and how it is not good to accept gain from every source. You will find more loss in evil than profit.

GUARD   May I speak? Or shall I just turn and go?

CREON   Know you not that even your voice is now an offense in my ears?

GUARD   In your ears or in your soul?

CREON   And would you define the location of my pain?

GUARD   I may offend your ears but the doer offends your soul.

CREON   You are a born babbler, that's clear.

GUARD   Maybe, but never the doer of the deed.

CREON   Yes, and more than that—the seller of your life for silver.

GUARD   Ah, me! It is sad, certainly, that a judge should misjudge.

CREON   Let your fancy play with the word "judgment" if you wish;—but, if you fail to catch the doers of these things, you shall swear that evil gains bring sorrows. [*Exit into Palace.*]

GUARD   Well, heaven send that he be found! But whether he is caught or not—fortune will decide that—you will not see me here again. Saved once, beyond my best hope, I owe the gods great thanks. [*Exit.*]

CHORUS   Wonders are many, and none is more wonderful than man: he has power to cross the white sea, driven by the stormy south-wind, plunging under surges that threaten to engulf him; and Earth, eldest of the gods, immortal, unwearied, does he master, turning the soil as the ploughs go to and fro year after year.

And the soaring race of birds, the tribes of savage beasts, and the brood of the sea, he traps in the meshes of his snares, man excellent in cunning. And he masters by his arts the beast whose den is in the wilderness, who roams the hills; he breaks the horse of shaggy mane and puts the yoke upon his neck; he tames the tireless mountain bull.

And speech, and lightning thought, and all the interweavings that shape a state has he taught himself; how to be sheltered from arrowy frost and the rushing rain. Yes, nothing is beyond his power; from baffling diseases he has devised escapes and only against Death shall he call for help in vain.

Cunning beyond fancy's dream is the fertile skill which now brings him to evil, now to good. When he honors the laws of the land and the justice which he has sworn by the gods to uphold, his city stands proud, but no city has he who, for his foolishness, lives with sin. Never may such a one share my hearth, or share my thoughts.

[*Enter the* GUARD *from the left, leading in* ANTIGONE.]

CHORUS   What sight is this? My soul stands amazed. I know her. It is Antigone. O, unhappy child and child of an unhappy father—Oedipus! What does this mean? *You* brought a prisoner? *You,* disloyal to the King's laws, and arrested for your folly?

GUARD   Here she is. She did it. We caught her burying him. But where is Creon?

CHORUS   He comes forth again from the Palace, at the right time.

CREON   What is it? What has happened that makes my coming timely?

GUARD   O King, men should be careful of their words, for second-thoughts may correct the first intention. I could have sworn that I should not soon be here again—scared by the threats by which you blasted me. But there is no pleasure like one unexpected, and I have returned, in spite of my oath, bringing this girl—who was taken doing grace to the dead. This time, be sure, there was no casting of lots, for this piece of luck belongs to me and to no one else. And now, Sire, take her yourself, question her, examine her as you will, but I hope I have gained the right to be free and completely rid of this trouble.

CREON   And your prisoner here—how and where did you take her?

GUARD   She was burying the man, as I said.

CREON   Do you mean what you say? Do you?

GUARD   I saw her burying the corpse that you had forbidden to bury. Is that plain and clear?

CREON   And how was she seen? how taken in the act?

GUARD   It happened this way. When we had come to the place—with your dreadful threats ringing in our ears—we swept away all the dust from the corpse and bared the dank body; and sat us down on the brow of the hill, to the windward to avoid the smell of him. Every man was wide awake and kept his neighbors awake with torrents of threats against anyone who shirked his task.

So it went, until the sun was straight overhead, and the heat began to burn: and then suddenly a whirlwind lifted a storm of dust, which filled the plain, covered the leaves of the trees, and choked the air. We closed our eyes and bore this plague of the gods.

And then, after a long time, the dust storm passed and the girl was seen. Like a bird bitter at finding its nest stripped of nestlings, she cried aloud when she saw the bare corpse. She wailed aloud and called down curses on the doers of the deed. Without hesitation she brought dust in her hands; and then from a bronze pitcher, three times she poured a drink-offering upon the corpse.

We rushed forward when we saw it and closed in on our quarry, who stood there undismayed. Then we charged her with her past and present doings and she denied nothing—a joy and a pain to me at the same time. To have escaped from one's own troubles is a great joy, but it is painful to bring troubles to others. However that may be, all such things mean less to me than my own safety.

CREON You—whose head is bowed—do you admit or do you deny the deed?

ANTIGONE I admit it; I make no denial.

CREON [*To the* GUARD.] You may go now, free and clear of a serious charge. [*Exit* GUARD.] [*To* ANTIGONE.] Now, tell me—in few words —did you know than an edict had forbidden this?

ANTIGONE I knew it—why shouldn't I? It was public.

CREON And you dared to transgress that law?

ANTIGONE Yes, for it was not Zeus that had issued that edict; nor was it a law given to men by Justice which lives with the gods below; nor did I consider your decrees so powerful as to override the unwritten and unfailing laws of heaven. For heaven's laws are eternal and no man knows when they were first put forth.

Not from dread of any human pride could I answer to the gods for breaking *these*. Die I must—I knew that well (how should I not know it?)—even without your edict. But if I am to die before my time, I count that gain, for when one lives, as I do, boxed in by evils, can one count death as anything but gain?

Therefore for me to meet this doom is a trifling grief, but if I had allowed my mother's son to remain unburied, that would have grieved me; for death, I am not grieved. And if my deeds are foolhardy in your sight, perhaps a foolish judge condemns my folly.

CHORUS She shows herself the passionate child of a passionate father and does not know how to bend before trouble.

CREON Yet I would have you know that stubbornness is most often humbled. It is the hardest iron, baked to brittleness in the fire, that you shall oftenest see snapped and shivered; and I have known wild horses brought tame by a little curbing; there is no room for pride among slaves.—This girl became versed in violence when she broke the laws that have been set forth; and, that done, behold a second insult as she boasts of this and exults in her defiance.

Now, truly I am no man—she is the man —if victory in this rests with her and brings no penalty. No! be she sister's child, or even nearer to me in blood than any that worship Zeus at the altar of the house, she and her kinfolk shall not avoid direst punishment, for I charge also her sister with a full share in plotting this burial.

Summon Ismene—for I saw her within just now—raving as if out of her mind. So often, before the deed, the mind convicts itself in its treason while plotting dark evil. But this, too, is truly hateful, when one has been caught in a crime and makes that crime a glory.

ANTIGONE Would you do more than kill me?

CREON Nothing more, no. That done, I am satisfied.

ANTIGONE Why, then, do you delay? In all your talk there is nothing pleasing to me—may there never be!—and my words, I suppose, are unpleasant to you. And yet, for glory— how could I have won greater glory than by giving burial to my own brother? All here would agree to this were they not afraid to say so. But royalty—blessed in so many ways —has the power to do and say what it will.

CREON You are in error. No citizens of Thebes agree with you.

ANTIGONE Yes they do. But fear of you seals their mouths.

CREON And are not you ashamed to be so different?

ANTIGONE No, for there is nothing shameful in honoring a brother.

CREON Was it not a brother, too, who died in the opposite cause?

ANTIGONE   Brother by the same mother and the same father.

CREON   Why then do you do honor which is impious in the sight of Eteocles?

ANTIGONE   Eteocles would not think my act impious.

CREON   He would think so, if you make him but equal in honor with the wicked.

ANTIGONE   It was his brother—not his slave—that perished.

CREON   Laying waste this land, while *he* fell defending it.

ANTIGONE   No matter. Duty must be paid the dead.

CREON   But good deserves more than evil.

ANTIGONE   Who can know such things? In the land of the dead that may not be the law.

CREON   A foe is never a friend—not even in death.

ANTIGONE   It is not my nature to hate but to love.

CREON   Join the dead, then, and love them. While I live, no woman shall rule me.

[*Enter* ISMENE, *led in by two* ATTENDANTS.]

CHORUS   Ismene comes, shedding the tears of a loving sister; her darkened brow casts a shadow over her cheeks as tears break in rain over her fair face.

CREON   And you, who, lurking like a viper in my house, were secretly sucking my life-blood, while I knew not I was nurturing two traitors to rise against my throne—come, tell me, will you confess your part in this burial, or will you deny knowledge of it?

ISMENE   I have done the deed—if my sister allows my claim—and share the guilt with her.

ANTIGONE   No. Justice will not allow that. You did not consent to the deed and neither did I allow you a part in it.

ISMENE   But, now that you are in it, I am not ashamed to take my place by your side.

ANTIGONE   Whose was the deed, Hades and the dead know. A friend in words has not my love.

ISMENE   But, Antigone, do not reject me. Let me die with you and thereby honor the dead.

ANTIGONE   You shall not die with me, nor claim a deed you had no part in. My death is enough.

ISMENE   If I lose you, what will life mean to me?

ANTIGONE   Ask Creon; you care only for him.

ISMENE   Why do you mock me to no purpose?

ANTIGONE   If, indeed, I mock you, it is with pain that I do so.

ISMENE   Tell me—how can I help you, even now?

ANTIGONE   Save yourself. I shall not mind.

ISMENE   Have pity, Antigone. May I not die with you?

ANTIGONE   Your choice was to live; mine, to die.

ISMENE   At least your choice was made over my protest.

ANTIGONE   One world approved your choice; another approved mine.

ISMENE   Yes, the offense is the same for both of us.

ANTIGONE   Be reconciled. Live . . . My life has long been given to death so that I might serve the dead.

CREON   One of these creatures, it appears, is newly mad; the other has been mad from the beginning.

ISMENE   Yes, O King, for the mind of the unfortunate often goes astray.

CREON   Yours did when you joined your sister.

ISMENE   How could I endure life without her?

CREON   She lives no more. Speak not as though she did.

ISMENE   But will you put to death the betrothed of your son?

CREON   Never mind that. There are other fields for him to plough.

ISMENE   But not such a love as bound him to her.

CREON   I will not countenance an evil wife for a son of mine.

ANTIGONE   Haemon, dearest. How your father wrongs you!

CREON   Enough and too much of you and your marriage!

CHORUS   Would you indeed take this girl from your son?

CREON   Not I, but Death.

CHORUS   It is determined that she shall die?

CREON   Determined, yes. [*To the* ATTENDANTS.] No more delay. Take them inside, the proper place for women, for even the bold seek to escape when life stands face to face with Death. [*Exit* ATTENDANTS, *guarding* ANTIGONE *and* ISMENE.]

CHORUS   Blessed are they whose days have never tasted of evil. When a house has once been shaken from heaven, the curse passes from generation to generation of the race;

even as, when the surge is driven from the deep by the fierce breath of Thracian gales, it roils the black sands from the depths, and there is a sullen roar from wind-vexed headlands that front the blows of the storm.

In the house of Labdacus[1] sorrows are heaped upon the sorrows of the dead, and generation is not freed by generation, but some god strikes them down, and the race has no deliverance.

For now that hope, the light of which had spread above the last root of the house of Oedipus—that hope, now, is brought low in blood-stained dust by the infernal gods, by folly in speech, and frenzy of heart.

Your power, O Zeus, what human trespass can limit? That power which is unquelled by sleep or the long march of months, as you dwell in dazzling splendor on Olympus, ageless but not aged.

And so, through the future, near or far, as through the past, shall this law stand: Nothing that is great comes into the life of man without a curse.

But hope is to many men a comfort, and to many a false lure of foolish desires; and man loses his awareness until suddenly his foot is burned against the hot fire. It is a wise and famous saying that evil comes to seem good to him whose mind the gods draw to mischief, and thus man fares not long free of suffering.

But Haemon comes, the last of your sons. Does he come to lament the doom of his promised bride, Antigone, and bitter over the loss of his marriage hopes?

[*Enter* HAEMON.]

CREON We shall know soon, better than prophets could tell us. My son, hearing the unalterable doom of your betrothed, are you come in anger against your father? Or do I still hold your love in spite of my action?

HAEMON Father, I am your son, and you in your wisdom trace rules for me that I shall follow. I cannot regard marriage as a greater gain than your good guidance.

CREON Yes, my son, your heart's fixed law should be to obey your father. Men pray to have loyal sons who will deal evil to their enemies and honor to their friends. But he who is father to unprofitable children has sown trouble for himself and comfort to his enemies. Therefore, my son, do not seize impulsively the pleasures offered by a woman, for know this: that joys grow cold if an evil woman shares your bed and home. For what wound could strike deeper than a false love? Loathe this girl as if she were your enemy and let her find a husband in Hades. For I have apprehended her, alone of all the city, in open disobedience. I will not make myself a liar to my people—I will put her to death.

Let her appeal as she will to the claims of kinship.[2] If I tolerate crime in my own kindred, I must bear the crimes of strangers. He who does his duty in his own household will be found righteous in matters of State too. But if anyone breaks the law and thinks to dictate to his rulers, such a one can win no praise from me. No, the one whom the State appoints must be obeyed, in little things and great, in just things and unjust. I am certain that that one who thus obeys would be a good ruler no less than a good subject, and in any battle would stand his ground where he was set, loyal and brave at his comrade's side.

But disobedience is the worst of evils. It ruins cities, desolates homes, and causes the defeat of armies; whereas unquestioning obedience saves the lives of multitudes. Consequently, we must support the cause of order and not allow a mere woman to worst us. If we must fall from power, it is better to fall before a man than to be called weaker than a woman.

CHORUS To us, unless the years have stolen our wits, you seem to say wisely what you say.

HAEMON Father, the gods implant reason in men, the highest of all things we have. I have not the skill nor the desire to prove you wrong; yet, what I have to say may be of some use. At least, as your son, I may report, for your good, all that men say or do, or find to blame. The dread of your displeasure forbids the citizens to speak up with words offensive to you; but I can hear the murmurs in the dark, the lamentings of the city for this maiden. The people say, "No woman ever

---

[1] Labdacus was the father of Laius, who was the father of Oedipus. See chart on p. 439.

[2] Antigone was Creon's niece. See chart on p. 439.

merited her doom less—none ever was to die shamefully for such glorious deeds; who when her own brother had fallen in bloody battle, would not leave him unburied to be eaten by dogs and birds. Does not *she* deserve golden reward?"

Such is the whispered rumor that spreads in secret. For me, father, no treasure is so precious as your welfare. What fairer exchange is there than a son's pride in his father and a father's pride in his son? Do not, therefore, keep to a single line of thought as though it were the only path. For if any man thinks that he alone is wise, that in speech and thought he has no equal, such a man when laid open to view will be found empty.

No, though a man be wise, it is not shameful for him to learn and to give way if need be. As you have seen, trees survive that bend to winter's torrents, while the unbending perish root and branch. So also, he who keeps the sheet of his sail taut and never slackens it before a gale, upsets the boat.

Father, forego your wrath. Permit yourself to change. For, if as young as I am I may say so, the next best thing to natural wisdom is wisdom acquired through accepting advice.

CHORUS   Sire, it would seem that Haemon has spoken wisely just as you also have spoken wisely. There seems much to be said on both sides.

CREON   Elders of Thebes—are we at our age to be schooled by this young fellow?

HAEMON   In nothing that is not right, but even if I am young, you should consider what I have said, not my years.

CREON   Is it right to be disobedient?

HAEMON   No one should respect evil-doers.

CREON   Is not your lady tainted with that malady?

HAEMON   The people of Thebes say no.

CREON   Shall the people of Thebes prescribe how I shall rule?

HAEMON   Surely that is a childish question.

CREON   Am I to rule this land by judgment other than my own?

HAEMON   No city belongs to one man.

CREON   Is not the city held to be the ruler's?

HAEMON   You would make a good ruler over a desert.

CREON   This boy, it appears, is the woman's champion.

HAEMON   Not at all—unless you are a woman. My concern is for you.

CREON   You show this by open feud with your father!

HAEMON   Only because you are offending against Justice.

CREON   Do I offend by respecting my own authority?

HAEMON   You show no respect by trampling on the rights of the gods.

CREON   What a coward—to give way to a woman!

HAEMON   You will not find me in league with baseness.

CREON   All your words, at least, plead for that girl.

HAEMON   And for you, and for me, and for the gods of the dead.

CREON   You will never marry her this side of the grave.

HAEMON   Then she must die, but she will not die alone.

CREON   Your boldness now runs to open threats?

HAEMON   What threat is it to argue against error?

CREON   You will regret this foolish effort to teach me wisdom.

HAEMON   If you were not my father, I should have said that you are not very wise.

CREON   Slave to this woman, don't go on chattering so!

HAEMON   Would you alone speak and hear no answer?

CREON   Do you say that? By the heaven above us—be sure of this: you shall suffer for taunting me in this outrageous way. Drag forth that hated thing that she may die now, in his presence—before his eyes—at his side!

HAEMON   No, not at my side—never shall that be; nor shall you ever set eyes again upon my face. Rave as you will to such followers as can endure you. [*Exit* HAEMON.]

CHORUS   He is gone, O King, in angry haste; a youthful mind, when stung, is dangerous.

CREON   Let him rave to the top of his bent and good speed to him, but he shall not save these two girls from their doom.

CHORUS   Indeed? Do you intend to slay them both?

CREON   No—you are right—not her who had no part in the matter.

CHORUS   And how will you slay the other?

CREON   I will take her where the path is loneliest and wall her up alive in a rocky cave, with food enough so we may not be responsible for her blood. There, let her pray to Hades, the only god she loves; perhaps she will obtain from him protection against death; or else she will learn, if a little late, how useless is reverence for the dead. [*Exit* CREON.]

CHORUS   Love, the unconquered, master of wealth, who keep your vigil on the soft cheeks of a maiden, you roam over the sea and among the dwellers of the wilds; no one escapes you, be he god or mortal man; and he who receives you is like a thing possessed.

The just themselves have their minds warped by you, to their ruin. You it is who have stirred the present strife of kinsmen. The light you kindled in the eyes of the fair bride is victorious; it is a power enthroned beside the eternal laws, and Aphrodite works her unconquerable will.

[ANTIGONE *enters, between* GUARDS.]

But now I am carried beyond the bounds of loyalty to my king, and I cannot keep back the streaming tears, as I see Antigone make her way to the bridal chamber of eternal sleep.

ANTIGONE   Look upon me, my countrymen, setting forth on my last way, gazing for the last time on the light of the sun, which for me shall be no more. For Hades, who offers sleep to all, is leading me, while yet alive, to the shore of Acheron. No wedding-chant will there be for me, no bridal day; but I am betrothed of the Lord of the Dark Lake.

CHORUS   But glory and praise will go with you to that deep place of the dead. Wasting sickness has not stricken you, nor were you taken away by the sword; but alive, mistress of your fate, you pass to Hades as has no other mortal.

ANTIGONE   I have heard that, long ago, Niobe,[3] daughter of Tantalus, was doomed to die a piteous death on the heights of Sipylus. There, rigid rocks encompassed her like ivy, and she was beaten upon by snow and rain, which even now—they say—mingle with her tears. Most like hers is the fate which brings me to my rest.

CHORUS   Yes, but she was a goddess, born of gods. We are mortal. Yet it is great renown for a woman to share the doom of a goddess both in her life and after death.

ANTIGONE   Oh, you are mocking me! In the name of our father's gods, cannot you wait till I am gone, but must taunt me to my face? You, at least, O fount of Dirce and many-charioted Thebes, will bear witness by what laws I pass to the rock-sealed tomb—unhappy me, unwept of friends, who have no home on earth nor in the shades, no home among the living or the dead!

CHORUS   But you stepped forth to the utmost limits of daring, my child; and you are now paying for that before the throne of Law. Yet I also think you are paying for your father's sins.

ANTIGONE   You have touched my bitterest thought, awakening the ever-new lament for my father and for the terrible doom visited on the house of Labdacus. Horrible thoughts!— the marriage of mother and son—a mother slumbering at the side of her son—my father! From what manner of parents did I take my miserable being! Now to them I go, accursed, unwed, to share their home! And, Polynices, ill-starred in marriage,[4] in death you have undone my life!

CHORUS   An act of reverence is worthy of some praise, but a challenge against authority will bring retribution. Your self-will has brought ruin upon you.

ANTIGONE   Unwept, without friends, without marriage-songs, I am led on a journey which cannot longer be delayed. I shall never see again the holy light of the sun, and for my fate no tear is shed, no friend laments.

[*Enter* CREON.]

CREON   Know you not that songs and wailings before death would never cease if it profited

---

[3] Niobe, an earlier queen of Thebes, had reared seven fine sons and seven lovely daughters. Pride in this accomplishment made Niobe consider herself above the gods, until one day she insulted Leto, the mother of Apollo and Diana. In punishment, all fourteen children were destroyed by the arrows of Apollo and Diana; and Niobe was turned into a stone on the side of Mount Sipylus. In summer, tears could be seen issuing from the stone.

[4] Polynices had married an Argive princess. The marriage opened the way to Argive backing for an assault on Thebes, during which Polynices lost his life and thereby brought on Antigone's defiance of Creon.

to utter them? Away with her! And when you have placed her, according to my order, in her vaulted grave, leave her there, alone; either to die, or to go on living in her tomb. In any case, our hands are clean. This, however, is certain: she shall henceforth be deprived of the light of day.

ANTIGONE   Tomb, bridal-chamber, eternal prison in the cave rock, there I must go to join my own—those many who have perished and dwell now with Persephone. Last of all, most miserable of all, before my time, I join the others. But I have good hope my coming will be welcome to my father and pleasant to my mother and more than welcome to you, my brothers, for when you died, with my own hands I washed and dressed you and poured libations at your graves. It is for tending your corpse, Polynices, that I have won this reward.

And yet I honored you rightly, the wise will say. [But I would not have taken this task upon me had I had a mother, or if a husband had been left unburied. What reason for this, you ask? The husband lost, another might have been found and another child might have replaced the first one; but with both my father and my mother dead, I could never have another brother. This is why I held you, Polynices, first in honor, but Creon held me guilty of a sin and outrage. And now I go alive to the vaults of death.]⁵

What law of heaven have I transgressed? Unfortunate that I am, why should I look to the gods any more—where is any ally for me —when by piety I have earned the name of impious? If my punishment is sanctioned by the gods, I shall soon know, but if the sin is with my judges, I could wish them no fuller measure of evil than they have heaped upon me.

CHORUS   Still the same tempest of the soul vexes this maiden with the same fierce gusts.

CREON   All the more reason for her guards to act at once!

ANTIGONE   Ah, that word has the sound of death.

CREON   Your doom will be fulfilled.

ANTIGONE   O city of my fathers, O eldest gods

of our race, they lead me away—now, now— they linger no longer! Look upon me, princes of Thebes, the last daughter of the house of your kings—see what has come upon me— and from whom, because I feared to cast away the fear of Heaven! [ANTIGONE *is led away by the* GUARDS.]

CHORUS   Even thus suffered Danaë, in her beauty exchanging the light of day for brass-bound walls; and in that dungeon, secret as the grave, she was held close prisoner. She, too, was of proud lineage, O Antigone, and she received into her in a golden shower the seed of Zeus. But dread is the mysterious power of fate. There is no deliverance from it by wealth or by war, by walled city, or dark sea-beaten ships.⁶

So suffered Lycurgus, too, when shackles tamed him, the son of Dryas, that King of the Edonians, so quick to anger. He paid for his frenzied taunts at the hands of Dionysus; for he too was shut away in a rocky prison. There the fierce exuberance of his madness slowly passed. He learned to know the power of the god whom in his frenzy he had mocked, when he angered the Muses by trying to quench the Bacchanalian fire of the Maenads.⁷

And by the waters of the Dark Rocks, the waters of the twofold sea, are the shores of Bosporus and Thracian Salmydessus. Here Ares, hard by the city, saw the blinding wounds inflicted by Idothea, fierce wife of Phineus, upon his two children. With weaving-needle she, bloody-handed, put out the light of their eyes, which craved for vengeance. They too were then entombed, as you; and deep in misery, they cried out against their cruel doom, those sons of a mother cursed by her marriage. Yet she was of Erechtheid blood, nursed amid her father's storms, a true child of Boreas, swift as wind, a daughter

⁵ This bracketed passage has been challenged as illogical and perhaps spurious—though all manuscripts contain it. Can it be defended?

⁶ Danaë's father, Acrisius, locked his daughter in a bronze tower to keep a prophecy from coming to pass, to wit, that Danaë would give birth to a son who would kill Acrisius. Zeus, however, descended in a golden shower through the roof and impregnated Danaë. She gave birth to Perseus who, later, at an athletic festival accidentally killed Acrisius with a discus.   ⁷ Lycurgus, opposed to Dionysus (Roman Bacchus), tried to stop revelry in the god's honor. For this he was shut up in a rocky prison. Soon afterward he went blind and died.

of the gods brought low by the gray Fates.[8] So it was, Antigone.

[*Enter from the right* TIRESIAS, *a blind seer, led by a* BOY.]

TIRESIAS Princes of Thebes, we have come with linked steps, both served by the eyes of one, for in this way the blind may walk.

CREON And what word do you bring, old man?

TIRESIAS I will tell you and you must take heed.

CREON Indeed, Tiresias, it has not been my custom to ignore your counsel.

TIRESIAS Thereby you have thus far steered well the city's course.

CREON I freely grant how much I owe to you.

TIRESIAS Hear this then: once more you stand on fate's fine edge.

CREON What mean you? Your words send a shudder through me.

TIRESIAS You will learn—you will learn when you hear my foretelling. As I sat in my accustomed place to read the voices of the birds, I heard a strange thing: they were screaming in feverish rage and their language was lost in jabber. And I knew from the whirr of their wings they were tearing murderously at each other.

In fear at what I had heard, I prepared a burnt-sacrifice, but the Fire-god offered no fire; a dank moisture oozed from the flesh and trickled upon the embers which smoked and sputtered. The gall of the sacrifice vanished into the air and the fat-larded thighs were bared of the fat. My boy assured me that no signs came, and my offering was a failure.

And who should be blamed for this failure? It is your evil counsel which has brought this sickness upon the city. The altars of Thebes have been tainted—all of them—by birds and dogs which have torn at the corpse of Oedipus' son; and therefore the gods no longer accept prayers and sacrifices at our hands or the flame of meat-offerings; nor does any bird give a clear sign by his shrill cry, for they have tasted a slain man's blood. Take heed of these things, my son. All men

may sin, but when a sin has been committed, the sinner is not forever lost if he will but heal the mischief he has done and not stubbornly cling to his error.

Self-will is folly. Give honor to the dead, for what courage is needed to slay the slain again? It is your good that I have sought, and for that reason you should accept what I have said.

CREON Old man, you join the others in the sport of shooting at me—a fair target for everyone's arrows. The tribe of seers has long made a business of me. Gain your gains, drive your trade, if you like, in the gold-mines of Sardis or India, but try not for advantage of me. You shall not hide that man in the grave—no, though the eagles of Zeus should carry morsels from the body to their Master's throne—no, not even for dread of such defilement will I allow his burial, for I know well enough no mortal can defile the gods. But you, aged Tiresias, how shameful the fall of wisdom when it dresses shameful thoughts in fair words—all for the sake of gain!

TIRESIAS Ah, does any man know, does any man consider . . . ?

CREON Go ahead. What sage comment do you have for us now?

TIRESIAS How precious, above all riches, is good counsel.

CREON True; as evil counsel is the worst of crimes.

TIRESIAS And you are tainted with that sickness.

CREON I would not answer the seer with a taunt.

TIRESIAS But you do by saying that I prophesy lies.

CREON Well, the tribe of prophets has always had an eye for money.

TIRESIAS And the race of tyrants loves base gain.

CREON Do you know you are speaking to your King?

TIRESIAS I know it. It was through me that you saved Thebes.

CREON You are a wise prophet, but not necessarily honest.

TIRESIAS You will taunt me into revealing a dread secret.

CREON Out with it!—only expect no profit for your words.

---

[8] Idothea was the second wife of the prophet Phineus. (She is called in other accounts Idaea, Dia, or Erytia.) Some versions have Phineus himself blinding his two children by a former marriage, because of charges made against them by their stepmother.

TIRESIAS As far as you're concerned, they'll bring no profit.

CREON You will not shake my determination.

TIRESIAS Then know this—and know it well—that the sun's swift chariot will not run many more courses before you shall have given a son of yours to death, a corpse in payment for corpses; because you have ruthlessly consigned a living soul to the tomb, and because you have kept from the tomb one who belongs there, and leave his corpse unburied, unhonored, unhallowed. These things are not for you to do, nor even for the gods. These are your crimes; and because of them avenging destroyers lie in wait for you; the Furies of Hell pursue you that you may suffer the ills you have brought to others.

Judge now if I speak these things as a hireling. Soon in your house shall rise the wailing of men and of women. And a tumult of hatred against you shall echo from all the cities nearby because some of their sons had their only burial-rites from dogs, or from wild beasts, or from carrion birds—a pollution to the hearths and altars of each city.

You have provoked me to launch these arrows at your heart, sure arrows from which you cannot escape.

Come boy, lead me home. Let him spend his rage on younger men or learn to control his tongue and sweeten his mind if he can. [*Exit* TIRESIAS.]

CHORUS He has gone, O King, and left behind his dread prophecies. In all the time it has taken to change my hair from dark to white, I have never known him to prophesy falsely.

CREON I, too, know it well and am troubled in soul. It is bad to give way, but it may be worse to stand firm.

CHORUS It would be well, son of Menoeceus, to accept advice.

CREON What advice? What should I do? Speak, and I will obey.

CHORUS Free Antigone from her rocky vault. And make a tomb for the unburied Polynices.

CREON And this is your advice? You would have me yield?

CHORUS Yes, Creon, and speedily. The gods strike swiftly and cut short the follies of men.

CREON It is hard to give way, but I do so. I obey. One must not wage a vain war against destiny.

CHORUS Do these things yourself. Do not leave them to others.

CREON I will go at once. Slaves! Take tools for digging and hurry to yonder hill. Since my mind is made up, I will myself unbind Antigone even as I myself bound her. But my mind is dark with foreboding. It had been best to keep the established laws, even to life's end. [*Exit* CREON *with* SERVANTS.]

CHORUS O god of many names, glory of the Cadmean bride, offspring of loud-thundering Zeus! You who watch over famed Italia and reign over the hospitable valley of Eleusis! O Bacchus, dweller in Thebes, mother-city of the Bacchantes, by the soft-gliding stream of Ismenus, on the soil where the fierce dragon's teeth were sown!

You have seen where torch-flames glare through smoke, and rise above the twin peaks, where dance the Corycian nymphs, your votaries, hard by Castalia's stream.

You come from the ivy-mantled slopes of Nysa's hills, from the green shore with many-clustered vines; and you hear your name in the streets of Thebes lifted up by immortal voices.

Thebes, of all cities, you hold first in honor, you, and also your mother whom the lightning struck. Now, when all our people bow before a violent plague, come with healing feet over the Parnassian height, over the moaning sea!

O you with whom the stars rejoice as they move, the stars whose breath is fire; O master of the voices of the night; son begotten of Zeus; come to us, O King, with your attendant Bacchantes, who in night-long frenzy dance before you, the Giver of Good Gifts, Bacchus!

[*Enter* MESSENGER *from the left of the stage.*]

MESSENGER Citizens of Thebes, the mortal life of man is never assured. Fortune raises and Fortune humbles the lucky or the unlucky from day to day, and no one can foretell what will be from what is. For Creon once was blessed, as I count bliss. He had saved Thebes from its enemies. He was clothed with sole authority in the land; he reigned, the glorious father of princely children. And now—all has been lost. For when a man has had life's pleasures taken from him, I count him as good as dead, a breathing corpse. Heap up riches, if you will, live like a king, but if there is no joy, I would not give the shadow of a shadow for such a life.

CHORUS   What new sorrow has come to our princes?

MESSENGER   Death. And the guilt is on those that live.

CHORUS   Who is the slayer and who the slain? Speak!

MESSENGER   Haemon is dead, his blood spilled by no stranger.

CHORUS   By his father's hand or by his own?

MESSENGER   By his own, in anger with his father for the murder.

CHORUS   O prophet, how true, then, have proved your words!

MESSENGER   So much you have heard. You must decide what to do.

CHORUS   Ah, Eurydice, Creon's unfortunate wife, approaches. Perhaps she comes by chance, or perhaps she has heard the news of her son.

[*Enter* EURYDICE.]

EURYDICE   People of Thebes, I heard what you were saying as I was going forth to salute with prayers the goddess Athena. Just as I was opening the gate, the messages of woe struck my ears. Filled with terror, I sank back into the arms of my handmaids, my senses numbed. Now, say again what you have already said. I shall hear it as one who is no stranger to sorrow.

MESSENGER   Dear lady, I will tell what I saw and leave no word of the truth untold. Why, indeed, should I soothe you with words which would soon be proved false? Truth is always best.

I attended your lord as his guide to the farthest part of the plain, where the body of Polynices, torn by dogs, still lay unhonored. We prayed to Hecate and to Pluto,[9] in mercy to restrain their anger. We washed the body with holy washing and with freshly broken boughs we solemnly burned such relics as there were. Then we raised a high mound of native earth. After that we turned away to enter the maiden's wedding chamber with its rocky couch, the caverned mansion of the bride of Death.

From far off, one of us heard loud wailing at the bride's unblessed bower, and came to tell our master Creon.

As the King drew nearer, uncertain sounds of bitter crying floated about him. He groaned. In anguish he muttered: "Wretched that I am, can my foreboding be true? Am I going on the saddest way that I ever went? My son's voice greets me. Go, my servants—hasten, and when you have reached the tomb, passed through the opening where the stones have been wrenched away to the cave's very mouth and look—see if it is Haemon's voice that I know—or if my ear is fooled by the gods."

This search, ordered by our despairing master, we went to make, and in the innermost part of the vault we saw Antigone hanging by the neck. The halter was fashioned from the fine linen thread of her dress. Haemon held his arms about her waist—crying out over the death of his bride, and his father's cruelty, and his own ill-starred love.

But his father, when he saw his son, raised a dreadful cry, and went in and called to him with the voice of despair: "O unhappy son, what have you done? What thoughts possess you? What kind of mischance has made you mad? Come away, my boy! I pray you—I implore!" But the boy glared at him with fierce eyes, spat in his face, and without a word of answer, drew forth his cross-fitted sword. His father fled, and the sword missed. Then, insane with anger, Haemon leaned with all his weight against the blade and drove it half its length into his side. While consciousness was fading, he clasped Antigone to his weak embrace and, gasping, spilled his blood on her pale cheek.

Corpse embracing corpse he lies. He has won his wedding rites, poor youth—not here, but in the halls of Death. He has shown to man that of all curses that plague mankind, ill counsel is the sovereign curse. [EURYDICE *retires into the Palace.*]

CHORUS   What do you make of this? She has left without a word.

MESSENGER   I, too, am startled; yet I feed on the hope that she simply wishes not to vent in public her grief over such sorrowful news. She will perhaps set her handmaids to mourn

[9] Hecate was a goddess of the underworld and Pluto its ruler.

in privacy. She has had many lessons in woe and may do nothing rash.

CHORUS   I do not know. But to me, at any rate, too much silence seems to bode evil, no less than loud lamenting.

MESSENGER   Well, I will go in, and learn whether in truth she is hiding some rash purpose in the depths of her passionate heart. Yes, you say true: too much silence may have a dangerous meaning. [*Exit* MESSENGER.]

[*Enter* CREON *from the left, with* ATTENDANTS, *carrying in a shroud the body of* HAEMON.]

CHORUS   See, yonder the King himself draws near, bearing that which tells too clear a tale —the work (if one may say so) not of a stranger's madness but of his own misdeeds.

CREON   Woe for the sins of a darkened soul, stubborn sins, shadowed by Death. Look on us —the father who has slain—the son who has perished! Darkest sorrow is mine for the wretched blindness of my stubborn will! Oh, my poor son, you have died in your youth, victim of an ill-timed doom—woe to me! Fled is your spirit, not by your folly but because of mine.

CHORUS   Ah, too late you seem to see the right.

CREON   I have learned the bitter lesson. But then, oh then, some god—I think—struck me from above with heavy weight, and hurled me into the ways of cruelty—overthrowing and trampling on my joy. Bitter woe comes to the labors of man.

[*Enter* MESSENGER *from the Palace.*]

MESSENGER   Sire, you come bearing sorrow; you are soon to look upon more within your Palace.

CREON   What more? What pain is yet to be added?

MESSENGER   Your queen has died, true mother of that corpse. Unhappy lady, her blows are newly dealt.

CREON   O Death, is there no end to your greed? Have you no mercy? You bearer of these evil, bitter words, what do you say? Already I was dead, yet you have struck me anew! What said you, my son? What is this new message —of my wife's death—of slaughter heaped on slaughter! [*The central door of the Palace is opened revealing the corpse of* EURYDICE.]

CHORUS   You can see for yourself—for now nothing is hidden.

CREON   Still another horror! What fate, ah what, can yet await me? I have just lifted my son in my arms, and now another corpse lies before me. Unhappy mother! Unhappy son!

MESSENGER   There at the altar she lay, stabbed with the sharp knife, and as her eyes grew dim she wailed for the noble sacrifice of Megareus, and then for the fate of Haemon who lies there. With her last breath, she invoked a curse upon you, the slayer of your sons.

CREON   O terror! I shake with dread! Is there no one to strike me to the heart with two-edged sword? Miserable, miserable, overwhelmed by anguish!

MESSENGER   Yes, both deaths—your son's, your wife's—are charged to you by her whose corpse you see.

CREON   Her last act—how—how did she it?

MESSENGER   When she had learned the fate of her son, with her own hand she drove the sharp knife home to her heart.

CREON   No man can be found guilty of this but I. Wretched that I am, I own the crime—it was I who murdered you. Take me away, my servants. My life is as death. Lead me away with all speed.

CHORUS   This were best, if best can be found in evil. Swiftness is best when only trouble is before us.

CREON   Let it come, I say. Let it appear, that fairest of fates for me that brings my last day. Yes! best fate of all. Let it come, that never may I look on tomorrow's light.

CHORUS   These things are for the future which is not known. Present tasks claim our care.

CREON   These, at any rate, are my fervent prayers.

CHORUS   Pray no more, for mortals have no escape from what will be.

CREON   Lead me away, I beg you, a rash, foolish man who has unwittingly murdered a son and a wife. I know not where to cast my eyes or where to seek support, for all has gone amiss with everything I have touched, and upon my head a crushing fate has fallen. [*Exit* CREON.]

CHORUS   Wisdom is the crown of happiness and reverence for the gods must be inviolate. The great words of prideful men are punished with great blows, which, in old age, teach the chastened to be wise.

Pronunciation of Proper Names in
Antigone

Antigone	Ăn-tǐ′-gō-nē
Ares	Ā′-rēz
Bacchantes	Băc-căn′-tēz
Corycian	Cŏr-ĭsh′-yăn
Creon	Crē′-ŏn
Danaë	Dăn′-ā-ē
Dirce	Dŭr′-sē
Eleusis	Ĕl-yū′-sis
Eteocles	Ē-tē′-ō-klēz
Eurydice	Yū-rĭ′-dĭ-sē
Haemon	Hē′-mŏn
Hecate	Hĕ-că-tē
Ismene	Īz-mē′-nē
Ismenus	Īz-mē′-nŭs
Labdacus	Lăb′-dă-cŭs
Laius	Lāy′-ŭs
Lycurgus	Lȳ-cŭr′-gŭs
Megareus	Mĕ-gă′-rē-ŭs
Menoeceus	Men-ē′-sē-us
Niobe	Nī′-ō-bé
Nysa	Nĭ′-suh
Oedipus	Ē′-dĭ-pŭs
Phineus	Fĭn′-ē-us
Polynices	Pōlē-nĭ-sēz
Salmydessus	Săl-mĭ-dĕs′-sus
Thebes	Thēb′z
Tiresias	Tĭ-rē′-sē-ăs

Comments and Questions

1. FIRST IMPRESSIONS. Was the play difficult to understand? Did you like it? If so, why? If not, why not? Is the action credible? Here first impressions may be misleading, and you may wish to answer two other questions: credible for twenty-four hundred years ago? credible for our time? Hasty answers to these last two questions are likely to be wrong. Answer them anyway and then, after analyzing the play more thoroughly, see whether or not you wish to modify your answers.

2. THE FACTS OF THE PLAY. The facts are simple enough, but you should record them as completely as possible. The problem here is to find the precise event which has any bearing on the present action. Does one need to go back farther than the duel be-tween Eteocles and Polynices which resulted in the deaths of these two brothers of Antigone?

3. EXPOSITION AND ANTECEDENT ACTION. Sophocles, as we have said, depended upon the fact that his audience knew the history of the Theban royal house. He, therefore, allows Ismene to say to Antigone:

> Remember how our father perished, amid hate and scorn, when sins, self-revealed, moved him to strike out his eyes with his own hands.

The Greek audience knew that "our father" was Oedipus and that his "awful sin" had been the murder of his father and marriage to his mother. This allusion and the ones which follow in Ismene's speech were simple reminders to the Greeks and did not tell them what they did not already know. The point of course is that the problem of exposition was simplified for the Greek dramatist.

4. SETTING. Greek drama, for the most part, preserved what Aristotle and Renaissance writers on drama identified as the three unities; that is, the unities of time, place, and action. Unity of time required that all the action should be completed in one day; unity of place that the action should occur in one place. *Antigone,* of course, observes these unities. Of how much importance, then, is setting to this play? Discuss. In what sense does time become of the essence? Consider Creon's actions after he capitulates to the gods. (Compare O'Neill's treatment of time in *Ile.* See Action Line, p. 427.)

5. PLOT. List the sequence of actions which make up the plot. In what way does the plot represent unity of action? What is the essential conflict? Do all actions rise out of this conflict? At what point is the conflict resolved? When, in other words, does Creon realize the terrible implications of his defiance of the gods? What happens after Creon decides to reverse his decrees concerning Polynices and Antigone? Why does Creon bury Polynices before attempting to save Antigone? Explain carefully.

6. CHARACTER. In spite of the title of this play, is Antigone the chief character? Discuss. Although you may find the comparison

a curious one, consider the likenesses and differences between Captain Keeney (*Ile*) and Creon. (You may look forward to comparing Creon and Madame Zachanassian in *The Visit,* p. 676.) What are Creon's strengths and weaknesses? Antigone's? Ismene's? Haemon's? Eurydice's? What sort of character does the Chorus have? Consider its wisdom, its doubts, its waverings, its decisions. Can a case be made for identifying the chorus with public opinion?

7. THE SUMMING PROCESS. What does your analysis add up to? What is the meaning of the play? Is the play concerned only with the question of whether or not Polynices should be buried? Or is it concerned with a conflict between the claims of the State and the claims of the gods? Or does it go beyond even this large issue to an even larger one—man's fate?

How does one get at such questions? Perhaps by asking a few others. Would every man have acted as Creon did? every woman as Antigone? A king other than Creon might have refused burial to both Eteocles and Polynices on the grounds that both were guilty of fratricide. Still someone else in Creon's place might have refused burial to Eteocles and granted it to Polynices on the grounds that Polynices through ridding Thebes of Eteocles had made way for a better man to mount the throne. And what of Antigone? Another daughter might have seen the justice in Creon's action or, like Ismene, might have bent to his will. We are forced to see that because Creon and Antigone acted as they did and not in some other way, they are *individuals responsible for what happened to them.*

Perhaps this conclusion is clear enough, but what of Ismene, Haemon, and Eurydice? What is their guilt? Ismene seems cautious. Is that her weakness or her strength? Haemon is dragged into conflict and destroyed by it. Could he have avoided destruction? Think carefully before you answer. Eurydice seems the most innocent of the bystanders. If she is without fault, how is her suicide to be explained?

If we pull things together now, we may glimpse a vastly disturbing conclusion about man's fate. (Compare with Frost's "A Masque of Reason," p. 358, and MacLeish's "Trespass on a Monument," p. 882.) Creon is guilty of a murderous drive to have his own way. He is crushed. Antigone is stubborn but ranges herself on the side of the gods. She is crushed. Haemon speaks with the voice of reason, stands for principles, but fails. He is crushed. Eurydice, without any part in the struggle, is overwhelmed by it. She is crushed. Ismene, timid and willing to accept what she assumes cannot be changed, survives, but survives without any of the persons she loves.

What is the pattern for this wholesale laying-low of the mighty and the near-mighty? Consider the last lines of the play:

> Wisdom is the crown of happiness and reverence for the gods must be inviolate. The great words of prideful men are punished with great blows, which, in old age, teach the chastened to be wise.

Do these statements account for what has happened to each of the characters?

Many other approaches to this play are possible, but whatever the approach, full meaning is to be realized only after each part of the play has been related to all the other parts.

The Tragedy of Othello
The Moor of Venice

WILLIAM SHAKESPEARE
1564–1616

A critical essay on *Othello,* prepared especially for this book, appears on pp. 867–875. The play, it is suggested, should be read first, then Norman Sanders' critical essay, after which the play should be reviewed. It is also suggested that a first reading of the play should be uninterrupted by reference to the many footnotes. The gist will be clear. Since, however, Elizabethan English differs from modern English just enough to require some "translation," it will be useful to check all annotations during the second reading.

DRAMATIS PERSONAE

DUKE OF VENICE
BRABANTIO, *a Senator, father to Desdemona*
SENATORS
GRATIANO, *brother to Brabantio* } two noble
LODOVICO, *kinsman to Brabantio* } Venetians
OTHELLO, *The Moor*
CASSIO, *his honorable Lieutenant*
IAGO, *Othello's Ancient, a villain*
RODERIGO, *a gulled gentleman*
MONTANO, *retiring Governor of Cyprus*
CLOWN, *servant to Othello*
DESDEMONA, *daughter to Brabantio and wife to Othello*
EMILIA, *wife to Iago*
BIANCA, *a courtesan*
SAILOR, MESSENGER, HERALD, OFFICERS, GENTLE-
MEN, MUSICIANS, ATTENDANTS

SCENES
Venice; Cyprus

ACT I

Scene I [*Venice. A street.*]

[*Enter* RODERIGO *and* IAGO.]

RODERIGO Tush, never tell me! I take it much
    unkindly
That thou, Iago, who hast had my purse
As if the strings were thine, shouldst know of
    this.   5
IAGO 'S blood, but you'll not hear me!
If ever I did dream of such a matter,
Abhor me.
RODERIGO Thou told'st me thou didst hold him
    in thy hate.   10
IAGO Despite me if I do not. Three great ones
    of the city,
In personal suit to make me his lieutenant,
Off-capped to him; and, by the faith of man,
I know my price, I am worth no worse a   15
    place.
But he, as loving his own pride and purposes,
Evades them with a bombast circumstance,
Horribly stuffed with epithets of war;
And, in conclusion,   20

6 *'S blood,* by God's blood.

Nonsuits my mediators; for, "Certes," says he,
"I have already chose my officer."
And what was he?
Forsooth, a great arithmetician,
One Michael Cassio, a Florentine   25
(A fellow almost damned in a fair wife),
That never set a squadron in the field,
Nor the division of a battle knows
More than a spinster; unless the bookish
    theoric,   30
Wherein the toged consuls can propose
As masterly as he. Mere prattle, without prac-
    tice,
Is all his soldiership. But he, sir, had th'
    election;   35
And I (of whom his eyes had seen the proof
At Rhodes, at Cyprus, and on other grounds
Christian and heathen) must be be-leed and
    calmed
By debitor and creditor, this counter-   40
    caster.
He (in good time!) must his lieutenant be,
And I (God bless the mark!) his Moorship's
    ancient.
RODERIGO By heaven, I rather would have   45
    been his hangman.
IAGO Why, there's no remedy; 'tis the curse of
    service.
Preferment goes by letter and affection,
And not by old gradation, where each   50
    second
Stood heir to the first. Now, sir, be judge your-
    self,
Whether I in any just term am affined
To love the Moor.   55
RODERIGO   I would not follow him then.

---

21 *Nonsuits,* dismisses. 24 *Arithmetician,* theoretical (military) tactician; *i.e.,* without practical battle
experience. 26 *a fair wife,* since Cassio, in this version, has no wife, scholars speculate that the line
appeared in a lost version of the play and, through
oversight, was not deleted when Shakespeare
changed the plot; less likely is the theory that *wife*
simply means *woman.* 29–30 *theoric,* theory. 31
toged consuls, consuls (officials) dressed in togas.
34–35 *had th' election,* was chosen (by Othello).
37 *at Rhodes, at Cyprus,* Aegean islands contended
for by Turkey and Venice. 39 *calmed,* becalmed.
40–41 *debitor and creditor, . . . counter caster,*
bookkeeping clerk . . . cashier. 44 *ancient,* ensign,
i.e., low-ranking military attendant. 49 *affection,*
personal liking (divorced from merit). 50 *old gradation,* advancement through seniority. 54 *affined,*
duty bound.

IAGO   O, sir, content you.
     I follow him to serve my turn upon him.
     We cannot all be masters, nor all masters
     Cannot be truly followed. You shall mark   60
     Many a duteous and knee-crooking knave
     That, doting on his own obsequious bond-
          age,
     Wears out his time, much like his master's ass,
     For naught but provender; and when he's   65
          old, cashiered.
     Whip me such honest knaves! Others there are
     Who, trimmed in forms and visages of duty,
     Keep yet their hearts attending on themselves;
     And, throwing but shows of service on   70
          their lords,
     Do well thrive by them, and when they have
          lined their coats,
     Do themselves homage. These fellows have
          some soul,   75
     And such a one do I profess myself.
          For, sir,
     It is as sure as you are Roderigo,
     Were I the Moor, I would not be Iago.
     In following him, I follow but myself.   80
     Heaven is my judge, not I for love and duty,
     But seeming so, for my peculiar end;
     For when my outward action doth demon-
          strate
     The native act and figure of my heart
     In compliment extern, 'tis not long after   85
     But I will wear my heart upon my sleeve
     For daws to peck at. I am not what I am.

RODERIGO   What a full fortune does the thick-
          lips owe
     If he can carry't thus!   90

IAGO   Call up her father:
     Rouse him, make after him, poison his de-
          light,
     Proclaim him in the streets, incense her kins-
          men,   95
     And though he in a fertile climate dwell,
     Plague him with flies; though that his joy be
          joy,
     Yet throw such changes of vexation on't
     As it may lose some color.   100

RODERIGO   Here is her father's house. I'll call
          aloud.

IAGO   Do, with like timorous accent and dire yell
     As when, by night and negligence, the fire
     Is spied in populous cities.   105

RODERIGO   What, ho, Brabantio! Signior Braban-
          tio, ho!

IAGO   Awake! What, ho, Brabantio! Thieves!
          thieves! thieves!
     Look to your house, your daughter, and   110
          your bags! Thieves! thieves!
     [Enter BRABANTIO, above, at a window.]

BRABANTIO   What is the reason of this terrible
          summons?
     What is the matter there?

RODERIGO   Signior, is all your family with-   115
          in?

IAGO   Are your doors locked?

BRABANTIO   Why, wherefore ask you
          this?

IAGO   Zounds, sir, y'are robbed! For shame,   120
          put on your gown!
     Your heart is burst; you have lost half your
          soul.
     Even now, now, very now, an old black ram
     Is tupping your white ewe. Arise, arise!   125
     Awake the snorting citizens with the bell,
     Or else the devil will make a grandsire of you.
     Arise, I say!

BRABANTIO   What, have you lost your wits?

RODERIGO   Most reverend signior, do you   130
          know my voice?

BRABANTIO   Not I. What are you?

RODERIGO   My name is Roderigo.

BRABANTIO   The worser welcome!
     I have charged thee not to haunt about   135
          my doors.
     In honest plainness thou hast heard me say
     My daughter is not for thee; and now, in mad-
          ness,
     Being full of supper and distemp'ring   140
          draughts,
     Upon malicious bravery dost thou come
     To start my quiet.

RODERIGO   Sir, sir, sir—

BRABANTIO   But thou must needs be sure   145

---

61 *knave,* servant. 66 *cashiered,* dismissed. 73
lined their coats, made their fortunes. 82 *peculiar
end,* unique purpose. 85 *compliment extern,* outward show of loyalty. 89 *owe,* own. 90 *carry't
thus,* put over (his) wishes in this manner.

103 *timorous accent,* a cry at a pitch to produce
timorousness. 120 *zounds,* God's wounds. 126
snorting, snoring. 142 *bravery,* bravado. 143 *start,*
disturb.

My spirit and my place have in their power
To make this bitter to thee.

RODERIGO   Patience, good sir.

BRABANTIO   What tell'st thou me of robbing?
    This is Venice;   150
My house is not a grange.

RODERIGO   Most grave Brabantio,
    In simple and pure soul I come to you.

IAGO   Zounds, sir, you are one of those that will
    not serve God if the devil bid you. Be-   155
    cause we come to do you service, and you
    think we are ruffians, you'll have your daugh-
    ter covered with a Barbary horse; you'll have
    your nephews neigh to you; you'll have courses
    for cousins, and gennets for germans.   160

BRABANTIO   What profane wretch art thou?

IAGO   I am one, sir, that comes to tell you your
    daughter and the Moor are now making the
    beast with two backs.

BRARANTIO   Thou art a villain.   165

IAGO   You are a senator.

BRABANTIO   This thou shalt answer. I know
    thee, Roderigo.

RODERIGO   Sir, I will answer anything. But I
    beseech you,   170
    If't be your pleasure and most wise consent
    (As partly I find it is) that your fair
        daughter,
    At this odd-even and dull watch o' the night,
    Transported, with no worse nor better   175
        guard
    But with a knave of common hire, a gondolier,
    To the gross clasps of a lascivious
        Moor—
    If this be known to you, and your   180
        allowance,
    We then have done you bold and saucy wrongs;
    But if you know not this, my manners tell me
    We have your wrong rebuke. Do not
        believe   185
    That, from the sense of all civility,
    I thus would play and trifle with your rev-
        erence.
    Your daughter, if you have not given her
        leave,   190

I say again, hath made a gross revolt,
Tying her duty, beauty, wit, and fortunes
In an extravagant and wheeling stranger
Of here and everywhere. Straight satisfy
    yourself   195
If she be in her chamber, or your house,
Let loose on me the justice of the state
For thus deluding you.

BRABANTIO   Strike on the tinder, ho!
Give me a taper! Call up all my people!   200
This accident is not unlike my dream:
Belief of it oppresses me already.
Light, I say! light! [Exit, above.]

IAGO   Farewell, for I must leave you.
It seems not meet, nor wholesome to my   205
    place,
To be produced (as, if I stay, I shall)
Against the Moor. For I do know, the state,
However this may gall him with some check,
Cannot with safety cast him; for he's em-   210
    barked
With such loud reason to the Cyprus wars,
Which even now stand in act, that for their
    souls
Another of his fadom they have none   215
To lead their business; in which regard,
Though I do hate him as I do hell pains,
Yet, for necessity of present life,
I must show out a flag and sign of love,
Which is indeed but sign. That you shall   220
    surely find him,
Lead to the Sagittary the raised search;
And there will I be with him. So farewell.
    [Exit.]

[Enter, below, BRABANTIO, in his nightgown,
    and SERVANTS with torches.]

BRABANTIO   It is true an evil. Gone she   225
    is;
And what's to come of my despised time
Is naught but bitterness. Now, Roderigo,
Where didst thou see her?—O unhappy girl!—
With the Moor, say'st thou?—Who   230
    would be a father? —
How didst thou know 'twas she?—O, she
    deceives me

---

151 *grange,* isolated farmhouse.   159 *nephews,* sons.
160 *cousins . . . gennets . . . germans,* kinsmen . . .
small Spanish horses . . . kinsmen.   163–164 *making
the beast with two backs,* copulating.   174 *odd-
even,* between one day and the morrow.   180–181
your allowance, by your permission.   186 *from the
sense,* in defiance of.

193 *extravagant and wheeling,* flamboyant and roam-
ing.   201 *accident,* occurrence.   207 *produced,* asked
to testify.   209 *gall . . . check,* chafe . . . reprimand.   210 *cast him,* discharge him.   213 *stand in
act,* is now going on.   215 *fadom,* ability.   222 *Sagittary,* inn with a sign of a Centaur with a bent bow.

Past thought!——What said she to you?—
    Get more tapers!
Raise all my kindred—Are they married,   235
    think you?
RODERIGO   Truly I think they are.
BRABANTIO   O heaven! How got she out? O
    treason of the blood!
Fathers, from hence trust not your   240
    daughters' minds
By what you see them act. Is there not charms
By which the property of youth and maidhood
May be abused? Have you not read,
    Roderigo,   245
Of some such thing?
RODERIGO   Yes, sir, I have indeed.
BRABANTIO   Call up my brother.—O, would
    you had had her!—
Some one way, some another.—Do you   250
    know
Where we may apprehend her and the Moor?
RODERIGO   I think I can discover him, if you
    please
To get good guard and go along with me.   255
BRABANTIO   Pray you lead on. At every house
    I'll call;
I may command at most.—Get weapons, ho!
And raise some special officers of night.—
On, good Roderigo. I'll deserve your   260
    pains. [*Exeunt.*]

Scene II   [*Venice. Before the Sagittary.*]

[*Enter* OTHELLO, IAGO, ATTENDANTS, *with
    torches.*]

IAGO   Though in the trade of war I have slain
    men,
Yet do I hold it very stuff o' the conscience
To do no contrived murder. I lack iniquity
Sometimes to do me service. Nine or ten   5
    times
I had thought t' have yerked him here under
    the ribs.
OTHELLO   'Tis better as it is.
IAGO   Nay, but he prated,   10
And spoke such scurvy and provoking terms
Against your honor,
That with the little godliness I have
I did full hard forbear him. But I pray you, sir,

Are you fast married? Be assured of this,   15
That the magnifico is much beloved,
And hath in his effect a voice potential
As double as the Duke's. He will divorce you,
Or put upon you what restraint and grievance
The law, with all his might to enforce it on,   20
Will give him cable.
OTHELLO   Let him do his spite.
My services which I have done the signiory
Shall out-tongue his complaints. 'Tis yet to
    know—   25
Which, when I know that boasting is an honor,
I shall promulgate—I fetch my life and being
From men of royal siege; and by demerits
May speak (unbonneted) to as proud a fortune
As this that I have reached. For know,   30
    Iago,
But that I love the gentle Desdemona,
I would not my unhoused free condition
Put into circumscription and confine
For the sea's worth.   35
[*Enter* CASSIO, *and* OFFICERS *with torches.*]
                    But look what lights come yond.
IAGO   Those are the raised father and his friends.
You were best go in.
OTHELLO   Not I. I must be found.
My parts, my title, and my perfect soul   40
Shall manifest me rightly. Is it they?
IAGO   By Janus, I think no.
OTHELLO   The servants of the Duke? and my
    lieutenant?
The goodness of the night upon you,   45
    friends!
What is the news?
CASSIO   The Duke does greet you, General;
And he requires your haste-post-haste appear-
    ance   50
Even on the instant.
OTHELLO   What's the matter, think you?
CASSIO   Something from Cyprus, as I may divine.
It is a business of some heat. The galleys
Have sent a dozen sequent messengers   55

16 *magnifico*, great nobleman (Brabantio). 18 *double as the Duke's* (the Doge of Venice was mistakenly thought by Elizabethans to have two votes;
thus Iago means that Brabantio on this occasion
would have a double vote.) 24–25 *'tis yet to know
. . .*, not yet revealed. (Othello here states that
his lineage is royal and therefore superior to Brabantio's.) 28 *seige . . . demerits*, position . . . deserts. 29 (*unbonneted*), with cap off (courteously).
33 *unhoused*, free from home duties. 40 *parts . . .
perfect soul*, qualities . . . good conscience.

243 *property*, nature. 244 *abused*, deceived. 260
deserve, reward.
7 *yerked*, jabbed.

This very night at one another's heels;
And many of the consuls, raised and met,
Are at the Duke's already. You have been
   hotly called for;
When, being not at your lodging to be   60
   found,
The Senate hath sent about three several quests
To search you out.
OTHELLO   'Tis well I am found by you.
I will but spend a word here in the house,   65
And go with you. [*Exit.*]
CASSIO   Ancient, what makes he here?
IAGO   Faith, he tonight hath boarded a land car-
   rack.
If it prove lawful prize, he's made for ever.   70
CASSIO   I do not understand.
IAGO   He's married.
CASSIO   To who?
        [*Enter* OTHELLO.]
IAGO   Marry, to—Come, Captain, will you go?
OTHELLO   Have with you.   75
CASSIO   Here comes another troop to seek for
   you.
[*Enter* BRABANTIO, RODERIGO, *and* OFFICERS *with*
      torches and weapons.]
IAGO   It is Brabantio. General, be advised;
He comes to bad intent.
OTHELLO   Holla! stand there!
RODERIGO   Signior, it is the Moor.   80
BRABANTIO   Down with him, thief!
     [*Both parties draw swords.*]
IAGO   You, Roderigo! Come, sir, I am for you.
OTHELLO   Keep up your bright swords, for the
   dew will rust them.   85
Good signior, you shall more command
   with years
Than with your weapons.
BRABANTIO   O thou foul thief, where hast thou
   stowed my daughter?   90
Damned as thou art, thou hast enchanted
   her!
For I'll refer me to all things of sense,
If she in chains of magic were not bound,
Whether a maid so tender, fair, and happy,   95
So opposite to marriage that she shunned
The wealthy curled darlings of our nation,
Would ever have (t' incur a general mock)
Run from her guardage to the sooty bosom
Of such a thing as thou—to fear, not   100
   to delight.

68–69 *carrack,* a ship (bearing treasure).

Judge me the world if 'tis not gross in sense
That thou hast practiced on her with foul
   charms,
Abused her delicate youth with drugs or   105
   minerals
That weaken motion. I'll have't disputed on.
'Tis probable, and palpable to thinking.
I therefore apprehend and do attach thee
For an abuser of the world, a practicer   110
Of arts inhibited and out of warrant.
Lay hold upon him. If he do resist,
Subdue him at his peril.
OTHELLO   Hold your hands,
Both you of my inclining and the rest.   115
Were it my cue to fight, I should have
   known it
Without a prompter. Where will you that I go
To answer this your charge?
BRABANTIO   To prison, till fit time   120
Of law and course of direct session
Call thee to answer.
OTHELLO   What if I do obey?
How may the Duke be therewith satisfied,
Whose messengers are here about my side   125
Upon some present business of the state
To bring me to him?
OFFICER   'Tis true, most worthy signior.
The Duke's in council, and your noble self,
I am sure, is sent for.   130
BRABANTIO   How? The Duke in council?
In this time of the night? Bring him away!
Mine's not an idle cause. The Duke himself,
Or any of my brothers of the state,
Cannot but feel this wrong as 'twere their   135
   own;
For if such actions may have passage
   free,
Bondslaves and pagans shall our statesmen be.
   [*Exeunt.*]

Scene III   [*Venice. A Chamber in the
          Senate House.*]

[*Enter* DUKE *and* SENATORS, *set at a table, with
     lights and* ATTENDANTS.]
DUKE   There is no composition in these news
That gives them credit.

102 *gross,* obvious. 107 *that weaken motion,* that
disturb judgment. 111 *out of warrant,* illegal. 115
of my inclining, on my side.
1 *composition,* consistency. 2 *credit,* credibility.

FIRST SENATOR   Indeed they are disproportioned.
My letters say a hundred and seven galleys.
DUKE   And mine hundred forty.   5
SECOND SENATOR   And mine two hundred.
But though they jump not on a just account
(As in these cases where the aim reports
'Tis oft with difference), yet do they all confirm
A Turkish fleet, and bearing up to Cyprus.   10
DUKE   Nay, it is possible enough to judgment.
I do not so secure me in the error
But the main article I do approve
In fearful sense.
SAILOR   [Within.] What, ho! What, ho!   15
   what, ho!
                    [Enter SAILOR.]
OFFICER   A messenger from the galleys.
DUKE   Now, what's the business?
SAILOR   The Turkish preparation makes for
   Rhodes.   20
So was I bid report here to the state
By Signior Angelo.
DUKE   How say you by this change?
FIRST SENATOR   This cannot be
By no assay of reason. 'Tis a pageant   25
To keep us in false gaze. When we consider
Th' importancy of Cyprus to the Turk,
And let ourselves again but understand
That, as it more concerns the Turk than
   Rhodes,   30
So may he with more facile question bear it,
For that it stands not in such warlike brace,
But altogether lacks th' abilities
That Rhodes is dressed in—if we make
   thought of this,   35
We must not think the Turk is so unskilful
To leave that latest which concerns him first,
Neglecting an attempt to ease and gain
To wake and wage a danger profitless.
DUKE   Nay, in all confidence he's not for   40
   Rhodes.
OFFICER   Here is more news.
                 [Enter a MESSENGER.]
MESSENGER   The Ottomites, reverend and gra-
   cious,

7 jump . . . just, agree . . . exact. 8 aim, guess.
12 I do not so secure me in the error, I do not feel
safe just because the reports err (are inconsistent).
25 assay of reason, reasonable test. 26 in false gaze,
looking the wrong way. 31 more facile question
bear it, capture it with less difficulty. 32 brace,
preparedness. 33 abilities, war-preparation. 39 wage,
risk.

Steering with due course toward the isle of   45
   Rhodes,
Have there injointed them with an after fleet.
FIRST SENATOR   Ay, so I thought. How many, as
   you guess?
MESSENGER   Of thirty sail; and now they   50
   do re-stem
Their backward course, bearing with frank
   appearance
Their purposes toward Cyprus. Signior Mon-
   tano,   55
Your trusty and most valiant servitor,
With his free duty recommends you thus,
And prays you to believe him.
DUKE   'Tis certain then for Cyprus.
Marcus Luccios, is not he in town?   60
FIRST SENATOR   He's now in Florence.
DUKE   Write from us to him; post-post-haste
   dispatch.
   [ENTER BRABANTIO, OTHELLO, CASSIO, IAGO,
             RODERIGO, and OFFICERS.]
FIRST SENATOR   Here comes Brabantio and
   the valiant Moor.   65
DUKE   Valiant Othello, we must straight employ
   you
Against the general enemy Ottoman.
   [To BRABANTIO.]   I did not see you.
   Welcome, gentle signior.   70
We lacked your counsel and your help tonight.
BRABANTIO   So did I yours. Good your Grace,
   pardon me.
Neither my place, nor aught I heard of
   business,   75
Hath raised me from my bed; nor doth the
   general care
Take hold on me; for my particular grief
Is of so floodgate and o'erbearing nature
That it engluts and swallows other sorrows,   80
And it is still itself.
DUKE   Why, what's the matter?
BRABANTIO   My daughter! O, my daughter!
ALL   Dead?
BRABANTIO   Ay, to me!   85
She is abused, stol'n from me, and corrupted
By spells and medicines bought of
   mountebanks;
For nature so prepost'rously to err,
Being not deficient, blind, or lame of sense,   90
Sans witchcraft could not.

47 injointed, joined. 51 re-stem, steer again. 57
recommends, reports duteously to. 90 deficient, de-
ranged.

DUKE   Whoe'er he be that in this foul
    proceeding
    Hath thus beguiled your daughter of herself,
    And you of her, the bloody book of law   95
    You shall yourself read in the bitter letter
    After your own sense; yea, though our
    proper son
    Stood in your action.

BRABANTIO   Humbly I thank your Grace.   100
    Here is the man—this Moor, whom now, it
    seems,
    Your special mandate, for the state affairs,
    Hath hither brought.

ALL   We are very sorry for't.   105

DUKE   [*To* OTHELLO.] What, in your own part,
    can you say to this?

BRABANTIO   Nothing, but this is so.

OTHELLO   Most potent, grave, and reverend
    signiors,   110
    My very noble, and approved good masters:
    That I have ta'en away this old man's
    daughter,
    It is most true; true that I have married
    her.   115
    The very head and front of my offending
    Hath this extent, no more. Rude am I in my
    speech,
    And little blessed with the soft phrase of
    peace;   120
    For since these arms of mine had seven years'
    pith
    Till now some nine moons wasted, they have
    used
    Their dearest action in the tented field;   125
    And little of this great world can I speak
    More than pertains to feats of broil and battle;
    And therefore little shall I grace my cause
    In speaking for myself. Yet, by your gracious
    patience,   130
    I will a round unvarnished tale deliver
    Of my whole course of love—what drugs,
    what charms,
    What conjuration, and what mighty
    magic   135
    (For such proceeding am I charged withal)
    I won his daughter.

BRABANTIO   A maiden never bold;
    Of spirit so still and quiet that her motion

Blushed at herself; and she—in spite of   140
    nature,
Of years, of country, credit, everything—
To fall in love with what she feared to look on!
It is a judgment maimed and most imperfect
That will confess perfection so could err   145
Against all rules of nature, and must be driven
To find out practices of cunning hell
Why this should be. I therefore vouch again
That with some mixtures pow'rful o'er the
    blood,   150
Or with some dram, conjured to this effect,
He wrought upon her.

DUKE   To vouch this is no proof,
Without more certain and more overt test
Than these thin habits and poor likelihoods   155
Of modern seeming do prefer against
    him.

FIRST SENATOR   But, Othello, speak.
Did you by indirect and forced courses
Subdue and poison this young maid's   160
    affections?
Or came it by request, and such fair question
As soul to soul affordeth?

OTHELLO   I do beseech you,
Send for the lady to the Sagittary   165
And let her speak of me before her father.
If you do find me foul in her report,
The trust, the office, I do hold of you
Not only take away, but let your sentence
Even fall upon my life.   170

DUKE   Fetch Desdemona hither.

OTHELLO   Ancient, conduct them; you best
    know the place.
    [*Exeunt* IAGO *and two or three* ATTENDANTS.]
    And till she come, as truly as to heaven
    I do confess the vices of my blood,   175
    So justly to your grave ears I'll present
    How I did thrive in this fair lady's love,
    And she in mine.

DUKE   Say it, Othello.

OTHELLO   Her father loved me, oft invited   180
    me;
    Still questioned me the story of my life
    From year to year—the battles, sieges, fortunes
    That I have passed.
    I ran it through, even from my boyish days   185

---

99 *stood in your action,* were subject of your charges. 117 *Rude,* inexpert. 122 *pith,* strength. 123 *wasted,* gone by. 131 *round,* straightforward. 139 *motion,* emotion.

142 *credit,* reputation. 148 *vouch,* assert. 154 *overt test,* tangible evidence. 155 *thin habits,* flimsy garb. 156 *modern,* ordinary. 159 *indirect and forced courses,* illegal and violent means.

To the very moment that he bade me tell it.
Wherein I spake of most disastrous chances,
Of moving accidents by flood and field;
Of hairbreadth scapes i' th' imminent deadly
    breach!   190
Of being taken by the insolent foe
And sold to slavery; of my redemption thence
And portance in my travel's history;
Wherein of antres vast and deserts idle,
Rough quarries, rocks, and hills whose   195
    heads touch heaven,
It was my hint to speak—such was the process;
And of the Cannibals that each other eat,
The Anthropophagi, and men whose heads
Do grow beneath their shoulders. This to   200
    hear
Would Desdemona seriously incline;
But still the house affairs would draw her
    thence;
Which ever as she could with haste   205
    dispatch,
She'd come again, and with a greedy ear
Devour up my discourse. Which I observing,
Took once a pliant hour, and found good means
To draw from her a prayer of earnest heart   210
That I would all my pilgrimage dilate,
Whereof by parcels she had something heard,
But not intentively. I did consent,
And often did beguile her of her tears
When I did speak of some distressful   215
    stroke
That my youth suffered. My story being done,
She gave me for my pains a world of sighs.
She swore, in faith, 'twas strange, 'twas pass-
    ing strange;   220
'Twas pitiful, 'twas wondrous pitiful.
She wished she had not heard it; yet she
    wished
That heaven had made her such a man.
    She thanked me;   225
And bade me, if I had a friend that loved her,
I should but teach him how to tell my
    story,

And that would woo her. Upon this hint I
    spake.   230
She loved me for the dangers I had passed,
And I loved her that she did pity them.
This only is the witchcraft I have used.
Here comes the lady: let her witness it.
   [*Enter* DESDEMONA, IAGO, ATTENDANTS.]
DUKE   I think this tale would win my   235
    daughter too.
Good Brabantio,
Take up this mangled matter at the best.
Men do their broken weapons rather use
Than their bare hands.   240
BRABANTIO   I pray you hear her speak.
If she confess that she was half the wooer,
Destruction on my head if my bad blame
Light on the man! Come hither, gentle
    mistress.   245
Do you perceive in all this noble company
Where most you owe obedience?
DESDEMONA   My noble father,
I do perceive here a divided duty.
To you I am bound for life and   250
    education;
My life and education both do learn me
How to respect you: you are the lord of duty;
I am hitherto your daughter. But here's
    my husband;   255
And so much duty as my mother showed
To you, preferring you before her father,
So much I challenge that I may profess
Due to the Moor my lord.
BRABANTIO   God be with   260
    you! I have done.
Please it your Grace, on to the state affairs.
I had rather to adopt a child than get it.
Come hither, Moor.
I here do give thee that with all my heart   265
Which, but thou hast already, with all my
    heart
I would keep from thee. For your sake, jewel,
I am glad at soul I have no other child;
For thy escape would teach me tyranny,   270
To hang clogs on them. I have done, my lord.
DUKE   Let me speak like yourself and lay a
    sentence
Which, as a grise or step, may help these lovers
Into your favor.   275

188 *moving accidents . . . flood,* exciting events . . .
sea. 189–190 *th' imminent deadly breach,* death-
threat at the breach (in a fortress). 193 *portance*
carried on. 194 *antres . . . idle,* caves . . . empty.
197 *hint . . . process,* occasion . . . tale. 199 *Anthropophagi,* eaters of men. 209 *pliant hour,* opportune time. 211 *dilate,* expand upon. 213 *intentively,* without distraction.

229 *hint,* opportunity. 268 *For your sake,* because
of you. 270 *escape,* escapade. 274 *grise,* start.

When remedies are past, the griefs are ended
By seeing the worst, which late on hopes de-
    pended.
To mourn a mischief that is past and gone
Is the next way to draw new mischief on.   280
What cannot be preserved when fortune takes,
Patience her injury a mock'ry makes.
The robbed that smiles steals something from
    the thief;
He robs himself that spends a bootless   285
    grief.
BRABANTIO   So let the Turk of Cyprus us beguile:
We lose it not, so long as we can smile.
He bears the sentence well that nothing bears
But the free comfort which from thence   290
    he hears;
But he bears both the sentence and the sorrow
That to pay grief must of poor patience borrow.
These sentences, to sugar, or to gall,
Being strong on both sides, are equivocal.   295
But words are words: I never yet did hear
That the bruised heart was pierced through
    the ear.
I humbly beseech you, proceed to the affairs
    of state.   300
DUKE   The Turk with a most mighty preparation
makes for Cyprus. Othello, the fortitude of the
place is best known to you; and though we
have there a substitute of most allowed suffi-
ciency, yet opinion, a sovereign mistress of   305
effects, throws a more safer voice on you. You
must therefore be content to slubber the gloss
of your new fortunes with this more stubborn
and boist'rous expedition.
OTHELLO   The tyrant custom, most grave   310
    senators,
Hath made the flinty and steel couch of war
My thrice-driven bed of down. I do agnize
A natural and prompt alacrity
I find in hardness; and do undertake   315
These present wars against the Ottomites.
Most humbly, therefore, bending to your state,
I crave fit disposition for my wife;
Due reference of place, and exhibition,

With such accommodation and besort   320
As levels with her breeding.
DUKE   If you please,
Be't at her father's.
BRABANTIO   I'll not have it so.
OTHELLO   Nor I.   325
DESDEMONA   Nor would I there reside,
To put my father in impatient thoughts
By being in his eye. Most gracious Duke,
To my unfolding lend your prosperous ear,
And let me find a charter in your voice,   330
T' assist my simpleness.
DUKE   What would you, Desdemona?
DESDEMONA   That I did love the Moor to live
    with him,
My downright violence, and storm of   335
    fortunes,
May trumpet to the world. My heart's subdued
Even to the very quality of my lord.
I saw Othello's visage in his mind,
And to his honors and his valiant parts   340
Did I my soul and fortunes consecrate.
So that, dear lords, if I be left behind,
A moth of peace, and he go to the war,
The rights for which I love him are bereft me,
And I a heavy interim shall support   345
By his dear absence. Let me go with him.
OTHELLO   Let her have your voice.
Vouch with me heaven, I therefore beg it not
To please the palate of my appetite,
Nor to comply with heat, the young   350
    affects
In my defunct and proper satisfaction;
But to be free and bounteous to her mind.
And heaven defend your good souls that you
    think   355
I will your serious and great business scant
For she is with me. No, when light-winged
    toys
Of feathered Cupid seel with wanton dullness
My speculative and officed instruments,   360
That my disports corrupt and taint my
    business,
Let housewives make a skillet of my helm,

---

294 *to gall,* to embitter. 302 *fortitude,* strength (military).   304 *substitute,* representative (of the Duke—
Montano, Governor of Cyprus).   307 *slubber,* smear.
313 *thrice-driven . . . agnize,* thoroughly winnowed
(to guarantee softness) . . . acknowledge.   315
hardness, hardship. 317 *state,* authority. 319 *reference . . . exhibition,* assignment . . . allowance
(of money).

320 *besort,* appropriateness. 329 *prosperous,* sympathetic. 330 *charter,* assent. 350 *heat,* passion.
353 *mind,* wishes. 357 *For,* because. 359 *seel . . .
wanton dullness,* close . . . drowsiness brought on
by wantonness. 360 *speculative and officed instruments,* eyes charged with duty of watching. 361
disports, dalliance (with Desdemona).

And all indign and base adversities
Make head against my estimation!   365
DUKE   Be it as you shall privately determine,
Either for her stay or going. Th' affair cries
haste,
And speed must answer it. You must away
tonight.   370
OTHELLO   With all my heart.
DUKE   At nine i' th' morning here we'll meet
again.
Othello, leave some officer behind,
And he shall our commission bring   375
to you;
With such things else of quality and respect
As doth import you.
OTHELLO   So please your Grace, my
ancient.   380
A man he is of honesty and trust.
To his conveyance I assign my wife,
With what else needful your good Grace
shall think
To be sent after me.   385
DUKE   Let it be so.
Good night to everyone. [*To* BRABANTIO.]
And, noble signior,
If virtue no delighted beauty lack,
Your son-in-law is far more fair than   390
black.
FIRST SENATOR   Adieu, brave Moor. Use Desde-
mona well.
BRABANTIO   Look to her, Moor, if thou hast
eyes to see.   395
She has deceived her father, and may thee.
[*Exit with* DUKE, SENATORS, OFFICERS, *etc.*]
OTHELLO   My life upon her faith!—Honest Iago,
My Desdemona must I leave to thee.
I prithee let thy wife attend on her,
And bring them after in the best advan-   400
tage.
Come, Desdemona. I have but an hour
Of love, of worldly matters and direction,
To spend with thee. We must obey the time.
[*Exeunt* MOOR *and* DESDEMONA.]
RODERIGO   Iago.   405
IAGO   What say'st thou, noble heart?
RODERIGO   What will I do, think'st thou?
IAGO   Why, go to bed and sleep.

RODERIGO   I will incontinently drown myself.
IAGO   If thou dost, I shall never love thee   410
after. Why, thou silly gentleman!
RODERIGO   It is silliness to live when to live is
torment; and then have we a prescription to
die when death is our physician.
IAGO   O villainous! I have looked upon the   415
world for four times seven years; and since I
could distinguish betwixt a benefit and an
injury, I never found man that knew how to
love himself. Ere I would say I would drown
myself for the love of a guinea hen, I   420
would change my humanity with a baboon.
RODERIGO   What should I do? I confess it is my
shame to be so fond, but it is not in my virtue
to amend it.
IAGO   Virtue? a fig! 'Tis in ourselves that   425
we are thus or thus. Our bodies are our gardens, to the which our wills are gardeners; so
that if we will plant nettles or sow lettuce, set
hyssop and weed up thyme, supply it with one
gender of herbs or distract it with many—   430
either to have it sterile with idleness or ma-
nured with industry—why, the power and corrigible authority of this lies in our wills. If the
balance of our lives had not one scale of reason
to poise another of sensuality, the blood   435
and baseness of our natures would conduct us
to most prepost'rous conclusions. But we have
reason to cool our raging motions, our carnal
stings, our unbitted lusts; whereof I take this
that you call love to be a sect or scion.   440
RODERIGO   It cannot be.
IAGO   It is merely a lust of the blood and a permission of the will. Come, be a man! Drown
thyself? Drown cats and blind puppies! I have
professed me thy friend, and I confess me   445
knit to thy deserving with cables of perdurable
toughness. I could never better stead thee than
now. Put money in thy purse. Follow thou the
wars; defeat thy favor with an usurped beard.
I say, put money in thy purse. It cannot   450
be that Desdemona should long continue her
love to the Moor—put money in thy purse—

---

364 *indign,* disgraceful.   365 *estimation,* reputation.
378 *import,* concern.   382 *conveyance,* escort.   389
delighted, delight-giving.   400–401 *best advantage*
first opportunity.

409 *incontinently,* at once.   420 *guinea hen,* boorish
term for women; (cp. modern use of pigeon, chicken,
quail.)   423 *virtue,* power.   432–433 *corrigible,* reg-
ulative.   435 *poise,* counterbalance.   440 *sect or
scion,* cutting or graft.   449 *defeat thy favor with
an usurped beard,* change your appearance by growing a beard.

nor he his to her. It was a violent commencement, and thou shalt see an answerable sequestration. Put but money in thy purse. 455 These Moors are changeable in their wills. Fill thy purse with money. The food that to him now is as luscious as locusts shall be to him shortly as bitter as coloquintida. She must change for youth. When she is sated with 460 his body, she will find the error of her choice. She must have change, she must. Therefore put money in thy purse. If thou wilt needs damn thyself, do it a more delicate way than drowning. Make all the money thou canst. 465 If sanctimony and a frail vow betwixt an erring barbarian and a supersubtle Venetian be not too hard for my wits and all the tribe of hell, thou shalt enjoy her. Therefore make money. A pox of drowning thyself! It is clean out 470 of the way. Seek thou rather to be hanged in compassing thy joy than to be drowned and go without her.

RODERIGO Wilt thou be fast to my hopes, if I depend on the issue? 475

IAGO Thou art sure of me. Go, make money. I have told thee often, and I re-tell thee again and again, I hate the Moor. My cause is hearted; thine hath no less reason. Let us be conjunctive in our revenge against him. If 480 thou canst cuckold him, thou dost thyself a pleasure, me a sport. There are many events in the womb of time, which will be delivered. Traverse! go! provide thy money! We will have more of this tomorrow. Adieu. 485

RODERIGO Where shall we meet i' the morning?

IAGO At my lodging.

RODERIGO I'll be with thee betimes.

IAGO Go to, farewell.—Do you hear, Roderigo?

RODERIGO What say you? 490

IAGO No more of drowning, do you hear?

RODERIGO I am changed. I'll go sell all my land.
[*Exit.*]

IAGO Thus do I ever make my fool my purse;
For I mine own gained knowledge 495
should profane
If I would time expend with such a snipe
But for my sport and profit. I hate the Moor;

454–455 *answerable sequestration*, abrupt (as the elopement) estrangement. 459 *coloquintida*, medicine. 465 *make*, raise. 466–467 *erring, wandering*. 479 *hearted*, emotionally strong. 484 *traverse*, march. 497 *snipe*, silly fool.

And it is thought abroad that 'twixt my sheets 500
'Has done my office. I know not if't be true;
Yet I, for mere suspicion in that kind,
Will do as if for surety. He holds me well;
The better shall my purpose work on him.
Cassio's a proper man. Let me see now: 505
To get his place, and to plume up my will
In double knavery—How, how? Let's see.
After some time, to abuse Othello's ear
That he is too familiar with his wife.
He hath a person and a smooth dispose 510
To be suspected—framed to make women false.
The Moor is of a free and open nature
That thinks men honest that but seem to be so, 515
And will as tenderly be led by the nose
As asses are.
I have't! It is engend'red! Hell and night
Must bring this monstrous birth to the world's light. [*Exit.*] 520

ACT II

Scene I [*A seaport in Cyprus. An open place near the harbor.*]

[*Enter* MONTANO *and two* GENTLEMEN.]

MONTANO What from the cape can you discern at sea?

FIRST GENTLEMAN Nothing at all, it is a high-wrought flood;
I cannot 'twixt the heaven and the main 5
Descry a sail.

MONTANO Methinks the wind hath spoke aloud at land;
A fuller blast ne'er shook our battlements.
If it hath ruffianed so upon the sea, 10
What ribs of oak, when mountains melt on them,
Can hold the mortise? What shall we hear of this?

SECOND GENTLEMEN A segregation of the 15
Turkish fleet.
For do but stand upon the foaming shore,
The chidden billow seems to pelt the clouds;
The wind-shaked surge, with high and monstrous mane, 20

506 *plume up*, give status to.
5 *main*, sea. 15 *segregation*, dispersal.

Seems to cast water on the burning Bear
And quench the Guards of th' ever-fixed pole.
I never did like molestation view
On the enchafed flood.

MONTANO   If that the Turkish 25
fleet
Be not ensheltered and embayed, they are
drowned.
It is impossible they bear it out.

[*Enter a* THIRD GENTLEMAN.]

THIRD GENTLEMAN   News, lads! Our wars 30
are done.
The desperate tempest hath so banged the
Turks
That their designment halts. A noble ship of
Venice   35
Hath seen a grievous wrack and sufferance
On most part of their fleet.

MONTANO   How? Is this true?

THIRD GENTLEMAN   The ship is here
put in,   40
A Veronesa; Michael Cassio,
Lieutenant to the warlike Moor Othello,
Is come on shore; the Moor himself at sea,
And is in full commission here for Cyprus.

MONTANO   I am glad on't. 'Tis a worthy 45
governor.

THIRD GENTLEMAN   But this same Cassio,
though he speak of comfort
Touching the Turkish loss, yet he looks sadly
And prays the Moor be safe, for they 50
were parted
With foul and violent tempest.

MONTANO   Pray heaven he
be;
For I have served him, and the man 55
commands
Like a full soldier. Let's to the seaside, ho!
As well to see the vessel that's come in
As to throw out our eyes for brave Othello,
Even till we make the main and th' 60
aerial blue
An indistinct regard.

THIRD GENTLEMAN   Come, let's do so;
For every minute is expectancy

Of more arrivance.   65

[*Enter* CASSIO.]

CASSIO   Thanks you, the valiant of this warlike
isle,
That so approve the Moor! O, let the heavens
Give him defense against the elements,
For I have lost him on a dangerous sea! 70

MONTANO   Is he well shipped?

CASSIO   His bark is stoutly timbered, and his
pilot
Of very expert and approved allowance.
Therefore my hopes (not surfeited to 75
death)
Stand in bold cure.

[*Within.*] "A sail, a sail, a sail!"

[*Enter a* MESSENGER.]

CASSIO   What noise?

MESSENGER   The town is empty; on the 80
brow o' the sea
Stand ranks of people, and they cry "A sail!"

CASSIO   My hopes do shape him for the Governor. [*A shot.*]

SECOND GENTLEMAN   They do discharge 85
their shot of courtesy.
Our friends at least.

CASSIO   I pray you, sir, go forth
And give us truth who 'tis that is arrived.

SECOND GENTLEMAN   I shall. [*Exit.*] 90

MONTANO   But, good Lieutenant, is your general
wived?

CASSIO   Most fortunately. He hath achieved a
maid
That paragons description and wild fame; 95
One that excels the quirks of blazoning pens,
And in th' essential vesture of creation
Does tire the ingener.

[*Enter* SECOND GENTLEMAN.]

                              How now? Who has put in?

SECOND GENTLEMAN   'Tis one Iago, 100
ancient to the General.

CASSIO   Has had most favorable and happy
speed.
Tempests themselves, high seas, and howling
winds,   105

22 *Guards,* stars in the Little Bear constellation.
23 *molestation,* violent disturbance. 24 *enchafed,* en-
raged. 34 *designment halts,* intentions are stopped.
36 *sufferance,* disaster. 60–62 (The blue of the
water and the blue of the sky cannot be distinctly
separated.)

75–77 (Cassio's hopes for Othello's safety have not
been overfed—*surfeited*—and, therefore, may soon
be realized.) 95 *paragons,* surpasses. 96–98 (Desdemona in her essential qualities—*essential vesture
of creation*—is superior to whatever ingenuities—
quirks—of praise—*blazoning*—can be bestowed
upon her by a professional praiser—*ingener.*)

The guttered rocks and congregated sands,
Traitors ensteeped to clog the guiltless keel,
As having sense of beauty, do omit
Their mortal natures, letting go safely by
The divine Desdemona.   110
MONTANO   What is she?
CASSIO   She that I spake of, our great captain's
   captain,
Left in the conduct of the bold Iago,
Whose footing here anticipates our   115
   thoughts
A se'nnight's speed. Great Jove, Othello guard,
And swell his sail with thine own pow'rful
   breath,
That he may bless this bay with his   120
   tall ship,
Make love's quick pants in Desdemona's arms,
Give renewed fire to our extincted spirits,
And bring all Cyprus comfort!
[*Enter* DESDEMONA, IAGO, RODERIGO, *and* EMILIA
   with ATTENDANTS.]
                              O, behold!   125
The riches of the ship is come on shore!
You men of Cyprus, let her have your knees.
Hail to thee, lady! and the grace of heaven,
Before, behind thee, and on every hand,
Enwheel thee round!   130
DESDEMONA   I thank you, valiant Cassio.
What tidings can you tell me of my lord?
CASSIO   He is not yet arrived; nor know I aught
But that he's well and will be shortly here.
DESDEMONA   O, but I fear! How lost you   135
   company?
CASSIO   The great contention of the sea and skies
Parted our fellowship.
            [*Within.*] "A sail, a sail!" [*A shot.*]
But hark. A sail!   140
SECOND GENTLEMAN   They gave their greeting
   to the citadel.
This likewise is a friend.
CASSIO   See for the news.
   [*Exit* GENTLEMAN.]   145
Good ancient, you are welcome. [*To* EMELIA.]
   Welcome, mistress.
Let it not gall your patience, good Iago,
That I extend my manners. 'Tis my breeding
That gives me this bold show of cour-   150
   tesy. [*Kisses her.*]

IAGO   Sir, would she give you so much of her lips
As of her tongue she oft bestows on me,
You would have enough.
DESDEMONA   Alas, she has no speech!   155
IAGO   In faith, too much.
I find it still when I have list to sleep.
Marry, before your ladyship, I grant,
She puts her tongue a little in her heart
And chides with thinking.   160
EMILIA   You have little cause to say so.
IAGO   Come on, come on! You are pictures out
   of doors,
Bells in your parlors, wildcats in your kitchens,
Saints in your injuries, devils being of-   165
   fended,
Players in your housewifery, and housewives
   in your beds.
DESDEMONA   O, fie upon thee, slanderer!
IAGO   Nay, it is true, or else I am a Turk.   170
You rise to play, and go to bed to work.
EMILIA   You shall not write my praise.
IAGO   No, let me not.
DESDEMONA   What wouldst thou write of me, if
   thou shouldst praise me?   175
IAGO   O gentle lady, do not put me to't,
For I am nothing if not critical.
DESDEMONA   Come on, assay.—There's one gone
   to the harbor?
IAGO   Ay, madam.   180
DESDEMONA   I am not merry; but I do beguile
The thing I am by seeming otherwise.
Come, how wouldst thou praise me?
IAGO   I am about it; indeed my invention
Comes from my pate as birdlime does   185
   from frieze—
It plucks out brains and all. But my Muse la-
   bors,
And thus she is delivered:

If she be fair and wise, fairness and   190
   wit—
The one's for use, the other useth it.
DESDEMONA   Well praised! How if she be black
   and witty?

IAGO   195
If she be black, and thereto have a wit,
She'll find a white that shall her blackness fit.

117 *se'nnight's,* seven-night's (week's).   123 *ex-tincted,* dropping.   130 *Enwheel,* circle.   149 *extend,* show.

157 *list,* desire.   167 *housewifery . . . housewives,* housework . . . hussies.   178 *assay,* try.   185–186 *birdlime . . . frieze,* sticky substance . . . nubby cloth.   193 *black,* brunette.

DESDEMONA   Worse and worse!

EMILIA   How if fair and foolish?

IAGO   200

  She never yet was foolish that was fair,
  For even her folly helped her to an heir.

DESDEMONA   These are old fond paradoxes to make fools laugh i' th' alehouse. What miserable praise hast thou for her that's foul 205 and foolish?

IAGO

  There's none so foul, and foolish thereunto,
  But does foul pranks which fair and wise
    ones do.   210

DESDEMONA   O heavy ignorance! Thou praisest the worst best. But what praise couldst thou bestow on a deserving woman indeed—one that, in the authority of her merit, did justly put on the vouch of very malice 215 itself?

IAGO

  She that was ever fair, and never proud;
  Had tongue at will, and yet was never loud;
  Never lacked gold, and yet went   220
    never gay;
  Fled from her wish, and yet said "Now I
    may";
  She that, being angered, her revenge being
    nigh,   225
  Bade her wrong stay, and her displeasure fly;
  She that in wisdom never was so frail
  To change the cod's head for the
    salmon's tail;
  She that could think, and ne'er   230
    disclose her mind;
  See suitors following, and not look behind:
  She was a wight (if ever such wight were)—

DESDEMONA   To do what?

IAGO   235

  To suckle fools and chronicle small beer.

DESDEMONA   O most lame and impotent conclusion! Do not learn of him, Emilia, though

he be thy husband. How say you, Cassio? Is he not a most profane and liberal 240 counsellor?

CASSIO   He speaks home, madam. You may relish him more in the soldier than in the scholar.

IAGO   [*Aside.*] He takes her by the palm. 245 Ay, well said, whisper! With as little a web as this will I ensnare as great a fly as Cassio. Ay, smile upon her, do! I will gyve thee in thine own courtship. You say true; 'tis so, indeed! If such tricks as these strip you out of your 250 lieutenantry, it had been better you had not kissed your three fingers so oft—which now again you are most apt to play the sir in. Very good! well kissed! an excellent curtsy! 'Tis so, indeed. Yet again your fingers to 255 your lips? Would they were clyster pipes for your sake! [*Trumpet within.*] The Moor! I know his trumpet.

CASSIO   'Tis truly so.

DESDEMONA   Let's meet him and receive 260 him.

CASSIO   Lo, where he comes!
    [*Enter* OTHELLO *and* ATTENDANTS.]

OTHELLO   O my fair warrior!

DESDEMONA   My dear Othello!

OTHELLO   It gives me wonder great as my 265
    content
  To see you here before me. O my soul's joy!
  If after every tempest come such calms,
  May the winds blow till they have wakened
    death!   270
  And let the laboring bark climb hills of seas
  Olympus-high, and duck again as low
  As hell's from heaven! If it were now to die,
  'Twere now to be most happy; for I fear
  My soul hath her content so absolute 275
  That not another comfort like to this
  Succeeds in unknown fate.

DESDEMONA   The heavens forbid
  But that our loves and comforts should in-
    crease   280
  Even as our days do grow!

OTHELLO   Amen to that, sweet powers!
  I cannot speak enough of this content;

---

202 *folly*, unchastity. 203 *fond*, foolish. 205 *foul*, ugly. 215 *put on the vouch*, compel the approval. 236 *chronicle small beer*, keep petty accounts.

240 *profane and liberal*, gross and licentious. 242 *home*, frankly. 248–249 *gyve . . . courtship*, fetter . . . courtesy. 252 *kissed your three fingers* (a courtly formality). 253 *to play the sir*, act the chivalrous gentleman. 256 *clyster*, syringe.

It stops me here; it is too much of joy.
And this, and this, the greatest discords   285
    be [*They kiss.*]
That e'er our hearts shall make!

IAGO   [*Aside.*] O, you are well tuned now!
But I'll set down the pegs that make this
    music,   290
As honest as I am.

OTHELLO   Come, let us to the castle.
News, friends! Our wars are done; the Turks
    are drowned.
How does my old acquaintance of this   295
    isle?—
Honey, you shall be well desired in Cyprus;
I have found great love amongst them. O my
    sweet,
I prattle out of fashion, and I dote   300
In mine own comforts. I prithee, good Iago,
Go to the bay and disembark my coffers.
Bring thou the master to the citadel.
He is a good one, and his worthiness
Does challenge much respect.—Come,   305
    Desdemona,
Once more well met at Cyprus. [*Exeunt all
    but* IAGO *and* RODERIGO.]

IAGO   Do thou meet me presently at the harbor.
Come hither. If thou be'st valiant (as they   310
say base men being in love have then a nobility in their natures more than is native to
them), list me. The Lieutenant tonight watches
on the court of guard. First, I must tell thee
this: Desdemona is directly in love with   315
him.

RODERIGO   With him? Why, 'tis not possible.

IAGO   Lay thy finger thus, and let thy soul be instructed. Mark me with what violence she first
loved the Moor, but for bragging and   320
telling her fantastical lies; and will she love
him still for prating? Let not thy discreet heart
think it. Her eye must be fed; and what delight shall she have to look on the devil? When
the blood is made dull with the act of   325
sport, there should be, again to inflame it and
to give satiety a fresh appetite, loveliness in
favor, sympathy in years, manners, and beauties; all which the Moor is defective in. Now
for want of these required conveniences,   330

her delicate tenderness will find itself abused,
begin to heave the gorge, disrelish and abhor
the Moor. Very nature will instruct her in it
and compel her to some second choice. Now,
sir, this granted (as it is a most pregnant   335
and unforced position), who stands so eminent
in the degree of this fortune as Cassio does? A
knave very voluble; no further conscionable
than in putting on the mere form of civil and
humane seeming for the better compass   340
of his salt and most hidden loose affection?
Why, none! why, none! A slipper and subtle
knave; a finder of occasion; that has an eye
can stamp and counterfeit advantages, though
true advantage never present itself; a   345
devilish knave! Besides, the knave is handsome,
young, and hath all those requisites in him that
folly and green minds look after. A pestilent
complete knave! and the woman hath found
him already.   350

RODERIGO   I cannot believe that in her. She's
full of most blessed condition.

IAGO   Blessed fig's-end! The wine she drinks is
made of grapes. If she had been blessed, she
would never have loved the Moor.   355
Blessed pudding! Didst thou not see her paddle
with the palm of his hand? Didst not mark
that?

RODERIGO   Yes, that I did; but that was but
courtesy.   360

IAGO   Lechery, by this hand! an index and obscure prologue to the history of lust and foul
thoughts. They met so near with their lips that
their breaths embraced together. Villainous
thoughts, Roderigo! When these mutuali-   365
ties so marshal the way, hard at hand comes
the master and main exercise, th' incorporate
conclusion. Pish! But, sir, be you ruled by me.
I have brought you from Venice. Watch you
tonight; for the command, I'll lay't upon   370
you. Cassio knows you not. I'll not be far from
you. Do you find some occasion to anger Cassio, either by speaking too loud, or tainting his
discipline, or from what other course you
please which the time shall more favor-   375
ably minister.

289 *set down the pegs,* change the turning (to produce disharmony). 328 *favor, sympathy,* features,
similarity. 330 *conveniences,* necessary features.

332 *heave the gorge,* become nauseated. 336 *position,* assertion. 338 *conscionable,* conscientious.
340–341 *humane . . . salt,* courteous . . . lustful.
342 *slipper,* slippery, tricky. 348 *green,* young, inex-
perienced. 352 *condition,* character. 356–366 *mu-
tualities,* familiarities. 367 *incorporate,* drawing of
two bodies together. 373 *tainting,* casting aspersions.

RODERIGO   Well.

IAGO   Sir, he is rash and very sudden in choler, and haply with his truncheon may strike at you. Provoke him that he may; for even,   380 out of that will I cause these of Cyprus to mutiny; whose qualification shall come into no true taste again but by the displanting of Cassio. So shall you have a shorter journey to your desires by the means I shall then have to   385 prefer them; and the impediment most profitably removed without the which there were no expectation of our prosperity.

RODERIGO   I will do this if I can bring it to any opportunity.   390

IAGO   I warrant thee. Meet me by-and-by at the citadel. I must fetch his necessaries ashore. Farewell.

RODERIGO   Adieu. [*Exit.*]

IAGO   That Cassio loves her, I do well   395
    believe it;
That she loves him, 'tis apt and of great credit.
The Moor (howbeit that I endure him not)
Is of a constant, loving, noble nature,
And I dare think he'll prove to   400
    Desdemona
A most dear husband. Now I do love her too;
Not out of absolute lust (though peradventure
I stand accountant for as great a sin)
But partly led to diet my revenge,   405
For that I do suspect the lusty Moor
Hath leaped into my seat; the thought whereof
Doth, like a poisonous mineral, gnaw my inwards;
And nothing can or shall content my soul   410
Till I am evened with him, wife for wife;
Or failing so, yet that I put the Moor
At least into a jealousy so strong
That judgment cannot cure. Which thing to do
If this poor trash of Venice, whom I   415
    trace
For his quick hunting, stand the putting on,
I'll have our Michael Cassio on the hip,
Abuse him to the Moor in the right garb
(For I fear Cassio with my nightcap too),   420
Make the Moor thank me, love me, and reward me
For making him egregiously an ass

---

382 *qualification,* pacification.   415-416 *whom I trace,* whom I restrain.   417 *putting on,* stirring up.   419 *garb,* fashion.

And practicing upon his peace and quiet
Even to madness. 'Tis here, but yet   425
    confused.
Knavery's plain face is never seen till used.
    [*Exit.*]

Scene II   [*Cyprus.   Before   Othello's Castle.*]

[*Enter Othello's* HERALD, *with a proclamation; people following.*]

HERALD   It is Othello's pleasure, our noble and valiant general, that, upon certain tidings now arrived, importing the mere perdition of the Turkish fleet, every man put himself into triumph; some to dance, some to make   5 bonfires, each man to what sport and revels his addiction leads him. For, besides these beneficial news, it is the celebration of his nuptial. So much was his pleasure should be proclaimed. All offices are open, and there is full   10 liberty of feasting from this present hour of five till the bell have told eleven. Heaven bless the isle of Cyprus and our noble general Othello! [*Exeunt.*]

Scene III   [*Cyprus. Within the Castle.*]

[*Enter* OTHELLO, DESDEMONA, CASSIO, *and* ATTENDANTS.]

OTHELLO   Good Michael, look you to the guard tonight.
Let's teach ourselves that honorable stop,
Not to outsport discretion.

CASSIO   Iago hath direction what to do;   5
But notwithstanding, with my personal eye
Will I look to't.

OTHELLO   Iago is most honest.
Michael, good night. Tomorrow with your
    earliest   10
Let me have speech with you.—Come, my
    dear love.
The purchase made, the fruits are to ensue;
That profit's yet to come 'tween me and you.—
Good night. [*Exeunt* OTHELLO *and* DESDE-   15
MONA *with* ATTENDANTS.]
    [*Enter* IAGO.]

CASSIO   Welcome, Iago. We must to the watch.

IAGO   Not this hour, Lieutenant; 'tis not yet ten

---

3 *mere perdition,* complete ruin.

o' the clock. Our general cast us thus early for
the love of his Desdemona; who let us not
therefore blame. He hath not yet made   20
wanton the night with her, and she is sport for
Jove.

CASSIO   She's a most exquisite lady.

IAGO   And I'll warrant her, full of game.

CASSIO   Indeed, she's a most fresh and deli-   25
cate creature.

IAGO   What an eye she has! Methinks it sounds
a parley to provocation.

CASSIO   An inviting eye; and yet methinks right
modest.   30

IAGO   And when she speaks, is it not an alarum
to love?

CASSIO   She is indeed perfection.

IAGO   Happiness to their sheets! Come, Lieutenant, I have a stoup of wine, and here   35
without are a brace of Cyprus gallants that
would fain have a measure to the health of
black Othello.

CASSIO   Not tonight, good Iago. I have very poor
and unhappy brains for drinking. I could   40
well wish courtesy would invent some other
custom of entertainment.

IAGO   O, they are our friends. But one cup! I'll
drink for you.

CASSIO   I have drunk but one cup tonight,   45
and that was craftily qualified too; and behold
what innovation it makes here. I am unfortunate in the infirmity and dare not task my
weakness with any more.

IAGO   What, man! 'Tis a night of revels.   50
The gallants desire it.

CASSIO   Where are they?

IAGO   Here at the door. I pray you call them in.

CASSIO   I'll do't, but it dislikes me. [Exit.]

IAGO   If I can fasten but one cup upon him   55
With that which he hath drunk tonight al-
ready,
He'll be as full of quarrel and offense
As my young mistress' dog. Now my sick fool
Roderigo,   60
Whom love hath turned almost the wrong side
out,
To Desdemona hath tonight caroused
Potations pottle-deep; and he's to watch.
Three lads of Cyprus—noble swelling   65
spirits,

18 *cast*, got rid of.   24 *full of game*, full of lust.
31 *alarum*, urgent invitation.   35 *stoup*, tankard.
46 *craftily qualified*, slyly weakened, diluted.

That hold their honors in a wary distance,
The very elements of this warlike isle—
Have I tonight flustered with flowing cups,
And they watch too. Now, 'mongst this   70
flock of drunkards
Am I to put out Cassio in some action
That may offend the isle.

[*Enter* CASSIO, MONTANO, *and* GENTLEMEN;
SERVANT *with wine*.]

But here they come.

If consequence do but approve my dream,   75
My boat sails freely, both with wind and
stream.

CASSIO   Fore God, they have given me a rouse already.

MONTANO   Good faith, a little one; not past   80
a pint, as I am a soldier.

IAGO   Some wine, ho!

[*Sings.*]
And let me the canakin clink, clink;
And let me the canakin clink.
A soldier's a man;   85
A life's but a span,
Why then, let a soldier drink.

Some wine, boys!

CASSIO   Fore God, an excellent song!

IAGO   I learned it in England, where indeed   90
they are most potent in potting. Your Dane,
your German, and your swag-bellied Hollander—Drink, ho!—are nothing to your
English.

CASSIO   Is your Englishman so expert in   95
his drinking?

IAGO   Why, he drinks you with facility your
Dane dead drunk; he sweats not to overthrow
your Almain; he gives your Hollander a vomit
ere the next pottle can be filled.   100

CASSIO   To the health of our General!

MONTANO   I am for it, Lieutenant, and I'll do
you justice.

IAGO   O sweet England!

[*Sings.*]
King Stephen was and a worthy peer;   105
His breeches cost him but a crown;
He held 'em sixpence all too dear,
With that he called the tailor lown.

67 *in a wary distance*, on guard (against any offense).   99 *Almain*, German.   108 *lown*, cheat.

He was a wight of high renown,
   And thou art but of low degree.   110
'Tis pride that pulls the country down;
   Then take thine auld cloak about thee.

Some wine, ho!

CASSIO   Fore God, this is a more exquisite song
than the other.   115

IAGO   Will you hear't again?

CASSIO   No, for I hold him unworthy of his
place that does those things. Well, God's above
all; and there be souls must be saved, and there
be souls must not be saved.   120

IAGO   It's true, good Lieutenant.

CASSIO   For mine own part—no offense to the
General, nor any man of quality—I hope to be
saved.

IAGO   And so do I too, Lieutenant.   125

CASSIO   Ay, but, by your leave, not before me.
The lieutenant is to be saved before the
ancient. Let's have no more of this; let's to
our affairs. God forgive us our sins! Gentlemen,
let's look to our business. Do you think,   130
gentlemen, I am drunk. This is my ancient.
This is my right hand, and this is my left. I
am not drunk now. I can stand well enough,
and speak well enough.

ALL   Excellent well!   135

CASSIO   Why, very well then. You must not think
then that I am drunk. [*Exit.*]

MONTANO   To the platform, masters. Come, let's
set the watch.

IAGO   You see this fellow that is gone be-   140
fore.

He is a soldier fit to stand by Caesar
And give direction; and do but see his vice.
'Tis to his virtue a just equinox,
The one as long as th' other. 'Tis pity   145
   of him.
I fear the trust Othello puts him in,
On some odd time of his infirmity,
Will shake this island.

MONTANO   But is he often thus?   150

IAGO   'Tis evermore the prologue to his sleep.
He'll watch the horologe a double set
If drink rock not his cradle.

MONTANO   It were well
The General were put in mind of it.   155

144 *just equinox,* precisely equal. 152 *horologe a
double set,* clock twice around (Cassio cannot sleep
without the aid of drinking).

Perhaps he sees it not, or his good nature
Prizes the virtue that appears in Cassio
And looks not on his evils. Is not this true?
   [*Enter* RODERIGO.]

IAGO   [*Aside to him.*] How now, Roderigo?
I pray you after the Lieutenant, go!   160
   [*Exit* RODERIGO.]

MONTANO   And 'tis great pity that the noble
   Moor
Should hazard such a place as his own second
With one of an engraffed infirmity.
It were an honest action to say   165
So to the Moor.

IAGO   Not I, for this fair island!
I do love Cassio well and would do much
To cure him of this evil.
   [*Within.*] "Help! Help!"   170
   But hark! What noise?
   [*Enter* CASSIO, *driving in* RODERIGO.]

CASSIO   Zounds, you rogue! you rascal!

MONTANO   What's the matter, Lieutenant?

CASSIO   A knave teach me my duty?
I'll beat the knave into a twiggen bottle.   175

RODERIGO   Beat me?

CASSIO   Dost thou prate, rogue? [*Strikes him.*]

MONTANO   Nay, good Lieutenant! [*Takes his
arm.*] I pray you, sir, hold your hand.

CASSIO   Let me go, sir,   180
Or I'll knock you o'er the mazzard.

MONTANO   Come, come, you're drunk!

CASSIO   Drunk?   [*They fight.*]

IAGO   [*Aside to* RODERIGO.] Away, I say! Go
out and cry a mutiny! [*Exit   185
Roderigo.*]
Nay, good Lieutenant. God's will, gentlemen!
Help, ho!—Lieutenant—sir—Montano—sir—
Help, masters!—Here's a goodly watch indeed!
   [*A bell rung.*]
Who's that which rings the bell? Diablo,   190
   ho!
The town will rise. God's will, Lieutenant,
   hold!
You will be shamed for ever.
   [*Enter* OTHELLO *and* ATTENDANTS.]

OTHELLO   What is the matter here?   195

MONTANO   I bleed still. I am hurt to death. He
   dies!

OTHELLO   Hold for your lives!

IAGO   Hold, hold! Lieutenant—sir—
Montano—gentlemen!   200

175 *twiggen,* wicker-covered. 181 *mazzard,* head.

Have you forgot all sense of place and duty?
Hold! The General speaks to you. Hold, hold,
for shame!

OTHELLO   Why, how now, ho? From whence
ariseth this?   205

Are we turned Turks, and to ourselves do that
Which heaven hath forbid the Ottomites?
For Christian shame put by this barbarous
brawl!
He that stirs next to carve for his own rage   210
Holds his soul light; he dies upon his motion.
Silence that dreadful bell! It frights the isle
From her propriety. What's the matter,
masters?
Honest Iago, that looks dead with grieving,   215
Speak. Who began this? On thy love, I charge
thee.

IAGO   I do not know. Friends all but now, even
now,
In quarter, and in terms like bride and   220
groom
Devesting them for bed; and then, but now
(As if some planet had unwitted men)
Swords out, and tilting one at other's breast
In opposition bloody. I cannot speak   225
Any beginning to this peevish odds,
And would in action glorious I had lost
Those legs that brought me to a part of it!

OTHELLO   How comes it, Michael, you are thus
forgot?   230

CASSIO   I pray you pardon me; I cannot speak.

OTHELLO   Worthy Montano, you were wont be
civil;
The gravity and stillness of your youth
The world hath noted, and your name is   235
great
In mouths of wisest censure. What's the matter
That you unlace your reputation thus
And spend your rich opinion for the name
Of a night-brawler? Give me answer to't.   240

MONTANO   Worthy Othello, I am hurt to
danger.
Your officer, Iago, can inform you,
While I spare speech, which something now
offends me,   245
Of all that I do know; nor know I aught
By me that's said or done amiss this night,
Unless self-charity be sometimes a vice,
And to defend ourselves it be a sin
When violence assails us.   250

OTHELLO   Now, by heaven,
My blood begins my safer guides to rule,
And passion, having my best judgment collied,
Assays to lead the way. If I once stir
Or do but lift this arm, the best of you   255
Shall sink in my rebuke. Give me to know
How this foul rout began, who set it on;
And he that is approved in this offense,
Though he had twinned with me, both at a
birth,   260
Shall lose me. What! in a town of war,
Yet wild, the people's hearts brimful of fear,
To manage private and domestic quarrel?
In night, and on the court and guard of safety?
'Tis monstrous. Iago, who began 't?   265

MONTANO   If partially affined, or leagued in
office,
Thou dost deliver more or less than truth,
Thou art no soldier.

IAGO   Touch me not so near.   270
I had rather have this tongue cut from my
mouth
Than it should do offense to Michael Cassio.
Yet I persuade myself, to speak the truth
Shall nothing wrong him. Thus it is,   275
General.
Montano and myself being in speech,
There comes a fellow crying out for help,
And Cassio following him with determined
sword   280
To execute upon him. Sir, this gentleman
Steps in to Cassio and entreats his pause.
Myself the crying fellow did pursue,
Lest by his clamor (as it so fell out)
The town might fall in fright. He, swift   285
of foot,
Outran my purpose; and I returned the rather
For that I heard the clink and fall of swords,
And Cassio high in oath; which till tonight
I ne'er might say before. When I came   290
back
(For this was brief) I found them close together
At blow and thrust, even as again they were
When you yourself did part them.
More of this matter cannot I report;   295
But men are men; the best sometimes forget.
Though Cassio did some little wrong to him,

---

237 *censure*, judgment.

252 *blood*, passion.   253 *collied*, obscured.   257 *rout*,
brawl.   263 *manage*, engage in.   266 *partial affined*,
made partial by friendship.

As men in rage strike those that wish them
    best,
Yet surely Cassio I believe received   300
From him that fled some strange indignity,
Which patience could not pass.

OTHELLO   I know, Iago,
Thy honesty and love doth mince this matter,
Making it light to Cassio. Cassio, I love   305
    thee;
But never more be officer of mine.
    [*Enter* DESDEMONA, *attended.*]
Look if my gentle love be not raised up!
I'll make thee an example.

DESDEMONA   What's the matter, dear?   310

OTHELLO   All's well now, sweeting; come away
    to bed.
    [*To* MONTANO.] Sir, for your hurts, myself
    will be your surgeon.
Lead him off. [*Exit* MONTANO,   315
    attended.]
Iago, look with care about the town
And silence those whom this vile brawl dis-
    tracted.
Come, Desdemona. 'Tis the soldiers' life
To have their balmy slumbers waked with   320
    strife. [*Exeunt all but* IAGO *and* CASSIO.]

IAGO   What, are you hurt, Lieutenant?

CASSIO   Ay, past all surgery.

IAGO   Marry, God forbid!

CASSIO   Reputation, reputation, reputation!   325
O, I have lost my reputation! I have lost the
immortal part of myself, and what remains is
bestial. My reputation, Iago, my reputation!

IAGO   As I am an honest man, I thought you had
received some bodily wound; there is   330
more sense in that than in reputation. Reputation is an idle and most false imposition; oft
got without merit and lost without deserving.
You have lost no reputation at all unless you
repute yourself such a loser. What, man!   335
there are ways to recover the General again.
You are but now cast in his mood—a punishment more in policy than in malice, even so as
one would beat his offenseless dog to affright
an imperious lion. Sue to him again, and   340
he's yours.

CASSIO   I will rather sue to be despised than to
deceive so good a commander with so slight,
so drunken, and so indiscreet an officer. Drunk?

and speak parrot? and squabble? swag-   345
ger? swear? and discourse fustian with one's
own shadow? O thou invisible spirit of wine, if
thou hast no name to be known by, let us call
thee devil!

IAGO   What was he that you followed with   350
your sword? What had he done to you?

CASSIO   I know not.

IAGO   Is't possible?

CASSIO   I remember a mass of things, but nothing
distinctly; a quarrel, but nothing where-   355
fore. O God, that men should put an enemy in
their mouths to steal away their brains! that
we should with joy, pleasance, revel, and applause transform ourselves into beasts!

IAGO   Why, but you are now well enough.   360
How came you thus recovered?

CASSIO   It hath pleased the devil drunkenness to
give place to the devil wrath. One unperfect-
ness shows me another, to make me frankly
despise myself.   365

IAGO   Come, you are too severe a moraler. As
the time, the place, and the condition of this
country stands, I could heartily wish this had
not so befall'n; but since it is as it is, mend it
for your own good.   370

CASSIO   I will ask him for my place again: he
shall tell me I am a drunkard! Had I as many
mouths as Hydra, such an answer would stop
them all. To be now a sensible man, by-and-by
a fool, and presently a beast! O strange!   375
Every inordinate cup is unblest, and the ingredient is a devil.

IAGO   Come, come, good wine is a good familiar
creature if it be well used. Exclaim no more
against it. And, good Lieutenant, I think   380
you think I love you.

CASSIO   I have well approved it, sir. I drunk?

IAGO   You or any man living may be drunk at a
time, man. I'll tell you what you shall do. Our
General's wife is now the General. I may   385
say so in this respect, for that he hath devoted
and given up himself to the contemplation,
mark, and denotement of her parts and graces.
Confess yourself freely to her. Importune her
help to put you in your place again.   390
She is of so free, so kind, so apt, so blessed a
disposition she holds it a vice in her goodness
not to do more than she is requested. This

---

346 *fustian*, nonsense. 358–359 *applause*, wish to
please. 373 *Hydra*, creature of many heads. 378
familiar, friendly.

332 *imposition*, attribute. 337 *mood*, (temporary)
anger.

broken joint between you and her husband entreat her to splinter; and my fortunes 395 against any lay worth naming, this crack of your love shall grow stronger than 'twas before.

CASSIO   You advise me well.

IAGO   I protest, in the sincerity of love and honest kindness. 400

CASSIO   I think it freely; and betimes in the morning will I beesech the virtuous Desdemona to undertake for me. I am desperate of my fortunes if they check me here.

IAGO   You are in the right. Good night, 405 Lieutenant; I must to the watch.

CASSIO   Good night, honest Iago. [*Exit.*]

IAGO   And what's he then that says I play the villain,
When this advice is free I give and honest, 410
Probal to thinking, and indeed the course
To win the Moor again? For 'tis most easy
Th' inclining Desdemona to subdue
In any honest suit. She's framed as fruitful
As the free elements. And then for her 415
To win the Moor—were't to renounce his baptism,
All seals and symbols of redeemed sin—
His soul is so enfettered to her love
That she may make, unmake, do what 420
she list,
Even as her appetite shall play the god
With his weak function. How am I then a
villain
To counsel Cassio to this parallel course, 425
Directly to his good? Divinity of hell!
When devils will the blackest sins put on,
They do suggest at first with heavenly shows,
As I do now. For whiles this honest fool
Plies Desdemona to repair his fortune, 430
And she for him pleads strongly to the Moor,
I'll pour this pestilence into his ear—
That she repeals him for her body's lust;
And by how much she strives to do him good, 435
She shall undo her credit with the Moor.
So will I turn her virtue into pitch,
And out of her own goodness make the net
That shall enmesh them all.

[*Enter* RODERIGO.]

395 *splinter,* bind with splints.   411 *probal,* expedient.   422 *appetite,* wishes.   423 *weak function,* easily controlled actions.   425 *parallel course,* a course in line (with Cassio's good).   433 *repeals,* seeks reversal of the sentence.

How now, Roderigo? 440

RODERIGO   I do follow here in the chase, not like a hound that hunts, but one that fills up the cry. My money is almost spent; I have been tonight exceedingly well cudgelled; and I think the issue will be, I shall have so much 445 experience for my pains; and so, with no money at all, and a little more wit, return again to Venice.

IAGO   How poor are they that have not patience! 450
What wound did ever heal but by degrees?
Thou know'st we work by wit, and not by witchcraft;
And wit depends on dilatory time.
Does't not go well? Cassio hath beaten 455
thee,
And thou by that small hurt hast cashiered Cassio.
Though other things grow fair against the sun,
Yet fruits that blossom first will first be 460
ripe.
Content thyself awhile. By th' mass, 'tis morning!
Pleasure and action make the hours seem short.
Retire thee; go where thou are billeted. 465
Away, I say! Thou shalt know more hereafter.
Nay, get thee gone! [*Exit* RODERIGO.]
Two things are to be done:
My wife must move for Cassio to her mistress;
Ill set her on; 470
Myself a while to draw the Moor apart
And bring him jump when he may Cassio find
Soliciting his wife. Ay, that's the way!
Dull not device by coldness and delay. [*Exit.*]

ACT III

Scene I   [*Cyprus. Within the Castle.*]

[*Enter* CASSIO, *with* MUSICIANS.]

CASSIO   Masters, play here, I will content your pains:
Something that's brief; and bid "Good morrow, General."

[*They play.*]

[*Enter the* CLOWN.]

CLOWN   Why, masters, have your instru- 5

457 *cashiered,* caused the discharge of.   472 *jump,* exactly.
1 *content,* reward.

ments been at Naples, that they speak i' th'
nose thus?

MUSICIANS   How, sir, how?

CLOWN   Are these, I pray, called wind instru-   10
ments?

MUSICIANS   Ay, marry, are they, sir.

CLOWN   O, thereby hangs a tail.

MUSICIANS   Whereby hangs a tale, sir?

CLOWN   Marry, sir, by many a wind instrument
that I know. But, masters, here's money   15
for you; and the General so likes your music
that he desires you, of all loves, to make no
more noise with it.

MUSICIANS   Well, sir, we will not.

CLOWN   If you have any music that may not   20
be heard, to't again. But, as they say, to hear
music the General does not greatly care.

MUSICIANS   We have none such, sir.

CLOWN   Then put up your pipes in your bag, for
I'll away. Go, vanish into air, away!   25
[Exeunt MUSICIANS.]

CASSIO   Dost thou hear, my honest friend?

CLOWN   No, I hear not your honest friend. I
hear you.

CASSIO   Prithee keep up thy quillets. There's a
poor piece of gold for thee. If the gentle-   30
woman that attends the General's wife be
stirring, tell her there's one Cassio entreats her
a little favor of speech. Wilt thou do this?

CLOWN   She is stirring, sir. If she will stir hither,
I shall seem to notify unto her.   35

CASSIO   Do, good my friend. [Exit CLOWN.]
[Enter IAGO.]
                        In happy time, Iago.

IAGO   You have not been abed then?

CASSIO   Why, no. The day had broke
Before we parted. I have made bold, Iago,   40
To send in to your wife. My suit to her
Is that she will to virtuous Desdemona
Procure me some access.

IAGO   I'll send her to you presently;
And I'll devise a mean to draw the Moor   45
Out of the way, that your converse and business
May be more free.

CASSIO   I humbly thank you for't. [Exit IAGO.]
                          I never knew
A Florentine more kind and honest.   50
[Enter EMILIA.]

EMILIA   Good morrow, good Lieutenant. I am
sorry

For your displeasure; but all will sure be well.
The General and his wife are talking of it,
And she speaks for you stoutly. The Moor   55
replies
That he you hurt is of great fame in Cyprus
And great affinity, and that in wholesome wis-
dom
He might not but refuse you. But he pro-   60
tests he loves you,
And needs no other suitor but his likings
To take the safest occasion by the front
To bring you in again.

CASSIO   Yet I beseech you,   65
If you think fit, or that it may be done,
Give me advantage of some brief discourse
With Desdemona alone.

EMILIA   Pray you come in.
I will bestow you where you shall have   70
time
To speak your bosom freely.

CASSIO   I am much bound to you.
[Exeunt.]

Scene II   [Cyprus. Within the Castle.]

[Enter OTHELLO, IAGO, and GENTLEMEN.]

OTHELLO   These letters give, Iago, to the pilot
And by him do my duties to the senate.
That done, I will be walking on the works.
Repair there to me.

IAGO   Well, my good lord, I'll do't.   5

OTHELLO   This fortification, gentlemen, shall we
see't?

GENTLEMEN   We'll wait upon your lordship.
[Exeunt.]

Scene III   [Cyprus. The garden of the Castle.]

[Enter DESDEMONA, CASSIO, and EMILIA.]

DESDEMONA   Be thou assured, good Cassio, I
will do
All my abilities in thy behalf.

EMILIA   Good madam, do. I warrant it grieves
my husband   5
As if the cause were his.

DESDEMONA   O, that's an honest fellow. Do not
doubt, Cassio,
But I will have my lord and you again

---

29 *quillets,* word play.   44 *presently,* immediately.

58 *affinity,* kinspeople.
3 *works,* breastworks (fortifications).

As friendly as you were.   10

CASSIO   Bounteous madam,
Whatever shall become of Michael Cassio,
He's never anything but your true servant.

DESDEMONA   I know't; I thank you. You do love
    my lord;   15
You have known him long; and be you well
    assured
He shall in strangeness stand no further off
Than in a politic distance.

CASSIO   Ay, but, lady,   20
That policy may either last so long,
Or feed upon such nice and waterish diet,
Or breed itself so out of circumstance,
That, I being absent, and my place supplied,
My General will forget my love and service.   25

DESDEMONA   Do not doubt that. Before Emilia
    here
I give thee warrant of thy place. Assure thee,
If I do vow a friendship, I'll perform it
To the last article. My lord shall never rest;   30
I'll watch him tame and talk him out of pa-
    tience;
His bed shall seem a school, his board a shrift;
I'll intermingle everything he does
With Cassio's suit. Therefore be merry,   35
    Cassio,
For thy solicitor shall rather die
Than give thy cause away.
           [*Enter* OTHELLO *and* IAGO.]

EMILIA   Madam, here comes my lord.

CASSIO   Madam, I'll take my leave.   40

DESDEMONA   Why, stay, and hear me speak.

CASSIO   Madam, not now. I am very ill at ease,
Unfit for mine own purposes.

DESDEMONA   Well, do your discretion. [*Exit*
    CASSIO.]

IAGO   Ha! I like not that.   45

OTHELLO   What dost thou say?

IAGO   Nothing, my lord; or if—I know not what.

OTHELLO   Was not that Cassio parted from my
    wife?

IAGO   Cassio, my lord? No, sure, I cannot   50
    think it,
That he would steal away so guilty-like,
Seeing you coming.

OTHELLO   I do believe 'twas he.

DESDEMONA   How now, my lord?   55

I have been talking with a suitor here,
A man that languishes in your displeasure.

OTHELLO   Who is't you mean?

DESDEMONA   Why, your lieutenant, Cassio.
    Good my lord,   60
If I have any grace or power to move you,
His present reconciliation take;
For if he be not one that truly loves you,
That errs in ignorance, and not in cunning,
I have no judgment in an honest face.   65
I prithee call him back.

OTHELLO   Went he hence now?

DESDEMONA   Yes, faith; so humbled
That he hath left part of his grief with me
To suffer with him. Good love, call him back.   70

OTHELLO   Not now, sweet Desdemon; some
    other time.

DESDEMONA   But shall't be shortly?

OTHELLO   The sooner, sweet, for you.

DESDEMONA   Shall't be tonight at supper?   75

OTHELLO   No, not tonight.

DESDEMONA   Tomorrow dinner then?

OTHELLO   I shall not dine at home.
I meet the captains at the citadel.

DESDEMONA   Why then, tomorrow night, or   80
    Tuesday morn,
Or Tuesday noon or night, or Wednesday
    morn.
I prithee name the time, but let it not
Exceed three days. I' faith, he's penitent;   85
And yet his trespass, in our common reason
(Save that, they say, the wars must make ex-
    amples
Out of their best) is not almost a fault
T' incur a private check. When shall he   90
    come?
Tell me, Othello. I wonder in my soul
What you could ask me that I should deny
Or stand so mamm'ring on. What? Michael
    Cassio,   95
That came a-wooing with you, and so many a
    time,
When I have spoke of you dispraisingly,
Hath ta'en your part—to have so much to do
To bring him in? Trust me, I could do   100
    much—

OTHELLO   Prithee no more. Let him come when
    he will!
I will deny thee nothing.

---

19 *politic,* expedient.   **22** *nice and waterish diet,* coy
and weak urgings.   **26** *doubt,* fear.   **31** *watch him
tame,* keep him awake until he gives in.   **33** *shrift,*
confessional.

62 *present,* immediate.   **90** *check,* rebuke.   **94** *mam-
m'ring,* hesitant.

DESDEMONA   Why, this is not a boon;   105
    'Tis as I should entreat you wear your gloves,
    Or feed on nourishing dishes, or keep you
       warm,
    Or sue to you to do a peculiar profit
    To your own person. Nay, when I have   110
       a suit
    Wherein I mean to touch your love indeed,
    It shall be full of poise and difficult weight,
    And fearful to be granted.
OTHELLO   I will deny thee nothing!   115
    Whereon I do beseech thee grant me this,
    To leave me but a little to myself.
DESDEMONA   Shall I deny you? No. Farewell,
    my lord.
OTHELLO   Farewell, my Desdemona. I'll   120
    come to thee straight.
DESDEMONA   Emilia, come.—Be as your fancies
    teach you.
    Whate'er you be, I am obedient. [*Exeunt*
    DESDEMONA *and* EMILIA.]
OTHELLO   Excellent   wretch!   Perdition   125
    catch my soul
    But I do love thee! and when I love thee not,
    Chaos is come again.
IAGO   My noble lord—
OTHELLO   What dost thou say, Iago?   130
IAGO   Did Michael Cassio, when you wooed my
    lady,
    Know of your love?
OTHELLO   He did, from first to last. Why dost
    thou ask?   135
IAGO   But for a satisfaction of my thought;
    No further harm.
OTHELLO   Why of thy thought, Iago?
IAGO   I did not think he had been acquainted
    with her.   140
OTHELLO   O, yes, and went between us very oft.
IAGO   Indeed?
OTHELLO   Indeed? Ay, indeed! Discern'st thou
    aught in that?
    Is he not honest?   145
IAGO   Honest, my lord?
OTHELLO   Honest? Ay, honest.
IAGO   My lord, for aught I know.
OTHELLO   What dost thou think?
IAGO   Think, my lord?   150
OTHELLO   Think, my lord?
    By heaven, he echoes me,
    As if there were some monster in his thought

    Too hideous to be shown. Thou dost mean
      something.   155
    I heard thee say even now, thou lik'st not that,
    When Cassio left my wife. What didst not like?
    And when I told thee he was of my counsel
    In my whole course of wooing, thou cried'st
      "Indeed?"   160
    And didst contract and purse thy brow to-
      gether,
    As if thou then hadst shut up in thy brain
    Some horrible conceit. If thou dost love
      me,   165
    Show me thy thought.
IAGO   My lord, you know I love you.
OTHELLO   I think thou dost;
    And, for I know thou'rt full of love and
      honesty   170
    And weigh'st thy words before thou giv'st
      them breath,
    Therefore these stops of thine fright me
      the more;
    For such things in a false disloyal knave   175
    Are tricks of custom; but in a man that's just
    They are close dilations, working from the
      heart
    That passion cannot rule.
IAGO   For Michael Cassio,   180
    I dare be sworn I think that he is honest.
OTHELLO   I think so too.
IAGO   Men should be what they seem;
    Or those that be not, would they might seem
      none!   185
OTHELLO   Certain, men should be what they
    seem.
IAGO   Why then, I think Cassio's an honest man.
OTHELLO   Nay, yet there's more in this.
    I prithee speak to me, as to thy   190
      thinkings,
    As thou dost ruminate, and give thy worst
      of thoughts
    The worst of words.
IAGO   Good my lord, pardon me.   195
    Though I am bound to every act of duty,
    I am not bound to that all slaves are free to.
    Utter my thoughts? Why, say they are vile
      and false,
    As where's that place whereinto foul   200
      things

112 *touch*, test.

158 *of my counsel*, my confidant.   164 *conceit*, idea.
177 *close dilations*, secret emotions.   179 *that passion cannot rule*, that cannot hide its emotion.

Sometimes intrude not? Who has a breast so pure
But some uncleanly apprehensions
Keep leets and law days, and in session sit 205
With meditations lawful?

OTHELLO   Thou dost conspire against thy friend, Iago,
If thou but think'st him wronged, and mak'st his ear 210
A stranger to thy thoughts.

IAGO   I do beseech you—
Though I perchance am vicious in my guess
(As I confess it is my nature's plague 215
To spy into abuses, and oft my jealousy
Shapes faults that are not)—that your wisdom
From one that so imperfectly conceits
Would take no notice, nor build yourself a trouble 220
Out of his scattering and unsure observance.
It were not for your quiet nor your good,
Nor for my manhood, honesty, or wisdom,
To let you know my thoughts.

OTHELLO   What dost thou mean? 225

IAGO   Good name in man and woman, dear my lord,
Is the immediate jewel of their souls.
Who steals my purse steals trash; 'tis something, nothing; 230
'Twas mine, 'tis his, and has been slave to thousands;
But he that filches from me my good name
Robs me of that which not enriches him
And makes me poor indeed. 235

OTHELLO   By heaven, I'll know thy thoughts!

IAGO   You cannot, if my heart were in your hand;
Nor shall not whilst 'tis in my custody.

OTHELLO   Ha! 240

IAGO   O, beware, my lord, of jealousy!
It is the green-eyed monster, which doth mock
The meat it feeds on. That cuckold lives in bliss
Who, certain of his fate, loves not his wronger; 245
But O, what damned minutes tells he o'er
Who dotes, yet doubts; suspects, yet strongly loves!

OTHELLO   O misery! 250

IAGO   Poor and content is rich, and rich enough;
But riches fineless is as poor as winter
To him that ever fears he shall be poor.
Good heaven, the souls of all my tribe defend 255
From jealousy!

OTHELLO   Why, why is this?
Think'st thou I'd make a life of jealousy,
To follow still the changes of the moon
With fresh suspicions? No! To be once 260
in doubt
Is once to be resolved. Exchange me for a goat
When I shall turn the business of my soul
To such exsufflicate and blown surmises,
Matching thy inference. 'Tis not to make 265
me jealous
To say my wife is fair, feeds well, loves company,
Is free of speech, sings, plays, and dances well.
Where virtue is, these are more virtuous. 270
Nor from mine own weak merits will I draw
The smallest fear or doubt of her revolt,
For she had eyes, and chose me. No, Iago;
I'll see before I doubt; when I doubt, prove;
And on the proof there is no more but 275
this—
Away at once with love or jealousy!

IAGO   I am glad of it; for now I shall have reason
To show the love and duty that I bear 280
you
With franker spirit. Therefore, as I am bound,
Receive it from me. I speak not yet of proof.
Look to your wife; observe her well with Cassio; 285
Wear your eye thus, not jealous nor secure.
I would not have your free and noble nature,
Out of self-bounty, be abused. Look to't.
I know our country disposition well:
In Venice they do let heaven see the 290
pranks
They dare not show their husbands; their best conscience
Is not to leave't undone, but keep't unknown.

204 *apprehensions,* imaginings. 205 *leets and law days,* sessions of the court. 214 *vicious,* mistaken. 216 *jealousy,* suspicious nature. 252 *fineless,* without bounds. 262 *to be resolved,* to have the doubt cleared up. 264 *exsufflicate and blown,* abominable and fly-blown (rotten). 265 *inference,* statement (about jealousy). 272 *revolt,* infidelity. 274 *prove,* test. 288 *self-bounty,* inner goodness.

OTHELLO   Dost thou say so?   295

IAGO   She did deceive her father, marrying you;
And when she seemed to shake and fear your
    looks,
She loved them most.

OTHELLO   And so she did.   300

IAGO   Why, go to then!
She that, so young, could give out such a
    seeming
To seel her father's eyes up close as oak—
He thought 'twas witchcraft—but I am   305
    much to blame.
I humbly do beseech you of your pardon
For too much loving you.

OTHELLO   I am bound to thee for ever.

IAGO   I see this hath a little dashed your   310
    spirits.

OTHELLO   Not a jot, not a jot.

IAGO   I' faith, I fear it has.
I hope you will consider what is spoke
Comes from my love. But I do see y'are   315
    moved.
I am to pray you not to strain my speech
To grosser issues nor to larger reach
Than to suspicion.

OTHELLO   I will not.   320

IAGO   Should you do so, my lord,
My speech should fall into such vile success
As my thoughts aim not at. Cassio's my worthy
    friend—
My lord, I see y'are moved.   325

OTHELLO   No, not much moved.
I do not think but Desdemona's honest.

IAGO   Long live she so! and long live you to
    think so!

OTHELLO   And yet, how nature erring from   330
    itself—

IAGO   Ay, there's the point! as (to be bold with
    you)
Not to affect many proposed matches
Of her own clime, complexion, and   335
    degree,
Whereto we see in all things nature tends—
Foh! one may smell in such a will most rank,
Foul disproportion, thoughts unnatural—
But pardon me—I do not in position   340

Distinctly speak of her; though I may fear
Her will, recoiling to her better judgment,
May fall to match you with her country
    forms,
And happily repent.   345

OTHELLO   Farewell, farewell!
If more thou dost perceive, let me know more.
Set on thy wife to observe. Leave me, Iago.

IAGO   My lord, I take my leave.   [Walks away.]

OTHELLO   Why did I marry? This honest   350
    creature doubtless
Sees and knows more, much more, than he
    unfolds.

IAGO   [Returns.] My lord, I would I might en-
    treat your Honor   355
To scan this thing no further. Leave it to time.
Although 'tis fit that Cassio have his place,
For sure he fills it up with great ability,
Yet, if you please to hold him off awhile,
You shall by that perceive him and his   360
    means.
Note if your lady strain his entertainment
With any strong or vehement importunity.
Much will be seen in that. In the mean time
Let me be thought too busy in my fears   365
(As worthy cause I have to fear I am)
And hold her free, I do beseech your Honor.

OTHELLO   Fear not my government.

IAGO   I once more take my leave.   [Exit.]

OTHELLO   This fellow's of exceeding   370
    honesty,
And knows all qualities, with a learned spirit
Of human dealings. If I do prove her hag-
    gard,
Though that her jesses were my dear   375
    heart-strings,
I'd whistle her off and let her down the wind
To prey at fortune. Haply, for I am black
And have not those soft parts of conver-
    sation   380
That chamberers have, or for I am declined
Into the vale of years (yet that's not much),
She's gone. I am abused, and my relief
Must be to loathe her. O curse of marriage,

---

304 *close as oak*, close as oak grain. 318 *grosser*,
exaggerated. 322 *vile success*, odious consequence.
327 *honest*, chaste. 334 *affect*, care for. 338 *will
. . . rank*, carnal desire . . . unhealthy. 340 *position*, positive statement.

341 *distinctly*, specifically. 342 *recoiling*, returning.
345 *happily*, perhaps. 361 *means*, method (of gaining reinstatement). 362 *strain . . . entertainment*,
push too hard . . . reinstatement. 365 *too busy*, too
great a busy body. 367 *free*, innocent. 373–374
haggard, unfaithful. 375 *jesses*, leash for hawks.
378 *prey at fortune* (shift for herself).

That we can call these delicate creatures 385
   ours,
And not their appetites! I had rather be a
   toad
And live upon the vapor of a dungeon
Than keep a corner in the thing I love 390
For others' uses. Yet 'tis the plague of great
   ones;
Prerogatived are they less than the base.
'Tis destiny unshunnable, like death:
Even then this forkéd plague is fated to us 395
When we do quicken. Desdemona comes.
      [*Enter* DESDEMONA *and* EMILIA.]
If she be false, O, then heaven mocks itself!
I'll not believe't.
DESDEMONA   How now, my dear Othello?
Your dinner, and the generous islanders 400
By you invited, do attend your presence.
OTHELLO   I am to blame.
DESDEMONA   Why do you speak so faintly?
Are you not well?
OTHELLO   I have a pain upon my forehead, 405
   here.
DESDEMONA   Faith, that's with watching; 'twill
   away again.
Let me but bind it hard, within this hour
It will be well. 410
OTHELLO   Your napkin is too little. [*He
pushes it away and it drops.*]
Let it alone. Come, I'll go in with you.
DESDEMONA   I am very sorry that you are not
   well. [*Exeunt* OTHELLO *and* DESDE- 415
   MONA.]
EMILIA   I am glad I have found this napkin.
This was her first remembrance from the
   Moor.
My wayward husband hath a hundred 420
   times
Wooed me to steal it; but she so loves the
   token
(For he conjured her she should ever keep it)
That she reserves it evermore about her 425
To kiss and talk to. I'll have the work ta'en out
And give't Iago.
What he will do with it heaven knows, not I;
I nothing but to please his fantasy.

[*Enter* IAGO.]
IAGO   How now? What do you here alone? 430
EMILIA   Do not you chide; I have a thing for
   you.
IAGO   A thing for me? It is a common thing—
EMILIA   Ha?
IAGO   To have a foolish wife. 435
EMILIA   O, is that all? What will you give me
   now
For that same handkerchief?
IAGO   What handkerchief?
EMILIA   What handkerchief? 440
Why that the Moor first gave to Desdemona;
That which so often you did bid me steal.
IAGO   Hast stol'n it from her?
EMILIA   No, faith; she let it drop by negligence,
And to th' advantage, I, being here, 445
   took't up.
Look, here it is.
IAGO   A good wench! Give it me.
EMILIA   What will you do with't, that you have
   been so earnest 450
To have me filch it?
IAGO   Why, what's that to you? [*Snatches it.*]
EMILIA   If it be not for some purpose of im-
   port,
Give't me again. Poor lady, she'll run 455
   mad
When she shall lack it.
IAGO   Be not you acknown on't; I have use for
   it.
Go, leave me. [*Exit* EMILIA.] 460
I will in Cassio's lodging lose this napkin
And let him find it. Trifles light as air
Are to the jealous confirmations strong
As proofs of holy writ. This may do some-
   thing. 465
The Moor already changes with my poison.
Dangerous conceits are in their natures poisons
Which at the first are scarce found to distaste,
But with a little act upon the blood
Burn like the mines of sulphur. 470
      [*Enter* OTHELLO.]
                I did say so.
Look where he comes! Not poppy nor man-
   dragora,
Nor all the drowsy syrups of the world,

---

393 *Prerogatived are they less than the base,* exempt
less than the lowly. 395 *forkéd plague,* horns (for
the cuckold). 396 *quicken,* start to live. 411 *napkin,* handkerchief. 413 *Let it alone* (never mind
about my head.) 420 *wayward,* whimsical. 426
work ta'en out, embroidery copied.

458 *Be not you acknown on't,* don't admit knowing
anything about it. 467 *conceits,* notions. 472–473
mandragora, sleep inducing medicine.

Shall ever medicine thee to that sweet   475
    sleep
Which thou ow'dst yesterday.
OTHELLO   Ha! ha! false to me?
IAGO   Why, how now, General? No more of that!
OTHELLO   Avaunt! be gone! Thou hast   480
    set me on the rack.
I swear 'tis better to be much abused
Than but to know't a little.
IAGO   How now, my lord?
OTHELLO   What sense had I of her stol'n   485
    hours of lust?
I saw't not, thought it not, it harmed not me.
I slept the next night well, was free and merry;
I found not Cassio's kisses on her lips.
He that is robbed, not wanting what is   490
    stol'n,
Let him not know't, and he's not robbed at
    all.
IAGO   I am sorry to hear this.
OTHELLO   I had been happy if the general   495
    camp,
Pioners and all, had tasted her sweet body,
So I had nothing known. O, now for ever
Farewell the tranquil mind! farewell content!
Farewell the plumed troop, and the big   500
    wars
That make ambition virtue! O, farewell!
Farewell the neighing steed and the shrill
    trump,
The spirit-stirring drum, th' ear-piercing   505
    fife,
The royal banner, and all quality,
Pride, pomp, and circumstance of glorious
    war!
And O ye mortal engines whose rude   510
    throats
Th' immortal Jove's dread clamors counter-
    feit,
Farewell! Othello's occupation's gone!
IAGO   Is't possible, my lord?   515
OTHELLO   Villain, be sure thou prove my love a
    whore!
Be sure of it; give me the ocular proof;
Or, by the worth of man's eternal soul,
Thou hadst been better have been born a   520
    dog
Than answer my waked wrath!

IAGO   Is't come to this?
OTHELLO   Make me to see't; or at the least so
    prove it   525
That the probation bear no hinge nor loop
To hang a doubt on—or woe upon thy life!
IAGO   My noble lord—
OTHELLO   If thou dost slander her and torture
    me,   530
Never pray more; abandon all remorse;
On horror's head horrors accumulate;
Do deeds to make heaven weep, all earth
    amazed;
For nothing canst thou to damnation   535
    add
Greater than that.
IAGO   O grace! O heaven forgive me!
Are you a man? Have you a soul or sense?—
God b' wi' you! take mine office. O   540
    wretched fool,
That liv'st to make thine honesty a vice!
O monstrous world! Take note, take note, O
    world,
To be direct and honest is not safe.   545
I thank you for this profit; and from hence
I'll love no friend, sith love breeds such offense.
OTHELLO   Nay, stay. Thou shouldst be honest.
IAGO   I should be wise; for honesty's a fool
And loses that it works for.   550
OTHELLO   By the world,
I think my wife be honest, and think she is not;
I think that thou are just, and think thou art
    not.
I'll have some proof. Her name, that was   555
    as fresh
As Dian's visage, is now begrimed and black
As mine own face. If there be cords, or knives,
Poison, or fire, or suffocating streams,
I'll not endure it. Would I were satisfied!   560
IAGO   I see, sir, you are eaten up with passion.
I do repent me that I put it to you.
You would be satisfied?
OTHELLO   Would? Nay, I will.
IAGO   And may. But how? how satisfied, my   565
    lord?
Would you, the supervisor, grossly gape on?
Behold her topped?
OTHELLO   Death and damnation! O!
IAGO   It were a tedious difficulty, I think,   570

---

477 *ow'dst*, hadst.   482 *abused*, deceived.   485 *sense*,
feeling.   497 *pioners*, military dirt-diggers.

526 *probation*, proof.   531 *remorse*, pity.   540 *God
b' wi' you!* God be with you (good-bye).   567 *supervisor*, witness.

To bring them to that prospect. Damn them
   then,
If ever mortal eyes do see them bolster
More than their own! What then? How then?
What shall I say? Where's satisfaction?   575
It is impossible you should see this,
Were they as prime as goats, as hot as
   monkeys,
As salt as wolves in pride, and fools as
   gross   580
As ignorance made drunk. But yet, I say,
If imputation and strong circumstances
Which lead directly to the door of truth
Will give you satisfaction, you may have't.

OTHELLO Give me a living reason she's   585
   disloyal.

IAGO   I do not like the office.
But sith I am entered in this cause so far,
Pricked to't by foolish honesty and love,
I will go on. I lay with Cassio lately,   590
And being troubled with a raging tooth,
I could not sleep.
There are a kind of men so loose of soul
That in their sleeps will mutter their affairs.
One of this kind is Cassio.   595
In sleep I heard him say, "Sweet Desdemona,
Let us be wary, let us hide our loves!"
And then, sir, would he gripe and wring my
   hand,
Cry "O sweet creature!" and then kiss   600
   me hard,
As if he plucked up kisses by the roots
That grew upon my lips; then laid his leg
Over my thigh, and sighed, and kissed, and
   then   605
Cried "Cursed fate that gave thee to the
   Moor!"

OTHELLO O monstrous! monstrous!

IAGO   Nay, this was but his dream.

OTHELLO But this denoted a foregone   610
   conclusion.
'Tis a shrewd doubt, though it be but a dream.

IAGO   And this may help to thicken other proofs
That do demonstrate thinly.

OTHELLO   I'll tear her all to pieces!   615

IAGO   Nay, but be wise. Yet we see nothing
   done;

She may be honest yet. Tell me but this—
Have you not sometimes seen a handkerchief
Spotted with strawberries in your wive's   620
   hand?

OTHELLO I gave her such a one; 'twas my first
   gift.

IAGO   I know not that; but such a handkerchief
(I am sure it was your wive's) did I   625
   today
See Cassio wipe his beard with.

OTHELLO   If't be that—

IAGO   If it be that, or any that was hers,
It speaks against her, with the other   630
   proofs.

OTHELLO O, that the slave had forty thousand
   lives!
One is too poor, too weak for my revenge.
Now do I see 'tis true. Look here, Iago: 635
All my fond love thus do I blow to heaven.
'Tis gone.
Arise, black vengeance, from the hollow hell!
Yield up, O love, thy crown and hearted throne
To tyrannous hate! Swell, bosom, with   640
   thy fraught,
For 'tis of aspics' tongues!

IAGO   Yet be content.

OTHELLO O, blood, blood, blood!

IAGO   Patience, I say. Your mind perhaps   645
   may change.

OTHELLO Never, Iago. Like to the Pontic sea,
Whose icy current and compulsive course
Ne'er feels retiring ebb, but keeps due on
To the Propontic and the Hellespont;   650
Even so my bloody thoughts, with violent pace,
Shall ne'er look back, ne'er ebb to humble love,
Till that a capable and wide revenge
Swallow them up. [*He kneels.*] Now, by yon
   marble heaven,   655
In the due reverence of a sacred vow
I here engage my words.

IAGO   Do not rise yet. [IAGO *kneels.*]
Witness, you ever-burning lights above,
You elements that clip us round about,   660
Witness that here Iago doth give up
The execution of his wit, hands, heart
To wronged Othello's service! Let him com-
   mand,
And to obey shall be in me remorse,   665
What bloody business ever. [*They rise.*]

---

571 *prospect,* view. 573 *bolster,* lie together. 579
salt . . . pride, lustful . . . heat. 610–611 *foregone
conclusion,* past experience. 612 *shrewd doubt,* terribly suspicious thing.

642 *aspics',* serpents'. 653 *capable,* all-embracing.
657 *engage,* pledge. 660 *clip,* embrace.

OTHELLO   I greet thy love,
Not with vain thanks but with acceptance
     bounteous,
And will upon the instant put thee to't.   670
Within these three days let me hear thee say
That Cassio's not alive.

IAGO   My friend is dead; 'tis done at your re-
     quest.
But let her live.   675

OTHELLO   Damn her, lewd minx! O, damn her!
Come, go with me apart. I will withdraw
To furnish me with some swift means of death
For the fair devil. Now art thou my lieutenant.

IAGO   I am your own for ever. [*Exeunt.*]   680

Scene IV   [*Cyprus. Before the Castle.*]

[*Enter* DESDEMONA, EMILIA, *and* CLOWN.]

DESDEMONA   Do you know, sirrah, where Lieutenant Cassio lies?

CLOWN   I dare not say he lies anywhere.

DESDEMONA   Why man?

CLOWN   He's a soldier; and for one to say a   5
soldier lies is stabbing.

DESDEMONA   Go to. Where lodges he?

CLOWN   To tell you where he lodges is to tell
you where I lie.

DESDEMONA   Can anything be made of this?   10

CLOWN   I know not where he lodges; and for
me to devise a lodging, and say he lies here
or he lies there, were to lie in mine own
throat.

DESDEMONA   Can you enquire him out, and   15
be edified by report?

CLOWN   I will catechize the world for him;
that is, make questions, and by them answer.

DESDEMONA   Seek him, bid him come   20
hither. Tell him I have moved my lord on
his behalf and hope all will be well.

CLOWN   To do this is within the compass of
man's wit, and therefore I'll attempt the doing
it.   [*Exit.*]   25

DESDEMONA   Where should I lose that handkerchief, Emilia?

EMILIA   I know not, madam.

DESDEMONA   Believe me, I had rather have lost
my purse   30

Full of crusadoes; and but my noble Moor
Is true of mind, and made of no such base-
     ness
As jealous creatures are, it were enough
To put him to ill thinking.   35

EMILIA   Is he not jealous?

DESDEMONA   Who? he? I think the sun where
he was born
Drew all such humors from him.

          [*Enter* OTHELLO.]

EMILIA   Look where he comes.   40

DESDEMONA   I will not leave him now till Cassio
Be called to him.—How is't with you, my
     lord?

OTHELLO   Well, my good lady. [*Aside.*] O, hardness to dissemble!—   45
How do you, Desdemona?

DESDEMONA   Well, my good lord.

OTHELLO   Give me your hand. This hand is
moist, my lady.

DESDEMONA   It yet hath felt no age nor   50
known no sorrow.

OTHELLO   This argues fruitfulness and liberal
     heart.
Hot, hot, and moist. This hand of yours re-
     quires   55
A sequester from liberty, fasting and prayer,
Much castigation, exercise devout;
For here's a young and sweating devil
     here
That commonly rebels. 'Tis a good hand,   60
A frank one.

DESDEMONA   You may, indeed, say so;
For 'twas that hand that gave away my
     heart.

OTHELLO   A liberal hand! The hearts of   65
old gave hands;
But our new heraldry is hands, not hearts.

DESDEMONA   I cannot speak of this. Come now,
your promise!

OTHELLO   What promise, chuck?   70

DESDEMONA   I have sent to bid Cassio come
speak with you.

OTHELLO   I have a salt and sorry rheum offends
me.
Lend me thy handkerchief.   75

DESDEMONA   Here, my lord.

OTHELLO   That which I gave you.

DESDEMONA   I have it not about me.

---

16 *edified,* instructed.   21 *moved,* spoken to.

32 *crusadoes,* gold coins.   56 *sequester,* retirement.
73 *sorry rheum,* bad cold.

OTHELLO   Not?

DESDEMONA   No indeed, my lord.   80

OTHELLO   That is a fault.
That handkerchief
Did an Egyptian to my mother give.
She was a charmer, and could almost read
The thoughts of people. She told her,   85
while she kept it,
'Twould make her amiable and subdue my
father
Entirely to her love; but if she lost it
Or made a gift of it, my father's eye   90
Should hold her loathed, and his spirits should
hunt
After new fancies. She, dying, gave it me,
And bid me, when my fate would have me
wive,   95
To give it her. I did so; and take heed
on't;
Make it a darling like your precious eye.
To lose't or give't away were such perdition
As nothing else could match.   100

DESDEMONA   Is't possible?

OTHELLO   'Tis true. There's magic in the web
of it.
A sibyl that had numb'red in the world
The sun to course two hundred com-   105
passes,
In her prophetic fury sewed the work;
The worms were hallowed that did breed the
silk;
And it was dyed in mummy which the   110
skilful
Conserved of maidens' hearts.

DESDEMONA   I' faith? Is't true?

OTHELLO   Most veritable. Therefore look to't
well.   115

DESDEMONA   Then would to God that I had
never seen't!

OTHELLO   Ha! Wherefore?

DESDEMONA   Why do you speak so startingly
and rash?   120

OTHELLO   Is't lost? Is't gone? Speak, is it out
o' th' way?

DESDEMONA   Heaven bless us!

OTHELLO   Say you?

DESDEMONA   It is not lost. But what an if it   125
were?

OTHELLO   How?

DESDEMONA   I say it is not lost.

OTHELLO   Fetch't, let me see't!

DESDEMONA   Why, so I can, sir; but I will   130
not now.
This is a trick to put me from my suit.
Pray you let Cassio be received again.

OTHELLO   Fetch me the handkerchief! My mind
misgives.   135

DESDEMONA   Come, come!
You'll never meet a more sufficient man.

OTHELLO   The handkerchief!

DESDEMONA   I pray talk me of Cassio.

OTHELLO   The handkerchief!   140

DESDEMONA   A man that all his time
Hath founded his good fortunes on your love,
Shared dangers with you—

OTHELLO   The handkerchief!

DESDEMONA   In sooth, you are to blame.   145

OTHELLO   Away!   [Exit.]

EMILIA   Is not this man jealous?

DESDEMONA   I ne'er saw this before.
Sure there's some wonder in this handker-
chief.   150
I am most unhappy in the loss of it.

EMILIA   'Tis not a year or two shows us a man,
They are all but stomachs, and we all but
food;
They eat us hungerly, and when they are   155
full,
They belch us.
[Enter IAGO and CASSIO.]
Look you—Cassio and my husband!

IAGO   There is no other way; 'tis she must do't.
And lo the happiness! Go and importune   160
her.

DESDEMONA   How now, good Cassio? What's the
news with you?

CASSIO   Madam, my former suit. I do beseech
you   165
That by your virtuous means I may again
Exist, and be a member of his love
Whom I with all the office of my heart
Entirely honor. I would not be delayed.
If my offense be of such mortal kind   170
That neither service past, nor present sorrows,
Nor purposed merit in futurity,
Can ransom me into his love again,
But to know so must be my benefit.
So shall I clothe me in a forced content,   175

---

83 *Egyptian*, gypsy. 93 *fancies*, loves. 99 *perdition*,
disaster. 105–106 *compasses*, yearly circuits. 110
mummy, dye from dried flesh.

151 *unhappy*, unlucky. 160 *happiness*, good luck.
174 *But*, only.

And shut myself up in some other course;
To fortune's alms.

DESDEMONA   Alas, thrice-gentle Cassio!
My advocation is not now in tune.
My lord is not my lord; nor should I know   180
   him,
Were he in favor as in humor altered.
So help me every spirit sanctified
As I have spoken for you all my best
And stood within the blank of his dis-   185
   pleasure
For my free speech! You must awhile be pa-
   tient.
What I can do I will; and more I will
Than for myself I dare. Let that suffice   190
   you.

IAGO   Is my lord angry?

EMILIA   He went hence but now,
And certainly in strange unquietness.

IAGO   Can he be angry? I have seen the   195
   cannon
When it hath blown his ranks into the air
And, like the devil, from his very arm
Puffed his own brother—and can he be angry?
Something of moment then. I will go meet   200
   him.
There's matter in't indeed if he be angry.

DESDEMONA   I prithee do so. [Exit IAGO.]
                       Something sure of state,
Either from Venice or some unhatched   205
   practice
Made demonstrable here in Cyprus to him,
Hath puddled his clear spirit; and in such
   cases
Men's natures wrangle with inferior   210
   things,
Though great ones are their object. 'Tis even
   so.
For let our finger ache, and it endues
Our other healthful members even to   215
   that sense
Of pain. Nay, we must think men are not
   gods,
Nor of them look for such observancy
As fits the bridal. Beshrew me much,   220
   Emilia,

I was (unhandsome warrior as I am!)
Arraigning his unkindness with my soul;
But now I find I had suborned the witness,
And he's indicted falsely.   225

EMILIA   Pray heaven it be state matters, as you
   think,
And no conception nor no jealous toy
Concerning you.

DESDEMONA   Alas the day! I never gave   230
   him cause.

EMILIA   But jealous souls will not be answered
   so.
They are not ever jealous for the cause,
But jealous for they are jealous. 'Tis a   235
   monster
Begot upon itself, born on itself.

DESDEMONA   Heaven keep that monster from
   Othello's mind!

EMILIA   Lady, amen.   240

DESDEMONA   I will go seek him. Cassio, walk
   here about.
If I do find him fit, I'll move your suit
And seek to effect it to my uttermost.

CASSIO   I humbly thank your ladyship.   245
   [Exeunt DESDEMONA and EMILIA.]
        [Enter BIANCA.]

BIANCA   Save you, friend Cassio!

CASSIO   What make you from home?
How is it with you, my most fair Bianca?
I' faith, sweet love, I was coming to   250
   your house.

BIANCA   And I was going to your lodging,
   Cassio.
What, keep a week away? seven days and
   nights?   255
Eightscore eight hours? and lovers' absent
   hours,
More tedious than the dial eightscore times?
O weary reck'ning!

CASSIO   Pardon me, Bianca,   260
I have this while with leaden thoughts been
   pressed;
But I shall in a more convenient time
Strike off this score of absence. Sweet Bianca,
   [Gives her DESDEMONA's handkerchief.] 265
Take me this work out.

BIANCA   O Cassio, whence came this?
This is some token from a newer friend.

---

177 *To fortune's alms,* to Fate's hand-out.   182 *favor
. . . humor,* physical appearance . . . disposition.
185 *within the blank,* center of direct fire.   205–206
unhatched practice, unmatured plot.   208 *puddled,*
muddied.   214 *endues,* brings.   219 *observancy,* devotion.

222 *unhandsome,* unfair.   228 *toy,* fancy.   258 *dial,*
clock.

To the felt absence now I feel a cause.
Is't come to this? Well, well.   270

CASSIO   Go to, woman!
Throw your vile guesses in the devil's teeth,
From whence you have them. You are
    jealous now
That this is from some mistress, some   275
    remembrance.
No, by my faith, Bianca.

BIANCA   Why, whose is it?

CASSIO   I know not, sweet. I found it in my
    chamber.   280
I like the work well. Ere it be demanded,
As like enough it will, I would have it copied.
Take it and do't, and leave me for this
    time.

BIANCA   Leave you? Wherefore?   285

CASSIO   I do attend here on the General
And think it no addition, nor my wish,
To have him see me womaned.

BIANCA   Why, I pray you?

CASSIO   Not that I love you not.   290

BIANCA   But that you do not love me!
I pray you bring me on the way a little,
And say if I shall see you soon at night.

CASSIO   'Tis but a little way that I can bring you,
For I attend here; but I'll see you soon.   295

BIANCA   'Tis very good. I must be circumstanced.
    [Exeunt.]

ACT IV

Scene I   [Cyprus. Before the Castle.]

[Enter OTHELLO and IAGO.]

IAGO   Will you think so?

OTHELLO   Think so, Iago?

IAGO   What,
To kiss in private?

OTHELLO   An unauthorized kiss.   5

IAGO   Or to be naked with her friend in bed
An hour, or more, not meaning any harm?

OTHELLO   Naked in bed, Iago, and not mean
    harm?
It is hypocrisy against the devil.   10
They that mean virtuously, and yet do so,
The devil their virtue tempts, and they tempt
    heaven.

IAGO   So they do nothing, 'tis a venial slip.
But if I give my wife a handkerchief—   15

OTHELLO   What then?

IAGO   Why, then 'tis hers, my lord; and being
    hers,
She may, I think, bestow't on any man.

OTHELLO   She is protectress of her honor too.   20
May she give that?

IAGO   Her honor is an essence that's not seen;
They have it very oft that have it not.
But for the handkerchief—

OTHELLO   By heaven, I would most gladly   25
    have forgot it!
Thou said'st (O, it comes o'er my memory
As doth the raven o'er the infected house,
Boding to all!) he had my handkerchief.

IAGO   Ay, what of that?   30

OTHELLO   That's not so good now.

IAGO   What
If I had said I had seen him do you wrong?
Or heard him say—as knaves be such abroad
Who having, by their own importunate suit,   35
Or voluntary dotage of some mistress,
Convinced or supplied them, cannot choose
But they must blab—

OTHELLO   Hath he said anything?

IAGO   He hath, my lord; but be you well-   40
    assured,
No more than he'll unswear.

OTHELLO   What hath he said?

IAGO   Faith, that he did—I know not what he
    did.   45

OTHELLO   What? what?

IAGO   Lie—

OTHELLO   With her?

IAGO   With her, on her; what you
    will.   50

OTHELLO   Lie with her? lie on her?—We say lie
on her when they belie her.—Lie with her!
Zounds, that's fulsome.—Handkerchief—confessions—handkerchief!—To confess, and be
hanged for his labor—first to be hanged,   55
and then to confess! I tremble at it. Nature
would not invest herself in such shadowing
passion without some instruction. It is not
words that shakes me thus.—Pish! Noses, ears,

---

287 addition, advantage.   292 bring, go with.   296
be circumstanced, accept the situation.

28 infected, plague-ridden.   29 Boding, foreboding.
37 convinced or supplied, prevailed upon or satisfied.
52 belie, slander.   57–58 invest herself in such
shadowing passion . . . instruction, feel such high
passion . . . authority.

and lips? Is't possible?—Confess?—hand- 60
kerchief?—O devil! [*Falls in a trance.*]

IAGO   Work on,
My medicine, work! Thus credulous fools are
caught,
And many worthy and chaste dames even 65
thus,
All guiltless, meet reproach.—What, ho! my
lord!
My lord, I say! Othello!
              [*Enter* CASSIO.]
                          How now, Cassio? 70

CASSIO   What's the matter?

IAGO   My lord is fall'n into an epilepsy.
This is his second fit; he had one yesterday.

CASSIO   Rub him about the temples.

IAGO   No, for- 75
bear.
The lethargy must have his quiet course.
If not, he foams at mouth, and by-and-by
Breaks out to savage madness. Look, he stirs.
Do you withdraw yourself a little while. 80
He will recover straight. When he is gone,
I would on great occasion speak with you.
              [*Exit* CASSIO.]
How is it, General? Have you not hurt your
head?

OTHELLO   Dost thou mock me? 85

IAGO   I mock you? No,
by heaven.
Would you would bear your fortune like a
man!

OTHELLO   A horned man's a monster and 90
a beast.

IAGO   There's many a beast then in a populous
city,
And many a civil monster.

OTHELLO   Did he confess it? 95

IAGO   Good sir, be a man.
Think every bearded fellow that's but yoked
May draw with you. There's millions now alive
That nightly lie in those unproper beds
Which they dare swear peculiar. Your 100
case is better.
O, 'tis the spite of hell, the fiend's arch-mock,
To lip a wanton in a secure couch,
And to suppose her chaste! No, let me
know; 105

And knowing what I am, I know what she shall
be.

OTHELLO   O, thou art wise! 'Tis certain.

IAGO   Stand you
awhile apart; 110
Confine yourself but in a patient list.
Whilst you were here, o'erwhelmed with your
grief
(A passion most unfitting such a man),
Cassio came hither. I shifted him away 115
And laid good 'scuse upon your ecstasy;
Bade him anon return, and here speak with
me;
The which he promised. Do but encave your-
self 120
And mark the fleers, the gibes, and notable
scorns
That dwell in every region of his face;
For I will make him tell the tale anew—
Where, how, how oft, how long ago, and 125
when
He hath, and is again to cope your wife.
I say, but mark his gesture. Marry, patience!
Or I shall say you are all in all in spleen,
And nothing of a man. 130

OTHELLO   Dost thou hear, Iago?
I will be found most cunning in my patience;
But (dost thou hear?) most bloody.

IAGO   That's not amiss;
But yet keep time in all. Will you with- 135
draw? [OTHELLO *retires.*]
Now will I question Cassio of Bianca,
A huswife that by selling her desires
Buys herself bread and clothes. It is a creature
That dotes on Cassio, as 'tis the strumpet's 140
plague
To beguile many and be beguiled by one.
He, when he hears of her, cannot refrain
From the excess of laughter. Here he comes.
              [*Enter* CASSIO.]
As he shall smile, Othello shall go mad; 145
And his unbookish jealousy must conster
Poor Cassio's smiles, gestures, and light be-
havior
Quite in the wrong. How do you now, Lieu-
tenant? 150

---

90 *horned man's*, cuckold's.   94 *civil*, civilized.   99
unproper, not exclusively their own.   100 *peculiar*,
reserved for themselves.   103 *secure*, free from
anxiety.

111 *patient list*, restrained bounds.   116 *ecstasy*, fit.
119 *encave*, hide. 121 *fleers*, sneers. 127 *cope*, have
assignation with.   129 *spleen*, uncontrolled anger.
146 *unbookish . . . conster*, ignorant . . . construe.

CASSIO   The worser that you give me the addition
Whose want even kills me.

IAGO   Ply Desdemona well, and you are sure
on't.

Now, if this suit lay in Bianca's power,   155
How quickly should you speed!

CASSIO   Alas, poor caitiff!

OTHELLO   Look how he laughs already!

IAGO   I never knew woman love man so.

CASSIO   Alas, poor rogue! I think, i' faith,   160
she loves me.

OTHELLO   Now he denies it faintly, and laughs
it out.

IAGO   Do you hear, Cassio?

OTHELLO   Now he   165
importunes him
To tell it o'er. Go to! Well said, well said!

IAGO   She gives it out that you shall marry her.
Do you intend it?

CASSIO   Ha, ha, ha!   170

OTHELLO   Do you triumph, Roman? Do you
triumph?

CASSIO   I marry her? What, a customer? Prithee
bear some charity to my wit; do not think it
so unwholesome. Ha, ha, ha!   175

OTHELLO   So, so, so, so! Laugh that wins!

IAGO   Faith, the cry goes that you shall marry
her.

CASSIO   Prithee say true.

IAGO   I am a very villain else.   180

OTHELLO   Have you scored me? Well.

CASSIO   This is the monkey's own giving out. She
is persuaded I will marry her out of her own
love and flattery, not out of my promise.

OTHELLO   Iago beckons me. Now he begins   185
the story.

CASSIO   She was here even now; she haunts me
in every place. I was t'other day talking on
the sea bank with certain Venetians, and
thither comes the bauble, and, by this   190
hand, she falls me thus about my neck—

OTHELLO   Crying "O dear Cassio!" as it were.
His gesture imports it.

CASSIO   So hangs, and lolls, and weeps upon me;
so hales and pulls me! Ha, ha, ha!   195

OTHELLO   Now he tells how she plucked him to
my chamber. O, I see that nose of yours, but
not that dog I shall throw't to.

CASSIO   Well, I must leave her company.
[Enter BIANCA.]

IAGO   Before me! Look where she comes.   200

CASSIO   'Tis such another fitchew! marry, a perfumed one. What do you mean by this haunting of me?

BIANCA   Let the devil and his dam haunt you!
What did you mean by that same hand-   205
kerchief you gave me even now? I was a fine
fool to take it. I must take out the work? A
likely piece of work that you should find it in
your chamber and know not who left it there!
This is some minx's token, and I must   210
take out the work? There! give it your hobby-
horse. Wheresoever you had it, I'll take out no
work on't.

CASSIO   How now, my sweet Bianca? How now?
how now?   215

OTHELLO   By heaven, that should be my handkerchief!

BIANCA   An you'll come to supper tonight, you
may; an you will not, come when you are next
prepared for. [Exit.]   220

IAGO   After her, after her!

CASSIO   Faith, I must; she'll rail i' the street else.

IAGO   Will you sup there?

CASSIO   Yes, I intend so.

IAGO   Well, I may chance to see you; for I   225
would very fain speak with you.

CASSIO   Prithee come. Will you?

IAGO   Go to! say no more. [Exit CASSIO.]

OTHELLO   [Comes forward.] How shall I murder him, Iago?   230

IAGO   Did you perceive how he laughed at his
vice?

OTHELLO   O Iago!

IAGO   And did you see the handkerchief?

OTHELLO   Was that mine?   235

IAGO   Yours, by this hand! And to see how he
prizes the foolish woman your wife! She gave
it him, and he hath giv'n it his whore.

OTHELLO   I would have him nine years a-killing!
—A fine woman! a fair woman! a sweet   240
woman!

IAGO   Nay, you must forget that.

OTHELLO   Ay, let her rot, and perish, and be
damned tonight, for she shall not live. No, my
heart is turned to stone: I strike it, and it   245

151 *addition*, title (of lieutenant). 157 *caitiff*, thing.
173 *customer*, harlot. 177 *cry*, rumor. 181 *scored*,
summed me up (by cuckolding). 190 *bauble*, play-
thing.

201 *fitchew*, polecat. 211–212 *hobby-horse*, whore.

hurts my hand. O, the world hath not a sweeter creature! She might lie by an emperor's side and command him tasks.

IAGO   Nay, that's not your way.

OTHELLO   Hang her! I do but say what   250
she is. So delicate with her needle! an admirable musician! O, she will sing the savageness out of a bear! Of so high and plenteous wit and invention!

IAGO   She's the worse for all this.   255

OTHELLO   O, a thousand thousand times! And then, of so gentle a condition!

IAGO   Ay, too gentle.

OTHELLO   Nay, that's certain. But yet the pity of it, Iago! O Iago, the pity of it, Iago!   260

IAGO   If you are so fond over her iniquity, give her patent to offend; for if it touch not you, it comes near nobody.

OTHELLO   I will chop her into messes! Cuckold me!   265

IAGO   O, 'tis foul in her.

OTHELLO   With mine officer!

IAGO   That's fouler.

OTHELLO   Get me some poison, Iago, this night. I'll not expostulate with her, lest her body   270
and beauty unprovide my mind again. This night, Iago!

IAGO   Do it not with poison. Strangle her in her bed, even the bed she hath contaminated.

OTHELLO   Good, good! The justice of it   275
pleases. Very good!

IAGO   And for Cassio, let me be his undertaker. You shall hear more by midnight.

OTHELLO   Excellent good! [A trumpet.]
                                    What trumpet is   280
that same?

IAGO   Something from Venice, sure.

[Enter LODOVICO, DESDEMONA, and ATTENDANTS.]
                                    'Tis Lodovico,
Come from the Duke; and see, your wife is with him.   285

LODOVICO   God save you, worthy General!

OTHELLO   With all my heart, sir.

LODOVICO   The Duke and Senators of Venice greet you. [Gives him a letter.]

OTHELLO   I kiss the instrument of their   290
pleasures. [Opens the letter and reads.]

DESDEMONA   And what's the news, good cousin Lodovico?

IAGO   I am very glad to see you, signior. Welcome to Cyprus.   295

LODOVICO   I thank you. How does Lieutenant Cassio?

IAGO   Lives, sir.

DESDEMONA   Cousin, there's fall'n between him and my lord   300
An unkind breach; but you shall make all well.

OTHELLO   Are you sure of that?

DESDEMONA   My lord?

OTHELLO   [Reads.] "This fail you not to do, as you will—"   305

LODOVICO   He did not call; he's busy in the paper.
Is there division 'twixt thy lord and Cassio?

DESDEMONA   A most unhappy one. I would do much   310
T' atone them, for the love I bear to Cassio.

OTHELLO   Fire and brimstone!

DESDEMONA   My lord?

OTHELLO   Are you wise?

DESDEMONA   What, is he angry?   315

LODOVICO   Maybe the letter moved him;
For, as I think, they do command him home, Deputing Cassio in his government.

DESDEMONA   By my troth, I am glad on't.   320

OTHELLO   Indeed?

DESDEMONA   My lord?

OTHELLO   I am glad to see you mad.

DESDEMONA   Why, sweet Othello!   325

OTHELLO   Devil! [Strikes her.]

DESDEMONA   I have not deserved this.

LODOVICO   My lord, this would not be believed in Venice,
Though I should swear I saw't. 'Tis very   330
much.
Make her amends; she weeps.

OTHELLO   O devil, devil!
If that the earth could teem with woman's tears,   335
Each drop she falls would prove a crocodile.
Out of my sight!

DESDEMONA   I will not stay to offend you.
                                    [Going.]

LODOVICO   Truly, an obedient lady.
I do beseech your lordship call her back.   340

OTHELLO   Mistress!

---

262 *patent*, license.   264 *messes*, little pieces.   311 *atone*, reconcile.   334 *teem*, breed.

DESDEMONA   My lord?

OTHELLO   What would you
with her, sir?

LODOVICO   Who? I, my lord?   345

OTHELLO   Ay! You did wish that I would make
her turn.

Sir, she can turn, and turn, and yet go on,
And turn again; and she can weep, sir, weep;
And she's obedient; as you say, obedient,   350
Very obedient.—Proceed you in your tears.—
Concerning this, sir (O well-painted passion!),
I am commanded home.—Get you away;
I'll send for you anon.—Sir, I obey the man-
date   355
And will return to Venice.—Hence, avaunt!
[*Exit* DESDEMONA.]

Cassio shall have my place. And, sir, tonight
I do entreat that we may sup together.
You are welcome, sir, to Cyprus.—
Goats and monkeys! [*Exit.*]   360

LODOVICO   Is this the noble Moor whom our
full senate

Call all in all sufficient? Is this the nature
Whom passion could not shake? whose solid
virtue   365
The shot of accident nor dart of chance
Could neither graze nor pierce?

IAGO   He is much changed.

LODOVICO   Are his wits safe? Is he not light of
brain?   370

IAGO   He's that he is. I may not breathe my
censure.

What he might be—if what he might he is
not—
I would to heaven he were!   375

LODOVICO   What, strike his wife?

IAGO   Faith, that was not so well; yet would I
knew
That stroke would prove the worst!

LODOVICO   Is it his use?   380
Or did the letters work upon his blood
And new-create this fault?

IAGO   Alas, alas!
It is not honesty in me to speak
What I have seen and known. You shall   385
observe him,
And his own courses will denote him so
That I may save my speech. Do but go after
And mark how he continues.

352 *passion,* emotion.

LODOVICO   I am sorry that I am deceived in   390
him. [*Exeunt.*]

Scene II   [*Cyprus. Within the Castle.*]

[*Enter* OTHELLO *and* EMILIA.]

OTHELLO   You have seen nothing then?

EMILIA   Nor ever heard, nor ever did suspect.

OTHELLO   Yes, you have seen Cassio and she
together.

EMILIA   But then I saw no harm, and then   5
I heard
Each syllable that breath made up between
them.

OTHELLO   What, did they never whisper?

EMILIA   Never, my lord.   10

OTHELLO   Nor send you out o' the way?

EMILIA   Never.

OTHELLO   To fetch her fan, her gloves, her mask,
nor nothing?

EMILIA   Never, my lord.   15

OTHELLO   That's strange.

EMILIA   I durst, my lord, to wager she is honest,
Lay down my soul at stake. If you think other,
Remove your thought; it doth abuse your
bosom.   20
If any wretch have put this in your head,
Let heaven requite it with the serpent's curse!
For if she be not honest, chaste, and true,
There's no man happy; the purest of their
wives   25
Is foul as slander.

OTHELLO   Bid her come hither. Go. [*Exit*
EMILIA.]
She says enough; yet she's a simple bawd
That cannot say as much. This is a subtle
whore,   30
A closet lock and key of villainous secrets;
And yet she'll kneel and pray; I have seen her
do't.
[*Enter* DESDEMONA *and* EMILIA.]

DESDEMONA   My lord, what is your will?

OTHELLO   Pray, chuck, come hither.   35

DESDEMONA   What is your pleasure?

OTHELLO   Let me see your eyes.
Look in my face.

DESDEMONA   What horrible fancy's this?

OTHELLO   [*To* EMILIA.] Some of your   40
function, mistress.
Leave procreants alone and shut the door;
Cough or cry hem if anybody come.

Your mystery, your mystery! Nay, dis-
    patch! [*Exit* EMILIA.]   45
DESDEMONA   Upon my knees, what doth your
    speech import?
I understand a fury in your words,
But not the words.
OTHELLO   Why, what art thou?   50
DESDEMONA   Your wife, my lord; your true
And loyal wife.
OTHELLO   Come, swear it, damn thyself;
Lest, being like one of heaven, the devils
    themselves   55
Should fear to seize thee. Therefore be double-
    damned—
Swear thou art honest.
DESDEMONA   Heaven doth truly know it.
OTHELLO   Heaven truly knows that thou art   60
    false as hell.
DESDEMONA   To whom, my lord? With whom?
    How am I false?
OTHELLO   Ah, Desdemon! away! away!
    away!   65
DESDEMONA   Alas the heavy day! Why do you
    weep?
Am I the motive of these tears, my lord?
If haply you my father do suspect
An instrument of this your calling back,   70
Lay not your blame on me. If you have lost
    him,
Why, I have lost him too.
OTHELLO   Had it pleased
    heaven   75
To try me with affliction, had they rained
All kinds of sores and shames on my bare
    head,
Steeped me in poverty to the very lips,
Given to captivity me and my utmost hopes,   80
I should have found in some place of my soul
A drop of patience. But, alas, to make me
A fixed figure for the time of scorn
To point his slow and moving finger at!
Yet could I bear that too; well, very well.   85
But there where I have garnered up my heart,
Where either I must live or bear no life,
The fountain from the which my current runs
Or else dries up—to be discarded thence,
Or keep it as a cistern for foul toads   90

To knot and gender in—turn thy complexion
    there,
Patience, thou young and rose-lipped cherubin!
I here look grim as hell!
DESDEMONA   I hope my noble lord esteems   95
    me honest.
OTHELLO   O, ay! as summer flies are in the
    shambles,
That quicken even with blowing. O thou
    weed,   100
Who are so lovely fair, and smell'st so sweet,
That the sense aches at thee, would thou hadst
    ne'er been born!
DESDEMONA   Alas, what ignorant sin have
    I committed?   105
OTHELLO   Was this fair paper, this most goodly
    book,
Made to write "whore" upon? What com-
    mitted?
Committed? O thou public commoner!   110
I should make very forges of my cheeks
That would to cinders burn up modesty,
Did I but speak thy deeds. What committed?
Heaven stops the nose at it, and the
    moon winks;   115
The bawdy wind, that kisses all it meets,
Is hushed within the hollow mine of earth
And will not hear it. What committed?
Impudent strumpet!
DESDEMONA   By heaven, you do me   120
    wrong!
OTHELLO   Are not you a strumpet?
DESDEMONA   No, as I am a Christian!
If to preserve this vessel for my lord
From any other foul unlawful touch   125
Be not to be a strumpet, I am none.
OTHELLO   What, not a whore?
DESDEMONA   No, as I shall be saved!
OTHELLO   Is't possible?
DESDEMONA   O, heaven forgive us!   130
OTHELLO   I cry you mercy then.
I took you for that cunning whore of Venice
That married with Othello.—You, mistress,
That have the office opposite to Saint Peter
And keep the gate of hell!   135
    [*Enter* EMILIA.]

---

44 *mystery*, profession. 70 *An instrument of*, responsible for. 83 *time of scorn*, scornful world.
90 *cistern*, cesspool.

91 *knot and gender*, breed. 99 *quicken even with
blowing*, come to life in the rot of fly-blown meat.
110 *commoner*, whore. 115 *winks*, shuts eyes. 124
vessel, body. 131 *cry you mercy*, beg your pardon.

You, you, ay you!
We have done our course. There's money for
    your pains.
I pray you turn the key, and keep our coun-
    sel. [*Exit.*]   140
EMILIA   Alas, what does this gentleman con-
    ceive?
How do you, madam? How do you, my good
    lady?
DESDEMONA   Faith, half asleep.   145
EMILIA   Good madam, what's the matter with
    my lord?
DESDEMONA   With who?
EMILIA   Why, with my lord, madam.
DESDEMONA   Who is thy lord?   150
EMILIA   He that is yours, sweet lady.
DESDEMONA   I have none. Do not talk to me,
    Emilia.
I cannot weep; nor answer have I none
But what should go by water. Prithee   155
    tonight
Lay on my bed my wedding sheets, remember;
And call thy husband hither.
EMILIA   Here's a change indeed! [*Exit.*]
DESDEMONA   'Tis meet I should be used   160
    so, very meet.
How have I been behaved, that he might stick
The small'st opinion on my least misuse?
    [*Enter* IAGO *and* EMILIA.]
IAGO   What is your pleasure, madam? How is't
    with you?   165
DESDEMONA   I cannot tell. Those that do teach
    young babes
Do it with gentle means and easy tasks.
He might have chid me so; for, in good faith,
I am a child to chiding.   170
IAGO   What is the matter, lady?
EMILIA   Alas, Iago, my lord hath so bewhored
    her,
Thrown such despite and heavy terms upon
    her   175
As true hearts cannot bear.
DESDEMONA   Am I that name, Iago?
IAGO   What name, fair lady?
DESDEMONA   Such as she says my lord did say
    I was.   180
EMILIA   He called her whore. A beggar in his
    drink

Could not have laid such terms upon his callet.
IAGO   Why did he so?
DESDEMONA   I do not know. I am sure I am   185
    none such.
IAGO   Do not weep, do not weep. Alas the day!
EMILIA   Hath she forsook so many noble
    matches,
Her father and her country, all her   190
    friends,
To be called whore? Would it not make one
    weep?
DESDEMONA   It is my wretched fortune.
IAGO   Beshrew him for't!   195
How comes this trick upon him?
DESDEMONA   Nay, heaven doth know.
EMILIA   I will be hanged if some eternal villain,
Some busy and insinuating rogue,
Some cogging, cozening slave, to get   200
    some office,
Have not devised this slander. I'll be hanged
    else.
IAGO   Fie, there is no such man! It is impossible.
DESDEMONA   If any such there be, heaven   205
    pardon him!
EMILIA   A halter pardon him! and hell gnaw
    his bones!
Why should he call her whore? Who keeps
    her company?   210
What place? what time? what form? what
    likelihood?
The Moor's abused by some most villainous
    knave,
Some base notorious knave, some scurvy   215
    fellow.
O heaven, that such companions thou'dst un-
    fold,
And put in every honest hand a whip
To lash the rascals naked through the   220
    world
Even from the East to the West!
IAGO   Speak within door.
EMILIA   O, fie upon them! Some such squire
    he was   225
That turned your wit the seamy side without
And made you to suspect me with the Moor.
IAGO   You are a fool. Go to.
DESDEMONA   O good Iago,

139–140 *counsel*, secret. 155 *go by water*, be expressed by tears. 163 *opinion . . . least misuse*, suspicion . . . smallest error. 174 *despite*, contempt.

183 *callet*, whore. 196 *trick*, odd conduct. 199 *busy*,
prying. 200 *cogging, cozening*, cheating (both
words). 215 *notorious*, infamous. 223 *within door*,
calmly.

What shall I do to win my lord again?   230
Good friend, go to him; for, by this light of
    heaven,
I know not how I lost him. Here I kneel.
If e'er my will did trespass 'gainst his love
Either in discourse of thought or actual   235
    deed,
Or that mine eyes, mine ears, or any sense
Delighted them in any other form,
Or that I do not yet, and ever did,
And ever will (though he do shake me off   240
To beggarly divorcement) love him dearly,
Comfort forswear me! Unkindness may do
    much;
And his unkindness may defeat my life,
But never taint my love. I cannot say   245
    "whore."
It doth abhor me now I speak the word;
To do the act that might th' addition earn
Not the world's mass of vanity could make me.
IAGO   I pray you be content. 'Tis but his   250
    humor.
The business of the state does him offense,
And he does chide with you.
DESDEMONA   If 'twere no other—
IAGO   'Tis but so, I warrant. [*Trumpets*   255
    within.]
Hark how these instruments summon you to
    supper.
The messengers of Venice stay the meat.
Go in, and weep not. All things shall be   260
    well. [*Exeunt* DESDEMONA *and* EMILIA.]
        [*Enter* RODERIGO.]
How now, Roderigo?
RODERIGO   I do not find that thou deal'st justly
    with me.
IAGO   What in the contrary?   265
RODERIGO   Every day thou daff'st me with some
    device, Iago, and rather, as it seems to me
    now, keep'st from me all conveniency than
    suppliest me with the least advantage of hope.
    I will indeed no longer endure it; nor am   270
    I yet persuaded to put up in peace what al-
    ready I have foolishly suffered.
IAGO   Will you hear me, Roderigo?
RODERIGO   Faith, I have heard too much; for
    your words and performances are no kin   275
    together.

IAGO   You charge me most unjustly.
RODERIGO   With naught but truth. I have wasted
    myself out of means. The jewels you have had
    from me to deliver to Desdemona would   280
    half have corrupted a votarist. You have told
    me she hath received them, and returned me
    expectations and comforts of sudden respect
    and acquaintance; but I find none.
IAGO   Well, go to; very well.   285
RODERIGO   Very well! go to! I cannot go to,
    man; nor 'tis not very well. Nay, I think it is
    scurvy, and begin to find myself fopped in it.
IAGO   Very well.
RODERIGO   I tell you 'tis not very well. I   290
    will make myself known to Desdemona. If she
    will return me my jewels, I will give over my
    suit and repent my unlawful solicitation. If
    not, assure yourself I will seek satisfaction of
    you.   295
IAGO   You have said now.
RODERIGO   Ay, and said nothing but what I pro-
    test intendment of doing.
IAGO   Why, now I see there's mettle in thee; and
    even from this instant do build on thee a   300
    better opinion than ever before. Give me thy
    hand, Roderigo. Thou hast taken against me
    a most just exception; but yet I protest I have
    dealt most directly in thy affair.
RODERIGO   It hath not appeared.   305
IAGO   I grant indeed it hath not appeared; and
    your suspicion is not without wit and judg-
    ment. But, Roderigo, if thou hast that in thee
    indeed which I have greater reason to believe
    now than ever (I mean purpose, cour-   310
    age, and valor), this night show it. If thou the
    next night following enjoy not Desdemona,
    take me from this world with treachery and
    devise engines for my life.
RODERIGO   Well, what is it? Is it within   315
    reason and compass?
IAGO   Sir, there is especial commission come
    from Venice to depute Cassio in Othello's
    place.
RODERIGO   Is that true? Why, then Othello   320
    and Desdemona return again to Venice.
IAGO   O, no. He goes into Mauritania and takes
    away with him the fair Desdemona, unless

---

235 *discourse*, process.   242 *Comfort forswear*, happiness abandon.   244 *defeat*, ruin.   266 *daff'st me*,
put me off.   268 *conveniency*, opportunity.

281 *votarist*, nun.   283 *sudden respect*, immediate
contact.   288 *fopped*, fooled.   303 *exception*, criticism.   314 *engines for*, plots against.

his abode be lingered here by some accident;
wherein none can be so determinate as   325
the removing of Cassio.

RODERIGO   How do you mean removing of him?

IAGO   Why, by making him uncapable of Othello's place—knocking out his brains.

RODERIGO   And that you would have me   330
to do?

IAGO   Ay, if you dare do yourself a profit and a
right. He sups tonight with a harlotry, and
thither will I go to him. He knows not yet of
his honorable fortune. If you will watch   335
his going thence, which I will fashion to fall
out between twelve and one, you may take
him at your pleasure. I will be near to second
your attempt, and he shall fall between us.
Come, stand not amazed at it, but go   340
along with me. I will show you such a necessity in his death that you shall think yourself
bound to put it on him. It is now high supper
time, and the night grows to waste. About it!

RODERIGO   I will hear further reason for   345
this.

IAGO   And you shall be satisfied. [*Exeunt.*]

Scene III   [*Cyprus. Another room in the
Castle.*]

[*Enter* OTHELLO, LODOVICO, DESDEMONA, EMILIA,
and ATTENDANTS.]

LODOVICO   I do beseech you, sir, trouble yourself no further.

OTHELLO   O, pardon me; 'twill do me good to
walk.

LODOVICO   Madam, good night. I humbly   5
thank your ladyship.

DESDEMONA   Your Honor is most welcome.

OTHELLO   Will you walk, sir?
O, Desdemona—

DESDEMONA   My lord?   10

OTHELLO   Get you to bed on th' instant. I will
be returned forthwith. Dismiss your attendant
there. Look 't be done.

DESDEMONA   I will, my lord. [*Exeunt* OTHELLO,
LODOVICO, *and* ATTENDANTS.]

EMILIA   How goes it now? He looks gentler   15
than he did.

DESDEMONA   He says he will return incontinent.

He hath commanded me to go to bed,
And bid me to dismiss you.

EMILIA   Dismiss me?   20

DESDEMONA   It was his bidding. Therefore, good
Emilia,
Give me my nightly wearing, and adieu.
We must not now displease him.

EMILIA   I would you had never seen him!   25

DESDEMONA   So would not I. My love doth so
approve him
That even his stubbornness, his checks, his
frowns
(Prithee unpin me) have grace and favor   30
in them.

EMILIA   I have laid those sheets you bade me
on the bed.

DESDEMONA   All's one. Good faith, how foolish
are our minds!   35
If I do die before thee, prithee shroud me
In one of those same sheets.

EMILIA   Come, come! You talk.

DESDEMONA   My mother had a maid called
Barbary.   40
She was in love; and he she loved proved mad
And did forsake her. She had a song of "Wil-
low."
An old thing 'twas; but it expressed her
fortune,   45
And she died singing it. That song tonight
Will not go from my mind. I have much to do
But to go hang my head all at one side
And sing it like poor Barbary. Prithee dis-
patch.   50

EMILIA   Shall I go fetch your nightgown?

DESDEMONA   No, unpin me here.
This Lodovico is a proper man.

EMILIA   A very handsome man.

DESDEMONA   He speaks well.   55

EMILIA   I know a lady in Venice would have
walked barefoot to Palestine for a touch of
his nether lip.

DESDEMONA   [*Sings.*]

The poor soul sat sighing by a sycamore   60
tree,
    Sing all a green willow;
Her hand on her bosom, her head on her
knee,
    Sing willow, willow, willow.   65

324 *abode be lingered,* stay be extended.
17 *incontinent,* immediately.

28 *stubbornness . . . checks,* roughness . . . rebukes.
41 *mad,* unfaithful.

The fresh streams ran by her and murmured
   her moans;
   Sing willow, willow, willow;
   Her salt tears fell from her, and soft'ned the
     stones.   70
   Sing willow—

Lay by these.

          willow, willow;

Prithee hie thee; he'll come anon.

   Sing all a green willow must be my gar-   75
     land.
   Let nobody blame him; his scorn I ap-
     prove—

Nay, that's not next. Hark! who is't that
   knocks?
EMILIA   It is the wind.   80
DESDEMONA

   I called my love false love; but what said he
     then?
   Sing willow, willow, willow:
   If I court moe women, you'll couch with   85
     moe men.

So, get thee gone; good night. Mine eyes do
   itch.
Doth that bode weeping?
EMILIA   'Tis neither here nor there.   90
DESDEMONA   I have heard it said so. O, these
   men, these men!
Dost thou in conscience think—tell me,
   Emilia—
That there be women do abuse their hus-   95
   bands
In such gross kind?
EMILIA   There be some such, no question.
DESDEMONA   Wouldst thou do such a deed for
   all the world?   100
EMILIA   Why, would not you?
DESDEMONA   No, by this heavenly light!
EMILIA   Nor I neither by this heavenly light.
I might do't as well i' the dark.
DESDEMONA   Wouldst thou do such a deed   105
   for all the world?

EMILIA   The world's a huge thing. It is a great
   price for a small vice.
DESDEMONA   In troth, I think thou wouldst not.
EMILIA   In troth, I think I should; and   110
   undo't when I had done it. Marry, I would
   not do such a thing for a joint-ring, nor for
   measures of lawn, nor for gowns, petticoats,
   nor caps, nor any petty exhibition; but, for all
   the whole world—'Ud's pity! who would   115
   not make her husband a cuckold to make him
   a monarch? I should venture purgatory for't.
DESDEMONA   Beshrew me if I would do such a
   wrong
For the whole world.   120
EMILIA   Why, the wrong is but a wrong i' the
   world; and having the world for your labor,
   'tis a wrong in your own world, and you might
   quickly make it right.
DESDEMONA   I do not think there is any   125
   such woman.
EMILIA   Yes, a dozen; and as many to the van-
   tage as would store the world they played
   for.
But I do think it is their husbands' faults   130
If wives do fall. Say that they slack their duties
And pour our treasures into foreign laps;
Or else break out in peevish jealousies,
Throwing restraint upon us; or say they strike
   us,   135
Or scant our former having in despite—
Why, we have galls; and though we have some
   grace,
Yet have we some revenge. Let husbands
   know   140
Their wives have sense like them. They see,
   and smell,
And have their palates both for sweet and
   sour,
As husbands have. What is it that they do   145
When they change us for others? Is it sport?
I think it is. And doth affection breed it?
I think it doth. Is't frailty that thus errs?
It is so too. And have not we affections,
Desires for sport, and frailty, as men   150
   have?
Then let them use us well; else let them know,
The ills we do, their ills instruct us so.

---

114 *exhibition,* present.   127–128 *to the vantage,* in
addition.   128 *store,* populate.   136 *having,* allowance.   137–138 *galls . . . grace,* resentments . . .
goodness.   147 *affection,* sudden desire.

85 *moe,* more.

DESDEMONA   Good night, good night. Heaven me such uses send,   155

Not to pick bad from bad, but by bad mend! [*Exeunt.*]

ACT V

Scene I   [*Cyprus. A street.*]

[*Enter* IAGO *and* RODERIGO.]

IAGO   Here, stand behind this bulk; straight will he come.

Wear thy good rapier bare, and put it home.

Quick, quick! Fear nothing; I'll be at thy elbow.   5

It makes us, or it mars us—think on that,

And fix most firm thy resolution.

RODERIGO   Be near at hand. I may miscarry in't.

IAGO   Here, at thy hand. Be bold, and take thy stand. [*Stands aside.*]   10

RODERIGO   I have no great devotion to the deed,

And yet he hath given me satisfying reasons.

'Tis but a man gone. Forth my sword! He dies!

IAGO   I have rubbed this young quat almost   15 to the sense,

And he grows angry. Now whether he kill Cassio,

Or Cassio him, or each do kill the other,

Every way makes my gain. Live   20 Roderigo,

He calls me to a restitution large

Of gold and jewels that I bobbed from him

As gifts to Desdemona.

It must not be. If Cassio do remain,   25

He hath a daily beauty in his life

That makes me ugly; and besides, the Moor

May unfold me to him! there stand I in much peril.

No, he must die. But so! I hear him   30 coming.

[*Enter* CASSIO.]

RODERIGO   I know his gait. 'Tis he. Villain, thou diest! [*Makes a pass at* CASSIO.]

CASSIO   That thrust had been mine enemy indeed   35

But that my coat is better than thou know'st.

I will make proof of thine. [*Draws, and wounds* RODERIGO.]

RODERIGO   O, I am slain! [IAGO *comes forward, wounds* CASSIO *from behind, and exits.*]

CASSIO   I am maimed for ever. Help, ho! Murder! murder! [*Falls.*]   40

[*Enter* OTHELLO.]

OTHELLO   The voice of Cassio. Iago keeps his word.

RODERIGO   O, villain that I am!

OTHELLO   It is even so.

CASSIO   O, help, ho! light! a surgeon!   45

OTHELLO   'Tis he. O brave Iago, honest and just,

That hast such noble sense of thy friend's wrong!

Thou teachest me. Minion, your dear lies   50 dead,

And your unblest fate hies. Strumpet, I come.

Forth of my heart those charms, thine eyes, are blotted.   55

Thy bed, lust-stained, shall with lust's blood be spotted. [*Exit.*]

[*Enter* LODOVICO *and* GRATIANO.]

CASSIO   What, ho? No watch? No passage? Murder! murder!

GRATIANO   'Tis some mischance. The cry is   60 very direful.

CASSIO   O, help!

LODOVICO   Hark!

RODERIGO   O wretched villain!

LODOVICO   Two or three groan. It is a   65 heavy night.

These may be counterfeits. Let's think't unsafe

To come in to the cry without more help.

RODERIGO   Nobody come? Then shall I   70 bleed to death.

LODOVICO   Hark!

[*Enter* IAGO.]

GRATIANO   Here's one comes in his shirt, with light and weapons.

IAGO   Who's there? Whose noise is this   75 that cries on murder?

LODOVICO   We do not know.

IAGO   Did not you hear a cry?

---

155 *uses,* conduct.
1 *bulk,* shop front.   15–16 *quat . . . sense,* pimple . . . quick.   23 *bobbed,* cheated.

50 *Minion,* small pet.   52 *hies,* comes soon.   58 *No passage?,* nobody passing?   66 *heavy,* dark.

CASSIO   Here, here! For heaven's sake, help me!

IAGO   What's the matter?   80

GRATIANO   This is Othello's ancient, as I take it.

LODOVICO   The same indeed, a very valiant
   fellow.

IAGO   What are you here that cry so grievously?   85

CASSIO   Iago? O, I am spoiled, undone by
   villains!
   Give me some help.

IAGO   O me, Lieutenant! What villains have
   done this?   90

CASSIO   I think that one of them is hereabout
   And cannot make away.

IAGO   O treacherous villains!
   What are you there? Come in, and give some
   help. [*To* LODOVICO   95
   and GRATIANO.]

RODERIGO   O, help me here!

CASSIO   That's one of them.

IAGO   O murd'rous slave! O villain!
   [*Stabs* RODERIGO.]

RODERIGO   O damned Iago! O inhuman dog!

IAGO   Kill men i' the dark? Where be these   100
   bloody thieves?
   How silent is this town! Ho! murder! murder!
   What may you be? Are you of good or evil?

LODOVICO   As you shall prove us, praise us.

IAGO   Signior Lodovico?   105

LODOVICO   He, sir.

IAGO   I cry you mercy. Here's Cassio hurt by
   villains.

GRATIANO   Cassio?

IAGO   How is it, brother?   110

CASSIO   My leg is cut in two.

IAGO   Marry, heaven forbid!
   Light, gentlemen. I'll bind it with my shirt.
                [*Enter* BIANCA.]

BIANCA   What is the matter, ho? Who is't that
   cried?   115

IAGO   Who is't that cried?

BIANCA   O my dear Cassio! my sweet Cassio!
   O Cassio, Cassio, Cassio!

IAGO   O notable strumpet!—Cassio, may you
   suspect   120
   Who they should be that thus have mangled
   you?

CASSIO   No.

GRATIANO   I am sorry to find you thus. I have
   been to seek you.   125

IAGO   Lend me a garter. So. O for a chair
   To bear him easily hence!

BIANCA   Alas, he faints! O Cassio, Cassio,
   Cassio!

IAGO   Gentlemen all, I do suspect this trash   130
   To be a party in this injury.—
   Patience awhile, good Cassio.—Come, come!
   Lend me a light. Know we this face or no?
   Alas, my friend and my dear countryman
   Roderigo? No. Yes, sure. O heaven!   135
   Roderigo.

GRATIANO   What, of Venice?

IAGO   Even he, sir. Did you know him?

GRATIANO   Know him? Ay.

IAGO   Signior Gratiano? I cry you gentle   140
   pardon.
   These bloody accidents must excuse my
   manners
   That so neglected you.

GRATIANO   I am glad to see you.   145

IAGO   How do you, Cassio?—O, a chair, a chair!

GRATIANO   Roderigo?

IAGO   He, he, 'tis he! [*A chair brought in.*]
   O, that's well said! the chair.
   Some good man bear him carefully from   150
   hence.
   I'll fetch the General's surgeon. [*To* BIANCA.]
   For you, mistress,
   Save you your labor.—He that lies slain here,
   Cassio,   155
   Was my dear friend. What malice was between
   you?

CASSIO   None in the world; nor do I know the
   man.

IAGO   [*To* BIANCA.] What, look you pale?   160
   O, bear him out o' th' air. [CASSIO *and*
   RODERIGO *are borne off.*]
   Stay you, good gentlemen.—Look you pale,
   mistress?—
   Do you perceive the gastness of her eye?—
   Nay, an you stare, we shall hear more   165
   anon.
   Behold her well; I pray you look upon her.
   Do you see, gentlemen? Nay, guiltiness will
   speak,
   Though tongues were out of use.   170
                [*Enter* EMILIA.]

EMILIA   'Las, whats the matter? What's the
   matter, husband?

IAGO   Cassio hath here been set on in the
   dark

---

164 *gastness*, fear.

By Roderigo, and fellows that are scaped.   175
He's almost slain, and Roderigo dead.

EMILIA   Alas,   good   gentleman! alas, good
    Cassio!

IAGO   This is the fruit of whoring. Prithee,
    Emilia,   180
    Go know of Cassio where he supped tonight.
    [*To* BIANCA.] What, do you shake at
    that?

BIANCA   He supped at my house; but I therefore
    shake not.   185

IAGO   O, did he so? I charge you go with me.

EMILIA   Fie, fie upon thee, strumpet!

BIANCA   I am no strumpet, but of life as honest
    As you that thus abuse me.

EMILIA   As I? Foh! fie upon   190
    thee!

IAGO   Kind gentlemen, let's go see poor Cassio
    dressed.
    [*To* BIANCA.] Come, mistress, you must tell's
    another tale.—   195
    Emilia, run you to the citadel
    And tell my lord and lady what hath happed.—
    Will you go on afore? [*Aside*.] This is the
    night
    That either makes me or fordoes me   200
    quite. [*Exeunt*.]

Scene II   [*Cyprus. A bedchamber in
    the Castle*.]

[DESDEMONA *in her bed. Enter* OTHELLO *with
    a light*.]

OTHELLO   It is the cause, it is the cause, my soul.
    Let me not name it to you, you chaste stars!
    It is the cause. Yet I'll not shed her blood,
    Nor scar that whiter skin of hers than snow,
    And smooth as monumental alabaster.   5
    Yet she must die, else she'll betray more men.
    Put out the light, and then put out the light.
    If I quench thee, thou flaming minister,
    I can again thy former light restore,
    Should I repent me; but once put out thy   10
    light,
    Thou cunning'st pattern of excelling nature,
    I know not where is that Promethean heat
    That can thy light relume. When I have
    plucked the rose,   15
    I cannot give it vital growth again;
    It needs must wither. I'll smell it on the tree.
    [*He kisses her*.]

200 *fordoes*, ruins.   8 *minister*, servant.

O balmy breath, that dost almost persuade
Justice to break her sword! One more, one
    more!   20
Be thus when thou art dead, and I will kill thee,
And love thee after. One more, and this the
    last!
So sweet was ne'er so fatal. I must weep,
But they are cruel tears. This sorrow's   25
heavenly,
It strikes where it doth love. She wakes.

DESDEMONA   Who's there? Othello?

OTHELLO   Ay, Desdemona.

DESDEMONA   Will you come to bed, my lord?   30

OTHELLO   Have you prayed tonight, Desdemona?

DESDEMONA   Ay, my lord.

OTHELLO   If you bethink yourself of any crime
Unreconciled as yet to heaven and grace,
Solicit for it straight.   35

DESDEMONA   Alack my lord, what may you mean
    by that?

OTHELLO   Well, do it, and be brief; I will walk
    by.
I would not kill thy unprepared spirit.   40
No, heaven forfend! I would not kill thy soul.

DESDEMONA   Talk you of killing?

OTHELLO   Ay, I do.

DESDEMONA   Then heaven
Have mercy on me!   45

OTHELLO   Amen, with all my heart!

DESDEMONA   If you say so, I hope you will not
    kill me.

OTHELLO   Humh!

DESDEMONA   And yet I fear you; for you   50
    are fatal then
When your eyes roll so. Why I should fear
    I know not,
Since guiltiness I know not; but yet I feel I
    fear.   55

OTHELLO   Think on thy sins.

DESDEMONA   They are loves I bear to you.

OTHELLO   Ay, and for that thou diest.

DESDEMONA   That death's unnatural that kills
    for loving.   60
Alas, why gnaw you so your nether lip?
Some bloody passion shakes your very frame.
These are portents; but yet I hope, I hope,
They do not point on me.

OTHELLO   Peace and be still!   65

DESDEMONA   I will so. What's the matter?

OTHELLO   That handkerchief which I so loved
    and gave thee
Thou gav'st to Cassio.

DESDEMONA   No, by my life and soul! 70
Send for the man and ask him.
OTHELLO   Sweet soul, take heed,
Take heed of perjury; thou art on thy death-
    bed.
DESDEMONA   Ay, but not yet to die. 75
OTHELLO   Yes, presently.
Therefore confess thee freely of thy sin;
For to deny each article with oath
Cannot remove nor choke the strong
    conception   80
That I do groan withal. Thou art to die.
DESDEMONA   Then Lord have mercy on me!
OTHELLO   I say amen.
DESDEMONA   And have you mercy too! I never
    did   85
Offend you in my life; never loved Cassio
But with such general warranty of heaven
As I might love. I never gave him token.
OTHELLO   By heaven, I saw my handkerchief
    in's hand!   90
O perjured woman! thou dost stone my heart,
And mak'st me call what I intend to do
A murder, which I thought a sacrifice.
I saw the handkerchief.
DESDEMONA   He found it then. 95
I never gave it him. Send for him hither.
Let him confess a truth.
OTHELLO   He hath confessed.
DESDEMONA   What, my lord?
OTHELLO   That he hath used thee.   100
DESDEMONA   How? unlawfully?
OTHELLO   Ay.
DESDEMONA   He will not say so.
OTHELLO   No, his mouth is stopped.
Honest Iago hath ta'en order for't.   105
DESDEMONA   O, my fear interprets. What, is he
    dead?
OTHELLO   Had all his hairs been lives, my great
    revenge
Had stomach for them all.   110
DESDEMONA   Alas, he is betrayed, and I un-
    done!
OTHELLO   Out, strumpet! Weep'st thou for him
    to my face?
DESDEMONA   O, banish me, my lord, but   115
    kill me not!
OTHELLO   Down, strumpet!

DESDEMONA   Kill me tomorrow; let me live to-
    night!
OTHELLO   Nay, an you strive—   120
DESDEMONA   But half an hour!
OTHELLO   Being done, there is no pause.
DESDEMONA   But while I say one prayer!
OTHELLO   It is too late.
[*He smothers her.* EMILIA *calls within, at the
    door.*]
EMILIA   My lord, my lord! What, ho, my   125
    lord, my lord!
OTHELLO   What noise is this? Not dead?
    not yet quite dead?
I that am cruel am yet merciful;
I would not have thee linger in thy pain.   130
So, so.
EMILIA   [*Within.*] What, ho! my lord, my lord!
OTHELLO   Who's there?
EMILIA   [*Within.*] O, good my lord, I would
    speak a word with you!   135
OTHELLO   Yes.—'Tis Emilia.—By-and-by.—
    She's dead.—
'Tis like she comes to speak of Cassio's
    death:
The noise was high. Ha! no more moving?   140
Still as the grave.—Shall she come in? Were't
    good?—
I think she stirs again. No.—What's best to do?
If she come in, she'll sure speak to my wife.
My wife! my wife! what wife? I have no   145
    wife.
O, insupportable! O heavy hour!
Methinks it should be now a huge
    eclipse
Of sun and moon, and that th' affrighted   150
    globe
Should yawn at alteration.
EMILIA   [*Within.*] I do beseech you
That I may speak with you, O good my
    lord!   155
OTHELLO   I had forgot thee: O, come in, Emilia.
Soft, by-and-by.—Let me the curtains draw.
—Where art thou? [*Opens the door.*]
            [*Enter* EMILIA.]
                What's the matter with thee now?
EMILIA   O my good lord, yonder's foul   160
    murder done!
OTHELLO   What? Now?
EMILIA   But now, my lord.

---

76 *presently,* at once. 80 *conception,* conviction.
86 *offend,* wrong. 91 *stone,* turn to stone.

140 *high,* loud. 152 *yawn,* quake.

OTHELLO   It is the very error of the moon.
   She comes more near the earth than she   165
     was wont
   And makes men mad.

EMILIA   Cassio, my lord, hath killed a young
     Venetian
   Called Roderigo.   170

OTHELLO   Roderigo killed?
   And Cassio killed?

EMILIA   No, Cassio is not killed.

OTHELLO   Not Cassio killed? Then murder's out
     of tune,   175
   And sweet revenge grows harsh.

DESDEMONA   O, falsely, falsely murdered!

EMILIA   O Lord! what cry is that?

OTHELLO   That? What?

EMILIA   Out and alas! that was my lady's   180
     voice.
   Help! help, ho! help! O lady, speak again!
   Sweet Desdemona! O sweet mistress, speak!

DESDEMONA   A guiltless death I die.

EMILIA   O, who hath done this deed?   185

DESDEMONA   Nobody—I myself. Farewell.
   Commend me to my kind lord. O, farewell!
   [*She dies.*]

OTHELLO   Why, how should she be murd'red?

EMILIA   Alas, who knows?

OTHELLO   You heard her say herself, it was   190
     not I.

EMILIA   She said so. I must needs report a
   truth.

OTHELLO   She's like a liar gone to burning
     hell!   195
   'Twas I that killed her.

EMILIA   O, the more angel she,
   And you the blacker devil!

OTHELLO   She turned to folly, and she was a
     whore.   200

EMILIA   Thou dost belie her, and thou art a
   devil.

OTHELLO   She was false as water.

EMILIA   Thou art rash as fire to say
   That she was false. O, she was heavenly   205
     true!

OTHELLO   Cassio did top her. Ask thy husband
     else.
   O, I were damned beneath all depth in
     hell   210
   But that I did proceed upon just grounds

To this extremity. Thy husband knew it all.

EMILIA   My husband?

OTHELLO   Thy husband.

EMILIA   That she was false to wedlock?   215

OTHELLO   Ay, with Cassio. Nay, had she been
     true,
   If heaven would make me such another world
   Of one entire and perfect chrysolite,
   I'd not have sold her for it.   220

EMILIA   My husband?

OTHELLO   Ay, 'twas he that told me first.
   An honest man he is, and hates the slime
   That sticks on filthy deeds.

EMILIA   My husband?   225

OTHELLO   What needs this iterance, woman?
   I say, thy husband.

EMILIA   O mistress, villainy hath made mocks
     with love!
   My husband say that she was false?   230

OTHELLO   He, woman.
   I say, thy husband. Dost understand the word?
   My friend, thy husband; honest, honest Iago.

EMILIA   If he say so, may his pernicious soul
   Rot half a grain a day! he lies to the heart.   235
   She was too fond of her most filthy bargain.

OTHELLO   Ha!

EMILIA   Do thy worst.
   This deed of thine is no more worthy heaven
   Than thou wast worthy her.   240

OTHELLO   Peace, you were best.

EMILIA   Thou hast not half the power to do me
     harm
   As I have to be hurt. O gull! O dolt!
   As ignorant as dirt! thou hast done a   245
     deed—
   I care not for thy sword; I'll make thee known,
   Though I lost twenty lives. Help! help, ho!
     help!
   The Moor hath killed my mistress! Mur-   250
     der! murder!

[*Enter* MONTANO, GRATIANO, IAGO, *and others.*]

MONTANO   What is the matter? How now,
     General?

EMILIA   O, are you come, Iago? You have done
     well,   255
   That men must lay their murders on your
     neck.

GRATIANO   What is the matter?

EMILIA   Disprove this villain, if thou be'st a
     man: 260

---

164 *error*, wandering (out of phase). 187 *commend*, give my love.

226 *iterance*, repetition. 244 *gull*, dupe.

He says thou told'st him that his wife was false.

I know thou didst not; thou'rt not such a villain.

Speak, for my heart is full.   265

IAGO   I told him what I thought, and told no more

Than what he found himself was apt and true.

EMILIA   But did you ever tell him she was   270
false?

IAGO   I did.

EMILIA   You told a lie, an odious damned lie!
Upon my soul, a lie! a wicked lie!

She false with Cassio? Did you say with   275
Cassio?

IAGO   With Cassio, mistress. Go to, charm your
tongue.

EMILIA   I will not charm my tongue; I am bound
to speak: 280

My mistress here lies murdered in her bed—

ALL   O heavens forfend!

EMILIA   And your reports have set the murder
on.

OTHELLO   Nay, stare not, masters. It is true   285
indeed.

GRATIANO   'Tis a strange truth.

MONTANO   O monstrous act!

EMILIA   Villainy, villainy, villainy!
I think upon't, I think! I smell't! O vil-   290
lainy!

I thought so then. I'll kill myself for grief.

O villainy, villainy!

IAGO   What, are you mad? I charge you get you
home.   295

EMILIA   Good gentlemen, let me have leave to
speak.

'Tis proper I obey him, but not now.

Perchance, Iago, I will ne'er go home.

OTHELLO   O! O! O! [Falls on the bed.]   300

EMILIA   Nay, lay thee down and roar!

For thou hast killed the sweetest innocent
That e'er did lift up eye.

OTHELLO   O' she was foul! [Rises.]
I scarce did know you, uncle. There lies   305
your niece,

Whose breath, indeed, these hands have newly
stopped.

I know this act shows horrible and grim.

GRATIANO   Poor Desdemon! I am glad thy   310
father's dead.

Thy match was mortal to him, and pure grief
Shore his old thread in twain. Did he live now,
This sight would make him do a desperate
turn;   315

Yea, curse his better angel from his side,
And fall to reprobance.

OTHELLO   'Tis pitiful; but yet Iago knows
That she with Cassio hath the act of shame
A thousand times committed. Cassio con-   320
fessed it;

And she did gratify his amorous works
With that recognizance and pledge of love
Which I first gave her; I saw it in his hand:
It was a handkerchief, an antique token   325
My father gave my mother.

EMILIA   O God! O heavenly pow'rs!

IAGO   Zounds, hold your peace!

EMILIA   'Twill out, 'twill out! I peace?
No, I will speak as liberal as the North.   330
Let heaven and men and devils, let them all,
All, all, cry shame against me, yet I'll speak.

IAGO   Be wise, and get you home.

EMILIA   I will not. [IAGO draws and threatens
EMILIA.]   335

GRATIANO   Fie!
Your sword upon a woman?

EMILIA   O thou dull Moor, that handkerchief
thou speak'st of

I found by fortune, and did give my   340
husband;

For often with a solemn earnestness
(More than indeed belonged to such a trifle)
He begged of me to steal't.

IAGO   Villainous whore!   345

EMILIA   She give it Cassio? No, alas, I found it,
And I did give't my husband.

IAGO   Filth, thou liest!

EMILIA   By heaven, I do not, I do not, gentle-
men.   350

O murd'rous coxcomb! what should such a
fool

Do with so good a wife?

OTHELLO   Are there no stones in heaven
But what serves for the thunder? Pre-   355
cious villain!

---

268 apt, probable.   277 charm, silence.

313 Shore . . . in twain, cut . . . in two.   317 reprobance, God's rejection.   323 recognizance, bond.
330 liberal as the North, free as the north wind.
351 coxcomb, fool.   354 stones, thunderbolts.   355–
356 precious, unsurpassed.

[*The Moor runs at* IAGO, *but is disarmed by*
MONTANO. IAGO *kills his wife.*]

GRATIANO   The woman falls. Sure he hath killed
his wife.

EMILIA   Ay, ay. O, lay me by my mistress' side.
[*Exit* IAGO.]   360

GRATIANO   He's gone, but his wife's killed.

MONTANO   'Tis a notorious villain. Take you
this weapon,

Which I have here recovered from the Moor.

Come, guard the door without. Let him   365
not pass,

But kill him rather. I'll after that same villain,

For 'tis a damned slave. [*Exeunt* MONTANO
and GRATIANO *with others. Manent*
OTHELLO *and* EMILIA.]   370

OTHELLO   I am not valiant neither;

But every puny whipster gets my sword.

But why should honor outlive honesty?

Let it go all.

EMILIA   What did thy song bode, lady?   375

Hark, canst thou hear me? I will play the
swan,

And die in music. [*Sings.*] "Willow, willow,
willow."

Moor, she was chaste; she loved thee,   380
cruel Moor.

So come my soul to bliss as I speak true.

So speaking as I think, I die, I die. [*She dies.*]

OTHELLO   I have another weapon in this
chamber;   385

It is a sword of Spain, the ice-brook's temper.

O, here it is—Uncle, I must come forth.

GRATIANO   [*Within.*] If thou attempt it, it will
cost thee dear.

Thou hast no weapon, and perforce must   390
suffer.

OTHELLO   Look in upon me then and speak with
me,

Or, naked as I am, I will assault thee.

[*Enter* GRATIANO.]

GRATIANO   What is the matter?   395

OTHELLO   Behold, I have a weapon.

A better never did itself sustain

Upon a soldier's thigh. I have seen the day

That with this little arm and this good sword

I have made my way through more   400
impediments

Than twenty times your stop. But O vain boast!

Who can control his fate? 'Tis not so now.

Be not afraid, though you do see me weaponed.

Here is my journey's end, here is my butt,   405

And very seamark of my utmost sail.

Do you go back dismayed? 'Tis a lost fear.

Man but a rush against Othello's breast,

And he retires. Where should Othello go?—

Now, how dost thou look now? O   410
ill-starred wench!

Pale as thy smock! When we shall meet at
compt,

This look of thine will hurl my soul from
heaven,   415

And fiends will snatch at it. Cold, cold, my girl?

Even like thy chastity.—O cursed slave!

Whip me, ye devils,

From the possession of this heavenly
sight!   420

Blow me about in winds! roast me in sulphur!

Wash me in steep-down gulfs of liquid fire!

O Desdemona, Desdemona! dead!

O! O! O!   425

[*Enter* LODOVICO, CASSIO, MONTANO, *and* IAGO,
with OFFICERS.]

LODOVICO   Where is this rash and most unfortunate man?

OTHELLO   That's he that was Othello. Here I am.

LODOVICO   Where is that viper? Bring the villain
forth.   430

OTHELLO   I look down towards his feet—but
that's a fable.

If that thou be'st a devil, I cannot kill thee.
[*Wounds* IAGO.]

LODOVICO   Wrench his sword from him.
[OTHELLO *is disarmed.*]

IAGO   I bleed, sir, but not killed. 435

OTHELLO   I am not sorry neither. I'd have thee
live;

For in my sense, 'tis happiness to die.

LODOVICO   O thou Othello that wert once so
good,   440

Fall'n in the practice of a damned slave,

What shall be said to thee?

OTHELLO   Why, anything:

An honorable murderer, if you will;

---

364 *recovered,* taken from.   373 *honesty,* probity.
386 *ice-brook's temper,* tempered in cold water.   394
naked, unarmed.

402 *stop,* ability to hinder. 405 *butt,* limit. 406 *sea-mark,* beacon.   408 *Man but a rush,* attach with only
a bulrush.   412–413 *at compt,* at the (final) account-ing.   441 *practice,* plotting.

For naught did I in hate, but all in   445
  honor.
LODOVICO   This wretch hath part confessed his
  villainy.
Did you and he consent in Cassio's death?
OTHELLO   Ay.   450
CASSIO   Dear General, I never gave you cause.
OTHELLO   I do believe it, and I ask your par-
  don.
Will you, I pray, demand that demi-devil
Why he hath thus ensnared my soul   455
  and body?
IAGO   Demand me nothing. What you know,
  you know.
From this time forth I never will speak word.
LODOVICO   What, not to pray?   460
GRATIANO   Torments will ope your lips.
OTHELLO   Well, thou dost best.
LODOVICO   Sir, you shall understand what hath
  befall'n,
Which, as I think, you know not. Here   465
  is a letter
Found in the pocket of the slain Roderigo;
And here another. The one of them
  imports
The death of Cassio to be undertook   470
By Roderigo.
OTHELLO   O villain!
CASSIO   Most heathenish and
  most gross!
LODOVICO   Now here's another discontented   475
  paper
Found in his pocket too; and this, it seems,
Roderigo meant t' have sent this damned
  villain;
But that, belike, Iago in the interim   480
Came in and satisfied him.
OTHELLO   O thou pernicious caitiff!—
How came you, Cassio, by that handker-
  chief
That was my wife's?   485
CASSIO   I found it in my chamber;
And he himself confessed but even now
That there he dropped it for a special
  purpose
Which wrought to his desire.   490
OTHELLO   O fool! fool! fool!
CASSIO   There is besides in Roderigo's letter,
How he upbraids Iago that he made him
Brave me upon the watch; whereon it came

That I was cast; and even but now he   495
  spake,
After long seeming dead—Iago hurt him,
Iago set him on.
LODOVICO   You must forsake this room and go
  with us.   500
Your power and your command is taken
  off,
And Cassio rules in Cyprus. For this slave,
If there be any cunning cruelty
That can torment him much and hold   505
  him long,
It shall be his. You shall close prisoner rest
Till that the nature of your fault be known
To the Venetian state. Come, bring away.
OTHELLO   Soft you! a word or two before   510
  you go.
I have done the state some service, and they
  know't—
No more of that. I pray you, in your letters,
When you shall these unlucky deeds   515
  relate,
Speak of me as I am. Nothing extenuate,
Nor set down aught in malice. Then must
  you speak
Of one that loved not wisely, but too well;   520
Of one not easily jealous, but, being wrought,
Perplexed in the extreme; of one whose hand
(Like the base Indian) threw a pearl away
Richer than all his tribe; of one whose
  subdued eyes,   525
Albeit unused to the melting mood,
Drop tears as fast as the Arabian trees
Their med'cinable gum. Set you down this;
And say besides that in Aleppo once,
Where a malignant and a turbaned Turk   530
Beat a Venetian and traduced the state,
I took by the throat the circumcised dog
And smote him—thus. [*He stabs himself.*]
LODOVICO   O bloody period!
GRATIANO   All that's spoke is marred.   535
OTHELLO   I kissed thee ere I killed thee. No
  way but this—
Killing myself, to die upon a kiss. [*He falls
  across* DESDEMONA *and dies.*]
CASSIO   This did I fear, but thought he had no
  weapon;   540
For he was great of heart.
LODOVICO   O Spartan dog,

449 *consent in,* plot together.   474 *gross,* blatant.

More fell than anguish, hunger, or the
    sea!
Look on the tragic loading of this bed.   545
This is thy work. The object poisons sight;
Let it be hid. Gratiano, keep the house,
And seize upon the fortunes of the Moor,
For they succeed on you. To you, Lord
    Governor,   550
Remains the censure of this hellish villain.
The time, the place, the torture—O, enforce
    it!
Myself will straight aboard, and to the state
This heavy act with heavy heart relate.   555
    [*Exeunt omnes.*]

Comments and Questions

T. S. Eliot has observed that in Shakespeare's plays there are "several levels of significance. For the simplest auditors there is the plot, for the more thoughtful the characters and conflict of characters, for the more literary the words and phrasing, for the more musically sensitive the rhythm, and for auditors of greater sensitivity and understanding a meaning which reveals itself gradually." He adds that this classification is not clear cut and that "the sensitiveness of every auditor is acted upon by all these elements at once, though in different degrees of consciousness." (*The Use of Poetry and the Use of Criticism,* Cambridge, Mass.: Harvard University Press, 1933.) The chief point here is that by digging deep into a Shakespearian play one may discover how virtually inexhaustible are the treasures. Explorations into *Othello,* one of the richest of plays, will reveal all the layers of interest observed by T. S. Eliot. One may start by looking next at Norman Sanders' essay on *Othello,* p. 867. After reading Sanders' analysis, one may profitably use the outline for play dissection as set forth on pp. 430–431.

1. The working out of the action in *Othello* is fairly intricate, but the large design is simple: an essentially noble but gullible husband is skillfully molded into the murderer of his innocent wife. How does Shakespeare lift this cheap story into greatness?

2. Iago, perhaps even more than Othello,

543 *fell,* cruel.

has fascinated generations of critics. Is he simply, as Roderigo calls him, an "inhuman dog"? Or is he only a vindictive man who plotted, not wisely, but too well? How was he regarded by everyone at the beginning of the play? Record estimations of Iago as spoken by each of the other characters throughout the play. What may one conclude from this record? Othello perhaps is something of a puzzle too. Is it reasonable that he should have submitted so completely to the machinations of Iago? At what points in the play did you perhaps say to yourself: "Ah, here Othello could easily have found out the truth"? (Consider, for example, scene i of Act IV in which Othello observes Iago and Cassio in conversation.)

3. Shakespeare rarely neglected his minor characters. What sort of individuals are Brabantio, Roderigo, Cassio, Emilia? Is Desdemona a major character? Discuss carefully.

4. Does one have the feeling that inevitable doom hangs over Othello as it did over Antigone? Discuss the differences.

5. In Act II, scene i while the newly arrived Venetians are waiting at the Cyprus harbor for Othello to arrive, a great deal of apparently incongruous bantering goes on between Iago and Desdemona. Can this scene be justified, either dramatically or psychologically?

6. Read and interpret John Peale Bishop's "Speaking of Poetry," p. 380. What sort of commentary is this on *Othello?*

The Physician in Spite of Himself
MOLIÈRE (JEAN-BAPTISTE POQUELIN)
1622–1673

CHARACTERS (in order of appearance)

SGANARELLE, *Martine's husband*
MARTINE, *Sganarelle's wife*
M. ROBERT, *Sganarelle's neighbour*
VALÈRE, *Géronte's servant*
LUCAS, *Jacqueline's husband*
GÉRONTE, *Lucinde's father*
JACQUELINE, *Lucas's wife*
LÉANDRE, *Lucinde's lover*
THIBAUT, *peasant*

PERRIN, *Thibaut's son*

LUCINDE, *Géronte's daughter, in love with Léandre*

ACT I [*A Forest.*]

Scene I [SGANARELLE, MARTINE *appearing on the stage, quarrelling*]

SGANARELLE No; I tell you that I will do nothing of the kind. It is for me to speak, and to be master.

MARTINE And I tell you that I will have you live as I like, and that I am not married to you to put up with your freaks.

SGANARELLE Oh! what a nuisance it is to have a wife! Aristotle is perfectly right in saying that a woman is worse than a devil.

MARTINE Look at the clever man with his silly Aristotle!

SGANARELLE Yes, clever indeed. Find me another faggot-binder who can argue upon things as I can, who has served a famous physician for six years, and who, when only a boy, knew his grammar by heart!

MARTINE Plague on the arrant fool.

SGANARELLE Plague on the slut!

MARTINE Cursed be the hour and the day when I took it into my head to say yes.

SGANARELLE Cursed be the cuckold of a notary that made me sign my own ruination.

MARTINE Certainly it well becomes you to complain on that score. Ought you not rather to thank Heaven every minute of the day that you have me for a wife? Did you deserve to marry a woman like me?

SGANARELLE It is true you did me too much honour, and I had great occasion to be satisfied with my wedding-night. Zounds! do not make me open my mouth too wide: I might say certain things . . .

MARTINE Well! What could you say?

SGANARELLE Enough; let us drop the subject. It is enough that we know what we know, and that you were very lucky to meet with me.

MARTINE What do you call very lucky to meet with you? A fellow who will drive me to the hospital—a debauched, deceitful wretch, who gobbles up every farthing I have got!

SGANARELLE That is a lie: I drink part of it.

MARTINE Who sells piecemeal every stick of furniture in the house!

SGANARELLE That is living upon one's means.

MARTINE Who has taken the very bed from under me!

SGANARELLE You will get up all the earlier.

MARTINE In short, who does not leave me a stick in the whole house.

SGANARELLE There will be less trouble in moving.

MARTINE And who from morning to night does nothing but gamble and guzzle.

SGANARELLE That is done in order not to get in the dumps.

MARTINE And what am I to do all the while with my family?

SGANARELLE Whatever you like.

MARTINE I have got four poor children on my hands.

SGANARELLE Put them down.

MARTINE Who keep asking me every moment for bread.

SGANARELLE Whip them. When I have had enough to eat and to drink, every one in the house ought to be satisfied.

MARTINE And do you mean to tell me, you sot, that things can always go on so?

SGANARELLE Wife, let us proceed gently, if you please.

MARTINE That I am to bear forever with your insolence and your debauchery?

SGANARELLE Do not let us get into a passion, wife.

MARTINE And that I do not know the way to bring you back to your duty?

SGANARELLE Wife, you know that I am not very patient, and that my arm is somewhat heavy.

MARTINE I laugh at your threats.

SGANARELLE My sweet wife, my pet, your skin is itching as usual.

MARTINE I will let you see that I am not afraid of you.

SGANARELLE My dearest rib, you have set your heart upon a thrashing.

MARTINE Do you think that I am frightened at your talk?

SGANARELLE Sweet object of my affections, I shall box your ears for you.

MARTINE Drunkard!

SGANARELLE I shall thrash you.

MARTINE Wine-cask!

SGANARELLE I shall pummel you.

MARTINE Infamous wretch!

SGANARELLE   I shall curry your skin for you.

MARTINE   Wretch! villain! deceiver! cur! scoundrel! gallows-bird! churl! rogue! scamp! thief! . . .

SGANARELLE   You will have it, will you? [*Takes a stick and beats her.*]

MARTINE   [*Shrieking.*] Help! help! help! help!

SGANARELLE   That is the best way of quieting you.

Scene II [M. ROBERT, SGANARELLE, MARTINE.]

M. ROBERT   Hulloa, hulloa, hulloa! Fie! What is this? What a disgraceful thing! Plague take the scamp to beat his wife so.

MARTINE   [*Her arms akimbo, speaks to* M. ROBERT, *and makes him draw back; at last she gives him a slap on the face.*] I like him to beat me, I do.

M. ROBERT   If that is the case, I consent with all my heart.

MARTINE   What are you interfering with?

M. ROBERT   I am wrong.

MARTINE   Is it any of your business?

M. ROBERT   You are right.

MARTINE   Just look at this impertinent fellow, who wishes to hinder husbands from beating their wives!

M. ROBERT   I apologize.

MARTINE   What have you got to say to it?

M. ROBERT   Nothing.

MARTINE   Is it for you to poke your nose into it?

M. ROBERT   No.

MARTINE   Mind your own business.

M. ROBERT   I shall not say another word.

MARTINE   It pleases me to be beaten.

M. ROBERT   Agreed.

MARTINE   It does not hurt you.

M. ROBERT   That is true.

MARTINE   And you are a fool to interfere with what does not concern you.

M. ROBERT   Neighbour, I ask your pardon with all my heart. Go on, thrash and beat your wife as much as you like; I shall help you, if you wish it. [*He goes towards* SGANARELLE, *who also speaks to him, makes him draw back, and beats him with the stick he has been using.*]

SGANARELLE   I do not wish it.

M. ROBERT   Ah! that is a different thing.

SGANARELLE   I will beat her if I like; and I will not beat her if I do not like.

M. ROBERT   Very good.

SGANARELLE   She is my wife, and not yours.

M. ROBERT   Undoubtedly.

SGANARELLE   It is not for you to order me about.

M. ROBERT   Just so.

SGANARELLE   I do not want your help.

M. ROBERT   Exactly so.

SGANARELLE   And it is like your impertinence to meddle with other people's business. Remember that Cicero says that between the tree and the finger you should not put the bark. [*He drives him away, then comes back to his wife, and says to her, squeezing her hand:*]

Scene III [SGANARELLE, MARTINE.]

SGANARELLE   Come, let us make it up. Shake hands.

MARTINE   Yes, after having beaten me thus!

SGANARELLE   Never mind that. Shake hands.

MARTINE   I will not.

SGANARELLE   Eh?

MARTINE   No.

SGANARELLE   Come, wife!

MARTINE   I shall not.

SGANARELLE   Come, I tell you.

MARTINE   I will do nothing of the kind.

SGANARELLE   Come, come, come.

MARTINE   No; I will be angry.

SGANARELLE   Bah! it is a trifle. Do.

MARTINE   Leave me alone.

SGANARELLE   Shake hands, I tell you.

MARTINE   You have treated me too ill.

SGANARELLE   Well! I beg your pardon; put your hand there.

MARTINE   I forgive you [*Aside, softly.*]; but I shall make you pay for it.

SGANARELLE   You are silly to take notice of it; these are trifles that are necessary now and then to keep up good feeling; and five or six strokes of a cudgel between people who love each other, only brighten the affections. There now! I am going to the wood, and I promise you that you shall have more than a hundred faggots to-day.

Scene IV [MARTINE, *alone.*]

Go, my lad, whatever look I may put on, I shall not forget to pay you out; and I am dying to hit upon something to punish you for the blows you gave me. I know well enough that a wife has always the means of being avenged upon her husband; but that is too delicate a punishment for my hangdog; I want a revenge that shall strike home a little more, or it will not pay me for the insult which I have received.

Scene V [VALÈRE, LUCAS, MARTINE.]

LUCAS [*To* VALÈRE, *without seeing* MARTINE.] I'll be blowed but we have undertaken a curious errand; and I do not know, for my part, what we shall get by it.

VALÈRE [*To* LUCAS, *without seeing* MARTINE.] What is the use of grumbling, good foster-father? We are bound to do as our master tells us; and, besides, we have both of us some interest in the health of his daughter, our mistress; for her marriage, which is put off through her illness, will no doubt bring us in something. Horace, who is generous, is the most likely to succeed among her suitors; and although she has shown some inclination for a certain Léandre, you know well enough that her father would never consent to receive him for his son-in-law.

MARTINE [*Musing on one side, thinking herself alone.*] Can I not find out some way of avenging myself?

LUCAS [*To* VALÈRE.] But what an idea has he taken into his head, since the doctors are quite at a loss.

VALÈRE [*To* LUCAS.] You may sometimes find by dint of seeking, what cannot be found at once; and often in the most unlikely spots you may . . .

MARTINE [*Still thinking herself alone.*] Yes; I must pay him out, no matter at what cost. Those cudgel blows lie heavy on my stomach; I cannot digest them; and . . . [*She is saying all this musingly, and as she moves, she comes in contact with the two men.*] Ah, gentlemen, I beg your pardon, I did not notice you, and was puzzling my brain about something that perplexes me.

VALÈRE Every one has his troubles in this world, and we also are looking for something that we should be very glad to find.

MARTINE Is it something in which I can assist you?

VALÈRE Perhaps. We are endeavouring to meet with some clever man, some special physician, who could give some relief to our master's daughter, seized with an illness which has at once deprived her of the use of her tongue. Several physicians have already exhausted all their knowledge on her behalf; but sometimes one may find people with wonderful secrets, and certain peculiar remedies, who very often succeed where others have failed; and that is the sort of man we are looking for.

MARTINE [*Softly and aside.*] Ah! This is an inspiration from Heaven to revenge myself on my rascal. [*Aloud.*] You could never have addressed yourselves to any one more able to find what you want; and we have a man here, the most wonderful fellow in the world for desperate maladies.

VALÈRE Ah! for mercy's sake, where can we meet with him?

MARTINE You will find him just now in that little spot yonder, where he is amusing himself in cutting wood.

LUCAS A doctor who cuts wood!

VALÈRE Who is amusing himself in gathering some simples, you mean to say?

MARTINE No; he is a strange fellow who takes delight in this; a fantastic, eccentric, whimsical man, whom you would never take to be what he really is. He goes about dressed in a most extraordinary fashion, pretends sometimes to be very ignorant, keeps his knowledge to himself, and dislikes nothing so much every day as using the marvellous talents which God has given him for the healing art.

VALÈRE It is a wonderful thing that all these great men have always some whim, some slight grain of madness mixed with their learning.

MARTINE The madness of this man is greater than can be imagined, for sometimes he has to be beaten before he will own his ability; and I warn you beforehand that you will not succeed, that he will never own that he is a physician, unless you take each a stick, and compel him, by dint of blows, to admit at last what he will conceal at first. It is thus that we act when we have need of him.

VALÈRE   What a strange delusion!

MARTINE   That is true; but, after that, you shall see that he works wonders.

VALÈRE   What is his name?

MARTINE   His name is Sganarelle. But it is very easy to recognise him. He is a man with a large black beard, and wears a ruff, and a yellow and green coat.

LUCAS   A yellow and green coat! He is then a parrot-doctor?

VALÈRE   But is it really true that he is as clever as you say?

MARTINE   As clever. He is a man who works miracles. About six months ago, a woman was given up by all the other physicians; she was considered dead at least six hours, and they were going to bury her, when they dragged by force the man we are speaking of to her bedside. Having seen her, he poured a small drop of something into her mouth; and at that very instant she rose from her bed, and began immediately to walk in her room as if nothing had happened.

LUCAS   Ah!

VALÈRE   It must have been a drop of liquid gold.

MARTINE   Possibly so. Not more than three weeks ago, a young child, twelve years old, fell from the top of the belfry, and smashed his head, arms, and legs on the stones. No sooner took they our man to it, than he rubbed the whole body with a certain ointment, which he knows how to prepare; and the child immediately rose on its legs, and ran away to play at chuck-farthing.

LUCAS   Hah!

VALÈRE   This man must have the universal cure-all.

MARTINE   Who doubts it?

LUCAS   Odds-bobs! that is the very man we want. Let us go quickly and fetch him.

VALÈRE   We thank you for the service you have rendered us.

MARTINE   But do not fail to remember the warning I have given you.

LUCAS   Hey! Zooks! leave it to us. If he wants nothing but a thrashing, we will gain our point.

VALÈRE   [To LUCAS.] We are very glad to have met with this woman; and I conceive the best hopes in the world from it.

Scene VI [SGANARELLE, VALÈRE, LUCAS.]

SGANARELLE   [Singing behind the Scene.] La, la, la . . .

VALÈRE   I hear someone singing and cutting wood.

SGANARELLE   [Coming on, with a bottle in his hand, without perceiving VALÈRE or LUCAS.] La, la, la. . . . Really I have done enough to deserve a drink. Let us take a little breath. [He drinks.] This wood is as salt as the very devil. [Sings.]

> What pleasure's so sweet as the bottle can give,
> What music's so good as thy little gull-gull!
> My fate might be envied by all on the earth
> Were my dear jolly flask but constantly full.
> Say why, my sweet bottle, I pray thee, say why
> Since, full you're delightful, you ever are dry?

Come! Zounds! we must take care not to get the blues.

VALÈRE   [Softly to LUCAS.] This is the very man.

LUCAS   [Softly to VALÈRE.] I think you are right, and that we have just hit upon him.

VALÈRE   Let us look a little closer.

SGANARELLE   [Hugging the bottle.] Ah! you little rogue! I love you, my pretty dear! [He sings; but perceiving LUCAS and VALÈRE, who are examining him, he lowers his voice.] My fate . . . might be envied . . . by all . . . on the earth. [Seeing that they examine him more closely.] Whom the deuce do these people want?

VALÈRE   [To LUCAS.] It is surely he.

LUCAS   [To VALÈRE.] There he is, exactly as he has been described to us.

SGANARELLE   [Aside. At this point he puts down his bottle; and when VALÈRE stoops down to bow to him, he thinks that it is in order to snatch it away, and puts it on the other side. As LUCAS is doing the same thing as VALÈRE, SGANARELLE takes it up again, and hugs it to his breast, with various grimaces which make a great deal of by-play.] They are consulting each other, while looking at me. What can be their intentions!

VALÈRE   Sir, is not your name Sganarelle?

SGANARELLE   Hey! What!

VALÈRE   I ask you if your name is not Sganarelle.

SGANARELLE   [*Turning first to* VALÈRE, *then to* LUCAS.] Yes, and no. It depends on what you want with him.

VALÈRE   We want nothing with him, but to offer him our utmost civilities.

SGANARELLE   In that case my name is Sganarelle.

VALÈRE   We are delighted to see you, Sir. We have been recommended to you for what we are in search of; and we have come to implore your help, of which we are in want.

SGANARELLE   If it be anything, gentlemen, that belongs to my little trade, I am quite ready to oblige you.

VALÈRE   You are too kind to us, Sir. But put your hat on, Sir, if you please; the sun might hurt you.

LUCAS   Pray, Sir, put it on.

SGANARELLE   [*Aside.*] What a deal of ceremony these people use. [*He puts his hat on.*]

VALÈRE   You must not think it strange, Sir, that we have addressed ourselves to you. Clever people are always much sought after, and we have been informed of your capacity.

SGANARELLE   It is true, gentlemen, that I am the best hand in the world at making faggots.

VALÈRE   Oh! Sir . . .

SGANARELLE   I spare no pains, and make them in a fashion that leaves nothing to be desired.

VALÈRE   That is not the question we have come about, Sir.

SGANARELLE   But I charge a hundred and ten sous the hundred.

VALÈRE   Let us not speak about that, if you please.

SGANARELLE   I pledge you my word that I could not sell them for less.

VALÈRE   We know what is what, Sir.

SGANARELLE   If you know what is what, you know that I charge that price.

VALÈRE   This is a joke, Sir, but . . .

SGANARELLE   It is no joke at all, I cannot bate a farthing.

VALÈRE   Let us talk differently, please.

SGANARELLE   You may find some elsewhere for less; there be faggots and faggots; but for those which I make . . .

VALÈRE   Let us change the conversation, pray, Sir.

SGANARELLE   I take my oath that you shall not have them for less, not a fraction.

VALÈRE   Fie! Fie!

SGANARELLE   No, upon my word, you shall have to pay that price. I am speaking frankly, and I am not the man to overcharge.

VALÈRE   Ought a gentleman like you, Sir, to amuse himself with those clumsy pretences, to lower himself to talk thus? Ought so learned a man, such a famous physician as you are, wish to disguise himself in the eyes of the world and keep buried his great talents?

SGANARELLE   [*Aside.*] He is mad.

VALÈRE   Pray, Sir, do not dissemble with us.

SGANARELLE   What do you mean?

LUCAS   All this beating about the bush is useless. We know what we know.

SGANARELLE   What do you know? What do you want with me? For whom do you take me?

VALÈRE   For what you are, a great physician.

SGANARELLE   Physician yourself; I am not one, and I have never been one.

VALÈRE   [*Aside.*] Now the fit is on him. [*Aloud.*] Sir, do not deny things any longer, and do not, if you please, make us have recourse to unpleasant extremities.

SGANARELLE   Have recourse to what?

VALÈRE   To certain things that we should be sorry for.

SGANARELLE   Zounds! Have recourse to whatever you like. I am not a physician, and do not understand what you mean.

VALÈRE   [*Aside.*] Well, I perceive that we shall have to apply the remedy. [*Aloud.*] Once more, Sir, I pray you to confess what you are.

LUCAS   Odds-bobs, do not talk any more nonsense; and confess plainly that you are a physician.

SGANARELLE   [*Aside.*] I am getting in a rage.

VALÈRE   What is the good of denying what all the world knows?

LUCAS   Why all these funny falsehoods? What is the good of it?

SGANARELLE   One word is as good as a thousand, gentlemen. I tell you that I am not a physician.

VALÈRE   You are not a physician?

SGANARELLE   No.

LUCAS You are not a physician?

SGANARELLE No, I tell you.

VALÈRE Since you will have it so, we must make up our minds to do it. [*They each take a stick, and thrash him.*]

SGANARELLE Hold! hold! hold, gentlemen! I will be anything you like.

VALÈRE Why, Sir, do you oblige us to use this violence?

LUCAS Why do you make us take the trouble of giving you a beating?

VALÈRE I assure you that I regret it with all my heart.

LUCAS Upon my word I am sorry for it, too.

SGANARELLE What the devil does it all mean, gentlemen? For pity's sake, is it a joke, or are you both gone out of your minds, to wish to make me out a physician?

VALÈRE What! you do not give in yet, and you still deny being a physician?

SGANARELLE The devil take me if I am one!

LUCAS Are you not a physician?

SGANARELLE No, plague choke me! [*They begin to thrash him again.*] Hold! hold! Well, gentlemen, yes, since you will have it so, I am a physician, I am a physician—an apothecary into the bargain, if you like. I prefer saying yes to everything to being knocked about so.

VALÈRE Ah! that is right, Sir; I am delighted to see you so reasonable.

LUCAS It does my heart good to hear you speak in this way.

VALÈRE I beg your pardon with all my heart.

LUCAS I hope you will forgive me for the liberty I have taken.

SGANARELLE [*Aside.*] Bless my soul! Am I perhaps myself mistaken, and have I become a physician without being aware of it?

VALÈRE You shall not regret, Sir, having shown us what you are; and you shall certainly be satisfied.

SGANARELLE But, tell me, gentlemen, may you not be yourselves mistaken? Is it quite certain that I am a physician?

LUCAS Yes, upon my word!

SGANARELLE Really and truly?

VALÈRE Undoubtedly.

SGANARELLE The devil take me if I knew it!

VALÈRE Nonsense! You are the cleverest physician in the world.

SGANARELLE Ha, ha!

LUCAS A physician who has cured I do not know how many complaints.

SGANARELLE The dickens I have!

VALÈRE A woman was thought dead for six hours; she was ready to be buried when you, with a drop of something, brought her to again, and made her walk at once about the room.

SGANARELLE The deuce I did!

LUCAS A child of twelve fell from the top of the belfry, by which he had his head, his legs, and his arms smashed; and you, with I do not know what ointment, made him immediately get up on his feet, and off he ran to play chuck-farthing.

SGANARELLE The deuce I did!

VALÈRE In short, Sir, you will be satisfied with us, and you shall earn whatever you like, if you allow us to take you where we intend.

SGANARELLE I shall earn whatever I like?

VALÈRE Yes.

SGANARELLE In that case I am a physician: there is no doubt of it. I had forgotten it; but I recollect it now. What is the matter? Where am I to go?

VALÈRE We will conduct you. The matter is to see a girl who has lost her speech.

SGANARELLE Indeed! I have not found it.

VALÈRE [*Softly to* LUCAS.] How he loves his joke! [*To* SGANARELLE.] Come along, Sir!

SGANARELLE Without a physician's gown!

VALÈRE We will get one.

SGANARELLE [*Presenting his bottle to* VALÈRE.] You carry this: I put my juleps in there. [*Turning round to* LUCAS *and spitting on the ground.*] And you, stamp on this, by order of the physician.

LUCAS Odds sniggers! this is a physician I like. I think he will do, for he is a comical fellow.

ACT II [*A room in* GÉRONTE's *house.*]

Scene I [GÉRONTE, VALÈRE, LUCAS, JACQUELINE.]

VALERE Yes, Sir, I think you will be satisfied; we have brought the greatest physician in the world with us.

LUCAS Oh! Zooks! this one beats everything; all the others are not worthy to hold the candle to him.

VALÈRE   He is a man who has performed some marvellous cures.

LUCAS   Who has put dead people on their legs again.

VALÈRE   He is somewhat whimsical, as I have told you; and at times there are moments when his senses wander, and he does not seem what he really is.

LUCAS   Yes, he loves a joke, and one would say sometimes that he has got a screw loose somewhere.

VALÈRE   But in reality he is quite scientific; and very often he says things quite beyond anyone's comprehension.

LUCAS   When he sets about it, he talks as finely as if he were reading a book.

VALÈRE   He has already a great reputation hereabout, and everybody comes to consult him.

GÉRONTE   I am very anxious to see him; send him to me quickly.

VALÈRE   I am going to fetch him.

Scene II [GÉRONTE, JACQUELINE, LUCAS.]

JACQUELINE   Upon my word, Sir, this one will do just the same as all the rest. I think it will be six of the one and half-a-dozen of the others; and the best medicine to give to your daughter would, in my opinion, be a handsome strapping husband, for whom she could have some love.

GÉRONTE   Lord bless my soul, nurse dear, you are meddling with many things.

LUCAS   Hold your tongue, mother Jacqueline; it is not for you to poke your nose there.

JACQUELINE   I tell you, and a dozen more of you, that all these physicians do her no good; that your daughter wants something else than rhubarb and senna, and that a husband is a plaster which cures all girls' complaints.

GÉRONTE   Would any one have her in her present state, with that affliction on her? and when I intended her to marry, has she not opposed my wishes?

JACQUELINE   No wonder. You wished to give her a man whom she does not like. Why did you not give her to Monsieur Léandre, who takes her fancy? She would have been very obedient, and I vouch for it that he will take her as she is, if you but give her to him.

GÉRONTE   Léandre is not the man we want; he has not got a fortune like the other.

JACQUELINE   He has got an uncle who is so rich, and he is the heir.

GÉRONTE   All these expectations seem to me but moonshine. Brag is a good dog, but Holdfast is a better; and we run a great risk in waiting for dead men's shoes. Death is not always at the beck and call of gentlemen heirs; and while the grass grows, the cow starves.

JACQUELINE   That is all well and good, but I have always heard that in marriage, as in everything else, happiness excels riches. Fathers and mothers have this cursed habit of asking always, "How much has he got?" and "How much has she got?" And gaffer Peter has married his Simonette to that lout Thomas, because he has got a few more vineyards than young Robin, for whom the girl had a fancy; and now the poor creature is as yellow as a guinea, and has not looked like herself ever since. That is a good example for you, Sir. After all, folks have but their pleasure in this world; and I would sooner give my daughter a husband whom she likes than have all the riches in the country.

GÉRONTE   Bless, me, nurse, how you chatter! Hold your tongue, let me beg of you; you take too much upon yourself, and you will spoil your milk.

LUCAS   [*Slapping* GÉRONTE's *shoulder at every word.*]   Indeed, be silent; you are too saucy. The master does not want your speeches, and he knows what he is about. All you have got to do is to suckle your baby, without arguing so much. Our master is the girl's father, and he is good and clever enough to know what she wants.

GÉRONTE   Gently, gently.

LUCAS   [*Still slapping* GÉRONTE's *shoulder.*]   I wish to show her her place, and teach her the respect due to you, Sir.

GÉRONTE   Very well. But it does not need all this gesticulating.

Scene III [VALÈRE, SGANARELLE, GÉRONTE, LUCAS, JACQUELINE.]

VALÈRE   Look out, Sir, here is our physician coming.

GÉRONTE   [*To* SGANARELLE.] I am delighted to see you, Sir, at my house, and we have very great need of you.

SGANARELLE   [*In a physician's gown with a very pointed cap.*] Hippocrates says . . . that we should both put our hats on.

GÉRONTE   Hippocrates says that?

SGANARELLE   Yes.

GÉRONTE   In which chapter, if you please?

SGANARELLE   In his chapter . . . on hats.

GÉRONTE   Since Hippocrates says so, we must obey.

SGANARELLE   Doctor, having heard of the marvellous things . . .

GÉRONTE   To whom are you speaking, pray?

SGANARELLE   To you.

GÉRONTE   I am not a physician.

SGANARELLE   You are not a physician?

GÉRONTE   Indeed I am not.

SGANARELLE   Really?

GÉRONTE   *Really.* [SGANARELLE *takes a stick and thrashes* GÉRONTE.] Oh! Oh! Oh!

SGANARELLE   Now you are a physician, I have never taken any other degree.

GÉRONTE   [*To* VALÈRE.] What a devil of a fellow you have brought me here!

VALÈRE   Did I tell you that he was a funny sort of a physician?

GÉRONTE   Yes; but I shall send him about his business with his fun.

LUCAS   Do not take any notice of it, Sir. It is only his joking.

GÉRONTE   The joking does not suit me.

SGANARELLE   Sir, I beg your pardon for the liberty I have taken.

GÉRONTE   I am your humble servant, Sir.

SGANARELLE   I am sorry . . .

GÉRONTE   It is nothing.

SGANARELLE   For the cudgelling I . . .

GÉRONTE   There is no harm done.

SGANARELLE   Which I have had the honour to give you.

GÉRONTE   Do not say any more about it, Sir. I have a daughter who is suffering from a strange complaint.

SGANARELLE   I am delighted, Sir, that your daughter has need of my skill; and I wish, with all my heart, that you stood in the same need of it, you and all your family, in order to show you my wish to serve you.

GÉRONTE   I am obliged to you for these kind feelings.

SGANARELLE   I assure you that I am speaking from my very heart.

GÉRONTE   You really do me too much honour.

SGANARELLE   What is your daughter's name?

GÉRONTE   Lucinde.

SGANARELLE   Lucinde! Ah! a pretty name to physic! Lucinde!

GÉRONTE   I will just see what she is doing.

SGANARELLE   Who is that tall woman?

GÉRONTE   She is my baby's nurse.

Scene IV [SGANARELLE, JACQUELINE, LUCAS.]

SGANARELLE   [*Aside.*] The deuce! that is a fine piece of household furniture. [*Aloud.*] Ah, nurse! Charming nurse! my physic is the very humble slave of your nurseship, and I should like to be the fortunate little nursling to suck the milk of your good graces. [*He puts his hand on her bosom.*] All my nostrums, all my skill, all my cleverness, is at your service; and . . .

LUCAS   By your leave, M. Doctor; leave my wife alone, I pray you.

SGANARELLE   What! is she your wife?

LUCAS   Yes.

SGANARELLE   Oh! indeed! I did not know that, but I am very glad of it for the love of both. [*He pretends to embrace* LUCAS, *but embraces the nurse.*]

LUCAS   [*Pulling* SGANARELLE *away, and placing himself between him and his wife.*] Gently, if you please.

SGANARELLE   I assure you that I am delighted that you should be united together. I congratulate her upon having such a husband as you; and I congratulate you upon having a wife so handsome, so discreet, and so well shaped as she is. [*He pretends once more to embrace* LUCAS, *who holds out his arms, he slips under them and embraces the nurse.*]

LUCAS   [*Pulling him away again.*] Do not pay so many compliments, I beg of you.

SGANARELLE   Shall I not rejoice with you about such a lovely harmony?

LUCAS   With me as much as you like; but a truce to compliments with my wife.

SGANARELLE   I have both your happiness equally at heart; and if I embrace you to show my delight in you, I embrace her to show my delight in her. [*Same by-play.*]

LUCAS [*Pulling him away for the third time.*] Odds boddikins, Doctor, what capers you cut!

Scene V [GÉRONTE, SGANARELLE, LUCAS, JACQUELINE.]

GÉRONTE   My daughter will be here directly, Sir.

SGANARELLE   I am awaiting her, Sir, with all my physic.

GÉRONTE   Where is it?

SGANARELLE   [*Touching his forehead.*] In there.

GÉRONTE   That is good.

SGANARELLE   But as I feel much interested in your family, I should like to test the milk of your nurse, and examine her breasts. [*He draws close to* JACQUELINE.]

LUCAS   [*Pulling him away, and swinging him round.*] Nothing of the sort, nothing of the sort. I do not wish it.

SGANARELLE   It is the physician's duty to see the breasts of the nurse.

LUCAS   Duty or no duty, I will not have it.

SGANARELLE   Have you the audacity to contradict a physician? Out with you.

LUCAS   I do not care a straw about a physician.

SGANARELLE   [*Looking askance at him.*] I will give you a fever.

JACQUELINE   [*Taking* LUCAS *by the arm, and swinging him around also.*] Get out of the way. Am I not big enough to take my own part, if he does anything to me which he ought not to do?

LUCAS   I will not have him touch you, I will not.

SGANARELLE   For shame you rascal, to be jealous of your wife.

GÉRONTE   Here comes my daughter.

Scene VI [LUCINDE, GÉRONTE, SGANARELLE, VALÈRE, LUCAS, JACQUELINE.]

SGANARELLE   Is this the patient?

GÉRONTE   Yes, I have but one daughter; and I would never get over it if she were to die.

SGANARELLE   Do not let her do anything of the kind. She must not die without a prescription of the physician.

GÉRONTE   A chair here!

SGANARELLE   [*Seated between* GÉRONTE *and* LUCINDE.] This is not at all an unpleasant patient, and I am of the opinion that she would not be at all amiss for a man in very good health.

GÉRONTE   You have made her laugh, Sir.

SGANARELLE   So much the better. It is the best sign in the world when a physician makes the patient laugh. [*To* LUCINDE.] Well, what is the matter? What ails you? What is it you feel?

LUCINDE   [*Replies by motions, by putting her hands to her mouth, her head, and under her chin.*] Ha, hi, ho, ha!

SGANARELLE   What do you say?

LUCINDE   [*Continues the same motions.*] Ha, hi, ho, ha, ha, hi, ho!

SGANARELLE   What is that?

LUCINDE   Ha, hi, ho!

SGANARELLE   [*Imitating her.*] Ha, hi, ho, ha, ha! I do not understand you. What sort of language do you call that?

GÉRONTE   That is just where her complaint lies, Sir. She has become dumb, without our having been able till now to discover the cause. This accident has obliged us to postpone her marriage.

SGANARELLE   And why so?

GÉRONTE   He whom she is going to marry wishes to wait for her recovery to conclude the marriage.

SGANARELLE   And who is this fool that does not want his wife to be dumb? Would to Heaven that mine had that complaint! I should take particular care not to have her cured.

GÉRONTE   To the point, Sir. We beseech you to use all your skill to cure her of this affliction.

SGANARELLE   Do not make yourself uneasy. But tell me, does this pain oppress her much?

GÉRONTE   Yes, Sir.

SGANARELLE   So much the better. Is the suffering very acute?

GÉRONTE   Very acute.

SGANARELLE   That is right. Does she go to . . . you know where?

GÉRONTE   Yes.

SGANARELLE   Freely?

GÉRONTE   That I know nothing about.

SGANARELLE   Is the matter healthy?

GÉRONTE   I do not understand these things.

SGANARELLE   [*Turning to the patient.*] Give me your hand. [*To* GÉRONTE.] The pulse tells me that your daughter is dumb.

GÉRONTE   Sir, that is what is the matter with her; ah! yes, you have found it out at the first touch.

SGANARELLE   Of course!

JACQUELINE   See how he has guessed her complaint.

SGANARELLE   We great physicians, we know matters at once. An ignoramus would have been nonplussed, and would have told you: it is this, that, or the other; but I hit the nail on the head from the very first, and I tell you that your daughter is dumb.

GÉRONTE   Yes; but I should like you to tell me whence it arises.

SGANARELLE   Nothing is easier; it arises from loss of speech.

GÉRONTE   Very good. But the reason of her having lost her speech, pray?

SGANARELLE   Our best authorities will tell you that it is because there is an impediment in the action of her tongue.

GÉRONTE   But, once more, your opinion upon this impediment in the action of her tongue.

SGANARELLE   Aristotle on this subject says . . . a great many clever things.

GÉRONTE   I dare say.

SGANARELLE   Ah! He was a great man!

GÉRONTE   No doubt.

SGANARELLE   Yes, a very great man. [*Holding out his arm, and putting a finger of the other hand in the bend.*] A man who was, by this, much greater than I. But to come back to our argument: I hold that this impediment in the action of her tongue is caused by certain humours, which among us learned men, we call peccant humours; peccant—that is to say . . . peccant humours; inasmuch as the vapours formed by the exhalations of the influences which rise in the very region of diseases, coming, . . . as we may say to. . . . Do you understand Latin?

GÉRONTE   Not in the least.

SGANARELLE   [*Suddenly rising.*] You do not understand Latin?

GÉRONTE   No.

SGANARELLE   [*Assuming various comic attitudes.*] *Cabricias arci thuram, catalamus, singulariter, nominativo, hœc musa,* the muse, *bonus, bona, bonum. Deus sanctus, estne oratio latinas? Etiam.* Yes. *Quare?* Why? *Quia substantivo et adjectivum, concordat in generi, numerum, et casus.*

GÉRONTE   Ah! Why did I not study?

JACQUELINE   What a clever man!

LUCAS   Yes, it is so beautiful that I do not understand a word of it.

SGANARELLE   Thus these vapours which I speak of, passing from the left side, where the liver is, to the right side, where we find the heart, it so happens that the lungs, which in Latin we call *armyan,* having communication with the brain, which in Greek we style *nasmus,* by means of *vena cava,* which in Hebrew, is termed *cubile,* meet in their course the said vapours, which fill the ventricles of the omoplata; and because the said vapours . . . now understand well this argument, pray . . . and because these said vapours are endowed with a certain malignity . . . listen well to this, I beseech you.

GÉRONTE   Yes.

SGANARELLE   Are endowed with a certain malignity which is caused . . . pay attention here, if you please.

GÉRONTE   I do.

SGANARELLE   Which is caused by the acridity of these humours engendered in the concavity of the diaphragm, it happens that these vapours. . . . *Ossabandus, nequeis, nequer, potarinum, puipsa milus.* That is exactly the reason that your daughter is dumb.

JACQUELINE   Ah! How well this gentleman explains all this.

LUCAS   Why does not my tongue wag as well as his?

GÉRONTE   It is undoubtedly impossible to argue better. There is but one thing that I cannot exactly make out: that is the whereabouts of the liver and the heart. It appears to me that you place them differently from where they are; that the heart is on the left side, and the liver on the right.

SGANARELLE   Yes; this was formerly; but we have changed all that, and we now-a-days practice the medical art on an entirely new system.

GÉRONTE   I did not know that, and I pray you pardon my ignorance.

SGANARELLE   There is no harm done; and you are not obliged to be so clever as we are.

GÉRONTE   Certainly not. But what think you, Sir, ought to be done for this complaint?

SGANARELLE   What do I think ought to be done?

GÉRONTE   Yes.

SGANARELLE   My advice is to put her to bed again, and make her, as a remedy, take plenty of bread soaked in wine.

GÉRONTE   Why so, sir?

SGANARELLE   Because there is in bread and wine mixed together a sympathetic virtue which produces speech. Do you not see that they give nothing else to parrots, and that, by eating it, they learn to speak?

GÉRONTE   That is true. Oh! the great man! Quick, plenty of bread and wine.

SGANARELLE   I shall come back to-night to see how the patient is getting on.

Scene VII [GÉRONTE, SGANARELLE, JACQUELINE.]

SGANARELLE   [To JACQUELINE.] Stop a little, you. [To GÉRONTE.] Sir, I must give some medicine to your nurse.

JACQUELINE   To me, Sir? I am as well as can be.

SGANARELLE   So much the worse, nurse, so much the worse. This excess of health is dangerous, and it would not be amiss to bleed you a little gently, and to administer some little soothing injection.

GÉRONTE   But, my dear Sir, that is a method which I cannot understand. Why bleed folks when they are not ill?

SGANARELLE   It does not matter, the method is salutary; and as we drink for the thirst to come, so must we bleed for the disease to come.

JACQUELINE   [Going.] I do not care a fig for all this, and I will not have my body made an apothecary's shop.

SGANARELLE   You object to my remedies; but we shall know how to bring you to reason.

Scene VIII [GÉRONTE, SGANARELLE.]

SGANARELLE   I wish you good day.

GÉRONTE   Stay a moment, if you please.

SGANARELLE   What are you going to do?

GÉRONTE   Give you your fee, Sir.

SGANARELLE   [Putting his hands behind him, from under his gown, while GÉRONTE opens his purse.] I shall not accept it, Sir.

GÉRONTE   Sir.

SGANARELLE   Not at all.

GÉRONTE   One moment.

SGANARELLE   On one consideration.

GÉRONTE   Pray!

SGANARELLE   You are jesting.

GÉRONTE   That is settled.

SGANARELLE   I shall do nothing of the kind.

GÉRONTE   What!

SGANARELLE   I do not practise for money's sake.

GÉRONTE   I am convinced of that.

SGANARELLE   [After having taken the money.] Are they good weight?

GÉRONTE   Yes, Sir.

SGANARELLE   I am not a mercenary physician.

GÉRONTE   I am well aware of it.

SGANARELLE   I am not actuated by interest.

GÉRONTE   I do not for a moment think so.

SGANARELLE   [Alone, looking at the money he has received.] Upon my word, this does not promise badly; and provided . . .

Scene IX [LÉANDRE, SGANARELLE.]

LÉANDRE   I have been waiting some time for you, Sir, and I have come to beg your assistance.

SGANARELLE   [Feeling his pulse.] That is a very bad pulse.

LÉANDRE   I am not ill, Sir; and it is not for that I am come to you.

SGANARELLE   If you are not ill, why the devil do you not tell me so?

LÉANDRE   No. To tell you the matter in a few words, my name is Léandre. I am in love with Lucinde to whom you have just paid a visit; and as all access to her is denied to me, through the ill-temper of her father, I venture to beseech you to serve me in my love affair, and to assist me in a stratagem that I have invented, so as to say a few words to her, on which my whole life and happiness absolutely depend.

SGANARELLE   [In apparent anger.] Whom do you take me for? How dare you address yourself to me to assist you in your love affair, and to wish me to lower the dignity of a physician by an affair of that kind!

LÉANDRE   Do not make a noise, Sir!

SGANARELLE   [Driving him back.] I will make a noise. You are an impertinent fellow.

LÉANDRE   Ah! gently, Sir.

SGANARELLE   An ill-mannered jackanapes.

LÉANDRE   Pray!

SGANARELLE   I will teach you that I am not the kind of man you take me for, and that it is the greatest insolence . . .

LÉANDRE   [*Taking out a purse.*] Sir . . .

SGANARELLE   To wish to employ me . . . [*Taking the purse.*] I am not speaking about you, for you are a gentleman; and I should be delighted to be of any use to you; but there are certain impertinent people in this world who take folks for what they are not; and I tell you candidly that this puts me in a passion.

LÉANDRE   I ask your pardon, Sir, for the liberty I have . . .

SGANARELLE   You are jesting. What is the affair in question?

LÉANDRE   You must know then, Sir, that this disease which you wish to cure is a feigned complaint. The physicians have argued about it, as they ought to do, and they have not failed to give it as their opinion—this one, that it arose from the brain; that one, from the intestines; another, from the spleen; another, again, from the liver; but the fact is that love is its real cause, and that Lucinde has only invented this illness in order to free herself from a marriage with which she has been harassed. But for fear that we may be seen together, let us retire; and I will tell you as we go along, what I wish you to do.

SGANARELLE   Come along, then, Sir. You have inspired me with an inconceivable interest in your love; and if all my medical science does not fail me, the patient shall either die or be yours.

ACT III   [A *place near* GÉRONTE's *house.*]

Scene I   [LÉANDRE, SGANARELLE.]

LÉANDRE   I think that I am not at all badly got up for an apothecary; and as her father has scarcely ever seen me, this change of dress and wig is likely enough, I think, to disguise me.

SGANARELLE   There is no doubt of it.

LÉANDRE   Only I should like to know five or six big medical words to leaven my conversation with, and to give me the air of a learned man.

SGANARELLE   Go along, go along; it is not at all necessary. The dress is sufficient; and I know no more about it than you do.

LÉANDRE   How is that!

SGANARELLE   The devil take me if I understand anything about medicine! You are a gentleman, and I do not mind confiding in you, as you have confided in me.

LÉANDRE   What! Then you are not really . . .

SGANARELLE   No, I tell you. They have made me a physician in the teeth of my protests. I have never attempted to be so learned as that; and all my studies did not go farther than the lowest class at school. I do not know how the idea has come to them; but when I saw that in spite of everything they would have it that I was a physician, I made up my mind to be so at somebody's expense. You would not believe, however, how this error has spread, and how everyone is possessed, and believes me to be a learned man. They come seeking me on all sides; and if things go on in this way, I am resolved to stick to the profession all my life. I find that it is the best trade of all; for, whether we manage well or ill, we are paid just the same. Bad workmanship never recoils on us; and we cut the material we have to work with pretty much as we like. A shoemaker, in making a pair of shoes, cannot spoil a scrap of leather without having to bear the loss; but in our business we may spoil a man without its costing us a farthing. The blunders are never put down to us, and it is always the fault of the fellow who dies. The best of this profession is, that there is the greatest honesty and discretion among the dead; for you never find them complain of the physician who has killed them.

LÉANDRE   It is true that the dead are very honourable in that respect.

SGANARELLE   [*Seeing some people advancing towards him.*] There come some people, who seem anxious to consult me. [*To* LÉANDRE.] Go and wait for me near the house of your ladylove.

Scene II   [THIBAUT, PERRIN, SGANARELLE.]

THIBAUT   Sir, we come to look for you, my son Perrin and myself.

SGANARELLE   What is the matter?

THIBAUT   His poor mother, whose name is Perrette, has been on a bed of sickness for the last six months.

SGANARELLE [*Holding out his hand as if to receive money.*] What would you have me do to her?

THIBAUT I would like you to give me some little doctor's stuff to cure her.

SGANARELLE We must first see what is the matter with her.

THIBAUT She is ill with the hypocrisy, Sir.

SGANARELLE With the hypocrisy?

THIBAUT Yes; I mean she is swollen everywhere. They say that there is a lot of seriosities in her inside, and that her liver, her belly, or her spleen, as you would call it, instead of making blood makes nothing but water. She has, every other day, the quotiguian fever, with lassitude and pains in the muscles of her legs. We can hear in her throat phlegms that are ready to choke her, and she is often taken with syncoles and conversions, so that we think she is going off the hooks. We have got in our village an apothecary—with respect be it said—who has given her, I do not know how much stuff; and it has cost me more than a dozen good crowns in clysters, saving your presence, in apostumes which he has made her swallow, in infections of hyacinth, and in cordial potions. But all this, as people say, was nothing but an ointment of fiddle-faddle. He wanted to give her a certain drug called ametile wine; but I was downright afeard that this would send her to the other world altogether; because they tell me that those big physicians kill, I do not know how many, with that new-fangled potion.

SGANARELLE [*Still holding out his hand, and moving it about to show that he wants money.*] Let us come to the point, friend, let us come to the point.

THIBAUT The point is, Sir, that we have come to beg of you to tell us what we must do.

SGANARELLE I do not understand you at all.

PERRIN My mother is ill, Sir, and here are two corwns which we have brought you to give us some stuff.

SGANARELLE Ah! you I do understand. There is a lad who speaks clearly, and explains himself as he should. You say that your mother is ill with the dropsy; that she is swollen all over her body; that she has a fever, with pains in the legs; that she sometimes is taken with

syncopes and convulsions, that is to say with fainting fits.

PERRIN Indeed, Sir! that is just it.

SGANARELLE I understand you at once. Your father does not know what he says. And now you ask me for a remedy?

PERRIN Yes sir.

SGANARELLE A remedy to cure her?

PERRIN That is just what I mean.

SGANARELLE Take this then. It is a piece of cheese which you must make her take.

PERRIN A piece of cheese, Sir?

SGANARELLE Yes; it is a kind of prepared cheese, in which there is gold, coral, and pearls, and a great many other precious things.

PERRIN I am very much obliged to you, Sir, and I shall go and make her take it directly.

SGANARELLE Go, and if she dies, do not fail to bury her in the best style you can.

Scene III [*The scene changes, and represents, as in the Second Act, a room in* GÉRONTE'S *house.* JACQUELINE, SGANARELLE, LUCAS, *at the far end of the stage.*]

SGANARELLE Here is the pretty nurse. Ah! you darling nurse, I am delighted at this meeting; and the sight of you is like rhubarb, cassia, and senna to me, which purges all melancholy from my mind.

JACQUELINE Upon my word, M. Physician, it is no good talking to me in that style, and I do not understand your Latin at all.

SGANARELLE Get ill, nurse, I beg of you; get ill for my sake. I shall have all the pleasure in the world of curing you.

JACQUELINE I am your humble servant; I would much rather not be cured.

SGANARELLE How I grieve for you, beautiful nurse, in having such a jealous and troublesome husband.

JACQUELINE What am I to do, Sir? It is as a penance for my sins; and where the goat is tied down she must browse.

SGANARELLE What! Such a clod-hopper as that! a fellow who is always watching you, and will let no one speak to you!

JACQUELINE Alas! you have seen nothing yet; and that is only a small sample of his bad temper.

SGANARELLE Is it possible? and can a man have so mean a spirit as to ill-use a woman like you? Ah! I know some, sweet nurse, and who are not very far off, who would only be too glad to kiss your little feet! Why should such a handsome woman have fallen into such hands! and a mere animal, a brute, a stupid, a fool. . . . Excuse me, nurse, for speaking in that way of your husband.

JACQUELINE   Oh! Sir, I know full well that he deserves all these names.

SGANARELLE   Undoubtedly, nurse, he deserves them; and he also deserves that you should plant something on his head to punish him for his suspicions.

JACQUELINE   It is true enough that if I had not his interest so much at heart, he would drive me to do some strange things.

SGANARELLE   Indeed it would just serve him right if you were to revenge yourself upon him with some one. The fellow richly deserves it all, I tell you, and if I were fortunate enough, fair nurse, to be chosen by you . . . [*While* SGANARELLE *is holding out his arms to embrace* JACQUELINE, LUCAS *passes his head under them, and comes between the two.* SGANARELLE *and* JACQUELINE *stare at* LUCAS, *and depart on opposite sides, but the doctor does so in a very comic manner.*]

Scene IV [GÉRONTE, LUCAS.]

GÉRONTE   I say, Lucas, have not you seen our physician here?

LUCAS   Indeed I have seen him, by all the devils, and my wife, too.

GÉRONTE   Where can he be?

LUCAS   I do not know; but I wish he were with the devil.

GÉRONTE   Just go and see what my daughter is doing.

Scene V
[SGANARELLE, LÉANDRE, GERONTE.]

GÉRONTE   I was just inquiring after you, Sir.

SGANARELLE   I have just been amusing myself in your court with expelling the superfluity of drink. How is the patient?

GÉRONTE   Somewhat worse since your remedy.

SGANARELLE   So much the better; it shows that it takes effect.

GÉRONTE   Yes; but while it is taking effect, I am afraid it will choke her.

SGANARELLE   Do not make yourself uneasy; I have some remedies that will make it all right! and I will wait until she is at death's door.

GÉRONTE   [*Pointing to* LÉANDRE.] Who is this man that is with you?

SGANARELLE   [*Intimates by motions of his hands that it is an apothecary.*] It is . . .

GÉRONTE   What?

SGANARELLE   He who . . .

GÉRONTE   Oh!

SGANARELLE   Who . . .

GÉRONTE   I understand.

SGANARELLE   Your daughter will want him.

Scene VI   [LUCINDE, GÉRONTE, LÉANDRE, JACQUELINE, SGANARELLE.]

JACQUELINE   Here is your daughter, Sir, who wishes to stretch her limbs a little.

SGANARELLE   That will do her good. Go to her, M. Apothecary, and feel her pulse, so that I may consult with you presently about her complaint. [*At this point he draws* GÉRONTE *to one end of the stage, and putting one arm upon his shoulder, he places his hand under his chin, with which he makes him turn towards him, each time that* GÉRONTE *wants to look at what is passing between his daughter and the apothecary, while he holds the following discourse with him.*] Sir, it is a great and subtle question among physicians to know whether women or men are more easily cured. I pray you to listen to this, if you please. Some say "no," others say "yes": I say both "yes" and "no"; inasmuch as the incongruity of the opaque humours, which are found in the natural temperament of women, causes the brutal part to struggle for the mastery over the sensitive, we find that the conflict of their opinion depends on the oblique motion of the circle of the moon; and as the sun, which darts its beams on the concavity of the earth, meets . . .

LUCINDE   [*To* LÉANDRE.] No; I am not at all likely to change my feelings.

GÉRONTE   Hark! my daughter speaks! O great virtue of the remedy! O excellent physician! How deeply am I obliged to you, Sir, for this marvellous cure! And what can I do for you after such a service?

SGANARELLE   [*Strutting about the stage, fanning*

himself with his hat.] This case has given me some trouble.

LUCINDE   Yes, father, I have recovered my speech; but I have recovered it to tell you that I will never have any other husband than Léandre, and that it is in vain for you to wish to give me to Horace.

GÉRONTE   But . . .

LUCINDE   Nothing will shake the resolution I have taken.

GÉRONTE   What . . .

LUCINDE   All your fine arguments will be in vain.

GÉRONTE   If . . .

LUCINDE   All your talking will be of no use.

GÉRONTE   I . . .

LUCINDE   I have made up my mind about the matter.

GÉRONTE   But . . .

LUCINDE   No paternal authority can compel me to marry against my will.

GÉRONTE   I have . . .

LUCINDE   You may try as much as you like.

GÉRONTE   It . . .

LUCINDE   My heart cannot submit to this tyranny.

GÉRONTE   The . . .

LUCINDE   And I will sooner go into a convent than marry a man I do not love.

GÉRONTE   But . . .

LUCINDE   [*In a loud voice.*] No. By no means. It is of no use. You waste your time. I shall do nothing of the kind. I am fully determined.

GÉRONTE   Ah! what a torrent of words! One cannot hold out against it. [*To* SGANARELLE.] I beseech you, Sir, to make her dumb again.

SGANARELLE   That is impossible. All that I can do in your behalf is to make you deaf, if you like.

GÉRONTE   I thank you. [*To* LUCINDE.] Do you think . . .

LUCINDE   No; all your reasoning will not have the slightest effect upon me.

GÉRONTE   You shall marry Horace this very evening.

LUCINDE   I would sooner marry death itself.

SGANARELLE   [*To* GÉRONTE.] Stop, for Heaven's sake! stop. Let me doctor this matter; it is a disease that has got hold of her, and I know the remedy to apply to it.

GÉRONTE   Is it possible, indeed, Sir, that you can cure this disease of the mind also?

SGANARELLE   Yes; let me manage it. I have remedies for everything; and our apothecary will serve us capitally for this cure. [*To* LÉANDRE.] A word with you. You perceive that the passion she has for this Léandre is altogether against the wishes of the father; that there is no time to lose; that the humours are very acrimonious; and that it becomes necessary to find speedily a remedy for this complaint, which may get worse by delay. As for myself, I see but one, which is a dose of purgative flight, mixed, as it should be, with two drachms of matrimonium, made up into pills. She may, perhaps, make some difficulty about taking this remedy; but as you are a clever man in your profession, you must induce her to consent to it, and make her swallow the thing as best you can. Go and take a little turn in the garden with her to prepare the humours, while I converse here with her father; but, above all, lose not a moment. Apply the remedy quick! apply the specific!

Scene VII [GÉRONTE, SGANARELLE.]

GÉRONTE   What drugs are those you have just mentioned, Sir? It seems to me that I never heard of them before.

SGANARELLE   They are drugs which are used only in urgent cases.

GÉRONTE   Did you ever see such insolence as hers?

SGANARELLE   Daughters are a little headstrong at times.

GÉRONTE   You would not believe how she is infatuated with this Léandre.

SGANARELLE   The heat of the blood produces those things in young people.

GÉRONTE   As for me, the moment I discovered the violence of this passion, I took care to keep my daughter under lock and key.

SGANARELLE   You have acted wisely.

GÉRONTE   And I have prevented the slightest communication between them.

SGANARELLE   Just so.

GÉRONTE   They would have committed some folly, if they had been permitted to see each other.

SGANARELLE   Undoubtedly.

GÉRONTE   And I think she would have been the girl to run away with him.

SGANARELLE   You have argued very prudently.

GÉRONTE   I was informed that he tried every means to get speech of her.

SGANARELLE   The rascal!

GÉRONTE   But he will waste his time.

SGANARELLE   Aye! Aye!

GÉRONTE   And I will effectually prevent him from seeing her.

SGANARELLE   He has no fool to deal with, and you know some tricks of which he is ignorant. One must get up very early to catch you asleep.

Scene VIII [LUCAS, GÉRONTE, SGANARELLE.]

LUCAS   Odds-bobs, Sir, here is a pretty to do. Your daughter has fled with her Léandre. It was he that played the apothecary, and this is the physician who has performed this nice operation.

GÉRONTE   What! to murder me in this manner! Quick, fetch a magistrate, and take care that he does not get away. Ah villain! I will have you punished by the law.

LUCAS   I am afraid, Master Doctor, that you will be hanged. Do not stir a step, I tell you.

Scene IX [MARTINE, SGANARELLE, LUCAS.]

MARTINE   [_To_ LUCAS.] Good gracious! what a difficulty I have had to find this place! Just tell me what has become of the physician I recommended to you?

LUCAS   Here he is; just going to be hanged.

MARTINE   What! my husband hanged! Alas, and for what?

LUCAS   He has helped some one to run away with master's daughter.

MARTINE   Alas, my dear husband, is it true that you are going to be hanged?

SGANARELLE   Judge for yourself. Ah!

MARTINE   And must you be made an end of in the presence of such a crowd.

SGANARELLE   What am I to do?

MARTINE   If you had only finished cutting our wood, I should be somewhat consoled.

SGANARELLE   Leave me, you break my heart.

MARTINE   No, I will remain to encourage you to die; and I will not leave you until I have seen you hanged.

SGANARELLE   Ah!

Scene X [GÉRONTE, SGANARELLE, MARTINE.]

GÉRONTE   [_To_ SGANARELLE.] The magistrate will be here directly, and we shall put you in a place of safety where they will be answerable for you.

SGANARELLE   [_On his knees, hat in hand._] Alas! will not a few strokes with a cudgel do instead?

GÉRONTE   No; no; the law shall decide. But what do I see?

Scene XI GÉRONTE, LÉANDRE, LUCINDE, SGANARELLE, LUCAS, MARTINE.]

LÉANDRE   Sir, I appear before you as Léandre, and am come to restore Lucinde to your authority. We intended to run away, and get married; but this design has given away to a more honourable proceeding. I will not presume to steal away your daughter, and it is from your hands alone that I will obtain her. I must at the same time acquaint you, that I have just now received some letters informing me of the death of my uncle, and that he has left me heir to all his property.

GÉRONTE   Really, Sir, your virtue is worthy of my utmost consideration, and I give you my daughter with the greatest pleasure in the world.

SGANARELLE   [_Aside._] The physician has had a narrow escape!

MARTINE   Since you are not going to be hanged, you may thank me for being a physician; for I have procured you this honour.

SGANARELLE   Yes, it is you who procured me, I do not know how many thwacks with a cudgel.

LÉANDRE   [_To_ SGANARELLE.] The result has proved too happy to harbour any resentment.

SGANARELLE   Be it so. [_To_ MARTINE.] I forgive you the blows on account of the dignity to which you have elevated me; but prepare yourself henceforth to behave with great respect towards a man of my consequence; and consider that the anger of a physician is more to be dreaded than people imagine.

Comments and Questions

This play, along with many others by Molière, represents the laughing theater at its best. It is all sunlight and no shadows. For this reason, serious analysis may seem out of place. The greatness of the art, however, has challenged critics for three hundred years, and serious analysis does help one to enter more fully into the pure fun; to laugh again at what he has laughed at before.

1. You may have been mildly puzzled by the many scenes. What occurs when a new scene is indicated? How does Molière's practice in this respect differ from modern practice? Compare, for example, the scenes in *An Enemy of the People,* next.

2. The facts of the play are preposterous, even more so than the facts set forth in *The Boor* (p. 432). What are the literal facts? How does each bit of action grow out of the preceding action?

3. How does the plot involving Sganarelle and Martine encompass the plot involving Léandre, Lucinde and Géronte? Outline both plots.

4. Discuss the by-play, that is, the action which the author through stage directions indicates for the actors. How much of the play's effect must depend upon the ability and agility of the actors? Consider particularly the scene in which Sganarelle makes advances to Jacqueline in the presence of Lucas, her husband (see II, iv).

5. Make a careful comparison of *The Boor* and this play. How much does the humor of both plays depend upon the age-old theme of male versus female?

6. Point out the passages in which Molière satirizes practitioners of medicine. Is the satire directed as much at the gullibility of people as at physicians? Is any of the satire still applicable today? Discuss.

An Enemy of the People

HENRIK IBSEN
1828–1906

Characters

DR. THOMAS STOCKMANN, *Medical Officer of the Municipal Baths*

MRS. STOCKMANN, *his wife*

PETRA, *their daughter, a teacher*

EJLIF, *aged 13, their son*

MORTEN, *aged 10, their son*

PETER STOCKMANN, *Dr. Stockmann's elder brother; Mayor of the town and Chief Constable, Chairman of the Baths' Committee, etc.*

MORTEN KIIL, *a tanner and Mrs. Stockmann's adoptive father*

HOVSTAD, *editor of "The People's Messenger"*

BILLING, *sub-editor*

CAPTAIN HORSTER

ASLAKSEN, *a printer*

Men of various conditions and occupations, some few women, and a troop of schoolboys—the audience at a public meeting

The action takes place in a coast town in southern Norway.

ACT I

SCENE: DR. STOCKMANN'S *sitting-room. It is evening. The room is plainly but neatly appointed and furnished. In the right-hand wall are two doors; the farther leads out to the hall, the nearer to the doctor's study. In the left-hand wall, opposite the door leading to the hall, is a door leading to the other rooms occupied by the family. In the middle of the same wall stands the stove, and, further forward, a couch with a looking-glass hanging over it and an oval table in front of it. On the table, a lighted lamp, with a lampshade. At the back of the room, an open door leads to the dining-room.* BILLING *is seen sitting at the dining table, on which a lamp is burning. He has a napkin tucked under his chin, and* MRS. STOCKMANN *is standing by the table handing him a large plate-full of roast beef. The other places at the table are empty, and the table somewhat in disorder, a meal having evidently recently been finished.*

MRS. STOCKMANN You see, if you come an hour late, Mr. Billing, you have to put up with cold meat.

BILLING [*As he eats.*] It is uncommonly good, thank you—remarkably good.

MRS. STOCKMANN My husband makes such a point of having his meals punctually, you know—

BILLING That doesn't affect me a bit. Indeed, I almost think I enjoy a meal all the better when I can sit down and eat all by myself and undisturbed.

MRS. STOCKMANN Oh well, as long as you are enjoying it—.[*Turns to the hall door, listening.*] I expect that is Mr. Hovstad coming too.

BILLING Very likely.

[PETER STOCKMANN *comes in. He wears an overcoat and his official hat, and carries a stick.*]

PETER STOCKMANN Good evening, Katherine.

MRS. STOCKMANN [*Coming forward into the sitting-room.*] Ah, good evening—is it you? How good of you to come up and see us!

PETER STOCKMANN I happened to be passing, and so— [*Looks into the dining-room.*] But you have company with you, I see.

MRS. STOCKMANN [*A little embarrassed.*] Oh, no—it was quite by chance he came in. [*Hurriedly.*] Won't you come in and have something, too?

PETER STOCKMANN I! No, thank you. Good gracious—hot meat at night! Not with my digestion.

MRS. STOCKMANN Oh, but just once in a way—

PETER STOCKMANN No, no, my dear lady; I stick to my tea and bread and butter. It is much more wholesome in the long run—and a little more economical, too.

MRS. STOCKMANN [*Smiling.*] Now you mustn't think that Thomas and I are spendthrifts.

PETER STOCKMANN Not you, my dear; I would never think that of you. [*Points to the* DOCTOR's *study.*] Is he not at home?

MRS. STOCKMANN No, he went out for a little turn after supper—he and the boys.

PETER STOCKMANN I doubt if that is a wise thing to do. [*Listens.*] I fancy I hear him coming now.

MRS. STOCKMANN No, I don't think it is he. [*A knock is heard at the door.*] Come in! [HOVSTAD *comes in from the hall.*] Oh, it is you, Mr. Hovstad!

HOVSTAD Yes, I hope you will forgive me, but I was delayed at the printer's. Good evening, Mr. Mayor.

PETER STOCKMANN [*Bowing a little distantly.*] Good evening. You have come on business, no doubt.

HOVSTAD Partly. It's about an article for the paper.

PETER STOCKMANN So I imagined. I hear my brother has become a prolific contributor to "The People's Messenger."

HOVSTAD Yes, he is good enough to write in "The People's Messenger" when he has any home truths to tell.

MRS. STOCKMANN [*To* HOVSTAD.] But won't you—? [*Points to the dining-room.*]

PETER STOCKMANN Quite so, quite so. I don't blame him in the least, as a writer, for addressing himself to the quarters where he will find the readiest sympathy. And, besides that, I personally have no reason to bear any ill will to your paper, Mr. Hovstad.

HOVSTAD I quite agree with you.

PETER STOCKMANN Taking one thing with another, there is an excellent spirit of toleration in the town—an admirable municipal spirit. And it all springs from the fact of our having a great common interest to unite us—an interest that is in an equally high degree the concern of every right-minded citizen—

HOVSTAD The Baths, yes.

PETER STOCKMANN Exactly—our fine, new, handsome Baths. Mark my words, Mr. Hovstad—the Baths will become the focus of our municipal life! Not a doubt of it!

MRS. STOCKMANN That is just what Thomas says.

PETER STOCKMANN Think how extraordinarily the place has developed within the last year or two! Money has been flowing in, and there is some life and some business doing in the town. Houses and landed property are rising in value every day.

HOVSTAD And unemployment is diminishing.

PETER STOCKMANN Yes, that is another thing. The burden of the poor-rates has been lightened, to the great relief of the propertied classes; and that relief will be even greater if only we get a really good summer this year, and lots of visitors—plenty of invalids, who will make the Baths talked about.

HOVSTAD   And there is a good prospect of that, I hear.

PETER STOCKMANN   It looks very promising. Enquiries about apartments and that sort of thing are reaching us every day.

HOVSTAD   Well, the doctor's article will come in very suitably.

PETER STOCKMANN   Has he been writing something just lately?

HOVSTAD   This is something he wrote in the winter, a recommendation of the Baths—an account of the excellent sanitary conditions here. But I held the article over, temporarily.

PETER STOCKMANN   Ah—some little difficulty about it, I suppose?

HOVSTAD   No, not at all; I thought it would be better to wait till the spring, because it is just at this time that people begin to think seriously about their summer quarters.

PETER STOCKMANN   Quite right; you were perfectly right, Mr. Hovstad.

MRS. STOCKMANN   Yes, Thomas is really indefatigable when it is a question of the Baths.

PETER STOCKMANN   Well—remember, he is the Medical Officer to the Baths.

HOVSTAD   Yes, and what is more, they owe their existence to him.

PETER STOCKMANN   To him? Indeed! It is true I have heard from time to time that some people are of that opinion. At the same time I must say I imagined that I took a modest part in the enterprise.

MRS. STOCKMANN   Yes, that is what Thomas is always saying.

HOVSTAD   But who denies it, Mr. Stockmann? You set the thing going and made a practical concern of it; we all know that. I only meant that the idea of it came first from the doctor.

PETER STOCKMANN   Oh, ideas—yes! My brother has had plenty of them in his time—unfortunately. But when it is a question of putting an idea into practical shape, you have to apply to a man of different mettle, Mr. Hovstad. And I certainly should have thought that in this house at least—

MRS. STOCKMANN   My dear Peter—

HOVSTAD   How can you think that—?

MRS. STOCKMANN   Won't you go in and have something, Mr. Hovstad? My husband is sure to be back directly.

HOVSTAD   Thank you, perhaps just a morsel.

[*Goes into the dining-room.*]

PETER STOCKMANN   [*Lowering his voice a little.*] It is a curious thing that these farmers' sons never seem to lose their want of tact.

MRS. STOCKMANN   Surely it is not worth bothering about! Cannot you and Thomas share the credit as brothers?

PETER STOCKMANN   I should have thought so; but apparently some people are not satisfied with a share.

MRS. STOCKMANN   What nonsense! You and Thomas get on so capitally together. [*Listens.*] There he is at last. I think. [*Goes out and opens the door leading to the hall.*]

DR. STOCKMANN   [*Laughing and talking outside.*] Look here—here is another guest for you, Katherine. Isn't that jolly? Come in, Captain Horster; hang your coat up on this peg. Ah, you don't wear an overcoat. Just think, Katherine; I met him in the street and could hardly persuade him to come up! [CAPTAIN HORSTER *comes into the room and greets* MRS. STOCKMANN. *He is followed by* DR. STOCKMANN.] Come along in, boys. They are ravenously hungry again, you know. Come along, Captain Horster; you must have a slice of beef. [*Pushes* HORSTER *into the dining-room.* EJLIF *and* MORTEN *go in after them.*]

MRS. STOCKMANN   But, Thomas, don't you see—?

DR. STOCKMANN   [*Turning in the doorway.*] Oh, is it you, Peter? [*Shakes hands with him.*] Now that is very delightful.

PETER STOCKMANN   Unfortunately I must go in a moment—

DR. STOCKMANN   Rubbish! There is some toddy just coming in. You haven't forgotten the toddy, Katherine?

MRS. STOCKMANN   Of course not; the water is boiling now. [*Goes into the dining-room.*]

PETER STOCKMANN   Toddy too!

DR. STOCKMANN   Yes, sit down and we will have it comfortably.

PETER STOCKMANN   Thanks, I never care about an evening's drinking.

DR. STOCKMANN   But this isn't an evening's drinking.

PETER STOCKMANN   It seems to me—. [*Looks towards the dining-room.*] It is extraordinary how they can put away all that food.

DR. STOCKMANN   [*Rubbing his hands.*] Yes, isn't

it splendid to see young people eat? They have always got an appetite, you know! That's as it should be. Lots of food—to build up their strength! They are the people who are going to stir up the fermenting forces of the future, Peter.

PETER STOCKMANN   May I ask what they will find here to "stir up," as you put it?

DR. STOCKMANN   Ah, you must ask the young people that—when the time comes. We shan't be able to see it, of course. That stands to reason—two old fogies, like us—

PETER STOCKMANN   Really, really! I must say that is an extremely odd expression to—

DR. STOCKMANN   Oh, you mustn't take me too literally, Peter. I am so heartily happy and contented, you know. I think it is such an extraordinary piece of good fortune to be in the middle of all this growing, germinating life. It is a splendid time to live in! It is as if a whole new world were being created around one.

PETER STOCKMANN   Do you really think so?

DR. STOCKMANN   Ah, naturally you can't appreciate it as keenly as I. You have lived all your life in these surroundings, and your impressions have got blunted. But I, who have been buried all these years in my little corner up north, almost without ever seeing a stranger who might bring new ideas with him—well, in my case it has the same effect as if I had been transported into the middle of a crowded city.

PETER STOCKMANN   Oh, a city—!

DR. STOCKMANN   I know, I know; it is all cramped enough here, compared with many other places. But there is life here—there is promise—there are innumerable things to work for and fight for; and that is the main thing. [Calls.] Katherine, hasn't the postman been here?

MRS. STOCKMANN   [From the dining-room.] No.

DR. STOCKMANN   And then to be comfortably off, Peter! That is something one learns to value, when one has been on the brink of starvation, as we have.

PETER STOCKMANN   Oh, surely—

DR. STOCKMANN   Indeed I can assure you we have often been very hard put to it, up there. And now to be able to live like a lord! Today, for instance, we had roast beef for dinner—and, what is more, for supper too. Won't you come and have a little bit? Or let me show it to you, at any rate? Come here—

PETER STOCKMANN   No, no—not for worlds!

DR. STOCKMANN   Well, but just come here then. Do you see, we have got a table-cover?

PETER STOCKMANN   Yes, I noticed it.

DR. STOCKMANN   And we have got a lamp-shade too. Do you see? All out of Katherine's savings! It makes the room so cosy. Don't you think so? Just stand here for a moment—no, no, not there—just here, that's it! Look now, when you get the light on it altogether—I really think it looks very nice, doesn't it?

PETER STOCKMANN   Oh, if you can afford luxuries of this kind—

DR. STOCKMANN   Yes, I can afford it now. Katherine tells me I earn almost as much as we spend.

PETER STOCKMANN   Almost—yes!

DR. STOCKMANN   But a scientific man must live in a little bit of style. I am quite sure an ordinary civil servant spends more in a year than I do.

PETER STOCKMANN   I daresay. A civil servant—a man in a well-paid position—

DR. STOCKMANN   Well, any ordinary merchant, then! A man in that position spends two or three times as much as—

PETER STOCKMANN   It just depends on circumstances.

DR. STOCKMANN   At all events I assure you I don't waste money unprofitably. But I can't find it in my heart to deny myself the pleasure of entertaining my friends. I need that sort of thing, you know. I have lived for so long shut out of it all that it is a necessity of life to me to mix with young, eager, ambitious men, men of liberal and active minds; and that describes every one of those fellows who are enjoying their supper in there. I wish you knew more of Hovstad—

PETER STOCKMANN   By the way, Hovstad was telling me he was going to print another article of yours.

DR. STOCKMANN   An article of mine?

PETER STOCKMANN   Yes, about the Baths. An article you wrote in the winter.

DR. STOCKMANN   Oh, that one! No, I don't intend that to appear just for the present.

PETER STOCKMANN   Why not? It seems to me that this would be the most opportune moment.

DR. STOCKMANN Yes, very likely—under normal conditions. [*Crosses the room.*]

PETER STOCKMANN [*Following him with his eyes.*] Is there anything abnormal about the present conditions?

DR. STOCKMANN [*Standing stiff.*] To tell you the truth, Peter, I can't say just at this moment— at all events not tonight. There may be much that is very abnormal about the present conditions—and it is possible there may be nothing abnormal about them at all. It is quite possible it may be merely my imagination.

PETER STOCKMANN I must say it all sounds most mysterious. Is there something going on that I am to be kept in ignorance of? I should have imagined that I, as Chairman of the governing body of the Baths—

DR. STOCKMANN And I should have imagined that I—. Oh, come, don't let us fly out at one another, Peter.

PETER STOCKMANN Heaven forbid! I am not in the habit of flying out at people, as you call it. But I am entitled to request most emphatically that all arrangements shall be made in a business-like manner, through the proper channels, and shall be dealt with by the legally constituted authorities. I can allow no going behind our backs by any roundabout means.

DR. STOCKMANN Have I ever at any time tried to go behind your backs?

PETER STOCKMANN You have an ingrained tendency to take your own way, at all events; and that is almost equally inadmissible in a well-ordered community. The individual ought undoubtedly to acquiesce in subordinating himself to the community—or, to speak more accurately, to the authorities who have the care of the community's welfare.

DR. STOCKMANN Very likely. But what the deuce has all this got to do with me?

PETER STOCKMANN That is exactly what you never appear to be willing to learn, my dear Thomas. But, mark my words, some day you will have to suffer for it—sooner or later. Now I have told you. Good-bye.

DR. STOCKMANN Have you taken leave of your senses? You are on the wrong scent altogether.

PETER STOCKMANN I am not usually that. You must excuse me now if I—[*Calls into the dining-room.*] Good night, Katherine. Good night, gentlemen. [*Goes out.*]

MRS. STOCKMANN [*Coming from the dining-room.*] Has he gone?

DR. STOCKMANN Yes, and in such a bad temper.

MRS. STOCKMANN But, dear Thomas, what have you been doing to him again?

DR. STOCKMANN Nothing at all. And, anyhow, he can't oblige me to make my report before the proper time.

MRS. STOCKMANN What have you got to make a report to him about?

DR. STOCKMANN Hm! Leave that to me, Katherine.—It is an extraordinary thing that the postman doesn't come.

[HOVSTAD, BILLING, *and* HORSTER *have got up from the table and come into the sitting-room.* EJLIF *and* MORTEN *come in after them.*]

BILLING [*Stretching himself.*] Ah!—one feels a new man after a meal like that.

HOVSTAD The mayor wasn't in a very sweet temper tonight, then.

DR. STOCKMANN It is his stomach; he has a wretched digestion.

HOVSTAD I rather think it was us two of "The People's Messenger" that he couldn't digest.

MRS. STOCKMANN I thought you came out of it pretty well with him.

HOVSTAD Oh yes; but it isn't anything more than a sort of truce.

BILLING That is just what it is! That word sums up the situation.

DR. STOCKMANN We must remember that Peter is a lonely man, poor chap. He has no home comforts of any kind; nothing but everlasting business. And all that infernal weak tea wash that he pours into himself! Now then, my boys, bring chairs up to the table. Aren't we going to have that toddy, Katherine?

MRS. STOCKMANN [*Going into the dining-room.*] I am just getting it.

DR. STOCKMANN Sit down here on the couch beside me, Captain Horster. We so seldom see you—. Please sit down, my friends.

[*They sit down at the table.* MRS. STOCKMANN *brings a tray, with a spirit-lamp, glasses, bottles, etc., upon it.*]

MRS. STOCKMANN There you are! This is arrack, and this is rum, and this one is the brandy. Now every one must help himself.

DR. STOCKMANN [*Taking a glass.*] We will. [*They all mix themselves some toddy.*] And let us have the cigars. Ejlif, you know where the box is. And you, Morten, can fetch my pipe. [*The two boys go into the room on the right.*] I have a suspicion that Ejlif pockets a cigar now and then!—but I take no notice of it. [*Calls out.*] And my smoking-cap too, Morten. Katherine, you can tell him where I left it. Ah, he has got it. [*The boys bring the various things.*] Now, my friends, I stick to my pipe, you know. This one has seen plenty of bad weather with me up north. [*Touches glasses with them.*] Your good health! Ah! it is good to be sitting snug and warm here.

MRS. STOCKMANN [*Who sits knitting.*] Do you sail soon, Captain Horster?

HORSTER I expect to be ready to sail next week.

MRS. STOCKMANN I suppose you are going to America?

HORSTER Yes, that is the plan.

MRS. STOCKMANN Then you won't be able to take part in the coming election.

HORSTER Is there going to be an election?

BILLING Didn't you know?

HORSTER No, I don't mix myself up with those things.

BILLING But do you not take an interest in public affairs?

HORSTER No, I don't know anything about politics.

BILLING All the same, one ought to vote, at any rate.

HORSTER Even if one doesn't know anything about what is going on?

BILLING Doesn't know! What do you mean by that? A community is like a ship; every one ought to be prepared to take the helm.

HORSTER Maybe that is all very well on shore, but on board ship it wouldn't work.

HOVSTAD It is astonishing how little most sailors care about what goes on on shore.

BILLING Very extraordinary.

DR. STOCKMANN Sailors are like birds of passage; they feel equally at home in any latitude. And that is only an additional reason for our being all the more keen, Hovstad. Is there to be anything of public interest in tomorrow's "Messenger"?

HOVSTAD Nothing about municipal affairs. But the day after to-morrow I was thinking of printing your article—

DR. STOCKMANN Ah, devil take it—my article! Look here, that must wait a bit.

HOVSTAD Really? We have just got convenient space for it, and I thought it was just the opportune moment—

DR. STOCKMANN Yes, yes, very likely you are right; but it must wait all the same. I will explain to you later.

[PETRA *comes in from the hall, in hat and cloak and with a bundle of exercise books under her arm.*]

PETRA Good evening.

DR. STOCKMANN Good evening, Petra; come along.

[*Mutual greetings;* PETRA *takes off her things and puts them down on a chair by the door.*]

PETRA And you have all been sitting here enjoying yourselves, while I have been out slaving!

DR. STOCKMANN Well, come and enjoy yourself too!

BILLING May I mix a glass for you?

PETRA [*Coming to the table.*] Thanks, I would rather do it; you always mix it too strong. But I forgot, father—I have a letter for you. [*Goes to the chair where she has laid her things.*]

DR. STOCKMANN A letter? From whom?

PETRA [*Looking in her coat pocket.*] The postman gave it to me just as I was going out—

DR. STOCKMANN [*Getting up and going to her.*] And you only give it to me now!

PETRA I really had not time to run up again. There it is!

DR. STOCKMANN [*Seizing the letter.*] Let's see, let's see, child! [*Looks at the address.*] Yes, that's all right!

MRS. STOCKMANN Is it the one you have been expecting so anxiously, Thomas?

DR. STOCKMANN Yes, it is. I must go to my room now and—. Where shall I get a light, Katherine? Is there no lamp in my room again?

MRS. STOCKMANN Yes, your lamp is all ready lit on your desk.

DR. STOCKMANN Good, good. Excuse me for a moment—. [*Goes into his study.*]

PETRA What do you suppose it is, mother?

MRS. STOCKMANN I don't know; for the last day or two he has always been asking if the postman has not been.

BILLING Probably some country patient.

PETRA Poor old dad!—he will overwork himself soon. [*Mixes a glass for herself.*] There, that will taste good!

HOVSTAD   Have you been teaching in the evening school again today?

PETRA   [*Sipping from her glass.*] Two hours.

BILLING   And four hours of school in the morning—

PETRA   Five hours.

MRS. STOCKMANN   And you have still got exercises to correct, I see.

PETRA   A whole heap, yes.

HORSTER   You are pretty full up with work too, it seems to me.

PETRA   Yes—but that is good. One is so delightfully tired after it.

BILLING   Do you like that?

PETRA   Yes, because one sleeps so well then.

MORTEN   You must be dreadfully wicked, Petra.

PETRA   Wicked?

MORTEN   Yes, because you work so much. Mr. Rörlund says work is a punishment for our sins.

EJLIF   Pooh, what a duffer you are, to believe a thing like that!

MRS. STOCKMANN   Come, come, Ejlif!

BILLING   [*Laughing.*] That's capital!

HOVSTAD   Don't you want to work as hard as that, Morten?

MORTEN   No, indeed I don't.

HOVSTAD   What do you want to be, then?

MORTEN   I should like best to be a Viking.

EJLIF   You would have to be a pagan then.

MORTEN   Well, I could become a pagan, couldn't I?

BILLING   I agree with you, Morten! My sentiments, exactly.

MRS. STOCKMANN   [*Signalling to him.*] I am sure that is not true, Mr. Billing.

BILLING   Yes, I swear it is! I am a pagan, and I am proud of it. Believe me, before long we shall all be pagans.

MORTEN   And then shall be allowed to do anything we like?

BILLING   Well, you see, Morten—.

MRS. STOCKMANN   You must go to your room now, boys; I am sure you have some lessons to learn for tomorrow.

EJLIF   I should like so much to stay a little longer—

MRS. STOCKMANN   No, no; away you go, both of you.

[*The boys say good-night and go into the room on the left.*]

HOVSTAD   Do you really think it can do the boys any harm to hear such things?

MRS. STOCKMANN   I don't know, but I don't like it.

PETRA   But you know, mother, I think you really are wrong about it.

MRS. STOCKMANN   Maybe, but I don't like it—not in our own home.

PETRA   There is so much falsehood both at home and at school. At home one must not speak, and at school we have to stand and tell lies to the children.

HORSTER   Tell lies?

PETRA   Yes, don't you suppose we have to teach them all sorts of things that we don't believe?

BILLING   That is perfectly true.

PETRA   If only I had the means I would start a school of my own, and it would be conducted on very different lines.

BILLING   Oh, bother the means—!

HORSTER   Well, if you are thinking of that, Miss Stockmann, I shall be delighted to provide you with a school-room. The great big old house my father left me is standing almost empty; there is an immense dining-room downstairs—

PETRA   [*Laughing.*] Thank you very much; but I am afraid nothing will come of it.

HOVSTAD   No, Miss Petra is much more likely to take to journalism, I expect. By the way, have you had time to do anything with that English story you promised to translate for us?

PETRA   No, not yet; but you shall have it in good time.

[DR. STOCKMANN *comes in from his room with an open letter in his hand.*]

DR. STOCKMANN   [*Waving the letter.*] Well, now the town will have something new to talk about, I can tell you!

BILLING   Something new?

MRS. STOCKMANN   What is this?

DR. STOCKMANN   A great discovery, Katherine.

HOVSTAD   Really?

MRS. STOCKMANN   A discovery of yours?

DR. STOCKMANN   A discovery of mine. [*Walks up and down.*] Just let them come saying, as usual, that it is all fancy and a crazy man's imagination! But they will be careful what they say this time, I can tell you!

PETRA   But, father, tell us what it is.

DR. STOCKMANN   Yes, yes—only give me time, and you shall know all about it. If only I had Peter here now! It just shows how we men can go about forming our judgments, when in reality we are as blind as any moles—

HOVSTAD What are you driving at, Doctor?

DR. STOCKMANN [*Standing still by the table.*] Isn't it the universal opinion that our town is a healthy spot?

HOVSTAD Certainly.

DR. STOCKMANN Quite an unusually healthy spot, in fact—a place that deserves to be recommended in the warmest possible manner either for invalids or for people who are well—

MRS. STOCKMANN Yes, but my dear Thomas—

DR. STOCKMANN And we have been recommending it and praising it—I have written and written, both in "The Messenger" and in pamphlets—

HOVSTAD Well, what then?

DR. STOCKMANN And the Baths—we have called them the "main artery of the town's life-blood," the "nerve-centre of our town," and the devil knows what else—

BILLING "The town's pulsating heart" was the expression I once used on an important occasion—

DR. STOCKMANN Quite so. Well, do you know what they really are, these great, splendid, much praised Baths, that have cost so much money—do you know what they are?

HOVSTAD No, what are they?

MRS. STOCKMANN Yes, what are they?

DR. STOCKMANN The whole place is a pest-house!

PETRA The Baths, father?

MRS. STOCKMANN [*At the same time.*] Our Baths!

HOVSTAD But, Doctor—

BILLING Absolutely incredible!

DR. STOCKMANN The whole Bath establishment is a whited, poisoned sepulchre, I tell you— the gravest possible danger to the public health! All the nastiness up at Mölledal, all that stinking filth, is infecting the water in the conduit-pipes leading to the reservoir; and the same cursed, filthy poison oozes out on the shore too—

HORSTER Where the bathing-place is?

DR. STOCKMANN Just there.

HOVSTAD How do you come to be so certain of all this, Doctor?

DR. STOCKMANN I have investigated the matter most conscientiously. For a long time past I have suspected something of the kind. Last year we had some very strange cases of illness among the visitors—typhoid cases, and cases of gastric fever—

MRS. STOCKMANN Yes, that is quite true.

DR. STOCKMANN At the time, we supposed the visitors had been infected before they came; but later on, in the winter, I began to have a different opinion; and so I set myself to examine the water, as well as I could.

MRS. STOCKMANN Then that is what you have been so busy with?

DR. STOCKMANN Indeed I have been busy, Katherine. But here I had none of the necessary scientific apparatus, so I sent samples, both of the drinking-water and of the sea-water, up to the University, to have an accurate analysis made by a chemist.

HOVSTAD And have you got that?

DR. STOCKMANN [*Showing him the letter.*] Here it is! It proves the presence of decomposing organic matter in the water—it is full of infusoria. The water is absolutely dangerous to use, either internally or externally.

MRS. STOCKMANN What a mercy you discovered it in time.

DR. STOCKMANN You may say so.

HOVSTAD And what do you propose to do now, Doctor?

DR. STOCKMANN To see the matter put right— naturally.

HOVSTAD Can that be done?

DR. STOCKMANN It must be done. Otherwise the Baths will be absolutely useless and wasted. But we need not anticipate that; I have a very clear idea what we shall have to do.

MRS. STOCKMANN But why have you kept this all so secret, dear?

DR. STOCKMANN Do you suppose I was going to run about the town gossiping about it, before I had absolute proof? No, thank you. I am not such a fool.

PETRA Still, you might have told us—

DR. STOCKMANN Not a living soul. But to-morrow you may run round to the old Badger—

MRS. STOCKMANN Oh, Thomas! Thomas!

DR. STOCKMANN Well, to your grandfather, then. The old boy will have something to be astonished at! I know he thinks I am cracked —and there are lots of other people think so too, I have noticed. But now these good folks shall see—they shall just see—! [*Walks about, rubbing his hands.*] There will be a nice upset in the town, Katherine; you can't imagine what it will be. All the conduit-pipes will have to be relaid.

HOVSTAD [*Getting up.*] All the conduit-pipes—?

DR. STOCKMANN Yes, of course. The intake is too low down; it will have to be lifted to a position much higher up.

PETRA Then you were right after all.

DR. STOCKMANN Ah, you remember, Petra—I wrote opposing the plans before the work was begun. But at that time no one would listen to me. Well, I am going to let them have it, now! Of course I have prepared a report for the Baths Committee; I have had it ready for a week, and was only waiting for this to come. [*Shows the letter.*] Now it shall go off at once. [*Goes into his room and comes back with some papers.*] Look at that! Four closely written sheets!—and the letter shall go with them. Give me a bit of paper, Katherine—something to wrap them up in. That will do! Now give it to—to—[*Stamps his foot.*]—what the deuce is her name?—give it to the maid, and tell her to take it at once to the Mayor.

[MRS. STOCKMANN *takes the packet and goes out through the dining-room.*]

PETRA What do you think uncle Peter will say, father?

DR. STOCKMANN What is there for him to say? I should think he would be very glad that such an important truth has been brought to light.

HOVSTAD Will you let me print a short note about your discovery in "The Messenger?"

DR. STOCKMANN I shall be very much obliged if you will.

HOVSTAD It is very desirable that the public should be informed of it without delay.

DR. STOCKMANN Certainly.

MRS. STOCKMANN [*Coming back.*] She has just gone with it.

BILLING Upon my soul, Doctor, you are going to be the foremost man in the town!

DR. STOCKMANN [*Walking about happily.*] Nonsense! As a matter of fact I have done nothing more than my duty. I have only made a lucky find—that's all. Still, all the same—

BILLING Hovstad, don't you think the town ought to give Dr. Stockmann some sort of testimonial?

HOVSTAD I will suggest it, anyway.

BILLING And I will speak to Aslaksen about it.

DR. STOCKMANN No, my good friends, don't let us have any of that nonsense. I won't hear of anything of the kind. And if the Baths Committee should think of voting me an increase of salary, I will not accept it. Do you hear, Katherine?—I won't accept it.

MRS. STOCKMANN You are quite right, Thomas.

PETRA [*Lifting her glass.*] Your health, father!

HOVSTAD *and* BILLING Your health, Doctor! Good health!

HORSTER [*Touches glasses with* DR. STOCKMANN.] I hope it will bring you nothing but good luck.

DR. STOCKMANN Thank you, thank you, my dear fellows! I feel tremendously happy! It is a splendid thing for a man to be able to feel that he has done a service to his native town and to his fellow-citizens. Hurrah, Katherine!

[*He puts his arms round her and whirls her round and round, while she protests with laughing cries. They all laugh, clap their hands and cheer the* DOCTOR. *The boys put their heads in at the door to see what is going on.*]

[*Curtain.*]

ACT II

SCENE: *The same. The door into the dining-room is shut. It is morning.* MRS. STOCKMANN, *with a sealed letter in her hand, comes in from the dining-room, goes to the door of the* DOCTOR's *study and peeps in.*

MRS. STOCKMANN Are you in, Thomas?

DR. STOCKMANN [*From within his room.*] Yes, I have just come in. [*Comes into the room.*] What is it?

MRS. STOCKMANN A letter from your brother.

DR. STOCKMANN Aha, let us see! [*Opens the letter and reads:*] "I return herewith the manuscript you sent me"—[*reads on in a low murmur.*] Hm!—

MRS. STOCKMANN What does he say?

DR. STOCKMANN [*Putting the papers in his pocket.*] Oh, he only writes that he will come up here himself about midday.

MRS. STOCKMANN Well, try and remember to be at home this time.

DR. STOCKMANN That will be all right; I have got through all my morning visits.

MRS. STOCKMANN I am extremely curious to know how he takes it.

DR. STOCKMANN You will see he won't like its having been I, and not he, that made the discovery.

MRS. STOCKMANN Aren't you a little nervous about that?

DR. STOCKMANN Oh, he really will be pleased enough, you know. But, at the same time, Peter is so confoundedly afraid of anyone's doing any service to the town except himself.

MRS. STOCKMANN I will tell you what, Thomas—you should be good-natured, and share the credit of this with him. Couldn't you make out that it was he who set you on the scent of discovery?

DR. STOCKMANN I am quite willing. If only I can get the thing set right. I—

[MORTEN KIIL *puts his head through the door leading from the hall, looks around in an enquiring manner and chuckles.*]

MORTEN KIIL [*Slyly.*] Is it—is it true?

MRS. STOCKMANN [*Going to the door.*] Father! —is it you?

DR. STOCKMANN Ah, Mr. Kiil—good morning, good morning!

MRS. STOCKMANN But come along in.

MORTEN KIIL If it is true, I will; if not, I am off.

DR. STOCKMANN If what is true?

MORTEN KIIL This tale about the water-supply. Is it true?

DR. STOCKMANN Certainly it is true. But how did you come to hear it?

MORTEN KIIL [*Coming in.*] Petra ran in on her way to the school—

DR. STOCKMANN Did she?

MORTEN KIIL Yes; and she declares that—. I thought she was only making a fool of me, but it isn't like Petra to do that.

DR. STOCKMANN Of course not. How could you imagine such a thing?

MORTEN KIIL Oh well, it is better never to trust anybody; you may find you have been made a fool of before you know where you are. But it is really true, all the same?

DR. STOCKMANN You can depend upon it that it is true. Won't you sit down? [*Settles him on the couch.*] Isn't it a real bit of luck for the town—

MORTEN KIIL [*Suppressing his laughter.*] A bit of luck for the town?

DR. STOCKMANN Yes, that I made the discovery in good time.

MORTEN KIIL [*As before.*] Yes, yes, yes!—But I should never have thought you the sort of man to pull your own brother's leg like this!

DR. STOCKMANN Pull his leg!

MRS. STOCKMANN Really, father dear—

MORTEN KIIL [*Resting his hands and his chin on the handle of his stick and winking slyly at the* DOCTOR.] Let me see, what was the story? Some kind of beast that had got into the waterpipes, wasn't it?

DR. STOCKMANN Infusoria—yes.

MORTEN KIIL And a lot of these beasts had got in, according to Petra—a tremendous lot.

DR. STOCKMANN Certainly; hundreds of thousands of them, probably.

MORTEN KIIL But no one can see them—isn't that so?

DR. STOCKMANN Yes; you can't see them.

MORTEN KIIL [*With a quiet chuckle.*] Damn—it's the finest story I have ever heard!

DR. STOCKMANN What do you mean?

MORTEN KIIL But you will never get the Mayor to believe a thing like that.

DR. STOCKMANN We shall see.

MORTEN KIIL Do you think he will be fool enough to—?

DR. STOCKMANN I hope the whole town will be fools enough.

MORTEN KIIL The whole town! Well, it wouldn't be a bad thing. It would just serve them right, and teach them a lesson. They think themselves so much cleverer than we old fellows. They hounded me out of the council; they did, I tell you—they hounded me out. Now they shall pay for it. You pull their legs too, Thomas!

DR. STOCKMANN Really, I—

MORTEN KIIL You pull their legs! [*Gets up.*] If you can work it so that the Mayor and his friends all swallow the same bait, I will give ten pounds to charity—like a shot!

DR. STOCKMANN That is very kind of you.

MORTEN KIIL Yes, I haven't got much money to throw away, I can tell you; but if you can work this, I will give five pounds to charity at Christmas.

[HOVSTAD *comes in by the hall door.*]

HOVSTAD Good morning! [*Stops.*] Oh, I beg your pardon—

DR. STOCKMANN Not at all; come in.

MORTEN KIIL [*With another chuckle.*] Oho!—is he in this too?

HOVSTAD What do you mean?

DR. STOCKMANN Certainly he is.

MORTEN KIIL I might have known it! It must get into the papers. You know how to do it, Thomas! Set your wits to work. Now I must go.

DR. STOCKMANN Won't you stay a little while?

MORTEN KIIL No, I must be off now. You keep up this game for all it is worth; you won't repent it, I'm damned if you will!

[*He goes out;* MRS. STOCKMANN *follows him into the hall.*]

DR. STOCKMANN [*Laughing.*] Just imagine—the old chap doesn't believe a word of all this about the water-supply.

HOVSTAD Oh, that was it, then?

DR. STOCKMANN Yes, that was what we were talking about. Perhaps it is the same thing that brings you here?

HOVSTAD Yes, it is. Can you spare me a few minutes, Doctor?

DR. STOCKMANN As long as you like, my dear fellow.

HOVSTAD Have you heard from the Mayor yet?

DR. STOCKMANN Not yet. He is coming here later.

HOVSTAD I have given the matter a great deal of thought since last night.

DR. STOCKMANN Well?

HOVSTAD From your point of view, as a doctor and a man of science, this affair of the water-supply is an isolated matter. I mean, you do not realise that it involves a great many other things.

DR. STOCKMANN How do you mean?—Let us sit down, my dear fellow. No, sit here on the couch. [HOVSTAD *sits down on the couch,* DR. STOCKMANN *on a chair on the other side of the table.*] Now then. You mean that—?

HOVSTAD You said yesterday that the pollution of the water was due to impurities in the soil.

DR. STOCKMANN Yes, unquestionably it is due to that poisonous morass up at Mölledal.

HOVSTAD Begging your pardon, Doctor, I fancy it is due to quite another morass altogether.

DR. STOCKMANN What morass?

HOVSTAD The morass that the whole life of our town is built on and is rotting in.

DR. STOCKMANN What the deuce are you driving at, Hovstad?

HOVSTAD The whole of the town's interests have, little by little, got into the hands of a pack of officials.

DR. STOCKMANN Oh, come!—they are not all officials.

HOVSTAD No, but those that are not officials are at any rate the officials' friends and adherents; it is the wealthy folk, the old families in the town, that have got us entirely in their hands.

DR. STOCKMANN Yes, but after all they are men of ability and knowledge.

HOVSTAD Did they show any ability or knowledge when they laid the conduit-pipes where they are now?

DR. STOCKMANN No, of course that was a great piece of stupidity on their part. But that is going to be set right now.

HOVSTAD Do you think that will be all such plain sailing?

DR. STOCKMANN Plain sailing or no, it has got to be done, anyway.

HOVSTAD Yes, provided the press takes up the question.

DR. STOCKMANN I don't think that will be necessary, my dear fellow; I am certain my brother—

HOVSTAD Excuse me, Doctor; I feel bound to tell you I am inclined to take the matter up.

DR. STOCKMANN In the paper?

HOVSTAD Yes. When I took over "The People's Messenger," my idea was to break up this ring of self-opinionated old fossils who had got hold of all the influence.

DR. STOCKMANN But you know you told me yourself what the result had been; you nearly ruined your paper.

HOVSTAD Yes, at the time we were obliged to climb down a peg or two, it is quite true, because there was a danger of the whole project of the Baths coming to nothing if they failed us. But now the scheme has been carried through, and we can dispense with these grand gentlemen.

DR. STOCKMANN   Dispense with them, yes; but we owe them a great debt of gratitude.

HOVSTAD   That shall be recognized ungrudgingly. But a journalist of my democratic tendencies cannot let such an opportunity as this slip. The bubble of official infallibility must be pricked. The superstition must be destroyed, like any other.

DR. STOCKMANN   I am whole-heartedly with you in that, Mr. Hovstad; if it is a superstition, away with it!

HOVSTAD   I should be very reluctant to bring the Mayor into it, because he is your brother. But I am sure you will agree with me that truth should be the first consideration.

DR. STOCKMANN   That goes without saying. [*With sudden emphasis.*] Yes, but—but—

HOVSTAD   You must not misjudge me. I am neither more self-interested nor more ambitious than most men.

DR. STOCKMANN   My dear fellow—who suggests anything of the kind?

HOVSTAD   I am of humble origin, as you know; and that has given me opportunities of knowing what is the most crying need in the humbler ranks of life. It is that they should be allowed some part of the direction of public affairs, Doctor. That is what will develop their faculties and intelligence and self-respect—

DR. STOCKMANN   I quite appreciate that.

HOVSTAD   Yes—and in my opinion a journalist incurs a heavy responsibility if he neglects a favorable opportunity of emancipating the masses—the humble and oppressed. I know well enough that in exalted circles I shall be called an agitator, and all that sort of thing; but they may call what they like. If only my conscience doesn't reproach me, then—

DR. STOCKMANN   Quite right! Quite right, Mr. Hovstad. But all the same—devil take it! [*A knock is heard at the door.*] Come in!

[ASLAKSEN *appears at the door. He is poorly but decently dressed, in black, with a slightly crumpled white neckcloth; he wears gloves and has a felt hat in his hand.*]

ASLAKSEN   [*Bowing.*] Excuse my taking the liberty, Doctor—

DR. STOCKMANN   [*Getting up.*]   Ah, it is you, Aslaksen!

ASLAKSEN   Yes, Doctor.

HOVSTAD   [*Standing up.*] Is it me you want, Aslaksen?

ASLAKSEN   No; I didn't know I should find you here. No, it was the Doctor I—

DR. STOCKMANN   I am quite at your service. What is it?

ASLAKSEN   Is what I heard from Mr. Billing true, sir—that you mean to improve our water-supply?

DR. STOCKMANN   Yes, for the Baths.

ASLAKSEN   Quite so, I understand. Well, I have come to say that I will back that up by every means in my power.

HOVSTAD   [*To the* DOCTOR.] You see!

DR. STOCKMANN   I shall be very grateful to you but—

ASLAKSEN   Because it may be no bad thing to have us small tradesmen at your back. We form, as it were, a compact majority in the town—if we choose. And it is always a good thing to have the majority with you, Doctor.

DR. STOCKMANN   That is undeniably true; but I confess I don't see why such unusual precautions should be necessary in this case. It seems to me that such a plain, straightforward thing—

ASLAKSEN   Oh, it may be very desirable, all the same. I know our local authorities so well; officials are not generally very ready to act on proposals that come from other people. That is why I think it would not be at all amiss if we made a little demonstration.

HOVSTAD   That's right.

DR. STOCKMANN   Demonstration, did you say? What on earth are you going to make a demonstration about?

ASLAKSEN   We shall proceed with the greatest moderation, Doctor. Moderation is always my aim; it is the greatest virtue in a citizen—at least, I think so.

DR. STOCKMANN   It is well known to be a characteristic of yours, Mr. Aslaksen.

ASLAKSEN   Yes, I think I may pride myself on that. And this matter of the water-supply is of the greatest importance to us small tradesmen. The Baths promise to be a regular gold-mine for the town. We shall all make our living out of them, especially those of us who are householders. That is why we will back up the project as strongly as possible. And as I am at present Chairman of the Householders' Association—

DR. STOCKMANN   Yes—?

ASLAKSEN   And, what is more, local secretary of

the Temperance Society—you know, sir, I suppose, that I am a worker in the temperance cause?

DR. STOCKMANN   Of course, of course.

ASLAKSEN   Well, you can understand that I come into contact with a great many people. And as I have the reputation of a temperate and law-abiding citizen—like yourself, Doctor —I have a certain influence in the town, a little bit of power, if I may be allowed to say so.

DR. STOCKMANN   I know that quite well, Mr. Aslaksen.

ASLAKSEN   So you see it would be an easy matter for me to set on foot some testimonial, if necessary.

DR. STOCKMANN   A testimonial?

ASLAKSEN   Yes, some kind of address of thanks from the townsmen for your share in a matter of such importance to the community. I need scarcely say that it would have to be drawn up with the greatest regard to moderation, so as not to offend the authorities—who, after all, have the reins in their hands. If we pay strict attention to that, no one can take it amiss, I should think!

HOVSTAD   Well, and even supposing they didn't like it—

ASLAKSEN   No, no, no; there must be no discourtesy to the authorities, Mr. Hovstad. It is no use falling foul of those upon whom our welfare so closely depends. I have done that in my time, and no good ever comes of it. But no one can take exception to a reasonable and frank expression of a citizen's views.

DR. STOCKMANN   [Shaking him by the hand.] I can't tell you, dear Mr. Aslaksen, how extremely pleased I am to find such hearty support among my fellow-citizens. I am delighted —delighted! Now you will take a small glass of sherry, eh?

ASLAKSEN   No, thank you; I never drink alcohol of that kind.

DR. STOCKMANN   Well, what do you say to a glass of beer, then?

ASLAKSEN   Nor that either, thank you, Doctor. I never drink anything as early as this. I am going into town now to talk this over with one or two householders, and prepare the ground.

DR. STOCKMANN   It is tremendously kind of you, Mr. Aslaksen; but I really cannot understand the necessity for all these precautions. It seems to me that the thing should go by itself.

ASLAKSEN   The authorities are somewhat slow to move, Doctor. Far be it from me to seem to blame them—

HOVSTAD   We are going to stir them up in the paper tomorrow, Aslaksen.

ASLAKSEN   But not violently, I trust, Mr. Hovstad. Proceed with moderation, or you will do nothing with them. You may take my advice; I have gathered my experience in the school of life. Well, I must say good-bye, Doctor. You know now that we small tradesmen are at your back at all events, like a solid wall. You have the compact majority on your side, Doctor.

DR. STOCKMANN   I am very much obliged, dear Mr. Aslaksen. [Shakes hands with him.] Good-bye, good-bye.

ASLAKSEN   Are you going my way, towards the printing-office, Mr. Hovstad?

HOVSTAD   I will come later; I have something to settle up first.

ASLAKSEN   Very well.

[Bows and goes out; STOCKMANN follows him into the hall.]

HOVSTAD   [As STOCKMANN comes in again.] Well, what do you think of that, Doctor? Don't you think it is high time we stirred a little life into all this slackness and vacillation and cowardice?

DR. STOCKMANN   Are you referring to Aslaksen?

HOVSTAD   Yes, I am. He is one of those who are floundering in a bog—decent enough fellow though he may be, otherwise. And most of the people here are in just the same case—seesawing and edging first to one side and then to the other, so overcome with caution and scruple that they never dare to take any decided step.

DR. STOCKMANN   Yes, but Aslaksen seemed to me so thoroughly well-intentioned.

HOVSTAD   There is one thing I esteem higher than that; and that is for a man to be self-reliant and sure of himself.

DR. STOCKMANN   I think you are perfectly right there.

HOVSTAD   That is why I want to seize this opportunity, and try if I cannot manage to put a little virility into these well-intentioned people for once. The idol of Authority must be shattered in this town. This gross and inexcusable blunder about the water-supply must be brought home to the mind of every municipal voter.

DR. STOCKMANN Very well; if you are of the opinion that it is for the good of the community, so be it. But not until I have had a talk with my brother.

HOVSTAD Anyway, I will get a leading article ready; and if the Mayor refuses to take the matter up—

DR. STOCKMANN How can you suppose such a thing possible?

HOVSTAD It is conceivable. And in that case—

DR. STOCKMANN In that case I promise you—. Look here, in that case you may print my report—every word of it.

HOVSTAD May I? Have I your word for it?

DR. STOCKMANN [*Giving him the MS.*] Here it is; take it with you. It can do no harm for you to read it through, and you can give it back to me later on.

HOVSTAD Good, good! That is what I will do. And now good-bye, Doctor.

DR. STOCKMANN Good-bye, good-bye. You will see everything will run quite smoothly, Mr. Hovstad—quite smoothly.

HOVSTAD Hm!—we shall see. [*Bows and goes out.*]

DR. STOCKMANN [*Opens the dining-room door and looks in.*] Katherine! Oh, you are back, Petra?

PETRA [*Coming in.*] Yes, I have just come from the school.

MRS. STOCKMANN [*Coming in.*] Has he not been here yet?

DR. STOCKMANN Peter? No. But I have had a long talk with Hovstad. He is quite excited about my discovery. I find it has a much wider bearing than I at first imagined. And he has put his paper at my disposal if necessity should arise.

MRS. STOCKMANN Do you think it will?

DR. STOCKMANN Not for a moment. But at all events it makes me feel proud to know that I have the liberal-minded independent press on my side. Yes, and—just imagine—I have had a visit from the Chairman of the Householders' Association!

MRS. STOCKMANN Oh! What did he want?

DR. STOCKMANN To offer me his support too. They will support me in a body if it should be necessary. Katherine—do you know what I have got behind me?

MRS. STOCKMANN Behind you? No, what have you got behind you?

DR. STOCKMANN The compact majority.

MRS. STOCKMANN Really? Is that a good thing for you, Thomas?

DR. STOCKMANN I should think it was a good thing. [*Walks up and down rubbing his hands.*] By Jove, it's a fine thing to feel this bond of brotherhood between oneself and one's fellow-citizens!

PETRA And to be able to do so much that is good and useful, father!

DR. STOCKMANN And for one's own native town into the bargain, my child!

MRS. STOCKMANN That was a ring at the bell.

DR. STOCKMANN It must be he, then. [*A knock is heard at the door.*] Come in!

PETER STOCKMANN [*Comes in from the hall.*] Good morning.

DR. STOCKMANN Glad to see you, Peter!

MRS. STOCKMANN Good morning, Peter. How are you?

PETER STOCKMANN So so, thank you. [*To* DR. STOCKMANN.] I received from you yesterday, after office-hours, a report dealing with the condition of the water at the Baths.

DR. STOCKMANN Yes. Have you read it?

PETER STOCKMANN Yes, I have.

DR. STOCKMANN And what have you to say to it?

PETER STOCKMANN [*With a sidelong glance.*] Hm!—

MRS. STOCKMANN Come along, Petra. [*She and* PETRA *go into the room on the left.*]

PETER STOCKMANN [*After a pause.*] Was it necessary to make all these investigations behind my back?

DR. STOCKMANN Yes, because until I was absolutely certain about it—

PETER STOCKMANN Then you mean that you are absolutely certain now?

DR. STOCKMANN Surely you are convinced of that.

PETER STOCKMANN Is it your intention to bring this document before the Baths Committee as a sort of official communication?

DR. STOCKMANN Certainly. Something must be done in the matter—and that quickly.

PETER STOCKMANN As usual, you employ violent expressions in your report. You say, amongst other things, that what we offer visitors in our Baths is a permanent supply of poison.

DR. STOCKMANN Well, can you describe it any other way, Peter? Just think—water that is poisonous, whether you drink it or bathe in it! And this we offer to the poor sick folk who come to us trustfully and pay us at an exorbitant rate to be made well again!

PETER STOCKMANN And your reasoning leads you to this conclusion, that we must build a sewer to draw off the alleged impurities from Mölledal and must re-lay the water conduits.

DR. STOCKMANN Yes. Do you see any other way out of it? I don't.

PETER STOCKMANN I made a pretext this morning to go and see the town engineer, and, as if only half seriously, broached the subject of these proposals as a thing we might perhaps have to take under consideration some time later on.

DR. STOCKMANN Some time later on!

PETER STOCKMANN He smiled at what he considered to be my extravagance, naturally. Have you taken the trouble to consider what your proposed alterations would cost? According to the information I obtained, the expenses would probably mount up to fifteen or twenty thousand pounds.

DR. STOCKMANN Would it cost so much?

PETER STOCKMANN Yes; and the worst part of it would be that the work would take at least two years.

DR. STOCKMANN Two years? Two whole years?

PETER STOCKMANN At least. And what are we to do with the Baths in the meantime? Close them? Indeed we should be obliged to. And do you suppose any one would come near the place after it had got about that the water was dangerous?

DR. STOCKMANN Yes, but Peter, that is what it is.

PETER STOCKMANN And all this at this juncture—just as the Baths are beginning to be known. There are other towns in the neighborhood with qualifications to attract visitors for bathing purposes. Don't you suppose they would immediately strain every nerve to divert the entire stream of strangers to themselves? Unquestionably they would; and then

where should we be? We should probably have to abandon the whole thing, which has cost us so much money—and then you would have ruined your native town.

DR. STOCKMANN I—should have ruined—!

PETER STOCKMANN It is simply and solely through the Baths that the town has before it any future worth mentioning. You know that just as well as I.

DR. STOCKMANN But what do you think ought to be done, then?

PETER STOCKMANN Your report has not convinced me that the condition of the water at the Baths is as bad as you represent it to be.

DR. STOCKMANN I tell you it is even worse!—or at all events it will be in summer, when the warm weather comes.

PETER STOCKMANN As I said, I believe you exaggerate the matter considerably. A capable physician ought to know what measures to take—he ought to be capable of preventing injurious influences or of remedying them if they become obviously persistent.

DR. STOCKMANN Well? What more?

PETER STOCKMANN The water-supply for the Baths is now an established fact, and in consequence must be treated as such. But probably the Committee, at its discretion, will not be disinclined to consider the question of how far it might be possible to introduce certain improvements consistent with a reasonable expenditure.

DR. STOCKMANN And do you suppose that I will have anything to do with such a piece of trickery as that?

PETER STOCKMANN Trickery!!

DR. STOCKMANN Yes, it would be a trick—a fraud, a lie, a downright crime towards the public, towards the whole community!

PETER STOCKMANN I have not, as I remarked before, been able to convince myself that there is actually any imminent danger.

DR. STOCKMANN You have not! It is impossible that you should not be convinced. I know I have represented the facts absolutely truthfully and fairly. And you know it very well, Peter, only you won't acknowledge it. It was owing to your action that both the Baths and the water conduits were built where they are; and that is what you won't acknowledge—

that damnable blunder of yours. Pooh!—do you suppose I don't see through you?

PETER STOCKMANN   And even if that were true? If I perhaps guard my reputation somewhat anxiously, it is in the interests of the town. Without moral authority I am powerless to direct public affairs as seems, to my judgment, to be best for the common good. And on that account—and for various other reasons, too—it appears to me to be a matter of importance that your report should not be delivered to the Committee. In the interests of the public, you must withhold it. Then, later on, I will raise the question and we will do our best, privately; but nothing of this unfortunate affair —not a single word of it—must come to the ears of the public.

DR. STOCKMANN   I am afraid you will not be able to prevent that now, my dear Peter.

PETER STOCKMANN   It must and shall be prevented.

DR. STOCKMANN   It is no use, I tell you. There are too many people that know about it.

PETER STOCKMANN   That know about it? Who? Surely you don't mean those fellows on "The People's Messenger"?

DR. STOCKMANN   Yes, they know. The liberal-minded independent press is going to see that you do your duty.

PETER STOCKMANN   [*After a short pause.*] You are an extraordinarily independent man, Thomas. Have you given no thought to the consequences this may have for yourself?

DR. STOCKMANN   Consequences?—for me?

PETER STOCKMANN   For you and yours, yes.

DR. STOCKMANN   What the deuce do you mean?

PETER STOCKMANN   I believe I have always behaved in a brotherly way to you—have always been ready to oblige or to help you?

DR. STOCKMANN   Yes, you have, and I am grateful to you for it.

PETER STOCKMANN   There is no need. Indeed, to some extent I was forced to do so—for my own sake. I always hoped that, if I helped to improve your financial position, I should be able to keep some check on you.

DR. STOCKMANN   What!! Then it was only for your own sake—!

PETER STOCKMANN   Up to a certain point, yes. It is painful for a man in an official position to have his nearest relative compromising himself time after time.

DR. STOCKMANN   And do you consider that I do that?

PETER STOCKMANN   Yes, unfortunately, you do, without even being aware of it. You have a restless, pugnacious, rebellious disposition. And then there is that disastrous propensity of yours to want to write about every sort of possible and impossible thing. The moment an idea comes into your head, you must needs go and write a newspaper article or a whole pamphlet about it.

DR. STOCKMANN   Well, but is it not the duty of a citizen to let the public share in any new ideas he may have?

PETER STOCKMANN   Oh, the public doesn't require any new ideas. The public is best served by the good, old-established ideas it already has.

DR. STOCKMANN   And that is your honest opinion?

PETER STOCKMANN   Yes, and for once I must talk frankly to you. Hitherto I have tried to avoid doing so, because I know how irritable you are; but now I must tell you the truth, Thomas. You have no conception what an amount of harm you do yourself by your impetuosity. You complain of the authorities, you even complain of the government—you are always pulling them to pieces; you insist that you have been neglected and persecuted. But what else can such a cantankerous man as you expect?

DR. STOCKMANN   What next! Cantankerous, am I?

PETER STOCKMANN   Yes, Thomas, you are an extremely cantankerous man to work with—I know that to my cost. You disregard everything that you ought to have consideration for. You seem completely to forget that it is me you have to thank for your appointment here as medical officer to the Baths—

DR. STOCKMANN   I was entitled to it as a matter of course!—I and nobody else! I was the first person to see that the town could be made into a flourishing watering-place, and I was the only one who saw it at that time. I had to fight single-handed in support of the idea for many years; and I wrote and wrote—

PETER STOCKMANN   Undoubtedly. But things were not ripe for the scheme then—though, of course, you could not judge of that in your out-of-the-way corner up north. But as soon as the opportune moment came I—and the others—took the matter into our hands—

DR. STOCKMANN   Yes, and made this mess of all my beautiful plans. It is pretty obvious now what clever fellows you were!

PETER STOCKMANN   To my mind the whole thing only seems to mean that you are seeking another outlet for your combativeness. You want to pick a quarrel with your superiors— an old habit of yours. You cannot put up with any authority over you. You look askance at anyone who occupies a superior official position; you regard him as a personal enemy, and then any stick is good enough to beat him with. But now I have called your attention to the fact that the town's interests are at stake —and, incidentally, my own too. And therefore I must tell you, Thomas, that you will find me inexorable with regard to what I am about to require you to do.

DR. STOCKMANN   And what is that?

PETER STOCKMANN   As you have been so indiscreet as to speak of this delicate matter to outsiders, despite the fact that you ought to have treated it as entirely official and confidential, it is obviously impossible to hush it up now. All sorts of rumors will get about directly, and everybody who has a grudge against us will take care to embellish these rumors. So it will be necessary for you to refute them publicly.

DR. STOCKMANN   I! How? I don't understand.

PETER STOCKMANN   What we shall expect is that, after making further investigations, you will come to the conclusion that the matter is not by any means as dangerous or as critical as you imagined in the first instance.

DR. STOCKMANN   Oho!—so that is what you expect!

PETER STOCKMANN   And, what is more, we shall expect you to make public profession of your confidence in the Committee and in their readiness to consider fully and consciously what steps may be necessary to remedy any possible defects.

DR. STOCKMANN   But you will never be able to do that by patching and tinkering at it—never! Take my word for it, Peter; I mean what I say, as deliberately and emphatically as possible.

PETER STOCKMANN   As an officer under the Committee, you have no right to any individual opinion.

DR. STOCKMANN   [Amazed.] No right?

PETER STOCKMANN   In your official capacity, no. As a private person, it is quite another matter. But as a subordinate member of the staff of the Baths, you have no right to express any opinion which runs contrary to that of your superiors.

DR. STOCKMANN   This is too much! I, a doctor, a man of science, have no right to—!

PETER STOCKMANN   The matter in hand is not simply a scientific one. It is a complicated matter, and has its economic as well as technical side.

DR. STOCKMANN   I don't care what it is! I intend to be free to express my opinion on any subject under the sun.

PETER STOCKMANN   As you please—but not on any subject concerning the Baths. That we forbid.

DR. STOCKMANN   [Shouting.] You forbid—! You! A pack of—

PETER STOCKMANN   I forbid it—I, your chief; and if I forbid it, you have to obey.

DR. STOCKMANN   [Controlling himself.] Peter— if you were not my brother—

PETRA   [Throwing open the door.] Father, you shan't stand this!

MRS. STOCKMANN   [Coming in after her.] Petra, Petra!

PETER STOCKMANN   Oh, so you have been eavesdropping.

MRS. STOCKMANN   You were talking so loud, we couldn't help—

PETRA   Yes, I was listening.

PETER STOCKMANN   Well, after all, I am very glad—

DR. STOCKMANN   [Going up to him.] You were saying something about forbidding and obeying?

PETER STOCKMANN   You obliged me to take that tone with you.

DR. STOCKMANN   And so I am to give myself the lie, publicly?

PETER STOCKMANN   We consider it absolutely necessary that you should make some such public statement as I have asked for.

DR. STOCKMANN   And if I do not—obey?

PETER STOCKMANN   Then we shall publish a statement ourselves to reassure the public.

DR. STOCKMANN   Very well; but in that case I shall use my pen against you. I stick to what I have said; I will show that I am right and that you are wrong. And what will you do then?

PETER STOCKMANN   Then I shall not be able to prevent your being dismissed.

DR. STOCKMANN   What—?

PETRA   Father—dismissed!

MRS. STOCKMANN   Dismissed!

PETER STOCKMANN   Dismissed from the staff of the Baths. I shall be obliged to propose that you shall immediately be given notice, and shall not be allowed any further participation in the Baths' affairs.

DR. STOCKMANN   You would dare to do that!

PETER STOCKMANN   It is you that are playing the daring game.

PETRA   Uncle, that is a shameful way to treat a man like father!

MRS. STOCKMANN   Do hold your tongue, Petra!

PETER STOCKMANN   [*Looking at* PETRA.] Oh, so we volunteer our opinions already, do we? Of course. [*To* MRS. STOCKMANN.] Katherine, I imagine you are the most sensible person in this house. Use any influence you may have over your husband, and make him see what this will entail for his family as well as—

DR. STOCKMANN   My family is my own concern and nobody else's!

PETER STOCKMANN   —for his own family, as I was saying, as well as for the town he lives in.

DR. STOCKMANN   It is I who have the real good of the town at heart; I want to lay bare the defects that sooner or later must come to the light of day. I will show whether I love my native town.

PETER STOCKMANN   You, who in your blind obstinacy want to cut off the most important source of the town's welfare?

DR. STOCKMANN   The source is poisoned, man! Are you mad? We are making our living by retailing filth and corruption! The whole of our flourishing municipal life derives its sustenance from a lie!

PETER STOCKMANN   All imagination—or something even worse. The man who can throw out such offensive insinuations about his native town must be an enemy of our community.

DR. STOCKMANN   [*Going up to him.*] Do you dare to—!

MRS. STOCKMANN   [*Throwing herself between them.*] Thomas!

PETRA   [*Catching her father by the arm.*] Don't lose your temper, father!

PETER STOCKMANN   I will not expose myself to violence. Now you have had a warning; so reflect on what you owe to yourself and your family. Good-bye. [*Goes out.*]

DR. STOCKMANN   [*Walking up and down.*] Am I to put up with such treatment as this? In my own house, Katherine! What do you think of that!

MRS. STOCKMANN   Indeed it is both shameful and absurd, Thomas—

PETRA   If only I could give uncle a piece of my mind—

DR. STOCKMANN   It is my own fault. I ought to have flown out at him long ago—shown my teeth!—bitten! To hear him call me an enemy of our community! Me! I shall not take that lying down, upon my soul!

MRS. STOCKMANN   But, dear Thomas, your brother has power on his side—

DR. STOCKMANN   Yes, but I have right on mine, I tell you.

MRS. STOCKMANN   Oh yes, right—right. What is the use of having right on your side if you have not got might?

PETRA   Oh, mother!—how can you say such a thing!

DR. STOCKMANN   Do you imagine that in a free country it is no use having right on your side? You are absurd, Katherine. Besides, haven't I got the liberal-minded, independent press to lead the way, and the compact majority behind me? That is might enough, I should think!

MRS. STOCKMANN   But, good heavens, Thomas, you don't mean to—?

DR. STOCKMANN   Don't mean to what?

MRS. STOCKMANN   To set yourself up in opposition to your brother.

DR. STOCKMANN   In God's name, what else do you suppose I should do but take my stand on right and truth?

PETRA   Yes, I was just going to say that.

MRS. STOCKMANN   But it won't do you any earthly good. If they won't do it, they won't.

DR. STOCKMANN   Oho, Katherine! Just give me time, and you will see how I will carry the war into their camp.

MRS. STOCKMANN   Yes, you carry the war into

their camp, and you get your dismissal—that is what you will do.

DR. STOCKMANN   In any case I shall have done my duty towards the public—towards the community. I, who am called its enemy!

MRS. STOCKMANN   But towards your family, Thomas? Towards your own home! Do you think that is doing your duty towards those you have to provide for?

PETRA   Ah, don't think always first of us, mother.

MRS. STOCKMANN   Oh, it is easy for you to talk; you are able to shift for yourself if need be. But remember the boys, Thomas; and think a little, too, of yourself, and of me—

DR. STOCKMANN   I think you are out of your senses, Katherine! If I were to be such a miserable coward as to go on my knees to Peter and his damned crew, do you suppose I should ever know an hour's peace of mind all my life afterwards?

MRS. STOCKMANN   I don't know anything about that; but God preserve us from the peace of mind we shall have, all the same, if you go on defying him! You will find yourself again without the means of subsistence, with no income to count upon. I should think we had had enough of that in the old days. Remember that, Thomas; think what that means.

DR. STOCKMANN   [Collecting himself with a struggle and clenching his fists.] And this is what this slavery can bring upon a free, honorable man! Isn't it horrible, Katherine?

MRS. STOCKMANN   Yes, it is sinful to treat you so, it is perfectly true. But, good heavens, one has to put up with so much injustice in this world.—There are the boys, Thomas! Look at them! What is to become of them? Oh, no, no, you can never have the heart—.

[EJLIF and MORTEN have come in while she was speaking, with their school books in their hands.]

DR. STOCKMANN   The boys—! [Recovers himself suddenly.] No, even if the whole world goes to pieces, I will never bow my neck to this yoke! [Goes towards his room.]

MRS. STOCKMANN   [Following him.] Thomas—what are you going to do!

DR. STOCKMANN   [At his door.] I mean to have the right to look my sons in the face when they are grown men. [Goes into his room.]

MRS. STOCKMANN   [Bursting into tears.] God help us all!

PETRA   Father is splendid! He will not give in. [The boys look on in amazement; PETRA signs to them not to speak.]

[Curtain.]

ACT III

SCENE: *The editorial office of "The People's Messenger." The entrance door is on the left-hand side of the back wall; on the right-hand side is another door with glass panels through which the printing-room can be seen. Another door in the right-hand wall. In the middle of the room is a large table covered with papers, newspapers, and books. In the foreground on the left a window, before which stand a desk and a high stool. There are a couple of easy chairs by the table, and other chairs standing along the wall. The room is dingy and uncomfortable; the furniture is old, the chairs stained and torn. In the printing-room the compositors are seen at work, and a printer is working a hand-press. HOVSTAD is sitting at the desk, writing. BILLING comes in from the right with DR. STOCKMANN's manuscript in his hand.*

BILLING   Well, I must say!

HOVSTAD   [Still writing.] Have you read it through?

BILLING   [Laying the MS. on the desk.] Yes, indeed I have.

HOVSTAD   Don't you think the Doctor hits them pretty hard?

BILLING   Hard? Bless my soul, he's crushing! Every word falls like—how shall I put it?—like the blow of a sledgehammer.

HOVSTAD   Yes, but they are not the people to throw up the sponge at the first blow.

BILLING   That is true; and for that reason we must strike blow upon blow until the whole of this aristocracy tumbles to pieces. As I sat in there reading this, I almost seemed to see a revolution in being.

HOVSTAD   [Turning round.] Hush!—Speak so that Aslaksen cannot hear you.

BILLING   [Lowering his voice.] Aslaksen is a

chicken-hearted chap, a coward; there is nothing of the man in him. But this time you will insist on your own way, won't you? You will put the Doctor's article in?

HOVSTAD Yes, and if the Mayor doesn't like it—

BILLING That will be the devil of a nuisance.

HOVSTAD Well, fortunately we can turn the situation to good account, whatever happens. If the Mayor will not fall in with the Doctor's project, he will have all the same tradesmen down on him—the whole of the Householders' Association and the rest of them. And if he does fall in with it, he will fall out with the whole crowd of large shareholders in the Baths, who up to now have been his most valuable supporters—

BILLING Yes, because they will certainly have to fork out a pretty penny—

HOVSTAD Yes, you may be sure they will. And in this way the ring will be broken up, you see, and then in every issue of the paper we will enlighten the public on the Mayor's incapability on one point and another, and make it clear that all the positions of trust in the town, the whole control of municipal affairs, ought to be put in the hands of the Liberals.

BILLING That is perfectly true! I see it coming—I see it coming; we are on the threshold of a revolution! [*A knock is heard at the door.*]

HOVSTAD Hush! [*Calls out.*] Come in! [DR. STOCKMANN *comes in by the street door.* HOVSTAD *goes to meet him.*] Ah, it is you, Doctor! Well?

DR. STOCKMANN You may set to work and print it, Mr. Hovstad!

HOVSTAD Has it come to that, then?

BILLING Hurrah!

DR. STOCKMANN Yes, print away. Undoubtedly it has come to that. Now they must take what they get. There is going to be a fight in the town, Mr. Billing!

BILLING War to the knife, I hope! We will get our knives to their throats, Doctor!

DR. STOCKMANN This article is only a beginning. I have already got four or five more sketched out in my head. Where is Aslaksen?

BILLING [*Calls into the printing-room.*] Aslaksen, just come here for a minute!

HOVSTAD Four or five more articles, did you say? On the same subject?

DR. STOCKMANN No—far from it, my dear fellow. No, they are about quite another matter. But they all spring from the question of the water-supply and the drainage. One thing leads to another, you know. It is like beginning to pull down an old house, exactly.

BILLING Upon my soul, it's true; you find you are not done till you have pulled all the old rubbish down.

ASLAKSEN [*Coming in.*] Pulled down? You are not thinking of pulling down the Baths surely, Doctor?

HOVSTAD Far from it; don't be afraid.

DR. STOCKMANN No, we meant something quite different. Well, what do you think of my article, Mr. Hovstad?

HOVSTAD I think it is simply a masterpiece—

DR. STOCKMANN Do you really think so? Well, I am very pleased, very pleased.

HOVSTAD It is so clear and intelligible. One need have no special knowledge to understand the bearing of it. You will have every enlightened man on your side.

ASLAKSEN And every prudent man too, I hope?

BILLING The prudent and the imprudent—almost the whole town.

ASLAKSEN In that case we may venture to print it.

DR. STOCKMANN I should think so!

HOVSTAD We will put it in tomorrow morning.

DR. STOCKMANN Of course—you must not lose a single day. What I wanted to ask you, Mr. Aslaksen, was if you would supervise the printing of it yourself.

ASLAKSEN With pleasure.

DR. STOCKMANN Take care of it as if it were a treasure! No misprints—every word is important. I will look in again a little later; perhaps you will be able to let me see a proof. I can't tell you how eager I am to see it in print, and see it burst upon the public—

BILLING Burst upon them—yes, like a flash of lightning!

DR. STOCKMANN —and to have it submitted to the judgment of my intelligent fellow-townsmen. You cannot imagine what I have gone through today. I have been threatened first with one thing and then with another; they have tried to rob me of my most elementary rights as a man—

BILLING What! Your rights as a man!

DR. STOCKMANN —they have tried to degrade me, to make a coward of me, to force me to put personal interests before my most sacred convictions—

BILLING   That is too much—I'm damned if it isn't.

HOVSTAD   Oh, you mustn't be surprised at anything from that quarter.

DR. STOCKMANN   Well, they will get the worst of it with me; they may assure themselves of that. I shall consider "The People's Messenger" my sheet-anchor now, and every single day I will bombard them with one article after another like bombshells—

ASLAKSEN   Yes, but—

BILLING   Hurrah!—it is war, it is war!

DR. STOCKMANN   I shall smite them to the ground—I shall crush them—I shall break down all their defences, before the eyes of the honest public! That is what I shall do!

ASLAKSEN   Yes, but in moderation, Doctor—proceed with moderation—

BILLING   Not a bit of it, not a bit of it! Don't spare the dynamite!

DR. STOCKMANN   Because it is not merely a question of water-supply and drains now, you know. No—it is the whole of our social life that we have got to purify and disinfect—

BILLING   Spoken like a deliverer!

DR. STOCKMANN   All the incapables must be turned out, you understand—and that in every walk of life! Endless vistas have opened themselves to my mind's eye today. I cannot see it all quite clearly yet, but I shall in time. Young and vigorous standard-bearers—those are what we need and must seek, my friends; we must have new men in command at all our outposts.

BILLING   Hear, hear!

DR. STOCKMANN   We only need to stand by one another, and it will all be perfectly easy. The revolution will be launched like a ship that runs smoothly off the stocks. Don't you think so?

HOVSTAD   For my part I think we have now a prospect of getting the municipal authority into the hands where it should lie.

ASLAKSEN   And if only we proceed with moderation, I cannot imagine that there will be any risk.

DR. STOCKMANN   Who the devil cares whether there is any risk or not? What I am doing, I am doing in the name of truth and for the sake of my conscience.

HOVSTAD   You are a man who deserves to be supported, Doctor.

ASLAKSEN   Yes, there is no denying that the Doctor is a true friend to the town—a real friend to the community, that he is.

BILLING   Take my word for it, Aslaksen, Dr. Stockmann is a friend of the people.

ASLAKSEN   I fancy the Householders' Association will make use of that expression before long.

DR. STOCKMANN   [Affected, grasps their hands.] Thank you, thank you, my dear staunch friends. It is very refreshing to me to hear you say that; my brother called me something quite different. By Jove, he shall have it back, with interest! But now I must be off to see a poor devil—. I will come back, as I said. Keep a very careful eye on the manuscript, Aslaksen, and don't for worlds leave out any of my notes of exclamation! Rather put one or two more in! Capital, capital! Well, good-bye for the present—good-bye, good-bye! [They show him to the door, and bow him out.]

HOVSTAD   He may prove an invaluably useful man to us.

ASLAKSEN   Yes, so long as he confines himself to this matter of the Baths. But if he goes farther afield, I don't think it would be advisable to follow him.

HOVSTAD   Hm!—that all depends—

BILLING   You are so infernally timid, Aslaksen!

ASLAKSEN   Timid? Yes, when it is a question of the local authorities, I am timid, Mr. Billing; it is a lesson I have learnt in the school of experience, let me tell you. But try me in higher politics, in matters that concern the government itself, and then see if I am timid.

BILLING   No, you aren't, I admit. But this is simply contradicting yourself.

ASLAKSEN   I am a man with conscience, and that is the whole matter. If you attack the government, you don't do the community any harm, anyway; those fellows pay no attention to attacks, you see—they go on just as they are, in spite of them. But local authorities are different; they can be turned out, and then perhaps you may get an ignorant lot into office who may do irreparable harm to the householders and everybody else.

HOVSTAD   But what of the education of citizens by self-government—don't you attach any importance to that?

ASLAKSEN   When a man has interests of his own to protect, he cannot think of everything, Mr. Hovstad.

HOVSTAD   Then I hope I shall never have interests of my own to protect!

BILLING   Hear, hear!

ASLAKSEN   [*With a smile.*] Hm! [*Points to the desk.*] Mr. Sheriff Stensgaard was your predecessor at that editorial desk.

BILLING   [*Spitting.*] Bah! That turncoat.

HOVSTAD   I am not a weathercock—and never will be.

ASLAKSEN   A politician should never be too certain of anything, Mr. Hovstad. And as for you, Mr. Billing, I should think it is time for you to be taking in a reef or two in your sails, seeing that you are applying for the post of secretary to the Bench.

BILLING   I—!

HOVSTAD   Are you, Billing?

BILLING   Well, yes—but you must clearly understand I am doing it only to annoy the bigwigs.

ASLAKSEN   Anyhow, it is no business of mine. But if I am to be accused of timidity and of inconsistency in my principles, this is what I want to point out: my political past is an open book. I have never changed, except perhaps to become a little more moderate, you see. My heart is still with the people; but I don't deny that my reason has a certain bias towards the authorities—the local ones, I mean. [*Goes into the printing-room.*]

BILLING   Oughtn't we to try and get rid of him, Hovstad?

HOVSTAD   Do you know anyone else who will advance the money for our paper and printing bill?

BILLING   It is an infernal nuisance that we don't possess some capital to trade on.

HOVSTAD   [*Sitting down at his desk.*] Yes, if we only had that, then—

BILLING   Suppose you were to apply to Dr. Stockmann?

HOVSTAD   [*Turning over some papers.*] What is the use? He has got nothing.

BILLING   No, but he has got a warm man in the background, old Morten Kiil—"the Badger," as they call him.

HOVSTAD   [*Writing.*] Are you so sure *he* has got anything?

BILLING   Good Lord, of course he has! And some of it must come to the Stockmanns. Most probably he will do something for the children, at all events.

HOVSTAD   [*Turning half round.*] Are you counting on that?

BILLING   Counting on it? Of course I am not counting on anything.

HOVSTAD   That is right. And I should not count on the secretaryship to the Bench either, if I were you; for I can assure you—you won't get it.

BILLING   Do you think I am not quite aware of that? My object is precisely *not* to get it. A slight of that kind stimulates a man's fighting power—it is like getting a supply of fresh bile—and I am sure one needs that badly enough in a hole-and-corner place like this, where so seldom anything happens to stir one up.

HOVSTAD   [*Writing.*] Quite so, quite so.

BILLING   Ah, I shall be heard of yet!—Now I shall go and write the appeal to the Householders' Association. [*Goes into the room on the right.*]

HOVSTAD   [*Sitting at his desk, biting his penholder, says slowly.*] Hm!—that's it, is it? [*A knock is heard.*] Come in! [PETRA *comes in by the outer door.* HOVSTAD *gets up.*] What, you!—here?

PETRA   Yes, you must forgive me—

HOVSTAD   [*Pulling a chair forward.*] Won't you sit down?

PETRA   No, thank you; I must go again in a moment.

HOVSTAD   Have you come with a message from your father, by any chance?

PETRA   No, I have come on my own account. [*Takes a book out of her coat pocket.*] Here is the English story.

HOVSTAD   Why have you brought it back?

PETRA   Because I am not going to translate it.

HOVSTAD   But you promised me faithfully—

PETRA   Yes, but then I had not read it. I don't suppose you have read it either?

HOVSTAD   No, you know quite well I don't understand English; but—

PETRA   Quite so. That is why I wanted to tell you that you must find something else. [*Lays the book on the table.*] You can't use this for "The People's Messenger."

HOVSTAD   Why not?

PETRA   Because it conflicts with all your opinions.

HOVSTAD   Oh, for that matter—

PETRA   You don't understand me. The burden of this story is that here is a supernatural power that looks after the so-called good people in this world and makes everything happen for the best in their case—while all the so-called bad people are punished.

HOVSTAD   Well, but that is all right. That is just what our readers want.

PETRA   And are you going to be the one to give it to them? For myself, I do not believe a word of it. You know quite well that things do not happen so in reality.

HOVSTAD   You are perfectly right, but an editor cannot always act as he would prefer. He is often obliged to bow to the wishes of the public in unimportant matters. Politics are the most important thing in life—for a newspaper, anyway; and if I want to carry my public with me on the path that leads to liberty and progress, I must not frighten them away. If they find a moral tale of this sort in the serial at the bottom of the page, they will be all the more ready to read what is printed above it; they feel more secure, as it were.

PETRA   For shame! You would never go and set a snare like that for your readers; you are not a spider!

HOVSTAD   [*Smiling.*] Thank you for having such a good opinion of me. No; as a matter of fact that is Billing's idea and not mine.

PETRA   Billing's!

HOVSTAD   Yes; anyway he propounded that theory here one day. And it is Billing who is so anxious to have that story in the paper; I don't know anything about the book.

PETRA   But how can Billing, with his emancipated views—

HOVSTAD   Oh, Billing is a many-sided man. He is applying for the post of secretary to the Bench, too, I hear.

PETRA   I don't believe it, Mr. Hovstad. How could he possibly bring himself to do such a thing?

HOVSTAD   Ah, you must ask him that.

PETRA   I should never have thought it of him.

HOVSTAD   [*Looking more closely at her.*] No? Does it really surprise you so much?

PETRA   Yes. Or perhaps not altogether. Really, I don't quite know—

HOVSTAD   We journalists are not worth much, Miss Stockmann.

PETRA   Do you really mean that?

HOVSTAD   I think so sometimes.

PETRA   Yes, in the ordinary affairs of everyday life, perhaps; I can understand that. But now, when you have taken a weighty matter in hand—

HOVSTAD   This matter of your father's, you mean?

PETRA   Exactly. It seems to me that now you must feel you are a man worth more than most.

HOVSTAD   Yes, today I do feel something of that sort.

PETRA   Of course you do, don't you? It is a splendid vocation you have chosen—to smooth the way for the march of unappreciated truths and new and courageous lines of thought. If it were nothing more than because you stand fearlessly in the open and take up the cause of an injured man—

HOVSTAD   Especially when that injured man is —ahem!—I don't rightly know how to—

PETRA   When that man is so upright and so honest, you mean?

HOVSTAD   [*More gently.*] Especially when he is your father, I meant.

PETRA   [*Suddenly checked.*] *That?*

HOVSTAD   Yes, Petra—Miss Petra.

PETRA   Is it *that*, that is first and foremost with you? Not the matter itself? Not the truth?— not my father's big generous heart?

HOVSTAD   Certainly—of course—that too.

PETRA   No, thank you; you have betrayed yourself, Mr. Hovstad, and now I shall never trust you again in anything.

HOVSTAD   Can you really take it so amiss in me that it is mostly for your sake—?

PETRA   I am angry with you for not having been honest with my father. You talked to him as if the truth and the good of the community were what lay nearest to your heart. You have made fools of both my father and me. You are not the man you made yourself out to be. And that I shall never forgive you —never!

HOVSTAD   You ought not to speak so bitterly, Miss Petra—least of all now.

PETRA   Why not now, especially?

HOVSTAD   Because your father cannot do without my help.

PETRA   [*Looking him up and down.*] Are you that sort of man too? For shame!

HOVSTAD   No, no, I am not. This came upon me so unexpectedly—you must believe that.

PETRA   I know what to believe. Good-bye.

ASLAKSEN   [*Coming from the printing-room, hurriedly and with an air of mystery.*] Damnation, Hovstad!—[*Sees* PETRA.] Oh, this is awkward—

PETRA   There is the book; you must give it to some one else. [*Goes towards the door.*]

HOVSTAD   [*Following her.*] But, Miss Stockmann—

PETRA   Good-bye. [*Goes out.*]

ASLAKSEN   I say—Mr. Hovstad—

HOVSTAD   Well, well!—what is it?

ASLAKSEN   The Mayor is outside in the printing-room.

HOVSTAD   The Mayor, did you say?

ASLAKSEN   Yes, he wants to speak to you. He came in by the back door—didn't want to be seen, you understand.

HOVSTAD   What can he want? Wait a bit—I will go myself. [*Goes to the door of the printing-room, opens it, bows and invites* PETER STOCKMANN *in.*] Just see, Aslaksen, that no one—

ASLAKSEN   Quite so. [*Goes into the printing-room.*]

PETER STOCKMANN   You did not expect to see me here, Mr. Hovstad?

HOVSTAD   No, I confess I did not.

PETER STOCKMANN   [*Looking round.*] You are very snug in here—very nice indeed.

HOVSTAD   Oh—

PETER STOCKMANN   And here I come, without any notice, to take up your time!

HOVSTAD   By all means, Mr. Mayor. I am at your service. But let me relieve you of your— [*Takes* STOCKMANN's *hat and stick and puts them on a chair.*] Won't you sit down?

PETER STOCKMANN   [*Sitting down by the table.*] Thank you. [HOVSTAD *sits down.*] I have had an extremely annoying experience today, Mr. Hovstad.

HOVSTAD   Really? Ah well, I expect with all the various business you have to attend to—

PETER STOCKMANN   The Medical Officer of the Baths is responsible for what happened today.

HOVSTAD   Indeed? The Doctor?

PETER STOCKMANN   He has addressed a kind of report to the Baths Committee on the subject of certain supposed defects in the Baths.

HOVSTAD   Has he indeed?

PETER STOCKMANN   Yes—has he not told you? I thought he said—

HOVSTAD   Ah, yes—it is true he did mention something about—

ASLAKSEN   [*Coming from the printing-room.*] I ought to have that copy—

HOVSTAD   [*Angrily.*] Ahem!—there it is on the desk.

ASLAKSEN   [*Taking it.*] Right.

PETER STOCKMANN   But look there—that is the thing I was speaking of!

ASLAKSEN   Yes, that is the Doctor's article, Mr. Mayor.

HOVSTAD   Oh, is *that* what you were speaking about?

PETER STOCKMANN   Yes, that is it. What do you think of it?

HOVSTAD   Oh, I am only a layman—and I have only taken a very cursory glance at it.

PETER STOCKMANN   But you are going to print it?

HOVSTAD   I cannot very well refuse a distinguished man—

ASLAKSEN   I have nothing to do with editing the paper, Mr. Mayor—

PETER STOCKMANN   I understand.

ASLAKSEN   I merely print what is put into my hands.

PETER STOCKMANN   Quite so.

ASLAKSEN   And so I must— [*Moves off towards the printing-room.*]

PETER STOCKMANN   No, but wait a moment, Mr. Aslaksen. You will allow me, Mr. Hovstad?

HOVSTAD   If you please, Mr. Mayor.

PETER STOCKMANN   You are a discreet and thoughtful man, Mr. Aslaksen.

ASLAKSEN   I am delighted to hear you think so, sir.

PETER STOCKMANN   And a man of very considerable influence.

ASLAKSEN   Chiefly among the small tradesmen, sir.

PETER STOCKMANN   The small taxpayers are the majority—here as everywhere else.

ASLAKSEN   That is true.

PETER STOCKMANN   And I have no doubt you know the general trend of opinion among them, don't you?

ASLAKSEN   Yes, I think I may say I do, Mr. Mayor.

PETER STOCKMANN   Yes. Well, since there is such a praiseworthy spirit of self-sacrifice among the less wealthy citizens of our town—

ASLAKSEN   What?

HOVSTAD   Self-sacrifice?

PETER STOCKMANN   It is pleasing evidence of a public-spirited feeling, extremely pleasing evidence. I might almost say I hardly expected it. But you have a closer knowledge of public opinion than I.

ASLAKSEN   But, Mr. Mayor—

PETER STOCKMANN   And indeed it is no small sacrifice that the town is going to make.

HOVSTAD   The town?

ASLAKSEN   But I don't understand. Is it the Baths—?

PETER STOCKMANN   At a provisional estimate, the alterations that the Medical Officer asserts are desirable will cost somewhere about twenty thousand pounds.

ASLAKSEN   That is a lot of money, but—

PETER STOCKMANN   Of course it will be necessary to raise a municipal loan.

HOVSTAD   [*Getting up.*] Surely you never mean that the town must pay—?

ASLAKSEN   Do you mean that it must come out of the municipal funds?—out of the ill-filled pockets of the small tradesmen?

PETER STOCKMANN   Well, my dear Mr. Aslaksen, where else is the money to come from?

ASLAKSEN   The gentlemen who own the Baths ought to provide that.

PETER STOCKMANN   The proprietors of the Baths are not in a position to incur any further expense.

ASLAKSEN   Is that absolutely certain, Mr. Mayor?

PETER STOCKMANN   I have satisfied myself that it is so. If the town wants these very extensive alterations, it will have to pay for them.

ASLAKSEN   But, damn it all— I beg your pardon—this is quite another matter, Mr. Hovstad!

HOVSTAD   It is, indeed.

PETER STOCKMANN   The most fatal part of it is that we shall be obliged to shut the Baths for a couple of years.

HOVSTAD   Shut them? Shut them altogether?

ASLAKSEN   For two years?

PETER STOCKMANN   Yes, the work will take as long as that—at least.

ASLAKSEN   I'm damned if we will stand that, Mr. Mayor! What are we householders to live upon in the meantime?

PETER STOCKMANN   Unfortunately, that is an extremely difficult question to answer, Mr. Aslaksen. But what would you have us do? Do you suppose we shall have a single visitor in the town, if we go about proclaiming that our water is polluted, that we are living over a plague spot, that the entire town—

ASLAKSEN   And the whole thing is merely imagination?

PETER STOCKMANN   With the best will in the world, I have not been able to come to any other conclusion.

ASLAKSEN   Well then, I must say it is absolutely unjustifiable of Dr. Stockmann—I beg your pardon, Mr. Mayor—

PETER STOCKMANN   What you say is lamentably true, Mr. Aslaksen. My brother has, unfortunately, always been a headstrong man.

ASLAKSEN   After this, do you mean to give him your support, Mr. Hovstad?

HOVSTAD   Can you suppose for a moment that I—?

PETER STOCKMANN   I have drawn up a short *résumé* of the situation as it appears from a reasonable man's point of view. In it I have indicated how certain possible defects might suitably be remedied without outrunning the resources of the Baths Committee.

HOVSTAD   Have you got it with you, Mr. Mayor?

PETER STOCKMANN   [*Fumbling in his pocket.*] Yes, I brought it with me in case you should—

ASLAKSEN   Good Lord, there he is!

PETER STOCKMANN   Who? My brother?

HOVSTAD   Where? Where?

ASLAKSEN   He has just gone through the printing-room.

PETER STOCKMANN   How unlucky! I don't want to meet him here, and I had still several things to speak to you about.

HOVSTAD   [*Pointing to the door on the right.*] Go in there for the present.

PETER STOCKMANN   But—?

HOVSTAD   You will only find Billing in there.

ASLAKSEN   Quick, quick, Mr. Mayor—he is just coming.

PETER STOCKMANN   Yes, very well; but see that you get rid of him quickly.

[*Goes out through the door on the right, which* ASLAKSEN *opens for him and shuts after him.*]

HOVSTAD   Pretend to be doing something, Aslaksen.

[*Sits down and writes.* ASLAKSEN *begins foraging among a heap of newspapers that are lying on a chair.*]

DR. STOCKMANN   [*Coming in from the printing-room.*] Here I am again. [*Puts down his hat and stick.*]

HOVSTAD   [*Writing.*] Already, Doctor? Hurry up with what we were speaking about, Aslaksen. We are very pressed for time today.

DR. STOCKMANN   [*To* ASLAKSEN.] No proof for me to see yet, I hear.

ASLAKSEN   [*Without turning around.*] You couldn't expect it yet, Doctor.

DR. STOCKMANN   No, no; but I am impatient, as you can understand. I shall not know a moment's peace of mind till I see it in print.

HOVSTAD   Hm!—it will take a good while yet, won't it, Aslaksen?

ASLAKSEN   Yes, I am almost afraid it will.

DR. STOCKMANN   All right, my dear friends; I will come back. I do not mind coming back twice if necessary. A matter of such great importance—the welfare of the town at stake—it is no time to shirk trouble. [*Is just going, but stops and comes back.*] Look here—there is one thing more I want to speak to you about.

HOVSTAD   Excuse me, but could it not wait till some other time?

DR. STOCKMANN   I can tell you in half a dozen words. It is only this. When my article is read tomorrow and it is realized that I have been quietly working the whole winter for the welfare of the town—

HOVSTAD   Yes, but, Doctor—

DR. STOCKMANN   I know what you are going to say. You don't see how on earth it was any more than my duty—my obvious duty as a citizen. Of course it wasn't; I know that as well as you. But my fellow-citizens, you know—! Good Lord, think of all the good souls who think so highly of me—!

ASLAKSEN   Yes, our townsfolk have had a very high opinion of you so far, Doctor.

DR. STOCKMANN   Yes, and that is just why I am afraid they—. Well, this is the point; when this reaches them, especially the poorer classes, and sounds in their ears like a summons to take the town's affairs into their own hands for the future—

HOVSTAD   [*Getting up.*] Ahem! Doctor, I won't conceal from you the fact—

DR. STOCKMANN   Ah! I knew there was something in the wind! But I won't hear a word of it. If anything of that sort is being set on foot—

HOVSTAD   Of what sort?

DR. STOCKMANN   Well, whatever it is—whether it is a demonstration in my honor, or a banquet, or a subscription list for some presentation to me—whatever it is, you must promise me solemnly and faithfully to put a stop to it. You, too, Mr. Aslaksen; do you understand?

HOVSTAD   You must forgive me, Doctor, but sooner or later we must tell you the plain truth—

[*He is interrupted by the entrance of* MRS. STOCKMANN, *who comes in from the street door.*]

MRS. STOCKMANN   [*Seeing her husband.*] Just as I thought!

HOVSTAD   [*Going towards her.*] You too, Mrs. Stockmann?

DR. STOCKMANN   What on earth do *you* want here, Katherine?

MRS. STOCKMANN   I should think you know very well what I want.

HOVSTAD   Won't you sit down? Or perhaps—

MRS. STOCKMANN   No, thank you; don't trouble. And you must not be offended at my coming to fetch my husband; I am the mother of three children, you know.

DR. STOCKMANN   Nonsense!—we know all about that.

MRS. STOCKMANN   Well, one would not give you credit for much thought for your wife and children today; if you had had that, you would not have gone and dragged us all into misfortune.

DR. STOCKMANN   Are you out of your senses, Katherine? Because a man has a wife and children, is he not to be allowed to proclaim the truth—is he not to be allowed to be an actively useful citizen—is he not to be allowed to do a service to his native town?

MRS. STOCKMANN   Yes, Thomas—in reason.

ASLAKSEN   Just what I say. Moderation is everything.

MRS. STOCKMANN   And that is why you wrong us, Mr. Hovstad, in enticing my husband away from his home and making a dupe of him in all this.

HOVSTAD   I certainly am making a dupe of no one—

DR. STOCKMANN   Making a dupe of me! Do you suppose *I* should allow myself to be duped?

MRS. STOCKMANN   It is just what you do. I know quite well you have more brains than anyone in the town, but you are extremely easily duped, Thomas. [*To* HOVSTAD.] Please realize that he loses his post at the Baths if you print what he has written—

ASLAKSEN   What!

HOVSTAD   Look here, Doctor—

DR. STOCKMANN   [*Laughing.*] Ha—ha!—just let them try! No, no—they will take good care not to. I have got the compact majority behind me, let me tell you!

MRS. STOCKMANN   Yes, that is just the worst of it—your having any such horrid thing behind you.

DR. STOCKMANN   Rubbish, Katherine! Go home and look after your house and leave me to look after the community. How can you be so afraid, when I am so confident and happy? [*Walks up and down, rubbing his hands.*] Truth and the People will win the fight, you may be certain! I see the whole of the broad-minded middle class marching like a victorious army—! [*Stops beside a chair.*] What the deuce is that lying there?

ASLAKSEN   Good Lord!

HOVSTAD   Ahem!

DR. STOCKMANN   Here we have the topmost pinnacle of authority!

[*Takes the* MAYOR's *official hat carefully between his finger-tips and holds it up in the air.*]

MRS. STOCKMANN   The Mayor's hat!

DR. STOCKMANN   And here is the staff of office too. How in the name of all that's wonderful—?

HOVSTAD   Well, you see—

DR. STOCKMANN   Oh, I understand. He has been here trying to talk you over. Ha—ha!—he made rather a mistake there! And as soon as he caught sight of me in the printing-room—. [*Bursts out laughing.*] Did he run away, Mr. Aslaksen?

ASLAKSEN   [*Hurriedly.*] Yes, he ran away, Doctor.

DR. STOCKMANN   Ran away without his stick or his.—Fiddlesticks! Peter doesn't run away and leave his belongings behind him. But what the deuce have you done with him? Ah!—in

there, of course. Now you shall see, Katherine.

MRS. STOCKMANN   Thomas—please don't—!

ASLAKSEN   Don't be rash, Doctor.

[DR. STOCKMANN *has put on the* MAYOR's *hat and taken his stick in his hand. He goes up to the door, opens it and stands with his hand to his hat at the salute.* PETER STOCKMANN *comes in, red with anger.* BILLING *follows him.*]

PETER STOCKMANN   What does this tomfoolery mean?

DR. STOCKMANN   Be respectful, my good Peter. I am the chief authority in the town now. [*Walks up and down.*]

MRS. STOCKMANN   [*Almost in tears.*] Really, Thomas!

PETER STOCKMANN   [*Following him about.*] Give me my hat and stick.

DR. STOCKMANN   [*In the same tone as before.*] If you are chief constable, let me tell you that I am the Mayor—I am the master of the whole town, please understand!

PETER STOCKMANN   Take off my hat, I tell you. Remember it is part of an official uniform.

DR. STOCKMANN   Pooh! Do you think the newly awakened lion-hearted people are going to be frightened by an official hat? There is going to be a revolution in the town tomorrow, let me tell you. You thought you could turn me out; but now I shall turn you out—turn you out of all your various offices. Do you think I cannot? Listen to me. I have triumphant social forces behind me. Hovstad and Billing will thunder in "The People's Messenger," and Aslaksen will take the field at the head of the whole Householders' Association—

ASLAKSEN   That I won't, Doctor.

DR. STOCKMANN   Of course you will—

PETER STOCKMANN   Ah!—may I ask then if Mr. Hovstad intends to join this agitation?

HOVSTAD   No, Mr. Mayor.

ASLAKSEN   No, Mr. Hovstad is not such a fool as to go and ruin his paper and himself for the sake of an imaginary grievance.

DR. STOCKMANN   [*Looking round him.*] What does this mean?

HOVSTAD   You have represented your case in a false light, Doctor, and therefore I am unable to give you my support.

BILLING   And after what the Mayor was so kind as to tell me just now, I—

DR. STOCKMANN   A false light! Leave that part

of it to me. Only print my article; I am quite capable of defending it.

HOVSTAD   I am not going to print it. I cannot and will not and dare not print it.

DR. STOCKMANN   You dare not? What nonsense! —you are the editor; and an editor controls his paper, I suppose!

ASLAKSEN   No, it is the subscribers, Doctor.

PETER STOCKMANN   Fortunately, yes.

ASLAKSEN   It is public opinion—the enlightened public—householders and people of that kind; they control the newspapers.

DR. STOCKMANN   [*Composedly.*] And I have all these influences against me?

ASLAKSEN   Yes, you have. It would mean the absolute ruin of the community if your article were to appear.

DR. STOCKMANN   Indeed.

PETER STOCKMANN   My hat and stick, if you please. [DR. STOCKMANN *takes off the hat and lays it on the table with the stick.* PETER STOCKMANN *takes them up.*] Your authority as Mayor has come to an untimely end.

DR. STOCKMANN   We have not got to the end yet. [*To* HOVSTAD.] Then it is quite impossible for you to print my article in "The People's Messenger"?

HOVSTAD   Quite impossible—out of regard for your family as well.

MRS. STOCKMANN   You need not concern yourself about his family, thank you, Mr. Hovstad.

PETER STOCKMANN   [*Taking a paper from his pocket.*] It will be sufficient, for the guidance of the public, if this appears. It is an official statement. May I trouble you?

HOVSTAD   [*Taking the paper.*] Certainly; I will see that it is printed.

DR. STOCKMANN   But not mine. Do you imagine that you can silence me and stifle the truth? You will not find it so easy as you suppose. Mr. Aslaksen, kindly take my manuscript at once and print it as a pamphlet—at my expense. I will have four hundred copies—no, five—six hundred.

ASLAKSEN   If you offered me its weight in gold, I could not lend my press for any such purpose, Doctor. It would be flying in the face of public opinion. You will not get it printed anywhere in the town.

DR. STOCKMANN   Then give it back to me.

HOVSTAD   [*Giving him the MS.*] Here it is.

DR. STOCKMANN   [*Taking his hat and stick.*] It shall be made public all the same. I will read it out at a mass meeting of the townspeople. All my fellow-citizens shall hear the voice of truth!

PETER STOCKMANN   You will not find any public body in the town that will give you the use of their hall for such a purpose.

ASLAKSEN   Not a single one, I am certain.

BILLING   No, I'm damned if you will find one.

MRS. STOCKMANN   But this is too shameful! Why should every one turn against you like that?

DR. STOCKMANN   [*Angrily.*] I will tell you why. It is because all the men in this town are old women—like you; they all think of nothing but their families, and never of the community.

MRS. STOCKMANN   [*Putting her arm into his.*] Then I will show them that an—an old woman can be a man for once. I am going to stand by you, Thomas!

DR. STOCKMANN   Bravely said, Katherine! It shall be made public—as I am a living soul! If I can't hire a hall, I shall hire a drum, and parade the town with it and read it at every street corner.

PETER STOCKMANN   You are surely not such an arrant fool as that!

DR. STOCKMANN   Yes, I am.

ASLAKSEN   You won't find a single man in the whole town to go with you.

BILLING   No, I'm damned if you will.

MRS. STOCKMANN   Don't give in, Thomas. I will tell the boys to go with you.

DR. STOCKMANN   That is a splendid idea!

MRS. STOCKMANN   Morten will be delighted; and Ejlif will do whatever he does.

DR. STOCKMANN   Yes, and Petra!—and you too, Katherine!

MRS. STOCKMANN   No, I won't do that; but I will stand at the window and watch you, that's what I will do.

DR. STOCKMANN   [*Puts his arms round her and kisses her.*] Thank you, my dear! Now you and I are going to try a fall, my fine gentlemen! I am going to see whether a pack of cowards can succeed in gagging a patriot who wants to purify society! [*He and his wife go out by the street door.*]

PETER STOCKMANN   [*Shaking his head seri-*

ously.] Now he has sent *her* out of her senses, too.

[*Curtain.*]

ACT IV

SCENE: A *big old-fashioned room in* CAP-TAIN HORSTER'S *house. At the back folding-doors, which are standing open, lead to an ante-room. Three windows in the left-hand wall. In the middle of the opposite wall a platform has been erected. On this a small table with two candles, a water-bottle and glass, and a bell. The room is lit by lamps placed between the windows. In the foreground on the left there is a table with candles and a chair. To the right is a door and some chairs standing near it. The room is nearly filled with a crowd of townspeople of all sorts, a few women and schoolboys being amongst them. People are still streaming in from the back, and the room is soon filled.*

FIRST CITIZEN [*Meeting another.*] Hullo, Lamstad! You here too?

SECOND CITIZEN I go to every public meeting, I do.

THIRD CITIZEN Brought your whistle too, I expect!

SECOND CITIZEN I should think so. Haven't you?

THIRD CITIZEN Rather! And old Evensen said he was going to bring a cow-horn, he did.

SECOND CITIZEN Good old Evensen!

[*Laughter among the crowd.*]

FOURTH CITIZEN [*Coming up to them.*] I say, tell me what is going on here tonight.

SECOND CITIZEN Dr. Stockmann is going to deliver an address attacking the Mayor.

FOURTH CITIZEN But the Mayor is his brother.

FIRST CITIZEN That doesn't matter; Dr. Stockmann's not the chap to be afraid.

THIRD CITIZEN But he is in the wrong; it said so in "The People's Messenger."

SECOND CITIZEN Yes, I expect he must be in the wrong this time, because neither the Householders' Association nor the Citizens' Club would lend him their hall for the meeting.

FIRST CITIZEN He couldn't even get the loan of the hall at the Baths.

SECOND CITIZEN No, I should think not.

A MAN IN ANOTHER PART OF THE CROWD I say —who are we to back up in this?

ANOTHER MAN, BESIDE HIM Watch Aslaksen, and do as he does.

BILLING [*Pushing his way through the crowd, with a writing-case under his arm.*] Excuse me, gentlemen—do you mind letting me through? I am reporting for "The People's Messenger." Thank you very much! [*He sits down at the table on the left.*]

A WORKMAN Who was that?

SECOND WORKMAN Don't you know him? It's Billing, who writes for Aslaksen's paper.

[CAPTAIN HORSTER *brings in* MRS. STOCKMANN *and* PETRA *through the door on the right.* EJLIF *and* MORTEN *follow them in.*]

HORSTER I thought you might all sit here; you can slip out easily from here, if things get too lively.

MRS. STOCKMANN Do you think there will be a disturbance?

HORSTER One can never tell—with such a crowd. But sit down, and don't be uneasy.

MRS. STOCKMANN [*Sitting down.*] It was extremely kind of you to offer my husband the room.

HORSTER Well, if nobody else would—

PETRA [*Who has sat down beside her mother.*] And it was a plucky thing to do, Captain Horster.

HORSTER Oh, it is not such a great matter as all that.

[HOVSTAD *and* ASLAKSEN *make their way through the crowd.*]

ASLAKSEN [*Going up to* HORSTER.] Has the Doctor not come yet?

HORSTER He is waiting in the next room.

[*Movement in the crowd by the door at the back.*]

HOVSTAD Look—here comes the Mayor!

BILLING Yes. I'm damned if he hasn't come after all!

[PETER STOCKMANN *makes his way gradually through the crowd, bows courteously and takes up a position by the wall on the left. Shortly afterwards* DR. STOCKMANN *comes in by the right-hand door. He is dressed in a black frockcoat, with a white tie. There is a little feeble applause, which is hushed down. Silence is obtained.*]

DR. STOCKMANN [*In an undertone.*] How do you feel, Katherine?

MRS. STOCKMANN All right, thank you. [*Lowering her voice.*] Be sure not to lose your temper, Thomas.

DR. STOCKMANN Oh, I know how to control myself. [*Looks at his watch, steps on to the platform and bows.*] It is a quarter past—so I will begin. [*Takes his MS. out of his pocket.*]

ASLAKSEN I think we ought to elect a chairman first.

DR. STOCKMANN No, it is quite unnecessary.

SOME OF THE CROWD Yes—yes!

PETER STOCKMANN I certainly think, too, that we ought to have a chairman.

DR. STOCKMANN But I have called this meeting to deliver a lecture, Peter.

PETER STOCKMANN Dr. Stockmann's lecture may possibly lead to a considerable conflict of opinion.

VOICES IN THE CROWD A chairman! A chairman!

HOVSTAD The general wish of the meeting seems to be that a chairman should be elected.

DR. STOCKMANN [*Restraining himself.*] Very well—let the meeting have its way.

ASLAKSEN Will the Mayor be good enough to undertake the task?

THREE MEN [*Clapping their hands.*] Bravo! Bravo!

PETER STOCKMANN For various reasons, which you will easily understand, I must beg to be excused. But fortunately we have amongst us a man who I think will be acceptable to you all. I refer to the President of the Householders' Association, Mr. Aslaksen!

SEVERAL VOICES Yes—Aslaksen! Bravo, Aslaksen!

[DR. STOCKMANN *takes up his MS. and walks up and down the platform.*]

ASLAKSEN Since my fellow-citizens choose to entrust me with this duty, I cannot refuse.

[*Loud applause.* ASLAKSEN *mounts the platform.*]

BILLING [*Writing.*] "Mr. Aslaksen was elected with enthusiasm."

ASLAKSEN And now, as I am in this position, I should like to say a few brief words. I am a quiet and peaceable man, who believes in discreet moderation, and—and—in moderate discretion. All my friends can bear witness to that.

SEVERAL VOICES That's right! That's right, Aslaksen!

ASLAKSEN I have learnt in the school of life and experience that moderation is the most valuable virtue a citizen can possess—

PETER STOCKMANN Hear, hear!

ASLAKSEN —and moreover that discretion and moderation are what enable a man to be of most service to the community. I would therefore suggest to our esteemed fellow-citizen, who has called this meeting, that he should strive to keep strictly within the bounds of moderation.

A MAN BY THE DOOR Three cheers for the Moderation Society!

A VOICE Shame!

SEVERAL VOICES Sh!—Sh!

ASLAKSEN No interruptions, gentlemen, please! Does anyone wish to make any remarks?

PETER STOCKMANN Mr. Chairman.

ASLAKSEN The Mayor will address the meeting.

PETER STOCKMANN In consideration of the close relationship in which, as you all know, I stand to the present Medical Officer of the Baths, I should have preferred not to speak this evening. But my official position with regard to the Baths and my solicitude for the vital interests of the town compel me to bring forward a motion. I venture to presume that there is not a single one of our citizens present who considers it desirable that unreliable and exaggerated accounts of the sanitary condition of the Baths and the town should be spread abroad.

SEVERAL VOICES No, no! Certainly not! We protest against it!

PETER STOCKMANN Therefore I should like to propose that the meeting should not permit the Medical Officer either to read or to comment on his proposed lecture.

DR. STOCKMANN [*Impatiently.*] Not permit—! What the devil—!

MRS. STOCKMANN [*Coughing.*] Ahem!—ahem!

DR. STOCKMANN [*Collecting himself.*] Very well. Go ahead!

PETER STOCKMANN In my communication to "The People's Messenger," I have put the essential facts before the public in such a way that every fair-minded citizen can easily form his own opinion. From it you will see that the main result of the Medical Officer's proposals

—apart from their constituting a vote of censure on the leading men of the town—would be to saddle the taxpayers with an unnecessary expenditure of at least some thousands of pounds.

[*Sounds of disapproval among the audience, and some catcalls.*]

ASLAKSEN [*Ringing his bell.*] Silence, please, gentlemen! I beg to support the Mayor's motion. I quite agree with him that there is something behind this agitation started by the Doctor. He talks about the Baths; but it is a revolution he is aiming at—he wants to get the administration of the town put into new hands. No one doubts the honesty of the Doctor's intentions—no one will suggest that there can be any two opinions as to that. I myself am a believer in self-government for the people, provided it does not fall too heavily on the taxpayers. But that would be the case here; and that is why I will see Dr. Stockmann damned—I beg your pardon—before I go with him in the matter. You can pay too dearly for a thing sometimes; that is my opinion. [*Loud applause on all sides.*]

HOVSTAD I, too, feel called upon to explain my position. Dr. Stockmann's agitation appeared to be gaining a certain amount of sympathy at first, so I supported it as impartially as I could. But presently we had reason to suspect that we had allowed ourselves to be misled by misrepresentation of the state of affairs—

DR. STOCKMANN Misrepresentation—!

HOVSTAD Well, let us say a not entirely trustworthy representation. The Mayor's statement has proved that. I hope no one here has any doubt as to my liberal principles; the attitude of "The People's Messenger" towards important political questions is well known to everyone. But the advice of experienced and thoughtful men has convinced me that in purely local matters a newspaper ought to proceed with a certain caution.

ASLAKSEN I entirely agree with the speaker.

HOVSTAD And, in the matter before us, it is now an undoubted fact that Dr. Stockmann has public opinion against him. Now, what is an editor's first and most obvious duty, gentlemen? Is it not to work in harmony with his readers? Has he not received a sort of tacit mandate to work persistently and assiduously for the welfare of those whose opinions he represents? Or is it possible I am mistaken in that?

VOICES FROM THE CROWD No, no! You are quite right!

HOVSTAD It has cost me a severe struggle to break with a man in whose house I have been lately a frequent guest—a man who till today has been able to pride himself on the undivided goodwill of his fellow-citizens—a man whose only, or at all events whose essential, failing is that he is swayed by his heart rather than his head.

A FEW SCATTERED VOICES That is true! Bravo, Stockmann!

HOVSTAD But my duty to the community obliged me to break with him. And there is another consideration that impels me to oppose him, and, as far as possible, to arrest him on the perilous course he has adopted; that is, consideration for his family—

DR. STOCKMANN Please stick to the water-supply and drainage!

HOVSTAD —consideration, I repeat, for his wife and his children for whom he has made no provision.

MORTEN Is that us, mother?

MRS. STOCKMANN Hush!

ASLAKSEN I will now put the Mayor's proposition to the vote.

DR. STOCKMANN There is no necessity! Tonight I have no intention of dealing with all that filth down at the Baths. No; I have something quite different to say to you.

PETER STOCKMANN [*Aside.*] What is coming now?

A DRUNKEN MAN [*By the entrance door.*] I am a taxpayer! And therefore I have a right to speak too! And my entire—firm—inconceivable opinion is—

A NUMBER OF VOICES Be quiet at the back there!

OTHERS He is drunk! Turn him out! [*They turn him out.*]

DR. STOCKMANN Am I allowed to speak?

ASLAKSEN [*Ringing his bell.*] Dr. Stockmann will address the meeting.

DR. STOCKMANN I should like to have seen anyone, a few days ago, dare to attempt to silence me as has been done tonight! I would have defended my sacred rights as a man, like a lion! But now it is all one to me; I have something of even weightier importance to say to you.

[*The crowd presses nearer to him,* MORTEN KIIL *conspicuous among them.*]

DR. STOCKMANN [*Continuing.*] I have thought and pondered a great deal, these last few days—pondered over such a variety of things that in the end my head seemed too full to hold them—

PETER STOCKMANN [*With a cough.*] Ahem!

DR. STOCKMANN —but I got them clear in my mind at last, and then I saw the whole situation lucidly. And that is why I am standing here tonight. I have a revelation to make to you, my fellow-citizens! I will impart to you a discovery of a far wider scope than the trifling matter that our water-supply is poisoned and our medicinal Baths are standing on pestiferous soil.

A NUMBER OF VOICES [*Shouting.*] Don't talk about the Baths! We won't hear you! None of that!

DR. STOCKMANN I have already told you that what I want to speak about is the great discovery I have made lately—the discovery that all the sources of our *moral* life are poisoned and that the whole fabric of our civic community is founded on the pestiferous soil of falsehood.

VOICES OF DISCONCERTED CITIZENS What is that he says?

PETER STOCKMANN Such an insinuation—!

ASLAKSEN [*With his hand on his bell.*] I call upon the speaker to moderate his language.

DR. STOCKMANN I have always loved my native town as a man only can love the home of his youthful days. I was not old when I went away from here; and exile, longing, and memories cast, as it were, an additional halo over both the town and its inhabitants. [*Some clapping and applause.*] And there I stayed, for many years, in a horrible hole far away up north. When I came into contact with some of the people that lived scattered about among the rocks, I often thought it would have been more service to the poor half-starved creatures if a veterinary doctor had been sent up there, instead of a man like me.

[*Murmurs among the crowd.*]

BILLING [*Laying down his pen.*] I'm damned if I have ever heard—!

HOVSTAD It is an insult to a respectable population!

DR. STOCKMANN Wait a bit! I do not think anyone will charge me with having forgotten my native town up there. I was like one of the eider-ducks brooding on its nest, and what I hatched was—the plans for these Baths. [*Applause and protests.*] And then when fate at last decreed for me the great happiness of coming home again—I assure you, gentlemen, I thought I had nothing more in the world to wish for. Or rather, there was one thing I wished for—eagerly, untiringly, ardently—and that was to be able to be of service to my native town and the good of the community.

PETER STOCKMANN [*Looking at the ceiling.*] You chose a strange way of doing it—ahem!

DR. STOCKMANN And so, with my eyes blinded to the real facts, I revelled in happiness. But yesterday morning—no, to be precise, it was yesterday afternoon—the eyes of my mind were opened wide, and the first thing I realized was the colossal stupidity of the authorities—.

[*Uproar, shouts, and laughter.* MRS. STOCKMANN *coughs persistently.*]

PETER STOCKMANN Mr. Chairman!

ASLAKSEN [*Ringing his bell.*] By virtue of my authority—!

DR. STOCKMANN It is a petty thing to catch me up on a word, Mr. Aslaksen. What I mean is only that I got scent of the unbelievable piggishness our leading men had been responsible for down at the Baths. I can't stand leading men at any price!—I have had enough of such people in my time. They are like billy-goats in a young plantation; they do mischief everywhere. They stand in a free man's way, whichever way he turns, and what I should like best would be to see them exterminated like any other vermin—.[*Uproar.*]

PETER STOCKMANN Mr. Chairman, can we allow such expressions to pass?

ASLAKSEN [*With his hand on his bell.*] Doctor—!

DR. STOCKMANN I cannot understand how it is that I have only now acquired a clear conception of what these gentry are, when I had almost daily before my eyes in this town such an excellent specimen of them—my brother Peter—slow-witted and hidebound in prejudice.

[*Laughter, uproar, and hisses.* MRS. STOCKMANN *sits coughing assiduously.* ASLAKSEN *rings his bell violently.*]

THE DRUNKEN MAN [*Who has got in again.*] Is it me he is talking about? My name's Petersen, all right—but devil take me if I—

ANGRY VOICES Turn out that drunken man! Turn him out. [*He is turned out again.*]

PETER STOCKMANN Who was that person?

FIRST CITIZEN I don't know who he is, Mr. Mayor.

SECOND CITIZEN He doesn't belong here.

THIRD CITIZEN I expect he is a lumberman from over at [*The rest is inaudible.*]

ASLAKSEN He had obviously had too much beer.—Proceed, Doctor; but please strive to be moderate in your language.

DR. STOCKMANN Very well, gentlemen, I will say no more about our leading men. And if anyone imagines, from what I have just said, that my object is to attack these people this evening, he is wrong—absolutely wide of the mark. For I cherish the comforting conviction that these parasites—all these venerable relics of a dying school of thought—are most admirably paving the way for their own extinction; they need no doctor's help to hasten their end. Nor is it folk of that kind who constitute the most pressing danger to the community. It is not they who are most instrumental in poisoning the sources of our moral life and infecting the ground on which we stand. It is not they who are the most dangerous enemies of truth and freedom amongst us.

SHOUTS FROM ALL SIDES Who then? Who is it? Name! Name!

DR. STOCKMANN You may depend upon it I shall name them! That is precisely the great discovery I made yesterday. [*Raises his voice.*] The most dangerous enemy of truth and freedom amongst us is the compact majority—yes, the damned compact Liberal majority—that is it! Now you know!

[*Tremendous uproar. Most of the crowd are shouting, stamping, and hissing. Some of the older men among them exchange stolen glances and seem to be enjoying themselves.* MRS. STOCKMANN *gets up, looking anxious.* EJLIF *and* MORTEN *advance threateningly upon some schoolboys who are playing pranks.* ASLAKSEN *rings his bell and begs for silence.* HOVSTAD *and* BILLING *both talk at once, but are inaudible. At last quiet is restored.*]

ASLAKSEN As chairman, I call upon the speaker to withdraw the ill-considered expressions he has just used.

DR. STOCKMANN Never, Mr. Aslaksen! It is the majority in our community that denies me my freedom and seeks to prevent my speaking the truth.

HOVSTAD The majority always has right on its side.

BILLING And truth too, by God!

DR. STOCKMANN The majority *never* has right on its side. Never, I say! That is one of these social lies against which an independent, intelligent man must wage war. Who constitutes the majority of the population in a country? Is it the clever folk or the stupid? I don't imagine you will dispute the fact that at present the stupid people are in an absolutely overwhelming majority all the world over. But, good Lord!—you can never pretend that it is right that the stupid folk should govern the clever ones! [*Uproar and cries.*] Oh, yes—you can shout me down, I know! but you cannot answer me. The majority has *might* on its side—unfortunately; but *right* it has *not*. I am in the right—I and a few other scattered individuals. The minority is always in the right. [*Renewed uproar.*]

HOVSTAD Aha—so Dr. Stockmann has become an aristocrat since the day before yesterday!

DR. STOCKMANN I have already said that I don't intend to waste a word on the puny, narrow-chested, short-winded crew whom we are leaving astern. Pulsating life no longer concerns itself with them. I am thinking of the few, the scattered few amongst us, who have absorbed new and vigorous truths. Such men stand, as it were, at the outposts, so far ahead that the compact majority has not yet been able to come up with them; and there they are fighting for truths that are too newly-born into the world of consciousness to have any considerable number of people on their side as yet.

HOVSTAD So the Doctor is a revolutionary now!

DR. STOCKMANN Good heavens—of course I am, Mr. Hovstad! I propose to raise a revolution against the lie that the majority has the monopoly of the truth. What sort of truths are they that the majority usually supports? They are the truths that are of such advanced age that they are beginning to break up. And if a truth is as old as that, it is also in a fair way to become a lie, gentlemen. [*Laughter and mocking cries.*] Yes, believe me or not, as you like; but truths are by no means as long-lived as Methuselah—as some folk imagine. A normally constituted truth lives, let us say, as a rule seventeen or eighteen, or at the most twenty years; seldom longer. But truths as aged as that are often worn frightfully thin, and nevertheless it is only then that the majority recognizes them and recommends them to the community as wholesome moral nourishment. There is no great nutritive value in that sort of fare, I can assure you; and, as a doctor, I ought to know. These "majority truths" are like last year's cured meat—like rancid, tainted ham; and they are the origin of the moral scurvy that is rampant in our communities.

ASLAKSEN It appears to me that the speaker is wandering a long way from his subject.

PETER STOCKMANN I quite agree with the Chairman.

DR. STOCKMANN Have you gone clean out of your senses, Peter? I am sticking as closely to my subject as I can; for my subject is precisely this, that it is the masses, the majority—this infernal compact majority—that poisons the sources of our moral life and infects the ground we stand on.

HOVSTAD And all this because the great, broad-minded majority of the people is prudent enough to show deference only to well-ascertained and well-approved truths?

DR. STOCKMANN Ah, my good Mr. Hovstad, don't talk nonsense about well-ascertained truths! The truths of which the masses now approve are the very truths that the fighters at the outposts held to in the days of our grandfathers. We fighters at the outposts nowadays no longer approve of them; and I do not believe there is any other well-ascertained truth except this, that no community can live a healthy life if it is nourished only on such old marrowless truths.

HOVSTAD But instead of standing there using vague generalities, it would be interesting if you would tell us what these old marrowless truths are, that we are nourished on. [*Applause from many quarters.*]

DR. STOCKMANN Oh, I could give you a whole string of such abominations; but to begin with I will confine myself to one well-approved truth, which at bottom is a foul lie, but upon which nevertheless M. Hovstad and "The People's Messenger" and all the "Messenger's" supporters are nourished.

HOVSTAD And that is—?

DR. STOCKMANN That is, the doctrine you have inherited from your forefathers and proclaim thoughtlessly far and wide—the doctrine that the public, the crowd, the masses are the essential part of the population—that they constitute the People—that the common folk, the ignorant and incomplete element in the community, have the same right to pronounce judgment and to approve, to direct, and to govern, as the isolated, intellectually superior personalities in it.

BILLING Well, damn me if ever I—

HOVSTAD [*At the same time, shouting out.*] Fellow-citizens, take good note of that!

A NUMBER OF VOICES [*Angrily.*] Oho! we are not the People! Only the superior folks are to govern, are they?

A WORKMAN Turn the fellow out, for talking such rubbish!

ANOTHER Out with him!

ANOTHER [*Calling out.*] Blow your horn, Evensen!

[*A horn is blown loudly, amidst hisses and an angry uproar.*]

DR. STOCKMANN [*When the noise has somewhat abated.*] Be reasonable! Can't you stand hearing the voice of truth for once? I don't in the least expect you to agree with me all at once; but I must say I did expect Mr. Hovstad to admit I was right, when he had recovered his composure a little. He claims to be a freethinker—

VOICES [*In murmurs of astonishment.*] Freethinker, did he say? Is Hovstad a freethinker?

HOVSTAD [*Shouting.*] Prove it, Dr. Stockmann! When have I said so in print?

DR. STOCKMANN [*Reflecting.*] No, confound it, you are right!—you have never had the courage to. Well, I won't put you in a hole, Mr. Hovstad. Let us say it is I that am the freethinker, then. I am going to prove to you, scientifically, that "The People's Messenger" leads you by the nose in a shameful manner when it tells you that you—that the common people, the crowd, the masses are the real essence of the People. That is only a newspaper lie, I tell you! The common people are nothing more than the raw material of which a People is made. [*Groans, laughter and uproar.*] Well, isn't that the case? Isn't there an enormous difference between a well-bred and an ill-bred strain of animals? Take, for instance, a common barn-door hen. What sort of eating do you get from a shrivelled up old scrag of fowl like that? Not much, do you? And what sort of eggs does it lay? A fairly good crow or a raven can lay pretty nearly as good an egg. But take a well-bred Spanish or Japanese hen; or a good pheasant or a turkey—then you will see the difference. Or take the case of dogs, with whom we humans are on such intimate terms. Think first of an ordinary common cur—I mean one of the horrible, coarse-haired, low-bred curs that do nothing but run the streets and befoul the walls of the houses. Compare one of these curs with a poodle whose sires for many generations have been bred in a gentleman's house, where they have had the best of food and had the opportunity of hearing soft voices and music. Do you not think that the poodle's brain is developed to quite a different degree from that of the cur? Of course it is. It is puppies of well-bred poodles like that that showmen train to do incredibly clever tricks—things that a common cur could never learn to do even if it stood on its head. [*Uproar and mocking cries.*]

A CITIZEN [*Calls out.*] Are you going to make out we are dogs, now?

ANOTHER CITIZEN We are not animals, Doctor!

DR. STOCKMANN Yes, but, bless my soul, we *are*, my friend! It is true we are the finest animals anyone could wish for; but, even amongst us, exceptionally fine animals are rare. There is a tremendous difference between poodle-men and cur-men. And the amusing part of it is that Mr. Hovstad quite agrees with me as long as it is a question of four-footed animals—

HOVSTAD Yes, it is true enough as far as they are concerned.

DR. STOCKMANN Very well. But as soon as I extend the principle and apply it to two-legged animals, Mr. Hovstad stops short. He no longer dares to think independently, or to pursue his ideas to their logical conclusion; so he turns the whole theory upside down and proclaims in "The People's Messenger" that it is the barndoor hens and street curs that are the finest specimens in the menagerie. But that is always the way, as long as a man retains the traces of common origin and has not worked his way up to intellectual distinction.

HOVSTAD I lay no claim to any sort of distinction. I am the son of humble countryfolk, and I am proud that the stock I came from is rooted deep among the common people he insults.

VOICES Bravo, Hovstad! Bravo! Bravo!

DR. STOCKMANN The kind of common people I mean are not only to be found low down in the social scale; they crawl and swarm all around us—even in the highest social positions. You have only to look at your own fine, distinguished Mayor! My brother Peter is every bit as plebeian as anyone that walks in two shoes—[*Laughter and hisses.*]

PETER STOCKMANN I protest against personal allusions of this kind.

DR. STOCKMANN [*Imperturbably.*]—and that, not because he is, like myself, descended from some old rascal of a pirate from Pomerania or thereabouts—because that is who we are descended from—

PETER STOCKMANN An absurd legend. I deny it!

DR. STOCKMANN —but because he thinks what his superiors think and holds the same opinions as they. People who do that are, intellectually speaking, common people; and that is why my magnificent brother Peter is in reality so very far from any distinction—and consequently also so far from being liberal-minded.

PETER STOCKMANN Mr. Chairman—!

HOVSTAD So it is only the distinguished men that are liberal-minded in this country? We are learning something quite new! [*Laughter.*]

DR. STOCKMANN Yes, that is part of my new discovery too. And another part of it is that broad-mindedness is almost precisely the same thing as morality. That is why I maintain that it is absolutely inexcusable in "The People's Messenger" to proclaim, day in and day out, the false doctrine that the masses, the crowd, the compact majority have the monopoly of broad-mindedness and morality—and that vice and corruption and every kind of intellectual depravity are the result of culture, just as all the filth that is draining into our Baths is the result of the tanneries up at Mölledal! [*Uproar and interruptions.* DR. STOCKMANN *is undisturbed, and goes on, carried away by his ardor, with a smile.*] And yet this same "People's Messenger" can go on preaching that the masses ought to be elevated to higher conditions of life! But, bless my soul, if the "Messenger's" teaching is to be depended upon, this very raising up the masses would mean nothing more or less than setting them straightway upon the paths of depravity! Happily the theory that culture demoralizes is only an old falsehood that our forefathers believed in and we have inherited. No, it is ignorance, poverty, ugly conditions of life that do the devil's work! In a house which does not get aired and swept every day—my wife Katherine maintains that the floor ought to be scrubbed as well, but that is a debatable question—in such a house, let me tell you, people will lose within two or three years the power of thinking or acting in a moral manner. Lack of oxygen weakens the conscience. And there must be a plentiful lack of oxygen in very many houses in this town, I should think, judging from the fact that the whole compact majority can be unconscientious enough to wish to build the town's prosperity on a quagmire of falsehood and deceit.

ASLAKSEN   We cannot allow such a grave accusation to be flung at a citizen community.

A CITIZEN   I move that the Chairman direct the speaker to sit down.

VOICES   [*Angrily.*] Hear, hear! Quite right! Make him sit down!

DR. STOCKMANN   [*Losing his self-control.*] Then I will go and shout the truth at every street corner. I will write it in other towns' newspapers! The whole country shall know what is going on here!

HOVSTAD   It almost seems as if Dr. Stockmann's intentions were to ruin the town.

DR. STOCKMANN   Yes, my native town is so dear to me that I would rather ruin it than see it flourishing upon a lie.

ASLAKSEN   This is really serious.

[*Uproar and cat-calls.* MRS. STOCKMANN *coughs, but to no purpose; her husband does not listen to her any longer.*]

HOVSTAD   [*Shouting above the din.*] A man must be a public enemy to wish to ruin a whole community!

DR. STOCKMANN   [*With growing fervor.*] What does the destruction of a community matter, if it lives on lies! It ought to be razed to the ground, I tell you! All who live by lies ought to be exterminated like vermin! You will end by infecting the whole country; you will bring about such a state of things that the whole country will deserve to be ruined. And if things come to that pass, I shall say from the bottom of my heart: Let the whole country perish, let all these people be exterminated!

VOICES FROM THE CROWD   That is talking like an out-and-out enemy of the people!

BILLING   There sounded the voice of the people, by all that's holy!

THE WHOLE CROWD   [*Shouting.*] Yes, yes! He is an enemy of the people! He hates his country! He hates his own people!

ASLAKSEN   Both as a citizen and as an individual, I am profoundly disturbed by what we have had to listen to. Dr. Stockmann has shown himself in a light I should never have dreamed of. I am unhappily obliged to subscribe to the opinion which I have just heard my estimable fellow-citizens utter; and I propose that we should give expression to that opinion in a resolution. I propose a resolution as follows: "This meeting declares that it considers Dr. Thomas Stockmann, Medical Officer of the Baths, to be an enemy of the people."

[*A storm of cheers and applause. A number of men surround the* DOCTOR *and hiss him.* MRS. STOCKMANN *and* PETRA *have got up from their seats.* MORTEN *and* EJLIF *are fighting the other schoolboys for hissing; some of their elders separate them.*]

DR. STOCKMANN   [*To the men who are hissing him.*] Oh, you fools! I tell you that—

ASLAKSEN   [*Ringing his bell.*] We cannot hear you now, Doctor. A formal vote is about to be taken; but, out of regard for personal feelings, it shall be by ballot and not verbal. Have you any clean paper, Mr. Billing?

BILLING   I have both blue and white here.

ASLAKSEN   [*Going to him.*] That will do nicely; we shall get on more quickly that way. Cut it up into small strips—yes, that's it. [*To the meeting.*] Blue means no; white means yes. I will come round myself and collect votes.

[PETER STOCKMANN *leaves the hall.* ASLAKSEN *and one or two others go round the room with the slips of paper in their hats.*]

FIRST CITIZEN   [*To* HOVSTAD] I say, what has come to the Doctor? What are we to think of it?

HOVSTAD   Oh, you know how headstrong he is.

SECOND CITIZEN [*To* BILLING.] Billing, you go to their house—have you ever noticed if the fellow drinks?

BILLING Well, I'm hanged if I know what to say. There are always spirits on the table when you go.

THIRD CITIZEN I rather think he goes quite off his head sometimes.

FIRST CITIZEN I wonder if there is any madness in his family?

BILLING I shouldn't wonder if there were.

FOURTH CITIZEN No, it is nothing more than sheer malice; he wants to get even with somebody for something or other.

BILLING Well certainly he suggested a rise in his salary on one occasion lately, and did not get it.

THE CITIZENS [*Together.*] Ah!—then it is easy to understand how it is!

THE DRUNKEN MAN [*Who has got amongst the audience again.*] I want a blue one, I do! And I want a white one too!

VOICES It's that drunken chap again! Turn him out!

MORTEN KIIL [*Going up to* DR. STOCKMANN.] Well, Stockmann, do you see what these monkey tricks of yours lead to?

DR. STOCKMANN I have done my duty.

MORTEN KIIL What was that you said about the tanneries at Mölledal?

DR. STOCKMANN You heard well enough. I said they were the source of all the filth.

MORTEN KIIL My tannery too?

DR. STOCKMANN Unfortunately your tannery is by far the worst.

MORTEN KIIL Are you going to put that in the papers?

DR. STOCKMANN I shall conceal nothing.

MORTEN KIIL That may cost you dear, Stockmann. [*Goes out.*]

A STOUT MAN [*Going up to* CAPTAIN HORSTER, *without taking any notice of the ladies.*] Well, Captain, so you lend your house to enemies of the people?

HORSTER I imagine I can do what I like with my own possessions, Mr. Vik.

THE STOUT MAN Then you can have no objection to my doing the same with mine.

HORSTER What do you mean, sir?

THE STOUT MAN You shall hear from me in the morning. [*Turns his back on him and moves off.*]

PETRA Was that not your owner, Captain Horster?

HORSTER Yes, that was Mr. Vik, the ship-owner.

ASLAKSEN [*With the voting-papers in his hands, gets up on the platform and rings his bell.*] Gentlemen, allow me to announce the result. By the votes of every one here except one person—

A YOUNG MAN That is the drunk chap!

ASLAKSEN By the votes of every one here except a tipsy man, this meeting of citizens declares Dr. Thomas Stockmann to be an enemy of the people. [*Shouts and applause.*] Three cheers for our ancient and honorable citizen community! [*Renewed applause.*] Three cheers for our able and energetic Mayor, who has so loyally suppressed the promptings of family feeling! [*Cheers.*] The meeting is dissolved. [*Gets down.*]

BILLING Three cheers for the Chairman!

THE WHOLE CROWD Three cheers for Aslaksen! Hurrah!

DR. STOCKMANN My hat and coat, Petra! Captain, have you room on your ship for passengers to the New World?

HORSTER For you and yours we will make room, Doctor.

DR. STOCKMANN [*As* PETRA *helps him into his coat.*] Good. Come, Katherine! Come, boys!

MRS. STOCKMANN [*In an undertone.*] Thomas, dear, let us go out by the back way.

DR. STOCKMANN No back ways for me, Katherine. [*Raising his voice.*] You will hear more of this enemy of the people, before he shakes the dust off his shoes upon you! I am not so forgiving as a certain Person; I do not say: "I forgive you, for ye know not what ye do."

ASLAKSEN [*Shouting.*] That is a blasphemous comparison, Dr. Stockmann!

BILLING It is, by God! It's dreadful for an earnest man to listen to.

A COARSE VOICE Threatens us now, does he?

OTHER VOICES [*Excitedly.*] Let's go and break his windows! Duck him in the fjord!

ANOTHER VOICE Blow your horn, Evensen! Pip, pip!

[*Horn-blowing, hisses, and wild cries.* DR. STOCKMANN *goes out through the hall with his family,* HORSTER *elbowing a way for them.*]

THE WHOLE CROWD [*Howling after them as they go.*] Enemy of the People! Enemy of the People!

BILLING [*As he puts his papers together.*] Well, I'm damned if I go and drink toddy with the Stockmanns tonight!

[*The crowd press towards the exit. The uproar continues outside; shouts of "Enemy of the People!" are heard from without.*]

[*Curtain.*]

ACT V

SCENE: DR. STOCKMANN's *study. Bookcases and cabinets containing specimens line the walls. At the back is a door leading to the hall; in the foreground on the left, a door leading to the sitting-room. In the right-hand wall are two windows, of which all the panes are broken. The* DOCTOR's *desk, littered with books and papers, stands in the middle of the room, which is in disorder. It is morning.* DR. STOCKMANN *in dressing-gown, slippers, and a smoking-cap, is bending down and raking with an umbrella under one of the cabinets. After a little while he rakes out a stone.*

DR. STOCKMANN [*Calling through the open sitting-room door.*] Katherine, I have found another one.

MRS. STOCKMANN [*From the sitting-room.*] Oh, you will find a lot more yet, I expect.

DR. STOCKMANN [*Adding the stone to a heap of others on the table.*] I shall treasure these stones as relics. Ejlif and Morten shall look at them every day, and when they are grown up they shall inherit them as heirlooms. [*Rakes about under a bookcase.*] Hasn't—what the deuce is her name?—the girl, you know—hasn't she been to fetch the glazier yet?

MRS. STOCKMANN [*Coming in.*] Yes, but he said he didn't know if he would be able to come today.

DR. STOCKMANN You will see he won't dare to come.

MRS. STOCKMANN Well, that is just what Randine thought—that he didn't dare to, on account of the neighbors. [*Calls into the sitting-room.*] What is it you want, Randine? Give it to me. [*Goes in, and comes out again directly.*] Here is a letter for you, Thomas.

DR. STOCKMANN Let me see it. [*Opens and reads it.*] Ah!—of course.

MRS. STOCKMANN Who is it from?

DR. STOCKMANN From the landlord. Notice to quit.

MRS. STOCKMANN Is it possible? Such a nice man—

DR. STOCKMANN [*Looking at the letter.*] Does not dare to otherwise, he says. Doesn't like doing it, but dare not do otherwise—on account of his fellow-citizens—out of regard for public opinion. Is in a dependent position—dare not offend certain influential men—

MRS. STOCKMANN There, you see, Thomas!

DR. STOCKMANN Yes, yes, I see well enough; the whole lot of them in the town are cowards; not a man among them dares do anything for fear of the others. [*Throws the letter onto the table.*] But it doesn't matter to us, Katherine. We are going to sail away to the New World, and—

MRS. STOCKMANN But, Thomas, are you sure we are well advised to take this step?

DR. STOCKMANN Are you suggesting that I should stay here, where they have pilloried me as an enemy of the people—branded me—broken my windows! And just look here, Katherine—they have torn a great rent in my black trousers too!

MRS. STOCKMANN Oh, dear—and they are the best pair you have got!

DR. STOCKMANN You should never wear your best trousers when you go out to fight for freedom and truth. It is not that I care so much about the trousers, you know; you can always sew them up again for me. But that the common herd should dare to make this attack on me, as if they were my equals—that is what I cannot, for the life of me, swallow!

MRS. STOCKMANN There is no doubt they have behaved very ill to you, Thomas; but is that sufficient reason for our leaving our native country for good and all?

DR. STOCKMANN If we went to another town, do you suppose we should not find the common people just as insolent as they are here? Depend upon it, there is not much to choose between them. Oh, well, let the curs snap—that is not the worst part of it. The worst is that, from one end of this country to the other, every man is the slave of his Party. Although, as far as that goes, I daresay it is not much better in the free West either; the compact majority, and liberal public opinion, and all that infernal old bag of tricks are probably rampant there too. But there things are done on a larger scale, you see. They may kill you, but they won't put you to death by slow torture. They don't squeeze a free man's soul in a vice, as they do here. And, if need be, one can live in solitude. [*Walks up and down.*] If only I knew where there was a virgin forest or a small South Sea island for sale, cheap—

MRS. STOCKMANN But think of the boys, Thomas.

DR. STOCKMANN [*Standing still.*] What a strange woman you are, Katherine! Would you prefer to have the boys grow up in a society like this? You saw for yourself last night that half the population are out of their minds; and if the other half have not lost their senses, it is because they are mere brutes, with no sense to lose.

MRS. STOCKMANN But, Thomas dear, the imprudent things you said had something to do with it, you know.

DR. STOCKMANN Well, isn't what I said perfectly true? Don't they turn every idea topsy-turvy? Don't they make a regular hotch-potch of right and wrong? Don't they say that the things I know are true are lies? The craziest part of it all is the fact of these "liberals," men of full age, going about in crowds imagining that they are the broad-minded party! Did you ever hear anything like it, Katherine?

MRS. STOCKMANN Yes, yes, it's mad enough of them, certainly; but—[PETRA *comes in from the sitting-room.*] Back from school already?

PETRA Yes. I have been given notice of dismissal.

MRS. STOCKMANN Dismissal?

DR. STOCKMANN You too?

PETRA Mrs. Busk gave me my notice; so I thought it best to go at once.

DR. STOCKMANN You were perfectly right, too!

MRS. STOCKMANN Who would have thought Mrs. Busk was a woman like that?

PETRA Mrs. Busk isn't a bit like that, mother; I saw quite plainly how it hurt her to do it. But she didn't dare do otherwise, she said; and so I got my notice.

DR. STOCKMANN [*Laughing and rubbing his hands.*] She didn't dare to do otherwise, either! It's delicious!

MRS. STOCKMANN Well, after the dreadful scenes last night—

PETRA It was not only that. Just listen to this, father!

DR. STOCKMANN Well?

PETRA Mrs. Busk showed me no less than three letters she received this morning—

DR. STOCKMANN Anonymous, I suppose?

PETRA Yes.

DR. STOCKMANN Yes, because they didn't dare to risk signing their names, Katherine!

PETRA And two of them were to the effect that a man, who has been our guest here, was declaring last night at the Club that my views on various subjects are extremely emancipated—

DR. STOCKMANN You did not deny that, I hope?

PETRA No, you know I wouldn't. Mrs. Busk's own views are tolerably emancipated, when we are alone together; but now that this report about me is being spread, she dare not keep me on any longer.

MRS. STOCKMANN And some one who had been a guest of ours! That shows you the return you get for your hospitality, Thomas!

DR. STOCKMANN We won't live in such a disgusting hole any longer. Pack up as quickly as you can, Katherine; the sooner we can get away the better.

MRS. STOCKMANN Be quiet—I think I hear some one in the hall. See who it is, Petra.

PETRA [*Opening the door.*] Oh, it's you, Captain Horster! Do come in.

HORSTER [*Coming in.*] Good morning. I thought I would just come in and see how you were.

DR. STOCKMANN [*Shaking his hand.*] Thanks—that is really kind of you.

MRS. STOCKMANN And thank you, too, for helping us through the crowd, Captain Horster.

PETRA How did you manage to get home again?

HORSTER Oh, somehow or other. I am fairly strong, and there is more sound than fury about these folk.

DR. STOCKMANN Yes, isn't their swinish cowardice astonishing? Look here, I will show you something! There are all the stones they have thrown through my windows. Just look at them! I'm hanged if there are more than two decently large bits of hardstone in the whole heap; the rest are nothing but gravel—wretched little things. And yet they stood out there bawling and swearing that they would do me some violence; but as for *doing* anything—you don't see much of that in this town.

HORSTER   Just as well for you this time, Doctor!

DR. STOCKMANN   True enough. But it makes one angry all the same; because if some day it should be a question of a national fight in real earnest, you will see that public opinion will be in favor of taking to one's heels, and the compact majority will turn tail like a flock of sheep, Captain Horster. That is what is so mournful to think of; it gives me so much concern, that—. No, devil take it, it is ridiculous to care about it! They have called me an enemy of the people, so an enemy of the people let me be!

MRS. STOCKMANN   You will never be that, Thomas.

DR. STOCKMANN   Don't swear to that, Katherine. To be called an ugly name may have the same effect as a pin-scratch in the lung. And that hateful name—I can't get quit of it. It is sticking here in the pit of my stomach, eating into me like a corrosive acid. And no magnesia will remove it.

PETRA   Bah!—you should only laugh at them, father.

HORSTER   They will change their minds some day, Doctor.

MRS. STOCKMANN   Yes, Thomas, as sure as you are standing here.

DR. STOCKMANN   Perhaps, when it is too late. Much good may it do them! They may wallow in their filth then and rue the day when they drove a patriot into exile. When do you sail, Captain Horster?

HORSTER   Hm!—that was just what I had come to speak about—

DR. STOCKMANN   Why, has anything gone wrong with the ship?

HORSTER   No; but what has happened is that I am not to sail in it.

PETRA   Do you mean that you have been dismissed from your command?

HORSTER   [Smiling.] Yes, that's just it.

PETRA   You too.

MRS. STOCKMANN   There, you see, Thomas!

DR. STOCKMANN   And that for the truth's sake! Oh! if I thought such a thing possible—

HORSTER   You mustn't take it to heart; I shall be sure to find a job with some ship-owner or other, elsewhere.

DR. STOCKMANN   And that is this man Vik—a wealthy man, independent of every one and everything—! Shame on him!

HORSTER   He is quite an excellent fellow otherwise; he told me himself he would willingly have kept me on, if only he had dared—

DR. STOCKMANN   But he didn't dare? No, of course not.

HORSTER   It is not such an easy matter, he said, for a party man—

DR. STOCKMANN   The worthy man spoke the truth. A party is like a sausage machine; it mashes up all sorts of heads together into the same mincemeat—fatheads and blockheads, all in one mush!

MRS. STOCKMANN   Come, come, Thomas dear!

PETRA   [To HORSTER.] If only you had not come home with us, things might not have come to this pass.

HORSTER   I do not regret it.

PETRA   [Holding out her hand to him.] Thank you for that!

HORSTER   [To DR. STOCKMANN.] And so what I came to say was that if you are determined to go away, I have thought of another plan—

DR. STOCKMANN   That's splendid!—if only we can get away at once.

MRS. STOCKMANN   Hush—wasn't that some one knocking?

PETRA   This is uncle, surely.

DR. STOCKMANN   Aha! [Calls out.] Come in!

MRS. STOCKMANN   Dear Thomas, promise me definitely— [PETER STOCKMANN comes in from the hall.]

PETER STOCKMANN   Oh, you are engaged. In that case, I will—

DR. STOCKMANN   No, no, come in.

PETER STOCKMANN   But I wanted to speak to you alone.

MRS. STOCKMANN   We will go into the sitting-room in the meanwhile.

HORSTER   And I will look in again later.

DR. STOCKMANN   No, go in there with them, Captain Horster; I want to hear more about—

HORSTER   Very well, I will wait, then.

[He follows MRS. STOCKMANN and PETRA into the sitting-room.]

DR. STOCKMANN   I daresay you find it rather draughty here today. Put your hat on.

PETER STOCKMANN   Thank you, if I may. [Does so.] I think I caught cold last night; I stood and shivered—

DR. STOCKMANN Really? I found it warm enough.

PETER STOCKMANN I regret that it was not in my power to prevent those excesses last night.

DR. STOCKMANN Have you anything particular to say to me besides that?

PETER STOCKMANN [*Taking a big letter from his pocket.*] I have this document for you, from the Baths Committee.

DR. STOCKMANN My dismissal?

PETER STOCKMANN Yes, dating from today. [*Lays the letter on the table.*] It gives us pain to do it; but, to speak frankly, we dared not do otherwise on account of public opinion.

DR. STOCKMANN [*Smiling.*] Dared not? I seem to have heard that word before, today.

PETER STOCKMANN I must beg you to understand your position clearly. For the future you must not count on any practice whatever in the town.

DR. STOCKMANN Devil take the practice! But why are you so sure of that?

PETER STOCKMANN The Householders' Association is circulating a list from house to house. All right-minded citizens are being called upon to give up employing you; and I can assure you that not a single head of a family will risk refusing his signature. They simply dare not.

DR. STOCKMANN No, no; I don't doubt it. But what then?

PETER STOCKMANN If I might advise you, it would be best to leave the place for a little while—

DR. STOCKMANN Yes, the propriety of leaving the place *has* occurred to me.

PETER STOCKMANN Good. And then, when you have had six months to think things over, if, after mature consideration, you can persuade yourself to write a few words of regret, acknowledging your error—

DR. STOCKMANN I might have my appointment restored to me, do you mean?

PETER STOCKMANN Perhaps. It is not at all impossible.

DR. STOCKMANN But what about public opinion, then? Surely you would not dare to do it on account of public feeling.

PETER STOCKMANN Public opinion is an extremely mutable thing. And, to be quite candid with you, it is a matter of great impor-

tance to us to have some admission of that sort from you in writing.

DR. STOCKMANN Oh, that's what you are after, is it? I will just trouble you to remember what I said to you lately about foxy tricks of that sort!

PETER STOCKMANN Your position was quite different then. At that time you had reason to suppose you had the whole town at your back—

DR. STOCKMANN Yes, and now I feel I have the whole town *on* my back—[*Flaring up.*] I would not do it if I had the devil and his dam on my back—! Never—never I tell you!

PETER STOCKMANN A man with a family has no right to behave as you do. You have no right to do it, Thomas.

DR. STOCKMANN I have no right! There is only one single thing in the world a free man has no right to do. Do you know what that is?

PETER STOCKMANN No.

DR. STOCKMANN Of course you don't, but I will tell you. A free man has no right to soil himself with filth; he has no right to behave in a way that would justify his spitting in his own face.

PETER STOCKMANN This sort of thing sounds extremely plausible, of course; and if there were no other explanation for your obstinacy—. But as it happens there is.

DR. STOCKMANN What do you mean?

PETER STOCKMANN You understand very well what I mean. But, as your brother and as a man of discretion, I advise you not to build too much upon expectations and prospects that may so very easily fail you.

DR. STOCKMANN What in the world is all this about?

PETER STOCKMANN Do you really ask me to believe that you are ignorant of the terms of Mr. Kiil's will?

DR. STOCKMANN I know that the small amount he possesses is to go to an institution for indigent old work-people. How does that concern me?

PETER STOCKMANN In the first place, it is by no means a small amount that is in question. Mr. Kiil is a fairly wealthy man.

DR. STOCKMANN I had no notion of that!

PETER STOCKMANN Hm!—hadn't you really? Then I suppose you had no notion, either, that a considerable portion of his wealth will come to your children, you and your wife having a life-income from the capital. Has he never told you so?

DR. STOCKMANN Never, on my honor! Quite the reverse; he has consistently done nothing but fume at being so unconscionably heavily taxed. But are you perfectly certain of this, Peter?

PETER STOCKMANN I have it from an absolutely reliable source.

DR. STOCKMANN Then, thank God, Katherine is provided for—and the children too! I must tell her this at once— [*Calls out.*] Katherine, Katherine!

PETER STOCKMANN [*Restraining him.*] Hush, don't say a word yet!

MRS. STOCKMANN [*Opening the door.*] What is the matter?

DR. STOCKMANN Oh, nothing, nothing; you can go back. [*She shuts the door.* DR. STOCKMANN *walks up and down in his excitement.*] Provided for!—Just think of it, we are all provided for! And for life! What a blessed feeling it is to know one is provided for!

PETER STOCKMANN Yes, but that is just exactly what you are not. Mr. Kiil can alter his will any day he likes.

DR. STOCKMANN But he won't do that, my dear Peter. The "Badger" is much too delighted at my attack on you and your wise friends.

PETER STOCKMANN [*Starts and looks intently at him.*] Ah, that throws a light on various things.

DR. STOCKMANN What things?

PETER STOCKMANN I see that the whole thing was a combined manœuvre on your part and his. These violent, reckless attacks that you have made against the leading men of the town, under the pretence that it was in the name of the truth—

DR. STOCKMANN What about them?

PETER STOCKMANN I see that they were nothing else than the stipulated price for that vindictive old man's will.

DR. STOCKMANN [*Almost speechless.*] Peter— you are the most disgusting plebeian I have ever met in all my life.

PETER STOCKMANN All is over between us. Your dismissal is irrevocable—we have a weapon against you now.—[*Goes out.*]

DR. STOCKMANN For shame! For shame! [*Calls out.*] Katherine, you must have the floor

scrubbed after him! Let—what's her name— devil take it, the girl who has always got soot on her nose—

MRS. STOCKMANN [*In the sitting-room.*] Hush, Thomas, be quiet!

PETRA [*Coming to the door.*] Father, grandfather is here, asking if he may speak to you alone.

DR. STOCKMANN Certainly he may. [*Going to the door.*] Come in, Mr. Kiil. [MORTEN KIIL *comes in.* DR. STOCKMANN *shuts the door after him.*] What can I do for you? Won't you sit down?

MORTEN KIIL I won't sit. [*Looks around.*] You look very comfortable here today, Thomas.

DR. STOCKMANN Yes, don't we?

MORTEN KIIL Very comfortable—plenty of fresh air. I should think you have got enough today of that oxygen you were talking about yesterday. Your conscience must be in splendid order today, I should think.

DR. STOCKMANN It is.

MORTEN KIIL So I should think. [*Taps his chest.*] Do you know what I have got here?

DR. STOCKMANN A good conscience, too, I hope.

MORTEN KIIL Bah!—No, it is something better than that.

[*He takes a thick pocket-book from his breast-pocket, opens it, and displays a packet of papers.*]

DR. STOCKMANN [*Looking at him in astonishment.*] Shares in the Baths?

MORTEN KIIL They were not difficult to get today.

DR. STOCKMANN And you have been buying—?

MORTEN KIIL As many as I could pay for.

DR. STOCKMANN But, my dear Mr. Kiil—consider the state of the Baths' affairs!

MORTEN KIIL If you behave like a reasonable man, you can soon set the Baths on their feet again.

DR. STOCKMANN Well, you can see for yourself that I have done all I can, but—. They are all mad in this town!

MORTEN KIIL You said yesterday that the worst of this pollution came from my tannery. If that is true, then my grandfather and my father before me, and I myself, for many years past, have been poisoning the town like three destroying angels. Do you think I am going to sit quiet under that reproach?

DR. STOCKMANN Unfortunately, I am afraid you will have to.

MORTEN KIIL No, thank you. I am jealous of my name and reputation. They call me "the Badger," I am told. A badger is a kind of pig, I believe; but I am not going to give them the right to call me that. I mean to live and die a clean man.

DR. STOCKMANN And how are you going to set about it?

MORTEN KIIL You shall cleanse me, Thomas.

DR. STOCKMANN I!

MORTEN KIIL Do you know what money I have bought these shares with? No, of course you can't know—but I will tell you. It is the money that Katherine and Petra and the boys will have when I am gone. Because I have been able to save a little bit after all, you know.

DR. STOCKMANN [Flaring up.] And you have gone and taken Katherine's money for this!

MORTEN KIIL Yes, the whole of the money is invested in the Baths now. And now I just want to see whether you are quite stark, staring mad, Thomas! If you still make out that these animals and other nasty things of that sort come from my tannery, it will be exactly as if you were to flay broad strips of skin from Katherine's body, and Petra's, and the boys'; and no decent man would do that—unless he were mad.

DR. STOCKMANN [Walking up and down.] Yes, but I am mad, I am mad!

MORTEN KIIL You cannot be so absurdly mad as all that, when it is a question of your wife and children.

DR. STOCKMANN [Standing still in front of him.] Why couldn't you consult me about it, before you went and bought all that trash?

MORTEN KIIL What is done cannot be undone.

DR. STOCKMANN [Walks about uneasily.] If only I were not so certain about it—! But I am absolutely convinced that I am right.

MORTEN KIIL [Weighing the pocket-book in his hand.] If you stick to your mad idea, this won't be worth much, you know. [Puts the pocket-book in his pocket.]

DR. STOCKMANN But, hang it all! it might be possible for science to discover some prophylactic, I should think—or some antidote of some kind—

MORTEN KIIL To kill these animals, do you mean?

DR. STOCKMANN Yes, or to make them innocuous.

MORTEN KIIL Couldn't you try some rat's-bane?

DR. STOCKMANN Don't talk nonsense! They all say it is only imagination, you know. Well, let it go at that! Let them have their own way about it! Haven't the ignorant, narrow-minded curs reviled me as an enemy of the people?—and haven't they been ready to tear the clothes off my back too?

MORTEN KIIL And broken all your windows to pieces!

DR. STOCKMANN And then there is my duty to my family. I must talk it over with Katherine; she is great on those things.

MORTEN KIIL That is right; be guided by a reasonable woman's advice.

DR. STOCKMANN [Advancing towards him.] To think you could do such a preposterous thing! Risking Katherine's money in this way, and putting me in such a horribly painful dilemma! When I look at you, I think I see the devil himself—.

MORTEN KIIL Then I had better go. But I must have an answer from you before two o'clock—yes or no. If it is no, the shares go to a charity, and that this very day.

DR. STOCKMANN And what does Katherine get?

MORTEN KIIL Not a halfpenny. [The door leading to the hall opens, and HOVSTAD and ASLAKSEN make their appearance.] Look at those two!

DR. STOCKMANN [Staring at them.] What the devil!—have you actually the face to come into my house?

HOVSTAD Certainly.

ASLAKSEN We have something to say to you, you see.

MORTEN KIIL [In a whisper.] Yes or no—before two o'clock.

ASLAKSEN [Glancing at HOVSTAD.] Aha!

[MORTEN KIIL goes out.]

DR. STOCKMANN Well, what do you want with me? Be brief.

HOVSTAD I can quite understand that you are annoyed with us for our attitude at the meeting yesterday—

DR. STOCKMANN Attitude, do you call it? Yes, it was a charming attitude! I call it weak, womanish—damnably shameful!

HOVSTAD Call it what you like; we could not do otherwise.

DR. STOCKMANN   You *dared* not do otherwise—isn't that it?

HOVSTAD   Well, if you like to put it that way.

ASLAKSEN   But why did you not let us have word of it beforehand?—just a hint to Mr. Hovstad or to me?

DR. STOCKMANN   A hint? Of what?

ASLAKSEN   Of what was behind it all.

DR. STOCKMANN   I don't understand you in the least.

ASLAKSEN   [*With a confidential nod.*] Oh, yes, you do, Dr. Stockmann.

HOVSTAD   It is no good making a mystery of it any longer.

DR. STOCKMANN   [*Looking first at one of them and then at the other.*] What the devil do you both mean?

ASLAKSEN   May I ask if your father-in-law is not going round the town buying up all the shares in the baths?

DR. STOCKMANN   Yes, he has been buying Baths' shares today; but—

ASLAKSEN   It would have been more prudent to get some one else to do it—some one less nearly related to you.

HOVSTAD   And you should not have let your name appear in the affair. There was no need for anyone to know that the attack on the Baths came from you. You ought to have consulted me, Dr. Stockmann.

DR. STOCKMANN   [*Looks in front of him; then a light seems to dawn on him and he says in amazement:*] Are such things conceivable? Are such things possible?

ASLAKSEN   [*With a smile.*] Evidently they are. But it is better to use a little finesse, you know.

HOVSTAD   And it is much better to have several persons in a thing of that sort, because the responsibility of each individual is lessened, when there are others with him.

DR. STOCKMANN   [*Composedly.*] Come to the point, gentlemen. What do you want?

ASLAKSEN   Perhaps Mr. Hovstad had better—

HOVSTAD   No, you tell him, Aslaksen.

ASLAKSEN   Well, the fact is that, now we know the bearings of the whole affair, we think we might venture to put "The People's Messenger" at your disposal.

DR. STOCKMANN   Do you dare do that now? What about public opinion? Are you not afraid of a storm breaking upon our heads?

HOVSTAD   We will try to weather it.

ASLAKSEN   And you must be ready to go off quickly on a new tack, Doctor. As soon as your invective has done its work—

DR. STOCKMANN   Do you mean, as soon as my father-in-law and I have got hold of the shares at a low figure?

HOVSTAD   Your reasons for wishing to get the control of the Baths are mainly scientific, I take it.

DR. STOCKMANN   Of course; it was for scientific reasons that I persuaded the old "Badger" to stand in with me in the matter. So we will tinker at the conduit-pipes a little, and dig up a little bit of the shore, and it shan't cost the town a sixpence. That will be all right—eh?

HOVSTAD   I think so—if you have "The People's Messenger" behind you.

ASLAKSEN   The Press is a power in a free community, Doctor.

DR. STOCKMANN   Quite so. And so is public opinion. And you, Mr. Aslaksen—I suppose you will be answerable for the Householders' Association?

ASLAKSEN   Yes, and for the Temperance Society. You may rely on that.

DR. STOCKMANN   But, gentlemen—I really am ashamed to ask the question—but, what return do you—?

HOVSTAD   We should prefer to help you without any return whatever, believe me. But "The People's Messenger" is in rather a shaky condition; it doesn't go really well; and I should be very unwilling to suspend the paper now, when there is so much work to do here in the political way.

DR. STOCKMANN   Quite so; that would be a great trial to such a friend of the people as you are. [*Flares up.*] But I am an enemy of the people, remember! [*Walks about the room.*] Where have I put my stick? Where the devil is my stick?

HOVSTAD   What's that?

ASLAKSEN   Surely you never mean—?

DR. STOCKMANN   [*Standing still.*] And suppose I don't give you a single penny of all I get out of it? Money is not very easy to get out of us rich folks, please to remember!

HOVSTAD   And you please to remember that this affair of the shares can be represented in two ways!

DR. STOCKMANN   Yes, and you are just the man to do it. If I don't come to the rescue of "The

People's Messenger," you will certainly take an evil view of the affair; you will hunt me down, I can well imagine—pursue me—try to throttle me as a dog does a hare.

HOVSTAD It is a natural law; every animal must fight for its own livelihood.

ASLAKSEN And get its food where it can, you know.

DR. STOCKMANN [*Walking about the room.*] Then you go and look for yours in the gutter, because I am going to show you which is the strongest animal of us three! [*Finds an umbrella and brandishes it above his head.*] Ah, now—!

HOVSTAD You are surely not going to use violence!

ASLAKSEN Take care what you are doing with that umbrella.

DR. STOCKMANN Out of the window with you, Mr. Hovstad!

HOVSTAD [*Edging to the door.*] Are you quite mad?

DR. STOCKMANN Out of the window, Mr. Aslaksen! Jump, I tell you! You will have to do it, sooner or later.

ASLAKSEN [*Running round the writing-table.*] Moderation, Doctor—I am a delicate man—I can stand so little—[*Calls out.*] Help, help!

[MRS. STOCKMANN, PETRA, *and* HORSTER *come in from the sitting-room.*]

MRS. STOCKMANN Good gracious, Thomas! What is happening?

DR. STOCKMANN [*Brandishing the umbrella.*] Jump out, I tell you! Out into the gutter!

HOVSTAD An assault on an unoffending man! I call you to witness, Captain Horster. [*Hurries out through the hall.*]

ASLAKSEN [*Irresolutely.*] If only I knew the way about here—. [*Steals out through the sitting-room.*]

MRS. STOCKMANN [*Holding her husband back.*] Control yourself, Thomas!

DR. STOCKMANN [*Throwing down the umbrella.*] Upon my soul, they have escaped after all.

MRS. STOCKMANN What did they want you to do?

DR. STOCKMANN I will tell you later on; I have something else to think about now. [*Goes to the table and writes something on a calling-card.*] Look there, Katherine; what is written there?

MRS. STOCKMANN Three big No's; what does that mean?

DR. STOCKMANN I will tell you that too, later on. [*Holds out the card to* PETRA.] There, Petra; tell sooty-face to run over to the "Badger's" with that, as quickly as she can. Hurry up! [PETRA *takes the card and goes out to the hall.*]

DR. STOCKMANN Well, I think I have had a visit from every one of the devil's messengers today! But now I am going to sharpen my pen till they can feel its point; I shall dip it in venom and gall; I shall hurl my ink-pot at their heads!

MRS. STOCKMANN Yes, but we are going away, you know, Thomas. [PETRA *comes back.*]

DR. STOCKMANN Well?

PETRA She has gone with it.

DR. STOCKMANN Good.—Going away, did you say? No, I'll be hanged if we are going away! We are going to stay where we are, Katherine!

PETRA Stay here?

MRS. STOCKMANN Here, in the town?

DR. STOCKMANN Yes, here. This is the field of battle—this is where the fight will be. This is where I shall triumph! As soon as I have had my trousers sewn up I shall go out and look for another house. We must have a roof over our heads for the winter.

HORSTER That you shall have in my house.

DR. STOCKMANN Can I?

HORSTER Yes, quite well. I have plenty of room, and I am almost never at home.

MRS. STOCKMANN How good of you, Captain Horster!

PETRA Thank you!

DR. STOCKMANN [*Grasping his hand.*] Thank you, thank you! That is one trouble over! Now I can set to work in earnest at once. There is an endless amount of things to look through here, Katherine! Luckily I shall have all my time at my disposal, because I have been dismissed from the Baths, you know.

MRS. STOCKMANN [*With a sigh.*] Oh, yes, I expected that.

DR. STOCKMANN And they want to take my practice away from me, too. Let them! I have got the poor people to fall back upon, anyway —those that don't pay anything; and, after all, they need me most, too. But, by Jove, they will have to listen to me; I shall preach to them in season and out of season, as it says somewhere.

MRS. STOCKMANN   But, dear Thomas, I should have thought events had showed you what use it is to preach.

DR. STOCKMANN   You are really ridiculous, Katherine. Do you want me to let myself be beaten off the field by public opinion and the compact majority and all that devilry? No, thank you! And what I want to do is so simple and clear and straightforward. I only want to drum into the heads of these curs the fact that the liberals are the most insidious enemies of freedom—that party programmes strangle every young and vigorous truth—that considerations of expediency turn morality and justice upside down—and that they will end by making life here unbearable. Don't you think, Captain Horster, that I ought to be able to make people understand that?

HORSTER   Very likely; I don't know much about such things myself.

DR. STOCKMANN   Well, look here—I will explain! It is the party leaders that must be exterminated. A party leader is like a wolf, you see—like a voracious wolf. He requires a certain number of smaller victims to prey upon each year, if he is to live. Just look at Hovstad and Aslaksen! How many smaller victims have they not put an end to—or at any rate maimed and mangled until they are fit for nothing except to be householders or subscribers to "The People's Messenger"! [*Sits down on the edge of the table.*] Come here, Katherine—look how beautifully the sun shines today! And this lovely spring air I am drinking in!

MRS. STOCKMANN   Yes, if only we could live on sunshine and spring air, Thomas.

DR. STOCKMANN   Oh, you will have to pinch and save a bit—then we shall get along. That gives me very little concern. What is much worse is that I know of no one who is liberal-minded and high-minded enough to venture to take up my work after me.

PETRA   Don't think about that, father; you have plenty of time before you.—Hullo, here are the boys already!

[EJLIF *and* MORTEN *come in from the sitting-room.*]

MRS. STOCKMANN   Have you got a holiday?

MORTEN   No; but we were fighting with the other boys between lessons—

EJLIF   That isn't true; it was the other boys were fighting with us.

MORTEN   Well, and then Mr. Rörlund said we had better stay at home for a day or two.

DR. STOCKMANN   [*Snapping his fingers and getting up from the table.*] I have it! I have it, by Jove! You shall never set foot in the school again!

THE BOYS   No more school!

MRS. STOCKMANN   But, Thomas—

DR. STOCKMANN   Never, I say. I will educate you myself; that is to say, you shan't learn a blessed thing—

MORTEN   Hooray!

DR. STOCKMANN   —but I will make liberal-minded and high-minded men of you. You must help me with that, Petra.

PETRA   Yes, father, you may be sure I will.

DR. STOCKMANN   And my school shall be in the room where they insulted me and called me an enemy of the people. But we are too few as we are; I must have at least twelve boys to begin with.

MRS. STOCKMANN   You will certainly never get them in this town.

DR. STOCKMANN   We shall. [*To the boys.*] Don't you know any street urchins—regular ragamuffins—?

MORTEN   Yes, father, I know lots!

DR. STOCKMANN   That's capital! Bring me some specimens of them. I am going to experiment with curs, just for once; there may be some exceptional heads amongst them.

MORTEN   And what are we going to do, when you have made liberal-minded and high-minded men of us?

DR. STOCKMANN   Then you shall drive all the wolves out of the country, my boys!

[EJLIF *looks rather doubtful about it;* MORTEN *jumps about crying "Hurrah!"*]

MRS. STOCKMANN   Let us hope it won't be the wolves that will drive you out of the country, Thomas.

DR. STOCKMANN   Are you out of your mind, Katherine? Drive me out! Now—when I am the strongest man in the town!

MRS. STOCKMANN   The strongest—now?

DR. STOCKMANN   Yes, and I will go so far as to say that now I am the strongest man in the whole world.

MORTEN   I say!

DR. STOCKMANN   [*Lowering his voice.*] Hush! You mustn't say anything about it yet, but I have made a great discovery.

MRS. STOCKMANN   Another one?

DR. STOCKMANN   Yes. [*Gathers them round him, and says confidentially.*] It is this, let me tell you—that the strongest man in the world is he who stands most alone.

MRS. STOCKMANN   [*Smiling and shaking her head.*] Oh, Thomas, Thomas!

PETRA   [*Encouragingly, as she grasps her father's hands.*] Father!

[*Curtain.*]

Comments and Questions

This play is an early example of realistic drama. Although Dr. Stockmann, the central character, is an extraordinary man, he is involved in no world-shaking events. The action takes place in a small town in southern Norway, and repercussions from what happens could not extend very far.

Two things are readily apparent about realistic drama: heroes are not completely heroic and villains are not completely villainous. Dr. Stockmann is the hero, but he is vain and flawed more than a little by an uncontrollable temper. Peter Stockmann, Dr. Stockmann's brother, is the villain, but he talks the good sense of expediency and does not lose his temper. The purpose of the realistic dramatist, then, is to expose people as they are, not as puppets representing good opposed to evil.

A writer of rare thrift, Ibsen makes each speech count and yet manages to maintain the casualness of ordinary conversation. Because of the economy and naturalness of the dialogue, it is necessary to make an especially careful summary of the plain facts before attempting to assess the meaning of the play. In other words, first impressions are likely to be false impressions. For example, one may be surprised at the turn given the plot when Mr. Kiil in Act V reveals what he has done with the money intended for the Stockmanns. Yet as early as Act II, Ibsen has begun the preparation for this revelation.

1. How much actual time elapses from the beginning to the end of the play? Is there any way to pinpoint how far back the antecedent action goes? References to antecedent action occur throughout the play and are not concentrated in Act I. You will observe that after a present action is completed, it becomes the antecedent (the motivating) action of a succeeding event. Note Dr. Stockmann's final confrontation with his brother, Peter Stockmann, in Act V. Here one may feel that Ibsen has resorted to a rigged ending (*deus ex machina*) when he reveals through the mayor the contents of Mr. Kiil's will. Study the antecedents to this revelation and decide whether or not Ibsen has properly prepared the reader (or the audience) for this revelation. One further point: the action moves in a wavelike motion, or like tide rolling in on a seashore. It advances, then coils back on itself. At the end, Dr. Stockmann stands alone with his family, and his isolation is the result of all the preceding action.

2. What ground is there for calling this a play of reversals? A reversal occurs when two characters change places. To answer this question, examine the relationships between Dr. Stockmann and his brother, and between Hovstad-Billing and Peter Stockmann.

3. Do you think Ibsen was tempted to include a love element in the play? Discuss.

4. For the insignificant parts they play, is the presence of the two boys, Ejlif and Morten, justifiable? What function, if any, do they perform?

5. It has been stated that Ibsen himself was somewhat like Dr. Stockmann, that, indeed, the play grew out of the author's resentment over public and critical rejection of two of his plays: *A Doll's House* and *Ghosts.* On the evidence in *An Enemy of the People,* can it be reasoned that Dr. Stockmann is only a partial portrait of Ibsen?

6. Mrs. Stockmann opposes her husband's hardheadedness and intemperate speech. What drew her to his side?

7. This is unquestionably a play of theme worked out through the interplay of realistic characters. Does the play have more than a single theme? State the chief one and then search out minor themes. If these exist, are they related to the major issue? In this connection, does Ibsen make it completely clear that Dr. Stockmann is right about the Baths? To what is the issue of the Baths subordi-

nated? Logically, does Dr. Stockmann's position depend entirely on whether or not he is right about the Baths? Discuss.

8. *Dramatic irony* is present when the audience or reader is aware of a situation of which at least one character on the stage is ignorant. Point out at least one striking example of dramatic irony in this play. In what way does *irony* differ from *dramatic* irony? Cite examples of irony.

9. What do you think of Dr. Stockmann's accusations against the common man? against newspapers? against authorities? We are living now in the age of the Common Man. We insist that by adding votes, with every vote equal to every other vote, we can determine how we wish to be governed. Does Dr. Stockmann make a convincing case against this system? Discuss.

Arms and the Man

GEORGE BERNARD SHAW
1856–1951

CHARACTERS (in the order of their appearance)

RAINA PETKOFF, *a young Bulgarian lady*
CATHERINE PETKOFF, *her mother*
LOUKA, *Raina's maid*
CAPTAIN BLUNTSCHLI, *a Swiss in the Serbian Army*
A RUSSIAN OFFICER, *in the Bulgarian Army*
NICOLA, *the Petkoffs' manservant*
MAJOR PETKOFF, *Raina's father*
MAJOR SERGIUS SARANOFF, *Raina's fiancé*

PLACE
Home of MAJOR PETKOFF, *in a small Bulgarian town*
TIME
1885–1886.

ACT I

Night. A lady's bedchamber in Bulgaria, in a small town near the Dragoman Pass, late in November in the year 1885. Through an open window with a little balcony a peak of the Balkans, wonderfully white and beautiful in the starlit snow, seems quite close at hand, though it is really miles away. The interior of the room is not like anything to be seen in the west of Europe. It is half rich Bulgarian, half cheap Viennese. Above the head of the bed, which stands against a little wall cutting off the left hand corner of the room, is a painted wooden shrine, blue and gold, with an ivory image of Christ, and a light hanging before it in a pierced metal ball suspended by three chains. The principal seat, placed toward the other side of the room and opposite the window, is a Turkish ottoman. The counterpane and hangings of the bed, the window curtains, the little carpet, and all the ornamental textile fabrics in the room are oriental and gorgeous: the paper on the walls is occidental and paltry. The washstand, against the wall on the side nearest the ottoman and window, consists of an enamelled iron basin with a pail beneath it in a painted metal frame, and a single towel on the rail at the side. The dressing table, between the bed and the window, is a common pine table, covered with a cloth of many colors, with an expensive toilet mirror on it. The door is on the side nearest the bed; and there is a chest of drawers between. This chest of drawers is also covered by a variegated native cloth; and on it there is a pile of paper-backed novels, a box of chocolate creams, and a miniature easel with a large photograph of an extremely handsome officer, whose lofty bearing and magnetic glance can be felt even from the portrait. The room is lighted by a candle on the chest of drawers, and another on the dressing table with a box of matches beside it.

The window is hinged doorwise and stands wide open. Outside, a pair of wooden shutters opening outwards, also stand open. On the balcony a young lady, intensely conscious of the romantic beauty of the night, and of the fact that her own youth and beauty are part of it, is gazing at the snowy Balkans. She is in her nightgown, well covered by a long mantle of furs, worth, on a moderate estimate, about three times the furniture of her room.

Her reverie is interrupted by her mother, CATHERINE PETKOFF, *a woman over forty, imperiously energetic, with magnificent black hair and eyes, who might be a very splendid specimen of the wife of a mountain farmer, but is determined to be a Viennese lady, and to that end wears a fashionable tea gown on all occasions.*

CATHERINE [*Entering hastily, full of good news.*] Raina! [*She pronounces it Raheena, with the stress on the ee.*] Raina! [*She goes to the bed, expecting to find* RAINA *there.*] Why, where—? [RAINA *looks into the room.*] Heavens, child! are you out in the night air instead of in your bed? You'll catch your death. Louka told me you were asleep.

RAINA [*Dreamily.*] I sent her away. I wanted to be alone. The stars are so beautiful! What is the matter?

CATHERINE Such news! There has been a battle.

RAINA [*Her eyes dilating.*] Ah! [*She comes eagerly to* CATHERINE.]

CATHERINE A great battle at Slivnitza! A victory! And it was won by Sergius.

RAINA [*With a cry of delight.*] Ah! [*They embrace rapturously.*] Oh, mother! [*Then, with sudden anxiety.*] Is father safe?

CATHERINE Of course: he sends me the news. Sergius is the hero of the hour, the idol of the regiment.

RAINA Tell me, tell me. How was it? [*Ecstatically.*] Oh, mother! mother! mother! [*She pulls her mother down on the ottoman; and they kiss one another frantically.*]

CATHERINE [*With surging enthusiasm.*] You cant guess how splendid it is. A cavalry charge! think of that! He defied our Russian commanders—acted without orders—led a charge on his own responsibility—headed it himself—was the first man to sweep through their guns. Cant you see it, Raina: our gallant splendid Bulgarians with their swords and eyes flashing, thundering down like an avalanche and scattering the wretched Serbs and their dandified Austrian officers like chaff. And you! you kept Sergius waiting a year before you would be betrothed to him. Oh, if you have a drop of Bulgarian blood in your veins, you will worship him when he comes back.

RAINA What will he care for my poor little worship after the acclamations of a whole army of heroes? But no matter: I am so happy! so proud! [*She rises and walks about excitedly.*] It proves that all our ideas were real after all.

CATHERINE [*Indignantly.*] Our ideas real! What do you mean?

RAINA Our ideas of what Sergius would do. Our patriotism. Our heroic ideas. I sometimes used to doubt whether they were anything but dreams. Oh, what faithless little creatures girls are! When I buckled on Sergius's sword he looked so noble: it was treason to think of disillusion or humiliation or failure. And yet—and yet—[*She sits down again suddenly.*] Promise me youll never tell him.

CATHERINE Dont ask me for promises until I know what I'm promising.

RAINA Well, it came into my head just as he was holding me in his arms and looking into my eyes, that perhaps we only had our heroic ideas because we are so fond of reading Byron and Pushkin, and because we were so delighted with the opera that season at Bucharest. Real life is so seldom like that! indeed never, as far as I knew it then. [*Remorsefully.*] Only think, mother: I doubted him: I wondered whether all his heroic qualities and his soldiership might not prove mere imagination when he went into a real battle. I had an uneasy fear that he might cut a poor figure there beside all those clever officers from the Tsar's court.

CATHERINE A poor figure! Shame on you! The Serbs have Austrian officers who are just as clever as the Russians; but we have beaten them in every battle for all that.

RAINA [*Laughing and snuggling against her mother.*] Yes: I was only a prosaic little coward. Oh, to think that it was all true! that Sergius is just as splendid and noble as he looks! that the world is really a glorious world for women who can see its glory and men who can act its romance! What happiness! what unspeakable fulfilment!

[*They are interrupted by the entry of* LOUKA, *a handsome proud girl in a pretty Bulgarian peasant's dress with a double apron, so defiant that her servility to* RAINA *is almost insolent. She is afraid of* CATHERINE, *but even with her goes as far as she dares.*]

LOUKA If you please, madam, all the windows are to be closed and the shutters made fast. They say there may be shooting in the streets. [RAINA *and* CATHERINE *rise together, alarmed.*] The Serbs are being chased right back through the pass; and they say they may run into the town. Our cavalry will be after them; and our people will be ready for them, you may be sure, now theyre running away. [*She goes out on the balcony, and pulls the outside shutters to; then steps back into the room.*]

CATHERINE [*Businesslike, her housekeeper instincts aroused.*] I must see that everything is made safe downstairs.

RAINA I wish our people were not so cruel. What glory is there in killing wretched fugitives?

CATHERINE Cruel! Do you suppose they would hesitate to kill you or worse?

RAINA [*To* LOUKA.] Leave the shutters so that I can close them if I hear any noise.

CATHERINE [*Authoritatively, turning on her way to the door.*] Oh no, dear: you must keep them fastened. You would be sure to drop off to sleep and leave them open. Make them fast, Louka.

LOUKA Yes, madam. [*She fastens them.*]

RAINA Dont be anxious about me. The moment I hear a shot, I shall blow out the candles and roll myself up in bed with my ears well covered.

CATHERINE Quite the wisest thing you can do, my love. Goodnight.

RAINA Goodnight. [*Her emotion comes back for a moment.*] Wish me joy. [*They kiss.*] This is the happiest night of my life—if only there are no fugitives.

CATHERINE Go to bed, dear; and dont think of them. [*She goes out.*]

LOUKA [*Secretly, to* RAINA.] If you would like the shutters open, just give them a push like this. [*She pushes them: they open: she pulls them again.*] One of them ought to be bolted at the bottom; but the bolt's gone.

RAINA [*With dignity, reproving her.*] Thanks, Louka; but we must do what we are told. [LOUKA *makes a grimace.*] Goodnight.

LOUKA [*Carelessly.*] Goodnight. [*She goes out, swaggering.*]

[RAINA, *left alone, takes off her fur cloak and throws it on the ottoman. Then she goes to the chest of drawers, and adores the portrait there with feelings that are beyond all expression. She does not kiss it or press it to her breast, or shew it any mark of bodily affection; but she takes it in her hands and elevates it, like a priestess.*]

RAINA [*Looking up at the picture.*] Oh, I shall never be unworthy of you any more, my soul's hero: never, never, never. [*She replaces it reverently. Then she selects a novel from the lit-*] tle pile of books. She turns over the leaves dreamily; finds her page; turns the book inside out at it; and, with a happy sigh, gets into bed and prepares to read herself to sleep. But before abandoning herself to fiction, she raises her eyes once more, thinking of the blessed reality, and murmurs.*] My hero! my hero!

[*A distant shot breaks the quiet of the night. She starts, listening; and two more shots, much nearer, follow, startling her so that she scrambles out of bed, and hastily blows out the candle on the chest of drawers. Then, putting her fingers in her ears, she runs to the dressing table, blows out the light there, and hurries back to bed in the dark, nothing being visible but the glimmer of the light in the pierced ball before the image, and the starlight seen through the slits at the top of the shutters. The firing breaks out again: there is a startling fusillade quite close at hand. Whilst it is still echoing, the shutters disappear, pulled open from without; and for an instant the rectangle of snowy starlight flashes out with the figure of a man silhouetted in black upon it. The shutters close immediately; and the room is dark again. But the silence is now broken by the sound of panting. Then there is a scratch; and the flame of a match is seen in the middle of the room.*]

RAINA [*Crouching on the bed.*] Who's there? [*The match is out instantly.*] Who's there? Who is that?

A MAN'S VOICE [*In the darkness, subduedly, but threateningly.*] Sh—sh! Dont call out; or youll be shot. Be good; and no harm will happen to you. [*She is heard leaving her bed, and making for the door.*] Take care: it's no use trying to run away.

RAINA But who—

THE VOICE [*Warning.*] Remember: if you raise your voice my revolver will go off. [*Commandingly.*] Strike a light and let me see you. Do you hear. [*Another moment of silence and darkness as she retreats to the chest of drawers. Then she lights a candle; and the mystery is at an end. He is a man of about 35, in a deplorable plight, bespattered with mud and blood and snow, his belt and the strap of his revolver-case keeping together the torn ruins of the blue tunic of a Serbian artillery officer. All that the candlelight and his un-*]

washed unkempt condition make it possible to discern is that he is of middling stature and undistinguished appearance, with strong neck and shoulders, roundish obstinate looking head covered with short crisp bronze curls, clear quick eyes and good brows and mouth, hopelessly prosaic nose like that of a strong minded baby, trim soldierlike carriage and energetic manner, and with all his wits about him in spite of his desperate predicament: even with a sense of the humor of it, without, however, the least intention of trifling with it or throwing away a chance. Reckoning up what he can guess about RAINA: *her age, her social position, her character, and the extent to which she is frightened, he continues, more politely but still most determinedly.*] Excuse my disturbing you; but you recognize my uniform? Serb! If I'm caught I shall be killed. [*Menacingly.*] Do you understand that?

RAINA   Yes.

THE MAN   Well, I dont intend to get killed if I can help it. [*Still more formidably.*] Do you understand that? [*He locks the door quickly but quietly.*]

RAINA   [*Disdainfully.*] I suppose not. [*She draws herself up superbly, and looks him straight in the face, adding, with cutting emphasis.*] Some soldiers, I know, are afraid to die.

THE MAN   [*with grim goodhumor.*] All of them, dear lady, all of them, believe me. It is our duty to live as long as we can. Now, if you raise an alarm—

RAINA   [*Cutting him short.*] You will shoot me. How do you know that *I* am afraid to die?

THE MAN   [*Cunningly.*] Ah; but suppose I dont shoot you, what will happen then? A lot of your cavalry will burst into this pretty room of yours and slaughter me here like a pig; for I'll fight like a demon: they shant get me into the street to amuse themselves with: I know what they are. Are you prepared to receive that sort of company in your present undress? [RAINA, *suddenly conscious of her nightgown, instinctively shrinks, and gathers it more closely about her neck. He watches her, and adds, pitilessly.*] Hardly presentable, eh? [*She turns to the ottoman. He raises his pistol instantly, and cries:*] Stop! [*She stops.*] Where are you going?

RAINA   [*With dignified patience.*] Only to get my cloak.

THE MAN   [*Passing swiftly to the ottoman and snatching the cloak.*] A good idea! I'll keep the cloak; and youll take care that nobody comes in and sees you without it. This is a better weapon than the revolver: eh? [*He throws the pistol down on the ottoman.*]

RAINA   [*Revolted.*] It is not the weapon of a gentleman!

THE MAN   It's good enough for a man with only you to stand between him and death. [*As they look at one another for a moment,* RAINA *hardly able to believe that even a Serbian officer can be so cynically and selfishly unchivalrous, they are startled by a sharp fusillade in the street. The chill of imminent death hushes the man's voice as he adds.*] Do you hear? If you are going to bring those blackguards in on me you shall receive them as you are.

[*Clamor and disturbance. The pursuers in the street batter at the house door, shouting* Open the door! Open the door! Wake up, will you! *A man servant's voice calls to them angrily from within* This is Major Petkoff's house: you cant come in here; *but a renewal of the clamor, and a torrent of blows on the door, end with his letting a chain down with a clank, followed by a rush of heavy footsteps and a din of triumphant yells, dominated at last by the voice of* CATHERINE, *indignantly addressing an officer with* What does this mean, sir? Do you know where you are? *The noise subsides suddenly.*]

LOUKA   [*Outside, knocking at the bedroom door.*] My lady! my lady! get up quick and open the door. If you dont they will break it down.

[*The fugitive throws up his head with the gesture of a man who sees that it is all over with him, and drops the manner he has been assuming to intimidate* RAINA.]

THE MAN   [*Sincerely and kindly.*] No use, dear: I'm done for. [*Flinging the cloak to her.*] Quick! wrap yourself up: theyre coming.

RAINA   Oh, thank you. [*She wraps herself up with intense relief.*]

THE MAN   [*Between his teeth.*] Dont mention it.

RAINA   [*Anxiously.*] What will you do?

THE MAN   [*Grimly.*] The first man in will find out. Keep out of the way; and dont look. It wont last long; but it will not be nice. [*He draws his sabre and faces the door, waiting.*]

RAINA [*Impulsively.*] I'll help you. I'll save you.

THE MAN You cant.

RAINA I can. I'll hide you. [*She drags him towards the window.*] Here! behind the curtains.

THE MAN [*Yielding to her.*] Theres just half a chance, if you keep your head.

RAINA [*Drawing the curtain before him.*] S-sh! [*She makes for the ottoman.*]

THE MAN [*Putting out his head.*] Remember—

RAINA [*Running back to him.*] Yes?

THE MAN —nine soldiers out of ten are born fools.

RAINA Oh! [*She draws the curtain angrily before him.*]

THE MAN [*Looking out at the other side.*] If they find me, I promise you a fight: a devil of a fight.

[*She stamps at him. He disappears hastily. She takes off her cloak, and throws it across the foot of the bed. Then, with a sleepy, disturbed air, she opens the door.* LOUKA *enters excitedly.*]

LOUKA One of those beasts of Serbs has been seen climbing up the waterpipe to your balcony. Our men want to search for him; and they are so wild and drunk and furious. [*She makes for the other side of the room to get as far from the door as possible.*] My lady says you are to dress at once, and to—[*She sees the revolver lying on the ottoman, and stops, petrified.*]

RAINA [*As if annoyed at being disturbed.*] They shall not search here. Why have they been let in?

CATHERINE [*Coming in hastily.*] Raina, darling: are you safe? Have you seen anyone or heard anything?

RAINA I heard the shooting. Surely the soldiers will not dare come in here?

CATHERINE I have found a Russian officer, thank Heaven: he knows Sergius. [*Speaking through the door to someone outside.*] Sir: will you come in now. My daughter will receive you.

[*A young Russian officer, in Bulgarian uniform, enters, sword in hand.*]

THE OFFICER [*With soft feline politeness and stiff military carriage.*] Good evening, gracious lady. I am sorry to intrude; but there is a Serb hiding on the balcony. Will you and the gracious lady your mother please to withdraw whilst we search?

RAINA [*Petulantly.*] Nonsense, sir: you can see that there is no one on the balcony. [*She throws the shutters wide open and stands with her back to the curtain where the man is hidden, pointing to the moonlit balcony. A couple of shots are fired right under the window; and a bullet shatters the glass opposite* RAINA, *who winks and gasps, but stands her ground; whilst* CATHERINE *screams, and the officer, with a cry of* Take care! *rushes to the balcony.*]

THE OFFICER [*On the balcony, shouting savagely down to the street.*] Cease firing there, you fools: do you hear? Cease firing, damn you! [*He glares down for a moment; then turns to* RAINA, *trying to resume his polite manner.*] Could anyone have got in without your knowledge? Were you asleep?

RAINA No: I have not been to bed.

THE OFFICER [*Impatiently, coming back into the room.*] Your neighbors have their heads so full of runaway Serbs that they see them everywhere. [*Politely.*] Gracious lady: a thousand pardons. Goodnight. [*Military bow, which* RAINA *returns coldly. Another to* CATHERINE, *who follows him out.*]

[RAINA *closes the shutters. She turns and sees* LOUKA, *who has been watching the scene curiously.*]

RAINA Dont leave my mother, Louka, until the soldiers go away.

[LOUKA *glances at* RAINA, *at the ottoman, at the curtain; then purses her lips secretively, laughs insolently, and goes out.* RAINA, *highly offended by this demonstration, follows her to the door, and shuts it behind her with a slam, locking it violently. The man immediately steps out from behind the curtain, sheathing his sabre, and closes the shutters. Then, dismissing the danger from his mind in a businesslike way, he comes affably to* RAINA.]

THE MAN A narrow shave; but a miss is as good as a mile. Dear young lady, your servant to the death. I wish for your sake I had joined the Bulgarian army instead of the other one. I am not a native Serb.

RAINA [*Haughtily.*] No: you are one of the Austrians who set the Serbs on to rob us of our national liberty, and who officer their army for them. We hate them!

THE MAN Austrian! not I. Dont hate me, dear young lady. I am a Swiss, fighting merely as a professional soldier. I joined the Serbs because they came first on the road from Switzerland. Be generous: youve beaten us hollow.

RAINA Have I not been generous?

THE MAN Noble! Heroic! But I'm not saved yet. This particular rush will soon pass through; but the pursuit will go on all night by fits and starts. I must take my chance to get off in a quiet interval. [*Pleasantly.*] You don't mind my waiting just a minute or two, do you?

RAINA [*Putting on her most genteel society manner.*] Oh, not at all. Wont you sit down?

THE MAN Thanks. [*He sits on the foot of the bed.*]

[RAINA *walks with studied elegance to the ottoman and sits down. Unfortunately she sits on the pistol, and jumps up with a shriek. The man, all nerves, shies like a frightened horse to the other side of the room.*]

THE MAN [*Irritably.*] Dont frighten me like that. What is it?

RAINA Your revolver! It was staring that officer in the face all the time. What an escape!

THE MAN [*Vexed at being unnecessarily terrified.*] Oh, is that all?

RAINA [*Staring at him rather superciliously as she conceives a poorer and poorer opinion of him, and feels proportionately more and more at her ease.*] I am sorry I frightened you. [*She takes up the pistol and hands it to him.*] Pray take it to protect yourself against me.

THE MAN [*Grinning wearily at the sarcasm as he takes the pistol.*] No use, dear young lady: theres nothing in it. It's not loaded. [*He makes a grimace at it, and drops it disparagingly into his revolver case.*]

RAINA Load it by all means.

THE MAN Ive no ammunition. What use are cartridges in battle? I always carry chocolate instead; and I finished the last cake of that hours ago.

RAINA [*Outraged in her most cherished ideals of manhood.*] Chocolate! Do you stuff your pockets with sweets—like a schoolboy—even in the field?

THE MAN [*Grinning.*] Yes: isnt it contemptible? [*Hungrily.*] I wish I had some now.

RAINA Allow me. [*She sails away scornfully to the chest of drawers, and returns with a box of confectionery in her hand.*] I am sorry I

have eaten them all except these. [*She offers him the box.*]

THE MAN [*Ravenously.*] Youre an angel! [*He gobbles the contents.*] Creams! Delicious! [*He looks anxiously to see whether there are any more. There are none: he can only scrape the box with his fingers and suck them. When that nourishment is exhausted he accepts the inevitable with pathetic goodhumor, and says, with grateful emotion.*] Bless you, dear lady! You can always tell an old soldier by the inside of his holsters and cartridge boxes. The young ones carry pistols and cartridges: the old ones, grub. Thank you. [*He hands back the box. She snatches it contemptuously from him and throws it away. He shies again, as if she had meant to strike him.*] Ugh! Dont do things so suddenly, gracious lady. It's mean to revenge yourself because I frightened you just now.

RAINA [*Loftily.*] Frighten me! Do you know, sir, that though I am only a woman, I think I am at heart as brave as you.

THE MAN I should think so. You havnt been under fire for three days as I have. I can stand two days without shewing it much; but no man can stand three days: I'm as nervous as a mouse. [*He sits down on the ottoman, and takes his head in his hands.*] Would you like to see me cry?

RAINA [*Alarmed.*] No.

THE MAN If you would, all you have to do is to scold me just as if I were a little boy and you my nurse. If I were in camp now, theyd play all sorts of tricks on me.

RAINA [*A little moved.*] I'm sorry. I wont scold you. [*Touched by the sympathy in her tone, he raises his head and looks gratefully at her: she immediately draws back and says stiffly.*] You must excuse me: our soldiers are not like that. [*She moves away from the ottoman.*]

THE MAN Oh yes they are. There are only two sorts of soldiers: old ones and young ones. Ive served fourteen years: half of your fellows never smelt powder before. Why, how is it that youve just beaten us? Sheer ignorance of the art of war, nothing else. [*Indignantly.*] I never saw anything so unprofessional.

RAINA [*Ironically.*] Oh! was it unprofessional to beat you?

THE MAN Well, come! is it professional to throw a regiment of cavalry on a battery of machine guns, with the dead certainty that if the guns go off not a horse or man will ever get within fifty yards of the fire? I couldnt believe my eyes when I saw it.

RAINA [*Eagerly turning to him, as all her enthusiasm and her dreams of glory rush back on her.*] Did you see the great cavalry charge? Oh, tell me about it. Describe it to me.

THE MAN You never saw a cavalry charge, did you?

RAINA How could I?

THE MAN Ah, perhaps not. No: of course not! Well, it's a funny sight. It's like slinging a handful of peas against a window pane: first one comes; then two or three close behind him; and then all the rest in a lump.

RAINA [*Her eyes dilating as she raises her clasped hands ecstatically.*] Yes, first One! the bravest of the brave!

THE MAN [*Prosaically.*] Hm! you should see the poor devil pulling at his horse.

RAINA Why should he pull at his horse?

THE MAN [*Impatient of so stupid a question.*] It's running away with him, of course: do you suppose the fellow wants to get there before the others and be killed? Then they all come. You can tell the young ones by their wildness and their slashing. The old ones come bunched up under the number one guard: they know that theyre mere projectiles, and that it's no use trying to fight. The wounds are mostly broken knees, from the horses cannoning together.

RAINA Ugh! But I dont believe the first man is a coward. I know he is a hero!

THE MAN [*Goodhumoredly.*] Thats what youd have said if youd seen the first man in the charge today.

RAINA [*Breathless, forgiving him everything.*] Ah, I knew it! Tell me. Tell me about him.

THE MAN He did it like an operatic tenor. A regular handsome fellow, with flashing eyes and lovely moustache, shouting his war-cry and charging like Don Quixote at the windmills. We did laugh.

RAINA You dared to laugh!

THE MAN Yes; but when the sergeant ran up as white as a sheet, and told us theyd sent us the wrong ammunition, and that we couldnt fire a round for the next ten minutes, we laughed on the other side of our mouths. I never felt so sick in my life; though Ive been in one or two very tight places. And I hadnt even a revolver cartridge: only chocolate. We'd no bayonets: nothing. Of course, they just cut us to bits. And there was Don Quixote flourishing like a drum major, thinking he'd done the cleverest thing ever known, whereas he ought to be courtmartialled for it. Of all the fools ever let loose on a field of battle, that man must be the very maddest. He and his regiment simply committed suicide; only the pistol missed fire: thats all.

RAINA [*Deeply wounded, but steadfastly loyal to her ideals.*] Indeed! Would you know him again if you saw him?

THE MAN Shall I ever forget him!

[*She again goes to the chest of drawers. He watches her with a vague hope that she may have something more for him to eat. She takes the portrait from its stand and brings it to him.*]

RAINA That is a photograph of the gentleman —the patriot and hero—to whom I am betrothed.

THE MAN [*Recognizing it with a shock.*] I'm really very sorry. [*Looking at her.*] Was it fair to lead me on? [*He looks at the portrait again.*] Yes: thats Don Quixote: not a doubt of it. [*He stifles a laugh.*]

RAINA [*Quickly.*] Why do you laugh?

THE MAN [*Apologetic, but still greatly tickled.*] I didnt laugh, I assure you. At least I didnt mean to. But when I think of him charging the windmills and imagining he was doing the finest thing—[*He chokes with suppressed laughter.*]

RAINA [*Sternly.*] Give me back the portrait, sir.

THE MAN [*With sincere remorse.*] Of course. Certainly. I'm really very sorry. [*He hands her the picture. She deliberately kisses it and looks him straight in the face before returning to the chest of drawers to replace it. He follows her, apologizing.*] Perhaps I'm quite wrong, you know: no doubt I am. Most likely he had got wind of the cartridge business somehow, and knew it was a safe job.

RAINA That is to say, he was a pretender and a coward! You did not dare say that before.

THE MAN [*With a comic gesture of despair.*] It's no use, dear lady: I cant make you see it from the professional point of view. [*As he turns away to get back to the ottoman, a couple of distant shots threaten renewed trouble.*]

RAINA [*Sternly, as she sees him listening to the shots.*] So much the better for you!

THE MAN [*Turning.*] How?

RAINA You are my enemy; and you are at my mercy. What would I do if I were a professional soldier?

THE MAN Ah, true, dear young lady: youre always right. I know how good youve been to me: to my last hour I shall remember those three chocolate creams. It was unsoldierly; but it was angelic.

RAINA [*Coldly.*] Thank you. And now I will do a soldierly thing. You cannot stay here after what you have just said about my future husband; but I will go out on the balcony and see whether it is safe for you to climb down into the street. [*She turns to the window.*]

THE MAN [*Changing countenance.*] Down that waterpipe! Stop! Wait! I cant! I darent! The very thought of it makes me giddy. I came up it fast enough with death behind me. But to face it now in cold blood—! [*He sinks on the ottoman.*] It's no use: I give up: I'm beaten. Give the alarm. [*He drops his head on his hands in the deepest dejection.*]

RAINA [*Disarmed by the pity.*] Come: dont be disheartened. [*She stoops over him almost maternally: he shakes his head.*] Oh, you are a very poor soldier: a chocolate cream soldier! Come, cheer up! it takes less courage to climb down than to face capture: remember that.

THE MAN [*Dreamily, lulled by her voice.*] No: capture only means death; and death is sleep: oh, sleep, sleep, sleep, undisturbed sleep! Climbing down the pipe means doing something—exerting myself—thinking! Death ten times over first.

RAINA [*Softly and wonderingly, catching the rhythm of his weariness.*] Are you as sleepy as that?

THE MAN Ive not had two hours undisturbed sleep since I joined. I havnt closed my eyes for forty-eight hours.

RAINA [*At her wit's end.*] But what am I to do with you?

THE MAN [*Staggering up, roused by her desperation.*] Of course. I must do something. [*He shakes himself; pulls himself together; and speaks with rallied vigor and courage.*] You see, sleep or no sleep, hunger or no hunger, tired or not tired, you can always do a thing when you know it must be done. Well, that pipe must be got down: [*He hits himself on the chest.*] do you hear that, you chocolate cream soldier? [*He turns to the window.*]

RAINA [*Anxiously.*] But if you fall?

THE MAN I shall sleep as if the stones were a feather bed. Goodbye. [*He makes boldly for the window; and his hand is on the shutter when there is a terrible burst of firing in the street beneath.*]

RAINA [*Rushing to him.*] Stop! [*She seizes him recklessly, and pulls him quite round.*] Theyll kill you.

THE MAN [*Coolly, but attentively.*] Never mind: this sort of thing is all in my day's work. I'm bound to take my chance. [*Decisively.*] Now do what I tell you. Put out the candles; so that they shant see the light when I open the shutters. And keep away from the window, whatever you do. If they see me theyre sure to have a shot at me.

RAINA [*Clinging to him.*] Theyre sure to see you: it's bright moonlight. I'll save you. Oh, how can you be so indifferent! You want me to save you, dont you?

THE MAN I really dont want to be troublesome. [*She shakes him in her impatience.*] I am not indifferent, dear young lady, I assure you. But how is it to be done?

RAINA Come away from the window. [*She takes him firmly back to the middle of the room. The moment she releases him he turns mechanically towards the window again. She seizes him and turns him back, exclaiming.*] Please! [*He becomes motionless, like a hypnotized rabbit, his fatigue gaining fast on him. She releases him, and addresses him patronizingly.*] Now listen. You must trust to our hospitality. You do not yet know in whose house you are. I am a Petkoff.

THE MAN A pet what?

RAINA [*Rather indignantly.*] I mean that I belong to the family of the Petkoffs, the richest and best known in our country.

THE MAN Oh yes, of course. I beg your pardon. The Petkoffs, to be sure. How stupid of me!

RAINA You know you never heard of them until this moment. How can you stoop to pretend!

THE MAN Forgive me: I'm too tired to think; and the change of subject was too much for me. Dont scold me.

RAINA   I forgot. It might make you cry. [*He nods, quite seriously. She pouts and then resumes her patronizing tone.*] I must tell you that my father holds the highest command of any Bulgarian in our army. He is [*Proudly.*] a Major.

THE MAN   [*Pretending to be deeply impressed.*] A Major! Bless me! Think of that!

RAINA   You shewed great ignorance in thinking that it was necessary to climb up to the balcony because ours is the only private house that has two rows of windows. There is a flight of stairs inside to get up and down by.

THE MAN   Stairs! How grand! You live in great luxury indeed, dear young lady.

RAINA   Do you know what a library is?

THE MAN   A library? A roomful of books?

RAINA   Yes. We have one, the only one in Bulgaria.

THE MAN   Actually a real library! I should like to see that.

RAINA   [*Affectedly.*] I tell you these things to shew you that you are not in the house of ignorant country folk who would kill you the moment they saw your Serbian uniform, but among civilized people. We go to Bucharest every year for the opera season; and I have spent a whole month in Vienna.

THE MAN   I saw that, dear young lady. I saw at once that you knew the world.

RAINA   Have you ever seen the opera of Ernani?

THE MAN   Is that the one with the devil in it in red velvet, and a soldiers' chorus?

RAINA   [*Contemptuously.*] No!

THE MAN   [*Stifling a heavy sigh of weariness.*] Then I dont know it.

RAINA   I thought you might have remembered the great scene where Ernani, flying from his foes just as you are tonight, takes refuge in the castle of his bitterest enemy, an old Castilian noble. The noble refuses to give him up. His guest is sacred to him.

THE MAN   [*Quickly, waking up a little.*] Have your people got that notion?

RAINA   [*With dignity.*] My mother and I can understand that notion, as you call it. And if instead of threatening me with your pistol as you did you had simply thrown yourself as a fugitive on our hospitality, you would have been as safe as in your father's house.

THE MAN   Quite sure?

RAINA   [*Turning her back on him in disgust.*] Oh, it is useless to try to make you understand.

THE MAN   Dont be angry: you see how awkward it would be for me if there was any mistake. My father is a very hospitable man: he keeps six hotels; but I couldnt trust him as far as that. What about your father?

RAINA   He is away at Slivnitza fighting for his country. I answer for your safety. There is my hand in pledge of it. Will that reassure you? [*She offers him her hand.*]

THE MAN   [*Looking dubiously at his own hand.*] Better not touch my hand, dear young lady. I must have a wash first.

RAINA   [*Touched.*] That is very nice of you. I see that you are a gentleman.

THE MAN   [*Puzzled.*] Eh?

RAINA   You must not think I am surprised. Bulgarians of really good standing—people in our position—wash their hands nearly every day. So you see I can appreciate your delicacy. You may take my hand. [*She offers it again.*]

THE MAN   [*Kissing it with his hands behind his back.*] Thanks, gracious young lady: I feel safe at last. And now would you mind breaking the news to your mother? I had better not stay here secretly longer than is necessary.

RAINA   If you will be so good as to keep perfectly still whilst I am away.

THE MAN   Certainly. [*He sits down on the ottoman.*]

[RAINA *goes to the bed and wraps herself in the fur cloak. His eyes close. She goes to the door. Turning for a last look at him, she sees that he is dropping off to sleep.*]

RAINA   [*At the door.*] You are not going asleep, are you? [*He murmurs inarticulately: she runs to him and shakes him.*] Do you hear? Wake up: you are falling asleep.

THE MAN   Eh? Falling aslee—? Oh no: not the least in the world. I was only thinking. It's all right: I'm wide awake.

RAINA   [*Severely.*] Will you please stand up while I am away. [*He rises reluctantly.*] All the time, mind.

THE MAN   [*Standing unsteadily.*] Certainly. Certainly: you may depend on me.

[RAINA *looks doubtfully at him. He smiles weakly. She goes reluctantly, turning again at the door, and almost catching him in the act of yawning. She goes out.*]

THE MAN   [*Drowsily.*] Sleep, sleep, sleep, sleep,

slee—[*The words trail off into a murmur. He wakes again with a shock on the point of falling.*] Where am I? Thats what I want to know: where am I? Must keep awake. Nothing keeps me awake except danger: remember that: [*Intently.*] danger, danger, danger, dan— [*Trailing off again: another shock.*] Wheres danger? Mus' find it. [*He starts off vaguely round the room in search of it.*] What am I looking for? Sleep—danger—dont know. [*He stumbles against the bed.*] Ah yes: now I know. All right now. I'm to go to bed, but not to sleep. Be sure not to sleep, because of danger. Not to lie down either, only sit down. [*He sits on the bed. A blissful expression comes into his face.*] Ah! [*With a happy sigh he sinks back at full length; lifts his boots into the bed with a final effort; and falls fast asleep instantly.*]

[CATHERINE *comes in, followed by* RAINA.]

RAINA [*Looking at the ottoman.*] He's gone! I left him here.

CATHERINE Here! Then he must have climbed down from the—

RAINA [*Seeing him.*] Oh! [*She points.*]

CATHERINE [*Scandalized.*] Well! [*She strides to the bed,* RAINA *following until she is opposite her on the other side.*] He's fast asleep. The brute!

RAINA [*Anxiously.*] Sh!

CATHERINE [*Shaking him.*] Sir! [*Shaking him again, harder.*] Sir!! [*Vehemently, shaking very hard.*] Sir!!!

RAINA [*Catching her arm.*] Dont, mamma: the poor darling is worn out. Let him sleep.

CATHERINE [*Letting him go, and turning amazed to* RAINA.] The poor darling! Raina!!! [*She looks sternly at her daughter.*]

[*The man sleeps profoundly.*]

ACT II

The sixth of March, 1886. In the garden of MAJOR PETKOFF's *house. It is a fine spring morning: the garden looks fresh and pretty. Beyond the paling the tops of a couple of minarets can be seen, shewing that there is a valley there, with the little town in it. A few miles further the Balkan mountains rise and shut in the landscape. Looking towards them from within the garden, the side of the house is seen on the left, with a* garden door reached by a little flight of steps. On the right the stable yard, with its gateway, encroaches on the garden. There are fruit bushes along the paling and house, covered with washing spread out to dry. A path runs by the house, and rises by two steps at the corner, where it turns out of sight. In the middle, a small table, with two bent wood chairs at it, is laid for breakfast with Turkish coffee pot, cups, rolls, etc.; but the cups have been used and the bread broken. There is a wooden garden seat against the wall on the right.*

LOUKA, *smoking a cigaret, is standing between the table and the house, turning her back with angry disdain on a man servant who is lecturing her. He is a middle-aged man of cool temperament and low but clear and keen intelligence, with the complacency of the servant who values himself on his rank in servitude, and the imperturbability of the accurate calculator who has no illusions. He wears a white Bulgarian costume: jacket with embroidered border, sash, wide knickerbockers, and decorated gaiters. His head is shaved up to the crown, giving him a high Japanese forehead. His name is* NICOLA.

NICOLA Be warned in time, Louka: mend your manners. I know the mistress. She is so grand that she never dreams that any servant could dare be disrespectful to her; but if she once suspects that you are defying her, out you go.

LOUKA I do defy her. I will defy her. What do I care for her?

NICOLA If you quarrel with the family, I never can marry you. It's the same as if you quarrelled with me!

LOUKA You take her part against me, do you?

NICOLA [*Sedately.*] I shall always be dependent on the good will of the family. When I leave their service and start a shop in Sofia, their custom will be half my capital: their bad word would ruin me.

LOUKA You have no spirit. I should like to catch them saying a word against me!

NICOLA [*Pityingly.*] I should have expected more sense from you, Louka. But youre young: youre young!

LOUKA Yes; and you like me the better for it, dont you? But I know some family secrets they wouldnt care to have told, young as I am. Let them quarrel with me if they dare!

NICOLA [*With compassionate superiority.*] Do you know what they would do if they heard you talk like that?

LOUKA What could they do?

NICOLA Discharge you for untruthfulness. Who would believe any stories you told after that? Who would give you another situation? Who in this house would dare be seen speaking to you ever again? How long would your father be left on his little farm? [*She impatiently throws away the end of her cigaret, and stamps on it.*] Child: you dont know the power such high people have over the like of you and me when we try to rise out of our poverty against them. [*He goes close to her and lowers his voice.*] Look at me, ten years in their service. Do you think I know no secrets? I know things about the mistress that she wouldnt have the master know for a thousand levas. I know things about him that she wouldnt let him hear the last of for six months if I blabbed them to her. I know things about Raina that would break off her match with Sergius if——

LOUKA [*Turning on him quickly.*] How do you know? I never told you!

NICOLA [*Opening his eyes cunningly.*] So thats your little secret, is it? I thought it might be something like that. Well, you take my advice and be respectful; and make the mistress feel that no matter what you know or dont know, she can depend on you to hold your tongue and serve the family faithfully. Thats what they like; and thats how youll make most out of them.

LOUKA [*With searching scorn.*] You have the soul of a servant, Nicola.

NICOLA [*Complacently.*] Yes: thats the secret of success in service.

[*A loud knocking with a whip handle on a wooden door is heard from the stable yard.*]

MALE VOICE OUTSIDE Hollo! Hollo there! Nicola!

LOUKA Master! back from the war!

NICOLA [*Quickly.*] My word for it, Louka, the war's over. Off with you and get some fresh coffee. [*He runs out into the stable yard.*]

LOUKA [*As she collects the coffee pot and cups on the tray, and carries it into the house.*] Youll never put the soul of a servant into me.

[MAJOR PETKOFF *comes from the stable yard, followed by* NICOLA. *He is a cheerful, excitable, insignificant, unpolished man of about 50, naturally unambitious except as to his income and his importance in local society, but just now greatly pleased with the military rank which the war has thrust on him as a man of consequence in his town. The fever of plucky patriotism which the Serbian attack roused in all the Bulgarians has pulled him through the war; but he is obviously glad to be home again.*]

PETKOFF [*Pointing to the table with his whip.*] Breakfast out here, eh?

NICOLA Yes, sir. The mistress and Miss Raina have just gone in.

PETKOFF [*Sitting down and taking a roll.*] Go in and say Ive come; and get me some fresh coffee.

NICOLA It's coming, sir. [*He goes to the house door.* LOUKA, *with fresh coffee, a clean cup, and a brandy bottle on her tray, meets him.*] Have you told the mistress?

LOUKA Yes: she's coming.

[NICOLA *goes into the house.* LOUKA *brings the coffee to the table.*]

PETKOFF Well: the Serbs havnt run away with you, have they?

LOUKA No, sir.

PETKOFF Thats right. Have you brought me some cognac?

LOUKA [*Putting the bottle on the table.*] Here, sir.

PETKOFF Thats right. [*He pours some into his coffee.*]

[CATHERINE *who, having at this early hour made only a very perfunctory toilet, wears a Bulgarian apron over a once brilliant but now half wornout dressing gown, and a colored hankerchief tied over her thick black hair, comes from the house with Turkish slippers on her bare feet, looking astonishingly handsome and stately under all the circumstances.* LOUKA *goes into the house.*]

CATHERINE My dear Paul: what a surprise for us! [*She stoops over the back of his chair to kiss him.*] Have they brought you fresh coffee?

PETKOFF Yes: Louka's been looking after me. The war's over. The treaty was signed three days ago at Bucharest; and the decree for our army to demobilize was issued yesterday.

CATHERINE [*Springing erect, with flashing eyes.*] Paul: have you let the Austrians force you to make peace?

PETKOFF [*Submissively.*] My dear; they didn't consult me. What could *I* do? [*She sits down and turns away from him.*] But of course we saw to it that the treaty was an honorable one. It declares peace—

CATHERINE [*Outraged.*] Peace!

PETKOFF [*Appeasing her.*] —but not friendly relations: remember that. They wanted to put that in; but I insisted on its being struck out. What more could I do?

CATHERINE You could have annexed Serbia and made Prince Alexander Emperor of the Balkans. Thats what I would have done.

PETKOFF I dont doubt it in the least, my dear. But I should have had to subdue the whole Austrian Empire first; and that would have kept me too long away from you. I missed you greatly.

CATHERINE [*Relenting.*] Ah! [*She stretches her hand affectionately across the table to squeeze his.*]

PETKOFF And how have you been, my dear?

CATHERINE Oh, my usual sore throats: thats all.

PETKOFF [*With conviction.*] That comes from washing your neck every day. Ive often told you so.

CATHERINE Nonsense, Paul!

PETKOFF [*Over his coffee and cigaret.*] I dont believe in going too far with these modern customs. All this washing cant be good for the health: it's not natural. There was an Englishman at Philippopolis who used to wet himself all over with cold water every morning when he got up. Disgusting! It all comes from the English: their climate makes them so dirty that they have to be perpetually washing themselves. Look at my father! he never had a bath in his life; and he lived to be ninety-eight, the healthiest man in Bulgaria. I dont mind a good wash once a week to keep up my position; but once a day is carrying the thing to a ridiculous extreme.

CATHERINE You are a barbarian at heart still, Paul. I hope you behaved yourself before all those Russian officers.

PETKOFF I did my best. I took care to let them know that we have a library.

CATHERINE Ah; but you didnt tell them that we have an electric bell in it? I have had one put up.

PETKOFF Whats an electric bell?

CATHERINE You touch a button; something tinkles in the kitchen; and then Nicola comes up.

PETKOFF Why not shout for him?

CATHERINE Civilized people never shout for their servants. Ive learnt that while you were away.

PETKOFF Well, I'll tell you something Ive learnt too. Civilized people dont hang out their washing to dry where visitors can see it; so youd better have all that [*Indicating the clothes on the bushes.*] put somewhere else.

CATHERINE Oh, thats absurd, Paul: I dont believe really refined people notice such things.

SERGIUS [*Knocking at the stable gates.*] Gate, Nicola!

PETKOFF Theres Sergius. [*Shouting.*] Hollo, Nicola!

CATHERINE Oh, dont shout, Paul: it really isnt nice.

PETKOFF Bosh! [*He shouts louder than before.*] Nicola!

NICOLA [*Appearing at the house door.*] Yes, sir.

PETKOFF Are you deaf? Dont you hear Major Saranoff knocking? Bring him round this way. [*He pronounces the name with the stress on the second syllable: Sarahnoff.*]

NICOLA Yes, major. [*He goes into the stable yard.*]

PETKOFF You must talk to him, my dear, until Raina takes him off our hands. He bores my life out about our not promoting him. Over my head, if you please.

CATHERINE He certainly ought to be promoted when he marries Raina. Besides, the country should insist on having at least one native general.

PETKOFF Yes; so that he could throw away whole brigades instead of regiments. It's no use, my dear: he hasnt the slightest chance of promotion until we're quite sure that the peace will be a lasting one.

NICOLA [*At the gate, announcing.*] Major Sergius Saranoff! [*He goes into the house and returns presently with a third chair, which he places at the table. He then withdraws.*]

[MAJOR SERGIUS SARANOFF, *the original of the*

portrait in RAINA's *room, is a tall romantically handsome man, with the physical hardihood, the high spirit, and the susceptible imagination of an untamed mountaineer chieftain. But his remarkable personal distinction is of a characteristically civilized type. The ridges of his eyebrows, curving with an interrogative twist round the projections at the outer corners; his jealously observant eye; his nose, thin, keen, and apprehensive in spite of the pugnacious high bridge and large nostril; his assertive chin would not be out of place in a Parisian salon, shewing that the clever imaginative barbarian has an acute critical faculty which has been thrown into intense activity by the arrival of western civilization in the Balkans. The result is precisely what the advent of nineteenth century thought first produced in England: to wit, Byronism. By his brooding on the perpetual failure, not only of others, but of himself, to live up to his ideals; by his consequent cynical scorn for humanity; by his jejune credulity as to the absolute validity of his concepts and the unworthiness of the world in disregarding them; by his wincings and mockeries under the sting of the petty disillusions which every hour spent among men brings to his sensitive observation, he has acquired the half tragic, half ironic air, the mysterious moodiness, the suggestion of a strange and terrible history that has left nothing but undying remorse, by which Childe Harold fascinated the grandmothers of his English contemporaries. It is clear that here or nowhere is* RAINA's *ideal hero.* CATHERINE *is hardly less enthusiastic about him than her daughter, and much less reserved in shewing her enthusiasm. As he enters from the stable gate, she rises effusively to greet him.* PETKOFF *is distinctly less disposed to make a fuss about him.*]

PETKOFF   Here already, Sergius! Glad to see you.

CATHERINE   My dear Sergius! [*She holds out both her hands.*]

SERGIUS   [*Kissing them with scrupulous gallantry.*] My dear mother, if I may call you so.

PETKOFF   [*Drily.*]   Mother-in-law, Sergius: mother-in-law! Sit down; and have some coffee.

SERGIUS   Thank you: none for me. [*He gets away from the table with a certain distaste for* PETKOFF's *enjoyment of it, and posts himself*

with conscious dignity against the rail of the steps leading to the house.]

CATHERINE   You look superb. The campaign has improved you, Sergius. Everybody here is mad about you. We were all wild with enthusiasm about that magnificent cavalry charge.

SERGIUS   [*With grave irony.*] Madam: it was the cradle and the grave of my military reputation.

CATHERINE   How so?

SERGIUS   I won the battle the wrong way when our worthy Russian generals were losing it the right way. In short, I upset their plans, and wounded their self-esteem. Two Cossack colonels had their regiments routed on the most correct principles of scientific warfare. Two major-generals got killed strictly according to military etiquette. The two colonels are now major-generals; and I am still a simple major.

CATHERINE   You shall not remain so, Sergius. The women are on your side; and they will see that justice is done you.

SERGIUS   It is too late. I have only waited for the peace to send in my resignation.

PETKOFF   [*Dropping his cup in his amazement.*] Your resignation!

CATHERINE   Oh, you must withdraw it!

SERGIUS   [*With resolute measured emphasis, folding his arms.*] I never withdraw.

PETKOFF   [*Vexed.*] Now who could have supposed you were going to do such a thing?

SERGIUS   [*With fire.*] Everyone that knew me. But enough of myself and my affairs. How is Raina; and where is Raina?

RAINA   [*Suddenly coming round the corner of the house and standing at the top of the steps in the path.*] Raina is here.

[*She makes a charming picture as they turn to look at her. She wears an underdress of pale green silk, draped with an overdress of thin ecru canvas embroidered with gold. She is crowned with a dainty eastern cap of gold tinsel.* SERGIUS *goes impulsively to meet her. Posing regally, she presents her hand: he drops chivalrously on one knee and kisses it.*]

PETKOFF   [*Aside to* CATHERINE, *beaming with parental pride.*] Pretty, isnt it? She always appears at the right moment.

CATHERINE   [*Impatiently.*] Yes: she listens for it. It is an abominable habit.

[SERGIUS *leads* RAINA *forward with splendid gallantry. When they arrive at the table, she turns to him with a bend of the head: he bows; and thus they separate, he coming to his place, and she going behind her father's chair.*]

RAINA [*Stooping and kissing her father.*] Dear father! Welcome home!

PETKOFF [*Patting her cheek.*] My little pet girl. [*He kisses her. She goes to the chair left by* NICOLA *for* SERGIUS, *and sits down.*]

CATHERINE And so youre no longer a soldier, Sergius.

SERGIUS I am no longer a soldier. Soldiering, my dear madam, is the coward's art of attacking mercilessly when you are strong, and keeping out of harm's way when you are weak. That is the whole secret of successful fighting. Get your enemy at a disadvantage; and never, on any account, fight him on equal terms.

PETKOFF They wouldnt let us make a fair stand-up fight of it. However, I suppose soldiering has to be a trade like any other trade.

SERGIUS Precisely. But I have no ambition to shine as a tradesman; so I have taken the advice of that bagman of a captain that settled the exchange of prisoners with us at Pirot, and given it up.

PETKOFF What! that Swiss fellow? Sergius, Ive often thought of that exchange since. He over-reached us about those horses.

SERGIUS Of course he over-reached us. His father was a hotel and livery stable keeper; and he owed his first step to his knowledge of horse-dealing. [*With mock enthusiasm.*] Ah, he was a soldier, every inch a soldier! If only I had bought the horses for my regiment instead of foolishly leading it into danger, I should have been a field-marshal now!

CATHERINE A Swiss? What was he doing in the Serbian army?

PETKOFF A volunteer, of course: keen on picking up his profession. [*Chuckling.*] We shouldnt have been able to begin fighting if these foreigners hadnt shewn us how to do it: we knew nothing about it; and neither did the Serbs. Egad, there'd have been no war without them!

RAINA Are there many Swiss officers in the Serbian army?

PETKOFF No. All Austrians, just as our officers were all Russians. This was the only Swiss I came across. I'll never trust a Swiss again. He humbugged us into giving him fifty able-bodied men for two hundred worn out chargers. They werent even eatable!

SERGIUS We were two children in the hands of that consummate soldier, Major: simply two innocent little children.

RAINA What was he like?

CATHERINE Oh, Raina, what a silly question!

SERGIUS He was like a commercial traveller in uniform. Bourgeois to his boots!

PETKOFF [*Grinning.*] Sergius, tell Catherine that queer story his friend told us about how he escaped after Slivnitza. You remember. About his being hid by two women.

SERGIUS [*With bitter irony.*] Oh yes: quite a romance! He was serving in the very battery I so unprofessionally charged. Being a thorough soldier, he ran away like the rest of them, with our cavalry at his heels. To escape their sabres he climbed a waterpipe and made his way into the bedroom of a young Bulgarian lady. The young lady was enchanted by his persuasive commercial traveller's manners. She very modestly entertained him for an hour or so, and then called in her mother lest her conduct should appear unmaidenly. The old lady was equally fascinated; and the fugitive was sent on his way in the morning, disguised in an old coat belonging to the master of the house, who was away at the war.

RAINA [*Rising with marked stateliness.*] Your life in the camp has made you coarse, Sergius. I did not think you would have repeated such a story before me. [*She turns away coldly.*]

CATHERINE [*Also rising.*] She is right, Sergius. If such women exist, we should be spared the knowledge of them.

PETKOFF Pooh! nonsense! what does it matter?

SERGIUS [*Ashamed.*] No, Petkoff: I was wrong. [*To* RAINA, *with earnest humility.*] I beg your pardon. I have behaved abominably. Forgive me, Raina. [*She bows reservedly.*] And you too, madam. [CATHERINE *bows graciously and sits down. He proceeds solemnly, again addressing* RAINA.] The glimpses I have had of the seamy side of life during the last few months have made me cynical; but I should not have brought my cynicism here: least of all in your presence, Raina. I—[*Here, turn ing to the others, he is evidently going to begin a long speech when the* MAJOR *interrupts him*]

PETKOFF Stuff and nonsense, Sergius! Thats quite enough fuss about nothing: a soldier's daughter should be able to stand up without flinching to a little strong conversation. [*He rises.*] Come: it's time for us to get to business. We have to make up our minds how those three regiments are to get back to Philippopolis: theres no forage for them on the Sofia route. [*He goes towards the house.*] Come along. [SERGIUS *is about to follow him when* CATHERINE *rises and intervenes.*]

CATHERINE Oh, Paul, cant you spare Sergius for a few moments? Raina has hardly seen him yet. Perhaps I can help you to settle about the regiments.

SERGIUS [*Protesting.*] My dear madam, impossible: you—

CATHERINE [*Stopping him playfully.*] You stay here, my dear Sergius: theres no hurry. I have a word or two to say to Paul. [SERGIUS *instantly bows and steps back.*] Now, dear [*Taking* PETKOFF'S *arm.*], come and see the electric bell.

PETKOFF Oh, very well, very well.

[*They go into the house together affectionately.* SERGIUS, *left alone with* RAINA, *looks anxiously at her, fearing that she is still offended. She smiles, and stretches out her arms to him.*]

SERGIUS [*Hastening to her.*] Am I forgiven?

RAINA [*Placing her hands on his shoulders as she looks up at him with admiration and worship.*] My hero! My king!

SERGIUS My queen! [*He kisses her on the forehead.*]

RAINA How I have envied you, Sergius! You have been out in the world, on the field of battle, able to prove yourself there worthy of any woman in the world; whilst I have had to sit at home inactive—dreaming—useless—doing nothing that could give me the right to call myself worthy of any man.

SERGIUS Dearest, all my deeds have been yours. You inspired me. I have gone through the war like a knight in a tournament with his lady looking down at him!

RAINA And you have never been absent from my thoughts for a moment. [*Very solemnly.*] Sergius, I think we two have found the higher love. When I think of you, I feel that I could never do a base deed or think an ignoble thought.

SERGIUS My lady and my saint. [*He clasps her reverently.*]

RAINA [*Returning his embrace.*] My lord and my—

SERGIUS Sh—sh! Let me be the worshipper, dear. You little know how unworthy even the best man is of a girl's pure passion!

RAINA I trust you. I love you. You will never disappoint me, Sergius. [LOUKA *is heard singing within the house. They quickly release each other.*] I cant pretend to talk indifferently before her: my heart is too full. [LOUKA *comes from the house with her tray. She goes to the table, and begins to clear it, with her back turned to them.*] I will get my hat; and then we can go out until lunch time. Wouldnt you like that?

SERGIUS Be quick. If you are away five minutes, it will seem five hours [RAINA *runs to the top of the steps, and turns there to exchange looks with him and wave him a kiss with both hands. He looks after her with emotion for a moment; then turns slowly away, his face radiant with the loftiest exaltation. The movement shifts his field of vision, into the corner of which there now comes the tail of* LOUKA'S *double apron. His attention is arrested at once. He takes a stealthy look at her, and begins to twirl his moustache mischievously, with his left hand akimbo on his hip. Finally, striking the ground with his heels in something of a cavalry swagger, he strolls over to the other side of the table, opposite her, and says.*] Louka, do you know what the higher love is?

LOUKA [*Astonished.*] No, sir.

SERGIUS Very fatiguing thing to keep up for any length of time, Louka. One feels the need of some relief after it.

LOUKA [*Innocently.*] Perhaps you would like some coffee, sir? [*She stretches her hand across the table for the coffee pot.*]

SERGIUS [*Taking her hand.*] Thank you, Louka.

LOUKA [*Pretending to pull.*] Oh, sir, you know I didnt mean that. I am surprised at you.

SERGIUS [*Coming clear of the table and drawing her with him.*] I am surprised at myself, Louka. What would Sergius, the hero of Slivnitza, say if he saw me now? What would Sergius, the apostle of the higher love, say if he saw me now? What would the half dozen

Sergiuses who keep popping in and out of this handsome figure of mine say if they caught us here? [*Letting go her hand and slipping his arm dexterously round her waist.*] Do you consider my figure handsome, Louka?

LOUKA   Let me go, sir. I shall be disgraced. [*She struggles: he holds her inexorably.*] Oh, will you let go?

SERGIUS   [*Looking straight into her eyes.*] No.

LOUKA   Then stand back where we cant be seen. Have you no common sense?

SERGIUS   Ah! thats reasonable. [*He takes her into the stableyard gateway, where they are hidden from the house.*]

LOUKA   [*Plaintively.*] I may have been seen from the windows: Miss Raina is sure to be spying about after you.

SERGIUS   [*Stung: letting her go.*] Take care, Louka. I may be worthless enough to betray the higher love; but do not you insult it.

LOUKA   [*Demurely.*] Not for the world, sir, I'm sure. May I go on with my work, please, now?

SERGIUS   [*Again putting his arm round her.*] You are a provoking little witch, Louka. If you were in love with me, would you spy out of windows on me?

LOUKA   Well, you see, sir, since you say you are half a dozen different gentlemen all at once, I should have a great deal to look after.

SERGIUS   [*Charmed.*] Witty as well as pretty. [*He tries to kiss her.*]

LOUKA   [*Avoiding him.*] No: I dont want your kisses. Gentlefolk are all alike: you making love to me behind Miss Raina's back; and she doing the same behind yours.

SERGIUS   [*Recoiling a step.*] Louka!

LOUKA   It shews how little you really care.

SERGIUS   [*Dropping his familiarity, and speaking with freezing politeness.*] If our conversation is to continue, Louka, you will please remember that a gentleman does not discuss the conduct of the lady he is engaged to with her maid.

LOUKA   It's so hard to know what a gentleman considers right. I thought from your trying to kiss me that you had given up being so particular.

SERGIUS   [*Turning from her and striking his forehead as he comes back into the garden from the gateway.*] Devil! devil!

LOUKA   Ha! ha! I expect one of the six of you is very like me, sir; though I am only Miss Raina's maid. [*She goes back to her work at the table, taking no further notice of him.*]

SERGIUS   [*Speaking to himself.*] Which of the six is the real man? thats the question that torments me. One of them is a hero, another a buffoon, another a humbug, another perhaps a bit of a blackguard. [*He pauses, and looks furtively at* LOUKA *as he adds, with deep bitterness.*] And one, at least, is a coward: jealous, like all cowards. [*He goes to the table.*] Louka.

LOUKA   Yes?

SERGIUS   Who is my rival?

LOUKA   You shall never get that out of me, for love or money.

SERGIUS   Why?

LOUKA   Never mind why. Besides, you would tell that I told you; and I should lose my place.

SERGIUS   [*Holding out his right hand in affirmation.*] No! on the honor of a—[*He checks himself; and his hand drops, nerveless, as he concludes sardonically.*]—of a man capable of behaving as I have been behaving for the last five minutes. Who is he?

LOUKA   I dont know. I never saw him. I only heard his voice through the door of her room.

SERGIUS   Damnation! How dare you?

LOUKA   [*Retreating.*] Oh, I mean no harm: youve no right to take up my words like that. The mistress knows all about it. And I tell you that if that gentleman ever comes here again, Miss Raina will marry him, whether he likes it or not. I know the difference between the sort of manner you and she put on before one another and the real manner.

[SERGIUS *shivers as if she had stabbed him. Then, setting his face like iron, he strides grimly to her, and grips her above the elbows with both hands.*]

SERGIUS   Now listen you to me.

LOUKA   [*Wincing.*] Not so tight: youre hurting me.

SERGIUS   That doesnt matter. You have stained my honor by making me a party to your eavesdropping. And you have betrayed your mistress.

LOUKA   [*Writhing.*] Please—

SERGIUS   That shews that you are an abominable little clod of common clay, with the soul of a servant. [*He lets her go as if she were an unclean thing, and turns away, dusting his hands of her, to the bench by the wall, where he sits down with averted head, meditating gloomily.]*

LOUKA [*Whimpering angrily with her hands up her sleeves, feeling her bruised arms.*] You know how to hurt with your tongue as well as with your hands. But I dont care, now Ive found out that whatever clay I'm made of, youre made of the same. As for her, she's a liar; and her fine airs are a cheat; and I'm worth six of her. [*She shakes the pain off hardily; tosses her head; and sets to work to put the things on the tray.*]

[*He looks doubtfully at her. She finishes packing the tray, and laps the cloth over the edges, so as to carry all out together. As she stoops to lift it, he rises.*]

SERGIUS Louka! [*She stops and looks defiantly at him.*] A gentleman has no right to hurt a woman under any circumstances. [*With profound humility, uncovering his head.*] I beg your pardon.

LOUKA That sort of apology may satisfy a lady. Of what use is it to a servant?

SERGIUS [*Rudely crossed in his chivalry, throws it off with a bitter laugh, and says slightingly.*] Oh, you wish to be paid for the hurt? [*He puts on his shako, and takes some money from his pocket.*]

LOUKA [*Her eyes filling with tears in spite of herself.*] No: I want my hurt made well.

SERGIUS [*Sobered by her tone.*] How?

[*She rolls up her left sleeve; clasps her arm with the thumb and fingers of her right hand; and looks down at the bruise. Then she raises her head and looks straight at him. Finally, with a superb gesture, she presents her arm to be kissed. Amazed, he looks at her; at the arm; at her again; hesitates; and then, with shuddering intensity, exclaims* Never! *and gets away as far as possible from her.*

Her arm drops. Without a word, and with unaffected dignity, she takes her tray, and is approaching the house when RAINA *returns, wearing a hat and jacket in the height of the Vienna fashion of the previous year, 1885.* LOUKA *makes way proudly for her, and then goes into the house.*]

RAINA I'm ready. Whats the matter? [*Gaily.*] Have you been flirting with Louka?

SERGIUS [*Hastily.*] No, no. How can you think such a thing?

RAINA [*Ashamed of herself.*] Forgive me, dear: it was only a jest. I am so happy to-day.

[*He goes quickly to her, and kisses her hand remorsefully.* CATHERINE *comes out and calls to them from the top of the steps.*]

CATHERINE [*Coming down to them.*] I am sorry to disturb you, children; but Paul is distracted over those three regiments. He doesnt know how to send them to Philippopolis; and he objects to every suggestion of mine. You must go and help him Sergius. He is in the library.

RAINA [*Disappointed.*] But we are just going out for a walk.

SERGIUS I shall not be long. Wait for me just five minutes. [*He runs up the steps to the door.*]

RAINA [*Following him to the foot of the steps and looking up at him with timid coquetry.*] I shall go round and wait in full view of the library windows. Be sure you draw father's attention to me. If you are a moment longer than five minutes, I shall go in and fetch you, regiments or no regiments.

SERGIUS [*Laughing.*] Very well. [*He goes in.*]

[RAINA *watches him until he is out of sight. Then, with a perceptible relaxation of manner, she begins to pace up and down the garden in a brown study.*]

CATHERINE Imagine their meeting that Swiss and hearing the whole story! The very first thing your father asked for was the old coat we sent him off in. A nice mess you have got us into!

RAINA [*Gazing thoughtfully at the gravel as she walks.*] The little beast!

CATHERINE Little beast! What little beast?

RAINA To go and tell! Oh, if I had him here, I'd cram him with chocolate creams till he couldnt ever speak again!

CATHERINE Dont talk such stuff. Tell me the truth, Raina. How long was he in your room before you came to me?

RAINA [*Whisking round and recommencing her march in the opposite direction.*] Oh, I forget.

CATHERINE You cannot forget! Did he really climb up after the soldiers were gone; or was he there when that officer searched the room?

RAINA No. Yes: I think he must have been there then.

CATHERINE   You think! Oh, Raina! Raina! Will anything ever make you straightforward? If Sergius finds out, it will be all over between you.

RAINA   [*With cool impertinence.*] Oh, I know Sergius is your pet. I sometimes wish you could marry him instead of me. You would just suit him. You would pet him, and spoil him, and mother him to perfection.

CATHERINE   [*Opening her eyes very widely indeed.*] Well, upon my word!

RAINA   [*Capriciously: half to herself.*] I always feel a longing to do or say something dreadful to him—to shock his propriety—to scandalize the five senses out of him. [*To* CATHERINE, *perversely.*] I dont care whether he finds out about the chocolate cream soldier or not. I half hope he may. [*She again turns and strolls flippantly away up the path to the corner of the house.*]

CATHERINE   And what should I be able to say to your father, pray?

RAINA   [*Over her shoulder, from the top of the two steps.*] Oh, poor father! As if he could help himself! [*She turns the corner and passes out of sight.*]

CATHERINE   [*Looking after her, her fingers itching.*] Oh, if you were only ten years younger! [LOUKA *comes from the house with a salver, which she carries hanging down by her side.*] Well?

LOUKA   Theres a gentleman just called, madam. A Serbian officer.

CATHERINE   [*Flaming.*] A Serb! And how dare he—[*Checking herself bitterly.*] Oh, I forgot. We are at peace now. I suppose we shall have them calling every day to pay their compliments. Well: if he is an officer why dont you tell your master? He is in the library with Major Saranoff. Why do you come to me?

LOUKA   But he asks for you, madam. And I dont think he knows who you are: he said the lady of the house. He gave me this little ticket for you. [*She takes a card out of her bosom; puts it on the salver; and offers it to* CATHERINE.]

CATHERINE   [*Reading.*] "Captain Bluntschli"? Thats a German name.

LOUKA   Swiss, madam, I think.

CATHERINE   [*With a bound that makes* LOUKA *jump back.*] Swiss! What is he like?

LOUKA   [*Timidly.*] He has a big carpet bag, madam.

CATHERINE   Oh Heavens! He's come to return the coat. Send him away: say we're not at home: ask him to leave his address and I'll write to him. Oh stop: that will never do. Wait! [*She throws herself into a chair to think it out.* LOUKA *waits.*] The master and Major Saranoff are busy in the library, arnt they?

LOUKA   Yes, madam.

CATHERINE   [*Decisively.*] Bring the gentleman out here at once. [*Peremptorily.*] And be very polite to him. Dont delay. Here [*Impatiently snatching the salver from her.*]: leave that here; and go straight back to him.

LOUKA   Yes, madam. [*Going.*]

CATHERINE   Louka!

LOUKA   [*Stopping.*] Yes, madam.

CATHERINE   Is the library door shut?

LOUKA   I think so, madam.

CATHERINE   If not, shut it as you pass through.

LOUKA   Yes, madam. [*Going.*]

CATHERINE   Stop! [*Louka stops.*] He will have to go that way. [*Indicating the gate of the stable yard.*] Tell Nicola to bring his bag here after him. Dont forget.

LOUKA   [*Surprised.*] His bag?

CATHERINE   Yes: here: as soon as possible. [*Vehemently.*] Be quick! [LOUKA *runs into the house.* CATHERINE *snatches her apron off and throws it behind a bush. She then takes up the salver and uses it as a mirror, with the result that the hankerchief tied round her head follows the apron. A touch to her hair and a shake to her dressing gown make her presentable.*] Oh, how? how? how can a man be such a fool! Such a moment to select! [LOUKA *appears at the door of the house, announcing* CAPTAIN BLUNTSCHLI. *She stands aside at the top of the steps to let him pass before she goes in again. He is the man of the midnight adventure in* RAINA's *room, clean, well brushed, smartly uniformed, and out of trouble, but still unmistakably the same man. The moment* LOUKA's *back is turned,* CATHERINE *swoops on him with impetuous, urgent, coaxing appeal.*] Captain Bluntschli, I am very glad to see you; but you must leave this house at once. [*He raises his eyebrows.*] My husband has just returned with my future son-in-law; and they know nothing. If they did, the consequences would be terrible. You are a foreigner: you do not feel our national animosities as we do. We still hate the Serbs: the effect of the peace on my husband has been to make him feel like a lion baulked of his prey. If he discovers our secret, he will never forgive me; and my daughter's life will hardly be safe. Will you, like the chivalrous gentleman and soldier you are, leave at once before he finds you here?

BLUNTSCHLI [*Disappointed, but philosophical.*] At once, gracious lady. I only came to thank you and return the coat you lent me. If you will allow me to take it out of my bag and leave it with your servant as I pass out, I need detain you no further. [*He turns to go into the house.*]

CATHERINE [*Catching him by the sleeve.*] Oh, you must not think of going back that way. [*Coaxing him across to the stable gates.*] This is the shortest way out. Many thanks. So glad to have been of service to you. Good-bye.

BLUNTSCHLI But my bag?

CATHERINE It shall be sent on. You will leave me your address.

BLUNTSCHLI True. Allow me. [*He takes out his card-case, and stops to write his address, keeping* CATHERINE *in an agony of impatience. As he hands her the card,* PETKOFF, *hatless, rushes from the house in a fluster of hospitality, followed by* SERGIUS.]

PETKOFF [*As he hurries down the steps.*] My dear Captain Bluntschli—

CATHERINE Oh Heavens! [*She sinks on the seat against the wall.*]

PETKOFF [*Too preoccupied to notice her as he shakes* BLUNTSCHLI's *hand heartily.*] Those stupid people of mine thought I was out here, instead of in the—haw!—library. [*He cannot mention the library without betraying how proud he is of it.*] I saw you through the window. I was wondering why you didnt come in. Saraanoff is with me: you remember him, dont you?

SERGIUS [*Saluting humorously, and then offering his hand with great charm of manner.*] Welcome, our friend the enemy!

PETKOFF No longer the enemy, happily. [*Rather anxiously.*] I hope youve called as a friend, and not about horses or prisoners.

CATHERINE Oh, quite as a friend, Paul. I was just asking Captain Bluntschli to stay to lunch; but he declares he must go at once.

SERGIUS [*Sardonically.*] Impossible, Bluntschli. We want you here badly. We have to send on three cavalry regiments to Philippopolis; and we dont in the least know how to do it.

BLUNTSCHLI [*Suddenly attentive and business-like.*] Philippopolis? The forage is the trouble, I suppose.

PETKOFF [*Eagerly.*] Yes, thats it. [*To* SERGIUS.] He sees the whole thing at once.

BLUNTSCHLI I think I can shew you how to manage that.

SERGIUS Invaluable man! Come along! [*Towering over* BLUNTSCHLI, *he puts his hand on his shoulder and takes him to the steps,* PETKOFF *following.*]

[RAINA *comes from the house as* BLUNTSCHLI *puts his foot on the first step.*]

RAINA Oh! The chocolate cream soldier!

[BLUNTSCHLI *stands rigid.* SERGIUS, *amazed, looks at* RAINA, *then at* PETKOFF, *who looks back at him and then at his wife.*]

CATHERINE [*With commanding presence of mind.*] My dear Raina, dont you see that we have a guest here? Captain Bluntschli, one of our new Serbian friends.

[RAINA *bows:* BLUNTSCHLI *bows.*]

RAINA How silly of me! [*She comes down into the center of the group, between* BLUNTSCHLI *and* PETKOFF.] I made a beautiful ornament this morning for the ice pudding; and that stupid Nicola has just put down a pile of plates on it and spoilt it. [*To* BLUNTSCHLI, *winningly.*] I hope you didnt think that you were the chocolate cream soldier, Captain Bluntschli.

BLUNTSCHLI [*Laughing.*] I assure you I did. [*Stealing a whimsical glance at her.*] Your explanation was a relief.

PETKOFF [*Suspiciously, to* RAINA.] And since when, pray, have you taken to cooking?

CATHERINE Oh, whilst you were away. It is her latest fancy.

PETKOFF [*Testily.*] And has Nicola taken to drinking? He used to be careful enough. First he shews Captain Bluntschli out here when he knew quite well I was in the library; and then he goes downstairs and breaks Raina's chocolate soldier. He must— [NICOLA *appears at the top of the steps with the bag. He descends; places it respectfully before* BLUNTSCHLI; *and waits for further orders. General amazement.* NICOLA, *unconscious of the effect he is produc-*

ing, *looks perfectly satisfied with himself. When* PETKOFF *recovers his power of speech, he breaks out at him with.*] Are you mad, Nicola?

NICOLA [*Taken aback.*] Sir?

PETKOFF What have you brought that for?

NICOLA My lady's orders, major. Louka told me that—

CATHERINE [*Interrupting him.*] My orders! Why should I order you to bring Captain Bluntschli's luggage out here? What are you thinking of, Nicola?

NICOLA [*After a moment's bewilderment, picking up the bag as he addresses* BLUNTSCHLI *with the very perfection of servile discretion.*] I beg your pardon, captain, I am sure. [*To* CATHERINE.] My fault, madam. I hope youll overlook it. [*He bows, and is going to the steps with the bag, when* PETKOFF *addresses him angrily.*]

PETKOFF Youd better go and slam that bag, too, down on Miss Raina's ice pudding! [*This is too much for* NICOLA. *The bag drops from his hand almost on his master's toes, eliciting a roar of:*] Begone, you butter-fingered donkey.

NICOLA [*Snatching up the bag, and escaping into the house.*] Yes, major.

CATHERINE Oh, never mind, Paul: dont be angry.

PETKOFF [*Blustering.*] Scoundrel! He's got out of hand while I was away. I'll teach him. Infernal blackguard! The sack next Saturday! I'll clear out the whole establishment— [*He is stifled by the caresses of his wife and daughter, who hang round his neck, petting him.*]

CATHERINE Now, now, now, it mustnt be angry. He meant no harm. Be good to please me, dear. Sh-sh-sh-sh!

RAINA [*Simultaneously with* CATHERINE.] Wow, wow, wow: not on your first day at home. I'll make another ice pudding. Tch-ch-ch!

PETKOFF [*Yielding.*] Oh well, never mind. Come, Bluntschli: let's have no more nonsense about going away. You know very well youre not going back to Switzerland yet. Until you do go back youll stay with us.

RAINA Oh, do, Captain Bluntschli.

PETKOFF [*To* CATHERINE.] Now, Catherine, it's of you he's afraid. Press him; and he'll stay.

CATHERINE Of course I shall be only too delighted if [*Appealingly.*] Captain Bluntschli really wishes to stay. He knows my wishes.

BLUNTSCHLI [*In his driest military manner.*] I am at madam's orders.

SERGIUS [*Cordially.*] That settles it!

PETKOFF [*Heartily.*] Of course!

RAINA You see you must stay.

BLUNTSCHLI [*Smiling.*] Well, if I must, I must. [*Gesture of despair from* CATHERINE.]

ACT III

In the library after lunch. It is not much of a library. Its literary equipment consists of a single fixed shelf stocked with old paper covered novels, broken backed, coffee stained, torn and thumbed; and a couple of little hanging shelves with a few gift books on them: the rest of the wall space being occupied by trophies of war and the chase. But it is a most comfortable sitting room. A row of three large windows shews a mountain panorama, just now seen in one of its friendliest aspects in the mellowing afternoon light. In the corner next the right hand window a square earthenware stove, a perfect tower of glistening pottery, rises nearly to the ceiling and guarantees plenty of warmth. The ottoman is like that in RAINA'S *room, and similarly placed; and the window seats are luxurious with decorated cushions. There is one object, however, hopelessly out of keeping with its surroundings. This is a small kitchen table, much the worse for wear, fitted as a writing table with an old canister full of pens, an eggcup filled with ink, and a deplorable scrap of heavily used pink blotting paper.*

At the side of this table, which stands to the left of anyone facing the window, BLUNTSCHLI *is hard at work with a couple of maps before him, writing orders. At the head of it sits* SERGIUS, *who is supposed to be also at work, but is actually gnawing the feather of a pen, and contemplating* BLUNTSCHLI'S *quick, sure, businesslike progress with a mixture of envious irritation at his own incapacity and awestruck wonder at an ability which seems to him almost miraculous, though its prosaic character forbids him to esteem it. The* MAJOR *is comfortably established on the ottoman, with a newspaper in his hand and the tube of his hookah within easy reach.* CATHERINE *sits at the stove, with her back to them, embroidering.* RAINA, *reclining on the divan, is gazing in a daydream out at the Balkan landscape, with a neglected novel in her lap.*

The door is on the same side as the stove, farther from the window. The button of the electric bell is at the opposite side, behind BLUNTSCHLI.

PETKOFF [*Looking up from his paper to watch how they are getting on at the table.*] Are you sure I cant help you in any way, Bluntschli?

BLUNTSCHLI [*Without interrupting his writing or looking up.*] Quite sure, thank you. Saranoff and I will manage it.

SERGIUS [*Grimly.*] Yes: we'll manage it. He finds out what to do; draws up the orders; and I sign em. Division of labor! [BLUNTSCHLI *passes him a paper.*] Another one? Thank you. [*He plants the paper squarely before him; sets his chair carefully parallel to it; and signs with his cheek on his elbow and his protruded tongue following the movements of his pen.*] This hand is more accustomed to the sword than to the pen.

PETKOFF It's very good of you, Bluntschli: it is indeed, to let yourself be put upon in this way. Now are you quite sure I can do nothing?

CATHERINE [*In a low warning tone.*] You can stop interrupting, Paul.

PETKOFF [*Starting and looking round at her.*] Eh? Oh! Quite right, my love: quite right. [*He takes his newspaper up again, but presently lets it drop.*] Ah, you havnt been campaigning, Catherine: you dont know how pleasant it is for us to sit here, after a good lunch, with nothing to do but enjoy ourselves. Theres only one thing I want to make me thoroughly comfortable.

CATHERINE What is that?

PETKOFF My old coat. I'm not at home in this one: I feel as if I were on parade.

CATHERINE My dear Paul, how absurd you are about that old coat! It must be hanging in the blue closet where you left it.

PETKOFF My dear Catherine, I tell you Ive looked there. Am I to believe my own eyes or not? [CATHERINE *rises and crosses the room to press the button of the electric bell.*] What are you shewing off that bell for? [*She looks at him majestically and silently resumes her chair and her needlework.*] My dear, if you think the obstinacy of your sex can make a coat out

of two old dressing gowns of Raina's, your waterproof, and my mackintosh, youre mistaken. Thats exactly what the blue closet contains at present.

[NICOLA *presents himself.*]

CATHERINE Nicola: go to the blue closet and bring your master's old coat here: the braided one he wears in the house.

NICOLA Yes, madame. [*He goes out.*]

PETKOFF Catherine.

CATHERINE Yes, Paul?

PETKOFF I bet you any piece of jewellery you like to order from Sofia against a week's housekeeping money that the coat isnt there.

CATHERINE Done, Paul!

PETKOFF [*Excited by the prospect of a gamble.*] Come: here's an opportunity for some sport. Wholl bet on it? Bluntschli, I'll give you six to one.

BLUNTSCHLI [*Imperturbably.*] It would be robbing you, major. Madame is sure to be right. [*Without looking up, he passes another batch of papers to* SERGIUS.]

SERGIUS [*Also excited.*] Bravo, Switzerland! Major, I bet my best charger against an Arab mare for Raina that Nicola finds the coat in the blue closet.

PETKOFF [*Eagerly.*] Your best char—

CATHERINE [*Hastily interrupting him.*] Dont be foolish, Paul. An Arabian mare will cost you 50,000 levas.

RAINA [*Suddenly coming out of her picturesque revery.*] Really, mother, if you are going to take the jewellery, I dont see why you should grudge me my Arab.

[NICOLA *comes back with the coat, and brings it to* PETKOFF, *who can hardly believe his eyes.*]

CATHERINE Where was it, Nicola?

NICOLA Hanging in the blue closet, madame.

PETKOFF Well, I am d—

CATHERINE [*Stopping him.*] Paul!

PETKOFF I could have sworn it wasnt there. Age is beginning to tell on me. I'm getting hallucinations. [*To* NICOLA.] Here: help me to change. Excuse me, Bluntschli. [*He begins changing coats,* NICOLA *acting as valet.*] Remember: I didnt take that bet of yours, Sergius. Youd better give Raina that Arab steed yourself, since youve roused her expectations. Eh, Raina? [*He looks round at her; but she is again rapt in the landscape. With a little gush of parental affection and pride, he points her out to them, and says.*] She's dreaming, as usual.

SERGIUS   Assuredly she shall not be the loser.

PETKOFF   So much the better for her. *I* shant come off so cheaply, I expect. [*The change is now complete.* NICOLA *goes out with the discarded coat.*] Ah, now I feel at home at last. [*He sits down and takes his newspaper with a grunt of relief.*]

BLUNTSCHLI   [*To* SERGIUS, *handing a paper.*] That's the last order.

PETKOFF   [*Jumping up.*] What! Finished?

BLUNTSCHLI   Finished.

PETKOFF   [*With childlike envy.*] Havnt you anything for me to sign?

BLUNTSCHLI   Not necessary. His signature will do.

PETKOFF   [*Inflating his chest and thumping it.*] Ah well, I think weve done a thundering good day's work. Can I do anything more?

BLUNTSCHLI   You had better both see the fellows that are to take these. [SERGIUS *rises.*] Pack them off at once; and shew them that Ive marked on the orders the time they should hand them in by. Tell them that if they stop to drink or tell stories—if theyre five minutes late, theyll have the skin taken off their backs.

SERGIUS   [*Stiffening indignantly.*] I'll say so. [*He strides to the door.*] And if one of them is man enough to spit in my face for insulting him, I'll buy his discharge and give him a pension. [*He goes out.*]

BLUNTSCHLI   [*Confidentially.*] Just see that he talks to them properly, major, will you?

PETKOFF   [*Officiously.*] Quite right, Bluntschli, quite right. I'll see to it. [*He goes to the door importantly, but hesitates on the threshold.*] By the bye, Catherine, you may as well come too. Theyll be far more frightened of you than of me.

CATHERINE   [*Putting down her embroidery.*] I daresay I had better. You would only splutter at them. [*She goes out,* PETKOFF *holding the door for her and following her.*]

BLUNTSCHLI   What an army! They make cannons out of cherry trees; and the officers send for their wives to keep discipline! [*He begins to fold and docket the papers.*]

[RAINA, *who has risen from the divan, marches slowly down the room with her hands clasped behind her, and looks mischievously at him.*]

RAINA   You look ever so much nicer than when we last met. [*He looks up, surprised.*] What have you done to yourself?

BLUNTSCHLI   Washed; brushed; good night's sleep and breakfast. Thats all.

RAINA   Did you get back safely that morning?

BLUNTSCHLI   Quite, thanks.

RAINA   Were they angry with you for running away from Sergius's charge?

BLUNTSCHLI   [*Grinning.*] No: they were glad; because theyd all just run away themselves.

RAINA   [*Going to the table, and leaning over it towards him.*] It must have made a lovely story for them: all that about me and my room.

BLUNTSCHLI   Capital story. But I only told it to one of them: a particular friend.

RAINA   On whose discretion you could absolutely rely?

BLUNTSCHLI   Absolutely.

RAINA   Hm! He told it all to my father and Sergius the day you exchanged the prisoners. [*She turns away and strolls carelessly across to the other side of the room.*]

BLUNTSCHLI   [*Deeply concerned, and half incredulous.*] No! You dont mean that, do you?

RAINA   [*Turning, with sudden earnestness.*] I do indeed. But they dont know that it was in this house you took refuge. If Sergius knew, he would challenge you and kill you in a duel.

BLUNTSCHLI   Bless me! then dont tell him.

RAINA   Please be serious, Captain Bluntschli. Can you not realize what it is to me to deceive him? I want to be quite perfect with Sergius: no meanness, no smallness, no deceit. My relation to him is the one really beautiful and noble part of my life. I hope you can understand that.

BLUNTSCHLI   [*Sceptically.*] You mean that you wouldnt like him to find out that the story about the ice pudding was a—a—a—You know.

RAINA   [*Wincing.*] Ah, dont talk of it in that flippant way. I lied: I know it. But I did it to save your life. He would have killed you. That was the second time I ever uttered a falsehood. [BLUNTSCHLI *rises quickly and looks doubtfully and somewhat severely at her.*] Do you remember the first time?

BLUNTSCHLI   I! No. Was I present?

RAINA   Yes; and I told the officer who was searching for you that you were not present.

BLUNTSCHLI   True. I should have remembered it.

RAINA   [*Greatly encouraged.*] Ah, it is natural that you should forget it first. It cost you nothing: it cost me a lie! A lie!

[*She sits down on the ottoman, looking straight before her with her hands clasped round her knee.* BLUNTSCHLI, *quite touched, goes to the ottoman with a particularly reassuring and considerate air, and sits down beside her.*]

BLUNTSCHLI   My dear young lady, dont let this worry you. Remember: I'm a soldier. Now what are the two things that happen to a soldier so often that he comes to think nothing of them? One is hearing people tell lies [RAINA *recoils.*]: the other is getting his life saved in all sorts of ways by all sorts of people.

RAINA   [*Rising in indignant protest.*] And so he becomes a creature incapable of faith and of gratitude.

BLUNTSCHLI   [*Making a wry face.*] Do you like gratitude? I dont. If pity is akin to love, gratitude is akin to the other thing.

RAINA   Gratitude! [*Turning on him.*] If you are incapable of gratitude you are incapable of any noble sentiment. Even animals are grateful. Oh, I see now exactly what you think of me! You were not surprised to hear me lie. To you it was something I probably did every day! every hour!! That is how men think of women. [*She paces the room tragically.*]

BLUNTSCHLI   [*Dubiously.*] Theres reason in everything. You said youd told only two lies in your whole life. Dear young lady: isnt that rather a short allowance? I'm quite a straightforward man myself; but it wouldnt last me a whole morning.

RAINA   [*Staring haughtily at him.*] Do you know, sir, that you are insulting me?

BLUNTSCHLI   I cant help it. When you strike that noble attitude and speak in that thrilling voice, I admire you; but I find it impossible to believe a single word you say.

RAINA   [*Superbly.*] Captain Bluntschli!

BLUNTSCHLI   [*Unmoved.*] Yes?

RAINA   [*Standing over him, as if she could not believe her senses.*] Do you mean what you said just now? Do you know what you said just now?

BLUNTSCHLI   I do.

RAINA   [*Gasping.*] I! I!!! [*She points to herself incredulously, meaning "I, Raina Petkoff, tell lies!" He meets her gaze unflinchingly. She suddenly sits down beside him, and adds, with a complete change of manner from the heroic to a babyish familiarity.*] How did you find me out?

BLUNTSCHLI   [*Promptly.*] Instinct, dear young lady. Instinct, and experience of the world.

RAINA   [*Wonderingly.*] Do you know, you are the first man I ever met who did not take me seriously?

BLUNTSCHLI   You mean, dont you, that I am the first man that has ever taken you quite seriously?

RAINA   Yes: I suppose I do mean that. [*Cosily, quite at her ease with him.*] How strange it is to be talked to in such a way! You know, Ive always gone on like that.

BLUNTSCHLI   You mean the—?

RAINA   I mean the noble attitude and the thrilling voice. [*They laugh together.*] I did it when I was a tiny child to my nurse. She believed in it. I do it before my parents. They believe in it. I do it before Sergius. He believes in it.

BLUNTSCHLI   Yes: he's a little in that line himself, isnt he?

RAINA   [*Startled.*] Oh! Do you think so?

BLUNTSCHLI   You know him better than I do.

RAINA   I wonder—I wonder is he? If I thought that—! [*Discouraged.*] Ah, well: what does it matter? I suppose, now youve found me out, you despise me.

BLUNTSCHLI   [*Warmly, rising.*] No, my dear young lady, no, no, no a thousand times. It's part of your youth: part of your charm. I'm like all the rest of them: the nurse, your parents, Sergius: I'm your infatuated admirer.

RAINA   [*Pleased.*] Really?

BLUNTSCHLI   [*Slapping his breast smartly with his hand, German fashion.*] Hand aufs Herz! Really and truly.

RAINA   [*Very happy.*] But what did you think of me for giving you my portrait.

BLUNTSCHLI   [*Astonished.*] Your portrait! You never gave me your portrait.

RAINA   [*Quickly.*] Do you mean to say you never got it?

BLUNTSCHLI   No. [*He sits down beside her, with renewed interest, and says, with some complacency*.] When did you send it to me?

RAINA [*Indignantly.*] I did not send it to you. [*She turns her head away, and adds, reluctantly.*] It was in the pocket of that coat.

BLUNTSCHLI [*Pursing his lips and rounding his eyes.*] Oh-o-oh! I never found it. It must be there still.

RAINA [*Springing up.*] There still! for my father to find the first time he puts his hand in his pocket! Oh, how could you be so stupid?

BLUNTSCHLI [*Rising also.*] It doesnt matter: I suppose it's only a photograph: how can he tell who it was intended for? Tell him he put it there himself.

RAINA [*Bitterly.*] Yes: that is so clever! isnt it? [*Distractedly.*] Oh! what shall I do?

BLUNTSCHLI Ah, I see. You wrote something on it. That was rash.

RAINA [*Vexed almost to tears.*] Oh, to have done such a thing for you, who care no more —except to laugh at me—oh! Are you sure nobody has touched it?

BLUNTSCHLI Well, I cant be quite sure. You see, I couldnt carry it about with me all the time: one cant take much luggage on active service.

RAINA What did you do with it?

BLUNTSCHLI When I got through to Pirot I had to put it in safe keeping somehow. I thought of the railway cloak room; but that the surest place to get looted in modern warfare. So I pawned it.

RAINA Pawned it!!!

BLUNTSCHLI I know it doesnt sound nice; but it was much the safest plan. I redeemed it the day before yesterday. Heaven only knows whether the pawnbroker cleared out the pockets or not.

RAINA [*Furious: throwing the words right into his face.*] You have a low shopkeeping mind. You think of things that would never come into a gentleman's head.

BLUNTSCHLI [*Phlegmatically.*] Thats the Swiss national character, dear lady. [*He returns to the table.*]

RAINA Oh, I wish I had never met you. [*She flounces away, and sits at the window fuming.*]

[LOUKA *comes in with a heap of letters and telegrams on her salver, and crosses, with her bold free gait, to the table. Her left sleeve is looped up to the shoulder with a brooch, shewing her naked arm, with a broad gilt bracelet covering the bruise.*]

LOUKA [*To* BLUNTSCHLI.] For you. [*She empties the salver with a fling on to the table.*] The messenger is waiting. [*She is determined not to be civil to an enemy, even if she must bring him his letters.*]

BLUNTSCHLI [*To* RAINA.] Will you excuse me: the last postal delivery that reached me was three weeks ago. These are the subsequent accumulations. Four telegrams: a week old. [*He opens one.*] Oho! Bad news!

RAINA [*Rising and advancing a little remorsefully.*] Bad news?

BLUNTSCHLI My father's dead. [*He looks at the telegram with his lips pursed, musing on the unexpected change in his arrangements.* LOUKA *crosses herself hastily.*]

RAINA Oh, how very sad!

BLUNTSCHLI Yes: I shall have to start for home in an hour. He has left a lot of big hotels behind him to be looked after. [*He takes up a fat letter in a long blue envelope.*] Here's a whacking letter from the family solicitor. [*He pulls out the enclosures and glances over them.*] Great Heavens! Seventy! Two hundred! [*In a crescendo of dismay.*] Four hundred! Four thousand!! Nine thousand six hundred!!! What on earth am I to do with them all?

RAINA [*Timidly.*] Nine thousand hotels?

BLUNTSCHLI Hotels! nonsense. If you only knew! Oh, it's too ridiculous! Excuse me: I must give my fellow orders about starting. [*He leaves the room hastily, with the documents in his hand.*]

LOUKA [*Knowing instinctively that she can annoy* RAINA *by disparaging* BLUNTSCHLI.] He has not much heart, that Swiss. He has not a word of grief for his poor father.

RAINA [*Bitterly.*] Grief! A man who has been doing nothing but killing people for years! What does he care? What does any soldier care? [*She goes to the door, restraining her tears with difficulty.*]

LOUKA Major Saranoff has been fighting too; and he has plenty of heart left. [RAINA, *at the door, draws herself up haughtily and goes out.*] Aha! I thought you wouldnt get much feeling out of your soldier. [*She is following* RAINA *when* NICOLA *enters with an armful of logs for the stove.*]

NICOLA [*Grinning amorously at her.*] Ive been

trying all the afternoon to get a minute alone with you, my girl. [*His countenance changes as he notices her arm.*] Why, what fashion is that of wearing your sleeve, child?

LOUKA   [*Proudly.*] My own fashion.

NICOLA   Indeed! If the mistress catches you, she'll talk to you. [*He puts the logs down, and seats himself comfortably on the ottoman.*]

LOUKA   Is that any reason why you should take it on yourself to talk to me?

NICOLA   Come! dont be so contrary with me. Ive some good news for you. [*She sits down beside him. He takes out some paper money.* LOUKA, *with an eager gleam in her eyes, tries to snatch it; but he shifts it quickly to his left hand, out of her reach.*] See! a twenty leva bill! Sergius gave me that, out of pure swagger. A fool and his money are soon parted. Theres ten levas more. The Swiss gave me that for backing up the mistress's and Raina's lies about him. He's no fool, he isnt. You should have heard old Catherine downstairs as polite as you please to me, telling me not to mind the Major being a little impatient; for they knew what a good servant I was—after making a fool and a liar of me before them all! The twenty will go to our savings; and you shall have the ten to spend if youll only talk to me so as to remind me I'm a human being. I get tired of being a servant occasionally.

LOUKA   Yes: sell your manhood for 30 levas, and buy me for 10! [*Rising scornfully.*] Keep your money. You were born to be a servant. I was not. When you set up your shop you will only be everybody's servant instead of somebody's servant. [*She goes moodily to the table and seats herself regally in* SERGIUS's *chair.*]

NICOLA   [*Picking up his logs, and going to the stove.*] Ah, wait til you see. We shall have our evenings to ourselves; and I shall be master in my own house, I promise you. [*He throws the logs down and kneels at the stove.*]

LOUKA   You shall never be master in mine.

NICOLA   [*Turning, still on his knees, and squatting down rather forlornly on his calves, daunted by her implacable disdain.*] You have a great ambition in you, Louka. Remember: if any luck comes to you, it was I that made a woman of you.

LOUKA   You!

NICOLA   [*Scrambling up and going at her.*] Yes, me. Who was it made you give up wearing a couple of pounds of false black hair on your head and reddening your lips and cheeks like any other Bulgarian girl? I did. Who taught you to trim your nails, and keep your hands clean, and be dainty about yourself, like a fine Russian lady? Me: do you hear that? me! [*She tosses her head defiantly; and he turns away, adding, more coolly.*] Ive often thought that if Raina were out of the way, and you just a little less of a fool and Sergius just a little more of one, you might come to be one of my grandest customers, instead of only being my wife and costing me money.

LOUKA   I believe you would rather be my servant than my husband. You would make more out of me. Oh, I know that soul of yours.

NICOLA   [*Going closer to her for greater emphasis.*] Never you mind my soul; but just listen to my advice. If you want to be a lady, your present behavior to me wont do at all, unless when we're alone. It's too sharp and impudent; and impudence is a sort of familiarity: it shews affection for me. And dont you try being high and mighty with me, either. Youre like all country girls: you think it's genteel to treat a servant the way I treat a stableboy. Thats only your ignorance; and dont you forget it. And dont be so ready to defy everybody. Act as if you expected to have your own way, not as if you expected to be ordered about. The way to get on as a lady is the same as the way to get on as a servant: youve got to know your place: thats the secret of it. And you may depend on me to know my place if you get promoted. Think over it, my girl. I'll stand by you: one servant should always stand by another.

LOUKA   [*Rising impatiently.*] Oh, I must behave in my own way. You take all the courage out of me with your cold-blooded wisdom. Go and put those logs on the fire: thats the sort of thing you understand.

[*Before* NICOLA *can retort,* SERGIUS *comes in. He checks himself a moment on seeing* LOUKA; *then goes to the stove.*]

SERGIUS   [*To* NICOLA.] I am not in the way of your work, I hope.

NICOLA   [*In a smooth, elderly manner.*] Oh no, sir: thank you kindly. I was only speaking to this foolish girl about her habit of running up here to the library whenever she gets a chance, to look at the books. Thats the worst of her education, sir: it gives her habits above her station. [*To* LOUKA.] Make that table tidy, Louka, for the Major. [*He goes out sedately.*]

[LOUKA, *without looking at* SERGIUS, *pretends to arrange the papers on the table. He crosses slowly to her, and studies the arrangement of her sleeve reflectively.*]

SERGIUS   Let me see: is there a mark there? [*He turns up the bracelet and sees the bruise made by his grasp. She stands motionless, not looking at him: fascinated, but on her guard.*] Ffff! Does it hurt?

LOUKA   Yes.

SERGIUS   Shall I cure it?

LOUKA   [*Instantly withdrawing herself proudly, but still not looking at him.*] No. You cannot cure it now.

SERGIUS   [*Masterfully.*] Quite sure? [*He makes a movement as if to take her in his arms.*]

LOUKA   Dont trifle with me, please. An officer should not trifle with a servant.

SERGIUS   [*Indicating the bruise with a merciless stroke of his forefinger.*] That was no trifle, Louka.

LOUKA   [*Flinching; then looking at him for the first time.*] Are you sorry?

SERGIUS   [*With measured emphasis, folding his arms.*] I am never sorry.

LOUKA   [*Wistfully.*] I wish I could believe a man could be as unlike a woman as that. I wonder are you really a brave man?

SERGIUS   [*Unaffectedly, relaxing his attitude.*] Yes: I am a brave man. My heart jumped like a woman's at the first shot; but in the charge I found that I was brave. Yes: that at least is real about me.

LOUKA   Did you find in the charge that the men whose fathers are poor like mine were any less brave than the men who are rich like you?

SERGIUS   [*With bitter levity.*] Not a bit. They all slashed and cursed and yelled like heroes. Psha! the courage to rage and kill is cheap. I have an English bull terrier who has as much of that sort of courage as the whole Bulgarian nation, and the whole Russian nation at its back. But he lets my groom thrash him, all the same. Thats your soldier all over! No, Louka: your poor men can cut throats; but they are afraid of their officers; they put up with insults and blows; they stand by and see one another punished like children: aye, and help to do it when they are ordered. And the officers!!! Well, [*With a short harsh laugh.*] I am an officer. Oh, [*Fervently.*] give me the man who will defy to the death any power on earth or in heaven that sets itself up against his own will and conscience: he alone is the brave man.

LOUKA   How easy it is to talk! Men never seem to me to grow up; they all have schoolboy's ideas. You dont know what true courage is.

SERGIUS   [*Ironically.*] Indeed! I am willing to be instructed. [*He sits on the ottoman, sprawling magnificently.*]

LOUKA   Look at me! how much am I allowed to have my own will? I have to get your room ready for you: to sweep and dust, to fetch and carry. How could that degrade me if it did not degrade you to have it done for you? But [*With subdued passion.*] if I were Empress of Russia, above everyone in the world, then!! Ah then, though according to you I could shew no courage at all, you should see, you should see.

SERGIUS   What would you do, most noble Empress?

LOUKA   I would marry the man I loved, which no other queen in Europe has the courage to do. If I loved you, though you would be as far beneath me as I am beneath you, I would dare to be the equal of my inferior. Would you dare as much if you loved me? No: if you felt the beginnings of love for me you would not let it grow. You would not dare· you would marry a rich man's daughter because you would be afraid of what other people would say of you.

SERGIUS   [*Bounding up.*] You lie: it is not so, by all the stars! If I loved you, and I were the Czar himself, I would set you on the throne by my side. You know that I love another woman, a woman as high above you as heaven is above earth. And you are jealous of her.

LOUKA   I have no reason to be. She will never marry you now. The man I told you of has come back. She will marry the Swiss.

SERGIUS   [*Recoiling.*] The Swiss!

LOUKA   A man worth ten of you. Then you can come to me; and I will refuse you. You are not good enough for me. [*She turns to the door.*]

SERGIUS   [*Springing after her and catching her*

fiercely in his arms.] I will kill the Swiss; and afterwards I will do as I please with you.

LOUKA [*In his arms, passive and steadfast.*] The Swiss will kill you, perhaps. He has beaten you in love. He may beat you in war.

SERGIUS [*Tormentedly.*] Do you think I believe that she—she! whose worst thoughts are higher than your best ones, is capable of trifling with another man behind my back?

LOUKA Do you think she would believe the Swiss if he told her now that I am in your arms?

SERGIUS [*Releasing her in despair.*] Damnation! Oh, damnation! Mockery! mockery everywhere! everything I think is mocked by everything I do. [*He strikes himself frantically on the breast.*] Coward! liar! fool! Shall I kill myself like a man, or live and pretend to laugh at myself? [*She again turns to go.*] Louka! [*She stops near the door.*] Remember: you belong to me.

LOUKA [*Turning.*] What does that mean? An insult?

SERGIUS [*Commandingly.*] It means that you love me, and that I have had you here in my arms, and will perhaps have you there again. Whether that is an insult I neither know nor care: take it as you please. But [*Vehemently.*] I will not be a coward and a trifler. If I choose to love you, I dare marry you, in spite of all Bulgaria. If these hands ever touch you again, they shall touch my affianced bride.

LOUKA We shall see whether you dare keep your word. And take care. I will not wait long.

SERGIUS [*Again folding his arms and standing motionless in the middle of the room.*] Yes: we shall see. And you shall wait my pleasure.

[BLUNTSCHLI, *much preoccupied, with his papers still in his hand, enters, leaving the door open for* LOUKA *to go out. He goes across to the table, glancing at her as he passes.* SERGIUS, *without altering his resolute attitude, watches him steadily.* LOUKA *goes out, leaving the door open.*]

BLUNTSCHLI [*Absently, sitting at the table as before, and putting down his papers.*] Thats a remarkable looking young woman.

SERGIUS [*Gravely, without moving.*] Captain Bluntschli.

BLUNTSCHLI Eh?

SERGIUS You have deceived me. You are my rival. I brook no rivals. At six o'clock I shall be in the drilling-ground on the Klissoura road, alone, on horseback, with my sabre. Do you understand?

BLUNTSCHLI [*Staring, but sitting quite at his ease.*] Oh, thank you: thats a cavalry man's proposal. I'm in the artillery; and I have the choice of weapons. If I go, I shall take a machine gun. And there shall be no mistake about the cartridges this time.

SERGIUS [*Flushing, but with deadly coldness.*] Take care, sir. It is not our custom in Bulgaria to allow invitations of that kind to be trifled with.

BLUNTSCHLI [*Warmly.*] Pooh! dont talk to me about Bulgaria. You dont know what fighting is. But have it your own way. Bring your sabre along. I'll meet you.

SERGIUS [*Fiercely delighted to find his opponent a man of spirit.*] Well said, Switzer. Shall I lend you my best horse?

BLUNTSCHLI No: damn your horse! thank you all the same my dear fellow. [RAINA *comes in, and hears the next sentence.*] I shall fight you on foot. Horseback's too dangerous: I dont want to kill you if I can help it.

RAINA [*Hurrying forward anxiously.*] I have heard what Captain Bluntschli said, Sergius. You are going to fight. Why? [SERGIUS *turns away in silence, and goes to the stove, where he stands watching her as she continues, to* BLUNTSCHLI.] What about?

BLUNTSCHLI I dont know: he hasnt told me. Better not interfere, dear young lady. No harm will be done: Ive often acted as sword instructor. He wont be able to touch me; and I'll not hurt him. It will save explanations. In the morning I shall be off home; and youll never see me or hear of me again. You and he will then make it up and live happily ever after.

RAINA [*Turning away deeply hurt, almost with a sob in her voice.*] I never said I wanted to see you again.

SERGIUS [*Striding forward.*] Ha! That is a confession.

RAINA [*Haughtily.*] What do you mean?

SERGIUS You love that man!

RAINA [*Scandalized.*] Sergius!

SERGIUS You allow him to make love to you behind my back, just as you treat me as your affianced husband behind his. Bluntschli, you knew our relations; and you deceived me. It is for that that I call you to account, not for having received favors *I* never enjoyed.

BLUNTSCHLI [*Jumping up indignantly.*] Stuff! Rubbish! I have received no favors. Why, the young lady doesnt even know whether I'm married or not.

RAINA [*Forgetting herself.*] Oh! [*Collapsing on the ottoman.*] Are you?

SERGIUS You see the young lady's concern, Captain Bluntschli. Denial is useless. You have enjoyed the privilege of being received in her own room, late at night—

BLUNTSCHLI [*Interrupting him pepperily.*] Yes, you blockhead! she received me with a pistol at her head. Your cavalry were at my heels. I'd have blown out her brains if she'd uttered a cry.

SERGIUS [*Taken aback.*] Bluntschli! Raina, is this true?

RAINA [*Rising in wrathful majesty.*] Oh, how dare you, how dare you?

BLUNTSCHLI Apologize, man: apologize. [*He resumes his seat at the table.*]

SERGIUS [*With the old measured emphasis, folding his arms.*] I never apologize!

RAINA [*Passionately.*] This is the doing of that friend of yours, Captain Bluntschli. It is he who is spreading this horrible story about me. [*She walks about excitedly.*]

BLUNTSCHLI No: he's dead. Burnt alive!

RAINA [*Stopping, shocked.*] Burnt alive!

BLUNTSCHLI Shot in the hip in a woodyard. Couldnt drag himself out. Your fellows' shells set the timber on fire and burnt him, with half a dozen other poor devils in the same predicament.

RAINA How horrible!

SERGIUS And how ridiculous! Oh, war! war! the dream of patriots and heroes! A fraud, Bluntschli. A hollow sham, like love.

RAINA [*Outraged.*] Like love! You say that before me!

BLUNTSCHLI Come, Saranoff: that matter is explained.

SERGIUS A hollow sham, I say. Would you have come back here if nothing had passed between you except at the muzzle of your pistol? Raina is mistaken about your friend who was burnt. He was not my informant.

RAINA Who then? [*Suddenly guessing the truth.*] Ah, Louka! my maid! my servant! You were with her this morning all that time after

—after—Oh, what sort of god is this I have been worshipping! [*He meets her gaze with sardonic enjoyment of her disenchantment. Angered all the more, she goes closer to him, and says, in a lower, intenser tone.*] Do you know that I looked out of the window as I went upstairs, to have another sight of my hero; and I saw something I did not understand then. I know now that you were making love to her.

SERGIUS [*With grim humor.*] You saw that?

RAINA Only too well. [*She turns away, and throws herself on the divan under the centre window, quite overcome.*]

SERGIUS [*Cynically.*] Raina, our romance is shattered. Life's a farce.

BLUNTSCHLI [*To Raina, whimsically.*] You see: he's found himself out now.

SERGIUS [*Going to him.*] Bluntschli, I have allowed you to call me a blockhead. You may now call me a coward as well. I refuse to fight you. Do you know why?

BLUNTSCHLI No; but it doesn't matter. I didnt ask the reason when you cried on; and I dont ask the reason now that you cry off. I'm a professional soldier: I fight when I have to, and am very glad to get out of it when I havnt to. Youre only an amateur: you think fighting's an amusement.

SERGIUS [*Sitting down at the table, nose to nose with him.*] You shall hear the reason all the same, my professional. The reason is that it takes two men— real men—men of heart, blood and honor—to make a genuine combat. I could no more fight with you than I could make love to an ugly woman. Youve no magnetism: youre not a man: youre a machine.

BLUNTSCHLI [*Apologetically.*] Quite true, quite true. I always was that sort of chap. I'm very sorry.

SERGIUS Psha!

BLUNTSCHLI But now that youve found that life isnt a farce, but something quite sensible and serious, what further obstacle is there to your happiness?

RAINA [*Rising.*] You are very solicitous about my happiness and his. Do you forget his new love—Louka? It is not you that he must fight now, but his rival, Nicola.

SERGIUS Rival!! [*Bounding half across the room.*]

RAINA Dont you know that theyre engaged?

SERGIUS Nicola! Are fresh abysses opening? Nicola!!

RAINA [*Sarcastically.*] A shocking sacrifice, isnt it? Such beauty! such intellect! such modesty! wasted on a middle-aged servant man. Really, Sergius, you cannot stand by and allow such a thing. It would be unworthy of your chivalry.

SERGIUS [*Losing all self-control.*] Viper! Viper! [*He rushes to and fro, raging.*]

BLUNTSCHLI Look here, Saranoff, youre getting the worst of this.

RAINA [*Getting angrier.*] Do you realize what he has done, Captain Bluntschli? He has set this girl as a spy on us; and her reward is that he makes love to her.

SERGIUS False! Monstrous!

RAINA Monstrous! [*Confronting him.*] Do you deny that she told you about Captain Bluntschli being in my room?

SERGIUS No; but—

RAINA [*Interrupting.*] Do you deny that you were making love to her when she told you?

SERGIUS No; but I tell you—

RAINA [*Cutting him short contemptuously.*] It is unnecessary to tell us anything more. That is quite enough for us. [*She turns away from him and sweeps majestically back to the window.*]

BLUNTSCHLI [*Quietly, as* SERGIUS, *in an agony of mortification, sinks on the ottoman, clutching his averted head between his fists.*] I told you you were getting the worst of it, Saranoff.

SERGIUS Tiger cat!

RAINA [*Running excitedly to* BLUNTSCHLI.] You hear this man calling me names, Captain Bluntschli?

BLUNTSCHLI What else can he do, dear lady? He must defend himself somehow. Come [*Very persuasively.*]: dont quarrel. What good does it do?

[RAINA, *with a gasp, sits down on the ottoman, and after a vain effort to look vexedly at* BLUNTSCHLI, *falls a victim to her sense of humor, and actually leans back babyishly against the writhing shoulder of* SERGIUS.]

SERGIUS Engaged to Nicola! Ha! ha! Ah well, Bluntschli, you are right to take this huge imposture of a world coolly.

RAINA [*Quaintly to* BLUNTSCHLI, *with an intuitive guess at his state of mind.*] I daresay you think us a couple of grown-up babies, dont you?

SERGIUS [*Grinning savagely.*] He does: he does. Swiss civilization nursetending Bulgarian barbarism, eh?

BLUNTSCHLI [*Blushing.*] Not at all, I assure you. I'm only very glad to get you two quieted. There! there! let's be pleasant and talk it over in a friendly way. Where is this other young lady?

RAINA Listening at the door, probably.

SERGIUS [*Shivering as if a bullet had struck him, and speaking with quiet but deep indignation.*] I will prove that that, at least, is a calumny. [*He goes with dignity to the door and opens it. A yell of fury bursts from him as he looks out. He darts into the passage, and returns dragging in* LOUKA, *whom he flings violently against the table, exclaiming.*] Judge her, Bluntschli. You, the cool impartial man: judge the eavesdropper.

[LOUKA *stands her ground, proud and silent.*]

BLUNTSCHLI [*Shaking his head.*] I mustnt judge her. I once listened myself outside a tent when there was a mutiny brewing. It's all a question of the degree of provocation. My life was at stake.

LOUKA My love was at stake. I am not ashamed.

RAINA [*Contemptuously.*] Your love! Your curiosity, you mean.

LOUKA [*Facing her and retorting her contempt with interest.*] My love, stronger than anything you can feel, even for your chocolate cream soldier.

SERGIUS [*With quick suspicion, to* LOUKA.] What does that mean?

LOUKA [*Fiercely.*] It means—

SERGIUS [*Interrupting her slightingly.*] Oh, I remember: the ice pudding. A paltry taunt, girl!

[MAJOR PETKOFF *enters, in his shirt-sleeves.*]

PETKOFF Excuse my shirtsleeves, gentlemen. Raina, somebody has been wearing that coat of mine: I'll swear it. Somebody with a differently shaped back. It's all burst open at the sleeve. Your mother is mending it. I wish she'd make haste: I shall catch cold. [*He looks more attentively at them.*] Is anything the matter?

RAINA No. [*She sits down at the stove, with a tranquil air.*]

SERGIUS Oh no. [*He sits down at the end of the table, as at first.*]

BLUNTSCHLI [*Who is already seated.*] Nothing. Nothing.

PETKOFF [*Sitting down on the ottoman in his old place.*] Thats all right. [*He notices* LOUKA.] Anything the matter, Louka?

LOUKA No, sir.

PETKOFF [*Genially.*] Thats all right. [*He sneezes.*] Go and ask your mistress for my coat, like a good girl, will you?

[NICOLA *enters with the coat.* LOUKA *makes a pretence of having business in the room by taking the little table with the hookah away to the wall near the windows.*]

RAINA [*Rising quickly as she sees the coat on* NICOLA's *arm.*] Here it is, papa. Give it to me, Nicola; and do you put some more wood on the fire. [*She takes the coat, and brings it to the* MAJOR, *who stands up to put it on.* NICOLA *attends to the fire.*]

PETKOFF [*To* RAINA, *teasing her affectionately.*] Aha! Going to be very good to poor old papa just for one day after his return from the wars, eh?

RAINA [*With solemn reproach.*] Ah, how can you say that to me, father?

PETKOFF Well, well, only a joke, little one. Come: give me a kiss. [*She kisses him.*] Now give me the coat.

RAINA No: I am going to put it on for you. Turn your back. [*He turns his back and feels behind him with his arms for the sleeves. She dexterously takes the photograph from the pocket and throws it on the table before* BLUNTSCHLI, *who covers it with a sheet of paper under the very nose of* SERGIUS, *who looks on amazed, with his suspicions roused in the highest degree. She then helps* PETKOFF *on with his coat.*] There, dear! Now are you comfortable?

PETKOFF Quite, little love. Thanks. [*He sits down; and* RAINA *returns to her seat near the stove.*] Oh, by the bye, Ive found something funny. Whats the meaning of this? [*He puts his hand into the picked pocket.*] Eh? Hallo! [*He tries the other pocket.*] Well, I could have sworn—! [*Much puzzled, he tries the breast pocket.*] I wonder—[*Trying the original pocket.*] Where can it—? [*He rises, exclaiming.*] Your mother's taken it!

RAINA [*Very red.*] Taken what?

PETKOFF Your photograph, with the inscription: "Raina, to her Chocolate Cream Soldier: a Souvenir." Now you know theres something more in this than meets the eye; and I'm going to find it out. [*Shouting.*] Nicola!

NICOLA [*Coming to him.*] Sir!

PETKOFF Did you spoil any pastry of Miss Raina's this morning?

NICOLA You heard Miss Raina say that I did, sir.

PETKOFF I know that, you idiot. Was it true?

NICOLA I am sure Miss Raina is incapable of saying anything that is not true, sir.

PETKOFF Are you? Then I'm not. [*Turning to the others.*] Come: do you think I dont see it all? [*He goes to* SERGIUS, *and slaps him on the shoulder.*] Sergius, youre the chocolate cream soldier, arnt you?

SERGIUS [*Starting up.*] I! A chocolate cream soldier! Certainly not.

PETKOFF Not! [*He looks at them. They are all very serious and very conscious.*] Do you mean to tell me that Raina sends things like that to other men?

SERGIUS [*Enigmatically.*] The world is not such an innocent place as we used to think, Petkoff.

BLUNTSCHLI [*Rising.*] It's all right, Major. I'm the chocolate cream soldier. [PETKOFF *and* SERGIUS *are equally astonished.*] The gracious young lady saved my life by giving me chocolate creams when I was starving: shall I ever forget their flavour! My late friend Stolz told you the story at Pirot. I was the fugitive.

PETKOFF You! [*He gasps.*] Sergius, do you remember how those two women went on this morning when we mentioned it? [SERGIUS *smiles cynically.* PETKOFF *confronts* RAINA *severely.*] Youre a nice young woman, arnt you?

RAINA [*Bitterly.*] Major Saranoff has changed his mind. And when I wrote that on the photograph, I did not know that Captain Bluntschli was married.

BLUNTSCHLI [*Startled into vehement protest.*] I'm not married.

RAINA [*With deep reproach.*] You said you were.

BLUNTSCHLI I did not. I positively did not. I never was married in my life.

PETKOFF [*Exasperated.*] Raina, will you kindly inform me, if I am not asking too much, which of these gentlemen you are engaged to?

RAINA To neither of them. This young lady [*Introducing* LOUKA, *who faces them all proudly.*] is the object of Major Saranoff's affections at present.

PETKOFF Louka! Are you mad, Sergius? Why, this girl's engaged to Nicola.

NICOLA I beg your pardon, sir. There is a mistake. Louka is not engaged to me.

PETKOFF Not engaged to you, you scoundrel! Why, you had twenty-five levas from me on the day of your betrothal; and she had that gilt bracelet from Miss Raina.

NICOLA [*With cool unction.*] We gave it out so, sir. But it was only to give Louka protection. She had a soul above her station; and I have been no more than her confidential servant. I intend, as you know, sir, to set up a shop later on in Sofia; and I look forward to her custom and recommendation should she marry into the nobility. [*He goes out with impressive discretion, leaving them all staring after him.*]

PETKOFF [*Breaking the silence.*] Well, I am—hm!

SERGIUS This is either the finest heroism or the most crawling baseness. Which is it, Bluntschli?

BLUNTSCHLI Never mind whether it's heroism or baseness. Nicola's the ablest man Ive met in Bulgaria. I'll make him manager of a hotel if he can speak French and German.

LOUKA [*Suddenly breaking out at* SERGIUS.] I have been insulted by everyone here. You set them the example. You owe me an apology.

[SERGIUS, *like a repeating clock of which the spring has been touched, immediately begins to fold his arms.*]

BLUNTSCHLI [*Before he can speak.*] It's no use. He never apologizes.

LOUKA Not to you, his equal and his enemy. To me, his poor servant, he will not refuse to apologize.

SERGIUS [*Approving.*] You are right. [*He bends his knee in his grandest manner.*] Forgive me.

LOUKA I forgive you. [*She timidly gives him her hand, which he kisses.*] That touch makes me your affianced wife.

SERGIUS [*Springing up.*] Ah, I forgot that.

LOUKA [*Coldly.*] You can withdraw if you like.

SERGIUS Withdraw! Never! You belong to me. [*He puts his arm about her.*]

[CATHERINE *comes in and finds* LOUKA *in Sergius's arms, with all the rest gazing at them in bewildered astonishment.*]

CATHERINE What does this mean?

[SERGIUS *releases* LOUKA.]

PETKOFF Well, my dear, it appears that Sergius is going to marry Louka instead of Raina. [*She is about to break out indignantly at him; he stops her by exclaiming testily.*] Dont blame me: Ive nothing to do with it. [*He retreats to the stove.*]

CATHERINE Marry Louka! Sergius, you are bound by your word to us!

SERGIUS [*Folding his arms.*] Nothing binds me.

BLUNTSCHLI [*Much pleased by this piece of common sense.*] Saranoff, your hand. My congratulations. These heroics of yours have their practical side after all. [*To* LOUKA.] Gracious young lady: the best wishes of a good Republican! [*He kisses her hand, to* RAINA's *great disgust, and returns to his seat.*]

CATHERINE Louka, you have been telling stories.

LOUKA I have done Raina no harm.

CATHERINE [*Haughtily.*] Raina!

[RAINA, *equally indignant, almost snorts at the liberty.*]

LOUKA I have a right to call her Raina: she calls me Louka. I told Major Saranoff she would never marry him if the Swiss gentleman came back.

BLUNTSCHLI [*Rising, much surprised.*] Hallo!

LOUKA [*Turning to* RAINA.] I thought you were fonder of him than of Sergius. You know best whether I was right.

BLUNTSCHLI What nonsense! I assure you, my dear Major, my dear Madame, the gracious young lady simply saved my life, nothing else. She never cared two straws for me. Why, bless my heart and soul, look at the young lady and look at me. She, rich, young, beautiful, with her imagination full of fairy princes and noble natures and cavalry charges and goodness knows what! And I, a commonplace Swiss soldier who hardly knows what a decent life is after fifteen years of barracks and battles: a vagabond, a man who has spoiled all his chances in life through an incurably romantic disposition, a man—

SERGIUS [*Starting as if a needle had pricked him and interrupting* BLUNTSCHLI *in incredulous amazement.*] Excuse me, Bluntschli:

what did you say had spoiled your chances in life?

BLUNTSCHLI [*Promptly.*] An incurably romantic disposition. I ran away from home twice when I was a boy. I went into the army instead of into my father's business. I climbed the balcony of this house when a man of sense would have dived into the nearest cellar. I came sneaking back here to have another look at the young lady when any other man of my age would have sent the coat back—

PETKOFF My coat!

BLUNTSCHLI —yes: thats the coat I mean—would have sent it back and gone quietly home. Do you suppose I am the sort of fellow a young girl falls in love with? Why, look at our ages! I'm thirty-four: I dont suppose the young lady is much over seventeen. [*This estimate produces a marked sensation, all the rest turning and staring at one another. He proceeds innocently.*] All that adventure which was life or death to me, was only a schoolgirl's game to her—chocolate creams and hide and seek. Heres the proof! [*He takes the photograph from the table.*] Now, I ask you, would a woman who took the affair seriously have sent me this and written on it "Raina, to her Chocolate Cream Soldier: a Souvenir"? [*He exhibits the photograph triumphantly, as if it settled the matter beyond all possibility of refutation.*]

PETKOFF Thats what I was looking for. How the deuce did it get there? [*He comes from the stove to look at it, and sits down on the ottoman.*]

BLUNTSCHLI [*To* RAINA, *complacently.*] I have put everything right, I hope, gracious young lady.

RAINA [*Going to the table to face him.*] I quite agree with your account of yourself. You are a romantic idiot. [BLUNTSCHLI *is unspeakably taken aback.*] Next time, I hope you will know the difference between a schoolgirl of seventeen and a woman of twenty-three.

BLUNTSCHLI [*Stupefied.*] Twenty-three!

[RAINA *snaps the photograph contemptuously from his hand; tears it up; throws the pieces in his face; and sweeps back to her former place.*]

SERGIUS [*With grim enjoyment of his rival's discomfiture.*] Bluntschli, my one last belief is gone. Your sagacity is a fraud, like everything else. You have less sense than even I.

BLUNTSCHLI [*Overwhelmed.*] Twenty-three! Twenty-three!! [*He considers.*] Hm! [*Swiftly making up his mind and coming to his host.*] In that case, Major Petkoff, I beg to propose formally to become a suitor for your daughter's hand, in place of Major Saranoff retired.

RAINA You dare!

BLUNTSCHLI If you were twenty-three when you said those things to me this afternoon, I shall take them seriously.

CATHERINE [*Loftily polite.*] I doubt, sir, whether you quite realize either my daughter's position or that of Major Sergius Saranoff, whose place you propose to take. The Petkoffs and the Saranoffs are known as the richest and most important families in the country. Our position is almost historical: we can go back for twenty years.

PETKOFF Oh, never mind that, Catherine. [*To* BLUNTSCHLI.] We should be most happy, Bluntschli, if it were only a question of your position; but hang it, you know, Raina is accustomed to a very comfortable establishment. Sergius keeps twenty horses.

BLUNTSCHLI But who wants twenty horses? We're not going to keep a circus.

CATHERINE [*Severely.*] My daughter, sir, is accustomed to a first-rate stable.

RAINA Hush, mother: youre making me ridiculous.

BLUNTSCHLI Oh well, if it comes to a question of an establishment, here goes! [*He darts impetuously to the table; seizes the papers in the blue envelope; and turns to* SERGIUS.] How many horses did you say?

SERGIUS Twenty, noble Switzer.

BLUNTSCHLI I have two hundred horses. [*They are amazed.*] How many carriages?

SERGIUS Three.

BLUNTSCHLI I have seventy. Twenty-four of them will hold twelve inside, besides two on the box, without counting the driver and conductor. How many tablecloths have you?

SERGIUS How the deuce do I know?

BLUNTSCHLI Have you four thousand?

SERGIUS No.

BLUNTSCHLI I have. I have nine thousand six hundred pairs of sheets and blankets, with two thousand four hundred eider-down quilts.

I have ten thousand knives and forks, and the same quantity of dessert spoons. I have three hundred servants. I have six palatial establishments, besides two livery stables, a tea garden, and a private house. I have four medals for distinguished services; I have the rank of an officer and the standing of a gentleman; and I have three native languages. Shew me any man in Bulgaria that can offer as much!

PETKOFF [*With childish awe.*] Are you Emperor of Switzerland?

BLUNTSCHLI My rank is the highest in Switzerland: I am a free citizen.

CATHERINE Then, Captain Bluntschli, since you are my daughter's choice—

RAINA [*Mutinously.*] He's not.

CATHERINE [*Ignoring her.*]—I shall not stand in the way of her happiness. [PETKOFF *is about to speak.*] That is Major Petkoff's feeling also.

PETKOFF Oh, I shall be only too glad. Two hundred horses! Whew!

SERGIUS What says the lady?

RAINA [*Pretending to sulk.*] The lady says that he can keep his tablecloths and his omnibuses. I am not here to be sold to the highest bidder. [*She turns her back on him.*]

BLUNTSCHLI I wont take that answer. I appealed to you as a fugitive, a beggar, and a starving man. You accepted me. You gave me your hand to kiss, your bed to sleep in, and your roof to shelter me.

RAINA I did not give them to the Emperor of Switzerland.

BLUNTSCHLI Thats just what I say. [*He catches her by the shoulders and turns her face to face with him.*] Now tell us whom you did give them to.

RAINA [*Succumbing with a shy smile.*] To my chocolate cream soldier.

BLUNTSCHLI [*With a boyish laugh of delight.*] Thatll do. Thank you. [*He looks at his watch and suddenly becomes businesslike.*] Time's up, Major. Youve managed those regiments so well that youre sure to be asked to get rid of some of the infantry of the Timok division. Send them home by way of Lom Palanka. Saranoff, dont get married until I come back: I shall be here punctually at five in the evening on Tuesday fortnight. Gracious ladies [*His heels click.*] good evening. [*He makes them a military bow, and goes.*]

SERGIUS What a man! Is he a man?

The Glass Menagerie
TENNESSEE WILLIAMS*
1914–

THE AUTHOR'S PRODUCTION NOTES

Being a "memory play," *The Glass Menagerie* can be presented with unusual freedom of convention. Because of its considerably delicate or tenuous material, atmospheric touches and subtleties of direction play a particularly important part. Expressionism and all other unconventional techniques in drama have only one valid aim, and that is a closer approach to truth. When a play employs unconventional techniques, it is not, or certainly shouldn't be, trying to escape its responsibility of dealing with reality, or interpreting experience, but is actually, or should be, attempting to find a closer approach, a more penetrating and vivid expression of things as they are. The straight realistic play with its genuine frigidaire and authentic ice-cubes, its characters that speak exactly as its audience speaks, corresponds to the academic landscape and has the same virtue of a photographic likeness. Everyone should know nowadays the unimportance of the photographic in art: that truth, life, or reality is an organic thing which the poetic imagination can represent or suggest, in essence, only through transformation, through changing into other forms than those which were merely present in appearance.

These remarks are not meant as a preface only to this particular play. They have to do with a conception of a new, plastic theatre which must take the place of the exhausted theatre of realistic conventions if the theatre is to resume vitality as a part of our culture.

The Screen Device

There is *only one important difference between the original and acting version of the play* and that is the *omission* in the latter of the device which I tentatively included in my *original* script. This device was the use of a screen on which were projected magic-lantern slides bear-

---

* See Lincoln Barnett's sketch, p. 784, particularly the part that discusses *The Glass Menagerie*.

ing images or titles. I do not regret the omission of this device from the present Broadway production. The extraordinary power of Miss Taylor's* performance made it suitable to have the utmost simplicity in the physical production. But I think it may be interesting to some readers to see how this device was conceived. So I am putting it into the published manuscript. These images and legends, projected from behind, were cast on a section of wall between the front-room and dining-room areas, which should be indistinguishable from the rest when not in use.

The purpose of this will probably be apparent. It is to give accent to certain values in each scene. Each scene contains a particular point (or several) which is structurally the most important. In an episodic play, such as this, the basic structure or narrative line may be obscured from the audience; the effect may seem fragmentary rather than architectural. This may not be the fault of the play so much as a lack of attention in the audience. The legend or image upon the screen will strengthen the effect of what is merely allusion in the writing and allow the primary point to be made more simply and lightly than if the entire responsibility were on the spoken lines. Aside from this structural value, I think the screen will have a definite emotional appeal, less definable but just as important. An imaginative producer or director may invent many other uses for this device than those indicated in the present script. In fact the possibilities of the device seem much larger to me than the instance of this play can possibly utilize.

The Music

Another extra-literary accent in this play is provided by the use of music. A single recurring tune, "The Glass Menagerie," is used to give emotional emphasis to suitable passages. This tune is like circus music, not when you are on the grounds or in the immediate vicinity of the parade, but when you are at some distance and very likely thinking of something else. It seems under those circumstances to continue almost interminably and it weaves in and out of your preoccupied consciousness; then it is the lightest, most delicate music in the world and perhaps

the saddest. It expresses the surface vivacity of life with the underlying strain of immutable and inexpressible sorrow. When you look at a piece of delicately spun glass you think of two things: how beautiful it is and how easily it can be broken. Both of those ideas should be woven into the recurring tune, which dips in and out of the play as if it were carried on a wind that changes. It serves as a thread of connection and allusion between the narrator with his separate point in time and space and the subject of his story. Between each episode it returns as reference to the emotion, nostalgia, which is the first condition of the play. It is primarily Laura's music and therefore comes out most clearly when the play focuses upon her and the lovely fragility of glass which is her image.

The Lighting

The lighting in the play is not realistic. In keeping with the atmosphere of memory, the stage is dim. Shafts of light are focused on selected areas or actors, sometimes in contradistinction to what is the apparent center. For instance, in the quarrel scene between Tom and Amanda, in which Laura has no active part, the clearest pool of light is on her figure. This is also true of the supper scene, when her silent figure on the sofa should remain the visual center. The light upon Laura should be distinct from the others, having a peculiar pristine clarity such as light used in early religious portraits of female saints or madonnas. A certain correspondence to light in religious paintings, such as El Greco's, where the figures are radiant in atmosphere that is relatively dusky, could be effectively used throughout the play. (It will also permit a more effective use of the screen.) A free, imaginative use of light can be of enormous value in giving a mobile, plastic quality to plays of a more or less static nature.

CHARACTERS

AMANDA WINGFIELD, *the mother*
A little woman of great but confused vitality clinging frantically to another time and place. Her characterization must be carefully created, not copied from type. She is not paranoiac, but her life is paranoia. There is much to admire in

* Laurette Taylor, who played memorably the part of Amanda in the Broadway production, 1945.

Amanda, and as much to love and pity as there is to laugh at. Certainly she has endurance and a kind of heroism, and though her foolishness makes her unwittingly cruel at times, there is tenderness in her slight person.

LAURA WINGFIELD, *her daughter*

Amanda, having failed to establish contact with reality, continues to live vitally in her illusions, but Laura's situation is even graver. A childhood illness has left her crippled, one leg slightly shorter than the other, and held in a brace. This defect need not be more than suggested on the stage. Stemming from this, Laura's separation increases till she is like a piece of her own glass collection, too exquisitely fragile to move from the shelf.

TOM WINGFIELD, *her son*

And the narrator of the play. A poet with a job in a warehouse. His nature is not remorseless, but to escape from a trap he has to act without pity.

JIM O'CONNOR, *the gentleman caller*

A nice, ordinary, young man.

SCENE

An Alley in St. Louis

PART I

Preparation for a Gentleman Caller

PART II

The Gentleman Calls

TIME

Now [c. 1944] and the Past

SCENE ONE

The Wingfield apartment is in the rear of the building, one of those vast hive-like conglomerations of cellular living-units that flower as warty growths in overcrowded urban centers of lower middle-class population and are symptomatic of the impulse of this largest and fundamentally enslaved section of American society to avoid fluidity and differentiation and to exist and function as one interfused mass of automatism.

The apartment faces an alley and is entered by a fire escape, a structure whose name is a touch of accidental poetic truth, for all of these huge buildings are always burning with the slow and implacable fires of human desperation. The fire escape is included in the set—that is, the landing of it and steps descending from it.

The scene is memory and is therefore nonrealistic. Memory takes a lot of poetic license. It omits some details; others are exaggerated, according to the emotional value of the articles it touches, for memory is seated predominantly in the heart. The interior is therefore rather dim and poetic.

At the rise of the curtain, the audience is faced with the dark, grim rear wall of the Wingfield tenement. This building, which runs parallel to the footlights, is flanked on both sides by dark, narrow alleys which run into murky canyons of tangled clotheslines, garbage cans, and the sinister lattice-work of neighboring fire escapes. It is up and down these side alleys that exterior entrances and exits are made, during the play. At the end of TOM's *opening commentary, the dark tenement wall slowly reveals (by means of a transparency) the interior of the ground floor Wingfield apartment.*

Downstage is the living room, which also serves as a sleeping room for LAURA, *the sofa unfolding to make her bed. Upstage, center, and divided by a wide arch or second proscenium with transparent faded portieres (or second curtain), is the dining room. In an old-fashioned what-not in the living room are seen scores of transparent glass animals. A blown-up photograph of the father hangs on the wall of the living room, facing the audience, to the left of the archway. It is the face of a very handsome young man in a doughboy's First World War cap. He is gallantly smiling, ineluctably smiling, as if to say, "I will be smiling forever."*

The audience hears and sees the opening scene in the dining room through both the transparent fourth wall of the building and the transparent gauze portieres of the dining-room arch. It is during this revealing scene that the fourth wall slowly ascends, out of sight. This transparent exterior wall is not brought down again until the very end of the play, during TOM's *final speech.*

The narrator is an undisguised convention of the play. He takes whatever license with dramatic convention is convenient to his purposes.

TOM *enters dressed as a merchant sailor from alley, stage left, and strolls across the front of the stage to the fire escape. There he stops and lights a cigarette. He addresses the audience.*

TOM Yes, I have tricks in my pocket, I have things up my sleeve. But I am the opposite of a stage magician. He gives you illusion that has the appearance of truth. I give you truth in the pleasant disguise of illusion.

To begin with, I turn back time. I reverse it to that quaint period, the thirties, when the huge middle class of America was matriculating in a school for the blind. Their eyes had failed them, or they had failed their eyes, and so they were having their fingers pressed forcibly down on the fiery Braille alphabet of a dissolving economy.

In Spain there was revolution. Here there was only shouting and confusion.

In Spain there was Guernica. Here there were disturbances of labor, sometimes pretty violent, in otherwise peaceful cities such as Chicago, Cleveland, Saint Louis . . .

This is the social background of the play.
[MUSIC]

The play is memory.

Being a memory play, it is dimly lighted, it is sentimental, it is not realistic.

In memory everything seems to happen to music. That explains the fiddle in the wings.

I am the narrator of the play, and also a character in it.

The other characters are my mother, Amanda, my sister, Laura, and a gentleman caller who appears in the final scenes.

He is the most realistic character in the play, being an emissary from a world of reality that we were somehow set apart from.

But since I have a poet's weakness for symbols, I am using this character also as a symbol; he is the long delayed but always expected something that we live for.

There is a fifth character in the play who doesn't appear except in this larger-than-life-size photograph over the mantel.

This is our father who left us a long time ago.

He was a telephone man who fell in love with long distances; he gave up his job with the telephone company and skipped the light fantastic out of town . . .

The last we heard of him was a picture post-card from Mazatlan, on the Pacific coast of Mexico, containing a message of two words—

"Hello—Good-bye!" and no address.

I think the rest of the play will explain itself. . . .
[AMANDA's *voice becomes audible through the portieres.*]

[LEGEND ON SCREEN: "OÙ SONT LES NEIGES" [1]]

[*He divides the portieres and enters the upstage area.*]
[AMANDA *and* LAURA *are seated at a drop-leaf table. Eating is indicated by gestures without food or utensils.* AMANDA *faces the audience,* TOM *and* LAURA *are seated in profile. The interior has lit up softly and through the scrim we see* AMANDA *and* LAURA *seated at the table in the upstage area.*]
AMANDA [*Calling.*] Tom?
TOM Yes, Mother.
AMANDA We can't say grace until you come to the table!
TOM Coming, Mother. [*He bows slightly and withdraws, reappearing a few moments later in his place at the table.*]
AMANDA [*To her son.*] Honey, don't push with your *fingers.* If you have to push with something, the thing to push with is a crust of bread. And chew—chew! Animals have sections in their stomachs which enable them to digest food without mastication, but human beings are supposed to chew their food before they swallow it down. Eat food leisurely, son, and really enjoy it. A well-cooked meal has lots of delicate flavors that have to be held in the mouth for appreciation. So chew your food and give your salivary glands a chance to function!
[TOM *deliberately lays his imaginary fork down and pushes his chair back from the table.*]
TOM I haven't enjoyed one bite of this dinner because of your constant directions on how to eat it. It's you that make me rush through meals with your hawk-like attention to every bite I take. Sickening—spoils my appetite—

1 "Where are the snows [of yesteryear]?" part of the refrain of François Villon's "Ballade of Dead Ladies."

all this discussion of—animals' secretion—salivary glands—mastication!

AMANDA [*Lightly.*] Temperament like a Metropolitan star! [*He rises and crosses downstage.*] You're not excused from the table.

TOM I'm getting a cigarette.

AMANDA You smoke too much.

[LAURA *rises.*]

LAURA I'll bring in the blanc mange.

[*He remains standing with his cigarette by the portieres during the following.*]

AMANDA [*Rising.*] No, sister, no, sister—you be the lady this time and I'll be the darky.

LAURA I'm already up.

AMANDA Resume your seat, little sister—I want you to stay fresh and pretty—for gentlemen callers!

LAURA I'm not expecting any gentlemen callers.

AMANDA [*Crossing out to kitchenette. Airily.*] Sometimes they come when they are least expected! Why, I remember one Sunday afternoon in Blue Mountain—[*Enters kitchenette.*]

TOM I know what's coming!

LAURA Yes. But let her tell it.

TOM Again?

LAURA She loves to tell it.

[AMANDA *returns with bowl of dessert.*]

AMANDA One Sunday afternoon in Blue Mountain—your mother received—*seventeen!*—gentlemen callers! Why, sometimes there weren't chairs enough to accommodate them all. We had to send the nigger over to bring in folding chairs from the parish house.

TOM [*Remaining at portieres.*] How did you entertain those gentlemen callers?

AMANDA I understood the art of conversation!

TOM I bet you could talk.

AMANDA Girls in those days *knew* how to talk, I can tell you.

TOM Yes?

[IMAGINE: AMANDA AS A GIRL ON A PORCH, GREETING CALLERS]

AMANDA They knew how to entertain their gentlemen callers. It wasn't enough for a girl to be possessed of a pretty face and a graceful figure—although I wasn't slighted in either respect. She also needed to have a nimble wit and a tongue to meet all occasions.

TOM What did you talk about?

AMANDA Things of importance going on in the world! Never anything coarse or common or vulgar. [*She addresses* TOM *as though he were seated in the vacant chair at the table though he remains by portieres. He plays this scene as though he held the book.*] My callers were gentlemen—all! Among my callers were some of the most prominent young planters of the Mississippi Delta—planters and sons of planters!

[TOM *motions for music and a spot of light on* AMANDA.]

[*Her eyes lift, her face glows, her voice becomes rich and elegiac.*]

[SCREEN LEGEND: "OÙ SONT LES NEIGES"]

There was young Champ Laughlin who later became vice-president of the Delta Planters Bank.

Hadley Stevenson who was drowned in Moon Lake and left his widow one hundred and fifty thousand in Government bonds.

There were the Cutrere brothers, Wesley and Bates. Bates was one of my bright particular beaux! He got in a quarrel with that wild Wainwright boy. They shot it out on the floor of Moon Lake Casino. Bates was shot through the stomach . Died in the ambulance on his way to Memphis. His widow was also well-provided for, came into eight or ten thousand acres, that's all. She married him on the rebound—never loved her—carried my picture on him the night he died!

And there was that boy that every girl in the Delta had set her cap for! That beautiful, brilliant young Fitzhugh boy from Greene County!

TOM What did he leave his widow?

AMANDA He never married! Gracious, you talk as though all of my old admirers had turned up their toes to the daisies!

TOM Isn't this the first you've mentioned that still survives?

AMANDA That Fitzhugh boy went North and made a fortune—came to be known as the Wolf of Wall Street! He had the Midas touch, whatever he touched turned to gold!

And I could have been Mrs. Duncan J. Fitzhugh, mind you! But—I picked your *father!*

LAURA [*Rising.*] Mother, let me clear the table.

AMANDA No, dear, you go in front and study your typewriter chart. Or practice your shorthand a little. Stay fresh and pretty!—It's almost time for our gentlemen callers to start arriving. [*She flounces girlishly toward the kitchenette.*] How many do you suppose we're going to entertain this afternoon?

[TOM *throws down the paper and jumps up with a groan.*]

LAURA [*Alone in the dining room.*] I don't believe we're going to receive any, Mother.

AMANDA [*Reappearing, airily.*] What? No one —not one? You must be joking! [LAURA *nervously echoes her laugh. She slips in a fugitive manner through the half-open portieres and draws them gently behind her. A shaft of very clear light is thrown on her face against the faded tapestry of the curtains.* MUSIC: "THE GLASS MENAGERIE" UNDER FAINTLY. *Lightly.*] Not one gentleman caller? It can't be true! There must be a flood, there must have been a tornado!

LAURA It isn't a flood, it's not a tornado, Mother. I'm just not popular like you were in Blue Mountain. . . . [TOM *utters another groan.* LAURA *glances at him with a faint, apologetic smile Her voice catching a little.*] Mother's afraid I'm going to be an old maid.

[*The Scene Dims Out with "Glass Menagerie" Music.*]

SCENE TWO

"Laura, Haven't You Ever Liked Some Boy?" On the dark stage the screen is lighted with the image of blue roses.

Gradually LAURA'S *figure becomes apparent and the screen goes out.*

The music subsides.

LAURA *is seated in the delicate ivory chair at the small clawfoot table.*

She wears a dress of soft violet material for a kimono—her hair tied back from her forehead with a ribbon.

She is washing and polishing her collection of glass.

AMANDA *appears on the fire-escape steps. At the sound of her ascent,* LAURA *catches her breath, thrusts the bowl of ornaments away and seats herself stiffly before the diagram of the typewriter keyboard as though it held her spellbound.*

Something has happened to AMANDA. *It is written in her face as she climbs to the landing: a look that is grim and hopeless and a little absurd.*

She has on one of those cheap or imitation velvety-looking cloth coats with imitation fur collar. Her hat is five or six years old, one of those dreadful cloche hats that were worn in the late twenties and she is clasping an enormous black patent-leather pocketbook with nickle clasps and initials. This is her full-dress outfit, the one she usually wears to the D.A.R.

Before entering she looks through the door.

She purses her lips, opens her eyes very wide, rolls them upward and shakes her head.

Then she slowly lets herself in the door. Seeing her mother's expression LAURA *touches her lips with a nervous gesture.*

LAURA Hello, Mother, I was—[*She makes a nervous gesture toward the chart on the wall.* AMANDA *leans against the shut door and stares at* LAURA *with a martyred look.*]

AMANDA Deception? Deception? [*She slowly removes her hat and gloves, continuing the sweet suffering stare. She lets the hat and gloves fall on the floor—a bit of acting.*]

LAURA [*Shakily.*] How was the D.A.R. meeting? [AMANDA *slowly opens her purse and removes a dainty white handkerchief which she shakes out delicately and delicately touches to her lips and nostrils.*] Didn't you go to the D.A.R. meeting, Mother?

AMANDA [*Faintly, almost inaudibly.*]—No—No. [*Then more forcibly.*] I did not have the strength—to go to the D.A.R. In fact, I did not have the courage! I wanted to find a hole in the ground and hide myself in it forever! [*She crosses slowly to the wall and removes the diagram of the typewriter keyboard. She holds it in front of her for a second, staring at it sweetly and sorrowfully—then bites her lips and tears it in two pieces.*]

LAURA [*Faintly.*] Why did you do that, Mother? [AMANDA *repeats the same procedure with the chart of the Gregg Alphabet.*] Why are you—

AMANDA Why? Why? How old are you, Laura?

LAURA Mother, you know my age.

AMANDA I thought that you were an adult; it seems that I was mistaken. [*She crosses slowly to the sofa and sinks down and stares at* LAURA.]

LAURA Please don't stare at me, Mother.

[AMANDA *closes her eyes and lowers her head. Count ten.*]

AMANDA   What are we going to do, what is going to become of us, what is the future? [*Count ten.*]

LAURA   Has something happened, Mother? [AMANDA *draws a long breath and takes out the handkerchief again. Dabbing process.*] Mother, has—something happened?

AMANDA   I'll be all right in a minute, I'm just bewildered—[*Count five.*]—by life. . . .

LAURA   Mother, I wish that you would tell me what's happened!

AMANDA   As you know, I was supposed to be inducted into my office at the D.A.R. this afternoon. [IMAGE: A SWARM OF TYPEWRITERS] But I stopped off at Rubicam's Business College to speak to your teachers about your having a cold and ask them what progress they thought you were making down there.

LAURA   Oh. . . .

AMANDA   I went to the typing instructor and introduced myself as your mother. She didn't know who you were. Wingfield, she said. We don't have any such student enrolled at the school!

I assured her she did, that you had been going to classes since early in January.

"I wonder," she said, "if you could be talking about that terribly shy little girl who dropped out of school after only a few days' attendance?"

"No," I said, "Laura, my daughter, has been going to school every day for the past six weeks!"

"Excuse me," she said. She took the attendance book out and there was your name, unmistakably printed, and all the dates you were absent until they decided that you had dropped out of school.

I still said, "No, there must have been some mistake! There must have been some mix-up in the records!"

And she said, "No—I remember her perfectly now. Her hands shook so that she couldn't hit the right keys! The first time we gave a speed-test, she broke down completely —was sick at the stomach and almost had to be carried into the wash-room! After that morning she never showed up any more. We phoned the house but never got any answer"

—while I was working at Famous and Barr, I suppose, demonstrating those—Oh!

I felt so weak I could barely keep on my feet!

I had to sit down while they got me a glass of water!

Fifty dollars' tuition, all of our plans—my hopes and ambitions for you—just gone up the spout, just gone up the spout like that. [LAURA *draws a long breath and gets awkwardly to her feet. She crosses to the victrola and winds it up.*] What are you doing?

LAURA   Oh! [*She releases the handle and returns to her seat.*]

AMANDA   Laura, where have you been going when you've gone out pretending that you were going to business college?

LAURA   I've just been going out walking.

AMANDA   That's not true.

LAURA   It is. I just went walking.

AMANDA   Walking? Walking? In winter? Deliberately courting pneumonia in that light coat? Where did you walk to, Laura?

LAURA   All sorts of places—mostly in the park.

AMANDA   Even after you'd started catching that cold?

LAURA   It was the lesser of two evils, Mother.

[IMAGE: WINTER SCENE IN PARK]

I couldn't go back up. I—threw up—on the floor!

AMANDA   From half past seven till after five every day you mean to tell me you walked around in the park, because you wanted to make me think that you were still going to Rubicam's Business College?

LAURA   It wasn't as bad as it sounds. I went inside places to get warmed up.

AMANDA   Inside where?

LAURA   I went in the art museum and the bird-houses at the Zoo. I visited the penguins every day! Sometimes I did without lunch and went to the movies. Lately I've been spending most of my afternoons in the Jewel-box, that big glass house where they raise the tropical flowers.

AMANDA   You did all this to deceive me, just for deception? [LAURA *looks down.*] Why?

LAURA   Mother, when you're disappointed, you get that awful suffering look on your face, like the picture of Jesus' mother in the museum!

AMANDA Hush!

LAURA I couldn't face it.

[*Pause. A whisper of strings.*]

[LEGEND: "THE CRUST OF HUMILITY"]

AMANDA [*Hopelessly fingering the huge pocketbook.*] So what are we going to do the rest of our lives? Stay home and watch the parades go by? Amuse ourselves with the glass menagerie, darling? Eternally play those worn-out phonograph records your father left as a painful reminder of him?

We won't have a business career—we've given that up because it gave us nervous indigestion! [*Laughs wearily.*] What is there left but dependency all our lives? I know so well what becomes of unmarried women who aren't prepared to occupy a position. I've seen such pitiful cases in the South—barely tolerated spinsters living upon the grudging patronage of sister's husband or brother's wife! —stuck away in some little mouse-trap of a room—encouraged by one in-law to visit another—little birdlike women without any nest —eating the crust of humility all their life!

Is that the future that we've mapped out for ourselves?

I swear it's the only alternative I can think of!

It isn't a very pleasant alternative, is it?

Of course—some girls *do marry*.

[LAURA *twists her hands nervously.*]

Haven't you ever liked some boy?

LAURA Yes. I liked one once. [*Rises.*] I came across his picture a while ago.

AMANDA [*With some interest.*] He gave you his picture?

LAURA No, it's in the year-book.

AMANDA [*Disappointed.*] Oh—a high-school boy.

[SCREEN IMAGE: JIM AS A HIGH-SCHOOL HERO BEARING A SILVER CUP]

LAURA Yes. His name was Jim. [LAURA *lifts the heavy annual from the claw-foot table.*] Here he is in *The Pirates of Penzance*.

AMANDA [*Absently.*] The what?

LAURA The operetta the senior class put on. He had a wonderful voice and we sat across the aisle from each other Mondays, Wednesdays, and Fridays in the Aud. Here he is with the silver cup for debating! See his grin?

AMANDA [*Absently.*] He must have had a jolly disposition.

LAURA He used to call me—Blue Roses.

[IMAGE: BLUE ROSES]

AMANDA Why did he call you such a name as that?

LAURA When I had that attack of pleurosis—he asked me what was the matter when I came back. I said pleurosis—he thought that I said Blue Roses! So that's what he always called me after that. Whenever he saw me, he'd holler, "Hello, Blue Roses!" I didn't care for the girl that he went out with. Emily Meisenbach. Emily was the best-dressed girl at Soldan.[2] She never struck me, though, as being sincere. . . . It says in the Personal Section —they're engaged. That's—six years ago! They must be married by now.

AMANDA Girls that aren't cut out for business careers usually wind up married to some nice man. [*Gets up with a spark of revival.*] Sister, that's what you'll do!

[LAURA *utters a startled, doubtful laugh. She reaches quickly for a piece of glass.*]

LAURA But, Mother—

AMANDA Yes? [*Crossing to photograph.*]

LAURA [*In a tone of frightened apology.*] I'm— crippled!

[IMAGE: SCREEN]

AMANDA Nonsense! Laura, I've told you never, never to use that word. Why, you're not crippled, you just have a little defect—hardly noticeable, even! When people have some slight disadvantage like that, they cultivate other things to make up for it—develop charm— and vivacity—and—*charm!* That's all you have to do! [*She turns again to the photograph.*] One thing your father had *plenty of*— was *charm!*

[TOM *motions to the fiddle in the wings.*]

[*The Scene Fades Out with Music.*]

---

[2] A large, centrally located St. Louis high school.

SCENE THREE

LEGEND ON SCREEN: "AFTER THE FIASCO—"

TOM *speaks from the fire-escape landing.*

TOM After the fiasco at Rubicam's Business College, the idea of getting a gentleman caller for Laura began to play a more and more important part in Mother's calculations.

It became an obsession. Like some archetype of the universal unconscious, the image of the gentleman caller haunted our small apartment. . . .

[IMAGE: YOUNG MAN AT DOOR WITH FLOWERS]

An evening at home rarely passed without some allusion to this image, this specter, this hope. . . .

Even when he wasn't mentioned, his presence hung in Mother's preoccupied look and in my sister's frightened, apologetic manner—hung like a sentence passed upon the Wingfields!

Mother was a woman of action as well as words.

She began to take logical steps in the planned direction.

Late that winter and in the early spring—realizing that extra money would be needed to properly feather the nest and plume the bird—she conducted a vigorous campaign on the telephone, roping in subscribers to one of those magazines for matrons called *The Homemaker's Companion,* the type of journal that features the serialized sublimations of ladies of letters who think in terms of delicate cuplike breasts, slim, tapering waists, rich, creamy thighs, eyes like wood-smoke in autumn, fingers that soothe and caress like strains of music, bodies as powerful as Etruscan sculpture.

[SCREEN IMAGE: GLAMOR MAGAZINE COVER]

[AMANDA *enters with phone on long extension cord. She is spotted in the dim stage.*]

AMANDA Ida Scott? This is Amanda Wingfield! We *missed* you at the D.A.R. last Monday! I said to myself: She's probably suffering with that sinus condition! How is that sinus condition?

Horrors! Heaven have mercy!—You're a Christian martyr, yes, that's what you are, a Christian martyr!

Well, I just now happened to notice that your subscription to the *Companion's* about to expire! Yes, it expires with the next issue, honey!—just when that wonderful new serial by Bessie Mae Hopper is getting off to such an exciting start. Oh, honey, it's something that you can't miss! You remember how *Gone With the Wind* took everybody by storm? You simply couldn't go out if you hadn't read it. All everybody *talked* was Scarlett O'Hara. Well, this is a book that critics already compare to *Gone With the Wind.* It's the *Gone With the Wind* of the post-World War generation!—What?—Burning?—Oh, honey, don't let them burn, go take a look in the oven and I'll hold the wire! Heavens—I think she's hung up!

DIM OUT

[LEGEND ON SCREEN: "YOU THINK I'M IN LOVE WITH CONTINENTAL SHOEMAKERS?"]

[*Before the stage is lighted, the violent voices of* TOM *and* AMANDA *are heard.*]

[*They are quarreling behind the portieres. In front of them stands* LAURA *with clenched hands and panicky expression.*]

[*A clear pool of light on her figure throughout this scene.*]

TOM What in Christ's name am I—

AMANDA [*Shrilly.*] Don't you use that—

TOM Supposed to do!

AMANDA Expression! Not in my—

TOM Ohhh!

AMANDA Presence! Have you gone out of your senses?

TOM I have, that's true, *driven* out!

AMANDA What is the matter with you, you—big—big—*idiot!*

TOM Look!—I've got *no thing,* no single thing—

AMANDA Lower your voice!

TOM In my life here that I can call my *own!* Everything is—

AMANDA Stop that shouting!

TOM Yesterday you confiscated my books! You had the nerve to—

AMANDA I took that horrible novel back to the library—yes! That hideous book by that insane Mr. Lawrence. [TOM *laughs wildly.*] I cannot control the output of diseased minds or people who cater to them—[TOM *laughs still more wildly.*] BUT I WON'T ALLOW SUCH FILTH BROUGHT INTO MY HOUSE! No, no, no, no, no!

TOM   House, house! Who pays rent on it, who makes a slave of himself to—

AMANDA   [*Fairly screeching.*] Don't you DARE to—

TOM   No, no, *I* mustn't say things! *I've* got to just—

AMANDA   Let me tell you—

TOM   I don't want to hear any more! [*He tears the portieres open. The upstage area is lit with a turgid smoky red glow.*]

[AMANDA'S *hair is in metal curlers and she wears a very old bathrobe, much too large for her slight figure, a relic of the faithless Mr. Wingfield.*]

[*An upright typewriter and a wild disarray of manuscripts is on the drop-leaf table. The quarrel was probably precipitated by* AMANDA'S *interruption of his creative labor. A chair lying overthrown on the floor.*]

[*Their gesticulating shadows are cast on the ceiling by the fiery glow.*]

AMANDA   You *will* hear more, you—

TOM   No, I won't hear more, I'm going out!

AMANDA   You come right back in—

TOM   Out, out, out! Because I'm—

AMANDA   Come back here, Tom Wingfield! I'm not through talking to you!

TOM   Oh, go—

LAURA   [*Desperately.*]—Tom!

AMANDA   You're going to listen, and no more insolence from you! I'm at the end of my patience!

[*He comes back toward her.*]

TOM   What do you think I'm at? Aren't I supposed to have any patience to reach the end of, Mother? I know, I know. It seems unimportant to you, what I'm *doing*—what I *want* to do—having a little *difference* between them! You don't think that—

AMANDA   I think you've been doing things that you're ashamed of. That's why you act like this. I don't believe that you go every night to the movies. Nobody goes to the movies night after night. Nobody in their right minds goes to the movies as often as you pretend to. People don't go to the movies at nearly midnight, and movies don't let out at two A.M. Come in

stumbling. Muttering to yourself like a maniac! You get three hours' sleep and then go to work. Oh, I can picture the way you're doing down there. Moping, doping, because you're in no condition.

TOM   [*Wildly.*] I'm in no condition!

AMANDA   What right have you got to jeopardize your job? Jeopardize the security of us all? How do you think we'd manage if you were—

TOM   Listen! You think I'm crazy *about the warehouse?* [*He bends fiercely toward her slight figure.*] You think I'm in love with the Continental Shoemakers? You think I want to spend fifty-five *years* down there in that— *celotex interior!* with—*fluorescent—tubes!* Look! I'd rather somebody picked up a crowbar and battered out my brains—than go back mornings! I *go!* Every time you come in yelling that God damn *"Rise and Shine!" "Rise and Shine!"* I say to myself, "How *lucky dead* people are!" But I get up. I *go!* For sixty-five dollars a month I give up all that I dream of doing and being *ever!* And you say self—*self's* all I ever think of. Why, listen, if self is what I thought of, Mother, I'd be where he is— GONE! [*Pointing to father's picture.*] As far as the system of transportation reaches! [*He starts past her. She grabs his arm.*] Don't grab at me, Mother!

AMANDA   Where are you going?

TOM   I'm going to the *movies!*

AMANDA   I don't believe that lie!

TOM   [*Crouching toward her, overtowering her tiny figure. She backs away, gasping.*] I'm going to opium dens! Yes, opium dens, dens of vice and criminals' hang-outs, Mother. I've joined the Hogan gang, a hired assassin, I carry a tommy-gun in a violin case! I run a string of cat-houses in the Valley! They call me Killer, Killer Wingfield, I'm leading a double-life, a simple, honest warehouse worker by day, by night a dynamic *czar* of the *underworld*, Mother. I go to gambling casinos, I spin away fortunes on the roulette table! I wear a patch over one eye and a false mustache, sometimes I put on green whiskers. On those occasions they call me—*El Diablo!* Oh, I could tell you things to make you sleepless! My enemies plan to dynamite this place. They're going to blow us all sky-high some night! I'll be glad, very happy, and so will you! You'll go up, up on a broomstick, over

Blue Mountain with seventeen gentlemen callers! You ugly—babbling old—*witch.* . . . [*He goes through a series of violent, clumsy movements, seizing his overcoat, lunging to the door, pulling it fiercely open. The women watch him, aghast. His arm catches in the sleeve of the coat as he struggles to pull it on. For a moment he is pinioned by the bulky garment. With an outraged groan he tears the coat off again, splitting the shoulder of it, and hurls it across the room. It strikes against the shelf of* LAURA's *glass collection, there is a tinkle of shattering glass.* LAURA *cries out as if wounded.*]

[MUSIC. LEGEND: "THE GLASS MENAGERIE"]

LAURA   [*Shrilly.*] My glass!—menagerie. . . . [*She covers her face and turns away.*]
[*But* AMANDA *is still stunned and stupefied by the "ugly witch" so that she barely notices this occurrence. Now she recovers her speech.*]

AMANDA   [*In an awful voice.*] I won't speak to you—until you apologize! [*She crosses through portieres and draws them together behind her.* TOM *is left with* LAURA. LAURA *clings weakly to the mantel with her face averted.* TOM *stares at her stupidly for a moment. Then he crosses to shelf. Drops awkwardly on his knees to collect the fallen glass, glancing at* LAURA *as if he would speak but couldn't.*]

[*"The Glass Menagerie" steals in as the Scene Dims Out.*]

SCENE FOUR

The interior is dark. Faint light in the alley. A deep-voiced bell in a church is tolling the hour of five as the scene commences.

TOM *appears at the top of the alley. After each solemn boom of the bell in the tower, he shakes a little noise-maker or rattle as if to express the tiny spasm of man in contrast to the sustained power and dignity of the Almighty. This and the unsteadiness of his advance make it evident that he has been drinking.*

As he climbs the few steps to the fire-escape landing light steals up inside. LAURA *appears in night-dress, observing* TOM's *empty bed in the front room.*

TOM *fishes in his pockets for door key, removing a motley assortment of articles in the* search, *including a perfect shower of movie-ticket stubs and an empty bottle. At last he finds the key, but just as he is about to insert it, it slips from his fingers. He strikes a match and crouches below the door.*

TOM   [*Bitterly.*] One crack—and it falls through!
[LAURA *opens the door.*]

LAURA   Tom, Tom, what are you doing?

TOM   Looking for a door key.

LAURA   Where have you been all this time?

TOM   I have been to the movies.

LAURA   All this time at the movies?

TOM   There was a very long program. There was a Garbo picture and a Mickey Mouse and a travelogue and a newsreel and a preview of coming attractions. And there was an organ solo and a collection for the milk-fund—simultaneously—which ended up in a terrible fight between a fat lady and an usher!

LAURA   [*Innocently.*] Did you have to stay through everything?

TOM   Of course! And, oh, I forgot! There was a big stage show! The headliner on this stage show was Malvolio the Magician. He performed wonderful tricks, many of them, such as pouring water back and forth between pitchers. First it turned to wine and then it turned to beer and then it turned to whiskey. I know it was whiskey it finally turned into because he needed somebody to come up out of the audience to help him, and I came up—both shows! It was Kentucky Straight Bourbon. A very generous fellow, he gave souvenirs. [*He pulls from his back pocket a shimmering rainbow-colored scarf.*] He gave me this. This is his magic scarf. You can have it, Laura. You wave it over a canary cage and you get a bowl of gold-fish. You wave it over the gold-fish bowl and they fly away canaries. . . . But the wonderfullest trick of all was the coffin trick. We nailed him into a coffin and he got out of the coffin without removing one nail. [*He has come inside.*] There is a trick that would come in handy for me—get me out of this 2 by 4 situation! [*Flops onto bed and starts removing shoes.*]

LAURA   Tom—Shhh!

TOM   What're you shushing me for?

LAURA   You'll wake up Mother.

TOM   Goody, goody! Pay 'er back for all those

"Rise an' Shines." [*Lies down, groaning.*] You know it don't take much intelligence to get yourself into a nailed-up coffin, Laura. But who in hell ever got himself out of one without removing one nail?

[*As if in answer, the father's grinning photograph lights up.*]

SCENE DIMS OUT

[*Immediately following: The church bell is heard striking six. At the sixth stroke the alarm clock goes off in* AMANDA's *room, and after a few moments we hear her calling: "Rise and Shine! Rise and Shine! Laura, go tell your brother to rise and shine!"*]

TOM [*Sitting up slowly.*] I'll rise—but I won't shine. [*The light increases.*]

AMANDA Laura, tell your brother his coffee is ready. [LAURA *slips into front room.*]

LAURA Tom!—It's nearly seven. Don't make Mother nervous. [*He stares at her stupidly. Beseechingly.*] Tom, speak to Mother this morning. Make up with her, apologize, speak to her!

TOM She won't to me. It's her that started not speaking.

LAURA If you just say you're sorry she'll start speaking.

TOM Her not speaking—is that such a tragedy?

LAURA Please—please!

AMANDA [*Calling from the kitchenette.*] Laura, are you going to do what I asked you to do, or do I have to get dressed and go out myself?

LAURA Going, going—soon as I get on my coat! [*She pulls on a shapeless felt hat with nervous, jerky movement, pleadingly glancing at* TOM. *Rushes awkwardly for coat. The coat is one of* AMANDA's, *inaccurately made-over, the sleeves too short for* LAURA.] Butter and what else?

AMANDA [*Entering upstage.*] Just butter. Tell them to charge it.

LAURA Mother, they make such faces when I do that.

AMANDA Sticks and stones can break our bones, but the expression on Mr. Garfinkel's face won't harm us! Tell your brother his coffee is getting cold.

LAURA [*At door.*] Do what I asked you, will you, will you, Tom?

[*He looks sullenly away.*]

AMANDA Laura, go now or just don't go at all!

LAURA [*Rushing out.*] Going—going! [*A second later she cries out.* TOM *springs up and crosses to door.* AMANDA *rushes anxiously in.* TOM *opens the door.*]

TOM Laura?

LAURA I'm all right. I slipped, but I'm all right.

AMANDA [*Peering anxiously after her.*] If anyone breaks a leg on those fire-escape steps, the landlord ought to be sued for every cent he possesses! [*She shuts door. Remembers she isn't speaking and returns to other room.*]

[*As* TOM *enters listlessly for his coffee, she turns her back to him and stands rigidly facing the window on the gloomy gray vault of the areaway. Its light on her face with its aged but childish features is cruelly sharp, satirical as a Daumier print.*]

[MUSIC UNDER: "AVE MARIA"]

[TOM *glances sheepishly but sullenly at her averted figure and slumps at the table. The coffee is scalding hot; he sips it and gasps and spits it back in the cup. At his gasp,* AMANDA *catches her breath and half turns. Then catches herself and turns back to window.*]

[TOM *blows on his coffee, glancing sidewise at his mother. She clears her throat.* TOM *clears his. He starts to rise. Sinks back down again, scratches his head, clears his throat again.* AMANDA *coughs.* TOM *raises his cup in both hands to blow on it, his eyes staring over the rim of it at his mother for several moments. Then he slowly sets the cup down and awkwardly and hesitantly rises from the chair.*]

TOM [*Hoarsely.*] Mother. I—I apologize, Mother. [AMANDA *draws a quick, shuddering breath. Her face works grotesquely. She breaks into childlike tears.*] I'm sorry for what I said, for everything that I said, I didn't mean it.

AMANDA [*Sobbingly.*] My devotion has made me a witch and so I make myself hateful to my children!

TOM *No,* you *don't.*

AMANDA I worry so much, don't sleep, it makes me nervous!

TOM [*Gently.*] I understand that.

AMANDA I've had to put up a solitary battle all these years. But you're my right-hand bower! Don't fall down, don't fall!

TOM [*Gently.*] I try, Mother.

AMANDA [*With great enthusiasm.*] Try and you

will SUCCEED! [*The notion makes her breathless.*] Why, you—you're just *full* of natural endowments! Both my children—they're *unusual* children! Don't you think I know it? I'm so—*proud!* Happy and—feel I've—so much to be thankful for but—Promise me one thing, Son!

TOM What, Mother?

AMANDA Promise, Son, you'll—never be a drunkard!

TOM [*Turns to her grinning.*] I will never be a drunkard, Mother.

AMANDA That's what frightened me so, that you'd be drinking! Eat a bowl of Purina!

TOM Just coffee, Mother.

AMANDA Shredded wheat biscuit?

TOM No. No, Mother, just coffee.

AMANDA You can't put in a day's work on an empty stomach. You've got ten minutes—don't gulp! Drinking too-hot liquids makes cancer of the stomach. . . . Put cream in.

TOM No, thank you.

AMANDA To cool it.

TOM No! No, thank you, I want it black.

AMANDA I know, but it's not good for you. We have to do all that we can to build ourselves up. In these trying times we live in, all that we have to cling to is—each other. . . . That's why it's so important to—Tom, I—I sent out your sister so I could discuss something with you. If you hadn't spoken I would have spoken to you. [*Sits down.*]

TOM [*Gently.*] What is it, Mother, that you want to discuss?

AMANDA *Laura!*

[TOM *puts his cup down slowly.*]

[LEGEND ON SCREEN: "LAURA"]

[MUSIC: "THE GLASS MENAGERIE"]

TOM —Oh—Laura . . .

AMANDA [*Touching his sleeve.*] You know how Laura is. So quiet but—still water runs deep! She notices things and I think she—broods about them. [TOM *looks up.*] A few days ago I came in and she was crying.

TOM What about?

AMANDA You.

TOM Me?

AMANDA She has an idea that you're not happy here.

TOM What gave her that idea?

AMANDA What gives her any idea? However, you do act strangely. I—I'm not criticizing, understand *that!* I know your ambitions do not lie in the warehouse, that like everybody in the whole wide world—you've had to—make sacrifices, but—Tom—Tom—life's not easy, it calls for—Spartan endurance! There's so many things in my heart that I cannot describe to you! I've never told you but I—*loved* your father. . . .

TOM [*Gently.*] I know that, Mother.

AMANDA And you—when I see you taking after his ways! Staying out late—and—well, you *had* been drinking the night you were in that —terrifying condition! Laura says that you hate the apartment and that you go out nights to get away from it! Is that true, Tom?

TOM No. You say there's so much in your heart that you can't describe to me. That's true of me, too. There's so much in my heart that I can't describe to *you!* So let's respect each other's—

AMANDA But, why—*why*, Tom—are you always so *restless?* Where do you *go* to, nights?

TOM I—go to the movies.

AMANDA Why do you go to the movies so much, Tom?

TOM I go to the movies because—I like adventure. Adventure is something I don't have much of at work, so I go to the movies.

AMANDA But, Tom, you go to the movies *entirely* too *much!*

TOM I like a lot of adventure.

[AMANDA *looks baffled, then hurt. As the familiar inquisition resumes he becomes hard and impatient again.* AMANDA *slips back into her querulous attitude toward him.*]

[IMAGE ON SCREEN: SAILING VESSEL WITH JOLLY ROGER]

AMANDA Most young men find adventure in their careers.

TOM Then most young men are not employed in a warehouse.

AMANDA The world is full of young men employed in warehouses and offices and factories.

TOM Do all of them find adventure in their careers?

AMANDA They do or they do without it! Not everybody has a craze for adventure.

TOM Man is by instinct a lover, a hunter, a

fighter, and none of those instincts are given much play at the warehouse!

AMANDA   Man is by instinct! Don't quote instinct to me! Instinct is something that people have got away from! It belongs to animals! Christian adults don't want it!

TOM   What do Christian adults want, then, Mother?

AMANDA   Superior things! Things of the mind and the spirit! Only animals have to satisfy instincts! Surely your aims are somewhat higher than theirs! Than monkeys—pigs—

TOM   I reckon they're not.

AMANDA   You're joking! However, that isn't what I wanted to discuss.

TOM   [*Rising.*] I haven't much time.

AMANDA   [*Pushing his shoulders.*] Sit down.

TOM   You want me to punch in red at the warehouse, Mother?

AMANDA   You have five minutes. I want to talk about Laura.

[LEGEND: "PLANS AND PROVISIONS"]

TOM   All right! What about Laura?

AMANDA   We have to be making some plans and provisions for her. She's older than you, two years, and nothing has happened. She just drifts along doing nothing. It frightens me terribly how she just drifts along.

TOM   I guess she's the type that people call home girls.

AMANDA   There's no such type, and if there is, it's a pity! That is, unless the home is hers, with a husband!

TOM   What?

AMANDA   Oh, I can see the handwriting on the wall as plain as I see the nose in front of my face! It's terrifying!

More and more you remind me of your father! He was out all hours without explanation!—Then *left! Good-bye!*

And me with the bag to hold. I saw that letter you got from the Merchant Marine. I know what you're dreaming of. I'm not standing here blindfolded.

Very well, then. Then *do* it!

But not till there's somebody to take your place.

TOM   What do you mean?

AMANDA   I mean that as soon as Laura has got somebody to take care of her, married, a home of her own, independent—why, then you'll be free to go wherever you please, on land, on sea, whichever way the wind blows you!

But until that time you've got to look out for your sister. I don't say me because I'm old and don't matter! I say for your sister because she's young and dependent.

I put her in business college—a dismal failure! Frightened her so it made her sick at the stomach.

I took her over to the Young People's League at the church. Another fiasco. She spoke to nobody, nobody spoke to her. Now all she does is fool with those pieces of glass and play those worn-out records. What kind of a life is that for a girl to lead?

TOM   What can I do about it?

AMANDA   Overcome selfishness! Self, self, self is all that you ever think of! [TOM *springs up and crosses to get his coat. It is ugly and bulky. He pulls on a cap with earmuffs.*] Where is your muffler? Put your wool muffler on! [*He snatches it angrily from the closet and tosses it around his neck and pulls both ends tight.*]

Tom! I haven't said what I had in mind to ask you.

TOM   I'm too late to—

AMANDA   [*Catching his arm—very importunately. Then shyly.*] Down at the warehouse, aren't there some—nice young men?

TOM   No!

AMANDA   There *must* be—*some* . . .

TOM   Mother—[*Gesture.*]

AMANDA   Find out one that's clean-living—doesn't drink and—ask him out for sister!

TOM   What?

AMANDA   For *sister!* To *meet!* Get *acquainted!*

TOM   [*Stamping to door.*] Oh, my go-osh!

AMANDA   Will you? [*He opens door. Imploringly.*] Will you? [*He starts down.*] Will you? *Will* you, dear?

TOM   [*Calling back.*] YES!

[AMANDA *closes the door hesitantly and with a troubled but faintly hopeful expression.*]

[SCREEN IMAGE: GLAMOR MAGAZINE COVER]

[*Spot* AMANDA *at phone.*]

AMANDA   Ella Cartwright? This is Amanda Wingfield!

How are you, honey?

How is that kidney condition? [*Pause.*] *Horrors!* [*Pause.*]

You're a Christian martyr, yes, honey, that's what you are, a Christian martyr!

Well I just now happened to notice in my little red book that your subscription to the *Companion* has just run out! I knew that you wouldn't want to miss out on the wonderful serial starting in this new issue. It's by Bessie Mae Hopper, the first thing she's written since *Honeymoon for Three*.

Wasn't that a strange and interesting story? Well, this one is even lovelier, I believe. It has a sophisticated, society background. It's all about the horsey set on Long Island!

[*Fade Out.*]

SCENE FIVE

LEGEND ON SCREEN: "ANNUNCIATION." *Fade with music.*

It is early dusk of a spring evening. Supper has just been finished in the Wingfield apartment. AMANDA *and* LAURA *in light-colored dresses are removing dishes from the table, in the up-stage area, which is shadowy, their movements formalized almost as a dance or ritual, their moving forms as pale and silent as moths.*

TOM, *in white shirt and trousers, rises from the table and crosses toward the fire-escape.*

AMANDA　[*As he passes her.*] Son, will you do me a favor?

TOM　What?

AMANDA　Comb your hair! You look so pretty when your hair is combed! [TOM *slouches on sofa with evening paper. Enormous caption "Franco Triumphs."*] There is only one respect in which I would like you to emulate your father.

TOM　What respect is that?

AMANDA　The care he always took of his appearance. He never allowed himself to look untidy. [*He throws down the paper and crosses to fire-escape.*] Where are you going?

TOM　I'm going out to smoke.

AMANDA　You smoke too much. A pack a day at fifteen cents a pack. How much would that amount to in a month? Thirty times fifteen is how much, Tom? Figure it out and you will be astounded at what you could save. Enough to give you a night-school course in account-ing at Washington U! Just think what a wonderful thing that would be for you, Son!

[TOM *is unmoved by the thought.*]

TOM　I'd rather smoke. [*He steps out on landing, letting the screen door slam.*]

AMANDA　[*Sharply.*] I know! That's the tragedy of it. . . . [*Alone, she turns to look at her husband's picture.*]

[DANCE MUSIC: "ALL THE WORLD IS WAIT-ING FOR THE SUNRISE!"]

TOM　[*To the audience.*] Across the alley from us was the Paradise Dance Hall. On evenings in spring the windows and doors were open and the music came outdoors. Sometimes the lights were turned out except for a large glass sphere that hung from the ceiling. It would turn slowly about and filter the dusk with delicate rainbow colors. Then the orchestra played a waltz or a tango, something that had a slow and sensuous rhythm. Couples would come outside, to the relative privacy of the alley. You could see them kissing behind ash-pits and telephone poles.

This was the compensation for lives that passed like mine, without any change or ad-venture.

Adventure and change were imminent in this year. They were waiting around the corner for all these kids.

Suspended in the mist over Berchtesgaden, caught in the folds of Chamberlain's um-brella—

In Spain there was Guernica!

But here there was only hot swing music and liquor, dance halls, bars, and movies, and sex that hung in the gloom like a chandelier and flooded the world with brief, deceptive rainbows. . . .

All the world was waiting for bombard-ments!

[AMANDA *turns from the picture and comes outside.*]

AMANDA　[*Sighing.*] A fire-escape landing's a poor excuse for a porch. [*She spreads a news-paper on a step and sits down, gracefully and demurely as if she were settling into a swing on a Mississippi veranda.*] What are you look-ing at?

TOM　The moon.

AMANDA　Is there a moon this evening?

TOM　It's rising over Garfinkel's Delicatessen.

AMANDA　So it is! A little silver slipper of a

moon. Have you made a wish on it yet?

TOM   Um-hum.

AMANDA   What did you wish for?

TOM   That's a secret.

AMANDA   A secret, huh? Well, I won't tell mine either. I will be just as mysterious as you.

TOM   I bet I can guess what yours is.

AMANDA   Is my head so transparent?

TOM   You're not a sphinx.

AMANDA   No, I don't have secrets. I'll tell you what I wished for on the moon. Success and happiness for my precious children! I wish for that whenever there's a moon, and when there isn't a moon, I wish for it, too.

TOM   I thought perhaps you wished for a gentleman caller.

AMANDA   Why do you say that?

TOM   Don't you remember asking me to fetch one?

AMANDA   I remember suggesting that it would be nice for your sister if you brought home some nice young man from the warehouse. I think that I've made that suggestion more than once.

TOM   Yes, you have made it repeatedly.

AMANDA   Well?

TOM   We are going to have one.

AMANDA   *What?*

TOM   A gentleman caller!

[THE ANNUNCIATION IS CELEBRATED WITH MUSIC]
[AMANDA *rises.*]

[IMAGE ON SCREEN: CALLER WITH BOUQUET]

AMANDA   You mean you have asked some nice young man to come over?

TOM   Yep. I've asked him to dinner.

AMANDA   You really did?

TOM   I did!

AMANDA   You did, and did he—*accept?*

TOM   He did!

AMANDA   Well, well—well, well! That's—lovely!

TOM   I thought that you would be pleased.

AMANDA   It's definite, then?

TOM   Very definite.

AMANDA   Soon?

TOM   Very soon.

AMANDA   For heaven's sake, stop putting on and tell me some things, will you?

TOM   What things do you want me to tell you?

AMANDA   *Naturally* I would like to know when he's *coming!*

TOM   He's coming tomorrow.

AMANDA   *Tomorrow?*

TOM   Yep. Tomorrow.

AMANDA   But, Tom!

TOM   Yes, Mother?

AMANDA   Tomorrow gives me no time!

TOM   Time for what?

AMANDA   Preparations! Why didn't you phone me at once, as soon as you asked him, the minute that he accepted? Then, don't you see, I could have been getting ready!

TOM   You don't have to make any fuss.

AMANDA   Oh, Tom, Tom, Tom, of course I have to make a fuss! I want things nice, not sloppy! Not thrown together. I'll certainly have to do some fast thinking, won't I?

TOM   I don't see why you have to think at all.

AMANDA   You just don't know. We can't have a gentleman caller in a pig-sty! All my wedding silver has to be polished, the monogrammed table linen ought to be laundered! The windows have to be washed and fresh curtains put up. And how about clothes? We have to *wear* something, don't we?

TOM   Mother, this boy is no one to make a fuss over!

AMANDA   Do you realize he's the first young man we've introduced to your sister?

  It's terrible, dreadful, disgraceful that poor little sister has never received a single gentleman caller! Tom, come inside! [*She opens the screen door.*]

TOM   What for?

AMANDA   I want to ask you some things.

TOM   If you're going to make such a fuss, I'll call it off, I'll tell him not to come!

AMANDA   You certainly won't do anything of the kind. Nothing offends people worse than broken engagements. It simply means I'll have to work like a Turk! We won't be brilliant, but we will pass inspection. Come on inside. [TOM *follows, groaning.*] Sit down.

TOM   Any particular place you would like me to sit?

AMANDA   Thank heavens I've got that new sofa! I'm also making payments on a floor lamp I'll have sent out! And put the chintz covers on, they'll brighten things up! Of course I'd hoped to have these walls repapered. . . . What is the young man's name?

TOM   His name is O'Connor.

AMANDA   That, of course, means fish—tomorrow is Friday! I'll have that salmon loaf—with

Durkee's dressing! What does he do? He works at the warehouse?

TOM   Of course! How else would I—

AMANDA   Tom, he—doesn't drink?

TOM   Why do you ask me that?

AMANDA   Your father *did!*

TOM   Don't get started on that!

AMANDA   He *does* drink, then?

TOM   Not that I know of!

AMANDA   Make sure, be certain! The last thing I want for my daughter's a boy who drinks!

TOM   Aren't you being a little bit premature? Mr. O'Connor has not yet appeared on the scene!

AMANDA   But will tomorrow. To meet your sister, and what do I know about his character? Nothing! Old maids are better off than wives of drunkards!

TOM   Oh, my God!

AMANDA   Be still!

TOM   [*Leaning forward to whisper.*] Lots of fellows meet girls whom they don't marry!

AMANDA   Oh, talk sensibly, Tom—and don't be sarcastic! [*She has gotten a hairbrush.*]

TOM   What are you doing?

AMANDA   I'm brushing that cow-lick down!
   What is this young man's position at the warehouse?

TOM   [*Submitting grimly to the brush and the interrogation.*] This young man's position is that of a shipping clerk, Mother.

AMANDA   Sounds to me like a fairly responsible job, the sort of a job *you* would be in if you just had more *get-up.*
   What is his salary? Have you any idea?

TOM   I would judge it to be approximately eighty-five dollars a month.

AMANDA   Well—not princely, but—

TOM   Twenty more than I make.

AMANDA   Yes, how well I know! But for a family man, eighty-five dollars a month is not much more than you can just get by on. . . .

TOM   Yes, but Mr. O'Connor is not a family man.

AMANDA   He might be, mightn't he? Some time in the future?

TOM   I see. Plans and provisions.

AMANDA   You are the only young man that I know of who ignores the fact that the future becomes the present, the present the past, and the past turns into everlasting regret if you don't plan for it!

TOM   I will think that over and see what I can make of it.

AMANDA   Don't be supercilious with your mother! Tell me some more about this—what do you call him?

TOM   James D. O'Connor. The D. is for Delaney.

AMANDA   Irish on *both* sides! *Gracious!* And doesn't drink?

TOM   Shall I call him up and ask him right this minute?

AMANDA   The only way to find out about those things is to make discreet inquiries at the proper moment. When I was a girl in Blue Mountain and it was suspected that a young man drank, the girl whose attentions he had been receiving, if any girl *was,* would sometimes speak to the minister of his church, or rather her father would if her father was living, and sort of feel him out on the young man's character. That is the way such things are discreetly handled to keep a young woman from making a tragic mistake!

TOM   Then how did you happen to make a tragic mistake?

AMANDA   That innocent look of your father's had everyone fooled!
   He *smiled*—the world was *enchanted!*
   No girl can do worse than put herself at the mercy of a handsome appearance!
   I hope that Mr. O'Connor is not too good-looking.

TOM   No, he's not too good-looking. He's covered with freckles and hasn't too much of a nose.

AMANDA   He's not right-down homely, though?

TOM   Not right-down homely. Just medium homely, I'd say.

AMANDA   Character's what to look for in a man.

TOM   That's what I've always said, Mother.

AMANDA   You've never said anything of the kind and I suspect you would never give it a thought.

TOM   Don't be so suspicious of me.

AMANDA   At least I hope he's the type that's up and coming.

TOM   I think he really goes in for self-improvement.

AMANDA   What reason have you to think so?

TOM   He goes to night school.

AMANDA   [*Beaming.*] Splendid! What does he do, I mean study?

TOM   Radio engineering and public speaking!

AMANDA   Then he has visions of being advanced in the world!

Any young man who studies public speaking is aiming to have an executive job some day!

And radio engineering? A thing for the future!

Both of these facts are very illuminating. Those are the sort of things that a mother should know concerning any young man who comes to call on her daughter. Seriously or—not.

TOM   One little warning. He doesn't know about Laura. I didn't let on that we had dark ulterior motives. I just said, why don't you come and have dinner with us? He said okay and that was the whole conservation.

AMANDA   I bet it was! You're eloquent as an oyster.

However, he'll know about Laura when he gets here. When he sees how lovely and sweet and pretty she is, he'll thank his lucky stars he was asked to dinner.

TOM   Mother, you mustn't expect too much of Laura.

AMANDA   What do you mean?

TOM   Laura seems all those things to you and me because she's ours and we love her. We don't even notice she's crippled any more.

AMANDA   Don't say crippled! You know that I never allow that word to be used!

TOM   But face facts, Mother. She is and—that's not all—

AMANDA   What do you mean "not all"?

TOM   Laura is very different from other girls.

AMANDA   I think the difference is all to her advantage.

TOM   Not quite all—in the eyes of others—strangers—she's terribly shy and lives in a world of her own and those things make her seem a little peculiar to people outside the house.

AMANDA   Don't say peculiar.

TOM   Face the facts. She is.

[THE DANCE-HALL MUSIC CHANGES TO A TANGO THAT HAS A MINOR AND SOMEWHAT OMINOUS TONE.]

AMANDA   In what way is she peculiar—may I ask?

TOM   [*Gently.*] She lives in a world of her own —a world of—little glass ornaments, Mother.

. . . [*Gets up.* AMANDA *remains holding brush, looking at him, troubled.*] She plays old phonograph records and—that's about all—[*He glances at himself in the mirror and crosses to door.*]

AMANDA   [*Sharply.*] Where are you going?

TOM   I'm going to the movies. [*Out screen door.*]

AMANDA   Not to the movies, every night to the movies! [*Follows quickly to screen door.*] I don't believe you always go to the movies! [*He is gone.* AMANDA *looks worriedly after him for a moment. Then vitality and optimism return and she turns from the door. Crossing to portieres.*] Laura! Laura! [LAURA *answers from kitchenette.*]

LAURA   Yes, Mother.

AMANDA   Let those dishes go and come in front! [LAURA *appears with dish towel. Gaily.*] Laura, come here and make a wish on the moon!

[SCREEN IMAGE: MOON]

LAURA   [*Entering.*] Moon—moon?

AMANDA   A little silver slipper of a moon.

Look over your left shoulder, Laura, and make a wish!

[LAURA *looks faintly puzzled as if called out of sleep.* AMANDA *seizes her shoulders and turns her at an angle by the door.*]

Now!

Now, darling, *wish!*

LAURA   What shall I wish for, Mother?

AMANDA   [*Her voice trembling and her eyes suddenly filling with tears.*] Happiness! Good fortune!

[*The violin rises and the stage dims out.*]

[*The Curtain Falls.*]

SCENE SIX

[IMAGE: HIGH SCHOOL HERO]

TOM   And so the following evening I brought Jim home to dinner. I had known Jim slightly in high school. In high school Jim was a hero. He had tremendous Irish good nature and vitality with the scrubbed and polished look of white chinaware. He seemed to move in a continual spotlight. He was a star in basketball, captain of the debating club, president of the senior class and the glee club, and he sang the male lead in the annual light operas. He was always running or bounding, never just walking. He seemed always at the point of defeating the law of gravity. He was shooting with such velocity through his adolescence that you would logically expect him to arrive at nothing short of the White House by the time he was thirty. But Jim apparently ran into more interference after his graduation from Soldan. His speed had definitely slowed. Six years after he left high school he was holding a job that wasn't much better than mine.

[IMAGE: CLERK]

He was the only one at the warehouse with whom I was on friendly terms. I was valuable to him as someone who could remember his former glory, who had seen him win basketball games and the silver cup in debating. He knew of my secret practice of retiring to a cabinet of the wash-room to work on poems when business was slack in the warehouse. He called me Shakespeare. And while the other boys in the warehouse regarded me with suspicious hostility, Jim took a humorous attitude toward me. Gradually his attitude affected the others, their hostility wore off and they also began to smile at me as people smile at an oddly fashioned dog who trots across their path at some distance.

I knew that Jim and Laura had known each other at Soldan, and I had heard Laura speak admiringly of his voice. I didn't know if Jim remembered her or not. In high school Laura had been as unobtrusive as Jim had been astonishing. If he did remember Laura, it was not as my sister, for when I asked him to dinner, he grinned and said, "You know, Shakespeare, I never thought of you as having folks!"

He was about to discover that I did. . . .

[LIGHT UP STAGE]

[LEGEND ON SCREEN: "THE ACCENT OF A COMING FOOT"]

[*Friday evening. It is about five o'clock of a late spring evening which comes "scattering poems in the sky."*]

[*A delicate lemony light is in the Wingfield apartment.*]

[AMANDA *has worked like a Turk in preparation for the gentleman caller. The results are astonishing. The new floor lamp with its rose-silk shade is in place, a colored paper lantern conceals the broken light fixture in the ceiling, new billowing white curtains are at the windows, chintz covers are on chairs and sofa, a pair of new sofa pillows make their initial appearance.*]

[*Open boxes and tissue paper are scattered on the floor.*]

[LAURA *stands in the middle with lifted arms while* AMANDA *crouches before her, adjusting the hem of the new dress, devout and ritualistic. The dress is colored and designed by memory. The arrangement of* LAURA's *hair is changed; it is softer and more becoming. A fragile, unearthly prettiness has come out in* LAURA: *she is like a piece of translucent glass touched by light, given a momentary radiance, not actual, not lasting.*]

AMANDA   [*Impatiently.*] Why are you trembling?

LAURA   Mother, you've made me so nervous!

AMANDA   How have I made you nervous?

LAURA   By all this fuss! You make it seem so important!

AMANDA   I don't understand you, Laura. You couldn't be satisfied with just sitting home, and yet whenever I try to arrange something for you, you seem to resist it.
[*She gets up.*]
Now take a look at yourself.
No, wait! Wait just a moment—I have an idea!

LAURA   What is it now?
[AMANDA *produces two powder puffs which she wraps in handkerchiefs and stuffs in* LAURA's *bosom.*]

LAURA   Mother, what are you doing?

AMANDA   They call them "Gay Deceivers"!

LAURA   I won't wear them!

AMANDA   You will!

LAURA   Why should I?

AMANDA   Because, to be painfully honest, your chest is flat.

LAURA   You make it seem like we were setting a trap.

AMANDA   All pretty girls are a trap, a pretty trap, and men expect them to be.

[LEGEND: "A PRETTY TRAP"]

Now look at yourself, young lady. This is the prettiest you will ever be!

I've got to fix myself now! You're going to be surprised by your mother's appearance! [*She crosses through portieres, humming gaily.*]

[LAURA *moves slowly to the long mirror and stares solemnly at herself.*]

[*A wind blows the white curtains inward in a slow, graceful motion and with a faint, sorrowful sighing.*]

AMANDA   [*Off stage.*] It isn't dark enough yet. [*She turns slowly before the mirror with a troubled look.*]

[LEGEND ON SCREEN: "THIS IS MY SISTER: CELEBRATE HER WITH STRINGS!" MUSIC]

AMANDA   [*Laughing, off.*] I'm going to show you something. I'm going to make a spectacular appearance!

LAURA   What is it, Mother?

AMANDA   Possess your soul in patience—you will see! Something I've resurrected from that old trunk! Styles haven't changed so terribly much after all. . . .

[*She parts the portieres.*]

Now just look at your mother!

[*She wears a girlish frock of yellowed voile with a blue silk sash. She carries a bunch of jonquils—the legend of her youth is nearly revived. Feverishly.*]

This is the dress in which I led the cotillion. Won the cakewalk twice at Sunset Hill, wore one spring to the Governor's ball in Jackson!

See how I sashayed around the ballroom, Laura?

[*She raises her skirt and does a mincing step around the room.*]

I wore it on Sundays for my gentlemen callers! I had it on the day I met your father—

I had malaria fever all that spring. The change of climate from East Tennessee to the Delta—weakened resistance—I had a little temperature all the time—not enough to be serious—just enough to make me restless and giddy!—Invitations poured in—parties all over the Delta!—"Stay in bed," said Mother, "you have fever!"—but I just wouldn't—I took quinine but kept on going, going!—Evenings, dances!—Afternoons, long, long rides! Picnics —lovely!—So lovely, that country in May— All lacy with dogwood, literally flooded with jonquils!—That was the spring I had the craze for jonquils. Jonquils became an absolute obsession. Mother said, "Honey, there's no more room for jonquils." And still I kept on bringing in more jonquils. Whenever, wherever I saw them, I'd say, "Stop! Stop! I see jonquils!" I made the young men help me gather the jonquils! It was a joke, Amanda and her jonquils! Finally there were no more vases to hold them, every available space was filled with jonquils. No vases to hold them? All right, I'll hold them myself! And then I— [*She stops in front of the picture.* MUSIC.] met your father!

Malaria fever and jonquils and then—this —boy. . . .

[*She switches on the rose-colored lamp.*]

I hope they get here before it starts to rain.

[*She crosses upstage and places the jonquils in bowl on table.*]

I gave your brother a little extra change so he and Mr. O'Connor could take the service car home.

LAURA   [*With altered look.*] What did you say his name was?

AMANDA   O'Connor.

LAURA   What is his first name?

AMANDA   I don't remember. Oh, yes, I do. It was—Jim!

[LAURA *sways slightly and catches hold of a chair.*]

[LEGEND ON SCREEN: "NOT JIM!"]

LAURA   [*Faintly.*] Not—Jim.

AMANDA   Yes, that was it, it was Jim! I've never known a Jim that wasn't nice!

[MUSIC: OMINOUS]

LAURA   Are you sure his name is Jim O'Connor?

AMANDA   Yes. Why?

LAURA   Is he the one that Tom used to know in high school?

AMANDA   He didn't say so. I think he just got to know him at the warehouse.

LAURA   There was a Jim O'Connor we both knew in high school—[*Then, with effort.*] If that is the one that Tom is bringing to dinner —you'll have to excuse me, I won't come to the table.

AMANDA   What sort of nonsense is this?

LAURA   You asked me once if I'd ever liked a boy. Don't you remember I showed you this boy's picture?

AMANDA   You mean the boy you showed me in the year book?

LAURA   Yes, that boy.

AMANDA   Laura, Laura, were you in love with that boy?

LAURA   I don't know, Mother. All I know is I couldn't sit at the table if it was him!

AMANDA   It won't be him! It isn't the least bit likely. But whether it is or not, you will come to the table. You will not be excused.

LAURA   I'll have to be, Mother.

AMANDA   I don't intend to humor your silliness, Laura. I've had too much from you and your brother, both!

So just sit down and compose yourself till they come. Tom has forgotten his key so you'll have to let them in, when they arrive.

LAURA   [*Panicky.*] Oh, Mother—*you* answer the door!

AMANDA   [*Lightly.*] I'll be in the kitchen—busy!

LAURA   Oh, Mother, please answer the door, don't make me do it!

AMANDA   [*Crossing into kitchenette.*] I've got to fix the dressing for the salmon. Fuss, fuss—silliness!—over a gentleman caller!

[*Door swings shut.* LAURA *is left alone.*]

[LEGEND: "TERROR!"]

[*She utters a low moan and turns off the lamp—sits stiffly on the edge of the sofa, knotting her fingers together.*]

[LEGEND ON SCREEN: "THE OPENING OF A DOOR!"]

[TOM *and* JIM *appear on the fire-escape steps and climb to landing. Hearing their approach,* LAURA *rises with a panicky gesture. She retreats to the portieres.*]

[*The doorbell.* LAURA *catches her breath and touches her throat. Low drums.*]

AMANDA   [*Calling.*] Laura, sweetheart! The door!

[LAURA *stares at it without moving.*]

JIM   I think we just beat the rain.

TOM   Uh-huh. [*He rings again, nervously.* JIM *whistles and fishes for a cigarette.*]

AMANDA   [*Very, very gaily.*] Laura, that is your brother and Mr. O'Connor! Will you let them in, darling?

[LAURA *crosses toward kitchenette door.*]

LAURA   [*Breathlessly.*] Mother—you go to the door!

[AMANDA *steps out of kitchenette and stares furiously at* LAURA. *She points imperiously at the door.*]

LAURA   Please, please!

AMANDA   [*In a fierce whisper.*] What is the matter with you, you silly thing?

LAURA   [*Desperately.*] Please, you answer it, *please!*

AMANDA   I told you I wasn't going to humor you, Laura. Why have you chosen this moment to lose your mind?

LAURA   Please, please, please, you go!

AMANDA   You'll have to go to the door because I can't!

LAURA   [*Despairingly.*] I can't either!

AMANDA   *Why?*

LAURA   I'm *sick!*

AMANDA   I'm sick, too—of your nonsense! Why can't you and your brother be normal people? Fantastic whims and behavior!

[TOM *gives a long ring.*]

Preposterous goings on! Can you give me one reason—[*Calls out lyrically.*] COMING! JUST ONE SECOND!—why you should be afraid to open a door? Now you answer it, Laura!

LAURA   Oh, oh, oh . . . [*She returns through the portieres. Darts to the victrola and winds it frantically and turns it on.*]

AMANDA   Laura Wingfield, you march right to that door!

LAURA   Yes—yes, Mother!

[*A faraway, scratchy rendition of "Dardanella" softens the air and gives her strength to move through it. She slips to the door and draws it cautiously open.*]

[TOM *enters with the caller,* JIM O'CONNOR.]

TOM   Laura, this is Jim. Jim, this is my sister, Laura.

JIM   [*Stepping inside.*] I didn't know that Shakespeare had a sister!

LAURA   [*Retreating stiff and trembling from the door.*] How—how do you do?

JIM   [*Heartily extending his hand.*] Okay!

[LAURA *touches it hesitantly with hers.*]

JIM   Your hand's cold, Laura!

LAURA   Yes, well—I've been playing the victrola. . . .

JIM   Must have been playing classical music on it! You ought to play a little hot swing music to warm you up!

LAURA   Excuse me—I haven't finished playing the victrola. . . .

[*She turns awkwardly and hurries into the front room. She pauses a second by the victrola. Then catches her breath and darts through the portieres like a frightened deer.*]

JIM   [*Grinning.*] What was the matter?

TOM   Oh—with Laura? Laura is—terribly shy.

JIM   Shy, huh? It's unusual to meet a shy girl nowadays. I don't believe you ever mentioned you had a sister.

TOM   Well, now you know. I have one. Here is the *Post Dispatch*. You want a piece of it?

JIM   Uh-huh.

TOM   What piece? The comics?

JIM   Sports! [*Glances at it.*] Ole Dizzy Dean is on his bad behavior.

TOM   [*Disinterest.*] Yeah? [*Lights cigarette and crosses back to fire-escape door.*]

JIM   Where are *you* going?

TOM   I'm going out on the terrace.

JIM   [*Goes after him.*] You know, Shakespeare —I'm going to sell you a bill of goods!

TOM   What goods?

JIM   A course I'm taking.

TOM   Huh?

JIM   In public speaking! You and me, we're not the warehouse type.

TOM   Thanks—that's good news.
But what has public speaking got to do with it?

JIM   It fits you for—executive positions!

TOM   Awww.

JIM   I tell you it's done a helluva lot for me.

[IMAGE: EXECUTIVE AT DESK]

TOM   In what respect?

JIM   In every! Ask yourself what is the difference between you an' me and men in the office down front? Brains?—No!—Ability?—No! Then what? Just one little thing—

TOM   What is that one little thing?

JIM   Primarily it amounts to—social poise! Being able to square up to people and hold your own on any social level!

AMANDA   [*Off stage.*] Tom?

TOM   Yes, Mother?

AMANDA   Is that you and Mr. O'Connor?

TOM   Yes, Mother.

AMANDA   Well, you just make yourselves comfortable in there.

TOM   Yes, Mother.

AMANDA   Ask Mr. O'Connor if he would like to wash his hands.

JIM   Aw, no—no—thank you—I took care of that at the warehouse. Tom—

TOM   Yes?

JIM   Mr. Mendoza was speaking to me about you.

TOM   Favorably?

JIM   What do you think?

TOM   Well—

JIM   You're going to be out of a job if you don't wake up.

TOM   I am waking up—

JIM   You show no signs.

TOM   The signs are interior.

[IMAGE ON SCREEN: THE SAILING VESSEL WITH JOLLY ROGER AGAIN]

TOM   I'm planning to change. [*He leans over the rail speaking with quiet exhilaration. The incandescent marquees and signs of the first-run movie houses light his face from across the alley. He looks like a voyager.*] I'm right at the point of committing myself to a future that doesn't include the warehouse and Mr. Mendoza or even a night-school course in public speaking.

JIM   What are you gassing about?

TOM   I'm tired of the movies.

JIM   Movies!

TOM   Yes, movies! Look at them— [*A wave toward the marvels of Grand Avenue.*] All of those glamorous people—having adventures— hogging it all, gobbling the whole thing up! You know what happens? People go to the *movies* instead of *moving!* Hollywood characters are supposed to have all the adventures for everybody in America, while everybody in America sits in a dark room and watches them have them! Yes, until there's a war. That's when adventure becomes available to the masses! *Everyone's* dish, not only Gable's! Then the people in the dark room come out of the dark room to have some adventures themselves—Goody, goody!—It's our turn now, to go to the South Sea Island—to make a safari —to be exotic, far-off!—But I'm not patient. I don't want to wait till then. I'm tired of the *movies* and I am *about to move*!

JIM [*Incredulously.*] Move?

TOM Yes.

JIM When?

TOM Soon!

JIM Where? Where?

[THEME THREE MUSIC SEEMS TO ANSWER THE QUESTION, WHILE TOM THINKS IT OVER. HE SEARCHES AMONG HIS POCKETS.]

TOM I'm starting to boil inside. I know I seem dreamy, but inside—well, I'm boiling!—Whenever I pick up a shoe, I shudder a little thinking how short life is and what I am doing!—Whatever that means, I know it doesn't mean shoes—except as something to wear on a traveler's feet! [*Finds paper.*] Look—

JIM What?

TOM I'm a member.

JIM [*Reading.*] The Union of Merchant Seamen.

TOM I paid my dues this month, instead of the light bill.

JIM You will regret it when they turn the lights off.

TOM I won't be here.

JIM How about your mother?

TOM I'm like my father. The bastard son of a bastard! See how he grins? And he's been absent going on sixteen years!

JIM You're just talking, you drip. How does your mother feel about it?

TOM Shhh!—Here comes Mother! Mother is not acquainted with my plans!

AMANDA [*Enters portieres.*] Where are you all?

TOM On the terrace, Mother.

[*They start inside. She advances to them.* TOM *is distinctly shocked at her appearance. Even* JIM *blinks a little. He is making his first contact with girlish Southern vivacity and in spite of the night-school course in public speaking is somewhat thrown off the beam by the unexpected outlay of social charm.*]

[*Certain responses are attempted by* JIM *but are swept aside by* AMANDA's *gay laughter and chatter.* TOM *is embarrassed but after the first shock* JIM *reacts very warmly, grins and chuckles, is altogether won over.*]

[IMAGE: AMANDA AS A GIRL]

AMANDA [*Coyly smiling, shaking her girlish ringlets.*] Well, well, well, so this is Mr. O'Connor. Introductions entirely unnecessary. I've heard so much about you from my boy. I finally said to him, Tom—good gracious!—why don't you bring this paragon to supper? I'd like to meet this nice young man at the warehouse!—Instead of just hearing him sing your praises so much!

I don't know why my son is so stand-offish—that's not Southern behavior!

Let's sit down and—I think we could stand a little more air in here! Tom, leave the door open. I felt a nice fresh breeze a moment ago. Where has it gone to?

Mmm, so warm already! And not quite summer, even. We're going to burn up when summer really gets started.

However, we're having—we're having a very light supper. I think light things are better fo' this time of year. The same as light clothes are. Light clothes an' light food are what warm weather calls fo'. You know our blood gets so thick during th' winter—it takes a while fo' us to *adjust* ou'selves!—when the season changes. . . .

It's come so quick this year. I wasn't prepared. All of a sudden—heavens! Already summer!—I ran to the trunk an' pulled out this light dress— Terribly old! Historical almost! But feels so good—so good an' co-ol, y' know. . . .

TOM Mother—

AMANDA Yes, honey?

TOM How about—supper?

AMANDA Honey, you go ask Sister if supper is ready! You know that Sister is in full charge of supper!

Tell her you hungry boys are waiting for it.

[*To* JIM.]

Have you met Laura?

JIM She—

AMANDA Let you in? Oh, good, you've met already! It's rare for a girl as sweet an' pretty as Laura to be domestic! But Laura is, thank heavens, not only pretty but also very domestic. I'm not at all. I never was a bit. I never could make a thing but angel-food cake. Well, in the South we had so many servants. Gone, gone, gone. All vestige of gracious living! Gone completely! I wasn't prepared for what the future brought me. All of my gentlemen callers were sons of planters and so of course

I assumed that I would be married to one and raise my family on a large piece of land with plenty of servants. But man proposes—and woman accepts the proposal!—To vary that old, old saying a little bit—I married no planter! I married a man who worked for the telephone company!—That gallantly smiling gentleman over there! [*Points to the picture.*] A telephone man who—fell in love with long-distance!—Now he travels and I don't even know where!—But what am I going on for about my—tribulations?

Tell me yours—I hope you don't have any! Tom?

TOM [*Returning.*] Yes, Mother?

AMANDA Is supper nearly ready?

TOM It looks to me like supper is on the table.

AMANDA Let me look— [*She rises prettily and looks through portieres.*] Oh, lovely!—But where is Sister?

TOM Laura is not feeling well and she says that she thinks she'd better not come to the table.

AMANDA What? — Nonsense! — Laura? Oh, Laura!

LAURA [*Off stage, faintly.*] Yes, Mother.

AMANDA You really must come to the table. We won't be seated until you come to the table!

Come in, Mr. O'Connor. You sit over there, and I'll—

Laura? Laura Wingfield!

You're keeping us waiting, honey! We can't say grace until you come to the table!

[*The back door is pushed weakly open and* LAURA *comes in. She is obviously quite faint, her lips trembling, her eyes wide and staring. She moves unsteadily toward the table.*]

[LEGEND: "TERROR!"]

[*Outside a summer storm is coming abruptly. The white curtains billow inward at the windows and there is a sorrowful murmur and deep blue dusk.*]

[LAURA *suddenly stumbles—she catches at a chair with a faint moan.*]

TOM Laura!

AMANDA Laura!

[*There is a clap of thunder.*]

[LEGEND: "AH!"]

[*Despairingly.*]

Why, Laura, you *are* sick, darling! Tom, help your sister into the living room, dear!

Sit in the living room, Laura—rest on the sofa.

Well!

[*To the gentleman caller.*]

Standing over the hot stove made her ill!—I told her that it was just too warm this evening, but—

[TOM *comes back in.* LAURA *is on the sofa.*]

Is Laura all right now?

TOM Yes.

AMANDA What *is* that? Rain? A nice cool rain has come up!

[*She gives the gentleman caller a frightened look.*]

I think we may—have grace—now. . . .

[TOM *looks at her stupidly.*]

Tom, honey—you say grace!

TOM Oh . . .

"For these and all thy mercies—"

[*They bow their heads,* AMANDA *stealing a nervous glance at* JIM. *In the living room* LAURA, *stretched on the sofa, clenches her hand to her lips, to hold back a shuddering sob.*]

God's Holy Name be praised—

[*The Scene Dims Out.*]

SCENE SEVEN

A Souvenir.

Half an hour later. Dinner is just being finished in the upstage area which is concealed by the drawn portieres.

As the curtain rises LAURA *is still huddled upon the sofa, her feet drawn under her, her head resting on a pale blue pillow, her eyes wide and mysteriously watchful. The new floor lamp with its shade of rose-colored silk gives a soft, becoming light to her face, bringing out the fragile, unearthly prettiness which usually escapes attention. There is a steady murmur of rain, but it is slackening and stops soon after the scene begins; the air outside becomes pale and luminous as the moon breaks out.*

A moment after the curtain rises, the lights in both rooms flicker and go out.

JIM   Hey, there, Mr. Light Bulb!
    [AMANDA *laughs nervously.*]

[LEGEND: "SUSPENSION OF A PUBLIC SERVICE"]

AMANDA   Where was Moses when the lights went out? Ha-ha. Do you know the answer to that one, Mr. O'Connor?

JIM   No, Ma'am, what's the answer?

AMANDA   In the dark!
    [JIM *laughs appreciatively.*]
    Everybody sit still. I'll light the candles. Isn't it lucky we have them on the table? Where's a match? Which of you gentlemen can provide a match?

JIM   Here.

AMANDA   Thank you, sir.

JIM   Not at all, Ma'am!

AMANDA   I guess the fuse has burnt out. Mr. O'Connor, can you tell a burnt-out fuse? I know I can't and Tom is a total loss when it comes to mechanics.
    [SOUND: GETTING UP: VOICES RECEDE A LITTLE TO KITCHENETTE]
    Oh, be careful you don't bump into something. We don't want our gentleman caller to break his neck. Now wouldn't that be a fine howdy-do?

JIM   Ha-ha!
    Where is the fuse-box?

AMANDA   Right here next to the stove. Can you see anything?

JIM   Just a minute.

AMANDA   Isn't electricity a mysterious thing? Wasn't it Benjamin Franklin who tied a key to a kite?
    We live in such a mysterious universe, don't we? Some people say that science clears up all the mysteries for us. In my opinion it only creates more!
    Have you found it yet?

JIM   No, Ma'am. All these fuses look okay to me.

AMANDA   Tom!

TOM   Yes, Mother?

AMANDA   That light bill I gave you several days ago. The one I told you we got the notices about?

[LEGEND: "HA!"]

TOM   Oh—Yeah.

AMANDA   You didn't neglect to pay it by any chance?

TOM   Why, I—

AMANDA   Didn't! I might have known it!

JIM   Shakespeare probably wrote a poem on that light bill, Mrs. Wingfield.

AMANDA   I might have known better than to trust him with it! There's such a high price for negligence in this world!

JIM   Maybe the poem will win a ten-dollar prize.

AMANDA   We'll just have to spend the remainder of the evening in the nineteenth century, before Mr. Edison made the Mazda lamp!

JIM   Candlelight is my favorite kind of light.

AMANDA   That shows you're romantic! But that's no excuse for Tom.
    Well, we got through dinner. Very considerate of them to let us get through dinner before they plunged us into everlasting darkness, wasn't it, Mr. O'Connor?

JIM   Ha-ha!

AMANDA   Tom, as a penalty for your carelessness you can help me with the dishes.

JIM   Let me give you a hand.

AMANDA   Indeed you will not!

JIM   I ought to be good for something.

AMANDA   Good for something? [*Her tone is rhapsodic.*] *You?* Why, Mr. O'Connor, nobody, *nobody's* given me this much entertainment in years—as you have!

JIM   Aw, now, Mrs. Wingfield!

AMANDA   I'm not exaggerating, not one bit! But Sister is all by her lonesome. You go keep her company in the parlor!
    I'll give you this lovely old candelabrum that used to be on the altar at the Church of the Heavenly Rest. It was melted a little out of shape when the church burnt down. Lightning struck it one spring. Gypsy Jones was holding a revival at the time and he intimated that the church was destroyed because the Episcopalians gave card parties.

JIM   Ha-ha!

AMANDA   And how about you coaxing Sister to drink a little wine? I think it would be good for her! Can you carry both at once?

JIM   Sure. I'm Superman!

AMANDA   Now, Thomas, get into this apron!

[*The door of kitchenette swings closed on* AMANDA's *gay laughter; the flickering light approaches the portieres.*]

[LAURA *sits up nervously as he enters. Her speech at first is low and breathless from the almost intolerable strain of being alone with a stranger.*]

[THE LEGEND: "I DON'T SUPPOSE YOU REMEMBER ME AT ALL!"]

[*In her first speeches in this scene, before* JIM's *warmth overcomes her paralyzing shyness,* LAURA's *voice is thin and breathless as though she has just run up a steep flight of stairs.*]

[JIM's *attitude is gently humorous. In playing this scene it should be stressed that while the incident is apparently unimportant, it is to* LAURA *the climax of her secret life.*]

JIM   Hello, there, Laura.

LAURA   [*Faintly.*] Hello. [*She clears her throat.*]

JIM   How are you feeling now? Better?

LAURA   Yes. Yes, thank you.

JIM   This is for you. A little dandelion wine. [*He extends it toward her with extravagant gallantry.*]

LAURA   Thank you.

JIM   Drink it—but don't get drunk!
    [*He laughs heartily.* LAURA *takes the glass uncertainly; laughs shyly.*]
    Where shall I set the candles?

LAURA   Oh—oh, anywhere . . .

JIM   How about here on the floor? Any objections?

LAURA   No.

JIM   I'll spread a newspaper under to catch the drippings. I like to sit on the floor. Mind if I do?

LAURA   Oh, no.

JIM   Give me a pillow?

LAURA   What?

JIM   A pillow!

LAURA   Oh . . . [*Hands him one quickly.*]

JIM   How about you? Don't you like to sit on the floor?

LAURA   Oh—yes.

JIM   Why don't you, then?

LAURA   I—will.

JIM   Take a pillow! [LAURA *does. Sits on the other side of the candelabrum.* JIM *crosses his legs and smiles engagingly at her.*] I can't hardly see you sitting way over there.

LAURA   I can—see you.

JIM   I know, but that's not fair, I'm in the limelight. [LAURA *moves her pillow closer.*] Good! Now I can see you! Comfortable?

LAURA   Yes.

JIM   So am I. Comfortable as a cow! Will you have some gum?

LAURA   No, thank you.

JIM   I think that I will indulge, with your permission. [*Musingly unwraps it and holds it up.*] Think of the fortune made by the guy that invented the first piece of chewing gum. Amazing, huh? The Wrigley Building is one of the sights of Chicago—I saw it summer before last when I went up to the Century of Progress. Did you take in the Century of Progress?

LAURA   No, I didn't.

JIM   Well, it was quite a wonderful exposition. What impressed me most was the Hall of Science. Gives you an idea of what the future will be in America, even more wonderful than the present time is! [*Pause. Smiling at her.*] Your brother tells me you're shy. Is that right, Laura?

LAURA   I—don't know.

JIM   I judge you to be an old-fashioned type of girl. Well, I think that's a pretty good type to be. Hope you don't think I'm being too personal—do you?

LAURA   [*Hastily, out of embarrassment.*] I believe I *will* take a piece of gum, if you—don't mind. [*Clearing her throat.*] Mr. O'Connor, have you—kept up with your singing?

JIM   Singing? Me?

LAURA   Yes. I remember what a beautiful voice you had.

JIM   When did you hear me sing?
    [VOICE OFF STAGE IN THE PAUSE]

VOICE   [*Off stage.*]

    O blow, ye winds, heigh-ho,
    A-roving I will go!
       I'm off to my love
       With a boxing glove—
    Ten thousand miles away!

JIM   You say you've heard me sing?

LAURA   Oh, yes! Yes, very often. . . . I—don't suppose—you remember me—at all?

JIM   [*Smiling doubtfully.*] You know I have an idea I've seen you before. I had that idea soon as you opened the door. It seemed almost like I was about to remember your name. But the name that I started to call you—wasn't a name! And so I stopped myself before I said it.

LAURA   Wasn't it—Blue Roses?

JIM [*Springs up. Grinning.*] Blue Roses!—My gosh, yes—Blue Roses!

That's what I had on my tongue when you opened the door!

Isn't it funny what tricks your memory plays? I didn't connect you with high school somehow or other.

But that's where it was; it was high school. I didn't even know you were Shakespeare's sister!

Gosh, I'm sorry.

LAURA I didn't expect you to. You—barely knew me!

JIM But we did have a speaking acquaintance, huh?

LAURA Yes, we—spoke to each other.

JIM When did you recognize me?

LAURA Oh, right away!

JIM Soon as I came in the door?

LAURA When I heard your name I thought it was probably you. I knew that Tom used to know you a little in high school. So when you came in the door—Well, then I was—sure.

JIM Why didn't you *say* something, then?

LAURA [*Breathlessly.*] I didn't know what to say, I was—too surprised!

JIM For goodness' sakes! You know, this sure is funny!

LAURA Yes! Yes, isn't it, though . . .

JIM Didn't we have a class in something together?

LAURA Yes, we did.

JIM What class was that?

LAURA It was—singing—Chorus!

JIM Aw!

LAURA I sat across the aisle from you in the Aud.

JIM Aw.

LAURA Mondays, Wednesdays, and Fridays.

JIM Now I remember—you always came in late.

LAURA Yes, it was so hard for me, getting upstairs. I had that brace on my leg—it clumped so loud!

JIM I never heard any clumping.

LAURA [*Wincing at the recollection.*] To me it sounded like—thunder!

JIM Well, well, well, I never even noticed.

LAURA And everybody was seated before I came in. I had to walk in front of all those people. My seat was in the back row. I had to go clumping all the way up the aisle with everyone watching!

JIM You shouldn't have been self-conscious.

LAURA I know, but I was. It was always such a relief when the singing started.

JIM Aw, yes, I've placed you now! I used to call you Blue Roses. How was it that I got started calling you that?

LAURA I was out of school a little while with pleurosis. When I came back you asked me what was the matter. I said I had pleurosis—you thought I said Blue Roses. That's what you always called me after that!

JIM I hope you didn't mind.

LAURA Oh, no—I liked it. You see, I wasn't acquainted with many—people. . . .

JIM As I remember you sort of stuck by yourself.

LAURA I—I—never have had much luck at—making friends.

JIM I don't see why you wouldn't.

LAURA Well, I—started out badly.

JIM You mean being—

LAURA Yes, it sort of—stood between me—

JIM You shouldn't have let it!

LAURA I know, but it did, and—

JIM You were shy with people!

LAURA I tried not to be but never could—

JIM Overcome it?

LAURA No, I—I never could!

JIM I guess being shy is something you have to work out of kind of gradually.

LAURA [*Sorrowfully.*] Yes—I guess it—

JIM Takes time!

LAURA Yes.

JIM People are not so dreadful when you know them. That's what you have to remember! And everybody has problems, not just you, but practically everybody has got some problems.

You think of yourself as having the only problems, as being the only one who is disappointed. But just look around you and you will see lots of people as disappointed as you are. For instance, I hoped when I was going to high school that I would be further along at this time, six years later, than I am now—You remember that wonderful write-up I had in *The Torch*?

LAURA Yes! [*She rises and crosses to table.*]

JIM It said I was bound to succeed in anything I went into! [LAURA *returns with the annual.*]

Holy Jeez! *The Torch!* [*He accepts it reverently. They smile across it with mutual wonder.* LAURA *crouches beside him and they begin to turn through it.* LAURA'S *shyness is dissolving in his warmth.*]

LAURA Here you are in *The Pirates of Penzance!*

JIM [*Wistfully.*] I sang the baritone lead in that operetta.

LAURA [*Raptly.*] So—*beautifully!*

JIM [*Protesting.*] Aw—

LAURA Yes, yes—beautifully—beautifully!

JIM You heard me?

LAURA All three times!

JIM No!

LAURA Yes!

JIM All three performances?

LAURA [*Looking down.*] Yes.

JIM Why?

LAURA I—wanted to ask you to—autograph my program.

JIM Why didn't you ask me to?

LAURA You were always surrounded by your own friends so much that I never had a chance to.

JIM You should have just—

LAURA Well, I—thought you might think I was—

JIM Thought I might think you was—what?

LAURA Oh—

JIM [*With reflective relish.*] I was beleaguered by females in those days.

LAURA You were terribly popular!

JIM Yeah—

LAURA You had such a—friendly way—

JIM I was spoiled in high school.

LAURA Everybody—liked you!

JIM Including you?

LAURA I—yes, I—I did, too— [*She gently closes the book in her lap.*]

JIM Well, well, well!—Give me that program, Laura. [*She hands it to him. He signs it with a flourish.*] There you are—better late than never!

LAURA Oh, I—what a—surprise!

JIM My signature isn't worth very much right now. But some day—maybe—it will increase in value!

Being disappointed is one thing and being discouraged is something else. I am disappointed but I am not discouraged.

I'm twenty-three years old.
How old are you?

LAURA I'll be twenty-four in June.

JIM That's not old age!

LAURA No, but—

JIM You finished high school?

LAURA [*With difficulty.*] I didn't go back.

JIM You mean you dropped out?

LAURA I made bad grades in my final examinations. [*She rises and replaces the book and the program. Her voice strained.*] How is—Emily Meisenbach getting along?

JIM Oh, that kraut-head!

LAURA Why do you call her that?

JIM That's what she was.

LAURA You're not still—going with her?

JIM I never see her.

LAURA It said in the Personal Section that you were—engaged!

JIM I know, but I wasn't impressed by that—propaganda!

LAURA It wasn't—the truth?

JIM Only in Emily's optimistic opinion!

LAURA Oh—

[LEGEND: "WHAT HAVE YOU DONE SINCE HIGH SCHOOL?"]

[JIM *lights a cigarette and leans indolently back on his elbows, smiling at* LAURA *with a warmth and charm which lights her inwardly with altar candles. She remains by the table and turns in her hands a piece of glass to cover her tumult.*]

JIM [*After several reflective puffs on a cigarette.*] What have you done since high school? [*She seems not to hear him.*] Huh? [LAURA *looks up.*] I said what have you done since high school, Laura?

LAURA Nothing much.

JIM You must have been doing something these six long years.

LAURA Yes.

JIM Well, then, such as what?

LAURA I took a business course at business college—

JIM How did that work out?

LAURA Well, not very—well—I had to drop out, it gave me—indigestion—
[JIM *laughs gently.*]

JIM What are you doing now?

LAURA   I don't do anything—much. Oh, please don't think I sit around doing nothing! My glass collection takes up a good deal of time. Glass is something you have to take good care of.

JIM   What did you say—about glass?

LAURA   Collection I said—I have one—[*She clears her throat and turns away again, acutely shy.*]

JIM   [*Abruptly.*] You know what I judge to be the trouble with you?

Inferiority complex! Know what that is? That's what they call it when someone low-rates himself!

I understand it because I had it, too. Although my case was not so aggravated as yours seems to be. I had it until I took up public speaking, developed my voice, and learned that I had an aptitude for science. Before that time I never thought of myself as being outstanding in any way whatsoever!

Now I've never made a regular study of it, but I have a friend who says I can analyze people better than doctors that make a profession of it. I don't claim that to be necessarily true, but I can sure guess a person's psychology. Laura! [*Takes out his gum.*] Excuse me, Laura. I always take it out when the flavor is gone. I'll use this scrap of paper to wrap it in. I know how it is to get it stuck on a shoe.

Yep—that's what I judge to be your principal trouble. A lack of confidence in yourself as a person. You don't have the proper amount of faith in yourself. I'm basing that fact on a number of your remarks and also on certain observations I've made. For instance that clumping you thought was so awful in high school. You say that you even dreaded to walk into class. You see what you did? You dropped out of school, you gave up an education because of a clump, which as far as I know was practically nonexistent! A little physical defect is what you have. Hardly noticeable even! Magnified thousands of times by imagination!

You know what my strong advice to you is? Think of yourself as *superior* in some way!

LAURA   In what way would I think?

JIM   Why, man alive, Laura! Just look about you a little. What do you see? A world full of common people! All of 'em born and all of 'em going to die!

Which of them has one-tenth of your good points! Or mine! Or anyone else's, as far as that goes—Gosh!

Everybody excels in some one thing. Some in many!

[*Unconsciously glances at himself in the mirror.*]

All you've got to do is discover in *what*! Take me, for instance.

[*He adjusts his tie at the mirror.*]

My interest happens to lie in electrodynamics. I'm taking a course in radio engineering at night school, Laura, on top of a fairly responsible job at the warehouse. I'm taking that course and studying public speaking.

LAURA   Ohhhh.

JIM   Because I believe in the future of television!

[*Turning back to her.*]

I wish to be ready to go up right along with it. Therefore I'm planning to get in on the ground floor. In fact I've already made the right connections and all that remains is for the industry itself to get under way! Full steam—

[*His eyes are starry.*]

Knowledge—Zzzzzp! Money—Zzzzzzp!—Power!

That's the cycle democracy is built on!

[*His attitude is convincingly dynamic. LAURA stares at him, even her shyness eclipsed in her absolute wonder. He suddenly grins.*]

I guess you think I think a lot of myself!

LAURA   No—o-o-o, I—

JIM   Now how about you? Isn't there something you take more interest in than anything else?

LAURA   Well, I do—as I said—have my—glass collection—

[*A peal of girlish laughter from the kitchen.*]

JIM   I'm not right sure I know what you're talking about.

What kind of glass is it?

LAURA   Little articles of it, they're ornaments mostly!

Most of them are little animals made out of glass, the tiniest little animals in the world. Mother calls them a glass menagerie!

Here's an example of one, if you'd like to see it!

This one is one of the oldest. It's nearly thirteen.

[MUSIC: "THE GLASS MENAGERIE"]

[*He stretches out his hand.*]

Oh, be careful—if you breathe, it breaks!

JIM I'd better not take it. I'm pretty clumsy with things.

LAURA Go on, I trust you with him!

[*Places it in his palm.*]

There now—you're holding him gently!

Hold him over the light, he loves the light! You see how the light shines through him?

JIM It sure does shine!

LAURA I shouldn't be partial, but he is my favorite one.

JIM What kind of a thing is this one supposed to be?

LAURA Haven't you noticed the single horn on his forehead?

JIM A unicorn, huh?

LAURA Mmm-hmmm!

JIM Unicorns, aren't they extinct in the modern world?

LAURA I know!

JIM Poor little fellow, he must feel sort of lonesome.

LAURA [*Smiling.*] Well, if he does he doesn't complain about it. He stays on a shelf with some horses that don't have horns and all of them seem to get along nicely together.

JIM How do you know?

LAURA [*Lightly.*] I haven't heard any arguments among them!

JIM [*Grinning.*] No arguments, huh? Well, that's a pretty good sign! Where shall I set him?

LAURA Put him on the table. They all like a change of scenery once in a while!

JIM [*Stretching.*] Well, well, well, well—

Look how big my shadow is when I stretch!

LAURA Oh, oh, yes—it stretches across the ceiling!

JIM [*Crossing to door.*] I think it's stopped raining. [*Opens fire-escape door.*] Where does the music come from?

LAURA From the Paradise Dance Hall across the alley.

JIM How about cutting the rug a little, Miss Wingfield?

LAURA Oh, I—

JIM Or is your program filled up? Let me have a look at it. [*Grasps imaginary card.*] Why, every dance is taken! I'll just have to scratch some out. [WALTZ MUSIC: "LA GOLONDRINA"]

Ahhh, a waltz! [*He executes some sweeping turns by himself then holds his arms toward* LAURA.]

LAURA [*Breathlessly.*] I—can't dance!

JIM There you go, that inferiority stuff!

LAURA I've never danced in my life!

JIM Come on, try!

LAURA Oh, but I'd step on you!

JIM I'm not made out of glass.

LAURA How—how—how do we start?

JIM Just leave it to me. You hold your arms out a little.

LAURA Like this?

JIM A little bit higher. Right. Now don't tighten up, that's the main thing about it—relax.

LAURA [*Laughing breathlessly.*] It's hard not to.

JIM Okay.

LAURA I'm afraid you can't budge me.

JIM What do you bet I can't? [*He swings her into motion.*]

LAURA Goodness, yes, you can!

JIM Let yourself go, now, Laura, just let yourself go.

LAURA I'm—

JIM Come on!

LAURA Trying!

JIM Not so stiff—Easy does it!

LAURA I know but I'm—

JIM Loosen th' backbone! There now, that's a lot better.

LAURA Am I?

JIM Lots, lots better! [*He moves her about the room in a clumsy waltz.*]

LAURA Oh, my!

JIM Ha-ha!

LAURA Oh, my goodness!

JIM Ha-ha-ha! [*They suddenly bump into the table.* JIM *stops.*] What did we hit on?

LAURA Table.

JIM Did something fall off it? I think—

LAURA Yes.

JIM I hope it wasn't the little glass horse with the horn!

LAURA Yes.

JIM Aw, aw, aw. Is it broken?

LAURA Now it is just like all the other horses.

JIM It's lost its—

LAURA Horn!

It doesn't matter. Maybe it's a blessing in disguise.

JIM   You'll never forgive me. I bet that that was your favorite piece of glass.

LAURA   I don't have favorites much. It's no tragedy, Freckles. Glass breaks so easily. No matter how careful you are. The traffic jars the shelves and things fall off them.

JIM   Still I'm awfully sorry that I was the cause.

LAURA   [*Smiling.*] I'll just imagine he had an operation.

The horn was removed to make him feel less—freakish!

[*They both laugh.*]

Now he will feel more at home with the other horses, the ones that don't have horns.

. . .

JIM   Ha-ha, that's very funny!

[*They both laugh.*]

I'm glad to see that you have a sense of humor.

You know—you're—well—very different! Surprisingly different from anyone else I know!

[*His voice becomes soft and hesitant with a genuine feeling.*]

Do you mind me telling you that?

[LAURA *is abashed beyond speech.*]

I mean it in a nice way. . . .

[LAURA *nods shyly, looking away.*]

You make me feel sort of—I don't know how to put it!

I'm usually pretty good at expressing things, but—

This is something that I don't know how to say!

[LAURA *touches her throat and clears it— turns the broken unicorn in her hands.*]

[*Even softer.*]

Has anyone ever told you that you were pretty?

[PAUSE: MUSIC]

[LAURA *looks up slowly, with wonder, and shakes her head.*]

Well, you are! In a very different way from anyone else.

And all the nicer because of the difference, too.

[*His voice becomes low and husky.* LAURA *turns away, nearly faint with the novelty of her emotion.*]

I wish that you were my sister. I'd teach you to have some confidence in yourself. The different people are not like other people, but being different is nothing to be ashamed of. Because other people are not such wonderful people. They're one hundred times one thousand. You're one times one! They walk all over the earth. You just stay here. They're common as—weeds, but—you—well you're—*Blue Roses!*

[IMAGE ON SCREEN: BLUE ROSES]
  [MUSIC CHANGES]

LAURA   But blue is wrong for—roses. . . .

JIM   It's right for you!—You're—pretty!

LAURA   In what respect am I pretty?

JIM   In all respects—believe me! Your eyes— your hair—are pretty! Your hands are pretty!

[*He catches hold of her hand.*]

You think I'm making this up because I'm invited to dinner and have to be nice. Oh, I could do that! I could put on an act for you, Laura, and say lots of things without being very sincere. But this time I am. I'm talking to you sincerely. I happened to notice you had this inferiority complex that keeps you from feeling comfortable with people. Somebody needs to build your confidence up and make you proud instead of shy and turning away and—blushing—

Somebody—ought to—

Ought to—*kiss* you, Laura!

[*His hand slips slowly up her arm to her shoulder.*]

[MUSIC SWELLS TUMULTUOUSLY]

[*He suddenly turns her about and kisses her on the lips.*]

[*When he releases her,* LAURA *sinks on the sofa with a bright, dazed look.*]

[JIM *backs away and fishes in his pocket for a cigarette.*]

[LEGEND ON SCREEN: "SOUVENIR"]

Stumble-john!

[*He lights the cigarette, avoiding her look.*]

[*There is a peal of girlish laughter from* AMANDA *in the kitchen.*]

[LAURA *slowly raises and opens her hand. It still contains the little broken glass animal. She looks at it with a tender, bewildered expression.*]

Stumble-john!

I shouldn't have done that— That was way off the beam. You don't smoke, do you?

[*She looks up, smiling, not hearing the question.*]

[*He sits beside her a little gingerly. She looks at him speechlessly—waiting.*]

[*He coughs decorously and moves a little farther aside as he considers the situation and senses her feelings, dimly with perturbation.*]

[*Gently.*]

Would you—care for a—mint?

[*She doesn't seem to hear him but her look grows brighter even.*]

Peppermint—Life-Saver?

My pocket's a regular drug store—wherever I go . . .

[*He pops a mint in his mouth. Then gulps and decides to make a clean breast of it. He speaks slowly and gingerly.*]

Laura, you know, if I had a sister like you, I'd do the same thing as Tom. I'd bring out fellows and—introduce her to them. The right type of boys of a type to—appreciate her.

Only—well—he made a mistake about me.

Maybe I've got no call to be saying this. That may not have been the idea in having me over. But what if it was?

There's nothing wrong about that. The only trouble is that in my case—I'm not in a situation to—do the right thing.

I can't take down your number and say I'll phone.

I can't call up next week and—ask for a date.

I thought I had better explain the situation in case you—misunderstood it and—hurt your feelings. . . .

[*Pause.*]

[*Slowly, very slowly, LAURA's look changes, her eyes returning slowly from his to the ornament in her palm.*]

[*AMANDA utters another gay laugh in the kitchen.*]

LAURA [*Faintly.*] You—won't—call again?

JIM No, Laura, I can't.

[*He rises from the sofa.*]

As I was just explaining, I've—got strings on me.

Laura, I've—been going steady!

I go out all of the time with a girl named Betty. She's a home-girl like you, and Catholic, and Irish, and in a great many ways we—get along fine.

I met her last summer on a moonlight boat trip up the river to Alton, on the *Majestic*.

Well—right away from the start it was—love!

[LEGEND: LOVE!]

[*LAURA sways slightly forward and grips the arm of the sofa. He fails to notice, now enrapt in his own comfortable being.*]

Being in love has made a new man of me!

[*Leaning stiffly forward, clutching the arm of the sofa, LAURA struggles visibly with her storm. But JIM is oblivious, she is a long way off.*]

The power of love is really pretty tremendous!

Love is something that—changes the whole world, Laura!

[*The storm abates a little and LAURA leans back. He notices her again.*]

It happened that Betty's aunt took sick, she got a wire and had to go to Centralia. So Tom—when he asked me to dinner—I naturally just accepted the invitation, not knowing that you—that he—that I—

[*He stops awkwardly.*]

Huh—I'm a stumble-john!

[*He flops back on the sofa.*]

[*The holy candles in the altar of LAURA's face have been snuffed out. There is a look of almost infinite desolation.*]

[*JIM glances at her uneasily.*]

I wish that you would—say something.

[*She bites her lip which was trembling and then bravely smiles. She opens her hand again on the broken glass ornament. Then she gently takes his hand and raises it level with her own. She carefully places the unicorn in the palm of his hand, then pushes his fingers closed upon it.*] What are you—doing that for? You want me to have him?—Laura? [*She nods.*] What for?

LAURA A—souvenir . . .

[*She rises unsteadily and crouches beside the victrola to wind it up.*]

[LEGEND ON SCREEN: "THINGS HAVE A WAY OF TURNING OUT SO BADLY!"]

[OR IMAGE: "GENTLEMAN CALLER WAVING GOODBYE!—GAILY"]

[*At this moment AMANDA rushes brightly back in the front room. She bears a pitcher of fruit *punch in an old-fashioned cut-glass pitcher and a plate of macaroons. The plate has a gold border and poppies painted on it.]*

AMANDA   Well, well, well! Isn't the air delightful after the shower? I've made you children a little liquid refreshment.

[Turns gaily to the gentleman caller.]

Jim, do you know that song about lemonade?

"Lemonade, lemonade
Made in the shade and stirred with a spade—
Good enough for any old maid!"

JIM   *[Uneasily.]* Ha-ha! No—I never heard it.

AMANDA   Why, Laura! You look so serious!

JIM   We were having a serious conversation.

AMANDA   Good! Now you're better acquainted!

JIM   *[Uncertainly.]* Ha-ha! Yes.

AMANDA   You modern young people are much more serious-minded than my generation. I was so gay as a girl!

JIM   You haven't changed, Mrs. Wingfield.

AMANDA   Tonight I'm rejuvenated! The gaiety of the occasion, Mr. O'Connor!
[She tosses her head with a peal of laughter. Spills lemonade.]
Oooo! I'm baptizing myself!

JIM   Here—let me—

AMANDA   *[Setting the pitcher down.]* There now. I discovered we had some maraschino cherries. I dumped them in, juice and all!

JIM   You shouldn't have gone to that trouble, Mrs. Wingfield.

AMANDA   Trouble, trouble? Why, it was loads of fun!
Didn't you hear me cutting up in the kitchen? I bet your ears were burning! I told Tom how outdone with him I was for keeping you to himself so long a time! He should have brought you over much, much sooner! Well, now that you've found your way, I want you to be a very frequent caller! Not just occasional but all the time.
Oh, we're going to have a lot of gay times together! I see them coming!
Mmm, just breathe that air! So fresh, and the moon's so pretty!
I'll skip back out—I know where my place is when young folks are having a—serious conversation!

JIM   Oh, don't go out, Mrs. Wingfield. The fact of the matter is I've got to be going.

AMANDA   Going, now? You're joking! Why, it's only the shank of the evening, Mr. O'Connor!

JIM   Well, you know how it is.

AMANDA   You mean you're a young workingman and have to keep workingmen's hours. We'll let you off early tonight. But only on the condition that next time you stay later.
What's the best night for you? Isn't Saturday night the best night for you workingmen?

JIM   I have a couple of time-clocks to punch, Mrs. Wingfield. One at morning, another one at night!

AMANDA   My, but you *are* ambitious! You work at night, too?

JIM   No, Ma'am, not work but—Betty! *[He crosses deliberately to pick up his hat. The band at the Paradise Dance Hall goes into a tender waltz.]*

AMANDA   Betty? Betty? Who's—Betty!
[There is an ominous cracking sound in the sky.]

JIM   Oh, just a girl. The girl I go steady with!
[He smiles charmingly. The sky falls.]

[LEGEND: "THE SKY FALLS"]

AMANDA   *[A long-drawn exhalation.]* Ohhhh . . . Is it a serious romance, Mr. O'Connor?

JIM   We're going to be married the second Sunday in June.

AMANDA   Ohhhh—how nice!
Tom didn't mention that you were engaged to be married.

JIM   The cat's not out of the bag at the warehouse yet.
You know how they are. They call you Romeo and stuff like that.
[He stops at the oval mirror to put on his hat. He carefully shapes the brim and the crown to give a discreetly dashing effect.]
It's been a wonderful evening, Mrs. Wingfield. I guess this is what they mean by Southern hospitality.

AMANDA   It really wasn't anything at all.

JIM   I hope it don't seem like I'm rushing off. But I promised Betty I'd pick her up at the Wabash depot, an' by the time I get my jalopy down there her train'll be in. Some women are pretty upset if you keep 'em waiting.

AMANDA   Yes, I know— The tyranny of women!
[Extends her hand.]
Good-bye, Mr. O'Connor.
I wish you luck—and happiness—and suc-

cess! All three of them, and so does Laura!—
Don't you, Laura?

LAURA   Yes!

JIM   [*Taking her hand.*] Good-bye, Laura. I'm
certainly going to treasure that souvenir. And
don't you forget the good advice I gave you.
   [*Raises his voice to a cheery shout.*]
So long, Shakespeare!
Thanks again, ladies— Good night!
   [*He grins and ducks jauntily out.*]
   [*Still bravely grimacing,* AMANDA *closes the
   door on the gentleman caller. Then she
   turns back to the room with a puzzled expression. She and* LAURA *don't dare to face
   each other.* LAURA *crouches beside the victrola to wind it.*]

AMANDA   [*Faintly.*] Things have a way of turn-
ing out so badly.
   I don't believe that I would play the vic-
trola.
   Well, well—well—
   Our gentleman caller was engaged to be
married!
   Tom!

TOM   [*From back.*] Yes, Mother?

AMANDA   Come in here a minute. I want to tell
you something awfully funny.

TOM   [*Enters with macroon and a glass of the
lemonade.*] Has the gentleman caller gotten
away already?

AMANDA   The gentleman caller has made an
early departure.
   What a wonderful joke you played on us!

TOM   How do you mean?

AMANDA   You didn't mention that he was engaged to be married.

TOM   Jim? Engaged?

AMANDA   That's what he just informed us.

TOM   I'll be jiggered! I didn't know about that.

AMANDA   That seems very peculiar.

TOM   What's peculiar about it?

AMANDA   Didn't you call him your best friend
down at the warehouse?

TOM   He is, but how did I know?

AMANDA   It seems extremely peculiar that you
wouldn't know your best friend was going to
be married!

TOM   The warehouse is where I work, not
where I know things about people!

AMANDA   You don't know things anywhere! You
live in a dream; you manufacture illusions!
   [*He crosses to door.*]

Where are you going?

TOM   I'm going to the movies.

AMANDA   That's right, now that you've had us
make such fools of ourselves. The effort, the
preparations, all the expense! The new floor
lamp, the rug, the clothes for Laura! All for
what? To entertain some other girl's fiancé!
   Go to the movies, go! Don't think about
us, a mother deserted, an unmarried sister
who's crippled and has no job! Don't let anything interfere with your selfish pleasure!
   Just go, go—to the movies!

TOM   All right, I will! The more you shout
about my selfishness to me the quicker I'll go,
and I won't go to the movies!

AMANDA   Go, then! Then go to the moon—you
selfish dreamer!

[TOM *smashes his glass on the floor. He plunges
out on the fire escape, slamming the door.*
LAURA *screams—cut by door.*]

[*Dance-hall music up.* TOM *goes to the rail and
grips it desperately, lifting his face in the chill
white moonlight penetrating the narrow abyss
of the alley.*]

[LEGEND ON SCREEN: "AND SO GOOD-BYE . . ."]

[TOM'S *closing speech is timed with the interior
pantomime. The interior scene is played as
though viewed through soundproof glass.*
AMANDA *appears to be making a comforting
speech to* LAURA *who is huddled upon the
sofa. Now that we cannot hear the mother's
speech, her silliness is gone and she has dignity
and tragic beauty.* LAURA'S *dark hair hides her
face until at the end of the speech she lifts it
to smile at her mother.* AMANDA'S *gestures are
slow and graceful, almost dancelike, as she
comforts the daughter. At the end of her
speech she glances a moment at the father's
picture—then withdraws through the portieres. At close of* TOM'S *speech,* LAURA *blows
out the candles, ending the play.*]

TOM   I didn't go to the moon, I went much
further—for time is the longest distance between two places—
   Not long after that I was fired for writing
a poem on the lid of a shoe-box.
   I left Saint Louis. I descended the steps of
this fire escape for a last time and followed,
from then on, in my father's footsteps, attempting to find in motion what was lost in
space—

I traveled around a great deal. The cities swept about me like dead leaves, leaves that were brightly colored but torn away from the branches.

I would have stopped, but I was pursued by something.

It always came upon me unawares, taking me altogether by surprise. Perhaps it was a familiar bit of music. Perhaps it was only a piece of transparent glass—

Perhaps I am walking along a street at night, in some strange city, before I have found companions. I pass the lighted window of a shop where perfume is sold. The window is filled with pieces of colored glass, tiny transparent bottles in delicate colors, like bits of a shattered rainbow.

Then all at once my sister touches my shoulder. I turn around and look into her eyes . . .

Oh, Laura, Laura, I tried to leave you behind me, but I am more faithful than I intended to be!

I reach for a cigarette, I cross the street, I run into the movies or a bar, I buy a drink, I speak to the nearest stranger—anything that can blow your candles out!

[LAURA *bends over the candles.*]

—for nowadays the world is lit by lightning! Blow out your candles, Laura—and so goodbye. . . .

[*She blows the candles out.*]

[*The Scene Dissolves.*]

Comments and Questions

Perhaps the central technical fact about this play is the emphasis upon symbols. (The three plays which follow this one will demonstrate that use of symbols has become a twentieth-century passion.) We have observed that all the serious plays preceding this one have dealt with individuals who, through their attitudes and actions, have in a variety of ways represented certain universal truths. Physical objects, however, have been used for the most part simply as stage props. Even the handkerchief, of so much importance in *Othello,* is merely a prop with no significance except that which Othello attaches to it. The dish dropped in *Ile* is

merely a dish. In *The Glass Menagerie,* on the other hand, the fire escape, the glass unicorn, the pieces of chewing gum, the picture on the wall—to name just a few of the props —are physical representations of abstractions. The total setting equals *environment,* a potent force which in a sense has been created by the characters and the social order and, at the same time, acts upon the characters.

Tennessee Williams clearly wants his intentions understood and therefore gives the reader (any director of the play, too) an extraordinary amount of help. His descriptions of the three major characters are precise and full. He sets the stage with great care and, as mentioned above, endows each item with a meaning beyond itself. Tom, speaking for the author, says ingenuously, "I have a poet's weakness for symbols." Identify as many of these symbols as you can. The list will be long and will reveal a principal source of the play's power.

The Caucasian Chalk Circle
BERTOLT BRECHT
1898–1956

The Caucasian Chalk Circle was written as propaganda. The Prologue sets forth the notion that land should belong to those who can make best use of it. The characters are Russian communists who are assembled to reason together after the defeat of Hitler. Those described as *on the right* were the original occupants of the land under dispute; those *on the left* are those who claim the land by right of being able to make better use of it.

At first, American producers were afraid to stage the Prologue because it explores, superficially at least, a noncapitalistic method of determining who shall have the use of a piece of property. Recently the Prologue has been included in productions of Brecht's play with, as one critic has observed, "no untoward incidents." Few viewers and, one suspects, fewer readers will take the Prologue very seriously because, as with all propaganda, the cards are so obviously stacked that there is no argument, merely statement.

By being weak as sociopolitical doctrine, the Prologue and the play which follows have a chance to be strong in other ways. And strong they are as earthly folk tales. The Prologue is a bland, good-natured fantasy in which all the characters are good. The play, with some arresting exceptions, pits black (all persons with possessions and status) against white (all persons without possessions or status). The appeal of the play hardly lies in its argument. The reader will discover the warm attractiveness of the heroically motherly Grusha and her faithful lover Simon and of the marvelous eccentric, Azdak. Most appealing perhaps are the humor and wisdom of the folk sayings, some poetic, some rough and salty. (Compare Carl Sandburg's *The People, Yes,* pp. 313–317.)

CHARACTERS

OLD MAN *on the right*
PEASANT WOMAN
   on the right
YOUNG PEASANT
A VERY YOUNG WORKER
OLD MAN *on the left*
PEASANT WOMAN
   on the left
AGRICULTURIST KATO
GIRL TRACTORIST
WOUNDED SOLDIER
THE DELEGATE
   from the capital
THE SINGER

} CHARACTERS IN PROLOGUE

GEORGI ABASHWILI, *the Governor*
NATELLA, *the Governor's wife*
MICHAEL, *their son*
SHALVA, *an adjutant*
ARSEN KAZBEKI, *a fat prince*
MESSENGER, *from the capital*
NIKO MIKADZE *and* MIKA LOLADZE, *doctors*
SIMON SHASHAVA, *a soldier*
GRUSHA VASHNADZE, *a kitchen maid*
OLD PEASANT *with the milk*
CORPORAL *and* PRIVATE
PEASANT *and his wife*

LAVRENTI VASHNADZE, *Grusha's brother*
ANIKO, *his wife*
PEASANT WOMAN, *for a while Grusha's mother-in-law*
JUSSUP, *her son*
MONK
AZDAK, *village recorder*
SHAUWA, *a policeman*
GRAND DUKE
DOCTOR
INVALID
LIMPING MAN
BLACKMAILER
LUDOVICA
INNKEEPER, *her father-in-law*
STABLEBOY
POOR OLD PEASANT WOMAN
IRAKLI, *her brother-in-law, a bandit*
THREE WEALTHY FARMERS
ILLO SHUBOLADZE *and* SANDRO OBOLADZE, *lawyers*
OLD MARRIED COUPLE
SOLDIERS, SERVANTS, PEASANTS, BEGGARS, MUSICIANS, MERCHANTS, NOBLES, ARCHITECTS

THE JUDGE Officer, fetch a piece of chalk. You will trace below the bench a circle, in the center of which you will place the young child. Then you will order the two women to wait, each of them at opposite sides of the circle. When the real mother takes hold of him, it will be easy for the child to come outside the circle. But the pretended mother cannot lead him out.

[THE OFFICER *traces a circle with the chalk and motions the* CHILD *to stand in the center of it.* MRS. MA *takes the* CHILD's *hand and leads him out of the circle.* HAI-TANG *fails to contend with her.*]

THE JUDGE It is evident that Hai-Tang is not the mother of the child, since she did not come forward to draw him out of the circle.

HAI-TANG I supplicate you, Honored Sir, to calm your wrath. If I cannot obtain my son without dislocating his arm or bruising his baby flesh, I would rather perish under the blows than make the least effort to take him out of the circle.

THE JUDGE A sage of old once said: What man can hide what he really is? Behold the power of the Chalk Circle! In order to seize an inheritance, Mrs. Ma has raised a young child that is not her own. But the Chalk Circle augustly brought out the truth and the false-hood. Mrs. Ma has an engaging exterior but her heart is corrupt. The true mother—Hai-Tang—is at last recognized.

—From *The Chalk Circle*, an anonymous Chinese play written about 1300 A.D.

[*The time and the place: After a prologue, set in 1945, we move back perhaps 1000 years.*

The action of The Caucasian Chalk Circle *centers on Nuka (or Nukha), a town in Azerbaijan. However, the capital referred to in the prologue is not Baku (capital of Soviet Azerbaijan) but Tiflis (or Tbilisi), capital of Georgia. When Azdak, later, refers to "the capital" he means Nuka itself, though whether Nuka was ever capital of Georgia I do not know: in what reading I have done on the subject I have only found Nuka to be the capital of a Nuka Khanate.*

The word "Georgia" has not been used in this English version because of its American associations; instead, the alternative name "Grusinia" (in Russian, Gruziya) has been used.

The reasons for resettling the old Chinese story in Transcaucasia are not far to seek. The play was written when the Soviet chief of state, Joseph Stalin, was a Georgian, as was his favorite poet, cited in the Prologue, Mayakovsky. And surely there is a point in having this story acted out at the place where Europe and Asia meet, a place incomparably rich in legend and history. Here Jason found the Golden Fleece. Here Noah's Ark touched ground. Here the armies of both Genghis Khan and Tamerlane wrought havoc.]

—ERIC BENTLEY[1]

PROLOGUE

Among the ruins of a war-ravaged Caucasian village the members of two Kolkhoz villages, mostly women and older men, are sitting in a circle, smoking and drinking wine. With them is a DELEGATE *of the State Reconstruction Commission from Nuka, the capital.*

[1] Friend of Brecht's and original editor of this play.

PEASANT WOMAN, *left* [*Pointing.*] In those hills over there we stopped three Nazi tanks, but the apple orchard was already destroyed.

OLD MAN, *right* Our beautiful dairy farm: a ruin.

GIRL TRACTORIST I laid the fire, Comrade. [*Pause.*]

DELEGATE Nuka, capital of Grusinia. Delegation received from the goat-breeding Kolkhoz "Rosa Luxemburg." This is a collective farm which moved eastwards on orders from the authorities at the approach of Hitler's armies. They are now planning to return. Their delegates have looked at the village and the land and found a lot of destruction. [*Delegates on the right nod.*] But the neighboring fruit farm —Kolkhoz [*To the left.*] "Galinsk"—proposes to use the former grazing land of Kolkhoz "Rosa Luxemburg" for orchards and vineyards. This land lies in a valley where grass doesn't grow very well. As a delegate of the Reconstruction Commission in Nuka I request that the two Kolkhoz villages decide between themselves whether Kolkhoz "Rosa Luxemburg" shall return or not.

OLD MAN, *right* First of all, I want to protest against the time limit on discussion. We of Kolkhoz "Rosa Luxemburg" have spent three days and three nights getting here. And now discussion is limited to half a day.

WOUNDED SOLDIER, *left* Comrade, we haven't as many villages as we used to have. We haven't as many hands. We haven't as much time.

GIRL TRACTORIST All pleasures have to be rationed. Tobacco is rationed, and wine. Discussion should be rationed.

OLD MAN, *right* [*Sighing.*] Death to the fascists! But I will come to the point and explain why we want our valley back. There are a great many reasons, but I'll begin with one of the simplest. Makinä Abakidze, unpack the goat cheese. [*A peasant woman from right takes from a basket an enormous cheese wrapped in a cloth. Applause and laughter.*] Help yourselves, Comrades, start in!

OLD MAN, *left* [*Suspiciously.*] Is this a way of influencing us?

OLD MAN, *right* [*Amid laughter.*] How could it be a way of influencing you, Surab, you valley-thief? Everyone knows you'll take the cheese and the valley, too. [*Laughter.*] All I expect from you is an honest answer. Do you like the cheese?

OLD MAN, *left* The answer is: yes.

OLD MAN, *right* Really. [*Bitterly.*] I ought to have known you know nothing about cheese.

OLD MAN, *left* Why not? When I tell you I like it?

OLD MAN, *right* Because you can't like it. Because it's not what it was in the old days. And why not? Because our goats don't like the new grass as they did the old. Cheese is not cheese because grass is not grass, that's the thing. Please put that in your report.

OLD MAN, *left* But your cheese is excellent.

OLD MAN, *right* It isn't excellent. It's just passable. The new grazing land is no good, whatever the young people may say. One can't live there. It doesn't even smell of morning in the morning. [*Several people laugh.*]

DELEGATE Don't mind their laughing: they understand you. Comrades, why does one love one's country? Because the bread tastes better there, the air smells better, voices sound stronger, the sky is higher, the ground is easier to walk on. Isn't that so?

OLD MAN, *right* The valley has belonged to us from all eternity.

SOLDIER, *left* What does *that* mean—from all eternity? Nothing belongs to anyone from all eternity. When you were young you didn't even belong to yourself. You belonged to the Kazbeki princes.

OLD MAN, *right* Doesn't it make a difference, though, what kind of trees stand next to the house you are born in? Or what kind of neighbors you have? Doesn't that make a difference? We want to go back just to have you as our neighbors, valley-thieves! Now you can all laugh again.

OLD MAN, *left* [*Laughing.*] Then why don't you listen to what your neighbor, Kato Wachtang, our agriculturist, has to say about the valley?

PEASANT WOMAN, *right* We've not said all there is to be said about our valley. By no means. Not all the houses are destroyed. As for the dairy farm, at least the foundation wall is still standing.

DELEGATE You can claim State support—here and there—you know that. I have suggestions here in my pocket.

PEASANT WOMAN, *right* Comrade Specialist, we haven't come here to haggle. I can't take your cap and hand you another, and say "This one's better." The other one might *be* better, but you *like* yours better.

GIRL TRACTORIST A piece of land is not a cap—not in our country, Comrade.

DELEGATE Don't get mad. It's true we have to consider a piece of land as a tool to produce something useful, but it's also true that we must recognize love for a particular piece of land. As far as I'm concerned, I'd like to find out more exactly what you [*To those on the left.*] want to do with the valley.

OTHERS Yes, let Kato speak.

KATO [*Rising; she's in military uniform.*] Comrades, last winter, while we were fighting in these hills here as Partisans, we discussed how, once the Germans were expelled, we could build up our fruit culture to ten times its original size. I've prepared a plan for an irrigation project. By means of a cofferdam on our mountain lake, 300 hectares of unfertile land can be irrigated. Our Kolkhoz could not only cultivate more fruit, but also have vineyards. The project, however, would pay only if the disputed valley of Kolkhoz "Rosa Luxemburg" were also included. Here are the calculations. [*She hands* DELEGATE *a briefcase.*]

OLD MAN, *right* Write into the report that our Kolkhoz plans to start a new stud farm.

GIRL TRACTORIST Comrades, the project was conceived during days and nights when we had to take cover in the mountains. We were often without ammunition for our half-dozen rifles. Even finding a pencil was difficult. [*Applause from both sides.*]

OLD MAN, *right* Our thanks to the Comrades of Kolkhoz "Galinsk" and all those who've defended our country! [*They shake hands and embrace.*]

PEASANT WOMAN, *left* In doing this our thought was that our soldiers—both your men and our men—should return to a still more productive homeland.

GIRL TRACTORIST As the poet Mayakovsky said: "The home of the Soviet people shall also be the home of Reason"!

The delegates including the OLD MAN *have got up, and with the* DELEGATE *specified proceed to study the Agriculturist's drawings. Ex-*

clamations such as: "Why is the altitude of fall 22 meters?"—"This rock will have to be blown up"—"Actually, all they need is cement and dynamite"—"They force the water to come down here, that's clever!"

A VERY YOUNG WORKER, *right* [*To* OLD MAN, *right.*] They're going to irrigate all the fields between the hills, look at that, Aleko!

OLD MAN, *right* I'm not going to look. I knew the project would be good. I won't have a pistol pointed at me!

DELEGATE But they only want to point a pencil at you!
Laughter.

OLD MAN, *right* [*Gets up gloomily, and walks over to look at the drawing.*] These valley-thieves know only too well that we in this country are suckers for machines and projects.

PEASANT WOMAN, *right* Aleko Bereshwili, you have a weakness for new projects. That's well known.

DELEGATE What about my report? May I write that you will all support the cession of your old valley in the interests of this project when you get back to your Kolkhoz?

PEASANT WOMAN, *right* I will. What about you, Aleko?

OLD MAN, *right* [*Bent over drawings.*] I suggest that you give us copies of the drawings to take along.

PEASANT WOMAN, *right* Then we can sit down and eat. Once he has the drawings and he's ready to discuss them, the matter is settled. I know him. And it will be the same with the rest of us.
Delegates laughingly embrace again.

OLD MAN, *left* Long live the Kolkhoz "Rosa Luxemburg" and much luck to your horse-breeding project!

PEASANT WOMAN, *left* In honor of the visit of the delegates from Kolkhoz "Rosa Luxemburg" and of the Specialist, the plan is that we all hear a presentation of the Singer Arkadi Tscheidse.
Applause. GIRL TRACTORIST *has gone off to bring the* SINGER.

PEASANT WOMAN, *right* Comrades, your entertainment had better be good. It's going to cost us a valley.

PEASANT WOMAN, *left* Arkadi Tscheidse knows about our discussion. He's promised to perform

something that has a bearing on the problem.

KATO We wired Tiflis three times. The whole thing nearly fell through at the last minute because his driver had a cold.

PEASANT WOMAN, *left* Arkadi Tscheidse knows 21,000 lines of verse.

OLD MAN, *left* He's hard to get. You and the Planning Commission should persuade him to come north more often, Comrade.

DELEGATE We are more interested in economics, I'm afraid.

OLD MAN, *left* [*Smiling.*] You arrange the redistribution of vines and tractors, why not songs?
Enter the SINGER *Arkadi Tscheidse, led by* GIRL TRACTORIST. *He is a well-built man of simple manners, accompanied by* FOUR MUSICIANS *with their instruments. The artists are greeted with applause.*

GIRL TRACTORIST This is the Comrade Specialist, Arkadi.
The SINGER *greets them all.*

DELEGATE Honored to make your acquaintance. I heard about your songs when I was a boy at school. Will it be one of the old legends?

SINGER A very old one. It's called "The Chalk Circle" and comes from the Chinese. But we'll do it, of course, in a changed version. Comrades, it's an honor for me to entertain you after a difficult debate. We hope you will find that the voice of the old poet also sounds well in the shadow of Soviet tractors. It may be a mistake to mix different wines, but old and new wisdoms mix admirably. Now I hope we'll get something to eat before the performance begins—it would certainly help.

VOICES Surely. Everyone into the Club House!
While everyone begins to move, DELEGATE *turns to* GIRL TRACTORIST.

DELEGATE I hope it won't take long. I've got to get back tonight.

GIRL TRACTORIST How long will it last, Arkadi? The Comrade Specialist must get back to Tiflis tonight.

SINGER [*Casually.*] It's actually two stories. An hour or two.

GIRL TRACTORIST [*Confidentially.*] Couldn't you make it shorter?

SINGER No.

VOICE Arkadi Tscheidse's performance will take place here in the square after the meal.
And they all go happily to eat.

1

THE NOBLE CHILD

As the lights go up, the SINGER *is seen sitting on the floor, a black sheepskin cloak round his shoulders, and a little, well-thumbed notebook in his hand. A small group of listeners— the chorus—sits with him. The manner of his recitation makes it clear that he has told his story over and over again. He mechanically fingers the pages, seldom looking at them. With appropriate gestures, he gives the signal for each scene to begin.*

SINGER   In olden times, in a bloody time,
There ruled in a Caucasian city—
Men called it City of the Damned—
A Governor.
His name was Georgi Abashwili.
He was rich as Croesus
He had a beautiful wife
He had a healthy baby.
No other governor in Grusinia
Had so many horses in his stable
So many beggars on his doorstep
So many soldiers in his service
So many petitioners in his courtyard.
Georgi Abashwili—how shall I describe him
to you?
He enjoyed his life.
On the morning of Easter Sunday
The Governor and his family went to church.
At the left a large doorway, at the right an even larger gateway. BEGGARS *and* PETITIONERS *pour from the gateway, holding up thin* CHILDREN, *crutches, and petitions. They are followed by* IRONSHIRTS, *and then, expensively dressed, the* GOVERNOR'S FAMILY.

BEGGARS AND PETITIONERS   —Mercy! Mercy, Your Grace! The taxes are too high.
   —I lost my leg in the Persian War, where can I get . . .
   —My brother is innocent, Your Grace, a misunderstanding . . .
   —The child is starving in my arms!
   —Our petition is for our son's discharge from the army, our last remaining son!
   —Please, Your Grace, the water inspector takes bribes.
One servant collects the petitions. Another distributes coins from a purse. Soldiers push the crowd back, lashing at them with thick leather whips.

SOLDIER   Get back! Clear the church door!
   Behind the GOVERNOR, *his* WIFE, *and the* ADJUTANT, *the* GOVERNOR'S CHILD *is brought through the gateway in an ornate carriage.*

CROWD   —The baby!
   —I can't see it, don't shove so hard!
   —God bless the child, Your Grace!

SINGER   [*While the crowd is driven back with whips.*] For the first time on that Easter Sunday, the people saw the Governor's heir.
Two doctors never moved from the noble child, apple of the Governor's eye.
Even the mighty Prince Kazbeki bows before him at the church door.
   The FAT PRINCE *steps forwards and greets the* FAMILY.

FAT PRINCE   Happy Easter, Natella Abashwili! What a day! When it was raining last night, I thought to myself, gloomy holidays! But this morning the sky was gay. I love a gay sky, a simple heart, Natella Abashwili. And little Michael is a governor from head to foot! Tititi! [*He tickles the* CHILD.]

GOVERNOR'S WIFE   What do you think, Arsen, at last Georgi has decided to start building the east wing. All those wretched slums are to be torn down to make room for the garden.

FAT PRINCE   Good news after so much bad! What's the latest on the war, Brother Georgi? [*The* GOVERNOR *indicates a lack of interest.*] Strategical retreat, I hear. Well, minor reverses are to be expected. Sometimes things go well, sometimes not. Such is war. Doesn't mean a thing, does it?

GOVERNOR'S WIFE   He's coughing. Georgi, did you hear? [*She speaks sharply to the* DOCTORS, *two dignified men standing close to the little carriage.*] He's coughing!

FIRST DOCTOR   [*To the* SECOND.] May I remind you, Niko Mikadze, that I was against the lukewarm bath? [*To the* GOVERNOR'S WIFE.] There's been a little error over warming the bath water, Your Grace.

SECOND DOCTOR   [*Equally polite.*] Mika Loladze, I'm afraid I can't agree with you. The temperature of the bath water was exactly what our great, beloved Mishiko Oboladze prescribed. More likely a slight draft during the night, Your Grace.

GOVERNOR'S WIFE But do pay more attention to him. He looks feverish, Georgi.

FIRST DOCTOR [*Bending over the* CHILD.] No cause for alarm, Your Grace. The bath water will be warmer. It won't occur again.

SECOND DOCTOR [*With a venomous glance at the* FIRST.] I won't forget that, my dear Mika Loladze. No cause for concern, Your Grace.

FAT PRINCE Well, well, well! I always say. "A pain in my liver? Then the doctor gets fifty strokes on the soles of his feet." We live in a decadent age. In the old days one said: "Off with his head!"

GOVERNOR'S WIFE Let's go into church. Very likely it's the draft here.

The procession of FAMILY *and* SERVANTS *turns into the doorway. The* FAT PRINCE *follows, but the* GOVERNOR *is kept back by the* ADJUTANT, *a handsome young man. When the crowd of* PETITIONERS *has been driven off, a young dust-stained* RIDER, *his arm in a sling, remains behind.*

ADJUTANT [*Pointing at the* RIDER, *who steps forward.*] Won't you hear the messenger from the capital, Your Excellency? He arrived this morning. With confidential papers.

GOVERNOR Not before Service, Shalva. But did you hear Brother Kazbeki wish me a happy Easter? Which is all very well, but I don't believe it did rain last night.

ADJUTANT [*Nodding.*] We must investigate.

GOVERNOR Yes, at once. Tomorrow.

They pass through the doorway. The RIDER, *who has waited in vain for an audience, turns sharply round and, muttering a curse, goes off. Only one of the palace guards—*SIMON SHASHAVA—*remains at the door.*

SINGER The city is still.
Pigeons strut in the church square.
A soldier of the Palace Guard
Is joking with a kitchen maid
As she comes up from the river with a bundle.

*A girl—*GRUSHA VASHNADZE—*comes through the gateway with a bundle made of large green leaves under her arm.*

SIMON What, the young lady is not in church? Shirking?

GRUSHA I was dressed to go. But they needed another goose for the banquet. And they asked me to get it. I know about geese.

SIMON A goose? [*He feigns suspicion.*] I'd like to see that goose. [GRUSHA *does not understand.*] One must be on one's guard with women. "I only went for a fish," they tell you, but it turns out to be something else.

GRUSHA [*Walking resolutely toward him and showing him the goose.*] There! If it isn't a fifteen-pound goose stuffed full of corn, I'll eat the feathers.

SIMON A queen of a goose! The Governor himself will eat it. So the young lady has been down to the river again?

GRUSHA Yes, at the poultry farm.

SIMON Really? At the poultry farm, down by the river . . . not higher up maybe? Near those willows?

GRUSHA I only go to the willows to wash the linen.

SIMON [*Insinuatingly.*] Exactly.

GRUSHA Exactly what?

SIMON [*Winking.*] Exactly that.

GRUSHA Why shouldn't I wash the linen by the willows?

SIMON [*With exaggerated laughter.*] "Why shouldn't I wash the linen by the willows!" That's good, really good!

GRUSHA I don't understand the soldier. What's so good about it?

SIMON [*Slyly.*] "If something I know someone learns, she'll grow hot and cold by turns!"

GRUSHA I don't know what I could learn about those willows.

SIMON Not even if there was a bush opposite? That one could see everything from? Everything that goes on there when a certain person is—"washing linen"?

GRUSHA What does go on? Won't the soldier say what he means and have done?

SIMON Something goes on. Something can be seen.

GRUSHA Could the soldier mean I dip my toes in the water when it's hot? There's nothing else.

SIMON There's more. Your toes. And more.

GRUSHA More what? At most my foot?

SIMON Your foot. And a little more. [*He laughs heartily.*]

GRUSHA [*Angrily.*] Simon Shashava, you ought to be ashamed of yourself! To sit in a bush on a hot day and wait till a girl comes and dips her legs in the river! And I bet you bring a friend along too! [*She runs off.*]

SIMON [*Shouting after her.*] I didn't bring any friends along!

As the SINGER *resumes his tale, the* SOLDIER *steps into the doorway as though to listen to the service.*

SINGER The city lies still
But why are there armed men?
The Governor's palace is at peace
But why is it a fortress?
And the Governor returned to his palace
And the fortress was a trap
And the goose was plucked and roasted
But the goose was not eaten this time
And noon was no longer the hour to eat:
Noon was the hour to die.

From the doorway at the left the FAT PRINCE *quickly appears, stands still, looks around. Before the gateway at the right two* IRONSHIRTS *are squatting and playing dice. The* FAT PRINCE *sees them, walks slowly past, making a sign to them. They rise: one goes through the gateway, the other goes off at the right. Muffled voices are heard from various directions in the rear: "To your posts!" The palace is surrounded. The* FAT PRINCE *quickly goes off. Church bells in the distance. Enter, through the doorway, the Governor's family and procession, returning from church.*

GOVERNOR'S WIFE [*Passing the* ADJUTANT.] It's impossible to live in such a slum. But Georgi, of course, will only build for his little Michael. Never for me! Michael is all! All for Michael!

The procession turns into the gateway. Again the ADJUTANT *lingers behind. He waits. Enter the wounded* RIDER *from the doorway. Two* IRONSHIRTS *of the Palace Guard have taken up positions by the gateway.*

ADJUTANT [*To the* RIDER.] The Governor does not wish to receive military news before dinner—especially if it's depressing, as I assume. In the afternoon His Excellency will confer with prominent architects. They're coming to dinner too. And here they are! [*Enter three gentlemen through the doorway.*] Go to the kitchen and eat, my friend. [*As the* RIDER *goes, the* ADJUTANT *greets the* ARCHITECTS.] Gentlemen, His Excellency expects you at dinner. He will devote all his time to you and your great new plans. Come!

ONE OF THE ARCHITECTS We marvel that His Excellency intends to build. There are disquieting rumors that the war in Persia has taken a turn for the worse.

ADJUTANT All the more reason to build! There's nothing to those rumors anyway. Persia is a long way off, and the garrison here would let itself be hacked to bits for its Governor. [*Noise from the palace. The shrill scream of a woman. Someone is shouting orders. Dumbfounded, the* ADJUTANT *moves toward the gateway. An* IRONSHIRT *steps out, points his lance at him.*] What's this? Put down that lance, you dog.

ONE OF THE ARCHITECTS It's the Princes! Don't you know the Princes met last night in the capital? And they're against the Grand Duke and his Governors? Gentlemen, we'd better make ourselves scarce. [*They rush off. The* ADJUTANT *remains helplessly behind.*]

ADJUTANT [*Furiously to the Palace Guard.*] Down with those lances! Don't you see the Governor's life is threatened?

The IRONSHIRTS *of the Palace Guard refuse to obey. They stare coldly and indifferently at the* ADJUTANT *and follow the next events without interest.*

SINGER O blindness of the great!
They go their way like gods,
Great over bent backs,
Sure of hired fists,
Trusting in the power
Which has lasted so long.
But long is not forever.
O change from age to age!
Thou hope of the people!

Enter the GOVERNOR, *through the gateway, between two* SOLDIERS *armed to the teeth. He is in chains. His face is gray.*

Up, great sir, deign to walk upright!
From your palace the eyes of many foes follow you!
And now you don't need an architect, a carpenter will do.
You won't be moving into a new palace
But into a little hole in the ground.
Look about you once more, blind man!

The arrested man looks round.

Does all you had please you?
Between the Easter Mass and the Easter meal

You are walking to a place whence no one returns.

The GOVERNOR *is led off. A horn sounds an alarm. Noise behind the gateway.*

When the house of a great one collapses
Many little ones are slain.
Those who had no share in the *good* fortunes of the mighty
Often have a share in their *mis*fortunes.
The plunging wagon
Drags the sweating oxen down with it
Into the abyss.

The SERVANTS *come rushing through the gateway in panic.*

SERVANTS   [*Among themselves.*] —The baskets! —Take them all into the third courtyard! Food for five days!

—The mistress has fainted! Someone must carry her down.

—She must get away.

—What about us? We'll be slaughtered like chickens, as always.

—Goodness, what'll happen? There's bloodshed already in the city, they say.

—Nonsense, the Governor has just been asked to appear at a Princes' meeting. All very correct. Everything'll be ironed out. I heard this on the best authority . . .

The two DOCTORS *rush into the courtyard.*

FIRST DOCTOR   [*Trying to restrain the other.*] Niko Mikadze, it is your duty as a doctor to attend Natella Abashwili.

SECOND DOCTOR   My duty! It's yours!

FIRST DOCTOR   Whose turn is it to look after the child today, Niko Mikadze, yours or mine?

SECOND DOCTOR   Do you really think, Mika Loladze, I'm going to stay a minute longer in this accursed house on that little brat's account? [*They start fighting. All one hears is "You neglect your duty!" and "Duty, my foot!" Then the* SECOND DOCTOR *knocks the* FIRST *down.*] Go to hell! [*Exit.*]

Enter the soldier, SIMON SHASHAVA. *He searches in the crowd for* GRUSHA.

SIMON   Grusha! There you are at last! What are you going to do?

GRUSHA   Nothing. If worst comes to worst, I've a brother in the mountains. How about you?

SIMON   Forget about me. [*Formally again.*] Grusha Vashnadze, your wish to know my plans fills me with satisfaction. I've been ordered to accompany Madam Abashwili as her guard.

GRUSHA   But hasn't the Palace Guard mutinied?

SIMON   [*Seriously.*] That's a fact.

GRUSHA   Isn't it dangerous to go with her?

SIMON   In Tiflis, they say: Isn't the stabbing dangerous for the knife?

GRUSHA   You're not a knife, you're a man, Simon Shashava, what has that woman to do with you?

SIMON   That woman has nothing to do with me. I have my orders, and I go.

GRUSHA   The soldier is pigheaded: he is running into danger for nothing—nothing at all. I must get into the third courtyard, I'm in a hurry.

SIMON   Since we're both in a hurry we shouldn't quarrel. You need time for a good quarrel. May I ask if the young lady still has parents?

GRUSHA   No, just a brother.

SIMON   As time is short—my second question is this: Is the young lady as healthy as a fish in water?

GRUSHA   I may have a pain in the right shoulder once in a while. Otherwise I'm strong enough for my job. No one has complained. So far.

SIMON   That's well known. When it's Easter Sunday, and the question arises who'll run for the goose all the same, she'll be the one. My third question is this: Is the young lady impatient? Does she want apples in winter?

GRUSHA   Impatient? No. But if a man goes to war without any reason and then no message comes—that's bad.

SIMON   A message will come. And now my final question . . .

GRUSHA   Simon Shashava, I must get to the third courtyard at once. My answer is yes.

SIMON   [*Very embarrassed.*] Haste, they say, is the wind that blows down the scaffolding. But they also say: The rich don't know what haste is. I'm from . . .

GRUSHA   Kutsk . . .

SIMON   The young lady has been inquiring about me? I'm healthy, I have no dependents, I make ten piasters a month, as paymaster twenty piasters, and I'm asking—very sincerely—for your hand.

GRUSHA   Simon Shashava, it suits me well.

SIMON   [*Taking from his neck a thin chain with a little cross on it.*] My mother gave me this cross, Grusha Vashnadze. The chain is silver. Please wear it.

GRUSHA   Many thanks, Simon.

SIMON   [*Hangs it round her neck.*] It would be better to go to the third courtyard now. Or there'll be difficulties. Anyway, I must harness the horses. The young lady will understand?

GRUSHA   Yes, Simon.

They stand undecided.

SIMON   I'll just take the mistress to the troops that have stayed loyal. When the war's over, I'll be back. In two weeks. Or three. I hope my intended won't get tired, awaiting my return.

GRUSHA   Simon Shashava, I shall wait for you.
Go calmly into battle, soldier
The bloody battle, the bitter battle
From which not everyone returns:
When you return I shall be there.
I shall be waiting for you under the green elm
I shall be waiting for you under the bare elm
I shall wait until the last soldier has returned
And longer
When you come back from the battle
No boots will stand at my door
The pillow beside mine will be empty
And my mouth will be unkissed.
When you return, when you return
You will be able to say: It is just as it was.

SIMON   I thank you, Grusha Vashnadze. And good-bye!

He bows low before her. She does the same before him. Then she runs quickly off without looking round. Enter the ADJUTANT *from the gateway.*

ADJUTANT   [*Harshly.*] Harness the horses to the carriage! Don't stand there doing nothing, scum!

SIMON SHASHAVA *stands to attention and goes off. Two* SERVANTS *crowd from the gateway, bent low under huge trunks. Behind them, supported by her women, stumbles* NATELLA ABASHWILI. *She is followed by a* WOMAN *carrying the* CHILD.

GOVERNOR'S WIFE   I hardly know if my head's still on. Where's Michael? Don't hold him so clumsily. Pile the trunks onto the carriage. No news from the city, Shalva?

ADJUTANT   None. All's quiet so far, but there's not a minute to lose. No room for all those trunks in the carriage. Pick out what you need. [*Exit quickly.*]

GOVERNOR'S WIFE   Only essentials! Quick, open the trunks! I'll tell you what I need. [*The trunks are lowered and opened. She points at some brocade dresses.*] The green one! And, of course, the one with the fur trimming. Where are Niko Mikadze and Mika Loladze? I've suddenly got the most terrible migraine again. It always starts in the temples. [*Enter* GRUSHA.] Taking your time, eh? Go and get the hot water bottles this minute! [GRUSHA *runs off, returns later with hot water bottles; the* GOVERNOR'S WIFE *orders her about by signs.*] Don't tear the sleeves.

A YOUNG WOMAN   Pardon, madam, no harm has come to the dress.

GOVERNOR'S WIFE   Because I stopped you. I've been watching you for a long time. Nothing in your head but making eyes at Shalva Tzereteli. I'll kill you, you bitch! [*She beats the* YOUNG WOMAN.]

ADJUTANT   [*Appearing in the gateway.*] Please make haste, Natella Abashwili. Firing has broken out in the city. [*Exit.*]

GOVERNOR'S WIFE   [*Letting go of the* YOUNG WOMAN.] Oh dear, do you think they'll lay hands on us? Why should they? Why? [*She herself begins to rummage in the trunks.*] How's Michael? Asleep?

WOMAN WITH THE CHILD   Yes, madam.

GOVERNOR'S WIFE   Then put him down a moment and get my little saffron-colored boots from the bedroom. I need them for the green dress. [*The* WOMAN *puts down the* CHILD *and goes off.*] Just look how these things have been packed! No love! No understanding! If you don't give them every order yourself . . . At such moments you realize what kind of servants you have! They gorge themselves at your expense, and never a word of gratitude! I'll remember this.

ADJUTANT   [*Entering, very excited.*] Natella, you must leave at once!

GOVERNOR'S WIFE   Why? I've got to take this silver dress—it cost a thousand piasters. And that one there, and where's the wine-colored one?

ADJUTANT   [*Trying to pull her away.*] Riots have broken out! We must leave at once. Where's the baby?

GOVERNOR'S WIFE [*Calling to the* YOUNG WOMAN *who was holding the baby.*] Maro, get the baby ready! Where on earth are you?

ADJUTANT [*Leaving.*] We'll probably have to leave the carriage behind and go ahead on horseback.

The GOVERNOR'S WIFE *rummages again among her dresses, throws some onto the heap of chosen clothes, then takes them off again. Noises, drums are heard. The* YOUNG WOMAN *who was beaten creeps away. The sky begins to grow red.*

GOVERNOR'S WIFE [*Rummaging desperately.*] I simply cannot find the wine-colored dress. Take the whole pile to the carriage. Where's Asja? And why hasn't Maro come back? Have you all gone crazy?

ADJUTANT [*Returning.*] Quick! Quick!

GOVERNOR'S WIFE [*To the* FIRST WOMAN.] Run! Just throw them into the carriage!

ADJUTANT We're not taking the carriage. And if you don't come now, I'll ride off on my own.

GOVERNOR'S WIFE [*As the* FIRST WOMAN *can't carry everything.*] Where's that bitch Asja? [*The* ADJUTANT *pulls her away.*] Maro, bring the baby! [*To the* FIRST WOMAN.] Go and look for Masha. No, first take the dresses to the carriage. Such nonsense! I wouldn't dream of going on horseback!

Turning round, she sees the red sky, and starts back rigid. The fire burns. She is pulled out by the ADJUTANT. *Shaking, the* FIRST WOMAN *follows with the dresses.*

MARO [*From the doorway with the boots.*] Madam! [*She sees the trunks and dresses and runs toward the* CHILD, *picks it up, and holds it a moment.*] They left it behind, the beasts. [*She hands it to* GRUSHA.] Hold it a moment. [*She runs off, following the* GOVERNOR'S WIFE.] *Enter* SERVANTS *from the gateway.*

COOK Well, so they've actually gone. Without the food wagons, and not a minute too early. It's time for us to clear out.

GROOM This'll be an unhealthy neighborhood for quite a while. [*To one of the* WOMEN.] Suliko, take a few blankets and wait for me in the foal stables.

GRUSHA What have they done with the Governor?

GROOM [*Gesturing throat cutting.*] Ffffft.

A FAT WOMAN [*Seeing the gesture and becoming hysterical.*] Oh dear, oh dear, oh dear, oh dear! Our master Georgi Abashwili! A picture of health he was, at the morning Mass—and now! Oh, take me away, we're all lost, we must die in sin like our master, Georgi Abashwili!

OTHER WOMAN [*Soothing her.*] Calm down, Nina! You'll be taken to safety. You've never hurt a fly.

FAT WOMAN [*Being led out.*] Oh dear, oh dear, oh dear! Quick! Let's all get out before they come, before they come!

A YOUNG WOMAN Nina takes it more to heart than the mistress, that's a fact. They even have to have their weeping done for them.

COOK We'd better get out, all of us.

ANOTHER WOMAN [*Glancing back.*] That must be the East Gate burning.

YOUNG WOMAN [*Seeing the* CHILD *in* GRUSHA'S *arms.*] The baby! What are you doing with it?

GRUSHA It got left behind.

YOUNG WOMAN She simply left it there. Michael, who was kept out of all the drafts!

The SERVANTS *gather round the* CHILD.

GRUSHA He's waking up.

GROOM Better put him down, I tell you. I'd rather not think what'd happen to anybody who was found with that baby.

COOK That's right. Once they get started, they'll kill each other off, whole families at a time. Let's go.

Exeunt all but GRUSHA, *with the* CHILD *on her arm, and* TWO WOMEN.

TWO WOMEN Didn't you hear? Better put him down.

GRUSHA The nurse asked me to hold him a moment.

OLDER WOMAN She's not coming back, you simpleton.

YOUNGER WOMAN Keep your hands off it.

OLDER WOMAN [*Amiably.*] Grusha, you're a good soul, but you're not very bright, and you know it. I tell you, if he had the plague he couldn't be more dangerous.

GRUSHA [*Stubbornly.*] He hasn't got the plague. He looks at me! He's human!

OLDER WOMAN Don't look at *him.* You're a fool—the kind that always gets put upon. A person need only say, "Run for the salad, you have the longest legs," and you run. My husband has an ox cart—you can come with us if you hurry! Lord, by now the whole neighborhood must be in flames.

Both women leave, sighing. After some hesitation, GRUSHA *puts the sleeping* CHILD *down, looks at it for a moment, then takes a brocade blanket from the heap of clothes and covers it. Then both women return, dragging bundles.* GRUSHA *starts guiltily away from the* CHILD *and walks a few steps to one side.*

YOUNGER WOMAN   Haven't you packed anything yet? There isn't much time, you know. The Ironshirts will be here from the barracks.

GRUSHA   Coming!

She runs through the doorway. Both women go to the gateway and wait. The sound of horses is heard. They flee, screaming. Enter the FAT PRINCE *with drunken* IRONSHIRTS. *One of them carries the Governor's head on a lance.*

FAT PRINCE   Here! In the middle! [*One soldier climbs onto the other's back, takes the head, holds it tentatively over the door.*] That's not the middle. Farther to the right. That's it. What I do, my friends, I do well. [*While with hammer and nail, the soldier fastens the head to the wall by its hair.*] This morning at the church door I said to Georgi Abashwili: "I love a clear sky." Actually, I prefer the lightning that comes out of a clear sky. Yes, indeed. It's a pity they took the brat along, though, I need him, urgently.

Exit with IRONSHIRTS *through the gateway. Trumpling of horses again. Enter* GRUSHA *through the doorway looking cautiously about her. Clearly she has waited for the* IRONSHIRTS *to go. Carrying a bundle, she walks toward the gateway. At the last moment, she turns to see if the* CHILD *is still there. Catching sight of the head over the doorway, she screams. Horrified, she picks up her bundle again, and is about to leave when the* SINGER *starts to speak. She stands rooted to the spot.*

SINGER   As she was standing between courtyard and gate,
She heard or she thought she heard a low voice calling.
The child called to her,
Not whining, but calling quite sensibly,
Or so it seemed to her.
"Woman," it said, "help me."

And it went on, not whining, but saying quite sensibly:
"Know, woman, he who hears not a cry for help
But passes by with troubled ears will never hear
The gentle call of a lover nor the blackbird at dawn
Nor the happy sigh of the tired grape-picker as the Angelus rings."

She walks a few steps toward the CHILD *and bends over it.*

Hearing this she went back for one more look at the child:
Only to sit with him for a moment or two,
Only till someone should come,
His mother, or anyone.

Leaning on a trunk, she sits facing the CHILD.

Only till she would have to leave, for the danger was too great,
The city was full of flame and crying.

The light grows dimmer, as though evening and night were coming on.

Fearful is the seductive power of goodness!

GRUSHA *now settles down to watch over the* CHILD *through the night. Once, she lights a small lamp to look at it. Once, she tucks it in with a coat. From time to time she listens and looks to see whether someone is coming.*

And she sat with the child a long time,
Till evening came, till night came, till dawn came.
She sat too long, too long she saw
The soft breathing, the small clenched fists,
Till toward morning the seduction was complete
And she rose, and bent down and, sighing, took the child
And carried it away.

She does what the SINGER *says as he describes it.*

As if it was stolen goods she picked it up.
As if she was a thief she crept away.

2

THE FLIGHT INTO THE NORTHERN MOUNTAINS

SINGER   When Grusha Vashnadze left the city
On the Grusinian highway

On the way to the Northern Mountains
She sang a song, she bought some milk.

CHORUS   How will this human child escape
The bloodhounds, the trap-setters?
Into the deserted mountains she journeyed
Along the Grusinian highway she journeyed
She sang a song, she bought some milk.

GRUSHA VASHNADZE *walks on. On her back she carries the* CHILD *in a sack, in one hand is a large stick, in the other a bundle. She sings.*

THE SONG OF THE FOUR GENERALS

Four generals
Set out for Iran.
With the first one, war did not agree.
The second never won a victory.
For the third the weather never was right.
For the fourth the men would never fight.
Four generals
And not a single man!
Sosso Robakidse
Went marching to Iran
With him the war did so agree
He soon had won a victory.
For him the weather was always right.
For him the men would always fight.
Sosso Robakidse,
He is our man!

A peasant's cottage appears.

GRUSHA   [*To the* CHILD.] Noontime is meal time. Now we'll sit hopefully in the grass, while the good Grusha goes and buys a little pitcher of milk. [*She lays the* CHILD *down and knocks at the cottage door. An* OLD MAN *opens it.*] Grandfather, could I have a little pitcher of milk? And a corn cake, maybe?

OLD MAN   Milk? We have no milk. The soldiers from the city have our goats. Go to the soldiers if you want milk.

GRUSHA   But grandfather, you must have a little pitcher of milk for a baby?

OLD MAN   And for a God-bless-you, eh?

GRUSHA   Who said anything about a God-bless-you? [*She shows her purse.*] We'll pay like princes. "Head in the clouds, backside in the water." [*The peasant goes off, grumbling, for milk.*] How much for the milk?

OLD MAN   Three piasters. Milk has gone up.

GRUSHA   Three piasters for this little drop? [*Without a word the* OLD MAN *shuts the door*

in her face.] Michael, did you hear that? Three piasters! We can't afford it! [*She goes back, sits down again, and gives the* CHILD *her breasts.*] Suck. Think of the three piasters. There's nothing there, but you *think* you're drinking, and that's something. [*Shaking her head, she sees that the* CHILD *isn't sucking any more. She gets up, walks back to the door, and knocks again.*] Open, grandfather, we'll pay. [*Softly.*] May lightning strike you! [*When the* OLD MAN *appears.*] I thought it would be half a piaster. But the baby must be fed. How about one piaster for that little drop?

OLD MAN   Two.

GRUSHA   Don't shut the door again. [*She fishes a long time in her bag.*] Here are two piasters. The milk better be good. I still have two days' journey ahead of me. It's a murderous business you have here—and sinful, too!

OLD MAN   Kill the soldiers if you want milk.

GRUSHA   [*Giving the* CHILD *some milk.*] This is an expensive joke. Take a sip, Michael, it's a week's pay. Around here they think we earned our money just sitting around. Oh, Michael, Michael, you're a nice little load for a girl to take on! [*Uneasy, she gets up, puts the* CHILD *on her back, and walks on. The* OLD MAN, *grumbling, picks up the pitcher and looks after her unmoved.*]

SINGER   As Grusha Vashnadze went northward The Princes' Ironshirts went after her.

CHORUS   How will the barefoot girl escape the Ironshirts,
The bloodhounds, the trap-setters?
They hunt even by night.
Pursuers never tire.
Butchers sleep little.

Two IRONSHIRTS *are trudging along the highway.*

CORPORAL   You'll never amount to anything, blockhead, your heart's not in it. Your senior officer sees this in little things. Yesterday, when I made the fat gal, yes, you grabbed her husband as I commanded, and you did kick him in the belly, at my request, but did you *enjoy* it, like a loyal Private, or were you just doing your duty? I've kept an eye on you blockhead, you're a hollow reed and a tinkling cymbal, you won't get promoted. [*They walk a while in silence.*] Don't think I've forgotten how insubordinate you are, either. Stop limping! I forbid you to limp! You limp because I sold the horses, and I sold the horses because I'd never have got that price again. You limp to show me you don't like marching. I know you. It won't help. You wait. Sing!

TWO IRONSHIRTS [*Singing.*] Sadly to war I went my way

Leaving my loved one at her door.

My friends will keep her honor safe

Till from the war I'm back once more.

CORPORAL Louder!

TWO IRONSHIRTS [*Singing.*] When 'neath a headstone I shall be

My love a little earth will bring:

"Here rest the feet that oft would run to me

And here the arms that oft to me would cling."

They begin to walk again in silence.

CORPORAL A good soldier has his heart and soul in it. When he receives an order, he gets a hard-on, and when he drives his lance into the enemy's guts, he comes. [*He shouts for joy.*] He lets himself be torn to bits for his superior officer, and as he lies dying he takes note that his corporal is nodding approval, and that is reward enough, it's his dearest wish. *You* won't get any nod of approval, but you'll croak all right. Christ, how'm I to get my hands on the Governor's bastard with the help of a fool like you! [*They stay on stage behind.*]

SINGER When Grusha Vashnadze came to the River Sirra

Flight grew too much for her, the helpless child too heavy.

In the cornfields the rosy dawn

Is cold to the sleepless one, only cold.

The gay clatter of the milk cans in the farmyard where the smoke rises

Is only a threat to the fugitive.

She who carries the child feels its weight and little more.

GRUSHA stops in front of a farm. A fat PEASANT WOMAN is carrying a milk can through the door. GRUSHA waits until she has gone in, then approaches the house cautiously.

GRUSHA [*To the CHILD.*] Now you've wet yourself again, and you know I've no linen. Michael, this is where we part company. It's far enough from the city. They wouldn't want you *so* much that they'd follow you all *this* way, little good-for-nothing. The peasant woman is kind, and can't you just smell the milk? [*She bends down to lay the CHILD on the threshold.*] So farewell, Michael, I'll forget how you kicked

me in the back all night to make me walk faster. And you can forget the meager fare— it was meant well. I'd like to have kept you— your nose is so tiny—but it can't be. I'd have shown you your first rabbit, I'd have trained you to keep dry, but now I must turn around. My sweetheart the soldier might be back soon, and suppose he didn't find me? You can't ask that, can you? [*She creeps up to the door and lays the CHILD on the threshold. Then, hiding behind a tree, she waits until the PEASANT WOMAN opens the door and sees the bundle.*]

PEASANT WOMAN Good heavens, what's this? Husband!

PEASANT What is it? Let me finish my soup.

PEASANT WOMAN [*To the CHILD.*] Where's your mother then? Haven't you got one? It's a boy. Fine linen. He's from a good family, you can see that. And they just leave him on our doorstep. Oh, these are times!

PEASANT If they think we're going to feed it, they're wrong. You can take it to the priest in the village. That's the best we can do.

PEASANT WOMAN What'll the priest do with him? He needs a mother. There, he's waking up. Don't you think we could keep him, though?

PEASANT [*Shouting.*] No!

PEASANT WOMAN I could lay him in the corner by the armchair. All I need is a crib. I can take him into the fields with me. See him laughing? Husband, we have a roof over our heads. We can do it. Not another word out of you!

She carries the CHILD into the house. The PEASANT follows protesting. GRUSHA steps out from behind the tree, laughs, and hurries off in the opposite direction.

SINGER Why so cheerful, making for home?

CHORUS Because the child has won new parents with a laugh,

Because I'm rid of the little one, I'm cheerful.

SINGER And why so sad?

CHORUS Because I'm single and free, I'm sad

Like someone who's been robbed

Someone who's newly poor.

She walks for a short while, then meets the two IRONSHIRTS who point their lances at her.

CORPORAL Lady, you are running straight into the arms of the Armed Forces. Where are you coming from? And when? Are you having illicit relations with the enemy? Where is he hiding? What movements is he making in your rear? How about the hills? How about the valleys? How are your stockings held in position? [GRUSHA *stands there frightened.*] Don't be scared, we always stage a retreat, if necessary . . . what, blockhead? I always stage retreats. In that respect at least, I can be relied on. Why are you staring like that at my lance? In the field no soldier drops his lance, that's a rule. Learn it by heart, blockhead. Now, lady, where are you headed?

GRUSHA To meet my intended, one Simon Shashava, of the Palace Guard in Nuka.

CORPORAL Simon Shashava? Sure, I know him. He gave me the key so I could look you up once in a while. Blockhead, we are getting to be unpopular. We must make her realize we have honorable intentions. Lady, behind apparent frivolity I conceal a serious nature, so let me tell you officially: I want a child from you. [GRUSHA *utters a little scream.*] Blockhead, she understands me. Uh-huh, isn't it a sweet shock? "Then first I must take the noodles out of the oven, Officer. Then first I must change my torn shirt, Colonel." But away with jokes, away with my lance! We are looking for a baby. A baby from a good family. Have you heard of such a baby, from the city, dressed in fine linen, and suddenly turning up here?

GRUSHA No, I haven't heard a thing. [*Suddenly she turns round and runs back, panic-stricken. The* IRONSHIRTS *glance at each other, then follow her, cursing.*]

SINGER Run, kind girl! The killers are coming!
Help the helpless babe, helpless girl!
And so she runs!

CHORUS In the bloodiest times
There are kind people.

As GRUSHA *rushes into the cottage, the* PEASANT WOMAN *is bending over the* CHILD'S *crib.*

GRUSHA Hide him. Quick! The Ironshirts are coming! I laid him on your doorstep. But he isn't mine. He's from a good family.

PEASANT WOMAN Who's coming? What Ironshirts?

GRUSHA Don't ask questions. The Ironshirts that are looking for it.

PEASANT WOMAN They've no business in my house. But I must have a little talk with you, it seems.

GRUSHA Take off the fine linen. It'll give us away.

PEASANT WOMAN Linen, my foot! In this house I make the decisions! "*You* can't vomit in *my* room!" Why did you abandon it? It's a sin.

GRUSHA [*Looking out of the window.*] Look, they're coming out from behind those trees! I shouldn't have run away, it made them angry. Oh, what shall I do?

PEASANT WOMAN [*Looking out of the window and suddenly starting with fear.*] Gracious! Ironshirts!

GRUSHA They're after the baby.

PEASANT WOMAN Suppose they come in!

GRUSHA You mustn't give him to them. Say he's yours.

PEASANT WOMAN Yes.

GRUSHA They'll run him through if you hand him over.

PEASANT WOMAN But suppose they ask for it? The silver for the harvest is in the house.

GRUSHA If you let them have him, they'll run him through, right here in this room! You've got to say he's yours!

PEASANT WOMAN Yes. But what if they don't believe me?

GRUSHA You must be firm.

PEASANT WOMAN They'll burn the roof over our heads.

GRUSHA That's why you must say he's yours. His name's Michael. But I shouldn't have told you. [*The* PEASANT WOMAN *nods.*] Don't nod like that. And don't tremble—they'll notice.

PEASANT WOMAN Yes.

GRUSHA And stop saying yes, I can't stand it. [*She shakes the* WOMAN.] Don't you have any children?

PEASANT WOMAN [*Muttering.*] He's in the war.

GRUSHA Then maybe *he's* an Ironshirt? Do you want *him* to run children through with a lance? You'd bawl him out. "No fooling with lances in my house!" you'd shout, "is that what I've reared you for? Wash your neck before you speak to your mother!"

PEASANT WOMAN That's true, he couldn't get away with anything around here!

GRUSHA So you'll say he's yours?

PEASANT WOMAN Yes.

GRUSHA Look! They're coming!

There is a knocking at the door. The women don't answer. Enter IRONSHIRTS. The PEASANT WOMAN bows low.

CORPORAL Well, here she is. What did I tell you? What a nose I have! I *smelt* her. Lady, I have a question for you. Why did you run away? What did you think I would do to you? I'll bet it was something dirty. Confess!

GRUSHA [*While the* PEASANT WOMAN *bows again and again.*] I'd left some milk on the stove, and I suddenly remembered it.

CORPORAL Or maybe you imagined I looked at you in a dirty way? Like there could be something between us? A lewd sort of look, know what I mean?

GRUSHA I didn't see it.

CORPORAL But it's possible, huh? You admit that much. After all, I might be a pig. I'll be frank with you: I could think of all sorts of things if we were alone. [*To the* PEASANT WOMAN.] Shouldn't you be busy in the yard? Feeding the hens?

PEASANT WOMAN [*Falling suddenly to her knees.*] Soldier, I didn't know a thing about it. Please don't burn the roof over our heads.

CORPORAL What are you talking about?

PEASANT WOMAN I had nothing to do with it. She left it on my doorstep, I swear it!

CORPORAL [*Suddenly seeing the* CHILD *and whistling.*] Ah, so there's a little something in the crib! Blockhead, I smell a thousand piasters. Take the old girl outside and hold on to her. It looks like I have a little cross-examining to do. [*The* PEASANT WOMAN *lets herself be led out by the* PRIVATE, *without a word.*] So, you've got the child I wanted from you! [*He walks toward the crib.*]

GRUSHA Officer, he's mine. He's not the one you're after.

CORPORAL I'll just take a look. [*He bends over the crib.*]

GRUSHA *looks round in despair.*

GRUSHA He's mine! He's mine!

CORPORAL Fine linen!

GRUSHA *dashes at him to pull him away. He throws her off and again bends over the crib. Again looking round in despair, she sees a log of wood, seizes it, and hits the* CORPORAL *over the head from behind. The* CORPORAL *collapses. She quickly picks up the* CHILD *and rushes off.*

SINGER And in her flight from the Ironshirts
After twenty-two days of journeying
At the foot of the Janga-Tau Glacier
Grusha Vashnadze decided to adopt the child.

CHORUS The helpless girl adopted the helpless child.

GRUSHA *squats over a half-frozen stream to get the* CHILD *water in the hollow of her hand.*

GRUSHA Since no one else will take you, son,
I must take you.
Since no one else will take you, son,
You must take me.
O black day in a lean, lean year,
The trip was long, the milk was dear,
My legs are tired, my feet are sore:
But I wouldn't be without you any more.
I'll throw your silken shirt away
And dress you in rags and tatters.
I'll wash you, son, and christen you in glacier water.
We'll see it through together.

She has taken off the child's fine linen and wrapped it in a rag.

SINGER When Grusha Vashnadze
Pursued by the Ironshirts
Came to the bridge on the glacier
Leading to the villages of the Eastern Slope
She sang the Song of the Rotten Bridge
And risked two lives.

A wind has risen. The bridge on the glacier is visible in the dark. One rope is broken and half the bridge is hanging down the abyss.

MERCHANTS, *two men and a woman, stand undecided before the bridge as* GRUSHA *and the* CHILD *arrive. One man is trying to catch the hanging rope with a stick.*

FIRST MAN Take your time, young woman. You won't get across here anyway.

GRUSHA But I *have* to get the baby to the east side. To my brother's place.

MERCHANT WOMAN Have to? How d'you mean, "have to"? I have to get there, too—because I have to buy carpets in Atum—carpets a woman had to sell because her husband had to die. But can *I* do what I have to? Can she? Andrei's been fishing for that rope for hours. And I ask you, how are we going to fasten it, even if he gets it up?

FIRST MAN [*Listening.*] Hush, I think I hear something.

GRUSHA The bridge isn't quite rotted through. I think I'll try it.

MERCHANT WOMAN I wouldn't—if the devil himself were after me. It's suicide.

FIRST MAN [*Shouting.*] Hi!

GRUSHA Don't shout! [*To the* MERCHANT WOMAN.] Tell him not to shout.

FIRST MAN But there's someone down their calling. Maybe they've lost their way.

MERCHANT WOMAN Why shouldn't he shout? Is there something funny about you? Are they after you?

GRUSHA All right, I'll tell. The Ironshirts are after me. I knocked one down.

SECOND MAN Hide our merchandise!

The WOMAN *hides a sack behind a rock.*

FIRST MAN Why didn't you say so right away? [*To the others.*] If they catch her they'll make mincemeat out of her!

GRUSHA Get out of my way. I've got to cross that bridge.

SECOND MAN You can't. The precipice is two thousand feet deep.

FIRST MAN Even with the rope it'd be no use. We could hold it up with our hands. But then we'd have to do the same for the Ironshirts.

GRUSHA Go away.

There are calls from the distance: "Hi, up there!"

MERCHANT WOMAN They're getting near. But you can't take the child on that bridge. It's sure to break. And look!

GRUSHA *looks down into the abyss. The* IRONSHIRTS *are heard calling again from below.*

SECOND MAN Two thousand feet!

GRUSHA But those men are worse.

FIRST MAN You can't do it. Think of the baby. Risk your life but not a child's.

SECOND MAN With the child she's that much heavier!

MERCHANT WOMAN Maybe she's *really* got to get across. Give *me* the baby. I'll hide it. Cross the bridge alone!

GRUSHA I won't. We belong together. [*To the* CHILD.] "Live together, die together." [*She sings.*]

THE SONG OF THE ROTTEN BRIDGE

Deep is the abyss, son,
I see the weak bridge sway
But it's not for us, son,
To choose the way.

The way I know
Is the one you must tread,

And all you will eat
Is my bit of bread.

Of every four pieces
You shall have three.
Would that I knew
How big they will be!

Get out of my way, I'll try it without the rope.

MERCHANT WOMAN You are tempting God!

There are shouts from below.

GRUSHA Please, throw that stick away, or they'll get the rope and follow me. [*Pressing the* CHILD *to her, she steps onto the swaying bridge. The* MERCHANT WOMAN *screams when it looks as though the bridge is about to collapse. But* GRUSHA *walks on and reaches the far side.*]

FIRST MAN She made it!

MERCHANT WOMAN [*Who has fallen on her knees and begun to pray angrily.*] I still think it was a sin.

The IRONSHIRTS *appear; the* CORPORAL'S *head is bandaged.*

CORPORAL Seen a woman with a child?

FIRST MAN [*While the* SECOND MAN *throws the stick into the abyss.*] Yes, there! But the bridge won't carry you!

CORPORAL You'll pay for this, blockhead!

GRUSHA, *from the far bank, laughs and shows the* CHILD *to the* IRONSHIRTS. *She walks on. The wind blows.*

GRUSHA [*Turning to the* CHILD.] You mustn't be afraid of the wind. He's a poor thing too. He has to push the clouds along and he gets quite cold doing it. [*Snow starts falling.*] And the snow isn't so bad, either, Michael. It covers the little fir trees so they won't die in winter. Let me sing you a little song. [*She sings.*]

THE SONG OF THE CHILD

Your father is a bandit
A harlot the mother who bore you.
Yet honorable men
Shall kneel down before you.
Food to the baby horses
The tiger's son will take.
The mothers will get milk
From the son of the snake.

3

IN THE NORTHERN MOUNTAINS

SINGER   Seven days the sister, Grusha Vashnadze,

Journeyed across the glacier

And down the slopes she journeyed.

"When I enter my brother's house," she
thought,

"He will rise and embrace me."

"Is that you, sister?" he will say,

"I have long expected you.

This is my dear wife,

And this is my farm, come to me by marriage,

With eleven horses and thirty-one cows. Sit
down.

Sit down with your child at our table and eat."

The brother's house was in a lovely valley.

When the sister came to the brother,

She was ill from walking.

The brother rose from the table.

A fat peasant couple rise from the table.
LAVRENTI VASHNADZE *still has a napkin round
his neck, as* GRUSHA, *pale and supported by a*
SERVANT, *enters with the* CHILD.

LAVRENTI   Where've *you* come from, Grusha?

GRUSHA   [*Feebly.*] Across the Janga-Tau Pass,
Lavrenti.

SERVANT   I found her in front of the hay barn.
She has a baby with her.

SISTER-IN-LAW   Go and groom the mare.
Exit the SERVANT.

LAVRENTI   This is my wife Aniko.

SISTER-IN-LAW   I thought you were in service in
Nuka.

GRUSHA   [*Barely able to stand.*] Yes, I was.

SISTER-IN-LAW   Wasn't it a good job? We were
told it was.

GRUSHA   The Governor got killed.

LAVRENTI   Yes, we heard there were riots. Your
aunt told us. Remember, Aniko?

SISTER-IN-LAW   Here with us, it's very quiet.
City people always want something going on.
[*She walks toward the door, calling:*] Sosso,
Sosso, don't take the cake out of the oven yet,
d'you hear? Where on earth are you? [*Exit,
calling.*]

LAVRENTI   [*Quietly, quickly.*] Is there a father?
[*As she shakes her head:*] I thought not. We

must think up something. She's religious.

SISTER-IN-LAW   [*Returning.*] Those servants!
[*To* GRUSHA.] You have a child.

GRUSHA   It's mine. [*She collapses.* LAVRENTI
rushes to her assistance.]

SISTER-IN-LAW   Heavens, she's ill—what are we
going to do?

LAVRENTI   [*Escorting her to a bench near the
stove.*] Sit down, sit. I think it's just weakness,
Aniko.

SISTER-IN-LAW   As long as it's not scarlet fever!

LAVRENTI   She'd have spots if it was. It's only
weakness. Don't worry, Aniko. [*To* GRUSHA.]
Better, sitting down?

SISTER-IN-LAW   Is the child hers?

GRUSHA   Yes, mine.

LAVRENTI   She's on her way to her husband.

SISTER-IN-LAW   I see. Your meat's getting cold.
[LAVRENTI *sits down and begins to eat.*] Cold
food's not good for you, the fat mustn't get
cold, you know your stomach's your weak
spot. [*To* GRUSHA.] If your husband's not in
the city, where is he?

LAVRENTI   She got married on the other side of
the mountain, she says.

SISTER-IN-LAW   On the other side of the mountain. I see. [*She also sits down to eat.*]

GRUSHA   I think I should lie down somewhere,
Lavrenti.

SISTER-IN-LAW   If it's consumption we'll all get
it. [*She goes on cross-examining her.*] Has
your husband got a farm?

GRUSHA   He's a soldier.

LAVRENTI   But he's coming into a farm—a small
one—from his father.

SISTER-IN-LAW   Isn't he in the war? Why not?

GRUSHA   [*With effort.*] Yes, he's in the war.

SISTER-IN-LAW   Then why d'you want to go to
the farm?

LAVRENTI   When he comes back from the war,
he'll return to his farm.

SISTER-IN-LAW   But you're going there now?

LAVRENTI   Yes, to wait for him.

SISTER-IN-LAW   [*Calling shrilly.*] Sosso, the cake!

GRUSHA   [*Murmuring feverishly.*] A farm—a
soldier—waiting—sit down, eat.

SISTER-IN-LAW   It's scarlet fever.

GRUSHA   [*Starting up.*] Yes, he's got a farm!

LAVRENTI   I think it's just weakness, Aniko.
Would you look after the cake yourself, dear?

SISTER-IN-LAW   But when will he come back if
war's broken out again as people say? [*She

waddles off, shouting.] Sosso! Where on earth are you? Sosso!

LAVRENTI [*Getting up quickly and going to* GRUSHA.] You'll get a bed in a minute. She has a good heart. But wait till after supper.

GRUSHA [*Holding out the* CHILD *to him.*] Take him.

LAVRENTI [*Taking it and looking around.*] But you can't stay here long with the child. She's religious, you see.

GRUSHA *collapses.* LAVRENTI *catches her.*

SINGER   The sister was so ill,
The cowardly brother had to give her shelter.
Summer departed, winter came.
The winter was long, the winter was short
People mustn't know anything.
Rats mustn't bite,
Spring mustn't come.

GRUSHA *sits over the weaving loom in a workroom. She and the* CHILD, *who is squatting on the floor, are wrapped in blankets. She sings.*

THE SONG OF THE CENTER

And the lover started to leave
And his betrothed ran pleading after him
Pleading and weeping, weeping and teaching:
"Dearest mine, dearest mine
When you go to war as now you do
When you fight the foe as soon you will
Don't lead with the front line
And don't push with the rear line
At the front is red fire
In the rear is red smoke
Stay in the war's center
Stay near the standard bearer
The first always die
The last are also hit
Those in the center come home."

Michael, we must be clever. If we make ourselves as small as cockroaches, the sister-in-law will forget we're in the house, and then we can stay till the snow melts.

Enter LAVRENTI. *He sits down beside his sister.*

LAVRENTI   Why are you sitting there muffled up like coachmen, you two? Is it too cold in the room?

GRUSHA [*Hastily removing one shawl.*] It's not too cold, Lavrenti.

LAVRENTI   If it's too cold, you shouldn't be sitting here with the child. Aniko would never forgive herself! [*Pause.*] I hope our priest didn't question you about the child?

GRUSHA   He did, but I didn't tell him anything.

LAVRENTI   That's good. I wanted to speak to you about Aniko. She has a good heart but she's very, very sensitive. People need only mention our farm and she's worried. She takes everything hard, you see. One time our milkmaid went to church with a hole in her stocking. Ever since, Aniko has worn two pairs of stockings in church. It's the old family in her. [*He listens.*] Are you sure there are no rats around? If there are rats, you couldn't live here. [*There are sounds as of dripping from the roof.*] What's that, dripping?

GRUSHA   It must be a barrel leaking.

LAVRENTI   Yes, it must be a barrel. You've been here six months, haven't you? Was I talking about Aniko? [*They listen again to the snow melting.*] You can't imagine how worried she gets about your soldier-husband. "Suppose he comes back and can't find her!" she says and lies awake. "He can't come before the spring," I tell her. The dear woman! [*The drops begin to fall faster.*] When d'you think he'll come? What do *you* think? [GRUSHA *is silent.*] Not before the spring, you agree? [GRUSHA *is silent.*] You don't believe he'll come at all? [GRUSHA *is silent.*] But when the spring comes and the snow melts here and on the passes, you can't stay on. They may come and look for you. There's already talk of an illegitimate child. [*The "glockenspiel" of the falling drops has grown faster and steadier.*] Grusha, the snow is melting on the roof. Spring is here.

GRUSHA   Yes.

LAVRENTI [*Eagerly.*] I'll tell you what we'll do. You need a place to go, and, because of the child [*He sighs.*], you have to have a husband, so people won't talk. Now I've made cautious inquiries to see if we can find you a husband. Grusha, I *have* one. I talked to a peasant woman who has a son. Just the other side of the mountain. A small farm. And she's willing.

GRUSHA   But I *can't* marry! I must wait for Simon Shashava.

LAVRENTI   Of course. That's all been taken care of. You don't need a man in bed—you need a man on paper. And I've found you one. The son of this peasant woman is going to die.

Isn't that wonderful? He's at his last gasp. And all in line with our story—a husband from the other side of the mountain! And when you met him he was at the last gasp. So you're a widow. What do you say?

GRUSHA It's true I could use a document with stamps on it for Michael.

LAVRENTI Stamps make all the difference. Without something in writing the Shah couldn't prove he's a Shah. And you'll have a place to live.

GRUSHA How much does the peasant woman want?

LAVRENTI Four hundred piasters.

GRUSHA Where will you find it?

LAVRENTI [Guiltily.] Aniko's milk money.

GRUSHA No one would know us there. I'll do it.

LAVRENTI [Getting up.] I'll let the peasant woman know.
    Quick exit.

GRUSHA Michael, you cause a lot of fuss. I came to you as the pear tree comes to the sparrows. And because a Christian bends down and picks up a crust of bread so nothing will go to waste. Michael, it would have been better had I walked quickly away on that Easter Sunday in Nuka in the second courtyard. Now I am a fool.

SINGER The bridegroom was on his deathbed when the bride arrived.
The bridegroom's mother was waiting at the door, telling her to hurry.
The bride brought a child along.
The witness hid it during the wedding.
    On one side the bed. Under the mosquito net lies a very sick man. GRUSHA is pulled in at a run by her future mother-in-law. They are followed by LAVRENTI and the CHILD.

MOTHER-IN-LAW Quick! Quick! Or he'll die on us before the wedding. [To LAVRENTI.] I was never told she had a child already.

LAVRENTI What difference does it make? [Pointing toward the dying man.] It can't matter to him—in his condition.

MOTHER-IN-LAW To him? But I'll never survive the shame! We are honest people. [She begins to weep.] My Jussup doesn't have to marry a girl with a child!

LAVRENTI All right, make it another two hundred piasters. You'll have it in writing that the farm will go to you: but she'll have the right to live here for two years.

MOTHER-IN-LAW [Drying her tears.] It'll hardly cover the funeral expenses. I hope she'll really lend a hand with the work. And what's happened to the monk? He must have slipped out through the kitchen window. We'll have the whole village on our necks when they hear Jussup's end is come! Oh dear! I'll go get the monk. But he mustn't see the child!

LAVRENTI I'll take care he doesn't. But why only a monk? Why not a priest?

MOTHER-IN-LAW Oh, he's just as good. I only made one mistake: I paid half his fee in advance. Enough to send him to the tavern. I only hope . . . [She runs off.]

LAVRENTI She saved on the priest, the wretch! Hired a cheap monk.

GRUSHA You will send Simon Shashava to see me if he turns up after all?

LAVRENTI Yes. [Pointing at the SICK PEASANT.] Won't you take a look at him? [GRUSHA, taking MICHAEL to her, shakes her head.] He's not moving an eyelid. I hope we aren't too late.
    They listen. On the opposite side enter neighbors who look around and take up positions against the walls, thus forming another wall near the bed, yet leaving an opening so that the bed can be seen. They start murmuring prayers. Enter the MOTHER-IN-LAW with a MONK. Showing some annoyance and surprise, she bows to the guests.

MOTHER-IN-LAW I hope you won't mind waiting a few moments? My son's bride has just arrived from the city. An emergency wedding is about to be celebrated. [To the MONK in the bedroom.] I might have known you couldn't keep your trap shut. [To GRUSHA.] The wedding can take place at once. Here's the license. Me and the bride's brother [LAVRENTI tries to hide in the background, after having quietly taken MICHAEL back from GRUSHA. The MOTHER-IN-LAW waves him away.] are the witnesses.
    GRUSHA has bowed to the MONK. They go to the bed. The MOTHER-IN-LAW lifts the mosquito net. The MONK starts reeling off the marriage ceremony in Latin. Meanwhile the MOTHER-IN-LAW beckons to LAVRENTI to get rid of the CHILD, but fearing that it will cry he draws its attention to the ceremony, GRUSHA glances once at the CHILD, and LAVRENTI waves the CHILD's hand in a greeting.

MONK Are you prepared to be a faithful, obedient, and good wife to this man, and to cleave to him until death you do part?

GRUSHA [*Looking at the* CHILD.] I am.

MONK [*To the* SICK PEASANT.] Are you prepared to be a good and loving husband to your wife until death you do part? [*As the* SICK PEASANT *does not answer, the* MONK *looks inquiringly around.*]

MOTHER-IN-LAW Of course he is! Didn't you hear him say yes?

MONK All right. We declare the marriage contracted! How about extreme unction?

MOTHER-IN-LAW Nothing doing! The wedding cost quite enough. Now I must take care of the mourners. [*To* LAVRENTI.] Did we say seven hundred?

LAVRENTI Six hundred. [*He pays.*] Now I don't want to sit with the guests and get to know people. So farewell, Grusha, and if my widowed sister comes to visit me, she'll get a welcome from my wife, or I'll show my teeth. [*Nods, gives the* CHILD *to* GRUSHA, *and leaves. The mourners glance after him without interest.*]

MONK May one ask where this child comes from?

MOTHER-IN-LAW Is there a child? I don't see a child. And you don't see a child either—you understand? Or it may turn out I saw all sorts of things in the tavern! Now come on.

After GRUSHA *has put the* CHILD *down and told him to be quiet, they move over left,* GRUSHA *is introduced to the neighbors.*

This is my daughter-in-law. She arrived just in time to find dear Jussup still alive.

ONE WOMAN He's been ill now a whole year, hasn't he? When our Vassili was drafted he was there to say good-bye.

ANOTHER WOMAN Such things are terrible for a farm. The corn all ripe and the farmer in bed! It'll really be a blessing if he doesn't suffer too long, I say.

FIRST WOMAN [*Confidentially.*] You know why we thought he'd taken to his bed? Because of the draft! And now his end is come!

MOTHER-IN-LAW Sit yourselves down, please! And have some cakes!

She beckons to GRUSHA *and both women go into the bedroom, where they pick up the cake pans off the floor. The guests, among them the* MONK, *sit on the floor and begin conversing in subdued voices.*

ONE PEASANT [*To whom the* MONK *has handed the bottle which he has taken from his soutane.*] There's a child, you say! How can that have happened to Jussup?

A WOMAN She was certainly lucky to get herself hitched, with him so sick!

MOTHER-IN-LAW They're gossiping already. And wolfing down the funeral cakes at the same time! If he doesn't die today, I'll have to bake some more tomorrow!

GRUSHA I'll bake them for you.

MOTHER-IN-LAW Yesterday some horsemen rode by, and I went out to see who it was. When I came in again he was lying there like a corpse! So I sent for you. It can't take much longer. [*She listens.*]

MONK Dear wedding and funeral guests! Deeply touched, we stand before a bed of death and marriage. The bride gets a veil; the groom, a shroud: how varied, my children, are the fates of men! Alas! One man dies and has a roof over his head, and the other is married and the flesh turns to dust from which it was made. Amen.

MOTHER-IN-LAW He's getting his own back. I shouldn't have hired such a cheap one. It's what you'd expect. A more expensive monk would behave himself. In Sura there's one with a real air of sanctity about him, but of course he charges a fortune. A fifty piaster monk like that has no dignity, and as for piety, just fifty piasters' worth and no more! When I came to get him in the tavern he'd just made a speech and he was shouting: "The war is over, beware of the peace!" We must go in.

GRUSHA [*Giving* MICHAEL *a cake.*] Eat this cake, and keep nice and still, Michael.

The two women offer cakes to the guests. The dying man sits up in bed. He puts his head out from under the mosquito net, stares at the two women, then sinks back again. The MONK *takes two bottles from his soutane and offers them to the peasant beside him. Enter three* MUSICIANS *who are greeted with a sly wink by the* MONK.

MOTHER-IN-LAW [*To the* MUSICIANS.] What are you doing here? With instruments?

ONE MUSICIAN Brother Anastasius here [*Pointing at the* MONK.] told us there was a wedding on.

MOTHER-IN-LAW What? You brought them?

Three more on my neck! Don't you know there's a dying man in the next room?

MONK A very tempting assignment for a musician: something that could be either a subdued Wedding March or a spirited Funeral Dance.

MOTHER-IN-LAW Well, you might as well play. Nobody can stop you eating in any case.

The musicians play a potpourri. The women serve cakes.

MONK The trumpet sounds like a whining baby. And you, little drum, what have you got to tell the world?

DRUNKEN PEASANT [*Beside the* MONK, *sings.*] Miss Roundass took the old old man
And said that marriage was the thing
To everyone who met 'er.
She later withdrew from the contract because
Candles are better.

The MOTHER-IN-LAW *throws the* DRUNKEN PEASANT *out. The music stops. The guests are embarrassed.*

GUESTS [*Loudly.*]—Have you heard? The Grand Duke is back! But the Princes are against him.

—They say the Shah of Persia has lent him a great army to restore order in Grusinia.

—But how is that possible? The Shah of Persia is the enemy . . .

—The enemy of Grusinia, you donkey, not the enemy of the Grand Duke!

—In any case, the war's over, so our soldiers are coming back.

GRUSHA *drops a cake pan. Guests help her pick up the cake.*

AN OLD WOMAN [*To* GRUSHA.] Are you feeling bad? It's just excitement about dear Jussup. Sit down and rest a while, my dear. [GRUSHA *staggers.*]

GUESTS Now everything'll be the way it was. Only the taxes'll go up because now we'll have to pay for the war.

GRUSHA [*Weakly.*] Did someone say the soldiers are back?

A MAN I did.

GRUSHA It can't be true.

FIRST MAN [*To a woman.*] Show her the shawl. We bought it from a soldier. It's from Persia.

GRUSHA [*Looking at the shawl.*] They are here. [*She gets up, takes a step, kneels down in prayer, takes the silver cross and chain out of her blouse, and kisses it.*]

MOTHER-IN-LAW [*While the guests silently watch* GRUSHA.] What's the matter with you? Aren't you going to look after our guests? What's all this city nonsense got to do with us?

GUESTS [*Resuming conversation while* GRUSHA *remains in prayer.*]—You can buy Persian saddles from the soldiers too. Though many want crutches in exchange for them.

—The leaders on one side can win a war, the soldiers on both sides lose it.

—Anyway, the war's over. It's something they can't draft you any more.

The dying man sits bolt upright in bed. He listens.

—What we need is two weeks of good weather.

—Our pear trees are hardly bearing a thing this year.

MOTHER-IN-LAW [*Offering cakes.*] Have some more cakes and welcome! There are more!

The MOTHER-IN-LAW *goes to the bedroom with the empty cake pans. Unaware of the dying man, she is bending down to pick up another tray when he begins to talk in a hoarse voice.*

PEASANT How many more cakes are you going to stuff down their throats? D'you think I can shit money?

The MOTHER-IN-LAW *starts, stares at him aghast, while he climbs out from behind the mosquito net.*

FIRST WOMAN [*Talking kindly to* GRUSHA *in the next room.*] Has the young wife got someone at the front?

A MAN It's good news that they're on their way home, huh?

PEASANT Don't stare at me like that! Where's this wife you've saddled me with?

Receiving no answer, he climbs out of bed and in his nightshirt staggers into the other room. Trembling, she follows him with the cake pan.

GUESTS [*Seeing him and shrieking.*] Good God! Jussup!

Everyone leaps up in alarm. The women rush to the door. GRUSHA, *still on her knees, turns round and stares at the man.*

PEASANT A funeral supper! You'd enjoy that, wouldn't you? Get out before I throw you out! [*As the guests stampede from the house, gloomily to* GRUSHA.] I've upset the apple cart, huh? [*Receiving no answer, he turns round and takes a cake from the pan which his mother is holding.*]

SINGER   O confusion! The wife discovers she has a husband.

By day there's the child, by night there's the husband.

The lover is on his way both day and night.

Husband and wife look at each other.

The bedroom is small.

  Near the bed the PEASANT *is sitting in a high wooden bathtub, naked, the* MOTHER-IN-LAW *is pouring water from a pitcher. Opposite* GRUSHA *cowers with* MICHAEL, *who is playing at mending straw mats.*

PEASANT   [*To his mother.*] That's her work, not yours. Where's she hiding out now?

MOTHER-IN-LAW   [*Calling.*] Grusha! The peasant wants you!

GRUSHA   [*To* MICHAEL.] There are still two holes to mend.

PEASANT   [*When* GRUSHA *approaches.*] Scrub my back!

GRUSHA   Can't the peasant do it himself?

PEASANT   "Can't the peasant do it himself?" Get the brush! To hell with you! Are you the wife here? Or are you a visitor? [*To the* MOTHER-IN-LAW.] It's too cold!

MOTHER-IN-LAW   I'll run for hot water.

GRUSHA   Let me go.

PEASANT   You stay here. [*The* MOTHER-IN-LAW *exits.*] Rub harder. And no shirking. You've seen a naked fellow before. That child didn't come out of thin air.

GRUSHA   The child was not conceived in joy, if that's what the peasant means.

PEASANT   [*Turning and grinning.*] You don't look the type. [GRUSHA *stops scrubbing him, starts back. Enter the* MOTHER-IN-LAW.]

PEASANT   A nice thing you've saddled me with! A simpleton for a wife!

MOTHER-IN-LAW   She just isn't cooperative.

PEASANT   Pour—but go easy! Ow! Go easy, I said. [*To* GRUSHA.] Maybe you did something wrong in the city . . . I wouldn't be surprised. Why else should you be here? But I won't talk about that. I've not said a word about the illegitimate object you brought into my house either. But my patience has limits! It's against nature. [*To the* MOTHER-IN-LAW.] More! [*To* GRUSHA.] And even if your soldier does come back, you're married.

GRUSHA   Yes.

PEASANT   But your soldier won't come back. Don't you believe it.

GRUSHA   No.

PEASANT   You're cheating me. You're my wife and you're not my wife. Where you lie, nothing lies, and yet no other woman can lie there. When I go to work in the morning I'm tired—when I lie down at night I'm awake as the devil. God has given you sex—and what d'you do? I don't have ten piasters to buy myself a woman in the city. Besides, it's a long way. Woman weeds the fields and opens up her legs, that's what our calendar says. D'you hear?

GRUSHA   [*Quietly.*] Yes. I didn't mean to cheat you out of it.

PEASANT   She didn't mean to cheat me out of it! Pour some more water! [*The* MOTHER-IN-LAW *pours.*] Ow!

SINGER   As she sat by the stream to wash the linen

She saw his image in the water

And his face grew dimmer with the passing moons.

As she raised herself to wring the linen

She heard his voice from the murmuring maple

And his voice grew fainter with the passing moons.

Evasions and sighs grew more numerous,

Tears and sweat flowed.

With the passing moons the child grew up.

  GRUSHA *sits by a stream, dipping linen into the water. In the rear, a few children are standing.*

GRUSHA   [*To* MICHAEL.] You can play with them, Michael, but don't let them boss you around just because you're the littlest. [MICHAEL *nods and joins the children. They start playing.*]

BIGGEST BOY   Today it's the Heads-Off Game. [*To a* FAT BOY.] You're the Prince and you laugh. [*To* MICHAEL.] You're the Governor. [*To a* GIRL.] You're the Governor's wife and you cry when his head's cut off. And I do the cutting. [*He shows his wooden sword.*] With this. First, they lead the Governor into the yard. The Prince walks in front. The Governor's wife comes last.

  They form a procession. The FAT BOY *is*

first and laughs. Then comes MICHAEL, *then the* BIGGEST BOY, *and then the* GIRL, *who weeps.*

MICHAEL   [*Standing still.*] Me cut off head!

BIGGEST BOY   That's my job. You're the littlest. The Governor's the easy part. All you do is kneel down and get your head cut off—simple.

MICHAEL   Me want sword!

BIGGEST BOY   It's mine! [*He gives* MICHAEL *a kick.*]

GIRL   [*Shouting to* GRUSHA.] He won't play his part!

GRUSHA   [*Laughing.*] Even the little duck is a swimmer, they say.

BIGGEST BOY   You can be the Prince if you can laugh. [MICHAEL *shakes his head.*]

FAT BOY   I laugh best. Let him cut off the head just once. Then you do it, then me.

Reluctantly, the BIGGEST BOY *hands* MICHAEL *the wooden sword and kneels down. The* FAT BOY *sits down, slaps his thigh, and laughs with all his might. The* GIRL *weeps loudly.* MICHAEL *swings the big sword and "cuts off" the head. In doing so, he topples over.*

BIGGEST BOY   Hey! I'll show you how to cut heads off!

MICHAEL *runs away. The children run after him.* GRUSHA *laughs, following them with her eyes. On looking back, she sees* SIMON SHAS-HAVA *standing on the opposite bank. He wears a shabby uniform.*

GRUSHA   Simon!

SIMON   Is that Grusha Vashnadze?

GRUSHA   Simon!

SIMON   [*Formally.*] A good morning to the young lady. I hope she is well.

GRUSHA   [*Getting up gaily and bowing low.*] A good morning to the soldier. God be thanked he has returned in good health.

SIMON   They found better fish, so they didn't eat me, said the haddock.

GRUSHA   Courage, said the kitchen boy. Good luck, said the hero.

SIMON   How are things here? Was the winter bearable? The neighbor considerate?

GRUSHA   The winter was a trifle rough, the neighbor as usual, Simon.

SIMON   May one ask if a certain person still dips her toes in the water when rinsing the linen?

GRUSHA   The answer is no. Because of the eyes in the bushes.

SIMON   The young lady is speaking of soldiers. Here stands a paymaster.

GRUSHA   A job worth twenty piasters?

SIMON   And lodgings.

GRUSHA   [*With tears in her eyes.*] Behind the barracks under the date trees.

SIMON   Yes, there. A certain person has kept her eyes open.

GRUSHA   She has, Simon.

SIMON   And has not forgotten? [GRUSHA *shakes her head.*] So the door is still on its hinges as they say? [GRUSHA *looks at him in silence and shakes her head again.*] What's this? Is anything not as it should be?

GRUSHA   Simon Shashava, I can never return to Nuka. Something has happened.

SIMON   What can have happened?

GRUSHA   For one thing, I knocked an Ironshirt down.

SIMON   Grusha Vashnadze must have had her reasons for that.

GRUSHA   Simon Shashava, I am no longer called what I used to be called.

SIMON   [*After a pause.*] I do not understand.

GRUSHA   When do women change their names, Simon? Let me explain. Nothing stands between us. Everything is just as it was. You must believe that.

SIMON   Nothing stands between us and yet there's something?

GRUSHA   How can I explain it so fast and with the stream between us? Couldn't you cross the bridge there?

SIMON   Maybe it's no longer necessary.

GRUSHA   It is very necessary. Come over on this side, Simon. Quick!

SIMON   Does the young lady wish to say someone has come too late?

GRUSHA *looks up at him in despair, her face streaming with tears.* SIMON *stares before him. He picks up a piece of wood and starts cutting it.*

SINGER   So many words are said, so many left unsaid.

The soldier has come.

Where he comes from, he does not say.

Hear what he thought and did not say:

"The battle began, gray at dawn, grew bloody at noon.

The first man fell in front of me, the second
behind me, the third at my side.

I trod on the first, left the second behind, the
third was run through by the captain.

One of my brothers died by steel, the other by
smoke.

My neck caught fire, my hands froze in my
gloves, my toes in my socks.

I fed on aspen buds, I drank maple juice, I
slept on stone, in water."

SIMON I see a cap in the grass. Is there a little
one already?

GRUSHA There is, Simon. There's no keeping
that from you. But please don't worry, it is
not mine.

SIMON When the wind once starts to blow,
they say, it blows through every cranny. The
wife need say no more. [GRUSHA *looks into her
lap and is silent.*]

SINGER There was yearning but there was no
waiting.

The oath is broken. Neither could say why.

Hear what she thought but did not say:

"While you fought in the battle, soldier,

The bloody battle, the bitter battle

I found a helpless infant

I had not the heart to destroy him

I had to care for a creature that was lost

I had to stoop for breadcrumbs on the floor

I had to break myself for that which was not
mine

That which was other people's.

Someone must help!

For the little tree needs water

The lamb loses its way when the shepherd is
asleep

And its cry is unheard!"

SIMON Give me back the cross I gave you. Better still, throw it in the stream. [*He turns to
go.*]

GRUSHA [*Getting up.*] Simon Shashava, don't
go away! He isn't mine! He isn't mine! [*She
hears the children calling.*] What's the matter,
children?

VOICES Soldiers! And they're taking Michael
away!

GRUSHA *stands aghast as two* IRONSHIRTS,
with MICHAEL *between them, come toward
her.*

ONE OF THE IRONSHIRTS Are you Grusha? [*She
nods.*] Is this your child?

GRUSHA Yes. [SIMON *goes.*] Simon!

IRONSHIRT We have orders, in the name of the
law, to take this child, found in your custody,
back to the city. It is suspected that the child
is Michael Abashwili, son and heir of the late
Governor Georgi Abashwili, and his wife, Natella Abashwili. Here is the document and the
seal. [*They lead the* CHILD *away.*]

GRUSHA [*Running after them, shouting.*] Leave
him here. Please! He's mine!

SINGER The Ironshirts took the child, the beloved child.

The unhappy girl followed them to the city,
the dreaded city.

She who had borne him demanded the child.

She who had raised him faced trial.

Who will decide the case?

To whom will the child be assigned?

Who will the judge be? A good judge? A bad?

The city was in flames.

In the judge's seat sat Azdak.[1]

4

THE STORY OF THE JUDGE

SINGER Hear the story of the judge

How he turned judge, how he passed judgment, what kind of judge he was.

On that Easter Sunday of the great revolt,
when the Grand Duke was overthrown

And his Governor Abashwili, father of our
child, lost his head

The Village Scrivener Azdak found a fugitive
in the woods and hid him in his hut.

AZDAK, *in rags and slightly drunk, is helping
an old beggar into his cottage.*

AZDAK Stop snorting, you're not a horse. And
it won't do you any good with the police to
run like a snotty nose in April. Stand still, I
say. [*He catches the* OLD MAN, *who has
marched into the cottage as if he'd like to go
through the walls.*] Sit down. Feed. Here's a
hunk of cheese. [*From under some rags, in a
chest, he fishes out some cheese, and the* OLD
MAN *greedily begins to eat.*] Haven't eaten
in a long time, huh? [*The* OLD MAN *growls.*]
Why were you running like that, asshole? The
cop wouldn't even have seen you.

OLD MAN Had to! Had to!

---

[1] [The name Azdak should be accented on the second syllable.—E. B.]

AZDAK Blue funk? [*The* OLD MAN *stares, uncomprehending.*] Cold feet? Panic? Don't lick your chops like a Grand Duke. Or an old sow. I can't stand it. We have to accept respectable stinkers as God made them, but not you! I once heard of a senior judge who farted at a public dinner to show an independent spirit! Watching you eat like that gives me the most awful ideas. Why don't you say something? [*Sharply.*] Show me your hand. Can't you hear? [*The* OLD MAN *slowly puts out his hand.*] White! So you're not a beggar at all! A fraud, a walking swindle! And I'm hiding you from the cops like you were an honest man! Why were you running like that if you're a landowner? For that's what you are. Don't deny it! I see it in your guilty face! [*He gets up.*] Get out! [*The* OLD MAN *looks at him uncertainly.*] What are you waiting for, peasant-flogger?

OLD MAN Pursued. Need undivided attention. Make proposition . . .

AZDAK Make what? A proposition? Well, if that isn't the height of insolence. He's making me a proposition! The bitten man scratches his fingers bloody, and the leech that's biting him makes him a proposition! Get out, I tell out!

OLD MAN Understand point of view! Persuasion! Pay hundred thousand piasters one night! Yes?

AZDAK What, you think you can buy me? For a hundred thousand piasters? Let's say a hundred and fifty thousand. Where are they?

OLD MAN Have not them here. Of course. Will be sent. Hope do not doubt.

AZDAK Doubt very much. Get out!

The OLD MAN *gets up, waddles to the door. A* VOICE *is heard offstage.*

VOICE Azdak!

The OLD MAN *turns, waddles to the opposite corner, stands still.*

AZDAK [*Calling out.*] I'm not in! [*He walks to door.*] So *you're* sniffing here again, Shauwa?

SHAUWA [*Reproachfully.*] You caught another rabbit, Azdak. And you'd promised me it wouldn't happen again!

AZDAK [*Severely.*] Shauwa, don't talk about things you don't understand. The rabbit is a dangerous and destructive beast. It feeds on plants, especially on the species of plants known as weeds. It must therefore be exterminated.

SHAUWA Azdak, don't be so hard on me. I'll lose my job if I don't arrest you. I know you have a good heart.

AZDAK I do not have a good heart! How often must I tell you I'm a man of intellect?

SHAUWA [*Slyly.*] I know, Azdak. You're a superior person. You say so yourself. I'm just a Christian and an ignoramus. So I ask you: When one of the Prince's rabbits is stolen, and I'm a policeman, what should I do with the offending party?

AZDAK Shauwa, Shauwa, shame on you. You stand and ask me a question, than which nothing could be more seductive. It's like you were a woman—let's say that bad girl Nunowna, and you showed me your thigh—Nunowna's thigh, that would be—and asked me: "What shall I do with my thigh, it itches?" Is she as innocent as she pretends? Of course not. I catch a rabbit, but you catch a man. Man is made in God's image. Not so a rabbit, you know that. I'm a rabbit-eater, but you're a man-eater, Shauwa. And God will pass judgment on you. Shauwa, go home and repent. No, stop, there's something . . . [*He looks at the* OLD MAN *who stands trembling in the corner.*] No, it's nothing. Go home and repent. [*He slams the door behind* SHAUWA.] Now you're surprised, huh? Surprised I didn't hand you over? I couldn't hand over a bedbug to that animal. It goes against the grain. Now don't tremble because of a cop! So old and still so scared? Finish your cheese, but eat it like a poor man, or else they'll still catch you. Must I even explain how a poor man behaves? [*He pushes him down, and then gives him back the cheese.*] That box is the table. Lay your elbows on the table. Now, encircle the cheese on the plate like it might be snatched from you at any moment—what right have you to be safe, huh?—now, hold your knife like an undersized sickle, and give your cheese a troubled look because, like all beautiful things, it's already fading away. [AZDAK *watches him.*] They're after you, which speaks in your favor, but how can we be sure they're not mistaken about you? In Tiflis one time they hanged a landowner, a Turk, who could prove he quartered his peasants instead of merely cutting them in half, as is the custom, and he squeezed twice the usual amount of taxes out of them, his zeal was above suspicion. And yet they hanged him like a common criminal—because he was a Turk—a thing he couldn't do much about. What injustice! He got onto the gallows by a sheer fluke. In short, I don't trust you.

SINGER   Thus Azdak gave the old beggar a bed,
And learned that old beggar was the old butcher, the Grand Duke himself.
And was ashamed.
He denounced himself and ordered the policeman to take him to Nuka, to court, to be judged.

In the court of justice three IRONSHIRTS *sit drinking.*

From a beam hangs a man in judge's robes. Enter AZDAK, *in chains, dragging* SHAUWA *behind him.*

AZDAK   [*Shouting.*] I've helped the Grand Duke, the Grand Thief, the Grand Butcher, to escape! In the name of justice I ask to be severely judged in public trial!

FIRST IRONSHIRT   Who's this queer bird?

SHAUWA   That's our Village Scrivener, Azdak.

AZDAK   I am contemptible! I am a traitor! A branded criminal! Tell them, flatfoot, how I insisted on being tied up and brought to the capital. Because I sheltered the Grand Duke, the Grand Swindler, by mistake. And how I found out afterwards. See the marked man denounce himself! Tell them how I forced you to walk half the night with me to clear the whole thing up.

SHAUWA   And all by threats. That wasn't nice of you, Azdak.

AZDAK   Shut your mouth, Shauwa. You don't understand. A new age is upon us! It'll go thundering over you. You're finished. The police will be wiped out—poof! Everything will be gone into, everything will be brought into the open. The guilty will give themselves up. Why? They couldn't escape the people in any case. [*To* SHAUWA.] Tell them how I shouted all along Shoemaker Street [*With big gestures, looking at the* IRONSHIRTS.] "In my ignorance I let the Grand Swindler escape! So tear me to pieces, brothers!" I wanted to get it in first.

FIRST IRONSHIRT   And what did your brothers answer?

SHAUWA   They comforted him in Butcher Street, and they laughed themselves sick in Shoemaker Street. That's all.

AZDAK   But with you it's different. I can see you're men of iron. Brothers, where's the judge? I must be tried.

FIRST IRONSHIRT   [*Pointing at the hanged man.*] There's the judge. And please stop "brothering" us. It's rather a sore spot this evening.

AZDAK   "There's the judge." An answer never heard in Grusinia before. Townsmen, where's His Excellency the Governor? [*Pointing to the ground.*] There's His Excellency, stranger. Where's the Chief Tax Collector? Where's the official Recruiting Officer? The Patriarch? The Chief of Police? There, there, there—all there. Brothers, I expected no less of you.

SECOND IRONSHIRT   What? *What* was it you expected, funny man?

AZDAK   What happened in Persia, brother, what happened in Persia?

SECOND IRONSHIRT   What did happen in Persia?

AZDAK   Everybody was hanged. Viziers, tax collectors. Everybody. Forty years ago now. My grandfather, a remarkable man by the way, saw it all. For three whole days. Everywhere.

SECOND IRONSHIRT   And who ruled when the Vizier was hanged?

AZDAK   A peasant ruled when the Vizier was hanged.

SECOND IRONSHIRT   And who commanded the army?

AZDAK   A soldier, a soldier.

SECOND IRONSHIRT   And who paid the wages?

AZDAK   A dyer. A dyer paid the wages.

SECOND IRONSHIRT   Wasn't it a weaver, maybe?

FIRST IRONSHIRT   And why did all this happen, Persian?

AZDAK   Why did all this happen? Must there be a special reason? Why do you scratch yourself, brother? War! Too long a war! And no justice! My grandfather brought back a song that tells how it was. I will sing it for you. With my friend the policeman. [*To* SHAUWA.] And hold the rope tight. It's very suitable. [*He sings, with* SHAUWA *holding the rope tight around him.*]

THE SONG OF INJUSTICE IN PERSIA

Why don't our sons bleed any more? Why don't our daughters weep?

Why do only the slaughterhouse cattle have blood in their veins?

Why do only the willows shed tears on Lake Urmi?

The king must have a new province, the peasant must give up his savings.

That the roof of the world might be conquered, the roof of the cottage is torn down.

Our men are carried to the ends of the earth, so that great ones can eat at home.

The soldiers kill each other, the marshals salute each other.

They bite the widow's tax money to see if it's good, their swords break.

The battle was lost, the helmets were paid for.

Refrain: Is it so? Is it so?

SHAUWA [*Refrain.*] Yes, yes, yes, yes, yes it's so.

AZDAK Want to hear the rest of it? [*The* FIRST IRONSHIRT *nods.*]

SECOND IRONSHIRT [*To* SHAUWA.] Did he teach you that song?

SHAUWA Yes, only my voice isn't very good.

SECOND IRONSHIRT No. [*To* AZDAK.] Go on singing.

AZDAK The second verse is about the peace. [*He sings.*]

The offices are packed, the streets overflow with officials.

The rivers jump their banks and ravage the fields.

Those who cannot let down their own trousers rule countries.

They can't count up to four, but they devour eight courses.

The corn farmers, looking round for buyers, see only the starving.

The weavers go home from their looms in rags.

Refrain: Is it so? Is it so?

SHAUWA [*Refrain.*] Yes, yes, yes, yes, yes it's so.

AZDAK

That's why our sons don't bleed any more, that's why our daughters don't weep.

That's why only the slaughterhouse cattle have blood in their veins,

And only the willows shed tears by Lake Urmi toward morning.

FIRST IRONSHIRT Are you going to sing that song here in town?

AZDAK Sure. What's wrong with it?

FIRST IRONSHIRT Have you noticed that the sky's getting red? [*Turning round,* AZDAK *sees the sky red with fire.*] It's the people's quarters on the outskirts of town. The carpet weavers have caught the "Persian Sickness," too. And they've been asking if Prince Kazbeki isn't eating too many courses. This morning they strung up the city judge. As for us we beat them to pulp. We were paid one hundred piasters per man, you understand?

AZDAK [*After a pause.*] I understand. [*He glances shyly round and, creeping away, sits down in a corner, his head in his hands.*]

IRONSHIRTS [*To each other.*] If there ever was a troublemaker it's him.

—He must've come to the capital to fish in the troubled waters.

SHAUWA Oh, I don't think he's a really bad character, gentlemen. Steals a few chickens here and there. And maybe a rabbit.

SECOND IRONSHIRT [*Approaching* AZDAK.] Came to fish in the troubled waters, huh?

AZDAK [*Looking up.*] I don't know why I came.

SECOND IRONSHIRT Are you in with the carpet weavers maybe? [AZDAK *shakes his head.*] How about that song?

AZDAK From my grandfather. A silly and ignorant man.

SECOND IRONSHIRT Right. And how about the dyer who paid the wages?

AZDAK [*Muttering.*] That was in Persia.

FIRST IRONSHIRT And this denouncing of yourself? Because you didn't hang the Grand Duke with your own hands?

AZDAK Didn't I tell you I let him run? [*He creeps farther away and sits on the floor.*]

SHAUWA I can swear to that: he let him run.

The IRONSHIRTS *burst out laughing and slap* SHAUWA *on the back.* AZDAK *laughs loudest. They slap* AZDAK *too, and unchain him. They all start drinking as the* FAT PRINCE *enters with a young man.*

FIRST IRONSHIRT [*To* AZDAK, *pointing at the* FAT PRINCE.] There's your "new age" for you! [*More laughter.*]

FAT PRINCE Well, my friends, what is there to laugh about? Permit me a serious word. Yesterday morning the Princes of Grusinia overthrew the warmongering government of the

Grand Duke and did away with his Governors. Unfortunately the Grand Duke himself escaped. In this fateful hour our carpet weavers, those eternal troublemakers, had the effrontery to stir up a rebellion and hang the universally loved city judge, our dear Illo Orbeliani. Ts—ts—ts. My friends, we need peace, peace, peace in Grusinia! And justice! So I've brought along my dear nephew Bizergan Kazbeki. He'll be the new judge, hm? A very gifted fellow. What do you say? I want your opinion. Let the people decide!

SECOND IRONSHIRT   Does this mean *we* elect the judge?

FAT PRINCE   Precisely. Let the people propose some very gifted fellow! Confer among yourselves, my friends. [*The* IRONSHIRTS *confer.*] Don't worry, my little fox. The job's yours. And when we catch the Grand Duke we won't have to kiss this rabble's ass any longer.

IRONSHIRTS   [*Among themselves.*]—Very funny: they're wetting their pants because they haven't caught the Grand Duke.

—When the outlook isn't so bright, they say: "My friends!" and "Let the people decide!"

—Now he even wants justice for Grusinia! But fun is fun as long as it lasts! [*Pointing at* AZDAK.] *He* knows all about justice. Hey, rascal, would you like this nephew fellow to be the judge?

AZDAK   Are you asking me? You're not asking *me?!*

FIRST IRONSHIRT   Why not? Anything for a laugh!

AZDAK   You'd like to test him to the marrow, correct? Have you a criminal on hand? An experienced one? So the candidate can show what he knows?

SECOND IRONSHIRT   Let's see. We do have a couple of doctors downstairs. Let's use them.

AZDAK   Oh, no, that's no good, we can't take real criminals till we're sure the judge will be appointed. He may be dumb, but he must be appointed, or the law is violated. And the law is a sensitive organ. It's like the spleen, you mustn't hit it—that would be fatal. Of course you can hang those two without violating the law, because there was no judge in the vicinity. But judgment, when pronounced, must be pronounced with absolute gravity—it's all such nonsense. Suppose, for instance, a judge jails a woman—let's say she's stolen a corn cake to feed her child—and this judge isn't wearing his robes—or maybe he's scratching himself while passing sentence and half his body is uncovered—a man's thigh *will* itch once in a while—the sentence this judge passes is a disgrace and the law is violated. In short it would be easier for a judge's robe and a judge's hat to pass judgment than for a man with no robe and no hat. If you don't treat it with respect, the law just disappears on you. Now you don't try out a bottle of wine by offering it to a dog; you'd only lose your wine.

FIRST IRONSHIRT   Then what do you suggest, hairsplitter?

AZDAK   I'll be the defendant.

FIRST IRONSHIRT   You? [*He bursts out laughing.*]

FAT PRINCE   What have you decided?

FIRST IRONSHIRT   We've decided to stage a rehearsal. Our friend here will be the defendant. Let the candidate be the judge and sit there.

FAT PRINCE   It isn't customary, but why not? [*To the* NEPHEW.] A mere formality, my little fox. What have I taught you? Who got there first—the slow runner or the fast?

NEPHEW   The silent runner, Uncle Arsen.

The NEPHEW *takes the chair. The* IRONSHIRTS *and the* FAT PRINCE *sit on the steps. Enter* AZDAK, *mimicking the gait of the Grand Duke.*

AZDAK   [*In the Grand Duke's accent.*] Is any here knows me? Am Grand Duke.

IRONSHIRTS   —*What* is he?

—The Grand Duke. He knows him, too.

—Fine. So get on with the trial.

AZDAK   Listen! Am accused instigating war? Ridiculous! Am saying ridiculous! That enough? If not, have brought lawyers. Believe five hundred. [*He points behind him, pretending to be surrounded by lawyers.*] Requisition all available seats for lawyers! [*The* IRONSHIRTS *laugh; the* FAT PRINCE *joins in.*]

NEPHEW   [*To the* IRONSHIRTS.] You really wish me to try this case? I find it rather unusual. From the taste angle, I mean.

FIRST IRONSHIRT   Let's go!

FAT PRINCE   [*Smiling.*] Let him have it, my little fox!

NEPHEW All right. People of Grusinia versus Grand Duke. Defendant, what have you got to say for yourself?

AZDAK Plenty. Naturally, have read war lost. Only started on the advice of patriots. Like Uncle Arsen Kazbeki. Call Uncle Arsen as witness.

FAT PRINCE [*To the* IRONSHIRTS, *delightedly.*] What a screwball!

NEPHEW Motion rejected. One cannot be arraigned for declaring a war, which every ruler has to do once in a while, but only for running a war badly.

AZDAK Rubbish! Did not run it at all! Had it run! Had it run by Princes! Naturally, they messed it up.

NEPHEW Do you by any chance deny having been commander-in-chief?

AZDAK Not at all! Always was commander-in-chief. At birth shouted at wet nurse. Was trained drop turds in toilet, grew accustomed to command. Always commanded officials rob my cash box. Officers flog soldiers only on command. Landowners sleep with peasants' wives only on strictest command. Uncle Arsen here grew his belly at *my* command.

IRONSHIRTS [*Clapping.*] He's good! Long live the Grand Duke!

FAT PRINCE Answer him, my little fox: I'm with you.

NEPHEW I shall answer him according to the dignity of the law. Defendant, preserve the dignity of the law!

AZDAK Agreed. Command you proceed with trial!

NEPHEW It is not your place to command me. You claim that the Princes forced you to declare war. How can you claim, then, that they —er—"messed it up"?

AZDAK Did not send enough people. Embezzled funds. Sent sick horses. During attack, drinking in whorehouse. Call Uncle Arsen as witness.

NEPHEW Are you making the outrageous suggestion that the Princes of this country did not fight?

AZDAK No. Princes fought. Fought for war contracts.

FAT PRINCE [*Jumping up.*] That's too much! This man talks like a carpet weaver!

AZDAK Really? Told nothing but truth.

FAT PRINCE Hang him! Hang him!

FIRST IRONSHIRT [*Pulling the* PRINCE *down.*] Keep quiet! Go on, Excellency!

NEPHEW Quiet, I now render a verdict: You must be hanged! By the neck! Having lost war!

AZDAK Young man, seriously advise not fall publicly into jerky clipped speech. Cannot be watchdog if howl like wolf. Got it? If people realize Princes speak same language as Grand Duke, may hang Grand Duke *and Princes,* huh? By the way, must overrule verdict. Reason? War lost, but for not Princes. Princes won their war. Got 3,863,000 piasters for horses not delivered, 8,240,000 piasters for food supplies not produced. Are therefore victors. War lost only for Grusinia, which is not present in this court.

FAT PRINCE I think that will do, my friends. [*To* AZDAK.] You can withdraw, funny man. [*To the* IRONSHIRTS.] You may now ratify the new judge's appointment, my friends.

FIRST IRONSHIRT Yes, we can. Take down the judge's gown. [*One* IRONSHIRT *climbs on the back of the other, pulls the gown off the hanged man.*] [*To the* NEPHEW.] Now you run away so the right ass can get on the right chair. [*To* AZDAK.] Step forward! Go to the judge's seat! Now sit in it! [AZDAK *steps up, bows, and sits down.*] The judge was always a rascal! Now the rascal shall be a judge! [*The judge's gown is placed around his shoulders, the hat on his head.*] And what a judge!

SINGER And there was civil war in the land.
The mighty were not safe.
And Azdak was made a judge by the Ironshirts.
And Azdak remained a judge for two years.

SINGER AND CHORUS When the towns were set afire
And rivers of blood rose higher and higher,
Cockroaches crawled out of every crack.
And the court was full of schemers
And the church of foul blasphemers.
In the judge's cassock sat Azdak.

AZDAK *sits in the judge's chair, peeling an apple.* SHAUWA *is sweeping out the hall. On one side an* INVALID *in a wheelchair. Opposite, a young man accused of blackmail. An* IRONSHIRT *stands guard, holding the Ironshirts' banner.*

AZDAK In consideration of the large number of cases, the Court today will hear two cases at a time. Before I open the proceedings, a short announcement—I accept. [*He stretches out his hand. The* BLACKMAILER *is the only one to produce any money. He hands it to* AZDAK.] I reserve the right to punish one of the parties for contempt of court. [*He glances at the* INVALID.] You [*To the* DOCTOR.] are a doctor, and you [*To the* INVALID.] are bringing a complaint against him. Is the doctor responsible for your condition?

INVALID   Yes. I had a stroke on his account.

AZDAK   That would be professional negligence.

INVALID   Worse than negligence. I gave this man money for his studies. So far, he hasn't paid me back a cent. It was when I heard he was treating a patient free that I had my stroke.

AZDAK   Rightly. [*To a* LIMPING MAN.] And what are *you* doing here?

LIMPING MAN   I'm the patient, Your Honor.

AZDAK   He treated your leg for nothing?

LIMPING MAN   The wrong leg! My rheumatism was in the left leg, he operated on the right. That's why I limp.

AZDAK   And you were treated free?

INVALID   A five-hundred-piaster operation free! For nothing! For a God-bless-you! And I paid for this man's studies! [*To the* DOCTOR.] Did they teach you to operate free?

DOCTOR   Your Honor, it is the custom to demand the fee before the operation, as the patient is more willing to pay before an operation than after. Which is only human. In the case in question I was convinced, when I started the operation, that my servant had already received the fee. In this I was mistaken.

INVALID   He was mistaken! A good doctor doesn't make mistakes! He examines before he operates!

AZDAK   That's right: [SHAUWA.] Public Prosecutor, what's the other case about?

SHAUWA   [*Busily sweeping.*] Blackmail.

BLACKMAILER   High Court of Justice, I'm innocent. I only wanted to find out from the landowner concerned if he really *had* raped his niece. He informed me very politely that this was not the case, and gave me the money only so I could pay for my uncle's studies.

AZDAK   Hm. [*To the* DOCTOR.] You, on the other hand, can cite no extenuating circumstances for your offense, huh?

DOCTOR   Except that to err is human.

AZDAK   And you are aware that in money matters a good doctor is a highly responsible person? I once heard of a doctor who got a thousand piasters for a sprained finger by remarking that sprains have something to do with blood circulation, which after all a less good doctor might have overlooked, and who, on another occasion made a real gold mine out of a somewhat disordered gall bladder, he treated it with such loving care. You have no excuse, Doctor. The corn merchant Uxu had his son study medicine to get some knowledge of trade, our medical schools are so good. [*To the* BLACKMAILER.] What's the landowner's name?

SHAUWA   He doesn't want it mentioned.

AZDAK   In that case I will pass judgment. The Court considers the blackmail proved. And you [*To the* INVALID.] are sentenced to a fine of one thousand piasters. If you have a second stroke, the doctor will have to treat you free. Even if he has to amputate. [*To the* LIMPING MAN.] As compensation, you will receive a bottle of rubbing alcohol. [*To the* BLACKMAILER.] You are sentenced to hand over half the proceeds of your deal to the Public Prosecutor to keep the landowner's name secret. You are advised, moreover, to study medicine—you seem well suited to that calling. [*To the* DOCTOR.] You have perpetrated an unpardonable error in the practice of your profession: you are acquitted. Next cases!

SINGER AND CHORUS   Men won't do much for a shilling.
For a pound they may be willing.
For twenty pounds the verdict's in the sack.
As for the many, all too many,
Those who've only got a penny—
They've one single, sole recourse: Azdak.

Enter AZDAK *from the caravansary on the highroad, followed by an old bearded* INNKEEPER. *The judge's chair is carried by a stableman and* SHAUWA. *An* IRONSHIRT, *with a banner, takes up his position.*

AZDAK   Put me down. Then we'll get some air, maybe even a good stiff breeze from the lemon grove there. It does justice good to be done in the open: the wind blows her skirts up and you can see what she's got. Shauwa, we've been eating too much. These official journeys are exhausting. [*To the* INNKEEPER.]

It's a question of your daughter-in-law?

INNKEEPER   Your Worship, it's a question of the family honor. I wish to bring an action on behalf of my son, who's away on business on the other side the mountain. This is the offending stableman, and here's my daughter-in-law.

Enter the DAUGHTER-IN-LAW, *a voluptuous wench. She is veiled.*

AZDAK   [*Sitting down.*] I accept. [*Sighing, the* INNKEEPER *hands him some money.*] Good. Now the formalities are disposed of. This is a case of rape?

INNKEEPER   Your Honor, I caught the fellow in the act. Ludovica was in the straw on the stable floor.

AZDAK   Quite right, the stable. Lovely horses! I specially liked the little roan.

INNKEEPER   The first thing I did, of course, was to question Ludovica. On my son's behalf.

AZDAK   [*Seriously.*] I said I specially liked the little roan.

INNKEEPER   [*Coldly.*] Really? Ludovica confessed the stableman took her against her will.

AZDAK   Take your veil off, Ludovica. [*She does so.*] Ludovica, you please the Court. Tell us how it happened.

LUDOVICA   [*Well schooled.*] When I entered the stable to see the new foal the stableman said to me on his own accord: "It's hot today!" and laid his hand on my left breast. I said to him: "Don't do that!" But he continued to handle me indecently, which provoked my anger. Before I realized his sinful intentions, he got much closer. It was all over when my father-in-law entered and accidentally trod on me.

INNKEEPER   [*Explaining.*] On my son's behalf.

AZDAK   [*To the* STABLEMAN.] You admit you started it?

STABLEMAN   Yes.

AZDAK   Ludovica, you like to eat sweet things?

LUDOVICA   Yes, sunflower seeds!

AZDAK   You like to lie a long time in the bathtub?

LUDOVICA   Half an hour or so.

AZDAK   Public Prosecutor, drop your knife—there on the ground. [SHAUWA *does so.*] Ludovica, pick up that knife. [LUDOVICA, *swaying her hips, does so.*] See that? [*He points at her.*] The way it moves? The rape is now proven. By eating too much—sweet things, especially—by lying too long in warm water, by laziness and too soft a skin, you have raped

that unfortunate man. Think you can run around with a behind like that and get away with it in court? This is a case of intentional assault with a dangerous weapon! You are sentenced to hand over to the Court the little roan which your father liked to ride "on his son's behalf." And now, come with me to the stables, so the Court can inspect the scene of the crime, Ludovica.

SINGER AND CHORUS   When the sharks the sharks devour
Little fishes have their hour.
For a while the load is off their back.
On Grusinia's highways faring
Fixed-up scales of justice bearing
Strode the poor man's magistrate: Azdak.

And he gave to the forsaken
All that from the rich he'd taken.
And a bodyguard of roughnecks was Azdak's.
And our good and evil man, he
Smiled upon Grusinia's Granny.
His emblem was a tear in sealing wax.

All mankind should love each other
But when visiting your brother
Take an ax along and hold it fast.
Not in theory but in practice
Miracles are wrought with axes
And the age of miracles is not past.

AZDAK's judge's chair is in a tavern. Three rich FARMERS *stand before* AZDAK. SHAUWA *brings him wine. In a corner stands an* OLD PEASANT WOMAN. *In the open doorway, and outside, stand villagers looking on. An* IRONSHIRT *stands guard with a banner.*

AZDAK   The Public Prosecutor has the floor.

SHAUWA   It concerns a cow. For five weeks, the defendant has had a cow in her stable, the property of the farmer Suru. She was also found to be in possession of a stolen ham, and a number of cows belonging to Shutoff were killed after he asked the defendant to pay the rent on a piece of land.

FARMERS   —It's a matter of my ham, Your Honor.
   —It's a matter of my cow, Your Honor.
   —It's a matter of my land, Your Honor.

AZDAK   Well, Granny, what have *you* got to say to all this?

OLD WOMAN   Your Honor, one night toward morning, five weeks ago, there was a knock at my door, and outside stood a bearded man with a cow. "My dear woman," he said, "I am the miracle-working Saint Banditus and because your son has been killed in the war, I bring you this cow as a souvenir. Take good care of it."

FARMERS —The robber, Irakli, Your Honor!
—Her brother-in-law, Your Honor!
—The cow-thief!
—The incendiary!
—He must be beheaded!

Outside, a woman screams. The crowd grows restless, retreats. Enter the BANDIT *Irakli with a huge ax.*

BANDIT A very good evening, dear friends! A glass of vodka!

FARMERS [*Crossing themselves.*] Irakli!

AZDAK Public Prosecutor, a glass of vodka for our guest. And who are you?

BANDIT I'm a wandering hermit, Your Honor. Thanks for the gracious gift. [*He empties the glass which* SHAUWA *has brought.*] Another!

AZDAK I am Azdak. [*He gets up and bows. The* BANDIT *also bows.*] The Court welcomes the foreign hermit. Go on with your story, Granny.

OLD WOMAN Your Honor, that first night I didn't yet know Saint Banditus could work miracles, it was only the cow. But one night, a few days later, the farmer's servants came to take the cow away again. Then they turned round in front of my door and went off without the cow. And bumps as big as a fist sprouted on their heads. So I knew that Saint Banditus had changed their hearts and turned them into friendly people.

The BANDIT *roars with laughter.*

FIRST FARMER I know what changed them.

AZDAK That's fine. You can tell us later. Continue.

OLD WOMAN Your Honor, the next one to become a good man was the farmer Shutoff—a devil, as everyone knows. But Saint Banditus arranged it so he let me off the rent on the little piece of land.

SECOND FARMER Because my cows were killed in the field.

The BANDIT *laughs.*

OLD WOMAN [*Answering* AZDAK's *sign to continue.*] Then one morning the ham came flying in at my window. It hit me in the small of the back. I'm still lame. Your Honor, look. [*She limps a few steps. The* BANDIT *laughs.*] Your

Honor, was there ever a time when a poor old woman could get a ham *without* a miracle?

The BANDIT *starts sobbing.*

AZDAK [*Rising from his chair.*] Granny, that's a question that strikes straight at the Court's heart. Be so kind as to sit here. [*The* OLD WOMAN, *hesitating, sits in the judge's chair.*]

AZDAK [*Sits on the floor, glass in hand, reciting.*]
Granny
We could almost call you Granny Grusinia
The Woebegone
The Bereaved Mother
Whose sons have gone to war
Receiving the present of a cow
She bursts out crying.
When she is beaten
She remains hopeful.
When she's not beaten
She's surprised.
On us
Who are already damned
May you render a merciful verdict
Granny Grusinia!

[*Bellowing at the* FARMERS:] Admit you don't believe in miracles, you atheists! Each of you is sentenced to pay five hundred piasters! For godlessness! Get out! [*The* FARMERS *slink out.*] And you Granny, and you [*To the* BANDIT.] pious man, empty a pitcher of wine with the Public Prosecutor and Azdak!

SINGER AND CHORUS And he broke the rules to save them.
Broken law like bread he gave them,
Brought them to shore upon his crooked back.
At long last the poor and lowly
Had someone who was not too holy
To be bribed by empty hands: Azdak.

For two years it was his pleasure
To give the beasts of prey short measure:
He became a wolf to fight the pack.
From All Hallows to All Hallows
On his chair beside the gallows
Dispensing justice in his fashion sat Azdak.

SINGER But the era of disorder came to an end.
The Grand Duke returned.
The Governor's wife returned.
A trial was held.
Many died.
The people's quarters burned anew.
And fear seized Azdak.

AZDAK's *judge's chair stands again in the court of justice.* AZDAK *sits on the floor, shaving and talking to* SHAUWA. *Noises outside. In the rear the* FAT PRINCE's *head is carried by on a lance.*

AZDAK Shauwa, the days of your slavery are numbered, maybe even the minutes. For a long time now I have held you in the iron curb of reason, and it has torn your mouth till it bleeds. I have lashed you with reasonable arguments, I have manhandled you with logic. You are by nature a weak man, and if one slyly throws an argument in your path, you *have* to snap it up, you can't resist. It is your nature to lick the hand of some superior being. But superior beings can be of very different kinds. And now, with your liberation, you will soon be able to follow your natural inclinations, which are low. You will be able to follow your infallible instinct, which teaches you to plant your fat heel on the faces of men. Gone is the era of confusion and disorder, which I find described in the Song of Chaos. Let us now sing that song together in memory of those terrible days. Sit down and don't do violence to the music. Don't be afraid. It sounds all right. And it has a fine refrain. [*He sings.*]

THE SONG OF CHAOS

Sister, hide your face! Brother, take your knife!
The times are out of joint!
Big men are full of complaint
And small men full of joy.
The city says:
"Let us drive the strong ones from our midst!"
Offices are raided. Lists of serfs are destroyed.
They have set Master's nose to the grindstone.
They who lived in the dark have seen the light.
The ebony poor box is broken.
Sesnem[2] wood is sawed up for beds.

[2] [I do not know what kind of wood this is, so I have left the word exactly as it stands in the German original. The song is based on an Egyptian papyrus which Brecht cites as such in his essay, "Five Difficulties in the Writing of the Truth." I should think he must have come across it in Adolf Erman's *Die Literatur der Aegypter*, 1923, p. 130 ff. Erman too gives the word as Sesnem. The same papyrus is quoted in Karl Jaspers' *Man in the Modern Age* (Anchor edition, pp. 18–19) but without the sentence about the Sesnem wood.—E.B.]

Who had no bread have barns full.
Who begged for alms of corn now mete it out.

SHAUWA [*Refrain.*] Oh, oh, oh, oh.
AZDAK [*Refrain.*] Where are you, General, where are you?
Please, please, please, restore order!

The nobleman's son can no longer be recognized;
The lady's child becomes the son of her slave.
The councilors meet in a shed.
Once, this man was barely allowed to sleep on the wall;
Now, he stretches his limbs in a bed.
Once, this man rowed a boat; now, he owns ships.
Their owner looks for them, but they're his no longer.
Five men are sent on a journey by their master.
"Go yourself," they say, "we have arrived."

SHAUWA [*Refrain.*] Oh, oh, oh, oh.
AZDAK [*Refrain.*] Where are you, General, where are you?
Please, please, please, restore order!

Yes, so it might have been, had order been neglected much longer. But now the Grand Duke has returned to the capital, and the Persians have lent him an army to restore order with. The people's quarters are already aflame. Go and get me the big book I always sit on. [SHAUWA *brings the big book from the judge's chair.* AZDAK *opens it.*] This is the Statute Book and I've always used it, as you can testify. Now I'd better look in this book and see what they can do to me. I've let the down-and-outs get away with murder, and I'll have to pay for it. I helped poverty onto its skinny legs, so they'll hang me for drunkenness. I peeped into the rich man's pocket, which is bad taste. And I can't hide anywhere—everybody knows me because I've helped everybody.

SHAUWA Someone's coming!
AZDAK [*In panic, he walks trembling to the chair.*] It's the end. And now they'd enjoy seeing what a Great Man I am. I'll deprive them of that pleasure. I'll beg on my knees for

mercy. Spittle will slobber down my chin. The fear of death is in me.

Enter Natella Abashwili, the GOVERNOR'S WIFE, *followed by the* ADJUTANT *and an* IRONSHIRT.

GOVERNOR'S WIFE What sort of a creature is that, Shalva?

AZDAK A willing one, Your Highness, a man ready to oblige.

ADJUTANT Natella Abashwili, wife of the late Governor, has just returned. She is looking for her two-year-old son, Michael. She has been informed that the child was carried off to the mountains by a former servant.

AZDAK The child will be brought back, Your Highness, at your service.

ADJUTANT They say that the person in question is passing it off as her own.

AZDAK She will be beheaded, Your Highness, at your service.

ADJUTANT That is all.

GOVERNOR'S WIFE [*Leaving.*] I don't like that man.

AZDAK [*Following her to door, bowing.*] At your service, Your Highness, it will all be arranged.

5

THE CHALK CIRCLE

SINGER Hear now the story of the trial
Concerning Governor Abashwili's child
And the determination of the true mother
By the famous test of the Chalk Circle.

Law court in Nuka. IRONSHIRTS *lead* MICHAEL *across stage and out at the back.* IRONSHIRTS *hold* GRUSHA *back with their lances under the gateway until the child has been led through. Then she is admitted. She is accompanied by the former Governor's* COOK. *Distant noises and a fire-red sky.*

GRUSHA [*Trying to hide.*] He's brave, he can wash himself now.

COOK You're lucky. It's not a real judge. It's Azdak, a drunk who doesn't know what he's doing. The biggest thieves have got by through him. Because he gets everything mixed up and the rich never offer him big enough bribes, the like of us sometimes do pretty well.

GRUSHA I *need* luck right now.

COOK Touch wood. [*She crosses herself.*] I'd

better offer up another prayer that the judge may be drunk. [*She prays with motionless lips, while* GRUSHA *looks around, in vain, for the child.*] Why must you hold on to it at any price if it isn't yours? In days like these?

GRUSHA He's mine. I brought him up.

COOK Have you never thought what'd happen when she came back?

GRUSHA At first I thought I'd give him to her. Then I thought she wouldn't come back.

COOK And even a borrowed coat keeps a man warm, hm? [GRUSHA *nods.*] I'll swear to anything for you. You're a decent girl. [*She sees the soldier* SIMON SHASHAVA *approaching.*] You've done wrong by Simon, though. I've been talking with him. He just can't understand.

GRUSHA [*Unaware of* SIMON'S *presence.*] Right now I can't be bothered whether he understands or not!

COOK He knows the child isn't yours, but you married and not free "till death you do part" —he can't understand *that.*

GRUSHA *sees* SIMON *and greets him.*

SIMON [*Gloomily.*] I wish the lady to know I will swear I am the father of the child.

GRUSHA [*Low.*] Thank you, Simon.

SIMON At the same time I wish the lady to know my hands are not tied—nor are hers.

COOK You needn't have said that. You know she's married.

SIMON And it needs no rubbing in.

Enter an IRONSHIRT.

IRONSHIRT Where's the judge? Has anyone seen the judge?

ANOTHER IRONSHIRT [*Stepping forward.*] The judge isn't here yet. Nothing but a bed and a pitcher in the whole house!

Exeunt IRONSHIRTS.

COOK I hope nothing has happened to him. With any other judge you'd have as much chance as a chicken has teeth.

GRUSHA [*Who has turned away and covered her face.*] Stand in front of me. I shouldn't have come to Nuka. If I run into the Ironshirt, the one I hit over the head . . .

She screams. An IRONSHIRT *had stopped and, turning his back, had been listening to her. He now wheels around. It is the* CORPORAL, *and he has a huge scar across his face.*

IRONSHIRT [*In the gateway.*] What's the matter, Shotta? Do you know her?

CORPORAL   [*After staring for some time.*] No.

IRONSHIRT   She's the one who stole the Abash-wili child, or so they say. If you know anything about it you can make some money, Shotta.

Exit the CORPORAL, *cursing.*

COOK   Was it him? [GRUSHA *nods.*] I think he'll keep his mouth shut, or he'd be admitting he was after the child.

GRUSHA   I'd almost forgotten him.

Enter the GOVERNOR'S WIFE, *followed by the* ADJUTANT *and two* LAWYERS.

GOVERNOR'S WIFE   At least there are no common people here, thank God. I can't stand their smell. It always gives me migraine.

FIRST LAWYER   Madam, I must ask you to be careful what you say until we have another judge.

GOVERNOR'S WIFE   But I didn't say anything, Illo Shuboladze. I love the people with their simple straightforward minds. It's only that their smell brings on my migraine.

SECOND LAWYER   There won't be many spectators. The whole population is sitting at home behind locked doors because of the riots on the outskirts of town.

GOVERNOR'S WIFE   [*Looking at* GRUSHA.] Is that the creature?

FIRST LAWYER   Please, most gracious Natella Abashwili, abstain from invective until it is certain the Grand Duke has appointed a new judge and we're rid of the present one, who's about the lowest fellow ever seen in judge's gown. Things are all set to move, you see.

Enter IRONSHIRTS *from the courtyard.*

COOK   Her Grace would pull your hair out on the spot if she didn't know Azdak is for the poor. He goes by the face.

IRONSHIRTS *begin fastening a rope to a beam.* AZDAK, *in chains, is led in, followed by* SHAUWA, *also in chains. The three* FARMERS *bring up the rear.*

AN IRONSHIRT   Trying to run away, were you? [*He strikes* AZDAK.]

ONE FARMER   Off with his judge's gown before we string him up!

IRONSHIRTS *and* FARMERS *tear off Azdak's gown. His torn underwear is visible. Then someone kicks him.*

AN IRONSHIRT   [*Pushing him into someone else.*] Want a load of justice? Here it is!

Accompanied by shouts of "You take it!"

and "Let me have him, Brother!" *they throw* AZDAK *back and forth until he collapses. Then he is lifted up and dragged under the noose.*

GOVERNOR'S WIFE   [*Who, during this "ball-game," has clapped her hands hysterically.*] I disliked that man from the moment I first saw him.

AZDAK   [*Covered with blood, panting.*] I can't see. Give me a rag.

AN IRONSHIRT   What is it you want to see?

AZDAK   You, you dogs! [*He wipes the blood out of his eyes with his shirt.*] Good morning, dogs! How goes it, dogs! How's the dog world? Does it smell good? Got another for me to lick? Are you back at each other's throats, dogs?

Accompanied by a CORPORAL, *a dust-covered* RIDER *enters. He takes some documents from a leather case, looks at them, then interrupts.*

RIDER   Stop! I bring a dispatch from the Grand Duke, containing the latest appointments.

CORPORAL   [*Bellowing.*] Atten—shun!

RIDER   Of the new judge it says: "We appoint a man whom we have to thank for saving a life indispensable to the country's welfare—a certain Azdak of Nuka." Which is he?

SHAUWA   [*Pointing.*] That's him, Your Excellency.

CORPORAL   [*Bellowing.*] What's going on here?

AN IRONSHIRT   I beg to report that His Honor Azdak was already His Honor Azdak, but on these farmers' denunciation was pronounced the Grand Duke's enemy.

CORPORAL   [*Pointing at the* FARMERS.] March them off! [*They are marched off. They bow all the time.*] See to it that His Honor Azdak is exposed to no more violence.

Exeunt RIDER *and* CORPORAL.

COOK   [*To* SHAUWA.] She clapped her hands! I hope he saw it!

FIRST LAWYER   It's a catastrophe.

AZDAK *has fainted. Coming to, he is dressed again in judge's robes. He walks, swaying, toward the* IRONSHIRTS.

AN IRONSHIRT   What does Your Honor desire?

AZDAK   Nothing, fellow dogs, or just an occasional boot to lick. [*To* SHAUWA.] I pardon you.

[*He is unchained.*] Get me some red wine, the sweet kind. [SHAUWA *stumbles off.*] Get out of here, I've got to judge a case. [*Exeunt* IRON-

SHIRTS. SHAUWA *returns with a pitcher of wine.* AZDAK *gulps it down.*] Something for my backside. [SHAUWA *brings the Statute Book, puts it on the judge's chair.* AZDAK *sits on it.*] I accept.

The Prosecutors, among whom a worried council has been held, smile with relief. They whisper.

COOK Oh dear!

SIMON A well can't be filled with dew, they say.

LAWYERS [*Approaching* AZDAK, *who stands up, expectantly.*] A quite ridiculous case, Your Honor. The accused has abducted a child and refuses to hand it over.

AZDAK [*Stretching out his hand, glancing at* GRUSHA.] A most attractive person. [*He fingers the money, then sits down, satisfied.*] I declare the proceedings open and demand the whole truth. [*To* GRUSHA.] Especially from you.

FIRST LAWYER High Court of Justice! Blood, as the popular saying goes, is thicker than water. This old adage . . .

AZDAK [*Interrupting.*] The Court wants to know the laywers' fee.

FIRST LAWYER [*Surprised.*] I beg your pardon? [AZDAK, *smiling, rubs his thumb and index finger.*] Oh, I see. Five hundred piasters, Your Honor, to answer the Court's somewhat unusual question.

AZDAK Did you hear? The question is unusual. I ask it because I listen in quite a different way when I know you're good.

FIRST LAWYER [*Bowing.*] Thank you, Your Honor. High Court of Justice, of all ties the ties of blood are strongest. Mother and child— is there a more intimate relationship? Can one tear a child from its mother? High Court of Justice, she has conceived it in the holy ecstasies of love. She has carried it in her womb. She has fed it with her blood. She has borne it with pain. High Court of Justice, it has been observed that the wild tigress, robbed of her young, roams restless through the mountains, shrunk to a shadow. Nature herself . . .

AZDAK [*Interrupting, to* GRUSHA.] What's your answer to all this and anything else that lawyer might have to say?

GRUSHA He's mine.

AZDAK Is that all? I hope you can prove it. Why should I assign the child to you in any case?

GRUSHA I brought him up like the priest says "according to my best knowledge and con-

science." I always found him something to eat. Most of the time he had a roof over his head. And I went to such trouble for him. I had expenses too. I didn't look out for my own comfort. I brought the child up to be friendly with everyone, and from the beginning taught him to work. As well as he could, that is. He's still very little.

FIRST LAWYER Your Honor, it is significant that the girl herself doesn't claim any tie of blood between her and the child.

AZDAK The Court takes note of that.

FIRST LAWYER Thank you, Your Honor. And now permit a woman bowed in sorrow—who has already lost her husband and now has also to fear the loss of her child—to address a few words to you. The gracious Natella Abashwili is . . .

GOVERNOR'S WIFE [*Quietly.*] A most cruel fate, sir, forces me to describe to you the tortures of a bereaved mother's soul, the anxiety, the sleepless nights, the . . .

SECOND LAWYER [*Bursting out.*] It's outrageous the way this woman is being treated! Her husband's palace is closed to her! The revenue of her estates is blocked, and she is cold-bloodedly told that it's tied to the heir. She can't do a thing without that child. She can't even pay her lawyers!! [*To the* FIRST LAWYER, *who, desperate about this outburst, makes frantic gestures to keep him from speaking.*] Dear Illo Shuboladze, surely it can be divulged now that the Abashwili estates are at stake?

FIRST LAWYER Please, Honored Sandro Oboladze! We agreed . . . [*To* AZDAK.] Of course it is correct that the trial will also decide if our noble client can dispose of the Abashwili estates, which are rather extensive. I say "also" advisedly, for in the foreground stands the human tragedy of a mother, as Natella Abashwili very properly explained in the first words of her moving statement. Even if Michael Abashwili were not heir to the estates, he would still be the dearly beloved child of my client.

AZDAK Stop! The Court is touched by the mention of estates. It's a proof of human feeling.

SECOND LAWYER Thanks, Your Honor. Dear Illo Shuboladze, we can prove in any case that the woman who took the child is not the child's mother. Permit me to lay before the Court the bare facts. High Court of Justice, by unfortunate chain of circumstances, Michael Abashwili was left behind on that Easter Sunday while his mother was making her escape. Grusha, a palace kitchen maid, was seen with the baby . . .

COOK All her mistress was thinking of was what dresses she'd take along!

SECOND LAWYER [*Unmoved.*] Nearly a year later Grusha turned up in a mountain village with a baby and there entered into the state of matrimony with . . .

AZDAK How'd you get to that mountain village?

GRUSHA On foot, Your Honor. And he was mine.

SIMON I'm the father, Your Honor.

COOK I used to look after it for them, Your Honor. For five piasters.

SECOND LAWYER This man is engaged to Grusha, High Court of Justice: his testimony is suspect.

AZDAK Are you the man she married in the mountain village?

SIMON No.

AZDAK [*To* GRUSHA.] Why? [*Pointing at* SIMON.] Is he no good in bed? Tell the truth.

GRUSHA We didn't get that far. I married because of the baby. So he'd have a roof over his head. [*Pointing at* SIMON.] He was in the war, Your Honor.

AZDAK And now he wants you back again, huh?

SIMON I wish to state in evidence . . .

GRUSHA [*Angrily.*] I am no longer free, Your Honor.

AZDAK And the child, you claim, comes from whoring? [GRUSHA *doesn't answer.*] I'm going to ask you a question: What kind of child is he? A ragged little bastard? Or from a good family?

GRUSHA [*Angrily.*] He's an ordinary child.

AZDAK I mean—did he have refined features from the beginning?

GRUSHA He had a nose on his face.

AZDAK A very significant comment! It has been said of me that I went out one time and sniffed at a rosebush before rendering a verdict—tricks like that are needed nowadays. Well, I'll make it short, and not listen to any more lies. [*To* GRUSHA.] Especially yours. [*To all the accused.*] I can imagine what you've cooked up to cheat me! I know you people. You're swindlers.

GRUSHA [*Suddenly.*] I can understand your wanting to cut it short, now I've seen what you accepted!

AZDAK Shut up! Did I accept anything from you?

GRUSHA [*While the* COOK *tries to restrain her.*] I haven't got anything.

AZDAK True. Quite true. From starvelings I never get a thing. I might just as well starve, myself. You want justice, but do you want to pay for it, hm? When you go to a butcher you know you have to pay, but you people go to a judge as if you were off to a funeral supper.

SIMON [*Loudly.*] When the horse was shod, the horsefly held out its leg, as the saying is.

AZDAK [*Eagerly accepting the challenge.*] Better a treasure in manure than a stone in a mountain stream.

SIMON A fine day. Let's go fishing, said the angler to the worm.

AZDAK I'm my own master, said the servant, and cut off his foot.

SIMON I love you as a father, said the Czar to the peasants, and had the Czarevitch's head chopped off.

AZDAK A fool's worst enemy is himself.

SIMON However, a fart has no nose.

AZDAK Fined ten piasters for indecent language in court! That'll teach you what justice is.

GRUSHA [*Furiously.*] A fine kind of justice! You play fast and loose with us because we don't talk as refined as that crowd with their lawyers.

AZDAK That's true. You people are too dumb. It's only right you should get it in the neck.

GRUSHA You want to hand the child over to her, and she wouldn't even know how to keep it dry, she's so "refined"! You know about as much about justice as I do!

AZDAK There's something in that. I'm an ignorant man. Haven't even a decent pair of pants on under this gown. Look! With me, everything goes for food and drink—I was educated in a convent. Incidentally, I'll fine you ten piasters for contempt of court. And you're a very silly girl, to turn me against you, instead of making eyes at me and wiggling your backside a little to keep me in a good temper. Twenty piasters!

GRUSHA Even if it was thirty, I'd tell you what I think of your justice, you drunken onion! [*Incoherently.*] How dare you talk to me like the cracked Isaiah on the church window? As if you were somebody? For you weren't born to this. You weren't born to rap your own mother on the knuckles if she swipes a bowl of salt someplace. Aren't you ashamed of yourself when you see how I tremble before you? You've made yourself their servant so no one will take their houses from them—houses they had stolen! Since when have houses belonged to the bedbugs? But you're on the watch, or they couldn't drag our men into their wars! You bribetaker!

AZDAK *half gets up, starts beaming. With his little hammer he halfheartedly knocks on the table as if to get silence. As* GRUSHA'S *scolding continues, he only beats time with his hammer.*

I've no respect for you. No more than for a thief or a bandit with a knife! You can do what you want. You can take the child away from me, a hundred against one, but I tell you one thing: only extortioners should be chosen for a profession like yours, and men who rape children! As punishment! Yes, let *them* sit in judgment on their fellow creatures. It is worse than to hang from the gallows.

AZDAK [*Sitting down.*] Now it'll be thirty! And I won't go on squabbling with you—we're not in a tavern. What'd happen to my dignity as a judge? Anyway, I've lost interest in your case. Where's the couple who wanted a divorce? [*To* SHAUWA.] Bring 'em in. This case is adjourned for fifteen minutes.

FIRST LAWYER [*To the* GOVERNOR'S WIFE.] Even without using the rest of the evidence, Madam, we have the verdict in the bag.

COOK [*To* GRUSHA.] You've gone and spoiled your chances with him. You won't get the child now.

GOVERNOR'S WIFE Shalva, my smelling salts!
Enter a very old couple.

AZDAK I accept. [*The old couple don't understand.*] I hear you want to be divorced. How long have you been together?

OLD WOMAN Forty years, Your Honor.

AZDAK And why do you want a divorce?

OLD MAN We don't like each other, Your Honor.

AZDAK Since when?

OLD WOMAN Oh, from the very beginning, Your Honor.

AZDAK I'll think about your request and render my verdict when I'm through with the other

case. [SHAUWA *leads them back.*] I need the child. [*He beckons* GRUSHA *to him and bends not unkindly toward her.*] I've noticed you have a soft spot for justice. I don't believe he's your child, but if he *were* yours, woman, wouldn't you want him to be rich? You'd only have to say he wasn't yours, and he'd have a palace and many horses in his stable and many beggars on his doorstep and many soldiers in his service and many petitioners in his courtyard, wouldn't he? What do you say—don't you want him to be rich?

GRUSHA *is silent.*

SINGER Hear now what the angry girl thought but did not say:
Had he golden shoes to wear
He'd be cruel as a bear
Evil would his life disgrace.
He'd laugh in my face.

Carrying a heart of flint
Is too troublesome a stint.
Being powerful and bad
Is hard on a lad.

Then let hunger be his foe!
Hungry men and women, no.
Let him fear the darksome night
But not daylight!

AZDAK I think I understand you, woman.

GRUSHA [*Suddenly and loudly.*] I won't give him up. I've raised him, and he knows me.
Enter SHAUWA *with the* CHILD.

GOVERNOR'S WIFE He's in rags!

GRUSHA That's not true. But I wasn't given time to put his good shirt on.

GOVERNOR'S WIFE He must have been in a pigsty.

GRUSHA [*Furiously.*] I'm not a pig, but there are some who are! Where did you leave your baby?

GOVERNOR'S WIFE I'll show you, you vulgar creature! [*She is about to throw herself on* GRUSHA, *but is restrained by her lawyers.*] She's a criminal, she must be whipped. Immediately!

SECOND LAWYER [*Holding his hand over her mouth.*] Natella Abashwili, you promised . . . Your Honor, the plaintiff's nerves . . .

AZDAK Plaintiff and defendant! The Court has listened to your case, and has come to no decision as to who the real mother is; therefore, I, the judge, am obliged to *choose* a mother for the child. I'll make a test. Shauwa, get a piece of chalk and draw a circle on the floor. [SHAUWA *does so.*] Now place the child in the center. [SHAUWA *puts* MICHAEL, *who smiles at* GRUSHA, *in the center of the circle.*] Stand near the circle, both of you. [*The* GOVERNOR'S WIFE *and* GRUSHA *step up to the circle.*] Now each of you take the child by one hand. [*They do so.*] The true mother is she who can pull the child out of the circle.

SECOND LAWYER [*Quickly.*] High Court of Justice, I object! The fate of the great Abashwili estates, which are tied to the child, as the heir, should not be made dependent on such a doubtful duel. In addition, my client does not command the strength of this person, who is accustomed to physical work.

AZDAK She looks pretty well fed to me. Pull! [*The* GOVERNOR'S WIFE *pulls the* CHILD *out of the circle on her side;* GRUSHA *has let go and stands aghast.*] What's the matter with you? You didn't pull.

GRUSHA I didn't hold on to him.

FIRST LAWYER [*Congratulating the* GOVERNOR'S WIFE.] What did I say! The ties of blood!

GRUSHA [*Running to* AZDAK.] Your Honor, I take back everything I said against you. I ask your forgiveness. But could I keep him till he can speak all the words? He knows a few.

AZDAK Don't influence the Court. I bet you only know about twenty words yourself. All right, I'll make the test once more, just to be certain. [*The two women take up their positions again.*] Pull! [*Again* GRUSHA *lets go of the* CHILD.]

GRUSHA [*In despair.*] I brought him up! Shall I also tear him to bits? I can't!

AZDAK [*Rising.*] And in this manner the Court has established the true mother. [*To* GRUSHA.] Take your child and be off. I advise you not to stay in the city with him. [*To the* GOVERNOR'S WIFE.] And you disappear before I fine you for fraud. Your estates fall to the city. They'll be converted into a playground for the children. They need one, and I've decided it'll be called after me: Azdak's Garden.

The GOVERNOR'S WIFE *has fainted and is carried out by the* LAWYERS *and the* ADJUTANT. GRUSHA *stands motionless.* SHAUWA *leads the* CHILD *toward her.*

Now I'll take off this judge's gown—it's got too hot for me. I'm not cut out for a hero.

In token of farewell I invite you all to a little dance in the meadow outside. Oh, I'd almost forgotten something in my excitement . . . to sign the divorce decree. [*Using the judge's chair as a table, he writes something on a piece of paper, and prepares to leave. Dance music has started.*]

SHAUWA [*Having read what is on the paper.*] But that's not right. You've not divorced the old people. You've divorced Grusha!

AZDAK Divorced the wrong couple? What a pity! And I never retract! If I did, how could we keep order in the land? [*To the old couple.*] I'll invite you to my party instead. You don't mind dancing with each other, do you? [*To* GRUSHA *and* SIMON.] I've got forty piasters coming from you.

SIMON [*Pulling out his purse.*] Cheap at the price, Your Honor. And many thanks.

AZDAK [*Pocketing the cash.*] I'll be needing this.

GRUSHA [*To* MICHAEL.] So we'd better leave the city tonight, Michael. [*To* SIMON.] You like him?

SIMON With my respects, I like him.

GRUSHA Now I can tell you: I took him because on that Easter Sunday I got engaged to you. So he's a child of love. Michael, let's dance.

She dances with MICHAEL, SIMON *dances with the* COOK, *the old couple with each other.* AZDAK *stands lost in thought. The dancers soon hide him from view. Occasionally he is seen, but less and less as more couples join the dance.*

SINGER And after that evening Azdak vanished and was never seen again.

The people of Grusinia did not forget him but long remembered

The period of his judging as a brief golden age,

Almost an age of justice.

All the couples dance off. AZDAK *has disappeared.*

But you, you who have listened to the Story of the Chalk Circle,

Take note what men of old concluded:

That what there is shall go to those who are good for it,

Children to the motherly, that they prosper,

Carts to good drivers, that they be driven well,

The valley to the waterers, that it yield fruit.

The Visit

FRIEDRICH DUERRENMATT
1921–

(Adapted by Maurice Valency)

CHARACTERS (*In order of appearance*)

HOFBAUER, *first man*
HELMESBERGER, *second man*
WECHSLER, *third man*
VOGEL, *fourth man*
PAINTER
STATION MASTER
BURGOMASTER
TEACHER
PASTOR
ANTON SCHILL
CLAIRE ZACHANASSIAN
CONDUCTOR
PEDRO CABRAL
BOBBY
POLICEMAN
FIRST GRANDCHILD
SECOND GRANDCHILD
MIKE
MAX
FIRST BLIND MAN
SECOND BLIND MAN
ATHLETE
FRAU BURGOMASTER
FRAU SCHILL
DAUGHTER
SON
DOCTOR NÜSSLIN
FRAU BLOCK, *first woman*
TRUCK DRIVER
REPORTER
TOWNSMAN

The action of the play takes place in and around the little town of Güllen, somewhere in Europe.

There are three acts.

ACT ONE

A *railway-crossing bell starts ringing. Then is heard the distant sound of a locomotive whistle. The curtain rises.*

The scene represents, in the simplest possible manner, a little town somewhere in Central Europe. The time is the present. The town is shabby and ruined, as if the plague had passed there. Its name, Güllen, is inscribed on the shabby signboard which adorns the façade of the railway station. This edifice is summarily indicated by a length of rusty iron paling, a platform parallel to the proscenium, beyond which one imagines the rails to be, and a baggage truck standing by a wall on which a torn timetable, marked "Fahrplan," is affixed by three nails. In the station wall is a door with a sign: "Eintritt Verboten."[1] This leads to the STATION MASTER's office.

Left of the station is a little house of gray stucco, formerly whitewashed. It has a tile roof, badly in need of repair. Some shreds of travel posters still adhere to the windowless walls. A shingle hanging over the entrance, left, reads: "Männer."[2] On the other side of the shingle reads: "Damen."[3] Along the wall of the little house there is a wooden bench, backless, on which four men are lounging cheerlessly, shabbily dressed, with cracked shoes. A fifth man is busied with paintpot and brush. He is kneeling on the ground, painting a strip of canvas with the words: "Welcome, Clara."

The warning signal rings uninterruptedly. The sound of the approaching train comes closer and closer. The STATION MASTER issues from his office, advances to the center of the platform and salutes.

The train is heard thundering past in a direction parallel to the footlights, and is lost in the distance. The men on the bench follow its passing with a slow movement of their heads, from left to right.

FIRST MAN   The "Emperor." Hamburg-Naples.
SECOND MAN   Then comes the "Diplomat."
THIRD MAN   Then the "Banker."
FOURTH MAN   And at eleven twenty-seven the "Flying Dutchman." Venice-Stockholm.
FIRST MAN   Our only pleasure—watching trains.
   [*The station bell rings again. The* STATION MASTER *comes out of his office and salutes another train. The men follow its course, right to left.*]
FOURTH MAN   Once upon a time the "Emperor" and the "Flying Dutchman" used to

---

[1] No Entrance.   [2] Men.   [3] Ladies.

stop here in Güllen. So did the "Diplomat," the "Banker," and the "Silver Comet."

SECOND MAN   Now it's only the local from Kaffigen and the twelve-forty from Kalberstadt.

THIRD MAN   The fact is, we're ruined.

FIRST MAN   What with the Wagonworks shut down . . .

SECOND MAN   The Foundry finished . . .

FOURTH MAN   The Golden Eagle Pencil Factory all washed up . . .

FIRST MAN   It's life on the dole.

SECOND MAN   Did you say life?

THIRD MAN   We're rotting.

FIRST MAN   Starving.

SECOND MAN   Crumbling.

FOURTH MAN   The whole damn town.

[The station bell rings.]

THIRD MAN   Once we were a center of industry.

PAINTER   A cradle of culture.

FOURTH MAN   One of the best little towns in the country.

FIRST MAN   In the world.

SECOND MAN   Here Goethe slept.

FOURTH MAN   Brahms composed a quartet.

THIRD MAN   Here Berthold Schwarz invented gunpowder.[4]

PAINTER   And I once got first prize at the Dresden Exhibition of Contemporary Art. What am I doing now? Painting signs.

[The station bell rings. The STATION MASTER comes out. He throws away a cigarette butt. The men scramble for it.]

FIRST MAN   Well, anyway, Madame Zachanassian will help us.

FOURTH MAN   If she comes . . .

THIRD MAN   If she comes.

SECOND MAN   Last week she was in France. She gave them a hospital.

FIRST MAN   In Rome she founded a free public nursery.

THIRD MAN   In Leuthenaw, a bird sanctuary.

PAINTER   They say she got Picasso to design her car.

FIRST MAN   Where does she get all that money?

SECOND MAN   An oil company, a shipping line, three banks and five railways—

FOURTH MAN   And the biggest string of geisha houses in Japan.

4 Berthold Schwarz was a German monk who lived in the fourteenth century. The invention of gunpowder has been attributed to him and to many others.

[From the direction of the town come the BURGOMASTER, the PASTOR, the TEACHER and ANTON SCHILL. The BURGOMASTER, the TEACHER and SCHILL are men in their fifties. The PASTOR is ten years younger. All four are dressed shabbily and are sad-looking. The BURGOMASTER looks official. SCHILL is tall and handsome, but graying and worn; nevertheless a man of considerable charm and presence. He walks directly to the little house and disappears into it.]

PAINTER   Any news, Burgomaster? Is she coming?

ALL   Yes, is she coming?

BURGOMASTER   She's coming. The telegram has been confirmed. Our distinguished guest will arrive on the twelve-forty from Kalberstadt. Everyone must be ready.

TEACHER   The mixed choir is ready. So is the children's chorus.

BURGOMASTER   And the church bell, Pastor?

PASTOR   The church bell will ring. As soon as the new bell ropes are fitted. The man is working on them now.

BURGOMASTER   The town band will be drawn up in the market place and the Athletic Association will form a human pyramid in her honor—the top man will hold the wreath with her initials. Then lunch at the Golden Apostle. I shall say a few words.

TEACHER   Of course.

BURGOMASTER   I had thought of illuminating the town hall and the cathedral, but we can't afford the lamps.

PAINTER   Burgomaster—what do you think of this?

[He shows the banner.]

BURGOMASTER   [Calls.] Schill! Schill!

TEACHER   Schill!

[SCHILL comes out of the little house.]

SCHILL   Yes, right away. Right away.

BURGOMASTER   This is more in your line. What do you think of this?

SCHILL   [Looks at the sign.] No, no, no. That certainly won't do, Burgomaster. It's much too intimate. It shouldn't read: "Welcome, Clara." It should read: "Welcome Madame . . ."

TEACHER   Zachanassian.

BURGOMASTER   Zachanassian.

SCHILL   Zachanassian.

PAINTER   But she's Clara to us.

FIRST MAN   Clara Wäscher.

SECOND MAN   Born here.

THIRD MAN   Her father was a carpenter. He built this.

[*All turn and stare at the little house.*]

SCHILL   All the same . . .

PAINTER   If I . . .

BURGOMASTER   No, no, no. He's right. You'll have to change it.

PAINTER   Oh, well, I'll tell you what I'll do. I'll leave this and I'll put "Welcome, Madame Zachanassian" on the other side. Then if things go well, we can always turn it around.

BURGOMASTER   Good idea. [*To* SCHILL.] Yes?

SCHILL   Well, anyway, it's safer. Everything depends on the first impression.

[*The train bell is heard. Two clangs. The* PAINTER *turns the banner over and goes to work.*]

FIRST MAN   Hear that? The "Flying Dutchman" has just passed through Leuthenau.

FOURTH MAN   Eleven twenty.

BURGOMASTER   Gentlemen, you know that the millionairess is our only hope.

PASTOR   Under God.

BURGOMASTER   Under God. Naturally. Schill, we depend entirely on you.

SCHILL   Yes, I know. You keep telling me.

BURGOMASTER   After all, you're the only one who really knew her.

SCHILL   Yes, I knew her.

PASTOR   You were really quite close to one another, I hear, in those days.

SCHILL   Close? Yes, we were close, there's no denying it. We were in love. I was young—good-looking, so they said—and Clara—you know, I can still see her in the great barn coming toward me—like a light out of the darkness. And in the Konradsweil Forest she'd come running to meet me—barefooted—her beautiful red hair streaming behind her. Like a witch. I was in love with her, all right. But you know how it is when you're twenty.

PASTOR   What happened?

SCHILL   [*Shrugs.*] Life came between us.

BURGOMASTER   You must give me some points about her for my speech.

[*He takes out his notebook.*]

SCHILL   I think I can help you there.

TEACHER   Well, I've gone through the school records. And the young lady's marks were, I'm afraid to say, absolutely dreadful. Even in deportment. The only subject in which she was even remotely passable was natural history.

BURGOMASTER   Good in natural history. That's fine. Give me a pencil.

[*He makes a note.*]

SCHILL   She was an outdoor girl. Wild. Once, I remember, they arrested a tramp, and she threw stones at the policeman. She hated injustice passionately.

BURGOMASTER   Strong sense of justice. Excellent.

SCHILL   And generous . . .

ALL   Generous?

SCHILL   Generous to a fault. Whatever little she had, she shared—so good-heartedly. I remember once she stole a bag of potatoes to give to a poor widow.

BURGOMASTER   [*Writing in notebook.*] Wonderful generosity—

TEACHER   Generosity.

BURGOMASTER   That, gentlemen, is something I must not fail to make a point of.

SCHILL   And such a sense of humor. I remember once when the oldest man in town fell and broke his leg, she said, "Oh, dear, now they'll have to shoot him."

BURGOMASTER   Well, I've got enough. The rest, my friend, is up to you.

[*He put the notebook away.*]

SCHILL   Yes, I know, but it's not so easy. After all, to part a woman like that from her millions—

BURGOMASTER   Exactly. Millions. We have to think in big terms here.

TEACHER   If she's thinking of buying us off with a nursery school—

ALL   Nursery school!

PASTOR   Don't accept.

TEACHER   Hold out.

SCHILL   I'm not so sure that I can do it. You know, she may have forgotten me completely.

BURGOMASTER   [He exchanges a look with the TEACHER *and the* PASTOR.] Schill, for many years you have been our most popular citizen. The most respected and the best loved.

SCHILL   Why, thank you . . .

BURGOMASTER   And therefore I must tell you—last week I sounded out the political opposition, and they agreed. In the spring you will be elected to succeed me as Burgomaster. By unanimous vote.

[*The others clap their hands in approval.*]

SCHILL   But, my dear Burgomaster—!

BURGOMASTER   It's true.

TEACHER   I'm a witness. I was at the meeting.

SCHILL   This is—naturally, I'm terribly flattered —It's a completely unexpected honor.

BURGOMASTER   You deserve it.

SCHILL   Burgomaster! Well, well—! [*Briskly.*] Gentlemen, to business. The first chance I get, of course, I shall discuss our miserable position with Clara.

TEACHER   But tactfully, tactfully—

SCHILL   What do you take me for? We must feel our way. Everything must be correct. Psychologically correct. For example, here at the railway station, a single blunder, one false note, could be disastrous.

BURGOMASTER   He's absolutely right. The first impression colors all the rest. Madame Zachanassian sets foot on her native soil for the first time in many years. She sees our love and she sees our misery. She remembers her youth, her friends. The tears well up into her eyes. Her childhood companions throng about her. I will naturally not present myself like this, but in my black coat with my top hat. Next to me, my wife. Before me, my two grandchildren all in white, with roses. My God, if it only comes off as I see it! If only it comes off. [*The station bell begins ringing.*] Oh, my God! Quick! We must get dressed.

FIRST MAN   It's not her train. It's only the "Flying Dutchman."

PASTOR   [*Calmly.*] We have still two hours before she arrives.

SCHILL   For God's sake, don't let's lose our heads. We still have a full two hours.

BURGOMASTER   Who's losing their heads? [*To FIRST *and* SECOND MAN.*] When her train comes, you two, Helmesberger and Vogel, will hold up the banner with "Welcome Madame Zachanassian." The rest will applaud.

THIRD MAN   Bravo!

[*He applauds.*]

BURGOMASTER   But, please, one thing—no wild cheering like last year with the government relief committee. It made no impression at all and we still haven't received any loan. What we need is a feeling of genuine sincerity. That's how we greet with full hearts our beloved sister who has been away from us so long. Be sincerely moved, my friends, that's

the secret; be sincere. Remember you're not dealing with a child. Next a few brief words from me. Then the church bell will start pealing—

PASTOR   If he can fix the ropes in time.

[*The station bell rings.*]

BURGOMASTER   —Then the mixed choir moves in. And then—

TEACHER   We'll form a line down here.

BURGOMASTER   Then the rest of us will form in two lines leading from the station—

[*He is interrupted by the thunder of the approaching train. The men crane their heads to see it pass. The* STATION MASTER *advances to the platform and salutes. There is a sudden shriek of air brakes. The train screams to a stop. The four men jump up in consternation.*]

PAINTER   But the "Flying Dutchman" never stops!

FIRST MAN   It's stopping.

SECOND MAN   In Güllen!

THIRD MAN   In the poorest—

FIRST MAN   The dreariest—

SECOND MAN   The lousiest—

FOURTH MAN   The most God-forsaken hole between Venice and Stockholm.

STATION MASTER   It cannot stop!

[*The train noises stop. There is only the panting of the engine.*]

PAINTER   It's stopped!

[*The* STATION MASTER *runs out.*]

OFFSTAGE VOICES   What's happened? Is there an accident?

[*A hubbub of offstage voices, as if the passengers on the invisible train were alighting.*]

CLAIRE   [*Offstage.*] Is this Güllen?

CONDUCTOR   [*Offstage.*] Here, here, what's going on?

CLAIRE   [*Offstage.*] Who the hell are you?

CONDUCTOR   [*Offstage.*] But you pulled the emergency cord, madame!

CLAIRE   [*Offstage.*] I always pull the emergency cord.

STATION MASTER   [*Offstage.*] I must ask you what's going on here.

CLAIRE   [*Offstage.*] And who the hell are you?

STATION MASTER   [*Offstage.*] I'm the Station Master, madame, and I must ask you—

CLAIRE   [*Enters.*] No!

[*From the right* CLAIRE ZACHANASSIAN *appears. She is an extraordinary woman. She is in her fifties, red-haired, remarkably dressed,*] *with a face as impassive as that of an ancient idol, beautiful still, and with a singular grace of movement and manner. She is simple and unaffected, yet she has the haughtiness of a world power. The entire effect is striking to the point of the unbelievable. Behind her comes her fiancé,* PEDRO CABRAL, *tall, young, very handsome, and completely equipped for fishing, with creel and net, and with a rod case in his hand. An excited* CONDUCTOR *follows.*]

CONDUCTOR But, madame, I must insist! You have stopped the "Flying Dutchman." I must have an explanation.

CLAIRE Nonsense. Pedro.

PEDRO Yes, my love?

CLAIRE This is Güllen. Nothing has changed. I recognize it all. There's the forest of Konradsweil. There's a brook in it full of trout, where you can fish. And there's the roof of the great barn. Ha! God! What a miserable blot on the map.

[*She crosses the stage and goes off with* PEDRO.]

SCHILL My God! Clara!

TEACHER Claire Zachanassian!

ALL Claire Zachanassian!

BURGOMASTER And the town band? The town band! Where is it?

TEACHER The mixed choir! The mixed choir!

PASTOR The church bell! The church bell!

BURGOMASTER [*To the* FIRST MAN.] Quick! My dress coat. My top hat. My grandchildren. Run! Run! [FIRST MAN *runs off. The* BURGOMASTER *shouts after him.*] And don't forget my wife!

[*General panic. The* THIRD MAN *and* FOURTH MAN *hold up the banner, on which only part of the name has been painted:* "Welcome Mad—" CLAIRE *and* PEDRO *re-enter, right.*]

CONDUCTOR [*Mastering himself with an effort.*] Madame. The train is waiting. The entire international railway schedule has been disrupted. I await your explanation.

CLAIRE You're a very foolish man. I wish to visit this town. Did you expect me to jump off a moving train?

CONDUCTOR [*Stupefied.*] You stopped the "Flying Dutchman" because you wished to visit the town?

CLAIRE Naturally.

CONDUCTOR [*Inarticulate.*] Madame!

STATION MASTER Madame, if you wished to visit the town, the twelve forty from Kalberstadt was entirely at your service. Arrival in Güllen, one seventeen.

CLAIRE The local that stops at Loken, Beisenbach, and Leuthenau? Do you expect me to waste three-quarters of an hour chugging dismally through this wilderness?

CONDUCTOR Madame, you shall pay for this!

CLAIRE Bobby, give him a thousand marks.

[BOBBY, *her butler, a man in his seventies, wearing dark glasses, opens his wallet. The townspeople gasp.*]

CONDUCTOR [*Taking the money in amazement.*] But, madame!

CLAIRE And three thousand for the Railway Widows' Relief Fund.

CONDUCTOR [*With the money in his hands.*] But we have no such fund, madame.

CLAIRE Now you have.

[*The* BURGOMASTER *pushes his way forward.*]

BURGOMASTER [*He whispers to the* CONDUCTOR *and* TEACHER.] The lady is Madame Claire Zachanassian!

CONDUCTOR Claire Zachanassian? Oh, my God! But that's naturally quite different. Needless to say, we would have stopped the train if we'd had the slightest idea. [*He hands the money back to* BOBBY.] Here, please. I couldn't dream of it. Four thousand. My God!

CLAIRE Keep it. Don't fuss.

CONDUCTOR Would you like the train to wait, madame, while you visit the town? The administration will be delighted. The cathedral porch. The town hall—

CLAIRE You may take the train away. I don't need it any more.

STATION MASTER All aboard!

[*He puts his whistle to his lips.* PEDRO *stops him.*]

PEDRO But the press, my angel. They don't know anything about this. They're still in the dining car.

CLAIRE Let them stay there. I don't want the press in Güllen at the moment. Later they will come by themselves. [*To* STATION MASTER.] And now what are you waiting for?

STATION MASTER All aboard!

[*The* STATION MASTER *blows a long blast on his whistle. The train leaves. Meanwhile, the* FIRST MAN *has brought the* BURGOMAS-TER's *dress coat and top hat. The* BURGO-MASTER *puts on the coat, then advances slowly and solemnly.*

CONDUCTOR   I trust madame will not speak of this to the administration. It was a pure mis-understanding.

[*He salutes and runs for the train as it starts moving.*]

BURGOMASTER   [*Bows.*] Gracious lady, as Bur-gomaster of the town of Güllen, I have the honor—

[*The rest of the speech is lost in the roar of the departing train. He continues speaking and gesturing, and at last bows amid applause as the train noises end.*]

CLAIRE   Thank you, Mr. Burgomaster.

[*She glances at the beaming faces, and lastly at* SCHILL, *whom she does not recognize. She turns upstage.*]

SCHILL   Clara!

CLAIRE   [*Turns and stares.*] Anton?

SCHILL   Yes. It's good that you've come back.

CLAIRE   Yes. I've waited for this moment. All my life. Ever since I left Güllen.

SCHILL   [*A little embarrassed.*] That is very kind of you to say, Clara.

CLAIRE   And have you thought about me?

SCHILL   Naturally. Always. You know that.

CLAIRE   Those were happy times we spent to-gether.

SCHILL   Unforgettable.

[*He smiles reassuringly at the* BURGO-MASTER.]

CLAIRE   Call me by the name you used to call me.

SCHILL   [*Whispers.*] My kitten.

CLAIRE   What?

SCHILL   [*Louder.*] My kitten.

CLAIRE   And what else?

SCHILL   Little witch.

CLAIRE   I used to call you my black panther. You're gray now, and soft.

SCHILL   But you are still the same, little witch.

CLAIRE   I am the same? [*She laughs.*] Oh, no, my black panther, I am not at all the same.

SCHILL   [*Gallantly.*] In my eyes you are. I see no difference.

CLAIRE   Would you like to meet my fiancé? Pedro Cabral. He owns an enormous planta-tion in Brazil.

SCHILL   A pleasure.

CLAIRE   We're to be married soon.

SCHILL   Congratulations.

CLAIRE   He will be my eighth husband. [PEDRO *stands by himself downstage, right.*] Pedro, come here and show your face. Come along, darling—come here! Don't sulk. Say hello.

PEDRO   Hello.

CLAIRE   A man of few words! Isn't he charm-ing? A diplomat. He's interested only in fish-ing. Isn't he handsome, in his Latin way? You'd swear he was a Brazilian. But he's not —he's a Greek. His father was a White Rus-sian. We were betrothed by a Bulgarian priest. We plan to be married in a few days here in the cathedral.

BURGOMASTER   Here in the cathedral? What an honor for us!

CLAIRE   No. It was my dream, when I was seventeen, to be married in Güllen cathedral. The dreams of youth are sacred, don't you think so, Anton?

SCHILL   Yes, of course.

CLAIRE   Yes, of course. I think so, too. Now I would like to look at the town. [*The mixed choir arrives, breathless, wearing ordinary clothes with green sashes.*] What's all this? Go away. [*She laughs.*] Ha! Ha! Ha!

TEACHER   Dear lady—[*He steps forward, hav-ing put on a sash also.*] Dear lady, as Rector of the high school and a devotee of that noble muse, Music, I take pleasure in presenting the Güllen mixed choir.

CLAIRE   How do you do?

TEACHER   Who will sing for you an ancient folk song of the region, with specially amended words—if you will deign to listen.

CLAIRE   Very well. Fire away.

[*The* TEACHER *blows a pitch pipe. The mixed choir begins to sing the ancient folk song with the amended words. Just then the station bell starts ringing. The song is drowned in the roar of the passing express. The* STATION MASTER *salutes. When the train has passed, there is applause.*]

BURGOMASTER   The church bell! The church bell! Where's the church bell?

[*The* PASTOR *shrugs helplessly.*]

CLAIRE   Thank you, Professor. They sang beau-tifully. The big little blond bass—no, not that one—the one with the big Adam's apple—was most impressive. [*The* TEACHER *bows. The* POLICEMAN *pushes his way professionally through the mixed choir and comes to attention in front of* CLAIRE ZACHANASSIAN.] Now, who are you?

POLICEMAN [*Clicks heels.*] Police Chief Schultz. At your service.

CLAIRE [*She looks him up and down.*] I have no need of you at the moment. But I think there will be work for you by and by. Tell me, do you know how to close an eye from time to time?

POLICEMAN How else could I get along in my profession?

CLAIRE You might practice closing both.

SCHILL [*Laughs.*] What a sense of humor, eh?

BURGOMASTER [*Puts on the top hat.*] Permit me to present my grandchildren, gracious lady. Hermine and Adolphine. There's only my wife still to come.

[*He wipes the perspiration from his brow, and replaces the hat. The little girls present the roses with elaborate curtsies.*]

CLAIRE Thank you, my dears. Congratulations, Burgomaster. Extraordinary children.

[*She plants the roses in* PEDRO's *arms. The* BURGOMASTER *secretly passes his top hat to the* PASTOR, *who puts it on.*]

BURGOMASTER Our pastor, madame.

[*The* PASTOR *takes off the hat and bows.*]

CLAIRE Ah. The pastor. How do you do? Do you give consolation to the dying?

PASTOR [*A bit puzzled.*] That is part of my ministry, yes.

CLAIRE And to those who are condemned to death?

PASTOR Capital punishment has been abolished in this country, madame.

CLAIRE I see. Well, it could be restored, I suppose.

[*The* PASTOR *hands back the hat. He shrugs his shoulders in confusion.*]

SCHILL [*Laughs.*] What an original sense of humor!

[*All laugh, a little blankly.*]

CLAIRE Well, I can't sit here all day—I should like to see the town.

[*The* BURGOMASTER *offers his arm.*]

BURGOMASTER May I have the honor, gracious lady?

CLAIRE Thank you, but these legs are not what they were. This one was broken in five places.

SCHILL [*Full of concern.*] My kitten!

CLAIRE When my airplane bumped into a mountain in Afghanistan. All the others were killed. Even the pilot. But as you see, I survived. I don't fly any more.

SCHILL But you're as strong as ever now.

CLAIRE Stronger.

BURGOMASTER Never fear, gracious lady. The town doctor has a car.

CLAIRE I never ride in motors.

BURGOMASTER You never ride in motors?

CLAIRE Not since my Ferrari crashed in Hong Kong.

SCHILL But how do you travel, then, little witch? On a broom?

CLAIRE Mike—Max! [*She claps her hands. Two huge bodyguards come in, left, carrying a sedan chair. She sits in it.*] I travel this way— a bit antiquated, of course. But perfectly safe. Ha! Ha! Aren't they magnificent? Mike and Max. I bought them in America. They were in jail, condemned to the chair. I had them pardoned. Now they're condemned to my chair. I paid fifty thousand dollars apiece for them. You couldn't get them now for twice the sum. The sedan chair comes from the Louvre. I fancied it so much that the President of France gave it to me. The French are so impulsive, don't you think so, Anton? Go!

[MIKE *and* MAX *start to carry her off.*]

BURGOMASTER You wish to visit the cathedral? And the old town hall?

CLAIRE No. The great barn. And the forest of Konradsweil. I wish to go with Anton and visit our old haunts once again.

THE PASTOR Very touching.

CLAIRE [*To the butler.*] Will you send my luggage and the coffin to the Golden Apostle?

BURGOMASTER The coffin?

CLAIRE Yes. I brought one with me. Go!

TEACHER Hip-hip—

ALL Hurrah! Hip-hip, hurrah! Hurrah!

[*They bear off in the direction of the town. The* TOWNSPEOPLE *burst into cheers. The church bell rings.*]

BURGOMASTER Ah, thank God—the bell at last.

[*The* POLICEMAN *is about to follow the others, when the two* BLIND MEN *appear. They are not young, yet they seem childish— a strange effect. Though they are of different height and features, they are dressed exactly alike, and so create the effect of being twins. They walk slowly, feeling their way. Their* voices, when they speak, are curiously high and flutelike, and they have a curious trick of repetition of phrases.]

FIRST BLIND MAN We're in—

BOTH BLIND MEN Güllen.

FIRST BLIND MAN We breathe—

SECOND BLIND MAN We breathe—

BOTH BLIND MEN We breathe the air, the air of Güllen.

POLICEMAN [Startled.] Who are you?

FIRST BLIND MAN We belong to the lady.

SECOND BLIND MAN We belong to the lady. She calls us—

FIRST BLIND MAN Kobby.

SECOND BLIND MAN And Lobby.

POLICEMAN Madame Zachanassian is staying at the Golden Apostle.

FIRST BLIND MAN We're blind.

SECOND BLIND MAN We're blind.

POLICEMAN Blind? Come along with me, then. I'll take you there.

FIRST BLIND MAN Thank you, Mr. Policeman.

SECOND BLIND MAN Thanks very much.

POLICEMAN Hey! How do you know I'm a policeman, if you're blind?

BOTH BLIND MEN By your voice. By your voice.

FIRST BLIND MAN All policemen sound the same.

POLICEMAN You've had a lot to do with the police, have you, little men?

FIRST BLIND MAN Men he calls us!

BOTH BLIND MEN Men!

POLICEMAN What are you then?

BOTH BLIND MEN You'll see. You'll see.

[The POLICEMAN claps his hands suddenly. The BLIND MEN turn sharply toward the sound. The POLICEMAN is convinced they are blind.]

POLICEMAN What's your trade?

BOTH BLIND MEN We have no trade.

SECOND BLIND MAN We play music.

FIRST BLIND MAN We sing.

SECOND BLIND MAN We amuse the lady.

FIRST BLIND MAN We look after the beast.

SECOND BLIND MAN We feed it.

FIRST BLIND MAN We stroke it.

SECOND BLIND MAN We take it for walks.

POLICEMAN What beast?

BOTH BLIND MEN You'll see—you'll see.

SECOND BLIND MAN We give it raw meat.

FIRST BLIND MAN And she gives us chicken and wine.

SECOND BLIND MAN Every day—

BOTH BLIND MEN Every day.

POLICEMAN Rich people have strange tastes.

BOTH BLIND MEN Strange tastes—strange tastes.

[The POLICEMAN puts on his helmet.]

POLICEMAN Come along, I'll take you to the lady.

[The two BLIND MEN turn and walk off.]

BOTH BLIND MEN We know the way—we know the way.

[The station and the little house vanish. A sign representing the Golden Apostle descends. The scene dissolves into the interior of the inn. The Golden Apostle is seen to be in the last stages of decay. The walls are cracked and moldering, and the plaster is falling from the ancient lath. A table represents the café of the inn. The BURGOMASTER and the TEACHER sit at this table, drinking a glass together. A procession of townspeople, carrying many pieces of luggage, passes. Then comes a coffin, and, last, a large box covered with a canvas. They cross the stage from right to left.]

BURGOMASTER Trunks. Suitcases. Boxes. [He looks up apprehensively at the ceiling.] The floor will never bear the weight. [As the large covered box is carried in, he peers under the canvas, then draws back.] Good God!

TEACHER Why, what's in it?

BURGOMASTER A live panther. [They laugh. The BURGOMASTER lifts his glass solemnly.] Your health, Professor. Let's hope she puts the Foundry back on its feet.

TEACHER [Lifts his glass.] And the Wagonworks.

BURGOMASTER And the Golden Eagle Pencil Factory. Once that starts moving, everything else will go. Prosit.[5]

[They touch glasses and drink.]

TEACHER What does she need a panther for?

BURGOMASTER Don't ask me. The whole thing is too much for me. The Pastor had to go home and lie down.

TEACHER [Sets down his glass.] If you want to know the truth, she frightens me.

BURGOMASTER [Nods gravely.] She's a strange one.

TEACHER You understand, Burgomaster, a man who for twenty-two years has been correcting

[5] Your health.

the Latin compositions of the students of Güllen is not unaccustomed to surprises. I have seen things to make one's hair stand on end. But when this woman suddenly appeared on the platform, a shudder tore through me. It was as though out of the clear sky all at once a fury descended upon us, beating its black wings—

[*The* POLICEMAN *comes in. He mops his face.*]

POLICEMAN Ah! Now the old place is livening up a bit!

BURGOMASTER Ah, Schultz, come and join us.

POLICEMAN Thank you. [*He calls.*] Beer!

BURGOMASTER Well, what's the news from the front?

POLICEMAN I'm just back from Schiller's barn. My God! What a scene! She had us all tiptoeing around in the straw as if we were in church. Nobody dared to speak above a whisper. And the way she carried on! I was so embarrassed I let them go to the forest by themselves.

BURGOMASTER Does the fiancé go with them?

POLICEMAN With his fishing rod and his landing net. In full marching order. [*He calls again.*] Beer!

BURGOMASTER That will be her seventh husband.

TEACHER Her eighth.

BURGOMASTER But what does she expect to find in the Konradsweil forest?

POLICEMAN The same thing she expected to find in the old barn, I suppose. The—the—

TEACHER The ashes of her youthful love.

POLICEMAN Exactly.

TEACHER It's poetry.

POLICEMAN Poetry.

TEACHER Sheer poetry! It makes one think of Shakespeare, of Wagner. Of Romeo and Juliet.

[*The* SECOND MAN *comes in as a waiter. The* POLICEMAN *is served his beer.*]

BURGOMASTER Yes, you're right. [*Solemnly.*] Gentlemen, I would like to propose a toast. To our great and good friend, Anton Schill, who is even now working on our behalf.

POLICEMAN Yes! He's really working.

BURGOMASTER Gentlemen, to the best-loved citizen of this town. My successor, Anton Schill!

[*They raise their glasses. At this point an* unearthly scream is heard. It is the black panther howling offstage. The sign of the Golden Apostle rises out of sight. The lights go down. The inn vanishes. Only the wooden bench, on which the four men were lounging in the opening scene, is left on the stage, downstage right. The procession comes on upstage. The two bodyguards carry in CLAIRE's sedan chair. Next to it walks SCHILL. PEDRO walks behind, with his fishing rod. Last come the two BLIND MEN and the butler. CLAIRE alights.]

CLAIRE Stop! Take my chair off somewhere else. I'm tired of looking at you. [*The bodyguards and the sedan chair go off.*] Pedro darling, your brook is just a little further along down that path. Listen. You can hear it from here. Bobby, take him and show him where it is.

BOTH BLIND MEN We'll show him the way— we'll show him the way.

[*They go off, left.* PEDRO *follows.* BOBBY *walks off, right.*]

CLAIRE Look, Anton. Our tree. There's the heart you carved in the bark long ago.

SCHILL Yes. It's still there.

CLAIRE How it has grown! The trunk is black and wrinkled. Why, its limbs are twice what they were. Some of them have died.

SCHILL It's aged. But it's there.

CLAIRE Like everything else. [*She crosses, examining other trees.*] Oh, how tall they are. How long it is since I walked here, barefoot over the pine needles and the damp leaves! Look, Anton. A fawn.

SCHILL Yes, a fawn. It's the season.

CLAIRE I thought everything would be changed. But it's all just as we left it. This is the seat we sat on years ago. Under these branches you kissed me. And over there under the hawthorn, where the moss is soft and green, we would lie in each other's arms. It is all as it used to be. Only we have changed.

SCHILL Not so much, little witch. I remember the first night we spent together, you ran away and I chased you till I was quite breathless—

CLAIRE Yes.

SCHILL Then I was angry and I was going home, when suddenly I heard you call and I looked up, and there you were sitting in a tree, laughing down at me.

CLAIRE   No. It was in the great barn. I was in the hayloft.

SCHILL   Were you?

CLAIRE   Yes. What else do you remember?

SCHILL   I remember the morning we went swimming by the waterfall, and afterwards we were lying together on the big rock in the sun, when suddenly we heard footsteps and we just had time to snatch up our clothes and run behind the bushes when the old pastor appeared and scolded you for not being in school.

CLAIRE   No. It was the schoolmaster who found us. It was Sunday and I was supposed to be in church.

SCHILL   Really?

CLAIRE   Yes. Tell me more.

SCHILL   I remember the time your father beat you, and you showed me the cuts on your back, and I swore I'd kill him. And the next day I dropped a tile from a roof top and split his head open.

CLAIRE   You missed him.

SCHILL   No!

CLAIRE   You hit old Mr. Reiner.

SCHILL   Did I?

CLAIRE   Yes. I was seventeen. And you were not yet twenty. You were so handsome. You were the best-looking boy in town.

[*The two* BLIND MEN *begin playing mandolin music offstage, very softly.*]

SCHILL   And you were the prettiest girl.

CLAIRE   We were made for each other.

SCHILL   So we were.

CLAIRE   But you married Mathilde Blumhard and her store, and I married old Zachanassian and his oil wells. He found me in a whore-house in Hamburg. It was my hair that entangled him, the old golden beetle.

SCHILL   Clara!

CLAIRE   [*She claps her hands.*] Bobby! A cigar.

[BOBBY *appears with a leather case. He selects a cigar, puts it in a holder, lights it, and presents it to* CLAIRE.]

SCHILL   My kitten smokes cigars!

CLAIRE   Yes. I adore them. Would you care for one?

SCHILL   Yes, please. I've never smoked one of those.

CLAIRE   It's a taste I acquired from old Zachanassian. Among other things. He was a real connoisseur.

SCHILL   We used to sit on this bench once, you and I, and smoke cigarettes. Do you remember?

CLAIRE   Yes. I remember.

SCHILL   The cigarettes I bought from Mathilde.

CLAIRE   No. She gave them to you for nothing.

SCHILL   Clara—don't be angry with me for marrying Mathilde.

CLAIRE   She had money.

SCHILL   But what a lucky thing for you that I did!

CLAIRE   Oh?

SCHILL   You were so young, so beautiful. You deserved a far better fate than to settle in this wretched town without any future.

CLAIRE   Yes?

SCHILL   If you had stayed in Güllen and married me, your life would have been wasted, like mine.

CLAIRE   Oh?

SCHILL   Look at me. A wretched shopkeeper in a bankrupt town!

CLAIRE   But you have your family.

SCHILL   My family! Never for a moment do they let me forget my failure, my poverty.

CLAIRE   Mathilde has not made you happy?

SCHILL   [*Shrugs.*] What does it matter?

CLAIRE   And the children?

SCHILL   [*Shakes his head.*] They're so completely materialistic. You know, they have no interest whatever in higher things.

CLAIRE   How sad for you.

[*A moment's pause, during which only the faint tinkling of the music is heard.*]

SCHILL   Yes. You know, since you went away my life has passed by like a stupid dream. I've hardly once been out of this town. A trip to a lake years ago. It rained all the time. And once five days in Berlin. That's all.

CLAIRE   The world is much the same everywhere.

SCHILL   At least you've seen it.

CLAIRE   Yes. I've seen it.

SCHILL   You've lived in it.

CLAIRE   I've lived in it. The world and I have been on very intimate terms.

SCHILL   Now that you've come back, perhaps things will change.

CLAIRE   Naturally. I certainly won't leave my native town in this condition.

SCHILL   It will take millions to put us on our feet again.

CLAIRE   I have millions.

SCHILL   One, two, three.

CLAIRE   Why not?

SCHILL   You mean—you will help us?

CLAIRE   Yes.

[*A woodpecker is heard in the distance.*]

SCHILL   I knew it—I knew it. I told them you were generous. I told them you were good. Oh, my kitten, my kitten.

[*He takes her hand. She turns her head away and listens.*]

CLAIRE   Listen! A woodpecker.

SCHILL   It's all just the way it was in the days when we were young and full of courage. The sun high above the pines. White clouds, piling up on one another. And the cry of the cuckoo in the distance. And the wind rustling the leaves, like the sound of surf on a beach. Just as it was years ago. If only we could roll back time and be together always.

CLAIRE   Is that your wish?

SCHILL   Yes. You left me, but you never left my heart. [*He raises her hand to his lips.*] The same soft little hand.

CLAIRE   No, not quite the same. It was crushed in the plane accident. But they mended it. They mend everything nowadays.

SCHILL   Crushed? You wouldn't know it. See, another fawn.

CLAIRE   The old wood is alive with memories.

[PEDRO *appears, right, with a fish in his hand.*]

PEDRO   See what I've caught, darling. See? A pike. Over two kilos.

[*The* BLIND MEN *appear onstage.*]

BOTH BLIND MEN   [*Clapping their hands.*] A pike! A pike! Hurrah! Hurrah!

[*As the* BLIND MEN *clap their hands,* CLAIRE *and* SCHILL *exit, and the scene dissolves. The clapping of hands is taken up on all sides. The townspeople wheel in the walls of the café. A brass band strikes up a march tune. The door of the Golden Apostle descends. The townspeople bring in tables and set them with ragged tablecloths, cracked china, and glassware. There is a table in the center, upstage, flanked by two tables perpendicular to it, right and left. The* PASTOR *and the* BURGOMASTER *come in.* SCHILL *enters. Other townspeople filter in, left and right. One, the* ATHLETE, *is in gymnastic costume. The applause continues.*]

BURGOMASTER   She's coming! [CLAIRE *enters upstage, center, followed by* BOBBY.] The applause is meant for you, gracious lady.

CLAIRE   The band deserves it more than I. They blow from the heart. And the human pyramid was beautiful. You, show me your muscles. [*The* ATHLETE *kneels before her.*] Superb. Wonderful arms, powerful hands. Have you ever strangled a man with them?

ATHLETE   Strangled?

CLAIRE   Yes. It's perfectly simple. A little pressure in the proper place, and the rest goes by itself. As in politics.

[*The* BURGOMASTER'S *wife comes up, simpering.*]

BURGOMASTER   [*Presents her.*] Permit me to present my wife, Madame Zachanassian.

CLAIRE   Annette Dummermuth. The head of our class.

BURGOMASTER   [*He presents another sour-looking woman.*] Frau Schill.

CLAIRE   Mathilde Blumhard. I remember the way you used to follow Anton with your eyes, from behind the shop door. You've grown a little thin and dry, my poor Mathilde.

SCHILL   My daughter, Ottilie.

CLAIRE   Your daughter . . .

SCHILL   My son, Karl.

CLAIRE   Your son. Two of them!

[*The town* DOCTOR *comes in, right. He is a man of fifty, strong and stocky, with bristly black hair, a mustache, and a saber cut on his cheek. He is wearing an old cutaway.*]

DOCTOR   Well, well, my old Mercedes got me here in time after all!

BURGOMASTER   Dr. Nüsslin, the town physician. Madame Zachanassian.

DOCTOR   Deeply honored, madame.

[*He kisses her hand.* CLAIRE *studies him.*]

CLAIRE   It is you who signs the death certificates?

DOCTOR   Death certificates?

CLAIRE   When someone dies.

DOCTOR   Why certainly. That is one of my duties.

CLAIRE   And when the heart dies, what do you put down? Heart failure?

SCHILL   [*Laughing.*] What a golden sense of humor!

DOCTOR   Bit grim, wouldn't you say?

SCHILL   [*Whispers.*] Not at all, not at all. She's promised us a million.

BURGOMASTER [*Turns his head.*] What?

SCHILL A million!

ALL [*Whisper.*] A million!

[CLAIRE *turns toward them.*]

CLAIRE Burgomaster.

BURGOMASTER Yes?

CLAIRE I'm hungry. [*The girls and the waiter fill glasses and bring food. There is a general stir. All take their places at the tables.*] Are you going to make a speech?

[*The* BURGOMASTER *bows,* CLAIRE *sits next to the* BURGOMASTER. *The* BURGOMASTER *rises, tapping his knife on his glass. He is radiant with good will. All applaud.*]

BURGOMASTER Gracious lady and friends. Gracious lady, it is now many years since you first left your native town of Güllen, which was founded by the Elector Hasso and which nestles in the green slope between the forest of Konradsweil and the beautiful valley of Pückenried. Much has taken place in this time, much that is evil.

TEACHER That's true.

BURGOMASTER The world is not what it was; it has become harsh and bitter, and we too have had our share of harshness and bitterness. But in all this time, dear lady, we have never forgotten our little Clara. [*Applause.*] Many years ago you brightened the town with your pretty face as a child, and now once again you brighten it with your presence. [*Polite applause.*] We haven't forgotten you, and we haven't forgotten your family. Your mother, beautiful and robust even in her old age—[*He looks for his notes on the table.*] —although unfortunately taken from us in the bloom of her youth by an infirmity of the lungs. Your respected father, Siegfried Wäscher, the builder, an example whose work next to our railway station is often visited—[SCHILL *covers his face.*]—that is to say, admired—a lasting monument of local design and local workmanship. And you, gracious lady, whom we remember as a golden-haired—[*He looks at her.*]—little red-headed sprite romping about our peaceful streets—on your way to school—which of us does not treasure your memory? [*He pokes nervously at his notebook.*] We will remember your scholarly attainments—

TEACHER Yes.

BURGOMASTER Natural history . . . Extraordi-

nary sense of justice . . . And, above all, your supreme generosity. [*Great applause.*] We shall never forget how you once spent the whole of your little savings to buy a sack of potatoes for a poor starving widow who was in need of food. Gracious lady, ladies and gentlemen, today our little Clara has become the world-famous Claire Zachanassian who has founded hospitals, soup kitchens, charitable institutes, art projects, libraries, nurseries, and schools, and now that she has at last once more returned to the town of her birth, sadly fallen as it is, I say in the name of all her loving friends who have sorely missed her: Long live our Clara!

ALL Long live our Clara!

[*Cheers. Music. Fanfare. Applause.* CLAIRE *rises.*]

CLAIRE Mr. Burgomaster. Fellow townsmen. I am greatly moved by the nature of your welcome and the disinterested joy which you have manifested on the occasion of my visit to my native town. I was not quite the child the Burgomaster described in his gracious address . . .

BURGOMASTER Too modest, madame.

CLAIRE In school I was beaten—

TEACHER Not by me.

CLAIRE And the sack of potatoes which I presented to Widow Boll, I stole with the help of Anton Schill, not to save the old trull from starvation, but so that for once I might sleep with Anton in a real bed instead of under the trees of the forest. [*The townspeople look grave, embarrassed.*] Nevertheless, I shall try to deserve your good opinion. In memory of the seventeen years I spent among you, I am prepared to hand over as a gift to the town of Güllen the sum of one billion marks. Five hundred million to the town, and five hundred million to be divided per capita among the citizens.

[*There is a moment of dead silence.*]

BURGOMASTER A billion marks?

CLAIRE On one condition.

[*Suddenly a movement of uncontrollable joy breaks out. People jump on chairs, dance about, yell excitedly. The* ATHLETE *turns handsprings in front of the speaker's table.*]

SCHILL Oh, Clara, you astonishing, incredible, magnificent woman! What a heart! What a gesture! Oh—my little witch!

[*He kisses her hand.*]

BURGOMASTER   [*Holds up his arms for order.*] Quiet! Quiet, please! On one condition, the gracious lady said. Now, madame, may we know what that condition is?

CLAIRE   I will tell you. In exchange for my billion marks, I want justice.

[*Silence.*]

BURGOMASTER   Justice, madam?

CLAIRE   I wish to buy justice.

BURGOMASTER   But justice cannot be bought, madame.

CLAIRE   Everything can be bought.

BURGOMASTER   I don't understand at all.

CLAIRE   Bobby, step forward.

[*The butler goes to the center of the stage. He takes off his dark glasses and turns his face with a solemn air.*]

BOBBY   Does anyone here present recognize me?

FRAU SCHILL   Hofer! Hofer!

ALL   Who? What's that?

TEACHER   Not Chief Magistrate Hofer?

BOBBY   Exactly. Chief Magistrate Hofer. When Madame Zachanassian was a girl, I was presiding judge at the criminal court of Güllen. I served there until twenty-five years ago, when Madame Zachanassian offered me the opportunity of entering her service as butler. I accepted. You may consider it a strange employment for a member of the magistracy, but the salary—

[CLAIRE *bangs the mallet on the table.*]

CLAIRE   Come to the point.

BOBBY   You have heard Madame Zachanassian's offer. She will give you a billion marks—when you have undone the injustice that she suffered at your hands here in Güllen as a girl.

[*All murmur.*]

BURGOMASTER   Injustice at our hands? Impossible!

BOBBY   Anton Schill . . .

SCHILL   Yes?

BOBBY   Kindly stand.

[SCHILL *rises. He smiles, as if puzzled. He shrugs.*]

SCHILL   Yes?

BOBBY   In those days, a bastardly case was tried before me. Madame Claire Zachanassian, at that time called Clara Wäscher, charged you with being the father of her illegitimate child.

[*Silence.*] You denied the charge. And produced two witnesses in your support.

SCHILL   That's ancient history. An absurd business. We were children. Who remembers?

CLAIRE   Where are the blind men?

BOTH BLIND MEN   Here we are. Here we are. [MIKE *and* MAX *push them forward.*]

BOBBY   You recognize these men, Anton Schill?

SCHILL   I never saw them before in my life. What are they?

BOTH BLIND MEN   We've changed. We've changed.

BOBBY   What were your names in your former life?

FIRST BLIND MAN   I was Jacob Hueblein. Jacob Hueblein.

SECOND BLIND MAN   I was Ludwig Sparr. Ludwig Sparr.

BOBBY   [*To* SCHILL.] Well?

SCHILL   These names mean nothing to me.

BOBBY   Jacob Hueblein and Ludwig Sparr, do you recognize the defendant?

FIRST BLIND MAN   We're blind.

SECOND BLIND MAN   We're blind.

SCHILL   Ha-ha-ha!

BOBBY   By his voice?

BOTH BLIND MEN   By his voice. By his voice.

BOBBY   At that trial, I was the judge. And you?

BOTH BLIND MEN   We were the witnesses.

BOBBY   And what did you testify on that occasion?

FIRST BLIND MAN   That we had slept with Clara Wäscher.

SECOND BLIND MAN   Both of us. Many times.

BOBBY   And was it true?

FIRST BLIND MAN   No.

SECOND BLIND MAN   We swore falsely.

FIRST BLIND MAN   Anton Schill bribed us.

SECOND BLIND MAN   He bribed us.

BOBBY   With what?

BOTH BLIND MEN   With a bottle of schnapps.

BOBBY   And now tell the people what happened to you. [*They hesitate and whimper.*] Speak!

FIRST BLIND MAN   [*In a low voice.*] She tracked us down.

BOBBY   Madame Zachanassian tracked them down. Jacob Hueblein was found in Canada. Ludwig Sparr in Australia. And when she found you, what did she do to you?

SECOND BLIND MAN She handed us over to Mike and Max.

BOBBY And what did Mike and Max do to you?

FIRST BLIND MAN They made us what you see.

[*The* BLIND MEN *cover their faces.* MIKE *and* MAX *push them off.*]

BOBBY And there you have it. We are all present in Güllen once again. The plaintiff. The defendant. The two false witnesses. The judge. Many years have passed. Does the plaintiff have anything further to add?

CLAIRE There is nothing to add.

BOBBY And the defendant?

SCHILL Why are you doing this? It was all dead and buried.

BOBBY What happened to the child that was born?

CLAIRE [*In a low voice.*] It lived a year.

BOBBY And what happened to you?

CLAIRE I became a whore.

BOBBY Why?

CLAIRE The judgment of the court left me no alternative. No one would trust me. No one would give me work.

BOBBY So. And now, what is the nature of the reparation you demand?

CLAIRE I want the life of Anton Schill.

[FRAU SCHILL *springs to Anton's side. She puts her arms around him. The children rush to him. He breaks away.*]

FRAU SCHILL Anton! No! No!

SCHILL No— No— She's joking. That happened long ago. That's all forgotten.

CLAIRE Nothing is forgotten. Neither the mornings in the forest, nor the nights in the great barn, nor the bedroom in the cottage, nor your treachery at the end. You said this morning that you wished that time might be rolled back. Very well—I have rolled it back. And now it is I who will buy justice. You bought it with a bottle of schnapps. I am willing to pay one billion marks.

[*The* BURGOMASTER *stands up, very pale and dignified.*]

BURGOMASTER Madame Zachanassian, we are not in the jungle. We are in Europe. We may be poor, but we are not heathens. In the name of the town of Güllen, I decline your offer. In the name of humanity. We shall never accept.

[*All applaud wildly. The applause turns into a sinister rhythmic beat. As* CLAIRE *rises, it dies away. She looks at the crowd, then at the* BURGOMASTER.]

CLAIRE Thank you, Burgomaster. [*She stares at him a long moment.*] I can wait.

[*She turns and walks off.*]

[*Curtain.*]

ACT II

The façade of the Golden Apostle, with a balcony on which chairs and a table are set out. To the right of the inn is a sign which reads: "ANTON SCHILL, HANDLUNG."[1] *Under the sign the shop is represented by a broken counter. Behind the counter are some shelves with tobacco, cigarettes, and liquor bottles. There are two milk cans. The shop door is imaginary, but each entrance is indicated by a doorbell with a tinny sound.*

It is early morning.

SCHILL *is sweeping the shop. The son has a pan and brush and also sweeps. The* DAUGHTER *is dusting. They are singing "The Happy Wanderer."*

SCHILL Karl—

[KARL *crosses with a dustpan.* SCHILL *sweeps dust into the pan. The doorbell rings.* THE THIRD MAN *appears, carrying a crate of eggs.*]

THIRD MAN 'Morning.

SCHILL Ah, good morning, Wechsler.

THIRD MAN Twelve dozen eggs, medium brown. Right?

SCHILL Take them, Karl. [*The* SON *puts the crate in a corner.*] Did they deliver the milk yet?

SON Before you came down.

THIRD MAN Eggs are going up again, Herr Schill. First of the month.

[*He gives* SCHILL *a slip to sign.*]

SCHILL What? Again? And who's going to buy them?

THIRD MAN Fifty pfennig a dozen.

SCHILL I'll have to cancel my order, that's all.

THIRD MAN That's up to you, Herr Schill.

[SCHILL *signs the slip.*]

[1] "Anton Schill, Merchandise."

SCHILL   There's nothing else to do. [*He hands back the slip.*] And how's the family?

THIRD MAN   Oh, scraping along. Maybe now things will get better.

SCHILL   Maybe.

THIRD MAN   [*Going.*] 'Morning.

SCHILL   Close the door. Don't let the flies in. [*The children resume their singing.*] Now, listen to me, children. I have a little piece of good news for you. I didn't mean to speak of it yet awhile, but well, why not? Who do you suppose is going to be the next Burgomaster? Eh? [*They look up at him.*] Yes, in spite of everything. It's settled. It's official. What an honor for the family, eh? Especially at a time like this. To say nothing of the salary and the rest of it.

SON   Burgomaster!

SCHILL   Burgomaster. [*The* SON *shakes him warmly by the hand. The* DAUGHTER *kisses him.*] You see, you don't have to be entirely ashamed of your father. [*Silence.*] Is your mother coming down to breakfast soon?

DAUGHTER   Mother's tired. She's going to stay upstairs.

SCHILL   You have a good mother, at least. There you are lucky. Oh, well, if she wants to rest, let her rest. We'll have breakfast together, the three of us. I'll fry some eggs and open a tin of the American ham. This morning we're going to breakfast like kings.

SON   I'd like to, only—I can't.

SCHILL   You've got to eat, you know.

SON   I've got to run down to the station. One of the laborers is sick. They said they could use me.

SCHILL   You want to work on the rails in all this heat? That's no work for a son of mine.

SON   Look, Father, we can use the money.

SCHILL   Well, if you feel you have to.

[*The* SON *goes to the door. The* DAUGHTER *moves toward* SCHILL.]

DAUGHTER   I'm sorry, Father. I have to go too.

SCHILL   You too? And where is the young lady going, if I may be so bold?

DAUGHTER   There may be something for me at the employment agency.

SCHILL   Employment agency?

DAUGHTER   It's important to get there early.

SCHILL   All right. I'll have something nice for you when you get home.

SON *and* DAUGHTER   [*Salute.*] Good day, Burgomaster.

[*The* SON *and* DAUGHTER *go out. The* FIRST MAN *comes into* SCHILL's *shop. Mandolin and guitar music are heard offstage.*]

SCHILL   Good morning, Hofbauer.

FIRST MAN   Cigarettes. [SCHILL *takes a pack from the shelf.*] Not those. I'll have the green today.

SCHILL   They cost more.

FIRST MAN   Put it in the book.

SCHILL   What?

FIRST MAN   Charge it.

SCHILL   Well, all right, I'll make an exception this time—seeing it's you, Hofbauer.

[SCHILL *writes in his cash book.*]

FIRST MAN   [*Opening the pack of cigarettes.*] Who's that playing out there?

SCHILL   The two blind men.

FIRST MAN   They play well.

SCHILL   To hell with them.

FIRST MAN   They make you nervous? [SCHILL *shrugs. The* FIRST MAN *lights a cigarette.*] She's getting ready for the wedding, I hear.

SCHILL   Yes. So they say.

[*Enter the* FIRST *and* SECOND WOMAN. *They cross to the counter.*]

FIRST WOMAN   Good morning, good morning.

SECOND WOMAN   Good morning.

FIRST MAN   Good morning.

SCHILL   Good morning, ladies.

FIRST WOMAN   Good morning, Herr Schill.

SECOND WOMAN   Good morning.

FIRST WOMAN   Milk please, Herr Schill.

SCHILL   Milk.

SECOND WOMAN   And milk for me too.

SCHILL   A liter of milk each. Right away.

FIRST WOMAN   Whole milk, please, Herr Schill.

SCHILL   Whole milk?

SECOND WOMAN   Yes. Whole milk, please.

SCHILL   Whole milk, I can only give you half a liter each of whole milk.

FIRST WOMAN   All right.

SCHILL   Half a liter of whole milk here, and half a liter of whole milk here. There you are.

FIRST WOMAN   And butter please, a quarter kilo.

SCHILL   Butter, I haven't any butter. I can give you some very nice lard?

FIRST WOMAN   No. Butter.

SCHILL   Goose fat? [*The* FIRST WOMAN *shakes her head.*] Chicken fat?

FIRST WOMAN   Butter.

SCHILL   Butter. Now, wait a minute, though. I have a tin of imported butter here somewhere. Ah. There you are. No, sorry, she asked first, but I can order some for you from Kalkerstadt tomorrow.

SECOND WOMAN   And white bread.

SCHILL   White bread.

[*He takes a loaf and a knife.*]

SECOND WOMAN   The whole loaf.

SCHILL   But a whole loaf would cost . . .

SECOND WOMAN   Charge it.

SCHILL   Charge it?

FIRST WOMAN   And a package of milk chocolate.

SCHILL   Package of milk chocolate—right away.

SECOND WOMAN   One for me, too, Herr Schill.

SCHILL   And a package of milk chocolate for you, too.

FIRST WOMAN   We'll eat it here, if you don't mind.

SCHILL   Yes, please do.

SECOND WOMAN   It's so cool at the back of the shop.

SCHILL   Charge it?

WOMEN   Of course.

SCHILL   All for one, one for all.

[*The* SECOND MAN *enters.*]

SECOND MAN   Good morning.

THE TWO WOMEN   Good morning.

SCHILL   Good morning, Helmesberger.

SECOND MAN   It's going to be a hot day.

SCHILL   Phew!

SECOND MAN   How's business?

SCHILL   Fabulous. For a while no one came, and now all of a sudden I'm running a luxury trade.

SECOND MAN   Good!

SCHILL   Oh, I'll never forget the way you all stood by me at the Golden Apostle in spite of your need, in spite of everything. That was the finest hour of my life.

FIRST MAN   We're not heathens, you know.

SECOND MAN   We're behind you, my boy; the whole town's behind you.

FIRST MAN   As firm as a rock.

FIRST WOMAN   [*Munching her chocolate.*] As firm as a rock, Herr Schill.

BOTH WOMEN   As firm as a rock.

SECOND MAN   There's no denying it—you're the most popular man in town.

FIRST MAN   The most important.

SECOND MAN   And in the spring, God willing, you will be our Burgomaster.

FIRST MAN   Sure as a gun.

ALL   Sure as a gun.

[*Enter* PEDRO *with fishing equipment and a fish in his landing net.*]

PEDRO   Would you please weigh my fish for me?

SCHILL   [*Weighs it.*] Two kilos.

PEDRO   Is that all?

SCHILL   Two kilos exactly.

PEDRO   Two kilos!

[*He gives* SCHILL *a tip and exits.*]

SECOND WOMAN   The fiancé.

FIRST WOMAN   They're to be married this week. It will be a tremendous wedding.

SECOND WOMAN   I saw his picture in the paper.

FIRST WOMAN   [*Sighs.*] Ah, what a man!

SECOND MAN   Give me a bottle of schnapps.

SCHILL   The usual?

SECOND MAN   No, cognac.

SCHILL   Cognac? But cognac costs twenty-two marks fifty.

SECOND MAN   We all have to splurge a little now and again—

SCHILL   Here you are. Three Star.

SECOND MAN   And a package of pipe tobacco.

SCHILL   Black or blond?

SECOND MAN   English.

SCHILL   English! But that makes twenty-three marks eighty.

SECOND MAN   Chalk it up.

SCHILL   Now, look. I'll make an exception this week. Only, you will have to pay me the moment your unemployment check comes in. I don't want to be kept waiting. [*Suddenly.*] Helmesberger, are those new shoes you're wearing?

SECOND MAN   Yes, what about it?

SCHILL   You too. Hofbauer. Yellow shoes! Brand new!

FIRST MAN   So?

SCHILL   [*To the women.*] And you. You all have new shoes! New shoes!

FIRST WOMAN   A person can't walk around forever in the same old shoes.

SECOND WOMAN   Shoes wear out.

SCHILL   And the money. Where does the money come from?

FIRST WOMAN   We got them on credit, Herr Schill.

SECOND WOMAN   On credit.

SCHILL   On credit? And where all of a sudden do you get credit?

SECOND MAN   Everybody gives credit now.

FIRST WOMAN   You gave us credit yourself.

SCHILL   And what are you going to pay with? Eh? [*They are all silent.* SCHILL *advances upon them threateningly.*] With what? Eh? With what? With what?

[*Suddenly he understands. He takes his apron off quickly, flings it on the counter, gets his jacket, and walks off with an air of determination. Now the shop sign vanishes. The shelves are pushed off. The lights go up on the balcony of the Golden Apostle, and the balcony unit itself moves forward into the optical center.* CLAIRE *and* BOBBY *step out on the balcony.* CLAIRE *sits down.* BOBBY *serves coffee.*]

CLAIRE   A lovely autumn morning. A silver haze on the streets and a violet sky above. Count Holk would have liked this. Remember him, Bobby? My third husband?

BOBBY   Yes, madame.

CLAIRE   Horrible man!

BOBBY   Yes, madame.

CLAIRE   Where is Monsieur Pedro? Is he up yet?

BOBBY   Yes, madame. He's fishing.

CLAIRE   Already? What a singular passion!

[PEDRO *comes in with the fish.*]

PEDRO   Good morning, my love.

CLAIRE   Pedro! There you are.

PEDRO   Look, my darling. Four kilos!

CLAIRE   A jewel! I'll have it grilled for your lunch. Give it to Bobby.

PEDRO   Ah—it is so wonderful here! I like your little town.

CLAIRE   Oh, do you?

PEDRO   Yes. These people, they are all so— what is the word?

CLAIRE   Simple, honest, hard-working, decent.

PEDRO   But, my angel, you are a mind reader. That's just what I was going to say—however did you guess?

CLAIRE   I know them.

PEDRO   Yet when we arrived it was all so dirty, so—what is the word?

CLAIRE   Shabby.

PEDRO   Exactly. But now everywhere you go, you see them busy as bees, cleaning their streets—

CLAIRE   Repairing their houses, sweeping— dusting—hanging new curtains in the windows—singing as they work.

PEDRO   But you astonishing, wonderful woman! You can't see all that from here.

CLAIRE   I know them. And in their gardens—I am sure that in their gardens they are manuring the soil for the spring.

PEDRO   My angel, you know everything. This morning on my way fishing I said to myself, look at them all manuring their gardens. It is extraordinary—and it's all because of you. Your return has given them a new—what is the word?

CLAIRE   Lease on life?

PEDRO   Precisely.

CLAIRE   The town was dying, it's true. But a town doesn't have to die. I think they realize that now. People die, not towns. Bobby! [BOBBY *appears.*] A cigar.

[*The lights fade on the balcony, which moves back upstage. Somewhat to the right, a sign descends. It reads: "Polizei." The* PO- LICEMAN *pushes a desk under it. This, with the bench, becomes the police station. He places a bottle of beer and a glass on the desk, and goes to hang up his coat offstage. The telephone rings.*]

POLICEMAN   Schultz speaking. Yes, we have a couple of rooms for the night. No, not for rent. This is not the hotel. This is the Güllen police station.

[*He laughs and hangs up.* SCHILL *comes in. He is evidently nervous.*]

SCHILL   Schultz.

POLICEMAN   Hello, Schill. Come in. Sit down. Beer?

SCHILL   Please.

[*He drinks thirstily.*]

POLICEMAN   What can I do for you?

SCHILL   I want you to arrest Madame Zachanassian.

POLICEMAN   Eh?

SCHILL   I said I want you to arrest Madame Zachanassian.

POLICEMAN   What the hell are you talking about?

SCHILL   I ask you to arrest this woman at once.

POLICEMAN   What offense has the lady committed?

SCHILL   You know perfectly well. She offered a billion marks—

POLICEMAN   And you want her arrested for that?

[*He pours beer into his glass.*]

SCHILL   Schultz! It's your duty.

POLICEMAN   Extraordinary! Extraordinary idea!

[*He drinks his beer.*]

SCHILL   I'm speaking to you as your next Burgomaster.

POLICEMAN   Schill, that's true. The lady offered us a billion marks. But that doesn't entitle us to take police action against her.

SCHILL   Why not?

POLICEMAN   In order to be arrested, a person must first commit a crime.

SCHILL   Incitement to murder.

POLICEMAN   Incitement to murder is a crime. I agree.

SCHILL   Well?

POLICEMAN   And such a proposal—if serious—constitutes an assault.

SCHILL   That's what I mean.

POLICEMAN   But her offer can't be serious.

SCHILL   Why?

POLICEMAN   The price is too high. In a case like yours, one pays a thousand marks, at the most two thousand. But not a billion! That's ridiculous. And even if she meant it, that would only prove she was out of her mind. And that's not a matter for the police.

SCHILL   Whether she's out of her mind or not, the danger to me is the same. That's obvious.

POLICEMAN   Look, Schill, you show us where anyone threatens your life in any way—say, for instance, a man points a gun at you—and we'll be there in a flash.

SCHILL   [*Gets up.*] So I'm to wait till someone points a gun at me?

POLICEMAN   Pull yourself together, Schill. We're all for you in this town.

SCHILL   I wish I could believe it.

POLICEMAN   You don't believe it?

SCHILL   No. No, I don't. All of a sudden my customers are buying white bread, whole milk, butter, imported tobacco. What does it mean?

POLICEMAN   It means business is picking up.

SCHILL   Helmesberger lives on the dole; he hasn't earned anything in five years. Today he bought French cognac.

POLICEMAN   I'll have to try your cognac one of these days.

SCHILL   And shoes. They all have new shoes.

POLICEMAN   And what have you got against new shoes? I'm wearing a new pair myself.

[*He holds out his foot.*]

SCHILL   You too?

POLICEMAN   Why not?

[*He pours out the rest of his beer.*]

SCHILL   Is that Pilsen you're drinking now?

POLICEMAN   It's the only thing.

SCHILL   You used to drink the local beer.

POLICEMAN   Hogwash.

[*Radio music is heard offstage.*]

SCHILL   Listen. You hear?

POLICEMAN   "The Merry Widow." Yes.

SCHILL   No. It's a radio.

POLICEMAN   That's Bergholzer's radio.

SCHILL   Bergholzer!

POLICEMAN   You're right. He should close his window when he plays it. I'll make a note to speak to him.

[*He makes a note in his notebook.*]

SCHILL   And how can Bergholzer pay for a radio?

POLICEMAN   That's his business.

SCHILL   And you, Schultz, with your new shoes and your imported beer—how are you going to pay for them?

POLICEMAN   That's my business. [*His telephone rings. He picks it up.*] Police Station, Güllen. What? What? Where? Where? How? Right, we'll deal with it.

[*He hangs up.*]

SCHILL   [*He speaks during the* POLICEMAN's *telephone conversation.*] Schultz, listen. No. Schultz, please—listen to me. Don't you see they're all . . . Listen, please. Look, Schultz. They're all running up debts. And out of these debts comes this sudden prosperity. And out of this prosperity comes the absolute need to kill me.

POLICEMAN   [*Putting on his jacket.*] You're imagining things.

SCHILL   All she has to do is to sit on her balcony and wait.

POLICEMAN   Don't be a child.

SCHILL   You're all waiting.

POLICEMAN   [*Snaps a loaded clip into the magazine of a rifle.*] Look, Schill, you can relax.

The police are here for your protection. They know their job. Let anyone, any time, make the slightest threat to your life, and all you have to do is let us know. We'll do the rest . . . Now, don't worry.

SCHILL   No, I won't.

POLICEMAN   And don't upset yourself. All right?

SCHILL   Yes. I won't. [*Then suddenly, in a low tone.*] You have a new gold tooth in your mouth!

POLICEMAN   What are you talking about?

SCHILL   [*Taking the* POLICEMAN's *head in his hands, and forcing his lips open.*] A brand new, shining gold tooth.

POLICEMAN   [*Breaks away and involuntarily levels the gun at* SCHILL.] Are you crazy? Look, I've no time to waste. Madame Zachanassian's panther's broken loose.

SCHILL   Panther?

POLICEMAN   Yes, it's at large. I've got to hunt it down.

SCHILL   You're not hunting a panther and you know it. It's me you're hunting!

[*The* POLICEMAN *clicks on the safety and lowers the gun.*]

POLICEMAN   Schill! Take my advice. Go home. Lock the door. Keep out of everyone's way. That way you'll be safe. Cheer up! Good times are just around the corner!

[*The lights dim in this area and light up on the balcony.* PEDRO *is lounging in a chair.* CLAIRE *is smoking.*]

PEDRO   Oh, this little town oppresses me.

CLAIRE   Oh, does it? So you've changed your mind?

PEDRO   It is true, I find it charming, delightful—

CLAIRE   Picturesque.

PEDRO   Yes. After all, it's the place where you were born. But it is too quiet for me. Too provincial. Too much like all small towns everywhere. These people—look at them. They fear nothing, they desire nothing, they strive for nothing. They have everything they want. They are asleep.

CLAIRE   Perhaps one day they will come to life again.

PEDRO   My God—do I have to wait for that?

CLAIRE   Yes, you do. Why don't you go back to your fishing?

PEDRO   I think I will.

[PEDRO *turns to go.*]

CLAIRE   Pedro.

PEDRO   Yes, my love?

CLAIRE   Telephone the president of Hambro's Bank.[2] Ask him to transfer a billion marks to my current account.

PEDRO   A billion? Yes, my love.

[*He goes. The lights fade on the balcony. A sign is flown in. It reads: "Rathaus."[3] The* THIRD MAN *crosses the stage, right to left, wheeling a new television set on a hand truck. The counter of* SCHILL's *shop is transformed into the* BURGOMASTER's *office. The* BURGOMASTER *comes in. He takes a revolver from his pocket, examines it and sets it down on the desk. He sits down and starts writing.* SCHILL *knocks.*]

BURGOMASTER   Come in.

SCHILL   I must have a word with you, Burgomaster.

BURGOMASTER   Ah, Schill. Sit down, my friend.

SCHILL   Man to man. As your successor.

BURGOMASTER   But of course. Naturally.

[SCHILL *remains standing. He looks at the revolver.*]

SCHILL   Is that a gun?

BURGOMASTER   Madame Zachanassian's black panther's broken loose. It's been seen near the cathedral. It's as well to be prepared.

SCHILL   Oh, yes. Of course.

BURGOMASTER   I've sent out a call for all able-bodied men with firearms. The streets have been cleared. The children have been kept in school. We don't want any accidents.

SCHILL   [*Suspiciously.*] You're making quite a thing of it.

BURGOMASTER   [*Shrugs.*] Naturally. A panther is a dangerous beast. Well? What's on your mind? Speak out. We're old friends.

SCHILL   That's a good cigar you're smoking, Burgomaster.

BURGOMASTER   Yes. Havana.

SCHILL   You used to smoke something else.

BURGOMASTER   Fortuna.

SCHILL   Cheaper.

BURGOMASTER   Too strong.

SCHILL   A new tie? Silk?

BURGOMASTER   Yes. Do you like it?

SCHILL   And have you also bought new shoes?

BURGOMASTER   [*Brings his feet out from under the desk.*] Why, yes. I ordered a new pair

---

[2] One of the principal banks of England.   [3] "City Hall."

from Kalberstadt. Extraordinary! However did you guess?

SCHILL   That's why I'm here.

[*The* THIRD MAN *knocks.*]

BURGOMASTER   Come in.

THIRD MAN   The new typewriter, sir.

BURGOMASTER   Put it on the table. [*The* THIRD MAN *sets it down and goes.*] What's the matter with you? My dear fellow, aren't you well?

SCHILL   It's you who don't seem well, Burgomaster.

BURGOMASTER   What do you mean?

SCHILL   You look pale.

BURGOMASTER   I?

SCHILL   Your hands are trembling. [*The* BURGOMASTER *involuntarily hides his hands.*] Are you frightened?

BURGOMASTER   What have I to be afraid of?

SCHILL   Perhaps this sudden prosperity alarms you.

BURGOMASTER   Is prosperity a crime?

SCHILL   That depends on how you pay for it.

BURGOMASTER   You'll have to forgive me, Schill, but I really haven't the slightest idea what you're talking about. Am I supposed to feel like a criminal every time I order a new typewriter?

SCHILL   Do you?

BURGOMASTER   Well, I hope you haven't come here to talk about a new typewriter. Now, what was it you wanted?

SCHILL   I have come to claim the protection of the authorities.

BURGOMASTER   Ei! Against whom?

SCHILL   You know against whom.

BURGOMASTER   You don't trust us?

SCHILL   That woman has put a price on my head.

BURGOMASTER   If you don't feel safe, why don't you go to the police?

SCHILL   I have just come from the police.

BURGOMASTER   And?

SCHILL   The chief has a new gold tooth in his mouth.

BURGOMASTER   A new—? Oh, Schill, really! You're forgetting. This is Güllen, the town of humane traditions. Goethe slept here. Brahms composed a quartet. You must have faith in us. This is a law-abiding community.

SCHILL   Then arrest this woman who wants to have me killed.

BURGOMASTER   Look here, Schill. God knows the lady has every right to be angry with you. What you did there wasn't very pretty. You forced two decent lads to perjure themselves and had a young girl thrown out on the streets.

SCHILL   That young girl owns half the world.

[*A moment's silence.*]

BURGOMASTER   Very well, then, we'll speak frankly.

SCHILL   That's why I'm here.

BURGOMASTER   Man to man, just as you said. [*He clears his throat.*] Now—after what you did, you have no moral right to say a word against this lady. And I advise you not to try. Also—I regret to have to tell you this—there is no longer any question of your being elected Burgomaster.

SCHILL   Is that official?

BURGOMASTER   Official.

SCHILL   I see.

BURGOMASTER   The man who is chosen to exercise the high post of Burgomaster must have, obviously, certain moral qualifications. Qualifications which, unhappily, you no longer possess. Naturally, you may count on the esteem and friendship of the town, just as before. That goes without saying. The best thing will be to spread the mantle of silence over the whole miserable business.

SCHILL   So I'm to remain silent while they arrange my murder?

[*The* BURGOMASTER *gets up.*]

BURGOMASTER   [*Suddenly noble.*] Now, who is arranging your murder? Give me the names and I will investigate the case at once. Unrelentingly. Well? The names?

SCHILL   You.

BURGOMASTER   I resent this. Do you think we want to kill you for money?

SCHILL   No. You don't want to kill me. But you want to have me killed.

[*The lights go down. The stage is filled with men prowling about with rifles, as if they were stalking a quarry. In the interval the* POLICEMAN's *bench and the* BURGOMASTER's *desk are shifted somewhat, so that they will compose the setting for the sacristy. The stage empties. The lights come up on the balcony.* CLAIRE *appears.*]

CLAIRE   Bobby, what's going on here? What are all these men doing with guns? Whom are they hunting?

BOBBY   The black panther has escaped, madame.

CLAIRE   Who let him out?

BOBBY   Kobby and Lobby, madame.

CLAIRE   How excited they are! There may be shooting?

BOBBY   It is possible, madame.

[*The lights fade on the balcony. The sacristan comes in. He arranges the set, and puts the altar cloth on the altar. Then* SCHILL *comes on. He is looking for the* PASTOR. *The* PASTOR *enters, left. He is wearing his gown and carrying a rifle.*]

SCHILL   Sorry to disturb you, Pastor.

PASTOR   God's house is open to all. [*He sees that* SCHILL *is staring at the gun.*] Oh, the gun? That's because of the panther. It's best to be prepared.

SCHILL   Pastor, help me.

PASTOR   Of course. Sit down. [*He puts the rifle on the bench.*] What's the trouble?

SCHILL   [*Sits on the bench.*] I'm frightened.

PASTOR   Frightened? Of what?

SCHILL   Of everyone. They're hunting me down like a beast.

PASTOR   Have no fear of man, Schill. Fear God. Fear not the death of the body. Fear the death of the soul. Zip up my gown behind, Sacristan.

SCHILL   I'm afraid, Pastor.

PASTOR   Put your trust in heaven, my friend.

SCHILL   You see, I'm not well. I shake. I have such pains around the heart. I sweat.

PASTOR   I know. You're passing through a profound psychic experience.

SCHILL   I'm going through hell.

PASTOR   The hell you are going through exists only within yourself. Many years ago you betrayed a girl shamefully, for money. Now you think that we shall sell you just as you sold her. No, my friend, you are projecting your guilt upon others. It's quite natural. But remember, the root of our torment lies always within ourselves, in our hearts, in our sins. When you have understood this, you can conquer the fears that oppress you; you have weapons with which to destroy them.

SCHILL   Siemethofer has bought a new washing machine.

PASTOR   Don't worry about the washing machine. Worry about your immortal soul.

SCHILL   Stockers has a television set.

PASTOR   There is also great comfort in prayer. Sacristan, the bands. [SCHILL *crosses to the altar and kneels. The sacristan ties on the* PASTOR's *bands.*] Examine your conscience, Schill. Repent. Otherwise your fears will consume you. Believe me, this is the only way. We have no other. [*The church bell begins to peal.* SCHILL *seems relieved.*] Now I must leave you. I have a baptism. You may stay as long as you like. Sacristan, the Bible, Liturgy, and Psalter. The child is beginning to cry. I can hear it from here. It is frightened. Let us make haste to give it the only security which this world affords.

SCHILL   A new bell?

PASTOR   Yes. It's tone is marvelous, don't you think? Full. Sonorous.

SCHILL   [*Steps back in horror.*] A new bell! You too, Pastor? You too?

[*The* PASTOR *clasps his hands in horror. Then he takes* SCHILL *into his arms.*]

PASTOR   Oh, God, God forgive me. We are poor, weak things, all of us. Do not tempt us further into the hell in which you are burning. Go Schill, my friend, go my brother, go while there is time.

[*The* PASTOR *goes.* SCHILL *picks up the rifle with a gesture of desperation. He goes out with it. As the lights fade, men appear with guns. Two shots are fired in the darkness. The lights come up on the balcony, which moves forward.*]

CLAIRE   Bobby! What was that shooting? Have they caught the panther?

BOBBY   He is dead, madame.

CLAIRE   There were two shots.

BOBBY   The panther is dead, madame.

CLAIRE   I loved him. [*Waves* BOBBY *away.*] I shall miss him.

[*The* TEACHER *comes in with two little girls, singing. They stop under the balcony.*]

TEACHER   Gracious lady, be so good as to accept our heartfelt condolences. Your beautiful panther is no more. Believe me, we are deeply pained that so tragic an event should mar your visit here. But what could we do? The panther was savage, a beast. To him our human laws could not apply. There was no other way—[SCHILL *appears with the gun. He looks dangerous. The girls run off, frightened. The* TEACHER *follows the girls.*] Children—children—children!

CLAIRE   Anton, why are you frightening the children?

[*He works the bolt, loading the chamber, and raises the gun slowly.*]

SCHILL   Go away, Claire—I warn you. Go away.

CLAIRE   How strange it is, Anton! How clearly it comes back to me! The day we saw one another for the first time, do you remember? I was on a balcony then. It was a day like today, a day in autumn without a breath of wind, warm as it is now—only lately I am always cold. You stood down there and stared at me without moving. I was embarrassed. I didn't know what to do. I wanted to go back into the darkness of the room, where it was safe, but I couldn't. You stared up at me darkly, almost angrily, as if you wished to hurt me, but your eyes were full of passion. [SCHILL *begins to lower the rifle involuntarily.*] Then, I don't know why, I left the balcony and I came down and stood in the street beside you. You didn't greet me, you didn't say a word, but you took my hand and we walked together out of the town into the fields, and behind us came Kobby and Lobby, like two dogs, sniveling and giggling and snarling. Suddenly you picked up a stone and hurled it at them, and they ran yelping back into the town, and we were alone. [SCHILL *has lowered the rifle completely. He moves forward toward her, as close as he can come.*] That was the beginning, and everything else had to follow. There is no escape.

[*She goes in and closes the shutters.* SCHILL *stands immobile. The* TEACHER *tiptoes in. He stares at* SCHILL, *who doesn't see him. Then he beckons to the children.*]

TEACHER   Come, children, sing. Sing.

[*They begin singing. He creeps behind* SCHILL *and snatches away the rifle.* SCHILL *turns sharply. The* PASTOR *comes in.*]

PASTOR   Go, Schill—go!

[SCHILL *goes out. The children continue singing, moving across the stage and off. The Golden Apostle vanishes. The crossing bell is heard. The scene dissolves into the railway-station setting, as in Act One. But there are certain changes. The timetable marked "Fahrplan" is now new, the frame freshly painted. There is a new travel poster on the station wall. It has a yellow sun and the words:* "Reist in den Süden." [4] *On the other side of the Fahrplan is another poster with the words:* "Die Passionsspiele Oberammergau." [5] *The sound of passing trains covers the scene change.* SCHILL *appears with an old valise in his hand, dressed in a shabby trench coat, his hat on his head. He looks about with a furtive air, walking slowly to the platform. Slowly, as if by chance, the townspeople enter, from all sides.* SCHILL *hesitates, stops.*]

BURGOMASTER   [*From upstage, center.*] Good evening, Schill.

SCHILL   Good evening.

POLICEMAN   Good evening.

SCHILL   Good evening.

PAINTER   [*Enters.*] Good evening.

SCHILL   Good evening.

DOCTOR   Good evening.

SCHILL   Good evening.

BURGOMASTER   So you're taking a little trip?

SCHILL   Yes. A little trip.

POLICEMAN   May one ask where to?

SCHILL   I don't know.

PAINTER   Don't know?

SCHILL   To Kalberstadt.

BURGOMASTER   [*With disbelief, pointing to the valise.*] Kalberstadt?

SCHILL   After that—somewhere else.

PAINTER   Ah. After that somewhere else.

[*The* FOURTH MAN *walks in.*]

SCHILL   I thought maybe Australia.

BURGOMASTER   Australia!

ALL   Australia!

SCHILL   I'll raise the money somehow.

BURGOMASTER   But why Australia?

POLICEMAN   What would you be doing in Australia?

SCHILL   One can't always live in the same town, year in, year out.

PAINTER   But Australia—

DOCTOR   It's a risky trip for a man of your age.

BURGOMASTER   One of the lady's little men ran off to Australia . . .

ALL   Yes.

POLICEMAN   You'll be much safer here.

PAINTER   Much!

---

[4] "Travel in the South."   [5] "The Oberammergau Passion Play," portraying the suffering and death of Jesus, is performed in the south German village every ten years.

[SCHILL *looks about him in anguish, like a beast at bay.*]

SCHILL [*Low voice.*] I wrote a letter to the administration at Kaffigen.

BURGOMASTER Yes? And?

[*They are all intent on the answer.*]

SCHILL They didn't answer.

[*All laugh.*]

DOCTOR Do you mean to say you don't trust old friends? That's not very flattering, you know.

BURGOMASTER No one's going to do you any harm here.

DOCTOR No harm here.

SCHILL They didn't answer because our postmaster held up my letter.

PAINTER Our postmaster? What an idea.

BURGOMASTER The postmaster is a member of the town council.

POLICEMAN A man of the utmost integrity.

DOCTOR He doesn't hold up letters. What an idea !

STATION MASTER [*Announcers.*] Local to Kalberstadt!

[*The townspeople all cross down to see the train arrive. Then they turn, with their backs to the audience, in a line across the stage.* SCHILL *cannot get through to reach the train.*]

SCHILL [*In a low voice.*] What are you all doing here? What do you want of me?

BURGOMASTER We don't like to see you go.

DOCTOR We've come to see you off.

[*The sound of the approaching train grows louder.*]

SCHILL I didn't ask you to come.

POLICEMAN But we have come.

DOCTOR As old friends.

ALL As old friends.

[*The* STATION MASTER *holds up his paddle. The train stops with a screech of brakes. We hear the engine panting offstage.*]

VOICE [*Offstage.*] Güllen!

BURGOMASTER A pleasant journey.

DOCTOR And long life!

PAINTER And good luck in Australia!

ALL Yes, good luck in Australia.

[*They press around him jovially. He stands motionless and pale.*]

SCHILL Why are you crowding me?

POLICEMAN What's the matter now?

[*The* STATION MASTER *blows a long blast on his whistle.*]

SCHILL Give me room.

DOCTOR But you have plenty of room.

[*They all move away from him.*]

POLICEMAN Better get aboard, Schill.

SCHILL I see. I see. One of you is going to push me under the wheels.

POLICEMAN Oh, nonsense. Go on, get aboard.

SCHILL Get away from me, all of you.

BURGOMASTER I don't know what you want. Just get on the train.

SCHILL No. One of you will push me under.

DOCTOR You're being ridiculous. Now, go on, get on the train.

SCHILL Why are you all so near me?

DOCTOR The man's gone mad.

STATION MASTER 'Board!

[*He blows his whistle. The engine bell clangs. The train starts.*]

BURGOMASTER Get aboard, man. Quick.

[*The following speeches are spoken all together until the train noises fade away.*]

DOCTOR The train's starting.

ALL Get aboard, man. Get aboard. The train's starting.

SCHILL If I try to get aboard, one of you will hold me back.

ALL No, no.

BURGOMASTER Get on the train.

SCHILL [*In terror, crouches against the wall of the* STATION MASTER'S *office.*] No—no—no. No. [*He falls on his knees. The others crowd around him. He cowers on the ground, abjectly. The train sounds fade away.*] Oh, no— no—don't push me, don't push me!

POLICEMAN There. It's gone off without you.

[*Slowly they leave him. He raises himself up to a sitting position, still trembling. A* TRUCK DRIVER *enters with an empty can.*]

TRUCK DRIVER Do you know where I can get some water? My truck's boiling over. [SCHILL *points to the station office.*] Thanks. [*He enters the office, gets the water and comes out. By this time,* SCHILL *is erect.*] Missed your train?

SCHILL Yes.

TRUCK DRIVER To Kalberstadt?

SCHILL Yes.

TRUCK DRIVER Well, come with me. I'm going that way.

SCHILL This is my town. This is my home. [*With strange new dignity.*] No, thank you. I've changed my mind. I'm staying.

TRUCK DRIVER [*Shrugs.*] All right.
> [*He goes out.* SCHILL *picks up his bag, looks right and left, and slowly walks off.*]

> [*Curtain.*]

ACT III

Music is heard. Then the curtain rises on the interior of the old barn, a dim, cavernous structure. Bars of light fall across the shadowy forms, shafts of sunlight from the holes and cracks in the walls and roof. Overhead hang old rags, decaying sacks, great cobwebs. Extreme left is a ladder leading to the loft. Near it, an old haycart. Left, CLAIRE ZACHANASSIAN *is sitting in her gilded sedan chair, motionless, in her magnificent bridal gown and veil. Near the chair stands an old keg.*

BOBBY [*Comes in, treading carefully.*] The doctor and the teacher from the high school to see you, madame.
CLAIRE [*Impassive.*] Show them in.
> [BOBBY *ushers them in as if they were entering a hall of state. The two grope their way through the litter. At last they find the lady, and bow. They are both well dressed in new clothes, but are very dusty.*]
BOBBY Dr. Nüsslin and Professor Müller.
DOCTOR Madame.
CLAIRE You look dusty, gentlemen.
DOCTOR [*Dusts himself off vigorously.*] Oh, forgive us. We had to climb over an old carriage.
TEACHER Our respects.
DOCTOR A fabulous wedding.
TEACHER Beautiful occasion.
CLAIRE It's stifling here. But I love this old barn. The smell of hay and old straw and axle grease—it is the scent of my youth. Sit down. All this rubbish—the haycart, the old carriage, the cask, even the pitchfork—it was all here when I was a girl.
TEACHER Remarkable place.
> [*He mops his brow.*]
CLAIRE I thought the pastor's text was very appropriate. The lesson a trifle long.
TEACHER I Corinthians 13.[1]

[1] See I *Corinthians* 13:13: "But now abideth faith, hope, love, these three; and the greatest of these is love."

CLAIRE Your choristers sang beautifully, Professor.
TEACHER Bach. From the *St. Matthew Passion*.
DOCTOR Güllen has never seen such magnificence! The flowers! The jewels! And the people.
TEACHER The theatrical world, the world of finance, the world of art, the world of science . . .
CLAIRE All these worlds are now back in their Cadillacs, speeding toward the capital for the wedding reception. But I'm sure you didn't come here to talk about them.
DOCTOR Dear lady, we should not intrude on your valuable time. Your husband must be waiting impatiently.
CLAIRE No, no, I've packed him off to Brazil.
DOCTOR To Brazil, madame?
CLAIRE Yes. For his honeymoon.
TEACHER *and* DOCTOR Oh! But your wedding guests?
CLAIRE I've planned a delightful dinner for them. They'll never miss me. Now what was it you wished to talk about?
TEACHER About Anton Schill, madame.
CLAIRE Is he dead?
TEACHER Madame, we may be poor. But we have our principles.
CLAIRE I see. Then what do you want?
TEACHER [*He mops his brow again.*] The fact is, madame, in anticipation of your well-known munificence, that is, feeling that you would give the town some sort of gift, we have all been buying things. Necessities . . .
DOCTOR With money we don't have.
> [*The* TEACHER *blows his nose.*]
CLAIRE You've run into debt?
DOCTOR Up to here.
CLAIRE In spite of your principles?
TEACHER We're human, madame.
CLAIRE I see.
TEACHER We have been poor for a long time. A long, long time.
DOCTOR [*He rises.*] The question is, how are we going to pay?
CLAIRE You already know.
TEACHER [*Courageously.*] I beg you, Madame Zachanassian, put yourself in our position for a moment. For twenty-two years I've been cudgeling my brains to plant a few seeds of knowledge in this wilderness. And all this time, my gallant colleague, Dr. Nüsslin, has

been rattling around in his ancient Mercedes, from patient to patient, trying to keep these wretches alive. Why? Why have we spent our lives in this miserable hole? For money? Hardly. The pay is ridiculous.

DOCTOR   And yet, the professor here has declined an offer to head the high school in Kalberstadt.

TEACHER   And Dr. Nüsslin has refused an important post at the University of Erlangen. Madame, the simple fact is, we love our town. We were born here. It is our life.

DOCTOR   That's true.

TEACHER   What has kept us going all these years is the hope that one day the community will prosper again as it did in the days when we were young.

CLAIRE   Good.

TEACHER   Madame, there is no reason for our poverty. We suffer here from a mysterious blight. We have factories. They stand idle. There is oil in the valley of Pückenried.

DOCTOR   There is copper under the Konradsweil Forest. There is power in our streams, in our waterfalls.

TEACHER   We are not poor, madame. If we had credit, if we had confidence, the factories would open, orders and commissions would pour in. And our economy would bloom together with our cultural life. We would become once again like the towns around us, healthy and prosperous.

DOCTOR   If the Wagonworks were put on its feet again—

TEACHER   The Foundry.

DOCTOR   The Golden Eagle Pencil Factory.

TEACHER   Buy these plants, madame. Put them in operation once more, and I swear to you, Güllen will flourish and it will bless you. We don't need a billion marks. Ten million, properly invested, would give us back our life, and incidentally return to the investor an excellent dividend. Save us, madame. Save us, and we will not only bless you, we will make money for you.

CLAIRE   I don't need money.

DOCTOR   Madame, we are not asking for charity. This is business.

CLAIRE   It's a good idea . . .

DOCTOR   Dear lady! I knew you wouldn't let us down.

CLAIRE   But it's out of the question. I cannot buy the Wagonworks. I already own them.

DOCTOR   The Wagonworks?

TEACHER   And the Foundry?

CLAIRE   And the Foundry.

DOCTOR   And the Golden Eagle Pencil Factory?

CLAIRE   Everything. The valley of Pückenried with its oil, the forest of Konradsweil with its ore, the barn, the town, the streets, the houses, the shops, everything. I had my agents buy up this rubbish over the years, bit by bit, piece by piece, until I had it all. Your hopes were an illusion, your vision empty, your self-sacrifice a stupidity, your whole life completely senseless.

TEACHER   Then the mysterious blight—

CLAIRE   The mysterious blight was I.

DOCTOR   But this is monstrous!

CLAIRE   Monstrous. I was seventeen when I left this town. It was winter. I was dressed in a sailor suit and my red braids hung down my back. I was in my seventh month. As I walked down the street to the station, the boys whistled after me, and someone threw something. I sat freezing in my seat in the Hamburg Express. But before the roof of the great barn was lost behind the trees, I had made up my mind that one day I would come back . . .

TEACHER   But, madame—

CLAIRE   [She smiles.] And now I have. [She claps her hands.] Mike. Max. Take me back to the Golden Apostle. I've been here long enough.

[MIKE and MAX start to pick up the sedan chair. The TEACHER pushes MIKE away.]

TEACHER   Madame. One moment. Please. I see it all now. I had thought of you as an avenging fury, a Medea, a Clytemnestra—but I was wrong. You are a warm-hearted woman who has suffered a terrible injustice, and now you have returned and taught us an unforgettable lesson. You have stripped us bare. But now that we stand before you naked, I know you will set aside these thoughts of vengeance. If we made you suffer, you too have put us through the fire. Have mercy, madame.

CLAIRE   When I have had justice. Mike!

[She signals to MIKE and MAX to pick up the sedan chair. They cross the stage. The TEACHER bars the way.]

TEACHER   But, madame, one injustice cannot

cure another. What good will it do to force us into crime? Horror succeeds horror, shame is piled on shame. It settles nothing.

CLAIRE It settles everything.

[*They move upstage toward the exit. The* TEACHER *follows.*]

TEACHER Madame, this lesson you have taught us will never be forgotten. We will hand it down from father to son. It will be a monument more lasting than any vengeance. Whatever we have been, in the future we shall be better because of you. You have pushed us to the extreme. Now forgive us. Show us the way to a better life. Have pity, madame—pity. That is the highest justice.

[*The sedan chair stops.*]

CLAIRE The highest justice has no pity. It is bright and pure and clear. The world made me into a whore; now I make the world into a brothel. Those who wish to go down, may go down. Those who wish to dance with me, may dance with me. [*To her porters.*] Go.

[*She is carried off. The lights black out. Downstage, right, appears* SCHILL's *shop. It has a new sign, a new counter. The doorbell, when it rings, has an impressive sound.* FRAU SCHILL *stands behind the counter in a new dress. The* FIRST MAN *enters, left. He is dressed as a prosperous butcher, a few bloodstains on his snowy apron, a gold watch chain across his open vest.*]

FIRST MAN What a wedding! I'll swear the whole town was there. Cigarettes.

FRAU SCHILL Clara is entitled to a little happiness after all. I'm happy for her. Green or white?

FIRST MAN Turkish. The bridesmaids! Dancers and opera singers. And the dresses! Down to here.

FRAU SCHILL It's the fashion nowadays.

FIRST MAN Reporters! Photographers! From all over the world! [*In a low voice.*] They will be here any minute.

FRAU SCHILL What have reporters to do with us? We are simple people, Herr Hofbauer. There is nothing for them here.

FIRST MAN They're questioning everybody. They're asking everything. [*The* FIRST MAN *lights a cigarette. He looks up at the ceiling.*] Footsteps.

FRAU SCHILL He's pacing the room. Up and down. Day and night.

FIRST MAN Haven't seen him all week.

FRAU SCHILL He never goes out.

FIRST MAN It's his conscience. That was pretty mean, the way he treated poor Madame Zachanassian.

FRAU SCHILL That's true. I feel very badly about it myself.

FIRST MAN To ruin a young girl like that— God doesn't forgive it. [FRAU SCHILL *nods solemnly with pursed lips. The butcher gives her a level glance.*] Look, I hope he'll have sense enough to keep his mouth shut in front of the reporters.

FRAU SCHILL I certainly hope so.

FIRST MAN You know his character.

FRAU SCHILL Only too well, Herr Hofbauer.

FIRST MAN If he tries to throw dirt at our Clara and tell a lot of lies, how she tried to get us to kill him, which anyway she never meant—

FRAU SCHILL Of course not.

FIRST MAN —Then we'll really have to do something! And not because of the money— [*He spits.*] But out of ordinary human decency. God knows Madame Zachanassian has suffered enough through him already.

FRAU SCHILL She has indeed.

[*The* TEACHER *comes in. He is not quite sober.*]

TEACHER [*Looks about the shop.*] Has the press been here yet?

FIRST MAN No.

TEACHER It's not my custom, as you know, Frau Schill—but I wonder if I could have a strong alcoholic drink?

FRAU SCHILL It's an honor to serve you, Herr Professor. I have a good Steinhäger.[2] Would you like to try a glass?

TEACHER A very small glass.

[FRAU SCHILL *serves bottle and glass. The* TEACHER *tosses off a glass.*]

FRAU SCHILL Your hand is shaking, Herr Professor.

TEACHER To tell the truth, I have been drinking a little already.

FRAU SCHILL Have another glass. It will do you good.

[*He accepts another glass.*]

---

[2] A kind of gin.

TEACHER   Is that he up there, walking?

FRAU SCHILL   Up and down. Up and down.

FIRST MAN   It's God punishing him.

[*The* PAINTER *comes in with the* SON *and the* DAUGHTER.]

PAINTER   Careful! A reporter just asked us the way to this shop.

FIRST MAN   I hope you didn't tell him.

PAINTER   I told him we were strangers here.

[*They all laugh. The door opens. The* SECOND MAN *darts into the shop.*]

SECOND MAN   Look out, everybody! The press! They are across the street in your shop, Hofbauer.

FIRST MAN   My boy will know how to deal with them.

SECOND MAN   Make sure Schill doesn't come down, Hofbauer.

FIRST MAN   Leave that to me.

[*They group themselves about the shop.*]

TEACHER   Listen to me, all of you. When the reporters come I'm going to speak to them. I'm going to make a statement. A statement to the world on behalf of myself as Rector of Güllen High School and on behalf of you all, for all your sakes.

PAINTER   What are you going to say?

TEACHER   I shall tell the truth about Claire Zachanassian.

FRAU SCHILL   You're drunk, Herr Professor; you should be ashamed of yourself.

TEACHER   I should be ashamed? You should all be ashamed!

SON   Shut your trap. You're drunk.

DAUGHTER   Please, Professor—

TEACHER   Girl, you disappoint me. It is your place to speak. But you are silent and you force your old teacher to raise his voice. I am going to speak the truth. It is my duty and I am not afraid. The world may not wish to listen, but no one can silence me. I'm not going to wait—I'm going over to Hofbauer's shop now.

ALL   No, you're not. Stop him. Stop him.

[*They all spring at the* TEACHER. *He defends himself. At this moment,* SCHILL *appears through the door upstage. In contrast to the others, he is dressed shabbily in an old black jacket, his best.*]

SCHILL   What's going on in my shop? [*The townsmen let go of the* TEACHER *and turn to stare at* SCHILL.] What's the trouble, Professor?

TEACHER   Schill, I am speaking out at last! I am going to tell the press everything.

SCHILL   Be quiet, Professor.

TEACHER   What did you say?

SCHILL   Be quiet.

TEACHER   You want me to be quiet?

SCHILL   Please.

TEACHER   But, Schill, if I keep quiet, if you miss this opportunity—they're over in Hofbauer's shop now . . .

SCHILL   Please.

TEACHER   As you wish. If you too are on their side, I have no more to say.

[*The doorbell jingles. A* REPORTER *comes in.*]

REPORTER   Herr Schill.

SCHILL   Er—no. Herr Schill's gone to Kalberstadt for the day.

REPORTER   Oh, thank you. Good day.

[*He goes out.*]

PAINTER   [*Mops his brow.*] Whew! Close shave.

[*He follows the* REPORTER *out.*]

SECOND MAN   [*Walking up to* SCHILL.] That was pretty smart of you to keep your mouth shut. You know what to expect if you don't.

[*He goes.*]

FIRST MAN   Give me a Havana. [SCHILL *serves him.*] Charge it. You bastard!

[*He goes.* SCHILL *opens his account book.*]

FRAU SCHILL   Come along, children—

[FRAU SCHILL, *the* SON *and the* DAUGHTER *go off, upstage.*]

TEACHER   They're going to kill you. I've known it all along, and you too, you must have known it. The need is too strong, the temptation too great. And now perhaps I too will join against you. I belong to them and, like them, I can feel myself hardening into something that is not human—not beautiful.

SCHILL   It can't be helped.

TEACHER   Pull yourself together, man. Speak to the reporters; you've no time to lose.

[SCHILL *looks up from his account book.*]

SCHILL   No. I'm not going to fight any more.

TEACHER   Are you so frightened that you don't dare open your mouth?

SCHILL   I made Claire what she is, I made myself what I am. What should I do? Should I pretend that I'm innocent?

TEACHER No, you can't. You are as guilty as hell.

SCHILL Yes.

TEACHER You are a bastard.

SCHILL Yes.

TEACHER But that does not justify your murder. [SCHILL *looks at him.*] I wish I could believe that for what they're doing—for what they're going to do—they will suffer for the rest of their lives. But it's not true. In a little while they will have justified everything and forgotten everything.

SCHILL Of course.

TEACHER Your name will never again be mentioned in this town. That's how it will be.

SCHILL I don't hold it against you.

TEACHER But I do. I will hold it against myself all my life. That's why—

[*The doorbell jingles. The* BURGOMASTER *comes in. The* TEACHER *stares at him, then goes out without another word.*]

BURGOMASTER Good afternoon, Schill. Don't let me disturb you. I've just dropped in for a moment.

SCHILL I'm just finishing my accounts for the week.

[*A moment's pause.*]

BURGOMASTER The town council meets tonight. At the Golden Apostle. In the auditorium.

SCHILL I'll be there.

BURGOMASTER The whole town will be there. Your case will be discussed and final action taken. You've put us in a pretty tight spot, you know.

SCHILL Yes. I'm sorry.

BURGOMASTER The lady's offer will be rejected.

SCHILL Possibly.

BURGOMASTER Of course I may be wrong.

SCHILL Of course.

BURGOMASTER In that case—are you prepared to accept the judgment of the town? The meeting will be covered by the press, you know.

SCHILL By the press?

BURGOMASTER Yes, and the radio and the newsreel. It's a very ticklish situation. Not only for you—believe me, it's even worse for us. What with the wedding, and all the publicity, we've become famous. All of a sudden our ancient democratic institutions have become of interest to the world.

SCHILL Are you going to make the lady's condition public?

BURGOMASTER No, no, of course not. Not directly. We will have to put the matter to a vote—that is unavoidable. But only those involved will understand.

SCHILL I see.

BURGOMASTER As far as the press is concerned, you are simply the intermediary between us and Madame Zachanassian. I have whitewashed you completely.

SCHILL That is very generous of you.

BURGOMASTER Frankly, it's not for your sake, but for the sake of your family. They are honest and decent people.

SCHILL Oh—

BURGOMASTER So far we've all played fair. You've kept your mouth shut and so have we. Now can we continue to depend on you? Because if you have any idea of opening your mouth at tonight's meeting, there won't be any meeting.

SCHILL I'm glad to hear an open threat at last.

BURGOMASTER We are not threatening you. You are threatening us. If you speak, you force us to act—in advance.

SCHILL That won't be necessary.

BURGOMASTER So if the town decides against you?

SCHILL I will accept their decision.

BURGOMASTER Good. [*A moment's pause.*] I'm delighted to see there is still a spark of decency left in you. But—wouldn't it be better if we didn't have to call a meeting at all? [*He pauses. He takes a gun from his pocket and puts it on the counter.*] I've brought you this.

SCHILL Thank you.

BURGOMASTER It's loaded.

SCHILL I don't need a gun.

BURGOMASTER [*He clears his throat.*] You see? We could tell the lady that we had condemned you in secret session and you had anticipated our decision. I've lost a lot of sleep getting to this point, believe me.

SCHILL I believe you.

BURGOMASTER Frankly, in your place, I myself would prefer to take the path of honor. Get it over with, once and for all. Don't you agree? For the sake of your friends! For the sake of our children, your own children—you have a daughter, a son—Schill, you know our need, our misery.

SCHILL   You've put me through hell, you and your town. You were my friends, you smiled and reassured me. But day by day I saw you change—your shoes, your ties, your suits—your hearts. If you had been honest with me then, perhaps I would feel differently toward you now. I might even use that gun you brought me. For the sake of my friends. But now I have conquered my fear. Alone. It was hard, but it's done. And now you will have to judge me. And I will accept your judgment. For me that will be justice. How it will be for you, I don't know. [*He turns away.*] You may kill me if you like. I won't complain, I won't protest, I won't defend myself. But I won't do your job for you either.

BURGOMASTER   [*Takes up his gun.*] There it is. You've had your chance and you won't take it. Too bad. [*He takes out a cigarette.*] I suppose it's more than we can expect of a man like you. [SCHILL *lights the* BURGOMASTER's *cigarette.*] Good day.

SCHILL   Good day. [*The* BURGOMASTER *goes.* FRAU SCHILL *comes in, dressed in a fur coat. The* DAUGHTER *is in a new red dress. The* SON *has a new sports jacket.*] What a beautiful coat, Mathilde!

FRAU SCHILL   Real fur. You like it?

SCHILL   Should I? What a lovely dress, Ottilie!

DAUGHTER   *C'est très chic, n'est-ce pas?* [3]

SCHILL   What?

FRAU SCHILL   Ottilie is taking a course in French.

SCHILL   Very useful. Karl—whose automobile is that out there at the curb?

SON   Oh, it's only an Opel. They're not expensive.

SCHILL   You bought yourself a car?

SON   On credit. Easiest thing in the world.

FRAU SCHILL   Everyone's buying on credit now, Anton. These fears of yours are ridiculous. You'll see. Clara has a good heart. She only means to teach you a lesson.

DAUGHTER   She means to teach you a lesson, that's all.

SON   It's high time you got the point, Father.

---

[3] It's very smart, isn't it?

SCHILL   I get the point. [*The church bells start ringing.*] Listen. The bells of Güllen. Do you hear?

SON   Yes, we have four bells now. It sounds quite good.

DAUGHTER   Just like Gray's Elegy.

SCHILL   What?

FRAU SCHILL   Ottilie is taking a course in English literature.

SCHILL   Congratulations! It's Sunday. I should very much like to take a ride in your car. Our car.

SON   You want to ride in the car?

SCHILL   Why not? I want to ride through the Konradsweil Forest. I want to see the town where I've lived all my life.

FRAU SCHILL   I don't think that will look very nice for any of us.

SCHILL   No—perhaps not. Well, I'll go for a walk by myself.

FRAU SCHILL   Then take us to Kalberstadt, Karl, and we'll go to a cinema.

SCHILL   A cinema? It's a good idea.

FRAU SCHILL   See you soon, Anton.

SCHILL   Good-bye, Ottilie. Good-bye, Karl. Good-bye, Mathilde.

FAMILY   Good-bye.

   [*They go out.*]

SCHILL   Good-bye. [*The shop sign flies off. The lights black out. They come up at once on the forest scene.*] Autumn. Even the forest has turned to gold.

   [SCHILL *wanders down to the bench in the forest. He sits.* CLAIRE's *voice is heard.*]

CLAIRE   [*Offstage.*] Stop. Wait here. [CLAIRE *comes in. She gazes slowly up at the trees, kicks at some leaves. Then she walks slowly down center. She stops before a tree, glances up the trunk.*] Bark-borers. The old tree is dying.

   [*She catches sight of* SCHILL.]

SCHILL   Clara.

CLAIRE   How pleasant to see you here. I was visiting my forest. May I sit by you?

SCHILL   Oh, yes. Please do. [*She sits next to him.*] I've just been saying good-bye to my family. They've gone to the cinema. Karl has bought himself a car.

CLAIRE   How nice.

SCHILL   Ottilie is taking French lessons. And a course in English literature.

CLAIRE   You see? They're beginning to take an interest in higher things.

SCHILL   Listen. A finch. You hear?

CLAIRE   Yes. It's a finch. And a cuckoo in the distance. Would you like some music?

SCHILL   Oh, yes. That would be very nice.

CLAIRE   Anything special?

SCHILL   "Deep in the Forest."

CLAIRE   Your favorite song. They know it.
[*She raises her hand. Offstage, the mandolin and guitar play the tune softly.*]

SCHILL   We had a child?

CLAIRE   Yes.

SCHILL   Boy or girl?

CLAIRE   Girl.

SCHILL   What name did you give her?

CLAIRE   I called her Genevieve.

SCHILL   That's a very pretty name.

CLAIRE   Yes.

SCHILL   What was she like?

CLAIRE   I saw her only once. When she was born. Then they took her away from me.

SCHILL   Her eyes?

CLAIRE   They weren't open yet.

SCHILL   And her hair?

CLAIRE   Black, I think. It's usually black at first.

SCHILL   Yes, of course. Where did she die, Clara?

CLAIRE   In some family. I've forgotten their name. Meningitis, they said. The officials wrote me a letter.

SCHILL   Oh, I'm so very sorry, Clara.

CLAIRE   I've told you about our child. Now tell me about myself.

SCHILL   About yourself?

CLAIRE   Yes. How I was when I was seventeen in the days when you loved me.

SCHILL   I remember one day you waited for me in the great barn. I had to look all over the place for you. At last I found you lying in the haycart with nothing on and a long straw between your lips . . .

CLAIRE   Yes. I was pretty in those days.

SCHILL   You were beautiful, Clara.

CLAIRE   You were strong. The time you fought with those two railwaymen who were following me, I wiped the blood from your face with my red petticoat. [*The music ends.*] They've stopped.

SCHILL   Tell them to play "Thoughts of Home."

CLAIRE   They know that too.

[*The music plays.*]

SCHILL   Here we are, Clara, sitting together in our forest for the last time. The town council meets tonight. They will condemn me to death, and one of them will kill me. I don't know who and I don't know where. Clara, I only know that in a little while a useless life will come to an end.
[*He bows his head on her bosom. She takes him in her arms.*]

CLAIRE   [*Tenderly.*] I shall take you in your coffin to Capri. You will have your tomb in the park of my villa, where I can see you from my bedroom window. White marble and onyx in a grove of green cypress. With a beautiful view of the Mediterranean.

SCHILL   I've always wanted to see it.

CLAIRE   Your love for me died years ago, Anton. But my love for you would not die. It turned into something strong, like the hidden roots of the forest; something evil, like white mushrooms that grow unseen in the darkness. And slowly it reached out for your life. Now I have you. You are mine. Alone. At last, and forever, a peaceful ghost in a silent house.
[*The music ends.*]

SCHILL   The song is over.

CLAIRE   Adieu, Anton.
[CLAIRE *kisses* ANTON, *a long kiss. Then she rises.*]

SCHILL   Adieu.
[*She goes.* SCHILL *remains sitting on the bench. A row of lamps descends from the flies. The townsmen come in from both sides, each bearing his chair. A table and chairs are set upstage, center. On both sides sit the townspeople. The* POLICEMAN, *in a new uniform, sits on the bench behind* SCHILL. *All the townsmen are in new Sunday clothes. Around them are technicians of all sorts, with lights, cameras, and other equipment. The townswomen are absent. They do not vote. The* BURGOMASTER *takes his place at the table, center. The* DOCTOR *and the* PASTOR *sit at the same table, at his right, and the* TEACHER *in his academic gown, at his left.*]

BURGOMASTER   [*At a sign from the radio technician, he pounds the floor with his wand of office.*] Fellow citizens of Güllen, I call this meeting to order. The agenda: there is only one matter before us. I have the honor to announce officially that Madame Claire Zachanassian, daughter of our beloved citizen, the famous architect Siegfried Wäscher, has decided to make a gift to the town of one billion marks. Five hundred million to the town, five hundred million to be divided per capita among the citizens. After certain necessary preliminaries, a vote will be taken, and you, as citizens of Güllen, will signify your will by a show of hands. Has anyone any objection to this mode of procedure? The pastor? [*Silence.*] The police? [*Silence.*] The town health official? [*Silence.*] The Rector of Güllen High School? [*Silence.*] The political opposition? [*Silence.*] I shall then proceed to the vote— [*The* TEACHER *rises. The* BURGOMASTER *turns in surprise and irritation.*] You wish to speak?

TEACHER   Yes.

BURGOMASTER   Very well.

[*He takes his seat. The* TEACHER *advances. The movie camera starts running.*]

TEACHER   Fellow townsmen. [*The photographer flashes a bulb in his face.*] Fellow townsmen. We all know that by means of this gift, Madame Claire Zachanassian intends to attain a certain object. What is this object? To enrich the town of her youth, yes. But more than that, she desires by means of this gift to reestablish justice among us. This desire expressed by our benefactress raises an all-important question. Is it true that our community harbors in its soul such a burden of guilt?

BURGOMASTER   Yes! True!

SECOND MAN   Crimes are concealed among us.

THIRD MAN   [*He jumps up.*] Sins!

FOURTH MAN   [*He jumps up also.*] Perjuries!

PAINTER   Justice!

TOWNSMEN   Justice! Justice!

TEACHER   Citizens of Güllen, this, then, is the simple fact of the case. We have participated in an injustice. I thoroughly recognize the material advantages which this gift opens to us —I do not overlook the fact that it is poverty which is the root of all this bitterness and evil. Nevertheless, there is no question here of money.

TOWNSMEN   No! no!

TEACHER   Here there is no question of our prosperity as a community, or our well-being as individuals—The question is—must be—

whether or not we wish to live according to the principles of justice, those principles for which our forefathers lived and fought and for which they died, those principles which form the soul of our Western culture.

TOWNSMEN   Hear! Hear!

[*Applause.*]

TEACHER   [*Desperately, realizing that he is fighting a losing battle, and on the verge of hysteria.*] Wealth has meaning only when benevolence comes of it, but only he who hungers for grace will receive grace. Do you feel this hunger, my fellow citizens, this hunger of the spirit, or do you feel only that other profane hunger, the hunger of the body? That is the question which I, as Rector of your high school, now propound to you. Only if you can no longer tolerate the presence of evil among you, only if you can in no circumstances endure a world in which injustice exists, are you worthy to receive Madame Zachanassian's billion and fulfill the condition bound up with this gift. If not—[*Wild applause. He gestures desperately for silence.*] If not, then God have mercy on us!

[*The townsmen crowd around him, ambiguously, in a mood somewhat between threat and congratulation. He takes his seat, utterly crushed, exhausted by his effort. The* BURGOMASTER *advances and takes charge once again. Order is restored.*]

BURGOMASTER   Anton Schill—[*The* POLICEMAN *gives* SCHILL *a shove.* SCHILL *gets up.*] Anton Schill, it is through you that this gift is offered to the town. Are you willing that this offer should be accepted?

[SCHILL *mumbles something.*]

RADIO REPORTER   [*Steps to his side.*] You'll have to speak up a little, Herr Schill.

SCHILL   Yes.

BURGOMASTER   Will you respect our decision in the matter before us?

SCHILL   I will respect your decision.

BURGOMASTER   Then I proceed to the vote. All those who are in accord with the terms on which this gift is offered will signify the same by raising their right hands. [*After a moment, the* POLICEMAN *raises his hand. Then one by one the others. Last of all, very slowly, the* TEACHER.] All against? The offer is accepted.

I now solemnly call upon you, fellow townsmen, to declare in the face of all the world that you take this action, not out of love for worldly gain . . .

TOWNSMEN [*In chorus.*] Not out of love for worldly gain . . .

BURGOMASTER But out of love for the right.

TOWNSMEN But out of love for the right.

BURGOMASTER [*Holds up his hand, as if taking an oath.*] We join together, now, as brothers . . .

TOWNSMEN [*Hold up their hands.*] We join together, now, as brothers . . .

BURGOMASTER To purify our town of guilt . . .

TOWNSMEN To purify our town of guilt . . .

BURGOMASTER And to reaffirm our faith . . .

TOWNSMEN And to reaffirm our faith . . .

BURGOMASTER In the eternal power of justice.

TOWNSMEN In the eternal power of justice.

[*The lights go off suddenly.*]

SCHILL [*A scream.*] Oh, God!

VOICE I'm sorry, Herr Burgomaster. We seem to have blown a fuse. [*The lights go on.*] Ah —there we are. Would you mind doing that last bit again?

BURGOMASTER Again?

THE CAMERAMAN [*Walks forward.*] Yes, for the newsreel.

BURGOMASTER Oh, the newsreel. Certainly.

THE CAMERAMAN Ready now? Right.

BURGOMASTER And to reaffirm our faith . . .

TOWNSMEN And to reaffirm our faith . . .

BURGOMASTER In the eternal power of justice.

TOWNSMEN In the eternal power of justice.

THE CAMERAMAN [*To his assistant.*] It was better before, when he screamed "Oh, God."

[*The assistant shrugs.*]

BURGOMASTER Fellow citizens of Güllen, I declare this meeting adjourned. The ladies and gentlemen of the press will find refreshments served downstairs, with the compliments of the town council. The exits lead directly to the restaurant.

THE CAMERAMAN Thank you.

[*The newsmen go off with alacrity. The townsmen remain on the stage. SCHILL gets up.*]

POLICEMAN [*Pushes SCHILL down.*] Sit down.

SCHILL Is it to be now?

POLICEMAN Naturally, now.

SCHILL I thought it might be best to have it at my house.

POLICEMAN It will be here.

BURGOMASTER Lower the lights. [*The lights dim.*] Are they all gone?

VOICE All gone.

BURGOMASTER The gallery?

SECOND VOICE Empty.

BURGOMASTER Lock the doors.

THE VOICE Locked here.

SECOND VOICE Locked here.

BURGOMASTER Form a lane. [*The men form a lane. At the end stands the ATHLETE in elegant white slacks, a red scarf around his singlet.*] Pastor. Will you be so good?

[*The PASTOR walks slowly to SCHILL.*]

PASTOR Anton Schill, your heavy hour has come.

SCHILL May I have a cigarette?

PASTOR Cigarette, Burgomaster.

BURGOMASTER Of course. With pleasure. And a good one.

[*He gives his case to the PASTOR, who offers it to SCHILL. The POLICEMAN lights the cigarette. The PASTOR returns the case.*]

PASTOR In the words of the prophet Amos—

SCHILL Please—

[*He shakes his head.*]

PASTOR You're no longer afraid?

SCHILL No. I'm not afraid.

PASTOR I will pray for you.

SCHILL Pray for us all.

[*The PASTOR bows his head.*]

BURGOMASTER Anton Schill, stand up!

[SCHILL *hesitates.*]

POLICEMAN Stand up, you swine!

BURGOMASTER Schultz, please.

POLICEMAN I'm sorry. I was carried away.

[SCHILL *gives the cigarette to the POLICEMAN. Then he walks slowly to the center of the stage and turns his back on the audience.*] Enter the lane.

[SCHILL *hesitates a moment. He goes slowly into the lane of silent men. The ATHLETE stares at him from the opposite end. SCHILL looks in turn at the hard faces of those who surround him, and sinks slowly to his knees. The lane contracts silently into a knot as the men close in and crouch over. Complete silence. The knot of men pulls back slowly, coming downstage. Then it opens. Only the* DOCTOR *is left in the center of the stage, kneeling by the corpse, over which the* TEACHER'S *gown has been spread. The* DOCTOR *rises and takes off his stethoscope.*]

PASTOR   Is it all over?

DOCTOR   Heart failure.

BURGOMASTER   Died of joy.

ALL   Died of joy.

[*The townsmen turn their backs on the corpse and at once light cigarettes. A cloud of smoke rises over them. From the left comes* CLAIRE ZACHANASSIAN, *dressed in black, followed by* BOBBY. *She sees the corpse. Then she walks slowly to center stage and looks down at the body of* SCHILL.]

CLAIRE   Uncover him. [BOBBY *uncovers* SCHILL'S *face. She stares at it a long moment. She sighs.*] Cover his face.

[BOBBY *covers it.* CLAIRE *goes out, up center.* BOBBY *takes the check from his wallet, holds it out peremptorily to the* BURGOMASTER, *who walks over from the knot of silent men. He holds out his hand for the check. The lights fade. At once the warning bell is heard, and the scene dissolves into the setting of the railway station. The gradual transformation of the shabby town into a thing of elegance and beauty is now accomplished. The railway station glitters with neon lights and is surrounded with garlands, bright posters, and flags. The townsfolk, men and women, now in brand new clothes, form themselves into a group in front of the station. The sound of the approaching train grows louder. The train stops.*]

STATION MASTER   Güllen-Rome Express. All aboard, please. [*The church bells start pealing. Men appear with trunks and boxes, a procession which duplicates that of the lady's arrival, but in inverse order. Then come the* TWO BLIND MEN, *then* BOBBY, *and* MIKE *and* MAX *carrying the coffin. Lastly* CLAIRE. *She is dressed in modish black. Her head is high, her face as impassive as that of an ancient idol. The procession crosses the stage and goes off. The people bow in silence as the coffin passes. When* CLAIRE *and her retinue have boarded the train, the* STATION MASTER *blows a long blast.*] 'Bo—ard!

[*He holds up his paddle. The train starts and moves off slowly, picking up speed. The crowd turns slowly, gazing after the departing train in complete silence. The train sounds fade.*]

[*The curtain falls slowly.*]

Comments and Questions

Duerrenmatt has said that "Claire Zachanassian represents neither justice nor the Marshall Plan nor even the Apocalypse; let her be only what she is: the richest woman in the world, whose fortune has put her in a position to act like the heroine of a Greek tragedy: absolute, cruel, something like Medea." It is possible, of course, to read this play as straight melodrama, as a kind of dark fairy tale with an unacceptable ending. The most literal-minded person, however, would feel uneasy in accepting Claire and the other characters in this play as individuals without allegorical significance.

1. What evidence may be adduced to identify Claire with justice? In what ways does this identification break down? An even weaker case may be made for equating Claire's actions with actions taken by the United States under the Marshall Plan, but a case of sorts can be made. What is it? Can Claire be equated with the Apocalypse? In what way does this suggested identification break down almost at once? Since none of these identifications fits perfectly, one may be tempted to try others—Nemesis, for example.

2. What about Anton Schill? Is the play as much his as it is Claire's, or is it more? Explain. Can a case be made for his being the only *individual* in the play? Consider the villagers. Consider Claire's entourage. What may one conclude about these groups? Also, what is the dramatic purpose of Claire's wedding? Why does the author have the world's great flock to Güllen for this affair?

3. Claire's entourage is a human menagerie plus a black panther. The whole village of Güllen is slowly disciplined, tamed, and corrupted. How does this view of human frailties fit the tenets of the Theater of the Absurd? See Martin Esslin's "The Absurdity of the Absurd," p. 862.

4. Compare the use of symbols in this play with their use in *The Glass Menagerie.*

Biedermann and the Firebugs

MAX FRISCH
1911–

(Adapted by Mordecai Gorlik)

Biedermann and the Firebugs is a tragicomedy with puppet characters. In technique and purpose it is a good representative of the Theater of the Absurd. (See Esslin's "The Absurdity of the Absurd," pp. 862–867.) Whereas *The Caucasian Chalk Circle* presents stereotypes plus a few individuals and *The Visit* gives embodiments of abstractions plus perhaps one individual, *Biedermann* offers only allegorical figures who move mechanically, helplessly toward an inescapable doom. Frisch's play was written specifically as a sardonic comment on the situation in Czechoslovakia when the democratic government tried to appease its enemies by giving them representation—by taking them into the house—even though it was known that these "arsonists" intended to burn down the democratic regime. The play also glances at the German intellectuals who refused to believe Hitler's announced plans to conquer the world—to burn it down if necessary.

The subtitle of Frisch's play, *A Learning Play without a Lesson,* implies that man might learn but he will not. If man will not learn, then surely his situation is absurd, and his life is meaningless. If Frisch's play exposes disastrous mistakes made by Czechoslovakia and Germany, what does it expose about current conditions in the United States?

CHARACTERS

GOTTLIEB BIEDERMANN
BABETTE, *his wife*
ANNA, *a maidservant*
SEPP SCHMITZ, *a wrestler*

WILLI EISENRING, *a waiter*
A POLICEMAN
A PH.D.
MRS. KNECHTLING
THE CHORUS OF FIREMEN

SCENE
A simultaneous setting, showing the living room and the attic of BIEDERMANN's *house.*

TIME
Now.

SCENE ONE

The stage is dark; then a match flares, illuminating the face of HERR BIEDERMANN. *He is lighting a cigar, and as the stage grows more visible he looks about him. He is surrounded by* FIREMEN *wearing their helmets.*

BIEDERMANN You can't even light a cigar any more without thinking of houses on fire . . . It's disgusting! [*He hides the burning cigar and exits. The* FIREMEN *come forward in the manner of an antique* CHORUS. *The town clock booms the quarter-hour.*]
CHORUS Fellow-citizens, we,
Guardians of the city.
Watchers, listeners,
Friends of the friendly town.
LEADER Which pays our salaries.
CHORUS Uniformed, equipped,
We guard your homes,
Patrol your streets,
Vigilant, tranquil.
LEADER Resting from time to time,
But alert, unsleeping.
CHORUS Watching, listening,
Lest hidden danger
Come to light
Too late.
[*The clock strikes half-hour.*]
LEADER Much goes up in flames,
But not always
Because of fate.
CHORUS Call it fate, they tell you,
And ask no questions.
But mischief alone
Can destroy whole cities.
LEADER Stupidity alone—

CHORUS   Stupidity, all-too-human—
LEADER   Can undo our citizens,
   Our all-too-mortal citizens.
      [*The clock strikes three-quarters.*]
CHORUS   Use your head;
   A stitch in time saves nine.
LEADER   Exactly.
CHORUS   Just because it happened,
   Don't put the blame on God,
   Nor on our human nature,
   Nor on our fruitful earth,
   Nor on our radiant sun . . .
   Just because it happened,
   Must you call the damned thing Fate?
      [*The clock strikes four-quarters.*]
LEADER   Our watch begins.
      [*The* CHORUS *sits. The clock strikes nine
o'clock.*]

SCENE TWO

The Living Room

   GOTTLIEB BIEDERMANN *is reading the paper
and smoking a cigar.* ANNA, *the maid-servant, in
a white apron, brings him a bottle of wine.*

ANNA   Herr Biedermann? [*No answer.*] Herr
   Biedermann—[*He puts down his paper.*]
BIEDERMANN   They ought to hang them! I've
   said so all along! Another fire! And always the
   same story: another peddler shoe-horning his
   way into somebody's attic—another "harmless" peddler—[*He picks up the bottle.*] They
   ought to hang every one of them! [*He picks
   up the corkscrew.*]
ANNA   He's still here, Herr Biedermann. The
   peddler. He wants to talk to you.
BIEDERMANN   I'm not in!
ANNA   Yes, sir, I told him—an hour ago. He
   says he knows you. I can't throw him out,
   Herr Biedermann.
BIEDERMANN   Why not?
ANNA   He's too strong.
BIEDERMANN   Let him come to the office tomor-
   row.
ANNA   Yes sir. I told him three times. He says
   he's not interested. He doesn't want any hair
   tonic.
BIEDERMANN   What *does* he want?
ANNA   Kindness, he says. Humanity.

BIEDERMANN   [*Sniffs at the cork.*] Tell him I'll
   throw him out myself if he doesn't get going
   at once. [*He fills his glass carefully.*] Humanity! [*He tastes the wine.*] Let him wait in
   the hall for me. If he's selling suspenders or
   razors . . . I'm not inhuman, you know,
   Anna. But they mustn't come into the house
   —I've told you that a hundred times! Even if
   we have three vacant beds, it's out of the
   question! Where a thing like that can lead to,
   these days—[ANNA *is about to go when*
   SCHMITZ *enters. He is athletic, in a costume
   reminiscent partly of the prison, partly of the
   circus; his arms are tattooed and there are
   leather straps on his wrists.* ANNA *edges out.*
   BIEDERMANN *sips his wine, unaware of*
   SCHMITZ, *who waits until he turns around.*]
SCHMITZ   Good evening. [BIEDERMANN *drops
   his cigar in surprise.*] Your cigar, Herr Bieder-
   mann. [*He picks up the cigar and hands it to*
   BIEDERMANN.]
BIEDERMANN   Look here—
SCHMITZ   Good evening.
BIEDERMANN   What is this? I told the girl dis-
   tinctly to have you wait in the hall.
SCHMITZ   My name is Schmitz.
BIEDERMANN   Without even knocking!
SCHMITZ   Sepp Schmitz. [*Silence.*] Good eve-
   ning.
BIEDERMANN   What do you want?
SCHMITZ   You needn't worry, Herr Biedermann.
   I'm not a peddler.
BIEDERMANN   No?
SCHMITZ   A heavyweight wrestler. I mean I
   used to be.
BIEDERMANN   And now?
SCHMITZ   Unemployed. [*Pause.*] Don't worry,
   sir, I'm not looking for a job—I'm fed up with
   wrestling. I came in here because it's raining
   hard outside. [*Pause.*] It's warm in here.
   [*Pause.*] I hope I'm not intruding . . .
   [*Pause.*]
BIEDERMANN   Cigar? [*He offers one.*]
SCHMITZ   You know, it's awful, Herr Bieder-
   mann—with a build like mine, everybody gets
   scared—Thank you. [BIEDERMANN *gives him
   a light.*] Thank you. [*They stand there, smok-
   ing.*]
BIEDERMANN   Get to the point.
SCHMITZ   My name is Schmitz.
BIEDERMANN   You've said that . . . Delighted.
SCHMITZ   I have no place to sleep. [*He holds*

the cigar to his nose, enjoying the aroma.] No place to sleep.

BIEDERMANN   Would you like—some bread?

SCHMITZ   If that's all there is.

BIEDERMANN   A glass of wine?

SCHMITZ   Bread and wine . . . If it's no trouble, sir; if it's no trouble. [BIEDERMANN *goes to the door.*]

BIEDERMANN   Anna! [*He comes back.*]

SCHMITZ   The girl said you were going to throw me out personally, Herr Biedermann, but I knew you didn't mean it. [ANNA *has entered.*]

BIEDERMANN   Anna, bring another glass.

ANNA   Yes sir.

BIEDERMANN   And some bread.

SCHMITZ   And if you don't mind, Fräulein, a little butter. Some cheese or cold cuts. Only don't go to any trouble. Some pickles, a tomato or something, some mustard—whatever you have, Fräulein.

ANNA   Yes sir.

SCHMITZ   If it's no trouble. [ANNA *exits.*]

BIEDERMANN   You told the girl you knew me.

SCHMITZ   That's right, sir.

BIEDERMANN   How do you know me?

SCHMITZ   I know you at your best, sir. Last night at the pub—you didn't see me; I was sitting in the corner. The whole place liked the way you kept banging at the table.

BIEDERMANN   What did I say?

SCHMITZ   Exactly the right thing, Herr Biedermann! [*He takes a puff at his cigar.*] "They ought to hang them all! The sooner the better—the whole bunch! All those firebugs!" [BIEDERMANN *offers him a chair.*]

BIEDERMANN   Sit down. [SCHMITZ *sits.*]

SCHMITZ   This country needs men like you, sir.

BIEDERMANN   I know, but—

SCHMITZ   No buts, Herr Biedermann, no buts. You're the old-time type of solid citizen. That's why your slant on things—

BIEDERMANN   Certainly, but—

SCHMITZ   That's why.

BIEDERMANN   Why what?

SCHMITZ   You have a conscience. Everybody in the pub could see that. A solid conscience.

BIEDERMANN   Naturally, but—

SCHMITZ   Herr Biedermann, it's not natural at all. Not these days. In the circus, where I did my wrestling, for instance—before it burned down, the whole damned circus—our manager, for instance; you know what he told me?

"Sepp," he says (They call me Sepp), "You know me. Will you tell me what I need a conscience for?" Just like that! "What my animals need is a whip," he says. That's the sort of character he is! "A conscience!" He'd laugh out loud. "If anybody has a conscience, you can make a bet it's a bad one." [*Enjoying his cigar.*] God rest him!

BIEDERMANN   Is he dead?

SCHMITZ   Burned to a frazzle, with everything he owned. [*A pendulum clock strikes nine.*]

BIEDERMANN   I don't know what's keeping that girl so long.

SCHMITZ   I've got time. [*Their eyes meet.*] You haven't an empty bed in the house, Herr Biedermann. The girl told me.

BIEDERMANN   Why do you laugh?

SCHMITZ   "Sorry, no empty bed." That's what they all say . . . What's the result? Somebody like me, with no place to sleep—Anyway I don't want a bed.

BIEDERMANN   No?

SCHMITZ   Oh, I'm used to sleeping on the floor. My father was a miner. I'm used to it. [*He puffs at his cigar.*] No apologies necessary, sir. You're not one of those birds who crap off in public—when *you* say something I believe it. What are things coming to if people can't believe each other any more? Nothing but suspicion all over! Am I right? But *you* still believe in yourself and others. Right? You're about the only man left in this town who doesn't say right off that people like us are firebugs.

BIEDERMANN   Here's an ash-tray.

SCHMITZ   Or am I wrong? [*He taps the ash off his cigar carefully.*] People don't believe in God any more—they believe in the Fire Department.

BIEDERMANN   What do you mean by that?

SCHMITZ   Nothing but the truth. [ANNA *comes in with a tray.*]

ANNA   We have no cold cuts.

SCHMITZ   This will do fine, Fräulein, this will do. Only you forgot the mustard.

ANNA   Excuse me. [*Exits.*]

BIEDERMANN   Eat. [*He fills the glasses.*]

SCHMITZ   You don't get a reception like this every place you go, Herr Biedermann, let me tell you that! I've had some experiences! Somebody like me comes to the door—no necktie, no place to stay, hungry; "Sit down," they say, "Have a seat"—and meanwhile they call the police. How do you like that? All I ask for is a place to sleep, that's all. A good wrestler who's wrestled all his life—and some bird who never wrestled at all grabs me by the collar! "What's this?" I ask myself. I turn around just to look, and first thing you know he's broken his shoulder! [*Picks up his glass.*] *Prosit!* [*They drink, and* SCHMITZ *starts eating.*]

BIEDERMANN That's how it goes, these days. You can't open a newspaper without reading about another arson case. The same old story: another peddler asking for a place to sleep, and next morning the house is in flames. I mean to say . . . well, frankly, I can understand a certain amount of distrust . . . [*Reaches for his newspaper.*] Look at this! [*He lays the paper next to* SCHMITZ's *plate.*]

SCHMITZ I saw it.

BIEDERMANN A whole district in flames. [*He gets up to show it to* SCHMITZ.] Just read that! [SCHMITZ *eats, reads and drinks.*]

SCHMITZ Is this wine Beaujolais?

BIEDERMANN Yes.

SCHMITZ Could be a little warmer. [*He reads, over his plate.*] "Apparently the fire was planned and executed in the same way as the previous one." [*They exchange a glance.*]

BIEDERMANN Isn't that the limit?

SCHMITZ That's why I don't care to read newspapers. Always the same thing.

BIEDERMANN Yes, yes, naturally . . . But that's no answer to the problem, to stop reading the papers. After all you have to know what you're up against.

SCHMITZ What for?

BIEDERMANN Why, because.

SCHMITZ It'll happen anyway, Herr Biedermann, it'll happen anyway. [*He sniffs the sausage.*] God's will. [*He slices the sausage.*]

BIEDERMANN You think so? [ANNA *brings the mustard.*]

SCHMITZ Thank you, Fräulein, thank you.

ANNA Anything else you'd like?

SCHMITZ Not today. [ANNA *stops at the door.*] Mustard is my favorite dish. [*He squeezes mustard out of the tube.*]

BIEDERMANN How do you mean, God's will?

SCHMITZ God knows . . . [*He continues to eat with his eye on the paper.*] "Expert opinion is that apparently the fire was planned and executed in the same way as the previous one." [*He laughs shortly, and fills his glass.*]

ANNA Herr Biedermann?

BIEDERMANN What is it now?

ANNA Herr Knechtling would like to speak to you.

BIEDERMANN Knechtling? Now? Knechtling?

ANNA He says—

BIEDERMANN Out of the question.

ANNA He says he simply can't understand you.

BIEDERMANN Why must he understand me?

ANNA He has a sick wife and three children, he says—

BIEDERMANN Out of the question! [*He gets up impatiently.*] Herr Knechtling! Herr Knechtling! Let Herr Knechtling leave me alone, dammit! Or let him get a lawyer! Please—let him! I'm through for the day . . . Herr Knechtling! All this to-do because I gave him his notice! Let him get a lawyer, by all means! I'll get one, too . . . Royalties on his invention! Let him put his head over the gas jet or get a lawyer! If Herr Knechtling can afford indulging in lawyers! Please—let him! [*Controlling himself, with a glance at* SCHMITZ.] Tell Herr Knechtling I have a visitor. [ANNA *exits.*] Excuse me.

SCHMITZ This is your house, Herr Biedermann.

BIEDERMANN How is the food? [*He sits, observing* SCHMITZ, *who attacks his food with enthusiasm.*]

SCHMITZ Who'd have thought you could still find it, these days?

BIEDERMANN Mustard?

SCHMITZ Humanity! [*He screws the top of the mustard tube back on.*] Here's what I mean: you don't grab me by the collar and throw me out in the rain, Herr Biedermann—*That's* what we need, Herr Biedermann! Humanity! [*He pours himself a drink.*] God will reward you! [*He drinks with gusto.*]

BIEDERMANN You mustn't think I'm inhuman, Herr Schmitz.

SCHMITZ Herr Biedermann!

BIEDERMANN That's what Frau Knechtling thinks.

SCHMITZ Would you be giving me a place to sleep tonight if you were inhuman?—Ridiculous!

BIEDERMANN Of course!

SCHMITZ Even if it's a bed in the attic. [*He*

puts down his glass.] Now our wine's the right temperature. [*The doorbell rings.*] Police?

BIEDERMANN My wife. [*The doorbell rings again.*] Come along, Herr Schmitz . . . But mind you, no noise! My wife has a heart condition—[WOMEN's *voices are heard offstage.* BIEDERMANN *motions to* SCHMITZ *to hurry. They pick up the tray, bottles and glasses and tiptoe toward stage right, where the* CHORUS *is sitting.*]

BIEDERMANN Excuse me! [*He steps over the bench.*]

SCHMITZ Excuse me! [*He steps over the bench. He and* BIEDERMANN *disappear.* FRAU BIEDERMANN *enters, left, accompanied by* ANNA, *who takes her wraps.*]

BABETTE Where's my husband? You know, Anna, we're not narrow-minded, and I don't mind your having a boy friend. But if you're going to park him in the house—

ANNA But I don't have a boy friend, Frau Biedermann.

BABETTE Then whose rusty bicycle is that, outside the front door? It scared me to death!

The Attic

[BIEDERMANN *switches on the light and gestures for* SCHMITZ *to come in. They speak in whispers.*]

BIEDERMANN Here's the light-switch. If you get cold there's an old sheepskin around here somewhere. Only for Heaven's sake be quiet! Take off your shoes! [SCHMITZ *puts down the tray, takes off one shoe.*] Herr Schmitz?

SCHMITZ Herr Biedermann?

BIEDERMANN You promise me, though, you're not a firebug? [SCHMITZ *starts to laugh.*] Sh!! [*He nods goodnight and exits, closing the door.* SCHMITZ *takes off his other shoe.*]

The Living Room

[BABETTE *has heard something; she listens, frightened. Then, relieved, she turns to the audience.*]

BABETTE Gottlieb, my husband, promised to go up to the attic every evening, personally, to see if there is any firebug up there. I'm so

thankful! Otherwise I'd lie awake half the night.

The Attic

[SCHMITZ, *now in his socks, goes to the light-switch and snaps out the light.*]

CHORUS Fellow-citizens, we,
Shield of the innocent.
Guardians ever-tranquil,
Shield of the sleeping city.
Standing or
Sitting,
Ever on guard.

LEADER Taking a quiet smoke, now and again, to pass the time.

CHORUS Watching,
Listening,
Lest malignant fire leap out
Above these cozy rooftops
To undo our city.
[*The town clock strikes three.*]

LEADER Everyone knows we're here,
Ready on call.
[*He fills his pipe.*]

CHORUS Who turns the light on at this wee, small hour?
Woe!
Nerve-shattered,
Uncomforted by sleep,
The wife appears.
[BABETTE *enters in a bathrobe.*]

BABETTE Somebody coughed! [*A snore.*] Gottlieb, did you hear that? [*A cough.*] Somebody's there! [*A snore.*] That's men for you! A sleeping pill is all they need!
[*The town clock strikes four.*]

LEADER Four o'clock.
[BABETTE *turns off the light again.*]
We were not called.
[*He puts away his pipe. The stage lightens.*]

CHORUS O radiant sun!
O godlike eye!
Light up the day above our cozy roofs!
Thanks be!
No harm has come to our sleeping town.
Not yet.
Thanks be!
[*The* CHORUS *sits.*]

SCENE THREE

The Living Room

BIEDERMANN, *his hat and coat on, his brief-case under his arm, is drinking a cup of coffee standing up, and is speaking to* BABETTE, *who is offstage.*

BIEDERMANN   For the last time—he's not a fire-bug!

BABETTE'S VOICE   How do you know?

BIEDERMANN   I asked him myself, point blank—Can't you think of anything else in this world? You and your firebugs—you're enough to drive a man insane! [BABETTE *enters with the cream pitcher.*]

BABETTE   Don't yell at me.

BIEDERMANN   I'm not yelling at you, Babette, I'm merely yelling. [*She pours cream into his cup.*] I have to go. [*He drinks his coffee. It's too hot.*] If everybody goes around thinking everybody else is an arsonist—You've got to have a little trust in people, Babette, just a little! [*He looks at his watch.*]

BABETTE   I don't agree. You're too good-hearted, Gottlieb. You listen to the promptings of your heart, but I'm the one who can't sleep all night . . . I'll give him some breakfast and then I'll send him on his way, Gottlieb.

BIEDERMANN   Do that.

BABETTE   In a nice way, of course, without offending him.

BIEDERMANN   Do that. [*He puts his cup down.*] I have to see my lawyer. [*He gives* BABETTE *a perfunctory kiss. They do not notice* SCHMITZ, *who enters, the sheepskin around his shoulders.*]

BABETTE   Why did you give Knechtling his notice?

BIEDERMANN   I don't need him any more.

BABETTE   But you were always so pleased with him!

BIEDERMANN   That's just what he's presuming on, now! Royalties on his invention—that's what he wants! Invention! Our hair tonic is merchandise, that's all—it's no invention! All those good folk who pour our tonic on their domes could use their own piss for all the good it does them!

BABETTE   Gottlieb!

BIEDERMANN   It's true, though. [*He checks to see if he has everything in his briefcase.*] I'm too goodhearted—you're right. But I'll take care of this Knechtling! [*He is about to go when he sees* SCHMITZ.]

SCHMITZ   Good morning, everybody.

BIEDERMANN   Herr Schmitz—[SCHMITZ *offers his hand.*]

SCHMITZ   Call me Sepp.

BIEDERMANN   [*Ignores his hand.*] My wife will speak with you, Herr Schmitz. I have to go, I'm sorry. Good luck . . . [*Changes his mind and shakes hands.*] Good luck, Sepp. [BIEDERMANN *exits.*]

SCHMITZ   Good luck, Gottlieb. [BABETTE *looks at him.*] That's your husband's name, isn't it—Gottlieb?

BABETTE   How did you sleep?

SCHMITZ   Thank you, madam—kind of freezing. But I made use of this sheepskin. Reminded me of old days in the mines. I'm used to the cold.

BABETTE   Your breakfast is ready.

SCHMITZ   Really, madam! [*She motions for him to sit.*] No, really, I—[*She fills his cup.*]

BABETTE   You must pitch in, Sepp. You have a long way to go, I'm sure.

SEPP   How do you mean? [*She points to the chair again.*]

BABETTE   Would you care for a soft-boiled egg?

SCHMITZ   Two.

BABETTE   Anna!

SCHMITZ   I feel right at home, madam. [*He sits.* ANNA *enters.*]

BABETTE   Two soft-boiled eggs.

ANNA   Yes ma'am.

SCHMITZ   Three and a half minutes.

ANNA   Very well. [ANNA *starts to leave.*]

SCHMITZ   Fräulein—[ANNA *stops at the door.*] Good morning.

ANNA   Morning. [*She exits.*]

SCHMITZ   The look she gave me! If it was up to her I'd still be out there in the pouring rain. [BABETTE *fills his cup.*]

BABETTE   Herr Schmitz—

SCHMITZ   Yeah?

BABETTE   If I may speak frankly—

SCHMITZ   Aren't you kind of shaky, madam?

BABETTE   Herr Schmitz—

SCHMITZ   What's troubling you?

BABETTE   Here's some cheese.

SCHMITZ   Thank you.

BABETTE   Marmalade.

SCHMITZ   Thank you.

BABETTE   Honey.

SCHMITZ   One at a time, madam, one at a time. [*He leans back, eating his bread and butter; attentively.*] Well?

BABETTE   Frankly, Herr Schmitz—

SCHMITZ   Just call me Sepp.

BABETTE   Frankly—

SCHMITZ   You'd like to get rid of me.

BABETTE   No, Herr Schmitz, no! I wouldn't put it that way—

SCHMITZ   How would you put it? [*He takes some cheese.*] Tilsit cheese is my dish. [*He leans back, eating; attentively.*] Madam thinks I'm a firebug.

BABETTE   Please don't misunderstand me. What did I say? The last thing I want to do is hurt your feelings, Herr Schmitz . . . You've got me all confused now. Who ever mentioned firebugs? Even your manners, Herr Schmitz; I'm not complaining.

SCHMITZ   I know. I have no manners.

BABETTE   That's not it, Herr Schmitz—

SCHMITZ   I smack my lips when I eat.

BABETTE   Nonsense.

SCHMITZ   That's what they used to tell me at the orphanage: "Schmitz, don't smack your lips when you eat!" [BABETTE *is about to pour more coffee.*]

BABETTE   You don't understand me. Really, you don't in the least! [SCHMITZ *places his hand over his cup.*]

SCHMITZ   I'm going.

BABETTE   Herr Schmitz—

SCHMITZ   I'm going.

BABETTE   Another cup of coffee? [*He shakes his head.*] Half a cup? [*He shakes his head.*] You mustn't take it like that, Herr Schmitz. I didn't mean to hurt your feelings. I didn't say a single word about you making noises while you eat. [*He gets up.*] Have I hurt your feelings? [*He folds his napkin.*]

SCHMITZ   It's not your lookout, madam, if I have no manners. My father was a coal-miner. Where would people like us get any manners? Starving and freezing, madam—that's something I don't mind; but no education, madam, no manners, madam, no refinement—

BABETTE   I understand.

SCHMITZ   I'm going.

BABETTE   Where?

SCHMITZ   Out in the rain.

BABETTE   Oh, no!

SCHMITZ   I'm used to it.

BABETTE   Herr Schmitz . . . don't look at me like that. Your father was a miner—I can understand it. You had an unfortunate childhood—

SCHMITZ   No childhood at all, madam. [*He looks down at his fingers.*] None at all. My mother died when I was seven . . . [*He turns away to wipe his eyes.*]

BABETTE   Sepp!—But Sepp—

[ANNA *brings the soft-boiled eggs.*]

ANNA   Anything else you'd like? [*She gets no answer; exits.*]

BABETTE   I haven't ordered you to leave, Herr Schmitz. I never said that. After all, what did I say? You misunderstand me, Herr Schmitz. Really, I mean it—won't you believe me? [*She takes his sleeve—with some hesitation.*] Come, Sepp—finish eating! [SCHMITZ *sits down again.*] What do you take us for? I haven't even noticed that you smack your lips. Honestly! Even if I did—we don't care a bit about external things. We're not like that at all, Herr Schmitz . . . [*He cracks his egg.*]

SCHMITZ   God will reward you!

BABETTE   Here's the salt. [*He eats the egg with a spoon.*]

SCHMITZ   It's true, madam, you didn't order me away. You didn't say a word about it. That's true. Pardon me, madam, for not understanding.

BABETTE   Is the egg all right?

SCHMITZ   A little soft . . . Do pardon me, won't you? [*He has finished the egg.*] What were you going to say, madam, when you started to say very frankly—

BABETTE   Well, I was going to say . . . [*He cracks the second egg.*]

SCHMITZ   God will reward you. [*He starts on the second egg.*] My friend Willi says you can't find it any more, he says. Private charity. No fine people left; everything State-controlled. No real people left, these days . . . He says. The world is going to the dogs—that's why! [*He salts his egg.*] Wouldn't he be surprised to get a breakfast like this! Wouldn't he open his eyes, my friend, Willi! [*The doorbell rings.*] That could be him. [*It rings again.*]

BABETTE   Who is Willi?

SCHMITZ   You'll see, madam. Willi's refined. Used to be a waiter at the Metropol. Before it burned down . . .

BABETTE   Burned down?

SCHMITZ   Head waiter. [ANNA *enters.*]

BABETTE   Who is it?

ANNA   A gentleman.

BABETTE   What does he want?

ANNA   From the fire insurance, he says. To look over the house. [BABETTE *gets up.*] He's wearing a frock coat—

SCHMITZ   My friend Willi!

CHORUS   Now two of them dismay us—
Two bicycles, both rusty.
To whom do they belong?

LEADER   One yesterday's arrival.
One today's.

CHORUS   Woe!

LEADER   Night once again, and our watch.
[*The town clock strikes.*]

CHORUS   How much the coward fears where nothing threatens!
Dreading his own shadow,
Whirling at each sound,
Until his fears overtake him
At his own bedside!
[*The town clock strikes.*]

LEADER   They never leave their room, these two. What is the reason?
[*The town clock strikes.*]

CHORUS   Blind, ah, blind is the weakling!
Trembling, expectant of evil,
Yet hoping somehow to avoid it!
Defenseless!
Ah, weary of menacing evil,
With open arms he receives it!
[*The town clock strikes.*]
Woe!
[*The* CHORUS *sits.*]

SCENE FOUR

The Attic

SCHMITZ *is dressed as before.* EISENRING *has removed the jacket of his frock coat and is in a white vest and shirtsleeves. He and* SCHMITZ *are rolling tin barrels into a corner of the attic. The barrels are the type used for storing gasoline. Both vagabonds are in their socks and are working as quietly as they can.*

EISENRING   Quiet! Quiet!

SCHMITZ   Suppose he calls the police?

EISENRING   Keep going.

SCHMITZ   What then?

EISENRING   Easy! Easy! [*They roll the barrels up to those already stacked in the shadows.* EISENRING *wipes his fingers with some cotton waste.*]

EISENRING   Why would he call the police?

SCHMITZ   Why not?

EISENRING   Because he's guilty himself—that's why. [*Doves are heard cooing.*] It's morning. Bed-time! [*He throws away the rag.*] Above a certain income every citizen is guilty one way or another. Have no fear. [*There is a sudden knocking on the locked door.*]

BIEDERMANN'S VOICE   Open up! Open up, there! [*He pounds on the door and shakes it.*]

EISENRING   That's no call for breakfast.

BIEDERMANN   Open, I say! Immediately!

SCHMITZ   He was never like that before. [*The banging on the door gets louder. Without haste, but briskly,* EISENRING *puts on his jacket, straightens his tie and flicks the dust from his trousers. Then he opens the door.* BIEDERMANN *enters. He is in his bathrobe. He does not see* EISENRING, *who is now behind the open door.*]

BIEDERMANN   Herr Schmitz!

SCHMITZ   Good morning, sir. I hope this noise didn't wake you.

BIEDERMANN   Herr Schmitz—

SCHMITZ   It won't happen again, I assure you.

BIEDERMANN   Leave this house! [*Pause.*] I say leave this house!

SCHMITZ   When?

BIEDERMANN   At once!

SCHMITZ   But—

BIEDERMANN   Or my wife will call the police. And I can't and won't stop her.

SCHMITZ   Hm . . .

BIEDERMANN   I said right away, and I mean it. What are you waiting for? [SCHMITZ *picks up his shoes.*] I'll have no discussion about it!

SCHMITZ   Did I say anything?

BIEDERMANN   If you think you can do as you like here because you're a wrestler—A racket like that, all night—[*Points to the door.*] Out, I say! Get out! [SCHMITZ *turns to* EISENRING.]

SCHMITZ   He was never like that before . . . [BIEDERMANN *sees* EISENRING *and is speechless.*]

EISENRING   My name is Eisenring.

BIEDERMANN   What's the meaning of this?

EISENRING   Willi Maria Eisenring.

BIEDERMANN   Why are there two of you suddenly? [SCHMITZ *and* EISENRING *look at each other.*] Without even asking!

EISENRING   There, you see!

BIEDERMANN   What's going on here?

EISENRING   [*To* SCHMITZ.] Didn't I tell you? Didn't I say it's no way to act, Sepp? Where are your manners? Without even asking! Suddenly two of us!

BIEDERMANN   I'm beside myself!

EISENRING   There, you see! [*He turns to* BIEDERMANN.] That's what I told him! [*Back to* SCHMITZ.] Didn't I? [SCHMITZ *hangs his head.*]

BIEDERMANN   Where do you think you are? Let's get one thing clear, gentlemen—I'm the owner of this house! I ask you—where do you think you are? [*Pause.*]

EISENRING   Answer when the gentleman asks you something! [*Pause.*]

SCHMITZ   Willi is a friend of mine . . .

BIEDERMANN   And so?

SCHMITZ   We were schoolmates together.

BIEDERMANN   And so?

SCHMITZ   And so I thought . . .

BIEDERMANN   What?

SCHMITZ   I thought . . . [*Pause.*]

EISENRING   You didn't think! [*He turns to* BIEDERMANN.] I understand fully, Herr Biedermann. All you want to do is what's right—let's get that clear! [*He shouts at* SCHMITZ.] You think the owner of this house is going to be pushed around? [*He turns to* BIEDERMANN *again.*] Sepp didn't consult you at all?

BIEDERMANN   Not one word!

EISENRING   Sepp—

BIEDERMANN   Not a word!

EISENRING   [*To* SEPP.] And then you're surprised when people throw you out in the street! [*He laughs contemptuously.*]

BIEDERMANN   There's nothing to laugh at, gentlemen! I'm serious! My wife has a heart condition—

EISENRING   There, you see!

BIEDERMANN   She didn't sleep half the night because of your noise. And anyway, what are you doing here? [*He looks around.*] What the devil are these barrels doing here? [SCHMITZ *and* EISENRING *look hard where there are no*

barrels.] If you don't mind—what are these? [*He raps on a barrel.*]

SCHMITZ   Barrels . . .

BIEDERMANN   Where did *they* come from?

SCHMITZ   Do you know, Willi? Where they came from?

EISENRING   It says "Imported" on the label.

BIEDERMANN   Gentlemen—

EISENRING   It says so on them somewhere! [EISENRING *and* SCHMITZ *look for a label.*]

BIEDERMANN   I'm speechless! What do you think you're doing? My whole attic is full of barrels—floor to ceiling! All the way from floor to ceiling!

EISENRING   I knew it! [EISENRING *swings around.*] Sepp had it figured out all wrong. [*To* SCHMITZ.] Twelve by fifteen meters, you said. There's not a hundred square meters in this attic!—I couldn't leave my barrels in the street, Herr Biedermann; you can understand that—

BIEDERMANN   I don't understand a thing! [SCHMITZ *shows him a label.*]

SCHMITZ   Here, Herr Biedermann—here's the label.

BIEDERMANN   I'm speechless! [*He inspects the label.*]

Downstairs

[ANNA *leads a* POLICEMAN *into the living room.*]

ANNA   I'll call him. [*She exits. The* POLICEMAN *waits.*]

Upstairs

BIEDERMANN   Gasoline?

Downstairs

[ANNA *returns.*]

ANNA   What's it about, officer?

POLICEMAN   Official business. [ANNA *goes out again. The* POLICEMAN *waits.*]

Upstairs

BIEDERMANN   Is it true, sirs? Is it true?

EISENRING   Is what true?

BIEDERMANN   What's printed on this label? [*He*

shows them the label.] What do you take me for? I've never in my life been through anything like this! Do you think I can't read? [*They look at the label.*] If you don't mind! [*He laughs sourly.*] Gasoline! [*In the voice of a district attorney.*] What is in those barrels?

EISENRING   Gasoline!

BIEDERMANN   Never mind your jokes! I'm asking you for the last time—what's in those barrels? You know as well as I do—this attic is no place for gasoline! [*He runs his finger over one of the barrels.*] If you don't mind—just smell that for yourselves! [*He waves his finger under their noses.*] Is that gasoline or isn't it? [*They sniff and exchange glances.*]

EISENRING   It is.

SCHMITZ   It is.

BOTH   No doubt whatever.

BIEDERMANN   Are you insane? My whole attic full of gasoline—

SCHMITZ   That's just why we don't smoke up here, Herr Biedermann.

BIEDERMANN   What do you think you're doing? A thing like that—when every single newspaper is warning people to watch out for fires! My wife will have a heart attack!

EISENRING   There, you see!

BIEDERMANN   Don't keep saying, "There, you see!"

EISENRING   You can't do that to a lady, Sepp. Not to a housewife. I know housewives. [ANNA *calls up the stairs.*]

ANNA   Herr Biedermann! Herr Biedermann! [BIEDERMANN *shuts the door.*]

BIEDERMANN   Herr Schmitz! Herr—

EISENRING   Eisenring.

BIEDERMANN   If you don't get these barrels out of the house this instant—and I mean this instant—

EISENRING   You'll call the police.

BIEDERMANN   Yes!

SCHMITZ   There, you see! [ANNA *calls up the stairs.*]

ANNA   Herr Biedermann!

BIEDERMANN   [*Lowers his voice.*] That's my last word.

EISENRING   What word?

BIEDERMANN   I won't stand for it! I won't stand for gasoline in my attic! Once for all! [*There is a knock at the door.*] I'm coming down! [*He opens the door. The* POLICEMAN *enters.*]

POLICEMAN   Ah, there you are, Herr Bieder-

mann! You don't have to come down; I won't take much of your time.

BIEDERMANN   Good morning!

POLICEMAN   Good morning!

EISENRING   Morning!

SCHMITZ   Morning! [SCHMITZ *and* EISENRING *nod courteously.*]

POLICEMAN   There's been an accident.

BIEDERMANN   Good Heavens!

POLICEMAN   An elderly man. His wife says he used to work for you . . . An inventor. Put his head over the gas jet of his kitchen stove last night. [*He consults his notebook.*] Knechtling, Johann. Number 11 Rossgasse. [*He puts his notebook away.*] Did you know anybody by that name?

BIEDERMANN   I—

POLICEMAN   Maybe you'd rather we talked about this privately, Herr Biedermann?

BIEDERMANN   Yes.

POLICEMAN   It doesn't concern these employees of yours.

BIEDERMANN   No . . . [*He stops at the door.*] If anyone wants me, gentlemen, I'll be at the police station. I'll be right back. [SCHMITZ *and* EISENRING *nod.*]

POLICEMAN   Herr Biedermann—

BIEDERMANN   I'm ready.

POLICEMAN   What have you got in those barrels?

BIEDERMANN   These?

POLICEMAN   If I may ask?

BIEDERMANN   . . . Hair tonic . . . [*He looks at* SCHMITZ *and* EISENRING.]

EISENRING   Hormotone.

SCHMITZ   Science's gift to the well-groomed.

EISENRING   Hormotone.

SCHMITZ   Try a bottle today.

EISENRING   You won't regret it.

BOTH   Hormotone. Hormotone. Hormotone. [*The* POLICEMAN *laughs.*]

BIEDERMANN   Is he dead? [BIEDERMANN *and the* POLICEMAN *exit.*]

EISENRING   A real sweetheart!

SCHMITZ   Didn't I tell you?

EISENRING   But he didn't mention breakfast.

SCHMITZ   He was never like that before. [EISENRING *reaches in his pants pocket.*]

EISENRING   Have you the detonator cap? [SCHMITZ *reaches in his pants pocket.*]

SCHMITZ   He was never that way before.

CHORUS   O radiant sun!
   O godlike eye!

Light up the day again above our cozy roofs!

LEADER   Today same as yesterday.

CHORUS   Hail!

LEADER   No harm has come to our sleeping city.

CHORUS   Hail!

LEADER   Not yet . . .

CHORUS   Hail!

[*Traffic noises offstage; honking, street-cars.*]

LEADER   Wise is man,
And able to ward off most perils,
If, sharp of mind and alert,
He heeds signs of coming disaster
In time.

CHORUS   And if he does not?

LEADER   He, who
Attentive to possible dangers,
Studies his newspaper daily—
Is daily, at breakfast, dismayed
By distant tidings, whose meaning
Is daily digested to spare him
Fatigue of his own stressful brain work—
Learning daily what's happened afar—
Can he so quickly discern
What is happening under his roof-tree?
Things that are—

CHORUS   Unpublished!

LEADER   Disgraceful!

CHORUS   Inglorious!

LEADER   Real!

CHORUS   Things not easy to face! For, if he—
[*The* LEADER *interrupts with a gesture.*]

LEADER   He's coming.
[*The* CHORUS *breaks formation.*]

CHORUS   No harm has come to the sleeping city.
No harm yesterday or today.
Ignoring all omens,
The freshly-shaved citizen
Speeds to his office . . .
[*Enter* BIEDERMANN *in hat and coat, his briefcase under his arm.*]

BIEDERMANN   Taxi! . . . Taxi! . . . Taxi! [*The* CHORUS *is in his way.*] What's the trouble?

CHORUS   Woe!

BIEDERMANN   What's up?

CHORUS   Woe!

BIEDERMANN   You've said that!

CHORUS   Three times woe!

BIEDERMANN   But why?

LEADER   All-too-strangely a fiery prospect
Unfolds to our eyes.
And to yours.

Shall I be plainer?
Gasoline in the attic—

BIEDERMANN   [*Shouts.*] Is that *your* business? [*Silence.*] Let me through—I have to see my lawyer—What do you want of me? I'm not guilty . . . [*Unnerved.*] What's this—an inquest? [*Masterfully.*] Let me through, please! [*The* CHORUS *remains motionless.*]

CHORUS   Far be it from us, the Chorus,
To judge a hero of drama—

LEADER   But we *do* see the oncoming peril,
See clearly the menacing danger!

CHORUS   Making a simple inquiry
About an impending disaster—
Uttering, merely, a warning—
Civic-minded, the Chorus comes forward,
Bathed, alas, in cold sweat,
In half-fainting fear of that moment
That calls for the hoses of firemen!
[BIEDERMANN *looks at his wrist watch.*]

BIEDERMANN   I'm in a hurry.

CHORUS   Woe!

LEADER   All that gasoline, Gottlieb
Biedermann!
How could you take it?

BIEDERMANN   Take it?

LEADER   You know very well,
The world is a brand for the burning!
Yet, knowing it, what did you think?

BIEDERMANN   Think? [*He appraises the* CHORUS.*] My dear sirs, I am a free and independent citizen. I can think anything I like. What are all these questions? I have the right, my dear sirs, not to think at all if I feel like it! Aside from the fact that whatever goes on under my own roof—Let's get one thing clear, gentlemen: I am the owner of the house!

CHORUS   Sacred, sacred to us
Is property,
Whatever befall!
Though we be scorched,
Though we be cindered—
Sacred, sacred to us!

BIEDERMANN   Well, then—[*Silence.*] Why can't I go through? [*Silence.*] Why must you always imagine the worst? Where will that get you? All I want is some peace and quiet, not a thing more . . . As for those two gentlemen—aside from the fact that I have other troubles right now . . . [BABETTE *enters in street clothes.*] What do *you* want here?

BABETTE   Am I interrupting?

BIEDERMANN   Can't you see I'm in conference? [BABETTE *nods to the* CHORUS, *then whispers in* BIEDERMANN's *ear.*] With ribbons, of course. Never mind the cost. As long as it's a wreath. [BABETTE *nods to the* CHORUS.]

BABETTE   Excuse me, sirs. [*She exits.*]

BIEDERMANN   To cut it short, gentlemen, I'm fed up! You and your firebugs! I don't even go to the pub any more—that's how fed up I am! Is there nothing else to talk about these days? Let's get one thing straight—if you go around thinking everybody except yourself is an arsonist, how are things ever going to improve? A little trust in people, for Heaven's sake! A little good will! Why keep looking at the bad side? Why go on the assumption that everybody else is a firebug? A little confidence, a little—[*Pause.*] You can't go on living in fear! [*Pause.*] You think I closed my eyes last night for one instant? I'm not an imbecile, you know! Gasoline is gasoline! I had the worst kind of thoughts running through my head last night . . . I climbed up on the table to listen—even got up on the bureau and put my ear to the ceiling! They were snoring, mind you—snoring! At least four times I climbed up on that bureau. Peacefully snoring! Just the same I got as far as the stairs, once—believe it or not—in my pajamas—and frantic, I tell you—frantic! I was all ready to wake up those two scoundrels and throw them out in the street, along with their barrels. Single-handedly, without compunction, in the middle of the night!

CHORUS   Single-handedly?

BIEDERMANN   Yes.

CHORUS   Without compunction?

BIEDERMANN   Yes.

CHORUS   In the middle of the night?

BIEDERMANN   Just about to! If my wife hadn't come after me, afraid I'd catch cold—[*Embarrassed, he reaches for a cigar.*]

LEADER   How shall I put it?
Sleepless he passed the night.
That they'd take advantage of a man's good
   nature—
Was that conceivable?
Suspicion came over him. Why?
   [BIEDERMANN *lights his cigar.*]

CHORUS   No it's not easy for the citizen,
Tough in business
But really soft of heart,

Always ready,
Ready always to do good.

LEADER   If that's how he happens to feel.

CHORUS   Hoping that goodness
Will come of goodness.
How mistaken can you be?

BIEDERMANN   What are you getting at?

CHORUS   It seems to us there's a stink of gasoline.
   [BIEDERMANN *sniffs.*]

BIEDERMANN   I don't smell anything.

CHORUS   Woe to us!

BIEDERMANN   Not a thing.

CHORUS   Woe to us!

LEADER   How soon he's got accustomed to bad smells!

CHORUS   Woe to us!

BIEDERMANN   And don't keep giving us that defeatism, gentlemen. Don't keep saying all the time, "Woe to us!" [*A car honks offstage*] Taxi!—Taxi! [*A car stops offstage.*] If you'll excuse me—[*He hurries off.*]

CHORUS   Citizen—where to?
   [*The car drives off.*]

LEADER   What is his recourse, poor wretch?
Forceful, yet fearful,
Milk-white of face,
Fearful yet firm—
Against what?
   [*The car is heard honking.*]

CHORUS   So soon accustomed to bad smells!
   [*The car is heard honking.*]
Woe to us!

LEADER   Woe to you!
   [*The* CHORUS *retires. All but the* LEADER, *who takes out his pipe.*]
He who dreads change
More than disaster,
How can he fight
When disaster impends?
   [*He follows the* CHORUS *out.*]

SCENE FIVE

The Attic

EISENRING *is alone, unwinding cord from a reel and singing "Lily Marlene" while he works. He stops whistling, wets his forefinger and holds it up to the dormer window to test the wind.*

The Living Room

[BIEDERMANN *enters, cigar in mouth, followed by* BABETTE. *He takes off his coat and throws down his briefcase.*]

BIEDERMANN   Do as I say.

BABETTE   A goose?

BIEDERMANN   A goose! [*He takes off his tie without removing his cigar.*]

BABETTE   Why are you taking off your necktie, Gottlieb?

BIEDERMANN   If I report those two boys to the police I'll make them my enemies. What good will that do me? Just one match and the whole house is up in flames! What good will that do us? On the other hand, if I go up there and invite them to dinner, why—

BABETTE   Why, what?

BIEDERMANN   Why, then we'll be friends. [*He takes off his jacket, hands it to* BABETTE *and exits.*]

BABETTE   [*Speaking to* ANNA, *offstage.*] Just so you'll know, Anna: you can't get off this evening—we're having company. Set places for four.

The Attic

[EISENRING *singing "Lily Marlene." There is a knock at the door.*]

EISENRING   Come in! [*He goes on singing. No one enters.*] Come in! [BIEDERMANN *enters in shirtsleeves, holding his cigar.*] Good day, Herr Biedermann!

BIEDERMANN   [*Tactfully.*] May I come in?

EISENRING   I hope you slept well last night?

BIEDERMANN   Thank you—miserably.

EISENRING   So did I. It's this wind. [*He goes on working with the reel.*]

BIEDERMANN   If I'm not disturbing you—

EISENRING   This is your house, Herr Biedermann.

BIEDERMANN   If I'm not in the way— [*The cooing of doves is heard.*] Where is our friend?

EISENRING   Sepp? He went to work this morning, the lazy dog—he didn't want to go without breakfast! I sent him out for some sawdust.

BIEDERMANN   Sawdust?

EISENRING   It helps spread the sparks.

[BIEDERMANN *laughs politely at what sounds like a poor joke.*]

BIEDERMANN   I was going to say, Herr Eisenring—

EISENRING   That you still want to kick us out?

BIEDERMANN   In the middle of the night—I'm out of sleeping pills—it suddenly struck me: you folks have no toilet facilities up here.

EISENRING   We have the roof gutter.

BIEDERMANN   Well, just as you like, of course. It merely struck me you might like to wash or take a shower— I kept thinking of that all night . . . You're very welcome to use my bathroom. I told Anna to hang up some towels for you there. [EISENRING *shakes his head.*] Why do you shake your head?

EISENRING   Where on earth did he put it?

BIEDERMANN   What?

EISENRING   You haven't seen a detonator cap? [*He searches around.*] Don't trouble yourself, Herr Biedermann. In jail, you know, we had no bathrooms either.

BIEDERMANN   In jail?

EISENRING   Didn't Sepp tell you I just came out of prison?

BIEDERMANN   No.

EISENRING   Not a word about it?

BIEDERMANN   No.

EISENRING   All he likes to talk about is himself. There *are* such people!— Is it our fault, after all, if his youth was tragic? Did *you* have a tragic youth, Herr Biedermann? *I* didn't. I could have gone to college; my father wanted me to be a lawyer . . . [*He stands at the attic window murmuring to the doves.*] Grrr! Grrr! Grrr! [BIEDERMANN *re-lights his cigar.*]

BIEDERMANN   Frankly, Herr Eisenring, I couldn't sleep all night. Is there really gasoline in those barrels?

EISENRING   You don't trust us.

BIEDERMANN   I'm merely asking.

EISENRING   Herr Biedermann, what do you take us for? Frankly, what sort of people—

BIEDERMANN   Herr Eisenring, you mustn't think I have no sense of humor. Only your idea of a joke—well—

EISENRING   That's something we've learned.

BIEDERMANN   What is?

EISENRING   That a joke is first-class camouflage. Next comes sentiment: like when Sepp talks about a childhood in the coal mines, orphanages, circuses and so forth. But the best camouflage of all—in my opinion—is the plain and simple truth. Because nobody ever believes it.

The Living Room

[ANNA *shows in the* WIDOW KNECHTLING, *dressed in black.*]

ANNA   Take a seat, please. [*The* WIDOW *sits.*] But if you are Frau Knechtling, it's no use. Herr Biedermann wants nothing to do with you, he said. [*The* WIDOW *gets up.*] Take a seat, please! [*The* WIDOW *sits down again.*] But don't get up any hopes. [ANNA *exits.*]

The Attic

[EISENRING *is busy with one thing or another.* BIEDERMANN *is smoking.*]

EISENRING   I wonder what's keeping Sepp. Sawdust can't be so hard to find. I hope they haven't nabbed him.

BIEDERMANN   Nabbed?

EISENRING   Why do you smile?

BIEDERMANN   When you use words like that, Herr Eisenring, it's as though you came from another world. Nab him! Like another world! *Our* kind of people seldom get nabbed!

EISENRING   Because your kind of people seldom steal sawdust. That's obvious, Herr Biedermann. That's the class difference.

BIEDERMANN   Absurd!

EISENRING   You don't mean to say, Herr Biedermann—

BIEDERMANN   I don't hold with class differences —you must have realized that by now, Herr Eisenring. I'm not old-fashioned—just the opposite, in fact. And I regret that the lower classes still talk about class differences. Aren't we all of us—rich or poor—the creation of one Creator? The middle class, too. Are we not—you and I—human beings, made of flesh and blood? . . . I don't know, sir, whether you smoke cigars— [*He offers one, but* EISENRING *shakes his head.*] I don't mean reducing people to a common level, you understand. There will always be rich and poor, Heaven knows—but why can't we just shake hands? A little good will, for Heaven's sake, a little idealism, a little—and we'd all

have peace and quiet, both the poor and the rich. Don't you agree?

EISENRING   If I may speak frankly, Herr Biedermann—

BIEDERMANN   Please do.

EISENRING   You won't take it amiss?

BIEDERMANN   The more frankly the better.

EISENRING   Frankly speaking, you oughtn't to smoke here. [BIEDERMANN, *startled, puts out his cigar.*] I can't make rules for you here, Herr Biedermann. After all, it's your house. Still and all—

BIEDERMANN   Naturally.

EISENRING   [*Looking down.*] There it is! [*He takes something off the floor and blows it clean before attaching it to the wire. He starts whistling "Lily Marlene."*]

BIEDERMANN   Tell me, Herr Eisenring, what is that you're doing? If I may ask? What is that thing?

EISENRING   A detonator.

BIEDERMANN   A——?

EISENRING   And this is a fuse.

BIEDERMANN   A——?

EISENRING   Sepp says they've developed better ones lately. But they don't have them yet, in the stores. Buying them's out of the question for us, of course. Anything that has to do with war is frightfully expensive. Always the best quality . . .

BIEDERMANN   A fuse, you say?

EISENRING   A time-fuse. [*He hands* BIEDERMANN *one end of the cord.*] If you'd be kind enough, Herr Biedermann, to hold this end— [BIEDERMANN *holds it for him.*]

BIEDERMANN   All joking aside, my friend—

EISENRING   One second— [*He whistles "Lily Marlene," measuring the fuse.*] Thank you, Herr Biedermann. [BIEDERMANN *suddenly laughs.*]

BIEDERMANN   Ha, ha! You can't put a scare into me, Willi! Though I must say, you count on people's sense of humor! The way you talk, I can understand your getting arrested now and then. You know, not everybody has my sense of humor!

EISENRING   You have to find the right man.

BIEDERMANN   At the pub, for instance—just say you believe in the natural goodness of man, and they have you marked down.

EISENRING   Ha!

BIEDERMANN   And still I won't mention how

much I donated to our Fire Department!

EISENRING Ha! [*He puts down the fuse.*] Those who have no sense of humor get what's coming to them just the same when the time comes—so don't let *that* worry you. [BIEDERMANN *sits down on a barrel. He has broken into a sweat.*] What's the trouble, Herr Biedermann? You've gone quite pale. [*He claps him on the shoulder.*] It's the smell. I know, if you're not used to it . . . I'll open the window for you, too. [*He opens the door.*]

BIEDERMANN Thanks . . . [ANNA *calls up the stairs.*]

ANNA Herr Biedermann! Herr Biedermann!

EISENRING The police again?

ANNA Herr Biedermann!

EISENRING It's a Police State!

ANNA Herr Biedermann—

BIEDERMANN I'm coming! [*They both whisper from here on.*] Herr Eisenring, do you like goose?

EISENRING Goose?

BIEDERMANN Roast goose.

EISENRING Why?

BIEDERMANN Stuffed with chestnuts?

EISENRING And red cabbage?

BIEDERMANN Yes . . . I was going to say: my wife and I—I, especially—if we may have the pleasure . . . I don't mean to obtrude, Herr Eisenring, but if you'd care to join us at a little supper, you and Sepp—

EISENRING Today?

BIEDERMANN Or tomorrow, if you prefer—

EISENRING We probably won't stay until tomorrow. But today—of course, Herr Biedermann, with pleasure.

BIEDERMANN Shall we say seven o'clock? [ANNA *calls up the stairs.*]

ANNA Herr Biedermann! [*They shake hands.*]

BIEDERMANN [*At the door with a twinkle.*] All set?

EISENRING All set! [BIEDERMANN *exits.* EISENRING *goes to work again, whistling. The* CHORUS *enters as for the end of the scene. They are interrupted by the sound of a crash, as of something falling in the attic.*]

The Attic

EISENRING You can come out, Professor. [*A* PH.D., *wearing horn-rimmed glasses, crawls out of the pile of barrels.*] You heard: we're invited to dinner, Sepp and me. You'll keep an eye on things. Nobody's to come in here and smoke, understand? Not before we're ready. [*The* PH.D. *polishes his glasses.*] I often ask myself, Professor, why in hell you hang around with us. You don't enjoy a good, crackling fire, or flames, or sparks. Or sirens that go off too late—or dogs barking—or people shrieking—or smoke. Or ashes . . . [*The* PH.D. *solemnly adjusts his glasses.* EISENRING *laughs.*] Do-gooder! [*He whistles gently to himself, surveying the* PROFESSOR.] I don't like you eggheads—I've told you that before, Professor. You get no real fun out of anything. You're all so idealistic, so solemn . . . You can't be trusted. That's no fun, Professor. [*He goes back to his work, whistling.*]

CHORUS Ready for action,
Axes and fire-hose;
Polished and oiled,
Every brass fitting.
Every man of us tested and ready.

LEADER We'll be facing a high wind.

CHORUS Every man of us tested and ready.
Our brass fire-pump
Polished and oiled,
Tested for pressure.

LEADER And the fire-hydrants?

CHORUS Everything ready.

LEADER Tested and ready for action.

[*Enter* BABETTE *with a goose, and the* PH.D.]

BABETTE Yes, Professor, I know, but my husband . . . Yes, I understand it's urgent, Professor. I'll tell him—[*She leaves the* PROFESSOR *and comes to the footlights.*] My husband ordered a goose. See, this is it. And I have to roast it, so we can be friends with those people upstairs. [*Church bells ring.*] It's Saturday night—you can hear the bells ringing. I have an odd feeling, somehow, that it may be the last time we'll hear them. [BIEDERMANN *calls, "Babette!"*] I don't know, ladies, if Gottlieb is always right . . . You know what he says? "Certainly they're scoundrels, Babette, but if I make enemies of them, it's goodbye to our hair tonic!" [BIEDERMANN *calls. "Babette!"*] Gottlieb's like that. Good-hearted. Always too good-hearted! [*She exits with the goose.*]

CHORUS This son of good family,
A wearer of glasses,

Pale, studious, trusting,
But trusting no longer
In power of goodness,
Will do anything now, for
Ends justify means.
(So he hopes.)
Ah, honest-dishonest!
Now wiping his glasses
To see things more clearly,
He sees no barrels—
No gasoline barrels!
It's an idea he sees—
An abstract conception—
Until it explodes!

PH.D. Good evening . . .

LEADER To the pumps!
The ladders!
The engines!
[*The* FIREMEN *rush to their posts.*]

LEADER Good evening.
[*To the audience, as shouts of "Ready!"
echo through the theatre.*]
We're ready.

SCENE SIX

The Living Room

The WIDOW KNECHTLING *is still there,
standing and waiting. Outside, the bells are ringing loudly.* ANNA *is setting the table.* BIEDER-
MANN *brings in two chairs.*

BIEDERMANN You can see, can't you, Frau
Knechtling? I haven't time now—no time to
think about the dead . . . I told you, go see
my lawyer. [*The* WIDOW KNECHTLING *leaves.*]
You can't hear yourself think, with that noise.
Close the window. [ANNA *shuts the window.
The sound of the bells is fainter.*] I said a
simple, informal dinner. What are those idiotic
candelabra for?

ANNA But, Herr Biedermann, we always have
those!

BIEDERMANN I said simple, informal—not
show-off! Fingerbowls! Knife-rests! Nothing
but crystal and silver! What does that look
like? [*He picks up the knife-rests and shoves
them into his pants pocket.*] Can't you see

I'm wearing my oldest jacket? And you . . .
Leave the carving knife, Anna—we'll need it;
but away with the rest of this silver! Those
two gentlemen must feel at home!—Where's
the corkscrew?

ANNA Here.

BIEDERMANN Don't we have anything simpler?

ANNA In the kitchen. But that one is rusty.

BIEDERMANN Bring it here. [*He takes a silver
ice-bucket off the table.*] What's this for?

ANNA For the wine.

BIEDERMANN Silver! [*He glares at the bucket,
then at* ANNA.] Do we always use that, too?

ANNA We're going to need it, Herr Biedermann.

BIEDERMANN Humanity, brotherhood—that's
what we need here! Away with that thing!
And what are those, will you tell me?

ANNA Napkins.

BIEDERMANN Damask napkins!

ANNA We don't have any others. [BIEDERMANN
shoves the napkins into the silver bucket.]

BIEDERMANN There are whole nations, Anna,
that live without napkins! [BABETTE *enters
with a large wreath.* BIEDERMANN, *standing
in front of the table, does not see her come
in.*] And why a cloth on the table?

BABETTE Gottlieb?

BIEDERMANN Let's have no class distinctions!
[*He sees* BABETTE.] What is that wreath?

BABETTE It's what we ordered—Gottlieb, what
do you think?! They sent the wreath here by
mistake! And I gave them the address myself
—Knechtling's address—I wrote it down,
even! And the ribbon and everything—they've
got it all backward!

BIEDERMANN What's wrong with the ribbon?

BABETTE And the clerk says they sent the bill
to Frau Knechtling! [*She shows him the ribbon:* "TO OUR DEAR, DEPARTED GOTT-
LIEB BIEDERMANN." *He considers the
ribbon.*]

BIEDERMANN We won't accept it, that's all! I
should say not! They've got to exchange it!
[*He goes back to the table.*] Don't upset, me,
will you, Babette? I can't think of everything—
[BABETTE *exits.*] Take that tablecloth away.
Help me, Anna. And remember—no serving!
You come in and put the pan on the table.

ANNA The roast-pan?! [*He takes away the
tablecloth.*]

BIEDERMANN That's better! A wooden table,

that's all. Just a table for supper. [*He hands* ANNA *the tablecloth.*]

ANNA   You mean that, Herr Biedermann—just bring in the goose in the pan? [*She folds up the tablecloth.*] What wine shall I bring?

BIEDERMANN   I'll get it myself.

ANNA   Herr Biedermann!

BIEDERMANN   What now?

ANNA   I don't have any sweater, sir—any old sweater, as if I belonged to the family.

BIEDERMANN   Borrow one of my wife's.

ANNA   The yellow or the red one?

BIEDERMANN   Don't be so fussy! No apron or cap, understand? And get rid of these candelabra. And make sure especially, Anna, that everything's not so neat!—I'll be in the cellar. [BIEDERMANN *exits.*]

ANNA   "Make sure especially, Anna, that everything's not so neat!" [*She throws the tablecloth down on the floor and stomps on it with both feet.*] How's that? [SCHMITZ *and* EISENRING *enter, each holding a rose.*]

BOTH   Good evening, Fräulein. [ANNA *exits without looking at them.*]

EISENRING   Why no sawdust?

SCHMITZ   Confiscated. Police measure. Precaution. They're picking up anybody who sells or owns sawdust without written permission. Precautions all over the place. [*He combs his hair.*]

EISENRING   Have you got matches?

SCHMITZ   No.

EISENRING   Neither have I. [SCHMITZ *blows his comb clean.*]

SCHMITZ   We'll have to ask him for them.

EISENRING   Biedermann?

SCHMITZ   Don't forget. [*He puts away his comb and sniffs.*] Mmm! That smells good!

SCENE SEVEN

BIEDERMANN *comes to the footlights with a bottle.*

BIEDERMANN   You can think what you like about me, gentlemen. But just answer one question— [*Laughter and loud voices offstage.*] I say to myself: as long as they're laughing and drinking, we're safe. The best bottles out of my cellar! I tell you, if anybody had told me a week ago . . . When did *you*

guess they were arsonists, gentlemen? This sort of thing doesn't happen the way you think. It comes on you slowly—slowly, at first —then sudden suspicion! Though I was suspicious at once—one's always suspicious! But tell me the truth, sirs—what would *you* have done? If you were in my place, for God's sake? And when? *When* would you have done it? At what point? [*He waits for an answer. Silence.*] I've got to go. [*He leaves the stage quickly.*]

SCENE EIGHT

The Living Room

The dinner is in full swing. Laughter. BIEDERMANN, *especially, cannot contain himself at the joke he's just heard. Only* BABETTE *is not laughing.*

BIEDERMANN   Oil waste! Did you hear that, Babette? Oil waste, he says! Oil waste burns better!

BABETTE   I don't see what's funny.

BIEDERMANN   Oil waste! You know what that is?

BABETTE   Yes.

BIEDERMANN   You have no sense of humor, Babette. [*He puts the bottle on the table.*]

BABETTE   All right, then, explain it.

BIEDERMANN   Okay!—This morning Willi told Sepp to go out and steal some sawdust. Sawdust—get it? And just now, when I asked Sepp if he got any, he said he couldn't find any sawdust—he found some oil waste instead. Get it? And Willi says, "Oil waste burns better!"

BABETTE   I understood all that.

BIEDERMANN   You did?

BABETTE   What's funny about it? [BIEDERMANN *gives up.*]

BIEDERMANN   Let's drink, men! [BIEDERMANN *removes the cork from the bottle.*]

BABETTE   Is that the truth, Herr Schmitz? Did you bring oil waste up to our attic?

BIEDERMANN   This will kill you, Babette! This morning we even measured the fuse together, Willi and I!

BABETTE   The fuse?

BIEDERMANN The time-fuse. [*He fills the glasses.*]

BABETTE Seriously—what does that mean? [BIEDERMANN *laughs.*]

BIEDERMANN Seriously! You hear that? Seriously! . . . Don't let them kid you, Babette. I told you—our friends have their own way of kidding! Different company, different jokes —that's what I always say . . . All we need now is to have them ask me for matches! [SCHMITZ *and* EISENRING *exchange glances.*] These gentlemen took me for some Milquetoast, for some dope without humor— [*He lifts his glass.*] Prosit!

EISENRING Prosit!

SCHMITZ Prosit!

BIEDERMANN To our friendship! [*They drink the toast standing up, then sit down again.*] We're not doing serving. Just help yourselves, gentlemen.

SCHMITZ I can't eat any more.

EISENRING Don't restrain yourself, Sepp, you're not at the orphanage. [*He helps himself to more goose.*] Your goose is wonderful, madam.

BABETTE I'm glad to hear it.

EISENRING Roast goose and stuffing! Now all we need is a tablecloth.

BABETTE You hear that, Gottlieb?

EISENRING We don't have to have one. Not one of those tablecloths, white damask, with silverware on it—

BIEDERMANN [*Loudly.*] Anna!

EISENRING Damask, with flowers all over it—a white flower pattern—we don't have to have one. We didn't have any in prison.

BABETTE In prison?

BIEDERMANN Where is that girl?

BABETTE Have you been in prison? [ANNA *enters. She is wearing a bright red sweater.*]

BIEDERMANN A tablecloth here—immediately!

ANNA Yes sir.

BIEDERMANN And if you have some finger-bowls or something—

ANNA Yes sir.

EISENRING Madam, you may think it's childish, but that's how the little man is. Take Sepp, for instance—he grew up in the coal mines, but it's the dream of his miserable life, a table like this, with crystal and silver! Would you believe it? He never heard of a knife-rest!

BABETTE But, Gottlieb, we have all those things!

EISENRING Of course we don't *have* to have them here—

ANNA Very well.

EISENRING If you have any napkins, Fräulein, out with them!

ANNA But Herr Biedermann said—

BIEDERMANN Out with them!

ANNA Yes sir. [*She starts to bring back the table service.*]

EISENRING I hope you won't take it amiss, madam, but when you're just out of prison— months at a time with no refinement whatever — [*He shows the tablecloth to* SCHMITZ.] You know what this is? [BABETTE.] He never saw one before! [*He turns back to* SCHMITZ.] This is damask!

SCHMITZ What do you want me to do with it? [EISENRING *ties the tablecloth around his neck.*]

EISENRING There— [BIEDERMANN *tries to find this amusing. He laughs.*]

BABETTE Where are the knife-rests, Anna?

ANNA Herr Biedermann—

BIEDERMANN Out with them!

ANNA But you said "Take them away!" before!

BIEDERMANN Bring them here, I tell you! Where are they, goddamit?

ANNA In your pants pocket. [BIEDERMANN *reaches in his pants pocket and finds them.*]

EISENRING Don't get excited.

ANNA I can't help it!

EISENRING No excitement, now, Fräulein— [ANNA *bursts into sobs and runs out.*]

EISENRING It's this wind. [*Pause.*]

BIEDERMANN Drink up, friends! [*They drink. A silence.*]

EISENRING I ate roast goose every day when I was a waiter. I used to flit down those corridors holding a platter like this . . . How do you suppose, madam, waiters clean off their hands? In their hair, that's how—while there's others who use crystal fingerbowls. That's something I'll never forget. [*He dips his fingers in the fingerbowl.*] Have you ever heard of a trauma?

BIEDERMANN No.

EISENRING I learned all about it in jail. [*He wipes his fingers dry.*]

BABETTE   And how did you happen to be there, Herr Eisenring?

BIEDERMANN   Babette!

EISENRING   How did I get into jail?

BIEDERMANN   One doesn't ask questions like that!

EISENRING   I wonder at that myself . . . I was a waiter—a little head waiter. Suddenly they made me out a great arsonist.

BIEDERMANN   Hm.

EISENRING   They called for me at my own home.

BIEDERMANN   Hm.

EISENRING   I was so amazed, I gave in.

BIEDERMANN   Hm.

EISENRING   I had luck, madam—seven really charming policemen. I said, "I have no time —I have to go to work." They answered, "Your restaurant's burned to the ground."

BIEDERMANN   Burned to the ground?

EISENRING   Overnight, apparently.

BABETTE   Burned to the ground?

EISENRING   "Fine," I said. "Then I *have* time . . ." Just a black, smoking hulk—that's all that was left of that place. I saw it as we drove by. Through those windows, you know, the little barred windows they have in those prison vans— [*He sips his wine delicately.*]

BIEDERMANN   And then? [EISENRING *studies the wine-label.*]

EISENRING   We used to keep this, too: '49, Cave de l'Echannon . . . And then? Let Sepp tell you the rest—As I was sitting in that police station, playing with my handcuffs, who do you think they brought in?—That one, there! [SCHMITZ *beams.*] Prosit, Sepp!

SCHMITZ   Prosit, Willi! [*They drink.*]

BIEDERMANN   And then?

SCHMITZ   "Are you the firebug?" they asked him, and offered him cigarettes. He said, "Excuse me, I have no matches, Herr Commissioner, although you think I'm a firebug—" [*They laugh uproariously and slap each other's thighs.*]

BIEDERMANN   Hm. [ANNA *enters, in cap and apron again. She hands* BIEDERMANN *a visiting card.*]

ANNA   It's urgent, he says.

BIEDERMANN   When I have visitors— [SCHMITZ *and* EISENRING *clink glasses again.*]

SCHMITZ   Prosit, Willi!

EISENRING   Prosit, Sepp! [*They drink.* BIEDERMANN *studies the visiting card.*]

BABETTE   Who is it, Gottlieb?

BIEDERMANN   It's a professor . . . [ANNA *is busy at the sideboard.*]

EISENRING   And what are those other things, Fräulein—those silver things?

ANNA   The candlesticks?

EISENRING   Why do you hide them?

BIEDERMANN   Bring them here!

ANNA   But you said, yourself, Herr Biedermann—

BIEDERMANN   I say bring them here! [ANNA *places the candelabra on the table.*]

EISENRING   What do you say to that, Sepp? They have candlesticks and they hide them! Real silver candlesticks—what more do you want?—Have you a match? [*He reaches into his pants pocket.*]

SCHMITZ   Me? No. [*He reaches into his pants pocket.*]

EISENRING   Sorry, no matches, Herr Biedermann.

BIEDERMANN   I have some.

EISENRING   Let's have them.

BIEDERMANN   I'll light the candles. Let me—I'll do it. [*He begins lighting the candles.*]

BABETTE   [*To* ANNA.] What does the visitor want?

ANNA   I don't know, ma'am. He says he can no longer be silent. And he's waiting on the stoop.

BABETTE   It's private, he says?

ANNA   Yes, ma'am. He says he has a revelation to make.

BABETTE   A revelation?

ANNA   That's how he talks. I can't follow it, even when he repeats it. He wants to remove himself, so he says . . . [BIEDERMANN *is still lighting candles.*]

EISENRING   It creates an atmosphere, doesn't it, madam? Candlelight, I mean.

BABETTE   Yes, it does.

EISENRING   I'm all for atmosphere. Refined, candlelight atmosphere—

BIEDERMANN   I'm happy to know that. [*All the candles are lit.*]

EISENRING   Schmitz, don't smack your lips when you eat! [BABETTE *takes* EISENRING *aside.*]

BABETTE   Let him alone!

EISENRING   He has no manners, madam. Excuse me—it's awful. But where could he have picked up any manners? From the coal mines to the orphanage—

BABETTE   I know.

EISENRING   From the orphanage to the circus.

BABETTE   I know.

EISENRING   From the circus to the theatre—

BABETTE   I didn't know.

EISENRING   A football of fate, madam. [BABETTE *turns to* SCHMITZ.]

BABETTE   In the theatre! Were you, really? [SCHMITZ *gnaws on a drumstick and nods.*] Where?

SCHMITZ   Upstage.

EISENRING   Really talented, too! Sepp as a ghost! Can you imagine it?

SCHMITZ   Not any more, though.

EISENRING   Why not?

SCHMITZ   I was in the theatre only a week, madam, before it burned to the ground.

BABETTE   Burned to the ground?

EISENRING   [*To* SCHMITZ.] Don't be diffident!

BIEDERMANN   Burned to the ground?

EISENRING   Don't be so diffident! [*He unties the tablecloth* SCHMITZ *has been wearing and throws it over* SCHMITZ'S *head.*] Come on! [SCHMITZ *gets up with the tablecloth over him.*] Doesn't he look like a ghost?

ANNA   I'm frightened!

EISENRING   Come here, little girl! [*He pulls* ANNA *onto his lap. She hides her face in her hands.*]

SCHMITZ   "Who calleth?"

EISENRING   That's theatre language, madam. They call that a cue. He learned it in less than a week, before the theatre burned down.

BABETTE   Please don't keep talking of fires!

SCHMITZ   "Who calleth?"

EISENRING   Ready— [*Everybody waits expectantly.* EISENRING *has a tight grip on* ANNA.]

SCHMITZ   "EVERYMAN! EVERYMAN!"

BABETTE   Gottlieb?

BIEDERMANN   Quiet!

BABETTE   We saw that in Salzburg!

SCHMITZ   "BIEDERMANN! BIEDERMANN!"

EISENRING   He's teriffic!

SCHMITZ   "BIEDERMANN! BIEDERMANN!"

EISENRING   You must say, "Who are you?"

BIEDERMANN   Me?

EISENRING   Or he can't say his lines.

SCHMITZ   "EVERYMAN! BIEDERMANN!"

BIEDERMANN   All right, then—who am I?

BABETTE   No! You must ask him who *he* is.

BIEDERMANN   I see.

SCHMITZ   "DOST THOU HEAR ME?"

EISENRING   No, no, Sepp—start it again. [*They change their positions.*]

SCHMITZ   "EVERYMAN! BIEDERMANN!"

BABETTE   Are you the Angel of Death, maybe?

BIEDERMANN   Nonsense!

BABETTE   What else *could* he be?

BIEDERMANN   Ask him. He might be the ghost in "Hamlet." Or that other one—what's-his-name—in "Macbeth."

SCHMITZ   "WHO CALLS ME?"

EISENRING   Go on.

SCHMITZ   "GOTTLIEB BIEDERMANN!"

BABETTE   Go ahead, ask him. He's talking to you.

SCHMITZ   "DOST THOU HEAR ME?"

BIEDERMANN   Who are you?

SCHMITZ   "I AM THE GHOST OF—KNECHTLING." [BABETTE *springs up with a scream.*]

EISENRING   Stop! [*He pulls the tablecloth off* SCHMITZ.] Idiot! How could you do such a thing? Knechtling was buried today!

SCHMITZ   That's why I thought of him. [BABETTE *hides her face in her hands.*]

EISENRING   He's not Knechtling, madam. [*He shakes his head over* SCHMITZ.] What crudeness!

SCHMITZ   He was on my mind . . .

EISENRING   Of all things—Knechtling! Herr Biedermann's best old employee! Imagine it: buried today—cold and stiff—not yet mouldy —pale as this tablecloth—white and shiny as damask— To go and act Knechtling— [*He takes* BABETTE *by the shoulder.*] Honest to God, madam, it's Sepp—it's not Knechtling at all. [SCHMITZ *wipes off his sweat.*]

SCHMITZ   I'm sorry . . .

BIEDERMANN   Let's sit down again.

ANNA   Is it over?

BIEDERMANN   Would you care for cigars, sirs? [*He offers a box of cigars.*]

EISENRING   [*To* SCHMITZ.] Idiot! You see how Herr Biedermann is shaking! . . . Thank you, Herr Biedermann!—You think that's funny, Sepp? When you know very well that Knechtling laid his head over a gas jet? After everything Gottlieb did for him? He gave this

Knechtling fourteen years' work—and this is his thanks!

BIEDERMANN   Let's not talk about it.

EISENRING   [*To* SCHMITZ.] And that's your thanks for the goose! [*They attend to their cigars.*]

SCHMITZ   Would you like me to sing something?

EISENRING   What?

SCHMITZ   "Fox, you stole that lovely goosie . . ." [*He sings loudly.*]
"Fox, you stole that lovely goosie,
Give it back again!"

EISENRING   That's enough.

SCHMITZ   "Give it back again!
Or they'll get you in the shnoosie—"

EISENRING   He's drunk.

SCHMITZ   "With their shooting-gun!"

EISENRING   Pay no attention to him.

SCHMITZ   "Give it back again!
Or they'll get you in the shnoosie
With their shooting-gun!"

BIEDERMANN   "Shooting-gun!" That's good! [*The men all join in the song.*]
"Fox, you stole that lovely goosie . . ."
   [*They harmonize, now loudly, now softly. Laughter and loud cheer. There is a pause, and* BIEDERMANN *picks up again, leading the hilarity until they've all had it.*]

BIEDERMANN   So— Prosit! [*They raise their glasses. Fire sirens are heard near by.*] What was that?

EISENRING   Sirens.

BIEDERMANN   Joking aside—

BABETTE   Firebugs! Firebugs!

BIEDERMANN   Don't yell like that! [BABETTE *runs to the window and throws it open. The sound of the sirens comes nearer, with a howl that goes to the marrow. The fire engines roar past.*]

BIEDERMANN   At least it's not here.

BABETTE   I wonder where?

EISENRING   From where the wind is blowing.

BIEDERMANN   Not here, anyway.

EISENRING   That's how we generally work it. Coax the Fire Department out to some cheap suburb or other, and then, when things really let loose, they find their way blocked.

BIEDERMANN   No, gentlemen—all joking aside—

SCHMITZ   That's how we do it—joking aside—

BIEDERMANN   Please—enough of this nonsense!

Don't overdo it! Look at my wife—white as chalk!

BABETTE   And you too!

BIEDERMANN   Besides, a fire alarm is nothing to laugh at, gentlemen. Somewhere some place is burning, or the Fire Department wouldn't be rushing there. [EISENRING *looks at his watch.*]

EISENRING   We've got to go, now.

BIEDERMANN   Now?

EISENRING   Sorry.

SCHMITZ   "Or they'll get you in the schnoosie . . ." [*The sirens are heard again.*]

BIEDERMANN   Bring us some coffee, Babette! [BABETTE *goes out.*] And you, Anna—do you have to stand there and gape? [ANNA *goes out.*] Just between us, gentlemen: enough is enough. My wife has a heart condition. Let's have no more joking about fires.

SCHMITZ   We're not joking, Herr Biedermann.

EISENRING   We're firebugs.

BIEDERMANN   No, gentlemen, quite seriously—

EISENRING   Quite seriously.

SCHMITZ   Yeah, quite seriously. Why don't you believe us?

EISENRING   Your house is very favorably situated, Herr Biedermann, you must admit that. Five villas like yours around the gas works . . . It's true they keep a close watch on the gas works. Still, there's a good stiff wind blowing—

BIEDERMANN   It can't be—

SCHMITZ   Let's have plain talk! You think we're firebugs—

BIEDERMANN   [*Like a whipped dog.*] No, no, I don't think you are! You do me an injustice, gentlemen—I don't think you're firebugs . . .

EISENRING   You swear you don't?

BIEDERMANN   No! No! No! I don't believe it!

SCHMITZ   What *do* you think we are?

BIEDERMANN   You're my friends . . . [*They clap him on the shoulder and start to leave.*]

EISENRING   It's time to leave.

BIEDERMANN   Gentlemen, I swear to you by all that's holy—

EISENRING   By all that's holy?

BIEDERMANN   Yes. [*He raises his hand as though to take an oath.*]

SCHMITZ   Willi doesn't believe in anything holy, Herr Biedermann. Any more than you do. You'll waste your time swearing. [*They go to the door.*]

BIEDERMANN   What can I do to make you believe me? [*He blocks the doorway.*]

EISENRING   Give us some matches.

BIEDERMANN   Some—

EISENRING   We have no more matches.

BIEDERMANN   You want me to—

EISENRING   If you don't think we're firebugs.

BIEDERMANN   Matches—

SCHMITZ   To show your belief in us, he means. [BIEDERMANN *reaches in his pocket.*]

EISENRING   See how he hesitates?

BIEDERMANN   Sh! Not in front of my wife . . . [BABETTE *returns.*]

BABETTE   Your coffee will be ready in a minute. [*Pause.*] Must you go?

BIEDERMANN   [*Formally.*] At least you've felt, while here, my friends . . . I don't want to make a speech on this occasion, but may we not drink, before you go, to our eternal friendship? [*He picks up a bottle and the corkscrew.*]

EISENRING   Tell your very charming husband, madam, that he needn't open any more bottles on our account. It isn't worth the trouble any more.

BIEDERMANN   It's no trouble, my friends, no trouble at all. If there's anything else you'd like—anything at all— [*He fills the glasses once more and hands them out.*] My friends! [*They clink glasses.*] Sepp—Willi— [*He kisses them each on the cheek. All drink.*]

EISENRING   Just the same, we must go now.

SCHMITZ   Unfortunately.

EISENRING   Madam— [*Sirens.*]

BABETTE   It's been such a nice evening. [*Alarm bells.*]

EISENRING   Just one thing, now, Gottlieb—

BIEDERMANN   What is it?

EISENRING   I've mentioned it to you before.

BIEDERMANN   Anything you like. Just name it.

EISENRING   The matches. [ANNA *has entered with coffee.*]

BABETTE   Why, what is it, Anna?

ANNA   The coffee.

BABETTE   You're all upset, Anna!

ANNA   Back there—Frau Biedermann—the sky! You can see it from the kitchen—the whole sky is burning, Frau Biedermann. [*The scene is turning red as* SCHMITZ *and* EISENRING *make their bows and exit.* BIEDERMANN *is left pale and shaken.*]

BIEDERMANN   Not our house, fortunately . . .

Not our house . . . Not our . . . [*The* PH.D. *enters.*] Who are you, and what do you want?

PH.D.   I can no longer be silent. [*He takes out a paper and reads.*] "Cognizant of the events now transpiring, whose iniquitous nature must be readily apparent, the undersigned submits to the authorities the subsequent statement . . ." [*Amid the shrieking of sirens he reads an involved statement, of which no one understands a word. Dogs howl, bells ring, there is the scream of departing sirens and the crackling of flames. The* PH.D. *hands* BIEDERMANN *the paper.*] I remove myself . . .

BIEDERMANN   But—

PH.D.   I have said my say. [*He takes off and folds up his glasses.*] Sir, as a serious-minded uplifter, I knew what they were doing in your attic. I did *not* know, however, that they were doing it just for fun!

BIEDERMANN   Professor— [*The* PH.D. *removes himself.*] What will I do with this, Professor? [*The* PH.D. *climbs over the footlights and takes a seat in the audience.*]

BABETTE   Gottlieb—

BIEDERMANN   He's gone.

BABETTE   What did you give them? Matches? Not matches?

BIEDERMANN   Why not?

BABETTE   Not matches?

BIEDERMANN   If they really were firebugs, do you think they wouldn't have matches? Don't be foolish, Babette! [*The clock strikes. Silence. The red light onstage begins deepening into blackness. Sirens. Bells ring. Dogs howl. Cars honk . . . A crash of collapsing buildings. A crackling of flames. Screams and outcries . . . fading. The* CHORUS *comes on again.*]

CHORUS   Useless, quite useless.
  And nothing more useless
  Than this useless story.
  For arson, once kindled,
  Kills many,
  Leaves few,
  And accomplishes nothing.
    [*First detonation.*]

LEADER   That was the gas works.
    [*Second detonation.*]

CHORUS   Long foreseen, disaster
  Has reached us at last.
  Horrendous arson!
  Unquenchable fire!

Fate—so they call it!
[*Third detonation.*]

LEADER More gas tanks.
[*There is a series of frightful explosions.*]

CHORUS Woe to us! Woe to us! Woe!
[*The house lights go up.*]

SCENE NINE

Epilog

CHARACTERS OF THE EPILOG

HERR BIEDERMANN
BABETTE
ANNA
BEELZEBUB
A PERSONAGE
A POLICEMAN
A RING-TAILED MONKEY
THE WIDOW KNECHTLING
THE CHORUS

BABETTE *and* BIEDERMANN *are revealed, standing in the same positions as at the end of the previous scene.*

BABETTE Gottlieb?

BIEDERMANN Sh!

BABETTE Are we dead? [*A parrot screeches.*]

BIEDERMANN Why didn't you come down before the stairs caught fire? Why did you run to our bedroom again?

BABETTE I went back for my jewelry.

BIEDERMANN Of course we're dead. [*The parrot squawks.*]

BABETTE Gottlieb?

BIEDERMANN Quiet, now.

BABETTE Where are we?

BIEDERMANN In heaven, of course. Where else? [*A baby cries.*]

BABETTE I never imagined heaven was like this. [*The baby cries again.*]

BIEDERMANN Don't lose your faith at a time like this!

BABETTE Did *you* imagine it this way? [*The parrot screeches.*] Gottlieb?

BIEDERMANN Don't lose your faith at a time like this.

BABETTE We've been waiting half an eternity. [*The baby cries.*] And now that baby again! [*The parrot screeches.*] Gottlieb?

BIEDERMANN What now?

BABETTE How did that parrot get into heaven? [*A doorbell rings.*]

BIEDERMANN Don't upset me, Babette. Why can't a parrot go to heaven? If he's led a good life? [*The doorbell rings again.*] What was that?

BABETTE Our doorbell.

BIEDERMANN Who can *that* be? [*The baby, the bell and the parrot all sound off together.*]

BABETTE Who needs that parrot? And that baby, too! I won't be able to take it, Gottlieb—a racket like that, forever! Why, it's just like the slums!

BIEDERMANN Sh!

BABETTE They can't expect us to—

BIEDERMANN Calm down.

BABETTE People like us are not used to it.

BIEDERMANN [*Considering it.*] Why wouldn't we be in heaven? Everybody we know is there—even my lawyer. This *must* be heaven! We've done nothing wrong— [*The doorbell rings.*]

BABETTE Shouldn't we answer the doorbell? [*It rings again.*] How did they get hold of our bell? [*It rings again.*] Maybe an angel calling . . .

BIEDERMANN I'm perfectly innocent. I honored my father and mother—you know that, Babette. Especially Mother—you were sore about that often enough. I never made a graven image of God—never thought of it, even. I never stole; we always had what we needed. I never killed anybody. I never worked Sundays. I never coveted my neighbor's house. Or if I did, I paid cash for it. Buying's permitted, I'm sure. And I never caught myself lying. I never committed adultery, Babette—I mean it; compared with others, at least . . . You are my witness, Babette, before the angels. I had only one earthly fault: I was too good-hearted. [*The parrot screeches.*]

BABETTE Can you understand what it's saying?

BIEDERMANN Did *you* kill anybody, Babette? I'm only asking, that's all. Or worship other gods? Outside of a little Yoga? Did you ever commit adultery?

BABETTE With whom?

BIEDERMANN Well, then—[*The doorbell rings.*] We *must* be in heaven. [ANNA *enters in cap and apron.*]

BABETTE How did Anna get into heaven? [ANNA *walks past. She has long, green hair.*] I hope she didn't notice that you gave them the matches. She might report it.

BIEDERMANN The matches!

BABETTE I warned you they were firebugs, Gottlieb. I warned you from the beginning. [ANNA *comes back with a* POLICEMAN. *The* POLICEMAN *has little white wings.*]

ANNA I'll call him. [*She exits. The* POLICEMAN *waits.*]

BIEDERMANN You see? An angel. [*The* POLICEMAN *salutes.*]

BABETTE I thought angels looked different.

BIEDERMANN This isn't the Middle Ages.

BABETTE Didn't *you* think they looked different? [*The* POLICEMAN *turns around. Continues to wait.*] Should we kneel, do you think?

BIEDERMANN Ask him if this is heaven. [*Encouraging her with a nod.*] We've been waiting half an eternity, tell him.

BABETTE My husband and I—

BIEDERMANN Tell him we're victims.

BABETTE My husband and I are victims.

BIEDERMANN Our house is ruined.

BABETTE My husband and I—

BIEDERMANN Tell him!

BABETTE Ruined.

BIEDERMANN He simply can't imagine what we've gone through. Tell him! We've lost everything, tell him. And it's in no way our fault.

BABETTE You can't imagine—

BIEDERMANN What we've gone through.

BABETTE All my jewelry melted.

BIEDERMANN Tell him we're innocent.

BABETTE Besides, we're innocent.

BIEDERMANN Compared with others.

BABETTE Compared with others. [*The* ANGEL-POLICEMAN *takes out a cigar.*]

POLICEMAN Have you a match? [BIEDERMANN *turns pale.*]

BIEDERMANN I? A match? [*A tongue of flame shoots up from the ground.*]

POLICEMAN I've got a light, thanks. Never mind. [BABETTE *and* BIEDERMANN *stare at the flame, astonished.*]

BABETTE Gottlieb—

BIEDERMANN Quiet!

BABETTE What does all this mean? [*Enter a* RING-TAILED MONKEY.]

MONKEY Who are these people?

POLICEMAN A couple of the damned. [*He hands over a report. The* MONKEY *puts on his glasses.*]

BABETTE Gottlieb, we know him!

BIEDERMANN Where from?

BABETTE The professor. Don't you remember? [*The* MONKEY *leafs through the report.*]

MONKEY How are things upstairs?

POLICEMAN No use complaining. Nobody knows where God lives, but otherwise everything's fine. No use complaining, thank you.

MONKEY [*Indicating the report.*] Why was this bunch sent here? [*The* POLICEMAN *glances at the report.*]

POLICEMAN Freethinkers. [*The* MONKEY *has ten rubber stamps. He chooses from them, stamping each document.*]

MONKEY "THOU SHALT HAVE NO OTHER GODS BEFORE ME."

POLICEMAN A doctor who gave wrong injections.

MONKEY "THOU SHALT NOT KILL."

POLICEMAN A board chairman with seven secretaries—all blonde.

MONKEY "THOU SHALT NOT COMMIT ADULTERY."

POLICEMAN An abortionist.

MONKEY "THOU SHALT NOT KILL."

POLICEMAN A drunk driver.

MONKEY "THOU SHALT NOT KILL."

POLICEMAN Refugees.

MONKEY What's their sin?

POLICEMAN Fifty-two potatoes, one umbrella, two wool blankets.

MONKEY "THOU SHALT NOT STEAL."

POLICEMAN A tax consultant.

MONKEY "THOU SHALT NOT BEAR FALSE WITNESS."

POLICEMAN Another drunk driver. [*The* MONKEY *stamps the paper silently.*] Another freethinker. [*Ditto.*] Seven underground fighters. Sent to heaven by mistake. They were caught and shot by a firing squad; but it seems they did some so-called liberating before then.

MONKEY Hm.

POLICEMAN Liberating while out of uniform.

MONKEY "THOU SHALT NOT STEAL."

POLICEMAN Another abortionist.

MONKEY "THOU SHALT NOT KILL."

POLICEMAN And here's the rest.

MONKEY "THOU SHALT NOT COMMIT ADULTERY." [*He stamps at least thirteen more reports.*] Nothing but middle-class! Old

Nick will be furious! And all these juvenile delinquents! I'm almost afraid of turning in this report! No general, no cabinet minister— not one celebrity in the lot!

POLICEMAN   Ts. Ts.

MONKEY   Take them down below. Beelzebub's already got the heat turned on, I think, or is about to. [THE POLICEMAN *salutes and exits.*]

BABETTE   Gottlieb, we are in hell!

BIEDERMANN   Don't scream like that.

BABETTE   Gottlieb— [*She breaks into sobs.*]

BIEDERMANN   There's something wrong here, Professor—it's got to be changed. How is it we're in hell, my wife and I? [*To* BABETTE.] Keep calm, Babette, this *must* be a mistake. [*To the* MONKEY.] Let me speak with the Devil.

BABETTE   Gottlieb—

BIEDERMANN   May I speak with the Devil, please?

MONKEY   [*With a gesture.*] Sit down, please. [BIEDERMANN *and* BABETTE *see no seats to sit down on.*] What do you want to see him about? [BIEDERMANN *hands him a card.*] What is that?

BIEDERMANN   Driver's license—identification.

MONKEY   Not required. [*He returns it without looking at it.*] You're Gottlieb Biedermann? Manufacturer? Big bank account?

BIEDERMANN   How did you know?

MONKEY   Number 33 Rosenweg? The Devil knows you well. [BABETTE *and* BIEDERMANN *look at each other.*] Take seats, please. [*Two burned chairs appear onstage.*]

BABETTE   Gottlieb—our chairs!

MONKEY   Sit down, please. [*They sit.*] Do you smoke?

BIEDERMANN   Not any more.

MONKEY   Your own cigars, you know. [*He helps himself to a cigar.*] They were burned, too. I'm sure that doesn't surprise you. [*Flames shoot up from the floor.*] I have a light, thank you. [*He lights his cigar and takes a puff.*] Now come to the point—what is it you want? Some bread? Some wine, maybe?

BIEDERMANN   We have no place to sleep! [*The* MONKEY *calls.*]

MONKEY   Anna!

BABETTE   We're not beggars, we're victims.

BIEDERMANN   We don't want charity. We're not used to it.

BABETTE   And we don't need it. [ANNA *appears.*]

ANNA   Yes?

MONKEY   They don't want charity.

ANNA   That's all right, then. [*She exits.*]

BABETTE   We had our own home.

BIEDERMANN   We demand compensation! [*The* MONKEY *withdraws without answering, as is the way of bureaucrats.*]

BABETTE   What does he mean, "The Devil knows you"?

BIEDERMANN   How should *I* know? [*A pendulum clock strikes.*]

BABETTE   Our grandfather clock! [*It strikes nine.*]

BIEDERMANN   I shall insist that everything be put back where it was! We were insured! [*The* MONKEY *returns from stage left.*]

MONKEY   One moment, please. [*Exists stage right.*]

BIEDERMANN   These devils put on an act!

BABETTE   Sh!

BIEDERMANN   Next thing you know they'll ask for our fingerprints, like the police. To try and give us a bad conscience. [BABETTE *puts her hand on his arm comfortably.*] My conscience is clear. So is yours—

BABETTE   What if they ask about the matches?

BIEDERMANN   I gave those boys matches, that's true. But what of it? So did everybody else. Or the whole city wouldn't have burned down the way it did. I saw the flames spring out over every roof . . . And don't forget I acted in good faith!

BABETTE   You're too excited.

BIEDERMANN   And even if everybody did it, you can't throw everybody into hell! What about forgiveness? [*The* MONKEY *returns.*]

MONKEY   The Lord of the Underworld isn't back yet. Would you care to speak with Beelzebub instead?

BABETTE   Beelzebub?

MONKEY   He's around. But I warn you he smells something awful. He's the one with the horns, the hoofs and the tail . . . But don't expect much from *him*, madam—a poor devil like Sepp!

BIEDERMANN   Sepp? [BABETTE *jumps up in alarm.*]

BABETTE   Gottlieb, what did I tell you?

BIEDERMANN   Babette! [*He gives her a look that sits her down again.*] My wife couldn't sleep nights. That's when you toss and worry. But by day, Professor, we had no ground for suspicion—none whatever. [BABETTE *gives him a look.*] At least *I* didn't.

BABETTE Then why were you going to throw them out of the house?

BIEDERMANN I didn't throw them out.

BABETTE That's just it.

BIEDERMANN Why didn't *you* throw them out? Instead of feeding them toast and marmalade and soft-boiled eggs? [*The* MONKEY *puffs at his cigar.*] To be brief, Professor, we had no idea what was going on at home. No idea. [*Trumpets sound.*]

MONKEY That's him—the Lord of the Underworld. [*Trumpets.*] In a terrible temper, no doubt. He's been up to heaven; probably had another tough session.

BIEDERMANN On my account?

MONKEY On account of this last amnesty . . . [*He whispers in* BIEDERMANN'S *ear.*]

BIEDERMANN I've heard about that.

MONKEY And what do you say to this? [*He whispers again.*]

BIEDERMANN You think so?

MONKEY If heaven thinks we're going to stand for anything and everything— [*He whispers again.*]

BIEDERMANN You mean it? [*Trumpets.*]

MONKEY He's coming! [*The* MONKEY *exits.*]

BABETTE What did he say?

BIEDERMANN They may close the doors of hell; no more people admitted. Because hell is going on strike. [*Doorbell rings.*] He says they're furious down here. They've been expecting a whole army of big shots, and it seems heaven has pardoned them all. He says it's a hell of a crisis. [ANNA *crosses from left to right.*] What's Anna doing here?

BABETTE I didn't tell you: she stole a pair of my new nylons. [ANNA *comes in with the* WIDOW KNECHTLING.]

ANNA Sit down, please. But don't get up any hopes: your husband committed suicide, you know. [ANNA *exits. The* WIDOW *remains standing, there being no more seats.*]

BABETTE It's Frau Knechtling! What does she want here? [*She gives the* WIDOW *a smile.*] She's going to testify against us, Gottlieb.

BIEDERMANN Let her! [*The trumpets sound closer.*] Why couldn't Knechtling have waited a week or two? He could have taken me aside at a favorable moment and talked it over,

couldn't he? How could I know he was going to commit suicide just because I gave him his notice? [*The trumpets sound closer.*] I'm not worried. [*The trumpets sound closer.*] Those matches!

BABETTE Maybe nobody saw you.

BIEDERMANN There've always been disasters! Always were and always will be! . . . Besides, look at our city now—everything glass and aluminum! In fact it's a blessing, really, that the town burned down. From the standpoint of city planning . . . [*Trumpets, then organ music. Enter a* PERSONAGE, *pompous and resplendent, in a costume slightly reminiscent of a bishop.* BIEDERMANN *and* BABETTE *kneel at the footlights. The* PERSONAGE *takes center stage.*]

PERSONAGE [*Calls.*] Anna! [*He starts to take off his violet gloves.*] I'm back from heaven.

BIEDERMANN [*To* BABETTE.] You hear that?

PERSONAGE It's hopeless. [*He calls.*] Anna! [*He goes on taking off his gloves.*] I wonder if it really was heaven I saw—even though they told me it was. They had incense coming out of loudspeakers. And the medals on everybody! My old friends, the mass-murderers, with chests full of medals! And the angels hovering over them, full of smiles! Everybody chatting, strolling, drinking toasts! The saints had nothing to say; they're made of wood, on permanent loan from somewhere. As for the princes of the church—I tried to ask them where God lives, but they shut up, too, even though they're *not* made of wood . . . [*He calls.*] Anna! [*He removes his hood. It is* EISENRING.] I was disguised, of course. And the folks who are running things up there— and are busy blessing themselves—didn't recognize me. I added my blessing . . . [ANNA *and the* MONKEY *enter and bow.*] Remove this clothing. [*The* PERSONAGE *holds out his arms to permit his four silken garments, one over the other, to be unbuttoned. These are, in order, silver, gold, violet and blood-red. The organ music ends.* BIEDERMANN *and* BABETTE *continue to kneel.*] Bring my tail-coat.

ANNA Yes sir.

PERSONAGE And my head-waiter's wig. [ANNA *and the* MONKEY *remove his first garment.*] I have some doubts whether it was God Himself who received me. He knew everything, and when He spoke He said exactly what the newspapers say, word for word. [*The parrot shrieks.*] Where is Beelzebub?

MONKEY   At the furnaces.

PERSONAGE   Let him appear. [*The stage suddenly turns red.*] What is this glare?

MONKEY   He's heating the furnaces. A new batch of sinners; the usual kind. [*They remove the second garment.*]

PERSONAGE   Let him put out the furnaces.

MONKEY   Put them out?

PERSONAGE   Put them out! [*The parrot shrieks.*] How is my parrot? [*He notices* BABETTE *and* BIEDERMANN.] Ask those people why they're praying.

MONKEY   They're not praying.

PERSONAGE   They're kneeling.

MONKEY   They want their home back. Compensation. [*The parrot screeches.*]

PERSONAGE   My lovely parrot! I found him in a burning house. The only creature who doesn't change his tune! He's going to ride on my shoulder when I go up to earth again. [ANNA *and the* MONKEY *remove his third garment.*] Bring the bicycles, Professor. [*The* MONKEY *bows and exits.*]

BIEDERMANN   Willi, don't you know me? I'm your friend Gottlieb!

BABETTE   We're innocent, Herr Eisenring! [ANNA *removes the* PERSONAGE's *fourth garment.*] Why does he pretend not to know us?

PERSONAGE   Bring two velvet cushions, Anna, for these people who are kneeling.

ANNA   Yes sir. [*She exits.*]

PERSONAGE   I remember everything, Gottlieb. You went so far as to kiss the Devil. [*The parrot calls.*]

BABETTE   But, Willi, if we had known you were the Devil—if we had had the slightest inkling — [ANNA *brings the frock-coat and the cushions.*]

PERSONAGE   Thank you, Anna. They won't need those cushions now—Where's Beelzebub?

BEELZEBUB   [*Appears.*] Here. [*It is* SEPP, *wearing horns, hoofs and goat tail, and carrying a huge shovel.*]

PERSONAGE   Don't roar like that!—We're going back to earth, Sepp. [ANNA *is helping him dress.*] Have you put out the ovens?

BEELZEBUB   No. I've just shoveled more coal on. [*A reflection of flames flickers over the stage.*]

PERSONAGE   Do as I tell you. [*He calls.*] Professor! [*To* SEPP.] I got nowhere with heaven. They won't give up a single one of their sinners.

BEELZEBUB   Not even one? [*The* MONKEY *enters.*]

PERSONAGE   Call the Fire Department! [*The* MONKEY *bows and exits.*] Not one! They're all saved! Anybody who kills while in uniform. Or who promises to wear a uniform while killing. Or who orders killing by others in uniform— all are saved!

BEELZEBUB   Saved?!

PERSONAGE   Don't roar like that! [*An echo is heard from above.*]

ECHO   Saved! Saved! Saved! [BEELZEBUB *glares up at the sound.*]

PERSONAGE   Get your earthly clothes on, Sepp; we're going back to work. [*The* CHORUS *enters.*]

CHORUS   Woe!

BABETTE   Gottlieb, what are *they* doing here?

CHORUS   Fellow-citizens, see
Our pitiful helplessness!
Tested and ready were we,
Equipped with engines and hose;
Now we're forever condemned
To view the fires of hell
As they roast our citizens well.

PERSONAGE   Gentlemen, put out the fires of hell! [*The* CHORUS *is startled.*] I don't intend to run hell for the sake of middle-of-the-roaders, lowbrows, highbrows, liberals, pickpockets, adulterers, slackers and servant girls who steal nylon stockings! [*The* CHORUS *is motionless.*] What are you waiting for?

CHORUS   Ready for action
Axes and fire-hose;
Polished and oiled,
Every brass fitting;
Every man of us tested and ready.
Our brass fire-pump
Polished and oiled,
Tested for pressure.

LEADER   And the fire-hydrants?

CHORUS   Tested and ready for action.

PERSONAGE   Then get going! [*The flickering red light, which had begun to die down, blazes up again.*]

LEADER   To the hoses!
The pumps!

The ladders!

[*The* FIREMEN *quickly take places.*]

PERSONAGE   Ready! [*The hiss of water is heard. The flames start to go out.*] And now, my wig, my bicycle and my parrot!

BEELZEBUB   What have they done to my childhood belief? "Thou shalt not kill," they said. And I believed them! [*The* PERSONAGE *polishes his fingernails.*] I, Sepp Schmitz, son of a miner and a gipsy—I belong to the Devil. "Go to the devil, Sepp," they said, and I went. I told lies, because lies make things easier. I stole where I listed and whored where I lusted. The villages feared me, for I was strong with the strength of the Devil. I tripped up the villagers on their way to church. I burned down their barns on Sundays while they prayed. I laughed at their loving God, who had no love for me . . . Who closed the mine-shaft that buried my father? My mother, praying for me, died of grief at my capers . . . I burned down the orphans' home—for fun! I burned down the circus—for fun! I set fire to town after town—all for fun, for fun! [*The* PERSONAGE *laughs.*] There's nothing to laugh at, Willi! [ANNA *brings the wig. The* MONKEY *brings two rusty bicycles.*] There's nothing to laugh at. What have they done with my childhood belief? It's enough to make one throw up! [*The* PERSONAGE *has put on his wig.*]

PERSONAGE   Make ready! [*He takes one of the rusty bicycles.*] How I burn to see them again —the big boys who never get sent here . . . And a good, crackling fire—alarms that are always too late—smoke—the howling of dogs and of people—and ashes! [BEELZEBUB *takes off his hoofs and his tail.*] Are we ready? [*He jumps on his bicycle and rings the bell.*]

BEELZEBUB   One moment—

LEADER   Stop pumping!
Down hoses!
Turn off the water!

[*The red shimmer dies out completely.*]

PERSONAGE   Your horns, Sepp! [BEELZEBUB *removes his horns, jumps on the other bicycle and rings the bell.*]

PERSONAGE   [*To* ANNA.] Thank you, my girl . . . But you're always so gloomy! I heard you laugh only once—when we were singing that song. [ANNA *laughs.*] Some day we'll sing it again.

ANNA   Oh, please do! [*The* CHORUS *comes forward.*]

CHORUS   Fellow-citizens, we—

PERSONAGE   Make it short, please!

CHORUS   Hell's fires are out.

PERSONAGE   Thank you. [*He reaches in his pants pocket.*] Got any matches?

BEELZEBUB   No. Have you?

PERSONAGE   Never mind. Somebody'll give us some. [*The* MONKEY *enters with the parrot.*] My parrot! [*He perches the parrot on his right shoulder.*] Before I forget, Professor: we're taking in no more souls. Tell heaven hell is on strike. And if any angel comes looking for us, tell him we're back on earth. [BEELZEBUB *rings his bicycle bell.*] Let's go. [SCHMITZ *and* EISENRING *ride away, waving.*]

BOTH   Good luck, Gottlieb, good luck! [*The* CHORUS *comes forward.*]

CHORUS   O radiant sun!
O godlike eye!
Light up the day—

LEADER   Above our rebuilt city.

CHORUS   Hallelujah!

[*The parrot squawks far off.*]

BABETTE   Gottlieb?

BIEDERMANN   Sh!

BABETTE   Are we saved?

BIEDERMANN   Don't lose your faith at a time like this. [*The* WIDOW KNECHTLING *exits.*]

CHORUS   Hallelujah!

BABETTE   Frau Knechtling is gone—

CHORUS   Lovelier than before,
Risen from its ruins and its ashes
Is our city.
Removed and forgotten is the rubbish;
Forgotten, too, the men and women
Whose cries rose from the flames.

BIEDERMANN   Life goes on.

CHORUS   Historic are they now,
Those people.
And silent.

LEADER   Hallelujah!

CHORUS   Lovelier than before,
And richer,
Skyscraper-modern,
All chrome and glass,
Yet ever the same
At heart.
Hallelujah!
Reborn is our city!

[*Organ music.*]

BABETTE Gottlieb?
BIEDERMANN What is it?
BABETTE Do you think we're saved?
BIEDERMANN Yes, I think so . . .

[*The organ music swells.* BABETTE *and* BIEDERMANN *are on their knees.*]

Comments and Questions

1. Compare the use of a Chorus in this play with its use in *Antigone, The Caucasian Chalk Circle,* and *The Visit.* (For a list of functions the Greek Chorus performed, see p. 439.) Why, do you suppose, has this ancient device become popular again? Consider the matter of conformity. Do large segments of modern-day society think and speak as one? If so, how does the tendency toward conformity clash with today's emphasis upon permissiveness?

2. The central thesis of this play can be summarized by the word *appeasement,* a concept that had grave significance for the Western world in the late thirties. What steps does Biedermann take to ward off harm from the arsonists? What is the significance of Biedermann's final gesture in scene viii?

3. What does the Ph.D. represent? Trace the steps leading to his too-late awakening.

4. This play invites many speculations about current conditions in the world and particularly in the United States. Permissiveness, for example, is a mark of our times: everybody may do as he likes. This new "freedom" gives broad privileges to the responsible and to the irresponsible. The responsible fear to judge, to control, but instead, like Biedermann, attempt to placate. Against this abject attitude, the firebugs become bolder and bolder. Consider the way violence is handled in America.

BIOGRAPHY

No one can write a man's life but himself.
—ROUSSEAU

PRELIMINARIES

THE BIOGRAPHICAL URGE

The biographical urge is best illustrated by our daily habit of probing into the health, habits, and affairs of others. We ask many questions which we could summarize as one demand: "Bring me up to date on your biography." The asker frequently awaits eagerly his chance to be the answerer. We have here, therefore, a pleasant arrangement through which we can partly satisfy our natural desire to talk about ourselves and to hear others talk about themselves. Perhaps the question of where idle talk about others (gossip) leaves off and serious talk about others (biography) begins is a matter of motivation. In any event, there is a great deal of entertaining talk, gossip or not, in the best biographies from earliest to latest times.

We want first of all and perhaps last of all to find out about ourselves, but in order to do this, we soon realize that we must find out as much as possible about others. We are essentially lonely. We live exclusively with ourselves, but only rarely do we like this arrangement of life. Much of our effort is expended in an attempt to live sociably—to break through to other persons. Yet the most sociable, outgoing person collects in a lifetime not more than a few hundred acquaintances out of perhaps two billion persons theoretically available to him. Of the acquaintances, only a few become intimates. If, therefore, one wishes any real quantitative extension of himself, any considerable relief for his isolation, he cannot depend upon his limited sphere of social activity.

He may, of course, sit out his life contemplating his navel. He is more likely, however, to contemplate some form, or forms, of art to relieve his boredom with himself and to remove some of the uncertainty about himself. All arts, because they are communicative, are attacks on the loneliness of the individual. Literature makes the most direct attack, and biography pinpoints it.

"That's just a tale," we may say, and the teller may protest, "No, it's not. It really happened." We like what "really happened." We are real, and our first taste is to hear about real persons like or unlike ourselves. If they are like ourselves, we enjoy the recognition of the likeness; we feel greater confidence in what we may have only suspected from self-examination to be true. If they are unlike ourselves, we enjoy the strangeness of the differences; we are extended. After much pondering over the lives of others, we come to understand the force of John Donne's insistence on the oneness of man:

> No man is an Island, entire of itself; every man is a piece of the *Continent*, a part of the *main*, if a *Clod* be washed away by the *Sea*, *Europe* is the less, as well as if a *Promontory* were, as well as if a Manor of thy *friends* or of *thine own* were, any man's *death* diminishes *me*, because I am involved in *Mankind;* and therefore never send to know for whom the *bell* tolls; it tolls for *thee*. [*Devotions upon Emergent Occasions*, 1624, No. XVII.]

We are indeed involved in mankind, deeply and intricately involved; and if a death—any death—diminishes us, a life—any life—increases us. Biographical writings seek to suspend oblivion for certain individuals, and one has but to imagine a world without any life-records to realize how shrunken and parochial such a world would be.

THE IMPORTANCE OF FACTS

Biography, like science, begins with fact. It presents specifics about individuals and is not required to illustrate representative truth (see "General Preliminaries"). It is concerned with heredity and environment, with ancestry, birth, education, marriage, escapades, failures, and triumphs. At one level, facts exclude the biographer and make of him a mere recorder. He must respect verified dates and occurrences and, if he uses them, must set them down as they are. Here then is an important difference between nonfictional and fictional forms of literature: in nonfiction the writer deals with facts but does not create them; in fiction, the writer may create the facts with which he deals. It is possible to challenge a fictional fact on the ground that it does not jibe with comparable nonfictional facts. A biographical fact, once proved, is simply incontrovertible and is not subject to either belief or disbelief. It *is*.

Does the sort of interest one has in a narrative depend upon whether it is truth or fiction? Here is one way to test for an answer. Consider the following bare account:

A family consisting of a father, mother, daughter and son live together. The father, though fairly well off, neglects the family. The son is subject to mental disorders. His sister, ten years his senior and apparently more normal, one day in a sudden fit of insanity kills her mother with a table-knife. The brother becomes his sister's guardian and cares for her, with no recurrence of his own malady, until his death thirty-eight years later. Toward the end of his life his sister's mental disturbances become more frequent and of longer duration. After the brother's death, the sister lives on for thirteen years without further mental troubles.

Does it make any difference whether we are here dealing with fact or fiction, with what really happened or with what has been made up? If the facts were invented, we would give the author a chance to make his facts probable. We would not care very much what names he gave his characters but would care a great deal about the handling of what seems to be the big scene—the murder of the mother—and the explanation of how a man could be mad and then sane and a woman could be sane, then mad, then sane again. Although we know that sudden murders do occur and that temporary insanity is a common defense for such murders, we tend not to believe in them in fiction. Insanity itself is in general suspect as a fictional device. If there is method in the madness, we see that

as super-shrewdness and accept it—at least in Hamlet—but insist that nothing important in a story shall hinge on an insane (irresponsible) action.

We can see the difference immediately if the facts, as stated, are true. If the father, mother, daughter, and son are real people, we want to know at once *who* they are—what are their names? Suppose the answer is that these people are Mr. and Mrs. John Doe and Mary and Charles Doe. Accounts of such persons might appear in a psychiatrist's case book, or perhaps in the records of the hearing for murder. Our interest would center chiefly in the queerness of the case, and the names, as in a fictional account, would matter less. If, however, these people are famous *for other reasons*, if instead of Mr. and Mrs. John Doe, the father and mother are Mr. and Mrs. John Lamb, the daughter, Mary Lamb, and the key figure, Charles Lamb, our interest gains a new perspective.

A biographer may seek a logical motivation for Mary Lamb's brutal action, but if he fails to find it, the fact remains, and he must accept it, just as we must. Herein lies the truth of the observation that fact is stranger than fiction. Fact is stranger than good fiction or good drama dares to be, for facts stubbornly remain even when their logic is not apparent.

WHAT TO DO WITH THE FACTS: THREE PROBLEMS

Every life moves in an unbroken sequence from birth to death. Every action follows a previous action, every thought a previous thought in uninterrupted series. Let us suppose that a man of considerable interest to the public had a life span of fifty-two years, or, deducting time out for sleep, 303,680 waking hours. Something went on during each of those hours; all were significant in making up the total account of this man. The ideal biographer writing the ideal biography should know those hours, all of them. Of course, he never does. If his subject is Shakespeare—who lived fifty-two years—he has no problem of selection at all. He can put down with three drops of ink—though he may use a barrel—all that is surely known of this man from Stratford. A hampering lack of facts, then, may be and frequently is one of the biographer's problems.

The second problem, a reverse of the first, is that too many facts may prove an embarrassment. Queen Victoria lived for eighty-two years, and there are probably more records available for any one year of her life than have been found for all of Shakespeare's fifty-two years. It is staggering to imagine the lofty mountain of facts already accumulated about Queen Elizabeth II. Of course, the biographer is better off with abundance than with famine, but his problems as an artist are greatly increased. The essence of art is selection, the removal of the superfluous so that a convincing portrait remains. All the selections which follow illustrate this point. (Compare, also, "General Preliminaries.")

The third problem is an ethical one and exists whenever the facts are in adequate supply. It amounts to this: What shall be done with facts which may throw a bad light on an essentially good man or a good light on an essentially evil man? Suppose it could be determined—it seldom can—that a man is nine-tenths saint and one-tenth sinner. One biographer might make such a man all saint; another, with somewhat less justification, all scoundrel. The first biographer may have observed, as Somerset Maugham says, that "people turn away with dismay when candid biographers reveal the truth about famous persons." But the second biographer, the debunker, may also tilt the balance too far and produce false weight. We shall note with what skill Boswell, who idolized Samuel Johnson, handled the problem of keeping his great hero in perspective.

FACTS ARE NOT ENOUGH

If we regard facts as the bony structure of biography, we must next look for the flesh and blood. The facts about Charles and Mary Lamb, as given above, are momentarily arresting but tell only *what* happened. The questions of *when, where,* and *why* are not answered. More important, interpretive details are lacking, flesh for the bones. Let us look for a moment at a plain statement of fact: "Richard Rodgers wrote the music for 'Bali Ha'i' in five minutes." This, or

something like it, was doubtless one of Lincoln Barnett's notes when he sat down to write a close-up of the composer Richard Rodgers. From the following anecdote, we may see how appropriate is the word *close-up.*

To others who may labor for hours to evolve a usable phrase, the fluency with which music wells from Rodgers is profoundly discouraging. "He could write music to the telephone book," a friend once remarked. Where it may take Hammerstein two or three weeks to complete a single set of lyrics that satisfy his rigorous poetic standards, Rodgers often exudes his loveliest melodies in a matter of minutes. Asked to describe their methods of collaboration, Hammerstein once said: "I simply hand him a lyric and get out of the way." One evening a few weeks before *South Pacific* was due to enter rehearsal, several observers had an opportunity to witness this system of operation. Rodgers was dining with a few friends at the home of Joshua Logan, the director and playwright. Coffee had just been served when Hammerstein arrived, happily waving the completed lyrics to the final song that remained to be written for the show. It was "Bali Ha'i." Rodgers quickly scanned the typewritten verses. Then pushing his demitasse to one side, he took out a pencil, drew a staff on the paper Hammerstein had given him, and without visible hesitation began writing down notes. Five minutes later he laid down his pencil. The melody for "Bali Ha'i," which a few weeks hence was to be whistled across the land, was done. Not a note or an accent had to be changed after those first few minutes of swift creation. [*Writing on Life: Sixteen Close-Ups,* New York, 1951, pp. 293–294.]

What has happened to the plain fact? Obviously there are many more words in the anecdote: 11 for the plain fact and 240 for the anecdote. Of what use are these additional words? The fact was already clear; the extra words do not made it clearer. The anecdote does not seek out and illuminate a hidden meaning, for apparently there is no hidden meaning. Yet we certainly *feel* that the anecdote gave us a kind of pleasure which the plain statement did not. By discovering the source of this pleasure, we reveal a basic truth about all literature: *literature does not merely tell, it shows.* Although far removed from the actual experience, the reader participates in the recounting of the experience. In the anecdote, it is as though the author, operating a camera on a moving crane, had taken his first picture of the subject at a distance and then had moved steadily closer until the eye of the camera hovered over the composer's shoulder as he wrote his music. The plain fact *told* us something: the anecdote *showed* us something.

THE ANECDOTE

What It is

An anecdote, as we have seen, is a moment of biography, the shortest form of a complete narrative. In it something of interest happens. "I was at a lawn party and shook hands with the host, who said, 'I'm glad to see you.'" Is this an anecdote? Something happens, but is it interesting? It could be, of course, but much depends upon which lawn and which host. "I was at a party on the White House lawn and shook hands with the President, who said, 'I'm glad to see you.'" Further details would *show* us this meeting with the President and the result would be a satisfactory anecdote.

Its Uses

An anecdote may be told for its own sake, for one of its requirements is the ability to stand on its own merits. Nevertheless, it normally is used to illustrate some sort of generalization, to *show* what the generalization means. Anecdotes, even when they may not be true, make broad statements memorable. Generalization: George Washington was always truthful. Anecdote: the cherry tree episode. Generalization: Richard Rodgers is a rapid composer. Anecdote: the composition of "Bali Ha'i." Generalization: God takes care of His own. Anecdote: "God brought me safe." (See p. 757).

Generalizations such as those just cited are subject to comment and perhaps to argument. Biographical sketches frequently resemble the essay in that they support generalizations which invite discussion and, in some instances, argument. "The Oxford Method" (p. 747) does more than report the meeting between a student and an Oxford tutor. Many of the sketches which follow are really dramatized essays. They are related, on the one hand, to short stories and, on the other, to essays. As essays, they provide some excellent topics for discussion, written or oral.

Quotations

A decided characteristic of biographical writing is the frequent use of direct quotation. The writer of autobiography in particular is prone to tell his experiences through dialogue. Rather than tell the reader about the experience, he prefers to show it to him, to let him hear the actual words that were spoken. (Why does the autobiographer feel a greater freedom in the use of dialogue than a biographer may feel?) To bring the reader into the presence of people talking is a technique almost as important to the autobiographer as to the novelist or the writer of short stories. Later we shall see that dialogue represents only one sort of quotation and that biographers use quotations for at least three other purposes (see p. 791).

Allusion

An allusion is a passing or casual reference. In "The Oxford Method" Logan Pearsall Smith refers in passing to "Socratic irony" and does not elaborate because he assumes that the reader knows what the phrase means. We mention allusion here, not because it is a distinctive feature of biographical writing (it is not), but because readers can find it baffling. The passing references in the anecdotal selections are few and not very difficult; you can prepare for your later reading by examining these allusions and learning to solve them.

Its Technique

1. POINT OF VIEW. The position from which an experience is seen is the point of view. All the following anecdotes are autobiographical with the exception of those taken from Boswell's *Life of Johnson*, and one might assume that autobiography would, by definition, have a fixed point of view. The author is writing about himself, and it is from his point of view that the incidents are told. This statement is true but not the whole truth. Rousseau indicates the difficulty in separating fact from fiction. The autobiographer is frequently an older man trying to recapture an experience of his youth. If our bodies completely change every seven years, as

we are told they do, then the older man is really trying to recover an experience that happened to someone else. The older man may adopt any one of numerous possible points of view. You may see what the possibilities are by comparing "A Cub Pilot's Experience" (p. 764) and "Christmas" (p. 758).

2. TIMING. In conversation, good timing is the ability to come to the point before someone tells you to. In literature, it is the ability to come to the point before the reader wishes he could tell the writer to. When we say that a literary artist tries to measure out exactly the right number of words, in the right sequence, to achieve his purpose, we are talking about timing. It is clear that the anecdote about the composition of "Bali Ha'i" shows resistance to some tempting side excursions. For example, the author might have said more about Oscar Hammerstein II or Joshua Logan, both important men in the theater. He might have described Logan's home, the other guests, or even the dinner. By resisting such temptations he achieved effective timing.

3. FUSION OF FACT AND FORM. Facts are the basis of all selections in this section, but as we have said before, facts are not enough. Some facts, of course, are unalterable and can be put down in one way only. Most of the information which we carry about in our heads in the form of memory is definitely alterable; that is, it may be put down in many different ways, and *how* it is put down will largely determine its meaning. The basic question for all writers is this: How can I make my material mean to the reader what it means to me? Three closely related processes are involved in the answer to this question: *selection, arrangement,* and *choice of words.* It is through these processes that fact and form are blended or fused. Once the selecting, arranging, and wording have been settled, the result is unique. For better or for worse, the wedding is permanent. This does not mean that all marriages between What and How were made in heaven. It does mean that, so long as the author does not literally destroy what he has written or revise it into another union, What and How are dependent upon each other. For purposes of analysis, however, we may talk about content and form separately even though we know that they are really one.

The Principle of Autobiography[1]
JEAN JACQUES ROUSSEAU
1712–1778

No one can write a man's life but himself. The character of his inner being, his real life, is known only to himself; but, in writing it, he disguises it; under the name of his life, he makes an apology; he shows himself as he wishes to be seen, but not at all as he is. The sincerest persons are truthful at most in what they say, but they lie by their reticences, and that of which they say nothing so changes that which they pretend to confess, that in uttering only a part of the truth they say nothing. I put Montaigne at the head of these falsely-sincere persons who wish to deceive in telling the truth. He shows himself with his faults, but he gives himself none but amiable ones; there is no man who has not odious ones. Montaigne paints his likeness, but it is a profile. Who knows whether some scar on the cheek, or an eye put out, on the side which he conceals from us, would not have totally changed the physiognomy? . . .

If I wish to produce a work written with care, like the others, I shall not paint, I shall rouge myself. It is with my portrait that I am here concerned, and not with a book. I am going to work, so to speak, in the darkroom; there is no other art necessary than to follow exactly the traits which I see marked. I form my resolution then about the style as about the things. I shall not try at all to render it uniform; I shall write always that which comes to me, I shall change it, without scruple, according to my humour; I shall speak of everything as I feel it, as I see it, without care, without constraint, without being embarrassed by the medley. In yielding myself at once to the memory of the impression received and to the present sentiment, I shall doubly paint the state of my soul, namely, at the moment when the event happened to me and the moment when I describe it; my style, unequal and natural, sometimes rapid and sometimes diffuse, sometimes wise and sometimes foolish, sometimes grave and sometimes gay, will itself make a part of my history. Finally, whatever may be the way in which this book

[1] From a rough draft of the introduction to Rousseau's *Confessions,* as quoted by Sainte-Beuve in his essay "Rousseau," first published in 1851.

may be written, it will be always, by its object, a book precious for philosophers; it is, I repeat, an illustrative piece for the study of the human heart, and it is the only one that exists.

Comments and Questions

Rousseau's fierce pride in writing with utmost frankness about himself is evident. The difficulty of writing in this manner is equally evident.

1. Why does Rousseau speculate that Montaigne, a French essayist, is a "falsely-sincere" person? How does Rousseau define "sincere"? What is basic to his conception of honest self-portrayal? What, probably, would his comment be on Aldous Huxley's "The Most Disgraceful Thing I Ever Did" (p. 746)? On Floyd Dell's "Christmas" (p. 758)?

2. What is meant to be conveyed by the words "rouge myself"? And the clause: "I shall doubly paint the state of my soul"?

3. Rousseau thought his *Confessions* would always be valuable to philosophers. Why?

Brandy

W. SOMERSET MAUGHAM
1874–1965

My second adventure was droll. I was being driven round the country by a woman who had been doing a great deal, as had a few charitable English and American women, to alleviate the lot of the unfortunate refugees, and latish in the afternoon I remarked that I must think about getting a room in some hotel for the night.

"You needn't bother about that," she said. "I have some distant cousins in this part of the country who'll be glad to put you up. They're very simple provincial people, but they're quite nice, and they'll give you a good dinner."

"That's very kind of them," I said.

She did not volunteer their name, and it did not occur to me to ask it. I gathered from what she said that they were poor relations who lived very modestly, so I was surprised when at nightfall we drove into a town and stopped at a house that in the darkness seemed quite imposing. We

were received by a shortish, fat man with a red, homely face. He was dressed in dark, somewhat ill-fitting clothes and looked the typical French bourgeois. He showed me to a warm and comfortably furnished room, and I was glad to see that there was a bathroom. He told me that dinner was at half past seven. I took a bath and, as I was very tired, had a nap. At the appointed hour I went downstairs and found my way to a living room in which a bright fire of logs was blazing. My host was sitting there and he offered me a glass of sherry. I sank into a large armchair.

"Did you find a bottle of brandy in your room?" he asked me.

"I didn't look," I said.

"I always keep a bottle of brandy in every bedroom in the house, even the children's rooms. They never touch it, but I like to know it's there."

I thought this an odd notion, but said nothing. Presently my driver of the day came in with a thin, dark woman to whom I was introduced. She was my host's sister, but I did not catch her name. I gathered from the conversation that my host was a bachelor and that she was staying with him with her two daughters, her husband being mobilized, for the duration of the war. We went in to dinner and found waiting for us two girls of perhaps fourteen and fifteen with a prim governess. We were waited on by an ancient butler and a maid. My host said: "I've opened for you my last magnum of claret, a Chateau Larose, 1874."

I had never seen a magnum of claret before, and I was impressed. It was delicious. For a poor relation I thought my host was doing very well. The food was excellent, real French country cooking, copious, slightly on the heavy side perhaps, and very rich, but extremely succulent. One dish was so good that I was forced to remark on it.

"I'm glad you like that," said my host. "Everything in this house is cooked in brandy."

I began to think it was a very strange house indeed, and I wished I knew who on earth this hospitable person was. We finished dinner and had coffee. Then the butler brought some large glasses and an immense bottle of brandy. I had done myself very well with the claret, I was among strangers, and thought it wise not to take any more alcohol, so when it was offered to me I refused.

"What," cried my host, throwing himself back in his chair, "have you come to spend the night in the house of Martell and you refuse a glass of brandy?"

I had been dining in the house of the greatest brandy merchant in the world.

Comments and Questions

In the telling of this little incident we know from almost the beginning that the author is deliberately creating mild suspense. Nearly the entire interest of the experience depends upon withholding, until the right moment, a name which he could have given to us at once. *Timing* here is all important. We are treated to a series of small surprises: the "simple provincial people" live in a house that "seemed quite imposing"; brandy is everywhere, even in "the children's rooms"; governess, butler, maid, magnum of claret, fine food—all are part of the careful build-up. At precisely the right moment the point of the incident is made clear.

1. If this were a fictional episode, would the author have told it the same way? See "Fiction: Preliminaries."

2. Is one's interest in this episode dependent upon the importance of the person whose name is revealed at the end? If one is not impressed by brandy merchants, would that fact reduce one's interest in the episode? Is any person sufficiently significant who for any reason qualifies as "greatest . . . in the world"? Discuss.

The Most Disgraceful Thing I Ever Did

ALDOUS HUXLEY
1894–1963

"I should like to show you," she said, and hesitated, blushing; embarrassed, she looked more ravishing than ever. "I should like to show you the little poem I wrote yesterday. I believe it's the best thing I've ever done."

I was only too delighted, of course. A man and a *bourgeois*—how could I fail to be de-lighted? This dazzling young aristocrat, so assured, so complete, so gloriously careless about everything and everyone except herself and her own fun, had actually, in our grandmother's phrase, "set her cap at me." She had taken the trouble to be charming. With what a delicious naïve sincerity and an obvious ignorance of all my works, she had flattered me. How much she had enjoyed all those books of mine, which she hadn't read! I basked in her radiance.

"Here it is." She pulled out of her bosom a folded paper. "Don't be too severe with it," she added, almost anxiously.

I adjusted my *pince-nez* and unfolded the document. "O Love," I began to read.

O Love is sweet when April showers fall,
And Love is lush when roses bloom in June,
And Love beneath the swelt'ring harvest
    moon
Is seldom pure; for love. . . .

I read it over twice slowly, wondering what on earth I should say. Why couldn't she be content with just living? And why, if she must *do* something, did she choose verse? There was the piano, there was the water-color sketching! . . . I looked up at her, and found myself confronted by her dark, intent eyes. She looked like Cleopatra, and twenty, and her body—oh, serpent of old Nile!—was sheathed in a skin of cloth-of-silver.

"What do you think of it?" she asked.

"I think it quite wonderful," I said with enthusiasm.

Her smile of pleasure was the loveliest thing in the world.

"I'm so glad," she said, with an air of detachment, "that you are compiling an anthology of the best modern verse."

A gloom suddenly descended on my spirit. I nodded. I couldn't deny it; everybody knew my anthology. It was going to be the very best of its kind—rigorously, austerely select.

"I thought," she said, and smiled at me again, "I thought that, perhaps, as you liked my little poem so much you might. . . ."

Questions

1. What does the author's *bourgeois* have to do with this episode?

2. Why did a "gloom suddenly descend" on Huxley's spirit?

3. Would Rousseau (p. 744) consider Huxley's act disgraceful?

The Oxford Method

LOGAN PEARSALL SMITH
1865–1946

The Oxford school of *Litterae humaniores* —or "Greats" as it is called—seems to my mature judgment the best scheme of education that I have ever heard of. It is based upon an accurate knowledge of Greek and Latin texts, especially the texts of Plato and Aristotle and Thucydides and Tacitus, and the subjects studied in it are the eternal problems of thought, of conduct, and of social organization. These are discussed, not by means of contemporary catchwords, but by translating them back into another world and another language. Nor could anything be more profitable from the pupil's point of view than the way in which this scheme of education was carried on. The student would prepare a paper on some special subject, and go with it, generally alone, and read it to his tutor, who would then discuss it and criticize it at length; or a group of two or three would meet in the tutor's room for a kind of Socratic discussion of some special point. These discussions were carried on much in the spirit of the Socratic dialogues; and the Socratic irony and assumed ignorance of the instructors, their deferential questions, as if the pupil were the teacher and they the learners, was a method which I found it hard at first to understand.

I remember, for instance, in reading a paper to Nettleship, I mentioned the distinction between form and matter. "Excuse me for interrupting you," Nettleship said, "but this distinction you make, though it is no doubt most important, is one that I find a little difficult to grasp. If it is not troubling you too much, it would be a real kindness if you would try to explain it to me."

"Oh, it's quite simple," I answered patronizingly. "There's the idea, say, in a poem, and there's the way in which it is expressed."

Nettleship still seemed puzzled. "Could you give me an instance?" he pleaded.

"Oh, nothing easier." I answered. "Take the lines, for instance, when Lovelace says,

I could not love thee, Dear, so much,
Loved I not Honour more.[1]

Now he might have said, 'I couldn't be nearly so fond of you, my dear, if I didn't care still more for my reputation.' The form, you see, is very different in both these sentences, but the subject of them—what they mean—is exactly the same."

Nettleship seemed greatly discouraged.

"I'm afraid," he said, "I can't see that the meaning of the two sentences is the same. I'm afraid I'm very stupid; but to me they seem to say quite different things."

He was, I thought, curiously stupid; but in my patient attempt to make my meaning clearer to him a dim suspicion began to waken in me that perhaps it was not Nettleship but myself who was playing the part of the fool in this dialogue.

Comments and Questions

1. How is the method of this anecdote similar to the method of "Brandy"? How is it different?

2. We are told that the Oxford method involves "a kind of Socratic discussion" between the student and the tutor, and then we are shown such a discussion. On the basis of what you find in the anecdote, how would you define a Socratic discussion?

3. What possible advantage does this Oxford method have over the teaching methods practiced in American universities? What advantage do you see in approaching "the eternal problems of thought, of conduct, and of social organization" through the works of Greek philosophers and Greek and Roman historians?

4. The young scholar and the tutor discuss the relation of form and matter. Show how their observations throw light on what has been said about this problem in "Biography: Preliminaries." (See pp. 740 ff.)

5. How well does the young scholar succeed in his prose paraphrase of the lines

---

[1] See p. 329 for the poem.

from Lovelace? What is the intent of his tutor's questions? What pertinence does the discussion have to the study of poetry? Compare "Poetry: Preliminaries" (pp. 236 ff.). If form and substance in poetry are inseparable, can a poem be paraphrased? Discuss.

Passages from
The Life of Johnson
JAMES BOSWELL
1740–1795

SUFFICIENTLY UNCOUTH

He [Dr. Johnson] received me very courteously; but, it must be confessed, that his apartment, and furniture, and morning dress, were sufficiently uncouth. His brown suit of clothes looked very rusty: he had on a little old shrivelled unpowdered wig, which was too small for his head; his shirtneck and knees of his breeches were loose; his black worsted stockings ill drawn up; and he had a pair of unbuckled shoes by way of slippers. But all these slovenly particularities were forgotten the moment that he began to talk.

I MIND MY BELLY VERY STUDIOUSLY

At supper this night he talked of good eating with uncommon satisfaction. "Some people (said he), have a foolish way of not minding, or pretending not to mind, what they eat. For my part, I mind my belly very studiously, and very carefully; for I look upon it, that he who does not mind his belly, will hardly mind anything else." He now appeared to me *Jean Bull philosophe*, and he was for the moment, not only serious but vehement. Yet I have heard him, upon other occasions, talk with great contempt of people who were anxious to gratify their palates; and the 206th number of his *Rambler* is a masterly essay against gulosity. His practice, indeed, I must acknowledge, may be considered as casting the balance of his different opinions upon this subject; for I never knew any man who relished good eating more than he did. When at table, he was totally absorbed in the business of the moment; his looks seemed riveted to his plate; nor would he, unless when in very high company, say one word, or even pay the least attention to what was said by others, till he had satisfied his appetite: which was so fierce, and indulged with such intenseness, that while in the act of eating, the veins of his forehead swelled, and generally a strong perspiration was visible. To those whose sensations were delicate, this could not but be disgusting; and it was doubtless not very suitable to the character of a philosopher, who should be distinguished by self-command. But it must be owned, that Johnson, though he could be rigidly *abstemious,* was not a *temperate* man either in eating or drinking. He could refrain, but he could not use moderately. He told me, that he had fasted two days without inconvenience, and that he had never been hungry but once. They who beheld with wonder how much he ate upon all occasions, when his dinner was to his taste, could not easily conceive what he must have meant by hunger.

Comments and Questions

1. Why does Boswell refer to Johnson as *Jean Bull philosophe?* Since this is simply the French for *John Bull as philosopher,* why did Boswell choose the French form? Review the subject of discussion, food, and you will see why. Context here would be all that could explain this allusion.

2. Does this excerpt sound as though it came from a journal? Explain.

A GOOD-HUMOURED FELLOW

As a curious instance how little a man knows, or wishes to know his own character in the world, or, rather as a convincing proof that Johnson's roughness was only external; and did not proceed from his heart, I insert the following dialogue. JOHNSON. "It is wonderful, Sir, how rare a quality good humor is in life. We meet with very few good-humored men." I mentioned four of our friends, none of whom he would allow to be good-humored. One was *acid,* another was *muddy,* and to the others he had objections which have escaped me. Then, shaking his head and stretching himself at ease in the coach, and smiling with much complacency, he turned to me and said, "I look upon *myself* as a good-humored fellow." The epithet *fellow,* applied to the great Lexicographer, the stately Moralist, the Masterly Critic, as if he had been *Sam* Johnson, a mere pleasant companion, was highly diverting; and this light notion of himself struck me with wonder. I answered, also smiling, "No, no, Sir; that will *not* do. You are good-natured, but not good-humored: you are irascible. You have not patience with folly and absurdity. I believe you would pardon them, if there were time to deprecate your vengeance; but punishment follows so quick after sentence, that they cannot escape."

VINOUS FLIGHTS

Johnson and I supped this evening at the Crown and Anchor tavern, in company with Sir Joshua Reynolds, Mr. Langton, Mr. Nairne, now one of the Scotch Judges, with the title of Lord Dunsinan, and my very worthy friend, Sir William Forbes, or Pitsligo.

We discussed the question, whether drinking improved conversation and benevolence. "No, Sir, before dinner men meet with great inequality of understanding; and those who are conscious of their inferiority have the modesty not to talk. When they have drunk wine, every man feels himself happy, and loses that modesty, and grows impudent and vociferous; but he is not improved: he is only not sensible of his defects." Sir Joshua said the Doctor was talking of the effects of excess in wine; but that a moderate glass enlivened the mind, by giving a proper circulation to the blood. "I am, (said he,) in very good spirits, when I get up in the morning. By dinner-time I am exhausted; wine puts me into the same state as when I got up: and I am sure that moderate drinking makes people talk better." JOHNSON. "No, Sir; wine gives not light, gay, ideal hilarity; but tumultuous, noisy, clamorous merriment. I have heard none of those drunken,—nay, drunken is a coarse word,—none of those *vinous* flights." SIR JOSHUA. "Because you have sat by, quite sober, and felt an envy of the happiness of those who were drinking." JOHNSON. "Perhaps, contempt.—And, Sir, it is not necessary to be drunk one's self, to relish the wit of drunkenness. Do we not judge of the drunken wit of the dialogue between Iago and Cassio, the most excellent of its kind, when we are quite sober? Wit is wit, by whatever means it is produced; and, if good, will appear so at all times. I admit that the spirits are raised by drinking, as by the common participation of any pleasure: cock-fighting, or bearbaiting, will raise the spirits of a company, as drinking does, though surely they will not improve conversation. I also admit, that there are some sluggish men who are improved by drinking; as there are fruits which are not good till they are rotten. There are such men, but they are medlars. I indeed allow that there have been a few men of talents who were improved by drinking; but I maintain that I am right about the effects of drinking in general: and let it be considered, that there is no position, however false in its universality, which is not true of some particular man."

Questions

From the context, can you guess what *medlars* are? (If the clause "There are such men" refers to the statement "There are some sluggish men who are improved by drinking," then to what statement does the word *medlars* refer?)

A DESIRE OF KNOWLEDGE

On Saturday, July 30, Dr. Johnson and I took a sculler at the Temple stairs, and set out for Greenwich. I asked him if he really thought a knowledge of the Greek and Latin languages an essential requisite to a good education. JOHNSON. "Most certainly, Sir; for those who know them have a very great advantage over those who do not. Nay, Sir, it is wonderful what a difference learning makes upon people even in the common intercourse of life, which does not appear to be much connected with it." "And yet, (said I) people go through the world very well, and carry on the business of life to good advantage, without learning." JOHNSON. "Why, Sir, that may be true in cases where learning cannot possibly be of use; for instance, this boy rows us as well without learning, as if he could sing the song of Orpheus to the Argonauts, who were the first sailors." He then called to the boy. "What would you give, my lad, to know about the Argonauts?" "Sir, (said the boy) I would give what I have." Johnson was much pleased with his answer, and we gave him a double fare. Dr. Johnson then turning to me, "Sir (said he) a desire of knowledge is the natural feeling of mankind; and every human being, whose mind is not debauched, will be willing to give all that he has, to get knowledge."

Comments and Questions

1. Allusions which refer to Greek or Roman culture are called *classical.* There are classical allusions in two of the preceding selections. In which ones?

2. Classical allusions normally disturb and sometimes baffle modern readers. Often, however, references to myth, as here in the naming of Orpheus and the Argonauts, are sufficiently self-explanatory. For the plain sense of this passage it is enough to know what Johnson tells: that Orpheus was a singer and the Argonauts the first sailors. But, as we have said before, allusions are intended to light up the text. Johnson and Boswell on the Thames river, far from the land and age of myth, take from that remote time a reference appropriate to their conversation. Two centuries later, we listen to their talk but understand it fully only if we understand the casual references. Look up *Orpheus* and *Argonauts* in your desk dictionary and see what extra light is then thrown on this anecdote.

A PROPENSITY TO PALTRY SAVING

The heterogeneous composition of human nature was remarkably exemplified in Johnson. His liberality in giving his money to persons in distress was extraordinary. Yet there lurked about him a propensity to paltry saving. One day I owned to him, that "I was occasionally troubled with a fit of *narrowness.*" "Why, Sir, (said he,) so am I. *But I do not tell it.*" He has now and then borrowed a shilling of me; and when I asked him for it again, seemed to be rather out of humor. A droll little circumstance once occurred: As if he meant to reprimand my minute exactness as a creditor, he thus addressed me;—"Boswell, *lend me sixpence—not to be repaid.*"

CLEAR YOUR MIND OF CANT

I have no minute of any interview with Johnson till Thursday, May 15th, when I find what follows: BOSWELL. "I wish much to be in Parliament, Sir." JOHNSON. "Why, Sir, unless you come resolved to support any administration, you would be the worse for being in Parliament, because you would be obliged to live more expensively." BOSWELL. "Perhaps, Sir, I should be the less happy for being in Parliament. I never would sell my vote, and I should be vexed if things went wrong." JOHNSON. "That's cant, Sir. It would not vex you more in the house than in the gallery; public affairs vex no man." BOSWELL. "Have not they vexed yourself a little, Sir? Have not you been vexed by all the turbulence of this reign, and by that absurd vote of the House of Commons, 'That the influence of the Crown has increased, is increasing, and ought to be diminished'?" JOHNSON. "Sir, I have never slept an hour less, nor eat an ounce less meat. I would have knocked the factious dogs on the head, to be sure; but I was *not vexed.*" BOSWELL. "I declare, Sir, upon my honour, I did imagine I was vexed, and took a pride in it; but it *was*, perhaps, cant; for I own I neither eat less, nor slept less." JOHNSON. "My dear friend, clear your *mind* of cant. You may *talk* as other people do; you may say to a man, 'Sir, I am your most humble servant.' You are *not* his most humble servant. You may say, 'These are bad times; it is a melancholy thing to be reserved to such times.' You don't mind the times. You tell a man, 'I am sorry you had such bad weather the last day of your journey, and were so much wet.' You don't care sixpence whether he is wet or dry. You may *talk* in this manner; it is a mode of talking in Society: but don't *think* foolishly."

Comments and Questions

1. Neither Johnson nor Boswell defines the word *cant,* but from what it is made to describe, can you define it?

2. If Johnson "would have knocked the factious dogs on the head" and yet was not vexed, what was he?

3. Johnson's political opinions are made clearer in passages quoted below, but there is a broad hint of his political beliefs here. What is the hint?

THE DIGNITY OF DANGER

We talked of war. JOHNSON. "Every man thinks meanly of himself for not having been a soldier, or not having been at sea." BOSWELL. "Lord Mansfield does not." JOHNSON. "Sir, if Lord Mansfield were in a company of General Officers and Admirals who have been in service, he would shrink; he'd wish to creep under the table." BOSWELL. "No; he'd think he could *try* them all." JOHNSON. "Yes, if he could catch them: but they'd try him much sooner. No, Sir: were Socrates and Charles the Twelfth of Sweden both present in any company, and Socrates to say, 'Follow me, and hear a lecture in philosophy'; and Charles, laying his hand on his sword, to say, 'Follow me, and dethrone the Czar'; a man would be ashamed to follow Socrates. Sir, the impression is universal: yet it is strange. As to the sailor, when you look down from the quarter-deck to the space below, you see the utmost extremity of human misery: such crowding, such filth, such stench!" BOSWELL. "Yet sailors are happy." JOHNSON. "They are happy as brutes are happy, with a piece of fresh meat, with the grossest sensuality. But, Sir, the profession of soldiers and sailors has the dignity of danger. Mankind reverence those who have got over fear, which is so general a weakness."

Comments and Questions

1. As in the passages above, there are here several self-revealing allusions. Few but specialists in the eighteenth century would know anything about Lord Mansfield but, by the information given and a bit of reasoning, any reader can sufficiently identify him. See if you can do so.

2. Is Johnson's use of the word *try* a pun? Explain.

3. Do you agree with Johnson's contention about soldiers and sailors?

DISMAL APPREHENSIONS

When we were alone, I introduced the subject of death, and endeavored to maintain that the fear of it might be got over. I told him that David Hume said to me, he was no more uneasy to think that he should *not be* after his life, than that he *had not been* before he began to exist. JOHNSON. "Sir, if he really thinks so, his perceptions are disturbed; he is mad; if he does not think so, he lies. He may tell you he holds his finger in the flame of a candle without feel-

ing pain; would you believe him? When he dies, he at least gives up all he has." BOSWELL. "Foote, Sir, told me, that when he was very ill he was not afraid to die." JOHNSON. "It is not true, Sir. Hold a pistol to Foote's breast, or to Hume's breast and threaten to kill them, and you'll see how they behave." BOSWELL. "But may we not fortify our minds for the approach of death?"—Here I am sensible I was in the wrong, to bring before his view what he ever looked upon with horror; for although when in a celestial frame of mind in his *Vanity of Human Wishes*, he has supposed death to be "kind Nature's signal for retreat," from this state of being to "a happier seat," his thoughts upon this awful change were in general full of dismal apprehensions. His mind resembled the vast amphitheatre, the Coliseum at Rome. In the centre stood his judgment, which like a mighty gladiator, combated those apprehensions that, like the wild beasts of the Arena, were all about in cells, ready to be let out upon him. After a conflict, he drives them back into their dens; but not killing them, they were still assailing him. To my question, whether we might not fortify our minds for the approach of death, he answered, in a passion, "No, Sir, let it alone. It matters not how a man dies, but how he lives. The act of dying is not of importance, it lasts so short a time." He added (with an earnest look), "A man knows it must be so, and submits. It will do him no good to whine."

I attempted to continue the conversation. He was so provoked, that he said: "Give us no more of this"; and was thrown into such a state of agitation, that he expressed himself in a way that alarmed and distressed me; showed an impatience that I should leave him, and when I was going away, called to me sternly, "Don't let us meet to-morrow."

I went home exceedingly uneasy. All the harsh observations which I had ever heard made upon his character, crowded into my mind, and I seemed to myself like the man who had put his head into the lion's mouth a great many times with perfect safety, but at last had it bit off.

THAT CELEBRATED LETTER

When the *Dictionary* was on the eve of publication, Lord Chesterfield, who, it is said, had flattered himself with the expectation that Johnson would dedicate the work to him, attempted, in a courtly manner, to soothe and insinuate himself with the Sage, conscious, as it should seem, of the cold indifference with which he had treated its learned author; and further attempted to conciliate him, by writing two papers in *The World,* in recommendation of the work; and it must be confessed, that they contain some studied compliments, so finely turned, that if there had been no previous offense, it is probable that Johnson would have been highly delighted. Praise, in general, was pleasing to him; but by praise from a man of rank and elegant accomplishments, he was peculiarly gratified.

This courtly device failed of its effect. Johnson, who thought that "all was false and hollow," despised the honeyed words, and was even indignant that Lord Chesterfield should, for a moment, imagine, that he could be the dupe of such an artifice. His expression to me concerning Lord Chesterfield, upon this occasion, was, "Sir, after making great professions, he had, for many years, taken no notice of me; but when my *Dictionary* was coming out, he fell a scribbling in *The World* about it. Upon which, I wrote him a letter expressed in civil terms, but such as might show him that I did not mind what he said or wrote, and that I had done with him."

This is that celebrated letter of which so much has been said, and about which curiosity has been so long excited, without being gratified. I for many years solicited Johnson to favor me with a copy of it, that so excellent a composition might not be lost to posterity. He delayed from time to time to give it to me; till at last in 1781, when we were on a visit at Mr. Dilly's, at South-hill, in Bedfordshire, he was pleased to dictate it to me from memory. He afterwards found among his papers a copy of it, which he had dictated to Mr. Baretti, with its title and corrections, in his own handwriting. This he gave to Mr. Langton; adding that if it were to come into print, he wished it to be from that copy. By Mr. Langton's kindness, I am enabled to enrich my work with a perfect transcript of what the world has so eagerly desired to see.

"To the Right Honorable the Earl of Chesterfield

"My Lord,   *February 7, 1755.*
"I have been lately informed, by the proprietor of the *World,* that two papers, in which my *Dictionary* is recommended to the public, were written by your Lordship. To be so distinguished, is an honor, which, being very little accustomed to favors from the great, I know not well how to receive, or in what terms to acknowledge.

"When, upon some slight encouragement, I first visited your Lordship, I was overpowered, like the rest of mankind, by the enchantment of your address, and could not forbear to wish that I might boast myself *Le vainqueur du vainqueur de la terre;*—that I might obtain that regard for which I saw the world contending; but I found my attendance so little encouraged, that neither pride nor modesty would suffer me to continue it. When I had once addressed your Lordship in public, I had exhausted all the art of pleasing which a retired and uncourtly scholar can possess. I had done all that I could; and no man is well pleased to have his all neglected, be it ever so little.

"Seven years, my Lord, have now passed, since I waited in your outward rooms, or was repulsed from your door; during which time I have been pushing on my work through difficulties, of which it is useless to complain, and have brought it, at last, to the verge of publication, without one act of assistance, one word of encouragement, or one smile of favor. Such treatment I did not expect, for I never had a Patron before.

"The shepherd in Virgil grew at last acquainted with Love, and found him a native of the rocks.

"Is not a Patron, my Lord, one who looks with unconcern on a man struggling for life in the water, and when he has reached ground, encumbers him with help? The notice which you have been pleased to take of my labors, had it been early, had been kind; but it has been delayed till I am indifferent, and cannot enjoy it; till I am solitary, and cannot impart it; till I am known, and do not want it. I hope it is no very cynical asperity, not to confess obligations where no benefit has been received, or to be unwilling that the Public should consider me as owing that to a Patron, which Providence has enabled me to do for myself.

"Having carried on my work thus far with so little obligation to any favorer of learning, I shall not be disappointed though I should conclude it, if less be possible, with less; for I have been long wakened from that dream of hope, in which I once boasted myself with so much exultation,

"*My Lord,*
"*Your Lordship's most humble,*
"*Most obedient servant,*
"*Sam. Johnson.*"

Comments and Questions

Boswell and others forgave or overlooked Johnson's uncouthness, but it is doubtful that the most elegant man of the century ever could have done so. In a letter to his son, Lord Chesterfield recommended "a genteel, easy manner and carriage, wholly free from those odd tricks, ill habits, and awkwardnesses, which even many very worthy and sensible people have in their behavior." He added: "I have known many a man, from his awkwardness, give people such a dislike of him at first, that all his merit could not get the better of it afterwards." Johnson was doubtless a worthy, sensible man of merit but not "wholly free from those odd tricks, ill habits, and awkwardnesses" which Lord Chesterfield found so distasteful. Johnson, for his part, had great respect for noblemen but more respect for his own integrity.

1. Explain the reference, in paragraph four of Johnson's letter, to the "shepherd in Virgil." Does one need to know this story more fully in order to understand the allusion?

2. Does any part of this letter contain a touch of sarcasm?

3. In the next-to-last paragraph, what does Johnson mean by the statement, "but it has been delayed . . . till I am solitary, and cannot impart it"?

4. What was "that dream of hope" referred to in the last paragraph?

THE SPIRIT OF CONTRADICTION

Notwithstanding the high veneration which I entertained for Dr. Johnson, I was sensible that he was sometimes a little actuated by the spirit of contradiction, and by means of that I hoped I should gain my point. I was persuaded that if I should come upon him with a direct proposal, "Sir, will you dine in company with Jack Wilkes?"

he would have flown into a passion, and probably would have answered, "Dine with Jack Wilkes, Sir! I'd as soon dine with Jack Ketch." I therefore, while we were sitting quietly by ourselves at his house in an evening, took occasion to open my plan thus: "Mr. Dilly, Sir, sends his respectful compliments to you, and would be happy if you would do him the honor to dine with him on Wednesday next along with me, as I must soon go to Scotland." JOHNSON. "Sir, I am obliged to Mr. Dilly. I will wait upon him—" BOSWELL. "Provided, Sir, I suppose, that the company which he is to have, is agreeable to you." JOHNSON. "What do you mean, Sir? What do you take me for? Do you think I am so ignorant of the world, as to imagine that I am to prescribe to a gentleman what company he is to have at his table?" BOSWELL. "I beg your pardon, Sir, for wishing to prevent you from meeting people whom you might not like. Perhaps he may have some of what he calls his patriotic friends with him." JOHNSON. "Well, Sir, and what then? What care *I* for his *patriotic friends?* Poh!" BOSWELL. "I should not be surprised to find Jack Wilkes there." JOHNSON. "And if Jack Wilkes *should* be there, what is that to *me,* Sir? My dear friend, let us have no more of this. I am sorry to be angry with you; but really it is treating me strangely to talk to me as if I could not meet any company whatever, occasionally." BOSWELL. "Pray, forgive me, Sir, I meant well. But you shall meet whoever comes, for me." Thus I secured him, and told Dilly that he would find him very well pleased to be one of his guests on the day appointed.

Comments and Questions

1. Jack Ketch was a name for the public hangman. How much do we find out about Jack Wilkes?

2. By inference, how much do we find out about Johnson's politics?

THE LEVELLING DOCTRINE

He again insisted on the duty of maintaining subordination of rank. "Sir, I would no more deprive a nobleman of his respect, than of his money. I consider myself as acting a part in the great system of society, and I do to others as I would have them do to me. I would behave to a nobleman as I should expect he would behave to me, were I a nobleman and he Sam Johnson. Sir, there is one Mrs. Macaulay in this town, a great republican. One day when I was at her house, I put on a very grave countenance, and said to her, 'Madam, I am now become a convert to your way of thinking. I am convinced that all mankind are upon an equal footing; and to give you an unquestionable proof, Madam, that I am in earnest, here is a very sensible, civil, well-behaved fellow-citizen, your footman; I desire that he may be allowed to sit down and dine with us.' I thus, Sir, showed her the absurdity of the levelling doctrine. She has never liked me since. Sir, your levellers wish to level *down* as far as themselves; but they cannot bear levelling *up* to themselves. They would all have some people under them; why not then have some people above them?" I mentioned a certain author who disgusted me by his forwardness, and by showing no deference to noblemen into whose company he was admitted. JOHNSON. "Suppose a shoemaker should claim an equality with him, as he does with a lord; how he would stare. 'Why, Sir, do you stare? (says the shoemaker,) I do great service to society. 'Tis true I am paid for doing it; but so are you, Sir: and I am sorry to say it, paid better than I am, for doing something not so necessary, for mankind could do better without your books, than without my shoes.' Thus, Sir, there would be a perpetual struggle for precedence, were there no fixed invariable rules for the distinction of rank, which creates no jealousy, as it is allowed to be accidental."

Questions

1. Is there anything *reasonable* in Johnson's doctrine? If noble birth is an accident —as obviously it is—upon what can respect be based? Is Johnson simply approving the *orderliness* of his society?

2. Do you think that Mrs. Macaulay should have called Johnson's bluff and invited the footman to dinner? If she had done so, what do you think Johnson would have done? Would a present-day Mrs. Macaulay act differently?

3. How far have we progressed toward leveling the humps out of society and reducing all to a flat plain? Is it true, as someone has said: "Mount Olympus is still there, and as one set of gods tumbles, the one who pushed them off take their places"?

THE SUBJECT OF TOLERATION

I introduced the subject of toleration. JOHNSON. "Every society has a right to preserve public peace and order, and therefore has a good right to prohibit the propagation of opinions which have a dangerous tendency. To say the *magistrate* has this right, is using an inadequate word: it is the *society* for which the magistrate is agent. He may be morally or theologically wrong in restraining the propagation of opinions which he thinks dangerous, but he is politically right." MAYO. "I am of opinion, Sir, that every man is entitled to liberty of conscience in religion; and that the magistrate cannot restrain the right." JOHNSON. "Sir, I agree with you. Every man has a right of liberty of conscience, and with that the magistrate cannot interfere. People confound liberty of thinking with liberty of talking; nay, with liberty of preaching. Every man has a physical right to think as he pleases; for it cannot be discovered how he thinks. He has not a moral right, for he ought to inform himself, and think justly. But, Sir, no member of society has a right to *teach* any doctrine contrary to what the society holds to be true. The magistrate, I say, may be wrong in what he thinks; but while he thinks himself right, he may and ought to enforce what he thinks." MAYO. "Then Sir, we are to remain always in error, and truth never can prevail; and the magistrate was right in persecuting the first Christians." JOHNSON. "Sir, the only method by which religious truth can be established is by martyrdom. The magistrate has a right to enforce what he thinks; and he who is conscious of the truth has a right to suffer. I am afraid there is no other way of ascertaining the truth but by persecution on the one hand and enduring it on the other." GOLDSMITH. "But how is a man to act, Sir? Though firmly convinced of the truth of his doctrine, may he not think it wrong to expose himself to persecution? Has he a right to do so? Is it not, as it were, committing voluntary suicide?" JOHNSON. "Sir, as to voluntary suicide, as you call it, there are twenty thousand men in an army who will go without scruple to be shot at, and mount a breach for five-pence a day." GOLDSMITH. "But have they a moral right to do this?" JOHNSON. "Nay, Sir, if you will not take the universal opinion of mankind, I have nothing to say. If mankind cannot defend their own way of thinking, I cannot defend it. Sir, if a man is in doubt whether it would be better to expose himself to martyrdom or not, he should not do it. He must be convinced that he has a delegation from heaven." GOLDSMITH. "I would consider whether there were a greater chance of good or evil upon the whole. If I see a man who had fallen into a well, I would wish to help him out: but if there is a greater probability that he shall pull me in, than that I shall pull him out, I would not attempt it. So were I to go to Turkey, I might wish to convert the Grand Signor to the Christian faith; but when I considered that I should probably be put to death without effectuating my purpose in any degree, I should keep myself quiet." JOHNSON. "Sir, you must consider that we have perfect and imperfect obligations. Perfect obligations, which are generally not to do something, are clear and positive: as, 'thou shalt not kill.' But charity, for instance, is not definable by limits. It is a duty to give to the poor; but no man can say how much another should give to the poor, or when a man has given too little to save his soul. In the same manner it is a duty to instruct the ignorant, and of consequence to convert infidels to Christianity; but no man in the common course of things is obliged to carry this to such a degree as to incur the danger of martyrdom, as no man is obliged to strip himself to the shirt in order to give charity. I have said that a man must be persuaded that he has a particular delegation from heaven." GOLDSMITH. "How is this to be known? Our first reformers, who were burnt for not believing bread and wine to be Christ—" JOHNSON (interrupting him). "Sir, they were not burnt for not believing bread and wine to be Christ, but for insulting those who did believe it. And, Sir, when the first reformers began, they did not intend to be martyred: as many of them ran away as could." BOSWELL. "But, Sir, there was your countryman, Elwal, who you told me challenged King George with

his black-guards, and his red-guards." JOHNSON. "My countryman, Elwal, Sir, should have been put in the stocks; a proper pulpit for him; and he'd have had a numerous audience. A man who preaches in the stocks will always have hearers enough." BOSWELL. "But Elwal thought himself in the right." JOHNSON. "We are not providing for mad people; there are places for them in the neighborhood" (meaning Moorfields). MAYO. "But, Sir, is it not very hard that I should not be allowed to teach my children what I believe to be the truth?" JOHNSON. "Why, Sir, you might contrive to teach your children *extrà scandalum;* but, Sir, the magistrate, if he knows it, has a right to restrain you. Suppose you teach your children to be thieves?" MAYO. "This is making a joke of the subject." JOHNSON. "Nay, Sir, take it thus:—that you teach them the community of goods; for which there are as many plausible arguments as for most erroneous doctrines. You teach them that all things at first were in common, and that no man had a right to anything but as he laid his hands upon it; and that this still is, or ought to be, the rule amongst mankind. Here, Sir, you sap a great principle in society,—property. And don't you think the magistrate would have a right to prevent you? Or, suppose you should teach your children the notion of the Adamites, and they should run naked into the streets, would not the magistrate have a right to flog 'em into their doublets?" MAYO. "I think the magistrate has no right to interfere till there is some overt act." BOSWELL. "So, Sir, though he sees an enemy to the state charging a blunderbuss, he is not to interfere till it is fired off?" MAYO. "He must be sure of its direction against the state." JOHNSON. "The magistrate is to judge of that.—He has no right to restrain your thinking, because the evil centers in yourself. If a man were sitting at this table, and chopping off his fingers, the magistrate, as guardian of the community, has no authority to restrain him, however he might do it from kindness as a parent.—Though, indeed, upon more consideration, I think he may; as it is probable, that he who is chopping off his own fingers, may soon proceed to chop off those of other people. If I think it right to steal Mr. Dilly's plate, I am a bad man; but he can say nothing to me. If I make an open declaration that I think so, he will keep me out of his house. If I put forth my hand, I shall be sent to Newgate. This is the gradation of thinking, preaching, and acting: if a man thinks erroneously, he may keep his thoughts to himself, and nobody will trouble him; if he preaches erroneous doctrine, society may expel him; if he acts in consequence of it, the law takes place, and he is hanged." MAYO. "But, Sir, ought not Christians to have liberty of conscience?" JOHNSON. "I have already told you so, Sir. You are coming back to where you were." BOSWELL. "Dr. Mayo is always taking a return post-chaise, and going the stage over again. He has it at half price." JOHNSON. "Dr. Mayo, like other champions for unlimited toleration, has got a set of words. Sir, it is no matter, politically, whether the magistrate be right or wrong. Suppose a club were to be formed, to drink confusion to King George the Third, and a happy restoration to Charles the Third, this would be very bad with respect to the state; but every member of that club must either conform to its rules, or be turned out of it. Old Baxter, I remember, maintains, that the magistrate should 'tolerate all things that are tolerable.' This is no good definition of toleration upon any principle; but it shows that he thought some things were not tolerable." TOPLADY. "Sir, you have untwisted this difficult subject with great dexterity."

During this argument, Goldsmith sat in restless agitation, from a wish to get in and *shine*. Finding himself excluded, he had taken his hat to go away, but remained for some time with it in his hand, like a gamester, who at the close of a long night, lingers for a little while, to see if he can have a favourable opening to finish with success. Once when he was beginning to speak, he found himself overpowered by the loud voice of Johnson, who was at the opposite end of the table, and did not perceive Goldsmith's attempt. Thus disappointed of his wish to obtain the attention of the company, Goldsmith in a passion threw down his hat, looking angrily at Johnson, and exclaiming in a bitter tone, *"Take it."* When Toplady was going to speak, Johnson uttered some sound, which led Goldsmith to think that he was beginning again, and taking the words from Toplady. Upon which, he seized this opportunity of venting his own envy and spleen, under the pretext of supporting another person: "Sir (said he to Johnson), the gentleman has heard you patiently for an hour; pray allow us now to hear him." JOHNSON (sternly). "Sir, I was not interrupting the gentleman. I was only giving him a signal of my attention. Sir, you are impertinent." Goldsmith made no reply, but continued in the company for some time.

Comments and Questions

1. If freedom of thought is not subject to control, is it a true freedom? (Is one condition of liberty that it could be taken away?)

2. This animated conversation of eighteenth-century men brings forcibly to mind current arguments, perhaps even more animated. Do you see some parallels?

3. Is Goldsmith on the track when he mentions "voluntary suicide"? Are both Goldsmith and Johnson, perhaps for the sake of argument, misusing the word *suicide*?

4. Is Johnson's argument sound about "perfect and imperfect obligations"? Does man recognize the injunction against killing as absolute? And what progress has man made toward reducing "charity" to a science? Is there any such thing as "the universal opinion of mankind"?

5. Do you agree that Johnson "untwisted" the difficult subject of toleration "with great dexterity"?

6. At the end are your sympathies with Goldsmith or with Johnson?

Questions on the passages as a whole

1. Suppose some holocaust had destroyed all we know of Boswell and Johnson except what we have in the passages quoted here. What would your estimate of the two men be? What would it be of other persons who appear briefly: Goldsmith, Sir Joshua Reynolds, Dr. Mayo?

2. There are three sharply defined attitudes toward Boswell: (1) that he attained literary eminence because he was "a great fool" (Macaulay); (2) that he attained literary eminence because, in spite of being a great fool, he had "an open loving heart" (Carlyle); (3) that he attained literary eminence because he was *not* a great fool but possibly a better man than Johnson. We have only glimpses of Boswell in the passages quoted here but what do you make of those

glimpses? What can be said about his sense of humor? his originality? his reasoning? his understanding of psychology—particularly Johnson's? Now look at a different sort of thing. What are his qualities as a reporter? as a literary artist? Is he simply one or the other or a blend of both?

3. There seems little doubt that without Boswell's *Life,* Johnson would have sunk into obscurity, for most of his writings have not stood up well. The *Life* has delayed obscurity indefinitely. One should remember, however, that Johnson created the original fascination; Boswell did not make it up. What is that fascination? His rightness in all his arguments? His club-wielding tactics in conversation? His tact or lack of it? The fact that he had a strong opinion on every subject and was willing, eager, to state it? His kindness? generosity? manliness? What combination of reasons accounts for our still whiffing with pleasure the Johnsonian ether?

4. One technical point: which of the passages quoted would you classify as anecdotes?

God Brought Me Safe
JOHN WESLEY
1703–1791

Up to this point we have been concerned with brief, single scenes from the lives of a variety of persons. This selection and the two following it are more than anecdotes and less than sketches. They involve several related occurrences which create a single impression.

[Oct. 1743.]

Thur. 20.—After preaching to a small, attentive congregation, I rode to Wednesbury. At twelve I preached in a ground near the middle of the town to a far larger congregation than was expected, on "Jesus Christ, the same yesterday, and to-day, and for ever." I believe every one present felt the power of God; and no creature offered to molest us, either going or coming; but the Lord fought for us, and we held our peace.

I was writing at Francis Ward's in the afternoon when the cry arose that the mob had beset the house. We prayed that God would disperse them, and it was so. One went this way, and another that; so that, in half an hour, not a man was left. I told our brethren, "Now is the time for us to go"; but they pressed me exceedingly to stay; so, that I might not offend them, I sat down, though I foresaw what would follow. Before five the mob surrounded the house again in greater numbers than ever. The cry of one and all was, "Bring out the minister; we will have the minister." I desired one to take their captain by the hand and bring him into the house. After a few sentences interchanged between us the lion became a lamb. I desired him to go and bring one or two more of the most angry of his companions. He brought in two, who were ready to swallow the ground with rage; but in two minutes they were as calm as he. I then bade them make way, that I might go out among the people. As soon as I was in the midst of them I called for a chair, and, standing up, asked, "What do any of you want with me?" Some said, "We want you to go with us to the Justice." I replied, "That I will with all my heart." I then spoke a few words, which God applied; so that they cried out with might and main, "The gentleman is an honest gentleman, and we will spill our blood in his defence." I asked, "Shall we go to the Justice to-night, or in the morning?" Most of them cried, "To-night, to-night"; on which I went before, and two or three hundred followed, the rest returning whence they came.

The night came on before we had walked a mile, together with heavy rain. However, on we went to Bentley Hall, two miles from Wednesbury. One or two ran before to tell Mr. Lane they had brought Mr. Wesley before his Worship. Mr. Lane replied, "What have I to do with Mr. Wesley? Go and carry him back again." By this time the main body came up, and began knocking at the door. A servant told them Mr. Lane was in bed. His son followed, and asked what was the matter. One replied, "Why an't please you, they sing psalms all day; nay, and make folks rise at five in the morning. And what would your Worship advise us to do?" "To go home," said Mr. Lane, "and be quiet."

Here they were at a full stop, till one advised to go to Justice Persehouse at Walsall. All agreed to this; so we hastened on, and about seven came to his house. But Mr. P. likewise sent word that he was in bed. Now they were at a stand again: but at last they all thought it the wisest course to make the best of their way home. About fifty of them undertook to convey me. But we had not gone a hundred yards when the mob of Walsall came, pouring in like a flood, and bore down all before them. The Darlaston mob made what defense they could; but they were weary, as well as outnumbered; so that in a short time, many being knocked down, the rest ran away, and left me in their hands.

To attempt speaking was vain, for the noise on every side was like the roaring of the sea. So they dragged me along till we came to the town, where, seeing the door of a large house open, I attempted to go in; but a man, catching me by the hair, pulled me back into the middle of the mob. They made no more stop till they had carried me through the main street, from one end of the town to the other. I continued speaking all the time to those within hearing, feeling no pain or weariness. At the west end of the town, seeing a door half open, I made toward it, and would have gone in, but a gentleman in the shop would not suffer me, saying they would pull the house down to the ground. However, I stood at the door and asked, "Are you willing to hear me speak?" Many cried out, "No, no! knock his brains out; down with him; kill him at once." Others said, "Nay, but we will hear him first." I began asking, "What evil have I done? Which of you all have I wronged in word or deed?" and continued speaking for above a quarter of an hour, till my voice suddenly failed. Then the floods began to lift up their voice again, many crying out, "Bring him away! Bring him away!"

In the meantime my strength and my voice returned, and I broke out aloud into prayer. And now the man who had just before headed the mob turned and said, "Sir, I will spend my life for you: follow me, and not one soul here shall touch a hair of your head." Two or three of his fellows confirmed his words, and got close to me immediately. At the same time, the gentleman in the shop cried out, "For shame, for shame! Let him go." An honest butcher, who was a little farther off, said it was a shame they should do thus; and pulled back four or five, one

after another, who were running on the most fiercely. The people then, as if it had been by common consent, fell to the right and left; while those three or four men took me between them, and carried me through them all. But on the bridge the mob rallied again: we therefore went on one side over the milldam, and thence through the meadows, till, a little before ten, God brought me safe to Wednesbury, having lost only one flap of my waistcoat and a little skin from one of my hands.

Comments and Questions

1. This excerpt was taken from John Wesley's *Journal.* How does a journal differ from autobiography? Consider the matter of intent to publish, to communicate with an expected reader.

2. Which one of the anecdotes preceding this one is most like the entry in a journal? How does a journal differ from a diary? Which form—diary, journal, or autobiography —is likely to be most self-conscious?

3. What can be learned of mob psychology from this account? Do we ever find out why the mobs attacked Wesley, what they held against him?

Christmas
FLOYD DELL
1887–1969

Memories of childhood are strange things. The obscurity of the past opens a little lighted space—a scene, unconnected with anything else. One must figure out when it happened. There may be anomalies in the scene, which need explanation. Sometimes the scenes are tiny fragments only. Again they are long dramas. Having once been remembered, they can be lived through again in every moment, with a detailed experiencing of movement and sensation and thought. One can start the scene in one's mind and see it all through again. Exactly so it was —clearer in memory than something that happened yesterday, though it was forty years ago.

And, oddly enough, if there is some detail skipped over, lost out of the memory picture, no repetition of the remembering process will supply it —the gap is always there.

That fall, before it was discovered that the soles of both my shoes were worn clear through, I still went to Sunday school. And one time the Sunday-school superintendent made a speech to all the classes. He said that these were hard times, and that many poor children weren't getting enough to eat. It was the first time that I had heard about it. He asked everybody to bring some food for the poor children next Sunday. I felt very sorry for the poor children.

Also little envelopes were distributed to all the classes. Each little boy and girl was to bring money for the poor, next Sunday. The pretty Sunday-school teacher explained that we were to write our names, or have our parents write them, up in the left-hand corner of the little envelopes. . . . I told my mother all about it when I came home. And my mother gave me, the next Sunday, a small bag of potatoes to carry to Sunday school. I supposed the poor children's mothers would make potato soup out of them. . . . Potato soup was good. My father, who was quite a joker, would always say, as if he were surprised, "Ah! I see we have some nourishing soup today!" It was so good that we had it every day. My father was at home all day long and every day, now; and I liked that, even if he was grumpy as he sat reading Grant's *Memoirs*. I had my parents all to myself, too; the others were away. My oldest brother was in Quincy, and memory does not reveal where the others were: perhaps with relatives in the country.

Taking my small bag of potatoes to Sunday school, I looked around for the poor children; I was disappointed not to see them. I had heard about poor children in stories. But I was told just to put my contribution with the others on the big table in the side room.

I had brought with me the little yellow envelope, with some money in it and sealed it up. My mother wouldn't tell me how much money she had put in it, but it felt like several dimes. Only she wouldn't let me write my name on the envelope. I had learned to write my name, and I was proud of being able to do it. But my mother said firmly, *no*, I must *not* write my name on the envelope; she didn't tell me why. On the

way to Sunday school I had pressed the envelope against the coins until I could tell what they were; they weren't dimes but pennies.

When I handed in my envelope, my Sunday-school teacher noticed that my name wasn't on it, and she gave me a pencil; I could write my own name, she said. So I did. But I was confused because my mother had said not to; and when I came home, I confessed what I had done. She looked distressed. "I told you not to!" she said. But she didn't explain why. . . .

I didn't go back to school that fall. My mother said it was because I was sick. I did have a cold the week that school opened; I had been playing in the gutters and had got my feet wet, because there were holes in my shoes. My father cut insoles out of cardboard, and I wore those in my shoes. As long as I had to stay in the house anyway, they were all right.

I stayed cooped up in the house, without any companionship. We didn't take a Sunday paper any more, but the *Barry Adage* came every week in the mails; and though I did not read small print, I could see the Santa Clauses and holly wreaths in the advertisements.

There was a calendar in the kitchen. The red days were Sundays and holidays; and that red 25 was Christmas. (It was on a Monday, and the two red figures would come right together in 1893; but this represents research in the *World Almanac*, not memory.) I knew when Sunday was, because I could look out of the window and see the neighbor's children, all dressed up, going to Sunday school. I knew just when Christmas was going to be.

But there was something queer! My father and mother didn't say a word about Christmas. And once, when I spoke of it, there was a strange silence; so I didn't say anything more about it. But I wondered, and was troubled. Why didn't they say anything about it? Was what I had said I wanted (memory refuses to supply that detail) too expensive?

I wasn't arrogant and talkative now. I was silent and frightened. What was the matter? Why didn't my father and mother say anything about Christmas? As the day approached, my chest grew tighter with anxiety.

Now it was the day before Christmas. I couldn't be mistaken. But not a word about it from my father and mother. I waited in painful bewilderment all day. I had supper with them, and was allowed to sit up for an hour. I was waiting for them to say something. "It's time for you to go to bed," my mother said gently. I *had* to say something.

"This is Christmas Eve, isn't it?" I asked, as if I didn't know. My father and mother looked at one another. Then my mother looked away. Her face was pale and stony. My father cleared his throat, and his face took on a joking look. He pretended he hadn't known it was Christmas Eve, because he hadn't been reading the papers. He said he would go downtown and find out.

My mother got up and walked out of the room. I didn't want my father to have to keep on being funny about it, so I got up and went to bed. I went by myself without having a light. I undressed in the dark and crawled into bed.

I was numb. As if I had been hit by something. It was hard to breathe. I ached all through. I was stunned—with finding out the truth.

My body knew before my mind quite did. In a minute, when I could think, my mind would know. And as the pain in my body ebbed, the pain in my mind began. I *knew*. I couldn't put it into words yet. But I knew why I had taken only a little bag of potatoes to Sunday school that fall. I knew why there had been only pennies in my little yellow envelope. I knew why I hadn't gone to school that fall—why I hadn't any new shoes—why we had been living on potato soup all winter. All these things, and others, many others, fitted themselves together in my mind, and meant something.

Then the words came into my mind and I whispered them into the darkness.

"*We're poor!*"

That was it. I was one of those poor children I had been sorry for, when I heard about them in Sunday school. My mother hadn't told me. My father was out of work, and we hadn't any money. That was why there wasn't going to be any Christmas at our house.

Then I remembered something that made me squirm with shame—a boast. (Memory will not yield this up. Had I said to some nice little boy, "I'm going to be President of the United States"? Or to a nice little girl: "I'll marry you when I grow up"? It was some boast as horribly shameful to remember.)

"*We're poor.*" There in bed in the dark, I whispered it over and over to myself. I was making myself get used to it. (Or—just torturing myself, as one pressed the tongue against a sore tooth? No, memory says not like that—but to keep myself from ever being such a fool again: suffering now, to keep this awful thing from ever happening again. Memory is clear on that; it was more like pulling the tooth, to get it over with—never mind the pain, this will be the end!)

It wasn't so bad, now that I knew. *I just hadn't known!* I had thought all sorts of foolish things; that I was going to Ann Arbor—going to be a lawyer—going to make speeches in the Square, going to be President! Now I knew better.

I had wanted (something) for Christmas. I didn't want it, now. I didn't want anything.

I lay there in the dark, feeling the cold emotion of renunciation. (The tendrils of desire unfold their clasp on the outer world of objects, withdraw, shrivel up. Wishes shrivel up, turn black, die. It is like that.)

It hurt. But nothing would ever hurt again. I would never let myself want anything again.

I lay there stretched out straight and stiff in the dark, my fists clenched hard upon Nothing. . . .

In the morning it had been like a nightmare that is not clearly remembered—that one wishes to forget. Though I hadn't hung up any stocking, there was one hanging at the foot of my bed. A bag of popcorn, and lead pencil, for me. They had done the best they could, now they realized that I knew about Christmas. But they needn't have thought they had to. I didn't want anything.

Comments

Try to imagine what would happen to the effect of this account if it were told differently. Here is a sample of a different telling of the first paragraph:

That autumn I still trudged manfully off to Sunday school even though my little shoes had long since seen their best days. On one memorable Sabbath, the Sunday-school superintendent made a very moving speech to all the classes. It wrung our little hearts when he reminded us that because of the difficult times many poverty-stricken children actually were not getting enough good wholesome food to fill their empty little stomachs. It was heartrending, and I was so innocent that I had never realized before that such conditions existed. Then we were told to help the poor little boys and girls by bringing them some food the next Sunday. I was filled with childish pity as I thought of those less fortunate (I imagined!) than myself.

If one compares this version with the original, two observations may be made: (1) *truth* itself may depend upon *how* something is said; (2) direct attempts to make a reader *feel* are self-defeating.

Let us examine for a moment this first observation. Floyd Dell was recalling events and feelings from a distance of years. His problem was to see and feel as a young boy had seen and felt. As a man his feelings towards what happened to the boy were doubtless quite different, but he rigorously excludes these mature emotions. Here, then, truth depends not entirely on *what* is said but also on *how* it is said. In the second version of the first paragraph, a false note is struck at once with the word *autumn,* and this sort of falseness continues throughout the paragraph in words and phrases which you can easily pick out.

We can restate the second observation this way: the greater the inherent emotional content of a situation, the less welcome are words which label it as emotional. A child's disappointment at Christmas time is a situation of this sort. Any direct attempt at drawing tears would result in sloppy sentimentality and no tears. Floyd Dell knew this pitfall and avoided it by sticking to a simple, straightforward account. As a result the pathos of the piece is powerful and authentic.

We have in "Christmas" our best example so far of the fusion of content and form, matter and manner. "Exactly so it was," says the author, and the matter-manner of the telling convinces us that so it was. This sort of fusion is characteristic of poetry, particularly lyric poetry (see "Poetry: Preliminaries"). All forms of literature seek this fusion; the great works always attain it.

Memories of Christmas

DYLAN THOMAS
1914–1953

One Christmas was so much like another, in those years, around the sea town corner now, and out of all sound except the distant speaking of the voices I sometimes hear a moment before sleep, that I can never remember whether it snowed for six days and six nights when I was twelve or whether it snowed for twelve days and twelve nights when I was six; or whether the ice broke and the skating grocer vanished like a snow man through a white trap-door on that same Christmas Day that the mince-pies finished Uncle Arnold and we tobogganed down the seaward hill, all the afternoon, on the best tea-tray, and Mrs. Griffiths complained, and we threw a snowball at her niece, and my hands burned so, with the heat and the cold, when I held them in front of the fire, that I cried for twenty minutes and then had some jelly.

All the Christmases roll down the hill towards the Welsh-speaking sea, like a snowball growing whiter and bigger and rounder, like a cold and headlong moon bundling down the sky that was our street; and they stop at the rim of the ice-edged, fish-freezing waves, and I plunge my hands in the snow and bring out whatever I can find; holly or robins or pudding, squabbles and carols and oranges and tin whistles, and the fire in the front room, and bang go the crackers, and holy, holy, holy, ring the bells, and the glass bells shaking on the tree, and Mother Goose, and Struwelpeter—oh! the baby-burning flames and the clacking scissorman!—Billy Bunter and Black Beauty, Little Women and boys who have three helpings, Alice and Mrs. Potter's badgers, penknives, teddy-bears—named after a Mr. Theodore Bear, their inventor, or father, who died recently in the United States—mouth-organs, tin-soldiers, and blanc-mange, and Auntie Bessie playing "Pop Goes the Weasel" and "Nuts in May" and "Oranges and Lemons" on the untuned piano in the parlour all through the thimble-hiding musical-chairing blindman's-buffing party at the end of the never-to-be-forgotten day at the end of the unremembered year.

In goes my hand into that wool-white bell-tongued ball of holidays resting at the margin of

the carol-singing sea, and out come Mrs. Prothero and the firemen.

It was on the afternoon of the day of Christmas Eve, and I was in Mrs. Prothero's garden,
waiting for cats, with her son Jim. It was snowing. It was always snowing at Christmas; December, in my memory, is white as Lapland, though
there were no reindeers. But there were cats.
Patient, cold, and callous, our hands wrapped in
socks, we waited to snowball the cats. Sleek and
long as jaguars and terrible-whiskered, spitting
and snarling they would slink and sidle over the
white back-garden walls, and the lynx-eyed
hunters, Jim and I, fur-capped and moccasined
trappers from Hudson's Bay off Eversley Road,
would hurl our deadly snowballs at the green
of their eyes. The wise cats never appeared. We
were so still, Eskimo-footed arctic marksmen in
the muffling silence of the eternal snows—eternal, ever since Wednesday—that we never heard
Mrs. Prothero's first cry from her igloo at the
bottom of the garden. Or, if we heard it at all,
it was, to us, like the far-off challenge of our
enemy and prey, the neighbour's Polar Cat. But
soon the voice grew louder. "Fire!" cried Mrs.
Prothero, and she beat the dinner-gong. And we
ran down the garden, with the snowballs in our
arms, towards the house, and smoke, indeed,
was pouring out of the dining-room, and the
gong was bombilating, and Mrs. Prothero was
announcing ruin like a town-crier in Pompeii.
This was better than all the cats in Wales standing on the wall in a row. We bounded into the
house, laden with snowballs, and stopped at the
open door of the smoke-filled room. Something
was burning all right; perhaps it was Mr. Prothero, who always slept there after midday dinner with a newspaper over his face; but he was
standing in the middle of the room, saying "A
fine Christmas!" and smacking at the smoke with
a slipper.

"Call the fire-brigade," cried Mrs. Prothero
as she beat the gong.

"They won't be there," said Mr. Prothero.
"It's Christmas."

There was no fire to be seen, only clouds of
smoke and Mr. Prothero standing in the middle
of them, waving his slipper as though he were
conducting.

"Do something," he said.

And we threw all our snowballs into the
smoke—I think we missed Mr. Prothero—and
ran out of the house to the telephone-box.

"Let's call the police as well," Jim said.

"And the ambulance."

"And Ernie Jenkins, he likes fires."

But we only called the fire-brigade, and soon
the fire-engine came and three tall men in helmets brought a hose into the house and Mr.
Prothero got out just in time before they turned
it on. Nobody could have had a noisier Christmas Eve. And when the firemen turned off the
hose and were standing in the wet and smoky
room, Jim's aunt, Miss Prothero, came downstairs and peered in at them. Jim and I waited,
very quietly, to hear what she would say to
them. She said the right thing, always. She
looked at the three tall firemen in their shining
helmets, standing among the smoke and cinders
and dissolving snowballs, and she said: "Would
you like something to read?"

Now out of that bright white snowball of
Christmas gone comes the stocking, the stocking
of stockings, that hung at the foot of the bed
with the arm of a golliwog dangling over the
top and small bells ringing in the toes. There was
a company, gallant and scarlet but never nice
to taste though I always tried when very young,
of belted and busbied and musketed lead soldiers so soon to lose their heads and legs in the
wars on the kitchen table after the tea-things,
the mince-pies, and the cakes that I helped to
make by stoning the raisins and eating them,
had been cleared away; and a bag of moist and
many-coloured jelly-babies and a folded flag
and a false nose and a tram-conductor's cap
and a machine that punched tickets and rang a
bell; never a catapult; once, by a mistake that
no one could explain, a little hatchet; and a
rubber buffalo, or it may have been a horse,
with a yellow head and haphazard legs; and a
celluloid duck that made, when you pressed it,
a most unducklike noise, a mewing moo that an
ambitious cat might make who wishes to be a
cow; and a painting-book in which I could make
the grass, the trees, the sea, and the animals
any colour I pleased: and still the dazzling sky-
blue sheep are grazing in the red field under a
flight of rainbow-beaked and pea-green birds.

Christmas morning was always over before
you could say Jack Frost. And look! suddenly
the pudding was burning! Bang the gong and

call the fire-brigade and the book-loving firemen! Someone found the silver three-penny-bit with a currant on it; and the someone was always Uncle Arnold. The motto in my cracker read:

Let's all have fun this Christmas Day,
Let's play and sing and shout hooray!

and the grownups turned their eyes towards the ceiling, and Auntie Bessie, who had already been frightened, twice, by a clock-work mouse, whimpered at the sideboard and had some elderberry wine. And someone put a glass bowl full of nuts on the littered table, and my uncle said, as he said once every year: "I've got a shoe-nut here. Fetch me a shoe-horn to open it, boy."

And dinner was ended.

And I remembered that on the afternoon of Christmas Day, when the others sat around the fire and told each other that this was nothing, no, nothing, to the great snow-bound and turkey-proud yule-log-crackling holly-berry-bedizened and kissing-under-the-mistletoe Christmas when *they* were children, I would go out, school-capped and gloved and mufflered, with my bright new boots squeaking, into the white world on to the seaward hill, to call on Jim and Dan and Jack and to walk with them through the silent snowscape of our town.

We went padding through the streets, leaving huge deep footprints in the snow, on the hidden pavements.

"I bet people'll think there's been hippoes."

"What would you do if you saw a hippo coming down Terrace Road?"

"I'd go like this, bang! I'd throw him over the railings and roll him down the hill and then I'd tickle him under the ear and he'd wag his tail . . ."

"What would you do if you saw *two* hippoes . . . ?"

Iron-flanked and bellowing he-hippoes clanked and blundered and battered through the scudding snow towards us as we passed by Mr. Daniel's house.

"Let's post Mr. Daniel a snowball through his letter box."

"Let's write 'Mr. Daniel looks like a spaniel' all over his lawn."

"Look," Jack said, "I'm eating snow-pie."

"What's it taste like?"

"Like snow-pie," Jack said.

Or we walked on the white shore.

"Can the fishes see it's snowing?"

"They think it's the sky falling down."

The silent one-clouded heavens drifted on to the sea.

"All the old dogs have gone."

Dogs of a hundred mingled makes yapped in the summer at the sea-rim and yelped at the trespassing mountains of the waves.

"I bet St. Bernards would like it now."

And we were snowblind travellers lost on the north hills, and the dewlapped dogs, with brandy-flasks round their necks, ambled and shambled up to us, baying "Excelsior."

We returned home through the desolate poor sea-facing streets where only a few children fumbled with bare red fingers in the thick wheel-rutted snow and cat-called after us, their voices fading away, as we trudged uphill, into the cries of the dock-birds and the hooters of ships out in the white and whirling bay.

Bring out the tall tales now that we told by the fire as we roasted chestnuts and the gaslight bubbled low. Ghosts with their heads under their arms trailed their chains and said "whooo" like owls in the long nights when I dared not look over my shoulder; wild beasts lurked in the cubby-hole under the stairs where the gas-meter ticked. "Once upon a time," Jim said, "there were three boys, just like us, who got lost in the dark in the snow, near Bethesda Chapel, and this is what happened to them. . . ." It was the most dreadful happening I had ever heard.

And I remember that we went singing carols once, a night or two before Christmas Eve, when there wasn't the shaving of a moon to light the secret, white-flying street. At the end of a long road was a drive that led to a large house, and we stumbled up the darkness of the drive that night, each one of us afraid, each one holding a stone in his hand in case, and all of us too brave to say a word. The wind made through the drive-trees noises as of old and unpleasant and maybe web-footed men wheezing in caves. We reached the black bulk of the house.

"What shall we give them?" Dan whispered.

"'Hark the Herald'? 'Christmas Comes but Once a Year'?"

"No," Jack said: "We'll sing 'Good King Wenceslas.' I'll count three."

One, two, three, and we began to sing, our voices high and seemingly distant in the snow-felted darkness round the house that was occupied by nobody we knew. We stood close together, near the dark door.

Good King Wenceslas looked out
On the Feast of Stephen.

And then a small, dry voice, like the voice of someone who has not spoken for a long time, suddenly joined our singing: a small, dry voice from the other side of the door: a small, dry voice through the keyhole. And when we stopped running we were outside *our* house; the front room was lovely and bright; the gramophone was playing; we saw the red and white balloons hanging from the gas-brackets; uncles and aunts sat by the fire; I thought I smelt our supper being fried in the kitchen. Everything was good again, and Christmas shone through all the familiar town.

"Perhaps it was a ghost," Jim said.

"Perhaps it was trolls," Dan said, who was always reading.

"Let's go in and see if there's any jelly left," Jack said.

And we did that.

Comments and Questions

1. What is the effect of the breathless opening paragraphs? When one thinks back to earlier experiences how do the impressions register, in orderly or in chaotic fashion?

2. Note the structure of this piece. Obviously memories of many Christmases are racing through the author's mind, but how is the impression of a single Christmas achieved?

3. Compare the mood and tone of this piece with Floyd Dell's "Christmas" (p. 758).

A Cub Pilot's Experience

SAMUEL L. CLEMENS
1835–1910

. . . The *Paul Jones* was now bound for St. Louis. I planned a siege against my pilot, and at the end of three hard days he surrendered. He agreed to teach me the Mississippi River from New Orleans to St. Louis for five hundred dollars, payable out of the first wages I should receive after graduating. I entered upon the small enterprise of "learning" twelve or thirteen hundred miles of the great Mississippi River with the easy confidence of my time of life. If I had really known what I was about to require of my faculties, I should not have had the courage to begin. I supposed that all a pilot had to do was to keep his boat in the river, and I did not consider that that could be much of a trick, since it was so wide.

The boat backed out from New Orleans at four in the afternoon, and it was "our watch" until eight. Mr. Bixby, my chief, "straightened her up," ploughed her along past the sterns of the other boats that lay at the Levee, and then said, "Here, take her; shave those steamships as close as you'd peel an apple." I took the wheel, and my heart-beat fluttered up into the hundreds; for it seemed to me that we were about to scrape the side off every ship in the line, we were so close. I held my breath and began to claw the boat away from the danger; and I had my own opinion of the pilot who had known no better than to get us into such peril, but I was too wise to express it. In half a minute I had a wide margin of safety intervening between the *Paul Jones* and the ships; and within ten seconds more I was set aside in disgrace, and Mr. Bixby was going into danger again and flaying me alive with abuse of my cowardice. I was stung, but I was obliged to admire the easy confidence with which my chief loafed from side to side of his wheel, and trimmed the ships so closely that disaster seemed ceaselessly imminent. When he had cooled a little he told me that the easy water was close ashore and the current outside, and therefore we must hug the bank, up-stream, to get the benefit of the former, and stay well out, down-stream, to take advantage of the latter. In my own mind I resolved to be a down-stream pilot and leave the up-streaming to people dead to prudence.

Now and then Mr. Bixby called my attention to certain things. Said he, "This is Six-Mile Point." I assented. It was pleasant enough information, but I could not see the bearing of it. I was not conscious that it was a matter of any interest to me. Another time he said, "This is Nine-Mile Point." Later he said, "This is Twelve-Mile Point." They were all about level with the water's edge; they all looked about alike to me; they were monotonously unpicturesque. I hoped Mr. Bixby would change the subject. But no; he would crowd up around a point, hugging the shore with affection, and then say: "The slack water ends here, abreast this bunch of China-trees; now we cross over." So he crossed over. He gave me the wheel once or twice, but I had no luck. I either came near chipping off the edge of a sugar plantation, or I yawed too far from shore, and so dropped back into disgrace again and got abused.

The watch was ended at last, and we took supper and went to bed. At midnight the glare of a lantern shone in my eyes, and the night watchman said: "Come, turn out!"

And then he left. I could not understand this extraordinary procedure; so I presently gave up trying to, and dozed off to sleep. Pretty soon the watchman was back again, and this time he was gruff. I was annoyed. I said:

"What do you want to come bothering around here in the middle of the night for? Now, as like as not, I'll not get to sleep again tonight."

The watchman said:

"Well, if this ain't good, I'm blessed."

The "off-watch" was just turning in, and I heard some brutal laughter from them, and such remarks as "Hello, watchman! ain't the new cub turned out yet? He's delicate, likely. Give him some sugar in a rag, and send for the chambermaid to sing 'Rock-a-by Baby,' to him."

About this time Mr. Bixby appeared on the scene. Something like a minute later I was climbing the pilothouse steps with some of my clothes on and the rest in my arms. Mr. Bixby was close behind, commenting. Here was something fresh—this thing of getting up in the middle of the night to go to work. It was a detail in piloting that had never occurred to me at all. I knew that boats ran all night, but somehow I had never happened to reflect that somebody had to get up out of a warm bed to run them. I began to fear that piloting was not quite so romantic as I had imagined it was; there was something very real and worklike about this new phase of it.

It was a rather dingy night, although a fair number of stars were out. The big mate was at the wheel, and he had the old tub pointed at a star and was holding her straight up the middle of the river. The shores on either hand were not much more than half a mile apart, but they seemed wonderfully far away and ever so vague and indistinct. The mate said:

"We've got to land at Jones's plantation, sir."

The vengeful spirit in me exulted. I said to myself, "I wish you joy of your job, Mr. Bixby; you'll have a good time finding Mr. Jones's plantation such a night as this; and I hope you never *will* find it as long as you live."

Mr. Bixby said to the mate:

"Upper end of the plantation, or the lower?"

"Upper."

"I can't do it. The stumps there are out of the water at this stage. It's no great distance to the lower, and you'll have to get along with that."

"All right, sir. If Jones don't like it, he'll have to lump it, I reckon."

And then the mate left. My exultation began to cool and my wonder to come up. Here was a man who not only proposed to find this plantation on such a night, but to find either end of it you preferred. I dreadfully wanted to ask a question, but I was carrying about as many short answers as my cargo-room would admit of, so I held my peace. All I desired to ask Mr. Bixby was the simple question whether he was ass enough to really imagine he was going to find that plantation on a night when all plantations were exactly alike and all of the same color. But I held in. I used to have fine inspirations of prudence in those days.

Mr. Bixby made for the shore and soon was scraping it, just the same as if it had been daylight. And not only that, but singing: "Father in heaven, the day is declining," etc. It seemed to me that I had put my life in the keeping of a peculiarly reckless outcast. Presently he turned on me and said:

"What's the name of the first point above New Orleans?"

I was gratified to be able to answer promptly, and I did. I said I didn't know.

"Don't *know?*"

This manner jolted me. I was down at the foot again, in a moment. But I had to say just what I had said before.

"Well, you're a smart one!" said Mr. Bixby. "What's the name of the *next* point?"

Once more I didn't know.

"Well, this beats anything. Tell me the name of *any* point or place I told you."

I studied a while and decided that I couldn't.

"Look here! What do you start out from, above Twelve-Mile Point, to cross over?"

"I—I—don't know."

"You—you—don't know?" mimicking my drawling manner of speech. "What *do* you know?"

"I—I—nothing, for certain."

"By the great Caesar's ghost, I believe you! You're the stupidest dunderhead I ever saw or ever heard of, so help me Moses! The idea of *you* being a pilot—*you*! Why, you don't know enough to pilot a cow down a lane."

Oh, but his wrath was up! He was a nervous man, and he shuffled from one side of his wheel to the other as if the floor was hot. He would boil a while to himself, and then overflow and scald me again.

"Look here! What do you suppose I told you the names of those points for?"

I tremblingly considered a moment, and then the devil of temptation provoked me to say:

"Well—to—to—be entertaining, I thought."

This was a red rag to the bull. He raged and stormed so (he was crossing the river at the time) that I judged it made him blind, because he ran over the steering-oar of a trading-scow. Of course the traders sent up a volley of red-hot profanity. Never was a man so grateful as Mr. Bixby was; because he was brimful, and here were subjects who could *talk back*. He threw open a window, thrust his head out, and such an irruption followed as I never had heard before. The fainter and farther away the scow-men's curses drifted, the higher Mr. Bixby lifted his voice and the weightier his adjectives grew. When he closed the window he was empty. You could have drawn a seine through his system and not caught curses enough to disturb your mother with. Presently he said to me in the gentlest way:

"My boy, you must get a little memorandum-book; and every time I tell you a thing, put it down right away. There's only one way to be a pilot, and that is to get this entire river by heart. You have to know it just like A B C."

This was a dismal revelation to me; for my memory was never loaded with anything but blank cartridges. However, I did not feel discouraged long. I judged that it was best to make some allowances, for doubtless Mr. Bixby was "stretching." Presently he pulled a rope and struck a few strokes on the big bell. The stars were all gone now, and the night was as black as ink. I could hear the wheels churn along the bank, but I was not entirely certain that I could see the shore. The voice of the invisible watchman called up from the hurricane-deck:

"What's this, sir?"

"Jones's plantation."

I said to myself, "I wish I might venture to offer a small bet that it isn't." But I did not chirp. I only waited to see. Mr. Bixby handled the engine-bells, and in due time the boat's nose came to the land, a torch glowed from the forecastle, a man skipped ashore, a darky's voice on the bank said, "Gimme de k'yarpetbag, Mass' Jones," and the next moment we were standing up the river again, all serene. I reflected deeply a while and then said—but not aloud—"Well, the finding of that plantation was the luckiest accident that ever happened; but it couldn't happen again in a hundred years." And I fully believed it *was* an accident, too.

By the time we had gone seven or eight hundred miles up the river, I had learned to be a tolerably plucky upstream steersman, in daylight, and before we reached St. Louis I had made a trifle of progress in night-work, but only a trifle. I had a note-book that fairly bristled with the names of towns, "points," bars, islands, bends, reaches, etc., but the information was to be found only in the note-book—none of it was in my head. It made my heart ache to think I had only got half the river set down; for as our watch was four hours off and four hours on, day and night, there was a long four-hour gap in my book for every time I had slept since the voyage began.

My chief was presently hired to go on a big New Orleans boat, and I packed my satchel and went with him. She was a grand affair. When I stood in her pilot-house I was so far above the water that I seemed perched on a mountain; and her decks stretched so far away, fore and aft, below me, that I wondered how I could ever have considered the little *Paul Jones* a large craft. There were other differences, too. The *Paul Jones's* pilot-house was a cheap, dingy, battered rattletrap, cramped for room; but here was a sumptuous glass temple; room enough to have a dance in; showy red and gold window curtains; an imposing sofa; leather cushions and a back to the high bench where visiting pilots sit, to spin yarns and "look at the river"; bright, fanciful "cuspidores," instead of a broad wooden box filled with sawdust; nice new oilcloth on the floor; a hospitable big stove for winter; a wheel as high as my head, costly with inlaid work; a wire tiller-rope; bright brass knobs for the bells; and a tidy, white-aproned black "texas-tender," to bring up tarts and ices and coffee during mid-watch, day and night. Now this was "something like"; and so I began to take heart once more to believe that piloting was a romantic sort of occupation after all. The moment we were under way I began to prowl about the great steamer and fill myself with joy. She was as clean and as dainty as a drawing-room; when I looked down her long, gilded saloon, it was like gazing through a splendid tunnel; she had an oil-picture, by some gifted signpainter, on every stateroom door; she glittered with no end of prism-fringed chandeliers; the clerk's office was elegant, the bar was marvellous, and the barkeeper had been barbered and upholstered at incredible cost. The boiler-deck (*i.e.*, the second story of the boat, so to speak) was as spacious as a church, it seemed to me; so with the forecastle; and there was no pitiful handful of deck-hands, firemen, and roustabouts down there, but a whole battalion of men. The fires were fiercely glaring from a long row of furnaces, and over them were eight huge boilers! This was unutterable pomp. The mighty engines—but enough of this. I had never felt so fine before. And when I found that the regiment of natty servants respectfully "sir'd" me, my satisfaction was complete.

Comments and Questions

1. Characterize Mr. Bixby. Was he an expert teacher? Describe his methods.

2. What attitude does Mark Twain, the cub pilot, take towards his experience? Is this the source of humor which pervades the account? Discuss. Cite several examples of obvious exaggeration.

Amazing Grace
ROBERT DRAKE
1930–

I didn't much want to go with Daddy and Mamma out to Salem Church that Sunday. They were going to have dinner on the ground after preaching, and then after that the Barlow County Singing Convention was going to meet. I was twelve years old, and it looked like to me that I never was going to get away from the country. Every Sunday afternoon we had to go out to Uncle Jim and Aunt Mary's at Maple Grove, where Pa Drake used to live. Pa had been dead for several years, but it looked like Daddy and Mamma didn't know how to quit going. And every time we had to sit around and listen to all those old tales about when the Drake boys were growing up and all the fun they used to have with their neighbors like the Powells and the Sweats.

Pa Drake had come from Virginia after the War and married Grandma, who had been a Sanders, and I think his folks always thought he had married beneath himself. But Daddy used to tell Mamma and she told *me* that they would all have starved to death if it hadn't been for Grandma. Pa had been raised with slaves to wait on him and had gone off to school and learned to read Latin and Greek before he went off to the War, and I reckon he wasn't ever about to learn how to do anything else.

But, anyhow, it looked like everybody in my family was from the country and wasn't ever going to be anywhere else. None of them had ever been off to college because they didn't have any money for *anything*, much less education. They just all went to school out at Maple Grove a few months every year and went to church every Sunday, and that was about as far as any of them got, except Uncle Buford; and he finished high school because Daddy quit school to let him go.

But I was bound and determined that wasn't going to happen to me. I was going to get all the education in the world so I never would have to be ashamed of saying *seen* and *done* and *taken*, and I was going to go places and do things. They needn't to think they were going to keep *me* in Barlow County all my life. I had already had a big argument with Daddy, though, because I said I wanted to go to school at Harvard, which was supposed to be the best school in the whole country. But Daddy said no, sir, I wasn't going to get above my raising and go up there to school with a lot of Yankees that all loved the Negroes so much; I was going to school in the South and like it. It made me mad because I thought he just couldn't stand for me to go off and do things nobody in the whole Drake family had ever done before.

Well, anyhow, somebody in the Salem community had asked us out that Sunday, so about ten o'clock we got in the car and drove off. It was laying-by time, after all the weeds had been chopped out of the cotton, and the cotton was growing like wildfire all along the road. But it was hot as a fox, and I wasn't looking forward to the prospect of eating off the ground with all those ants and worms crawling all over the food and you, too.

It didn't take us long to get out to Salem; it was only about five miles out from Woodville. The church, which was a Baptist church, sat back off the road under some great big oak trees, and people had parked all over the yard without any system at all. They just drove up and stopped wherever they got ready. Most of the cars were old and broken-down looking, and there were a lot of pick-up trucks, too. Daddy was always talking about how poor farmers were and what a hard time they had, so I was used to them looking pretty run-down. But what made me kind of tired was the way Daddy seemed to *enjoy* talking about how bad off they were, like there might be something good about having to work so hard and never having any money and never going anywhere and doing anything. For my part, I just couldn't wait to go to New York and see all the museums and theaters and famous people and everything that was going on. But nothing ever happened to any of the Drakes; they just went on year after year as slow as Christmas.

There were still a lot of people in the cars, like couples courting and women nursing babies and changing their diapers right there in your face. But then they began getting out to go in the church, and they were all laughing and hollering like they hadn't seen each other in a thousand years. I thought it was all pretty disgusting and common. It didn't look like any of them had any refinement, and I didn't see how Daddy could be so crazy about them. But he was. He was always talking about some old man out in the country who probably didn't know how to read and write and saying, "He's one of the best men that ever had on a pair of pants"; or he would mention some old woman that was ugly as homemade sin and say, "Yes, I know she's so cross-eyed, when she cries, the tears run down her back, but she's one of the best women you ever saw." That kind of thing worried me because it looked like you had to be ugly and ignorant in order to be good, just like if you really enjoyed something, like going to the picture show, it was probably a bad influence on you. Or at least that was the way a lot of people acted.

The sermon was a pretty regulation Baptist kind with lots of emphasis on whether you were a wise or a foolish virgin and whether you would be ready if Jesus should come tonight. It looked like to me I had more and more things to worry about all the time. It wasn't enough for you to worry about whether or not you were going to get all A's on your report card so you could go to the picture show on school nights and whether you had practiced your hour on the piano every day. Then, on top of all that, you had to worry about going to Heaven and all. It looked like some people just couldn't be satisfied.

So I was pretty glad when church was over and it was time to eat, even if we were going to eat off the ground. The women went on out in the yard and started unloading the food from the cars and spreading their white Sunday tablecloths out under the big oak trees. There was lots of fried chicken and country ham and sliced tomatoes and stuffed eggs and all kinds of cake and pie. And somebody had gone into Woodville right after church to get the ice for the iced tea. Then everybody got a paper plate and started going around and helping himself to everything. When we started around, Mamma whispered to me that we had to take some of everything so as not to hurt anybody's feelings. That was another thing you had to worry about—whether or not you were going to hurt somebody's feelings. But it didn't look like to me anybody was sitting up late at night worrying about whether or not he had hurt *my* feelings.

We went around helping ourselves to everything and trying to eat a little on the side. A cross-eyed woman with buckteeth and dyed hair came up to Mamma and said, "Have you had any of my *cormel* cake?" And Mamma said, "Why, it's Cousin Lucy Belle Sanders, isn't it? No, indeed, I must get some of your caramel cake right away." It seemed like it was always people like that that we had to be kin to, and you always had to be nice to them when you didn't really want to. I used to wonder sometimes whether it would hurt you as much to be nice to people with straight eyes and straight teeth; but then, of course, when they were like that, you didn't have to worry about being *nice* to them in the first place.

Brother Jernigan, the preacher, was stepping around, speaking to all the ladies and eating enough to kill a mule. It looked like I hadn't ever seen a preacher yet that wasn't a big eater and a big man with the ladies; it looked like that just sort of *went* with preaching. And *they* always acted like they had it coming to them just for getting up there once a week and making you wonder about whether or not you were worrying about all the things you should. But they didn't seem to worry much about anything themselves. I reckoned it was sort of like the ravens feeding Elijah or doctors never getting sick or something.

About two o'clock when everybody was full as he could be and all the babies had gone to sleep, everybody began to get up off the ground and brush themselves off and put away the food and everything before the singing convention started. There was going to be a Bette Davis movie on that afternoon at the Dixie Theater in Woodville, and I begged Daddy to let us go on back home so I could see it. But he said, "Now, Robert, we're not going to eat and run like that. That would be just plain ordinary." I didn't like it, but I had to stop and think. It never had occurred to me before that I could be ordinary; it was uneducated people out in the country that were ordinary. I didn't exactly know what to make of it, so I followed Mamma and Daddy on into the church without saying anything.

The church was just like an oven, and you could tell that a lot of those people in there weren't any too familiar with soap and water. The place was jam-packed, and there didn't seem to be a breath of air stirring anywhere. The

singing convention met only about four times a year, so they were always pretty sure to have a good crowd on hand. People came from all over the county to hear the different solos and quartets and things from every community. Daddy said, though, that they used to meet more often; it was just one more old thing that was dying out.

Everybody got real quiet, and then the Boyd's Landing Quartet got up to sing. They were supposed to be the best quartet in the county; and Daddy said that Mr. Tom Newman, who sang bass, had a voice like distant thunder. They started off with "Alas, and did my Savior bleed?" which was another one of those hymns where you had to low-rate yourself and say you were a worm. ("Would He devote that sacred head for such a worm as I?") It was just like everything else; you never could enjoy anything without thinking maybe you didn't have any right to and were probably going to have to pay for it some day.

I looked at Mamma to see how she was holding out, but she and Daddy were sitting there looking like they couldn't think of anywhere else in the world they would rather be than right there. So I decided I might as well make up my mind to sit there all afternoon, but I sure hoped God was taking notice of how good I was being and was putting it down by my name in the Lamb's Book of Life or wherever He kept all His records.

Finally, after they had sung "Near-o my God to Thee" (they always pronounced "nearer" that way out in the country) and "On Jordan's stormy banks I stand," they got to "Amazing Grace." That was the first hymn I had ever learned; my nurse, Louella, had taught it to me when I was five years old. And it was written by John Newton, who was a converted slave trader. So I followed right along with the Quartet in my mind.

The first verse went:

"Amazing grace! how sweet the sound,
That saved a wretch like me!
I once was lost, but now am found,
Was blind, but now I see."

There you were calling yourself a wretch again, and yet there was supposed to be something sweet about it. I looked around at all those people; and I could see, from the way they looked so far off from the world, so calm and peaceful, that they all thought there was something sweet about being a wretch, too. But why was it so sweet to be a wretch? If it was good to be a wretch, it might also be good to live out in the country and have nothing but lamps for light and have dinner on the ground. Did it mean that God didn't really care whether you said *taken* or got all A's on your report card or lived at Salem or in New York, and that maybe He sort of enjoyed some people saying *taken* and living out in the country, and that maybe He didn't really care whether or not you were worrying about Jesus coming tonight? Was grace maybe something like rain that just fell anyhow and didn't care where it was falling and that was why it was so amazing?

I looked around at Daddy, and his eyes were full—just like they always got whenever he talked about Grandma and Pa or whenever he told me he loved Mamma even more now than he did when they were married or whenever he said he wanted me to have all the opportunities he had never had. Then the Quartet went on to another verse and sang:

" 'Twas grace that taught my heart to fear,
And grace my fears relieved;
How precious did that grace appear,
The hour I first believed!"

I was sitting there thinking that grace must be about the most wonderful thing going if it could do all that and that that must have been the way John Newton felt when he wrote that hymn, when, all of a sudden, Daddy put his arm around me and whispered, "Son, you just don't know how much Daddy loves you." And then, right there, in front of all those people, I just reached up and hugged him around the neck.

Comments and Questions

1. The movement of this piece seems to be casual, as though the narrator were simply offering impressions of "dinner on the ground after preaching." Is the selection of details really haphazard or are they highly controlled?

2. What is the basic dissatisfaction of the twelve-year-old boy toward his parents, his relatives, and the whole situation of his home town? How does this attitude give point to the unrestrained gesture at the end of the episode?

A Child's Reasoning
FREDERICK DOUGLASS
ca. 1817–1895

The incidents related in the foregoing chapter[1] led me thus early to inquire into the origin and nature of slavery. Why am I a slave? Why are some people slaves and others masters? These were perplexing questions and very troublesome to my childhood. I was very early told by some one that *"God up in the sky"* had made all things, and had made black people to be slaves and white people to be masters. I was told too that God was good, and that He knew what was best for everybody. This was, however, less satisfactory than the first statement. It came point blank against all my notions of goodness. The case of Aunt Esther[2] was in my mind. Besides, I could not tell how anybody could know that God made black people to be slaves. Then I found, too, that there were puzzling exceptions to this theory of slavery, in the fact that all black people were not slaves, and all white people were not masters.

An incident occurred about this time that made a deep impression on my mind. My Aunt Jennie and one of the men slaves of Captain Anthony ran away. A great noise was made about it. Old master was furious. He said he would follow them and catch them and bring them back, but he never did, and somebody told me that Uncle Noah and Aunt Jennie had gone to the free states and were free. Besides this occurrence, which brought much light to my mind on the subject, there were several slaves on Mr. Lloyd's place who remembered being brought from Africa. There were others who told me that their fathers and mothers were stolen from Africa.

---

[1] Chapter 5 of *Life and Times of Frederick Douglass*, revised edition of 1892. [2] The little boy had witnessed "old master," as the slave owner was called, brutally whipping the bared back of his Aunt Esther.

This to me was important knowledge, but not such as to make me feel very easy in my slave condition. The success of Aunt Jennie and Uncle Noah in getting away from slavery was, I think, the first fact that made me seriously think of escape for myself. I could not have been more than seven or eight years old at the time of this occurrence, but young as I was, I was already, in spirit and purpose, a fugitive from slavery.

Up to the time of the brutal treatment of my Aunt Esther, already narrated, and the shocking plight in which I had seen my cousin from Tuckahoe, my attention had not been especially directed to the grosser and more revolting features of slavery. I had, of course, heard of whippings and savage mutilations of slaves by brutal overseers, but happily for me I had always been out of the way of such occurrences. My play time was spent outside of the corn and tobacco fields, where the overseers and slaves were brought together and in conflict. But after the case of my Aunt Esther I saw others of the same disgusting and shocking nature. The one of these which agitated and distressed me most was the whipping of a woman, not belonging to my old master, but to Col. Lloyd. The charge against her was very common and very indefinite, namely, *"impudence."* This crime could be committed by a slave in a hundred different ways, and depended much upon the temper and caprice of the overseer as to whether it was committed at all. He could create the offense whenever it pleased him. A look, a word, a gesture, accidental or intentional, never failed to be taken as impudence when he was in the right mood for such an offense. In this case there were all the necessary conditions for the commission of the crime charged. The offender was nearly white, to begin with; she was the wife of a favorite hand on board of Mr. Lloyd's sloop, and was, besides, the mother of five sprightly children. Vigorous and spirited woman that she was, a wife and a mother, with a predominating share of the blood of the master running in her veins, Nellie (for that was her name) had all the qualities essential to impudence to a slave overseer. My attention was called to the scene of the castigation by the loud screams and curses that proceeded from the direction of it. When I came near the parties engaged in the struggle the overseer had hold of Nellie, endeavoring

with his whole strength to drag her to a tree against her resistance. Both his and her faces were bleeding, for the woman was doing her best. Three of her children were present, and though quite small (from seven to ten years old, I should think), they gallantly took the side of their mother against the overseer, and pelted him well with stones and epithets. Amid the screams of the children, "Let my mammy go! Let my mammy go!" the hoarse voice of the maddened overseer was heard in terrible oaths that he would teach her how to give a white man *impudence*. The blood on his face and on hers attested her skill in the use of her nails, and his dogged determination to conquer. His purpose was to tie her up to a tree and give her, in slaveholding parlance, a "genteel flogging," and he evidently had not expected the stern and protracted resistance he was meeting, or the strength and skill needed to its execution. There were times when she seemed likely to get the better of the brute, but he finally overpowered her and succeeded in getting her arms firmly tied to the tree towards which he had been dragging her. The victim was now at the mercy of his merciless lash. What followed I need not here describe. The cries of the now helpless woman, while undergoing the terrible infliction, were mingled with the hoarse curses of the overseer and the wild cries of her distracted children. When the poor woman was untied her back was covered with blood. She was whipped, terribly whipped, but she was not subdued, and continued to denounce the overseer and to pour upon him every vile epithet of which she could think.

Such floggings are seldom repeated on the same persons by overseers. They prefer to whip those who are the most easily whipped. The doctrine that submission to violence is the best cure for violence did not hold good as between slaves and overseers. He was whipped oftener who was whipped easiest. That slave who had the courage to stand up for himself against the overseer, although he might have many hard stripes at first, became while legally a slave virtually a freeman. "You can shoot me," said a slave to Rigby Hopkins, "but you can't whip me," and the result was he was neither whipped nor shot. I do not know that Mr. Sevier ever attempted to whip Nellie again. He probably never did, for he was taken sick not long after and died. It was commonly said that his deathbed was a wretched one, and that, the ruling passion being strong in death, he died flourishing the slave whip and with horrid oaths upon his lips. This deathbed scene may only be the imagings of the slaves. One thing is certain, that when he was in health his profanity was enough to chill the blood of an ordinary man. Nature, or habit, had given to his face an expression of uncommon savageness. Tobacco and rage had ground his teeth short, and nearly every sentence that he uttered was commenced or completed with an oath. Hated for his cruelty, despised for his cowardice, he went to his grave lamented by nobody on the place outside of his own house, if, indeed, he was even lamented there.

In Mr. James Hopkins, the succeeding overseer, we had a different and a better man, as good perhaps as any man could be in the position of a slave overseer. Though he sometimes wielded the lash, it was evident that he took no pleasure in it and did it with much reluctance. He stayed but a short time here, and his removal from the position was much regretted by the slaves generally. Of the successor of Mr. Hopkins I shall have something to say at another time and in another place.

For the present we will attend to a further description of the businesslike aspect of Col. Lloyd's "Great House" farm. There was always much bustle and noise here on the two days at the end of each month, for then the slaves belonging to the different branches of this great estate assembled here by their representatives to obtain their monthly allowances of cornmeal and pork. These were gala days for the slaves of the outlying farms, and there was much rivalry among them as to who should be elected to go up to the Great House farm for the "Allowances," and indeed to attend to any other business at this great place, to them the capital of a little nation. Its beauty and grandeur, its immense wealth, its numerous population, and the fact that uncles Harry, Peter, and Jake, the sailors on board the sloop, usually kept on sale trinkets which they bought in Baltimore to sell to their less fortunate fellow-servants, made a visit to the Great House farm a high privilege, and eagerly sought. It was valued, too, as a

mark of distinction and confidence, but probably the chief motive among the competitors for the office was the opportunity it afforded to shake off the monotony of the field and to get beyond the overseer's eye and lash. Once on the road with an oxteam and seated on the tongue of the cart, with no overseer to look after him, one felt comparatively free.

Slaves were expected to sing as well as to work. A silent slave was not liked, either by masters or overseers. "Make a noise there! Make a noise there!" and "bear a hand," were words usually addressed to slaves when they were silent. This, and the natural disposition of the Negro to make a noise in the world, may account for the almost constant singing among them when at their work. There was generally more or less singing among the teamsters, at all times. It was a means of telling the overseer, in the distance, where they were and what they were about. But on the allowance days those commissioned to the Great House farm were peculiarly vocal. While on the way they would make the grand old woods for miles around reverberate with their wild and plaintive notes. They were indeed both merry and sad. Child as I was, these wild songs greatly depressed my spirits. Nowhere outside of dear old Ireland, in the days of want and famine, have I heard sounds so mournful.

In all these slave songs there was some expression of praise of the Great House farm—something that would please the pride of the Lloyds.

> I am going to the Great House farm,
>   O, yea! O, yea! O, yea!
> My old master is a good old master,
>   O, yea! O, yea! O, yea!

These words would be sung over and over again, with others, improvised as they went along—jargon, perhaps, to the reader, but full of meaning to the singers. I have sometimes thought that the mere hearing of these songs would have done more to impress the good people of the North with the soul-crushing character of slavery than whole volumes exposing the physical cruelties of the slave system, for the heart has no language like song. Many years ago, when recollecting my experience in this respect, I wrote of these slave songs in the following strain:

"I did not, when a slave, fully understand the deep meaning of those rude and apparently incoherent songs. I was, myself, within the circle, so that I could then neither hear nor see as those without might see and hear. They breathed the prayer and complaint of souls overflowing with the bitterest anguish. They depressed my spirits and filled my heart with ineffable sadness."

The remark in the olden time was not unfrequently made, that slaves were the most contented and happy laborers in the world, and the dancing and singing were referred to in proof of this alleged fact; but it was a great mistake to suppose them happy because they sometimes made those joyful noises. The songs of the slaves represented their sorrows, rather than their joys. Like tears, they were a relief to aching hearts. It is not inconsistent with the constitution of the human mind that it avails itself of one and the same method for expressing opposite emotions. Sorrow and desolation have their songs, as well as joy and peace.

It was the boast of slaveholders that their slaves enjoyed more of the physical comforts of life than the peasantry of any country in the world. My experience contradicts this. The men and the women slaves on Col. Lloyd's farm received, as their monthly allowance of food, eight pounds of pickled pork, or its equivalent in fish. The pork was often tainted, and the fish were of the poorest quality. With their pork or fish, they had given them one bushel of Indian meal, unbolted, of which quite fifteen per cent was more fit for pigs than for men. With this, one pint of salt was given, and this was the entire monthly allowance of a full-grown slave, working constantly in the open field from morning till night every day in the month except Sunday. There is no kind of work which really requires a better supply of food to prevent physical exhaustion than the field-work of a slave. The yearly allowance of clothing was not more ample than the supply of food. It consisted of two tow-linen shirts, one pair of trousers of the same coarse material, for summer, and a woolen pair of trousers and a woolen jacket for winter, with one pair of yarn stockings and a pair of shoes of the coarsest description. Children under ten years old had neither shoes, stockings, jackets,

nor trousers. They had two coarse tow-linen shirts per year, and when these were worn out they went naked till the next allowance day—and this was the condition of the little girls as well as of the boys.

As to beds, they had none. One coarse blanket was given them, and this only to the men and women. The children stuck themselves in holes and corners about the quarters, often in the corners of huge chimneys, with their feet in the ashes to keep them warm. The want of beds, however, was not considered a great privation by the field hands. Time to sleep was of far greater importance. For when the day's work was done most of these had their washing, mending, and cooking to do, and having few or no facilities for doing such things, very many of their needed sleeping hours were consumed in necessary preparations for the labors of the coming day. The sleeping apartments, if they could have been properly called such, had little regard to comfort or decency. Old and young, male and female, married and single, dropped down upon the common clay floor, each covering up with his or her blanket, their only protection from cold or exposure. The night, however, was shortened at both ends. The slaves worked often as long as they could see, and were late in cooking and mending for the coming day, and at the first gray streak of the morning they were summoned to the field by the overseer's horn. They were whipped for oversleeping more than for any other fault. Neither age nor sex found any favor. The overseer stood at the quarter door, armed with stick and whip, ready to deal heavy blows upon any who might be a little behind time. When the horn was blown there was a rush for the door, for the hindermost one was sure to get a blow from the overseer. Young mothers who worked in the field were allowed an hour about ten o'clock in the morning to go home to nurse their children. This was when they were not required to take them to the field with them, and leave them upon "turning row," or in the corner of the fences.

As a general rule the slaves did not come to their quarters to take their meals, but took their ashcake (called thus because baked in the ashes) and piece of pork, or their salt herrings, where they were at work.

But let us now leave the rough usage of the

field, where vulgar coarseness and brutal cruelty flourished as rank as weeds in the tropics and where a vile wretch, in the shape of a man, rides, walks, and struts about, with whip in hand, dealing heavy blows and leaving deep gashes on the flesh of men and women, and turn our attention to the less repulsive slave life as it existed in the home of my childhood. Some idea of the splendor of that place sixty years ago has already been given. The contrast between the condition of the slaves and that of their masters was marvelously sharp and striking. There were pride, pomp, and luxury on the one hand, servility, dejection, and misery on the other.

Comments and Questions

1. This selection was taken from *Life and Times of Frederick Douglass* (chapter 6). It is, therefore, only a small segment of a long autobiography, a work which centers in the person of one man but which, just as importantly, exposes the reality of a slave-owning society. Does the author succeed in his attempt to make his readers *feel* the condition of being a field hand slave? Note the stateliness of the prose. Note also the use of adjectives: *brutal, shocking, revolting, savage, terrible* and the like. Do these words evoke the response Douglass was seeking? Compare the style of Floyd Dell in "Christmas," p. 758.

2. Memories of childhood have also been the basis of the four pieces preceding this one. All five authors display distinctive styles. If style is the man, what may be concluded about Dell, Thomas, Clemens, Drake, and Douglass?

3. Chapter 7 of Douglass's autobiography is called "Luxuries of the Great House." It throws into sharp contrast the lives of the slave owners and their slaves; yet the observation is made that "the poor slave, on his hard pine plank, scantily covered with his thin blanket, slept more soundly than the feverish voluptuary who reclined upon his downy pillow." Comment.

4. Douglass looms large today as a black who overcame. See Robert Hayden's "Frederick Douglass," p. 400.

The Execution of a Queen
JAMES ANTHONY FROUDE
1818–1894

The point of view in all the preceding selections, even in the passages from the *Life of Johnson,* has been from the inside looking out, with each biographer his own interpreter. In "The Execution of a Queen" Froude acts as a detached observer, the skillful artist who swings the camera close to his subject and gives us an intimate view of the last hours of Mary, Queen of Scots.

Her last night was a busy one. As she said to herself, there was much to be done and the time was short. A few lines to the King of France were dated two hours after midnight. They were to insist for the last time that she was innocent of the conspiracy, that she was dying for religion, and for having asserted her right to the crown; and to beg that out of the sum which he owed her, her servants' wages might be paid and masses provided for her soul. After this she slept for three or four hours, and then rose and with the most elaborate care prepared to encounter the end.

At eight in the morning the provost-marshal knocked at the outer door which communicated with her suite of apartments. It was locked and no one answered, and he went back in some trepidation lest the fears might prove true which had been entertained the preceding evening. On his returning with the sheriff, however, a few minutes later, the door was open, and they were confronted with the tall majestic figure of Mary Stuart standing before them in splendour. The plain gray dress had been exchanged for a robe of black satin; her jacket was of black satin also, looped and slashed and trimmed with velvet. Her false hair was arranged studiously with a coif, and over her head and falling down over her back was a white veil of delicate lawn. A crucifix of gold hung over her neck. In her hand she held a crucifix of ivory, and a number of jewelled pater-nosters was attached to her girdle. Led by two of Paulet's gentlemen, the sheriff walking before her, she passed to the chamber of presence in which she had been tried, where Shrewsbury, Kent, Paulet, Drury, and others were waiting to receive her. Andrew Melville, Sir Robert's brother, who had been master of her household, was kneeling in tears. "Melville," she said, "you should rather rejoice than weep that the end of my troubles is come. Tell my friends I die a true Catholic. Commend me to my son. Tell him I have done nothing to prejudice his kingdom of Scotland, and so, good Melville, farewell." She kissed him, and turning asked for her chaplain Du Preau. He was not present. There had been a fear of some religious melodrama which it was thought well to avoid. Her ladies, who had attempted to follow her, had been kept back also. She could not afford to leave the account of her death to be reported by enemies and Puritans, and she required assistance for the scene which she meditated. Missing them she asked the reason of their absence, and said she wished them to see her die. Kent said he feared they might scream or faint, or attempt perhaps to dip their handkerchiefs in her blood. She undertook that they should be quiet and obedient. "The queen," she said, "would never deny her so slight a request"; and when Kent still hesitated, she added with tears, "You know I am cousin to your queen, of the blood of Henry VII, a married Queen of France, and anointed Queen of Scotland."

It was impossible to refuse. She was allowed to take six of her own people with her, and select them herself. She chose her physician Burgoyne, Andrew Melville, the apothecary Gorion, and her surgeon, with two ladies, Elizabeth Kennedy, and Curle's young wife Barbara Mowbray, whose child she had baptized.

Allons donc, she then said—"Let us go," and passing out attended by the earls, and leaning on the arm of an officer of the guard, she descended the great staircase to the hall. The news had spread far through the country. Thousands of people were collected outside the walls. About three hundred knights and gentlemen of the county had been admitted to witness the execution. The tables and forms had been removed, and a great wood fire was blazing in the chimney. At the upper end of the hall, above the fireplace, but near it, stood the scaffold, twelve feet square and two feet and a half high. It was covered with black cloth; a low rail ran around it covered with black cloth also, and the sheriff's

guard of halberdiers were ranged on the floor below on the four sides to keep off the crowd. On the scaffold was the block, black like the rest; a square black cushion was placed behind it, and behind the cushion a black chair; on the right were two other chairs for the earls. The ax leaned against the rail, and two masked figures stood like mutes on either side at the back. The Queen of Scots as she swept in seemed as if coming to take part in some solemn pageant. Not a muscle of her face could be seen to quiver; she ascended the scaffold with absolute composure, looked round her smiling, and sat down. Shrewsbury and Kent followed and took their places, the sheriff stood at her left hand, and Beale then mounted a platform and read the warrant aloud.

In all the assembly Mary Stuart appeared the person least interested in the words which were consigning her to death.

"Madam," said Lord Shrewsbury to her, when the reading was ended, "you hear what we are commanded to do."

"You will do your duty," she answered, and rose as if to kneel and pray.

The Dean of Peterborough, Dr. Fletcher, approached the rail. "Madam," he began, with a low obeisance, "the queen's most excellent majesty"—thrice he commenced his sentence, wanting words to pursue it. When he repeated the words a fourth time, she cut him short.

"Mr. Dean," she said, "I am a Catholic, and must die a Catholic. It is useless to attempt to move me, and your prayers will avail me but little."

"Change your opinion, madam," he cried, his tongue being loosed at last; "repent of your sins, settle your faith in Christ, by him to be saved."

"Trouble not yourself further, Mr. Dean," she answered; "I am settled in my own faith, for which I mean to shed my blood."

"I am sorry, madam," said Shrewsbury, "to see you so addicted to popery."

"That image of Christ you hold there," said Kent, "will not profit you if he be not engraved in your heart."

She did not reply, and turning her back on Fletcher, knelt for her own devotions.

He had been evidently instructed to impair the Catholic complexion of the scene, and the Queen of Scots was determined that he should not succeed. When she knelt he commenced an extempore prayer in which the assembly joined. As his voice was sounded out in the hall she raised her own, reciting with powerful deep-chested tones the penitential psalms in Latin, introducing English sentences at intervals that the audience might know what she was saying, and praying with especial distinctness for her Holy Father the Pope.

From time to time, with conspicuous vehemence, she struck the crucifix against her bosom, and then, as the Dean gave up the struggle, leaving her Latin, she prayed in English wholly, still clear and loud. She prayed for the Church which she had been ready to betray, for her son whom she had disinherited, for the queen whom she had endeavoured to murder. She prayed God to avert his wrath from England, that England which she had sent a last message to Philip to beseech him to invade. She forgave her enemies, whom she had invited Philip not to forget, and then, praying to the saints to intercede for her with Christ, and kissing the crucifix and crossing her own breast, "Even as thy arms, O Jesus," she cried, "were spread upon the cross, so receive me into thy mercy and forgive my sins."

With these words she rose; the black mutes stepped forward, and in the usual form begged her forgiveness.

"I forgive you," she said, "for now I hope you shall end all my troubles." They offered their help in arranging her dress. "Truly, my lords," she said with a smile to the earls, "I never had such grooms waiting on me before." Her ladies were allowed to come up upon the scaffold to assist her; for the work to be done was considerable, and had been prepared with no common thought.

She laid her crucifix on her chair. The chief executioner took it as a perquisite, but was ordered instantly to lay it down. The lawn veil was lifted carefully off, not to disturb the hair, and was hung upon the rail. The black robe was next removed. Below it was a petticoat of crimson velvet. The black jacket followed, and under the jacket was a body of crimson satin. One of her ladies handed her a pair of crimson sleeves, with which she hastily covered her arms; and thus she stood on the black scaffold with the black figures all around her, blood-red from head to foot.

Her reasons for adopting so extraordinary a costume must be left to conjecture. It is only certain that it must have been carefully studied, and that the pictorial effect must have been appalling.

The women, whose firmness had hitherto borne the trial, began now to give way, spasmodic sobs bursting from them which they could not check. *Ne criez vous*, she said, *j'ay promis pour vous*. Struggling bravely, they crossed their breasts again and again, she crossing them in turn and bidding them pray for her. Then she knelt on the cushion. Barbara Mowbray bound her eyes with a handkerchief. *Adieu*, she said, smiling for the last time and waving her hand to them. *Adieu, au revoir*. They stepped back from off the scaffold and left her alone. On her knees she repeated the psalm, *In te, Domine, confido*, "In Thee, O Lord, have I put my trust." Her shoulders being exposed, two scars became visible, one on either side, and the earls being now a little behind her, Kent pointed to them with his white wand and looked inquiringly at his companion. Shrewsbury whispered that they were the remains of two abcesses from which she had suffered while living with him at Sheffield.

When the psalm was finished she felt for the block, and laying down her head she muttered: *In manus, Domine tuas, commendo animam meam*. The hard wood seemed to hurt her, for she placed her hands under her neck. The executioners gently removed them, lest they should deaden the blow, and then one of them holding her slightly, the other raised the ax and struck. The scene had been too trying even for the practised headsman of the Tower. His arm wandered. The blow fell on the knot of the handkerchief, and scarcely broke the skin. She neither spoke nor moved. He struck again, this time effectively. The head hung by a shred of skin, which he divided without withdrawing the ax; and at once a metamorphosis was witnessed, strange as was ever wrought by wand of fabled enchanter. The coif fell off and the false plaits. The laboured illusion vanished. The lady who had knelt before the block was in the maturity of grace and loveliness. The executioner, when he raised the head, as usual, to show it to the crowd, exposed the withered features of a grizzled, wrinkled old woman.

"So perish all enemies of the queen," said the Dean of Peterborough. A loud Amen rose over the hall. "Such end," said the Earl of Kent, rising and standing over the body, "to the queen's and the Gospels' enemies."

Orders had been given that everything which she had worn should be immediately destroyed, that no relics should be carried off to work imaginary miracles. Sentinels stood at the doors who allowed no one to pass out without permission; and after the first pause, the earls still keeping their places, the body was stripped. It then appeared that a favourite lapdog had followed its mistress unperceived, and was concealed under her clothes; when discovered it gave a short cry, and seated itself between the head and the neck, from which the blood was still flowing. It was carried away and carefully washed, and then beads, Paternoster, handkerchief—each particle of dress which the blood had touched, with the cloth on the block and on the scaffold, was burned in the hall fire in the presence of the crowd. The scaffold itself was next removed: a brief account of the execution was drawn up, with which Henry Talbot, Lord Shrewsbury's son, was sent to London, and then everyone was dismissed. Silence settled down on Fotheringay, and the last scene of the life of Mary Stuart, in which tragedy and melodrama were so strangely intermingled, was over. . . .

Comments and Questions

1. What is the essential conflict in this episode? What purpose does the Queen hope to realize through her careful preparation for the execution scene?

2. Explain the metamorphosis "strange as was ever wrought by wand of fabled enchanter."

3. In what way is this account like fiction? How does it differ from fiction?

4. Much is made by some modern critics of what is called "aesthetic distance." Although this phrase is more fully discussed elsewhere (see p. 20), it may be briefly defined here as describing the distance an author thinks appropriate for separating the reader from an action. It is assumed that some scenes can be fully responded to only if the emotional aspects of the scene are tightly controlled. Several questions in this connection arise when one considers "The Execution of a Queen." In general should historians as opposed to, say, novelists be concerned with aesthetic distance? Discuss. Specifically, is Froude justified in writing the paragraph, third from the end of the selection, in which the actual execution is described? Even more specifically, should he have written the sentence beginning: "The head hung by a shred of skin. . . ."?

"The last thing I wanted was infinite security. . . ."
SYLVIA PLATH
1932–1963

Although all autobiography is inevitably fictionalized to some extent, the following selection is frankly a hybrid of fiction and fact. The essential truth of Sylvia Plath's "confessions," however, cannot be doubted. She admitted that in *The Bell Jar,* from which this excerpt (chapter 7) has been taken, "many people close to her" were only "slightly disguised." In her own words: "I've tried to picture my world and the people in it as seen through the distorting lens of a bell jar." (Quoted in Lois Ames' "A Biographical Note," which appeared in the first American edition of *The Bell Jar,* New York: Harper & Row, 1971.)

Of course, Constantin was much too short, but in his own way he was handsome, with light brown hair and dark blue eyes and a lively, challenging expression. He could almost have been an American, he was so tan and had such good teeth, but I could tell straight away that he wasn't. He had what no American man I've ever met has had, and that's intuition.

From the start Constantin guessed I wasn't any protégé of Mrs. Willard's. I raised an eyebrow here and dropped a dry little laugh there, and pretty soon we were both openly raking Mrs. Willard over the coals and I thought, "This Constantin won't mind if I'm too tall and don't know enough languages and haven't been to Europe, he'll see through all that stuff to what I really am."

Constantin drove me to the UN in his old green convertible with cracked, comfortable brown leather seats and the top down. He told me his tan came from playing tennis, and when we were sitting there side by side flying down the streets in the open sun he took my hand and squeezed it, and I felt happier than I had been since I was about nine and running along the hot white beaches with my father the summer before he died.

And while Constantin and I sat in one of those hushed plush auditoriums in the UN, next to a stern muscular Russian girl with no makeup who was a simultaneous interpreter like Constantin, I thought how strange it had never occurred to me before that I was only purely happy until I was nine years old.

After that—in spite of the Girl Scouts and the piano lessons and the water-color lessons and the dancing lessons and the sailing camp, all of which my mother scrimped to give me, and college, with crewing in the mist before breakfast and blackbottom pies and the little new firecrackers of ideas going off every day—I had never been really happy again.

I stared through the Russian girl in her double-breasted gray suit, rattling off idiom after idiom in her own unknowable tongue—which Constantin said was the most difficult part because the Russians didn't have the same idioms as our idioms—and I wished with all my heart I could crawl into her and spend the rest of my life barking out one idiom after another. It mightn't make me any happier, but it would be one more little pebble of efficiency among all the other pebbles.

Then Constantin and the Russian girl interpreter and the whole bunch of black and white and yellow men arguing down there behind their labeled microphones seemed to move off at a distance. I saw their mouths going up and down without a sound, as if they were sitting on the deck of a departing ship, stranding me in the middle of a huge silence.

I started adding up all the things I couldn't do.

I began with cooking.

My grandmother and my mother were such good cooks that I left everything to them. They were always trying to teach me one dish or another, but I would just look on and say, "Yes, yes, I see," while the instructions slid through my head like water, and then I'd always spoil what I did so nobody would ask me to do it again.

I remember Jody, my best and only girlfriend at college in my freshman year, making me scrambled eggs at her house one morning. They tasted unusual, and when I asked her if she had put in anything extra, she said cheese and garlic salt. I asked who told her to do that, and she said nobody, she just thought it up. But then, she was practical and a sociology major.

I didn't know shorthand either.

This meant I couldn't get a good job after college. My mother kept telling me nobody wanted a plain English major. But an English major who knew shorthand was something else again. Everybody would want her. She would be in demand among all the up-and-coming young men and she would transcribe letter after thrilling letter.

The trouble was, I hated the idea of serving men in any way. I wanted to dictate my own thrilling letters. Besides, those little shorthand symbols in the book my mother showed me seemed just as bad as let t equal time and let s equal the total distance.

My list grew longer.

I was a terrible dancer. I couldn't carry a tune. I had no sense of balance, and when we had to walk down a narrow board with our hands out and a book on our heads in gym class I always fell over. I couldn't ride a horse or ski, the two things I wanted to do most, because they cost too much money. I couldn't speak German or read Hebrew or write Chinese. I didn't even know where most of the old out-of-the-way countries the UN men in front of me represented fitted in on the map.

For the first time in my life, sitting there in the soundproof heart of the UN building between Constantin who could play tennis as well as simultaneously interpret and the Russian girl who knew so many idioms, I felt dreadfully inadequate. The trouble was, I had been inadequate all along. I simply hadn't thought about it.

The one thing I was good at was winning scholarships and prizes, and that era was coming to an end.

I felt like a racehorse in a world without racetracks or a champion college footballer suddenly confronted by Wall Street and a business suit, his days of glory shrunk to a little gold cup on his mantel with a date engraved on it like the date on a tombstone.

I saw my life branching out before me like the green fig tree in the story.

From the tip of every branch, like a fat purple fig, a wonderful future beckoned and winked. One fig was a husband and a happy home and children, and another fig was a famous poet and another fig was a brilliant professor, and another fig was Ee Gee, the amazing editor, and another fig was Europe and Africa and South America, and another fig was Constantin and Socrates and Attila and a pack of other lovers with queer names and offbeat professions, and another fig was an Olympic lady crew champion, and beyond and above these figs were many more figs I couldn't quite make out.

I saw myself sitting in the crotch of this fig tree, starving to death, just because I couldn't make up my mind which of the figs I would choose. I wanted each and every one of them, but choosing one meant losing all the rest, and, as I sat there, unable to decide, the figs began to wrinkle and go black, and, one by one, they plopped to the ground at my feet.

Constantin's restaurant smelt of herbs and spices and sour cream. All the time I had been in New York I had never found such a restaurant. I only found those Heavenly Hamburger places, where they serve giant hamburgers and soup-of-the-day and four kinds of fancy cake at a very clean counter facing a long glarey mirror.

To reach this restaurant we had to climb down seven dimly lit steps into a sort of cellar.

Travel posters plastered the smoke-dark walls, like so many picture windows overlooking Swiss lakes and Japanese mountains and African velds, and thick, dusty bottle-candles, that seemed for centuries to have wept their colored waxes red over blue over green in a fine, three-dimensional lace, cast a circle of light round each table where the faces floated, flushed and flamelike themselves.

I don't know what I ate, but I felt immensely better after the first mouthful. It occurred to me that my vision of the fig tree and all the fat figs that withered and fell to earth might well have arisen from the profound void of an empty stomach.

Constantin kept refilling our glasses with a sweet Greek wine that tasted of pine bark, and I found myself telling him how I was going to learn German and go to Europe and be a war correspondent like Maggie Higgins.

I felt so fine by the time we came to the yogurt and strawberry jam that I decided I would let Constantin seduce me.

Ever since Buddy Willard had told me about that waitress I had been thinking I ought to go out and sleep with somebody myself. Sleeping with Buddy wouldn't count, though, because he would still be one person ahead of me, it would have to be with somebody else.

The only boy I ever actually discussed going to bed with was a bitter, hawk-nosed Southerner from Yale, who came to college one weekend only to find his date had eloped with a taxi driver the day before. As the girl had lived in my house and I was the only one home that particular night, it was my job to cheer him up.

At the local coffee shop, hunched in one of the secretive, high-backed booths with hundreds of people's names gouged into the wood, we drank cup after cup of black coffee and talked frankly about sex.

This boy—his name was Eric—said he thought it disgusting the way all the girls at my college stood around on the porches under the lights and in the bushes in plain view, necking madly before the one o'clock curfew, so everybody passing by could see them. A million years of evolution, Eric said bitterly, and what are we? Animals.

Then Eric told me how he had slept with his first woman.

He went to a Southern prep school that specialized in building all-round gentlemen, and by the time you graduated it was an unwritten rule that you had to have known a woman. Known in the Biblical sense, Eric said.

So one Saturday Eric and a few of his classmates took a bus into the nearest city and visited a notorious whorehouse. Eric's whore hadn't even taken off her dress. She was a fat, middle-aged woman with dyed red hair and suspiciously thick lips and rat-colored skin and she wouldn't turn off the light, so he had had her under a fly-spotted twenty-five watt bulb, and it was nothing like it was cracked up to be. It was boring as going to the toilet.

I said maybe if you loved a woman it wouldn't seem so boring, but Eric said it would be spoiled by thinking this woman too was just an animal like the rest, so if he loved anybody he would never go to bed with her. He'd go to a whore if he had to and keep the woman he loved free of all that dirty business.

It had crossed my mind at the time that Eric might be a good person to go to bed with, since he had already done it and, unlike the usual run of boys, didn't seem dirty-minded or silly when he talked about it. But then Eric wrote me a letter saying he thought he might really be able to love me, I was so intelligent and cynical and yet had such a kind face, surprisingly like his older sister's; so I knew it was no use, I was the type he would never go to bed with, and wrote him I was unfortunately about to marry a childhood sweetheart.

The more I thought about it the better I liked the idea of being seduced by a simultaneous interpreter in New York City. Constantin seemed mature and considerate in every way. There were no people I knew he would want to brag to about it, the way college boys bragged about sleeping with girls in the backs of cars to their roommates or their friends on the basketball team. And there would be a pleasant irony in sleeping with a man Mrs. Willard had introduced me to, as if she were, in a roundabout way, to blame for it.

When Constantin asked if I would like to come up to his apartment to hear some balalaika records I smiled to myself. My mother had always told me never under any circumstances to go with a man to a man's rooms after an evening out, it could mean only one thing.

"I am very fond of balalaika music," I said.

Constantin's room had a balcony, and the bal-cony overlooked the river, and we could hear the hooing of the tugs down in the darkness. I felt moved and tender and perfectly certain about what I was going to do.

I knew I might have a baby, but that thought hung far and dim in the distance and didn't trouble me at all. There was no one hundred per cent sure way not to have a baby, it said in an article my mother cut out of the *Reader's Digest* and mailed to me at college. This article was written by a married woman lawyer with children and called "In Defense of Chastity."

It gave all the reasons a girl shouldn't sleep with anybody but her husband and then only after they were married.

The main point of the article was that a man's world is different from a woman's world and a man's emotions are different from a woman's emotions and only marriage can bring the two worlds and the two different sets of emotions together properly. My mother said this was something a girl didn't know about till it was too late, so she had to take the advice of people who were already experts, like a married woman.

This woman lawyer said the best men wanted to be pure for their wives, and even if they weren't pure, they wanted to be the ones to teach their wives about sex. Of course they would try to persuade a girl to have sex and say they would marry her later, but as soon as she gave in, they would lose all respect for her and start saying that if she did that with them she would do that with other men and they would end up by making her life miserable.

The woman finished her article by saying better be safe than sorry and besides, there was no sure way of not getting stuck with a baby and then you'd really be in a pickle.

Now the one thing this article didn't seem to me to consider was how a girl felt.

It might be nice to be pure and then to marry a pure man, but what if he suddenly confessed he wasn't pure after we were married, the way Buddy Willard had? I couldn't stand the idea of a woman having to have a single pure life and a man being able to have a double life, one pure and one not.

Finally I decided that if it was so difficult to find a red-blooded intelligent man who was still pure by the time he was twenty-one I might as well forget about staying pure myself and marry somebody who wasn't pure either. Then when he started to make my life miserable I could make his miserable as well.

When I was nineteen, pureness was the great issue.

Instead of the world being divided up into Catholics and Protestants or Republicans and Democrats or white men and black men or even men and women, I saw the world divided into people who had slept with somebody and people who hadn't, and this seemed the only really significant difference between one person and another.

I thought a spectacular change would come over me the day I crossed the boundary line.

I thought it would be the way I'd feel if I ever visited Europe. I'd come home, and if I looked closely into the mirror I'd be able to make out a little white Alp at the back of my eye. Now I thought that if I looked into the mirror tomorrow I'd see a doll-size Constantin sitting in my eye and smiling out at me.

Well, for about an hour we lounged on Constantin's balcony in two separate slingback chairs with the victrola playing and the balalaika records stacked between us. A faint milky light diffused from the street lights or the half moon or the cars or the stars, I couldn't tell what, but apart from holding my hand Constantin showed no desire to seduce me whatsoever.

I asked if he was engaged or had any special girlfriend, thinking maybe that's what was the matter, but he said no, he made a point of keeping clear of such attachments.

At last I felt a powerful drowsiness drifting through my veins from all the pine-bark wine I had drunk.

"I think I'll go in and lie down," I said.

I strolled casually into the bedroom and stooped over to nudge off my shoes. The clean bed bobbed before me like a safe boat. I stretched full length and shut my eyes. Then I heard Constantin sigh and come in from the balcony. One by one his shoes clonked on to the floor, and he lay down by my side.

I looked at him secretly from under a fall of hair.

He was lying on his back, his hands under his head, staring at the ceiling. The starched white sleeves of his shirt, rolled up to the elbows, glimmered eerily in the half dark and his tan skin seemed almost black. I thought he must be the most beautiful man I'd ever seen.

I thought if only I had a keen, shapely bone structure to my face or could discuss politics shrewdly or was a famous writer Constantin might find me interesting enough to sleep with.

And then I wondered if as soon as he came to like me he would sink into ordinariness, and if as soon as he came to love me I would find fault after fault, the way I did with Buddy Willard and the boys before him.

The same thing happened over and over:

I would catch sight of some flawless man off in the distance, but as soon as he moved closer I immediately saw he wouldn't do at all.

That's one of the reasons I never wanted to get married. The last thing I wanted was infinite security and to be the place an arrow shoots off from. I wanted change and excitement and to shoot off in all directions myself, like the colored arrows from a Fourth of July rocket.

I woke to the sound of rain.

It was pitch dark. After a while I deciphered the faint outlines of an unfamiliar window. Every so often a beam of light appeared out of thin air, traversed the wall like a ghostly, exploratory finger, and slid off into nothing again.

Then I heard the sound of somebody breathing.

At first I thought it was only myself, and that I was lying in the dark in my hotel room after being poisoned. I held my breath, but the breathing kept on.

A green eye glowed on the bed beside me. It was divided into quarters like a compass. I reached out slowly and closed my hand on it. I lifted it up. With it came an arm, heavy as a dead man's, but warm with sleep.

Constantin's watch said three o'clock.

He was lying in his shirt and trousers and stocking feet just as I had left him when I dropped asleep, and as my eyes grew used to the darkness I made out his pale eyelids and his straight nose and his tolerant, shapely mouth, but they seemed insubstantial, as if drawn on fog. For a few minutes I leaned over, studying him. I had never fallen asleep beside a man before.

I tried to imagine what it would be like if Constantin were my husband.

It would mean getting up at seven and cooking him eggs and bacon and toast and coffee and dawdling about in my nightgown and curlers after he'd left for work to wash up the dirty plates and make the bed, and then when he came home after a lively, fascinating day he'd expect a big dinner, and I'd spend the evening washing up even more dirty plates till I fell into bed, utterly exhausted.

This seemed a dreary and wasted life for a girl with fifteen years of straight A's, but I knew that's what marriage was like, because cook and clean and wash was just what Buddy Willard's mother did from morning till night, and she was the wife of a university professor and had been a private school teacher herself.

Once when I visited Buddy I found Mrs. Willard braiding a rug out of strips of wool from Mr. Willard's old suits. She'd spent weeks on that rug, and I had admired the tweedy browns and greens and blues patterning the braid, but after Mrs. Willard was through, instead of hanging the rug on the wall the way I would have done, she put it down in place of her kitchen mat, and in a few days it was soiled and dull and indistinguishable from any mat you could buy for under a dollar in the five and ten.

And I knew that in spite of all the roses and kisses and restaurant dinners a man showered on a woman before he married her, what he secretly wanted when the wedding service ended was for her to flatten out underneath his feet like Mrs. Willard's kitchen mat.

Hadn't my own mother told me that as soon as she and my father left Reno on their honeymoon—my father had been married before, so he needed a divorce—my father said to her, "Whew, that's a relief, now we can stop pretending and be ourselves"?—and from that day on my mother never had a minute's peace.

I also remembered Buddy Willard saying in a sinister, knowing way that after I had children I would feel differently, I wouldn't want to write poems any more. So I began to think maybe it was true that when you were married and had children it was like being brainwashed, and afterward you went about numb as a slave in some private, totalitarian state.

As I stared down at Constantin the way you stare down at a bright, unattainable pebble at the bottom of a deep well, his eyelids lifted and he looked through me, and his eyes were full of love. I watched dumbly as a shutter of recognition clicked across the blur of tenderness and the wide pupils went glossy and depthless as patent leather.

Constantin sat up, yawning. "What time is it?"

"Three," I said in a flat voice. "I better go home. I have to be at work first thing in the morning."

"I'll drive you."

As we sat back to back on our separate sides of the bed fumbling with our shoes in the horrid cheerful white light of the bed lamp, I sensed Constantin turn round. "Is your hair always like that?"

"Like what?"

He didn't answer but reached over and put his hand at the root of my hair and ran his fingers out slowly to the tip ends like a comb. A little electric shock flared through me and I sat quite still. Ever since I was small I loved feeling somebody comb my hair. It made me go all sleepy and peaceful.

"Ah, I know what it is," Constantin said. "You've just washed it."

And he bent to lace up his tennis shoes.

An hour later I lay in my hotel bed, listening to the rain. It didn't even sound like rain, it sounded like a tap running. The ache in the middle of my left shin bone came to life, and I abandoned any hope of sleep before seven, when my radio-alarm clock would rouse me with its hearty renderings of Sousa.

Every time it rained the old leg-break seemed to remember itself, and what it remembered was a dull hurt.

Then I thought, "Buddy Willard made me break that leg."

Then I thought, "No, I broke it myself. I broke it on purpose to pay myself back for being such a heel."

Comments and Questions

1. One notes an adolescent lighthearted frankness in the author's recounting of her experiences. A quite different mood pervades Plath's poems. Read "Two Views of a

Cadaver Room'' and ''Suicide off Egg Rock,'' p. 412, and compare the mood in these poems with the mood in the prose sketch.

2. Explain the metaphor of the figs. How does Plath, later in the chapter, make fun of the dark implications of the withering figs?

3. Lamb observed that all people fall into only two classes: borrowers and lenders. (See ''Two Races of Man,'' p. 803.) Into what two classes does Plath, at nineteen, divide human kind?

4. Plath is something of a hero to the women liberationists of today. Locate the passages in this selection which qualify her for this rôle. Locate others which do not.

BIOGRAPHY: SKETCHES

BIOGRAPHY IN THREE LENGTHS

The biographical sketch stands somewhere between encyclopedia accounts and full-length biographies. It is an expansion of the first and a distillation of the second. The encyclopedist works strictly by formula and within rigid space limitations. He presents highly selective, straight facts in chronological order, with a few details and little comment. Somewhat more informative than tombstone biography, his compilation serves the same sort of need that a map of routes through a city does in a travel book. The encyclopedist may safely assume the interest of the reader and does nothing to stimulate it. His one job is to include facts relating to the highlights of his subject's career: dates of birth and death, education, chief claim to fame, marital status, homes, travels, with perhaps a word about reputation yesterday and today, and the names of one or two authoritative books on his subject. The encyclopedist is a reporter, not an artist.

The writer of full-length biography is necessarily an artist. He may be a good one or a poor one, but he cannot escape most of the problems which the creative artist has to solve. Unlike the encyclopedist but like the creative writer, he cannot assume continuing interest on the part of readers. He must select and arrange his materials, which may be vast. More important, he must interpret and account for the pattern of his subject's life. Sometimes the biographer digs out the facts *and* writes the biography. Boswell, for example, was a searcher, researcher, and biographer, and great at all three. Many biographies are simply a reworking of known facts which are decked out in a new style, in a different arrangement, with a shifted emphasis— all of which constitutes a new interpretation. Often these biographies are fat tomes, as long or longer than novels.

The personal sketch has something of the same relation to full-length biography that the short story has to the novel. Differences, however, are greater than the surface similarities. The purpose of the sketcher is to provide a quickly readable, entertaining account. To achieve this goal, he too writes by formula—the formula of the artist, not the compiler. This formula consists of what may be called tricks of the trade—methods carefully worked out and tested by which the writer expects to seize and hold the attention of the reader. He assumes that the reader already knows something about the person being portrayed: his chief claim to fame, approximately when he lived, and perhaps other facts. His main task is to provide a focus, a way of looking at his subject. He gives information, but it is incidental to interpretation. He handles the facts so much as an essayist would that the term "biographical essay" could be accurately applied to most of these sketches.

SKETCHES OF THE QUICK AND THE DEAD

Portraits of living persons involve special difficulties, not the least of which is the restraining influence of the libel laws. For this reason, the sketch from life may give the appearance of a retouched photograph with all the wrinkles missing. Information may be abundant; it may include, and frequently does, personal contact between the subject and the sketcher. At such close range, however, accurate focusing is difficult, the problem of interpretation great. We have included one portrait of a living person, the playwright Tennessee Williams, as representative of this class of biography.

We have included one short interpretive account of a person who has been dead for nearly two centuries. The facts about Edward Gibbon, the subject of this sketch, have long been known and available. What do the facts mean? That is the question the portraitist of the dead has to answer. Besides finding the meaning, he has the problem of making this meaning interesting to readers. Like an expert chef, he manages the ingredients as best he can to produce a palatable result. How he manages is his technique.

As we read the following selections we shall be able to make two observations: (1) that certain techniques are common to all the sketches, and (2) that the results, in spite of this common ground, are different for each sketch.

GUIDE QUESTIONS BASIC TO ANALYSES OF BIOGRAPHICAL SKETCHES

How is the beginning handled?

Is a controlling idea for the whole sketch indicated?

At what point, if at all, does the chronological account of the life begin?

What parts of the account would you call interpretive?

How much quoted material is used and for what purpose?

Are all the allusions familiar to you?

How is the ending handled?

Tennessee Williams

LINCOLN BARNETT
1909–

One Sunday afternoon shortly after the opening of Tennessee Williams's remarkable new drama, *A Streetcar Named Desire*, a friend called on the playwright in his temporary lodging in midtown Manhattan. It was little more than a furnished room, a dusty, angular recess in an old brownstone house. Through its windows crept drafts and a view of other brown façades across the street. A small desk lamp cast pale rays across the unmade bed, across a moraine of movie magazines and books of philosophy, across a table littered with albums of Shostakovich and New Orleans jazz, and into the wild desolation of a kitchenette in the rear. Under the lamp was a portable typewriter. In the typewriter was a sheet of paper. On the paper was a passage of fresh dialogue.

The visitor waved some newspapers at Williams as he entered. "Say, Tenn," he said, shouting above the uproar of a singing commercial extruding from the radio, "did you see the *Times* and *Trib* today?"

Williams stared at the manuscript in his machine. His boyish, rather ovoid face was expressionless. "The thing I hate about starting a new play," he said mostly to himself, "is that there's always so much waste. So many things don't strike fire."

"Listen, if you didn't see the papers today, let me read you what—here it is, Howard Barnes in the *Herald Tribune*. Listen to this now, quote, 'A great new talent is at work in the theater to make one hope that the lean years are over. In *A Streetcar Named Desire*, Tennessee Williams more than justifies the promise of high dramatic imagination and craftsmanship which he held forth in *The Glass Menagerie*. His new work is a somber tragedy about frustration, but it has far more heroic dimensions than his earlier—' Hey, do you mind if I shut off that radio? Are you listening—I mean to me?"

Williams lowered his gaze from a section of molding in a far corner of the ceiling. "Listening to you?" he repeated. "Yes. Why?"

"I thought you were off in space somewhere. Well, Barnes goes on to say, quote, 'There is a maturity about'—wait a minute now, get this —'Williams is certainly the Eugene O'Neill of the present period on the stage! . . . It is not unlikely that he will lead the theater into a new and exciting era!'"

"Well," said Williams.

"Did you hear that? You're the Eugene O'Neill of today!"

"Well," said Williams, slumping on his bed with the hopeless air of one confronted with a problem too tough even to think about.

"Now, then, listen to what Brooks Atkinson says in the *Times*, quote, 'By common consent the finest new play on the boards just now is Tennessee Williams's *A Streetcar Named Desire*. As a tribute to the good taste of this community it is also a smash hit. . . . Although Mr. Williams does not write verse, nor escape into mysticism or grandeur, he is a poet. . . . Out of a few characters he can evoke the sense of life as a wide, endlessly flowing pattern of human needs and aspirations. . . . He is an incomparably beautiful writer. . . .' Now how do you like that?"

"Well," said Williams, "that's very good, isn't it? I reckon I'd better write and say thank you."

"Write! If I were you I'd take 'em both to dinner at Twenty-One."

"Would you?" A shadow of anxiety came into his bland blue eyes. "I'm scared to death of meeting critics. I'm so afraid of offending them some way." He got to his feet and put a blues record on the phonograph. Then he wandered over to the typewriter and contemplated the page of dialogue it contained. For several minutes he stood there, silent, abstracted, serene. Then without emotion, as though stating a broad philosophical principle, he said, "It's hard to get new subjects to write about."

The principal reason for Williams's apparent apathy lay in the fact that he was already at work on a new play—in itself an anomaly that differentiates him from more seasoned playwrights who usually tend to lie fallow for months following a profitable endeavor. Williams is a rarity among writers in that he cherishes the actual operation of writing. The exterior or active world which men call the world of reality is to him as evanescent as a dream. He feels wholly alive and tranquil only when he is submerged in his inner cosmos, apprehending the stimuli of his own invention. Although he is a compassionate man, sensitive to the moods and responses of other people, he has few really close friends. And although he enjoys random hours of drinking or conversation, it is always with a sense of relief that he returns to his typewriter and the comradeship of his introspection. Also, like many writers and most bachelors, he is a hypochondriac. He is continuously and unpleasantly conscious of the pulsations of his heart, the act of respiration, and the flow of blood in his arterial system. He forgets these functions of the flesh only in the make-believe world of which he writes.

Because of his withdrawal from the objective world, acquaintances often assume that Williams is egotistical or pompous. To some extent his appearance abets this impression. In the past two years he has gained weight, and this extra poundage, combined with a new-grown mustache and less-than-average height, invests him, at thirty-three, with a deceptive air of plump complacency. When people see him at a party, sitting in a corner by himself, his eyes remote and somnolent, they generally conclude that he is bored to death and perhaps contemptuous. There is little in his rather stolid and commonplace exterior to suggest the sensitive, poetic intellect within.

His conversation shows little kinship with the luminous dialogue that distinguishes his plays. With friends he reveals a certain shy charm, but lapses recurrently into long, detached silences; with others the silences are longer. He has no small talk; when people express admiration for his work he is likely to respond with an ambiguous grunt. For one thing, he has always regarded his work as important, but important principally to himself as a narcotic, as fulfillment and escape. He now finds himself surprised, even more than pleased, to discover that other people consider it important too.

Williams's plays have been compared with those of Anton Chekhov, and he readily acknowledges the great Russian as his dramaturgic mentor. Like Chekhov's, his plays imbue isolated and outwardly trivial events with a sense of spiritual significance. In mood the plays of both Chekhov and Williams are warm but unsentimental. In content both deal with the isolation of human beings and their tragic inability to understand one another. *A Streetcar Named Desire* is, by Williams's own definition, "a tragedy of incomprehension"; its protagonist, Blanche Du Bois, is, in the words of Brooks Atkinson, "one of the dispossessed whose experience has unfitted her for reality." The latter phrase could be applied with equal validity to the trio of principals in *The Glass Menagerie* or a score of characters in Williams's other works (which include several less successful three-act dramas and more than a dozen published one-act plays).

"Every artist has a basic premise pervading his whole life," Williams observes, "and that premise can provide the impulse to everything he creates. For me the dominating premise has been the need for understanding and tenderness and fortitude among individuals trapped by circumstance."

Williams once termed *The Glass Menagerie* a "memory play" and he is frank to admit that the character of Amanda Wingfield (enacted by Laurette Taylor just before her death) derives from his mother. By the same token Laura Wingfield is, with modifications, his sister. And Tom Wingfield, the unhappy young man who wanted beauty and adventure in his life but had to spend it working in a warehouse, is Tennessee Williams himself. He speaks indeed through the mouths of all his characters, for until three years ago Williams too was "one of the dispossessed."

Although Williams's antecedents are Southern, he was born in Mississippi, not Tennessee, and his real name is Thomas Lanier Williams. He abandoned his given name when he felt he had "compromised" it by the imperfections of his early writing, and he adopted Tennessee as a gesture to his ancestors who had fought the Indians in that state. His father was a traveling salesman for a shoe company. His maternal grandfather, with whom the Williamses lived, was a rector of an Episcopal church in Columbus, Mississippi. The first years of Williams's life were happy ones, spent for the most part in the South and marked by only two events of psychogenetic significance. The first involved a Negro nurse named Ozzie who dearly loved Williams and his elder sister and younger brother, and whose affection was reciprocated by them. One day in a moment of petulance, Williams called her "nigger," a word he had never heard used in his grandfather's house. Ozzie walked out and never returned, and although the family sought her for weeks afterward they never saw her again. The episode left Williams with a sensation of guilt which persists to this day and makes him especially sympathetic to all antidiscrimination causes. His contract for *Streetcar* contains a clause, inserted at his request, that the play will not be performed in any theater where race segregation is the rule.

The other formative event of Williams's childhood was an attack of diphtheria that injured his heart and confined him to his room for a year. During these months of immobility he became a bookish, solitary boy whose imagination contrived the adventures his illness denied him. He developed a curious faculty of visualizing scenes with his eyes closed in bed at night. When he finished a book that captured his fancy he would amplify and elaborate the story in his mind, with himself as hero, and the images he projected against his closed eyelids were as vivid as though he perceived them in color on a motion-picture screen. As the years passed, the ocular effects faded and dimmed, but he never entirely lost his odd aptitude. "I still beguile myself," he says, "with fantasies at night."

When Williams was still a small boy his father, who had done well on the road, was transferred to a desk job in St. Louis. The move had profound and tragic results for the family. Neither Williams nor his sister, who was the closest companion of his childhood, could adjust to urban life. They had loved Mississippi—"a dark wide spacious land that you can breathe in"—and they had never been aware of economic differences or their own slim circumstances, for their grandfather was the Rector, and they were aristocracy. "But in St. Louis," Williams recalled in later years, "we suddenly discovered that there were two kinds of people, the rich and the poor, and that we belonged more to the latter." The private-school children snubbed them and the public-school children ridiculed their Southern speech and manners. "I remember gangs of kids following me home yelling 'Sissy!'—and home was not a very pleasant refuge. It was a perpetually dim little apartment in a wilderness of identical brick and concrete structures. . . . If I had been born to this situation I might not have resented it deeply. But it was forced upon my consciousness at the most sensitive age of childhood. It produced a shock and rebellion that have grown into an inherent part of my work."

The room occupied by Williams's sister looked out on a narrow sunless areaway so dreary in aspect that she kept her curtains constantly drawn and immersed herself in twilit gloom. Williams named the areaway "Death Valley," for night after night stray cats, pursued by stray dogs, were cornered there and torn to pieces, screaming hideously; morning after morning new eviscerated corpses bled beneath her window. To alleviate the melancholy of her surroundings, together they painted the furniture white, hung white curtains across the window, and arrayed on shelves around the walls a collection of miniature animals and other objects made of glass, which suffused the room with a light and delicate enchantment. These little glass animals, Williams recalls, "came to represent in my memory all the softest emotions that belong to recollections of things past. They stood for all the small and tender things that relieve the austere pattern of life and make it endurable to the sensitive. The areaway where the cats were torn to pieces was one thing—my sister's white curtains and tiny menagerie of glass were another. Somewhere between them was the world that we lived in."

Williams's distaste for his new home soon flowered into a cluster of neuroses. He developed a fear of using his voice in public and sat mute when called on to recite in class. He blushed when anyone addressed him or caught his eye and, being ashamed of blushing, he blushed all the more. One night it occurred to him that falling asleep was akin to dying, so for months he fought off sleep each night, holding his eyes open and staring at the window with terrified intensity. Even now this specter recurrently haunts him, and he will find himself after midnight fearfully resisting the approach of oblivion. Yet somehow he finished school and three years at the University of Missouri. He won several prizes for prose and poetry and sold a few short stories to *Weird Tales*. He also joined a fraternity (Alpha Tau Omega), fell in love for a while with a girl in a sorority across the street, and discovered that alcohol was a good cure for shyness.

At the end of three years the depression persuaded his father to remove him from college and put him to work with the shoe company. He endured his job with a loathing that has never waned to this day. "The job was designed for insanity," he says. "It was a living death." Each morning he had to dust every shoe in the sample room; each afternoon he had to type endless factory orders consisting mostly of strings of numerals; each day was utterly monotonous and a repetition of the day before. "The lives of most people," he wrote one day in a vortex of despair, "are insulated against monotony by a corres-

ponding monotony in their own souls . . . alas for the poet, the dreamer . . . who has been cast into the world without this indispensable insulation." After work, to void his frustrations he shut himself in his room, gulped coffee to keep himself awake, and wrote innumerable short stories and poems which he could not sell.

Ultimately under this regime, which lasted two years, his health failed. One night while writing he felt his heart begin to pound and skip beats. Panic-stricken, he rushed from the house and walked the streets until dawn. Next day a doctor told him casually that he had a heart condition, but neglected to assure him it was nothing organic but simply a functional disorder that rest would cure. Williams immediately sank into an abyss of hypochondriacal fear. Several nights later when coming home from the movies in a taxi with his sister his fingers suddenly went rigid and a paralytic spasm immobilized his legs. He spent a week in the hospital, at the end of which time he was warned to stop worrying about his heart, to give up his job, and go away for a protracted rest.

No sooner was he delivered from the shoe company than Williams's health improved. He convalesced at the home of his grandparents and then, with their assistance, finished his education at the State University of Iowa, where he majored in drama and received his B.A. in 1938. During this interlude he wrote two full-length plays which were produced by a drama group in St. Louis. The first was a success, the second such an emphatic failure that at the end of the opening performance he tore the manuscript to shreds and, with friends on hand to intercept him, lunged desperately at an open window.

Upon his graduation he found his father still opposed to his literary ambitions and anxious to reinstate him in the shoe factory. Finding home intolerable, Williams resolved to strike out on his own, and from that day on he was "that common American phenomenon, a rootless wandering writer." He worked as a waiter in the French Quarter of New Orleans and picked feathers from squabs on a pigeon ranch in California. He traveled on his thumb, and once with an equally destitute friend who owned a Ford jalopy crossed the country by siphoning gasoline from parked cars. Meantime he wrote a number of one-act plays which won him a one-hundred-dollar prize in a competition for young play-wrights and, more importantly, caught the eye of a New York agent named Audrey Wood, who was to become his loyal friend and counselor.

For several bleak months he was forced back to St. Louis, where he worked in the attic of his parents' house on a three-act play called *Battle of Angels*. When it was finished he dispatched it to Miss Wood and began hunting despondently for a job. One morning the phone rang when he was still in bed. He heard his mother answer it and then gasp, "Long-distance from New York!" It was Miss Wood calling with the news that he had been awarded a one-thousand-dollar Dra-matists' Guild Fellowship for his previous work and that she had read *Battle of Angels* and was excited about it. When he hung up, his mother burst into tears. "What's the matter?" he asked in amazement. "I'm just so happy and relieved," she sobbed.

Fortified by new hope and his one thousand dollars, Williams went to New York and suddenly found himself in the midst of the professional theater, for soon after his arrival Miss Wood had relayed another bulletin: the Theatre Guild had taken an option on *Battle of Angels*. Later came the even more staggering news that Miriam Hopkins was flying from Hollywood to play the lead. "Probably no man has ever written for the theater with less foreknowledge of it," he re-flected. "I had never been back-stage, I had not seen more than two or three professional pro-ductions. . . . My conversion to the theater arrived as mysteriously as those impulses that enter the flesh at puberty." Had Williams been more experienced in the theater he might have been better armored against what was to follow. The technical difficulties of his play were enor-mous, particularly in the final scene, which in-volved a kind of Wagnerian holocaust. By the time the play opened in Boston on December 30, 1940, the company was so engulfed in produc-tion problems that no one had time to ponder how Bostonians might react to the script. It certainly had never occurred to Williams that he had written an immoral play. Admittedly it touched on "human longings" and "the some-times conflicting desires of the flesh and the spirit," yet he had always felt it to be idealistic. The response of the first-night audience, how-ever, was one of unmistakable and audible dis-

pleasure. At the beginning of the third act people began to whisper. "Subdued hissings and cluck-ings," Williams recalls, "were punctuated now and then by the banging up of a seat." To com-plete the rout, the stagehands outdid them-selves in the closing fire scene. Their over-loaded smokepots belched suffocating billows over the footlights and into the eyes and nostrils of the outraged audience. Had it not been so disastrous there might have been something almost comical, according to one witness, in the spectacle of "all the little ladies with black velvet ribbons about their throats gasping for breath." The notices next day were scarifying, and when the cen-sors stormed down demanding wholesale exci-sions, the Theatre Guild decided to close then and there without even trying to enter New York.

Stunned by the catastrophe, Williams decided his career was over. This was the nadir of na-dirs, for in the midst of his professional humilia-tion his draft board called him up for his physical examination. The doctor listened to his heart, and promptly told him, "You're 4-F," which in-stantly reactivated all his old cardiac ghosts. He had also at this time developed a cataract in his left eye, and although he expected his heart to stop any minute and almost wished it would, he entered a hospital and underwent the first of four operations that ultimately were required to repair his sight. When he emerged he was virtually penniless and without hope save for a vague promise that the Theatre Guild might consider *Battle of Angels* again if he rewrote it.

The next two years were as desolate as any he had known. For a while he subsisted in New Orleans on a thin trickle of revenue from his one-act plays and pawnshop loans on his watch, his clothes, his phonograph, everything but his typewriter. He came up with a new version of *Battle of Angels,* but the Guild's interest had cooled rapidly and they indicated the project was dead. Then the head of a New York drama school wired him that he was planning to revive *Battle of Angels* and forwarded train fare so that Williams could come north. But when he reached the city the production was called off. His life took on a bohemian color that winter. He was hired as a waiter in a Greenwich Village night club, primarily because he had just undergone another eye operation and the proprietor was enchanted by Williams's black patch on which a friend had drawn a fiercely libidinous eye in white chalk. In addition to serving drinks, Williams doubled as entertainer late at night by reciting bawdy verse of his own composition. When he lost this job following a dispute with his employer over tips, he was kept from starvation by a group of amiable alcoholics who liked his recitations. They wound up each evening at the home of an aging retired actress, and Williams found that if he stayed with them long enough somebody would eventually telephone for chicken sandwiches. For days he lived on nothing but highballs and chicken sandwiches and was wolfishly hungry most of the time. There was never any food in the actress's icebox because she never ate—whenever she sensed that a collapse was imminent she went to a hospital and had a blood transfusion; next day she would show up at her favorite bar, her thirst and hemoglobin count back to normal. Somehow during this period Williams managed to collaborate with a friend, Donald Windham, on a comedy called *You Touch Me!* suggested by a short story by D. H. Lawrence. But the play did not reach Broadway for three years and Williams still was destitute. During the winter and spring of 1942–43 he worked as night elevator operator in a New York hotel and as an usher in the Strand Theater on Broadway. He enjoyed the latter job, not because of the movies but because of the uniform which, as a 4-F, he regarded as better than no uniform at all.

Then once again his benign angel Audrey Wood brought him tidings—that by some necromancy she had sold his talents to Hollywood. "We got you a six months' contract and a salary of two hundred and fifty dollars!" she announced. Williams, who was then making seventeen dollars a week, was dazzled. "You mean two hundred and fifty dollars every month!" he gasped. "I mean two hundred and fifty dollars every week," Miss Wood said. The upturn in his luck was definitive. For after trying to write a picture for Lana Turner and after being told that his dialogue was magnificent but not quite right for Miss Turner, he was assigned to a script for Margaret O'Brien. And after announcing that child actors made him vomit he was released from all duties whatsoever. For the remainder of his stay in Hollywood he drew his $250 each

week and spent his waking hours writing *The Glass Menagerie.*

This fragile and beautiful play, into which he wove with tender artistry the memories of his troubled youth, at once established Williams as a playwright of foremost rank. Critics at the Chicago première on December 26, 1944, composed reviews that glowed with the reflected poetry of the script, and when the public seemed slow to respond they followed up their first notices with angry columns berating Chicagoans for their neglect of a distinguished work of art. It played to packed houses in Chicago for three months and then ran in New York for a year and a half.

The advent of success had a curious effect on Williams. The security and glory and opportunity for material indulgence were ashes in his mouth. He became even more diffident and vastly more cynical and unhappy than he had ever been during his years of struggle. It was some time before he understood the cause. His life prior to this success, he observed in a reminiscence in the New York *Times* several years afterward, "was one that required endurance, a life of clawing and scratching along a sheer surface and holding on tight with raw fingers. . . . I was not aware of how much vital energy had gone into this struggle until the struggle was removed. I was out on a level plateau with my arms still thrashing and my lungs still grabbing at air that no longer resisted. This was security at last. . . . [But] security is a kind of death, and it can come to you in a storm of royalty checks beside a kidney-shaped pool in Beverly Hills or anywhere at all that is removed from the conditions that made you an artist. . . ." Having discovered what he now recognizes as an organic truth—that he finds reality and satisfaction only in his work—Williams went back to it and to the conditions that made him an artist. He rented an apartment in a venerable house in the Vieux Carré of New Orleans, which he regards as his home, and from the world outside his windows and the more intense world of his creative imagination drew forth the trenchant drama of *A Streetcar Named Desire.*

To Williams the success of *Streetcar* has brought higher rewards by far than *The Glass Menagerie.* More than his royalties of over two thousand dollars a week he values the knowledge that he has transcended his first achievement. His insight into theatre mechanics had increased too, for he participated for the first time in his life in the business of producing a play. Formerly he had languished, like most playwrights, on the fringe of operations, unconsulted and unheard. But this time Producer Irene Selznick and Director Elia Kazan sought his opinion on each detail from music and lighting to the casting of bit parts. These varied factors have combined to draw Williams forth a little from his shell of isolation. A few days before the New York opening Mrs. Selznick asked him what he would do when the audience began yelling "Author!" Williams replied, "Why, I'll get right up on the stage as fast as I can, I'll be so proud and happy." As it turned out the audience did yell "Author!" and Williams did respond with a pleased and embarrassed bow.

He remained in New York for a month after the opening performance. During that interlude he displayed no symptoms of success. He avoided expensive hotels and remained in the furnished flat he had rented during the early days of rehearsal. He ignored opulent restaurants, eating for the most part at cafeterias and counters. His only sartorial indulgence took the form of a Burberry topcoat, and when his friend William Liebling, Miss Wood's husband, suggested he ought to invest in a dress suit, he replied, "No, I'd lose it." His recreations consisted of daily swims at the Y.M.C.A. (where he negotiated twenty laps in a leisurely crawl every afternoon) and poker games several times a week with the Negro musicians backstage at the theater. He busied himself most of the time with preparations for a trip to Europe, where he planned to spend an indefinite number of months traveling and writing. And in treasured moments he confronted his typewriter and worked blissfully on two new plays in progress.

Williams's friends feel that his distaste for profligate living and the chic professional society that have atrophied many a promising talent in New York and Hollywood is an auspicious omen for his career. But from time to time they wish he would reveal to them personally a fraction of the eloquence and emotional vitality he injects into his plays. On the night *Streetcar* opened, members of the company were invited, together with certain celebrities, to an after-theater party at Twenty-One. They were fairly tense until the late editions of the newspaper appeared; but as the notices began to come in, rave piling on rave, the air filled with elation. Williams wandered easily among the guests, accepting their congratulations with felicity and pleasure. But there came a moment later when he found himself temporarily alone, and as always his thoughts turned inward and his eyes gazed far away. Then someone appeared at his elbow and said, "Tenn, are you really happy?" It was Audrey Wood.

"Of course I am," Williams replied in surprise.

"Are you a completely fulfilled young man?" she asked sternly.

"Completely," said Williams. "Why do you ask me?"

Miss Wood looked at him searchingly. "I just wanted to hear you say it," she said.

Comments and Questions

In reading we should be guided by two attitudes of mind, the sympathetic and the skeptical. Sympathy (a positively friendly approach toward what the author has done) should dominate during a first reading. After that, in reviewing, it is time to be skeptical even if one's general impression is favorable. A skeptical, quizzing approach is a spur to analysis and may help as much to reveal the virtues of a piece as to discover its defects. We have read the sketch of "Tennessee Williams" with sympathy, let us hope, and now it is time to be skeptical.

We have three large questions to guide us here, just as they will guide us in the opening analysis of any piece of literature:

1. What has the author attempted to do?
2. Was it worth doing?
3. How well has he done what he attempted?

In this instance we may dispose of the first two questions quickly and concentrate on the third.

The author, writing for a magazine of large circulation (*Time*), has attempted in a limited space to reveal the personal and professional life of a successful American playwright. It seems clear that such a sketch or close-up, as it is called, was worth doing.

In answering the third question, we have the opportunity to discover some of the tricks of the biographical trade. Because we are looking at an example of expert journalistic biography, we expect the techniques to be appropriate to this popular medium and reasonably obvious. Later on in the other selection, we shall see these devices modified to the talents and purposes of the different biographers.

The Beginning

You have noticed that beginnings of all sorts are exciting: the beginning of the school term, the kick-off of a football game, the rise of the curtain at a play. Writers have learned to make use of the advantage they have at the moment a reader scans their first words. Some of the best lines of poetry are first lines. Most self-conscious about openings, however, is the modern writer of short biographies. It is part of his formula to open with a bang. Yet a good opening must be more than a firecracker. The sketch of Tennessee Williams opens with a scene, a somewhat spacious beginning which allows the author to *show* us his subject at an important moment in his career. By the time the anecdote ends we have seen enough to become interested in Tennessee Williams, both as a person and as a playwright. Now we are likely to respond, as the author intended we should respond, by wanting to know what led up to this rather curious scene of triumph.

A provocative opening is, no doubt, a trick, but skillfully used it is more than that. Frequently it is a distillation of the author's interpretation of his subject. It is almost always the key to the whole sketch, the statement which controls all that comes later. We shall be interested to see how different biographers handle the problem of getting started.

Quotations

What impression does the use of numerous quotations make? They certainly help us *to*

hear and *to hear about* Tennessee Williams. They do more. If we examine the quotations, we realize that they serve four purposes:

1. Some of them are used, as in the opening and closing anecdotes, to simulate actual conversation. Here the author employs a device of fiction. Since he cannot know, he invents part of the conversation between Williams and his unnamed friend about *A Streetcar Named Desire.* (Is this possibly a dangerous procedure on the part of a writer whose concern is with facts?)

2. Some quotations, such as those from the *Times* and the *Tribune,* give authority to the notion that Tennessee Williams is an important playwright.

3. Some phrases are quoted because they say strikingly what the author thinks he could not say so well. (Point out examples of this sort of quotation.)

4. Quotation marks are placed around certain words which the author questions and wishes the reader to question: "nigger," "compromise."

Since quotations are a staple of all biographical writing, one effective way to study biography is to examine and classify the quotations.

Treatment of Facts

Perhaps the strongest taboo in current writing of short biography may be stated in the commandment: "Thou shalt not say when a person was born." Hints are permitted but no such direct statement as this: "Tennessee Williams was born in Columbus, Mississippi, March 26, 1914." A birth date is not exciting, and readers may very well hurry over such information. For all sorts of reasons, however, they may have an interest in this vital statistic and feel cheated by its omission.

Even though we do not find out Tennessee William's exact birth date, we are given in a palatable form much hundrum information about his education and various homes. It would be an informing exercise to cull the facts from this account and set them up in chronological order. The result would show that more facts have been unobtrusively inserted than is immediately apparent.

Before we leave this subject of handling

facts, we should like to ask one question: Did you compare the beginning of this sketch with the ending? If you did, you may have been puzzled by references in both to newspaper criticisms of *A Streetcar Named Desire.* Name the apparent discrepancy and see if you can resolve it.

Allusions

We have briefly discussed allusions in "Biography: Preliminaries." The close-up of "Tennessee Williams" contains few allusions and perhaps only one without sufficient context to explain it. The reference is to "Wagnerian holocaust." For this phrase, the reader with no knowledge of either "Wagner" or "holocaust" would have to resort to reference books.

As an exercise in allowing context to throw light on an allusion, imagine that you do not know the following persons or places mentioned in the sketch of "Tennessee Williams" and see whether you can provide identifications solely from the context: "mid-town Manhattan"; "Shostakovich"; "Eugene O'Neill"; "Twenty-One"; "Beverly Hills." How did you arrive at each identification?

Gibbon, Edward
From *The Columbia Encyclopedia*

Gibbon, Edward (gĭ´ bun), 1737–1794, English historian, author of the monumental *Decline and Fall of the Roman Empire.* His childhood was sickly, and he had little formal education but read enormously and omnivorously. He went at 15 to Magdalen College, Oxford, but was forced to leave because of his conversion to Roman Catholicism. His father sent him (1753) to Lausanne, where he was formally reconverted to Protestantism. Actually he became a sceptic and later greatly offended the pious by his famous chapters of historical criticism of Christianity in his great work. In Lausanne he fell in love with the penniless daughter of a pastor, Suzanne Curchod (who was later to be the great intellectual, Mme. Necker). The two were engaged to be married, but Gibbon's father refused to consent. Gibbon

"sighed as a lover" but "obeyed as a son" and gave up the match. He left Lausanne in 1758. It was on a visit to Rome that he conceived the idea of his magnificent and panoramic history. This appeared as *The History of the Decline and Fall of the Roman Empire* (6 vols., 1776–88), and won immediate acclaim, despite some harsh criticism. Gibbon himself was assured of the greatness of his work, which is, indeed, one of the most-read historical works of modern times. Gibbon himself, was not, however, accorded much personal admiration. He moved in the high circles of society and was a member of the litarary circle of Samuel Johnson, but he was personally unprepossessing. Short (under 5 ft.), bulbously fat, always dressed in ornate and vivid clothes that flattered his vanity but not his appearance, and affected in manner and speech, he was a figure of ridicule. The salons buzzed with stories mocking him. He entered upon a short and highly inglorious political career, serving as a member of Parliament from 1774 to 1783. He violently opposed the American Revolution, though later he was to look with favor on the more radical French Revolution. In 1783 he withdrew to Lausanne, where he completed his great work. One of the fascinating things about Gibbon is the disparity between his personal character and his work, a disparity not resolved by his own *Memoirs of His Life and Writings,* commonly called the *Autobiography,* which first appeared in the edition of his miscellaneous works by Lord Sheffield in 1796. The autobiography is, however, one of the most subtle and interesting works of its kind in English. An edition of Gibbon's original six drafts appeared as *The Autobiographies* in 1896. Editions of the *Decline and Fall* are legion. The modern standard edition is that of J. B. Bury (7 vols., 1896–1900). A bibliography of the works of Gibbon by Jane E. Norton appeared in 1941. See biography by D. M. Low (1937).

Gibbon
LYTTON STRACHEY
1880–1932

Happiness is the word that immediately rises to the mind at the thought of Edward Gibbon:

and happiness in its widest connotation—including good fortune as well as enjoyment. Good fortune, indeed, followed him from the cradle to the grave in the most tactful way possible; occasionally it appeared to fail him, but its absence always turned out to be a blessing in disguise. Out of a family of seven he alone had the luck to survive—but only with difficulty; and the maladies of his childhood opened his mind to the pleasures of study and literature. His mother died; but her place was taken by a devoted aunt, whose care brought him through the dangerous years of adolescence to a vigorous manhood. His misadventures at Oxford saved him from becoming a don. His exile to Lausanne, by giving him a command of the French language, initiated him into European culture, and at the same time enabled him to lay the foundations of his scholarship. His father married again; but his stepmother remained childless and became one of his dearest friends. He fell in love; the match was forbidden; and he escaped the dubious joys of domestic life with the future Madame Necker. While he was allowed to travel on the Continent, it seemed doubtful for some time whether his father would have the resources or the generosity to send him over the Alps into Italy. His fate hung in the balance; but at last his father produced the necessary five hundred pounds, and, in the autumn of 1764 Rome saw her historian. His father died at exactly the right moment, and left him exactly the right amount of money. At the age of thirty-three Gibbon found himself his own master, with a fortune just sufficient to support him as an English gentleman of leisure and fashion. For ten years he lived in London, a member of Parliament, a place-man, and a diner-out, and during those ten years he produced the first three volumes of his History. After that he lost his place, failed to obtain another, and, finding his income unequal to his expenses, returned to Lausanne, where he took up his residence in the house of a friend, overlooking the Lake of Geneva. It was the final step in his career, and no less fortunate than all the others. In Lausanne he was rich once more, he was famous, he enjoyed a delightful combination of retirement and society. Before another ten years were out he had completed his History; and in ease, dignity, and absolute satisfaction his work in this world was accomplished.

One sees in such a life an epitome of the blessings of the eighteenth century—the wonderful μηδὲν ἄγαν [nothing in excess] of that most balmy time—the rich fruit ripening slowly on the sunwarmed wall, and coming inevitably to its delicious perfection. It is difficult to imagine, at any other period in history, such a combination of varied qualities, so beautifully balanced—the profound scholar who was also a brilliant man of the world—the votary of cosmopolitan culture, who never for a moment ceased to be a supremely English "character." The ten years of Gibbon's life in London afford an astonishing spectacle of interacting energies. By what strange power did he succeed in producing a masterpiece of enormous erudition and perfect form, while he was leading the gay life of a man about town, spending his evenings at White's or Boodle's or the Club, attending Parliament, oscillating between his house in Bentinck Street, his country cottage at Hampton Court, and his little establishment at Brighton, spending his summers in Bath or Paris, and even, at odd moments, doing a little work at the Board of Trade, to show that his place was not entirely a sinecure? Such a triumph could only have been achieved by the sweet reasonableness of the eighteenth century. "Monsieur Gibbon n'est point mon homme," said Rousseau. Decidedly! The prophet of the coming age of sentiment and romance could have nothing in common with such a nature. It was not that the historian was a mere frigid observer of the golden mean—far from it. He was full of fire and feeling. His youth had been at moments riotous—night after night he had reeled hallooing down St. James's Street. Old age did not diminish the natural warmth of his affections; the beautiful letter—a model of its kind—written on the death of his aunt, in his fiftieth year, is a proof of it. But the fire and the feeling were controlled and co-ordinated. Boswell was a Rousseauite, one of the first of the Romantics, an inveterate sentimentalist and nothing could be more complete than the contrast between his career and Gibbon's. He, too, achieved a glorious triumph; but it was by dint of the sheer force of native genius asserting itself over the extravagance and disorder of an agitated life—a life which, after a desperate struggle, seemed to end at last in darkness and shipwreck. With Gibbon there was never any struggle: everything came naturally to him—learning and dissipation, industry and indolence, affection and scepticism—in the correct proportions; and he enjoyed himself up to the very end.

To complete the picture one must notice another antithesis: the wit, the genius, the massive intellect, were housed in a physical mould that was ridiculous. A little figure, extraordinarily rotund, met the eye, surmounted by a top-heavy head, with a button nose, planted amid a vast expanse of cheek and ear, and chin upon chin rolling downward. Nor was this appearance only; the odd shape reflected something in the inner man. Mr. Gibbon, it was noticed, was always slightly over-dressed; his favourite wear was flowered velvet. He was a little vain, a little pompous; at the first moment one almost laughed; then one forgot everything under the fascination of that even flow of admirably intelligent, exquisitely turned, and most amusing sentences. Among all his other merits this obviously ludicrous egotism took its place. The astonishing creature was able to make a virtue of absurdity. Without that touch of nature he would have run the risk of being too much of good thing; as it was there was no such danger; he was preposterous and a human being.

It is not difficult to envisage the character and figure; what seems strange, and remote, and hard to grasp is the connection between this individual and the decline and fall of the Roman Empire. The paradox, indeed, is so complete as to be almost romantic. At a given moment—October 15, 1764—at a given place—the Capitoline Hill, outside the church of Aracoeli—the impact occurred between the serried centuries of Rome and Edward Gibbon. His life, his work, his fame, his place in the history of civilization, followed from that circumstance. The point of his achievement lay precisely in the extreme improbability of it. The utter incongruity of those combining elements produced the masterpiece—the gigantic ruin of Europe through a thousand years, mirrored in the mind of an eighteenth-century English gentleman.

How was the miracle accomplished? Needless to say, Gibbon was a great artist—one of those rare spirits, with whom a vital and penetrating imagination and a supreme capacity for general conceptions express themselves instinctively in an appropriate form. That the question has ever been not only asked but seriously debated, whether History was an art, is certainly one of the curiosities of human ineptitude. What else can it possibly be? It is obvious that History is not a science: it is obvious that History is not the accumulation of facts, but the relation of them. Only the pedantry of incomplete academic persons could have given birth to such a monstrous supposition. Facts relating to the past, when they are collected without art, are compilations; and compilations, no doubt, may be useful; but they are no more History than butter, eggs, salt and herbs are an omelette. That Gibbon was a great artist, therefore, is implied in the statement that he was a great historian; but what is interesting is the particular nature of his artistry. His whole genius was preëminently classical; order, lucidity, balance, precision—the great classical qualities—dominate his work; and his History is chiefly remarkable as one of the supreme monuments of Classic Art in European literature.

L'ordre est ce qu'il y a de plus rare dans les opérations de l'esprit. Gibbon's work is a magnificent illustration of the splendid dictum of Fénelon. He brought order out of the enormous chaos of his subject—a truly stupendous achievement! With characteristic good fortune, indeed, the material with which he had to cope was still just not too voluminous to be digested by a single extremely competent mind. In the following century even a Gibbon would have collapsed under the accumulated mass of knowledge at his disposal. As it was, by dint of a superb constructive vision, a serene self-confidence, a very acute judgment, and an astonishing facility in the manipulation of material, he was able to dominate the known facts. To dominate, nothing more; anything else would have been foreign to his purpose. He was a classicist; and his object was not comprehension but illumination. He drove a straight, firm road through the vast unexplored forest of Roman history; his readers could follow with easy pleasure along the wonderful way; they might glance, as far as their eyes could reach, into the entangled recesses on either side of them; but they were not invited to stop, or wander, or camp out, or make friends with the natives; they must be content to look and to pass on.

It is clear that Gibbon's central problem was

the one of exclusion: how much, and what, was he to leave out? This was largely a question of scale—always one of the major difficulties in literary composition—and it appears from several passages in the Autobiographies that Gibbon paid particular attention to it. Incidentally, it may be observed that the six Autobiographies were not so much excursions in egotism—though no doubt it is true that Gibbon was not without a certain fondness for what he himself called "the most disgusting of the pronouns"—as exercises on the theme of scale. Every variety of compression and expansion is visible among those remarkable pages; but apparently, since the manuscripts were left in an unfinished state, Gibbon still felt, after the sixth attempt, that he had not discovered the right solution. Even with the scale of the History he was not altogether satisfied; the chapters on Christianity, he thought, might, with further labour, have been considerably reduced. But, even more fundamental than the element of scale, there was something else that in reality, conditioned the whole treatment of his material, the whole scope and nature of his History; and that was the style in which it was written. The style once fixed, everything else followed. Gibbon was well aware of this. He wrote his first chapter three times over, his second and third twice; then at last he was satisfied, and after that he wrote on without a hitch. In particular the problem of exclusion was solved. Gibbon's style is probably the most exclusive in literature. By its very nature it bars out a great multitude of human energies. It makes sympathy impossible, it takes no cognizance of passion, it turns its back upon religion with a withering smile. But that was just what was wanted. Classic beauty came instead. By the penetrating influence of style—automatically, inevitably—lucidity, balance and precision were everywhere introduced; and the miracle of order was established over the chaos of a thousand years.

Of course, the Romantics raised a protest. "Gibbon's style," said Coleridge, "is detestable; but," he added, "it is not the worst thing about him." Critics of the later nineteenth century were less consistent. They admired Gibbon for everything except his style, imagining that his History would have been much improved if it had been written in some other way; they did not see that,

if it had been written in any other way, it would have ceased to exist; just as St. Paul's would cease to exist if it were rebuilt in Gothic. Obsessed by the colour and movement of romantic prose, they were blind to the subtlety, the clarity, the continuous strength of Gibbon's writing. Gibbon could turn a bold phrase with the best of them—"the fat slumbers of the Church," for instance—if he wanted to; but he very rarely wanted to; such effects would have disturbed the easy, close-knit, homogeneous surface of his work. His use of words is, in fact, extremely delicate. When, describing St. Simeon Stylites on his pillar, he speaks of "this last and lofty station," he succeeds, with the least possible emphasis, merely by the combination of those two alliterative epithets with that particular substantive, in making the whole affair ridiculous. One can almost see his shoulders shrug. The nineteenth century found him pompous; they did not relish the irony beneath the pomp. He produces some of his most delightful effects by rhythm alone. In the *Vindication*—a work which deserves to be better known, for it shows us Gibbon, as one sees him nowhere else, really letting himself go—there is an admirable example of this. "I still think," he says, in reply to a criticism by Dr. Randolph, "I still think that an hundred Bishops, with Athanasius at their head, were as competent judges of the discipline of the fourth century, as even the Lady Margaret's Professor of Divinity in the University of Oxford." Gibbon's irony, no doubt, is the salt of his work; but, like all irony, it is the product of style. It was not for nothing that he read through every year the *Lettres Provinciales* of Pascal. From this point of view it is interesting to compare him with Voltaire. The irony of the great Frenchman was a flashing sword—extreme, virulent, deadly—a terrific instrument of propaganda. Gibbon uses the weapon with far more delicacy; he carves his enemy "as a dish fit for the Gods"; his mocking is aloof, almost indifferent, and perhaps, in the long run, for that very reason, even more effective.

At every period of his life Gibbon is a pleasant thing to contemplate, but perhaps most pleasant of all in the closing weeks of it, during his last visit to England. He had hurried home from Lausanne to join his friend Lord Sheffield, whose wife had died suddenly, and who, he felt, was in need of his company. The journey was no small proof of his affectionate nature; old age was approaching; he was corpulent, gouty, and accustomed to every comfort; and the war of the French Revolution was raging in the districts through which he had to pass. But he did not hesitate; and after skirting the belligerent armies in his chaise, arrived safely in England. After visiting Lord Sheffield he proceeded to Bath, to stay with his stepmother. The amazing little figure, now almost spherical, bowled along the Bath Road in the highest state of exhilaration. "I am always," he told his friend, "so much delighted and improved with this union of ease and motion, that, were not the expense enormous, I would travel every year some hundred miles, more especially in England." Mrs. Gibbon, a very old lady, but still full of vitality, worshipped her stepson, and the two spent ten days together, talking, almost always *tête-à-tête,* for ten hours a day. Then the historian went off to Althorpe, where he spent a happy morning with Lord Spencer, looking at early editions of Cicero. And so back to London. In London a little trouble arose. A protuberance in the lower part of his person, which, owing to years of characteristic *insouciance,* had grown to extraordinary proportions, required attention; an operation was necessary; but it went off well, and there seemed to be no danger. Once more Mr. Gibbon dined out. Once more he was seen, in his accustomed attitude, with advanced forefinger, addressing the company, and rapping his snuff box at the close of each particularly pointed phrase. But illness came on again—nothing very serious. The great man lay in bed discussing how much longer he would live—he was fifty-six—ten years, twelve years, or perhaps twenty. He ate some chicken and drank three glasses of madeira. Life seemed almost as charming as usual. Next morning, getting out of bed for a necessary moment, "*Je suis plus adroit,*" he said with his odd smile to his French valet. Back in bed again, he muttered something more, a little incoherently, lay back among the pillows, dozed, half-woke, dozed again, and became unconscious—forever.

Comments and Questions

1. How much interpretive comment is offered in the *Encyclopedia* account of Gibbon?

2. Note Strachey's first paragraph. Besides length, what does it have in common with the *Encyclopedia* account? In what ways does it differ? Which provides more factual information? How does purpose account for this difference? Which is more interpretive?

3. What controls the selection of details in the *Encyclopedia* account? What controls Strachey's account? What controls Strachey's selection of details?

4. Show what happens in Strachey's "Gibbon" to each of the facts included in the *Encyclopedia* account. Does Strachey make use of all the facts? How do you account for specific omissions? Does he ever tell when Gibbon was born? What facts does he use which are not even summarized by the encyclopedist? Do these facts pertain chiefly to Gibbon's personal or to his professional life?

5. Consider Strachey's style. Style is a "characteristic mode of expression," which may be partly identified by answering certain questions. What is the pattern of the sketch as a whole? What are the main divisions? In what way does Strachey avoid monotony in his sentences? Consider any sequence of ten sentences and record what you find as to length and arrangement. Does each sentence move the sketch forward or do some of the sentences simply restate what has already been said? What comment can you make about word choice? Could you determine from the context the meanings of words you did not know? Could you do the same for the allusions? Are there many allusions? Are there many figures of speech? Are the transitions smoothly achieved? Consider, for example, the movement from paragraph to paragraph. Can you point to any memorable phrases, sentences, or passages? Now, after answering all these questions how would you summarize your impression of Strachey's style?

6. Follow up some of Strachey's casual references to Gibbon's activities or to those of his contemporaries. What were the "misadventures at Oxford"? What kind of person was Madame Necker that Strachey should have referred to "the dubious joy of domestic life" with her? Compare Gibbon and Boswell; Gibbon and Rousseau. (Strachey has written sketches of both Boswell and Rousseau.)

7. How much quoted material does Strachey use? For what purposes?

8. In what way does the last paragraph of the sketch offer a final comment on Strachey's thesis concerning Gibbon? Why does Strachey go into more detail at this point than he does elsewhere in the sketch?

_____

ESSAYS

**The essay does not pursue its theme like a pointer,
but goes hither and thither like a bird to find material for its nest,
or a bee to get honey for its comb.**

—ANONYMOUS

PRELIMINARIES

The essay as a form stands astride the line dividing literature as a tool and literature as an interpretive art. The essayist is chiefly interested in the interpretation of facts. He may wish to report a fact, explain it, correct a previous misinterpretation of it, or merely express an opinion concerning a fact. To further his effects he may use at will the devices and techniques associated with biography, fiction, poetry, or drama. This borrowing of devices is a sort of literary fair play since biographers, fiction writers, poets, and dramatists use as needed the devices of the essay. After observing the give-and-take between literary forms, we may be tempted to define the essay as almost any kind of writing which is not specifically something else.

Of all the forms of literature the essay is in its method the least complex. Anyone who can put pen to paper can compose an essay of a sort, something which very likely would be nearer the form attempted than would be the result of a similar effort to produce a poem, a play, or even a short story. The papers or themes written as high school or college exercises are in the tradition of the essay, if the word *essay* is broadly enough defined. Since, therefore, you have both read and written many essays, you are hardly unaware of the form's general characteristics. As a review of these characteristics let us examine excerpts from two very different essays: Thomas Henry Huxley's "The Nature of an Hypothesis" and Charles Lamb's "The Two Races of Men." First we shall observe the qualities of the essay as revealed in Huxley. Next we shall see how these qualities are repeated, modified, or added to in Lamb.

THE SERIOUS APPROACH

"The Nature of an Hypothesis" is an excerpt but will serve to illustrate the features of a serious essay written for a practical purpose. Before we read Huxley, let us look at the word "hypothesis" as a dictionary might define it:

> *hypothesis:* a supposition or unproved theory which may be provisionally accepted to explain or account for a group of facts; a *working hypothesis* provides a basis for continued investigation.

Does Huxley say anything more than this in the following paragraphs?

The Nature of an Hypothesis
THOMAS HENRY HUXLEY
1825–1895

When our means of observation of any natural fact fail to carry us beyond a certain point it is perfectly legitimate, and often extremely useful, to make a supposition as to what we should see, if we could carry direct observation a step farther. A supposition of this kind is called an *hypothesis*, and the value of any hypothesis depends upon the extent to which reasoning upon the assumption that it is true enables us to account for the phenomena with which it is concerned.

Thus, if a person is standing close behind you, and you suddenly feel a blow on your back, you have no direct evidence of the cause of the blow; and if you two were alone, you could not possibly attain any; but you immediately suppose that this person has struck you. Now that is an hypothesis, and it is a legitimate hypothesis, first, because it explains the fact; and, secondly, because no other explanation is probable; probable meaning in the ordinary course of nature. If your companion declared that you fancied you felt a blow, or that some invisible spirit struck you, you would probably decline to accept his explanation of the fact. You would say that both the hypotheses by which he professed to explain the phenomenon were extremely improbable or in other words, that in the ordinary course of nature fancies of this kind do not occur, nor spirits strike blows. In fact his hypotheses would be illegitimate, and yours would be legitimate; and, in all probability, you would act upon your own. In daily life nine-tenths of our actions are based upon suppositions or hypotheses, and our success or failure in practical affairs depends upon the legitimacy of these hypotheses. You believe a man on the hypothesis that he is always truthful; you give him pecuniary credit on the hypothesis that he is solvent.

Thus, everybody invents, and, indeed, is compelled to invent, hypotheses in order to account for phenomena of the cause of which he has no direct evidence; and they are just as legitimate and necessary in science as in common life. Only the scientific reasoner must be careful to remember that which is sometimes forgotten in daily life, that an hypothesis must be regarded as a means and not as an end; that we may cherish it so long as it helps us to explain the order of nature; and that we are bound to throw it away without hesitation as soon as it is shown to be inconsistent with any part of that order.

Telling and Showing

What has Huxley done to bring his definition within the scope of interpretive literature and within the compass of the essay form? In his first paragraph he *tells* us why suppositions are necessary; he *tells* us that a supposition is an hypothesis; he *tells* us that an hypothesis is valuable if it helps to account for other phenomena. If he had continued in this vein, he would have produced good, scientific prose, as lucid and exact as dictionary prose but more spacious. The cool tone of this paragraph is only slightly warmed by the use of the personal pronouns *our*, *us*, and *we*. All the remaining words are as impersonal as ciphers.

Now see what happens in the second paragraph. Persons appear. A little scene is suggested. *You*, the reader, are in the scene. What happens, happens to you. Huxley has gone straight to drama for his device, and in doing so has temporarily abandoned *telling* for *showing*. An action has brought an abstraction—the word *hypothe-*

sis—to life. This is the way of interpretive literature. (See "General Preliminaries, pp. 4 ff.")

Focus

Why, having borrowed from drama, did not Huxley create a full scene, complete with dialogue? Something like this:

(*You are standing, abstracted, looking off into space, when you feel a sudden blow on your back. You whirl and come face to face with the only other occupant of the room.*)
  You: What's the idea?
  Other Occupant: Idea of what?
  You: Idea of hitting me, that's what!
  O.O.: Who hit you?
  You: You hit me. Don't say you didn't.
  O.O.: Prove it.
  You: Why, you, you . . . I ought to . . .
  O.O.: Don't get excited. You're imagining things. Probably nobody hit you.
  You: Imagining, my eye! I felt the blow— right there—between the shoulder blades.
  O.O.: Right there? Well, maybe a spirit struck you.

And so on. If Huxley had so indulged himself, what would have happened to the focus on the word hypothesis? Clearly there was need for just so much drama and no more, for Huxley was intent upon making his definition memorable and not in creating a diversion. We have here revealed one fairly constant characteristic of the essay: it is chiefly aimed at explaining and uses sparingly the devices of showing as a means to that end.

Tone and Purpose

We can see that Huxley is not simply toying with an idea. He is serious. He is genuinely concerned that we shall understand what he is talking about. In the third paragraph he indicates why he, a scientist and a spokesman for science, wishes to have the conception of an hypothesis understood. "Everybody invents . . . hypotheses," he says, "and they are just as legitimate and necessary in science as in common life." Here is his central point. Because his point is a serious one and because he has treated it seriously, we call the result a formal essay.

Such essays, furthermore, are called formal because they are impersonal. Like a lecturer who turns a globe to indicate its shape, Huxley shows us the form of an hypothesis. We look at the object, not at the lecturer. We may admire the clarity of the lecturer's mind, his ability to use the right words in the right places, but our attention is where he wants it to be: on what he is talking about.

Directness

The essay is more direct than any other form of literature, except perhaps biography. In "Quality" Galsworthy tells us a story but not its meaning (see "Fiction: Preliminaries," p. 12). In *Ile* O'Neill tells a story in the form of a play, but he leaves it to us to find the meaning (see "Drama: Preliminaries," p. 416). If we fail to find the meaning of either of these works, the narrative or the plot remains. If we read an essay and fail to understand it, to know what it means, virtually nothing remains. The essayist, therefore, is seldom coy. He is intent upon revealing his meaning as directly as possible.

This directness is frequently apparent in the title he chooses: "The Nature of an Hypothesis"; "The Literature of Knowledge and the Literature of Power." He likes the flat, aphoristic statement: "The interests of a writer and the interests of his readers are never the same . . ." (W. H. Auden, "Reading"). He defines or partly defines whenever necessary and as he goes along: "A poem has many levels of meaning and none of them is prose." (Stephen Spender, "On Teaching Modern Poetry.") *

What effect does the direct approach have upon the appeal of the essay? Clearly it is farthest removed from the appeal of poetry, which depends upon indirection and which exercises both our understanding and our feelings. The essay appeals almost exclusively to the understanding and feeds most directly our desire to know.

Incompleteness

We gain from T. H. Huxley a clear but limited notion of the qualities and uses of hypotheses. He could have used many more examples. He could have developed a single hypothesis and carried it through its various stages from

* See the Index for the essays mentioned in this paragraph.

first observations through all the phases of testing, modifying, testing again, and so on to the establishment of a theory, or perhaps, a law. Why did not Huxley do this? For one thing he was writing for a general audience, not for scientists. He accepted the limitations of this fact and in so doing accepted the limiting scope of the essay. The essay, even when the subject itself is relatively narrow, does not pretend to completeness.

Is incompleteness characteristic of all forms of literature? In a sense it is. The plot structures of short stories have been described as open or closed (see "Fiction: Preliminaries," p. 23). The closed story is rounded at the end and is in a technical sense complete, for all the questions *posed by the author* of the particular story have been answered. No story, however, carries a comment upon itself, and no comments of readers and critics ever exhaust the story's implications. In this sense and others, then, any piece of writing is incomplete.

The essay, however, is by definition *an attempt*, a tentative examination of a single subject. In short, it offers a word, but far from the last word, on a given topic.

THE LIGHT APPROACH

Let us turn now to the opening paragraphs of another essay written with a different purpose and to a quite different effect than Huxley's. Before we examine Lamb's remarks on "The Two Races of Men," let us see how a dictionary defines the word "race":

> *race:* any of the major biological divisions of mankind, distinguished by color and texture of hair, color of skin and eyes, stature, bodily proportions, etc.: many ethnologists now consider that there are only three primary divisions, the Caucasian (loosely, *white race*), Negroid (loosely, *black race*) and Mongoloid (loosely, *yellow race*), each with various subdivisions.

Does Lamb say anything resembling this definition in his remarks on races?

The Two Races of Men

CHARLES LAMB
1775–1834

The human species, according to the best theory I can form of it, is composed of two distinct races, *the men who borrow, and the men who lend.* To these two original diversities may be reduced all those impertinent classifications of Gothic and Celtic tribes, white men, black men, red men. All the dwellers upon earth, "Parthians, and Medes, and Elamites," flock hither, and do naturally fall in with one or other of these primary distinctions. The infinite superiority of the former, which I choose to designate as the *great race,* is discernible in their figure, port, and a certain instinctive sovereignty. The latter are born degraded. "He shall serve his brethren." There is something in the air of one of this cast, lean and suspicious; contrasting with the open, trusting, generous manners of the other.

Observe who have been the greatest borrowers of all ages—Alcibiades—Falstaff—Sir Richard Steele—our late incomparable Brinsley— what a family likeness in all four!

What a careless, even deportment hath your borrower! what rosy gills! what a beautiful reliance on Providence doth he manifest,—taking no more thought than lilies! What contempt for money, accounting it (yours and mine especially) no better than dross! What a liberal confounding of those pedantic distinctions of *meum* and *tuum!* or rather what a noble simplification of language (beyond Tooke), resolving these supposed opposites into one clear, intelligible pronoun adjective!—What near approaches doth he make to the primitive *community,*—to the extent of one half of the principle at least.

He is the true taxer who "calleth all the world up to be taxed"; and the distance is as vast between him and *one of us,* as subsisted between the Augustan Majesty and the poorest obolary Jew that paid it tribute-pittance at Jerusalem!— His exactions, too, have such a cheerful, voluntary air! So far removed from your sour parochial or state-gatherers,—those ink-horn varlets, who carry their want of welcome in their faces! He cometh to you with a smile, and troubleth you with no receipt; confining himself to no set

season. Every day is his Candlemas, or his Feast of Holy Michael. He applieth the *lene tormentum* of a pleasant look to your purse,—which to that gentle warmth expands her silken leaves, as naturally as the cloak of the traveller, for which sun and wind contended! He is the true Propontic which never ebbeth! The sea which taketh handsomely at each man's hand. In vain the victim, whom he delighteth to honour, struggles with destiny; he is in the net. Lend therefore cheerfully, O man ordained to lend—that thou lose not in the end, with thy worldly penny, the reversion promised. Combine not preposterously in thine own person the penalties of Lazarus and of Dives!—but, when thou seest the proper authority coming, meet it smilingly, as it were half-way. Come, a handsome sacrifice! See how light *he* makes of it! Strain not courtesies with a noble enemy.

THE RANGE OF THE ESSAY FORM

We have recognized that Huxley was seriously intent upon making clear the nature of an hypothesis. Is Lamb equally serious in his attempt to make clear the distinction between his two "races"? Does his explanation bear any resemblance to the dictionary definition of the word race? He begins solemnly enough:

> The human species, according to the best theory I can form of it, is composed of two distinct races. . . .

These could be the first words of a treatise on ethnology (the science of races). Here in these sober words—except for the unscientific first person—we have the authentic tone of a serious speculation. Indeed, after reading Huxley, we anticipate an upcoming hypothesis. When Lamb tells us that the two races are *"the men who borrow and the men who lend,"* the matter-of-fact tone remains, but we know that the fact itself—the scientific substance—is not there. Yet Lamb, after announcing his theory, proceeds as though his speculation is so reasonable as to be self-evident. He waves aside all the "impertinent classifications" which have preceded his revelation. Having disposed of these impertinencies, he turns to the contrasts between his races. In the second paragraph he continues the "scientific approach." "Observe," he advises, and names four exemplars of the great race of borrowers. We note Falstaff in his list, a dramatic creation mingling with three historical characters. We know now, if we did not know immediately, that Lamb's intent is only superficially similar to Huxley's.

Yet both essayists depend chiefly upon telling rather than showing and use illustrations to highlight their main contention. Both maintain a focus on a single topic, although Lamb's beam of light wavers more than does Huxley's. Even the structure of the two excerpts is similar, as one may see by comparing the first two paragraphs of the two selections. In the matter of directness, Lamb seems as intent on driving home his point as is Huxley. And both essayists appeal to the understanding and hardly at all to the emotions.

All these points of similarity are matters of technique. In essence the selections are as different as beavers and squirrels, both of which are rodents. Huxley has the businesslike efficiency of the beaver; Lamb the frisky, darting playfulness of the squirrel. Both get their business done. The excerpts from these two writers suggest the range of the essay, from the practical and serious to the fanciful and playful. We would not wish the range to be less wide.

ALLUSIONS

Huxley entertained us, perhaps, but that was not his chief purpose. Entertainment is apparently Lamb's chief purpose. It is certain that he is only mildly concerned that even his main contention be accepted. We do learn something about human nature from him, or, if we do not learn, we are at least pleasantly reminded of something we already know. From our own experience we can testify to at least the limited validity of Lamb's thesis concerning rosy borrowers and submissive lenders. Even here, however, Lamb is only playing with an idea based upon random observation.

Since it was Lamb's purpose to amuse, his far-ranging allusions are devices for achieving his purpose. We may muse for a moment over the "family likeness" between the four great borrowers: an Athenian general (Alcibiades), a man with personal talent, enough to levy trib-

ute on friend and foe alike; the fat, lovable rascal (Falstaff), who forgave Mistress Quickly for his own offense so that she might feel free to lend him more; the lighthearted moralist (Sir Richard Steele) who plundered the dour lender, Addison; the gay and irresponsible playwright (Richard Brinsley Sheridan) who spent affably other persons' money. The family likeness is evident and it is a pleasure to recognize it. From paragraph three onward, Lamb frisks through a fast sequence of allusions and suggestions. When he exclaims, "what rosy gills!" a picture flashes before us of glowing confidence, good health, and something of the solemn rightness of a fish's countenance. Just this touch of an allusion—"Taking no more thought than the lilies!"—opens our memories: "Consider the lilies of the field, how they grow; they toil not, neither do they spin: And yet I say unto you, That even Solomon in all his glory was not arrayed like one of these." Through this allusion Lamb allows us *to show* ourselves the very substance of the borrower. For the remainder of this paragraph and on through the next, Lamb uses allusion after allusion to complete his picture.

Two sorts of pleasure may be found in allusions: recognition and application. Of course, if recognition fails, there is no opportunity for pleasure here—but some for annoyance. The second pleasure may be had, however, if one will look up the allusion and then apply what he finds to the context. The habit of investigating allusions is a good one to cultivate as one of the pleasantest and most purposeful ways to extend one's knowledge.

VALUES

If Lamb has not given us dependable information or even a separation of fictional from historical characters, if he has not been serious and practical, are we to conclude that what he has written is trivial and of less value than the sort of essay Huxley wrote? Most readers would say in answer to this question that both writers have been expert in carrying out their respective purposes and that the two samples of their work are to be weighed on different scales. Huxley's essay should be compared with one of comparably serious intentions, with, for example, Aldous Huxley's "Music at Night" (p. 810). One needs to come even closer than this for a valid comparison at all points—to an essay with similar subject matter. Lamb's essay should be compared with other essays written in a light and playful vein, with, for example, Thurber's "The Unicorn in the Garden" below. The point is that we do not need to make exclusive choices and forego Huxley if we like Lamb or forego Lamb if we like Huxley. Both have much to offer, just as the whole varied range of literature, from its most useful to its most fanciful forms, has much to offer.

The Unicorn in the Garden

JAMES THURBER
1894–1961

Once upon a sunny morning a man who sat in a breakfast nook looked up from his scrambled eggs to see a white unicorn with a gold horn quietly cropping the roses in the garden. The man went up to the bedroom where his wife was still asleep and woke her. "There's a unicorn in the garden," he said. "Eating roses." She opened one unfriendly eye and looked at him. "The unicorn is a mythical beast," she said, and turned her back on him. The man walked slowly downstairs and out into the garden. The unicorn was still there; he was now browsing among the tulips. "Here, unicorn," said the man, and he pulled up a lily and gave it to him. The unicorn ate it gravely. With a high heart, because there was a unicorn in his garden, the man went upstairs and roused his wife again. "The unicorn," he said, "ate a lily." His wife sat up in bed and looked at him, coldly. "You are a booby," she said, "and I am going to have you put in the booby-hatch." The man, who had never liked the words "booby" and "booby-hatch," and who liked them even less on a shining morning when there was a unicorn in the garden, thought for a moment. "We'll see about that," he said. He walked over to the door. "He has a golden horn in the middle of his forehead," he told her. Then he went back to the garden to watch the unicorn; but the unicorn had gone away. The man sat down among the roses and went to sleep.

As soon as the husband had gone out of the house, the wife got up and dressed as fast as she could. She was very excited and there was a gloat in her eye. She telephoned the police and she telephoned a psychiatrist; she told them to hurry to her house and bring a strait-jacket. When the police and the psychiatrist arrived they sat down in chairs and looked at her, with great interest. "My husband," she said, "saw a unicorn this morning." The police looked at the psychiatrist and the psychiatrist looked at the police. "He told me it ate a lily," she said. The psychiatrist looked at the police and the police looked at the psychiatrist. "He told me it had a golden horn in the middle of its forehead," she said. At a solemn signal from the psychiatrist, the police leaped from their chairs and seized the wife. They had a hard time subduing her, for she put up a terrific struggle, but they finally subdued her. Just as they got her into the strait-jacket, the husband came back into the house.

"Did you tell your wife you saw a unicorn?" asked the police. "Of course not," said the husband. "The unicorn is a mythical beast." "That's all I wanted to know," said the psychiatrist. "Take her away. I'm sorry, sir, but your wife is as crazy as a jay bird." So they took her away, cursing and screaming, and shut her up in an institution. The husband lived happily ever after.

Moral: Don't count your boobies until they are hatched.

Comments and Questions

1. Is this an essay? Think carefully, then justify your answer. (You may wish to compare Thurber's purpose with Galsworthy's in "Quality," pp. 12 ff. Is "Quality" a short story?)

2. This is a tightly knit piece in which every word counts. Note the matter of fact opening sentence. How can a man look "up from his scrambled eggs" and see "a white unicorn with a golden horn"? Why "scrambled eggs"? What is significant about the wife's being "still asleep"? Why does the husband not like "the words 'booby' and 'booby-hatch' "? Has he heard them before? What is the effect of the figure of speech: "There was a gloat in her eye"?

3. By suggestion, Thurber allows the reader to do at least three things: characterize the wife, characterize the husband, and judge the marriage. Do all three, with supporting evidence from the fable.

4. Lamb divides all the human race into

borrowers and lenders. (See "The Two Races of Men," p. 803.) Thurber makes a simple division, too. What is it?

An Extemporaneous Talk for Students[1]

ROBERT FROST
1874–1963

To the graduating class I address myself to I want to say first how much I admire you—from here. And I admire you for more than I see. I admire you for having completed a four-year plan, and I admire anybody or any nation that can complete one. I never could do that. I am too impatient. If I could complete a four-year plan I would write an epic for you. I never succeeded in writing an epic. I lost my interest.

And I want to say, after praising you that way, what I expect of you. From what I know of this College, what I have learned through the years and what I learned last night and this morning about you, I expect a good deal. I was relieved to hear it said in so many words that you weren't expected to go on thinking that learning was all—piling up knowledge is as bad as piling up money, indefinitely. You were expected at some point to begin to kick around what you know.

The word "freedom" is on everybody's lips. I never have valued any liberty conferred on me particularly. I value myself on the liberties I take, and I have learned to appreciate the word "unscrupulous." I am not a sticker at trifles. If I wrote the history of the world in jail like Nehru twenty years ago I would expect to take many liberties with the story. I should expect to bend the story somewhat the way I wanted it to go. There is a certain measure of unscrupulousness in this. I find the same thing in good scientists. An unscrupulous person for me in science, history or literature is a person who doesn't stick at trifles.

Now the freedom that I am asked to think about sometimes is the freedom to speak—to speak out—academic and in the press, or from

the platform like this. I say I have the right to tell anything—to talk about anything I am smart enough to find out about. Second, I am free to talk about anything I am deep enough to understand, and third, I am free to talk about anything I have the ability to talk about. The limitations on my freedom, you see, are more in myself than anywhere else.

The ability to find out, the ability to understand, the ability to express . . . But now that you have had more of that freedom here—and I compliment you on that—than you get in most colleges, you have reached the point of sweeping thoughts, sweeping thoughts like Toynbee's when he writes about the history of the world . . . you know, he leaves Vermont out—unscrupulous. But he has his point to make, and the point is the great thing, and that is the courage. There is no time when I talk or when you talk that we ought not to introduce ourselves with the expression, "I make bold to say." And making bold to say means leaving out what you don't want—no lies, that is corruption—but leave out what you don't want to say.

From now on what I expect of you is more than this. Freedom has already been inculcated to help you understand what it is. But I expect more than this. I expect that you have picked up in these years of your growth—not only here at college but in the world—some interests, say four, five, six, seven, eight, nine, ten—I don't know—main ones, chief ones. For instance, you are probably interested in the immortality of the soul, and you are interested in the subject of corruption in our affairs, the corruption that comes a good deal from the vastness of our population. You are interested in education. Now these interests lead you not to uncertainty. I want you to treat them as knitting which you keep to pick up at odd moments the rest of your lives. Not just to pick up with uncertainty, but to pick up to knit, to have ideas about. Not to opinionate about, but to have ideas about. That's something more.

Let me tell you what I mean. Opinion is just pro and con, having your nose counted. For instance, I don't believe women can write philosophy, and somebody says to me, "Why do you believe that?" Well, I believe that because I have an idea about it, not just an opinion. I believe it because no woman in the whole world's history has ever made a name for herself in philosophy. It just occurred to me the other day. I pick up the question of feminism and anti-feminism as one piece of knitting that I do something with every little while. I did a little knitting about it the other day.

Now the immortality of the soul, for instance. I pick up that one every so often. Is there a hereafter, am I thinking about a hereafter? Is a hereafter more to me than the present?—and so on. Am I so interested in the hereafter that I have no interest in any reform that is going on in education?

You, of course, would first prefer to think, to have the idea yourselves. I judge that from the kind of education you have had. I myself would. I am very selfish that way. I would rather think, have an idea myself, than have an idea given to me—second to my selfishness, there is an unselfishness I sometimes have, and so I pay attention to what somebody else says to me, as you are asked to listen to me now. But the main thing is to think of it first myself.

Now there is a word we've had that goes wrong. I don't know whether you have encountered it or not. The word is, "the dream." I wonder how much you have encountered it? I have it thrown in my face every little while, and always by somebody who thinks the dream has not come true. And then the next time I pick it up to knit I wonder what the dream is, or why. And the next time I pick it up, I wonder who dreamed it. Did Tom Paine dream it, did Thomas Jefferson dream it, did George Washington dream it? Gouverneur Morris? And lately I've decided the best dreamer of it was Madison. I have been reading the Federalist papers.

But anyway I am always concerned with the question, is it a dream that's gone by? Each age is a dream that is dying, they say, or one that is coming to birth. It depends on what you mean by an age. Is the age over in which that dream had its existence—has it gone by? Can we treat the Constitution as if it were something gone by? Can we interpret it out of existence? By calling it a living document, it means something different every day, something new every day, until it doesn't mean anything that it meant to Madison. And this thought occurred to me the other day when I picked it up. Has the dream, instead of having come true, has it done something that the witches talk about? Has it simply materialized?

Young writers that I know—novelists that I know—began as poets, most of them. They began more ethereal than substantial, and have ended up more substantial than ethereal. And is that what has happened to our country? Has the ethereal idealism of the founders materialized into something too material? In South America last year at a convention I heard everybody regretting or fearing or worrying about our materialism. Not for our own sake, but for their sake, because we were misleading them into a material future for the whole world, and anxiety for us. I told them we were anxious about that too. We have scales in our bathrooms to see how material we are getting.

Now I think the first thing I wanted to say to you is that women have not been philosophers. They have been too wise to be philosophers. They have the wisdom of all such sayings as "Misery loves company," or "We all must eat our peck of dirt." That is just a figurative way of saying we must all be a little—but I won't say that. Or else, in California, I learned to say we must all eat our peck of gold. That means we all must get a little rich . . . the country must get rich, and we must not fear that.

Now I know—I think I know, as of today—what Madison's dream was. It was just a dream of a new land to fulfill with people in self-control. In self-control. That is all through his thinking. And let me say that again to you. To fulfill this land—a new land—with people in self-control. And do I think that dream has failed? Has come to nothing, or has materialized too much? It is always the fear. We live in constant fear, of course. To cross the road, we live in fear of cars. But we can live in fear, if we want to, of too much education, too little education, too much of this, too little of that. But the thing is, the measure.

I am always pleased when I see someone making motions like this [gesture of conducting a chorus]—like a metronome. Seeing the music measured. Measure always reassures me. Measure in love, in government, measure in selfishness, measure in unselfishness. Measure in selfishness. My selfishness is in being the one to think of it first, and it is only just a little ahead of my unselfishness in listening to someone else who thinks of it ahead of me. But first comes the selfishness of being the one to think of it, and to take the liberty.

Now I thought I would say a poem to you— a poem about what Madison may have thought. This is called "The Gift Outright" and it is my story of the revolutionary war. My story of the revolutionary war might be about two little battles—one little battle called King's Mountain and another little battle called Bennington—but I'll leave battles out and give you the abstract:

> The land was ours before we were the land's.
> She was our land more than a hundred years
> Before we were her people. She was ours
> In Massachusetts, in Virginia.
> But we were England's, still colonials,
> Possessing what we still were unpossessed by,
> Possessed by what we now no more possessed.
> Something we were withholding left us weak
> Until we found out that it was ourselves
> We were withholding from our land of living,
> And forthwith found salvation in surrender.
> Such as we were we gave ourselves outright
> (The deed of gift was many deeds of war)
> To the land vaguely realizing westward,
> But still unstoried, artless, unenhanced,
> Such as she was, such as she would become.

. . . The dream was to occupy the land with character—that's another way to put it—to occupy a new land with character.

You must have these interests that you keep to knit. And you must not live in uncertainty about anything like that—just with no ideas at all about them. That's what I call being a Dover beachcomber—to wish the long uncertainty would end. It isn't that uncertainty, it's getting forward. Every time you have a fresh idea in the knitting, it's strengthening. It is life. It is courage. . . .

Comments and Questions

1. What meaning does Frost give to the word "unscrupulous"? Compare the dictionary meaning and Frost's.

2. What becomes of "the truth, the whole truth and nothing but the truth" if one follows the advice to "leave out what you don't want to say"? Carefully discuss.

3. How appropriate is the recurring figure of picking up ideas as one would knitting?

4. Comment on these questions: "Has the dream, instead of having come true, has it done something that the witches talk about? Has it simply materialized?" Note particularly the word "materialized."

5. What does Frost mean by "a Dover beachcomber"? Compare "Dover Beach" (p. 347).

The Literature of Knowledge and the Literature of Power[1]
THOMAS DE QUINCEY
1785–1859

In that great social organ which, collectively, we call literature, there may be distinguished two separate offices, that may blend and often *do* so, but capable, severally, of a severe insulation, and naturally fitted for reciprocal repulsion. There is, first, the literature of *knowledge,* and, secondly, the literature of *power.* The function of the first is to *teach;* the function of the second is to *move:* the first is a rudder; the second an oar or a sail. The first speaks to the *mere* discursive understanding; the second speaks ultimately, it may happen, to the higher understanding, or reason, but always *through* affections of pleasure and sympathy. Remotely it may travel towards an object seated in what Lord Bacon calls *dry* light; but proximately it does and must operate—else it ceases to be a literature of *power*—on and through that *humid* light which clothes itself in the mists and glittering *iris* of human passions, desires, and genial emotions. Men have so little reflected on the higher functions of literature as to find it a paradox if one should describe it as a mean or subordinate purpose of books to give information. But this is a paradox only in the sense which makes it honorable to be paradoxical. Whenever we talk in ordinary language of seeking information or gaining knowledge, we understand the words as connected with something of absolute novelty. But it is the grandeur of all truth which *can* occupy a very high place in human interests that it is never absolutely novel to the meanest of minds: it exists eternally, by way of germ or latent principle, in the lowest as in the highest, needing to be developed but never to be planted. To be capable of transplantation is the immediate criterion of a truth that ranges on a lower scale. Besides which, there is

[1] From *The Poetry of Pope,* 1848.

a rarer thing than truth, namely *power*, or deep sympathy with truth. What is the effect, for instance, upon society, of children? By the pity, by the tenderness, and by the peculiar modes of admiration, which connect themselves with the helplessness, with the innocence, and with the simplicity of children, not only are the primal affections strengthened and continually renewed, but the qualities which are dearest in the sight of heaven—the frailty, for instance, which appeals to forbearance, the innocence which symbolizes the heavenly, and the simplicity which is most alien from the worldly—are kept up in perpetual remembrance, and their ideals are continually refreshed. A purpose of the same nature is answered by the higher literature, viz., the literature of power. What do you learn from *Paradise Lost?* Nothing at all. What do you learn from a cookery-book? Something new, something that you did not know before, in every paragraph. But would you therefore put the wretched cookery-book on a higher level of estimation than the divine poem? What you owe to Milton is not any knowledge, of which a million separate items are still but a million of advancing steps on the same earthly level; what you owe is *power,* that is, exercise and expansion to your own latent capacity of sympathy with the infinite, where every pulse and each separate influx is a step upwards, a step ascending as upon a Jacob's ladder from earth to mysterious altitudes above the earth. *All* the steps of knowledge, from first to last, carry you further on the same plane, but could never raise you one foot above your ancient level of earth; whereas the very *first* step in power is a flight, is an ascending movement into another element where earth is forgotten.

Were it not that human sensibilities are ventilated and continually called out into exercise by the great phenomena of infancy, or of real life as it moves through chance and change, or of literature as it recombines these elements in the mimicries of poetry, romance, etc., it is certain that, like any animal power or muscular energy falling into disuse, all such sensibilities would gradually droop and dwindle. It is in relation to these great *moral* capacities of man that the literature of power, as contradistinguished from that of knowledge, lives and has its field of action. It is concerned with what is highest in man; for the Scriptures themselves never condescended to deal by suggestion or co-operation with the mere discursive understanding: when speaking of man in his intellectual capacity, the Scriptures speak, not of the understanding, but of *"the understanding heart,"* making the heart, —that is, the great *intuitive* (or nondiscursive) organ, to be the interchangeable formula for man in his highest state of capacity for the infinite. Tragedy, romance, fairy tale, or epopee, all alike restore to man's mind the ideals of justice, of hope, of truth, of mercy, of retribution, which else (left to the support of daily life in its realities) would languish for want of sufficient illustration. What is meant, for instance, by *poetic justice?* It does not mean a justice that differs by its object from the ordinary justice of human jurisprudence, for then it must be confessedly a very bad kind of justice; but it means a justice that differs from common forensic justice by the degree in which it *attains* its object, a justice that is more omnipotent over its own ends, as dealing, not with the refractory elements of earthly life, but with the elements of its own creation and with materials flexible to its own purest preconceptions. It is certain that, were it not for the literature of power, these ideals would often remain amongst us as mere arid notional forms; whereas, by the creative forces of man put forth in literature, they gain a vernal life of restoration and germinate into vital activities. The commonist novel, by moving in alliance with human fears and hopes, with human instincts of wrong and right, sustains and quickens those affections. Calling them into action, it rescues them from torpor. And hence the pre-eminency, over all authors that merely *teach,* of the meanest that moves, or that teaches, if at all, indirectly *by* moving. The very highest work that has ever existed in the literature of knowledge is but a provisional work, a book upon trial and sufferance, and *quamdiu bene se gesserit* [as long as it bore itself well]. Let its teaching be even partially revised, let it be but expanded, nay, even let its teaching be but placed in a better order, and instantly it is superseded. Whereas the feeblest works in the literature of power, surviving at all, survive as finished and unalterable among men. For instance, the *Principia* of Sir Isaac Newton was a book *militant* on earth from the first. In all stages of its progress it would have to fight for its existence: first, as regards absolute truth; secondly, when that combat was over, as regards its form, or mode of presenting the truth. And as soon as a La Place, or anybody else, builds higher upon the foundations laid by this book, effectually he throws it out of the sunshine into decay and darkness; by weapons won from this book he superannuates and destroys this book, so that soon the name of Newton remains as a mere *nominis umbra* [shadow of a name], but his book, as a living power, has transmigrated into other forms. Now, on the contrary, the *Iliad*, the *Prometheus* of Æschylus, the *Othello* or *King Lear*, the *Hamlet* or *Macbeth*, and the *Paradise Lost* are not militant but triumphant forever, as long as the languages exist in which they speak or can be taught to speak. They never *can* transmigrate into new incarnations. To reproduce these in new forms or variations, even if in some things they should be improved, would be to plagiarize. A good steam-engine is properly superseded by a better. But one lovely pastoral valley is not superseded by another, nor a statue of Praxiteles by a statue of Michelangelo. These things are separated, not by imparity, but by disparity. They are not thought of as unequal under the same standard, but as different in *kind*, and, if otherwise equal, as equal under a different standard. Human works of immortal beauty and works of nature in one respect stand on the same footing: they never absolutely repeat each other, never approach so near as not to differ; and they differ not as better and worse, or simply by more and less; they differ by undecipherable and incommunicable differences, that cannot be caught by mimicries, that cannot be reflected in the mirror of copies, that cannot become ponderable in the scales of vulgar comparison.

Comments and Questions

1. Why does De Quincey call literature a "social organ"? Does this suggest that the fundamental function of literature is communication? Discuss.

2. At one point the author calls the literature of knowledge a "rudder" and then adds further on that it is "a mean or subordinate purpose of books to give information." Does there seem to be a contradiction here? Discuss carefully.

3. Explain: "all truth . . . exists eternally, by way of germ or latent principle, in the lowest as in the highest, needing to be developed but never to be planted." Compare Emerson: "To believe your own thought, to believe that what is true for you in your private heart is true for all men,—that is genius." Now, contrast Ciardi, who has his Poet ask of the Citizen: "The point is why *should* I write for you?" (See "Dialogue with the Audience," p. 845.)

4. How does De Quincey use children to illustrate the function of the literature of power?

5. Define *poetic justice*. Compare your definition with De Quincey's.

6. Explain the term "militant" as applied to the literature of knowledge and contrast with the word "triumphant" as applied to the literature of power.

7. Which section of this book, *Interpreting Literature*, comes nearest to the literature of knowledge? Clearly the editorial material in an anthology of this sort belongs to the literature of knowledge. Why?

Music at Night
ALDOUS HUXLEY
1894–1963

Moonless, this June night is all the more alive with stars. Its darkness is perfumed with faint gusts from the blossoming lime trees, with the smell of wetted earth and the invisible greenness of the vines. There is silence; but a silence that breathes with the soft breathing of the sea, and the thin shrill noise of a cricket, insistently, incessantly harps on the fact of its own deep perfection. Far away, the passage of a train is like a long caress, moving gently, with an inexorable gentleness, across the warm living body of the night.

Music, you say; it would be a good night for music. But I have music here in a box, shut up, like one of those bottled djinns in the *Arabian Nights*, and ready at a touch to break out of its prison. I make the necessary mechanical magic, and suddenly, by some miraculously appropriate coincidence (for I had selected the record in the dark, without knowing what music the machine would play), suddenly the introduction to the

Benedictus in Beethoven's *Missa Solemnis* begins to trace its patterns on the moonless sky.

The *Benedictus*. Blessed and blessing, this music is in some sort the equivalent of the night, of the deep and living darkness, into which, now in a single jet, now in a fine interweaving of melodies, now in pulsing and almost solid clots of harmonious sound, it pours itself, stanchlessly pours itself, like time, like the rising and falling, falling trajectories of a life. It is the equivalent of the night in another mode of being, as an essence is the equivalent of the flowers, from which it is distilled.

There is, at least there sometimes seems to be, a certain blessedness lying at the heart of things, a mysterious blessedness, of whose existence occasional accidents or providences (for me, this night is one of them) make us obscurely, or it may be intensely, but always fleetingly, alas, always only for a few brief moments aware. In the *Benedictus* Beethoven gives expression to this awareness of blessedness. His music is the equivalent of this Mediterranean night, or rather of the blessedness at the heart of the night, of the blessedness as it would be if it could be sifted clear of irrelevance and accident, refined and separated out into its quintessential purity.

"*Benedictus, benedictus . . .*" One after another the voices take up the theme propounded by the orchestra and lovingly meditated through a long and exquisite solo (for the blessedness reveals itself most often to the solitary spirit) by a single violin. "*Benedictus, benedictus . . .*" And then, suddenly, the music dies; the flying djinn has been rebottled. With a stupid insect-like insistence, a steel point rasps and rasps the silence.

At school, when they taught us what was technically known as English, they used to tell us to "express in our own words" some passage from whatever play of Shakespeare was at the moment being rammed, with all its annotations —particularly the annotations—down our reluctant throats. So there we would sit, a row of inky urchins, laboriously translating "now silken dalliance in the wardrobe lies" into "now smart silk clothes lie in the wardrobe," or "To be or not to be" into "I wonder whether I ought to commit suicide or not." When we had finished, we would hand in our papers, and the presiding pedagogue would give us marks more or less

according to the accuracy with which "our own words" had "expressed" the meaning of the Bard.

He ought, of course, to have given us naught all round with a hundred lines to himself for ever having set us the silly exercise. Nobody's "own words," except those of Shakespeare himself, can possibly "express" what Shakespeare meant. The substance of a work of art is inseparable from its form; its truth and its beauty are two and yet, mysteriously, one. The verbal expression of even a metaphysic or a system of ethics is very nearly as much of a work of art as a love poem. The philosophy of Plato expressed in the "own words" of Jowett is not the philosophy of Plato; nor in the "own words" of, say, Billy Sunday, is the teaching of St. Paul St. Paul's teaching.

"Our own words" are inadequate even to express the meaning of other words; how much more inadequate, when it is a matter of rendering meanings which have their original expression in terms of music or one of the visual arts! What, for example, does music "say"? You can buy at almost any concert an analytical programme that will tell you exactly. Much too exactly; that is the trouble. Every analyst has his own version. Imagine Pharaoh's dream interpreted successively by Joseph, by the Egyptian soothsayers, by Freud, by Rivers, by Adler, by Jung, by Wohlgemuth: it would "say" a great many different things. Not nearly so many, however, as the Fifth Symphony has been made to say in the verbiage of its analysts. Not nearly so many as the Virgin of the Rocks and the Sistine Madonna have no less lyrically said.

Annoyed by the verbiage and this absurd multiplicity of attributed "meanings," some critics have protested that music and painting signify nothing but themselves; that the only things they "say" are things, for example, about modulations and fugues, about colour values and three-dimensional forms. That they say anything about human destiny or the universe at large is a notion which these purists dismiss as merely nonsensical.

If the purists were right, then we should have to regard painters and musicians as monsters. For it is strictly impossible to be a human being and not to have views of some kind about the universe at large, very difficult to be a human being and not to express those views, at any rate by implication. Now, it is a matter of observation that painters and musicians are *not* monsters. Therefore . . . The conclusion follows, unescapably.

It is not only in programme music and problem pictures that composers and painters express their views about the universe. The purest and most abstract artistic creations can be, in their own peculiar language, as eloquent in this respect as the most deliberately tendentious.

Compare, for example, a Virgin by Piero della Francesca with a Virgin by Tura. Two Madonnas—and the current symbolical conventions are observed by both artists. The difference, the enormous difference between the two pictures is a purely pictorial difference, a difference in the forms and their arrangement, in the disposition of the lines and planes and masses. To any one in the least sensitive to the eloquence of pure form, the two Madonnas say utterly different things about the world.

Piero's composition is a welding together of smooth and beautifully balanced solidities. Everything in his universe is endowed with a kind of supernatural substantiality, is much more "there" than any object of the actual world could possibly be. And how sublimely rational, in the noblest, the most humane acceptation of the world, how orderedly philosophical is the landscape, are all the inhabitants of this world! It is the creation of a god who "ever plays the geometer."

What does she say, this Madonna from San Sepolcro? If I have not wholly mistranslated the eloquence of Piero's forms, she is telling us of the greatness of the human spirit, of its power to rise above circumstance and dominate fate. If you were to ask her, "How shall I be saved?" "By Reason," she would probably answer. And, anticipating Milton, "Not only, not mainly upon the Cross," she would say, "is Paradise regained, but in those deserts of utter solitude where man puts forth the strength of his reason to resist the fiend." This particular mother of Christ is probably not a Christian.

Turn now to Tura's picture. It is fashioned out of a substance that is like the living embodiment of flame—flame-flesh, alive and sensitive and suffering. His surfaces writhe away from the eye, as though shrinking, as though in pain. The lines flow intricately with something of that disquieting and, you feel, magical calligraphy, which characterizes certain Tibetan paintings.

Look closely; feel your way into the picture, into the painter's thoughts and intuitions and emotions. This man was naked and at the mercy of destiny. To be able to proclaim the spirit's stoical independence, you must be able to raise your head above the flux of things; this man was sunk in it, overwhelmed. He could introduce no order into his world; it remained for him a mysterious chaos, fantastically marbled with patches, now of purest heaven, now of the most excruciating hell. A beautiful and terrifying world, is this Madonna's verdict; a world like the incarnation, the material projection, of Ophelia's madness. There are no certainties in it but suffering and occasional happiness. And as for salvation, who knows the way of salvation? There may perhaps be miracles, and there is always hope.

The limits of criticism are very quickly reached. When he has said "in his own words" as much, or rather as little, as "own words" can say, the critic can only refer his readers to the original work of art: let them go and see for themselves. Those who overstep the limit are either rather stupid, vain people, who love their "own words" and imagine that they can say in them more than "own words" are able in the nature of things to express. Or else they are intelligent people who happen to be philosophers or literary artists and who find it convenient to make the criticism of other men's work a jumping-off place for their own creativity.

What is true of painting is equally true of music. Music "says" things about the world, but in specifically musical terms. Any attempt to reproduce these musical statements "in our own words" is necessarily doomed to failure. We cannot isolate the truth contained in a piece of music; for it is a beauty-truth and inseparable from its partner. The best we can do is to indicate in the most general terms the nature of the musical beauty-truth under consideration and to refer curious truth-seekers to the original. Thus, the introduction to the *Benedictus* in the *Missa Solemnis* is a statement about the blessedness that is at the heart of things. But this is about as far as "own words" will take us. If we were to start describing in our "own words" exactly what Beethoven felt about this blessedness, how he conceived it, what he thought its nature to be, we should very soon find ourselves writing lyrical nonsense in the style of the analytical programme makers. Only music, and only Beethoven's music, and only this particular music of Beethoven, can tell us with any precision what Beethoven's conception of the blessedness at the heart of things actually was. If we want to know, we must listen—on a still June night, by preference, with the breathing of the invisible sea for background to the music and the scent of lime trees drifting through the darkness, like some exquisite soft harmony apprehended by another sense.

Comments and Questions

1. Note the structure of this essay. How does the author move from his lyrical tribute to Beethoven into his central statement? Then, at the end, how does he enforce what he has said by a return to Beethoven's music at night?

2. "The substance of a work is inseparable from its form." If this is strictly true, what becomes of the notion that music, painting, poetry—all art forms—can be interpreted? Compare "Poetry: Preliminaries" (pp. 236 ff.).

3. You might wish to look at the two pictures—Piero della Francesca's Virgin and Tura's Virgin—and compare your response to these paintings with Huxley's interpretations. This procedure would be following the author's advice to readers: "let them go and see for themselves."

4. Compare this essay with Malcolm Cowley's "Criticism: A Many-Windowed House" (p. 817).

Reading
W. H. AUDEN
1907–1973

A book is a mirror: if an ass peers into it, you can't expect an apostle to look out.

—C. G. LICHTENBERG

One only reads well that which one reads with some quite personal purpose. It may be to acquire some power. It can be out of hatred for the author.

—PAUL VALÉRY

The interests of a writer and the interests of his readers are never the same and if, on occasion, they happen to coincide, this is a lucky accident.

In relation to a writer, most readers believe in the Double Standard: they may be unfaithful to him as often as they like, but he must never, never be unfaithful to them.

To read is to translate, for no two persons' experiences are the same. A bad reader is like a bad translator: he interprets literally when he ought to paraphrase and paraphrases when he ought to interpret literally. In learning to read well, scholarship, valuable as it is, is less important than instinct; some great scholars have been poor translators.

We often derive much profit from reading a book in a different way from that which its author intended but only (once childhood is over) if we know that we are doing so.

As readers, most of us, to some degree, are like those urchins who pencil mustaches on the faces of girls in advertisements.

One sign that a book has literary value is that it can be read in a number of different ways. Vice versa, the proof that pornography has no literary value is that, if one attempts to read it in any other way than as a sexual stimulus, to read it, say, as a psychological case-history of the author's sexual fantasies, one is bored to tears.

Though a work of literature can be read in a number of ways, this number is finite and can be arranged in a hierarchical order; some readings are obviously "truer" than others, some doubtful, some obviously false, and some, like reading a novel backwards, absurd. That is why, for a desert island, one would choose a good dictionary rather than the greatest literary masterpiece imaginable, for, in relation to its readers, a dictionary is absolutely passive and may legitimately be read in an infinite number of ways.

We cannot read an author for the first time in the same way that we read the latest book by an established author. In a new author, we tend to see either only his virtues or only his defects and, even if we do see both, we cannot see the relation between them. In the case of an established author, if we can still read him at all, we know that we cannot enjoy the virtues we admire in him without tolerating the defects we deplore. Moreover, our judgment of an established author is never simply an aesthetic judgment. In addition to any literary merit it may have, a new book by him has a historic interest for us as the act of a person in whom we have long been interested. He is not only a poet or a novelist; he is also a character in our biography.

A poet cannot read another poet, nor a novelist another novelist, without comparing their work to his own. His judgments as he reads are of this kind: *My God! My Great-Grandfather! My Uncle! My Enemy! My Brother! My imbecile Brother!*

In literature, vulgarity is preferable to nullity, just as grocer's port is preferable to distilled water.

Good taste is much more a matter of discrimination than of exclusion, and when good taste feels compelled to exclude, it is with regret, not with pleasure.

Pleasure is by no means an infallible critical guide, but it is the least fallible.

A child's reading is guided by pleasure, but his pleasure is undifferentiated; he cannot distinguish, for example, between aesthetic pleasure and the pleasures of learning or daydreaming. In adolescence we realize that there are different kinds of pleasure, some of which cannot be enjoyed simultaneously, but we need help from others in defining them. Whether it be a matter of taste in food or taste in literature, the adolescent looks for a mentor in whose authority he can believe. He eats or reads what his mentor recommends and, inevitably, there are occasions when he has to deceive himself a little; he has to pretend that he enjoys olives or *War and Peace* a little more than he actually does. Between the ages of twenty and forty we are engaged in the process of discovering who we are, which involves learning the difference between accidental limitations which it is our duty to outgrow and the necessary limitations of our nature beyond which we cannot trespass with impunity. Few of us can learn this without making mistakes, without trying to become a little more of a universal man than we are permitted to be. It is during this period that a writer can most easily be led astray by another writer or by some ideology. When someone between twenty and forty says, apropos of a work of art, "I know what I like," he is really saying "I have no taste of my own but accept the taste of my cultural milieu," because, between twenty and forty, the surest sign that a man has a genuine taste of his own is that he is uncertain of it. After forty, if we have not lost our authentic selves altogether, pleasure can again become what it was when we were children, the proper guide to what *we* should read.

Though the pleasure which works of art give us must not be confused with other pleasures that we enjoy, it is related to all of them simply by being *our* pleasure and not someone else's. All the judgments, aesthetic or moral, that we pass, however objective we try to make them, are in part a rationalization and in part a corrective discipline of our subjective wishes. So long as a man writes poetry or fiction, his dream of Eden is his own business, but the moment he starts writing literary criticism, honesty demands that he describe it to his readers, so that they may be in the position to judge his judgments. Accordingly, I must now give my answers to a questionnaire I once made up which provides the kind of information I should like to have myself when reading other critics.

Eden

Landscape
Limestone uplands like the Pennines plus a small region of igneous rocks with at least one extinct volcano. A precipitous and indented sea-coast.

Climate
British.

Ethnic origin of inhabitants
Highly varied as in the United States, but with a slight nordic predominance.

Language
Of mixed origins like English, but highly inflected.

Weights & Measures
Irregular and complicated. No decimal system.

Religion
Roman Catholic in an easygoing Mediterranean sort of way. Lots of local saints.

Size of Capital
Plato's ideal figure, 5004, about right.

Form of Government
Absolute monarchy, elected for life by lot.

Sources of Natural Power
Wind, water, peat, coal. No oil.

Economic activities
Lead mining, coal mining, chemical factories, paper mills, sheep farming, truck farming, greenhouse horticulture.

Means of transport
Horses and horse-drawn vehicles, canal barges, balloons. No automobiles or airplanes.

Architecture
State: Baroque. Ecclesiastical: Romanesque or Byzantine. Domestic: Eighteenth Century British or American Colonial.

Domestic Furniture and Equipment
Victorian except for kitchens and bathrooms which are as full of modern gadgets as possible.

Formal Dress
The fashions of Paris in the 1830's and '40's.

Sources of Public Information
Gossip. Technical and learned periodicals but no newspapers.

Public Statues
Confined to famous defunct chefs.

Public Entertainments
Religious Processions, Brass Bands, Opera, Classical Ballet. No movies, radio or television.

If I were to attempt to write down the names of all the poets and novelists for whose work I am really grateful because I know that if I had not read them my life would be poorer, the list would take up pages. But when I try to think of all the critics for whom I am really grateful, I find myself with a list of thirty-four names. Of these, twelve are German and only two French. Does this indicate a conscious bias? It does.

If good literary critics are rarer than good poets or novelists, one reason is the nature of human egoism. A poet or a novelist has to learn to be humble in the face of his subject matter which is life in general. But the subject matter of a critic, before which he has to learn to be humble, is made up of authors, that is to say, of human individuals, and this kind of humility is much more difficult to acquire. It is far easier to say—"Life is more important than anything I can say about it"—than to say—"Mr. A's work is more important than anything I can say about it."

There are people who are too intelligent to become authors, but they do not become critics.

Authors can be stupid enough, God knows, but they are not always quite so stupid as a certain kind of critic seems to think. The kind of critic, I mean, to whom, when he condemns a work or a passage, the possibility never occurs that its author may have foreseen exactly what he is going to say.

What is the function of a critic? So far as I am concerned, he can do me one or more of the following services:

1. Introduce me to authors or works of which I was hitherto unaware.

2. Convince me that I have undervalued an author or a work because I had not read them carefully enough.

3. Show me relations between works of different ages and cultures which I could never have seen for myself because I do not know enough and never shall.

4. Give a "reading" of a work which increases my understanding of it.

5. Throw light upon the process of artistic "Making."

6. Throw light upon the relation of art to life, to science, economics, ethics, religion, etc.

The first three of these services demand scholarship. A scholar is not merely someone whose knowledge is extensive; the knowledge must be of value to others. One would not call a man who knew the Manhattan Telephone Directory by heart a scholar, because one cannot imagine circumstances in which he would acquire a pupil. Since scholarship implies a relation between one who knows more and one who knows less, it may be temporary; in relation to the public, every reviewer is, temporarily, a scholar, because he has read the book he is reviewing and the public have not. Though the knowledge a scholar possesses must be potentially valuable, it is not necessary that he recognize its value himself; it is always possible that the pupil to whom he imparts his knowledge has a better sense of its value than he. In general, when reading a scholarly critic, one profits more from his quotations than from his comments.

The last three services demand, not superior knowledge, but superior insight. A critic shows superior insight if the questions he raises are fresh and important, however much one may disagree with his answers to them. Few readers, probably, find themselves able to accept Tolstoi's conclusions in *What is Art?*, but, once one has read the book, one can never again ignore the questions Tolstoi raises.

The one thing I most emphatically do not ask of a critic is that he tell me what I *ought* to approve of or condemn. I have no objection to his telling me what works and authors he likes and dislikes; indeed, it is useful to know this for, from his expressed preferences about works which I have read, I learn how likely I am to agree or disagree with his verdicts on works which I have not. But let him not dare to lay down the law to me. The responsibility for what I choose to read is mine, and nobody else on earth can do it for me.

The critical opinions of a writer should always be taken with a large grain of salt. For the most part, they are manifestations of his debate with himself as to what he should do next and what he should avoid. Moreover, unlike a scientist, he is usually even more ignorant of what his colleagues are doing than is the general public. A poet over thirty may still be a voracious reader, but it is unlikely that much of what he reads is modern poetry.

Very few of us can truthfully boast that we have never condemned a book or even an author on hearsay, but quite a lot of us that we have never praised one we had not read.

The injunction "Resist not evil but overcome evil with good" may in many spheres of life be impossible to obey literally, but in the sphere of the arts it is common sense. Bad art is always with us, but any given work of art is always bad in a period way; the particular kind of badness it exhibits will pass away to be succeeded by some other kind. It is unnecessary, therefore, to attack it, because it will perish anyway. Had Macaulay never written his review of Robert Montgomery, we would not today be still under the illusion that Montgomery was a great poet. The only sensible procedure for a critic is to keep silent about works which he believes to be bad, while at the same time vigorously campaigning for those which he believes to be good, especially if they are being neglected or underestimated by the public.

Some books are undeservedly forgotten; none are undeservedly remembered.

Some critics argue that it is their moral duty to expose the badness of an author because, un-less this is done, he may corrupt other writers. To be sure, a young writer can be led astray, deflected, that is, from his true path, by an older, but he is much more likely to be seduced by a good writer than by a bad one. The more powerful and original a writer, the more dangerous he is to lesser talents who are trying to find themselves. On the other hand, works which were in themselves poor have often proved a stimulus to the imagination and become the indirect cause of good work in others.

You do not educate a person's palate by telling him that what he has been in the habit of eating—watery, overboiled cabbage, let us say—is disgusting, but by persuading him to try a dish of vegetables which have been properly cooked. With some people, it is true, you seem to get quicker results by telling them—"Only vulgar people like over-cooked cabbage; the best people like cabbage as the Chinese cook it"—but the results are less likely to be lasting.

If, when a reviewer whose taste I trust condemns a book, I feel a certain relief, this is only because so many books are published that it is a relief to think—"Well, here, at least, is one I do not have to bother about." But had he kept silent, the effect would have been the same.

Attacking bad books is not only a waste of time but also bad for the character. If I find a book really bad, the only interest I can derive from writing about it has to come from myself, from such display of intelligence, wit and malice as I can contrive. One cannot review a bad book without showing off.

There is one evil that concerns literature which should never be passed over in silence but be continually publicly attacked, and that is corruption of the language, for writers cannot invent their own language and are dependent upon the language they inherit so that, if it be corrupt, they must be corrupted. But the critic who concerns himself with this evil must attack it at its source, which is not in works of literature but in the misuse of language by the man-in-the-street, journalists, politicians, etc. Furthermore, he must be able to practice what he preaches. How many critics in England or America today are masters of their native tongue as Karl Kraus was a master of German?

One cannot blame the reviewers themselves. Most of them, probably, would much prefer to review only those books which, whatever their faults, they believe to be worth reading but, if a regular reviewer on one of the big Sunday papers were to obey his inclination, at least one Sunday in three his column would be empty. Again, any conscientious critic who has ever had to review a new volume of poetry in a limited space knows that the only fair thing to do would be to give a series of quotations without comment but, if he did so, his editor would complain that he was not earning his money.

Reviewers may justly be blamed, however, for their habit of labeling and packaging authors. At first critics classified authors as Ancients, that is to say, Greek and Latin authors, and Moderns, that is to say, every post-Classical Author. Then they classified them by eras, the Augustans, the Victorians, etc., and now they classify them by decades, the writers of the '30's, '40's, etc. Very soon, it seems, they will be labeling authors, like automobiles, by the year. Already the decade classification is absurd, for it suggests that authors conveniently stopped writing at the age of thirty-five or so.

"Contemporary" is a much abused term. My contemporaries are simply those who are on earth while I am alive, whether they be babies or centenarians.

A writer, or, at least, a poet, is always being asked by people who should know better: "Whom do you write for?" The question is, of course, a silly one, but I can give it a silly answer. Occasionally I come across a book which I feel has been written especially for me and for me only. Like a jealous lover, I don't want anybody else to hear of it. To have a million such readers, unaware of each other's existence, to be read with passion and never talked about, is the daydream, surely, of every author.

Comments and Questions

1. Does this essay have organization, or does it classify simply as a series of provocative observations on reading?

2. Compare Auden on the function of a critic with Aldous Huxley's remarks on this subject in "Music at Night." Also compare Auden with Cowley (see "Criticism: A Many-Windowed House," next).

3. Make a list of the startling—at least thought-provoking—statements in this essay

and show how apposite they are. Example: "As readers, most of us, to some degree, are like those urchins who pencil mustaches on the faces of girls in advertisements." What quality in a reader does this simile suggest?

Criticism: A Many-Windowed House
MALCOLM COWLEY
1898–

[1] Although I have been a literary critic for more than forty years, I must confess that I have not devoted much time to the basic theories of my profession. Partly, that oversight is due to indolence, but it is also the result of what might be called an incest taboo: I have tried to avoid critical endogamy and inbreeding. Instead of dealing critically with the critical critics of criticism, I have preferred to be a critic of poems and novels, or at most a literary historian. More recently, however, I have defied the taboo by reviewing several big critical works, and I have been dismayed to find that many of them were so badly written as to reveal a sort of esthetic deafness, that some of them were contemptuous of writers and writing—except as the raw material of critical works—and that most of them were episodes in the battle among critical systems, one or another of which we were being cannonaded into accepting as the only true critical faith.

[2] When I tried to compare the systems in order to find a faith for myself, it seemed to me that each of them led to a different but equally specialized and partial standard for judging works of art. Thus, for historical critics the best book is the one that either sums up a historical movement or else has directly influenced history. For biographical critics it is the one most intimately connected with the author's life. For psychoanalytical critics it is the one that reveals how the author sublimated his antisocial desires. For expressionist critics of the Crocean school, the standard is sincerity and spontaneity of expression. For moral critics—who were dominant in this country as late as the 1920s—the best books are those which embody philosophi-

cal truths or inculcate the highest moral lessons. For political critics they are the books that advance a political cause, and this, during the 1930s, was usually that of international revolution. Each of these standards is inescapable, being derived from the method itself. Often the critic says, "I do not judge, I merely explain," yet the standard is revealed, if nowhere else, in his choice of books for explication.

[3] In the 1960s all those standards have fallen into critical disfavor. The presently accepted system of approaching works of art is one that attempts to purify criticism by purging it of everything that might be regarded as an extraneous element or, to use the fashionable word, as a fallacy. Out go the historical fallacy, the social fallacy, the moral fallacy, the personal fallacy, the genetic fallacy, the effective fallacy. Out goes the author's life; out goes his social background; out goes the audience for which he wrote; out goes the political meaning of his work; out goes its moral effect. What is supposed to remain after this cathartic process is the work itself, as pure act without antecedents or relevance or results: simply the words in their naked glory. They are the purified subject of the system known as textual or integral criticism, or less exactly—since the term has several meanings—as the "new" criticism.

[4] Like all other systems, this one involves a standard of judgment derived from the method itself. Let me quote from an essay by John V. Hagopian, who is one of the ablest of the new critics. "The critic's duty," he says—and of course there is no question of the critic's or the reader's pleasure—"is to determine as nearly as he can what feeling-qualities are embodied in the form-content of the work, how they are embodied there, and how well. . . . He has no other task; evaluations of historical significance, autobiographical expression, moral goodness, or philosophical truths are purely gratuitous for criticism, even though"—a generous concession —"they may be valuable to other disciplines of the humanities." Then, after this rejection of other standards, Mr. Hagopian offers an effective but still, it seems to me, oversimplified standard of his own. "Given two literary works," he says, "which are equally successful in resolving an artistic problem, the critics can choose the more important one by determining which has integrated the greatest amount of complexity."

[5] To put Mr. Hagopian's statement in slightly different words, the critic pretends that every work of literature is completely autonomous, and then judges it by the complexity of its inner relations. He could find worse standards. The new or integral system of evaluating works has yielded some precious illuminations and has proved to be an effective method of teaching literature. It does, however, involve a disturbing amount of make-believe. Let's pretend that the poem or story was written at no particular date in no particular country. Let's pretend that it has no relation with any other work by the same author, or with any tendencies prevailing among a group of authors. Let's pretend that it can be interpreted and judged with no material except the text itself, and perhaps a few commentaries by other textual critics.

[6] All those pretenses are hard to maintain. Literature is not a pure art like music, or a relatively pure art like painting and sculpture. Its medium is not abstract like tones and colors, not inorganic like metal and stone. Instead it uses language, which is a social creation, changing with the society that created it. The study of any author's language carries us straight into history, institutions, moral questions, personal stratagems, and all the other esthetic impurities or fallacies that many new critics are trying to expunge.

[7] Nor is that the only reason why these critics cannot be consistently applying their own standard of judgment. As soon as they admit that a given work of literature was not self-produced but had an author—as soon as they admit that he wrote other works, some of which preceded and some followed the work in question—they are violating the purity of their method and are becoming, if ever so faintly, biographical critics. As soon as they admit that the work may have been affected by other authors, or may have exerted an effect on them, they are becoming historical. As soon as they admit that the work was written for an audience, they are deviating into sociology. As soon as they admit that it had or might have had an effect on the conduct of that audience, they have to introduce moral notions; there is no escaping them. As soon as they discuss or even hint at the author's intentions, they are becoming psychological. Criticism too is a literary art, and like other forms of literature it is impure by definition.

[8] Some critics have looked for a way out of this dilemma by denying that criticism is an art and by claiming a place for it among the sciences. In order to make it a science, however, they have to subject it to another process of purgation. This time they have to remove all its subjective elements, including the critic's feelings about the work and also including the author of the work, whose mere presence may be a source of nonconformity to scientific laws. Why not simply abolish the author—or if he can't be abolished, why not rule him out of consideration?

[9] That radical but, in the circumstances, necessary step was taken some years ago by professors W. K. Wimsatt, Jr., and M. D. Beardsley. In an essay called "The Intentional Fallacy" they asserted that "The design or intention of the author is neither available nor desirable as a standard for judging the success of a work of art." They admitted that the psychology of composition was sometimes a valid and useful study, but they described it as "an art separate from criticism . . . an individual and private culture, yoga, or system of self-development which the young poet would do well to notice, but different from"—and I italicize their words—"*the public science of evaluating poems.*"

[10] Now "public" implies that the critic should be objective and impersonal. "Science" implies that he administers a body of universal laws, the truth of which can be demonstrated by quantitative measurements. "Of evaluating poems" implies that judgment or evaluation is the critic's essential task. Each of these implications, it seems to me, is based on a radical misconception of what the critic is able or entitled to do.

[11] Since his judgment of a work starts with his own reaction to it, he cannot, in practice, be purely impersonal. He is not entitled to speak of criticism as a science. As Paul Valéry said many years ago, "There are sciences of exact things, and arts of inexact things." The best of criticism is inexact. In these days, however, everybody wants to be a scientist and move in the air of terrified respect that surrounds the men who split the atom. Every school of the humanities wants to share in the huge endowments of the new physics laboratories and cancer-research institutes. Inevitably some of the humanists begin to speak of their work in scientific language, as if it were performed with micrometric gauges, electronic computers, and balance pans in a vacuum. But there will never be a science of taste or of belief or of the arts of language. There will only be critics who talk like scientists and some of whom end by achieving the wooden arrogance of minor critics in the eighteenth century, who also thought they were expounding the laws of universal and unchanging wisdom.

[12] Evaluating poems and novels is not the central task of a critic. Rather than judgment that task is interpretation and definition. The first question for a critic to answer is not "How good is this poem?" but simply "What *is* this poem, in structure, in style, in meaning, and in its effect on the reader?" Judgment is the end of the critical process, but if the work has been defined and interpreted correctly, then judgment often follows as a matter of course. For example, if one defines a certain novel as "A rapid sequence of events that offers no opportunity to develop the characters in depth," one does not have to add that it is a minor work of fiction.

[13] In deciding what a novel or poem *is*, we cannot accept the author's testimony as final, knowing as we do that authors often intend one thing and end by producing another. We think of all the authors who intended masterpieces, as compared with the small number of masterpieces, and we also think of Mark Twain, who intended a boy's book and brought forth an epic. Nevertheless, if the author has offered his testimony—in letters, in outlines, in journals, in public statements—it is probative evidence and we cannot simply throw it out of court. If we fail to consider it we may, like many recent critics, fall into the opposite or unintentional fallacy by substituting our own story, our own creation, our own fantasy for the book that was actually written by the author.

[14] Some years ago Stanley Edgar Hyman, always a lively critic, wrote a long and favorable review of a book called *The Disguises of Love,* by Robie Macauley. He presented it as a novel in which "accounts of homosexual relations are disguised as accounts of heterosexual relations," since, the reviewer explained, owing to American prudishness "our authors have no choice but to metamorphose gender." Therefore the heroine's name, Frances feminine, should be altered to Francis masculine by any discerning reader. In the following issue of the *Hudson Review* the author protested against this distortion of his

meaning. No homosexuality was involved or implied in the story. Frances feminine was Frances completely female.

[15] The reviewer was not in the least disconcerted. He answered in part, "I am sorry that Mr. Macauley, for whatever reason, prefers not to have written the interesting and complicated novel I read and tried to describe, and prefers instead to have written the poor thin novel he describes. . . . Mr. Macauley is not the first novelist to have builded better than he knows or will admit; nor will he, probably, be the last." And then this manifesto, from Mr. Hyman, of complete critical independence: "I am not prepared," he said, "to be scared out of a critical reading of a novel by the author's waspish insistence that it is not *his* reading."

[16] Authors haven't much chance with critics who throw their evidence out of court as insubstantial, immaterial, and incompetent. What Stanley Hyman did for a single book (not without a gleam of mischief in his style), Leslie A. Fiedler has done solemnly for American fiction in general. In a work almost as long as Parrington's *Main Currents in American Thought,* he has proclaimed that all our great novelists were sexually immature, that their work represented an escape from a female-dominated world into male companionship, and that *The Last of the Mohicans, Moby-Dick* and *Huckleberry Finn* are almost identical fables of homosexual miscegenation. Mr. Fiedler's book is a final exploit of criticism cut loose from its moorings and sailing across the moon like a Halloween witch on her broomstick.

[17] Although it seems impossibly far from Mr. Wimsatt's sober and quasi-scientific type of criticism, still it results from the same doctrine, namely, that an author's intentions should be utterly disregarded. The effect of the doctrine is to deprive the author of all property in his work from the moment it is printed. It becomes the property of everybody and nobody, but it doesn't long remain in that situation. Soon it is seized upon by critics, who claim the privilege of reinterpreting and in fact rewriting it into something the author cannot recognize. If the author protests, the critic feels entitled to jeer at his "waspish insistence." The critic rules supreme, and his next step—which Mr. Fiedler and others have taken—is to present the author as an immature

neurotic whom the critic, disguised as a psychoanalyst, is not even attempting to cure, but is merely exposing to public shame.

[18] I do not propose to offer still another system of criticism to set against those I have questioned. But since this paper started as a confession, I had better state a few of my own beliefs.

[19] First of all I believe that a definition of criticism should be as simple and short as possible. Mightn't it be enough to say that it is *writing which deals with works of art?* Any narrower definition would restrict the liberty of the critic and might also restrict his usefulness.

[20] I believe that criticism should be approached as one of the literary arts. The word "literary" implies that it should be written in the language of English literature and not, like a great deal of recent criticism, in some variety of philosophical or social-scientific jargon. When a critic's language is awkward, involved, and inaccurate, we are entitled to question his ability to recognize good prose. As for the word "arts," it implies that criticism is not a science based on exact measurement. If it is going to be persuasive, however, it had better include a great deal of objectively verifiable information.

[21] I do not believe that it is one of the major literary arts. The major arts are poetry, fiction, drama, and also nonfictional or documentary writing so long as this last is regarded as a field for exercise of the interpretive imagination. Without those major arts, literary criticism would have no subject matter and would cease to exist. Therefore a critic cannot afford to be arrogant. He is dealing in most cases with better works than he has proved his capability of writing.

[22] I believe that the first of his functions is to select works of art worth writing about, with special emphasis on works that are new, not much discussed, or widely misunderstood. Incidentally, this task is neglected by academic critics, most of whom prefer to write about books already regarded as canonical. His second function is to describe or analyze or reinterpret the chosen works, as a basis for judgments which can often be merely implied. In practice his problem may be to explain why he enjoys a particular book, and perhaps to find new reasons for enjoying it, so as to deepen his readers' capacity for appreciation.

[23] In practice, again, I always start and end with the text itself, and I am willing to accept the notion of the textual or integral critics that the principal value of a work lies in the complexity and unity of its internal relations. But I also try to start with a sort of innocence, that is, with a lack of preconceptions about what I might or might not discover. To preserve the innocence, I try not to read the so-called secondary or critical sources until my own discoveries, if any, have been made.

[24] What I read after the text itself are other texts by the same author. It is a mistake to approach each work as if it were an absolutely separate production, a unique artifact, the last and only relic of a buried civilization. Why not approach it as the author does? It seems to me that any author of magnitude has his eye on something larger than the individual story or poem or novel. He wants each of these to be as good as possible, and self-subsistent, but he also wants it to serve as a chapter or aspect of the larger work that is his lifetime production, his *oeuvre*. This larger work is also part of the critic's subject matter.

[25] In this fashion the author's biography comes into the picture, and so do his notebooks and letters. They aren't part of the text to be criticized, but often they help us to find in it what we might otherwise have missed, and they serve as a warning against indulging in fantasies about the text or deforming it into a Gothic fable of love, death, and homoeroticism. We should read not to impose our meanings on a work, but to see what we can find.

[26] Innocence is the keynote, and ignorance that tries to become knowledge by asking questions. We know, for example, that Melville spent about a year on *Moby-Dick*, and that he rewrote the book from a lost early version concerned chiefly with the whaling industry. We also know that he wrote *Pierre* in about six weeks, working at top speed while on the edge of a nervous breakdown. That of course, is biographical knowledge, but aren't we justified in using it? Aren't critics losing their sense of proportion when they discuss both books, the masterpiece and the nightmare, in the same terms, especially if those terms make the nightmare seem more important than the masterpiece? Aren't they wrong to look for the same sort of symbols in

Pierre that Joyce put into *Finnegans Wake*, on which we know that he slaved for ten years?

[27] Innocence is the keynote, but not innocence that refrains from learning about an author's life on the ground that such knowledge would destroy the purity of one's critical method. A truly innocent search might lead us into studies of the society in which an author lived, if they were necessary to explain his meaning. Or again, remembering as we should that a novel or a poem is not merely a structure of words but also a device for producing a certain effect on an audience, as if it were a motionless machine for creating perpetual motion—remembering this, we might try to find the nature of the particular audience for which it was written. That would be deviating into the sociological or affective fallacy, but still it might be a useful and stimulating piece of, yes, critical research.

[28] I believe, in short, that criticism is a house with many windows.

Comments and Questions

We note the suggestion of the author's theme in the opening sentence:

> Although I have been a literary critic for more than forty years, I must confess that I have not devoted much time to the basic theories of my profession.

We assume that this essay will consider basic theories of criticism and will include a statement of the theory preferred by the author. The *tone*, sober, serious but not stodgy, is clearly different from the light heartedness of the essays by Lamb (p. 803), or by Thurber (p. 805). The author writes to convince.

For our part as readers, we have three tasks to perform in reading argumentative essays: (1) we must understand what is said; (2) we must judge the truth of what is said; (3) we must adopt or reject, in whole or in part, what is said. (Indifference would constitute a kind of rejection.) In reading "The Two Races of Men" (p. 803) and similar essays, we perform the first two of these tasks but feel no call to perform the third. We say of such essays that we understand them, that they are true—or partly true—

but beyond that we are not asked to go. Cowley clearly wishes us to go all the way, to convince us that his is the reasonable approach to critical theorizing.

Structure Analyzed

Cowley emphasizes a device to make his purpose clear and effective: the device of *obvious structure*. In the first paragraph, he explains why he has not written on this subject before and why he is writing on it now. Paragraph 2 ticks off the "different but equally specialized" systems of criticism, and paragraph 3 defines "the new criticism," which has tended to cast into disfavor all formerly accepted systems. To give authority to his own definition of the new criticism, the author in paragraph 4 quotes from "one of the ablest of the new critics." It is now clear that Mr. Cowley will contend with the tenets of one system called the new criticism.

After acknowledging in paragraph 5 that some virtues in integral criticism exist, the author proceeds in the remainder of this paragraph and on through paragraphs 6 and 7 to expose the weaknesses of the system. Paragraph 8 reduces the new criticism to an absurdity or at least to an untenable position. In the next four paragraphs (9 through 12) the author shows how two new critics had tried to escape from this position by identifying criticism as a science, not an art. He contends that criticism cannot be a science, for it cannot escape the personal in either the writer or the critic. He adds that evaluation grows out of analysis and is "not the central task of a critic."

In paragraph 13, Cowley cites the new critical principle that an author is to be ignored as an interpreter of his own works. Paragraphs 14 through 17 illustrate what happens when critics behave as though authors do not exist, as though their works are disembodied.

From paragraph 18 to the end of the essay, Cowley states his own critical credo, which he summarizes in the final sentence.

Now we may see the skeletal structure of the whole essay:

I. Statement of reasons for writing on this subject (paragraph 1).

II. Identification of topics not to be treated and the one which will be treated (paragraphs 2–4).

III. The negative: analysis and running refutation of points the author considers invalid (paragraphs 5–17.)

IV. The positive: what the author subscribes to as valid (paragraphs 18–28).

This is one pattern for the serious, argumentative essay. Not all essays will include these four parts, and few will preserve the same order, but most essays written with a sober purpose will necessarily adopt a pattern similar to this one.

Why is the serious essayist seriously concerned with logical structure? Perhaps more than any other writer he wishes to be precisely understood. Unless he is clearly understood, the truth of what he says cannot be judged. And if the truth cannot be judged, the position recommended would remain meaningless.

Because logical structure aids clarity, it does not necessarily follow that a clear argument is a true argument. A clear, wrong argument, however, is more serviceable than a fuzzy, wrong argument. We may be able to do something about the first and merely be baffled by the second. Being clearly wrong is the next best thing to being clearly right. Logical structure and lucid statement are the essayist's best devices for being effective.

1. Examine the structure of "The Two Races of Men" (p. 803) and account for the way it differs from the pattern of Cowley's essay. In what way are these essays alike?

2. What stimulated the author to examine his own critical tenets? Discuss.

3. Define "integral criticism" and list the arguments in favor of this approach to literature. What approach does Cowley recommend? How does this approach compare with the one adopted in this book, *Interpreting Literature?*

4. Do you agree, or disagree, that an author's interpretation of his own work is of no significance? Discuss.

5. Robert Frost has said that his poem, "Stopping by Woods on a Snowy Evening," does not suggest a death wish on the part of the speaker (see p. 238 *n*.). Should his contention be heeded?

Nobel Prize Acceptance Speech

ALBERT CAMUS
1913–1960
(translated by Justin O'Brien)

Upon receiving the distinction with which your free academy has seen fit to honor me, I measured the extent to which that reward exceeded my personal deserts, and this only increased my gratitude. Every man and, even more understandably, every artist, wants recognition. I want it too. But it was not possible for me to learn of your decision without comparing its repercussions with whatever merits I really have. How could a man still almost young, possessed only of his doubts and of a work still in progress, accustomed to living in the isolation of work or the seclusion of friendship—how could he have failed to feel a sort of panic upon learning of a choice that suddenly focused a harsh spotlight on him alone and reduced to himself? And in what spirit could he receive that honor at a moment when other European writers, often the greatest among them, are reduced to silence, and at a time when his native land is experiencing prolonged suffering?

I felt that shock and that perplexity. I could recover my peace of mind, in short, only by adapting myself to an overgenerous fate. And inasmuch as I could not measure up to it through my own merits, I could think of no other help than what has always comforted me throughout life, even in the most adverse circumstances: the idea I entertain of my art and of the writer's role. Please allow me to express my gratitude and friendship by telling you, as simply as I can, just what that idea is.

I cannot live as a person without my art. And yet I have never set that art above everything else. It is essential to me, on the contrary, because it excludes no one and allows me to live, just as I am, on a footing with all. To me art is not a solitary delight. It is a means of stirring the greatest number of men by providing them with a privileged image of our common joys and woes. Hence it forces the artist not to isolate himself; it subjects him to the humblest and most universal truth. And the man who, as often happens, chose the path of art because he was aware of his difference soon learns that he can nourish his art, and his difference, solely by admitting his resemblance to all. The artist fashions himself in that ceaseless oscillation from himself to others, midway between the beauty he cannot do without and the community from which he cannot tear himself. This is why true artists scorn nothing. They force themselves to understand instead of judging. And if they are to take sides in this world, they can do so only with a society in which, according to Nietzsche's profound words, the judge will yield to the creator, whether he be a worker or an intellectual.

By the same token, the writer's function is not without arduous duties. By definition, he cannot serve today those who make history; he must serve those who are subject to it. Otherwise he is alone and deprived of his art. All the armies of tyranny with their millions of men cannot people his solitude—even, and especially, if he is willing to fall into step with them. But the silence of an unknown prisoner subjected to humiliations at the other end of the world is enough to tear the writer from exile, at least whenever he manages, amid the privileges of freedom, not to forget that silence but to give it voice by means of art.

No one of us is great enough for such a vocation. Yet in all the circumstances of his life, unknown or momentarily famous, bound by tyranny or temporarily free to express himself, the writer can recapture the feeling of a living community that will justify him. But only if he accepts as completely as possible the two trusts that constitute the nobility of his calling: the service of truth and the service of freedom. Because his vocation is to unite the greatest possible number of men, it cannot countenance falsehood and slavery, which breed solitudes wherever they prevail. Whatever our personal frailties may be, the nobility of our calling will always be rooted in two commitments difficult to observe: refusal to lie about what we know and resistance to oppression.

For more than twenty years of absolutely insane history, lost hopelessly like all those of my age in the convulsions of the epoch, I derived comfort from the vague impression that writing was an honor today because the act itself obligated a man, obligated him to more than just writing. It obligated me in particular, such as I was, with whatever strength I possessed, to bear —along with all the others living the same history—the tribulation and hope we shared. Those men born at the beginning of World War I, who had reached the age of twenty just as Hitler was seizing power and the first revolutionary trials were taking place, who then had to complete their education by facing up to war in Spain, World War II, the regime of concentration camps, a Europe of torture and prisons, must today bring their children and their works to maturity in a world threatened with nuclear destruction. No one, I suppose, can expect them to be optimistic. I even go so far as to feel that, without ceasing to struggle against those who through an excess of despair insisted upon their right to dishonor and hurled themselves into the current nihilisms, we must understand their error. Nonetheless, most of us in my country and in Europe rejected that nihilism and strove to find some form of legitimacy. We had to fashion for ourselves an art of living in times of catastrophe in order to be reborn before fighting openly against the death instinct at work in our history.

Probably every generation sees itself as charged with remaking the world. Mine, however, knows that it will not remake the world. But its task is perhaps even greater, for it consists in keeping the world from destroying itself. As the heir of a corrupt history that blends blighted revolutions, misguided techniques, dead gods, and worn-out ideologies, in which second-rate powers can destroy everything today but are unable to win anyone over and in which intelligence has stooped to becoming the servant of hatred and oppression, that generation, starting from nothing but its own negations, has had to re-establish both within and without itself a little of what constitutes the dignity of life and death. Faced with a world threatened with disintegration, in which our grand inquisitors may set up once and for all the kingdoms of death, that generation knows that, in a sort of mad race against time, it ought to re-establish among nations a peace not based on slavery, to reconcile labor and culture again, and to reconstruct with all men an Ark of the Covenant. Perhaps it can never accomplish that vast undertaking, but most certainly throughout the world it has already accepted the double challenge of truth and liberty and, on occasion, has shown that it can lay down its life without hatred. That generation deserves to be acclaimed and encouraged wherever it happens to be, and especially wherever it is sacrificing itself. And to it, confident of your wholehearted agreement, I should like to transfer the honor you have just done me.

At the same time, after having extolled the nobility of the writer's calling, I should have taken the writer down a peg, showing him as he is, with no other rights than those he shares with his fellow fighters: vulnerable but stubborn, unjust and eager for justice, constructing his work without shame or pride within sight of all, constantly torn between pain and beauty, and devoted to extracting from his dual nature the creations he obstinately strives to raise up in the destructive fluctuation of history. Who, after that, could expect of him ready-made solutions and fine moral codes? Truth is mysterious, elusive, ever to be won anew. Liberty is dangerous, as hard to get along with as it is exciting. We must progress toward those two objectives, painfully but resolutely, sure in advance that we shall weaken and flinch on such a long road. Consequently, what writer would dare, with a clear conscience, to become a preacher of virtue? As for me, I must say once more that I am far from all that. I have never been able to forget the sunlight, the delight in life, the freedom in which I grew up. But although that nostalgia explains many of my mistakes and shortcomings, it doubtless helped me to understand my calling, and it still helps me to stand implicitly beside all those silent men who, throughout the world, endure the life that has been made for them only because they remember or fleetingly re-experience free moments of happiness.

Reduced in this way to what I am in reality, to my limits and to my liabilities, as well as to my difficult faith, I feel freer to show you in conclusion the extent and generosity of the distinction you have just granted me, freer likewise to tell you that I should like to receive it as a tribute paid to all those who, sharing the same fight, have received no reward, but on the contrary have known only woe and persecution. It remains for me then to thank you from the bottom of my heart and to make you publicly, as a personal token of gratitude, the same age-old promise of allegiance that every true artist, every day, makes to himself, in silence.

Comments and Questions

1. Comment on the statement that "true artists scorn nothing." Does Camus assign a

special meaning to the word *scorn?* What special dilemma for the artist does Camus recognize as resulting from current world unrest?

2. Discuss what Camus calls "the death instinct at work in our history." Cite examples of what Camus may have had in mind.

Brave Words for a Startling Occasion

RALPH ELLISON
1914–

First, as I express my gratitude for this honor which you have bestowed on me, let me say that I take it that you are rewarding my efforts rather than my not quite fully achieved attempt at a major novel. Indeed, if I were asked in all seriousness just what I considered to be the chief significance of *Invisible Man* as a fiction, I would reply: Its experimental attitude, and its attempt to return to the mood of personal moral responsibility for democracy which typified the best of our nineteenth-century fiction. That my first novel should win this most coveted prize must certainly indicate that there is a crisis in the American novel. You as critics have told us so, and current fiction sales would indicate that the reading public agrees. Certainly the younger novelists concur. The explosive nature of events mocks our brightest efforts. And the very "facts" which the naturalists assumed would make us free have lost the power to protect us from despair. Controversy now rages over just what aspects of American experience are suitable for novelistic treatment. The prestige of the theorists of the so-called novel of manners has been challenged. Thus after a long period of stability we find our assumptions concerning the novel being called into question. And though I was only vaguely aware, it was this growing crisis which shaped the writing of *Invisible Man*.

After the usual apprenticeship of imitation and seeking with delight to examine my experience through the discipline of the novel, I became gradually aware that the forms of so many of the works which impressed me were too restricted to contain the experience which I knew. The diversity of American life with its extreme flu-

idity and openness seemed too vital and alive to be caught for more than the briefest instant in the tight well-made Jamesian novel, which was, for all its artistic perfection, too concerned with "good taste" and stable areas. Nor could I safely use the forms of the "hard-boiled" novel, with its dedication to physical violence, social cynicism and understatement. Understatement depends, after all, upon commonly held assumptions and my minority status rendered all such assumptions questionable. There was also a problem of language, and even dialogue, which, with its hard-boiled stance and its monosyllabic utterance, is one of the shining achievements of twentieth-century American writing. For despite the notion that its rhythms were those of everyday speech, I found that when compared with the rich babel of idiomatic expression around me, a language full of imagery and gesture and rhetorical canniness, it was embarrassingly austere. Our speech I found resounding with an alive language swirling with over three hundred years of American living, a mixture of the folk, the Biblical, the scientific and the political. Slangy in one stance, academic in another, loaded poetically with imagery at one moment, mathematically bare of imagery in the next. As for the rather rigid concepts of reality which informed a number of the works which impressed me and to which I owe a great deal, I was forced to conclude that reality was far more mysterious and uncertain, and more exciting, and still, despite its raw violence and capriciousness, more promising. To attempt to express that American experience which has carried one back and forth and up and down the land and across, and across again the great river, from freight train to Pullman car, from contact with slavery to contact with a world of advanced scholarship, art and science, is simply to burst such neatly understated forms of the novel asunder.

A novel whose range was both broader and deeper was needed. And in my search I found myself turning to our classical nineteenth-century novelists. I felt that except for the work of William Faulkner something vital had gone out of American prose after Mark Twain. I came to believe that the writers of that period took a much greater responsibility for the condition of democracy and, indeed, their works were imaginative projections of the conflicts within the human heart which arose when the sacred principles of the Constitution and the Bill of Rights clashed with the practical exigencies of human greed and fear, hate and love. Naturally I was attracted to these writers as a Negro. Whatever they thought of my people per se, in their imaginative economy the Negro symbolized both the man lowest down and the mysterious, underground aspect of human personality. In a sense the Negro was the gauge of the human condition as it waxed and waned in our democracy. These writers were willing to confront the broad complexities of American life and we are the richer for their having done so.

Thus to see America with an awareness of its rich diversity and its almost magical fluidity and freedom, I was forced to conceive of a novel unburdened by the narrow naturalism which has led, after so many triumphs, to the final and unrelieved despair which marks so much of our current fiction. I was to dream of a prose which was flexible, and swift as American change is swift, confronting the inequalities and brutalities of our society forthrightly, but yet thrusting forth its images of hope, human fraternity and individual self-realization. It would use the richness of our speech, the idiomatic expression and the rhetorical flourishes from past periods which are still alive among us. And despite my personal failures, there must be possible a fiction which, leaving sociology to the scientists, can arrive at the truth about the human condition, here and now, with all the bright magic of a fairy tale.

What has been missing from so much experimental writing has been the passionate will to dominate reality as well as the laws of art. This will is the true source of the experimental attitude. We who struggle with form and with America should remember Eidothea's advice to Menelaus when in the *Odyssey* he and his friends are seeking their way home. She tells him to seize her father, Proteus, and to hold him fast "however he may struggle and fight. He will turn into all sorts of shapes to try you," she says, "into all the creatures that live and move upon the earth, into water, into blazing fire; but you must hold him fast and press him all the harder. When he is himself, and questions you in the same shape that he was when you saw him in his bed, let the old man go; and then, sir, ask which god it is who is angry, and how you shall make your way homewards over the fish-giving sea."

For the novelist, Proteus stands for both America and the inheritance of illusion through which all men must fight to achieve reality; the offended god stands for our sins against those principles we all hold sacred. The way home we seek is that condition of man's being at home in the world, which is called love, and which we term democracy. Our task then is always to challenge the apparent forms of reality—that is, the fixed manners and values of the few, and to struggle with it until it reveals its mad, variimplicated chaos, its false faces, and on until it surrenders its insight, its truth. We are fortunate as American writers in that with our variety of racial and national traditions, idioms and manners, we are yet one. On its profoundest level American experience is of a whole. Its truth lies in its diversity and swiftness of change. Through forging forms of the novel worthy of it, we achieve not only the promise of our lives, but we anticipate the resolution of those world problems of humanity which for a moment seem to those who are in awe of statistics completely insoluble.

Whenever we as Americans have faced serious crises we have returned to fundamentals; this, in brief, is what I have tried to do.

Comments and Questions

The occasion referred to in the title was a dinner at which Ralph Ellison received the National Book Award for his novel, *Invisible Man.*

1. Speeches which respond to an award, particularly one for literary merit, are usually both personal and reflective. Compare this short speech with Camus' (p. 823), equally short. Note the similarity in the opening sentences, models of modesty both. Camus' speech has no title. Explain Ellison's.

2. What does Ellison mean by "personal moral responsibility for democracy?" He ascribes this sort of responsibility to nineteenth-century fiction writers. Can you tell whether he is talking about American or British novelists?

3. Re-read "Fiction: Preliminaries," particularly the paragraph headed "The Meaning of the Story: The Parts and the Whole," p. 22. According to both Camus and Ellison, is there a place for writers of fiction as pure enter-

tainment? Do any of the short stories presented in this text qualify as simply pleasant narratives? "Roman Fever" (p. 26), perhaps?

Trends in Negro American Literature (1940–1965)

ARTHUR P. DAVIS
1904–

The course of Negro American literature has been highlighted by a series of social and political crises over the Negro's position in America. The Abolition Movement, the Civil War, Reconstruction, and the riot-lynching periods both before and after World War I have all radically influenced Negro writing. Each crisis has brought in new themes, new motivations, new character-types, new viewpoints; and as each crisis has passed, the Negro writer has tended to drop most of the special attitudes which the crisis produced and to move toward the so-called mainstream of American literature.

Between, roughly, 1940 and 1965, two new crises occurred: the Integration Movement (which was climaxed by the 1954 Supreme Court Decision), and the Civil Rights Revolution (which is still with us and which began to take on its present day characteristics around 1960). Each of these movements has affected Negro writing. Twenty-five years is obviously a short time in which to show literary changes resulting from *one* movement, to say nothing of two, but we live in stirring and fast-moving times. For example, within a single decade a supposedly well-established program of non-violence and passive resistance has given way to a new and militant nationalist movement that makes the work of Martin Luther King seem almost gradualistic. Riots have taken the place of "marches," and the objectives of Negroes have shifted from integration to goals entirely alien to anything the black middle class envisioned. These changes have been incredibly swift and phenomenal, but Negro literature during the period in question has reflected them to a greater extent than is commonly realized.

Let us examine the Integration Movement first. Forces of integration had been at work long before 1954, but it is convenient to date the movement from that year. And, of course, the official stamp given it by the Supreme Court accelerated the social changes already in progress. After 1954 the ferment of integration seemed to go to work immediately—not only in the public schools, but in the armed forces, in Southern state universities, and in several other areas as well. A few institutions and localities and segments of the nation naturally held out, and are still holding out, but even the harshest critics of American democracy had to admit that substantial progress towards integration had been made, that the nation had committed itself officially and spiritually to that ideal. And though the commitment was largely theoretical or at best token, it changed the racial climate of America.

This change of climate, however, inadvertently dealt the Negro writer of the fifties a crushing blow. Up to that decade, our literature had been predominantly a protest literature. Ironical though it may seem, we had capitalized on oppression (in a literary sense, of course). Although one may deplore and condemn the cause, there is great creative motivation in a movement which brings all members of a group together and cements them in a common bond. And that is just what segregation did for the Negro especially during the twenties and thirties when full segregation was not only practiced in the South but tacitly condoned by the whole nation. As long as there was this common enemy, we had a common purpose and a strong urge to transform into artistic terms our deep-rooted feelings of bitterness and scorn. When the enemy capitulated, he shattered our most fruitful literary tradition. The possibility of imminent integration tended to destroy during the fifties the protest element in Negro writing.

And one must always keep in mind the paradox involved. We did not have actual integration anywhere. There was surface and token integration in many areas, but the everyday pattern of life for the overwhelming majority was unchanged. But we did have—and this is of the utmost importance—the spiritual commitment and climate out of which full integration could develop. The Negro literary artist recognized and acknowledged that climate; he accepted it in good faith; and he resolved to work with it at all costs. In the meantime, he had to live between two worlds, and that for any artist is a disturbing experience. For the Negro writers of the fifties, especially those in their middle years, it became almost a tragic experience because it meant giving up a tradition in which they had done their apprentice and journeyman work, giving it up when they were prepared to make use of that tradition as master craftsmen.

Another disturbing factor which must be considered here is that this change of climate came about rather suddenly. Perhaps it would be more exact to say that the full awareness came suddenly because there were signs of its approach all during the forties, and Negro writers from time to time showed that they recognized these signs. But the full awareness did not come until the fifties, and it came with some degree of abruptness. For example, all through World War II, all through the forties, most Negro writers were still grinding out protest and problem novels, many of them influenced by *Native Son* (1940). The list of these works is impressive: Attaway's *Blood on the Forge* (1941), Offord's *The White Face* (1943), Himes' *If He Hollers* (1945), Petry's *The Street* (1946), Kaye's *Taffy* (1950), and there were others—practically all of them naturalistic novels with the same message of protest against America's treatment of its black minority.

The poets wrote in a similar view. Walker's *For My People* (1942), Hughes' *Freedom's Plow* (1943), Brooks' *A Street in Bronzeville* (1945), and Dodson's *Powerful Long Ladder* (1946) all had strong protest elements; all dealt in part with the Negro's fight against segregation and discrimination at home and in the armed services.

Noting the dates of these works—both fiction and poetry—one realizes that, roughly speaking, up to 1950 the protest tradition was in full bloom, and that most of our best writers were still using it. Then came this awareness of a radical change in the nation's climate and with it the realization that the old protest themes had to be abandoned. The new climate tended to *date* the problem works of the forties as definitely as time had dated the New Negro "lynching-passing" literature of the twenties and thirties. In other words, protest writing had become the first casualty of the new racial climate.

Faced with the loss of his oldest and most cherished tradition, the Negro writer was forced to seek fresh ways to use his material. First of all, he attempted to find new themes within the racial framework. Retaining the Negro character and background, he shifted his emphasis from the protest aspect of Negro living and placed it on the problems and conflicts within the group itself. For example, Chester Himes pursuing this course in *Third Generation*, explores school life in the Deep South. His main conflict in this work is not concerned with interracial protest but with discord within a Negro family caused by color differences and other problems. The whole racial tone of this novel is quite different from that of *If He Hollers*, a typical protest work. One came out in 1945, the other in 1953. The two books are a good index to the changes which took place in the years separating them.

In like manner, Owen Dodson and Gwendolyn Brooks in their novels, *Boy at the Window* (1951) and *Maud Martha* (1953), respectively, show this tendency to find new themes within the racial framework. Both publications are "little novels," giving intimate and subtle vignettes of middle class living. Their main stress is on life within the group, not on conflict with outside forces. Taking a different approach, William Demby in *Beetlecreek* (1950), completely reversed the protest pattern by showing the black man's inhumanity to his white brother. In *The Outsider* (1953), Richard Wright took an even more subtle approach. He used a Negro main character, but by adroitly and persistently minimizing that character's racial importance, he succeeded in divorcing him from any real association with the traditional protest alignment. And Langston Hughes in *Sweet Flypaper of Life* (1955), though using all Negro characters, does not touch on the matter of inter-racial protest. All of these authors, it seems to me, show their awareness of the new climate by either playing down or avoiding entirely the traditional protest approach.

Another group of writers (and there is some overlapping here) showed their awareness by avoiding the Negro character. Among them are William Gardner Smith (*Anger at Innocence*), Ann Petry (*Country Place*), Richard Wright (*Savage Holiday*), and Willard Motley (*Knock on Any Door*). None of these works has Negro main characters. With the exception of *Knock on Any Door*, each was a "second" novel, following a work written in the forties which had

Negro characters and background, and which was written in the protest vein. In each case, the first work was popular, and yet each of these novelists elected to avoid the theme which gave him his initial success.

So far I have spoken only of the novelists, but Negro poets also sensed the change of climate in America and reacted to it. Incidentally, several of our outstanding protest poets of the thirties and forties simply dropped out of the picture as poets. I cannot say, of course, that the new climate alone silenced them, but I do feel that it was a contributing cause. It is hard for a mature writer to slough off a tradition in which he has worked during all of his formative years. Acquiring a new approach in any field of art is a very serious and trying experience. One must also remember that the protest tradition was no mere surface fad with the Negro writer. It was part of his self-respect, part of his philosophy of life, part of his inner being. It was almost a religious experience with those of us who came up through the dark days of the twenties and thirties. When a tradition so deeply ingrained is abandoned, it tends to leave a spiritual numbness—a kind of void not easily filled with new interests or motivations. Several of our ablest poets—and novelists too, for that matter—did not try to fill that void.

A few of the poets, however, met the challenge of the new climate, among them the late M. B. Tolson and Gwendolyn Brooks. A comparison of the early and later works of these poets will show a tendency in the later works either to avoid protest themes entirely or to approach them more subtly and obliquely. Compare, for example, Tolson's *Rendezvous with America* (1944) with *A Libretto for the Republic of Liberia* (1953). The thumping rhythms of the protest verse in the former work gave way in the latter to a new technique, one that was influenced largely by Hart Crane. With this new work, Tolson successfully turned his back on the tradition in which he came to maturity. Concerning the work, Allen Tate felt that: "For the first time . . . a Negro poet has assimilated completely the full poetic language of his time and, by implication, the language of the Anglo-American poetic tradition." Two works of Gwendolyn Brooks also show a change in attitude. There is far more racial protest in *A Street in Bronzeville* (1945) than in her Pulitzer Prize-winning *Annie Allen* (1949). Moreover, the few pieces in the latter work which concern the "problem" are different in approach and technique from those in her first work.

Summing up then, I believe we can say that the Integration Movement influenced Negro writing in the following ways: it forced the black creative artist to play down his most cherished tradition; it sent him in search of new themes; it made him abandon, at least on occasion, the Negro character and background; and it possibly helped to silence a few of the older writers then living. But before the Integration Movement could come to full fruition, it was cut off by the Civil Rights Revolution, particularly the black nationalist elements in the revolution. I speak here, of course, of the literary tendencies of both movements. The main thrust, the principal tenets of black nationalism, in their very essence, negate the paramount aim of the integrationist writer which is to lose himself in the American literary mainstream.

During the 1925 New Negro Renaissance, there was an embryonic black nationalist movement, founded and led by Marcus Garvey. Though short-lived and abortive, it, nevertheless, influenced to some degree the works of Hughes, Cullen, McKay, and other New Negro poets. But Garveyism never achieved the popularity or possessed the civil and "spiritual" strength that the present day black nationalist program has. The influence of this movement goes far beyond the obvious and sensational evidences of it seen in the press or on the T.V. For better or worse, the ideas of black nationalism have influenced the thinking of far more Negroes than one would expect, and this influence has brought to recent Negro writing new themes and a new attitude on the part of the black author.

Perhaps the most important of these new attitudes is the repudiation of American middle class culture and all of the things—the good, on occasion, along with the bad—for which that culture stands. This repudiation may take various forms, and it appears in the poetry (that of LeRoi Jones, for example) as well as in the novels. One form of this attack concerns the Negro woman. She is accused of "emasculating" her husbands and lovers by insisting that they conform to middle class standards. This theme is found in Chester Himes' *Third Generation* (also in other recent works by him), and there is a strain of it in Kelley's *A Drop of Patience* (1965). In Fair's *Hog Butcher* (1966), the author not only attacks the Negro middle class in his story, but in the "Prologue to Part II," he steps into the work, after the manner of Fielding, and delivers a scathing lecture on the subject. The most striking statement of the repudiation of America's white middle class comes from Baldwin's "Letter to My Nephew" in *The Fire Next Time* (1963): "There is no reason for you to try to become like white people and there is no basis whatever for their impertinent assumption that *they* must accept *you*. The really terrible thing, old buddy, is that *you* must accept *them*. And I mean that very seriously. You must accept them and accept them with love. For these innocent people have no other hope."

The influence of the Black Revolt is also seen in the revival of the moribund protest theme in Negro writing. In some cases, the protest novel has returned practically unchanged in the matter of technique and point of view. Frank London Brown's *Trumbull Park* (1958) and Richard Wright's *The Long Dream* (1958) are very similar in spirit to the protest works of the forties. It is curious to note that Wright, after taking a sort of vacation from the protest tradition in *The Outsider* and *Savage Holiday*, comes back to it in *The Long Dream*. Though he deals with discrimination in the Army and though he moves his scene finally from America to Australia, Killens in *And Then We Heard the Thunder* (1963) is still using the old protest tradition. (This, of course, is no reflection on the quality of the novel.) And William Gardner Smith is doing the same thing although in *Stone Face* (1963) he deals primarily with French prejudice against Algerians. There are, however, two recent works in this neo-protest tradition which show freshness and originality. One of them is Kelley's *A Different Drummer* (1962). Making use of fantasy, symbol, and other modern devices and techniques, Kelley gives us not only a new, bitter, and effective type of protest novel, but also a new type of Negro character as well. Ronald Fair's *Many Thousands Gone* (1966) is equally as fresh in its approach and equally as effective. Through a morbidly exaggerated description of life in a mythical Southern locality, Fair tells us symbolically many things about the race situa-

tion in America today. He calls his work "An American Fable."

From the twenties on down to the present, the jazz musician has been popular with black writers, but he has never before received the kind and the amount of attention now given him. In these days of black nationalism and "negritude," the jazz musician has acquired a new significance. He has become for many Negro writers a symbol of the spontaneous creative impulse of the race; he represents black "original genius," something that is not indebted in any way to middle class culture. As depicted in recent works, the Negro jazz musician is often crude, sexy, uninhibited, uneducated, yet wise with a folk wisdom far superior to that which comes from schools and books. We find variants of this character in John A. Williams' *Night Song* (1961), in Kelley's *A Drop of Patience* (1965), and though the character is not fully developed, in Rufus in Baldwin's *Another Country*. On occasion these characters are based on the actual lives of famous jazz musicians.

Black Revolt literature takes an interesting and by no means simple attitude towards whites —an attitude which ranges from pity and contempt to the kind of sadistic love-hatred found in *Another Country*. In several of these novels, the black man–white woman love affair is portrayed. We find this not only in Baldwin's work, but also in *A Drop of Patience*, in *Then We Heard the Thunder*, and in *Night Song* (a very complex analysis of guilt-laden frustration on the part of the man). LeRoi Jones' *The Dutchman*, whatever else it may be saying, also comments on this theme. To see the new type of white woman and the new role she is playing in these affairs, one should compare a novel like Himes' *If He Hollers* with, let us say, *Night Song*. It is ironic that the white woman should figure as largely as she does in the literature of the Black Revolt.

A minor theme of Black Revolt literature deals with the Negro slum boy, usually depicted as the victim of our indifferent middle class society. Three excellent and intriguing studies of the ghetto kid are found in the following works: Kennedy's *The Pecking Order* (1953), Mayfield's *The Long Night* (1958), and Fair's *Hog Butcher* (1966). In delineating the "culturally deprived" boy, the authors naturally give a lot of space and attention to police brutality, relief, bad housing for Negroes, corrupt and prejudiced city officials, and all of the other evils that the present day militant protest groups attack.

Summing up again—these, then, are the trends I find in the literature of the Black Revolt: a repudiation of American middle class values; a revival of interest in protest writing; the glorification of the black jazz musician; a "mixed" attitude towards whites, particularly white women; and a tendency to depict through the ghetto kid the evils of the inner city. In the works of the period which I have read, I have found two or three highly competent productions but none of the caliber and scope of *Invisible Man*, the finest fruit of the Integration Movement. Perhaps it is far too soon to expect that kind of synthesis.

What about the future? Where will these tendencies lead? When America grants full equality to the Negro (as it will), several of these current attitudes and themes will be dropped. The Negro American writer will do then what he has always done after each crisis in the past—continue on his trek to the mainstream of American literature.

Comments and Questions

1. This critical-historical essay is an excellent survey of the most significant black literature produced during the years between 1940–65. The essay itself was published in 1967. Its value lies in the perceptive recognition of forces which have strongly influenced Negro writers. What are these forces?

2. Outline this essay, using the analysis of Cowley's "Criticism: A Many-Windowed House" (p. 822) as a model.

3. Davis classifies many novels and some poems as products of one set of circumstances or of another. A revealing project would be to compare, say, Richard Wright's *Native Son* with his *Savage Holiday*. Many other comparisons are suggested by Davis's classifications.

4. Do you know of any protest literature written by white authors? There are plenty of examples, but what distinguishes angry works by white authors from angry works by black authors? Consider what is called the black experience. Is there an experience called white?

Electric Orphic Circuit
BARBARA FARRIS GRAVES
1938–
and DONALD J. McBAIN
1945–

[1]

Don't listen to evil rumors; poetry is alive and well. While it is true that the era of T. S. Eliot,[1] Ezra Pound,[1] and Wallace Stevens[1] is over, and that some poets (and critics) are floundering in the wake of these giants, nevertheless more poetry is being written, read, spoken, sung, listened to, and generally appreciated today than perhaps at any time before. And more *kinds* of poetry. A reader looking for recently published poetry can step inside a bookstore and find anything from the word and picture games of John Lennon to the sprawling cosmic chants of Allen Ginsberg to the soft, semiconfessional sonnets of Robert Lowell.[1] Indeed, the post-World War II period has witnessed a parade of variously ephemeral poetic forms, styles, cliques, schools, and movements. Some of these have been highly innovative; some have returned to or developed past traditions. It is difficult to determine whether any have forged new major directions.

In the past decade, forces have gathered to generate a movement whose poets are united often by life style and personal philosophy but principally by the form in which they create —songs, the lyric form. As precursor, prophet, central figure, and sage, Bob Dylan[2] has managed so far to span the movement; at least he saw it through its incipient period, the decade of the sixties. Certainly, he was the first popular songwriter in quite some time to be considered as a poet, although his right to this title has been battered back and forth by all the people who enjoy that sort of thing. People whose po-

---

[1] See the Index for their poems.   [2] For two of Dylan's songs see pp. 263, 264.

etic backgrounds range from amateur to aesthete have reacted to the phenomenon that Dylan helped to set in motion and that his verse represents. Some have demeaned it for its illiteracy. Some have said that he is only a songwriter and not a poet, and that his art form is outside the realm of modern poetry. Others have proclaimed him the first poet laureate of mass media. Such divergent critical reactions, however, sometimes indicate more about the particular commentators or about the cultural divergences in our society than they do about either Dylan's verse or the movement.

Nevertheless, the movement has made inroads, even in academic circles. Significantly, the high schools were the first to teach current songs in English classes, though usually smuggled into the course by either a hip or a desperate teacher rather than as part of the regular curriculum. More recently, college poetry courses and texts have been including song lyrics, and some schools have offered seminars in "rock" poetry. This must mean the movement has arrived. The questions arise, though: Will it be a major direction? Is it new? Poet Allen Ginsberg, himself not completely accepted in the more highbrow academic strata, in a recent anthology called *Naked Poetry*, offered a key to the phenomenon:

. . . But young minstrels have now arisen on the airwaves whose poetic forms outwardly resemble antique verse including regular stanzas, refrains and rhymes: Dylan and Donovan[3] and some fragments of the Rolling Stones because they *think* not only in words but also in music simultaneously have out of the necessities of their own space-age media and electric machinery tunes evolved a natural use of—a personal realistic imaginative rhymed verse. Principle of composition here is, however, unlike antique literary form, primarily spontaneous and improvised (in the studio if need be at the last minute) and prophetic in character in that tune and language are invoked shamanistically on the spot from the unconscious. The new ear is not dead only for eye-page, it's connected with a voice improvising, with hesitancies aloud, a living musician's ear. The old library poets had lost their voices; natural voice was rediscovered, and now natural song

for physical voice. Oddly, this fits Pound's paradigm tracing the degeneration of Poesy from the Greek dance-foot-chorus thru minstrel song thru 1900 abstract voiceless pages. So now returned to song and song forms we yet anticipate inspired Creators like Shiva Krishna Chaitanya. . . .

Allen Ginsberg, "Some Metamorphoses of Personal Prosody," in *Naked Poetry: Recent American Poetry in Open Forms,* ed. Stephen Berg and Robert Mezey (New York: Bobbs-Merrill Co., Inc., 1969), p. 221.

"Returned to song and song forms": Ginsberg's words suggest a kind of cyclical pattern, one whose first "revolution" is just now being achieved. It is worthwhile to investigate this idea as an introduction to this book. Hopefully, our investigation will enable us to put these anthologized songs in a historical perspective that dates further back than the rockabilly days of Bill Haley and his Comets, and to establish inroads for further study in this area. In considering an evolutionary cycle of poetry, and specifically lyric poetry, there are four periods that demand our attention—the origins of poetry, the Greek lyric, the Renaissance, and the modern electric lyric. Although evolution is a continuous process, these are recognizable stages and focal points of the development of poetry as it meets us today.

[2]

The arts of poetry and music had a common origin in primitive song, in what the Greeks were later to call "lyric." These early songs probably consisted of many different kinds—work songs, love songs, lullabies, laments. Song, however, is essentially a public art. Historians, anthropologists, and linguists continue to speculate on the specific date and form of the first actual lyric. However, it is generally agreed on and sustained by the earliest findings of lyric poetry that the lyric grew out of ritualistic patterns surrounding primitive religious ceremonies, and was usually an expression of some kind of mystical experience that the poet was undergoing.

Certain key characteristics, then, should be noted concerning what can be considered the genesis of our poetry. The first is that words and music were conceived as a fused unit, evolv-

---

[3] For two of Donovan Leitch's songs see p. 265.

ing perhaps from spontaneous cries around the ceremonial fires, to chants, and eventually to the story-lyric or ballad. The poet, throughout this development, thought "not only in words but in music simultaneously." Second, since the poet was originally associated with mysticism and magic, poetry was rooted in the realm of the supernatural and the divine. Third, the emphasis was on performance; many of the songs were improvised "shamanistically on the spot from the unconscious." Finally, the entire group participated in the performance, echoing and answering the single voice (this function developed into the Greek "chorus" and, in our modern lyrical poetry, we see its remnant in the refrain, an atrophied, surrogate form of audience participation). Hence the beginnings, and perhaps the essence of poetry, can be found in the primitive lyric, a form that was intense, spontaneous, visceral, communal, magical, mystical . . . and music.

In the Greek period the lyric grew in number and complexity, developing into a profusion of types, such as the triumph, the dirge, the dance-song, the hymn, the processional, and culminating in the fully developed ode with its divisions of strophe and antistrophe. It was also at this time that the term "lyric" first came into use. The Greeks who were Aristotle's contemporaries made three fundamental distinctions. Elegiac and iambic poems were chanted; melic or lyric poems were sung by one voice to musical accompaniment (the lyre), and choric was for several voices. Notice that the distinctions were based on external differences and not subject matter. Eventually, "lyric" became a general name for any poem that was composed for singing, and the meaning did not change until the Renaissance.

In the lyric there is a basic tension between words and music. Although both are temporal forms, always throwing the attention forward, because words have semantic properties, we are tempted (at some times more than others) to stop and think about them; meanwhile the song's melody and rhythm continue to hurtle us on. In addition, there is a basic division in the function of these two components of the lyric. Some critics maintain that the words convey ideas and the music conveys emotion. Others differentiate between the intellectual appeal of music and that of poetry, saying that the former is

more related to structure and the latter to content. Whatever the differences of critical opinion as to what the separate functions are, the tension caused by their separateness is generally agreed upon. The ideal lyric profits from this tension, keeping a balance between the weight of the two.

In the primitive lyric the problem of conflict did not exist, since (as we mentioned earlier), the two forms were thought of as a fused unit, and within that unit they not only complemented each other but depended on each other for survival. As each art became more developed, however, the problem of rivalry arose. Words became music in themselves, music attempted to express ideas on its own—one began to outshine the other in virtuosity. In almost all lyric periods, one or the other form has been to some degree subordinated. During the Greek era, for example, the odes of Pindar and Bacchylides, the music was obviously subordinated to the words. The Elizabethan period, the great age of English lyricism, was a time when, at least in the early part, words and music were written in careful consideration of each other, either by the same artist or by joint contribution of the poet and composer. But the Renaissance brought with it a separation that has lasted for centuries and that has created the hybrid form known as lyrical poetry.

Several events combined in the Renaissance to produce breaches that affected the entire fabric of society and culture and, in turn, the lyric. In the latter part of the Elizabethan period the once nearly symbiotic relationship between poetry and music grew apart. During the late Middle Ages, music had become more sophisticated and was finally able to stand on its own. We can see a marked evolution in the difference between the simple music of the early Elizabethan lutanist, in which the composer was chiefly concerned with conveying the poet's meaning, and the complex patterns of the later madrigals, which were concerned chiefly with the music and which often drowned the words in complicated fugal progressions. So too with poetry. The poet grew weary of the rhyme, the refrain, the end stops, the exact stanza form of the lyric. All these things had once stimulated his art; now he felt shackled by them. Poetry too was becoming more sophisticated and profound. The complex analogies of metaphysical verse required an intellectual analysis, but the temporal experience of song prohibits such lingering. John Donne's poetry,[4] for example, demands reading and rereading. This brings us to a crucial point.

The invention of printing completely altered life in the Renaissance and in each succeeding age. It created the literate society, brought us out of the Dark Ages (the ages of magic, by the way), and spread uniformed knowledge and culture across the world. Marshall McLuhan, in *Understanding Media,* and more exhaustively in *The Gutenberg Galaxy,* explained the changes that the medium of print itself effected because of the kind of perspective it demanded (and still demands) from its audience.

Let's review the points that most concern our topic. First, printed, mass-produced books encouraged individualism and the fixed, personal, detached point of view. A book is an artifact. A person can open it or shut it. He can take it to his room to read (indeed, printing even changed architecture, demanding that houses have separate, closed-off rooms that one could go to in order to read his book). Since under normal circumstances books are read individually and privately, the reader's response is individual and private. Thus the communal quality of poetry was lost.

Also the medium is "hot"; it provides a large amount of specific information—information that can be reread as often as desired—thereby precluding the involvement that an oral form required, eliminating the sense of mystery necessary for the survival of magic, urging in, eventually, the Age of Reason. The linear form encouraged linear perspective and linear thought, which nurtured logic and scientific methodology. The line, which was segmented into separate words and separate letters, encouraged fragmentation. The mechanical age was now prepared for, with all its assembly lines and wheels and gadgets.

Since print dictated that poetry be seen[5] and not heard, poets began suiting their work to a visual rather than an auditory medium. Because of its strict pattern and traditionally conventional content, poetry written for music is usually monotonous to read. The rhyme and refrain

become wearisome. Sometimes a verbal rhythm seems lopsided when read, although it is even when put to the appropriate music. The poet Dryden[6] once complained, "I have been obliged to cramp my verses, and make them rugged to the reader, that they may be harmonious to the hearer." And so, as a result of all these conflicts, the sister arts went their separate ways. Consequently, although poets continued to be more or less knowledgeable about music, their knowledge resulted more from social contacts than from any close ties between the arts. Moreover, the gulf between them grew wider with time.

The advent of printing intensified another oncoming divorce. The minstrel was shoved out of his position as a disseminator of verse, as poems of all kinds became readily available in print. Also we begin to see a definitive split during this period between high and low art, or between art and folk. In the realm of the lyric, there was a growing distinction between the art or literary lyric and the folk lyric. From the close of the Renaissance the folk lyric continued to flourish on its own, however, through the days of the broadsheets and chapbooks, through the Victorian street ballads, the vaudeville and Broadway music halls, to the pop songs of our time. Its illiteracy has always been preserved; the folk lyric has been virtually unaffected by the literary fashion of the day. Usually, however, somewhat more influence has been felt the other way. Sophisticated poets from Swift to Eliot have at times borrowed the street manner for their poems.

The art lyric traveled another path. Except for Dryden, after the early seventeenth century no major English poet until Robert Burns[7] spent a large part of his poetic efforts writing songs that were intended for singing. Although poets continued to create many poems that were called "songs" and odes to music (plenty of them in the eighteenth century), most poets were not interested in its possibilities for poetry. Moreover, few poets besides Milton, Ireland's Thom Moore, and Gerard Manley Hopkins[8] could claim any solid musical training. Moore[9]

---

[4] For Donne's poems see the Index.   [5] E. E. Cummings' poems are often referred to as eye-poetry; for four examples, see the Index.

[6] For Dryden's "A Song for St. Cecilia's Day 1687," see p. 329.   [7] For three poems by Burns see pp. 249, 333.   [8] For two poems by Hopkins see pp. 281, 353.   [9] For Moore's "Believe Me, If All Those Endearing Young Charms," see p. 276.

and Burns, both excellent lyricists, stand out in the English poetic tradition, which was veering further and further away from song. The neoclassic couplet, for example, was about the most unsuitable verse for music in the history of poetry. And, finally, the decline in drama also influenced the lyric's decline, since so many of the best songs had been written for the stage. In 1798, *Lyrical Ballads*,[10] though attempting to return poetry to "real" speech, never approached bringing it back to song. The lyric had become the lyri*cal*. The subject and tone defined the poem. The term "lyric" no longer referred specifically to a song-poem, but rather to a particular kind of poetry that was, as the poet William Wordsworth defined it, "emotion recollected in tranquillity."

To emphasize the essential features of a strain that has undoubtedly influenced the writers represented here, let's take additional liberties with time and space. The following have played important roles in the completion of a lyric cycle.

William Blake[11] renewed the concept of the poet as magic-maker, as shaman. His association of the poem with a mystical experience recurs in the works of such spiritual-minded poets as Hopkins, Baudelaire, Yeats,[12] and Rilke. Also, Blake's "Songs of Innocence and Experience" (for which he reputedly had composed melodies that he sang to himself), in their blending of a simple, lyrical surface with deeper levels of mystery, allegory, and archetype, were ideal models for many of our current lyrics. Compare Blake's "Songs," for example, with Dylan's songs on his *John Wesley Harding* album.

Edgar Allan Poe,[13] in his subordination of thought to the music of his words, and in his concept and use of the grotesque, had a considerable influence on all of modern poetry. Much of his influence was directly absorbed and then rebounded by the *fin de siècle* French symbolist poets, especially Mallarmé and Valéry, who consciously aspired to produce in poetry the pure and absolute qualities of music.

The French surrealists, for whom André Breton was a chief spokesman, liberated the unconscious in poetry and for poetry. Among themselves they tried experiments invoking the creative unconscious in the spontaneous "automatic poem," and seeking to collect their creative consciousness in the communal "group poem."

During the twenties in America and elsewhere there was much experimental activity in poetry. E. E. Cummings[14] was in the vanguard of this activity, and in his verse we can see the seeds of two divergent strains in poetry. His concern with the formal and spatial arrangement of words (and parts of words) on the page helped to precipitate the concrete movement. Much of this poetry is not merely dependent on but is restricted to a visual orientation. Hence Ginsberg's reference to "abstract voiceless page."

On the other hand, Cummings was very much concerned with the oral form. Many of his visual patterns were aids to oral delivery, and he even made commercial recordings of his own poetry, as many poets have done since. These recordings gave him an infinitely greater listening audience, just as the invention of printing gave the Renaissance poet an infinitely greater reading audience. The differences between the two kinds of audience, as we have mentioned earlier, are significant. And it was the new electric technology that helped to create a new audience or rather, to recreate the audience in its primitive form.

The media of records, radio, television, and film have redirected our orientation toward the spoken and sung word. For example, electronic amplification is one factor in making rock concerts the huge communal gatherings that they are, since it enables the sound to be carried over large areas. These concerts are often recorded and filmed, so they can be replayed to other group audiences. The impact of these new media, and the involvement they demand, is total and continuous. Many observers feel that they are replacing the printed word, that society has become (or at least is still in the process of becoming) postliterate and thereby postliterary. Electric circuitry, McLuhan tells us, has become modern society's central nervous system. We share via radio and television the everyday experiences of our African and Asian brothers. We

---

[10] By Woodsworth and Coleridge. For their poems see the Index.   [11] For poems by Blake see the Index.   [12] For three poems by Yeats see the Index.   [13] For Poe's "The Conqueror Worm" see p. 341.

[14] See footnote 5.

are rapidly becoming, in a sense, all members of the same tribe, living in a "global village."

The new media made poets more interested in public readings. In America, the beat movement of the fifties accelerated this interest; readings developed into true communal experiences, complete with chanting and incantations. And once again, the emphasis was on performance, with poems often improvised and spontaneous. Kenneth Patchen and others tried experiments—live and on radio and records—with poetry read to a jazz background, and although the relationship between the two forms was at best contrapuntal, the effort was another major step toward the final fusion and return to song and song forms. As certain jazz forms are heavy influences on current rock music, the beats are the immediate poetic forbears of the current lyric movement.

Pop art has provided another kind of fusion. The pop revolution has proved to be a great cultural equalizer. Be it music, movies, painting, sculpture, or commercial art, pop has consistently shattered traditional boundaries between the sophisticated and the mundane, the art and the folk, the classical and the camp. A Dylan song called "Tombstone Blues" has Ma Rainey and Beethoven composing a song together. "Bob Dylan's 115th Dream" mixes various literary, historical and mythological sources in an absurd modern account of the discovery of America. The Beatles' songs and their bankbooks offer collective proof that there need be no distinction between art and public entertainment. Nor is there as much need for conscious cross-fertilization between sophisticated poetry and folk song, nor between culture and subcultures, as the global village becomes a tighter and tighter unit.

Dylan's work in the sixties heralded poetry's return to song and song forms. His songs were ingenious combinations of blues rhythms, surreal imagery, topical protest, fatalistic existentialism, a huge repertory of poetic devices, and colorful verbal idiom. His impact on the pop music scene is undeniable; he made so many musicians conscious of infusing their songs with poetry. But equally important, he has made a growing number of poets aware of the new possibilities of poetry and music together. A milieu, nurtured in the sixties, is now established. Leon-

ard Cohen,[15] already a successful novelist and linear poet, is writing songs and recording them personally. Ed Sanders and Tuli Kupferberg of the Fugs, both linear poets, both incorporate their verses into song, as did Richard Fariña. These poets are by no means ignorant of the literary tradition, but neither do they have to *borrow* the street idiom. Poets and musicians meet in Liverpool, in New York, in San Francisco, and blend their wares.

A significant number of the lyric writers whose works appear in this book [16] have written their own music and performed their own songs. Donovan is perhaps the best current example of both the primitive mystic poet and the early Renaissance minstrel poet. And he and Dylan and the others are reaching (through the electric circuits) millions of young people, some of whom are budding bards themselves. In his excellent study of the lyric, *The Lyric Impulse*, C. Day Lewis commented on this contemporary phenomenon:

> The mantle of the bard has fallen upon the shoulders of the pop singer—from which it is frequently torn off by a raving horde of his fans and distributed among them as souvenirs. Nothing new in this. The first pop singer, Orpheus, was torn in pieces by Maenads. And dare we feel superior about these rabid manifestations? Do they not indicate a psychological need, a spontaneity of emotion, which the higher levels of art in the West are today ignoring?
>
> C. Day Lewis, *The Lyric Impulse* (Cambridge: Harvard University Press, 1965), p. 2.

[3]

The minstrel has returned; his stringed instrument is now electric, and without traveling he can be heard across the world. And he will be heard—by everyone—since the human ear is not equipped with earlids.

Thus a cycle seems to be reaching completion. We are now in a position to consider again

[15] For two songs by Cohen see p. 261.   [16] By the authors of this essay, *Lyric Voices, Approaches to the Poetry of Contemporary Song*, New York; John Wiley & Sons, Inc. 1972.

the questions raised earlier: Will the current lyric movement be a major direction? Is it new? In view of the increasingly large dimensions of the lyric movement, there can be no doubt that it is, by sheer force of numbers, a major trend. The return to the roots of poetry demonstrated by the reemergence of the singer-poets makes this movement, in an even more significant sense, a major direction.

But as these two questions are answered, two further problems can be anticipated concerning the proposed cyclical theory, and so it must be clarified. One, we cannot say that *all* poetry is returning to song; as long as people continue to speak, there will be spoken poetry. As T. S. Eliot once warned, if poetry departs too far from common speech, it can wither and die of abstraction. We can propose, however, that the lyric movement is a major direction. And this brings up the second problem.

If the mainstream of poetry is returning to lyric form, and the lyric is by tradition a light, simple song, then what happens to poetry that is by nature sophisticated, complex, and profound? We spoke earlier of the tension between the forward-moving musical pace and the words whose meanings must sometimes be pondered. To preserve the balance, the lyric has traditionally been light and simple in meaning and thereby fast-moving. Although most current lyrics continue to be light, several important songs point toward a new kind of lyric. Dylan's "All Along the Watchtower" [17] is one example. The song has a simple narrative surface that moves along quickly but, in the style of Blake, it uses symbol, allegory, and archetype to suggest more profound meanings. Songs like Phil Och's "Crucifixion," [18] Carl Oglesby's "Black Panther," [19] Fariña's "Celebration for a Grey Day," [20] and Dylan's "Sad-Eyed Lady of the Lowlands" [21] are examples of a somewhat different type. These songs, with their intricate image patterns, their many-sided symbols and levels of meaning, are "heavy." They do not offer a contrast to the "higher levels of art."

And yet they are rapid. In each song the music keeps us moving toward the conclusion.

We cannot linger on the "meaning"; lingering is for later. In this electric age, things happen allatonce, and, sometimes, if we are to survive, we must let them happen and reflect on them later. So with the films of Fellini and Godard, so with the Joshua Light Show, so with "Sad-Eyed Lady of the Lowlands."

Still another possible explanation of the "heavy" lyric bears consideration. It may be that the electronic media are gradually conditioning us to the ability to respond to many different stimuli on many levels. As we continue to experience the perceptual expansion that the electronic media stimulate, it is possible that our ability to function simultaneously on the perceptual and intellectual levels will increase. Modern film techniques overwhelm us with a rapid series of visual images, while contemporary songs bombard us with an infinitely complex fusion of visual, auditory, and kinetic images and intellectual ideas.

These modern orphic voices are plugging us in to the times we actually live in.

Comments and Questions

1. Explain the title of this essay.
2. We have, in this text, made a feature of the new minstrelsy. See pp. 259–269. The footnotes to the present selection direct readers to many of the lyrics which represent the current vogue for folk and country music. After reading the two poems by Bob Dylan (pp. 263 and 264), comment on the observation that Dylan is "precursor, prophet, central figure, and sage" of a new movement in poetry.
3. The authors recognize four periods in the "evolutionary cycle of . . . lyric poetry." Examine the four. Note that there are some huge jumps in time. Comment.

On Teaching Modern Poetry
STEPHEN SPENDER
1909–

A poem has many levels of meaning, and none of them is prose. Are some of these "righter" than others? Is it altogether "wrong" to think

[17] See p. 264.   [18] See p. 266.   [19] See p. 267.   [20] See p. 262.   [21] See p. 263.

that a poem may be paraphrased? Can an appreciation of poetry be acquired? Does poetry have educational value for the student who is incapable of a complete experience of poetry but who can acquire a limited appreciation which may not seem to survive his years at school or college? This last question, which the reader may be inclined to answer with an immediate "No" is, in practice, not so easy to answer. For students who may never completely understand a poem, can often understand other things through the discussion of poetry. Those who prefer discussing poetry to reading poems, look to poetry for an illumination of some of the problems of living. One cannot afford to dismiss this as irrelevant when one is taking into consideration the whole picture of the education of an individual. Many people look to poetry today as an illumination of religious and philosophic problems. Although poetry is not and cannot be a substitute for religion and philosophy, nevertheless, it may lead people to think seriously about such things. It may lead them through poetry and out of it into their real interest or vocation.

Probably most modern critics would agree that a poem *means* the sum of everything which it *is*, in language used to suggest not just thought but also imagery and sound. It means a thought which can be paraphrased in prose, plus the sound of the words in which this thought is expressed and which add as much to the thought as color does to drawing in a painting, plus the imagery which becomes a sensory experience to the reader as he reads from line to line, plus the energy of the metre, plus the poet's taste or palate in words, plus even such things as the punctuation and spacing of the poem upon the printed page. All these things become an *experience* which the poem is and means.[1]

Most contemporary critics, as I say, would agree about this. On the whole, the tendency today is to judge the poem by the sacred order of the irreplaceable line, and not by the generalized reducible opinions and attitudes of the poet within his poem. This modern appreciation of the concreteness and texture of art is surely one of the characteristics of intellectual life in the twentieth century which we can consider to be an advance of the nineteenth.

Yet, if we do not feel the need to translate poetry into prose, nevertheless the need to explain and annotate it seems to remain. Why else those books explaining the philosophy of T. S. Eliot's *Four Quartets* or of Rilke's *Duino Elegies?* It is all very well for Mr. Robert Graves to declare that his poems are written only for poets, implying that all poems should be that and that only. But evidently, despite the modern purist desire not to lose the poem in the prose translation, poetry expresses complicated ideas and attitudes. This inevitably leads us on from a discussion of the best order of the best words to that of the ideas behind them. Robert Graves may be right in thinking that poetry should be for poets only. But despite his protestations, the overwhelming mass of contemporary criticism of poetry assumes that poetry is written for a reading public who are not just poets: or at least that there is a content of poetry which exists, as it were, apart from the pure esthetic experience which can only be communicated to people who think poetically, as the poet himself thinks.

The teacher of poetry finds that although it is important to stress that a poetry *is,* it is also true that poetry is about things. To a certain type of student the "about" ness will always be more important than the "is" ness: and perhaps this student may learn more from having poetry explained to him than the one who understands poetry intuitively and who therefore scarcely requires to be taught.

The teacher is not a poet teaching poets, nor even a literary critic concerned only with readers whose interest in poetry is "pure." He has to accept, I think, that the interest of most students in poetry, however serious it may be, will not be for the sake of that which is essentially the poetry in poetry. At the same time, poetry itself is ambiguous, and that which it is about is inseparably bound up with that which it is. If a critic as austere as Mr. T. S. Eliot can argue that a poet as pure as Blake is not a great poet because he has a "homemade philosophy," that means that one approach to Blake is certainly by way of his philosophy. And if many of Blake's readers never get beyond his philosophy to the center of his imagination, that does not mean that they have entirely missed the poetry in

---

[1] The point of view expressed in this paragraph, especially in the first sentence, is demonstrated in some detail in "Poetry Preliminaries," pp. 236 ff.

Blake: because Blake's thought, which can perhaps be paraphrased, nevertheless remains a part of his poetry. What a poem is about, even if it can be expressed in critics' prose, does take us some way toward understanding that which it is.

Many students undoubtedly try to *use* poetry to help them to develop attitudes towards things other than poetry. Sarah Lawrence College provided me with several examples of such a utilitarian attitude. One student, K., had difficulty with certain modern poems at the beginning of the course, because she disapproved of the views which the poets appeared to her to be expressing in their poems; for example, the pessimism of Thomas Hardy, the mysticism of T. S. Eliot, and the insistence on sexuality of D. H. Lawrence. She thought that poetry should in some way express ideas which contributed to the betterment of human society.

Perhaps I should have argued with K. that poetry had nothing to do with the views of poets and still less to do with improving the lot of humanity. But I only partly did this. I also argued against her views in themselves, quite apart from their relevance to poetry. I tried to point out that the search for a meaning in life, even if it seems to neglect the exigencies of social welfare, is not escapism. The result of allowing her to discuss aspects of poetry, such as the opinions and personalities of poets, which seemed on the face of it to have little to do with their work, was that she did, in the course of a year, develop powers of appreciation which I had not thought possible. A block to her appreciation was removed. She learned tolerance through tolerating poets. Having acquired a certain tolerance she experienced a certain release in her imaginative life which brought her to an appreciation of poetry for its own sake. Her prejudices were not just irrelevant: they were barriers which had to be removed before she could understand poetry at all. Her criticism of every poem—that it said something with which she disagreed—implied conviction that poetry ought to have a social message with which she did agree. It would have been useless to say that what a poem *said* was irrelevant to the poetry, because to her the saying something was what really mattered, and ultimately her objection was to the expression of any attitudes of mind which she did not consider socially responsible. To say to her that Thomas Hardy's pessimism was irrelevant to his poetry would only be a way of making her think that Hardy not only had the wrong opinions but also attempted to evade responsibility for them. Therefore it seemed best to accept her view that poetry was about opinions which she could not tolerate and to point out that those opinions, within the contexts in which they were expressed, might have a value which she could come to appreciate. When she had learned to tolerate these opinions she was well on the way to understanding the freedom of the imagination of the poet in his poetry. On the other hand, so long as she could not tolerate what she considered antisocial opinions, she would not tolerate the life of the imagination.

K., it transpired, was using poetry as a means of liberating herself from a narrow application of her social conscience to every situation. Her case was not rare. There is a fairly widespread tendency amongst students today to label a great deal of their reading "escapist," for the most superficial reasons. To them all the poetry of Walter de la Mare is "escapist," Mr. T. S. Eliot is not "escapist" in *The Waste Land* but becomes so in the *Four Quartets,* Mr. W. H. Auden has recently become an "escapist," D. H. Lawrence is escaping from social reality into "personal relationships and mysticism," and so on. Such readers seem to expect that it is the duty of literature to confront them with a social reality, which, in fact, they rarely face themselves in their lives. They wish poets to stop being what is called escapists and become scapegoats, punished and punishing in their work for all the ills of society. One might reasonably argue that if literature did do this, it might indeed be providing a facile escape in imagination from problems which people ought to be facing in their living. In fact, there is a case to be made for saying that people should be social realists in their lives but not in their literature. For living should certainly be pre-occupied with improving conditions, but literature should be concerned with enlarging our ideas of a significance beyond the paraphernalia of living. Without such a significance, improved conditions themselves become a burden. There must be a goal beyond the goal of social improvement—to give significance to better conditions of living when they have been achieved.

In an ideal world I suppose that living would be involved in problems of living, and that literature would be concerned with values which transcend living. It is these values which ultimately give living itself a purpose. Of course, as long as we do not live in an ideal world, some writers will insist on the necessity of using writing as a means of describing the problems of social reality and, if they are so inspired, they will be right to do so. But to call this kind of literature "realistic" and any other kind escapist is to sacrifice the pursuit of permanent values for immediate and pressing ones: and there is danger of the sense of that which endures being lost in the exigencies of the present.

If there is any such thing as "escapism" in poetry, it is the tendency of poets sometimes to assert that experiences contained in certain poems have some kind of consoling application to other experiences of a different nature. That a sunset, a rose, or a landscape can be evoked in language which compensates for poverty, social injustice, or war, is obviously a false proposition. To maintain it is to escape from the greater evil into the lesser prettiness. Poets, even in such a poet as Keats, have occasionally misled themselves and their readers in writing about poetry as though it were a housing project for happy dreamers. The mistake perhaps arises from confusing the objective standards by which poetry is made and judged with the subjective experience it provides. For the fact is that poetry is an art employing an objective medium and technique for the purpose of communicating the subjective insight of the poet to the subjective sensibility of the reader. It can express and communicate an experience which may be of great value to the individual reader, perhaps even providing him with a philosophy and helping him in his life. But this kind of individual experience conveyed from one individual to another by means of the objective medium of art, arises only as a possible rather irrelevant reaction of the reader to the subject matter of the poem. Poetry cannot preach social values as effectively as journalism or propaganda or systematized thought, even though it may indirectly have a social effect. Poetry does not provide a kind of reality which can either, on the one hand, console readers for the ills of society, or, on the other, by being "realistic," make people face up to social problems. All poetry may do, as an in-

cidental effect of its use of language, is to provide the reader with an experience which will affect him according to the laws of his own nature. The propagandist view that poetry can save society is just as irrelevant to the nature of poetry as the one that it can provide an escape from the ills of the modern age.

I have dwelt on "escapism" so long because one of the chief prejudices the teacher of students of poetry today has to fight is indicated by the word "escapist." However, I think the teacher should be sympathetic to the student who wants to know how poetry will be useful to him. After all, utility itself, in connection with poetry, is a somewhat complex concept, and there is every reason to consider it. For one thing, poetry is useful to anyone who appreciates it, in enabling him to enter into complex states of mind which should help him to understand his own nature and that of other people. The reader of a poem has the illusion, through the sensuous use of language, of being in the presence of the event which is the occasion of the poem. The subject of a poem is an event individually experienced; its method (sensuous language) creates the form which is the universal form of all experience for everyone of every event. The reader of a poem is made aware that the experience of every event by every individual is a unique occasion in the universe, and that at the same time, this uniqueness is the universal mode of experiencing all events. Poetry makes one realize that one is alone, and complex; and that to be alone is universal.

The fact that one cannot establish the value of the experience of a poem in a hierarchy of utilitarian values, does not mean that poetry is not useful. On the contrary, one can insist that poetry is of use to the individual who appreciates it, even while one may refuse to measure that utility. The teacher who thinks it is part of his integrity, or of the integrity of his subject, to refuse to admit the utility of spiritual values, may be in the position of offering art to his pupils in the form of significantly formed stones, when they are asking for bread. He should ask himself seriously whether there is not a sense in which poetry is indeed bread for those who can understand it, and even, to a lesser extent, to those who partially misunderstand it.

Poetry, as has often been said, reveals the familiar as unfamiliar. The inspiration of the poet is the moment in which he becomes aware of unfamiliarity. The unfamiliarity, the newness of things, the uniqueness of every contact of a mind with an event, is, indeed, everything. But there are certain experiences in life which are always unfamiliar for everyone, and these form a vast subject matter for poetry, the unfamiliarity of the unfamiliar. Such subjects are death, love, infinity, the idea of God, the smallness of man in relation to the vastness of the universe, the unknown. Religion, philosophy, and morals are also concerned with these fundamentals of the human condition, and it is here that the experiencing of life in poetry brings the poetic experience close to the reasoned processes of philosophers, theologians, and moralists. Thus the teaching of poetry leads the student to a discussion of conditions of human life, where man is alone with the strangeness of his situation in time and space.

Poets can only express their experiences in terms of other experiences, which men have experienced with their senses. Sensuous language means that the poet creates his poem from words which have associations, and these associations are of the experience of things with the senses. A love poem can only be expressed in words which have associations with actual loving, and in the same way a religious poem can only be created in the language of religious experience—however remote this may seem. For this reason, the teacher will find that a great deal of discussion of poetry in class will consist of inquiring into the connection between the poet's experience and his poem. Is the poet sincere? Did he really feel this? are questions often asked by students. When poetry goes beyond personal experience to the experience of belief, we are brought up against a more difficult question of sincerity. Can the poet really believe this? Does he know God? Can he believe in immortality? We are soon confronted with problems of tradition and belief which may seem far removed from a particular poem, but which may really be essential to an understanding of it.

Amongst our contemporaries today one finds that directly a poet ceases to write of some immediate human experience of an occasional nature, for which purposes he can draw on the simple associative language of the physical senses, one is up against the difficulty that a shared language of religious or philosophical experience, with associations which are as easily recognized as those of the senses, does not exist. In reading poetry such as T. S. Eliot's *Four Quartets* with students, one finds that for many of them there is no sensuous language associated with ideas of eternity. God, immortality, heaven, hell, and so on. Eliot's world is for them a world of abstract speculation, his language never, or almost never strikes the note of an experience of eternity in their own minds. Naturally they think of Eliot's preoccupations as "escapism," because they are about an experience of which they know nothing.

If one wishes to teach such students to appreciate the *Four Quartets* the only way to do so seems to be to build up by intellectual arguments the associations with experience on which the poetry is based. One can show that each of the four poems in the *Four Quartets* is connected with real places which have historic associations with certain disciplines of living dependent on certain metaphysical beliefs. One can discuss the use to which Eliot has deliberately put the influence of Dante in his poem, and one can discuss the time-philosophy and the theological ideas of the *Four Quartets*. All this will not give the student the immediate contact with the metaphysical searching which is as much the sensuous experience of this poetry as the color grey is sensuous experience in the line:

> Towards what shores what grey rocks and
>   what islands.

Consider such lines as:

> All manner of things shall be well
> When the tongues of flame are infolded
> Into the crowned knot of fire
> And the fire and the rose are one.

Here it is far easier to make the student understand the Dantesque imagery than the sensuous mystical perception of the life of the individual within eternity. Can one understand such writing without having had, consciously or unconsciously, a mystical experience which foreshadows the condition described? This is a baffling question for the teacher. All he can reasonably hope to do is make the student understand the traditional belief within which Eliot's recent poetry exists, and to argue against the view of the student who thinks that mystical experience is "escapist."

Teachers of Latin within the system of a classical education have always taught much poetry, partly because this branch of classical literature is supremely excellent, partly because the language of poetry taught the greatest mastery of all the uses of the language, and partly also because within poetry there exist all the ideas of Roman civilization. These reasons for teaching poetry remain in force today. Insistence on the esthetic aspect should not conceal from us that poetry remains the most instructive of the arts, being rooted in myth, being supremely the exercise by the poet of the historic sense within the tradition of literature, and involving often discussion of general ideas.

The most important thing to teach about modern poetry is that modern poetry is simply poetry, expressing what poets have tried to express at all times, but within modern conditions. The problem of the poet has always been to express inward experience in imagery and sound which communicate the significance of this experience to others. He can only communicate to other minds what is significant to him by involving an outward event symbolizing a significance which corresponds to his inner state of mind. If he is an Elizabethan, certain of his inner experiences may have a significance recognized by others when he attaches to these experiences the symbolism of the rose, the crown, or the cross. For a modern man who, as a human being, has an inner experience exactly similar to that of the Elizabethan, the symbol which corresponds to his experience will be one chosen from modern life, if it is to communicate itself in a way which will awaken the living experience of our time to his contemporaries. To select rose, crown, or cross would be for him to detach his experience from the present and place it in a literary past.

Our expansive, restless, materialist, explosive age does not easily provide us in our environment with outward symbols for inner states of mind. For our outer world has little accessible language of symbols to which we can attach the experiences of our lives. Instead of our minds being able to invade it with their inwardness, it invades us with its outwardness, almost persuading us that not the inner life of man, but non-human, geographical and mechanical events are all that is significant in the universe. However, the fact remains that a man's problem is that everything for him is a mental event in his own mind. This includes the whole extent of the universe, and all the achievements of scientists and generals. The external world is man's inner world and his problem is to organize this inner world within his own mind.

Therefore the eternal problem of poetry—to express inner experiences in terms of outer things—remains, although the apparent unresponsiveness of outer things in the modern world makes this appear difficult. Man has learned, invented, and organized his modern world. It is an object of his awareness, inventiveness, and will. He is not an object of it. Therefore the machine and the spatial distances which appear to impose their vastness on him are the material of his own inner spiritual life. Within his mind they are symbols. Perhaps they are symbols of the apparent powerlessness of his inner life. But his sanity depends on his mastering within himself what he has discovered and invented in his outer world. He has power to imagine the inner mastery of his own situation. Modern poetry is an aspect of the struggle to restore the balance of our inner with our outer world.

In view of this, it is a peculiarity of American education that it makes a division of literature into "creative," "critical," and "reading" functions. Some students will tell you that they expect to learn to write creatively, others to criticize, and others to read. An extreme example of this oversimple approach was given to me by a student who told me that I could not expect her to be interested in any of the poets she read: because she wished to learn to write poetry, not to read it. This was exceptional, but three other students whom I taught were only really interested in those poets whom they considered useful to them in their own writing.

The creative writing classes in the United States must be considered a very interesting educational experiment, but their advantages must be weighed against several disadvantages. One disadvantage is that they tend to divide literary studies into creative and non-creative. If this means also that the student thinks of writing as being an activity which has little to do with reading, or which has the effect of limiting the writer's reading to that which helps him in his own creative work, here is a further disadvantage. For one only has to read the lives of writers to see that an avaricious habit of reading everything that comes his way is the atmosphere in which most writers have developed and lived.

There is certainly a good deal in the writing of poetry which can be taught. Readers of the prose passages in Dante's *Vita Nuova* will see that Dante considered himself a member of a school who were inventing and propagating a particular style of poetry. Baudelaire, Mallarmé, and several other poets have considered the teaching of poetry as a theoretical possibility. At the beginning of this century the imagists held views about the writing of poetry, such as that the poet must concentrate entirely on producing a perfectly clear image, and that this can be taught and learned.

Poetry is written in various forms, and there is no doubt that these can be taught, just as musical technique can be. The parallel with music exists in theory, but actually it does not quite work out in practice. Music is concerned with notes measured in time. A sequence of notes producing the same tune can be invented to produce a slow or fast effect simply by lengthening the duration of each note, or variations can be made by sustaining some notes and quickening others, within the rhythm. Thus a musician can take a tune and produce a great many variations on it without altering the original idea. However, poetry uses words and not notes. A poet cannot alter the speed and mood of an idea simply by adding syllables and emphatic pauses with the ease which is possible to the composer. Thus the idea which in poetry corresponds to tune can only be created in one set of words in which meaning is inseparable from the form in which it is expressed. A poet is not like a composer in search for freedom of expression which he can achieve among a great variety of forms: he is in search for the few forms which correspond most exactly to that which he wishes to say. When he has discovered those forms, he interests himself in no others, except insofar as he is feeling his way towards those which may further his later development. Form in poetry is inseparable from thought: and the only form which the poet needs is that in which he can think. Thus from Walt Whitman, down to T. S. Eliot, one can think of dozens of poets who know far less in general about poetic forms than is taught in the creative writing courses: they are masters of their own particular forms, and probably even avoid thinking in other ones, through an instinctive discipline.

A sonnet, for example, is a poetic form for thinking a thought which is a sonnet. If a poet had no potentiality for thinking in sonnets, to write them may actually confuse him and prevent him from attaining so soon the form which is uniquely his. The poet W. B. Yeats once told me that he had learned to write in an overliterary poetic tradition and that he had spent his life trying to write poems in a simpler manner. To a lesser talent, nothing might seem simpler than Yeats's problem. All he had to do was to leave out some rhymes and prune away his imagery, one might think. But the ornament, the over-poetic style had become his poetic thought, and when he struggled to express ideas which were too bare and harsh for this form, he had great difficulty in adapting his style to his later subject-matter.

Thus, to teach students to write in a variety of poetic techniques would be a doubtful benefit. What one can do, perhaps, is criticize their work, with a view to helping them to discover their own form, teach them to relate as widely as possible the poetry of others to what they themselves are trying to do, teach them to think concretely and with their senses, and develop in their minds a sense of purpose independent of the literary market and literary fashions.

Young writers often forget that a poem should be as well written as a letter or diary or any other piece of prose, that is to say, as well written, considered simply as writing, as they can possibly make it. Perhaps the most reasonable method of writing a poem is first of all to write down rapidly those impressions, that rhythm, that shape which makes it seem a poetic experience, without regard to other considerations. But the second or third stage of writing should certainly be to take out the "bad writing," that is to say, the redundancies, the bad grammar, the linguistic inversions, and write the sense of the poem as well and clearly as possible. A teacher can certainly be of help here, because a good deal of potentially good poetry is lost under sheer bad writing.

A poet discovers his own formal qualities through learning to analyze the qualities of his own sensibility. He must know whether, for example, his gifts are predominantly of the eye or the ear. The visual writer cannot afford to sacrifice his eye to his ear: a preoccupation with rules of rhyme and strict metre could disintegrate the concentration on the image which is necessary to develop his gift.

In relating his own work to that of other poets, the student has to learn to avoid two dangers which have destroyed many talents: on the one hand, the danger of being absorbed into a greater talent; on the other, the danger of shutting out the greater talent for fear of being absorbed. One has to learn to relate one's own work to that of others and to learn from this relation by using other work for purposes of criticising one's own, or sometimes for interpreting the work of other poets in terms of one's own talent. The relation of Keats to Shakespeare, or, in our own time, of Eliot to Dante, is each a classic example of the power of a poet to interpret within his own sensibility the achievement of a past poet. Here it seems to me that the teacher should be of considerable help to the student. For example, I think it would be a good exercise for students to make free translations of poems in a foreign language, interpreting the particular significance for them of a poem which appeals to them into terms of their own technique and sensibility. They should seek in such free renderings, not for accuracy, but to create in their own language the general effect which appeals to them in the foreign poem.

Of course far and away the most important quality of a poet is his power of thinking sensuously in words. The test of sensuous thought is not the occasional striking image or well-sounding line, but the power as it were to *follow through* with the senses, just as in a game a player may have a perception of a whole sequence of moves following from one move, which affect him physically, as though he were at one moment feeling the muscular changes required by all these moves expanding through his blood and muscles. The power of the verbal eye to see the transformation from line to line of the image and sound in a poem: this is the central excitement of poetry, it is the real life, and everything else is fabrication. The teacher cannot of course teach sensuous energy: still less can he explain how this can clothe itself in vital words. But he can at least be an efficient guide; for it is in confused imagery, mixed metaphor, abstract expressions, that by far the greatest number of mistakes are made by poets. If he is able to see with intensity, even for the duration of a phrase or a line, there is the possibility of development. If he is able to understand the necessity of a certain consistency, a poetic logic in the development of imagery and sound, then he may well be capable of poetry.

Too often in schools of creative writing, the student's eye is directed towards the market of magazines and reviews. Perhaps it would be too idealistic to say that creative writing courses should be directed against rather than towards the standards of editorial offices; but at least it may be said that as far as possible independence from such standards should be taught. The period during a student's life when he is writing only for teachers and friends, is not only in itself one of liberty, but it should represent a freedom which he is able to value afterwards, and to which he should always return. In a sense a writer should always remain a student, should be writing only for himself and his friend. But if, when he is a student, he is already considered to be writing for publication, this standard is destroyed in his own mind. Therefore teachers should encourage students to indulge in that kind of writing which cannot be published: for example, the writing of journals and experiments, perhaps even of erotic and obscene poems. The habit of writing for the wastepaper basket is the most valuable one that a writer can acquire.

Despite the creative writing courses, teaching students to read poems seems more useful than teaching them to write them, for various reasons. Although the true readers of poetry are perhaps as rare as the poets themselves, the reading of poetry does lead to many other things. Poetry is, after all, a nerve center of the consciousness of a civilization, with responses to many of the important situations in that civilization. The reading of poetry within an education therefore justifies itself as a discipline of the humanities. Learning to write poetry is an interesting experiment and in some years' time a survey of the results of this education will be interesting. Perhaps it will be found that in place of the creative writing courses there should be a far greater emphasis on writing in all literary courses. It would seem that a very valuable development of the American experiment would be if the conception of written work in all English courses were extended considerably beyond the essay, to include poems and stories.

To sum up: the teacher of poetry has always to remember that he is not only a poet teaching poets or even a critic insisting on the purest and fullest appreciation. He is really filling several roles, of which these two are the easiest and perhaps not the most important, since writers and readers with a true vocation will probably find it without him.

His most important role is to teach poetry as a discipline of the imagination; a discipline which reveals the complexity of the experience of the individual human being isolated in time and place within the universe and experiencing everything at every moment of his life, as no one before or since has experienced or will ever experience it; which, when it has revealed this terrifying uniqueness and complexity, shows how the unique, which is also the universal form of experiencing, can be related through the understanding of poetry to the experiences of other men who have been able to express a similar sense of their isolation within time and space, at other times and other places; which shows that complexity and awareness only become creative when they can be disciplined within a formal pattern.

The student who is unable to attain complete appreciation can learn a great deal from the discipline of poetry. Modern poetry can teach above all that the poetic problem is the same, at all times, though it has to express itself in different forms; the same, because the problem of the poet is to relate his inner significant experiences to the outward world which impresses itself on him. The world of modern phenomena is as much a product of man's spiritual condition as the world in the past has been and the world in the future will be.

Comments and Questions

1. Mr. Spender, in his second paragraph, says that "a poem *means* the sum of everything which it *is.* . . ." Then he breaks up this possible sum into how many parts? Examine these parts and apply them to a poem that you like. (You may want to choose from the section on "Poetry.") After discussing the

parts, have you yet said anything about the poetic *experience?* Do you think this experience is of such complex impact that it can be realized only intuitively?

2. In what way does Mr. Spender support the view that limited appreciation of poetry is better than none at all?

3. What do you understand by the word "escapism"? How does Mr. Spender forward his definition of poetry by denying that it is escapist? At one point Mr. Spender implies that a poet's pessimism—Hardy's, for example—is not relevant to his poems as poems; elsewhere, he emphasizes the importance of a poet's sincerity. How does he reconcile these statements?

4. Comment on these significant passages:

Poetry makes one realize that one is alone, and complex; and that to be alone is universal.

Poetry . . . reveals the familiar as unfamiliar. . . . poetry remains the most instructive of the arts. . . .

Form in poetry is inseparable from thought: and the only form which the poet needs is that in which he can think.

Dialogue with the Audience
JOHN CIARDI
1916–

"I'm not exactly illiterate," says the Citizen. "I'm a pretty fair historian. I can read Freud—at least some of him—without being entirely in the dark. But I get nowhere with this modern poetry. I've given up trying."

The Poet has heard it all before, but the Citizen obviously wants to talk about it. The Poet, as a matter of fact, rather likes the Citizen. Maybe, the Poet thinks, if I can peg the talk to something specific it won't just ramble on aimlessly and forever. Aloud he says: "Just for the fun of it—who is the last particular poet you gave up on?"

"It was Wallace Stevens," says the Citizen. "I read your review of the *Collected Poems* and I shelled out $7.50 for it on your say-so." He reaches up to a shelf and hauls down the book. "Here it is," he says, tossing it on the table, "a big fat collection of unintelligibility."

"Sorry," says the Poet, "no refunds, if that's what you're getting at. But do me a favor: show me a specific poem that you take to be unintelligible."

The Citizen stares. "Do you mean to say you understand every poem in this book?"

The Poet shakes his head. "Far from it. I don't even understand White House news releases. But I like Stevens better."

"Without knowing what it is you like?"

"Let's keep the talk as specific as we can. I've asked you to cite a poem: turn around is fair play—find a poem called 'Asides on the Oboe.' Here, take this passage:

The obsolete fiction of the wide river in
An empty land; the gods that Boucher killed;
And the metal heroes that time granulates—
The philosophers' man alone still walks in
        dew,
Still by the sea-side mutters milky lines
Concerning an immaculate imagery.
If you say on the hautboy man is not enough,
Can never stand as god, is ever wrong
In the end, however naked, tall, there is still
The impossible possible philosophers' man,
The man who has had the time to think
        enough,
The central man, the human globe, respon-
        sive
As a mirror with a voice, the man of glass,
Who in a million diamonds sums us up."

"Let me get it straight," says the Citizen. "Is this an example of a passage you do understand, or of one you don't?"

"As a matter of fact, it's an example of both," says the Poet. "Suppose I were to say I found it elusive, yet clear—would that make any sense? I can't unravel it detail by detail. I encounter areas of obscurity in it. Yet the total force of the passage is both unmistakable and moving, and just beyond every momentary obscurity I keep emerging into areas of immediate clarity."

"No, in a word. It makes no sense to me."

"Well, what do you mean by sense? Stevens does not write for factual-information sense. Why should he? He picks up a theme and orchestrates it. His 'sense' is a structure. The reader must keep that total structure in mind in order to grasp Stevens's kind of sense. He does not,

moreover, 'mean' any one thing, but rather all the possibilities of all the relationships he is orchestrating."

"Clear as Navy coffee," says the Citizen. "Am I supposed to swallow it?"

"You do in music," says the Poet, glancing at the Citizen's collection of recordings, "why not in poetry?"

"Because, among other things, words have meanings."

"They have," says the Poet, "but far more meanings than anyone thinks about in reading factual prose. A word is not a meaning but a complex of meanings consisting of all its possibilities: its ability to identify something, the image it releases in making that identification, its sound, its history, its association-in-context with the other words of the passage. Good poets use *more* of the word than most readers are used to."

"Yes," says the Citizen, who is proud of being a fair-minded person, "I suppose that *is* true."

"But not only is the individual word a complex. It is used in a phrase that is itself a complex of complexes. And the phrase is in turn used in the complex of the total poem's structure."

"So a poem is a complex of complexes of complexes," says the Citizen, half-indignant now. "I'm beginning to get a complex myself."

"No," says the Poet, "that's a complex you've always had. You are used to words basically as denotations in statements intended or purporting to intend to convey facts. You have the 'practicality complex' and your basic symptom is 'why doesn't he say it straight'?"

"Well, why doesn't he?"

"As a matter of fact he does at times—even in your terms. Take the line, 'The man who has had the time to think enough.' How much 'straighter' could he make the phrase of that line?"

"I can agree there," says the Citizen. "But what about 'milky lines'? Why does he have to say it on 'the hautboy'? And what's all that about a mirror with a voice?"

"One at a time," says the Poet. "The 'milky lines' is one of those details I remain unsure of. I suspect that Stevens was thinking of the seas as a kind of mother-of-life and that he used 'milky' in that connection. If my guess is right that makes 'milky lines' mean something like 'lines fed by the essential life fluid of all-mothering nature.' But that is only a guess and I have no way of verifying it. In fact, some of what follows in the poem—not in this passage— troubles my guess. That is one of the obscurities I feel in the passage. One I feel and *welcome*, may I say.

"The hautboy, on the other hand, is a straightforward Stevens signature, a part of his personal idiom, like his blue-guitar. The hautboy is the kind of detail that reveals itself immediately as you get to know more about the way the poet writes. For the time being I can only suggest that you take the hautboy to be one of the instruments of art. On that instrument of artifice, Stevens must make the 'fiction' (always a special term in his writing) that can replace the 'obsolete fiction' of the gods. In Stevens, the rituals of art constantly take the place of the rituals of religion—themselves richly obscure.

"As for the 'mirror with voice,'—there I have to charge you with petulant misreading. Stevens has established the context of his statement clearly enough for any willing reader, and it is no reading at all to ignore the context. What he is saying is roughly 'that it is *as if* the responsive man were a mirror with a voice reflecting all of us in a heightened way, *as if* summing us up in the million-diamond-reflection of his artifice.' I am satisfied that the gist of it is about that, though I confess I am uncertain about it later when the poem becomes unmistakably Leibnizian. At that later point, I conclude I don't know Leibniz well enough to guess out Stevens's sense of him. I am left puzzled. But I am also left considerably richer. Certainly, I should be willing to read a much longer and much more obscure poem than this if only to meet that man 'who has had the time to think enough.' I want him in my mind."

"Yes," says the Citizen, "I can go along with some of that. Even with most of it. But why must he be so elusive about it?"

The Poet smiles. "We're back to the business of 'saying it straight' again. I suggest, first, that the thought itself is elusive. And, second, that it's a kind of thinking you're not used to, partly because you have not read enough Stevens to catch the flavor of his thinking, and partly because you're not really a reader of poetry and never have been."

The Citizen draws himself up. "Now I don't know about that," he says. "I took quite a lot of English courses in school and . . ."

"And you haven't read as many as three books of new poems a year since then."

"Well," says the Citizen more slowly, "I guess you have me there. Maybe if I were a more practised reader I'd see more. But isn't some of it the poets' fault? Why do they make it so hard for a man to read them? I'm no genius, but I'm reasonably intelligent."

"And rational," suggests the Poet.

"Certainly. What's wrong with rationality?"

"Ask yourself that question as you read through an issue of the *Reader's Digest* sometime," says the Poet. "Or let me ask you how rationally you got married? Or by what sequence of syllogisms you begot your children? Or what Certified Public Accountant writes the scripts of your dreamlife?"

The Poet is talking fast now, warming to his most fundamental sermon. "We all contain elements of rationality, but we're all much more than those elements. A poet thinks with his senses, his nerve endings, his whole body. He looks at his thought physically, and he looks from many directions at once. He *feels* what he thinks, and he feels it most in the act of making a poetic structure of it. Just as a composer feels himself into his musical structure. There is no auditing of rationalities in that process; there is, rather, the accomplishment into form of some part of a whole life."

The Citizen is being fair-minded again. "I can't grasp entirely your way of putting things," he says after a while, "but I can get a glimpse of what I think you're saying—especially when I try to feel it in terms of what a composer does inside his music." He rubs his jaw. "I don't know. There are too many ideas in it that are new to me. I suppose if you say so . . ."

"The last time you started supposing on my say-so it cost you $7.50," says the Poet. "Suppose me nothing on my say-so: I refuse to be trusted by any man who can trust himself, and I doubly refuse to be trusted by a man who can't trust himself. Make up your own mind on the basis of what makes sense in itself."

"That's just the trouble," says the Citizen. "You make it sound sensible enough, but then I turn to a poem and I just can't get my hooks into it."

"That's just what I started to ask you in the

beginning. There's the book: give me a for-instance."

"I remember one queer thing called 'Bantams in Pine-Woods'," says the Citizen, thumbing the pages. "I swear I spent a day trying to make sense of the first two lines. Here they are."

Chieftain Iffucan of Azcan in caftan
Of tan with henna hackles, halt!

"What's the problem?" says the Poet.

"No problem," says the Citizen. "Just gibberish. What the devil is all this henna-hackled Iffucan of Azcan trashcan stuff?"

"Ah!" says the Poet, "I see. To tell you the truth I hadn't ever thought of those lines as a difficulty: they're having such fun with themselves—all those lovely exaggerated sound-sequences and that big spoofing tone."

"Is all that—whatever it is—enough excuse for writing nonsense-syllables?"

"Ask Lewis Carroll," says the Poet. "But the fact is they're not nonsense syllables. Note the title. A bantam may certainly be taken as a pretentious and pompous bird strutting around in his half-pint ego as if he owned the world, and refusing to be dwarfed even by pine woods . . ."

"I'm still lost in the Azcan ashcan. And at this point I've had enough of your symbol-threading."

"But the Azcan business is a fact from the world," says the Poet. "Have you ever looked into a pedigree book? I assume this to be a pure-bred bantam and that he is registered as Chieftain Iffucan of Azcan. Stevens begins by reporting the fact, obviously relishing its pretentiousness. 'Caftan' is his first 'poetic' addition. But note this: a caftan is a garment that hangs down just about the way the leg-feathers of a bantam do. The detail is physically right. And the sound of the word itself is exactly right for the sound-sequence Stevens builds. That's always a sign of the poet—the ability to do more than one thing at once and to have his choices come out equally right on all levels."

The Citizen sits thoughtfully, turning it over in his mind. The Poet, watching the Citizen, once more has the impression of a painful fair-mindedness at work. Somehow that sense depresses him. He has a vision of the Citizen laboring to be open-minded and forever lost to the real life of the poem.

"I have to conclude that you're right," says the Citizen. "But I also know I could never have seen it that way. And I still don't understand the poem."

"Nor do I, completely," confesses the Poet. "But what of it? I don't understand 'Kubla Khan' nor 'Tiger, Tiger.' Not in detail. But I can certainly experience them as poems. I can, to put it metaphorically, identify their emotional frequencies and the areas into which they transmit."

The Citizen is not satisfied. "I'm still thinking of this Iffucan of Azcan business. There I bogged down on a detail I did not recognize. And perhaps I'll never be any better at identifying odd details. But what about the poem that comes right after it? This one—'Anecdote of the Jar.' Now there is a poem I spent a lot of time on and although I understand every word and every sentence, I'm blessed if I know what Stevens is talking about." He reads it over:

I placed a jar in Tennessee,
And round it was, upon a hill.
It made the slovenly wilderness
Surround that hill.

The wilderness rose up to it,
And sprawled around, no longer wild.
The jar was round upon the ground
And tall and of a port in air.

It took dominion everywhere.
The jar was gray and bare.
It did not give of bird or bush,
Like nothing else in Tennessee.

The Citizen finishes reading and looks up. "I was bothered at first by 'port,'" he says, "but I checked the word in the dictionary and I think I see what he's doing with it. But how am I supposed to understand 'It made the slovenly wilderness surround that hill'? How can a jar make a wilderness surround a hill? The wilderness was already surrounding the hill, and long before Stevens and his jar came along."

"In a sense, yes," says the Poet, "but only in the most usual prose-sense. Poetry constantly makes over that usual sense of things. The jar is a made-form; as such it stands for all artifice. The wilderness is nature as-it-happens, the opposite of made-form. But to 'surround' is 'to take position around a center.' And what is formless has no center. It is human artifice, the assertion of human artifice, that puts a center to the wilderness. Because the wilderness is formless it still 'sprawls' but now it sprawls 'up to' the jar. It approaches form, that is, and therefore it 'is no longer wild.' "

"Wait a minute," says the Citizen, "aren't you the one who is doing the paraphrasing now?"

"Yes, surely. I have no quarrel with paraphrase: only with paraphrase as a substitute for the poem. I am not trying to say 'this is what the poem comes to.' Far from it. I am trying to point out the symbolic areas in which the poem moves. The two poles of Stevens's thought seem clearly enough to be 'artifice' and 'formless nature.' Why shouldn't those poles be identified? But the poles are not the poem. The poem is much better seen as those poles plus the force-field they create."

"That does it!" says the Citizen and slams the book shut. "Symbolic areas, force-fields, artifice versus formless-nature—what is all this jargon? Didn't you write once that a poem is an emotion or nothing?"

"I certainly did."

"Then tell me how on earth I am supposed to get an emotion from this sort of haywire theorizing?"

The Poet smiles sadly. "I'm about ready to grant you that all criticism is in fact haywire, but would you grant me that criticism is not the poem? At that, one can still rig a weather-vane out of haywire, and that vane can point to the weather. The poem is not the vane, nor is it the haywire from which the vane is improvised: the poem is the weather that is pointed-to.

"Stevens, as it happens, had very strong feelings about form versus the formless. Those feelings crowd all his poems. They are fundamental to his very sense of reality. His emotions, to be sure, are intellectual things. If you refuse to think a sense of esthetic-reality as opposed to some other more common ideas of reality is worth an emotion, you are breaking no law but Stevens is obviously not for you. And that, I find myself thinking, is your loss rather than his."

"Maybe so," says the Citizen, but now he is sitting up as if squared for battle. "I'll even say he is obviously not for me. Who *is* he for? I'm the one who brought up Stevens, and I'll grant he may be a special case. But Stevens is not the only one who is obviously not for me. Who *are* you modern poets for? Is there no such thing as an audience?"

This charge, too, is a familiar one to the Poet.

"You've fired a lot of questions," he says, "and a full answer would call for a long sermon. Let me try the short form.

"What is the idea of 'the audience'? Is it enough to argue 'I have bought this book of poems and therefore I have certain audience-rights'? I think, first, one must distinguish between two ideas of 'the audience.'

"One idea may be called the horizontal audience and the other the vertical audience. The horizontal audience consists of everybody who is alive at this moment. The vertical audience consists of everyone, vertically through time, who will ever read a given poem.

"Isn't it immediately obvious that Stevens can only 'be for' a tiny percentage of the horizontal audience? Even Frost, who is the most seemingly-clear and the most widely loved of our good poets, certainly does not reach more than a small percentage of the total population, or even of that part of the population that thinks of itself as literate—as at least literate enough to buy a best-seller. The fact is that no horizontal audience since the age of folk-poetry has been much interested in good poetry. And you may be sure that a few spokesmen sounding off in the name of that horizontal audience are not going to persuade the poets.

"All good poets write for the vertical audience. The vertical audience for Dante, for example, is now six centuries old. And it is growing. If the human race has any luck at all, part of Dante's audience is still thousands of years short of being born.

"Now try a flight of fancy. Imagine that you held an election tomorrow and asked the horizontal audience to vote for Dante as opposed to Eddie Guest. Guest would certainly swamp Dante in such an election. More people in the horizontal audience have read Guest and even, God save the mark, been moved by him—if only to their own inanition. But moved, nevertheless. And we're a democracy, aren't we? The majority rules: bless the majority?

"Not in art. Not horizontally at least. The verdict in art is vertical. Take the idea of majority vote a step further. Imagine that you held the same election on Judgment Day, calling for a total vote of the human race down through time. Can you fail to believe that Dante would then swamp Eddie Guest plus all the horizontalists from Robert Service to Carl Sandburg?

"The point is that the horizontal audience always outnumbers the vertical at any one moment, but that the vertical audience for good poetry always outnumbers the horizontal in time-enough. And not only for the greatest poets. Andrew Marvell is certainly a minor poet, but given time enough, more people certainly will have read 'To His Coy Mistress' than will ever have subscribed to *Time, Life,* and *Fortune.* Compared to what a good poem can do, Luce is a piker at getting circulation."

"Impressive, if true," says the Citizen, "but how does any given poet get his divine sense of this vertical audience?"

"By his own ideal projection of his own best sense of himself. It's as simple as that," says the Poet. "He may be wrong, but he has nothing else to go by. And there is one thing more: all good poets are difficult when their work is new. And their work always becomes less difficult as their total shape becomes more and more visible. As that shape impresses itself upon time, one begins to know how to relate the parts to their total. Even Keats and Shelley confounded their contemporary critics as 'too difficult' and 'not for me'."

The Citizen throws his hands up. "All right, all right: I've been out-talked. But who *does* write for me?"

The Poet spread his hands palms out. "Keats and Shelley—now that they have lost their first difficulty."

"And are dead enough?" says the Citizen. "Well, may be. But why is it so impossible for *you* to think about writing for me? I'm willing to give it a try."

The Poet shrugs. "The sort of try you gave Stevens? But no matter. The point is why *should* I write for you?—you're going to be dead the next time anyone looks. We all are for that matter. But not the poem. Not if it's made right. If I make it for you I have to take the chance that it will die with you. I'm not sure you're that good an investment. Besides which, I have to invest in myself. If we happen to share some of the same sense of poetry, it may work out that I do happen to write for you. But that would be a happy bonus at best. I still cannot think of you as a main investment—not till you show a better 'vertical-sense'."

"We who are about to die," says the Citizen, "salute the poems we cannot grasp. Is that it?"

"Like nothing else in Tennessee," says the Poet bowing.

Comments and Questions

In "Poetry: Preliminaries" (p. 236) we have stated that understanding is basic to one's enjoyment of a poem—or of any work of art. We have suggested that a reader is wise to fix in his mind the literal statement of a poem as a necessary basis for realizing or comprehending all the poem has to offer. We have insisted that a poem is a whole and that a part should never be taken for the whole. If these things be true, it follows that areas of obscurity make it impossible to be sure—or even reasonably sure—what a poem is. Frustration results and frustration is uncomfortable.

1. How does Mr. Ciardi view this matter of alleged obscurity in modern poetry? He mentions "momentary obscurity" and "areas of immediate clarity." He seems pleased to be able to explain certain lines and also pleased when he cannot. Of the phrase "milky lines," he is "unsure" but says he welcomes such uncertainty. A bit later he says, "I am left puzzled. But I am left considerably richer." Does Mr. Ciardi make clear where this enrichment comes from? Discuss.

2. What does the phrase "personal idiom" mean?

3. Would you say Mr. Ciardi is trying to make the point that there are poets and that everybody else is not-a-poet? Discuss.

4. Explain the distinction made between the *horizontal* and the *vertical audience.* Comment on this use of words. For what the author intends, could these terms be reversed? Discuss the statement: "All good poets write for the vertical audience." List some "good poets" and try to determine what seems to have been their attitude towards the horizontal audience. You may wish to consider Shakespeare, Pope, Byron, Tennyson, Browning, Frost, T. S. Eliot, among many others.

5. Mr. Ciardi's Poet: "The point is why *should* I write for you [the Citizen]?" Perhaps you will wish to answer this question. Also, compare the last paragraph of Auden's "Reading" (p. 817).

6. Make a careful comparison of Spender's "On Teaching Modern Poetry," p. 837 and this essay of Ciardi's.

Notes for a Hypothetical Novel: An Address

JAMES BALDWIN
1924–

We've been talking about writing for the last two days, which is a very reckless thing to do, so that I shall be absolutely reckless tonight and pretend that I'm writing a novel in your presence. I'm going to ramble on a little tonight about my own past, not as though it were my own past exactly, but as a subject for fiction. I'm doing this in a kind of halting attempt to relate the terms of my experience to yours; and to find out what specific principle, if any, unites us in spite of the obvious disparities, some of which are superficial and some of which are profound, and most of which are entirely misunderstood. We'll come back to that, in any case, this misunderstanding, I mean, in a minute, but I want to warn you that I'm not pretending to be unbiased. I'm certain that there is something which unites all the Americans in this room, though I can't say what it is. But if I were to meet any one of you in some other country, England, Italy, France, or Spain, it would be at once apparent to everybody else, though it might not be to us, that we had something in common which scarcely any other people, or no other people could really share.

Let's pretend that I want to write a novel concerning the people or some of the people with whom I grew up, and since we are only playing let us pretend it's a very long novel. I want to follow a group of lives almost from the time they open their eyes on the world until some point of resolution, say, marriage, or childbirth, or death. And I want to impose myself on these people as little as possible. That means that I do not want to tell them or the reader what principle their lives illustrate, or what principle is activating their lives, but by examining their lives I hope to be able to make them convey to me and to the reader what their lives mean.

Now I know that this is not altogether possible. I mean that I know that my people are controlled by my point of view and that by the time I begin the novel I have some idea of what I want the novel to do, or to say, or to be. But just the same, whatever my point of view is and whatever my intentions, because I am an American writer my subject and my material inevitably has to be a handful of incoherent people in an incoherent country. And I don't mean incoherent in any light sense, and later on we'll talk about what I mean when I use that word.

Well, who are these people who fill my past and seem to clamor to be expressed? I was born on a very wide avenue in Harlem, and in those days that part of town was called The Hollow and now it's called Junkie's Hollow. The time was the 1920's, and as I was coming into the world there was something going on called The Negro Renaissance; and the most distinguished survivor of that time is Mr. Langston Hughes. This Negro Renaissance is an elegant term which means that white people had then discovered that Negroes could act and write as well as sing and dance and this Renaissance was not destined to last very long. Very shortly there was to be a depression and the artistic Negro, or the noble savage, was to give way to the militant or the new Negro; and I want to point out something in passing which I think is worth our time to look at, which is this: that the country's image of the Negro, which hasn't very much to do with the Negro, has never failed to reflect with a kind of frightening accuracy the state of mind of the country. This was the Jazz Age you will remember. It was the epoch of F. Scott Fitzgerald, Josephine Baker had just gone to France, Mussolini had just come to power in Italy, there was a peculiar man in Germany who was plotting and writing, and the lord knows what Lumumba's mother was thinking. And all of these things and a million more which are now known to the novelist, but not to his people, are to have a terrible effect on their lives.

There's a figure I carry in my mind's eye to this day and I don't know why. He can't really be the first person I remember, but he seems to be, apart from my mother and my father, and this is a man about as old perhaps as I am now who's coming up our street, very drunk, falling-down drunk, and it must have been a Saturday and I was sitting in the window. It must have been winter because I remember he had a black overcoat on—because his overcoat was open —and he's stumbling past one of those high, iron railings with spikes on top, and he falls and he bumps his head against one of these railings, and blood comes down his face, and there are kids behind him and they're tormenting him and laughing at him. And that's all I remember and I don't know why. But I only throw him in to dramatize this fact, that however solemn we writers, or myself, I, may sometimes sound, or how pontifical I may sometimes seem to be, on that level from which any genuine work of the imagination springs, I'm really, and we all are, absolutely helpless and ignorant. But this figure is important because he's going to appear in my novel. He can't be kept out of it. He occupies too large a place in my imagination.

And then, of course, I remember the church people because I was practically born in the church, and I seem to have spent most of the time that I was helpless sitting on someone's lap in the church and being beaten over the head whenever I fell asleep, which was usually. I was frightened of all those brothers and sisters of the church because they were all powerful, I thought they were. And I had one ally, my brother, who was a very undependable ally because sometimes I got beaten for things he did and sometimes he got beaten for things I did. But we were united in our hatred for the deacons and the deaconesses and the shouting sisters and of our father. And one of the reasons for this is that we were always hungry and he was always inviting those people over to the house on Sunday for an enormous banquet and we sat next to the icebox in the kitchen watching all those hams, and chickens, and biscuits go down those righteous bellies, which had no bottom.

Now so far, in this hypothetical sketch of an unwritten and probably unwritable novel, so good. From what we've already sketched we can begin to anticipate one of those long, warm, toasty novels. You know, those novels in which the novelist is looking back on himself, absolutely infatuated with himself as a child and everything is in sentimentality. But I think we ought to bring ourselves up short because we don't need another version of *A Tree Grows in Brooklyn* and we can do without another ver-

sion of *The Heart Is a Lonely Hunter*. This hypothetical book is aiming at something more implacable than that. Because no matter how ridiculous this may sound, that unseen prisoner in Germany is going to have an effect on the lives of these people. Two Italians are going to be executed presently in Boston, there's going to be something called the Scottsboro case which will give the Communist party hideous opportunities. In short, the social realities with which these people, the people I remember, whether they knew it or not, were really contending can't be left out of the novel without falsifying their experience. And—this is very important—this all has something to do with the sight of that tormented, falling down, drunken, bleeding man I mentioned at the beginning. Who is he and what does he mean?

Well, then I remember, principally I remember, the boys and girls in the streets. The boys and girls on the streets, at school, in the church. I remember in the beginning I only knew Negroes except for one Jewish boy, the only white boy in an all-Negro elementary school, a kind of survivor of another day in Harlem, and there was an Italian fruit vendor who lived next door to us who had a son with whom I fought every campaign of the Italian-Ethiopian war. Because, remember that we're projecting a novel, and Harlem is in the course of changing all the time, very soon there won't be any white people there, and this is also going to have some effect on the people in my story.

Well, more people now. There was a boy, a member of our church, and he backslid, which means he achieved a sex life and started smoking cigarettes, and he was therefore rejected from the community in which he had been brought up, because Harlem is also reduced to communities. And I've always believed that one of the reasons he died was because of this rejection. In any case, eighteen months after he was thrown out of the church he was dead of tuberculosis.

And there was a girl, who was a nice girl. She was a niece of one of the deaconesses. In fact, she was my girl. We were very young then, we were going to get married and we were always singing, praying and shouting, and we thought we'd live that way forever. But one day she was picked up in a nightgown on Lenox Avenue screaming and cursing and they carried her away to an institution where she still may be.

And by this time I was a big boy, and there were the friends of my brothers, my younger brothers and sisters. And I had danced to Duke Ellington, but they were dancing to Charlie Parker; and I had learned how to drink gin and whisky, but they were involved with marijuana and the needle. I will not really insist upon continuing this roster. I have not known many survivors. I know mainly about disaster, but then I want to remind you again of that man I mentioned in the beginning, who haunts the imagination of this novelist. The imagination of a novelist has everything to do with what happens to his material.

Now, we're a little beyond the territory of Betty Smith and Carson McCullers, but we are not quite beyond the territory of James T. Farrell or Richard Wright. Let's go a little bit farther. By and by I left Harlem. I left all those deaconesses, all those sisters, and all those churches, and all those tambourines, and I entered or anyway I encountered the white world. Now this white world which I was just encountering was, just the same, one of the forces that had been controlling me from the time I opened my eyes on the world. For it is important to ask, I think, where did these people I'm talking about come from and where did they get their peculiar school of ethics? What was its origin? What did it mean to them? What did it come out of? What function did it serve and why was it happening here? And why were they living where they were and what was it doing to them? All these things which sociologists think they can find out and haven't managed to do, which no chart can tell us. People are not, though in our age we seem to think so, endlessly manipulable. We think that once one has discovered that thirty thousand, let us say, Negroes, Chinese or Puerto Ricans or whatever have syphilis or don't, or are unemployed or not, that we've discovered something about the Negroes, Chinese or Puerto Ricans. But in fact, this is not so. In fact, we've discovered nothing very useful because people *cannot* be handled in that way.

Anyway, in the beginning I thought that the white world was very different from the world I was moving out of and I turned out to be entirely wrong. It seemed different. It seemed safer, at least the white people seemed safer. It seemed cleaner, it seemed more polite, and, of course, it seemed much richer from the material point of view. But I didn't meet anyone in that world who didn't suffer from the very same affliction that all the people I had fled from suffered from and that was that they didn't know who they were. They wanted to be something that they were not. And very shortly I didn't know who I was, either. I could not be certain whether I was really rich or really poor, really black or really white, really male or really female, really talented or a fraud, really strong or merely stubborn. In short, I had become an American. I had stepped into, I had walked right into, as I inevitably had to do, the bottomless confusion which is both public and private, of the American republic.

Now we've brought this hypothetical hero to this place, now what are we going to do with him, what does all of this mean, what can we make it mean? What's the thread that unites all these peculiar and disparate lives, whether it's from Idaho to San Francisco, from Idaho to New York, from Boston to Birmingham? Because there is something that unites all of these people and places. What does it mean to be an American? What nerve is pressed in you or me when we hear this word?

Earlier I spoke about the disparities and I said I was going to try and give an example of what I meant. Now the most obvious thing that would seem to divide me from the rest of my countrymen is the fact of color. The fact of color has a relevance objectively and some relevance in some other way, some emotional relevance and not only for the South. I mean that it persists as a problem in American life because it means something, it fulfills something in the American personality. It is here because the Americans in some peculiar way believe or think they need it. Maybe we can find out what it is that this problem fulfils in the American personality, what it corroborates and in what way this peculiar thing, until today, helps Americans to feel safe.

When I spoke about incoherence I said I'd try to tell you what I meant by that word. It's a kind of incoherence that occurs, let us say, when I am frightened, I am absolutely frightened to death, and there's something which is happening or about to happen that I don't want to face, or, let us say, which is an even better example, that I have a friend who has just murdered his mother and put her in the closet and I know it, but we're not going to talk about it. Now this means very shortly since, after all, I know the corpse is in the closet, and he knows I know it, and we're sitting around having a few drinks and trying to be buddy-buddy together, that very shortly, we can't talk about anything because we can't talk about that. No matter what I say I may inadvertently stumble on this corpse. And this incoherence which seems to afflict this country is analogous to that. I mean that in order to have a conversation with someone you have to reveal yourself. In order to have a real relationship with somebody you have got to take the risk of being thought, God forbid, "an oddball." You know, you have to take a chance which in some peculiar way we don't seem willing to take. And this is very serious in that it is not so much a writer's problem, that is to say, I don't want to talk about it from the point of view of a writer's problem, because, after all, you didn't ask me to become a writer, but it seems to me that the situation of the writer in this country is symptomatic and reveals, says something, very terrifying about this country. If I were writing hypothetically about a Frenchman I would have in a way a frame of reference and a point of view and in fact it is easier to write about Frenchmen, comparatively speaking, because they interest me so much less. But to try to deal with the American experience, that is to say to deal with this enormous incoherence, these enormous puddings, this shapeless thing, to try and make an American, well listen to them, and try to put that on a page. The truth about dialogue, for example, or the technical side of it, is that you try and make people say what they would say if they could and then you sort of dress it up to look like speech. That is to say that it's really an absolute height, people don't ever talk the way they talk in novels, but I've got to make you believe they do because I can't possibly do a tape recording.

But to try and find out what Americans mean is almost impossible because there are so many things they do not want to face. And not only the Negro thing which is simply the most obvious and perhaps the simplest example, but on the level of private life which is after all where we have to get to in order to write about any-

thing and also the level we have to get to in order to live, it seems to me that the myth, the illusion, that this is a free country, for example, is disastrous. Let me point out to you that freedom is not something that anybody can be given; freedom is something people take and people are as free as they want to be. One hasn't got to have an enormous military machine in order to be unfree when it's simpler to be asleep, when it's simpler to be apathetic, when it's simpler, in fact, not to want to be free, to think that something else is more important. And I'm not using freedom now so much in a political sense as I'm using it in a personal sense. It seems to me that the confusion is revealed, for example, in those dreadful speeches by Eisenhower, those incredible speeches by Nixon, they sound very much, after all, like the jargon of the Beat generation, that is, in terms of clarity. Not a pin to be chosen between them, both levels, that is, the highest level presumably, the administration in Washington, and the lowest level in our national life, the people who are called "beatniks" are both involved in saying that something which is really on their heels does not exist. Jack Kerouac says "Holy, holy" and we say Red China does not exist. But it really does. I'm simply trying to point out that it's the symptom of the same madness.

Now, in some way, somehow, the problem the writer has which is, after all, his problem and perhaps not yours is somehow to unite these things, to find the terms of our connection, without which we will perish. The importance of a writer is continuous; I think it's socially debatable and usually socially not terribly rewarding, but that's not the point; his importance, I think, is that he is here to describe things which other people are too busy to describe. It is a function, let's face it, it's a special function. There is no democracy on this level. It's a very difficult thing to do, it's a very special thing to do and people who do it cannot by that token do many other things. But their importance is, and the importance of writers in this country now is this, that this country is yet to be discovered in any real sense. There is an illusion about America, a myth about America to which we are clinging which has nothing to do with the lives we lead and I don't believe that anybody in this country who has really thought about it or really almost anybody who has been brought up against it—and almost all of us have one way or another—this collision between one's image of oneself and what one actually is is always very painful and there are two things you can do about it, you can meet the collision head-on and try and become what you really are or you can retreat and try to remain what you thought you were, which is a fantasy, in which you will certainly perish. Now, I don't want to keep you any longer. But I'd like to leave you with this, I think we have some idea about reality which is not quite true. Without having anything whatever against Cadillacs, refrigerators or all the paraphernalia of American life, I yet suspect that there is something much more important and much more real which produces the Cadillac, refrigerator, atom bomb, and what produces it, after all, is something which we don't seem to want to look at, and that is the person. A country is only as good—I don't care now about the Constitution and the laws, at the moment let us leave these things aside —a country is only as strong as the people who make it up and the country turns into what the people want it to become. Now, this country is going to be transformed. It will not be transformed by an act of God, but by all of us, by you and me. I don't believe any longer that we can afford to say that it is entirely out of our hands. We made the world we're living in and we have to make it over.

Comments and Questions

1. Note the informality, as though the speaker really does intend "to ramble on a little." Compare Frost's "An Extemporaneous Talk for Students," p. 806. What advantages are gained by the casual approach? Is is disarming? Does this essay ramble? Explain.

2. For the hypothetical novel, Baldwin says, "I want to impose myself on these people [characters] as little as possible." Comment.

3. Explain the term, "noble savage." When did it come into use and how did it serve what philosophical concept?

4. What sort of symbolism does the author see in the "tormented, falling down, drunken, bleeding man"? Does he equate this figure with the human experience? Discuss.

5. Carlyle invented a term: "organic filaments." By this term he meant fibers which organically connect all persons and objects on earth so intimately that nothing can happen to anybody, anywhere, which does not affect everybody, everywhere. Baldwin asks: "What's the thread that unites all these peculiar and disparate lives?" Is the answer, or attempted answer, to this question to be the theme of the hypothetical novel?

6. D. H. Lawrence once observed that "the mass of men have only the tiniest touch of individuality, if any." (See p. 875.) If this is true, what becomes of Baldwin's novel, of his "peculiar and disparate lives"? Discuss carefully.

The Tragic Fallacy
JOSEPH WOOD KRUTCH
1893–1970

. . . Tragedy, said Aristotle, is the "imitation of noble actions," and though it is some twenty-five hundred years since the dictum was uttered there is only one respect in which we are inclined to modify it. To us "imitation" seems a rather naïve word to apply to that process by which observation is turned into art, and we seek one which would define or at least imply the nature of that interposition of the personality of the artist between the object and the beholder which constitutes his function and by means of which he transmits a modified version, rather than a mere imitation, of the thing which he has contemplated.

In the search for this word the aestheticians of romanticism invented the term "expression" to describe the artistic purpose to which apparent imitation was subservient. Psychologists, on the other hand, feeling that the artistic process was primarily one by which reality is modified in such a way as to render it more acceptable to the desires of the artist, employed various terms in the effort to describe that distortion which the wish may produce in vision. And though many of the newer critics reject both romanticism and psychology, even they insist upon the fundamental fact that in art we are concerned, not with mere imitation but with the imposition of some form upon the material which it would not have if it were merely copied as a camera copies.

Tragedy is not, then, as Aristotle said, the *imitation* of noble actions, for, indeed, no one knows what a *noble* action is or whether or not such a thing as nobility exists in nature apart from the mind of man. Certainly the action of Achilles in dragging the dead body of Hector around the walls of Troy and under the eyes of Andromache, who had begged to be allowed to give it decent burial, is not to us a noble action, though it was such to Homer, who made it the subject of a noble passage in a noble poem. Certainly, too, the same action might conceivably be made the subject of a tragedy and the subject of a farce, depending upon the way in which it was treated; so that to say that tragedy is the *imitation* of a *noble* action is to be guilty of assuming, first, that art and photography are the same and, second, that there may be something inherently noble in an act as distinguished from the motives which prompted it or from the point of view from which it is regarded.

And yet, nevertheless, the idea of nobility is inseparable from the idea of tragedy, which cannot exist without it. If tragedy is not the imitation or even the modified representation of noble actions it is certainly a representation of actions *considered* as noble, and herein lies its essential nature, since no man can conceive it unless he is capable of believing in the greatness and importance of man. Its action is usually, if not always, calamitous, because it is only in calamity that the human spirit has the opportunity to reveal itself triumphant over the outward universe which fails to conquer it; but this calamity in tragedy is only a means to an end and the essential thing which distinguishes real tragedy from those distressing modern works sometimes called by its name is the fact that it is in the former alone that the artist has found himself capable of considering and of making us consider that his people and his actions have that amplitude and importance which make them noble. Tragedy arises then when, as in Periclean Greece or Elizabethan England, a people fully aware of the calamities of life is nevertheless serenely confident of the greatness of man, whose mighty passions and supreme fortitude are revealed when one of these calamities overtakes him.

To those who mistakenly think of it as something gloomy or depressing, who are incapable of recognizing the elation which its celebration of human greatness inspires, and who, therefore, confuse it with things merely miserable or pathetic, it must be a paradox that the happiest, most vigorous, and most confident ages which the world has ever known—the Periclean and the Elizabethan—should be exactly those which created and which most relished the mightiest tragedies; but the paradox is, of course, resolved by the fact that tragedy is essentially an expression, not of despair, but of the triumph over despair and of confidence in the value of human life. If Shakespeare himself ever had that "dark period" which his critics and biographers have imagined for him, it was at least no darkness like that bleak and arid despair which sometimes settles over modern spirits. In the midst of it he created both the elemental grandeur of Othello and the pensive majesty of Hamlet and, holding them up to his contemporaries, he said in the words of his own Miranda, "Oh, rare new world that hath *such* creatures in it."

All works of art which deserve their name have a happy end. This is indeed the thing which constitutes them art and through which they perform their function. Whatever the character of the events, fortunate or unfortunate, which they recount, they so mold or arrange or interpret them that we accept gladly the conclusion which they reach and would not have it otherwise. They may conduct us into the realm of pure fancy where wish and fact are identical and the world is remade exactly after the fashion of the heart's desire or they may yield some greater or less allegiance to fact; but they must always reconcile us in one way or another to the representation which they make and the distinctions between the genres are simply the distinctions between the means by which this reconciliation is effected.

Comedy laughs the minor mishaps of its characters away; drama solves all the difficulties which it allows to arise; and melodrama, separating good from evil by simple lines, distributes its rewards and punishments in accordance with the principles of a naïve justice which satisfies the simple souls of its audience, which are neither philosophical enough to question its primitive ethics nor critical enough to object to the way in which its neat events violate the laws of probability. Tragedy, the greatest and the most difficult of the arts, can adopt none of these methods; and yet it must reach its own happy end in its own way. Though its conclusion must be, by its premise, outwardly calamitous, though it must speak to those who know that the good man is cut off and that the fairest things are the first to perish, yet it must leave them, as *Othello* does, content that this is so. We must be and we are glad that Juliet dies and glad that Lear is turned out into the storm.

Milton set out, he said, to justify the ways of God to man, and his phrase, if it be interpreted broadly enough, may be taken as describing the function of all art, which must, in some way or other, make the life which it seems to represent satisfactory to those who see its reflection in the magic mirror, and it must gratify or at least reconcile the desires of the beholder, not necessarily, as the naïver exponents of Freudian psychology maintain, by gratifying individual and often eccentric wishes, but at least by satisfying the universally human desire to find in the world some justice, some meaning, or, at the very least, some recognizable order. Hence it is that every real tragedy, however tremendous it may be, is an affirmation of faith in life, a declaration that even if God is not in his Heaven, then at least Man is in his world.

We accept gladly the outward defeats which it describes for the sake of the inward victories which it reveals. Juliet died, but not before she had shown how great and resplendent a thing love could be; Othello plunged the dagger into his own breast, but not before he had revealed that greatness of soul which makes his death seem unimportant. Had he died in the instant when he struck the blow, had he perished still believing that the world was as completely black as he saw it before the innocence of Desdemona was revealed to him, then, for him at least, the world would have been merely damnable, but Shakespeare kept him alive long enough to allow him to learn his error and hence to die, not in despair, but in the full acceptance of the tragic reconciliation to life. Perhaps it would be pleasanter if men could believe what the child is taught—that the good are happy and that things turn out as they should—but it is far more important to be able to believe, as Shakespeare did, that however much things in the outward world may go awry, man has, never-

theless, splendors of his own and that, in a word, Love and Honor and Glory are not words but realities.

Thus for the great ages tragedy is not an expression of despair but the means by which they saved themselves from it. It is a profession of faith, and a sort of religion; a way of looking at life by virtue of which it is robbed of its pain. The sturdy soul of the tragic author seizes upon suffering and uses it only as a means by which joy may be wrung out of existence, but it is not to be forgotten that he is enabled to do so only because of his belief in the greatness of human nature and because, though he has lost the child's faith in life, he has not lost his far more important faith in human nature. A tragic writer does not have to believe in God, but he must believe in man.

And if, then, the Tragic Spirit is in reality the product of a religious faith in which, sometimes at least, faith in the greatness of God is replaced by faith in the greatness of man, it serves, of course, to perform the function of religion, to make life tolerable for those who participate in its beneficent illusion. It purges the souls of those who might otherwise despair and it makes endurable the realization that the events of the outward world do not correspond with the desires of the heart, and thus, in its own particular way, it does what all religions do, for it gives a rationality, a meaning, and a justification to the universe. But if it has the strength it has also the weakness of all faiths, since it may—nay, it must—be ultimately lost as reality, encroaching further and further into the realm of imagination, leaving less and less room in which the imagination can build its refuge.

It is, indeed, only at a certain stage in the development of the realistic intelligence of a people that the tragic faith can exist. A naïver people may have, as the ancient men of the north had, a body of legends which are essentially tragic, or it may have only (and need only) its happy and childlike mythology which arrives inevitably at its happy end, where the only ones who suffer "deserve" to do so and in which, therefore, life is represented as directly and easily acceptable. A too sophisticated society on the other hand —one which, like ours, has outgrown not merely the simple optimism of the child but also that vigorous, one might almost say adolescent, faith in the nobility of man which marks a Sophocles or a Shakespeare—has neither fairy tales to assure it that all is always right in the end nor tragedies to make it believe that it rises superior in soul to the outward calamities which befall it.

Distrusting its thought, despising its passions, realizing its impotent unimportance in the universe, it can tell itself no stories except those which make it still more acutely aware of its trivial miseries. When its heroes (sad misnomer for the pitiful creatures who people contemporary fiction) are struck down it is not, like Oedipus, by the gods that they are struck but only, like Oswald Alving, by syphilis, for they know that the gods, even if they existed, would not trouble with them, and they cannot attribute to themselves in art an importance in which they do not believe. Their so-called tragedies do not and cannot end with one of those splendid calamities which in Shakespeare seem to reverberate through the universe, because they cannot believe that the universe trembles when their love is, like Romeo's, cut off or when the place where they (small as they are) have gathered up their trivial treasure is, like Othello's sanctuary, defiled. Instead, mean misery piles on mean misery, petty misfortune follows petty misfortune, and despair becomes intolerable because it is no longer even significant or important.

Ibsen once made one of his characters say that he did not read much because he found reading "irrelevant," and the adjective was brilliantly chosen because it held implications even beyond those of which Ibsen was consciously aware. What is it that made the classics irrelevant to him and to us? Is it not just exactly those to him impossible premises which make tragedy what it is, those assumptions that the soul of man is great, that the universe (together with whatever gods may be) concerns itself with him and that he is, in a word, noble? Ibsen turned to village politics for exactly the same reason that his contemporaries and his successors have, each in his own way, sought out some aspect of the common man and his common life—because, that is to say, here was at least something small enough for him to be able to believe.

Bearing this fact in mind, let us compare a modern "tragedy" with one of the great works of a happy age, not in order to judge of their relative technical merits but in order to determine to what extent the former deserves its name by achieving a tragic solution capable of purging the soul or of reconciling the emotions to the life which it pictures. And in order to make the comparison as fruitful as possible let us choose *Hamlet* on the one hand and on the other a play like *Ghosts* which was not only written by perhaps the most powerful as well as the most typical of modern writers but which is, in addition, the one of his works which seems most nearly to escape that triviality which cannot be entirely escaped by anyone who feels, as all contemporary minds do, that man is relatively trivial.

In *Hamlet* a prince ("in understanding, how like a god!") has thrust upon him from the unseen world a duty to redress a wrong which concerns not merely him, his mother, and his uncle, but the moral order of the universe. Erasing all trivial fond records from his mind, abandoning at once both his studies and his romance because it has been his good fortune to be called upon to take part in an action of cosmic importance, he plunges (at first) not into action but into thought, weighing the claims which are made upon him and contemplating the grandiose complexities of the universe. And when the time comes at last for him to die he dies, not as a failure, but as a success. Not only has the universe regained the balance which had been upset by what *seemed* the monstrous crime of the guilty pair ("there is nothing either good nor ill but thinking makes it so"), but in the process by which that readjustment is made a mighty mind has been given the opportunity, first to contemplate the magnificent scheme of which it is a part and then to demonstrate the greatness of its spirit by playing a rôle in the grand style which it called for. We do not need to despair in *such* a world if it has *such* creatures in it.

Turn now to *Ghosts*—look upon this picture and upon that. A young man has inherited syphilis from his father. Struck by a to him mysterious malady he returns to his northern village, learns the hopeless truth about himself, and persuades his mother to poison him. The incidents prove, perhaps, that pastors should not endeavor to keep a husband and wife together unless they know what they are doing. But what a world is this in which a great writer can deduce nothing more than that from his greatest work and how are we to be purged or reconciled when we see it acted? Not only is the failure utter, but it is trivial and meaningless as well.

Yet the journey from Elsinore to Skien is precisely the journey which the human spirit has made, exchanging in the process princes for invalids and gods for disease. We say, as Ibsen would say, that the problems of Oswald Alving are more "relevant" to our life than the problems of Hamlet, that the play in which he appears is more "real" than the other more glamorous one, but it is exactly because we find it so that we are condemned. We can believe in Oswald but we cannot believe in Hamlet, and a light has gone out in the universe. Shakespeare justifies the ways of God to man, but in Ibsen there is no such happy end and with him tragedy, so called, has become merely an expression of our despair at finding that such justification is no longer possible.

Modern critics have sometimes been puzzled to account for the fact that the concern of ancient tragedy is almost exclusively with kings and courts. They have been tempted to accuse even Aristotle of a certain naïveté in assuming (as he seems to assume) that the "nobility" of which he speaks as necessary to a tragedy implies a nobility of rank as well as of soul, and they have sometimes regretted that Shakespeare did not devote himself more than he did to the serious consideration of those common woes of the common man which subsequent writers have exploited with increasing pertinacity. Yet the tendency to lay the scene of a tragedy at the court of a king is not the result of any arbitrary convention but of the fact that the tragic writers believed easily in greatness just as we believe easily in meanness. To Shakespeare, robes and crowns and jewels are the garments most appropriate to man because they are the fitting outward manifestation of his inward majesty, but to us they seem absurd because the man who bears them has, in our estimation, so pitifully shrunk. We do not write about kings because we do not believe that any man is worthy to be one and we do not write about courts because hovels seem to us to be dwellings more appropriate to the creatures who inhabit them. Any modern attempt to dress characters in robes ends only by making us aware of a comic incongruity and any modern attempt to furnish them

with a language resplendent like Shakespeare's ends only in bombast.

True tragedy capable of performing its function and of purging the soul by reconciling man to his woes can exist only by virtue of a certain pathetic fallacy far more inclusive than that to which the name is commonly given. The romantics, feeble descendants of the tragic writers to whom they are linked by their effort to see life and nature in grandiose terms, loved to imagine that the sea or the sky had a way of according itself with their moods, of storming when they stormed and smiling when they smiled. But the tragic spirit sustains itself by an assumption much more farreaching and no more justified. Man as it sees him lives in a world which he may not dominate but which is always aware of him. Occupying the exact center of a universe which would have no meaning except for him and being so little below the angels that, if he believes in God, he has no hesitation in imagining Him formed as he is formed and crowned with a crown like that which he or one of his fellows wears, he assumes that each of his acts reverberates through the universe. His passions are important to him because he believes them important throughout all time and all space; the very fact that he can sin (no modern can) means that this universe is watching his acts; and though he may perish, a God leans out from infinity to strike him down. And it is exactly because an Ibsen cannot think of man in any such terms as these that his persons have so shrunk and that his "tragedy" has lost that power which real tragedy always has of making that infinitely ambitious creature called man content to accept his misery if only he can be made to feel great enough and important enough. An Oswald is not a Hamlet chiefly because he has lost that tie with the natural and supernatural world which the latter had. No ghost will leave the other world to warn or encourage him, there is no virtue and no vice which he can possibly have which can be really important, and when he dies neither his death nor the manner of it will be, outside the circle of two or three people as unnecessary as himself, any more important than that of a rat behind the arras.

Perhaps we may dub the illusion upon which the tragic spirit is nourished the Tragic, as opposed to the Pathetic, Fallacy, but fallacy though it is, upon its existence depends not merely the writing of tragedy but the existence of that religious feeling of which tragedy is an expression and by means of which a people aware of the dissonances of life manages nevertheless to hear them as harmony. Without it neither man nor his passions can seem great enough or important enough to justify the sufferings which they entail, and literature, expressing the mood of a people, begins to despair where once it had exulted. Like the belief in love and like most of the other mighty illusions by means of which human life has been given a value, the Tragic Fallacy depends ultimately upon the assumption which man so readily makes that something outside his own being, some "spirit not himself"—be it God, Nature, or that still vaguer thing called a Moral Order —joins him in the emphasis which he places upon this or that and confirms him in his feeling that his passions and his opinions are important. When his instinctive faith in that correspondence between the outer and the inner world fades, his grasp upon the faith that sustained him fades also, and Love or Tragedy or what not ceases to be the reality which it was because he is never strong enough in his own insignificant self to stand alone in a universe which snubs him with its indifference.

In both the modern and the ancient worlds tragedy was dead long before writers were aware of the fact. Seneca wrote his frigid melodramas under the impression that he was following in the footsteps of Sophocles, and Dryden probably thought that his *All for Love* was an improvement upon Shakespeare, but in time we awoke to the fact that no amount of rhetorical bombast could conceal the fact that grandeur was not to be counterfeited when the belief in its possibility was dead, and turning from the hero to the common man we inaugurated the era of realism. For us no choice remains except that between mere rhetoric and the frank consideration of our fellow men, who may be the highest of the anthropoids but who are certainly too far below the angels to imagine either that these angels can concern themselves with them or that they can catch any glimpse of even the soles of angelic feet. We can no longer tell tales of the fall of noble men because we do not believe that noble men exist. The best that we can achieve is pathos and the most that we can

do is to feel sorry for ourselves. Man has put off his royal robes and it is only in sceptered pomp that tragedy can come sweeping by.

Nietzsche was the last of the great philosophers to attempt a tragic justification of life. His central and famous dogma—"Life is good *because* it is painful"—sums up in a few words the desperate and almost meaningless paradox to which he was driven in his effort to reduce to rational terms the far more imaginative conception which is everywhere present but everywhere unanalyzed in a Sophocles or a Shakespeare and by means of which they rise triumphant over the manifold miseries of life. But the very fact that Nietzsche could not even attempt to state in any except intellectual terms an attitude which is primarily unintellectual and to which, indeed, intellectual analysis is inevitably fatal is proof of the distance which he had been carried (by the rationalizing tendencies of the human mind) from the possibility of the tragic solution which he sought; and the confused, half-insane violence of his work will reveal, by the contrast which it affords with the serenity of the tragic writers whom he admired, how great was his failure.

Fundamentally this failure was, moreover, conditioned by exactly the same thing which has conditioned the failure of all modern attempts to achieve what he attempted—by the fact, that is to say, that tragedy must have a hero if it is not to be merely an accusation against, instead of a justification of, the world in which it occurs. Tragedy is, as Aristotle said, an imitation of noble actions, and Nietzsche, for all his enthusiasm for the Greek tragic writers, was palsied by the universally modern incapacity to conceive man as noble. Out of this dilemma, out of his need to find a hero who could give to life as he saw it the only possible justification, was born the idea of the Superman, but the Superman is, after all, only a hypothetical being, destined to become what man actually was in the eyes of the great tragic writers—a creature (as Hamlet said) "how infinite in capacities, in understanding how like a god." Thus Nietzsche lived half in the past through his literary enthusiasms and half in the future through his grandiose dreams, but for all his professed determination to justify existence he was no more able than the rest of us to find the present acceptable. Life, he said in effect, is not a Tragedy now but perhaps it will be when the Ape-man has been transformed into a hero (the *Übermensch*), and trying to find that sufficient, he went mad.

He failed, as all moderns must fail when they attempt, like him, to embrace the tragic spirit as a religious faith, because the resurgence of that faith is not an intellectual but a vital phenomenon, something not achieved by taking thought but born, on the contrary, out of an instinctive confidence in life which is nearer to the animal's unquestioning allegiance to the scheme of nature than it is to that critical intelligence characteristic of a fully developed humanism. And like other faiths it is not to be recaptured merely by reaching an intellectual conviction that it would be desirable to do so.

Modern psychology has discovered (or at least strongly emphasized) the fact that under certain conditions desire produces belief, and having discovered also that the more primitive a given mentality the more completely are its opinions determined by its wishes, modern psychology has concluded that the best mind is that which most resists the tendency to believe a thing simply because it would be pleasant or advantageous to do so. But justified as this conclusion may be from the intellectual point of view, it fails to take into account the fact that in a universe as badly adapted as this one to human as distinguished from animal needs, this ability to will a belief may bestow an enormous vital advantage as it did, for instance, in the case at present under discussion where it made possible for Shakespeare the compensations of a tragic faith completely inaccessible to Nietzsche. Pure intelligence, incapable of being influenced by desire and therefore also incapable of choosing one opinion rather than another simply because the one chosen is the more fruitful or beneficent, is doubtless a relatively perfect instrument for the pursuit of truth, but the question (likely, it would seem, to be answered in the negative) is simply whether or not the spirit of man can endure the literal and inhuman truth.

Certain ages and simple people have conceived of the action which passes upon the stage of the universe as of something in the nature of a Divine Comedy, as something, that is to say, which will reach its end with the words "and they lived happily ever after." Others, less naïve and therefore more aware of those maladjustments whose reality, at least so far as outward events are concerned, they could not escape, have imposed upon it another artistic form and called it a Divine Tragedy, accepting its catastrophe as we accept the catastrophe of an *Othello,* because of its grandeur. But a Tragedy, Divine or otherwise, must, it may again be repeated, have a hero, and from the universe as we see it both the Glory of God and the Glory of Man have departed. Our cosmos may be farcical or it may be pathetic but it has not the dignity of tragedy and we cannot accept it as such.

Yet our need for the consolations of tragedy has not passed with the passing of our ability to conceive it. Indeed, the dissonances which it was tragedy's function to resolve grow more insistent instead of diminishing. Our passions, our disappointments, and our sufferings remain important to us though important to nothing else and they thrust themselves upon us with an urgency which makes it impossible for us to dismiss them as the mere trivialities which, so our intellects tell us, they are. And yet, in the absence of tragic faith or the possibility of achieving it, we have no way in which we may succeed in giving them the dignity which would not only render them tolerable but transform them as they were transformed by the great ages into joys. The death of tragedy is, like the death of love, one of those emotional fatalities as the result of which the human as distinguished from the natural world grows more and more a desert.

Poetry, said Santayana in his famous phrase, is "religion which is no longer believed," but it depends, nevertheless, upon its power to revive in us a sort of temporary or provisional credence and the nearer it can come to producing an illusion of belief the greater is its power as poetry. Once the Tragic Spirit was a living faith and out of it tragedies were written. Today these great expressions of a great faith have declined, not merely into poetry, but into a kind of poetry whose premises are so far from any we can really accept that we can only partially and dimly grasp its meaning.

We read but we do not write tragedies. The

tragic solution of the problem of existence, the reconciliation to life by means of the tragic spirit is, that is to say, now only a fiction surviving in art. When that art itself has become, as it probably will, completely meaningless, when we have ceased not only to write but to *read* tragic works, then it will be lost and in all real senses forgotten, since the devolution from Religion to Art to Document will be complete.

Comments and Questions

Krutch's essay examines, in the light of twentieth-century shabbiness of spirit, Aristotle's definition of tragedy as "the imitation of noble actions." "The Tragic Fallacy" was written before the Theater of the Absurd came into being and is both an explication of traditional dramatic values and an accounting for the modern neglect of those values. The essay may be profitably read in conjunction with Martin Esslin's "The Absurdity of the Absurd," next, because man's spiritual incapability, pinpointed by Krutch, may be seen to have reached its logical conclusion: the meaningless absurd.

1. If one recalls *Antigone* (p. 438) and *Othello* (p. 455), it is obvious that Sophocles and Shakespeare believed in "the greatness and importance of man." What of Ibsen? What does he believe about man as may be deduced from *An Enemy of the People* (p. 523)? What of Tennessee Williams (p. 602)? Is he devoid of a tragic sense?

2. Consider the falling away of man's confidence in the worth of man by examining this sequence of characters: Othello, Dr. Stockmann (*An Enemy of the People,* p. 523), the townsmen of Güllen (*The Visit,* p. 676), and Biedermann (*Biedermann and the Firebugs,* p. 709).

3. What may be made of the statement that "no modern can" sin? Why not? Discuss.

4. At what point does Krutch make clear what he means by the Tragic Fallacy? Does the author contend that man is in fact worthy of tragedy or simply that man is lost without this illusion?

5. Comment upon the final statement in this essay: "the devolution from Religion to Art to Document will be complete."

The Absurdity of the Absurd
MARTIN ESSLIN
1918–

In every art form today the effect of a dissonant world is manifest, but in no form so palpably as in drama. Pop art in sculpture, a current fad, may use junkyard materials which are welded into odd shapes to express, presumably, the sculptor's low estimate of life. Poetry, which broke away earlier from the traditional, now appears to be returning to its moorings. Stream-of-consciousness fiction possibly has had its day, and writers, though still obsessed with low life, are producing stories with beginning, middle, and end. With Ibsen, drama first became realistic, then with his successors the settings against which ordinary people exposed their ordinary problems became ultrarealistic. As Krutch has observed, society, as interpreted by many twentieth-century playwrights, is disillusioned, "distrusting its thought, despising its passions, realizing its impotent unimportance in the universe" and accepts, as a consequence, "no stories except those which make it more acutely aware of its trivial miseries." (See "The Tragic Fallacy," p. 858.)

Since Krutch made the foregoing observation, triviality has become absurdity. Martin Esslin in the following essay gives a perceptive account of the movement.

On November 19, 1957, a group of worried actors were preparing to face their audience. The actors were members of the company of the San Francisco Actors' Workshop. The audience consisted of fourteen hundred convicts at the San Quentin penitentiary. No live play had been performed at San Quentin since Sarah Bernhardt appeared there in 1913. Now, forty-four years later, the play that had been chosen, largely because no woman appeared in it, was Samuel Beckett's *Waiting for Godot.*

No wonder the actors and Herbert Blau, the director, were apprehensive. How were they to face one of the toughest audiences in the world with a highly obscure, intellectual play that had produced near riots among a good many highly sophisticated audiences in Western Europe? Herbert Blau decided to prepare the San Quentin audience for what was to come. He stepped onto the stage and addressed the packed, darkened North Dining Hall—a sea of flickering matches that the convicts tossed over their shoulders after lighting their cigarettes. Blau compared the play to a piece of jazz music "to which one must listen for whatever one may find in it." In the same way, he hoped, there would be some meaning, some personal significance for each member of the audience in *Waiting for Godot*.

The curtain parted. The play began. And what had bewildered the sophisticated audiences of Paris, London, and New York was immediately grasped by an audience of convicts. As the writer of "Memos of a First-Nighter" put it in the columns of the prison paper, the *San Quentin News*:

> The trio of muscle-men, biceps overflowing, who parked all 642 lbs on the aisle and waited for the girls and funny stuff. When this didn't appear they audibly fumed and audibly decided to wait until the house lights dimmed before escaping. They made one error. They listened and looked two minutes too long—and stayed. Left at the end. All shook . . .

Or as the writer of the lead story of the same paper reported, under the headline, "San Francisco Group Leaves S.Q. Audience Waiting for Godot":

> From the moment Robin Wagner's thoughtful and limbolike set was dressed with light, until the last futile and expectant handclasp was hesitantly activated between the two searching vagrants, the San Francisco company had its audience of captives in its collective hand. . . . Those that had felt a less controversial vehicle should be attempted as a first play here had their fears allayed a short five minutes after the Samuel Beckett piece began to unfold.

A reporter from the San Francisco *Chronicle* who was present noted that the convicts did not find it difficult to understand the play. One prisoner told him, "Godot is society." Said another: "He's the outside." A teacher at the prison was quoted as saying, "They know what is meant by waiting . . . and they knew if Godot finally came, he would only be a disappointment." The leading article of the prison paper showed how clearly the writer had understood the meaning of the play:

> It was an expression, symbolic in order to avoid all personal error, by an author who expected each member of his audience to draw his own conclusions, make his own errors. It asked nothing in point, it forced no dramatized moral on the viewer, it held out no specific hope. . . . We're still waiting for Godot, and shall continue to wait. When the scenery gets too drab and the action too slow, we'll call each other names and swear to part forever—but then, there's no place to go!

It is said that Godot himself, as well as turns of phrase and characters from the play, have since become a permanent part of the private language, the institutional mythology of San Quentin.

Why did a play of the supposedly esoteric avant-garde make so immediate and so deep an impact on an audience of convicts? Because it confronted them with a situation in some ways analogous to their own? Perhaps. Or perhaps because they were unsophisticated enough to come to the theatre without any preconceived notions and ready-made expectations, so that they avoided the mistake that trapped so many established critics who condemned the play for its lack of plot, development, characterization, suspense, or plain common sense. Certainly the prisoners of San Quentin could not be suspected of the sin of intellectual snobbery, for which a sizable proportion of the audiences of *Waiting for Godot* have often been reproached; of pretending to like a play they did not even begin to understand, just to appear in the know.

The reception of *Waiting for Godot* at San Quentin, and the wide acclaim plays by Ionesco, Adamov, Pinter, and others have received, testify that these plays, which are so often superciliously dismissed as nonsense or mystification, *have* something to say and *can* be understood. Most of the incomprehension with which plays of this type are still being received by critics and theatrical reviewers, most of the bewilderment they have caused and to which they still give rise, come from the fact that they are part of a new, and still developing stage convention that has not yet been generally understood and has hardly ever been defined. Inevitably, plays written in this new convention will, when judged by the standards and criteria of another, be regarded as impertinent and outrageous impostures. If a good play must have a cleverly constructed story, these have no story or plot to speak of; if a good play is judged by subtlety of characterization and motivation, these are often without recognizable characters and present the audience with almost mechanical puppets; if a good play has to have a fully explained theme, which is neatly exposed and finally solved, these often have neither a beginning nor an end; if a good play is to hold the mirror up to nature and portray the manners and mannerisms of the age in finely observed sketches, these seem often to be reflections of dreams and nightmares; if a good play relies on witty repartee and pointed dialogue, these often consist of incoherent babblings.

But the plays we are concerned with here pursue ends quite different from those of the conventional play and therefore use quite different methods. They can be judged only by the standards of the Theatre of the Absurd, which it is the purpose of this book to define and clarify.

It must be stressed, however, that the dramatists whose work is here presented and discussed under the generic heading of the Theatre of the Absurd do not form part of any self-proclaimed or self-conscious school or movement. On the contrary, each of the writers in question is an individual who regards himself as a lone outsider, cut off and isolated in his private world. Each has his own personal approach to both subject matter and form; his own roots, sources, and background. If they also, very clearly and in spite of themselves, have a good deal in common, it is because their work most sensitively mirrors and reflects the preoccupations and anxieties, the emotions and thinking of an important segment of their contemporaries in the Western world.

This is not to say that their works are representative of mass attitudes. It is an oversimplification to assume that any age presents a homogeneous pattern. Ours being, more than most others, an age of transition, it displays a bewilderingly stratified picture: medieval beliefs still held and overlaid by eighteenth-century rationalism and mid-nineteenth-century Marxism, rocked by sudden volcanic eruptions of prehistoric fanaticisms and primitive tribal cults. Each of these components of the cultural pattern of the age finds its characteristic artistic expression. The Theatre of the Absurd, how-

ever, can be seen as the reflection of what seems the attitude most genuinely representative of our own time's contribution.

The hallmark of this attitude is its sense that the certitudes and unshakable basic assumptions of former ages have been swept away, that they have been tested and found wanting, that they have been discredited as cheap and somewhat childish illusions. The decline of religious faith was masked until the end of the Second World War by the substitute religions of faith in progress, nationalism, and various totalitarian fallacies. All this was shattered by the war. By 1942, Albert Camus[1] was calmly putting the question why, since life had lost all meaning, man should not seek escape in suicide. In one of the great, seminal heart-searchings of our time, *The Myth of Sisyphus*, Camus tried to diagnose the human situation in a world of shattered beliefs:

A world that can be explained by reasoning, however faulty, is a familiar world. But in a universe that is suddenly deprived of illusions and of light, man feels a stranger. His is an irremediable exile, because he is deprived of memories of a lost homeland as much as he lacks the hope of a promised land to come. This divorce between man and his life, the actor and his setting, truly constitutes the feeling of Absurdity.

"Absurd" originally means "out of harmony," in a musical context. Hence its dictionary definition: "out of harmony with reason or propriety; incongruous, unreasonable, illogical." In common usage in the English-speaking world, "absurd" may simply mean "ridiculous." But this is not the sense in which Camus uses the word, and in which it is used when we speak of the Theatre of the Absurd. In an essay on Kafka, Ionesco defined his understanding of the term as follows: "Absurd is that which is devoid of purpose. . . . Cut off from his religious, metaphysical, and transcendental roots, man is lost; all his actions become senseless, absurd, useless."

This sense of metaphysical anguish at the absurdity of the human condition is, broadly speaking, the theme of the plays of Beckett, Adamov, Ionesco, Genet, and the other writers discussed in this book. But it is not merely the

[1] For stories by Camus, Kafka, and Sartre, and related commentaries, see the Index.

subject matter that defines what is here called the Theatre of the Absurd. A similar sense of the senselessness of life, of the inevitable devaluation of ideals, purity, and purpose, is also the theme of much of the work of dramatists like Giraudoux, Anouilh, Salacrou, Sartre, and Camus himself. Yet these writers differ from the dramatists of the Absurd in an important respect: They present their sense of the irrationality of the human condition in the form of highly lucid and logically constructed reasoning, while the Theatre of the Absurd strives to express its sense of the senselessness of the human condition and the inadequacy of the rational approach by the open abandonment of rational devices and discursive thought. While Sartre or Camus express the new content in the old convention, the Theatre of the Absurd goes a step further in trying to achieve a unity between its basic assumptions and the form in which these are expressed. In some senses, the *theatre* of Sartre and Camus is less adequate as an expression of the *philosophy* of Sartre and Camus—in artistic, as distinct from philosophic, terms—than the Theatre of the Absurd.

If Camus argues that in our disillusioned age the world has ceased to make sense, he does so in the elegantly rationalistic and discursive style of an eighteenth-century moralist, in well-constructed and polished plays. If Sartre argues that existence comes before essence and that human personality can be reduced to pure potentiality and the freedom to choose itself anew at any moment, he presents his ideas in plays based on brilliantly drawn characters who remain wholly consistent and thus reflect the old convention that each human being has a core of immutable, unchanging essence—in fact, an immortal soul. And the beautiful phrasing and argumentative brilliance of both Sartre and Camus in their relentless probing still, by implication, proclaim a tacit conviction that logical discourse can offer valid solutions, that the analysis of language will lead to the uncovering of basic concepts—Platonic ideas.

This is an inner contradiction that the dramatists of the Absurd are trying, by instinct and intuition rather than by conscious effort, to overcome and resolve. The Theatre of the Absurd has renounced arguing *about* the absurdity of the human condition; it merely *presents* it in being—that is, in terms of concrete stage images

of the absurdity of existence. This is the difference between the approach of the philosopher and that of the poet; the difference, to take an example from another sphere, between the *idea* of God in the works of Thomas Aquinas or Spinoza and the *intuition* of God in those of St. John of the Cross or Meister Eckhart—the difference between theory and experience.

It is this striving for an integration between the subject matter and the form in which it is expressed that separates the Theatre of the Absurd from the Existentialist theatre.

The Theatre of the Absurd must also be distinguished from another important, and parallel, trend in the contemporary French theatre, which is equally preoccupied with the absurdity and uncertainty of the human condition: the "poetic avant-garde" theatre of dramatists like Michel de Ghelderode, Jacques Audiberti, Georges Neveux, and, in the younger generation, Georges Schehadé, Henri Pichette, and Jean Vauthier, to name only some of its most important exponents. This is an even more difficult dividing line to draw, for the two approaches overlap a good deal. The "poetic avant-garde" relies on fantasy and dream reality as much as the Theatre of the Absurd does; it also disregards such traditional axioms as that of the basic unity and consistency of each character or the need for a plot. Yet basically the "poetic avant-garde" represents a different mood; it is more lyrical, and far less violent and grotesque. Even more important is its different attitude toward language: the "poetic avant-garde" relies to a far greater extent on consciously "poetic" speech; it aspires to plays that are in effect poems, images composed of a rich web of verbal associations.

The Theatre of the Absurd, on the other hand, tends toward a radical devaluation of language, toward a poetry that is to emerge from the concrete and objectified images of the stage itself. The element of language still plays an important, yet subordinate, part in this conception, but what *happens* on the stage transcends, and often contradicts, the *words* spoken by the characters. In Ionesco's *The Chairs*, for example, the poetic content of a powerfully poetic play does not lie in the banal words that are uttered but in the fact that they are spoken to an ever-growing number of empty chairs.

The Theatre of the Absurd is thus part of the

"anti-literary" movement of our time, which has found its expression in abstract painting, with its rejection of "literary" elements in pictures; or in the "new novel" in France, with its reliance on the description of objects and its rejection of empathy and anthropomorphism. It is no coincidence that, like all these movements and so many of the efforts to create new forms of expression in all the arts, the Theatre of the Absurd should be centered in Paris.

This does not mean that the Theatre of the Absurd is essentially French. It is broadly based on ancient strands of the Western tradition and has its exponents in Britain, Spain, Italy, Germany, Switzerland, and the United States as well as in France. Moreover, its leading practitioners who live in Paris and write in French are not themselves Frenchmen.

As a powerhouse of the modern movement, Paris is an international rather than a merely French center: it acts as a magnet attracting artists of all nationalities who are in search of freedom to work and to live nonconformist lives unhampered by the need to look over their shoulder to see whether their neighbors are shocked. That is the secret of Paris as the capital of the world's individualists: here, in a world of cafés and small hotels, it is possible to live easily and unmolested.

That is why a cosmopolitan of uncertain origin like Apollinaire; Spaniards like Picasso or Juan Gris; Russians like Kandinsky and Chagall; Rumanians like Tzara and Brancusi; Americans like Gertrude Stein, Hemingway, and E. E. Cummings; an Irishman like Joyce; and many others from the four corners of the world could come together in Paris and shape the modern movement in the arts and literature. The Theatre of the Absurd springs from the same tradition and is nourished from the same roots: An Irishman, Samuel Beckett; a Rumanian, Eugène Ionesco; a Russian of Armenian origin, Arthur Adamov, not only found in Paris the atmosphere that allowed them to experiment in freedom, they also found there the opportunities to get their work produced in theatres.

The standards of staging and production in the smaller theatres of Paris are often criticized as slapdash and perfunctory; that may indeed sometimes be the case; yet the fact remains that there is no other place in the world where so many first-rate men of the theatre can be found

who are adventurous and intelligent enough to champion the experimental work of new playwrights and to help them acquire a mastery of stage technique—from Lugné-Poë, Copeau, and Dullin to Jean-Louis Barrault, Jean Vilar, Roger Blin, Nicolas Bataille, Jacques Mauclair, Sylvain Dhomme, Jean-Marie Serreau, and a host of others whose names are indissolubly linked with the rise of much that is best in the contemporary theatre.

Equally important, Paris also has a highly intelligent theatregoing public, which is receptive, thoughtful, and as able as it is eager to absorb new ideas. Which does not mean that the first productions of some of the more startling manifestations of the Theatre of the Absurd did not provoke hostile demonstrations or, at first, play to empty houses. What matters is that these scandals were the expression of passionate concern and interest, and that even the emptiest houses contained enthusiasts articulate enough to proclaim loudly and effectively the merits of the original experiments they had witnessed.

Yet in spite of these favorable circumstances, inherent in the fertile cultural climate of Paris, the success of the Theatre of the Absurd, achieved within a short span of time, remains one of the most astonishing aspects of this astonishing phenomenon of our age. That plays so strange and puzzling, so clearly devoid of the traditional attractions of the well-made drama, should within less than a decade have reached the stages of the world from Finland to Japan, from Norway to the Argentine, and that they should have stimulated a large body of work in a similar convention, are in themselves powerful and entirely empirical tests of the importance of the Theatre of the Absurd.

The study of this phenomenon as literature, as stage technique, and as a manifestation of the thinking of its age must proceed from the examination of the works themselves. Only then can they be seen as part of an old tradition that may at times have been submerged but one that can be traced back to antiquity, and only after the movement of today has been placed within its historical context can an attempt be made to assess its significance and to establish its importance and the part it has to play within the pattern of contemporary thought.

A public conditioned to an accepted convention tends to receive the impact of artistic experiences through a filter of critical standards, of predetermined expectations and terms of reference, which is the natural result of the schooling of its taste and faculty of perception. This framework of values, admirably efficient in itself, produces only bewildering results when it is faced with a completely new and revolutionary convention—a tug of war ensues between impressions that have undoubtedly been received and critical preconceptions that clearly exclude the possibility that any such impressions could have been felt. Hence the storms of frustration and indignation always caused by works in a new convention.

It is the purpose of this book to provide a framework of reference that will show the works of the Theatre of the Absurd within their own convention so that their relevance and force can emerge as clearly to the reader as *Waiting for Godot* did to the convicts of San Quentin.

Comments and Questions

1. If the absurdists, "very clearly and in spite of themselves, have a good deal in common, it is because their work most sensitively mirrors and reflects the preoccupations and anxieties, the emotions and thinking of an important segment of their contemporaries in the Western world." Compare this statement with the quotation from Krutch in the forenote to Esslin's essay.

2. Note the definitions of the Absurd. In what way does Duerrenmatt's *The Visit* (p. 676) qualify as an absurdist play? Frisch's *Biedermann and the Firebugs* (p. 709)? Discuss.

3. Esslin observes that absurdist plays are "anti-literary," really antidrama. Is there a paradox in this? Try to resolve it.

An Introduction to *Othello**

NORMAN SANDERS
1929–

Although Shakespeare is generally considered to be the greatest of English tragic dra-

* Professor Sanders (University of Tennessee), at our request, prepared this critique. We are grateful to him for his perceptive analysis.

matists, it is not really possible to speak of "Shakespearean tragedy" in the same sense as we can of "Attic tragedy." His tragic plays share neither a similarity of form, nor an adherence to any rules such as those defined by Aristotle in his *Poetics*,[1] nor are their subjects based on a body of historical or mythological knowledge common to the dramatist and audience alike. They exhibit a greater degree of difference in their structures, and contain a wider variety of dramatic materials than the great tragic masterpieces of, say, fifth-century Athens or seventeenth-century France. They are hybrid plays, which mingle comic with the tragic matter and happily blend naturalistic utterance and psychologically credible characters with large impressionistic effects and persons of symbolic or even vaguely mythical proportions.

The lack of uniformity they display has much to do with the fact that Shakespeare's tragedies are so easily called to mind as separate entities and not merely as variant examples of a single prodigious talent. The imagined worlds they create partake of none of the anonymity that surrounds their maker. Rather, each play has a unique and specific flavor, a special atmosphere that remains with the reader or viewer even after the details of plot and character may have become blurred. The very title of *Macbeth* conjures up the dense, suffocating metaphoric climate of primal evil, darkness, blood, violated sleep, and nature poisoned at its source. *Hamlet* offers a clearer, more civilized and populous world, dominated by the black-clothed Prince whose every thought and action raise complex intellectual issues that extend far beyond their immediate context. And *King Lear* evokes a different timeless realm with its erupting natural forces blasting superhuman figures in a landscape of legendary prehistory. Certainly, such impressions are vague, and they are invariably modified by both detailed study and attendance at theatrical performances; but any account of the final tragic vision these plays contain must take cognizance of the distinctive quality that each possesses—indeed, for every reader or viewer his dominant impression is the only gateway he has to their terrible worlds.

In the study and the theater those aspects of *Othello* that are immediately striking are very different in kind and range from the other tragedies. The play's grip upon the emotions is quickly effected and relentlessly sustained by the rapid pace of the action, by the severe concentration on a single household and its relationships, by the dramatic interest's being focused upon feelings and actions that have an awful relevance and consequence for the human beings who experience them and few, if any, implications on a wider social plane. It was Shakespeare's only attempt at "domestic tragedy," and this fact together with its theme of sexual jealousy account in part for the degree of personal involvement that audiences seem always to have experienced.

At the play's dramatic center is a naked conflict between two sharply contrasted men: between a noble, exotic Negro general of simple mind and powerful emotions, but newly wed to a white woman, and his Italian ensign, a consummate hypocrite, jealously goading and scheming, within a space of days, to destroy those who appear to his twisted mind to have a daily beauty in their lives. From this basic opposition, because the play is verse drama, there emerges also a rich poetic texture made up of juxtaposed extremes: of involved deceit and transparent honesty, of violent emotion and coldly vicious mental calculation, of animal sexuality and love based on a sympathy of minds, of the daily domestic round and highly colored adventure, and of blackness and whiteness in all their physical immediacy and their spiritual connotations.

The plot of *Othello* is a simple one, noticeably uncomplicated by either a subplot or any extraneous material that might serve to divert the audience's attention from the central issue. One critic has summed up this simplicity in this way:

A man, dissappointed of promotion which he thought he had the right to expect, determines on revenge, and in part secures it. Or, in expanded form: An ensign, expecting promotion to a vacant lieutenancy, is exasperated when his general appoints another man over his head. He determines to revenge himself on the general and secure the dismissal of his rival. By a series of adroit moves he persuades the general of the adultery of the general's wife with the lieutenant. As a result the general kills first his wife and then himself, but the ensign fails in the second part of his

design, since the plot is disclosed, the lieutenant receives yet further promotion, and he himself faces trial and torture.[2]

Shakespeare's source was a sordid and melodramatic story of intrigue and sexual jealousy, which he found in a collection of Italian tales called *Gli Hecatommithi* by Geraldi Cinthio. Although in Cinthio's original the events are spread over a far longer period of time, Shakespeare determined to dramatize only those happenings between the night of Othello's marriage to Desdemona and the night of their deaths; and, in doing so, reduce the period covered by even these in the source from years to weeks. In deciding to do this he was faced with certain technical problems, which he solved by methods unique to this play.

To begin with the audience had to be informed of events prior to the play's opening; and in this respect the first scene is of great importance. By using a quarrel between a young Venetian exquisite, Roderigo, and the villain Iago over the money the latter has received to act as go-between in the young man's attempt to win Desdemona's hand, the dramatist is able to display Iago's hatred for Othello and its reasons, his jealousy of Cassio, and his intention to revenge himself on the general for the slight he considers he has received. As a first gesture in this direction, he persuades Roderigo to tell Desdemona's father that his daughter has secretly married Othello. Finally, by means of Iago's soliloquy, the audience is assured that Iago's hatred for Othello is genuine and not assumed for the purpose of deceiving an irate Roderigo, and is informed of Othello's importance as general of the Venetian army at a time when the state is threatened.

Apart from simply giving the audience the necessary events of the antecedent action, this opening scene also fulfills another function in a way that is alien to Shakespeare's practice in his other tragedies. That is, it introduces us to the tragic hero but does so in a totally negative fashion as a man who loves "his own pride and purposes," who evades issues bombastically, whose speech is "horribly stuffed with epithets of war"; he is depicted as a "thick-lips," a "Barbary horse," and an "old black ram" tupping a white

[2] M. R. Ridley, ed. *Othello,* London: Methuen, 1962, p. xlv.

ewe. It is true, of course, that Iago is clearly shown to be speaking as a man convinced of having been wronged, and Roderigo as a disappointed suitor. Nevertheless, the caricature we are given of Othello is a vivid one; and it ensures that when the hero himself appears, the audience has to make up its own picture of him, and to do so by the gradual modification of Iago's crude version. As the play progresses the audience receives further knowledge of events preceding the opening, and all of it is linked by an awful relevance to the dramatic moment at which it is presented. For example, we learn of the story of Othello's life as he defends his marriage to Desdemona before the Senate (I. iii. 180 ff.); we hear that Cassio went wooing with Othello at the moment Iago is planting the seeds of his jealousy in his mind (III. iii. 131–141); and the vividly pictured incident of Othello slaying a Turk who "struck a Venetian and traduced the state" occurs to the Moor immediately before he stabs himself for striking down the Venetian Desdemona and traducing the state of man (V. ii. 529–533).

Shakespeare's fashioning of the events of his play has long raised problems in that he appears to be playing strange tricks with the clock. Obviously the acting time of *Othello* is not meant to correspond exactly to the time that is supposed to elapse in "real life"; but the difficulty is not solved by such a recognition of the necessity for dramatic telescoping. The first act represents a period of time little longer than that which it takes to perform on the stage. The opening scene is almost exact in its equation of theatrical and probable time. Scene ii can be observed to follow it without perceptible break, with the opening fifty-six lines covering the period during which Brabantio and his party are seeking Othello out at the inn. The movement of the two groups, after their exchange before the Sagittary, to the Senate Chamber is accounted for by the discussion of the war by the Duke and Senators at the opening of the third scene. In fact, the only obvious theatrical license Shakespeare employs in the first act is in having Othello's famous speech on his wooing (I. iii. 180 ff.) equal the time taken by Iago to fetch Desdemona from her lodging. But even here, because of the speech's leisurely descriptive movement, the number of years it accounts for, and its poetic evocation of time and geographical space, it possesses theatrical length far in excess of the two minutes it takes an actor to deliver. This close correspondence between stage and "real" time in the opening scenes is deliberate on Shakespeare's part because it persuades the audience of the rapid pace of the action necessary if the remainder of the play is to succeed.

The interval of time between Acts I and II is any we think appropriate; but after the arrival in Cyprus the gap between the two time schemes widens. Iago begins his temptation the morning after his arrival on the island, and at the end of the scene promises that Cassio will be dead within three days. The impression we get of the events leading up to the attempt on Cassio's life persuades us that he makes good this promise; and the happenings of the final act appear to hurry along without any perceptible pause. Yet despite this illusion of pace, there are many indications in the play that contradict it. For example, we know that the news of the dispersal of the Turkish fleet must be conveyed to Venice and that Lodovico must travel to Cyprus; Bianca accuses Cassio of having neglected her for a week; and most important, Iago's accusations against Desdemona and Cassio presuppose at least time for opportunity.

What Shakespeare is doing is using two clocks. He knew that rapidity of movement was not only desirable from the point of view of dramatic tension, but that it was absolutely necessary if Iago's plot was not to appear incredible to the audience. Yet he was simultaneously aware that certain aspects of the story required a much longer time in which to take place. He therefore depicts on the stage an unbroken series of actions taking place in a *short time,* and provides sufficient indications to set them in a context of related events, not presented in the play, which reminds the audience of a *longer time.*

Some understanding of the dramatist's methods in respect to time is necessary if the reader of the play is not to be plagued for longer than is necessary by the question that is asked by most readers of the play: When is Desdemona supposed to have committed the acts of adultery of which Iago accuses her and in which Othello believes? When it is asked, certain aspects of the drama should be taken into account. To begin with, Shakespeare wrote the play to be acted, and so skillful is his management of the plot that the question does not arise in the theater. Secondly, he is writing poetic and not naturalistic drama, and simply because the characterization draws the play close to what we know as psychological theater, we should not be lured into asking the play to be something it is not. Finally, the point that the question somehow avoids is that Othello's jealousy is wholly without foundation; it is a monstrous growth drawn by Iago out of the complex of strengths and weaknesses that make up the character of Othello; and its nature is perhaps best grasped by noting that the only concrete piece of "evidence" to support his charges that Iago offers is not even recognized by his victim when he sees it in Cassio's hand:

IAGO   And did you see the handkerchief?
OTHELLO   Was that mine?
IAGO   Yours, by this hand.   (IV. i. 234–236)

The earliest printed text of *Othello,* which was found in the First Folio of 1623, is headed both by the title by which the play is commonly known and also by a description of the hero: "the Moor of Venice." Both of the key words here furnished Shakespeare with certain associations held by his audience on which he could build poetically and dramatically. For the seventeenth-century Englishman, Italy had a double image: It was at once a world of romance, wit, pleasure, and refinement, the birthplace of Ariosto, Castiglione, and Petrarch; but it was also the home of Nicolai Machiavelli, of criminal intrigue in the various courts that made up the divided nation, a veritable sump of the most sophisticated of human vices. Venice, of all Italian cities, was almost a type-name for the commercial society *par excellence,* for the spirit of dynamic and often unscrupulous capitalism. It was a city which gazed in two directions: toward civilized and Christian Europe of which it was a part, and toward the remote Eastern world of blaspheming Jews, pagan infidels, Turks, and Moors, to which it was the gateway. Shakespeare could thus rely upon his audience accepting the Venice of his play as an appropriate place for his tale of a Moorish general, invading Turks, a poisonous villain, hints of witchcraft, and irate whores. But even a Venetian Moor would have a special connotation for the average Globe theatergoer. For him a Moor was "of all that bears man's shape, likest a divell," a creature from those outer-Christian lands who was "fearful in sight and bearing."

Shakespeare used these geographical and racial assumptions of his audience in his own way —a way which in no sense simply takes over the traditional associations. For his Moor is noble, heroic, courtly in speech and bearing, loving, loyal, and a Christian defender of a Christian state against the Turkish infidels. It is Iago who is the representative of Satan in the play and who is also the repository of the normal English viewpoint of the Moor as savage, as devil, as the emblem of hell and damnation. What his choice of place and his hero's race gave Shakespeare then was a starting point and a freedom to make vivid a dramatic exploration of certain moral problems; but more important, it gave him the opportunity to explore in tragic terms what one scholar has called "the image of the foreigner, the stranger, the outsider in a dimension which is at once terrestrial and spiritual";[3] even as he had done in the comic mode some seven years earlier with his great archetypal figure of Shylock the Jew—also of Venice.

One further point might be made about the setting of the play. It is noticeable that while the action has its origins in Venice, the results are worked out in Cyprus. This movement from the commercial city to a Mediterranean island is motivated on the story level by the continuing Christian crusade against the Turks. But the shift of place also enabled Shakespeare to have the ideal conditions for his domestic drama: an island still in a state of fear; a new wife isolated from friends and family; a new husband busy with a new command in which he is responsible for the safety of others; the villainous ensign moving in his own professional world of a military campaign. These conditions invest with a naturalness such things as Iago's management of Cassio's disgrace, the edginess of the soldiers, and the necessity for quick decisions. In short, it provided an atmosphere in which the plot would be credible. "A town of war/Yet wild, the people's hearts brimful of fear" is the perfect backcloth to a "private and domestic quarrel" between a man and wife whose love is seen poetically in terms of the husband's occupation. At the end of the play there is no return to

[3] G. K. Hunter, *Shakespeare Survey 17,* Cambridge, England: Cambridge University Press, 1964, p. 52.

Venice—to the "normal" world; but the city is present during the last act in the person of its emissary Lodovico, who shows us how far the Venetian Othello has fallen as he asks, "Is this the noble Moor, whom our full Senate/Call all in all sufficient?," and who also can reassert what order is possible at the end and deliver Iago to the punishment that society decrees.

Any final assessment of *Othello* rests ultimately on the view one takes of the two main characters, and it is about them that there has been most critical debate. Although many scholars have taken note of the fact that Iago is a stage descendant of The Vice or wicked intriguer of the early Tudor morality plays, much of the analysis devoted to his part in the play has been plagued by the question of his psychological credibility. The difficulty is best summed up (perhaps too memorably) in Coleridge's phrase "the motive-hunting of motiveless malignity"; and the Iago who emerges from many critical studies is an inhuman abstraction, a stage monstrosity, a Satanist for whom evil is his good. But before considering the implications of this view, what is the man whom he so successfully manipulates, corrupts, and destroys —Othello the noble Moor?

To begin with, he is a foreigner employed by some Venetians and a governor of others. From both of these groups he is set off by his race, and most importantly from the theatrical point of view, by his color. Whether Shakespeare had in mind a native of Morocco, an Arab, or a black-amoor, a Negro, when he conceived the play seems to me a problem that is largely academic. What is important is that all the other characters in the play are aware of Othello's color. To Iago he is an "old black ram"; to Emilia in the final scene he appears "the blacker devil"; Roderigo refers to him scornfully as "the thick-lips"; Brabantio's incredulity at Desdemona's action takes the form of refusing to see her flying to a "sooty bosom"; Othello himself talks of his reputation as being "begrimed and black/As mine own face"; and even Desdemona feels the necessity to excuse her choice of husband by asserting that she saw "Othello's visage in his mind." In addition to the racial difference between the man and wife, it should also be noticed that the marriage is also a January–May affair with Othello "somewhat declined into the vale of years."

Almost of equal importance with his race is Othello's profession. He is great and proud in the exercise of arms; and prior to his meeting with Desdemona, soldiering has been his whole life. On his first appearance the military note is struck at once as he recalls the services he has done the signory; and his confrontation with the angry Brabantio and his sword-wielding followers contains all the scorn of the professional soldier when faced with civilian brawlers:

> Keep up your bright swords for the dew will rust them . . .
> Were it my cue to fight, I should have known it
> Without a prompter.   (I. ii. 84–85, 116–118)

Later before the Senate, although he is a natural orator, Othello feels diffident about his ability to answer Brabantio's accusations because of his military background:

>   Rude am I in my speech
> And little blessed with the soft phrase of peace;
> For since these arms of mine had seven years' pith
> Till now some nine moons wasted, they have used
> Their dearest action in the tented field.
>   (I. iii. 117–125)

And it is his philosophical acceptance as a career soldier that enables him to accede to the Duke's command to sail for Cyprus on the night of his wedding:

> The tyrant custom, most grave Senators,
> Hath made the flinty and steel couch of war
> My thrice-driven bed of down. I do agnize
> A natural and prompt alacrity
> I find in hardness; and do undertake
> This present war against the Ottomites.
>   (I. iii. 310–316)

The military aspect of Othello's character is important also because of the poetic connections Shakespeare makes between it and his marriage to Desdemona. His wooing and proposal grew out of his occupation:

> Her father loved me, oft invited me,
> Still questioned me the story of my life
> From year to year—the battles, sieges, fortunes
> That I have passed . . .
>   this to hear

Would Desdemona seriously incline.
                    (I. iii. 180–183, 199–200)

Desdemona falls in love with him for his auto-biography:

> She loved me for the dangers I had passed,
> And I loved her that she did pity them.
>   (I. iii. 230–231)

The very idiom in which she describes her action in marrying the Moor is martial and violent:

> That I did love the Moor to live with him
> My downright violence and storm of fortunes
> May trumpet to the world. My heart's sub-
>   dued
> Even to the very quality of my lord.
>   (I. iii. 333–338)

Thus their marriage, begun in civil disorder in Venice and developed as the wife goes to war with her husband, is consummated in an island of fear where Othello has to teach his wife " 'tis a soldier's life,/To have their balmy slumbers waked with strife." Small wonder indeed that at times their roles seem to change so that the wife is seen to be the "fair warrior" and the husband "dear Othello."

Related to these circumstances of Othello's life are the strands that go to make up his nature, which Dr. Johnson has fairly summed up as "fiery openness . . . magnanimous, artless, credulous, boundless in his confidence, ardent in his affection, inflexible in his resolution, and obdurate in his revenge." Like every professional soldier Othello is a basically simple man; he is "of a free and open nature that thinks men honest who but seem to be so." Because of this simplicity, the worst mental state he can envisage is uncertainty in which the victim tells o'er "damned minutes" and "dotes yet doubts, suspects, yet strongly loves." For such a man, the feverish reaching out for the truth, even the painful truth, is natural. "Give me the ocular proof!" he demands of Iago; and in this state of mind any kind of proof will suffice that will obviate the necessity for thought and the doubt it brings. Thus a handkerchief, in reality a "trifle light as air," becomes for him a "confirmation strong as holy writ."

Ironically Othello finds a kind of agonizing comfort once he has decided on a course of action. His determination once taken is immovable, as the "three great ones of the city" found

when they attempted to change his mind on Cassio's appointment. The dismissal of Cassio, the ordering of his death, the immediate slaying of Desdemona, and his own suicide all flow from this characteristic which he well knows:

> IAGO   Patience I say, your mind perhaps may
>   change.
> OTHELLO   Never, Iago. Like to the Pontic
>   Sea,
> Whose icy current, and compulsive course,
> Ne'er feels retiring ebb, but keeps due on
> To the Propontic, and the Hellespont:
> Even so my bloody thoughts, with violent
>   pace
> Shall ne'er look back, ne'er ebb to humble
>   love
> Till that a capable and wide revenge
> Swallow them up.   (III. iii. 645–654)

While it is this quality that gives Othello his drive to act, it is another that gives him the power for action: namely, the strength of his natural passions. From the very start of the play we feel an enormous emotional force is being kept under strict control, and we realize on the night of Cassio's dismissal how tenuous the control is:

>   Now by heaven
> My blood begins my safer guides to rule,
> And passion having my best judgment collied
> Assays to lead the way.   (II. iii. 251–254)

This power when fixed on Desdemona who "would sing the roughness out of a bear" is safe enough; but when Iago plays on all Othello's weaknesses and strengths with a terrible skill, he not only removes all control, but unleashes the fury of emotion on the gentle cub herself.

Iago, the man who wreaks the havoc, is no obvious villain; and his role on the stage must not be played as a sneering Machiavellian. Rather it should be acted as Edwin Booth did in the nineteenth century and Ralph Richardson in the twentieth: that is, as the honest man that all characters in the play take him for and only the audience knows he is not. His power over Othello is derived from his ability to speak as a Venetian, from the fact that he is cerebral rather than emotional, and from his perception that Othello's weaknesses may be exploited for his particular ends. At every point in his temptation we may find examples of the way he uses his powers. For example, the Moor's free and open nature is at once the quality that Desdemona appears to have abused yet that ensures Iago a hearing; tokens to which Othello himself has given a special emotional connotation are turned to Iago's advantage; and even Desdemona's ultimate act of love in turning her back on her father and her race are transformed into a fault as Iago echoes Brabantio's words "Look to her, Moor, if thou hast eyes to see./She hath deceived her father and may thee."

In fact, Iago has only one quality to fear in Othello: his instinctive emotional response to people. Iago cannot pervert this, he can only prevent Othello's using it. When Othello follows his instinct he is invariably correct; it is only when he imagines he is acting rationally (like Iago) that his rightness deserts him. Perhaps the most painful moment in the play is that at which he lists the excellences of his wife at the moment he vows his revenge, simultaneously trying to persuade himself that he is only being intellectually fair.

Close analysis of the poetry of the play has demonstrated just how successful Iago is in infusing Othello with his own spirit. For example, two of the tricks of speech that Shakespeare gives Iago in the first two acts are the frequent recourse to the animal world for illustrations of the workings of human nature (he uses asses, daws, flies, rams, jennets, baboons, goats and monkeys, among others); and his ready allusions to hell and damnation. Neither of these speech characteristics is typical of Othello during the same part of the play; but once he falls a prey to jealousy, his lines become infected, as it were, by them; even as his sexual attitudes become a hideous caricature of Iago's own.

During the course of the play Shakespeare allows the villain the chance to give us a number of reasons for his actions: that he suspects that Othello and Cassio have cuckolded him; that his ambition has been disappointed; that he hates good people because they have a daily beauty in their lives that makes him seem ugly. Coleridge, Lamb, A. C. Bradley, and Granville-Barker among other great critics of the play have considered these "motives" insufficient. Yet because this information is given to the audience by the dramatist's use of the soliloquy convention, we must accept that Iago is telling the truth as he sees it.

Such motives seem insufficient only when the character is considered in psychological isolation. When the character is viewed as a part of the whole dramatic design, the villain's "reasons" take on a greater relevance. There is an obvious relationship between his and Othello's actions and attitudes. In fact, it would not be going too far to see in the interaction of the two the spectacle of one human being, inferior in every respect to the other, carefully working to have all his own preoccupations worked out to their logical emotional and personal conclusion on a scale far vaster than any he himself could manage. It is almost as if Iago were creating a giant version of his own obsessions, making a black and monstrous reality of his own mind, by reducing a finer nature than his own to the level of his spiritual lieutenant.

It is in the complexities of this relationship that the clue to Othello's terrible descent into barbarity can be found, and the only possible answer to his last anguished question: "Will you, I pray, demand of that demi-devil/Why he hath thus ensnared my soul and body?" One other critical decision also rests upon each reader's view of this relationship: this is one's reaction to the final scene to which critical response has ranged from Dr. Johnson's finding it unendurable through Bradley's depression and Granville-Barker's sense of meaninglessness, and on to Muir's claim for an Othello restored to his former grandeur and nobility.

The conflict of the characters and its endless psychological fascination should not make us forget that Shakespeare was writing poetic tragedy and not Ibsenian social drama. The dramatist certainly deploys his great range of poetic technique at the service of such things as character creation, the manipulation of the audience's mood, the management of pace, and so on. But poetry in drama accomplishes something more, what one critic has called the revelation of

the presence of a surrounding or accompanying universe of thought or experience which cannot otherwise be included, however essential to its poetic purpose, without forfeiting the rapidity and compression in which the artistic strength of drama chiefly lies. This is often effected by symbolism, setting or incidental description, but imagery, in the strict sense of metaphorical speech, is a more powerful means; more passionate than symbolism, more flexible than setting, more concentrated than descriptive digression.[4]

The way in which the poetry of the play evokes this "surrounding universe" is one means of grasping its universal significance. For it is poetically as well as physically that *Othello* embodies many of life's great oppositions: the instinctive and rational ways of responding, war and peace, hatred and love, honesty and falsehood, illusion and reality, reputation and disgrace, trust and suspicion, fidelity and betrayal, discord and harmony, the wife and the whore, proof and supposition, the noble and the despicable, beauty and ugliness, salvation and damnation. However, as we experience the play in the theater or the study, none of these opposites are as simple or as clearcut as the above listing suggests. At certain points the distinction between them may seem obvious enough; but far more frequently their poetic statement blurs the dividing-line between them, often seeing each element of the opposition in terms of the other. Perhaps the easiest way of seeing how this works is to consider the most striking of them that not only sums up or draws to it by association all the others, but challenges the very idea of opposition itself. This is, of course, the theme of light and darkness.

At its simplest level it is a contrast between the white skin of Desdemona and the black skin of Othello. But blackness cannot have here the traditional associations of hell, evil, damnation, and deceit; for the Moor is noble, he believes in love, in dedication, in ideals, in his profession, and he thinks in absolutes. The whiteness of Desdemona, on the other hand, is a fitting image of her purity, her innocent generosity, her gentle goodness, and her terrible truth. But Iago is white also and honest in everyone's eyes. Yet he believes in nothing; human beings have for him no value. Love to him is merely "a lust of the blood and a permission of the will"; truth is a means of telling a lie; love is an instrument of hatred; reputation is "an idle and most false imposition"; virtue an illusion that covers vice; and men are all fools to be used as an ever-open purse or to be "tenderly led by the nose as asses are." As the action of the play develops, these associations of black and white shuttle back and

forth as Desdemona's virtue is seen as pitch; as Iago gives the more memorable utterance to the ideal of a good name; as Othello grovels like an animal and mouths filth comparable with Iago's; and as the general is led by the ensign to make Desdemona's bedroom a brothel, then a court of unjust judgment, and finally a tomb.

Shakespeare's poetic and dramatic manipulation thus forces us to question the very fundamentals of existence. For in the last resort, the spirits of Othello and Iago grappling in the flickering light and darkness of the play's moral landscape must be recognized for what they are: not mighty opposites, not two ways of seeing life, but a terrible composite of the creative and destructive forces in man—forces that we all share.

Comments and Questions

The foregoing comments on *Othello* follow, in the main, the method of play analysis set forth in the Preliminaries to the Drama section. (See pp. 424–432.)

1. Note the emphasis Professor Sanders places upon setting. Does the modern reader lose something if he is unaware of the significance attached to Venice and Cyprus by an Elizabethan audience? In other words, are there at least two valid ways to read *Othello*? Which way helps more to generalize—universalize—the characters in the play? Discuss carefully.

2. "We must accept that Iago is telling the truth as he sees it." In what way is this a key interpretation of Shakespeare's most controversial character? Is Iago a devil or a misguided human being? Argue for or against Professor Sanders' interpretation. Be sure to take into account what the other characters say about Iago, what he says about himself and his motives—particularly in the soliloquies—and the significance of his last speech.

3. Compare what Professor Sanders says about *Othello* and what Krutch says about this play in "The Tragic Fallacy" (p. 855, passim).

[4] U. M. Ellis-Fermor, *The Frontiers of Drama*, London: Methuen, 1945, p. 8.

Lawrence's Quarrel with Christianity: "The Man Who Died"

GRAHAM HOUGH
1908–

After innumerable attempts at defining the basis of his objection to democracy, scattered through his work from *Women in Love* onwards, Lawrence gets it out most clearly at the eleventh hour in *Apocalypse*:

> The mass of men have only the tiniest touch of individuality, if any. The mass of men live and move, think and feel collectively, and have practically no individual emotions, feelings or thoughts at all. They are fragments of the collective or social consciousness. It has always been so, and it always will be so.

Which has not prevented him saying earlier that the end of all education and social life is the development of the individual. So it is—but only so far as the individual exists. And in most men the individual exists very little, the rest of them being realised in their share of the collectivity.

Most men are largely citizens, members of the community, collective men. And "as a citizen, as a collective being, man has his fulfilment in the gratification of his power sense." A man may wish to be a unit of pure altruistic love, but since he is inescapably a member of the political community, he is also inescapably a unit of worldly power. A man must be both a unit of love and a unit of power; he must satisfy himself both in the love-mode and the power-mode. This theme, appearing in almost the last words Lawrence wrote, goes back to a far earlier period of his career. It is expressed in almost similar terms in the last chapter of *Aaron's Rod*.

> I told you there were two urges—two great life-urges, didn't I? There may be more. But it comes on me so strongly, now, that there are two: love and power. And we've been trying to work ourselves, at least as individuals, from the love-urge exclusively, hating the power-urge and repressing it. And now I find we've got to accept the very thing we've hated.
>
> We've exhausted our love-urge, for the moment. And yet we try to force it to continue working. So we get inevitably anarchy and murder. It's no good. We've got to accept the power motive, accept it in deep responsibility.

And this is as good a point as any to enter Lawrence's long quarrel with Christianity. For Christianity as Lawrence sees it is the attempt to live from the love-motive alone—to make love, *caritas,* pure altruism, the only motive in life. "The essence of Christianity is a love of mankind." Of course this takes no account whatever of historic and doctrinal Christianity in all its developed complexity; still worse, from the Christian point of view, it takes no account of the *source* of that love, which should be the motive of all faith and all action. Still, in a thousand places in his fiction and expository writing Lawrence makes the identification between Christianity and the doctrine of pure, universal, altruistic love. It is against this doctrine of Kangaroo's that Somers revolts, exalts his own dark god and preserves his integrity. It is against this doctrine that Don Ramón revolts and triumphs over in the person of Doña Carlota. It is against this doctrine that the Ursula of *The Rainbow* revolts when she shakes the little sister who has slapped her face, and feels the better for it— "unchristian but clear." On every level from the prophetic to the trivial Lawrence sees Christianity as the love-ideal and rejects it.

Two thousand years ago Western man embarked on the attempt to live from the love-motive alone. Sometimes Lawrence puts it a few hundred years earlier, with Platonism and the rise of the higher religions. He refers to this momentous step in the history of humanity in at least two different ways. Sometimes he sees it as a great rejection, a failure of courage, a refusal of the responsibility of life, sometimes as a necessary development, living and valid for its time and for centuries to come, but now at an end. Perhaps the second judgment represents his steadiest and most central belief:

> I know the greatness of Christianity: it is a past greatness. I know that, but for those early Christians, we should never have emerged from the chaos and hopeless disaster of the Dark Ages. If I had lived in the year 400, pray God, I should have been a true and passionate Christian. The adventurer.
>
> But now I live in 1924, and the Christian venture is done. The adventure is gone out of Christianity. We must start on a new venture towards God.

In either case, the love-mode is exhausted. Christianity is kept going by a barren effort of will, it has no longer any connection with the deep sources of life; and the consequences of this continuing will-driven automatism of love is to be seen everywhere in the modern world.

The psychological and personal consequences have been touched on sufficiently often already. The withered and fluttering figure of Doña Carlota is supposed to represent the etiolation of spiritual love; and the unsleeping will behind it has strained her relation to Don Ramón beyond the breaking point. When Kangaroo proposes to love Somers, Somers reflects: "He doesn't love *me*, he just turns a great general emotion on me, like a tap. . . . Damn his love, he wants to *force* me." Hermione wants to love Birkin spiritually, and when Birkin, to preserve his integrity, has to reject her, she tries to knock his brains out. Farther back still, the unhappy Paul of *Sons and Lovers* is in the toils of a 'spiritual' love which should have been a happy physical relation, but can never become so because of Miriam's fixed spiritual will; and his situation is complicated because there is another woman, his mother, who also wants to possess his soul. The common element in all these admittedly complex and varying situations is a love which is cut off from the natural carnal roots of love, and continues to exist simply as a function of the will. It is sterile in itself and becomes life-exhausting to whoever exercises it. Since it is something imposed on the object of love, not a reciprocal relation, it becomes inevitably a kind of spiritual bullying, and must inevitably be rejected by anyone who wishes to preserve his individual being. And all this in Lawrence's eyes is an inevitable consequence in personal relations of the Christian love-doctrine, the Christian discipline of the heart.

There is an analogous development in public life. The universal sentiment of love for mankind is similarly cut off from the natural roots of human comradeship, the warm, carnal physical community; known, for instance, by men working together in a common manual task or playing together in a ritual dance. These are communities of power, and have behind them the inexhaustible vitality of a common physical life. The love of mankind offers only a community of sentiment, and can be maintained only as a fixed direction of the will. So, like private spiritual love, it becomes a kind of bullying. *Sois mon frère ou je te tue.* Hence the devastat-ing wars by which Christendom has been riven. Further, this kind of love is not a true communal feeling at all; it is a product of the individual will, of the ego, of all that is most personal and least deeply rooted in man. It demands that each man shall be an individual power-house of universal love. This has two consequences. The first, only clearly apparent late in the Christian cycle, but its inevitable and logical development, is democracy. Each individual must love all others, equally and impartially—the Whitmanesque universal brotherhood. The mysteries of power and lordship are denied—for they would be a break in the uniformity of universal love. So that universal love becomes a forcing of the same ideal sentiment on all alike; or looked at in reverse, a claim by each individual alike for the same universal consideration. And this claim is false, for all men do not possess individuality in the same measure. And this brings us to the second consequence of the demand for universal love—it involves the demand that all men shall be fully individuals, and that each shall be a separate individual source of universal spiritual love. It is a demand for the impossible, and it falsifies the whole relation of man to man;

> In democracy, bullying inevitably takes the place of power. Bullying is the negative form of power. The modern Christian state is a soul-destroying force, for it is made up of fragments which have no organic whole, only a collective whole. In a hierarchy each part is organic and vital, as my finger is an organic and vital part of me. But a democracy is bound in the end to be obscene, for it is composed of myriads of dis-united fragments, each fragment assuming to itself a false wholeness, a false individuality. Modern democracy is made up of millions of fractional parts all asserting their own wholeness.

Christianity, in fact, is designed for a world of free, pure, bodiless individuals, not for a world of men—men, who exist largely in their undifferentiated physical community, most of whom are capable of very little individual spiritual development. "Christianity, then, is the ideal, but it is impossible." Lawrence agrees with Dostoevsky's Grand Inquisitor, as he makes plain in an introduction that he wrote to that dialogue. Christ loved man, but loved him in the wrong way. The following words of the Inquisitor might almost have been written by Lawrence himself: "By showing him so much respect, thou didst, as it were, cease to feel for him—thou who hast loved him more than thyself. Respecting him less, thou wouldst have asked less of him. That would have been more like love, for his burden would have been lighter." Or, as Lawrence paraphrases it: "To be able to live at all, mankind must be loved more tolerantly and more contemptuously than Jesus loved it, loved for all that, more truly, since it is loved for itself, for what it is, not for what it ought to be, free and limitless."

But man is not free and limitless. He needs earthly bread, the satisfaction of his physical appetites, and he needs to acknowledge that satisfaction as a divine gift. And he needs authority, someone to bow down to, the acknowledgment of power—not the spiritual power of an unseen god, but embodied power in the flesh. To restore health to the community of men it is first necessary to accept the power-motive again, to acknowledge the legitimacy of both individual authority and collective power. The mass of undeveloped mankind will find their vicarious fulfilment in this acknowledgment. Lawrence worries constantly over this problem of power from *Aaron's Rod* to *The Plumed Serpent;* and never successfully. His negative analyses of the corruptions of 'white' love and democratic humanitarianism are piercing and profound; yet the dark god of power who is to be not destructive but life-giving is never successfully evoked. The attempts to embody him in fiction produce fascist leaders or posturing mountebanks. It might be said that this is exactly what such attempts produce in life—these are the only practical embodiments of the dark god. History since Lawrence's death might well seem to confirm the accusation. I think Lawrence could still reply that this is not so; it is precisely because the reality of power is shirked by the general "democratic" presuppositions that, like all realities that have been denied and suppressed, it reasserts itself in violent and terrible explosions. If the reality had always been admitted to its rightful place, the explosions would not have been necessary.

He would in part be right. The most committed liberal democrat would be free to admit that the calamities of the last thirty years are in part a result of the decadence of his own ideals, a decadence evident in the general loss of all sense both of the proper mode of exercising authority and the proper mode of submitting to it. This decay is not yet arrested, and Lawrence is one of its sharpest analysts. He was asking a real question, though he never found an answer.

It may be that Lawrence had himself too many relics of Christianity in his heart ever to be able to cope with the problem of earthly power, or even thoroughly to accept the necessity he asserted. Certainly he knew too little of how it works and how it is obtained. What could a man who had never had an ordinary job, never had a place in a community of men, never exercised or submitted to authority, know of political reality? His characters become steadily less convincing the nearer they come to exercising political power. The only way Lawrence can realise power and convey the sense of it, unhampered by ignorance or an inner resistance, is when it is displayed in nature. Lou Carrington submits to the "wild spirit" she finds in the mountains of Taos, but it is hard to see her submitting to any human embodiment of it. Lawrence becomes aware of this failure himself, for after *The Plumed Serpent* we hear less of the power-mode. He is still equally concerned with the failure of 'Christian' love, but he is now inclined to find the alternative in "a new tenderness," a fleshly tenderness. *Lady Chatterley* is supposed to be the illustration of this tenderness, and the story which explores its relation to Christianity is "The Man Who Died."

As Lawrence's attention shifts from power to sensual tenderness as the alternative to Christian love, the opposition becomes less intense; and it becomes easier for him to represent his doctrine as a completion of Christianity rather than a contradiction. Spiritual love and sensual love are, after all, both forms of love: and the Christian depreciation of sexuality[1] is an accident rather than the essence of its doctrine. "The Man Who Died." therefore, comes nearer to being a reconciliation with Christianity than anything else Lawrence wrote. In other places

[1] I take it for granted that Christianity does depreciate sexuality, or at most make reluctant concessions to it; and that Lawrence was right in believing this, wherever else he was wrong; and that the Chestertonian (and post-Chestertonian) trick of representing Christianity as a robustly Rabelaisian sort of faith is a vulgar propagandist perversion.

sensual love is seen as the negation of "white" love, *agape,* Christian love. Here we come near to seeing it as a transcendence, reached by death and re-birth. And this means that it represents, not the climax of his art, which it certainly is not, but a climactic point in the development of his thought.

This story of the rejected prophet, almost killed, left for dead, returning painfully to life, and finding it, not in the resumption of his mission but in the knowledge of a woman—this story of the resurrection is certainly Lawrence's most audacious enterprise. Many readers have found in it the final evidence of the arrogance, the ignorant presumption of which Lawrence has often been accused. To take a story so tremendous, so profoundly interwoven with the life of our civilisation, and "to try to improve on it," as I have heard it said, may well seem to suggest something of the kind. I think the charge can be dismissed if we are careful enough to see what Lawrence was trying to do. Although the prophet is unnamed, the identification with Jesus is not disguised. The Crucifixion, the Entombment, St. Mary Magdalen, the journey to Emmaus are all explicitly referred to. Yet what is the Jesus to whom the story refers? The "historical Jesus," the Lamb of God who takes away the sins of the world, the Christ who shall come again with glory to judge the living and the dead? Surely none of these. Lawrence had believed since he was twenty that Jesus was "as human as we are"; but he is not trying to provide a demythologised historical version of his end, more acceptable to positivists than a supernatural resurrection. George Moore attempts something of the kind in *The Brook Kerith;* but not Lawrence. And the cosmic and eschatological bearings of the Gospel story concern him even less. There is no suggestion anywhere in his tale that the death and resurrection of Jesus is a mystery of redemption or that it affects the destiny of mankind. Lawrence is concerned with two aspects of the Christian myth, and two only: one, the value of Christian love; the other, the personal destiny of Jesus the teacher. What he has done is not to vulgarise or reduce the splendours and mysteries of traditional Christology; he simply leaves them on one side. He has taken Jesus as what he believed him to be, a human teacher; he sees what he

believes to be the consequences of his teaching, and tries according to his own lights to push beyond it. Certainly an audacious attempt, possibly a misguided one, but to anyone who cares to read what Lawrence wrote, not to rest on a conceptual summary, it will not, I think, appear as an attempt made without due reverence.

The story was originally called *The Escaped Cock* and ended at Part I, with the prophet setting out alone to walk through the world, vividly aware of life in the flesh, but as yet without any active participation in it. The central symbol of this part of the story is the cock itself, tied by the leg by the vulgar peasant, released by the prophet. The first act of his re-born existence is to let it fly free; and its new-found freedom is a symbol of his own sensuous faculties, imprisoned during the years of his mission and almost extinguished during his passion and death. For it has been a real death. With great discretion Lawrence avoids the question of a miraculous resurrection. What does it matter? One who has suffered, as the prophet has done, the extremity of physical and spiritual torment has in effect died; and if his vital powers should, miraculously or unmiraculously, return, it is a real re-birth. In the concentration-camp world that we have produced after twenty centuries of Christian civilisation there are many people who know this. At first the prophet walks in the world like one who is still not of it.

> He felt the cool silkiness of the young wheat under his feet that had been dead, and the roughishness of its separate life was apparent to him. At the edges of rocks, he saw the silky, silvery-haired buds of the scarlet anemone bending downwards. And they too were in another world. In his own world he was alone, utterly alone.

He can feel no kinship with the tender life of the young spring; and this may serve to remind us how different Lawrence's nature religion is from the Wordsworthianism of the nineteenth century. Lawrence is more aware of the tormenting complexity of human experience, of the indirectness, even the contrariety of the relation between man and external nature. Man cannot learn of man by passively receiving impulses from a vernal wood, but only by adventures in the world of men. The prophet awakens to the new life of the body only when he realises that the peasant woman desires him. He does not desire her; he has died and does not desire anything; anyway, he knows that she is hard, short-sighted and greedy. But the knowledge of her desire awakens in him a new realisation.

Risen from the dead, he had realised at last that the body, too, has its little life; and beyond that, the greater life. He was virgin, in recoil from the little, greedy life of the body. But now he knew that virginity is a form of greed; and that the body rises again to give and to take, to take and to give, ungreedily.

So he does not reject her harshly—"he spoke a quiet pleasant word to her and turned away."

But he has another and a sterner rejection to make, the rejection of his own former mission, and of Madeleine, the woman who had believed in him. They meet, and she wishes him to come back to her and the disciples. But he only replies that the day of his interference with others is done, the teacher and the saviour are dead in him. In a sense he accepts this death: betrayal and death are the natural end of such a mission. "I wanted to be greater than the limits of my own hands and feet, so I brought betrayal on myself." This is what happens to the man who would embrace multitudes when he has never truly embraced even one. On his second meeting with Madeleine he again rejects her entreaties, saying that he must ascend to the Father. She does not understand, and he does not explain; but the reader will remember that in Lawrence's mythology the Father was also the Flesh.

Madeleine, who wants to devote everything to him, is also under the spell of a hard necessity. In her life as a carnal sinner she had taken more than she gave. Now she wants to give without taking, and that is denied her. The prophet prefers the society of the peasants, for their earthy inert companionship "would put no compulsion on him." He dreads the love of which he had once been the preacher, the love that compels.

The central symbol of the second part of the story is the priestess. She is a priestess of Isis, Isis in search of the dead Osiris, and like the prophet she is virgin. She had known many men in her youth, Caesar and Antony among them, but had remained always cool and untouched; and an old philosopher had told her that women such as she must reject the splendid and the assertive and wait for the re-born man.

The lovely description of her temple and its setting is a delicate Mediterranean landscape, nature at its most humane, friendly and responsive. At the moment when the stranger lands on her shores—the stranger who is the prophet on his travels—she is idly watching two slaves, a boy and a girl. The boy beats the girl, and in a moment of half-frightened excitement copulates with her, scared and shamefaced. The priestess turns away indifferently. These are the loves of slaves; whatever fulfilment she is to find has no more in common with these vulgar couplings that with the loves of Caesars. When the stranger-prophet asks for shelter he is given it, indifferently and impersonally. A slave suspects that he is an escaped malefactor, and the priestess goes to look at him as he sleeps.

She had no interest in men, particularly in the servile class. Yet she looked at the sleeping face. It was worn, hollow, and rather ugly. But, a true priestess, she saw the other kind of beauty in it, the sheer stillness of the deeper life.

. . . There was a beauty of much suffering, and the strange calm candour of finer life in the whole delicate ugliness of the face. For the first time, she was touched on the quick at the sight of a man, as if the tip of a fine flame of living had touched her. It was the first time.

Both the prophet and the priestess are separate, cut off from the common life around them. She is surrounded only by slaves, and she found slaves repellent. "They were so embedded in their lesser life, and their appetites and their small consciousness were a little disgusting." And as for the prophet—"He had come back to life, but not the same life that he had left, the life of the little people and the little day. Reborn, he was in the other life, the greater day of the human consciousness." Both are aristocrats of the spirit and both are incomplete—she because she is the living representative of Isis in search of Osiris; and he because he has died and come back to the world and still dreads its contact. She realises that she has not yet found her Osiris, and he realises that there is the whole vista of a new life before him that he has not yet been able to touch.

And when she becomes Isis to his Osiris (for there are no surprises in this story), we are to see it not only as the satisfaction of a long-denied bodily hunger (it is that, too), but as the consummation for each of them of a solitary life of spiritual exploration—a spiritual journey that can never be complete until it has reached carnal fruition that will alter its whole meaning. She who has played out her life as a drama of search has now found. "And she said to herself, 'He is Osiris. I wish to know no more'." And he who has died, returned to the world, but not yet felt himself to be living again, knows that he is risen from the dead when he feels desire for the woman and the power to satisfy it. When the life of the little world, in the shape of the slaves and the Roman soldiers, breaks in upon these Christian-Osirian mysteries, the prophet takes a boat and slips away, healed, whole, risen in the body, content to take what may come on another day.

Aesthetically, no doubt, the story was more satisfying in its first form, when it ended with the prophet's rejection of his old mission and his yet unfulfilled knowledge that a new life awaits him. The temptation to be explicit about what cannot properly be explained is always the *ignis fatuus* for which Lawrence is content to lose his way. The attempt to *present* the experience of one who has stepped inside the gates of death and come out again seems foredoomed to failure. As it turns out, the failure is of a different kind from that which might have been expected. It is a breakdown of continuity, not a breakdown of expression. The idyll of the stranger and the priestess is beautifully done; the balance between fabulous remoteness and concrete sensuous realisation is delicately held; and Lawrence convinces us as he rarely does that the conjunction he describes is that of two rare beings, each with an exquisitely specialised individual life, yet satisfying each other completely by meeting on a ground which is beyond the personal life of either. And over it all is shed like sunshine the warm tolerant beauty of the ancient Mediterranean world—a beauty which may be partly the product of Arcadian fantasy, but still forms a real and living part of European experience.

All this is true. But it is also true that it is hard to accept the stranger of the second part of the book as identical with the prophet of the first. In the first part the broad, unspecific outlines of fable are filled out with what we know of the Gospel narrative, which is still very close

to us. The invented myth is given density and immediacy by its dependence on the great public myth. In the second part the invented myth stands alone, and like all products of the pure personal imagination, it is thinner than what history or the mythopoeic faculty of a whole culture supplies. The stranger in the second part is not so much a different person as a person out of a different story; the change is a change in the mode of conception. For the tale has two kinds of significance, unequally distributed— the one more prominent in the first part, the other in the later addition.

It can be interpreted synchronically or diachronically, to borrow terms from the linguists. Synchronically, it is simply what Lawrence first called it—a story of the Resurrection, deriving much of its strength from its background of the Gospel narrative, passing over into a more rootless fantasy as this recedes into the distance. Its theme is the necessity of rejecting the Christian love-ideal for a man who has really risen in the flesh. And right or wrong, we recognise this as an integral part of the Laurentian thesis. The second part of the story is a more arbitrary invention, and as such abides our question. Should the fulfilment of the flesh, the obvious natural destiny of mortal creatures, be discovered so late and after such long wandering? Should it, for the sake of Lawrence's thesis, be a healer for creatures who have been so long estranged from the roots of life? Could it be so, for beings who have been so long specialised in other directions, one of whom has suffered to death? It would be absurd to press these questions too hard, but they do at least begin to obtrude themselves. They can be answered by seeing the tale in the second way, diachronically; not as the story of a particular man at a particular time, but as an allegory of the course of Christian civilisation. The death of the prophet is also a symbol of the death of the Christian dispensation. Christian civilisation is dying after two thousand years. But the story of man is a continuity, and no culture ever really dies: it comes to life again, to a new life, which it is at first incapable of realising and is unable to face. The passion and death of the prophet are the death-agonies of Christian culture ("Ours is a tragic age," as Lawrence said at the beginning of *Lady Chatterley*), and the second part of the story is a foreshadowing of the new dispensation that is to come. But it is a new dispensation only reached by death and re-birth. The fleshly tenderness that is to replace Christian love in the new order can never be the pristine, unembarrassed pagan delectation. The one thing a post-Christian can never be is a pagan, C. S. Lewis has remarked; and Lawrence is showing his sense of this. Christianity may be brought into touch again with the old nature-mysteries of death and re-birth, as it is in this tale; but they will be changed in the process. The fleshly healing is painfully, almost fearfully accepted by the priestess and the prophet, after years of deprivation and a season of anguish; and so it must be in the history of Western man. It will not be among *hommes moyens sensuels* that the new apprehension of life is born. Theirs is the "little day," as it always has been, under any dispensation. But to encompass this in the greater day will be the task precisely of those who have most completely submitted to the old spiritual disciplines. True, the mission of Christianity has to be rejected, but it has been lived through before it has been rejected, and nothing can ever be the same again. If a new order is to come into being, it will in all its splendour and joy be the inheritor of the Christian abnegation and suffering.

I believe that this, or something like it, is what Lawrence is saying in "The Man Who Died," and that this is the most developed state of his relation to Christianity. The hostility had, after all, never been unmitigated. "Give me the mystery and let the world live for me"—Kate's cry in *The Plumed Serpent* was Lawrence's own. And Christianity, at any rate Catholic Christianity, was at least a guardian of the mystery in the midst of the desert of mechanised civilisation. As Lawrence sees it, Catholicism had even preserved some of the old earthy pagan consciousness, and through the cycle of the liturgical year had kept in touch with the rhythm of the seasons, the essential rhythm of man's life on earth. As the inheritor of the sense of vital mystery which was the essence of religion, the Catholic Church seemed at times to him a vehicle of hope. It was a sympathy of sentiment only, not at all of dogma, intermittently awakened in Lawrence by his love for the Mediterranean world. Far stronger was the perpetual

intellectual and moral preoccupation with Christian civilisation and Christian ethics; a preoccupation so intense that he is able to orientate himself only by taking bearings on the Christian position he had abandoned.

For of course he had abandoned it; and the Christians (there are some) who would use Lawrence's stream to turn their own mills have need of caution. He often looks at Christianity with sympathy, but to do so he always has to turn it upside down. A choice had to be made, and Lawrence, in fact, made it in early life. However he may use Christian language, he uses it to a different end. For Christianity the life of the flesh receives its sanction and purpose from a life of the spirit which is eternal and transcendent. For Lawrence the life of the spirit has its justification in enriching and glorifying the life of the flesh of which it is in any case an epiphenomenon. It is at once an older and a newer religion that he is celebrating with what were almost his last words.

For man, the vast marvel is to be alive. For man, as for flower, beast and bird, the supreme triumph is to be most vividly, most perfectly alive. Whatever the unborn and the dead may know, they cannot know the beauty, the marvel of being alive in the flesh. The dead may look after the afterwards. But the magnificent here and now of life in the flesh is ours, and ours alone, and ours only for a time. We ought to dance with rapture that we should be alive and in the flesh, and part of the living, incarnate cosmos. I am part of the sun as my eye is part of me. That I am part of the earth my feet know perfectly, and my blood is part of the sea. My soul knows that I am part of the human race, my soul is an organic part of the great human soul, as my spirit is part of my nation. In my own very self I am part of my family. There is nothing of me that is alone and absolute except my mind, and we shall find that the mind has no existence by itself, it is only the glitter of the sun on the surface of the waters.

Comments and Questions

1. Hough's article is a perceptive commentary on one of D. H. Lawrence's most thoughtful pieces of fiction. Full commentary

and annotations accompany the text of "The Man Who Died," pp. 209–233.

2. Compare James Baldwin's "Notes for a Hypothetical Novel," pp. 851–855, and Camus' "Nobel Prize Acceptance Speech," pp. 823–824, with Hough's essay. Does "The Man Who Died" differ markedly from Baldwin's idea of what a novel should be? Camus' idea? Discuss.

3. In the light of the assertion so often made in the last two decades that "God is dead," may one consider Lawrence as prophetic when he says, "But now I live in 1924, and the Christian venture is done"? But then, what does one make of the recent extremism of the so-called "Jesus freaks"? Is the Christian venture done? Discuss carefully.

4. Even if you do not know French, can you deduce the meaning of the sentence: "Sois mon frère ou je te tue"?

5. Read carefully the quotation from Lawrence at the end of this essay. Compare this with MacLeish's thesis concerning Job in "Trespass on a Monument," below.

Trespass on a Monument
ARCHIBALD MacLEISH
1892–

Before MacLeish's play *J. B.* opened on Broadway (December 11, 1958), *The New York Times* asked the author to comment on his intentions in writing such a play. Mr. MacLeish's response is more than a comment on his drama. It is a deep probing into the most vexing question one can ask concerning God's relationship to His prime creation: man.

Many men have pondered the implications of Job's story. Compare, for example, what Robert Frost has to say on this subject in "A Masque of Reason" (p. 358).

If the invitation to write this piece means that the drama editor of *The New York Times* regards my play as crying out, like Job's boils, for justification, I can only agree. A man may be forgiven for dramatizing an incident from the Bible and even for modernizing it in the process. But what I have done is not so easy to excuse. I have constructed a modern play inside the ancient majesty of *The Book of Job* much as the Bedouins, thirty years ago, used to build within the towering ruins of Palmyra their shacks of gasoline tins roofed with fallen stones.

The Bedouins had the justification of necessity and I can think of nothing better for myself. When you are dealing with questions too large for you, which, nevertheless, will not leave you alone, you are obliged to house them somewhere —and an old wall helps. Which is perhaps why so many modern plays have proved, on critical examination, to be reconstructions of the myths of Greece. That appeal to precedent, however, is of little use to me, for my *J. B.* is not a reconstruction of *The Book of Job*—not, at least, a reconstruction of the kind presently familiar in which the discovery of the model is part of the adventure. My play is put in motion by two broken-down actors who believe, themselves, that the play is *The Book of Job* and that one of them is acting God and the other, Satan. When J. B. and his family appear, however, it is not out of the Bible that they come.

But justification is still necessary and necessity is still the only justification I can plead. I badly needed an ancient structure on which to build the contemporary play that has haunted me for five years past, and the structure of the poem of Job is the only one I know of which our modern history will fit. Job's search, like ours, was for the meaning of his afflictions—the loss of his children, the loss of everything he possessed, the loss of his wife's kindness, who turned upon him in his agony with those ineradicable words, surely the most dreadful ever spoken by wife to husband: "Curse God and die!" There was no reason for all this: no reason the mind, at least, could grasp. Job was, by witness of God himself and twice repeated, "a perfect and an upright man" and his destruction was, by the same unquestionable authority, "without cause." As for ourselves, there can be very few of us who are perfect, but the enormous, nameless disasters that have befallen whole cities, entire peoples, in two great wars and many small ones, have destroyed the innocent together with the guilty —and with no "cause" our minds can grasp.

Question of Guilt

We attribute these sufferings, except when it is we ourselves who inflicted them, to the malevolence of our enemies, but even so we are appalled by all this anguish. Hiroshima, in its terrible retrospect, appals us. And we attempt —millions of us, the psychiatrists say—to justify the inexplicable misery of the world by taking the guilt upon ourselves, as Job attempted to take it: "Show me my guilt, O God." We even listen, as Job did, to the Comforters—though our comforters are not like his. Where Job's Comforters undertook to persuade him, against the evidence of his own inner conviction, that he *was* guilty, ours attempt to persuade us that we are not—that we cannot be—that, for psychological reasons, or because everything is determined in advance by economic necessity anyway, or because we were damned before we started, guilt is impossible. Our Comforters are, if anything, less comfortable than Job's for they drive us from the last refuge in which our minds can hide from the enormous silence. If we cannot even be guilty then there are no reasons.

There are those, I know—because I have heard them—who will object that Job's story bears no true relationship to our own because God has changed in the interval. The God of Job is God the Creator of the Universe, and science, they say, now knows that there is no such Creator—that the events of time progress by an automatism of their own—that the watch winds itself and ticks by its own juggling. The modern God of the scientific age, that is to say, does not control events: not, at least, events in the world of here and now.

Question of Faith

I have no wish, and certainly no competence, to argue the questions of faith that underlie that attitude. But two things may be said from the merely human position. The first relates to the statement that science knows now there is no Creator. Does it? Einstein has told us that he had sometimes the sense that he was following, in his plumbings and probings of the universe, the track of an Intelligence far beyond the reaches of his own. The second thing to be said

of this: that there has been nothing in human history that has brought mankind closer to the immanence of an infinite creativity than the revelation that the minutest particles of inert matter contain an almost immeasurable power. To me, a man committed to no creed, and more uncertain than I should be of certain ultimate beliefs, the God of Job seems closer to this generation than he has to any other in centuries.

J. B. Himself

My hero, called J. B. after the current fashion in business address, bears little relation, perhaps, to that ancient owner of camels and oxen and sheep. He is not a particularly devout man. But he is, at the beginning of the play, prosperous, powerful, possessed of a lovely wife, fine children—everything the heart of man can desire—and he is aware, as he could hardly help being, that God has made "an hedge about him and about his house and about all that he hath on every side." Not that the name of God is often in his mouth. He is one of those vastly successful American business men—not as numerous now as they were before the Great Depression—who, having everything, believe as a matter of course that they have a right to have everything. They do not believe this out of vulgarity. They are not Babbitts: on the contrary, they are most often men of exuberance, of high animal spirits, of force and warmth. They believe it because they possess in large measure that characteristically American courage that has so often amused Asian and European visitors, the courage to believe in themselves. Which means to believe in their lives. Which means, if their tongues can shape the words, to believe in God's goodness to them. They are not hypocritical. They do not think that they deserve more at God's hands than others. They merely think that they have more —and that they have a right to have it.

Such a man is not better prepared than Job was for the sudden and inexplicable loss of everything. And such a man must ask, as our time does ask, Job's repeated question. Job wants *justice* of the universe. He needs to know the reason for his wretchedness. And it is in those repeated cries of his that we hear most clearly our own voices. For our age is an age haunted and driven by the need to know. Not only is our science full of it but our arts also. And it is here, or so it seems to me, that our story and the story of Job come closest to each other. Job is not *answered* in the Bible by the voice out of the whirling wind. He is *silenced* by it—silenced by some thirty or forty of the greatest lines in all literature—silenced by the might and majesty and magnificence of the creation. He is brought, not to *know*, but to *see*. As we also have been brought.

Troublesome Chapter

And what follows that *seeing* which cannot *know*? What follows is a chapter of *The Book of Job* the theologians have tried again and again to explain away. Job is given all he had before twice over—all but his children who are the same in number but more beautiful. And that is not all. Not only is Job *given* his life again: Job *accepts* his life again. The man who was once highest and happiest and has now been brought lowest and made most miserable, the man who has suffered every loss, every agony, and for no reason, moral or intelligible, the mind can grasp; the man who has cried out to God for death, begged over and over to die, regretted the womb that bore him, yearned never to have been, never to have breathed the air or seen the light—*this* man accepts his life again, accepts to live his life again, take back his wife again, beget new children mortal as those others, risk himself upon the very hazards on which, before, his hopes were wrecked. And why? Because his sufferings have been justified? They have not been justified. God has merely lifted into the blazing fire of the imagination his own power and Job's impotence; his own immeasurable knowledge and Job's poor, trembling, ridiculous ignorance. Job accepts to live his life again in spite of all he knows of life, in spite of all he knows now of himself, because he is a man.

Our own demand for justice and for reasons comes to the same unanswering answer. A few days before he died, the greatest of modern poets, and the most modern of great poets, William Butler Yeats, wrote to a friend that he had found what, all his life, he had been looking for. But when, in that letter, he went on to spell his answer out in words, it was not an answer made of words: it was an answer made of life: "When I try to put it all into a phrase I say, 'Man can

embody truth but he cannot know it.'" Which means, to me at least, that man can *live* his truth, his deepest truth, but cannot speak it. It is for this reason that love becomes the ultimate human answer to the ultimate human question. Love, in reason's terms, answers nothing. We say that *Amor vincit omnia* but in truth love conquers nothing—certainly not death—certainly not chance. What love does is to affirm. It affirms the worth of life in spite of life. It affirms the wonder and the beauty of the human creature, mortal and insignificant and ignorant though he be. It answers life with life and so justifies that bravely tolling line of Shakespeare's that declares that love "bears it out even to the edge of doom." [1] Love does: and for us no less than for that ancient man who took back his life again after all that wretchedness. J. B., like Job, covers his mouth with his hand; acquiesces in the vast indifference of the universe as all men must truly face it; takes back his life again. In love. To live.

I suppose, if I am really to justify my trespass, I must go on to say that, though human beings have taken back their lives over and over, generation after generation since time began, they have, perhaps, never done so with such desperate courage as in these past, strange years. Men, our own contemporaries, have already sat as Job did on an earth reduced to ash-heap, picking in agony at the cinders of a bomb-scorched skin, asking Job's eternal question. We know that they have sat there. We know that we may sit there too. But we know also something more. We know that even men like these can learn, in Yeats' words, to "live it all again."

Questions

1. Why does the author feel that *The Book of Job* has special applicability to our times? Is man now apparently more prone to undeserved or, at least, inexplicable disaster than heretofore? Discuss.

2. How do the Job's comforters of today differ from the original comforters? Is it no comfort to feel that "guilt is impossible"? Why or why not? What examples can you cite

[1] A reference to Sonnet 116, "Let Me Not to the Marriage of True Minds," p. 278.

to illustrate the modern trend towards a disbelief in individual guilt?

3. What does the author mean when he says that Job was brought "not to *know,* but to *see"?* Compare De Quincey's "The Literature of Knowledge and the Literature of Power" (p. 808).

4. How is it that "love becomes the ultimate answer to the ultimate human question"? How does the author relate love to Job's reacceptance of life?

5. It has been said that Job felt no sense of guilt. Is MacLeish right, then, in quoting Job as saying: "Show me my guilt, O God"? Discuss.

APPENDIX

FROM ARISTOTLE'S "POETICS" [1]

I

I propose to treat of Poetry in itself and of its various kinds, noting the essential quality of each; to inquire into the structure of the plot as requisite to a good poem; into the number and nature of the parts of which a poem is composed; and similarly into whatever else falls within the same inquiry. Following, then, the order of nature, let us begin with the principles which come first.

Epic poetry and Tragedy, Comedy also and Dithyrambic poetry, and the music of the flute and of the lyre in most of their forms, are all in their general conception modes of imitation. They differ, however, from one another in three respects—the medium, the objects, the manner or mode of imitation, being in each case distinct.

For as there are persons who, by conscious art or mere habit, imitate and represent various objects through the medium of colour and form, or again by the voice; so in the arts above mentioned, taken as a whole, the imitation is produced by rhythm, language, or "harmony," either singly or combined. . . .

II

Since the objects of imitation are men in action, and these men must be either of a higher or a lower type (for moral character mainly answers to these divisions, goodness and badness being the distinguishing marks of moral differences), it follows that we must represent men either as better than in real life, or as worse, or as they are. . . . Homer, for example, makes men better than they are; Cleophon as they are; Hegemon the Thasian, the inventor of parodies, and

[1] Butcher translation, 4th ed.

Nicochares, the author of the Deiliad, worse than they are. . . .

III

There is still a third difference—the manner in which each of these objects may be imitated. For the medium being the same, and the objects the same, the poet may imitate by narration—in which case he can either take another personality as Homer does, or speak in his own person, unchanged—or he may present all his characters as living and moving before us.

These, then, as we said at the beginning, are the three differences which distinguish artistic imitation—the medium, the objects, and the manner. So that from one point of view, Sophocles is an imitator of the same kind as Homer—for both imitate higher types of character; from another point of view, of the same kind as Aristophanes—for both imitate persons acting and doing. Hence, some say, the name of "drama" is given to such poems, as representing action. . . .

This may suffice as to the number and nature of the various modes of imitation.

IV

Poetry in general seems to have sprung from two causes, each of them lying deep in our nature. First, the instinct of imitation is implanted in man from childhood, one difference between him and other animals being that he is the most imitative of living creatures, and through imitation learns his earliest lessons; and no less universal is the pleasure felt in things imitated. We have evidence of this in the facts of experience. Objects which in themselves we view with pain, we delight to contemplate when reproduced with minute fidelity: such as the forms of the most ignoble animals and of dead bodies. The cause of this again is, that to learn gives the liveliest pleasure, not only to philosophers but to men in general; whose capacity, however, of learning is more limited. Thus the reason why men enjoy seeing a likeness is, that in contemplating it they find themselves learning or inferring, and saying perhaps, "Ah, that is he." For if you happen not to have seen the original, the pleasure will be due not to the imitation as such, but to the execution, the colouring, or some such other cause.

Imitation, then, is one instinct of our nature. Next, there is the instinct for "harmony" and rhythm, metres being manifestly sections of rhythm. Persons, therefore, starting with this natural gift developed by degrees their special aptitudes, till their rude improvisations gave birth to Poetry.

Poetry now diverged in two directions, according to the individual character of the writers. The graver spirits imitated noble actions, and the actions of good men. The more trivial sort imitated the actions of meaner persons, at first composing satires, as the former did hymns to the gods and the praises of famous men. . . . But when Tragedy and Comedy came to light, the two classes of poets still followed their natural bent: the lampooners became writers of Comedy, and the Epic poets were succeeded by Tragedians, since the drama was a larger and higher form of art. . . .

V

Comedy is, as we have said, an imitation of characters of a lower type—not, however, in the full sense of the word bad, the Ludicrous being merely a subdivision of the ugly. It consists in some defect or ugliness which is not painful or destructive. To take an obvious example, the comic mask is ugly and distorted, but does not imply pain. . . .

Epic poetry agrees with Tragedy in so far as it is an imitation in verse of characters of a higher type. They differ, in that Epic poetry admits but one kind of metre, and is narrative in form. They differ, again, in their length: for Tragedy endeavours, as far as possible, to confine itself to a single revolution of the sun, or but slightly to exceed this limit; whereas the Epic action has no limits of time. This, then, is a second point

of difference; though at first the same freedom was admitted in Tragedy as in Epic poetry.

Of their constituent parts some are common to both, some peculiar to Tragedy: whoever, therefore, knows what is good or bad Tragedy, knows also about Epic poetry. All the elements of an Epic poem are found in Tragedy, but the elements of a Tragedy are not all found in the Epic poem.

VI

. . . . Let us now discuss Tragedy, resuming its formal definition, as resulting from what has been already said.

Tragedy, then, is an imitation of an action that is serious, complete, and of a certain magnitude; in language embellished with each kind of artistic ornament, the several kinds being found in separate parts of the play; in the form of action, not of narrative; through pity and fear effecting the proper purgation of these emotions. By "language embellished," I mean language into which rhythm, "harmony," and song enter. By "the several kinds in separate parts," I mean, that some parts are rendered through the medium of verse alone, others again with the aid of song.

Now as tragic imitation implies persons acting, it necessarily follows, in the first place, that Spectacular equipment will be a part of Tragedy. Next, Song and Diction, for these are the medium of imitation. By "Diction" I mean the mere metrical arrangement of the words: as for "Song," it is a term whose sense every one understands.

Again, Tragedy is the imitation of an action; and an action implies personal agents, who necessarily possess certain distinctive qualities both of character and thought; for it is by these that we qualify actions themselves, and these—thought and character—are the two natural causes from which actions spring, and on actions again all success or failure depends. Hence, the Plot is the imitation of the action:—for by plot I here mean the arrangement of the incidents. By Character I mean that in virtue of which we ascribe certain qualities to the agents. Thought is required wherever a statement is proved, or, it may be, a general truth enunciated. Every Tragedy, therefore, must have six parts, which parts determine its quality—namely, Plot, Character, Diction, Thought, Spectacle, Song. Two of the parts constitute the medium of imitation, one the manner, and three the objects of imitation. And these complete the list. These elements have been employed, we may say, by the poets to a man; in fact, every play contains Spectacular elements as well as Character, Plot, Diction, Song, and Thought.

But most important of all is the structure of the incidents. For Tragedy is an imitation, not of men, but of an action and of life, and life consists in action, and its end is a mode of action, not a quality. Now character determines men's qualities, but it is by their actions that they are happy or the reverse. Dramatic action, therefore, is not with a view to the representation of character: character comes in as subsidiary to the actions. Hence the incidents and the plot are the end of a tragedy; and the end is the chief thing of all. Again, without action there cannot be a tragedy; there may be without character. . . . Again, if you string together a set of speeches expressive of character, and well finished in point of diction and thought, you will not produce the essential tragic effect nearly so well as with a play which, however deficient in these respects, yet has a plot and artistically constructed incidents. Besides which, the most powerful elements of emotional interest in Tragedy—Peripeteia or Reversal of the Situation, and Recognition scenes—are parts of the plot. A further proof is, that novices in the art attain to finish of diction and precision of portraiture before they can construct the plot. It is the same with almost all the early poets.

The Plot, then, is the first principle, and, as it were, the soul of a tragedy: Character holds the second place. . . .

Third in order is Thought,—that is, the faculty of saying what is possible and pertinent in given circumstances. In the case of oratory, this is the function of the political art and of the art of rhetoric: and so indeed the older poets make their characters speak the language of civic life; the poets of our time, the language of the rhetoricians. Character is that which reveals moral purpose, showing what kind of things a man chooses or avoids. Speeches, therefore, which do not make this manifest, or in which the speaker does not choose or avoid anything whatever, are not expressive of character. Thought, on the other hand, is found where something is proved to be or not to be, or a general maxim is enunciated. . . .

VII

These principles being established, let us now discuss the proper structure of the Plot, since this is the first and most important thing in Tragedy.

Now, according to our definition, Tragedy is an imitation of an action that is complete, and whole, and of a certain magnitude; for there may be a whole that is wanting in magnitude. A whole is that which has a beginning, a middle, and an end. A beginning is that which does not iself follow anything by causal necessity, but after which something naturally is or comes to be. An end, on the contrary, is that which itself naturally follows some other thing, either by necessity, or as a rule, but has nothing following it. A middle is that which follows something as some other thing follows it. A well constructed plot, therefore, must neither begin nor end at haphazard, but conform to these principles.

Again, a beautiful object, whether it be a living organism or any whole composed of parts, must not only have an orderly arrangement of parts, but must also be of a certain magnitude; for beauty depends on magnitude and order. Hence a very small animal organism cannot be beautiful; for the view of it is confused, the object being seen in an almost imperceptible moment of time. Nor, again, can one of vast size be beautiful; for as the eye cannot take it all in at once, the unity and sense of the whole is lost for the spectator; as for instance if there were one a thousand miles long. As, therefore, in the case of animate bodies and organisms a certain magnitude is necessary, and a magnitude which may be easily embraced in one view; so in the plot, a certain length is necessary, and a length which can be easily embraced by the memory. The limit of length in relation to dramatic competition and sensuous presentment, is no part of artistic theory. For had it been the rule for a hundred tragedies to compete together, the performance would have been regulated by the water-clock,—as indeed we are told was formerly done. But the limit as fixed by the nature of the drama itself is this:—the greater the length, the more beautiful will the piece be by reason of its size, provided that the whole be perspicuous. And to define the matter roughly, we may say that the proper magnitude is comprised within such limits, that the sequence of events, according to the law of probability or necessity, will admit of a change from bad fortune to good, or from good fortune to bad.

VIII

Unity of plot does not, as some persons think, consist in the unity of the hero. . . . In composing the Odyssey [Homer] did not include all the adventures of Odysseus—such as his wound on Parnassus, or his feigned madness at the mustering of the host—incidents between which there was no necessary or probable connection: but he made the Odyssey, and likewise the Iliad, to centre round an action that in our sense of the word is one. As therefore, in the other imitative arts, the imitation is one when the object imitated is one, so the plot, being an imitation of an action, must imitate one action and that a whole, the structural union of the parts being such that, if any one of them is displaced or removed, the whole will be disjointed and disturbed. For a thing whose presence or absence makes no visible difference, is not an organic part of the whole.

IX

It is, moreover, evident from what has been said, that it is not the function of the poet to relate what has happened, but what may happen,—what is possible according to the law of probability or necessity. The poet and the historian differ not by writing in verse or in prose. The work of Herodotus might be put into verse, and it would still be a species of history, with metre no less than without it. The true difference is that one relates what has happened, the other what may happen. Poetry, therefore, is a more philosophical and a higher thing than history: for poetry tends to express the universal, history the particular. By the universal I mean how a person of a certain type will on occasion speak or act, according to the law of probability or necessity; and it is this universality at which

poetry aims in the names she attaches to the personages. . . .

Of all plots and actions the epeisodic are the worst. I call a plot "epeisodic" in which the episodes or acts succeed one another without probable or necessary sequence. Bad poets compose such pieces by their own fault, good poets, to please the players; for, as they write show pieces for competition, they stretch the plot beyond its capacity, and are often forced to break the natural continuity.

But again, Tragedy is an imitation not only of a complete action, but of events inspiring fear or pity. Such an effect is best produced when the events come on us by surprise; and the effect is heightened when, at the same time, they follow as cause and effect. The tragic wonder will then be greater than if they happened of themselves or by accident; for even coincidences are most striking when they have an air of design. We may instance the statue of Mitys at Argos, which fell upon his murderer while he was a spectator at a festival, and killed him. Such events seem not to be due to mere chance. Plots, therefore, constructed on these principles are necessarily the best.

X

Plots are either Simple or Complex, for the actions in real life, of which the plots are an imitation, obviously show a similar distinction. An action which is one and continuous in the sense above defined, I call Simple, when the change of fortune takes place without Reversal of the Situation and without Recognition.

A Complex action is one in which the change is accompanied by such Reversal, or by Recognition, or by both. These last should arise from the internal structure of the plot, so that what follows should be the necessary or probable result of the preceding action. It makes all the difference whether any given event is a case of *propter hoc* or *post hoc*.

XI

Reversal of the Situation is a change by which the action veers round to its opposite, subject always to our rule of probability or necessity. Thus in the Oedipus the messenger comes to cheer Oedipus and free him from his alarms about his mother, but by revealing who he is, he produces the opposite effect. Again in the Lynceus, Lynceus is being led away to his death, and Danaus goes with him, meaning to slay him; but the outcome of the preceding incidents is that Danaus is killed and Lynceus saved.

Recognition, as the name indicates, is a change from ignorance to knowledge, producing love or hate between the persons destined by the poet for good or bad fortune. The best form of recognition is coincident with a Reversal of the Situation, as in the Oedipus. . . .

XIII

As the sequel to what has already been said, we must proceed to consider what the poet should aim at, and what he should avoid, in constructing his plots; and by what means the specific effect of Tragedy will be produced.

A perfect tragedy should, as we have seen, be arranged not on the simple but on the complex plan. It should, moreover, imitate actions which excite pity and fear, this being the distinctive mark of tragic imitation. It follows plainly, in the first place, that the change of fortune presented must not be the spectacle of a virtuous man brought from prosperity to adversity: for this moves neither pity nor fear; it merely shocks us. Nor, again, that of a bad man passing from adversity to prosperity: for nothing can be more alien to the spirit of Tragedy; it possesses no single tragic quality; it neither satisfies the moral sense nor calls forth pity or fear. Nor, again, should the downfall of the utter villain be exhibited. A plot of this kind would, doubtless, satisfy the moral sense, but it would inspire neither pity nor fear; for pity is aroused by unmerited misfortune, fear by the misfortune of a man like ourselves. Such an event, therefore, will be neither pitiful nor terrible. There remains, then, the character between these two extremes,—that of a man who is not eminently good and just, yet whose misfortune is brought about not by vice or depravity, but by some error or frailty. He must be one who is highly renowned and prosperous—a personage like Oedipus, Thyestes, or other illustrious men of such families.

A well constructed plot should, therefore, be single in its issue, rather than double as some maintain. The change of fortune should be not from bad to good, but, reversely, from good to bad. It should come about as the result not of vice, but of some great error or frailty, in a character either such as we have described, or better rather than worse. The practice of the stage bears out our view. At first the poets recounted any legend that came in their way. Now, the best tragedies are founded on the story of a few houses,—on the fortunes of Alcmaeon, Oedipus, Orestes, Meleager, Thyestes, Telephus, and those others who have done or suffered something terrible. A tragedy, then, to be perfect according to the rules of art should be of this construction. . . .

XIV

Fear and pity may be aroused by spectacular means; but they may also result from the inner structure of the piece, which is the better way, and indicates a superior poet. For the plot ought to be so constructed that, even without the aid of the eye, he who hears the tale told will thrill with horror and melt to pity at what takes place. This is the impression we should receive from hearing the story of the Oedipus. But to produce this effect by the mere spectacle is a less artistic method, and dependent on extraneous aids. Those who employ spectacular means to create a sense not of the terrible but only of the monstrous, are strangers to the purpose of Tragedy; for we must not demand of Tragedy any and every kind of pleasure, but only that which is proper to it. And since the pleasure which the poet should afford is that which comes from pity and fear through imitation, it is evident that this quality must be impressed upon the incidents.

Let us then determine what are the circumstances which strike us as terrible or pitiful.

Actions capable of this effect must happen between persons who are either friends or enemies or indifferent to one another. If an enemy kills an enemy, there is nothing to excite pity either in the act or the intention,—except so far as the suffering in itself is pitiful. So again with indifferent persons. But when the tragic incident occurs between those who are near or dear to one another—if, for example, a brother kills, or intends to kill, a brother, a son his father, a mother her son, a son his mother, or any other deed of the kind is done—these are the situations to be looked for by the poet. He may not indeed destroy the framework of the received legends —the fact, for instance, that Clytemnestra was slain by Orestes and Eriphyle by Alcmaeon— but he ought to show invention of his own, and skillfully handle the traditional material. Let us explain more clearly what is meant by skillful handling.

The action may be done unconsciously and with knowledge of the persons, in the manner of the older poets. It is thus too that Euripides makes Medea slay her children. Or, again, the deed of horror may be done, but done in ignorance, and the tie of kinship or friendship be discovered afterwards. The Oedipus of Sophocles is an example. Here, indeed, the incident is outside the drama proper; but cases occur where it falls within the action of the play: one may cite the Alcmaeon of Astydamas, or Telegonus in the Wounded Odysseus. Again, there is a third case,—to be about to act with knowledge of the persons and then not to act. The fourth case is when some one is about to do an irreparable deed through ignorance, and makes the discovery before it is done. These are the only possible ways. For the deed must either be done or not done,—and that wittingly or unwittingly. But of all these ways, to be about to act knowing the persons, and then not to act, is the worst. It is shocking without being tragic, for no disaster follows. It is, therefore, never, or very rarely, found in poetry. One instance, however, is in the Antigone, where Haemon threatens to kill Creon. The next and better way is that the deed should be perpetrated. Still better, that it should be perpetrated in ignorance, and the discovery made afterwards. There is then nothing to shock us, while the discovery produces a startling effect. The last case is the best, as when in the Cresphontes Merope is about to slay her son, but, recognising who he is, spares his life. So in the Iphigenia, the sister recognises the brother just in time. Again in the Helle, the son recognizes the mother when on the point of giving her up. This, then, is why a few families only, as has been already observed, furnish the subject of tragedy. It was not art, but happy chance, that led the poets in search of subjects to impress the tragic quality upon their plots. They are compelled, therefore, to have recourse to those houses whose history contains moving incidents like these.

Enough has now been said concerning the structure of the incidents, and the right kind of plot.

XV

In respect of Character there are four things to be aimed at. First, and most important, it must be good. Now any speech or action that manifests moral purpose of any kind will be expressive of character: the character will be good if the purpose is good. This rule is relative to each class. Even a woman may be good, and also a slave; though the woman may be said to be an inferior being, and the slave quite worthless. The second thing to aim at is propriety. There is a type of manly valour; but valour in a woman, or unscrupulous cleverness, is inappropriate. Thirdly, character must be true to life: for this is a distinct thing from goodness and propriety, as here described. The fourth point is consistency: for though the subject of the imitation, who suggested the type, be inconsistent, still he must be consistently inconsistent. . . .

As in the structure of the plot, so too in the portraiture of character, the poet should always aim either at the necessary or the probable. Thus a person of a given character should speak or act in a given way, by the rule either of necessity or of probability; just as this event should follow that by necessary or probable sequence. . . .

Again, since Tragedy is an imitation of persons who are above the common level, the example of good portrait-painters should be followed. They, while reproducing the distinctive form of the original, make a likeness which is true to life and yet more beautiful. So too the poet, in representing men who are irascible or indolent, or have other defects of character, should preserve the type and yet ennoble it. In this way Achilles is portrayed by Agathon and Homer. . . .

XVIII

Every tragedy falls into two parts,—Complication and Unravelling or *Dénouement*. Incidents extraneous to the action are frequently combined with a portion of the action proper, to form the Complication; the rest is the Unravelling. By the Complication I mean all that extends from the beginning of the action to the part which marks the turning-point to good or bad fortune. The Unravelling is that which extends from the beginning of the change to the end. . . .

XIX

. . . Under Thought is included every effect which has to be produced by speech, the subdivisions being—proof and refutation; the excitation of the feelings, such as pity, fear, anger, and the like; the suggestion of importance or its opposite. Now, it is evident that the dramatic incidents must be treated from the same points of view as the dramatic speeches, when the object is to evoke the sense of pity, fear, importance, or probability. The only difference is, that the incidents should speak for themselves without verbal exposition; while the effects aimed at in speech should be produced by the speaker, and as a result of the speech. For what were the business of a speaker, if the Thought were revealed quite apart from what he says? . . .

XXII

. . . But the greatest thing by far is to have a command of metaphor. This alone cannot be imported by another; it is the mark of genius, for to make good metaphors implies an eye for resemblances. . . .

XXIII

As to that poetic imitation which is narrative in form and employs a single metre, the plot manifestly ought, as in a tragedy, to be constructed on dramatic principles. It should have for its subject a single action, whole and complete, with a beginning, a middle, and an end. It will thus resemble a living organism in all its unity, and produce the pleasure proper to it. It will differ in structure from historical compositions, which of necessity present not a single action, but a single period, and all that happened within that period to one person or to many, little connected together as the events may be. For as the sea-fight at Salamis and the battle with the Carthaginians in Sicily took place at the same time, but did not tend to any one result, so in the sequence of events, one thing sometimes follows another, and yet no single result is thereby produced. Such is the practice, we may say, of most poets. . . .

XXIV

Again, Epic poetry must have as many kinds as Tragedy: it must be simple, or complex, or "ethical," or "pathetic." The parts also, with the exception of song and spectacle, are the same; for it requires Reversals of the Situation, Recognitions, and Scenes of Suffering. Moreover, the thoughts and the diction must be artistic. In all these respects Homer is our earliest and sufficient model. Indeed each of his poems has a twofold character. The Iliad is at once simple and "pathetic," and the Odyssey complex (for Recognition scenes run through it), and at the same time "ethical." Moreover, in diction and thought they are supreme.

Epic poetry differs from Tragedy in the scale on which it is constructed, and in its metre. As regards scale or length, we have already laid down an adequate limit:—the beginning and the end must be capable of being brought within a single view. This condition will be satisfied by poems on a smaller scale than the old epics, and answering in length to the group of tragedies presented at a single sitting.

Epic poetry has, however, a great—a special—capacity for enlarging its dimensions, and we can see the reason. In Tragedy we cannot imitate several lines of actions carried on at one and the same time; we must confine ourselves to the action on the stage and the part taken by the players. But in Epic poetry, owing to the narrative form, many events simultaneously transacted can be presented; and these, if relevant to the subject, add mass and dignity to the poem. The Epic has here an advantage, and one that conduces to grandeur of effect, to diverting the mind of the hearer, and relieving the story with varying episodes. For sameness of incident soon produces satiety, and makes tragedies fail on the stage. . . .

Homer, admirable in all respects, has the special merit of being the only poet who rightly appreciates the part he should take himself. The poet should speak as little as possible in his own person, for it is not this that makes him an imitator. Other poets appear themselves upon the scene throughout, and imitate but little and rarely. Homer, after a few prefatory words, at once brings in a man, or woman, or other personage; none of them wanting in characteristic qualities, but each with a character of his own.

The element of the wonderful is required in Tragedy. The irrational, on which the wonderful depends for its chief effects, has wider scope in Epic poetry, because there the person acting is not seen. Thus, the pursuit of Hector would be ludicrous if placed upon the stage—the Greeks standing still and not joining in the pursuit, and Achilles waving them back. But in the Epic poem the absurdity passes unnoticed. Now the wonderful is pleasing: as may be inferred from the fact that every one tells a story with some addition of his own, knowing that his hearers like it. . . .

Accordingly, the poet should prefer probable impossibilities to improbable possibilities. The tragic plot must not be composed of irrational parts. Everything irrational should, if possible, be excluded; or, at all events, it should lie outside the action of the play (as, in the Oedipus, the hero's ignorance as to the manner of Laius' death); not within the drama—as in the Electra, the messenger's account of the Pythian games; or, as in the Mysians, the man who has come from Tegea to Mysia and is still speechless. The plea that otherwise the plot would have been ruined, is ridiculous; such a plot should not in the first instance be constructed. But once the irrational has been introduced and an air of likelihood imparted to it, we must accept it in spite of the absurdity. Take even the irrational incidents in the Odyssey, where Odysseus is left upon the shore of Ithaca. How intolerable even these might have been would be apparent if an inferior poet were to treat the subject. As it is, the absurdity is veiled by the poetic charm with which the poet invests it.

The diction should be elaborated in the pauses of the action, where there is no expression of character or thought. For, conversely, character and thought are merely obscured by a diction that is over brilliant.

ACKNOWLEDGMENTS (Continued from copyright page)

The Dial Press for permission to reprint "Notes for a Hypothetical Novel" from the book, *Nobody Knows My Name* by James Baldwin. Copyright © 1961 by James Baldwin. Copyright © 1954, 1956, 1958, 1960 by James Baldwin. Reprinted by permission of the publisher, The Dial Press.

Doubleday & Company, Inc., for permission to reprint "The Colonel's Lady" from *Creatures of Circumstance* by W. Somerset Maugham; "Brandy" from *Strictly Personal* by W. Somerset Maugham, copyright 1940, 1941; "A Bottle of Milk for Mother" from *Neon Wilderness* by Nelson Algren. Copyright, 1941 by Nelson Algren; "The Absurdity of the Absurd" from *The Theatre of the Absurd* by Martin Esslin. Copyright © 1961 by Martin Esslin. Reprinted by permission of Doubleday & Company, Inc.; "Dolor" by Theodore Roethke, copyright 1943 by the Modern Poetry Association, Inc., from *The Collected Poems of Theodore Roethke* by Theodore Roethke. Reprinted by permission of Doubleday & Company, Inc.

Duckworth Press for permission to reprint "Lawrence's Quarrel with Christianity: The Man Who Died," copyright © 1956 The Duckworth Press.

Dwarf Music for permission to reprint "Sad-Eyed Lady of the Lowlands," copyright © 1966 Dwarf Music; "All Along the Watchtower," copyright © 1968 Dwarf Music.

James A. Emanuel for permission to reprint "A Pause for a Fine Phrase" and "Emmett Till."

Faber and Faber Limited for "Lullaby," "The Cultivation of Christmas Trees," reprinted with permission of Faber and Faber, Ltd.

Farrar, Straus & Giroux, Inc., for permission to reprint "The Magic Barrel" from *The Magic Barrel* by Bernard Malamud. Copyright © 1945, 1958 by Bernard Malamud; "The Lottery" from *The Lottery* by Shirley Jackson. Copyright 1948, 1949 by Shirley Jackson. First published in *The New Yorker;* "Sorrow Is the Only Faithful One" from *Powerful Long Ladder* by Owen Dodson, copyright 1946 by Owen Dodson; "Everything That Rises Must Converge," from *Everything That Rises Must Converge* by Flannery O'Connor, copyright © 1961, 1965 by the Estate of Mary Flannery O'Connor; "The Cultivation of Christmas Trees," from *The Cultivation of Christmas Trees,* by T.S. Eliot, copyright © 1954, 1956 by Thomas Stearns Eliot.

Samuel French, Inc., for permission to reprint *The Boor* by Anton Chekhov (trans. Hilmar Baukhage).

Harcourt Brace Jovanovich, Inc., for permission to reprint selections from *The People, Yes* by Carl Sandburg, copyright 1936, by Harcourt Brace Jovanovich, Inc., renewed, © 1964, by Carl Sandburg; "Candles" from *The Complete Poems of Cavafy* (trans. by Rae Dalven), copyright, 1948, 1949, © 1959, 1961, by Rae Dalven. Reprinted by permission of Harcourt Brace Jovanovich Inc.; "the Cambridge ladies" copyright, 1923, 1951, by E. E. Cummings. Reprinted from his volume, *Poems 1923–1954* by permission of Harcourt Brace Jovanovich Inc.; "a/mong crum/bling people" copyright, 1931, 1959, by E. E. Cummings. Reprinted from his volume, *Poems 1923–1954* by permission of Harcourt Brace Jovanovich, Inc.; "anyone lived in a pretty how town" copyright, 1940, by E. E. Cummings. Reprinted from his volume, *Poems 1923–1954* by permission of Harcourt Brace Jovanovich, Inc.; "pity this busy monster, manunkind," copyright, 1944, by E. E. Cummings, renewed 1972 by Nancy Andrews. Reprinted by permission of Harcourt Brace Jovanovich, Inc. "Edgar A. Guest Considers 'The Old Woman Who Lived in a Shoe' and the Good Old Verities at the Same Time" from *Collected Parodies* by Louis Untermeyer, copyright 1926; "The Love Song of J. Alfred Prufrock," "Morning at the Window," and "The Hollow Men" from *Collected Poems, 1909–1962* by T. S. Eliot, copyright 1936 by Harcourt Brace Jovanovich Inc., copyright, © 1963, 1964 by T. S. Eliot. Reprinted by permission of the publishers; "The Naming of Cats" from *Old Possum's Book of Practical Cats,* copyright, 1939, by T. S. Eliot, renewed, 1967, by Esme Valerie Eliot. Reprinted by permission of Harcourt Brace Jovanovich, Inc.; "Gibbon" from *Portraits in Minature and Other Essays,* by Lytton Strachey, copyright 1931 by Lytton Strachey, renewed © 1959, by James Strachey; "As a Plane Tree by the Water" and "The Dead in Europe" from *Lord Weary's Castle* by Robert Lowell, copyright, 1944, 1946 by Robert Lowell; "The Tragic Fallacy" from *The Modern Temper* by Joseph Wood Krutch, copyright, 1929, by Harcourt Brace Jovanovich, Inc., renewed, 1957, by Joseph Wood Krutch. Reprinted by permission of the publishers.

Harper & Row for permission to reprint "I Paint What I See" from *The Fox of the Peapack and Other Poems* by E. B. White, copyright 1933, 1961 by E. B. White. Originally appeared in *The New Yorker,* and reprinted by permission of Harper & Row, Publishers; "Music at Night" from *Music at Night* by Aldous Huxley. Copyright 1931, © 1959 by Aldous Huxley; "Yet Do I Marvel," copyright 1925 by Harper & Row, Publishers, Inc., "For John Keats, "copyright 1925 by Harper & Row, Publishers, Inc., "From the Dark Tower," copyright © 1927 by Harper & Row, Publishers, Inc., all from *On These I Stand* by Countee Cullen; "Kitchenette Building," p. 4, copyright 1945 by Gwendolyn Brooks Blakely, "The Ballad of Chocolate Mabbie," p. 14, copyright 1945 by Gwendolyn Brooks Blakely, "The Egg Boiler," p. 366, copyright © 1960 by Gwendolyn Brooks Blakely, "The Children of the Poor," p. 99, copyright 1949 by Gwendolyn Brooks Blakely, all from *The World of Gwendolyn Brooks;* "Miracles" by Arna Bontemps from *Golden Slippers* by Arna Bontemps, copyright, 1941 by Harper & Row, Publishers, Inc.; "Bright and Morning Star" from *Uncle Tom's Children* by Richard Wright, copyright 1938 by Richard Wright, by permission of Harper & Row, Publishers, Inc.; Chapter 7 (pp. 81–95, hardbound edition) from *The Bell Jar* by Sylvia Plath, copyright © 1971 by Harper & Row, Publishers, Inc. Reprinted by permission of the publishers.

Harvard University Press for permission to reprint the poems of Emily Dickinson. Reprinted by permission of the publishers and the Trustees of Amherst College from Thomas H. Johnson, Editor, *The Poems of Emily Dickinson,* Cambridge, Mass.: The Belknap Press of Harvard University Press, Copyright, 1951, 1955, by The President and Fellows of Harvard College.

James Hearst for permission to reprint "Truth" from *Limited View* by James Hearst (Prairie Press, Iowa City, Iowa), copyright © 1962 by James Hearst, and "Snake in the Strawberries."

Hill and Wang, Inc., for permission to reprint *The Firebugs* by Max Frisch, translated by Mordecai Gorelik. Original title *Herr Biedermann Und Die Brandstifter.* Copyright © 1958 by Suhrkamp Verlag, Frankfurt am Main. English translation as an unpublished work copyright © 1959 by Mordecai Gorelik. Reprinted by permission of Hill and Wang, Inc.

Holt, Rinehart and Winston, Inc., for permission to reprint "Stopping by the Woods on a Snowy Evening," "The Gift Outright," "The Secret Sits," "Acquainted with the Night," "Departmental," "Neither Out Far nor In Deep," "The Trial by Existence," "The Strong Are Saying Nothing" from *The Poetry of Robert Frost* edited by Edward Connery Lathem. Copyright 1923, 1928, 1930, 1934, 1939, © 1969 by Holt, Rinehart and Winston, Inc. Copyright 1936, 1942, 1951, © 1956, 1958, 1962 by Robert Frost. Copyright © 1964, 1967, 1970 by Lesley Frost Ballantine. Reprinted by permission of Holt, Rinehart and Winston, Inc. *A Masque of Reason* by Robert Frost, copyright 1945 by Holt, Rinehart and Winston, Inc.; "When I Was One-and-Twenty" and "To an Athlete Dy-ing Young" from "A Shropshire Lad"—Authorised Edition—from *The Collected Poems of A. E. Housman.* Copyright 1939, 1940, © 1965 by Holt, Rinehart and Winston, Inc. Copyright © 1967, 1968 by Robert E. Symons. Reprinted by permission of Holt, Rinehart and Winston, Inc.; "Christmas" from *Homecoming* by Floyd Dell, copyright 1933 by Floyd Dell; "An Extemporaneous Talk for Students" by Robert Frost, copyright © 1965 by Holt, Rinehart and Winston, Inc.

Houghton Mifflin Company for permission to reprint "Ars Poetica," " 'Not Marble nor the Gilded Monuments,' " and "You, Andrew Marvell," from *Collected Poems, 1917–1952* by Archibald MacLeish; "Frescoes for Mr. Rockefeller's City" by Archibald MacLeish; "The Dinner-Party" from *Men, Women and Ghosts* by Amy Lowell; "The Kiss" and "It Is a Spring Afternoon" from *Love Poems, 1969* by Anne Sexton.

Howard University Press for permission to reprint "Trends in Negro American Literature" by Arthur P. Davis.

Olwyn Hughes, Literary Agent, for permission to reprint "Two Views of a Cadaver Room" and "Suicide off Egg Rock" from *The Colossus* published by Faber and Faber, Ltd., London, copyright 1967 by Ted Hughes.

Mrs. Randall Jarrell for permission to reprint "The Emancipators" and "Second Air Force" by Randall Jarrell.

Margot Johnson Agency for permission to reprint "The Goose Fish" by Howard Nemerov.

Robert Lantz-Candida Donadio Literary Agency, Inc. for permission to reprint "A Bottle of Milk for Mother," copyright © Nelson Algren.

Little, Brown and Company for permission to reprint "For Esmé—With Love and Squalor" from *Nine Stories* by J. D. Salinger, copyright 1950 by J. D. Salinger (appeared originally in *The New Yorker*); "The Seven Spiritual Ages of Mrs. Marmaduke Moore." Copyright, 1933, by Ogden Nash; "The Oxford Method" from *Unforgotten Years* by Logan Pearsall Smith, copyright 1939.

Liveright Publishers for permission to reprint "North Labrador" and "To Brooklyn Bridge" from *The Collected Poems and Selected Letters and Prose of Hart Crane* by Hart Crane. Permission of LIVERIGHT, Publishers, N.Y. Copyright © 1933, 1958, 1966 by Liveright Publishing Corporation.

Mary McCarthy for permission to reprint "Cruel and Barbarous Treatment."

The Macmillan Company for permission to reprint "Three Deaths" from *A Treasury of Great Russian Short Stories* by Leo Tolstoy (trans. by Constance Garnett), copyright 1944; "On the Road" from *The Chorus Girl and Other Stories* by Anton

Chekhov. Copyright 1920 by The Macmillan Co. Renewed 1948 by David Garnett; "The Eagle That Is Forgotten" from *Collected Poems* by Vachel Lindsay. Copyright 1923 by The Macmillan Co. Renewed 1951 by Elizabeth C. Lindsay; "Among School Children," Copyright 1928 by The Macmillan Company, renewed 1956 by George Yeats. "The Wild Swans at Coole," Copyright 1919 by The Macmillan Company, renewed 1947 by Bertha Georgie Yeats and "The Second Coming," Copyright 1924 by The Macmillan Company, renewed 1952 by Bertha Georgie Yeats from *Collected Poems* by William Butler Yeats, copyright 1950; "Hap," "In Tenebris, II," "The Man He Killed," and "The Last Chrysanthemum" from *Collected Poems* by Thomas Hardy, copyright 1925 by The Macmillan Company; "Mr. Flood's Party" from *Collected Poems* by Edwin Arlington Robinson, copyright 1921 by Edwin Arlington Robinson, renewed 1949 by Ruth Nivison; "Lawrence's Quarrel with Christianity: *The Man Who Died*" from *The Dark Sun: A Study of D. H. Lawrence* by Graham Hough; copyright © Graham Gouldner Hough 1956, 1957.

Mrs. Edgar Lee Masters for permission to reprint "Carl Hamblin" from *Spoon River Anthology* by Edgar Lee Masters, published by The Macmillan Company.

Stephen Mooney for permission to reprint "Assassination at Memphis" © 1968 by Stephen Mooney, and "The Garden."

William Morns Agency, Inc. for permission to reprint "King of the Bingo Game," by Ralph Ellison, on behalf of author, Copyright © 1944 (renewed) by Ralph Ellison.

New Directions for permission to reprint "The force that through the green fuse" from *The Collected Poems of Dylan Thomas,* copyright 1939 by New Directions Publishing Corporation; "Do not go gentle" from *The Collected Poems of Dylan Thomas,* copyright 1952 by Dylan Thomas; "Memories of Chirstmas" (J. M. Dent version) by Dylan Thomas from *Quite Early One Morning.* All rights reserved. Copyright 1954 by New Directions Publishing Corp.; "Envoi (1919)" and "Ballad of the Goodly Fere" by Ezra Pound from *Personae.* Copyright 1926, 1954 by Ezra Pound. Reprinted by permission of the New Directions Publishing Corp.

The New York Times for permission to reprint "Emmett Till" by James A. Emanuel, copyright © 1963 by The New York Times Company. Reprinted by permission; "Trespass on a Monument" from *The New York Times,* December 7, 1958.

Harold Ober Associates, Inc. for permission to reprint "Southern Mansion" and "Reconnaissance" by Arna Bontemps, copyright © 1963 by Arna Bontemps; "On the Road" by Langston Hughes, copyright © 1952 by Langston Hughes. All reprinted by permission of Harold Ober Associates, Inc.

October House, Inc. for permission to reprint "Frederick Douglass" by Robert Hayden from *Selected Poems,* copyright © 1966 by Robert Hayden; reprinted with permission of October House, Inc.

Oxford University Press for permission to reprint "The Windhover" and "Spring and Fall" by Gerard Manley Hopkins; "The Fury of Aerial Bombardment" Richard Eberhart. © 1960 by Richard Eberhart. Reprinted by permission of Oxford University Press, Inc.

Peer—Southern Organization for permission to reprint "Hampstead Incident" by Donovan Leitch © Copyright 1967 by Donovan (Music) Ltd. Sole Selling Agent Peer International Corporation. Used by permission; "The Lullaby of Spring" by Donovan Leitch © Copyright 1967 by Donovan (Music) Ltd. Sole Selling Agent Peer International Corporation. Used by permission.

A. D. Peters and Company for permission to reprint "The Drunkard" by Frank O'Connor.

Nancy Price for permission to use "Centennial of Shiloh."

Dudley Randall for permission to reprint "Booker T. and W.E.B.," "Black Poet, White Critic," by Dudley Randall and "For Malcolm X" by Margaret A. Walker.

Random House, Inc., for permission to reprint "The Equilibrists" by John Crowe Ransom. Copyright 1927 by Alfred A. Knopf, Inc., and renewed 1955 by John Crowe Ransom. Reprinted from *Selected Poems,* by John Crowe Ransom by permission of the publishers; "Reading" from *The Dyer's Hand* by W. H. Auden; "The Unknown Citizen," "Lullaby," and "Musée des Beaux Arts" by W. H. Auden. Copyright 1940 and renewed 1968 by W. H. Auden Reprinted from *Collected Shorter Poems, 1927–1957,* by W. H. Auden by permission of Random House, Inc.; "Shine, Republic" from *Solstice* by Robinson Jeffers, copyright 1934, renewed © 1962 by Donnan Jeffers and Garth Jeffers; "Shine, Pershing Republic" and "Science." Copyright 1925 and renewed 1953 by Robinson Jeffers. Reprinted from *Selected Poetry of Robinson Jeffers* by permission of Random House, Inc.; "The Bloody Sire" from *Selected Poems,* by Robinson Jeffers. © Copyright 1965 by Donnan Jeffers and Garth Jeffers. Reprinted by permission of Random House, Inc.; "Landscape Near an Aerodrome," copyright 1934 and renewed 1962 by Stephen Spender. Reprinted from *Selected Poems,* by Stephen Spender by permission of Random House, Inc.; "A Rose for Emily" from *Collected Stories of William Faulkner,* copyright 1930 and renewed © 1958 by William Faulkner; "The Infant Prodigy" by Thomas Mann. Copyright 1936 by Alfred A. Knopf, Inc. Reprinted from *Stories of Three Decades,* by Thomas Mann, trans. by H. T. Lowe-Porter, by permission of the publisher; "The Guest" by Albert Camus. © Copyright 1957, 1958 by Alfred A. Knopf, Inc. Reprinted from *Exile and the Kingdom,* by Albert Camus, trans. by Justin O'Brien, by permission of the publisher; "The Wall" by Jean-Paul Sartre. Maria Jolas translation. Copyright 1945 by Random House, Inc. Reprinted from *Bedside Book of Famous French Stories* (B. Becker and R. N. Linscott, eds.) by permission of New Directions Publishing Corp. and Random House, Inc.; *The Glass Menagerie,* by Tennessee Williams. Copyright 1945 by Tennessee Williams and Edwina D. Williams. Reprinted from *Six Modern American Plays* by permission of Random House, Inc.; *Ile,* by Eugene O'Neill. Copyright 1919 and renewed 1947 by Eugene O'Neill. Reprinted from *The Long Voyage Home: Seven Plays of the Sea,* by Eugene O'Neill by permission of Random House, Inc.; *The Visit,* by Friedrich Duerrenmatt. © Copyright 1958 by Maurice Valency. © Copyright 1956 by Maurice Valency, as an unpublished work entitled "The Old Lady's Visit," adapted by Maurice Valency from *Der Besuch Der Alten Dame,* by Friedrich Duerrenmatt. Reprinted by permission of Random House, Inc.; "Nobel Prize Acceptance Speech" from *Camus at Stockholm,* trans. by Justin O'Brien. © Copyright 1958 by Alfred A. Knopf, Inc. Reprinted by permission of the publisher; "Sunday Morning," "Peter Quince at the Clavier," from *The Collected Poems of Wallace Stevens.* Copyright 1923, 1951 by Wallace Stevens. Reprinted by permission of Alfred A. Knopf, Inc.; "Movie Actress" from *V-Letter and Other Poems* by Karl Shapiro, copyright 1943 by Karl Shapiro; "Two Views of a Cadaver Room" and "Sucide Off Egg Rock," copyright © 1960 by Sylvia Plath. Reprinted from *The Colossus and Other Poems,* by Sylvia Plath; "Celebration for a Gray Day," copyright © 1961 by Margarita M. Fariña, Administratrix of the Estate of Richard G. Fariña. Reprinted from *Long Time Coming and a Long Time Gone,* by Richard Fariña; "The Negro Mother," copyright 1938 and renewed 1966 by Langston Hughes, reprinted from *Selected Poems* by Langston Hughes; "The Drunkard,"

copyright 1951 by Frank O'Connor, reprinted from *The Stories of Frank O'Connor,* by permission of Alfred A. Knopf, Inc., first appeared in *The New Yorker;* "The Man Who Died" from *St. Mawr and The Man Who Died,* by D. H. Lawrence, copyright 1928 by Alfred A. Knopf, Inc., reprinted by permission of the publisher; "Brave Words for a Startling Occasion," copyright © 1963, 1964 by Ralph Ellison, reprinted from *Shadow and Act,* by Ralph Ellison.

The Saturday Review for permission to reprint John Ciardi's "Dialogue with the Audience" from November 22, 1958, issue; "Criticism: A Many-Windowed House" by Malcolm Cowley from the August 12, 1961, issue. Reprinted by permission of the *Saturday Review* and the author.

Schocken Books Inc. for permission to reprint "A Hunger Artist" from *The Penal Colony* by Franz Kafka. Copyright © 1948 by Shocken Books Inc.

Charles Scribner's Sons for permission to reprint "Quality" from *The Inn of Tranquility* by John Galsworthy, copyright 1912 by Charles Scribner's Sons, 1940 by Ada Galsworthy; "Miniver Cheevy" from *The Town Down the River* by Edwin Arlington Robinson, copyright 1910 by Charles Scribner's Sons, 1938 by Ruth Nivinson; "Speaking of Poetry" from *Now With His Love* by John Peale Bishop. Copyright 1936, Charles Scribner's Sons, renewal copyright © 1961 Margaret G. H. Bronson; "A Clean, Well-Lighted Place" (Copyright 1933 Charles Scribner's Sons; renewal copyright © 1961 Ernest Hemingway) is reprinted by permission of Charles Scribner's Sons from *Winner Take Nothing* by Ernest Hemingway.

Stephen Spender for permission to reprint "On Teaching Modern Poetry" from *Essays on Teaching, edited* by Harold Taylor, by permission of the author and editor.

Helen Thurber for permission to reprint "The Unicorn in the Garden, copyright © 1940 James Thurber. Copyright © 1968 Helen Thurber. From Fables for Our Time, published by Harper & Row. Originally printed in *The New Yorker.*

Twayne Publishers for permission to reprint "Harlem Dancer," "The White House," "If We Must Die," by Claude McKay; from "Harlem Gallery," by Melvin B. Tolson.

University of Minnesota Press for permission to reprint Bertolt Brecht's "The Caucasian Chalk Circle," © copyright 1947, 1948, 1961, 1963 by Eric Bentley; Prologue © copyright 1959 by Eric Bentley; Introduction © copyright 1965 by Eric Bentley. Originally published in the volume *Parables for the Theatre: Two Plays by Bertolt Brecht* by the University of Minnesota Press. Reprinted by permission.

Vanguard Press for permission to reprint "In the Region of Ice," by Joyce Carol Oates from *The Wheel of Love and Other Stories* by Joyce Carol Oates. Copyright © 1970, 1969, 1968, 1967, 1966, 1965, by Joyce Carol Oates.

Vanguard Recording Society for permission to reprint "Black Panther" by Carl Oglesby, Copyright © 1968 by Fennario Music Publishers, Inc.

The Viking Press for permission to reprint "Piano" from *Collected Poems of D. H. Lawrence,* copyright 1929 by Jonathan Cape and Harrison Smith, Inc.; "Eveline" from *Dubliners* by James Joyce, originally published by B. W. Huebsch, Inc., in 1916. All rights reserved. Reprinted by permission of The Viking Press, Inc.; "The Horse-Dealer's Daughter" from *The Complete Short Stories of D. H. Lawrence,* Volume II, copyright 1922 by Thomas B. Seltzer, Inc., 1950 by Frieda Lawrence. Reprinted by permission of The Viking Press, Inc.; "The Day After Sunday" from *Times Three* by Phyllis McGinley, copyright 1952 by Phyllis McGinley. Originally appeared in *The New Yorker.* Reprinted by permission of The Viking Press, Inc.; "The Elephant Is Slow To Mate" from *The Complete Poems of D. H. Lawrence,* edited by Vivian De Sola Pinto and F. Warren Roberts, copyright 1929 by Frieda Lawrence Ravagali. All rights reserved. Reprinted by permission of The Viking Press, Inc.; "The Chrysanthemums," from *The Long Valley* by John Steinbeck, copyright 1937, © 1965 by John Steinbeck; reprinted by permission of The Viking Press, Inc.

A. Watkins, Inc., for permission to reprint "Roman Fever" from *The World Over* by Edith Wharton. Copyright 1934 Edith Wharton, renewed 1962 William R. Tyler.

A. P. Watt and Son for permission to reprint "The Colonel's Lady," by W. Somerset Maugham, also with permission of the Literary Executor of the late W. Somerset Maugham; "The Wild Swans at Coole," "The Second Coming," "Among School Children," by William Butler Yeats; "On the Road" by Anton Chekhov, translated by Constance Garnett.

Wesleyan University Press for permission to reprint "To the Western World," copyright © 1957 by Louis Simpson, by permission of Wesleyan University Press.

John Wiley and Sons for permission to reprint "Electric Orphic Circuit" from *Lyric Voices: Approaches to the Poetry of Contemporary Song,* by Barbara Farris Graves and Donald J. McBain. Copyright © 1972, by John Wiley & Sons, Inc.

Robley Wilson, Jr., for permission to reprint "The Great Teachers " and "War."

Yale University Press for permission to reprint "Molly Means" by Margaret Walker, copyright © 1942 by Yale University Press.

INDEX OF AUTHORS AND TITLES

INDEX OF LITERARY AND CRITICAL TERMS